The Java™ EE 5 Tutorial

Third Edition

Good luck in the new job!

Love & kisses...

Eric

The Java™ EE 5 Tutorial

Third Edition

For Sun Java System Application Server Platform Edition 9

Eric Jendrock
Jennifer Ball
Debbie Carson
Ian Evans
Scott Fordin
Kim Haase

Addison-Wesley

Upper Saddle River, NJ • Boston • Indianapolis • San Francisco
New York • Toronto • Montreal • London • Munich • Paris • Madrid
Capetown • Sydney • Tokyo • Singapore • Mexico City

The publisher offers excellent discounts on this book when ordered in quantity for bulk purchases or special sales, which may include electronic versions and/or custom covers and content particular to your business, training goals, marketing focus, and branding interests. For more information, please contact:

U.S. Corporate and Government Sales
(800) 382–3419
corpsales@pearsontechgroup.com

For sales outside the United States please contact:

International Sales
international@pearsoned.com

This Book Is Safari Enabled

The Safari® Enabled icon on the cover of your favorite technology book means the book is available through Safari Bookshelf. When you buy this book, you get free access to the online edition for 45 days.

Safari Bookshelf is an electronic reference library that lets you easily search thousands of technical books, find code samples, download chapters, and access technical information whenever and wherever you need it.

To gain 45-day Safari Enabled access to this book:

- Go to http://www.awprofessional.com/safarienabled
- Complete the brief registration form
- Enter the coupon code DTCF-3BXD-JXI5-GWDL-S4MT

If you have difficulty registering on Safari Bookshelf or accessing the online edition, please e-mail customer-service@safaribooksonline.com.

Visit us on the Web: www.awprofessional.com

Library of Congress Cataloging-in-Publication Data

The Java EE 5 tutorial / Eric Jendrock ... [et al.]. -- 3rd ed.
p. cm.
Previous ed: The J2EE Tutorial / by Stephanie Bodoff.
Includes index.
ISBN 0-321-49029-0 (pbk. : alk. paper)
1. Java (Computer program language) 2. Internet programming. I. Jendrock, Eric.

QA76.73.J38J3652 2006
005.13'3--dc22 2006029908

Pearson Education, Inc.
Rights and Contracts Department
75 Arlington Street, Suite 300
Boston, MA 02116
Fax: (617) 848-7047

Cover art by Nathan Clement.

ISBN 0–321–49029–0
Text printed in the United States on recycled paper at Courier in Stoughton, Massachusetts.
First printing, October 2006

Contents

Chapter 10: Using JavaServer Faces Technology in JSP Pages . . . 317

Chapter 16: Binding between XML Schema and Java Classes 519

About This Tutorial

THIS tutorial is a guide to developing enterprise applications for the Java Platform, Enterprise Edition 5 (Java EE 5). Here we cover all the things you need to know to make the best use of this tutorial.

Who Should Use This Tutorial

This tutorial is intended for programmers who are interested in developing and deploying Java EE 5 applications on the Sun Java System Application Server Platform Edition 9.

Prerequisites

Before proceeding with this tutorial, you should have a good knowledge of the Java programming language. A good way to get to that point is to work through *The Java™ Tutorial, Fourth Edition*, Sharon Zakhour et al. (Addison-Wesley, 2006). You should also be familiar with the relational database features described in *JDBC API Tutorial and Reference, Third Edition*, Maydene Fisher et al. (Addison-Wesley, 2003).

How to Read This Tutorial

The Java EE 5 platform is quite large, and this tutorial reflects this. However, you don't have to digest everything in it at once. The tutorial has been divided into parts to help you navigate the content more easily.

This tutorial opens with an introductory chapter, which you should read before proceeding to any specific technology area. Chapter 1 covers the Java EE 5 platform architecture and APIs along with the Sun Java System Application Server Platform Edition 9.

When you have digested the basics, you can delve into one or more of the five main technology areas listed next. Because there are dependencies between some of the chapters, Figure 1 contains a roadmap for navigating through the tutorial.

- The web-tier technology chapters cover the components used in developing the presentation layer of a Java EE 5 or stand-alone web application:
  - Java Servlet
  - JavaServer Pages (JSP)
  - JavaServer Pages Standard Tag Library (JSTL)
  - JavaServer Faces
  - Web application internationalization and localization
- The web services technology chapters cover the APIs used in developing standard web services:
  - The Java API for XML-based Web Services (JAX-WS)
  - The Java API for XML Binding (JAXB)
  - The Streaming API for XML (StAX)
  - The SOAP with Attachments API for Java (SAAJ)
  - The Java API for XML Registries (JAXR)
- The Enterprise JavaBeans (EJB) technology chapters cover the components used in developing the business logic of a Java EE 5 application:
  - Session beans
  - Message-driven beans
- The Persistence technology chapters cover the Java Persistence API, which is used for accessing databases from Java EE applications:
  - Introduction to the Java Persistence API
  - Persistence in the Web Tier
  - Persistence in the EJB Tier
  - The Java Persistence Query Language

- The platform services chapters cover the system services used by all the Java EE 5 component technologies:
  - Transactions
  - Resource connections
  - Security
  - Java Message Service
  - The Connector architecture

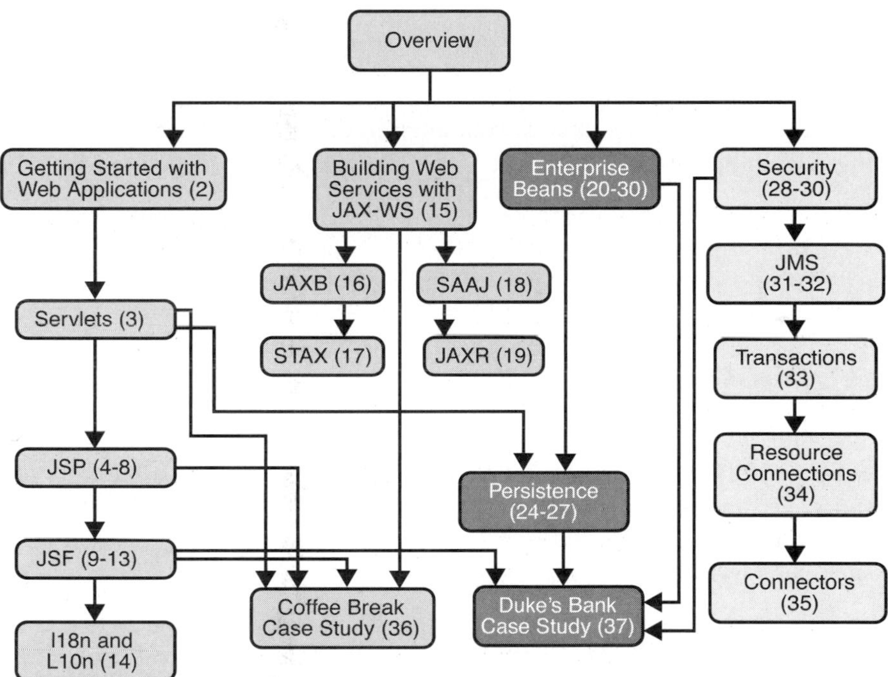

Figure 1 Roadmap to This Tutorial

After you have become familiar with some of the technology areas, you are ready to tackle the case studies, which tie together several of the technologies discussed in the tutorial. The Coffee Break Application describes an application that uses the web application and web services APIs. The Duke's Bank Application describes an application that employs web application technologies, enterprise beans, and the Java Persistence API.

Finally, the appendix contains information about Java encoding schemes that may be helpful to the Java EE 5 application developer.

About the Examples

This section tells you everything you need to know to install, build, and run the examples.

Required Software

The following software is required to run the examples.

Tutorial Bundle

The tutorial example source is contained in the tutorial bundle. If you are viewing this online, you need to click on the Download link at the top of any page.

After you have installed the tutorial bundle, the example source code is in the `<INSTALL>/javaeetutorial5/examples/` directory, with subdirectories for each of the technologies discussed in the tutorial.

Application Server

The Sun Java System Application Server Platform Edition 9 is targeted as the build and runtime environment for the tutorial examples. To build, deploy, and run the examples, you need a copy of the Application Server and Java 2 Platform, Standard Edition 5.0 (J2SE 5.0). If you already have a copy of the J2SE SDK, you can download the Application Server from:

```
http://java.sun.com/javaee/downloads/index.html
```

You can also download the Java EE 5 SDK—which contains the Application Server and the J2SE SDK—from the same site.

Application Server Installation Tips

In the Admin configuration pane of the Application Server installer:

- Select the Don't Prompt for Admin User Name radio button. This will save the user name and password so that you won't need to provide them when performing administrative operations with `asadmin`. You will still have to provide the user name and password to log in to the Admin Console.

- Note the HTTP port at which the server is installed. This tutorial assumes that you are accepting the default port of 8080. If 8080 is in use during installation and the installer chooses another port or if you decide to change it yourself, you will need to update the common build properties file (described in the next section) and the configuration files for some of the tutorial examples to reflect the correct port.

In the Installation Options pane, check the Add Bin Directory to PATH checkbox so that Application Server scripts (`asadmin`, `wsimport`, `wsgen`, `xjc`, and `schemagen`) override other installations.

NetBeans 5.5

The NetBeans integrated development environment (IDE) is a free, open-source IDE for developing Java applications, including enterprise applications. NetBeans 5.5 supports the Java EE 5 platform. You can build, package, deploy, and run the tutorial examples from within NetBeans 5.5, which you can download at `http://www.netbeans.org/downloads/index.html`. For information on creating enterprise applications in NetBeans 5.5, see `http://www.netbeans.org/kb/55/index.html`.

Apache Ant

Ant is a Java technology-based build tool developed by the Apache Software Foundation (`http://ant.apache.org`), and is used to build, package, and deploy the tutorial examples. Ant is included with the Application Server. To use the `ant` command, add `<JAVAEE_HOME>/lib/ant/bin` to your `PATH` environment variable.

Registry Server

You need a registry server to run the examples discussed in Chapter 19. Instructions for obtaining and setting up a registry server are provided in Chapter 19.

Building the Examples

The tutorial examples are distributed with a configuration file for either NetBeans 5.5 or Ant. Directions for building the examples are provided in each chapter. Either NetBeans 5.5 or Ant may be used to build, package, deploy, and run the examples.

Building the Examples Using NetBeans 5.5

To run the tutorial examples in NetBeans 5.5, you must register your Application Server installation as a NetBeans Server Instance. Follow these instructions to register the Application Server in NetBeans 5.5.

1. Select Tools→Server Manager to open the Server Manager dialog.
2. Click Add Server.
3. Under Server, select Sun Java System Application Server and click Next.
4. Under Platform Location, enter the location of your Application Server installation.
5. Select Register Local Default Domain and click Next.
6. Under Admin Username and Admin Password, enter the admin name and password you specified while installing the Application Server.
7. Click Finish.

Building the Examples on the Command-Line Using Ant

Build properties common to all the examples are specified in the `build.properties` file in the `<INSTALL>/javaeetutorial5/examples/bp-project/` directory. You must create this file before you can run the examples. We've included a sample file, `build.properties.sample`, that you should rename to `build.properties` and edit to reflect your environment. The tutorial examples use the Java BluePrints (`http://java.sun.com/reference/blueprints/`) build system and application layout structure.

To run the Ant scripts, you must set common build properties in the file `<INSTALL>/javaeetutorial5/examples/bp-project/build.properties` as follows:

- Set the `javaee.home` property to the location of your Application Server installation. The build process uses the `javaee.home` property to include the libraries in `<JAVAEE_HOME>/lib/` in the classpath. All examples that run on the Application Server include the Java EE library archive—`<JAVAEE_HOME>/lib/javaee.jar`—in the build classpath. Some examples use additional libraries in `<JAVAEE_HOME>/lib/`; the required libraries are enumerated in the individual technology chapters. *<JAVAEE_HOME>* refers to the directory where you have installed the Application Server.

Note: On Windows, you must escape any backslashes in the `javaee.home` property with another backslash or use forward slashes as a path separator. So, if your Application Server installation is `C:\Sun\AppServer`, you must set `javaee.home` as follows:

```
javaee.home = C:\\Sun\\AppServer
```

or

```
javaee.home=C:/Sun/AppServer
```

- Set the `javaee.tutorial.home` property to the location of your tutorial. This property is used for Ant deployment and undeployment.

  For example, on UNIX:

  ```
  javaee.tutorial.home=/home/username/javaeetutorial5
  ```

  On Windows:

  ```
  javaee.tutorial.home=C:/javaeetutorial5
  ```

  Do not install the tutorial to a location with spaces in the path.
- If you did not use the default value (`admin`) for the admin user, set the `admin.user` property to the value you specified when you installed the Application Server.
- If you did not use port 8080, set the `domain.resources.port` property to the value specified when you installed the Application Server.
- Set the admin user's password in the `admin-password.txt` file in the *<INSTALL>*`/javaeetutorial5/examples/common/` directory to the value you specified when you installed the Application Server. The format of this file is `AS_ADMIN_PASSWORD=`*`password`*. For example:

  ```
  AS_ADMIN_PASSWORD=mypassword
  ```

Tutorial Example Directory Structure

To facilitate iterative development and keep application source separate from compiled files, the tutorial examples use the Java BluePrints application directory structure.

Each application module has the following structure:

- `build.xml`: Ant build file
- `src/java`: Java source files for the module
- `src/conf`: configuration files for the module, with the exception of web applications
- `web`: JSP and HTML pages, style sheets, tag files, and images
- `web/WEB-INF`: configuration files for web applications
- `nbproject`: NetBeans project files

Examples that have multiple application modules packaged into an enterprise application archive (or EAR) have submodule directories that use the following naming conventions:

- <*EXAMPLE_NAME*>`-app-client`: Application clients
- <*EXAMPLE_NAME*>`-ejb`: Enterprise bean JARs
- <*EXAMPLE_NAME*>`-war`: web applications

The Ant build files (`build.xml`) distributed with the examples contain targets to create a `build` subdirectory and to copy and compile files into that directory; a `dist` subdirectory, which holds the packaged module file; and a `client-jar` directory, which holds the retrieved application client JAR.

Further Information

This tutorial includes the basic information that you need to deploy applications on and administer the Application Server.

See the *Sun Java™ System Application Server Platform Edition 9 Developer's Guide* at `http://docs.sun.com/doc/819-3659` for information about developer features of the Application Server.

See the *Sun Java™ System Application Server Platform Edition 9 Administration Guide* at `http://docs.sun.com/doc/819-3658` for information about administering the Application Server.

For information about the Java DB database included with the Application Server see the Apache web site at `http://db.apache.org/derby`.

Typographical Conventions

Table 1 lists the typographical conventions used in this tutorial.

Table 1 Typographical Conventions

Font Style	Uses
italic	Emphasis, titles, first occurrence of terms
`monospace`	URLs, code examples, file names, path names, tool names, application names, programming language keywords, tag, interface, class, method, and field names, properties
`italic monospace`	Variables in code, file paths, and URLs
<*`italic monospace`*>	User-selected file path components

Menu selections indicated with the right-arrow character →, for example, First→Second, should be interpreted as: select the First menu, then choose Second from the First submenu.

Acknowledgments

The Java EE tutorial team would like to thank the Java EE specification leads: Bill Shannon, Linda DeMichiel, Sekhar Vajjhala, Jan Luehe, Gregory Murray, Arun Gupta, Doug Kohlert, Ed Burns, V B Kumar Jayanti, Binod P. G., Sankara Rao, Dhiru Pandey, Rajiv Mordani, Farrukh Najmi, and Ron Monzillo. We would also like to thank the Java EE 5 SDK team members: Anil Gaur, Tony Ng, Inderjeet Singh, Carla Carlson, Nazrul Islam, Jerome Dochez, Jean-Francois Arcand, Chinmay Mehta, Suveen Nadipalli, Vipin Rajan, and Chinmayee Srivathsa.

The chapters on custom tags and the Coffee Break and Duke's Bank applications use a template tag library that first appeared in *Designing Enterprise Applica-*

tions with the J2EE™ Platform, Second Edition, Inderjeet Singh et al., (Addison-Wesley, 2002).

The JavaServer Faces technology and JSP Documents chapters benefited greatly from the invaluable documentation reviews and example code contributions of these engineers: Ed Burns, Roger Kitain, Jan Luehe, Craig McClanahan, and especially Ryan Lubke and Jayashri Visvanathan.

The EJB technology and Java Persistence API chapters were written with extensive input from Sun's EJB and Persistence teams. We'd like to thank Marina Vatkina, Ken Saks, Geoff Halliwell, Shelly MacGowan, Linda DeMichiel, Markus Fuchs, Rochelle Raccah, Lance Andersen, Vince Kraemer, Michael Bouschen, and Tim Quinn for their contributions to the material and code examples.

The security, JAXB, and StAX chapter writers greatly appreciate the input of Raja Perumal, Joseph Fialli, Ryan Shoemaker, Kohsuke Kawaguchi, Rebecca Searls, and Neeraj Bajaj, who were a key contributors both to the chapters and to the examples.

We'd like to thank the NetBeans engineering and documentation teams, particularly Petr Jiricka, Jan Chalupa, Ludovic Champenois, Petr Blaha, Peter Williams, Geertjan Wielenga, Jesse Glick, Tomasz Slota, John Jullion-Ceccarelli, and Patrick Keegan, for their help in enabling NetBeans support for the code examples.

Stephanie Bodoff and Dale Green contributed much content to the first and second editions of The J2EE Tutorial, and much of that content has been carried forward to the current edition.

We are extremely grateful to the many internal and external reviewers who provided feedback on the tutorial. Their feedback helped improve the technical accuracy and presentation of the chapters and eliminate bugs from the examples.

We would like to thank our manager, Alan Sommerer, for his support and steadying influence.

We also thank Dwayne Wolff for developing and updating the illustrations in record time and our editor, Julie Bettis, for improving the readability and flow of the book. Thanks are also due to our copy editor, Hartley Ferguson, for helping this multiauthor project achieve a common style.

Finally, we would like to express our profound appreciation to Greg Doench, Elizabeth Ryan, and the production team at Addison-Wesley for graciously seeing our large, complicated manuscript to publication.

Feedback

To send comments, broken link reports, errors, suggestions, and questions about this tutorial to the tutorial team, please use the feedback form at `http://java.sun.com/javaee/5/docs/tutorial/information/sendusmail.html`.

1

Overview

DEVELOPERS today increasingly recognize the need for distributed, transactional, and portable applications that leverage the speed, security, and reliability of server-side technology. In the world of information technology, enterprise applications must be designed, built, and produced for less money, with greater speed, and with fewer resources.

With the Java™ Platform, Enterprise Edition (Java EE), development of Java enterprise applications has never been easier or faster. The aim of the Java EE 5 platform is to provide developers a powerful set of APIs while reducing development time, reducing application complexity, and improving application performance.

The Java EE 5 platform introduces a simplified programming model. With Java EE 5 technology, XML deployment descriptors are now optional. Instead, a developer can simply enter the information as an annotation directly into a Java source file, and the Java EE server will configure the component at deployment and runtime. These annotations are generally used to embed in a program data that would otherwise be furnished in a deployment descriptor. With annotations, the specification information is put directly in your code next to the program element that it affects.

In the Java EE platform, dependency injection can be applied to all resources that a component needs, effectively hiding the creation and lookup of resources from application code. Dependency injection can be used in EJB containers, web containers, and application clients. Dependency injection allows the Java EE container to automatically insert references to other required components or resources using annotations.

The Java™ Persistence API is new to the Java EE 5 platform. The Java Persistence API provides an object/relational mapping for managing relational data in enterprise beans, web components, and application clients. It can also be used in Java SE applications, outside of the Java EE environment.

This tutorial uses examples to describe the features and functionalities available in the Java EE 5 platform for developing enterprise applications. Whether you are a new or experienced Enterprise developer, you should find the examples and accompanying text a valuable and accessible knowledge base for creating your own solutions.

If you are new to Java EE enterprise application development, this chapter is a good place to start. Here you will review development basics, learn about the Java EE architecture and APIs, become acquainted with important terms and concepts, and find out how to approach Java EE application programming, assembly, and deployment.

Java EE Application Model

The Java EE application model begins with the Java programming language and the Java virtual machine. The proven portability, security, and developer productivity they provide forms the basis of the application model. Java EE is designed to support applications that implement enterprise services for customers, employees, suppliers, partners, and others who make demands on or contributions to the enterprise. Such applications are inherently complex, potentially accessing data from a variety of sources and distributing applications to a variety of clients.

To better control and manage these applications, the business functions to support these various users are conducted in the middle tier. The middle tier represents an environment that is closely controlled by an enterprise's information technology department. The middle tier is typically run on dedicated server hardware and has access to the full services of the enterprise.

The Java EE application model defines an architecture for implementing services as multitier applications that deliver the scalability, accessibility, and manageability needed by enterprise-level applications. This model partitions the work needed to implement a multitier service into two parts: the business and presentation logic to be implemented by the developer, and the standard system services provided by the Java EE platform. The developer can rely on the platform to provide solutions for the hard systems-level problems of developing a multitier service.

Distributed Multitiered Applications

The Java EE platform uses a distributed multitiered application model for enterprise applications. Application logic is divided into components according to function, and the various application components that make up a Java EE application are installed on different machines depending on the tier in the multitiered Java EE environment to which the application component belongs. Figure 1–1 shows two multitiered Java EE applications divided into the tiers described in the following list. The Java EE application parts shown in Figure 1–1 are presented in Java EE Components (page 4).

- Client-tier components run on the client machine.
- Web-tier components run on the Java EE server.
- Business-tier components run on the Java EE server.
- Enterprise information system (EIS)-tier software runs on the EIS server.

Although a Java EE application can consist of the three or four tiers shown in Figure 1–1, Java EE multitiered applications are generally considered to be three-tiered applications because they are distributed over three locations: client machines, the Java EE server machine, and the database or legacy machines at the back end. Three-tiered applications that run in this way extend the standard two-tiered client and server model by placing a multithreaded application server between the client application and back-end storage.

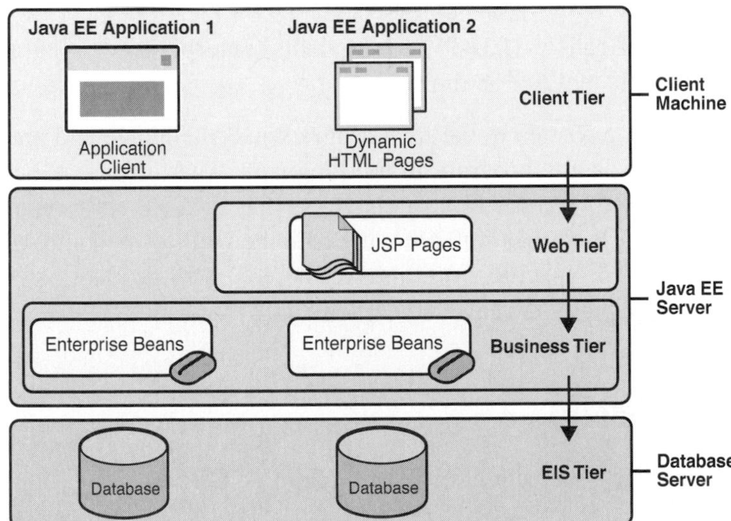

Figure 1–1 Multitiered Applications

Security

While other enterprise application models require platform-specific security measures in each application, the Java EE security environment enables security constraints to be defined at deployment time. The Java EE platform makes applications portable to a wide variety of security implementations by shielding application developers from the complexity of implementing security features.

The Java EE platform provides standard declarative access control rules that are defined by the developer and interpreted when the application is deployed on the server. Java EE also provides standard login mechanisms so application developers do not have to implement these mechanisms in their applications. The same application works in a variety of different security environments without changing the source code.

Java EE Components

Java EE applications are made up of components. A *Java EE component* is a self-contained functional software unit that is assembled into a Java EE application with its related classes and files and that communicates with other components. The Java EE specification defines the following Java EE components:

- Application clients and applets are components that run on the client.
- Java Servlet, JavaServer Faces, and JavaServer Pages™ (JSP™) technology components are web components that run on the server.
- Enterprise JavaBeans™ (EJB™) components (enterprise beans) are business components that run on the server.

Java EE components are written in the Java programming language and are compiled in the same way as any program in the language. The difference between Java EE components and "standard" Java classes is that Java EE components are assembled into a Java EE application, are verified to be well formed and in compliance with the Java EE specification, and are deployed to production, where they are run and managed by the Java EE server.

Java EE Clients

A Java EE client can be a web client or an application client.

Web Clients

A *web client* consists of two parts: (1) dynamic web pages containing various types of markup language (HTML, XML, and so on), which are generated by web components running in the web tier, and (2) a web browser, which renders the pages received from the server.

A web client is sometimes called a *thin client*. Thin clients usually do not query databases, execute complex business rules, or connect to legacy applications. When you use a thin client, such heavyweight operations are off-loaded to enterprise beans executing on the Java EE server, where they can leverage the security, speed, services, and reliability of Java EE server-side technologies.

Applets

A web page received from the web tier can include an embedded applet. An *applet* is a small client application written in the Java programming language that executes in the Java virtual machine installed in the web browser. However, client systems will likely need the Java Plug-in and possibly a security policy file for the applet to successfully execute in the web browser.

Web components are the preferred API for creating a web client program because no plug-ins or security policy files are needed on the client systems. Also, web components enable cleaner and more modular application design because they provide a way to separate applications programming from web page design. Personnel involved in web page design thus do not need to understand Java programming language syntax to do their jobs.

Application Clients

An *application client* runs on a client machine and provides a way for users to handle tasks that require a richer user interface than can be provided by a markup language. It typically has a graphical user interface (GUI) created from the Swing or the Abstract Window Toolkit (AWT) API, but a command-line interface is certainly possible.

Application clients directly access enterprise beans running in the business tier. However, if application requirements warrant it, an application client can open an HTTP connection to establish communication with a servlet running in the web tier. Application clients written in languages other than Java can interact with Java EE 5 servers, enabling the Java EE 5 platform to interoperate with legacy systems, clients, and non-Java languages.

The JavaBeans™ Component Architecture

The server and client tiers might also include components based on the JavaBeans component architecture (JavaBeans components) to manage the data flow between an application client or applet and components running on the Java EE server, or between server components and a database. JavaBeans components are not considered Java EE components by the Java EE specification.

JavaBeans components have properties and have `get` and `set` methods for accessing the properties. JavaBeans components used in this way are typically simple in design and implementation but should conform to the naming and design conventions outlined in the JavaBeans component architecture.

Java EE Server Communications

Figure 1–2 shows the various elements that can make up the client tier. The client communicates with the business tier running on the Java EE server either directly or, as in the case of a client running in a browser, by going through JSP pages or servlets running in the web tier.

Your Java EE application uses a thin browser-based client or thick application client. In deciding which one to use, you should be aware of the trade-offs between keeping functionality on the client and close to the user (thick client) and off-loading as much functionality as possible to the server (thin client). The more functionality you off-load to the server, the easier it is to distribute, deploy, and manage the application; however, keeping more functionality on the client can make for a better perceived user experience.

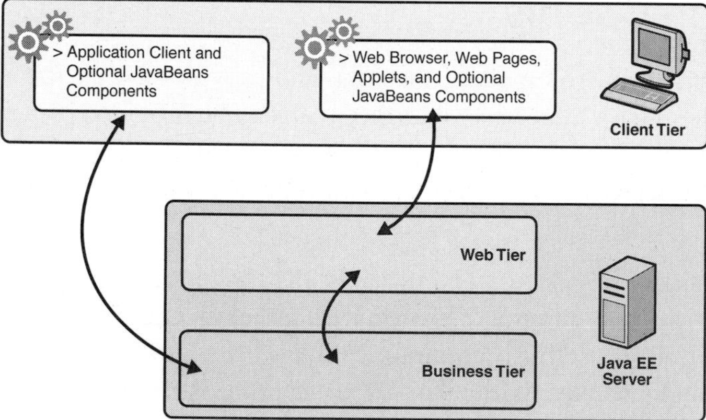

Figure 1–2 Server Communication

Web Components

Java EE web components are either servlets or pages created using JSP technology (JSP pages) and/or JavaServer Faces technology. *Servlets* are Java programming language classes that dynamically process requests and construct responses. *JSP pages* are text-based documents that execute as servlets but allow a more natural approach to creating static content. *JavaServer Faces* technology builds on servlets and JSP technology and provides a user interface component framework for web applications.

Static HTML pages and applets are bundled with web components during application assembly but are not considered web components by the Java EE specification. Server-side utility classes can also be bundled with web components and, like HTML pages, are not considered web components.

As shown in Figure 1–3, the web tier, like the client tier, might include a JavaBeans component to manage the user input and send that input to enterprise beans running in the business tier for processing.

Business Components

Business code, which is logic that solves or meets the needs of a particular business domain such as banking, retail, or finance, is handled by enterprise beans running in the business tier. Figure 1–4 shows how an enterprise bean receives data from client programs, processes it (if necessary), and sends it to the enterprise information system tier for storage. An enterprise bean also retrieves data from storage, processes it (if necessary), and sends it back to the client program.

Enterprise Information System Tier

The enterprise information system tier handles EIS software and includes enterprise infrastructure systems such as enterprise resource planning (ERP), mainframe transaction processing, database systems, and other legacy information systems. For example, Java EE application components might need access to enterprise information systems for database connectivity.

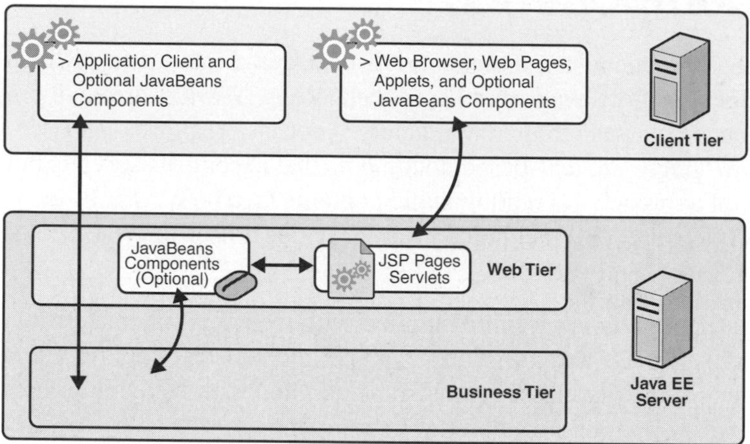

Figure 1–3 Web Tier and Java EE Applications

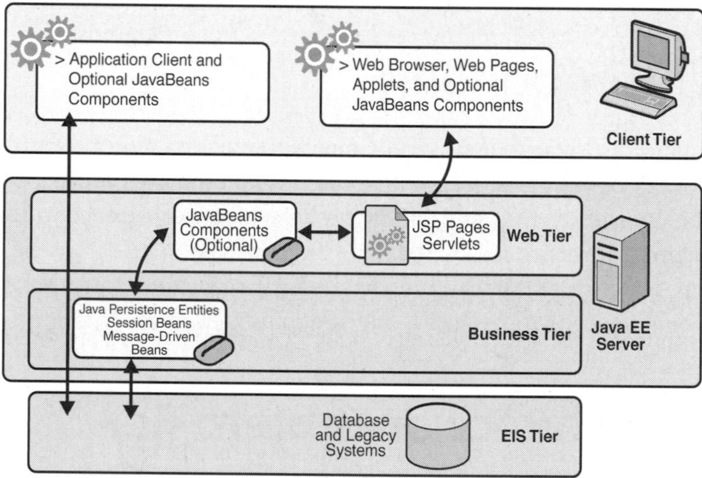

Figure 1–4 Business and EIS Tiers

Java EE Containers

Normally, thin-client multitiered applications are hard to write because they involve many lines of intricate code to handle transaction and state management, multithreading, resource pooling, and other complex low-level details. The component-based and platform-independent Java EE architecture makes Java EE applications easy to write because business logic is organized into reusable components. In addition, the Java EE server provides underlying services in the form of a container for every component type. Because you do not have to develop these services yourself, you are free to concentrate on solving the business problem at hand.

Container Services

Containers are the interface between a component and the low-level platform-specific functionality that supports the component. Before a web, enterprise bean, or application client component can be executed, it must be assembled into a Java EE module and deployed into its container.

The assembly process involves specifying container settings for each component in the Java EE application and for the Java EE application itself. Container settings customize the underlying support provided by the Java EE server, including services such as security, transaction management, Java Naming and Directory Interface™ (JNDI) lookups, and remote connectivity. Here are some of the highlights:

- The Java EE security model lets you configure a web component or enterprise bean so that system resources are accessed only by authorized users.
- The Java EE transaction model lets you specify relationships among methods that make up a single transaction so that all methods in one transaction are treated as a single unit.
- JNDI lookup services provide a unified interface to multiple naming and directory services in the enterprise so that application components can access these services.
- The Java EE remote connectivity model manages low-level communications between clients and enterprise beans. After an enterprise bean is created, a client invokes methods on it as if it were in the same virtual machine.

Because the Java EE architecture provides configurable services, application components within the same Java EE application can behave differently based on where they are deployed. For example, an enterprise bean can have security settings that allow it a certain level of access to database data in one production environment and another level of database access in another production environment.

The container also manages nonconfigurable services such as enterprise bean and servlet life cycles, database connection resource pooling, data persistence, and access to the Java EE platform APIs (see Java EE 5 APIs, page 18).

Container Types

The deployment process installs Java EE application components in the Java EE containers as illustrated in Figure 1–5.

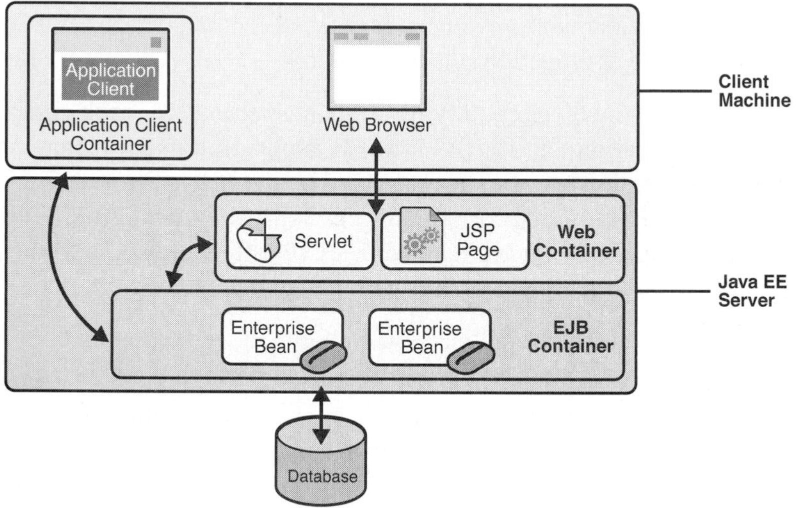

Figure 1–5 Java EE Server and Containers

- **Java EE server**: The runtime portion of a Java EE product. A Java EE server provides EJB and web containers.
- **Enterprise JavaBeans (EJB) container**: Manages the execution of enterprise beans for Java EE applications. Enterprise beans and their container run on the Java EE server.
- **Web container**: Manages the execution of JSP page and servlet components for Java EE applications. Web components and their container run on the Java EE server.
- **Application client container**: Manages the execution of application client components. Application clients and their container run on the client.
- **Applet container**: Manages the execution of applets. Consists of a web browser and Java Plug-in running on the client together.

Web Services Support

Web services are web-based enterprise applications that use open, XML-based standards and transport protocols to exchange data with calling clients. The Java EE platform provides the XML APIs and tools you need to quickly design, develop, test, and deploy web services and clients that fully interoperate with other web services and clients running on Java-based or non-Java-based platforms.

To write web services and clients with the Java EE XML APIs, all you do is pass parameter data to the method calls and process the data returned; or for document-oriented web services, you send documents containing the service data back and forth. No low-level programming is needed because the XML API implementations do the work of translating the application data to and from an XML-based data stream that is sent over the standardized XML-based transport protocols. These XML-based standards and protocols are introduced in the following sections.

The translation of data to a standardized XML-based data stream is what makes web services and clients written with the Java EE XML APIs fully interoperable. This does not necessarily mean that the data being transported includes XML tags because the transported data can itself be plain text, XML data, or any kind of binary data such as audio, video, maps, program files, computer-aided design (CAD) documents and the like. The next section introduces XML and explains how parties doing business can use XML tags and schemas to exchange data in a meaningful way.

XML

XML is a cross-platform, extensible, text-based standard for representing data. When XML data is exchanged between parties, the parties are free to create their own tags to describe the data, set up schemas to specify which tags can be used in a particular kind of XML document, and use XML stylesheets to manage the display and handling of the data.

For example, a web service can use XML and a schema to produce price lists, and companies that receive the price lists and schema can have their own stylesheets to handle the data in a way that best suits their needs. Here are examples:

- One company might put XML pricing information through a program to translate the XML to HTML so that it can post the price lists to its intranet.
- A partner company might put the XML pricing information through a tool to create a marketing presentation.
- Another company might read the XML pricing information into an application for processing.

SOAP Transport Protocol

Client requests and web service responses are transmitted as Simple Object Access Protocol (SOAP) messages over HTTP to enable a completely interoperable exchange between clients and web services, all running on different platforms and at various locations on the Internet. HTTP is a familiar request-and response standard for sending messages over the Internet, and SOAP is an XML-based protocol that follows the HTTP request-and-response model.

The SOAP portion of a transported message handles the following:

- Defines an XML-based envelope to describe what is in the message and how to process the message
- Includes XML-based encoding rules to express instances of application-defined data types within the message
- Defines an XML-based convention for representing the request to the remote service and the resulting response

WSDL Standard Format

The Web Services Description Language (WSDL) is a standardized XML format for describing network services. The description includes the name of the service, the location of the service, and ways to communicate with the service. WSDL service descriptions can be stored in UDDI registries or published on the web (or both). The Sun Java System Application Server Platform Edition 8 provides a tool for generating the WSDL specification of a web service that uses remote procedure calls to communicate with clients.

UDDI and ebXML Standard Formats

Other XML-based standards, such as Universal Description, Discovery and Integration (UDDI) and ebXML, make it possible for businesses to publish information on the Internet about their products and web services, where the information can be readily and globally accessed by clients who want to do business.

Java EE Application Assembly and Deployment

A Java EE application is packaged into one or more standard units for deployment to any Java EE platform-compliant system. Each unit contains:

- A functional component or components (enterprise bean, JSP page, servlet, applet, etc.)
- An optional deployment descriptor that describes its content

Once a Java EE unit has been produced, it is ready to be deployed. Deployment typically involves using a platform's deployment tool to specify location-specific information, such as a list of local users that can access it and the name of the local database. Once deployed on a local platform, the application is ready to run.

Packaging Applications

A Java EE application is delivered in an Enterprise Archive (EAR) file, a standard Java Archive (JAR) file with an `.ear` extension. Using EAR files and modules makes it possible to assemble a number of different Java EE applications using some of the same components. No extra coding is needed; it is only a matter of assembling (or packaging) various Java EE modules into Java EE EAR files.

An EAR file (see Figure 1–6) contains Java EE modules and deployment descriptors. A *deployment descriptor* is an XML document with an `.xml` extension that describes the deployment settings of an application, a module, or a component. Because deployment descriptor information is declarative, it can be changed without the need to modify the source code. At runtime, the Java EE server reads the deployment descriptor and acts upon the application, module, or component accordingly.

There are two types of deployment descriptors: Java EE and runtime. A *Java EE deployment descriptor* is defined by a Java EE specification and can be used to configure deployment settings on any Java EE-compliant implementation. A *runtime deployment descriptor* is used to configure Java EE implementation-specific parameters. For example, the Sun Java System Application Server Platform Edition 9 runtime deployment descriptor contains information such as the context root of a web application, the mapping of portable names of an application's resources to the server's resources, and Application Server implementation-specific parameters, such as caching directives. The Application Server runtime deployment descriptors are named `sun-`*`moduleType`*`.xml` and are located in the same directory as the Java EE deployment descriptor.

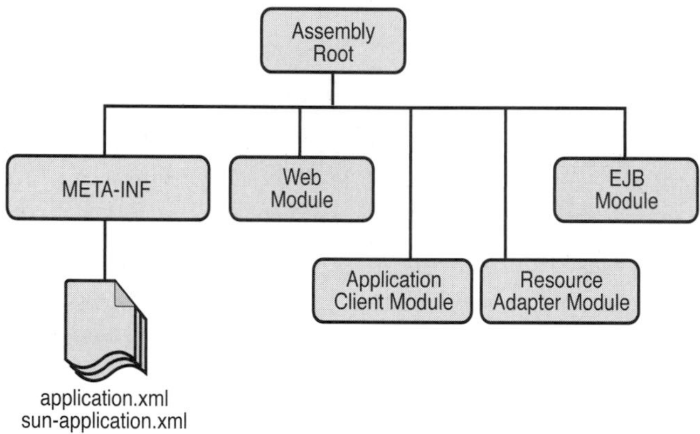

Figure 1–6 EAR File Structure

A *Java EE module* consists of one or more Java EE components for the same container type and one component deployment descriptor of that type. An enterprise bean module deployment descriptor, for example, declares transaction attributes and security authorizations for an enterprise bean. A Java EE module without an application deployment descriptor can be deployed as a *stand-alone* module. The four types of Java EE modules are as follows:

- EJB modules, which contain class files for enterprise beans and an EJB deployment descriptor. EJB modules are packaged as JAR files with a `.jar` extension.
- Web modules, which contain servlet class files, JSP files, supporting class files, GIF and HTML files, and a web application deployment descriptor. Web modules are packaged as JAR files with a `.war` (Web ARchive) extension.

- Application client modules, which contain class files and an application client deployment descriptor. Application client modules are packaged as JAR files with a `.jar` extension.
- Resource adapter modules, which contain all Java interfaces, classes, native libraries, and other documentation, along with the resource adapter deployment descriptor. Together, these implement the Connector architecture (see J2EE Connector Architecture, page 23) for a particular EIS. Resource adapter modules are packaged as JAR files with an `.rar` (resource adapter archive) extension.

Development Roles

Reusable modules make it possible to divide the application development and deployment process into distinct roles so that different people or companies can perform different parts of the process.

The first two roles involve purchasing and installing the Java EE product and tools. After software is purchased and installed, Java EE components can be developed by application component providers, assembled by application assemblers, and deployed by application deployers. In a large organization, each of these roles might be executed by different individuals or teams. This division of labor works because each of the earlier roles outputs a portable file that is the input for a subsequent role. For example, in the application component development phase, an enterprise bean software developer delivers EJB JAR files. In the application assembly role, another developer combines these EJB JAR files into a Java EE application and saves it in an EAR file. In the application deployment role, a system administrator at the customer site uses the EAR file to install the Java EE application into a Java EE server.

The different roles are not always executed by different people. If you work for a small company, for example, or if you are prototyping a sample application, you might perform the tasks in every phase.

Java EE Product Provider

The Java EE product provider is the company that designs and makes available for purchase the Java EE platform APIs, and other features defined in the Java EE specification. Product providers are typically application server vendors who implement the Java EE platform according to the Java EE 5 Platform specification.

Tool Provider

The tool provider is the company or person who creates development, assembly, and packaging tools used by component providers, assemblers, and deployers.

Application Component Provider

The application component provider is the company or person who creates web components, enterprise beans, applets, or application clients for use in Java EE applications.

Enterprise Bean Developer

An enterprise bean developer performs the following tasks to deliver an EJB JAR file that contains the enterprise bean(s):

- Writes and compiles the source code
- Specifies the deployment descriptor
- Packages the `.class` files and deployment descriptor into the EJB JAR file

Web Component Developer

A web component developer performs the following tasks to deliver a WAR file containing the web component(s):

- Writes and compiles servlet source code
- Writes JSP, JavaServer Faces, and HTML files
- Specifies the deployment descriptor
- Packages the `.class`, `.jsp`, and `.html` files and deployment descriptor into the WAR file

Application Client Developer

An application client developer performs the following tasks to deliver a JAR file containing the application client:

- Writes and compiles the source code
- Specifies the deployment descriptor for the client
- Packages the `.class` files and deployment descriptor into the JAR file

Application Assembler

The application assembler is the company or person who receives application modules from component providers and assembles them into a Java EE application EAR file. The assembler or deployer can edit the deployment descriptor directly or can use tools that correctly add XML tags according to interactive selections. A software developer performs the following tasks to deliver an EAR file containing the Java EE application:

- Assembles EJB JAR and WAR files created in the previous phases into a Java EE application (EAR) file
- Specifies the deployment descriptor for the Java EE application
- Verifies that the contents of the EAR file are well formed and comply with the Java EE specification

Application Deployer and Administrator

The application deployer and administrator is the company or person who configures and deploys the Java EE application, administers the computing and networking infrastructure where Java EE applications run, and oversees the runtime environment. Duties include such things as setting transaction controls and security attributes and specifying connections to databases.

During configuration, the deployer follows instructions supplied by the application component provider to resolve external dependencies, specify security settings, and assign transaction attributes. During installation, the deployer moves the application components to the server and generates the container-specific classes and interfaces.

A deployer or system administrator performs the following tasks to install and configure a Java EE application:

- Adds the Java EE application (EAR) file created in the preceding phase to the Java EE server
- Configures the Java EE application for the operational environment by modifying the deployment descriptor of the Java EE application
- Verifies that the contents of the EAR file are well formed and comply with the Java EE specification
- Deploys (installs) the Java EE application EAR file into the Java EE server

Java EE 5 APIs

Figure 1–7 illustrates the availability of the Java EE 5 platform APIs in each Java EE container type. The following sections give a brief summary of the technologies required by the Java EE platform, and the APIs used in Java EE applications.

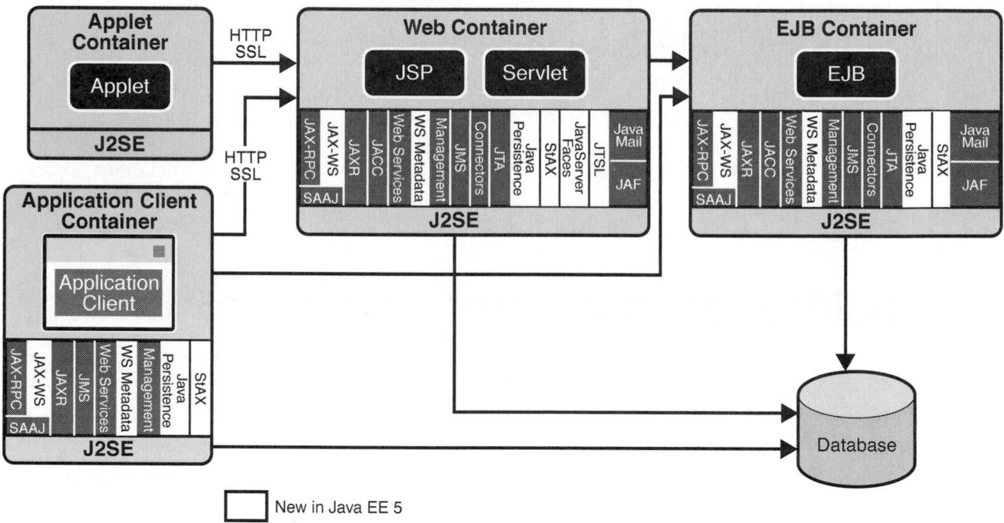

Figure 1–7 Java EE Platform APIs

Enterprise JavaBeans Technology

An Enterprise JavaBeans™ (EJB™) component, or *enterprise bean*, is a body of code having fields and methods to implement modules of business logic. You can think of an enterprise bean as a building block that can be used alone or with other enterprise beans to execute business logic on the Java EE server.

There are two kinds of enterprise beans: session beans and message-driven beans. A *session bean* represents a transient conversation with a client. When the client finishes executing, the session bean and its data are gone. A *message-driven bean* combines features of a session bean and a message listener, allowing a business component to receive messages asynchronously. Commonly, these are Java Message Service (JMS) messages.

In Java EE 5, entity beans have been replaced by Java™ persistence API entities. An entity represents persistent data stored in one row of a database table. If the client terminates, or if the server shuts down, the persistence manager ensures that the entity data is saved.

Java Servlet Technology

Java servlet technology lets you define HTTP-specific servlet classes. A servlet class extends the capabilities of servers that host applications that are accessed by way of a request-response programming model. Although servlets can respond to any type of request, they are commonly used to extend the applications hosted by web servers.

JavaServer Pages Technology

JavaServer Pages™ (JSP™) technology lets you put snippets of servlet code directly into a text-based document. A JSP page is a text-based document that contains two types of text: static data (which can be expressed in any text-based format such as HTML, WML, and XML) and JSP elements, which determine how the page constructs dynamic content.

JavaServer Pages Standard Tag Library

The JavaServer Pages Standard Tag Library (JSTL) encapsulates core functionality common to many JSP applications. Instead of mixing tags from numerous vendors in your JSP applications, you employ a single, standard set of tags. This standardization allows you to deploy your applications on any JSP container that supports JSTL and makes it more likely that the implementation of the tags is optimized.

JSTL has iterator and conditional tags for handling flow control, tags for manipulating XML documents, internationalization tags, tags for accessing databases using SQL, and commonly used functions.

JavaServer Faces

JavaServer Faces technology is a user interface framework for building web applications. The main components of JavaServer Faces technology are as follows:

- A GUI component framework.
- A flexible model for rendering components in different kinds of HTML or different markup languages and technologies. A `Renderer` object generates the markup to render the component and converts the data stored in a model object to types that can be represented in a view.
- A standard `RenderKit` for generating HTML/4.01 markup.

The following features support the GUI components:

- Input validation
- Event handling
- Data conversion between model objects and components
- Managed model object creation
- Page navigation configuration

All this functionality is available using standard Java APIs and XML-based configuration files.

Java Message Service API

The Java Message Service (JMS) API is a messaging standard that allows Java EE application components to create, send, receive, and read messages. It enables distributed communication that is loosely coupled, reliable, and asynchronous.

Java Transaction API

The Java Transaction API (JTA) provides a standard interface for demarcating transactions. The Java EE architecture provides a default auto commit to handle transaction commits and rollbacks. An *auto commit* means that any other applications that are viewing data will see the updated data after each database read or write operation. However, if your application performs two separate database access operations that depend on each other, you will want to use the JTA API to demarcate where the entire transaction, including both operations, begins, rolls back, and commits.

JavaMail API

Java EE applications use the JavaMail™ API to send email notifications. The JavaMail API has two parts: an application-level interface used by the application components to send mail, and a service provider interface. The Java EE platform includes JavaMail with a service provider that allows application components to send Internet mail.

JavaBeans Activation Framework

The JavaBeans Activation Framework (JAF) is included because JavaMail uses it. JAF provides standard services to determine the type of an arbitrary piece of data, encapsulate access to it, discover the operations available on it, and create the appropriate JavaBeans component to perform those operations.

Java API for XML Processing

The Java API for XML Processing (JAXP), part of the Java SE platform, supports the processing of XML documents using Document Object Model (DOM), Simple API for XML (SAX), and Extensible Stylesheet Language Transformations (XSLT). JAXP enables applications to parse and transform XML documents independent of a particular XML processing implementation.

JAXP also provides namespace support, which lets you work with schemas that might otherwise have naming conflicts. Designed to be flexible, JAXP lets you use any XML-compliant parser or XSL processor from within your application and supports the W3C schema. You can find information on the W3C schema at this URL: `http://www.w3.org/XML/Schema`.

Java API for XML Web Services (JAX-WS)

The JAX-WS specification provides support for web services that use the JAXB API for binding XML data to Java objects. The JAX-WS specification defines client APIs for accessing web services as well as techniques for implementing web service endpoints. The Web Services for J2EE specification describes the deployment of JAX-WS-based services and clients. The EJB and servlet specifications also describe aspects of such deployment. It must be possible to deploy JAX-WS-based applications using any of these deployment models.

The JAX-WS specification describes the support for message handlers that can process message requests and responses. In general, these message handlers execute in the same container and with the same privileges and execution context as the JAX-WS client or endpoint component with which they are associated. These message handlers have access to the same JNDI `java:comp/env` namespace as their associated component. Custom serializers and deserializers, if supported, are treated in the same way as message handlers.

Java Architecture for XML Binding (JAXB)

The Java Architecture for XML Binding (JAXB) provides a convenient way to bind an XML schema to a representation in Java language programs. JAXB can be used independently or in combination with JAX-WS, where it provides a standard data binding for web service messages. All Java EE application client containers, web containers, and EJB containers support the JAXB API.

SOAP with Attachments API for Java

The SOAP with Attachments API for Java (SAAJ) is a low-level API on which JAX-WS and JAXR depend. SAAJ enables the production and consumption of messages that conform to the SOAP 1.1 specification and SOAP with Attachments note. Most developers do not use the SAAJ API, instead using the higher-level JAX-WS API.

Java API for XML Registries

The Java API for XML Registries (JAXR) lets you access business and general-purpose registries over the web. JAXR supports the ebXML Registry and Repository standards and the emerging UDDI specifications. By using JAXR, developers can learn a single API and gain access to both of these important registry technologies.

Additionally, businesses can submit material to be shared and search for material that others have submitted. Standards groups have developed schemas for particular kinds of XML documents; two businesses might, for example, agree to use the schema for their industry's standard purchase order form. Because the schema is stored in a standard business registry, both parties can use JAXR to access it.

J2EE Connector Architecture

The J2EE Connector architecture is used by tools vendors and system integrators to create resource adapters that support access to enterprise information systems that can be plugged in to any Java EE product. A *resource adapter* is a software component that allows Java EE application components to access and interact with the underlying resource manager of the EIS. Because a resource adapter is specific to its resource manager, typically there is a different resource adapter for each type of database or enterprise information system.

The J2EE Connector architecture also provides a performance-oriented, secure, scalable, and message-based transactional integration of Java EE-based web services with existing EISs that can be either synchronous or asynchronous. Existing applications and EISs integrated through the J2EE Connector architecture into the Java EE platform can be exposed as XML-based web services by using JAX-WS and Java EE component models. Thus JAX-WS and the J2EE Connector architecture are complementary technologies for enterprise application integration (EAI) and end-to-end business integration.

Java Database Connectivity API

The Java™ Database Connectivity (JDBC) API lets you invoke SQL commands from Java programming language methods. You use the JDBC API in an enterprise bean when you have a session bean access the database. You can also use the JDBC API from a servlet or a JSP page to access the database directly without going through an enterprise bean.

The JDBC API has two parts: an application-level interface used by the application components to access a database, and a service provider interface to attach a JDBC driver to the Java EE platform.

Java Persistence API

The Java™ Persistence API is a Java standards-based solution for persistence. Persistence uses an object-relational mapping approach to bridge the gap between an object oriented model and a relational database. Java Persistence consists of three areas:

- The Java Persistence API
- The query language
- Object/relational mapping metadata

Java Naming and Directory Interface

The Java Naming and Directory Interface™ (JNDI) provides naming and directory functionality, enabling applications to access multiple naming and directory services, including existing naming and directory services such as LDAP, NDS, DNS, and NIS. It provides applications with methods for performing standard directory operations, such as associating attributes with objects and searching for objects using their attributes. Using JNDI, a Java EE application can store and retrieve any type of named Java object, allowing Java EE applications to coexist with many legacy applications and systems.

Java EE naming services provide application clients, enterprise beans, and web components with access to a JNDI naming environment. A *naming environment* allows a component to be customized without the need to access or change the component's source code. A container implements the component's environment and provides it to the component as a JNDI *naming context*.

A Java EE component can locate its environment naming context using JNDI interfaces. A component can create a `javax.naming.InitialContext` object and looks up the environment naming context in `InitialContext` under the name `java:comp/env`. A component's naming environment is stored directly in the environment naming context or in any of its direct or indirect subcontexts.

A Java EE component can access named system-provided and user-defined objects. The names of system-provided objects, such as JTA `UserTransaction` objects, are stored in the environment naming context, `java:comp/env`. The Java EE platform allows a component to name user-defined objects, such as enterprise beans, environment entries, JDBC `DataSource` objects, and message connections. An object should be named within a subcontext of the naming environment according to the type of the object. For example, enterprise beans are named within the subcontext `java:comp/env/ejb`, and JDBC `DataSource` references in the subcontext `java:comp/env/jdbc`.

Java Authentication and Authorization Service

The Java Authentication and Authorization Service (JAAS) provides a way for a Java EE application to authenticate and authorize a specific user or group of users to run it.

JAAS is a Java programming language version of the standard Pluggable Authentication Module (PAM) framework, which extends the Java Platform security architecture to support user-based authorization.

Simplified Systems Integration

The Java EE platform is a platform-independent, full systems integration solution that creates an open marketplace in which every vendor can sell to every customer. Such a marketplace encourages vendors to compete, not by trying to lock customers into their technologies but instead by trying to outdo each other in providing products and services that benefit customers, such as better performance, better tools, or better customer support.

The Java EE 5 APIs enable systems and applications integration through the following:

- Unified application model across tiers with enterprise beans
- Simplified request-and-response mechanism with JSP pages and servlets
- Reliable security model with JAAS
- XML-based data interchange integration with JAXP, SAAJ, and JAX-WS
- Simplified interoperability with the J2EE Connector architecture
- Easy database connectivity with the JDBC API
- Enterprise application integration with message-driven beans and JMS, JTA, and JNDI

Sun Java System Application Server Platform Edition 9

The Sun Java System Application Server Platform Edition 9 is a fully compliant implementation of the Java EE 5 platform. In addition to supporting all the APIs described in the previous sections, the Application Server includes a number of Java EE tools that are not part of the Java EE 5 platform but are provided as a convenience to the developer.

This section briefly summarizes the tools that make up the Application Server, and instructions for starting and stopping the Application Server, starting the Admin Console, and starting and stopping the Java DB database server. Other chapters explain how to use the remaining tools.

Tools

The Application Server contains the tools listed in Table 1–1. Basic usage information for many of the tools appears throughout the tutorial. For detailed information, see the online help in the GUI tools.

Table 1–1 Application Server Tools

Tool	Description
Admin Console	A web-based GUI Application Server administration utility. Used to stop the Application Server and manage users, resources, and applications.
`asadmin`	A command-line Application Server administration utility. Used to start and stop the Application Server and manage users, resources, and applications.
`asant`	A portable command-line build tool that is an extension of the Ant tool developed by the Apache Software Foundation (see `http://ant.apache.org/`). `asant` contains additional tasks that interact with the Application Server administration utility.
`appclient`	A command-line tool that launches the application client container and invokes the client application packaged in the application client JAR file.

Table 1–1 Application Server Tools (Continued)

Tool	Description
`capture-schema`	A command-line tool to extract schema information from a database, producing a schema file that the Application Server can use for container-managed persistence.
`package-appclient`	A command-line tool to package the application client container libraries and JAR files.
Java DB database	A copy of the Java DB database server.
`verifier`	A command-line tool to validate Java EE deployment descriptors.
`xjc`	A command-line tool to transform, or bind, a source XML schema to a set of JAXB content classes in the Java programming language.
`schemagen`	A command-line tool to create a schema file for each namespace referenced in your Java classes.
`wsimport`	A command-line tool to generate JAX-WS portable artifacts for a given WSDL file. After generation, these artifacts can be packaged in a WAR file with the WSDL and schema documents along with the endpoint implementation and then deployed.
`wsgen`	A command-line tool to read a web service endpoint class and generate all the required JAX-WS portable artifacts for web service deployment and invocation.

Starting and Stopping the Application Server

To start the Application Server, open a terminal window or command prompt and execute the following:

```
asadmin start-domain --verbose domain1
```

A *domain* is a set of one or more Application Server instances managed by one administration server. Associated with a domain are the following:

- The Application Server's port number. The default is 8080.
- The administration server's port number. The default is 4848.
- An administration user name and password.

You specify these values when you install the Application Server. The examples in this tutorial assume that you chose the default ports.

With no arguments, the `start-domain` command initiates the default domain, which is domain1. The `--verbose` flag causes all logging and debugging output to appear on the terminal window or command prompt (it will also go into the server log, which is located in `<JAVAEE_HOME>/domains/domain1/logs/server.log`).

Or, on Windows, you can choose:

Programs → Sun Microsystems → Application Server PE → Start Default Server

After the server has completed its startup sequence, you will see the following output:

```
Domain domain1 started.
```

To stop the Application Server, open a terminal window or command prompt and execute:

```
asadmin stop-domain domain1
```

Or, on Windows, choose:

Programs → Sun Microsystems → Application Server PE → Stop Default Server

When the server has stopped you will see the following output:

```
Domain domain1 stopped.
```

Starting the Admin Console

To administer the Application Server and manage users, resources, and Java EE applications, use the Admin Console tool. The Application Server must be running before you invoke the Admin Console. To start the Admin Console, open a browser at the following URL:

```
http://localhost:4848/asadmin/
```

On Windows, from the Start menu, choose:

Programs → Sun Microsystems → Application Server PE → Admin Console

Starting and Stopping the Java DB Database Server

The Application Server includes the Java DB database.

To start the Java DB database server, open a terminal window or command prompt and execute:

```
asadmin start-database
```

On Windows, from the Start menu, choose:

Programs → Sun Microsystem → Application Server PE → Start Java DB

To stop the Java DB server, open a terminal window or command prompt and execute:

```
asadmin stop-database
```

On Windows, from the Start menu, choose:

Programs → Sun Microsystems → Application Server PE → Stop Java DB

For information about the Java DB database included with the Application Server, see the Apache Derby Project web site at `http://db.apache.org/derby/`.

Debugging Java EE Applications

This section describes how to determine what is causing an error in your application deployment or execution.

Using the Server Log

One way to debug applications is to look at the server log in *<JAVAEE_HOME>*`/domains/domain1/logs/server.log`. The log contains output from the Application Server and your applications. You can log messages from any Java class in your application with `System.out.println` and the Java Logging APIs (documented at `http://java.sun.com/j2se/1.5.0/docs/guide/logging/index.html`) and from web components with the `ServletContext.log` method.

If you start the Application Server with the `--verbose` flag, all logging and debugging output will appear on the terminal window or command prompt and the server log. If you start the Application Server in the background, debugging information is only available in the log. You can view the server log with a text editor or with the Admin Console log viewer. To use the log viewer:

1. Select the Application Server node.
2. Select the Logging tab.
3. Click the Open Log Viewer button. The log viewer will open and display the last 40 entries.

If you wish to display other entries:

1. Click the Modify Search button.
2. Specify any constraints on the entries you want to see.
3. Click the Search button at the bottom of the log viewer.

Using a Debugger

The Application Server supports the Java Platform Debugger Architecture (JPDA). With JPDA, you can configure the Application Server to communicate debugging information using a socket. To debug an application using a debugger:

1. Enable debugging in the Application Server using the Admin Console:
   a. Select the Application Server node.
   b. Select the JVM Settings tab. The default debug options are set to:
      ```
      -Xdebug -Xrunjdwp:transport=dt_socket,server=y,
       suspend=n,address=9009
      ```
      As you can see, the default debugger socket port is 9009. You can change it to a port not in use by the Application Server or another service.
   c. Check the Enabled box of the Debug field.
   d. Click the Save button.
2. Stop the Application Server and then restart it.

Part One: The Web Tier

Part One explores the technologies in the web tier.

2

Getting Started with Web Applications

A web application is a dynamic extension of a web or application server. There are two types of web applications:

- *Presentation-oriented*: A presentation-oriented web application generates interactive web pages containing various types of markup language (HTML, XML, and so on) and dynamic content in response to requests. Chapters 3 through 14 cover how to develop presentation-oriented web applications.
- *Service-oriented*: A service-oriented web application implements the endpoint of a web service. Presentation-oriented applications are often clients of service-oriented web applications. Chapters 15 and 18 cover how to develop service-oriented web applications.

In the Java 2 platform, *web components* provide the dynamic extension capabilities for a web server. Web components are either Java servlets, JSP pages, or web service endpoints. The interaction between a web client and a web application is illustrated in Figure 2–1. The client sends an HTTP request to the web server. A web server that implements Java Servlet and JavaServer Pages technology converts the request into an `HTTPServletRequest` object. This object is delivered to a web component, which can interact with JavaBeans components or a database to generate dynamic content. The web component can then generate an `HTTPServletResponse` or it can pass the request to another web component. Eventually a web component generates a `HTTPServletResponse` object. The web server converts this object to an HTTP response and returns it to the client.

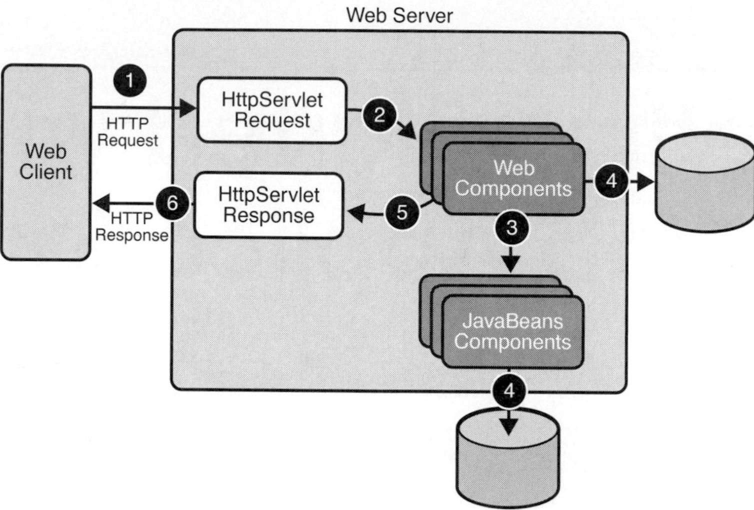

Figure 2–1 Java Web Application Request Handling

Servlets are Java programming language classes that dynamically process requests and construct responses. *JSP pages* are text-based documents that execute as servlets but allow a more natural approach to creating static content. Although servlets and JSP pages can be used interchangeably, each has its own strengths. Servlets are best suited for service-oriented applications (web service endpoints are implemented as servlets) and the control functions of a presentation-oriented application, such as dispatching requests and handling nontextual data. JSP pages are more appropriate for generating text-based markup such as HTML, Scalable Vector Graphics (SVG), Wireless Markup Language (WML), and XML.

Since the introduction of Java Servlet and JSP technology, additional Java technologies and frameworks for building interactive web applications have been developed. Figure 2–2 illustrates these technologies and their relationships.

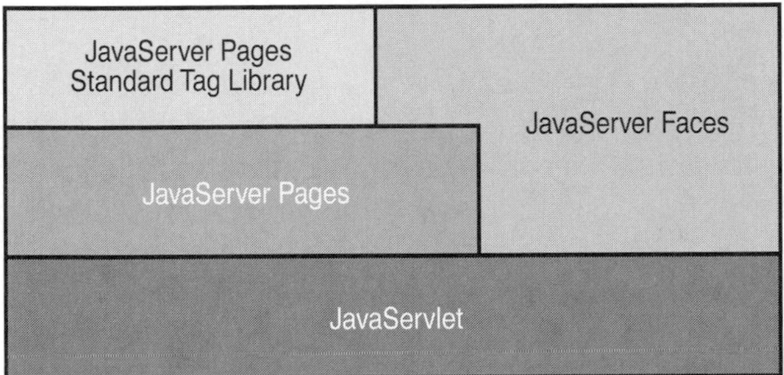

Figure 2–2 Java Web Application Technologies

Notice that Java Servlet technology is the foundation of all the web application technologies, so you should familiarize yourself with the material in Chapter 3 even if you do not intend to write servlets. Each technology adds a level of abstraction that makes web application prototyping and development faster and the web applications themselves more maintainable, scalable, and robust.

Web components are supported by the services of a runtime platform called a *web container.* A web container provides services such as request dispatching, security, concurrency, and life-cycle management. It also gives web components access to APIs such as naming, transactions, and email.

Certain aspects of web application behavior can be configured when the application is installed, or *deployed*, to the web container. The configuration information is maintained in a text file in XML format called a *web application deployment descriptor* (DD). A DD must conform to the schema described in the Java Servlet Specification.

This chapter gives a brief overview of the activities involved in developing web applications. First we summarize the web application life cycle. Then we describe how to package and deploy very simple web applications on the Application Server. We move on to configuring web applications and discuss how to specify the most commonly used configuration parameters. We then introduce an example—Duke's Bookstore—that we use to illustrate all the Java EE web-tier technologies, and we describe how to set up the shared components of this example. Finally we discuss how to access databases from web applications and set up the database resources needed to run Duke's Bookstore.

Web Application Life Cycle

A web application consists of web components, static resource files such as images, and helper classes and libraries. The web container provides many supporting services that enhance the capabilities of web components and make them easier to develop. However, because a web application must take these services into account, the process for creating and running a web application is different from that of traditional stand-alone Java classes. The process for creating, deploying, and executing a web application can be summarized as follows:

1. Develop the web component code.
2. Develop the web application deployment descriptor.
3. Compile the web application components and helper classes referenced by the components.
4. Optionally package the application into a deployable unit.
5. Deploy the application into a web container.
6. Access a URL that references the web application.

Developing web component code is covered in the later chapters. Steps 2 through 4 are expanded on in the following sections and illustrated with a Hello, World-style presentation-oriented application. This application allows a user to enter a name into an HTML form (Figure 2–3) and then displays a greeting after the name is submitted (Figure 2–4).

The Hello application contains two web components that generate the greeting and the response. This chapter discusses two versions of the application: a JSP version called `hello1`, in which the components are implemented by two JSP pages (`index.jsp` and `response.jsp`) and a servlet version called `hello2`, in which the components are implemented by two servlet classes (`GreetingServlet.java` and `ResponseServlet.java`). The two versions are used to illustrate tasks involved in packaging, deploying, configuring, and running an application that contains web components. The section About the Examples (page xxxiv) explains how to get the code for these examples. After you install the tutorial bundle, the source code for the examples is in the following directories:

- `<INSTALL>/javaeetutorial5/examples/web/hello1/`
- `<INSTALL>/javaeetutorial5/examples/web/hello2/`

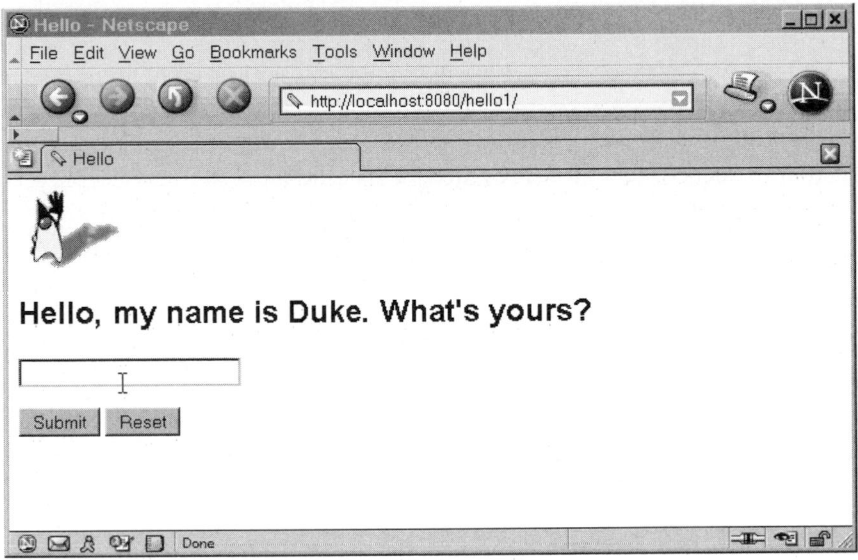

Figure 2–3 Greeting Form

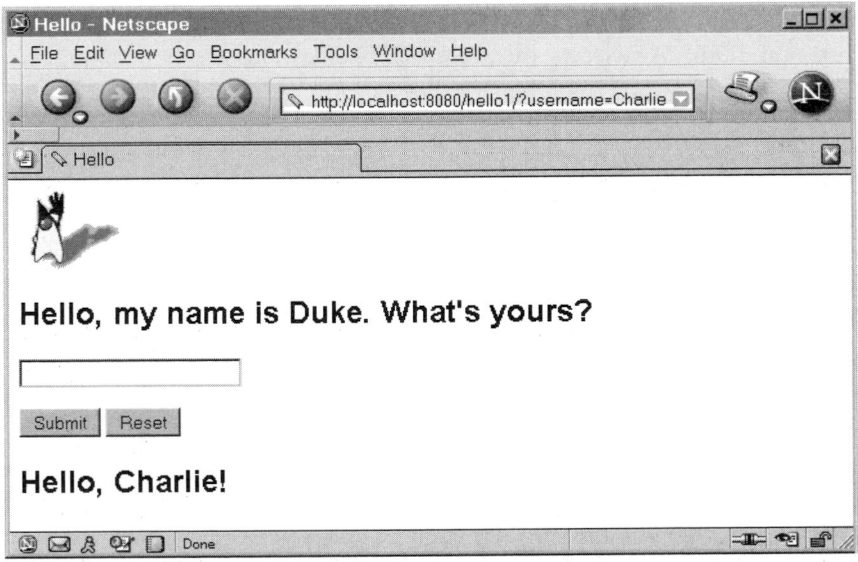

Figure 2–4 Response

Web Modules

In the Java EE architecture, web components and static web content files such as images are called *web resources*. A *web module* is the smallest deployable and usable unit of web resources. A Java EE web module corresponds to a *web application* as defined in the Java Servlet specification.

In addition to web components and web resources, a web module can contain other files:

- Server-side utility classes (database beans, shopping carts, and so on). Often these classes conform to the JavaBeans component architecture.
- Client-side classes (applets and utility classes).

A web module has a specific structure. The top-level directory of a web module is the *document root* of the application. The document root is where JSP pages, *client-side* classes and archives, and static web resources, such as images, are stored.

The document root contains a subdirectory named `/WEB-INF/`, which contains the following files and directories:

- `web.xml`: The web application deployment descriptor
- Tag library descriptor files (see Tag Library Descriptors, page 229)
- `classes`: A directory that contains *server-side classes*: servlets, utility classes, and JavaBeans components
- `tags`: A directory that contains tag files, which are implementations of tag libraries (see Tag File Location, page 214)
- `lib`: A directory that contains JAR archives of libraries called by server-side classes

If your web module does not contain any servlets, filter, or listener components then it does not need a web application deployment descriptor. In other words, if your web module only contains JSP pages and static files then you are not required to include a `web.xml` file. The `hello1` example, first discussed in Packaging Web Modules (page 39), contains only JSP pages and images and therefore does not include a deployment descriptor.

You can also create application-specific subdirectories (that is, package directories) in either the document root or the `/WEB-INF/classes/` directory.

A web module can be deployed as an unpacked file structure or can be packaged in a JAR file known as a web archive (WAR) file. Because the contents and use of WAR files differ from those of JAR files, WAR file names use a `.war` extension. The web module just described is portable; you can deploy it into any web container that conforms to the Java Servlet Specification.

To deploy a WAR on the Application Server, the file must also contain a runtime deployment descriptor. The runtime deployment descriptor is an XML file that contains information such as the context root of the web application and the mapping of the portable names of an application's resources to the Application Server's resources. The Application Server web application runtime DD is named `sun-web.xml` and is located in `/WEB-INF/` along with the web application DD. The structure of a web module that can be deployed on the Application Server is shown in Figure 2–5.

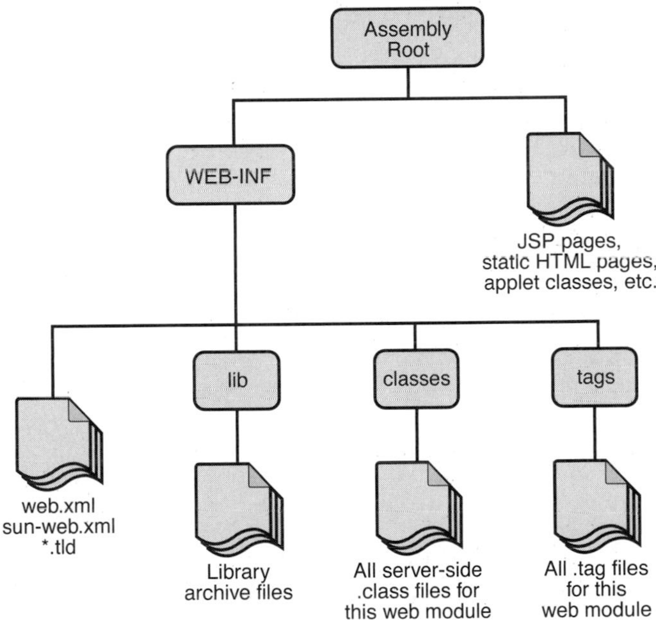

Figure 2–5 Web Module Structure

Packaging Web Modules

A web module must be packaged into a WAR in certain deployment scenarios and whenever you want to distribute the web module. You package a web module into a WAR by executing the `jar` command in a directory laid out in the format of a web module, by using the `ant` utility, or by using the IDE tool of your choice. This tutorial shows you how to use NetBeans 5.5 or `ant` to build, package, and deploy the sample applications.

To build the `hello1` application with NetBeans 5.5, follow these instructions:

1. In NetBeans 5.5, select File→Open Project.
2. In the Open Project dialog, navigate to:

   `<INSTALL>/javaeetutorial5/examples/web/`

3. Select the `hello1` folder.
4. Select the Open as Main Project checkbox.
5. Click Open Project Folder.
6. In the Projects tab, right-click the `hello1` project and select Build Project.

To build the `hello1` application using the `ant` utility, follow these steps:

1. In a terminal window, go to *<INSTALL>*`/javaeetutorial5/examples/web/hello1/`.
2. Run `ant`. This target will spawn any necessary compilations, copy files to the *<INSTALL>*`/javaeetutorial5/examples/web/hello1/build/` directory, create the WAR file, and copy it to the *<INSTALL>*`/javaeetutorial5/examples/web/hello1/dist/` directory.

Deploying a WAR File

You can deploy a WAR file to the Application Server in a few ways:

- Copying the WAR into the *<JavaEE_HOME>*`/domains/domain1/autodeploy/` directory.
- Using the Admin Console.
- By running `asadmin` or `ant` to deploy the WAR.

All these methods are described briefly in this chapter; however, throughout the tutorial, we use `ant` and NetBeans 5.5 for packaging and deploying.

Setting the Context Root

A *context root* identifies a web application in a Java EE server. You specify the context root when you deploy a web module. A context root must start with a forward slash (`/`) and end with a string.

In a packaged web module for deployment on the Application Server, the context root is stored in `sun-web.xml`.

To edit the context root, do the following:

1. Expand your project tree in the Projects pane of NetBeans 5.5.
2. Expand the Web Pages and WEB-INF nodes of your project.
3. Double-click `sun-web.xml`.
4. In the editor pane, click Edit As XML.
5. Edit the context root, which is enclosed by the `context-root` element.

Deploying a Packaged Web Module

If you have deployed the `hello1` application, before proceeding with this section, undeploy the application by following one of the procedures described in Undeploying Web Modules (page 45).

Deploying with the Admin Console

1. Expand the Applications node.
2. Select the Web Applications node.
3. Click the Deploy button.
4. Select the radio button labeled "Package file to be uploaded to the Application Server."
5. Type the full path to the WAR file (or click on Browse to find it), and then click the OK button.
6. Click Next.
7. Type the application name.
8. Type the context root.
9. Select the Enabled box.
10. Click the Finish button.

Deploying with asadmin

To deploy a WAR with `asadmin`, open a terminal window or command prompt and execute

```
asadmin deploy full-path-to-war-file
```

Deploying with ant

To deploy a WAR with `ant`, open a terminal window or command prompt in the directory where you built and packaged the WAR, and execute

```
ant deploy
```

Deploying with NetBeans 5.5

To deploy a WAR with NetBeans 5.5, do the following:

1. In NetBeans 5.5, select File→Open Project.
2. In the Open Project dialog, navigate to your project and open it.
3. In the Projects tab, right-click the project and select Deploy Project.

Testing Deployed Web Modules

Now that the web module is deployed, you can view it by opening the application in a web browser. By default, the application is deployed to host `localhost` on port 8080. The context root of the web application is `hello1`.

To test the application, follow these steps:

1. Open a web browser.
2. Enter the following URL in the web address box:

   `http://localhost:8080/hello1`
3. Enter your name, and click Submit.

The application should display the name you submitted as shown in Figure 2–3 and Figure 2–4.

Listing Deployed Web Modules

The Application Server provides two ways to view the deployed web modules:

- Admin Console

  a. Open the URL `http://localhost:4848/asadmin` in a browser.

  b. Expand the nodes Applications→Web Applications.

- `asadmin`
  a. Execute

     `asadmin list-components`

Updating Web Modules

A typical iterative development cycle involves deploying a web module and then making changes to the application components. To update a deployed web module, you must do the following:

1. Recompile any modified classes.
2. If you have deployed a packaged web module, update any modified components in the WAR.
3. Redeploy the module.
4. Reload the URL in the client.

Updating a Packaged Web Module

This section describes how to update the `hello1` web module that you packaged.

First, change the greeting in the file `<INSTALL>/javaeetutorial5/examples/web/hello1/web/index.jsp` to

```
<h2>Hi, my name is Duke. What's yours?</h2>
```

To update the project in NetBeans 5.5:

- Right-click on the project and select Build Project.
- Right-click on the project and select Deploy Project.

To update the project using the Ant build tool:

- Run `ant` to copy the modified JSP page into the `build` directory.
  - Run `ant deploy` to deploy the WAR file.

To view the modified module, reload the URL in the browser.

You should see the screen in Figure 2–6 in the browser.

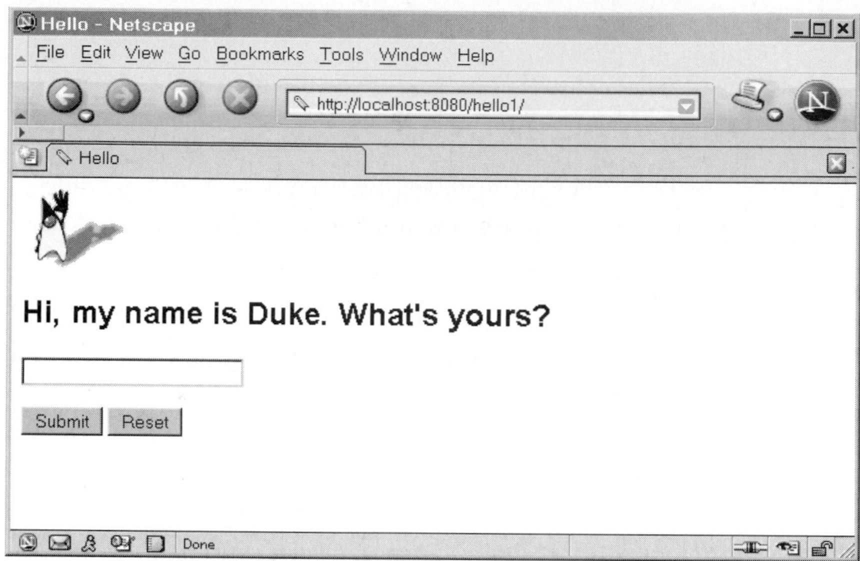

Figure 2–6 New Greeting

Dynamic Reloading

If dynamic reloading is enabled, you do not have to redeploy an application or module when you change its code or deployment descriptors. All you have to do is copy the changed JSP or class files into the deployment directory for the application or module. The deployment directory for a web module named `context_root` is `<JavaEE_HOME>/domains/domain1/applications/j2ee-modules/context_root`. The server checks for changes periodically and redeploys the application, automatically and dynamically, with the changes.

This capability is useful in a development environment, because it allows code changes to be tested quickly. Dynamic reloading is not recommended for a production environment, however, because it may degrade performance. In addition, whenever a reload is done, the sessions at that time become invalid and the client must restart the session.

To enable dynamic reloading, use the Admin Console:

1. Select the Applications Server node.
2. Select the Advanced tab.

3. Check the Reload Enabled box to enable dynamic reloading.
4. Enter a number of seconds in the Reload Poll Interval field to set the interval at which applications and modules are checked for code changes and dynamically reloaded.
5. Click the Save button.

In addition, to load new servlet files or reload deployment descriptor changes, you must do the following:

1. Create an empty file named `.reload` at the root of the module:

   `<JavaEE_HOME>/domains/domain1/applications/j2ee-modules/context_root/.reload`

2. Explicitly update the `.reload` file's time stamp each time you make these changes. On UNIX, execute

   ```
   touch .reload
   ```

For JSP pages, changes are reloaded automatically at a frequency set in the Reload Poll Interval field. To disable dynamic reloading of JSP pages, set the Reload Poll Interval field value to –1.

Undeploying Web Modules

You can undeploy web modules in four ways:

- NetBeans 5.5
  a. Ensure the Sun Java System Application Server is running.
  b. In the Runtime window, expand the Sun Java System Application Server instance and the node containing the application or module.
  c. Right-click the application or module and choose Undeploy.
- Admin Console
  a. Open the URL `http://localhost:4848/asadmin` in a browser.
  b. Expand the Applications node.
  c. Select Web Applications.
  d. Click the checkbox next to the module you wish to undeploy.
  e. Click the Undeploy button.
- `asadmin`
  a. Execute

     ```
     asadmin undeploy context_root
     ```

- `ant`
    a. In the directory where you built and packaged the WAR, execute
    ```
    ant undeploy
    ```

Configuring Web Applications

Web applications are configured via elements contained in the web application deployment descriptor.

The following sections give a brief introduction to the web application features you will usually want to configure. A number of security parameters can be specified; these are covered in Securing Web Applications (page 987).

In the following sections, examples demonstrate procedures for configuring the Hello, World application. If Hello, World does not use a specific configuration feature, the section gives references to other examples that illustrate how to specify the deployment descriptor element.

Mapping URLs to Web Components

When a request is received by the web container it must determine which web component should handle the request. It does so by mapping the URL path contained in the request to a web application and a web component. A URL path contains the context root and an alias:

```
http://host:port/context_root/alias
```

Setting the Component Alias

The *alias* identifies the web component that should handle a request. The alias path must start with a forward slash (/) and end with a string or a wildcard expression with an extension (for example, `*.jsp`). Since web containers automatically map an alias that ends with `*.jsp`, you do not have to specify an alias for a JSP page unless you wish to refer to the page by a name other than its file name.

The `hello2` application has two servlets that need to be mapped in the `web.xml` file. You can edit a web application's `web.xml` file in NetBeans 5.5 by doing the following:

1. In NetBeans 5.5, select File→Open Project.
2. In the Open Project dialog, navigate to:
   `<INSTALL>/javaeetutorial5/examples/web/`
3. Select the `hello2` folder.
4. Select the Open as Main Project checkbox.
5. Click Open Project Folder.
6. Expand the project tree in the Projects pane.
7. Expand the Web pages node and then the WEB-INF node in the project tree.
8. Double-click the `web.xml` file inside the WEB-INF node.

The following steps detail how we made the necessary edits to the `web.xml` file, including how to set the display name and how to map the servlet components. Because we've already made the edits, you can just use the steps to view the settings we've made.

To set the display name:

1. Click General at the top of the editor to open the general view.
2. Enter `hello2` in the Display Name field.

To perform the servlet mappings:

1. Click Servlets at the top of the editor to open the servlets view.
2. Click Add Servlet.
3. In the Add Servlet dialog, enter `GreetingServlet` in the Servlet Name field.
4. Enter `servlets.GreetingServlet` in the Servlet Class field.
5. Enter `/greeting` in the URL Pattern field.
6. Click OK.
7. Repeat the preceding steps, except enter `ResponseServlet` as the servlet name, `servlets.ResponseServlet` as the servlet class, and `/response` as the URL pattern.

If you are not using NetBeans 5.5, you can add these settings using a text editor.

To package the example with NetBeans 5.5, do the following:

1. In NetBeans 5.5, select File→Open Project.
2. In the Open Project dialog, navigate to:
   `<INSTALL>/javaeetutorial5/examples/web/`
3. Select the `hello2` folder.
4. Select the Open as Main Project checkbox.
5. Click Open Project Folder.
6. In the Projects tab, right-click the `hello2` project and select Build Project.

To package the example with the `ant` utility, do the following:

1. In a terminal window, go to `<INSTALL>/javaeetutorial5/examples/web/hello2/`.
2. Run `ant`. This target will build the WAR file and copy it to the `<INSTALL>/javaeetutorial5/examples/web/hello2/dist/` directory.

To deploy the example using NetBeans 5.5, right-click on the project in the Projects pane and select Deploy Project.

To deploy the example using `ant`, run `ant deploy`. The deploy target in this case gives you an incorrect URL to run the application. To run the application, please use the URL shown at the end of this section.

To run the application, first deploy the web module, and then open the URL `http://localhost:8080/hello2/greeting` in a browser.

Declaring Welcome Files

The *welcome files* mechanism allows you to specify a list of files that the web container will use for appending to a request for a URL (called a *valid partial request)* that is not mapped to a web component.

For example, suppose you define a welcome file `welcome.html`. When a client requests a URL such as *`host:port/webapp/directory`*, where *`directory`* is not mapped to a servlet or JSP page, the file *`host:port/webapp/directory/`*`welcome.html` is returned to the client.

If a web container receives a valid partial request, the web container examines the welcome file list and appends to the partial request each welcome file in the order specified and checks whether a static resource or servlet in the WAR is mapped to that request URL. The web container then sends the request to the first resource in the WAR that matches.

If no welcome file is specified, the Application Server will use a file named `index.`*XXX*, where *XXX* can be `html` or `jsp`, as the default welcome file. If there is no welcome file and no file named `index.`*XXX*, the Application Server returns a directory listing.

To specify a welcome file in the web application deployment descriptor using NetBeans 5.5, do the following:

1. Open the project if you haven't already.
2. Expand the project's node in the Projects pane.
3. Expand the Web Pages node and then the WEB-INF node.
4. Double-click `web.xml`.
5. Do one of the following, making sure that the JSP pages you specify are actually included in the WAR file:
   a. Click Pages at the top of the editor pane and enter the names of the JSP pages that act as welcome files in the Welcome Files field.
   b. Click XML at the top of the editor pane, specify the JSP pages using `welcome-file` elements and include these elements inside a `welcome-file-list` element. The `welcome-file` element defines the JSP page to be used as the welcome page.

The example discussed in Encapsulating Reusable Content Using Tag Files (page 212) has a welcome file.

Setting Initialization Parameters

The web components in a web module share an object that represents their application context (see Accessing the Web Context, page 88). You can pass initialization parameters to the context or to a web component.

To add a context parameter using NetBeans 5.5, do the following:

1. Open the project if you haven't already.
2. Expand the project's node in the Projects pane.
3. Expand the Web Pages node and then the WEB-INF node.
4. Double-click `web.xml`.
5. Click General at the top of the editor pane.

6. Select the Context Parameters node.
7. Click Add.
8. In the Add Context Parameter dialog, do the following:
   a. Enter the name that specifies the context object in the Param Name field.
   b. Enter the parameter to pass to the context object in the Param Value field.
   c. Click OK.

Alternatively, you can edit the XML of the `web.xml` directly by clicking XML at the top of the editor pane and using the following elements to add a context parameter:

- A `param-name` element that specifies the context object.
- A `param-value` element that specifies the parameter to pass to the context object.
- A `context-param` element that encloses the previous two elements.

For a sample context parameter, see the example discussed in The Example JSP Pages (page 101).

To add a web component initialization parameter using NetBeans 5.5, do the following:

1. Open the project if you haven't already.
2. Expand the project's node in the Projects pane.
3. Expand the Web Pages node and then the WEB-INF node.
4. Double-click `web.xml`.
5. Click Servlets at the top of the editor pane.
6. After entering the servlet's name, class, and URL pattern, click the Add button under the Initialization Parameters table.
7. In the Add Initialization Parameter dialog:
   a. Enter the name of the parameter in the Param Name field.
   b. Enter the parameter's value in the Param Value Field.
   c. Click OK.

Alternatively, you can edit the XML of the `web.xml` file directly by clicking XML at the top of the editor pane and using the following elements to add a context parameter:

- A `param-name` element that specifies the name of the initialization parameter
- A `param-value` element that specifies the value of the initialization parameter.
- An `init-param` element that encloses the previous two elements.

Mapping Errors to Error Screens

When an error occurs during execution of a web application, you can have the application display a specific error screen according to the type of error. In particular, you can specify a mapping between the status code returned in an HTTP response or a Java programming language exception returned by any web component (see Handling Errors, page 66) and any type of error screen.

To set up error mappings using NetBeans 5.5, do the following:

1. Open the project if you haven't already.
2. Expand the project's node in the Projects pane.
3. Expand the Web Pages node and then the WEB-INF node.
4. Double click `web.xml`.
5. Click Pages at the top of the editor pane.
6. Expand the Error Pages node.
7. Click Add.
8. In the Add Error Page dialog:
   a. Click Browse to locate the page that you want to act as the error page.
   b. Enter the HTTP status code that will cause the error page to be opened in the Error Code field.
   c. Enter the exception that will cause the error page to load in the Exception Type field.
   d. Click OK.

Alternatively, you can click XML at the top of the editor pane and enter the error page mapping by hand using the following elements:

- An `exception-type` element specifying either the exception or the HTTP status code that will cause the error page to be opened.
- A `location` element that specifies the name of a web resource to be invoked when the status code or exception is returned. The name should have a leading forward slash (`/`).
- An `error-page` element that encloses the previous two elements.

You can have multiple `error-page` elements in your deployment descriptor. Each one of the elements identifies a different error that causes an error page to open. This error page can be the same for any number of `error-page` elements.

Note: You can also define error screens for a JSP page contained in a WAR. If error screens are defined for both the WAR and a JSP page, the JSP page's error page takes precedence. See Handling Errors (page 109).

For a sample error page mapping, see the example discussed in The Example Servlets (page 60).

Declaring Resource References

If your web component uses objects such as enterprise beans, data sources, or web services, you use Java EE annotations to inject these resources into your application. Annotations eliminate a lot of the boilerplate lookup code and configuration elements that previous versions of Java EE required.

Although resource injection using annotations can be more convenient for the developer, there are some restrictions from using it in web applications. First, you can only inject resources into container-managed objects. This is because a container must have control over the creation of a component so that it can perform the injection into a component. As a result, you cannot inject resources into objects such as simple JavaBeans components. However, JavaServer Faces managed beans are managed by the container; therefore, they can accept resource injections.

Additionally, JSP pages cannot accept resource injections. This is because the information represented by annotations must be available at deployment time, but the JSP page is compiled after that; therefore, the annotation will not be seen when it is needed. Those components that can accept resource injections are listed in Table 2–1.

This section describes how to use a couple of the annotations supported by a servlet container to inject resources. Chapter 25 describes how web applications use annotations supported by the Java Persistence API. Chapter 30 describes how to use annotations to specify information about securing web applications.

Table 2–1 Web Components That Accept Resource Injections

Component	Interface/Class
Servlets	javax.servlet.Servlet
Servlet Filters	javax.servlet.ServletFilter
Event Listeners	javax.servlet.ServletContextListener javax.servlet.ServletContextAttributeListener javax.servlet.ServletRequestListener javax.servlet.ServletRequestAttributeListener javax.servlet.http.HttpSessionListener javax.servlet.http.HttpSessionAttributeListener javax.servlet.http.HttpSessionBindingListener
Taglib Listeners	same as above
Taglib Tag Handlers	javax.servlet.jsp.tagext.JspTag
Managed Beans	Plain Old Java Objects

Declaring a Reference to a Resource

The @Resource annotation is used to declare a reference to a resource such as a data source, an enterprise bean, or an environment entry. This annotation is equivalent to declaring a resource-ref element in the deployment descriptor.

The @Resource annotation is specified on a class, method or field. The container is responsible for injecting references to resources declared by the @Resource annotation and mapping it to the proper JNDI resources. In the following example, the @Resource annotation is used to inject a data source into a component that needs to make a connection to the data source, as is done when using JDBC technology to access a relational database:

```
@Resource javax.sql.DataSource catalogDS;
public getProductsByCategory() {
  // get a connection and execute the query
  Connection conn = catalogDS.getConnection();
  ..
}
```

The container injects this data source prior to the component being made available to the application. The data source JNDI mapping is inferred from the field name `catalogDS` and the type, `javax.sql.DataSource`.

If you have multiple resources that you need to inject into one component, you need to use the `@Resources` annotation to contain them, as shown by the following example:

```
@Resources ({
  @Resource (name="myDB" type=java.sql.DataSource),
  @Resource(name="myMQ" type=javax.jms.ConnectionFactory)
})
```

The web application examples in this tutorial use the Java Persistence API to access relational databases. This API does not require you to explicitly create a connection to a data source. Therefore, the examples do not use the `@Resource` annotation to inject a data source. However, this API supports the `@PersistenceUnit` and `@PersistenceContext` annotations for injecting `EntityManagerFactory` and `EntityManager` instances, respectively. Chapter 25 describes these annotations and the use of the Java Persistence API in web applications.

Declaring a Reference to a Web Service

The `@WebServiceRef` annotation provides a reference to a web service. The following example shows uses the `@WebServiceRef` annotation to declare a reference to a web service. WebServiceRef uses the wsdlLocation element to specify the URI of the deployed service's WSDL file:

```
...
import javax.xml.ws.WebServiceRef;
...
public class ResponseServlet extends HTTPServlet {
@WebServiceRef(wsdlLocation=
  "http://localhost:8080/helloservice/hello?wsdl")
static HelloService service;
```

Duke's Bookstore Examples

In Chapters 3 through 14 a common example—Duke's Bookstore—is used to illustrate the elements of Java Servlet technology, JavaServer Pages technology, the JSP Standard Tag Library, and JavaServer Faces technology. The example emulates a simple online shopping application. It provides a book catalog from which users can select books and add them to a shopping cart. Users can view and modify the shopping cart. When users are finished shopping, they can purchase the books in the cart.

The Duke's Bookstore examples share common classes and a database schema. These files are located in the directory *<INSTALL>*/javaeetutorial5/examples/web/bookstore/. The common classes are packaged into a JAR. Each of the Duke's Bookstore examples must include this JAR file in their WAR files. The process that builds and packages each application also builds and packages the common JAR file and includes it in the example WAR file.

The next section describes how to create the bookstore database tables and resources required to run the examples.

Accessing Databases from Web Applications

Data that is shared between web components and is persistent between invocations of a web application is usually maintained in a database. To maintain a catalog of books, the Duke's Bookstore examples described in Chapters 3 through 14 use the Java DB database included with the Application Server.

To access the data in a database, web applications use the new Java Persistence API (see chapter 24). See chapter 25 to learn how the Duke's Bookstore applications use this API to access the book data.

To run the Duke's Bookstore applications, you need to first populate the database with the book data and create a data source in the application server. The rest of this section explains how to perform these tasks.

Populating the Example Database

When you deploy any of the Duke's Bookstore applications using `ant deploy`, the database is automatically populated at the same time. If you want to populate the database separately from the deploy task or are using NetBeans 5.5 to deploy the application, follow these steps:

1. In a terminal window, go to the `books` directory or any one of the `bookstore1` through `bookstore6` example directories.
2. Start the Java DB database server. For instructions, see Starting and Stopping the Java DB Database Server (page 29). You don't have to do this if you are using NetBeans 5.5. It starts the database server automatically.
3. Run `ant create-tables`. This task runs a command to read the file `tutorial.sql` and execute the SQL commands contained in the file.
4. At the end of the processing, you should see the following output:

```
...
[sql] 185 of 185 SQL statements executed successfully
```

When you are running `create-tables`, don't worry if you see a message that an SQL statement failed. This usually happens the first time you run the command because it always tries to delete an existing database table first before it creates a new one. The first time through, there is no table yet, of course.

Creating a Data Source in the Application Server

A `DataSource` object has a set of properties that identify and describe the real world data source that it represents. These properties include information such as the location of the database server, the name of the database, the network protocol to use to communicate with the server, and so on.

Data sources in the Application Server implement connection pooling. To define the Duke's Bookstore data source, you use the installed Derby connection pool named DerbyPool.

You create the data source using the Application Server Admin Console, following this procedure:

1. Expand the Resources node.
2. Expand the JDBC node.
3. Select the JDBC Resources node.
4. Click the New... button.
5. Type `jdbc/BookDB` in the JNDI Name field.
6. Choose `DerbyPool` for the Pool Name.
7. Click OK.

Further Information

For more information about web applications, refer to the following:

- Java Servlet specification:
  `http://java.sun.com/products/servlet/download.html#specs`
- The Java Servlet web site:
  `http://java.sun.com/products/servlet`

3

Java Servlet Technology

As soon as the web began to be used for delivering services, service providers recognized the need for dynamic content. Applets, one of the earliest attempts toward this goal, focused on using the client platform to deliver dynamic user experiences. At the same time, developers also investigated using the server platform for this purpose. Initially, Common Gateway Interface (CGI) scripts were the main technology used to generate dynamic content. Although widely used, CGI scripting technology has a number of shortcomings, including platform dependence and lack of scalability. To address these limitations, Java servlet technology was created as a portable way to provide dynamic, user-oriented content.

What Is a Servlet?

A *servlet* is a Java programming language class that is used to extend the capabilities of servers that host applications access via a request-response programming model. Although servlets can respond to any type of request, they are commonly used to extend the applications hosted by web servers. For such applications, Java Servlet technology defines HTTP-specific servlet classes.

The `javax.servlet` and `javax.servlet.http` packages provide interfaces and classes for writing servlets. All servlets must implement the `Servlet` interface, which defines life-cycle methods. When implementing a generic service, you can use or extend the GenericServlet class provided with the Java Servlet API. The HttpServlet class provides methods, such as doGet and doPost, for handling HTTP-specific services.

This chapter focuses on writing servlets that generate responses to HTTP requests.

The Example Servlets

This chapter uses the Duke's Bookstore application to illustrate the tasks involved in programming servlets. Table 3–1 lists the servlets that handle each bookstore function. Each programming task is illustrated by one or more servlets. For example, BookDetailsServlet illustrates how to handle HTTP GET requests, BookDetailsServlet and CatalogServlet show how to construct responses, and CatalogServlet illustrates how to track session information.

Table 3–1 Duke's Bookstore Example Servlets

Function	Servlet
Enter the bookstore	BookStoreServlet
Create the bookstore banner	BannerServlet
Browse the bookstore catalog	CatalogServlet
Put a book in a shopping cart	CatalogServlet, BookDetailsServlet
Get detailed information on a specific book	BookDetailsServlet
Display the shopping cart	ShowCartServlet
Remove one or more books from the shopping cart	ShowCartServlet
Buy the books in the shopping cart	CashierServlet
Send an acknowledgment of the purchase	ReceiptServlet

The data for the bookstore application is maintained in a database and accessed through the database access class `database.BookDBAO`. The `database` package also contains the class `Book` which represents a book. The shopping cart and shopping cart items are represented by the classes `cart.ShoppingCart` and `cart.ShoppingCartItem`, respectively.

The source code for the bookstore application is located in the `<INSTALL>/javaeetutorial5javaeetutorial5/examples/web/bookstore1/` directory, which is created when you unzip the tutorial bundle (see Building the Examples, page xxxv).

To deploy and run the application using NetBeans 5.5, follow these steps:

1. Perform all the operations described in Accessing Databases from Web Applications (page 55).
2. In NetBeans 5.5, select File→Open Project Folder.
3. In the Open Project dialog, navigate to:

   `<INSTALL>/javaeetutorial5/examples/web/`
4. Select the `bookstore1` folder.
5. Select the Open as Main Project checkbox and the Open Required Projects checkbox.
6. Click Open Project Folder.
7. In the Projects tab, right-click the `bookstore1` project, and select Deploy Project.
8. To run the application, open the bookstore URL `http://localhost:8080/bookstore1/bookstore`.

To deploy and run the application using Ant, follow these steps:

1. In a terminal window, go to `<INSTALL>/javaeetutorial5/examples/web/bookstore1/`.
2. Run the command `ant`. This target will spawn any necessary compilations, copy files to the `<INSTALL>/javaeetutorial5/examples/web/bookstore1/build/` directory, and create a WAR file and copy it to the `<INSTALL>/javaeetutorial5/examples/web/bookstore1/dist/` directory.
3. Start the Application Server.
4. Perform all the operations described in Creating a Data Source in the Application Server (page 56).

5. To deploy the example, run `ant deploy`. The deploy target outputs a URL for running the application. Ignore this URL, and instead use the one shown in the next step.
6. To run the application, open the bookstore URL `http://localhost:8080/bookstore1/bookstore`.

To learn how to configure the example, refer to the deployment descriptor (the `web.xml` file), which includes the following configurations:

- A `display-name` element that specifies the name that tools use to identify the application.
- A set of `filter` elements that identify servlet filters contained in the application.
- A set of `filter-mapping` elements that identify which servlets will have their requests or responses filtered by the filters identified by the `filter` elements. A `filter-mapping` element can define more than one servlet mapping and more than one URL pattern for a particular filter.
- A set of `servlet` elements that identify all the servlet instances of the application.
- A set of `servlet-mapping` elements that map the servlets to URL patterns. More than one URL pattern can be defined for a particular servlet.
- A set of error-page mappings that map exception types to an HTML page, so that the HTML page opens when an exception of that type is thrown by the application.

Troubleshooting

The Duke's Bookstore database access object returns the following exceptions:

- `BookNotFoundException`: Returned if a book can't be located in the bookstore database. This will occur if you haven't loaded the bookstore database with data or the server has not been started or has crashed. You can populate the database by running `ant create-tables`.
- `BooksNotFoundException`: Returned if the bookstore data can't be retrieved. This will occur if you haven't loaded the bookstore database with data or if the database server hasn't been started or it has crashed.
- `UnavailableException`: Returned if a servlet can't retrieve the web context attribute representing the bookstore. This will occur if the database server hasn't been started.

Because we have specified an error page, you will see the message

```
The application is unavailable. Please try later.
```

If you don't specify an error page, the web container generates a default page containing the message

```
A Servlet Exception Has Occurred
```

and a stack trace that can help you diagnose the cause of the exception. If you use `errorpage.html`, you will have to look in the server log to determine the cause of the exception.

Servlet Life Cycle

The life cycle of a servlet is controlled by the container in which the servlet has been deployed. When a request is mapped to a servlet, the container performs the following steps.

1. If an instance of the servlet does not exist, the web container
   a. Loads the servlet class.
   b. Creates an instance of the servlet class.
   c. Initializes the servlet instance by calling the `init` method. Initialization is covered in Initializing a Servlet (page 70).
2. Invokes the `service` method, passing request and response objects. Service methods are discussed in Writing Service Methods (page 71).

If the container needs to remove the servlet, it finalizes the servlet by calling the servlet's `destroy` method. Finalization is discussed in Finalizing a Servlet (page 92).

Handling Servlet Life-Cycle Events

You can monitor and react to events in a servlet's life cycle by defining listener objects whose methods get invoked when life-cycle events occur. To use these listener objects you must define and specify the listener class.

Defining the Listener Class

You define a listener class as an implementation of a listener interface. Table 3–2 lists the events that can be monitored and the corresponding interface that must be implemented. When a listener method is invoked, it is passed an event that contains information appropriate to the event. For example, the methods in the `HttpSessionListener` interface are passed an `HttpSessionEvent`, which contains an `HttpSession`.

Table 3–2 Servlet Life-Cycle Events

Object	Event	Listener Interface and Event Class
Web context (see Accessing the Web Context, page 88)	Initialization and destruction	`javax.servlet.ServletContextListener` and `ServletContextEvent`
	Attribute added, removed, or replaced	`javax.servlet.ServletContextAttributeListener` and `ServletContextAttributeEvent`
Session (See Maintaining Client State, page 89)	Creation, invalidation, activation, passivation, and timeout	`javax.servlet.http.HttpSessionListener`, `javax.servlet.http.HttpSessionActivationListener`, and `HttpSessionEvent`
	Attribute added, removed, or replaced	`javax.servlet.http.HttpSessionAttributeListener` and `HttpSessionBindingEvent`
`Request`	A servlet request has started being processed by web components	`javax.servlet.ServletRequestListener` and `ServletRequestEvent`
	Attribute added, removed, or replaced	`javax.servlet.ServletRequestAttributeListener` and `ServletRequestAttributeEvent`

The `listeners.ContextListener` class creates and removes the database access and counter objects used in the Duke's Bookstore application. The methods retrieve the web context object from ServletContextEvent and then store (and remove) the objects as servlet context attributes.

```
import database.BookDBAO;
import javax.servlet.*;
import util.Counter;

import javax.ejb.*;
import javax.persistence.*;

public final class ContextListener
  implements ServletContextListener {
  private ServletContext context = null;

  @PersistenceUnit
  EntityManagerFactory emf;

  public void contextInitialized(ServletContextEvent event) {
    context = event.getServletContext();
    try {
      BookDBAO bookDB = new BookDBAO(emf);
      context.setAttribute("bookDB", bookDB);
    } catch (Exception ex) {
      System.out.println(
        "Couldn't create database: " + ex.getMessage());
    }
    Counter counter = new Counter();
    context.setAttribute("hitCounter", counter);
    counter = new Counter();
    context.setAttribute("orderCounter", counter);
  }

  public void contextDestroyed(ServletContextEvent event) {
    context = event.getServletContext();
    BookDBAO bookDB = context.getAttribute("bookDB");
    bookDB.remove();
    context.removeAttribute("bookDB");
    context.removeAttribute("hitCounter");
    context.removeAttribute("orderCounter");
  }
}
```

Specifying Event Listener Classes

You specify an event listener class using the `listener` element of the deployment descriptor. Review The Example Servlets (page 60) for information on how to specify the `ContextListener` listener class. You can specify an event listener using the deployment descriptor editor of NetBeans 5.5 by doing the following:

1. Expand your application's project node.
2. Expand the project's Web Pages and WEB-INF nodes.
3. Double-click `web.xml`.
4. Click General at the top of the `web.xml` editor.
5. Expand the Web Application Listeners node.
6. Click Add.
7. In the Add Listener dialog, click Browse to locate the listener class.
8. Click OK.

Handling Errors

Any number of exceptions can occur when a servlet executes. When an exception occurs, the web container generates a default page containing the message

```
A Servlet Exception Has Occurred
```

But you can also specify that the container should return a specific error page for a given exception. Review the deployment descriptor file included with the example to learn how to map the exceptions `exception.BookNotFound`, `exception.BooksNotFound`, and `exception.OrderException` returned by the Duke's Bookstore application to `errorpage.html`.

See Mapping Errors to Error Screens (page 51) for instructions on how to specify error pages using NetBeans 5.5.

Sharing Information

Web components, like most objects, usually work with other objects to accomplish their tasks. There are several ways they can do this. They can use private helper objects (for example, JavaBeans components), they can share objects that are attributes of a public scope, they can use a database, and they can invoke other web resources. The Java servlet technology mechanisms that allow a web component to invoke other web resources are described in Invoking Other Web Resources (page 84).

Using Scope Objects

Collaborating web components share information via objects that are maintained as attributes of four scope objects. You access these attributes using the `[get|set]Attribute` methods of the class representing the scope. Table 3–3 lists the scope objects.

Table 3–3 Scope Objects

Scope Object	Class	Accessible From
Web context	`javax.servlet.ServletContext`	Web components within a web context. See Accessing the Web Context (page 88).
Session	`javax.servlet.http.HttpSession`	Web components handling a request that belongs to the session. See Maintaining Client State (page 89).
Request	subtype of `javax.servlet.ServletRequest`	Web components handling the request.
Page	`javax.servlet.jsp.JspContext`	The JSP page that creates the object. See Using Implicit Objects (page 111).

Figure 3–1 shows the scoped attributes maintained by the Duke's Bookstore application.

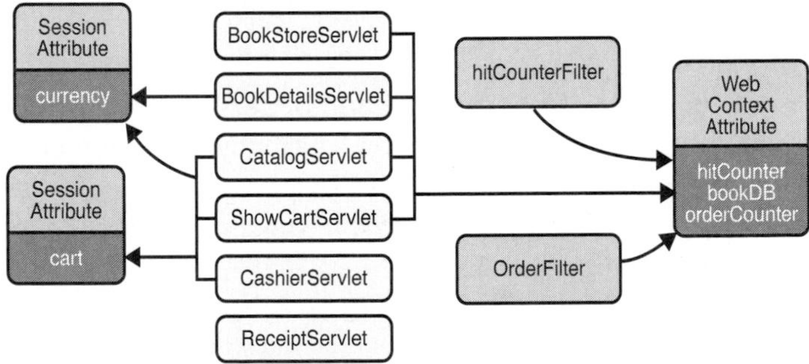

Figure 3–1 Duke's Bookstore Scoped Attributes

Controlling Concurrent Access to Shared Resources

In a multithreaded server, it is possible for shared resources to be accessed concurrently. In addition to scope object attributes, shared resources include in-memory data (such as instance or class variables) and external objects such as files, database connections, and network connections. Concurrent access can arise in several situations:

- Multiple web components accessing objects stored in the web context.
- Multiple web components accessing objects stored in a session.
- Multiple threads within a web component accessing instance variables. A web container will typically create a thread to handle each request. If you want to ensure that a servlet instance handles only one request at a time, a servlet can implement the `SingleThreadModel` interface. If a servlet implements this interface, you are guaranteed that no two threads will execute concurrently in the servlet's service method. A web container can implement this guarantee by synchronizing access to a single instance of the servlet, or by maintaining a pool of web component instances and dispatching each new request to a free instance. This interface does not prevent synchronization problems that result from web components accessing shared resources such as static class variables or external objects. In addition, the Servlet 2.4 specification deprecates the `SingleThreadModel` interface.

When resources can be accessed concurrently, they can be used in an inconsistent fashion. To prevent this, you must control the access using the synchronization techniques described in the Threads lesson in *The Java Tutorial, Fourth Edition*, by Sharon Zakhour et al. (Addison-Wesley, 2006).

In the preceding section we show five scoped attributes shared by more than one servlet: `bookDB`, `cart`, `currency`, `hitCounter`, and `orderCounter`. The `bookDB` attribute is discussed in the next section. The cart, currency, and counters can be set and read by multiple multithreaded servlets. To prevent these objects from being used inconsistently, access is controlled by synchronized methods. For example, here is the `util.Counter` class:

```
public class Counter {
  private int counter;
  public Counter() {
    counter = 0;
  }
```

```
    public synchronized int getCounter() {
      return counter;
    }
    public synchronized int setCounter(int c) {
      counter = c;
      return counter;
    }
    public synchronized int incCounter() {
      return(++counter);
    }
}
```

Accessing Databases

Data that is shared between web components and is persistent between invocations of a web application is usually maintained by a database. Web components use the Java Persistence API to access relational databases. The data for Duke's Bookstore is maintained in a database and is accessed through the database access class `database.BookDBAO`. For example, `ReceiptServlet` invokes the `BookDBAO.buyBooks` method to update the book inventory when a user makes a purchase. The `buyBooks` method invokes `buyBook` for each book contained in the shopping cart, as shown in the following code.

```
public void buyBooks(ShoppingCart cart) throws OrderException{

  Collection items = cart.getItems();
  Iterator i = items.iterator();

  try {
    while (i.hasNext()) {
      ShoppingCartItem sci = (ShoppingCartItem)i.next();
      Book bd = (Book)sci.getItem();
      String id = bd.getBookId();
      int quantity = sci.getQuantity();
      buyBook(id, quantity);
    }
  } catch (Exception ex) {
    throw new OrderException("Commit failed: " +
      ex.getMessage());
  }
}

public void buyBook(String bookId, int quantity)
  throws OrderException {
```

```
        try {
            Book requestedBook = em.find(Book.class, bookId);

            if (requestedBook != null) {
                int inventory = requestedBook.getInventory();
                if ((inventory - quantity) >= 0) {
                    int newInventory = inventory - quantity;
                    requestedBook.setInventory(newInventory);
                } else{
                    throw new OrderException("Not enough of "
                        + bookId + " in stock to complete order.");
                }
            }
        } catch (Exception ex) {
            throw new OrderException("Couldn't purchase book: "
                + bookId + ex.getMessage());
        }
    }
```

To ensure that the order is processed in its entirety, the call to `buyBooks` is wrapped in a single transaction. In the following code, the calls to the `begin` and `commit` methods of `UserTransaction` mark the boundaries of the transaction. The call to the `rollback` method of `UserTransaction` undoes the effects of all statements in the transaction so as to protect the integrity of the data.

```
try {
    utx.begin();
    bookDB.buyBooks(cart);
    utx.commit();
} catch (Exception ex) {
    try {
        utx.rollback();
    } catch(Exception e) {
        System.out.println("Rollback failed: "+e.getMessage());
    }
    System.err.println(ex.getMessage());
    orderCompleted = false;}
}
```

Initializing a Servlet

After the web container loads and instantiates the servlet class and before it delivers requests from clients, the web container initializes the servlet. To customize this process to allow the servlet to read persistent configuration data, initialize resources, and perform any other one-time activities, you override the `init` method of the `Servlet` interface. A servlet that cannot complete its initialization process should throw `UnavailableException`.

All the servlets that access the bookstore database (`BookStoreServlet`, `CatalogServlet`, `BookDetailsServlet`, and `ShowCartServlet`) initialize a variable in their `init` method that points to the database access object created by the web context listener:

```
public class CatalogServlet extends HttpServlet {
  private BookDBAO bookDB;
  public void init() throws ServletException {
    bookDB = (BookDBAO)getServletContext().
      getAttribute("bookDB");
    if (bookDB == null) throw new
      UnavailableException("Couldn't get database.");
  }
}
```

Writing Service Methods

The service provided by a servlet is implemented in the `service` method of a `GenericServlet`, in the `do`*`Method`* methods (where *`Method`* can take the value `Get`, `Delete`, `Options`, `Post`, `Put`, or `Trace`) of an `HttpServlet` object, or in any other protocol-specific methods defined by a class that implements the `Servlet` interface. In the rest of this chapter, the term *service method* is used for any method in a servlet class that provides a service to a client.

The general pattern for a service method is to extract information from the request, access external resources, and then populate the response based on that information.

For HTTP servlets, the correct procedure for populating the response is to first retrieve an output stream from the response, then fill in the response headers, and finally write any body content to the output stream. Response headers must always be set before the response has been committed. Any attempt to set or add headers after the response has been committed will be ignored by the web container. The next two sections describe how to get information from requests and generate responses.

Getting Information from Requests

A request contains data passed between a client and the servlet. All requests implement the `ServletRequest` interface. This interface defines methods for accessing the following information:

- Parameters, which are typically used to convey information between clients and servlets
- Object-valued attributes, which are typically used to pass information between the servlet container and a servlet or between collaborating servlets
- Information about the protocol used to communicate the request and about the client and server involved in the request
- Information relevant to localization

For example, in `CatalogServlet` the identifier of the book that a customer wishes to purchase is included as a parameter to the request. The following code fragment illustrates how to use the `getParameter` method to extract the identifier:

```
String bookId = request.getParameter("Add");
if (bookId != null) {
  Book book = bookDB.getBook(bookId);
```

You can also retrieve an input stream from the request and manually parse the data. To read character data, use the `BufferedReader` object returned by the request's `getReader` method. To read binary data, use the `ServletInputStream` returned by `getInputStream`.

HTTP servlets are passed an HTTP request object, `HttpServletRequest`, which contains the request URL, HTTP headers, query string, and so on.

An HTTP request URL contains the following parts:

```
http://[host]:[port][request path]?[query string]
```

The request path is further composed of the following elements:

- *Context path*: A concatenation of a forward slash (`/`) with the context root of the servlet's web application.
- *Servlet path*: The path section that corresponds to the component alias that activated this request. This path starts with a forward slash (`/`).

- *Path info*: The part of the request path that is not part of the context path or the servlet path.

If the context path is `/catalog` and for the aliases listed in Table 3–4, Table 3–5 gives some examples of how the URL will be parsed.

Table 3–4 Aliases

Pattern	Servlet
`/lawn/*`	`LawnServlet`
`/*.jsp`	`JSPServlet`

Table 3–5 Request Path Elements

Request Path	Servlet Path	Path Info
`/catalog/lawn/index.html`	`/lawn`	`/index.html`
`/catalog/help/feedback.jsp`	`/help/feedback.jsp`	`null`

Query strings are composed of a set of parameters and values. Individual parameters are retrieved from a request by using the `getParameter` method. There are two ways to generate query strings:

- A query string can explicitly appear in a web page. For example, an HTML page generated by the `CatalogServlet` could contain the link `<a href="/bookstore1/catalog?Add=101">Add To Cart</a>`. `CatalogServlet` extracts the parameter named `Add` as follows:

  ```
  String bookId = request.getParameter("Add");
  ```

- A query string is appended to a URL when a form with a `GET` HTTP method is submitted. In the Duke's Bookstore application, `CashierServlet` generates a form, then a user name input to the form is appended to the URL that maps to `ReceiptServlet`, and finally `ReceiptServlet` extracts the user name using the `getParameter` method.

Constructing Responses

A response contains data passed between a server and the client. All responses implement the `ServletResponse` interface. This interface defines methods that allow you to:

- Retrieve an output stream to use to send data to the client. To send character data, use the `PrintWriter` returned by the response's `getWriter` method. To send binary data in a MIME body response, use the `ServletOutputStream` returned by `getOutputStream`. To mix binary and text data, for example—to create a multipart response—use a `ServletOutputStream` and manage the character sections manually.
- Indicate the content type (for example, `text/html`) being returned by the response with the `setContentType(String)` method. This method must be called before the response is committed. A registry of content type names is kept by the Internet Assigned Numbers Authority (IANA) at:

  `http://www.iana.org/assignments/media-types/`
- Indicate whether to buffer output with the `setBufferSize(int)` method. By default, any content written to the output stream is immediately sent to the client. Buffering allows content to be written before anything is actually sent back to the client, thus providing the servlet with more time to set appropriate status codes and headers or forward to another web resource. The method must be called before any content is written or before the response is committed.
- Set localization information such as locale and character encoding. See Chapter 14 for details.

HTTP response objects, `HttpServletResponse`, have fields representing HTTP headers such as the following:

- Status codes, which are used to indicate the reason a request is not satisfied or that a request has been redirected.
- Cookies, which are used to store application-specific information at the client. Sometimes cookies are used to maintain an identifier for tracking a user's session (see Session Tracking, page 91).

In Duke's Bookstore, `BookDetailsServlet` generates an HTML page that displays information about a book that the servlet retrieves from a database. The servlet first sets response headers: the content type of the response and the buffer size. The servlet buffers the page content because the database access can generate an exception that would cause forwarding to an error page. By buffering the response, the servlet prevents the client from seeing a concatenation of part of a Duke's Bookstore page with the error page should an error occur. The `doGet` method then retrieves a `PrintWriter` from the response.

To fill in the response, the servlet first dispatches the request to `BannerServlet`, which generates a common banner for all the servlets in the application. This process is discussed in Including Other Resources in the Response (page 85). Then the servlet retrieves the book identifier from a request parameter and uses the identifier to retrieve information about the book from the bookstore database. Finally, the servlet generates HTML markup that describes the book information and then commits the response to the client by calling the `close` method on the `PrintWriter`.

```
public class BookDetailsServlet extends HttpServlet {
  ...
   public void doGet (HttpServletRequest request,
      HttpServletResponse response)
      throws ServletException, IOException {
    ...
    // set headers before accessing the Writer
    response.setContentType("text/html");
    response.setBufferSize(8192);
    PrintWriter out = response.getWriter();

    // then write the response
    out.println("<html>" +
      "<head><title>+
      messages.getString("TitleBookDescription")
      +</title></head>");

    // Get the dispatcher; it gets the banner to the user
    RequestDispatcher dispatcher =
      getServletContext().
      getRequestDispatcher("/banner");
    if (dispatcher != null)
      dispatcher.include(request, response);

    // Get the identifier of the book to display
    String bookId = request.getParameter("bookId");
    if (bookId != null) {
      // and the information about the book
      try {
        Book bd =
          bookDB.getBook(bookId);
        ...
        // Print the information obtained
        out.println("<h2>" + bd.getTitle() + "</h2>" +
```

```
            ...
          } catch (BookNotFoundException ex) {
            response.resetBuffer();
            throw new ServletException(ex);
          }
        }
        out.println("</body></html>");
        out.close();
      }
    }
```

`BookDetailsServlet` generates a page that looks like Figure 3–2.

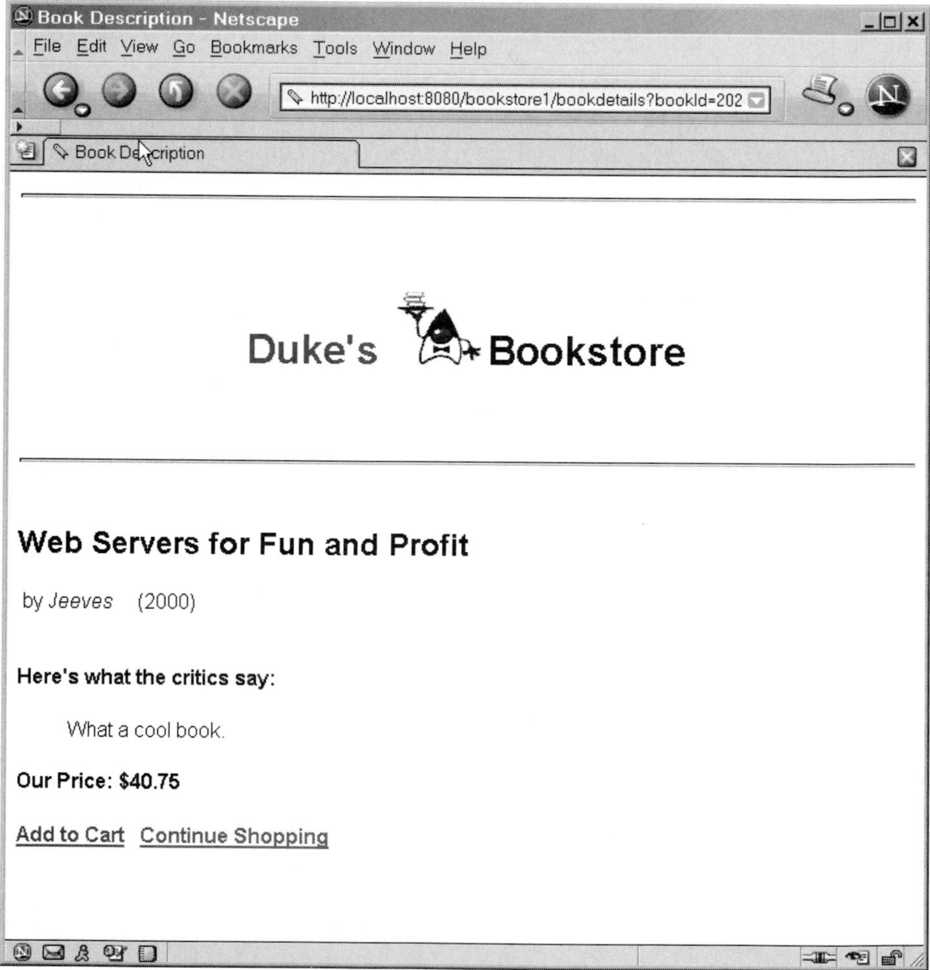

Figure 3–2 Book Details

Filtering Requests and Responses

A *filter* is an object that can transform the header and content (or both) of a request or response. Filters differ from web components in that filters usually do not themselves create a response. Instead, a filter provides functionality that can be "attached" to any kind of web resource. Consequently, a filter should not have any dependencies on a web resource for which it is acting as a filter; this way it can be composed with more than one type of web resource. The main tasks that a filter can perform are as follows:

- Query the request and act accordingly.
- Block the request-and-response pair from passing any further.
- Modify the request headers and data. You do this by providing a customized version of the request.
- Modify the response headers and data. You do this by providing a customized version of the response.
- Interact with external resources.

Applications of filters include authentication, logging, image conversion, data compression, encryption, tokenizing streams, XML transformations, and so on.

You can configure a web resource to be filtered by a chain of zero, one, or more filters in a specific order. This chain is specified when the web application containing the component is deployed and is instantiated when a web container loads the component.

In summary, the tasks involved in using filters are

- Programming the filter
- Programming customized requests and responses
- Specifying the filter chain for each web resource

Programming Filters

The filtering API is defined by the `Filter`, `FilterChain`, and `FilterConfig` interfaces in the `javax.servlet` package. You define a filter by implementing the `Filter` interface. The most important method in this interface is `doFilter`, which is passed request, response, and filter chain objects. This method can perform the following actions:

- Examine the request headers.
- Customize the request object if the filter wishes to modify request headers or data.
- Customize the response object if the filter wishes to modify response headers or data.
- Invoke the next entity in the filter chain. If the current filter is the last filter in the chain that ends with the target web component or static resource, the next entity is the resource at the end of the chain; otherwise, it is the next filter that was configured in the WAR. The filter invokes the next entity by calling the `doFilter` method on the chain object (passing in the request and response it was called with, or the wrapped versions it may have created). Alternatively, it can choose to block the request by not making the call to invoke the next entity. In the latter case, the filter is responsible for filling out the response.
- Examine response headers after it has invoked the next filter in the chain.
- Throw an exception to indicate an error in processing.

In addition to `doFilter`, you must implement the `init` and `destroy` methods. The `init` method is called by the container when the filter is instantiated. If you wish to pass initialization parameters to the filter, you retrieve them from the `FilterConfig` object passed to `init`.

The Duke's Bookstore application uses the filters `HitCounterFilter` and `OrderFilter` to increment and log the value of counters when the entry and receipt servlets are accessed.

In the `doFilter` method, both filters retrieve the servlet context from the filter configuration object so that they can access the counters stored as context attributes. After the filters have completed application-specific processing, they invoke `doFilter` on the filter chain object passed into the original `doFilter` method. The elided code is discussed in the next section.

```
public final class HitCounterFilter implements Filter {
  private FilterConfig filterConfig = null;

  public void init(FilterConfig filterConfig)
     throws ServletException {
     this.filterConfig = filterConfig;
  }
  public void destroy() {
```

```
        this.filterConfig = null;
    }
    public void doFilter(ServletRequest request,
        ServletResponse response, FilterChain chain)
        throws IOException, ServletException {
        if (filterConfig == null)
            return;
        StringWriter sw = new StringWriter();
        PrintWriter writer = new PrintWriter(sw);
        Counter counter = (Counter)filterConfig.
            getServletContext().
            getAttribute("hitCounter");
        writer.println();
        writer.println("===============");
        writer.println("The number of hits is: " +
            counter.incCounter());
        writer.println("===============");
        // Log the resulting string
        writer.flush();
        System.out.println(sw.getBuffer().toString());
        ...
        chain.doFilter(request, wrapper);
        ...
    }
}
```

Programming Customized Requests and Responses

There are many ways for a filter to modify a request or response. For example, a filter can add an attribute to the request or can insert data in the response. In the Duke's Bookstore example, `HitCounterFilter` inserts the value of the counter into the response.

A filter that modifies a response must usually capture the response before it is returned to the client. To do this, you pass a stand-in stream to the servlet that generates the response. The stand-in stream prevents the servlet from closing the original response stream when it completes and allows the filter to modify the servlet's response.

To pass this stand-in stream to the servlet, the filter creates a response wrapper that overrides the `getWriter` or `getOutputStream` method to return this stand-in stream. The wrapper is passed to the `doFilter` method of the filter chain. Wrapper methods default to calling through to the wrapped request or response object.

This approach follows the well-known Wrapper or Decorator pattern described in *Design Patterns, Elements of Reusable Object-Oriented Software*, by Erich Gamma et al. (Addison-Wesley, 1995). The following sections describe how the hit counter filter described earlier and other types of filters use wrappers.

To override request methods, you wrap the request in an object that extends `ServletRequestWrapper` or `HttpServletRequestWrapper`. To override response methods, you wrap the response in an object that extends `ServletResponseWrapper` or `HttpServletResponseWrapper`.

`HitCounterFilter` wraps the response in a `CharResponseWrapper`. The wrapped response is passed to the next object in the filter chain, which is `BookStoreServlet`. Then `BookStoreServlet` writes its response into the stream created by `CharResponseWrapper`. When `chain.doFilter` returns, `HitCounterFilter` retrieves the servlet's response from `PrintWriter` and writes it to a buffer. The filter inserts the value of the counter into the buffer, resets the content length header of the response, and then writes the contents of the buffer to the response stream.

```
PrintWriter out = response.getWriter();
CharResponseWrapper wrapper = new CharResponseWrapper(
  (HttpServletResponse)response);
chain.doFilter(request, wrapper);
CharArrayWriter caw = new CharArrayWriter();
caw.write(wrapper.toString().substring(0,
  wrapper.toString().indexOf("</body>")-1));
caw.write("<p>\n<center>" +
  messages.getString("Visitor") + "<font color='red'>" +
  counter.getCounter() + "</font></center>");
caw.write("\n</body></html>");
response.setContentLength(caw.toString().getBytes().length);
out.write(caw.toString());
out.close();

public class CharResponseWrapper extends
  HttpServletResponseWrapper {
  private CharArrayWriter output;
  public String toString() {
    return output.toString();
  }
  public CharResponseWrapper(HttpServletResponse response){
    super(response);
    output = new CharArrayWriter();
  }
```

```
    public PrintWriter getWriter(){
      return new PrintWriter(output);
    }
  }
```

Figure 3–3 shows the entry page for Duke's Bookstore with the hit counter.

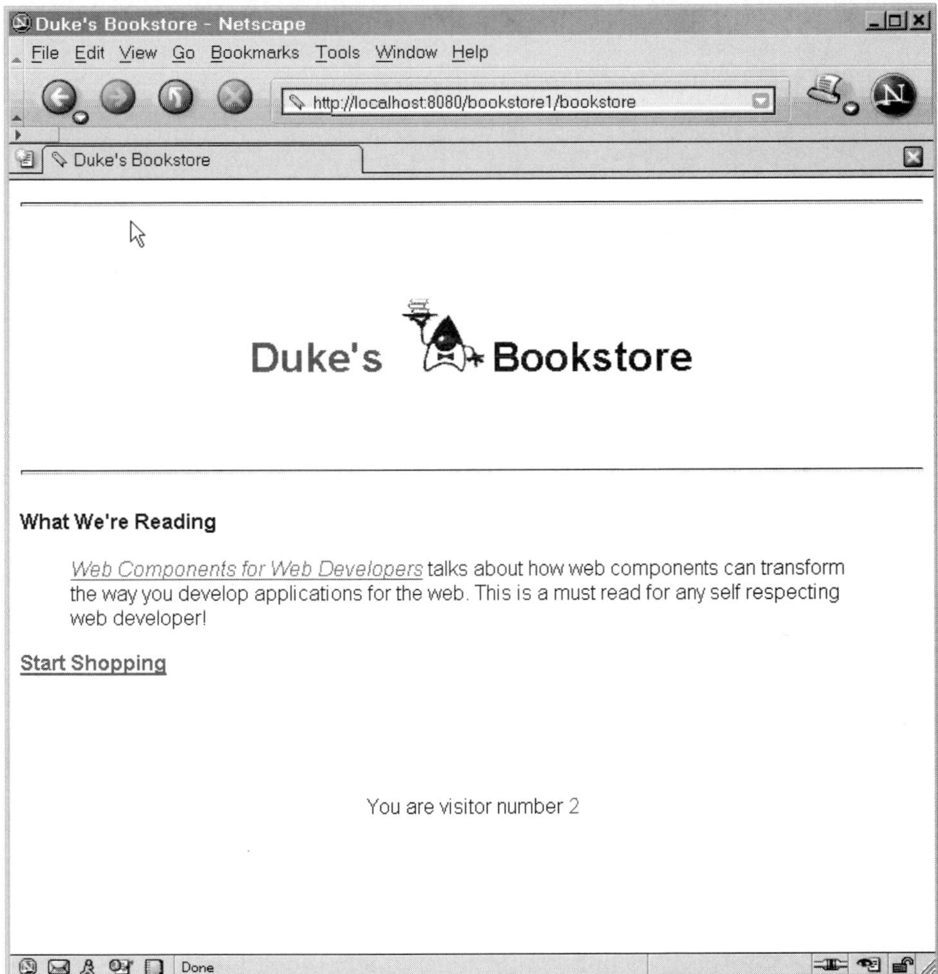

Figure 3–3 Duke's Bookstore with Hit Counter

Specifying Filter Mappings

A web container uses filter mappings to decide how to apply filters to web resources. A filter mapping matches a filter to a web component by name, or to web resources by URL pattern. The filters are invoked in the order in which filter mappings appear in the filter mapping list of a WAR. You specify a filter mapping list for a WAR in its deployment descriptor, either with NetBeans 5.5 or by coding the list by hand with XML.

To declare the filter and map it to a web resource using NetBeans 5.5, do the following:

1. Expand the application's project node in the Project pane.
2. Expand the Web Pages and WEB-INF nodes under the project node.
3. Double-click `web.xml`.
4. Click Filters at the top of the editor pane.
5. Expand the Servlet Filters node in the editor pane.
6. Click Add Filter Element to map the filter to a web resource by name or by URL pattern.
7. In the Add Servlet Filter dialog, enter the name of the filter in the Filter Name field.
8. Click Browse to locate the servlet class to which the filter applies. You can include wildcard characters so that you can apply the filter to more than one servlet.
9. Click OK.

To constrain how the filter is applied to requests, do the following:

1. Expand the Filter Mappings node in the Filters tab of the editor pane.
2. Select the filter from the list of filters.
3. Click Add.
4. In the Add Filter Mapping dialog, select one of the following dispatcher types:
    - `REQUEST`: Only when the request comes directly from the client
    - `FORWARD`: Only when the request has been forwarded to a component (see Transferring Control to Another Web Component, page 87)
    - `INCLUDE`: Only when the request is being processed by a component that has been included (see Including Other Resources in the Response, page 85)

- `ERROR`: Only when the request is being processed with the error page mechanism (see Handling Errors, page 66)

  You can direct the filter to be applied to any combination of the preceding situations by selecting multiple dispatcher types. If no types are specified, the default option is `REQUEST`.

You can declare, map, and constrain the filter by editing the XML in the web application deployment descriptor directly by following these steps:

1. While in the `web.xml` editor pane in NetBeans 5.5, click XML at the top of the editor pane.
2. Declare the filter by adding a `filter` element right after the `display-name` element. The `filter` element creates a name for the filter and declares the filter's implementation class and initialization parameters.
3. Map the filter to a web resource by name or by URL pattern using the `filter-mapping` element:
   a. Include a `filter-name` element that specifies the name of the filter as defined by the `filter` element.
   b. Include a `servlet-name` element that specifies to which servlet the filter applies. The `servlet-name` element can include wildcard characters so that you can apply the filter to more than one servlet.
4. Constrain how the filter will be applied to requests by specifying one of the enumerated dispatcher options (described in step 4 of the preceding set of steps) with the `dispatcher` element and adding the `dispatcher` element to the `filter-mapping` element.

   You can direct the filter to be applied to any combination of the preceding situations by including multiple `dispatcher` elements. If no elements are specified, the default option is `REQUEST`.

If you want to log every request to a web application, you map the hit counter filter to the URL pattern `/*`. Table 3–6 summarizes the filter definition and mapping list for the Duke's Bookstore application. The filters are matched by servlet name, and each filter chain contains only one filter.

You can map a filter to one or more web resources and you can map more than one filter to a web resource. This is illustrated in Figure 3–4, where filter F1 is mapped to servlets S1, S2, and S3, filter F2 is mapped to servlet S2, and filter F3 is mapped to servlets S1 and S2.

Table 3–6 Duke's Bookstore Filter Definition and Mapping List

Filter	Class	Servlet
`HitCounterFilter`	`filters.HitCounterFilter`	`BookStoreServlet`
`OrderFilter`	`filters.OrderFilter`	`ReceiptServlet`

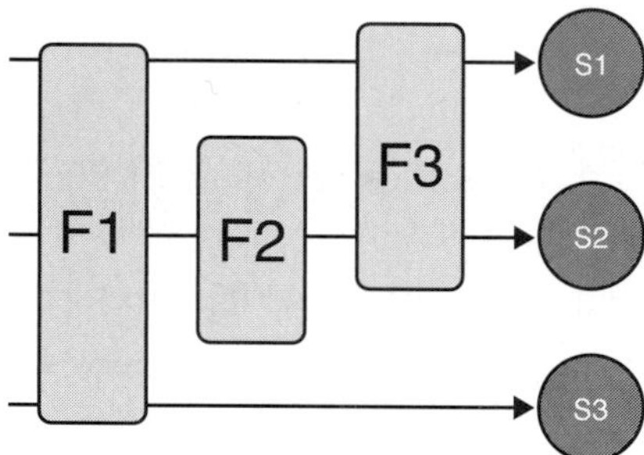

Figure 3–4 Filter-to-Servlet Mapping

Recall that a filter chain is one of the objects passed to the `doFilter` method of a filter. This chain is formed indirectly via filter mappings. The order of the filters in the chain is the same as the order in which filter mappings appear in the web application deployment descriptor.

When a filter is mapped to servlet S1, the web container invokes the `doFilter` method of F1. The `doFilter` method of each filter in S1's filter chain is invoked by the preceding filter in the chain via the `chain.doFilter` method. Because S1's filter chain contains filters F1 and F3, F1's call to `chain.doFilter` invokes the `doFilter` method of filter F3. When F3's `doFilter` method completes, control returns to F1's `doFilter` method.

Invoking Other Web Resources

Web components can invoke other web resources in two ways: indirectly and directly. A web component indirectly invokes another web resource when it embeds a URL that points to another web component in content returned to a client. In the Duke's Bookstore application, most web components contain embedded URLs that point to other web components. For example, `ShowCartServlet` indirectly invokes the `CatalogServlet` through the following embedded URL:

```
/bookstore1/catalog
```

A web component can also directly invoke another resource while it is executing. There are two possibilities: The web component can include the content of another resource, or it can forward a request to another resource.

To invoke a resource available on the server that is running a web component, you must first obtain a `RequestDispatcher` object using the `getRequestDispatcher("URL")` method.

You can get a `RequestDispatcher` object from either a request or the web context; however, the two methods have slightly different behavior. The method takes the path to the requested resource as an argument. A request can take a relative path (that is, one that does not begin with a `/`), but the web context requires an absolute path. If the resource is not available or if the server has not implemented a `RequestDispatcher` object for that type of resource, `getRequestDispatcher` will return null. Your servlet should be prepared to deal with this condition.

Including Other Resources in the Response

It is often useful to include another web resource—for example, banner content or copyright information—in the response returned from a web component. To include another resource, invoke the `include` method of a `RequestDispatcher` object:

```
include(request, response);
```

If the resource is static, the `include` method enables programmatic server-side includes. If the resource is a web component, the effect of the method is to send the request to the included web component, execute the web component, and then include the result of the execution in the response from the containing servlet. An included web component has access to the request object, but it is limited in what it can do with the response object:

- It can write to the body of the response and commit a response.
- It cannot set headers or call any method (for example, `setCookie`) that affects the headers of the response.

The banner for the Duke's Bookstore application is generated by `BannerServlet`. Note that both `doGet` and `doPost` are implemented because `BannerServlet` can be dispatched from either method in a calling servlet.

```
public class BannerServlet extends HttpServlet {
  public void doGet (HttpServletRequest request,
    HttpServletResponse response)
    throws ServletException, IOException {
      output(request, response);
  }
  public void doPost (HttpServletRequest request,
    HttpServletResponse response)
    throws ServletException, IOException {
      output(request, response);
}

private void output(HttpServletRequest request,
    HttpServletResponse response)
    throws ServletException, IOException {
    PrintWriter out = response.getWriter();
    out.println("<body bgcolor=\"#ffffff\">" +
    "<center>" + "<hr> <br>  " + "<h1>" +
    "<font size=\"+3\" color=\"#CC0066\">Duke's </font>" +
    <img src=\"" + request.getContextPath() +
    "/duke.books.gif\">" +
    "<font size=\"+3\" color=\"black\">Bookstore</font>" +
    "</h1>" + "</center>" + "<br>   <hr> <br> ");
  }
}
```

Each servlet in the Duke's Bookstore application includes the result from `BannerServlet` using the following code:

```
RequestDispatcher dispatcher =
  getServletContext().getRequestDispatcher("/banner");
if (dispatcher != null)
  dispatcher.include(request, response);
}
```

Transferring Control to Another Web Component

In some applications, you might want to have one web component do preliminary processing of a request and have another component generate the response. For example, you might want to partially process a request and then transfer to another component depending on the nature of the request.

To transfer control to another web component, you invoke the `forward` method of a `RequestDispatcher`. When a request is forwarded, the request URL is set to the path of the forwarded page. The original URI and its constituent parts are saved as request attributes `javax.servlet.forward.[request_uri|context-path|servlet_path|path_info|query_string]`. The `Dispatcher` servlet, used by a version of the Duke's Bookstore application described in The Example JSP Pages (page 204), saves the path information from the original URL, retrieves a `RequestDispatcher` from the request, and then forwards to the JSP page `template.jsp`.

```
public class Dispatcher extends HttpServlet {
  public void doGet(HttpServletRequest request,
    HttpServletResponse response) {
    RequestDispatcher dispatcher = request.
      getRequestDispatcher("/template.jsp");
    if (dispatcher != null)
      dispatcher.forward(request, response);
  }
  public void doPost(HttpServletRequest request,
  ...
}
```

The `forward` method should be used to give another resource responsibility for replying to the user. If you have already accessed a `ServletOutputStream` or `PrintWriter` object within the servlet, you cannot use this method; doing so throws an `IllegalStateException`.

Accessing the Web Context

The context in which web components execute is an object that implements the `ServletContext` interface. You retrieve the web context using the `getServletContext` method. The web context provides methods for accessing:

- Initialization parameters
- Resources associated with the web context
- Object-valued attributes
- Logging capabilities

The web context is used by the Duke's Bookstore filters `com.sun.bookstore1.filters.HitCounterFilter` and `OrderFilter`, which are discussed in Filtering Requests and Responses (page 77). Each filter stores a counter as a context attribute. Recall from Controlling Concurrent Access to Shared Resources (page 68) that the counter's access methods are synchronized to prevent incompatible operations by servlets that are running concurrently. A filter retrieves the counter object using the context's `getAttribute` method. The incremented value of the counter is recorded in the log.

```
public final class HitCounterFilter implements Filter {
  private FilterConfig filterConfig = null;
  public void doFilter(ServletRequest request,
    ServletResponse response, FilterChain chain)
    throws IOException, ServletException {
    ...
    StringWriter sw = new StringWriter();
    PrintWriter writer = new PrintWriter(sw);
    ServletContext context = filterConfig.
      getServletContext();
    Counter counter = (Counter)context.
      getAttribute("hitCounter");
    ...
    writer.println("The number of hits is: " +
      counter.incCounter());
    ...
    System.out.println(sw.getBuffer().toString());
    ...
  }
}
```

Maintaining Client State

Many applications require that a series of requests from a client be associated with one another. For example, the Duke's Bookstore application saves the state of a user's shopping cart across requests. Web-based applications are responsible for maintaining such state, called a *session*, because HTTP is stateless. To support applications that need to maintain state, Java servlet technology provides an API for managing sessions and allows several mechanisms for implementing sessions.

Accessing a Session

Sessions are represented by an `HttpSession` object. You access a session by calling the `getSession` method of a request object. This method returns the current session associated with this request, or, if the request does not have a session, it creates one.

Associating Objects with a Session

You can associate object-valued attributes with a session by name. Such attributes are accessible by any web component that belongs to the same web context *and* is handling a request that is part of the same session.

The Duke's Bookstore application stores a customer's shopping cart as a session attribute. This allows the shopping cart to be saved between requests and also allows cooperating servlets to access the cart. `CatalogServlet` adds items to the cart; `ShowCartServlet` displays, deletes items from, and clears the cart; and `CashierServlet` retrieves the total cost of the books in the cart.

```
public class CashierServlet extends HttpServlet {
  public void doGet (HttpServletRequest request,
     HttpServletResponse response)
     throws ServletException, IOException {

     // Get the user's session and shopping cart
     HttpSession session = request.getSession();
     ShoppingCart cart =
        (ShoppingCart)session.
```

```
        getAttribute("cart");
    ...
    // Determine the total price of the user's books
    double total = cart.getTotal();
```

Notifying Objects That Are Associated with a Session

Recall that your application can notify web context and session listener objects of servlet life-cycle events (Handling Servlet Life-Cycle Events, page 63). You can also notify objects of certain events related to their association with a session such as the following:

- When the object is added to or removed from a session. To receive this notification, your object must implement the `javax.servlet.http.HttpSessionBindingListener` interface.
- When the session to which the object is attached will be passivated or activated. A session will be passivated or activated when it is moved between virtual machines or saved to and restored from persistent storage. To receive this notification, your object must implement the `javax.servlet.http.HttpSessionActivationListener` interface.

Session Management

Because there is no way for an HTTP client to signal that it no longer needs a session, each session has an associated timeout so that its resources can be reclaimed. The timeout period can be accessed by using a session's `[get|set]MaxInactiveInterval` methods. You can also set the timeout period in the deployment descriptor using NetBeans 5.5:

1. Open the `web.xml` file in the `web.xml` editor.
2. Click General at the top of the editor.
3. Enter an integer value in the Session Timeout field. The integer value represents the number of minutes of inactivity that must pass before the session times out.

To ensure that an active session is not timed out, you should periodically access the session via service methods because this resets the session's time-to-live counter.

When a particular client interaction is finished, you use the session's invalidate method to invalidate a session on the server side and remove any session data. The bookstore application's ReceiptServlet is the last servlet to access a client's session, so it has the responsibility to invalidate the session:

```
public class ReceiptServlet extends HttpServlet {
  public void doPost(HttpServletRequest request,
           HttpServletResponse response)
           throws ServletException, IOException {
    // Get the user's session and shopping cart
    HttpSession session = request.getSession();
    // Payment received -- invalidate the session
    session.invalidate();
    ...
```

Session Tracking

A web container can use several methods to associate a session with a user, all of which involve passing an identifier between the client and the server. The identifier can be maintained on the client as a cookie, or the web component can include the identifier in every URL that is returned to the client.

If your application uses session objects, you must ensure that session tracking is enabled by having the application rewrite URLs whenever the client turns off cookies. You do this by calling the response's encodeURL(URL) method on all URLs returned by a servlet. This method includes the session ID in the URL only if cookies are disabled; otherwise, it returns the URL unchanged.

The doGet method of ShowCartServlet encodes the three URLs at the bottom of the shopping cart display page as follows:

```
out.println("<p>   <p><strong><a href=\"" +
  response.encodeURL(request.getContextPath() +
    "/bookcatalog") +
    "\">" + messages.getString("ContinueShopping") +
    "</a>      " +
    "<a href=\"" +
  response.encodeURL(request.getContextPath() +
    "/bookcashier") +
    "\">" + messages.getString("Checkout") +
    "</a>      " +
    "<a href=\"" +
```

```
response.encodeURL(request.getContextPath() +
  "/bookshowcart?Clear=clear") +
  "\">" + messages.getString("ClearCart") +
  "</a></strong>");
```

If cookies are turned off, the session is encoded in the Check Out URL as follows:

```
http://localhost:8080/bookstore1/cashier;
  jsessionid=c0o7fszeb1
```

If cookies are turned on, the URL is simply

```
http://localhost:8080/bookstore1/cashier
```

Finalizing a Servlet

When a servlet container determines that a servlet should be removed from service (for example, when a container wants to reclaim memory resources or when it is being shut down), the container calls the `destroy` method of the `Servlet` interface. In this method, you release any resources the servlet is using and save any persistent state. The following `destroy` method releases the database object created in the `init` method described in Initializing a Servlet (page 70):

```
public void destroy() {
  bookDB = null;
}
```

All of a servlet's service methods should be complete when a servlet is removed. The server tries to ensure this by calling the `destroy` method only after all service requests have returned or after a server-specific grace period, whichever comes first. If your servlet has operations that take a long time to run (that is, operations that may run longer than the server's grace period), the operations could still be running when `destroy` is called. You must make sure that any threads still handling client requests complete; the remainder of this section describes how to do the following:

- Keep track of how many threads are currently running the `service` method.
- Provide a clean shutdown by having the `destroy` method notify long-running threads of the shutdown and wait for them to complete.

- Have the long-running methods poll periodically to check for shutdown and, if necessary, stop working, clean up, and return.

Tracking Service Requests

To track service requests, include in your servlet class a field that counts the number of service methods that are running. The field should have synchronized access methods to increment, decrement, and return its value.

```
public class ShutdownExample extends HttpServlet {
  private int serviceCounter = 0;
  ...
  // Access methods for serviceCounter
  protected synchronized void enteringServiceMethod() {
     serviceCounter++;
  }
  protected synchronized void leavingServiceMethod() {
     serviceCounter--;
  }
  protected synchronized int numServices() {
     return serviceCounter;
  }
}
```

The `service` method should increment the service counter each time the method is entered and should decrement the counter each time the method returns. This is one of the few times that your `HttpServlet` subclass should override the `service` method. The new method should call `super.service` to preserve the functionality of the original `service` method:

```
protected void service(HttpServletRequest req,
             HttpServletResponse resp)
             throws ServletException,IOException {
  enteringServiceMethod();
  try {
     super.service(req, resp);
  } finally {
     leavingServiceMethod();
  }
}
```

Notifying Methods to Shut Down

To ensure a clean shutdown, your destroy method should not release any shared resources until all the service requests have completed. One part of doing this is to check the service counter. Another part is to notify the long-running methods that it is time to shut down. For this notification, another field is required. The field should have the usual access methods:

```
public class ShutdownExample extends HttpServlet {
  private boolean shuttingDown;
  ...
  //Access methods for shuttingDown
  protected synchronized void setShuttingDown(boolean flag) {
    shuttingDown = flag;
  }
  protected synchronized boolean isShuttingDown() {
    return shuttingDown;
  }
}
```

Here is an example of the destroy method using these fields to provide a clean shutdown:

```
public void destroy() {
  /* Check to see whether there are still service methods /*
  /* running, and if there are, tell them to stop. */
  if (numServices() > 0) {
    setShuttingDown(true);
  }

  /* Wait for the service methods to stop. */
  while(numServices() > 0) {
    try {
      Thread.sleep(interval);
    } catch (InterruptedException e) {
    }
  }
}
```

Creating Polite Long-Running Methods

The final step in providing a clean shutdown is to make any long-running methods behave politely. Methods that might run for a long time should check the value of the field that notifies them of shutdowns and should interrupt their work, if necessary.

```
public void doPost(...) {
   ...
   for(i = 0; ((i < lotsOfStuffToDo) &&
      !isShuttingDown()); i++) {
      try {
         partOfLongRunningOperation(i);
      } catch (InterruptedException e) {
         ...
      }
   }
}
```

Further Information

For further information on Java Servlet technology, see

- Java Servlet 2.4 specification:
  `http://java.sun.com/products/servlet/download.html#specs`
- The Java Servlet web site:
  `http://java.sun.com/products/servlet`

4

JavaServer Pages Technology

JAVASERVER Pages (JSP) technology allows you to easily create web content that has both static and dynamic components. JSP technology makes available all the dynamic capabilities of Java Servlet technology but provides a more natural approach to creating static content. The main features of JSP technology are as follows:

- A language for developing JSP pages, which are text-based documents that describe how to process a request and construct a response
- An expression language for accessing server-side objects
- Mechanisms for defining extensions to the JSP language

JSP technology also contains an API that is used by developers of web containers, but this API is not covered in this tutorial.

What Is a JSP Page?

A *JSP page* is a text document that contains two types of text: static data, which can be expressed in any text-based format (such as HTML, SVG, WML, and XML), and JSP elements, which construct dynamic content.

The recommended file extension for the source file of a JSP page is `.jsp`. The page can be composed of a top file that includes other files that contain either a complete JSP page or a fragment of a JSP page. The recommended extension for the source file of a fragment of a JSP page is `.jspf`.

The JSP elements in a JSP page can be expressed in two syntaxes—standard and XML—though any given file can use only one syntax. A JSP page in XML syntax is an XML document and can be manipulated by tools and APIs for XML documents. This chapter and Chapters 6 through 8 document only the standard syntax. The XML syntax is covered in Chapter 5.

Example

The web page in Figure 4–1 is a form that allows you to select a locale and displays the date in a manner appropriate to the locale.

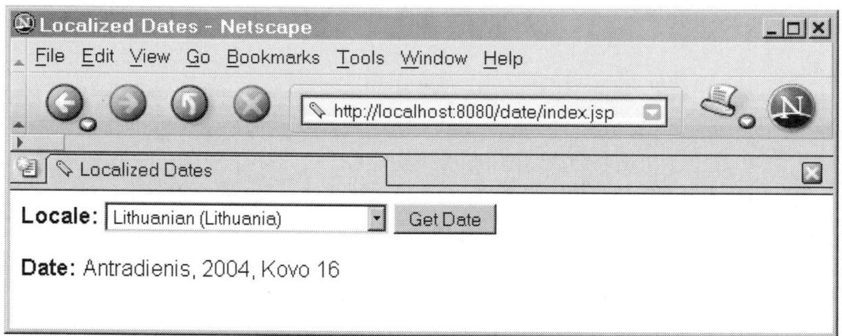

Figure 4–1 Localized Date Form

The source code for this example is in the `<INSTALL>/javaeetutorial5/examples/web/date/` directory. The JSP page, `index.jsp`, used to create the form appears in a moment; it is a typical mixture of static HTML markup and JSP elements. If you have developed web pages, you are probably familiar with the HTML document structure statements (`<head>`, `<body>`, and so on) and the HTML statements that create a form (`<form>`) and a menu (`<select>`).

The lines in bold in the example code contain the following types of JSP constructs:

- A page directive (**`<%@page ... %>`**) sets the content type returned by the page.
- Tag library directives (**`<%@taglib ... %>`**) import custom tag libraries.
- **`jsp:useBean`** creates an object containing a collection of locales and initializes an identifier that points to that object.

- JSP expression language expressions (**${ }**) retrieve the value of object properties. The values are used to set custom tag attribute values and create dynamic content.
- Custom tags set a variable (**c:set**), iterate over a collection of locale names (**c:forEach**), and conditionally insert HTML text into the response (**c:if**, **c:choose**, **c:when**, **c:otherwise**).
- **jsp:setProperty** sets the value of an object property.
- A function (**f:equals**) tests the equality of an attribute and the current item of a collection. (Note: A built-in == operator is usually used to test equality.)

Here is the JSP page:

```
<%@ page contentType="text/html; charset=UTF-8" %>
<%@ taglib uri="http://java.sun.com/jsp/jstl/core"
     prefix="c" %>
<%@ taglib uri="/functions" prefix="f" %>
<html>
<head><title>Localized Dates</title></head>
<body bgcolor="white">
<jsp:useBean id="locales" scope="application"
  class="mypkg.MyLocales"/>

<form name="localeForm" action="index.jsp" method="post">
<c:set var="selectedLocaleString" value="${param.locale}" />
<c:set var="selectedFlag"
  value="${!empty selectedLocaleString}" />
<b>Locale:</b>
<select name=locale>
<c:forEach var="localeString" items="${locales.localeNames}" >
<c:choose>
  <c:when test="${selectedFlag}">
    <c:choose>
      <c:when
        test="${f:equals(selectedLocaleString,
          localeString)}" >
        <option selected>${localeString}</option>
      </c:when>
      <c:otherwise>
        <option>${localeString}</option>
      </c:otherwise>
    </c:choose>
  </c:when>
  <c:otherwise>
    <option>${localeString}</option>
  </c:otherwise>
```

```
</c:choose>
</c:forEach>
</select>
<input type="submit" name="Submit" value="Get Date">
</form>

<c:if test="${selectedFlag}" >
  <jsp:setProperty name="locales"
    property="selectedLocaleString"
    value="${selectedLocaleString}" />
  <jsp:useBean id="date" class="mypkg.MyDate"/>
  <jsp:setProperty name="date" property="locale"
    value="${locales.selectedLocale}"/>
  <b>Date: </b>${date.date}
</c:if>
</body>
</html>
```

To deploy the date application with NetBeans 5.5, follow these steps:

1. Start the Application Server.
2. In NetBeans 5.5, select File→Open Project.
3. In the Open Project dialog, navigate to:

   <INSTALL>/javaeetutorial5/examples/web/
4. Select the date folder.
5. Select the Open as Main Project checkbox.
6. Click Open Project Folder.
7. In the Projects tab, right-click the date project, and select Deploy Project.

To deploy the date application with the Ant tool, follow these steps:

1. In a terminal window, go to *<INSTALL>*/javaeetutorial5/examples/web/date/.
2. Run the command ant. This target will spawn any necessary compilations, copy files to the *<INSTALL>*/javaeetutorial5/examples/web/date/build/ directory, and create a WAR file.
3. Start the Application Server.
4. Run ant deploy.

To run the example, do the following:

1. Set the character encoding in your browser to UTF-8.
2. Open your browser to http://localhost:8080/date.

3. You will see a combo box whose entries are locales. Select a locale and click Get Date. You will see the date expressed in a manner appropriate for that locale.

Some of the characters might not display properly if you don't have the appropriate language files installed on your machine. Consult the user guide or online help for your operating system to determine how you can install these language files.

The Example JSP Pages

To illustrate JSP technology, this chapter rewrites each servlet in the Duke's Bookstore application introduced in The Example Servlets (page 60) as a JSP page (see Table 4–1).

Table 4–1 Duke's Bookstore Example JSP Pages

Function	JSP Pages
Enter the bookstore.	`bookstore.jsp`
Create the bookstore banner.	`banner.jsp`
Browse the books offered for sale.	`bookcatalog.jsp`
Add a book to the shopping cart.	`bookcatalog.jsp` and `bookdetails.jsp`
Get detailed information on a specific book.	`bookdetails.jsp`
Display the shopping cart.	`bookshowcart.jsp`
Remove one or more books from the shopping cart.	`bookshowcart.jsp`
Buy the books in the shopping cart.	`bookcashier.jsp`
Receive an acknowledgment for the purchase.	`bookreceipt.jsp`

The data for the bookstore application is still maintained in a database and is accessed through `com.sun.bookstore2.database.BookDBAO`. However, the JSP pages access `BookDBAO` through the JavaBeans component com.sun.bookstore2.database.BookDB. This class allows the JSP pages to use JSP elements designed to work with JavaBeans components (see JavaBeans Component Design Conventions, page 136).

The implementation of the database bean follows. The bean has two instance variables: the current book and the data access object.

```
package database;
public class BookDB {
  private String bookId = "0";
  private BookDBAO database = null;

  public BookDB () throws Exception {
  }
  public void setBookId(String bookId) {
    this.bookId = bookId;
  }
  public void setDatabase(BookDAO database) {
    this.database = database;
  }
  public Book getBook()
    throws Exception {
    return (Book)database.getBook(bookId);
  }
  ...
}
```

This version of the Duke's Bookstore application is organized along the Model-View-Controller (MVC) architecture. The MVC architecture is a widely used architectural approach for interactive applications that distributes functionality among application objects so as to minimize the degree of coupling between the objects. To achieve this, it divides applications into three layers: model, view, and controller. Each layer handles specific tasks and has responsibilities to the other layers:

- The *model* represents business data, along with business logic or operations that govern access and modification of this business data. The model notifies views when it changes and lets the view query the model about its state. It also lets the controller access application functionality encapsulated by the model. In the Duke's Bookstore application, the shopping cart and database access object contain the business logic for the application.
- The *view* renders the contents of a model. It gets data from the model and specifies how that data should be presented. It updates data presentation when the model changes. A view also forwards user input to a controller.

The Duke's Bookstore JSP pages format the data stored in the session-scoped shopping cart and the page-scoped database bean.

- The *controller* defines application behavior. It dispatches user requests and selects views for presentation. It interprets user inputs and maps them into actions to be performed by the model. In a web application, user inputs are HTTP `GET` and `POST` requests. A controller selects the next view to display based on the user interactions and the outcome of the model operations. In the Duke's Bookstore application, the `Dispatcher` servlet is the controller. It examines the request URL, creates and initializes a session-scoped JavaBeans component—the shopping cart—and dispatches requests to view JSP pages.

Note: When employed in a web application, the MVC architecture is often referred to as a Model-2 architecture. The bookstore example discussed in Chapter 3, which intermixes presentation and business logic, follows what is known as a Model-1 architecture. The Model-2 architecture is the recommended approach to designing web applications.

In addition, this version of the application uses several custom tags from the JavaServer Pages Standard Tag Library (JSTL), described in Chapter 6:

- `c:if`, `c:choose`, `c:when`, and `c:otherwise` for flow control
- `c:set` for setting scoped variables
- `c:url` for encoding URLs
- `fmt:message`, `fmt:formatNumber`, and `fmt:formatDate` for providing locale-sensitive messages, numbers, and dates

Custom tags are the preferred mechanism for performing a wide variety of dynamic processing tasks, including accessing databases, using enterprise services such as email and directories, and implementing flow control. In earlier versions of JSP technology, such tasks were performed with JavaBeans components in conjunction with scripting elements (discussed in Chapter 8). Although still available in JSP 2.0 technology, scripting elements tend to make JSP pages more difficult to maintain because they mix presentation and logic, something that is discouraged in page design. Custom tags are introduced in Using Custom Tags (page 141) and described in detail in Chapter 7.

Finally, this version of the example contains an applet to generate a dynamic digital clock in the banner. See Including an Applet (page 147) for a description of the JSP element that generates HTML for downloading the applet.

To deploy and run the application using NetBeans 5.5, follow these steps:

1. Perform all the operations described in Accessing Databases from Web Applications (page 55).
2. In NetBeans 5.5, select File→Open Project.
3. In the Open Project dialog, navigate to:
   `<INSTALL>/javaeetutorial5/examples/web/`
4. Select the `bookstore2` folder.
5. Select the Open as Main Project checkbox and the Open Required Projects checkbox.
6. Click Open Project Folder.
7. In the Projects tab, right-click the `bookstore2` project, and select Deploy Project.
8. To run the application, open the bookstore URL `http://localhost:8080/bookstore2/books/bookstore`.

To deploy and run the application using Ant, follow these steps:

1. In a terminal window, go to `<INSTALL>/javaeetutorial5/examples/web/bookstore2/`.
2. Run the command `ant`. This target will spawn any necessary compilations, copy files to the `<INSTALL>/javaeetutorial5/examples/web/bookstore2/build/` directory, and create a WAR file and copy it to the `<INSTALL>/javaeetutorial5/examples/web/bookstore2/dist/` directory.
3. Start the Application Server.
4. Perform all the operations described in Creating a Data Source in the Application Server (page 56).
5. To deploy the example, run `ant deploy`. The deploy target outputs a URL for running the application. Ignore this URL, and instead use the one shown in the next step.
6. To run the application, open the bookstore URL `http://localhost:8080/bookstore2/books/bookstore`.

To learn how to configure the example, refer to the deployment descriptor (the `web.xml` file), which includes the following configurations:

- A `display-name` element that specifies the name that tools use to identify the application.
- A `context-param` element that specifies the JSTL resource bundle base name.
- A `listener` element that identifies the `ContextListener` class used to create and remove the database access.
- A `servlet` element that identifies the `Dispatcher` servlet instance.
- A set of `servlet-mapping` elements that map `Dispatcher` to URL patterns for each of the JSP pages in the application.
- Nested inside a `jsp-config` element are two `jsp-property-group` elements, which define the preludes and coda to be included in each page. See Setting Properties for Groups of JSP Pages (page 149) for more information.

Figure 4–2 shows the `bookcatalog.jsp` page from the Duke's Bookstore application. This page displays a list of all the books that are available for purchase.

See Troubleshooting (page 62) for help with diagnosing common problems related to the database server. If the messages in your pages appear as strings of the form `??? Key ???`, the likely cause is that you have not provided the correct resource bundle base name as a context parameter.

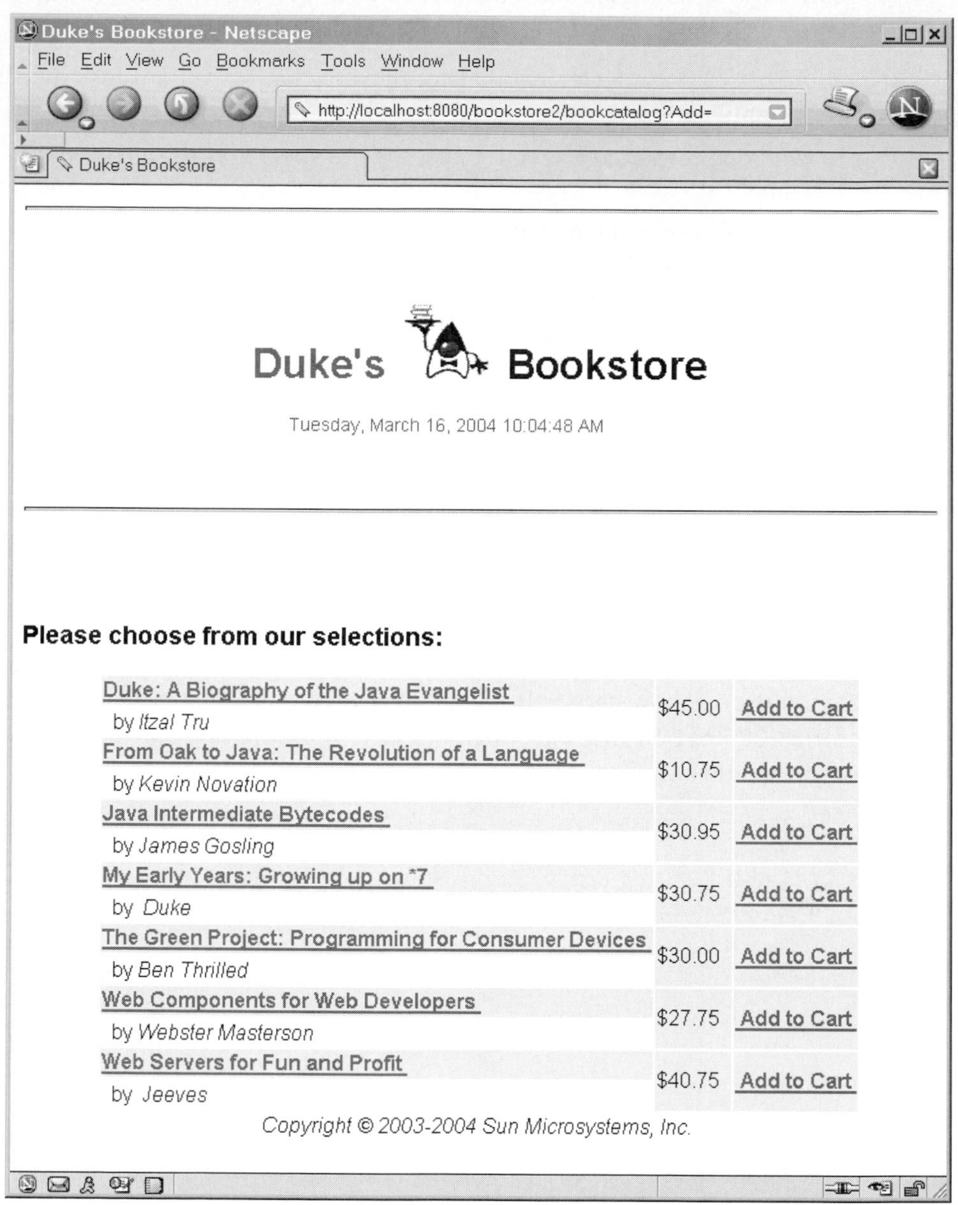

Figure 4–2 Book Catalog

The Life Cycle of a JSP Page

A JSP page services requests as a servlet. Thus, the life cycle and many of the capabilities of JSP pages (in particular the dynamic aspects) are determined by Java Servlet technology. You will notice that many sections in this chapter refer to classes and methods described in Chapter 3.

When a request is mapped to a JSP page, the web container first checks whether the JSP page's servlet is older than the JSP page. If the servlet is older, the web container translates the JSP page into a servlet class and compiles the class. During development, one of the advantages of JSP pages over servlets is that the build process is performed automatically.

Translation and Compilation

During the translation phase each type of data in a JSP page is treated differently. Static data is transformed into code that will emit the data into the response stream. JSP elements are treated as follows:

- Directives are used to control how the web container translates and executes the JSP page.
- Scripting elements are inserted into the JSP page's servlet class. See Chapter 8 for details.
- Expression language expressions are passed as parameters to calls to the JSP expression evaluator.
- `jsp:[set|get]Property` elements are converted into method calls to JavaBeans components.
- `jsp:[include|forward]` elements are converted into invocations of the Java Servlet API.
- The `jsp:plugin` element is converted into browser-specific markup for activating an applet.
- Custom tags are converted into calls to the tag handler that implements the custom tag.

In the Application Server, the source for the servlet created from a JSP page named *pageName* is in this file:

```
<JAVAEE_HOME>/domains/domain1/generated/jsp/j2ee-modules/
WAR_NAME/pageName_jsp.java
```

For example, the source for the index page (named `index.jsp`) for the `date` localization example discussed at the beginning of the chapter would be named:

```
<JAVAEE_HOME>/domains/domain1/generated/jsp/j2ee-modules/date/
index_jsp.java
```

Both the translation and the compilation phases can yield errors that are observed only when the page is requested for the first time. If an error is encountered during either phase, the server will return `JasperException` and a message that includes the name of the JSP page and the line where the error occurred.

After the page has been translated and compiled, the JSP page's servlet (for the most part) follows the servlet life cycle described in Servlet Life Cycle (page 63):

1. If an instance of the JSP page's servlet does not exist, the container:
   a. Loads the JSP page's servlet class
   b. Instantiates an instance of the servlet class
   c. Initializes the servlet instance by calling the `jspInit` method
2. The container invokes the `_jspService` method, passing request and response objects.

If the container needs to remove the JSP page's servlet, it calls the `jspDestroy` method.

Execution

You can control various JSP page execution parameters by using `page` directives. The directives that pertain to buffering output and handling errors are discussed here. Other directives are covered in the context of specific page-authoring tasks throughout the chapter.

Buffering

When a JSP page is executed, output written to the response object is automatically buffered. You can set the size of the buffer using the following page directive:

```
<%@ page buffer="none|xxxkb" %>
```

A larger buffer allows more content to be written before anything is actually sent back to the client, thus providing the JSP page with more time to set appropriate status codes and headers or to forward to another web resource. A smaller buffer decreases server memory load and allows the client to start receiving data more quickly.

Handling Errors

Any number of exceptions can arise when a JSP page is executed. To specify that the web container should forward control to an error page if an exception occurs, include the following `page` directive at the beginning of your JSP page:

```
<%@ page errorPage="file_name" %>
```

The Duke's Bookstore application page `preludeerrorpage.jspf` contains the directive:

```
<%@ page errorPage="errorpage.jsp"%>
```

The following page directive at the beginning of `errorpage.jsp` indicates that it is serving as an error page:

```
<%@ page isErrorPage="true" %>
```

This directive makes an object of type `javax.servlet.jsp.ErrorData` available to the error page so that you can retrieve, interpret, and possibly display information about the cause of the exception in the error page. You access the error data object in an EL (see Unified Expression Language, page 113) expression by way of the page context. Thus, `${pageContext.errorData.statusCode}` retrieves the status code, and `${pageContext.errorData.throwable}` retrieves the exception. You can retrieve the cause of the exception using this expression:

```
${pageContext.errorData.throwable.cause}
```

For example, the error page for Duke's Bookstore is as follows:

```
<%@ page isErrorPage="true" %>
<%@ taglib uri="http://java.sun.com/jsp/jstl/core"
  prefix="c" %>
<%@ taglib uri="http://java.sun.com/jsp/jstl/fmt"
  prefix="fmt" %>
<html>
```

```
<head>
<title><fmt:message key="ServerError"/></title>
</head>
<body bgcolor="white">
<h3>
<fmt:message key="ServerError"/>
</h3>
<p>
: ${pageContext.errorData.throwable.cause}
</body>
</html>
```

Note: You can also define error pages for the WAR that contains a JSP page. If error pages are defined for both the WAR and a JSP page, the JSP page's error page takes precedence.

Creating Static Content

You create static content in a JSP page simply by writing it as if you were creating a page that consisted only of that content. Static content can be expressed in any text-based format, such as HTML, Wireless Markup Language (WML), and XML. The default format is HTML. If you want to use a format other than HTML, at the beginning of your JSP page you include a `page` directive with the `contentType` attribute set to the content type. The purpose of the `contentType` directive is to allow the browser to correctly interpret the resulting content. So if you wanted a page to contain data expressed in WML, you would include the following directive:

```
<%@ page contentType="text/vnd.wap.wml"%>
```

A registry of content type names is kept by the IANA at:

```
http://www.iana.org/assignments/media-types/
```

Response and Page Encoding

You also use the `contentType` attribute to specify the encoding of the response. For example, the date application specifies that the page should be encoded using UTF-8, an encoding that supports almost all locales, using the following `page` directive:

```
<%@ page contentType="text/html; charset=UTF-8" %>
```

If the response encoding weren't set, the localized dates would not be rendered correctly.

To set the source encoding of the page itself, you would use the following `page` directive:

```
<%@ page pageEncoding="UTF-8" %>
```

You can also set the page encoding of a set of JSP pages. The value of the page encoding varies depending on the configuration specified in the JSP configuration section of the web application deployment descriptor (see Declaring Page Encodings, page 152).

Creating Dynamic Content

You create dynamic content by accessing Java programming language object properties.

Using Objects within JSP Pages

You can access a variety of objects, including enterprise beans and JavaBeans components, within a JSP page. JSP technology automatically makes some objects available, and you can also create and access application-specific objects.

Using Implicit Objects

Implicit objects are created by the web container and contain information related to a particular request, page, session, or application. Many of the objects are defined by the Java servlet technology underlying JSP technology and are discussed at length in Chapter 3. The section Implicit Objects (page 130) explains how you access implicit objects using the JSP expression language.

Using Application-Specific Objects

When possible, application behavior should be encapsulated in objects so that page designers can focus on presentation issues. Objects can be created by developers who are proficient in the Java programming language and in accessing databases and other services. The main way to create and use application-specific objects within a JSP page is to use JSP standard tags (discussed in JavaBeans Components, page 136) to create JavaBeans components and set their properties, and EL expressions to access their properties. You can also access JavaBeans components and other objects in scripting elements, which are described in Chapter 8.

Using Shared Objects

The conditions affecting concurrent access to shared objects (described in Controlling Concurrent Access to Shared Resources, page 68) apply to objects accessed from JSP pages that run as multithreaded servlets. You can use the following `page` directive to indicate how a web container should dispatch multiple client requests:

```
<%@ page isThreadSafe="true|false" %>
```

When the `isThreadSafe` attribute is set to `true`, the web container can choose to dispatch multiple concurrent client requests to the JSP page. This is the *default* setting. If using `true`, you must ensure that you properly synchronize access to any shared objects defined at the page level. This includes objects created within declarations, JavaBeans components with page scope, and attributes of the page context object (see Implicit Objects, page 130).

If `isThreadSafe` is set to `false`, requests are dispatched one at a time in the order they were received, and access to page-level objects does not have to be controlled. However, you still must ensure that access is properly synchronized to attributes of the `application` or `session` scope objects and to JavaBeans components with application or session scope. Furthermore, it is not recommended to set `isThreadSafe` to `false`. The JSP page's generated servlet will implement the `javax.servlet.SingleThreadModel` interface, and because the Servlet 2.4 specification deprecates `SingleThreadModel`, the generated servlet will contain deprecated code.

Unified Expression Language

The primary new feature of JSP 2.1 is the unified expression language (unified EL), which represents a union of the expression language offered by JSP 2.0 and the expression language created for JavaServer Faces technology (see Chapter 9) version 1.0.

The expression language introduced in JSP 2.0 allows page authors to use simple expressions to dynamically read data from JavaBeans components. For example, the test attribute of the following conditional tag is supplied with an EL expression that compares the number of items in the session-scoped bean named `cart` with 0.

```
<c:if test="${sessionScope.cart.numberOfItems > 0}">
  ...
</c:if>
```

As explained in The Life Cycle of a JSP Page (page 107), JSP supports a simple request/response life cycle, during which a page is executed and the HTML markup is rendered immediately. Therefore, the simple, read-only expression language offered by JSP 2.0 was well suited to the needs of JSP applications.

JavaServer Faces technology, on the other hand, features a multiphase life cycle designed to support its sophisticated UI component model, which allows for converting and validating component data, propagating component data to objects, and handling component events. To facilitate these functions, JavaServer Faces technology introduced its own expression language that included the following functionality:

- Deferred evaluation of expressions
- The ability to set data as well as get data
- The ability to invoke methods

See Using the Unified EL to Reference Backing Beans (page 307) for more information on how to use the unified EL in JavaServer Faces applications.

These two expression languages have been unified for a couple reasons. One reason is so that page authors can mix JSP content with JavaServer Faces tags without worrying about conflicts caused by the different life cycles these technologies support. Another reason is so that other JSP-based technologies could make use of the additional features similarly to the way JavaServer Faces technology uses them. In fact, although the standard JSP tags and static content continue to use only those features present in JSP 2.0, authors of JSP custom tags can create tags that take advantage of the new set of features in the unified expression language.

To summarize, the new, unified expression language allows page authors to use simple expressions to perform the following tasks:

- Dynamically read application data stored in JavaBeans components, various data structures, and implicit objects
- Dynamically write data—such as user input into forms—to JavaBeans components
- Invoke arbitrary static and public methods
- Dynamically perform arithmetic operations

The unified EL also allows custom tag developers to specify which of the following kinds of expressions that a custom tag attribute will accept:

- *Immediate evaluation expressions* or *deferred evaluation expressions*. An immediate evaluation expression is evaluated immediately by the JSP engine. A deferred evaluation expression can be evaluated later by the underlying technology using the expression language.
- *Value expression* or *method expression*. A value expression references data, whereas a method expression invokes a method.
- *Rvalue expression* or *Lvalue expression*. An rvalue expression can only read a value, whereas an lvalue expression can both read and write that value to an external object.

Finally, the unified EL also provides a pluggable API for resolving expressions so that application developers can implement their own resolvers that can handle expressions not already supported by the unified EL.

This section gives an overview of the unified expression language features by explaining the following topics:

- Immediate evaluation and deferred evaluation
- Value expressions and method expressions
- Defining Tag Attribute Types
- Deactivating Expression Evaluation
- Literal Expressions
- Resolving Expressions

- Implicit Objects
- Functions

Immediate and Deferred Evaluation Syntax

The unified EL supports both immediate and deferred evaluation of expressions. *Immediate evaluation* means that the JSP engine evaluates the expression and returns the result immediately when the page is first rendered. *Deferred evaluation* means that the technology using the expression language can employ its own machinery to evaluate the expression sometime later during the page's life cycle, whenever it is appropriate to do so.

Those expressions that are evaluated immediately use the `${}` syntax, which was introduced with the JSP 2.0 expression language. Expressions whose evaluation is deferred use the `#{}` syntax, which was introduced by JavaServer Faces technology.

Because of its multiphase life cycle, JavaServer Faces technology uses deferred evaluation expressions. During the life cycle, component events are handled, data is validated, and other tasks are performed, all done in a particular order. Therefore, it must defer evaluation of expressions until the appropriate point in the life cycle.

Other technologies using the unified EL might have different reasons for using deferred expressions.

Immediate Evaluation

All expressions using the `${}` syntax are evaluated immediately. These expressions can only be used within template text or as the value of a JSP tag attribute that can accept runtime expressions.

The following example shows a tag whose value attribute references an immediate evaluation expression that gets the total price from the session-scoped bean named cart:

```
<fmt:formatNumber value="${sessionScope.cart.total}"/>
```

The JSP engine evaluates the expression, `${sessionScope.cart.total}`, converts it, and passes the returned value to the tag handler.

Immediate evaluation expressions are always read-only value expressions. The expression shown above can only get the total price from the cart bean; it cannot set the total price.

Deferred Evaluation

Deferred evaluation expressions take the form `#{expr}` and can be evaluated at other phases of a page life cycle as defined by whatever technology is using the expression. In the case of JavaServer Faces technology, its controller can evaluate the expression at different phases of the life cycle depending on how the expression is being used in the page.

The following example shows a JavaServer Faces `inputText` tag, which represents a text field component into which a user enters a value. The `inputText` tag's `value` attribute references a deferred evaluation expression that points to the `name` property of the `customer` bean.

```
<h:inputText id="name" value="#{customer.name}" />
```

For an initial request of the page containing this tag, the JavaServer Faces implementation evaluates the `#{customer.name}` expression during the render response phase of the life cycle. During this phase, the expression merely accesses the value of `name` from the `customer` bean, as is done in immediate evaluation.

For a postback, the JavaServer Faces implementation evaluates the expression at different phases of the life cycle, during which the value is retrieved from the request, validated, and propagated to the `customer` bean.

As shown in this example, deferred evaluation expressions can be value expressions that can be used to both read and write data. They can also be method expressions. Value expressions (both immediate and deferred) and method expressions are explained in the next section.

Value and Method Expressions

The unified EL defines two kinds of expressions: value expressions and method expressions. Value expressions can either yield a value or set a value. Method expressions reference methods that can be invoked and can return a value.

Value Expressions

Value expressions can be further categorized into rvalue and lvalue expressions. *Rvalue expressions* are those that can read data, but cannot write it. *Lvalue expressions* can both read and write data.

All expressions that are evaluated immediately use the `${}` delimiters and are always rvalue expressions. Expressions whose evaluation can be deferred use the `#{}` delimiters and can act as both rvalue and lvalue expressions. Consider these two value expressions:

```
<taglib:tag value="${customer.name}" />

<taglib:tag value="#{customer.name}" />
```

The former uses immediate evaluation syntax, whereas the latter uses deferred evaluation syntax. The first expression accesses the `name` property, gets its value, and the value is added to the response and rendered on the page. The same thing can happen with the second expression. However, the tag handler can defer the evaluation of this expression to a later time in the page life cycle, if the technology using this tag allows it.

In the case of JavaServer Faces technology, the latter tag's expression is evaluated immediately during an initial request for the page. In this case, this expression acts as an rvalue expression. During a postback, this expression can be used to set the value of the `name` property with user input. In this situation, the expression acts as an lvalue expression.

Referencing Objects Using Value Expressions

Both rvalue and lvalue expressions can refer to the following objects and their properties or attributes:

- JavaBeans components
- Collections
- Java SE enumerated types
- Implicit objects.

See Implicit Objects (page 130) for more detail on the implicit objects available with JSP technology.

To refer to these objects, you write an expression using a variable name with which you created the object. The following expression references a JavaBeans component called customer.

```
${customer}
```

The web container evaluates a variable that appears in an expression by looking up its value according to the behavior of PageContext.findAttribute(String). For example, when evaluating the expression ${customer}, the container will look for customer in the page, request, session, and application scopes and will return its value. If customer is not found, null is returned. A variable that matches one of the implicit objects described in Implicit Objects (page 130) will return that implicit object instead of the variable's value.

You can alter the way variables are resolved with a custom EL resolver, which is a new feature of the unified EL. For instance, you can provide an ELResolver that intercepts objects with the name customer, so that ${customer} returns a value in the EL resolver instead. However, you cannot override implicit objects in this way. See EL Resolvers (page 128) for more information on EL resolvers.

You can set the variable name, customer, when you declare the bean. See Creating and Using a JavaBeans Component (page 138) for information on how to declare a JavaBeans component for use in your JSP pages.

To declare beans in JavaServer Faces applications, you use the managed bean facility. See Backing Beans (page 304) for information on how to declare beans for use in JavaServer Faces applications.

When referencing an enum constant with an expression, you use a String literal. For example, consider this Enum class:

```
public enum Suit {hearts, spades, diamonds, clubs}
```

To refer to the Suit constant, Suit.hearts with an expression, you use the String literal, "hearts". Depending on the context, the String literal is converted to the enum constant automatically. For example, in the following expression in which mySuit is an instance of Suit, "hearts" is first converted to a Suit.hearts before it is compared to the instance.

```
${mySuit == "hearts"}
```

Referring to Object Properties Using Value Expressions

To refer to properties of a bean or an Enum instance, items of a collection, or attributes of an implicit object, you use the `.` or `[]` notation, which is similar to the notation used by ECMAScript.

So, if you wanted to reference the `name` property of the `customer` bean, you could use either the expression `${customer.name}` or the expression `${customer["name"]}`. The part inside the square brackets is a `String` literal that is the name of the property to reference.

You can use double or single quotes for the `String` literal. You can also combine the `[]` and `.` notations, as shown here:

```
${customer.address["street"]}
```

Properties of an enum can also be referenced in this way. However, as with JavaBeans component properties, the Enum class's properties must follow JavaBeans component conventions. This means that a property must at least have an accessor method called `get<Property>`—where `<Property>` is the name of the property—so that an expression can reference it.

For example, say you have an Enum class that encapsulates the names of the planets of our galaxy and includes a method to get the mass of a planet. You can use the following expression to reference the method `getMass` of the `Planet` Enum class:

```
${myPlanet.mass}
```

If you are accessing an item in an array or list, you must use either a literal value that can be coerced to int or the `[]` notation with an int and without quotes. The following examples could all resolve to the same item in a list or array, assuming that `socks` can be coerced to `int`:

- `${customer.orders[1]}`
- `${customer.orders.socks}`

In contrast, an item in a `Map` can be accessed using a string literal key; no coercion is required:

```
${customer.orders["socks"]}
```

An rvalue expression also refers directly to values that are not objects, such as the result of arithmetic operations and literal values, as shown by these examples:

- `${"literal"}`
- `${customer.age + 20}`
- `${true}`
- `${57}`

The unified expression language defines the following literals:

- Boolean: `true` and `false`
- Integer: as in Java
- Floating point: as in Java
- String: with single and double quotes; `"` is escaped as `\"`, `'` is escaped as `\'`, and `\` is escaped as `\\`
- Null: `null`

You can also write expressions that perform operations on an enum constant. For example, consider the following Enum class:

```
public enum Suit {club, diamond, heart, spade }
```

After declaring an enum constant called `mySuit`, you can write the following expression to test if `mySuit` is `spade`:

```
${mySuit == "spade"}
```

When the EL resolving mechanism resolves this expression it will invoke the `valueOf` method of the Enum class with the `Suit` class and the `spade` type, as shown here:

```
mySuit.valueOf(Suit.class, "spade"}
```

See JavaBeans Components (page 136) for more information on using expressions to reference JavaBeans components and their properties.

Where Value Expressions Can Be Used

Value expressions using the `${}` delimiters can be used in the following places:

- In static text
- In any standard or custom tag attribute that can accept an expression

The value of an expression in static text is computed and inserted into the current output. Here is an example of an expression embedded in static text:

```
<some:tag>
  some text ${expr} some text
</some:tag>
```

If the static text appears in a tag body, note that an expression *will not* be evaluated if the body is declared to be `tagdependent` (see Tags with Attributes, page 207).

Lvalue expressions can only be used in tag attributes that can accept lvalue expressions.

There are three ways to set a tag attribute value using either an rvalue or lvalue expression:

- With a single expression construct:

  ```
  <some:tag value="${expr}"/>
  ```

  ```
  <another:tag value="#{expr}"/>
  ```

  These expressions are evaluated and the result is coerced to the attribute's expected type.

- With one or more expressions separated or surrounded by text:

  ```
  <some:tag value="some${expr}${expr}text${expr}"/>
  ```

  ```
  <another:tag value="some#{expr}#{expr}text#{expr}"/>
  ```

  These kinds of expression are called a *composite expressions*. They are evaluated from left to right. Each expression embedded in the composite expression is coerced to a `String` and then concatenated with any intervening text. The resulting `String` is then coerced to the attribute's expected type.

- With text only:

  ```
  <some:tag value="sometext"/>
  ```

  This expression is called a *literal expression*. In this case, the attribute's `String` value is coerced to the attribute's expected type. Literal value expressions have special syntax rules. See Literal Expressions (page 126) for more information. When a tag attribute has an enum type, the expression that the attribute uses must be a literal expression. For example, the tag attribute can use the expression `"hearts"` to mean `Suit.hearts`. The literal is coerced to `Suit` and the attribute gets the value `Suit.hearts`.

All expressions used to set attribute values are evaluated in the context of an expected type. If the result of the expression evaluation does not match the expected type exactly, a type conversion will be performed. For example, the expression `${1.2E4}` provided as the value of an attribute of type `float` will result in the following conversion:

```
Float.valueOf("1.2E4").floatValue()
```

See section 1.17 of the Expression Language specification for the complete type conversion rules.

Method Expressions

Another feature of the unified expression language is its support of deferred method expressions. A method expression is used to invoke an arbitrary public method, which can return a result. A similar feature of the unified EL is functions. Method expressions differ from functions in many ways. Functions (page 134) explains more about the differences between functions and method expressions.

Method expressions primarily benefit JavaServer Faces technology, but they are available to any technology that can support the unified expression language. Let's take a look at how JavaServer Faces technology employs method expressions.

In JavaServer Faces technology, a component tag represents a UI component on a page. The component tag uses method expressions to invoke methods that perform some processing for the component. These methods are necessary for handling events that the components generate and validating component data, as shown in this example:

```
<h:form>
  <h:inputText
    id="name"
    value="#{customer.name}"
    validator="#{customer.validateName}"/>
  <h:commandButton
    id="submit"
    action="#{customer.submit}" />
</h:form>
```

The `inputText` tag displays a `UIInput` component as a text field. The `validator` attribute of this `inputText` tag references a method, called `validateName`, in the bean, called `customer`. The TLD that defines the `inputText` tag specifies what signature the method referred to by the `validator` attribute must have. The same is true of the `customer.submit` method referenced by the `action` attribute of the `commandButton` tag. The TLD specifies that the `submit` method must return an `Object` instance that specifies which page to navigate to next after the button represented by the `commandButton` tag is clicked.

The `validation` method is invoked during the process validation phase of the life cycle, whereas the `submit` method is invoked during the invoke application phase of the life cycle. Because a method can be invoked during different phases of the life cycle, method expressions must always use the deferred evaluation syntax.

Similarly to lvalue expressions, method expressions can use the . and `[]` operators. For example, `#{object.method}` is equivalent to `#{object["method"]}`. The literal inside the `[]` is coerced to `String` and is used to find the name of the method that matches it. Once the method is found, it is invoked or information about the method is returned.

Method expressions can be used only in tag attributes and only in the following ways:

- With a single expression construct, where `bean` refers to a JavaBeans component and `method` refers to a method of the JavaBeans component:

  ```
  <some:tag value="#{bean.method}"/>
  ```

  The expression is evaluated to a method expression, which is passed to the tag handler. The method represented by the method expression can then be invoked later.

- With text only:

  ```
  <some:tag value="sometext"/>
  ```

  Method expressions support literals primarily to support `action` attributes in JavaServer Faces technology. When the method referenced by this method expression is invoked, it returns the `String` literal, which is then coerced to the expected return type, as defined in the tag's TLD.

Defining a Tag Attribute Type

As explained in the previous section, all kinds of expressions can be used in tag attributes. Which kind of expression and how that expression is evaluated—

whether immediately or deferred—is determined by the `type` attribute of the tag's definition in the TLD file that defines the tag.

If you plan to create custom tags (see Chapter 7), you need to specify for each tag in the TLD what kind of expression it accepts. Table 4–2 shows the three different kinds of tag attributes that accept EL expressions, and gives examples of expressions they accept and the type definitions of the attributes that must be added to the TLD. Note that it is illegal to use `#{}` syntax for a dynamic attribute or `${}` syntax for a deferred attribute.

Table 4–2 Definitions of Tag Attributes That Accept EL Expressions

Attribute Type	Example Expression	Type Attribute Definition
dynamic	`"literal"`	`<rtexprvalue>true</rtexprvalue>`
	`${literal}`	`<rtexprvalue>true</rtexprvalue>`

deferred value	`"literal"`	`<deferred-value>`
		`<type>java.lang.String</type>`
		`</deferred-value>`

	`#{customer.age}`	`<deferred-value>`
		`<type>int</type>`
		`</deferred-value>`

deferred method	`"literal"`	`<deferred-method>`
		`<method-signature>`
		`java.lang.String submit()`
		`</method-signature>`
		`<deferred-method>`

	`#{customer.calcTotal}`	`<deferred-method>`
		`<method-signature>`
		`double calcTotal(int, double)`
		`</method-signature>`
		`</deferred-method`

In addition to the tag attribute types shown in Table 4–2, you can also define an attribute to accept both dynamic and deferred expressions. In this case, the tag attribute definition contains both an `rtexprvalue` definition set to `true` and either a `deferred-value` or `deferred-method` definition.

Deactivating Expression Evaluation

Because the patterns that identify EL expressions—`${ }` and `#{ }`—were not reserved in the JSP specifications before JSP 2.0, there might exist applications in which such patterns are intended to pass through verbatim. To prevent the patterns from being evaluated, you can deactivate EL evaluation using one of the following methods:

- Escape the `#{` or `${` characters in the page.
- Configure the application with a JSP Property Group.
- Configure the page with the page directive.

To escape the `#{` or `${` characters in the page, you use the \ character as follows:

```
some text \#{ some more\${ text

<my:tag someAttribute="sometext\#{more\${text" />
```

Another way to deactivate EL evaluation is by using a JSP property group to either allow the `#{` characters as a String literal using the `deferred-syntax-allowed-as-literal` subelement, or to treat all expressions as literals using the `el-ignored` subelement:

```
<jsp-property-group>
  <deferred-syntax-allowed-as-literal>
    true
  </deferred-syntax-allowed-as-literal>
</jsp-property-group>
```

or

```
<jsp-property-group>
  <el-ignored>true</el-ignored>
</jsp-property-group>
```

Finally, you can configure the page with the `page` directive to either accept the `#{` characters as String literals with the `deferredSyntaxAllowedAsLiteral` attribute, or to ignore all EL expressions using the `isELIgnored` attribute:

```
<%@page ... deferredSyntaxAllowedAsLiteral="true" %>
```

or

```
<%@ page isELIgnored ="true" %>
```

The valid values of these attributes are `true` and `false`. If `isELIgnored` is `true`, EL expressions are ignored when they appear in static text or tag attributes. If it is `false`, EL expressions are evaluated by the container only if the attribute has `rtexprvalue` set to `true` or the expression is a deferred expression.

The default value of `isELIgnored` varies depending on the version of the web application deployment descriptor. The default mode for JSP pages delivered using a Servlet 2.3 or earlier descriptor is to ignore EL expressions; this provides backward compatibility. The default mode for JSP pages delivered with a Servlet 2.4 descriptor is to evaluate EL expressions; this automatically provides the default that most applications want.

Literal Expressions

A literal expression evaluates to the text of the expression, which is of type String. It does not use the `${}` or `#{}` delimiters.

If you have a literal expression that includes the reserved `${}` or `#{}` syntax, you need to escape these characters as follows.

- By creating a composite expression as shown here:

  ```
  ${'${'}exprA}
  ```

  ```
  #{'#{'}exprB}
  ```

  The resulting values would then be the strings `${exprA}` and `#{exprB}`.

- The escape characters `\$` and `\#` can be used to escape what would otherwise be treated as an eval-expression:

  ```
  \${exprA}
  ```

  ```
  \#{exprB}
  ```

  The resulting values would again be the strings `${exprA}` and `#{exprB}`.

When a literal expression is evaluated, it can be converted to another type. Table 4–3 shows examples of various literal expressions and their expected types and resulting values.

Table 4–3 Literal Expressions

Expression	Expected Type	Result
Hi	String	Hi
true	Boolean	Boolean.TRUE
42	int	42

Literal expressions can be evaluated immediately or deferred and can be either value or method expressions. At what point a literal expression is evaluated depends on where it is being used. If the tag attribute that uses the literal expression is defined as accepting a deferred value expression, then the literal expression references a value and is evaluated at a point in the life cycle that is determined by where the expression is being used and to what it is referring.

In the case of a method expression, the method that is referenced is invoked and returns the specified `String` literal. The `commandButton` tag of the Guess Number application uses a literal method expression as a logical outcome to tell the JavaServer Faces navigation system which page to display next. See Navigation Model (page 302) for more information on this example.

Resolving Expressions

The unified EL introduces a new, pluggable API for resolving expressions. The main pieces of this API are:

- The `ValueExpression` class, which defines a value expression
- The `MethodExpression` class, which defines a method expression
- An `ELResolver` class that defines a mechanism for resolving expressions
- A set of `ELResolver` implementations, in which each implementation is responsible for resolving expressions that reference a particular type of object or property

- An ELContext object that saves state relating to EL resolution, holds references to EL resolvers, and contains context objects (such as JspContext) needed by the underlying technology to resolve expressions

Most application developers will not need to use these classes directly unless they plan to write their own custom EL resolvers. Those writing JavaServer Faces custom components will definitely need to use ValueExpression and MethodExpression. This section details how expressions are resolved for the benefit of these developers. It does not explain how to create a custom resolver. For more information on creating custom resolvers, see the article *The Unified Expression Language*, Ryan Lubke et al., located at http://java.sun.com/products/jsp/reference/techart/unifiedEL.html. You can also refer to Request Processing (page 1249), which explains how the Duke's Bank application uses a custom resolver.

Process of Expression Evaluation

When a value expression that is included in a page is parsed during an initial request for the page, a ValueExpression object is created to represent the expression. Then, the ValueExpression object's getValue method is invoked. This method will in turn invoke the getValue method of the appropriate resolver. A similar process occurs during a postback when setValue is called if the expression is an lvalue expression.

In the case of a method expression, a BeanELResolver is used to find the object that implements the method to be invoked or queried. Similarly to the process for evaluating value expressions, when a method expression is encountered, a MethodExpression object is created. Subsequently, either the invoke or getMethodInfo method of the MethodExpression object is called. This method in turn invokes the BeanELResolver object's getValue method. The getMethodInfo is mostly for use by tools.

After a resolver completes resolution of an expression, it sets the propertyResolved flag of the ELContext to true so that no more resolvers are consulted.

EL Resolvers

At the center of the EL machinery is the extensible ELResolver class. A class that implements ELResolver defines how to resolve expressions referring to a particular type of object or property. In terms of the following expression, a BeanELResolver instance is called the first time to find the *base* object, employee, which is a JavaBeans component. Once the resolver finds the object, it is called again to resolve the *property*, lName of the employee object.

```
${employee.lName}
```

The unified EL includes a set of standard resolver implementations. Table 4–4 lists these standard resolvers and includes example expressions that they can resolve.

Table 4–4 Standard EL Resolvers

Resolver	Example Expression	Description
ArrayELResolver	${myArray[1]}	Returns the value at index 1 in the array called myArray
BeanELResolver	${employee.lName}	Returns the value of the lName property of the employee bean
ListELResolver	${myList[5]}	Returns the value at index 5 of myList list
MapELResolver	${myMap.someKey}	Returns the value stored at the key, someKey, in the Map, myMap
ResourceBundleELResolver	${myRB.myKey}	Returns the message at myKey in the resource bundle called myRB

Depending on the technology using the unified EL, other resolvers might be available. In addition, application developers can add their own implementations of ELResolver to support resolution of expressions not already supported by the unified EL by registering them with an application.

All of the standard and custom resolvers available to a particular application are collected in a chain in a particular order. This chain of resolvers is represented by a CompositeELResolver instance. When an expression is encountered, the CompositeELResolver instance iterates over the list of resolvers and consults each resolver until it finds one that can handle the expression.

If an application is using JSP technology, the chain of resolvers includes the ImplicitObjectELResolver and the ScopedAttributeELResolver. These are described in the following section.

See section JSP2.9 of the JavaServer Pages 2.1 specification to find out the order in which resolvers are chained together in a CompositeELResolver instance.

To learn how to create a custom EL resolver, see the article *The Unified Expression Language,* located at http://java.sun.com/products/jsp/reference/techart/unifiedEL.html.

Implicit Objects

The JSP expression language defines a set of implicit objects:

- pageContext: The context for the JSP page. Provides access to various objects including:
    - servletContext: The context for the JSP page's servlet and any web components contained in the same application. See Accessing the Web Context (page 88).
    - session: The session object for the client. See Maintaining Client State (page 89).
    - request: The request triggering the execution of the JSP page. See Getting Information from Requests (page 72).
    - response: The response returned by the JSP page. See Constructing Responses (page 74).

In addition, several implicit objects are available that allow easy access to the following objects:

- param: Maps a request parameter name to a single value
- paramValues: Maps a request parameter name to an array of values
- header: Maps a request header name to a single value
- headerValues: Maps a request header name to an array of values
- cookie: Maps a cookie name to a single cookie
- initParam: Maps a context initialization parameter name to a single value

Finally, there are objects that allow access to the various scoped variables described in Using Scope Objects (page 67).

- `pageScope`: Maps page-scoped variable names to their values
- `requestScope`: Maps request-scoped variable names to their values
- `sessionScope`: Maps session-scoped variable names to their values
- `applicationScope`: Maps application-scoped variable names to their values

JSP 2.1 provides two EL resolvers to handle expressions that reference these objects: `ImplicitObjectELResolver` and `ScopedAttributeELResolver`.

A variable that matches one of the implicit objects is evaluated by `ImplicitObjectResolver`, which returns the implicit object. This resolver only handles expressions with a base of `null`. What this means for the following expression is that the `ImplicitObjectResolver` resolves the `sessionScope` implicit object only. Once the implicit object is found, the `MapELResolver` instance resolves the `profile` attribute because the `profile` object represents a map.

```
${sessionScope.profile}
```

`ScopedAttributeELResolver` evaluates a single object that is stored in scope. Like `ImplicitObjectELResolver`, it also only evaluates expressions with a base of `null`. This resolver essentially looks for an object in all of the scopes until it finds it, according to the behavior of `PageContext.findAttribute(String)`. For example, when evaluating the expression `${product}`, the resolver will look for `product` in the page, request, session, and application scopes and will return its value. If `product` is not found, `null` is returned.

When an expression references one of the implicit objects by name, the appropriate object is returned instead of the corresponding attribute. For example, `${pageContext}` returns the `PageContext` object, even if there is an existing `pageContext` attribute containing some other value.

Operators

In addition to the `.` and `[]` operators discussed in Value and Method Expressions (page 116), the JSP expression language provides the following operators, which can be used in rvalue expressions only:

- Arithmetic: `+`, `-` (binary), `*`, `/` and `div`, `%` and `mod`, `-` (unary)
- Logical: `and`, `&&`, `or`, `||`, `not`, `!`

- Relational: ==, eq, !=, ne, <, lt, >, gt, <=, ge, >=, le. Comparisons can be made against other values, or against boolean, string, integer, or floating point literals.
- Empty: The empty operator is a prefix operation that can be used to determine whether a value is null or empty.
- Conditional: A ? B : C. Evaluate B or C, depending on the result of the evaluation of A.

The precedence of operators highest to lowest, left to right is as follows:

- [] .
- () - Used to change the precedence of operators.
- - (unary) not ! empty
- * / div % mod
- + - (binary)
- < > <= >= lt gt le ge
- == != eq ne
- && and
- || or
- ? :

Reserved Words

The following words are reserved for the JSP expression language and should not be used as identifiers.

```
and    eq    gt    true    instanceof
or     ne    le    false   empty
not    lt    ge    null    div    mod
```

Note that many of these words are not in the language now, but they may be in the future, so you should avoid using them.

Examples

Table 4–5 contains example EL expressions and the result of evaluating them.

Table 4–5 Example Expressions

EL Expression	Result
`${1 > (4/2)}`	`false`
`${4.0 >= 3}`	`true`
`${100.0 == 100}`	`true`
`${(10*10) ne 100}`	`false`
`${'a' < 'b'}`	`true`
`${'hip' gt 'hit'}`	`false`
`${4 > 3}`	`true`
`${1.2E4 + 1.4}`	`12001.4`
`${3 div 4}`	`0.75`
`${10 mod 4}`	`2`
`${!empty param.Add}`	True if the request parameter named `Add` is null or an empty string.
`${pageContext.request.contextPath}`	The context path.
`${sessionScope.cart.numberOfItems}`	The value of the `numberOfItems` property of the session-scoped attribute named `cart`.
`${param['mycom.productId']}`	The value of the request parameter named `mycom.productId`.
`${header["host"]}`	The host.
`${departments[deptName]}`	The value of the entry named `deptName` in the `departments` map.
`${requestScope['javax.servlet.forward.servlet_path']}`	The value of the request-scoped attribute named `javax.servlet.forward.servlet_path`.

Table 4–5 Example Expressions (Continued)

EL Expression	Result
`#{customer.lName}`	Gets the value of the property `lName` from the `customer` bean during an initial request. Sets the value of `lName` during a postback.
`#{customer.calcTotal}`	The return value of the method `calcTotal` of the `customer` bean.

Functions

The JSP expression language allows you to define a function that can be invoked in an expression. Functions are defined using the same mechanisms as custom tags (see Using Custom Tags, page 141 and Chapter 7).

At first glance, functions seem similar to method expressions, but they are different in the following ways:

- Functions refer to static methods that return a value. Method expressions refer to non-static, arbitrary public methods on objects.
- Functions are identified statically at translation time, whereas methods are identified dynamically at runtime.
- Function parameters and invocations are specified as part of an EL expression. A method expression only identifies a particular method. The invocation of that method is not specified by the EL expression; rather, it is specified in the tag attribute definition of the attribute using the method expression, as described in Defining a Tag Attribute Type (page 123).

Using Functions

Functions can appear in static text and tag attribute values.

To use a function in a JSP page, you use a `taglib` directive to import the tag library containing the function. Then you preface the function invocation with the prefix declared in the directive.

For example, the date example page index.jsp imports the /functions library and invokes the function equals in an expression:

```
<%@ taglib prefix="f" uri="/functions"%>
...
     <c:when
       test="${f:equals(selectedLocaleString,
          localeString)}" >
```

In this example, the expression referencing the function is using immediate evaluation syntax. A page author can also use deferred evaluation syntax to reference a function in an expression, assuming that the attribute that is referencing the function can accept deferred expressions.

If an attribute references a function with a deferred expression then the function is not invoked immediately; rather, it is invoked whenever the underlying technology using the function determines it should be invoked.

Defining Functions

To define a function, you program it as a public static method in a public class. The mypkg.MyLocales class in the date example defines a function that tests the equality of two Strings as follows:

```
package mypkg;
public class MyLocales {

  ...
  public static boolean equals( String l1, String l2 ) {
     return l1.equals(l2);
  }
}
```

Then you map the function name as used in the EL expression to the defining class and function signature in a TLD. The following functions.tld file in the date example maps the equals function to the class containing the implementation of the function equals and the signature of the function:

```
<function>
  <name>equals</name>
  <function-class>mypkg.MyLocales</function-class>
  <function-signature>boolean equals( java.lang.String,
     java.lang.String )</function-signature>
</function>
```

No two functions within a tag library can have the same name.

JavaBeans Components

JavaBeans components are Java classes that can be easily reused and composed together into applications. Any Java class that follows certain design conventions is a JavaBeans component.

JavaServer Pages technology directly supports using JavaBeans components with standard JSP language elements. You can easily create and initialize beans and get and set the values of their properties.

JavaBeans Component Design Conventions

JavaBeans component design conventions govern the properties of the class and govern the public methods that give access to the properties.

A JavaBeans component property can be:

- Read/write, read-only, or write-only
- Simple, which means it contains a single value, or indexed, which means it represents an array of values

A property does not have to be implemented by an instance variable. It must simply be accessible using public methods that conform to the following conventions:

- For each readable property, the bean must have a method of the form:

  ```
  PropertyClass getProperty() { ... }
  ```

- For each writable property, the bean must have a method of the form:

  ```
  setProperty(PropertyClass pc) { ... }
  ```

In addition to the property methods, a JavaBeans component must define a constructor that takes no parameters.

The Duke's Bookstore application JSP pages `bookstore.jsp`, `bookdetails.jsp`, `catalog.jsp`, and `showcart.jsp` use the following JavaBeans components:

- `com.sun.bookstore2.database.BookDB`
- `com.sun.bookstore2.database.BookDetails`

`BookDB` provides a JavaBeans component front end to the access object `BookDBAO`. The JSP pages `showcart.jsp` and `cashier.jsp` access the bean `com.sun.bookstore.cart.ShoppingCart`, which represents a user's shopping cart.

The `BookDB` bean has two writable properties, `bookId` and `database`, and three readable properties: `bookDetails`, `numberOfBooks`, and `books`. These latter properties do not correspond to any instance variables but rather are a function of the `bookId` and `database` properties.

```
package database;
public class BookDB {
  private String bookId = "0";
  private BookDBAO database = null;
  public BookDB () {
  }
  public void setBookId(String bookId) {
  this.bookId = bookId;
  }
  public void setDatabase(BookDBAO database) {
  this.database = database;
  }
  public Book getBook() throws
     BookNotFoundException {
     return (Book)database.getBook(bookId);
  }
  public List getBooks() throws BooksNotFoundException {
     return database.getBooks();
  }
  public void buyBooks(ShoppingCart cart)
     throws OrderException {
     database.buyBooks(cart);
  }
  public int getNumberOfBooks() throws BooksNotFoundException {
     return database.getNumberOfBooks();
  }
}
```

Creating and Using a JavaBeans Component

To declare that your JSP page will use a JavaBeans component, you use a jsp:useBean element. There are two forms:

```
<jsp:useBean id="beanName"
  class="fully_qualified_classname" scope="scope"/>
```

and

```
<jsp:useBean id="beanName"
  class="fully_qualified_classname" scope="scope">
  <jsp:setProperty .../>
</jsp:useBean>
```

The second form is used when you want to include jsp:setProperty statements, described in the next section, for initializing bean properties.

The jsp:useBean element declares that the page will use a bean that is stored within and is accessible from the specified scope, which can be application, session, request, or page. If no such bean exists, the statement creates the bean and stores it as an attribute of the scope object (see Using Scope Objects, page 67). The value of the id attribute determines the *name* of the bean in the scope and the *identifier* used to reference the bean in EL expressions, other JSP elements, and scripting expressions (see Chapter 8). The value supplied for the class attribute must be a fully qualified class name. Note that beans cannot be in the unnamed package. Thus the format of the value must be *package_name.class_name*.

The following element creates an instance of mypkg.myLocales if none exists, stores it as an attribute of the application scope, and makes the bean available throughout the application by the identifier locales:

```
<jsp:useBean id="locales" scope="application"
  class="mypkg.MyLocales"/>
```

Setting JavaBeans Component Properties

The standard way to set JavaBeans component properties in a JSP page is by using the `jsp:setProperty` element. The syntax of the `jsp:setProperty` element depends on the source of the property value. Table 4–6 summarizes the various ways to set a property of a JavaBeans component using the `jsp:setProperty` element.

Table 4–6 Valid Bean Property Assignments from String Values

Value Source	Element Syntax
String constant	<jsp:setProperty name="*beanName*" property="*propName*" value="*string constant*"/>
Request parameter	<jsp:setProperty name="*beanName*" property="*propName*" param="*paramName*"/>
Request parameter name that matches bean property	<jsp:setProperty name="*beanName*" property="*propName*"/> <jsp:setProperty name="*beanName*" property="*"/>
Expression	<jsp:setProperty name="*beanName*" property="*propName*" value="*expression*"/> <jsp:setProperty name="*beanName*" property="*propName*" > <jsp:attribute name="value"> *expression* </jsp:attribute> </jsp:setProperty>

Syntax rules of attribute values used in this table:
1. *beanName* must be the same as that specified for the `id` attribute in a `useBean` element.
2. There must be a *setPropName* method in the JavaBeans component.
3. *paramName* must be a request parameter name.

A property set from a constant string or request parameter must have one of the types listed in Table 4–7. Because constants and request parameters are strings, the web container automatically converts the value to the property's type; the conversion applied is shown in the table.

String values can be used to assign values to a property that has a PropertyEditor class. When that is the case, the setAsText(String) method is used. A conversion failure arises if the method throws an IllegalArgumentException.

The value assigned to an indexed property must be an array, and the rules just described apply to the elements.

You use an expression to set the value of a property whose type is a compound Java programming language type. The type returned from an expression must match or be castable to the type of the property.

Table 4–7 Valid Property Value Assignments from String Values

Property Type	Conversion on String Value
Bean Property	Uses setAsText(*string-literal*)
boolean or Boolean	As indicated in java.lang.Boolean.valueOf(String)
byte or Byte	As indicated in java.lang.Byte.valueOf(String)
char or Character	As indicated in java.lang.String.charAt(0)
double or Double	As indicated in java.lang.Double.valueOf(String)
int or Integer	As indicated in java.lang.Integer.valueOf(String)
float or Float	As indicated in java.lang.Float.valueOf(String)
long or Long	As indicated in java.lang.Long.valueOf(String)
short or Short	As indicated in java.lang.Short.valueOf(String)
Object	new String(*string-literal*)

The Duke's Bookstore application demonstrates how to use the setProperty element to set the current book from a request parameter in the database bean in bookstore2/web/bookdetails.jsp:

```
<c:set var="bid" value="${param.bookId}"/>
<jsp:setProperty name="bookDB" property="bookId"
  value="${bid}" />
```

The following fragment from the page bookstore2/web/bookshowcart.jsp illustrates how to initialize a BookDB bean with a database object. Because the initialization is nested in a useBean element, it is executed only when the bean is created.

```
<jsp:useBean id="bookDB" class="database.BookDB" scope="page">
  <jsp:setProperty name="bookDB" property="database"
    value="${bookDBAO}" />
</jsp:useBean>
```

Retrieving JavaBeans Component Properties

The main way to retrieve JavaBeans component properties is by using the unified EL expressions. Thus, to retrieve a book title, the Duke's Bookstore application uses the following expression:

```
${bookDB.bookDetails.title}
```

Another way to retrieve component properties is to use the jsp:getProperty element. This element converts the value of the property into a String and inserts the value into the response stream:

```
<jsp:getProperty name="beanName" property="propName"/>
```

Note that *beanName* must be the same as that specified for the id attribute in a useBean element, and there must be a get*PropName* method in the JavaBeans component. Although the preferred approach to getting properties is to use an EL expression, the getProperty element is available if you need to disable expression evaluation.

Using Custom Tags

Custom tags are user-defined JSP language elements that encapsulate recurring tasks. Custom tags are distributed in a *tag library*, which defines a set of related custom tags and contains the objects that implement the tags.

Custom tags have the syntax

```
<prefix:tag attr1="value" ... attrN="value" />
```

or

```
<prefix:tag attr1="value" ... attrN="value" >
  body
</prefix:tag>
```

where `prefix` distinguishes tags for a library, `tag` is the tag identifier, and `attr1 ... attrN` are attributes that modify the behavior of the tag.

To use a custom tag in a JSP page, you must

- Declare the tag library containing the tag
- Make the tag library implementation available to the web application

See Chapter 7 for detailed information on the different types of tags and how to implement tags.

Declaring Tag Libraries

To declare that a JSP page will use tags defined in a tag library, you include a `taglib` directive in the page before any custom tag from that tag library is used. If you forget to include the `taglib` directive for a tag library in a JSP page, the JSP compiler will treat any invocation of a custom tag from that library as static data and will simply insert the text of the custom tag call into the response.

```
<%@ taglib prefix="tt" [tagdir=/WEB-INF/tags/dir | uri=URI ] %>
```

The `prefix` attribute defines the prefix that distinguishes tags defined by a given tag library from those provided by other tag libraries.

If the tag library is defined with tag files (see Encapsulating Reusable Content Using Tag Files, page 212), you supply the `tagdir` attribute to identify the location of the files. The value of the attribute must start with `/WEB-INF/tags/`. A translation error will occur if the value points to a directory that doesn't exist or if it is used in conjunction with the `uri` attribute.

The `uri` attribute refers to a URI that uniquely identifies the tag library descriptor (TLD), a document that describes the tag library (see Tag Library Descriptors, page 229).

Tag library descriptor file names must have the extension .tld. TLD files are stored in the WEB-INF directory or subdirectory of the WAR file, or in the META-INF/ directory or subdirectory of a tag library packaged in a JAR. You can reference a TLD directly or indirectly.

The following taglib directive directly references a TLD file name:

```
<%@ taglib prefix="tlt" uri="/WEB-INF/iterator.tld"%>
```

This taglib directive uses a short logical name to indirectly reference the TLD:

```
<%@ taglib prefix="tlt" uri="/tlt"%>
```

The iterator example defines and uses a simple iteration tag. The JSP pages use a logical name to reference the TLD.

To deploy and run the iterator application with NetBeans 5.5, follow these steps:

1. In NetBeans 5.5, select File→Open Project.
2. In the Open Project dialog, navigate to:
   <INSTALL>/javaeetutorial5/examples/web/
3. Select the iterator folder.
4. Select the Open as Main Project checkbox.
5. Click Open Project Folder.
6. In the Projects tab, right-click the iterator project, and select Deploy Project.
7. To run the application, open the bookstore URL http://localhost:8080/iterator.

To deploy and run the iterator application with Ant, follow these steps:

1. In a terminal window, go to *<INSTALL>*/javaeetutorial5/examples/web/iterator/.
2. Run the command ant. This target will spawn any necessary compilations, copy files to the *<INSTALL>*/javaeetutorial5/examples/web/iterator/build/ directory, and create a WAR file.
3. Start the Application Server.
4. Run ant deploy.
5. To run the example, open your browser to http://localhost:8080/iterator.

To learn how to configure the example, refer to the deployment descriptor, which includes the following configurations:

- A `display-name` element that specifies the name that tools use to identify the application.
- Nested inside a `jsp-config` element is a `taglib` element, which provides information on a tag library used by the pages of the application. Inside the `taglib` element are the `taglib-uri` element and the `taglib-location` element. The `taglib-uri` element identifies the logical name of the tag library. The `taglib-location` element gives the absolute location or the absolute URI of the tag library.

The absolute URIs for the JSTL library are as follows:

- *Core*: `http://java.sun.com/jsp/jstl/core`
- *XML*: `http://java.sun.com/jsp/jstl/xml`
- *Internationalization*: `http://java.sun.com/jsp/jstl/fmt`
- *SQL*: `http://java.sun.com/jsp/jstl/sql`
- *Functions*: `http://java.sun.com/jsp/jstl/functions`

When you reference a tag library with an absolute URI that exactly matches the URI declared in the `taglib` element of the TLD (see Tag Library Descriptors, page 229), you do not have to add the `taglib` element to `web.xml`; the JSP container automatically locates the TLD inside the JSTL library implementation.

Including the Tag Library Implementation

In addition to declaring the tag library, you also must make the tag library implementation available to the web application. There are several ways to do this. Tag library implementations can be included in a WAR in an unpacked format: Tag files are packaged in the `/WEB-INF/tag/` directory, and tag handler classes are packaged in the `/WEB-INF/classes/` directory of the WAR. Tag libraries already packaged into a JAR file are included in the `/WEB-INF/lib/` directory of the WAR. Finally, an application server can load a tag library into all the web applications running on the server. For example, in the Application Server, the JSTL TLDs and libraries are distributed in the archive `appserv-jstl.jar` in *<JAVAEE_HOME>*`/lib/`. This library is automatically loaded into the classpath of all web applications running on the Application Server, so you don't need to add it to your web application.

The `iterator` tag library is implemented with tag handlers. Therefore, its implementation classes are packaged in the `/WEB-INF/classes/` directory.

Reusing Content in JSP Pages

There are many mechanisms for reusing JSP content in a JSP page. Three mechanisms that can be categorized as direct reuse—the `include` directive, preludes and codas, and the `jsp:include` element—are discussed here. An indirect method of content reuse occurs when a tag file is used to define a custom tag that is used by many web applications. Tag files are discussed in the section Encapsulating Reusable Content Using Tag Files (page 212) in Chapter 7.

The `include` directive is processed when the JSP page is *translated* into a servlet class. The effect of the directive is to insert the text contained in another file—either static content or another JSP page—into the including JSP page. You would probably use the `include` directive to include banner content, copyright information, or any chunk of content that you might want to reuse in another page. The syntax for the `include` directive is as follows:

```
<%@ include file="filename" %>
```

For example, all the Duke's Bookstore application pages could include the file `banner.jspf`, which contains the banner content, by using the following directive:

```
<%@ include file="banner.jspf" %>
```

Another way to do a static include is to use the prelude and coda mechanisms described in Defining Implicit Includes (page 152). This is the approach used by the Duke's Bookstore application.

Because you must put an `include` directive in each file that reuses the resource referenced by the directive, this approach has its limitations. Preludes and codas can be applied only to the beginnings and ends of pages. For a more flexible approach to building pages out of content chunks, see A Template Tag Library (page 253).

The `jsp:include` element is processed when a JSP page is *executed*. The `include` action allows you to include either a static or a dynamic resource in a JSP file. The results of including static and dynamic resources are quite different. If the resource is static, its content is inserted into the calling JSP file. If the resource is dynamic, the request is sent to the included resource, the included page is executed, and then the result is included in the response from the calling JSP page. The syntax for the jsp:include element is:

```
<jsp:include page="includedPage" />
```

The hello1 application discussed in Packaging Web Modules (page 39) uses the following statement to include the page that generates the response:

```
<jsp:include page="response.jsp"/>
```

Transferring Control to Another Web Component

The mechanism for transferring control to another web component from a JSP page uses the functionality provided by the Java Servlet API as described in Accessing a Session (page 89). You access this functionality from a JSP page by using the jsp:forward element:

```
<jsp:forward page="/main.jsp" />
```

Note that if any data has already been returned to a client, the jsp:forward element will fail with an IllegalStateException.

jsp:param Element

When an include or forward element is invoked, the original request object is provided to the target page. If you wish to provide additional data to that page, you can append parameters to the request object by using the jsp:param element:

```
<jsp:include page="..." >
  <jsp:param name="param1" value="value1"/>
</jsp:include>
```

When jsp:include or jsp:forward is executed, the included page or forwarded page will see the original request object, with the original parameters augmented with the new parameters and new values taking precedence over existing values when applicable. For example, if the request has a parameter

A=foo and a parameter A=bar is specified for forward, the forwarded request will have A=bar,foo. Note that the new parameter has precedence.

The scope of the new parameters is the jsp:include or jsp:forward call; that is, in the case of an jsp:include the new parameters (and values) will not apply after the include.

Including an Applet

You can include an applet or a JavaBeans component in a JSP page by using the jsp:plugin element. This element generates HTML that contains the appropriate client-browser-dependent construct (<object> or <embed>) that will result in the download of the Java Plug-in software (if required) and the client-side component, and in the subsequent execution of any client-side component. The syntax for the jsp:plugin element is as follows:

```
<jsp:plugin
  type="bean|applet"
  code="objectCode"
  codebase="objectCodebase"
  { align="alignment" }
  { archive="archiveList" }
  { height="height" }
  { hspace="hspace" }
  { jreversion="jreversion" }
  { name="componentName" }
  { vspace="vspace" }
  { width="width" }
  { nspluginurl="url" }
  { iepluginurl="url" } >
  { <jsp:params>
    { <jsp:param name="paramName" value= paramValue" /> }+
  </jsp:params> }
  { <jsp:fallback> arbitrary_text </jsp:fallback> }
</jsp:plugin>
```

The jsp:plugin tag is replaced by either an <object> or an <embed> tag as appropriate for the requesting client. The attributes of the jsp:plugin tag provide configuration data for the presentation of the element as well as the version of the plug-in required. The nspluginurl and iepluginurl attributes override the default URL where the plug-in can be downloaded.

The jsp:params element specifies parameters to the applet or JavaBeans component. The jsp:fallback element indicates the content to be used by the client browser if the plug-in cannot be started (either because `<object>` or `<embed>` is not supported by the client or because of some other problem).

If the plug-in can start but the applet or JavaBeans component cannot be found or started, a plug-in-specific message will be presented to the user, most likely a pop-up window reporting a `ClassNotFoundException`.

The Duke's Bookstore page `/template/prelude.jspf` creates the banner that displays a dynamic digital clock generated by `DigitalClock` (see Figure 4–3).

Figure 4–3 Duke's Bookstore with Applet

Here is the `jsp:plugin` element that is used to download the applet:

```
<jsp:plugin
  type="applet"
  code="DigitalClock.class"
  codebase="/bookstore2"
  jreversion="1.4"
  align="center" height="25" width="300"
  nspluginurl="http://java.sun.com/j2se/1.4.2/download.html"
  iepluginurl="http://java.sun.com/j2se/1.4.2/download.html" >
  <jsp:params>
    <jsp:param name="language"
      value="${pageContext.request.locale.language}" />
    <jsp:param name="country"
      value="${pageContext.request.locale.country}" />
    <jsp:param name="bgcolor" value="FFFFFF" />
    <jsp:param name="fgcolor" value="CC0066" />
  </jsp:params>
  <jsp:fallback>
    <p>Unable to start plugin.</p>
  </jsp:fallback>
</jsp:plugin>
```

Setting Properties for Groups of JSP Pages

It is possible to specify certain properties for a group of JSP pages:

- Expression language evaluation
- Treatment of scripting elements (see Disabling Scripting, page 264)
- Page encoding
- Automatic prelude and coda includes

A JSP property group is defined by naming the group and specifying one or more URL patterns; all the properties in the group apply to the resources that match any of the URL patterns. If a resource matches URL patterns in more than one group, the pattern that is most specific applies. To define a property group in a deployment descriptor using NetBeans 5.5, follow these steps:

1. In NetBeans 5.5, expand your project's folder in the Projects pane.
2. Expand the Web Pages node and then the WEB-INF node.
3. Double-click `web.xml` to open it in the editor pane.

4. Click Pages at the top of the editor pane.
5. Click Add JSP Property Group.
6. In the Add JSP Property Group dialog:
   a. Enter a name for the JSP property group in the Display Name field.
   b. Enter a URL pattern (a regular expression, such as *.jsp) or click Browse to indicate to which page or set of pages to apply the properties specified by the JSP property group.
   c. Click OK.

Instead of performing the preceding steps, you can define a JSP property group by editing the XML by hand using NetBeans 5.5 by doing the following:

1. Perform steps 1 through 3 in the preceding set of steps.
2. Click XML at the top of the editor pane.
3. Include a `jsp-config` element if the deployment descriptor doesn't already have one.
4. Add a `jsp-property-group` element inside the `jsp-config` element.
5. Add a `display-name` element inside the `jsp-property-group` element and give it a name.
6. Add a `url-pattern` element inside the `jsp-property-group` element and give it a URL pattern (a regular expression, such as `*.jsp`).

The following sections discuss the properties and explain how they are interpreted for various combinations of group properties, individual page directives, and web application deployment descriptor versions.

Deactivating EL Expression Evaluation

Each JSP page has a default mode for EL expression evaluation. The default value varies depending on the version of the web application deployment descriptor. The default mode for JSP pages delivered using a Servlet 2.3 or earlier descriptor is to ignore EL expressions; this provides backward compatibility. The default mode for JSP pages delivered with a Servlet 2.4 descriptor is to evaluate EL expressions; this automatically provides the default that most applications want. For tag files (see Encapsulating Reusable Content Using Tag Files, page 212), the default is to always evaluate expressions.

You can override the default mode through the `isELIgnored` attribute of the `page` directive in JSP pages and through the `isELIgnored` attribute of the `tag` directive in tag files. You can also explicitly change the default mode by doing one of the following:

- If you are using the Pages section of the `web.xml` editor pane in NetBeans 5.5:
  a. Expand the JSP Property Group node.
  b. Select the Ignore Expression Language checkbox.
- If you are editing the `web.xml` by hand:
  a. Add an `el-ignored` element to the `jsp-property-group` element in the deployment descriptor and set it to true.

Table 4–8 summarizes the EL evaluation settings for JSP pages.

Table 4–8 EL Evaluation Settings for JSP Pages

JSP Configuration	Page Directive `isELIgnored`	EL Encountered
Unspecified	Unspecified	Evaluated if 2.4 `web.xml` Ignored if <= 2.3 `web.xml`
`false`	Unspecified	Evaluated
`true`	Unspecified	Ignored
Overridden by page directive	`false`	Evaluated
Overridden by page directive	`true`	Ignored

Table 4–9 summarizes the EL evaluation settings for tag files.

Table 4–9 EL Evaluation Settings for Tag Files

Tag Directive `isELIgnored`	EL Encountered
Unspecified	Evaluated
`false`	Evaluated
`true`	Ignored

Declaring Page Encodings

You set the page encoding of a group of JSP pages using the JSP property group configuration in the deployment descriptor by doing one of the following:

- If you are using the Pages section of the `web.xml` editor pane in NetBeans 5.5:
  a. Expand the JSP Property Group node.
  b. Enter the page encoding in the Page Encoding field.
- If you are editing the `web.xml` by hand:
  a. Add a `page-encoding` element to the `jsp-property-group` element in the deployment descriptor and set it to one of the valid character encoding codes, which are the same as those accepted by the `pageEncoding` attribute of the `page` directive.

A translation-time error results if you define the page encoding of a JSP page with one value in the JSP configuration element and then give it a different value in a `pageEncoding` directive.

Defining Implicit Includes

You can implicitly include preludes and codas for a group of JSP pages by adding items to the Include Preludes and Codas lists. Their values are context-relative paths that must correspond to elements in the web application. When the elements are present, the given paths are automatically included (as in an `include` directive) at the beginning and end, respectively, of each JSP page in the property group. When there is more than one include or coda element in a group, they are included in the order they appear. When more than one JSP property group applies to a JSP page, the corresponding elements will be processed in the same order as they appear in the JSP configuration section.

For example, the Duke's Bookstore application uses the files `/template/prelude.jspf` and `/template/coda.jspf` to include the banner and other boilerplate in each screen. To add these files to the Duke's Bookstore property group using the deployment descriptor, follow these steps:

1. In NetBeans 5.5, expand your project's folder in the Projects pane.
2. Expand the Web Pages node and then the WEB-INF node.
3. Double-click `web.xml` to open it in the editor pane.
4. Click Pages at the top of the editor pane.

5. Add a new JSP property group if you haven't already (see Setting Properties for Groups of JSP Pages, page 149) and give it the name `bookstore2` and the URL pattern `*.jsp`.
6. Expand the JSP Property Group node.
7. Click the Browse button to the right of the Include Preludes field to locate the file that you want to include at the beginning of all pages matching the pattern in the URL pattern field. In this case, you want the `/template/prelude.jspf` file.
8. Click the Browse button to the right of the Include Codas field to locate the file that you want to include at the end of all pages matching the URL pattern. In this case, you want the `/template/coda.jspf` file.

Instead of performing the preceding steps, you can add preludes and codas by editing the XML by hand using NetBeans 5.5 by doing the following:

1. Perform steps 1 through 3 in the preceding set of steps.
2. Click XML at the top of the editor pane.
3. Add a new JSP property group (see Setting Properties for Groups of JSP Pages, page 149) and give it the name `bookstore2` and URL pattern `*.jsp`.
4. Add an `include-prelude` element to the `jsp-property-group` element and give it the name of the file to include, in this case, `/template/prelude.jspf`.
5. Add an `include-coda` element to the `jsp-property-group` element and give it the name of the file to include, in this case, `/template/coda.jspf`.

Preludes and codas can put the included code only at the beginning and end of each file. For a more flexible approach to building pages out of content chunks, see A Template Tag Library (page 253).

Eliminating Extra White Space

White space included in the template text of JSP pages is preserved by default. This can have undesirable effects. For example, a carriage return added after a `taglib` directive would be added to the response output as an extra line.

If you want to eliminate the extra white space from the page, you can add a `trim-directive-whitespaces` element to a `jsp-property-group` element in the deployment descriptor and set it to `true`.

Alternatively, a page author can set the value of the `trimDirectiveWhitespaces` attribute of the `page` directive to true or false. This will override the value specified in the deployment descriptor.

Custom tag authors can eliminate white space from the output generated by a tag file by setting the `trimDirectiveWhiteSpace` attribute of the `tag` directive to true.

Further Information

For further information on JavaServer Pages technology, see the following:

- JavaServer Pages 2.0 specification:

  `http://java.sun.com/products/jsp/download.html#specs`

- The JavaServer Pages web site:

  `http://java.sun.com/products/jsp`

- *The Unified Expression Language*, Ryan Lubke et al.:

  `http://java.sun.com/products/jsp/reference/techart/unifiedEL.html`

5

JavaServer Pages Documents

A *JSP document* is a JSP page written in XML syntax as opposed to the standard syntax described in Chapter 4. Because it is written in XML syntax, a JSP document is also an XML document and therefore gives you all the benefits offered by the XML standard:

- You can author a JSP document using one of the many XML-aware tools on the market, enabling you to ensure that your JSP document is well-formed XML.
- You can validate the JSP document against a document type definition (DTD).
- You can nest and scope namespaces within a JSP document.
- You can use a JSP document for data interchange between web applications and as part of a compile-time XML pipeline.

In addition to these benefits, the XML syntax gives the JSP page author less complexity and more flexibility. For example, a page author can use any XML document as a JSP document. Also, elements in XML syntax can be used in JSP pages written in standard syntax, allowing a gradual transition from JSP pages to JSP documents.

This chapter gives you details on the benefits of JSP documents and uses a simple example to show you how easy it is to create a JSP document.

You can also write tag files in XML syntax. This chapter covers only JSP documents. Writing tag files in XML syntax will be addressed in a future release of the tutorial.

The Example JSP Document

This chapter uses the Duke's Bookstore application, version `bookstore5`, and the `books` application to demonstrate how to write JSP pages in XML syntax. The JSP pages of the `bookstore5` application use the JSTL XML tags (see XML Tag Library, page 188) to manipulate the book data from an XML stream. The `books` application contains the JSP document `books.jspx`, which accesses the book data from the database and converts it into the XML stream. The `bookstore5` application accesses this XML stream to get the book data.

These applications show how easy it is to generate XML data and stream it between web applications. The `books` application can be considered the application hosted by the book warehouse's server. The `bookstore5` application can be considered the application hosted by the book retailer's server. In this way, the customer of the bookstore web site sees the list of books currently available, according to the warehouse's database.

The source for the Duke's Bookstore application is located in the `<INSTALL>/javaeetutorial5/examples/web/bookstore5/` directory, which is created when you unzip the tutorial bundle (see About the Examples, page xxx).

To deploy the `books` application using NetBeans 5.5, follow these steps:

1. Perform all the operations described in Accessing Databases from Web Applications (page 55).
2. In NetBeans 5.5, select File→Open Project.
3. In the Open Project dialog, navigate to:

   `<INSTALL>/javaeetutorial5/examples/web/`
4. Select the `books` folder.
5. Select the Open as Main Project checkbox and the Open Required Projects checkbox.
6. Click Open Project Folder.
7. In the Projects tab, right-click the `books` project, and select Deploy Project.

To deploy the `books` application using the `ant` utility, follow these steps:

1. In a terminal window, go to `<INSTALL>/javaeetutorial5/examples/web/books/`.
2. Run `ant build`. This target will spawn any necessary compilations, copy files to the `<INSTALL>/javaeetutorial5/examples/web/books/build/` directory, build a WAR file, and copy the WAR file to the `<INSTALL>/javaeetutorial5/examples/web/books/dist/` directory.
3. Deploy the application by running `ant deploy`.

To deploy and run the `bookstore5` application using NetBeans 5.5, follow these steps:

1. Perform all the operations described in Accessing Databases from Web Applications (page 55).
2. In NetBeans 5.5, select File→Open Project.
3. In the Open Project dialog, navigate to:
   `<INSTALL>/javaeetutorial5/examples/web/`
4. Select the `bookstore5` folder.
5. Select the Open as Main Project checkbox and the Open Required Projects checkbox.
6. Click Open Project Folder.
7. In the Projects tab, right-click the `bookstore5` project, and select Deploy Project.
8. To run the applications, open the bookstore URL `http://localhost:8080/bookstore5/books/bookstore`.

To deploy and run the application using `ant` follow these steps:

1. In a terminal window, go to `<INSTALL>/javaeetutorial5/examples/web/bookstore5/`.
2. Run `ant`. This target will spawn any necessary compilations, copy files to the `<INSTALL>/javaeetutorial5/examples/web/bookstore5/build/` directory, and create a WAR file and copy it to the `<INSTALL>/javaeetutorial5/examples/web/bookstore5/dist/` directory.
3. Start the Application Server.
4. Perform all the operations described in Creating a Data Source in the Application Server (page 56).

5. To deploy the example, run `ant deploy`. The deploy target outputs a URL for running the application. Ignore this URL, and instead use the one shown in the next step.
6. To run the applications, open the bookstore URL `http://localhost:8080/bookstore5/books/bookstore`.

To learn how to configure the `bookstore5` example, refer to the `web.xml` file, which includes the following configurations:

- A `display-name` element that specifies the name that tools use to identify the application.
- A `context-param` element that identifies the context path to the XML stream.
- A `context-param` element that specifies the JSTL resource bundle base name.
- A set of `servlet` elements that identify the JSP files in the application.
- A set of `servlet-mapping` elements that identify aliases to the JSP pages identified by the `servlet` elements.
- Nested inside a `jsp-config` element are two `jsp-property-group` elements, which define the preludes and coda to be included in each page. See Setting JavaBeans Component Properties (page 139) for more information.

To learn how to configure the `books` example, refer to the web.xml file, which includes the following configurations:

- A `display-name` element that specifies the name that tools use to identify the application.
- A `listener` element that identifies the `ContextListener` class used to create and remove the database access.
- A `servlet` element that identifies the JSP page.
- Nested inside a `jsp-config` element is a `jsp-property-group` element, which identifies the JSP page as an XML document. See Identifying the JSP Document to the Container (page 173) for more information.

Creating a JSP Document

A JSP document is an XML document and therefore must comply with the XML standard. Fundamentally, this means that a JSP document must be well formed, meaning that each start tag must have a corresponding end tag and that the document must have only one root element. In addition, JSP elements included in the JSP document must comply with the XML syntax.

Much of the standard JSP syntax is already XML-compliant, including all the standard actions. Those elements that are not compliant are summarized in Table 5–1 along with the equivalent elements in XML syntax. As you can see, JSP documents are not much different from JSP pages. If you know standard JSP syntax, you will find it easy to convert your current JSP pages to XML syntax and to create new JSP documents.

Table 5–1 Standard Syntax Versus XML Syntax

Syntax Elements	Standard Syntax	XML Syntax
Comments	`<%--.. --%>`	`<!-- .. -->`
Declarations	`<%! ..%>`	`<jsp:declaration> .. </jsp:declaration>`
Directives	`<%@ include .. %>`	`<jsp:directive.include .. />`
	`<%@ page .. %>`	`<jsp:directive.page .. />`
	`<%@ taglib .. %>`	`xmlns:prefix="tag library URL"`
Expressions	`<%= ..%>`	`<jsp:expression> .. </jsp:expression>`
Scriptlets	`<% ..%>`	`<jsp:scriptlet> .. </jsp:scriptlet>`

To illustrate how simple it is to transition from standard syntax to XML syntax, let's convert a simple JSP page to a JSP document. The standard syntax version is as follows:

```
<%@ taglib uri="http://java.sun.com/jsp/jstl/core"
  prefix="c" %>
<%@ taglib uri="http://java.sun.com/jsp/jstl/functions"
  prefix="fn" %>
<html>
  <head><title>Hello</title></head>
  <body bgcolor="white">
    <img src="duke.waving.gif">
    <h2>My name is Duke. What is yours?</h2>
    <form method="get">
```

```
            <input type="text" name="username" size="25">
            <p></p>
            <input type="submit" value="Submit">
            <input type="reset" value="Reset">
         </form>
         <jsp:useBean id="userNameBean" class="hello.UserNameBean"
              scope="request"/>
         <jsp:setProperty name="userNameBean" property="name"
              value="${param.username}" />
         <c:if test="${fn:length(userNameBean.name) > 0}" >
            <%@include file="response.jsp" %>
         </c:if>
      </body>
   </html>
```

Here is the same page in XML syntax:

```
<html
   xmlns:c="http://java.sun.com/jsp/jstl/core"
   xmlns:fn="http://java.sun.com/jsp/jstl/functions" >
   <head><title>Hello</title></head>
   <body bgcolor="white" />
   <img src="duke.waving.gif" />
   <h2>My name is Duke. What is yours?</h2>
   <form method="get">
      <input type="text" name="username" size="25" />
      <p></p>
      <input type="submit" value="Submit" />
      <input type="reset" value="Reset" />
   </form>
   <jsp:useBean id="userNameBean" class="hello.UserNameBean"
      scope="request"/>
   <jsp:setProperty name="userNameBean" property="name"
      value="${param.username}" />
   <c:if test="${fn:length(userNameBean.name) gt 0}" >
      <jsp:directive.include="response.jsp" />
   </c:if>
   </body>
</html>
```

As you can see, a number of constructs that are legal in standard syntax have been changed to comply with XML syntax:

- The `taglib` directives have been removed. Tag libraries are now declared using XML namespaces, as shown in the `html` element.
- The `img` and `input` tags did not have matching end tags and have been made XML-compliant by the addition of a / to the start tag.

- The > symbol in the EL expression has been replaced with `gt`.
- The `include` directive has been changed to the XML-compliant `jsp:directive.include` tag.

With only these few small changes, when you save the file with a `.jspx` extension, this page is a JSP document.

Using the example described in The Example JSP Document (page 156), the rest of this chapter gives you more details on how to transition from standard syntax to XML syntax. It explains how to use XML namespaces to declare tag libraries, include directives, and create static and dynamic content in your JSP documents. It also describes `jsp:root` and `jsp:output`, two elements that are used exclusively in JSP documents.

Declaring Tag Libraries

This section explains how to use XML namespaces to declare tag libraries.

In standard syntax, the `taglib` directive declares tag libraries used in a JSP page. Here is an example of a `taglib` directive:

```
<%@ taglib uri="http://java.sun.com/jsp/jstl/core"
  prefix="c" %>
```

This syntax is not allowed in JSP documents. To declare a tag library in a JSP document, you use the `xmlns` attribute, which is used to declare namespaces according to the XML standard:

```
...
xmlns:c="http://java.sun.com/jsp/jstl/core"
...
```

The value that identifies the location of the tag library can take three forms:

- A plain URI that is a unique identifier for the tag library. The container tries to match it against any `<taglib-uri>` elements in the application's `web.xml` file or the `<uri>` element of tag library descriptors (TLDs) in JAR files in `WEB-INF/lib` or TLDs under `WEB-INF`.
- A URN of the form `urn:jsptld:path`.
- A URN of the form `urn:jsptagdir:path`.

The URN of the form `urn:jsptld:path` points to one tag library packaged with the application:

```
xmlns:u="urn:jsptld:/WEB-INF/tlds/my.tld"
```

The URN of the form `urn:jsptagdir:path` must start with `/WEB-INF/tags/` and identifies tag extensions (implemented as tag files) installed in the `WEB-INF/tags/` directory or a subdirectory of it:

```
xmlns:u="urn:jsptagdir:/WEB-INF/tags/mytaglibs/"
```

You can include the `xmlns` attribute in any element in your JSP document, just as you can in an XML document. This capability has many advantages:

- It follows the XML standard, making it easier to use any XML document as a JSP document.
- It allows you to scope prefixes to an element and override them.
- It allows you to use `xmlns` to declare other namespaces and not just tag libraries.

The `books.jspx` page declares the tag libraries it uses with the `xmlns` attributes in the root element, `books`:

```
<books
  xmlns:jsp="http://java.sun.com/JSP/Page"
  xmlns:c="http://java.sun.com/jsp/jstl/core"
>
```

In this way, all elements within the `books` element have access to these tag libraries.

As an alternative, you can scope the namespaces:

```
<books>
...
  <jsp:useBean xmlns:jsp="http://java.sun.com/JSP/Page"
               id="bookDB"
               class="database.BookDB"
               scope="page">
    <jsp:setProperty name="bookDB"
               property="database" value="${bookDBAO}" />
  </jsp:useBean>
  <c:forEach xmlns:c="http://java.sun.com/jsp/jstl/core"
```

```
              var="book" begin="0" items="${bookDB.books}">
              ...
    </c:forEach>
  </books>
```

In this way, the tag library referenced by the `jsp` prefix is available only to the `jsp:useBean` element and its subelements. Similarly, the tag library referenced by the `c` prefix is only available to the `c:forEach` element.

Scoping the namespaces also allows you to override the prefix. For example, in another part of the page, you could bind the `c` prefix to a different namespace or tag library. In contrast, the `jsp` prefix must always be bound to the JSP namespace: `http://java.sun.com/JSP/Page`.

Including Directives in a JSP Document

Directives are elements that relay messages to the JSP container and affect how it compiles the JSP page. The directives themselves do not appear in the XML output.

There are three directives: `include`, `page`, and `taglib`. The `taglib` directive is covered in the preceding section.

The `jsp:directive.page` element defines a number of page-dependent properties and communicates these to the JSP container. This element must be a child of the root element. Its syntax is

```
<jsp:directive.page page_directive_attr_list />
```

The `page_directive_attr_list` is the same list of attributes that the `<@ page ...>` directive has. These are described in Chapter 4. All the attributes are optional. Except for the `import` and `pageEncoding` attributes, there can be only one instance of each attribute in an element, but an element can contain more than one attribute.

An example of a page directive is one that tells the JSP container to load an error page when it throws an exception. You can add this error page directive to the `books.jspx` page:

```
<books xmlns:jsp="http://java.sun.com/JSP/Page">
  <jsp:directive.page errorPage="errorpage.jsp" />
  ...
</books>
```

If there is an error when you try to execute the page (perhaps when you want to see the XML output of `books.jspx`), the error page is accessed.

The `jsp:directive.include` element is used to insert the text contained in another file—either static content or another JSP page—into the including JSP document. You can place this element anywhere in a document. Its syntax is:

```
<jsp:directive.include file="relativeURLspec" />
```

The XML view of a JSP document does not contain `jsp:directive.include` elements; rather the included file is expanded in place. This is done to simplify validation.

Suppose that you want to use an `include` directive to add a JSP document containing magazine data inside the JSP document containing the books data. To do this, you can add the following `include` directive to `books.jspx`, assuming that `magazines.jspx` generates the magazine XML data.

```
<jsp:root version="2.0" >
  <books ...>
  ...
  </books>
  <jsp:directive.include file="magazine.jspx" />
</jsp:root>
```

Note that `jsp:root` is required because otherwise `books.jspx` would have two root elements: `<books>` and `<magazines>`. The output generated from `books.jspx` will be a sequence of XML documents: one with `<books>` and the other with `<magazines>` as its root element.

The output of this example will not be well-formed XML because of the two root elements, so the client might refuse to process it. However, it is still a legal JSP document.

In addition to including JSP documents in JSP documents, you can also include JSP pages written in standard syntax in JSP documents, and you can include JSP documents in JSP pages written in standard syntax. The container detects the page you are including and parses it as either a standard syntax JSP page or a JSP document and then places it into the XML view for validation.

Creating Static and Dynamic Content

This section explains how to represent static text and dynamic content in a JSP document. You can represent static text in a JSP document using uninterpreted XML tags or the `jsp:text` element. The `jsp:text` element passes its content through to the output.

If you use `jsp:text`, all whitespace is preserved. For example, consider this example using XML tags:

```
<books>
  <book>
    Web Servers for Fun and Profit
  </book>
</books>
```

The output generated from this XML has all whitespace removed:

```
<books><book>
    Web Servers for Fun and Profit
</book></books>
```

If you wrap the example XML with a `<jsp:text>` tag, all whitespace is preserved. The whitespace characters are `#x20`, `#x9`, `#xD`,and `#xA`.

You can also use `jsp:text` to output static data that is not well formed. The `${counter}` expression in the following example would be illegal in a JSP document if it were not wrapped in a `jsp:text` tag.

```
<c:forEach var="counter" begin="1" end="${3}">
  <jsp:text>${counter}</jsp:text>
</c:forEach>
```

This example will output

```
123
```

The `jsp:text` tag must not contain any other elements. Therefore, if you need to nest a tag inside `jsp:text`, you must wrap the tag inside `CDATA`.

You also need to use `CDATA` if you need to output some elements that are not well-formed. The following example requires `CDATA` wrappers around the `blockquote` start and end tags because the `blockquote` element is not well formed. This is because the `blockquote` element overlaps with other elements in the example.

```
<c:forEach var="i" begin="1" end="${x}">
  <![CDATA[<blockquote>]]>
</c:forEach>
...
<c:forEach var="i" begin="1" end="${x}">
  <![CDATA[</blockquote>]]>
</c:forEach>
```

Just like JSP pages, JSP documents can generate dynamic content using expressions language (EL) expressions, scripting elements, standard actions, and custom tags. The `books.jspx` document uses EL expressions and custom tags to generate the XML book data.

As shown in this snippet from `books.jspx`, the `c:forEach` JSTL tag iterates through the list of books and generates the XML data stream. The EL expressions access the JavaBeans component, which in turn retrieves the data from the database:

```
<c:forEach var="book" begin="0" items="${bookDB.books}">
  <book id="${book.bookId}" >
    <surname>${book.surname}</surname>
    <firstname>${book.firstName}</firstname>
    <title>${book.title}</title>
    <price>${book.price}</price>
    <year>${book.year}</year>
    <description>${book.description}</description>
    <inventory>${book.inventory}</inventory>
  </book>
</c:forEach>
```

When using the expression language in your JSP documents, you must substitute alternative notation for some of the operators so that they will not be interpreted as XML markup. Table 5–2 enumerates the more common operators and their alternative syntax in JSP documents.

Table 5–2 EL Operators and JSP Document-Compliant Alternative Notation

EL Operator	JSP Document Notation
<	`lt`
>	`gt`
<=	`le`
>=	`ge`
!=	`ne`

You can also use EL expressions with `jsp:element` to generate tags dynamically rather than hardcode them. This example could be used to generate an HTML header tag with a `lang` attribute:

```
<jsp:element name="${content.headerName}"
    xmlns:jsp="http://java.sun.com/JSP/Page">
  <jsp:attribute name="lang">${content.lang}</jsp:attribute>
  <jsp:body>${content.body}</jsp:body>
</jsp:element>
```

The `name` attribute identifies the generated tag's name. The `jsp:attribute` tag generates the `lang` attribute. The body of the `jsp:attribute` tag identifies the value of the `lang` attribute. The `jsp:body` tag generates the body of the tag. The output of this example `jsp:element` could be

```
<h1 lang="fr">Heading in French</h1>
```

As shown in Table 5–1, scripting elements (described in Chapter 8) are represented as XML elements when they appear in a JSP document. The only exception is a scriptlet expression used to specify a request-time attribute value. Instead of using <%=`expr` %>, a JSP document uses %= `expr` % to represent a request-time attribute value.

The three scripting elements are declarations, scriptlets, and expressions.

A `jsp:declaration` element declares a scripting language construct that is available to other scripting elements. A `jsp:declaration` element has no attributes and its body is the declaration itself. Its syntax is

```
<jsp:declaration> declaration goes here </jsp:declaration>
```

A `jsp:scriptlet` element contains a Java program fragment called a scriptlet. This element has no attributes, and its body is the program fragment that constitutes the scriptlet. Its syntax is

```
<jsp:scriptlet> code fragment goes here </jsp:scriptlet>
```

The `jsp:expression` element inserts the value of a scripting language expression, converted into a string, into the data stream returned to the client. A `jsp:expression` element has no attributes and its body is the expression. Its syntax is

```
<jsp:expression> expression goes here </jsp:expression>
```

Using the jsp:root Element

The `jsp:root` element represents the root element of a JSP document. A `jsp:root` element is not required for JSP documents. You can specify your own root element, enabling you to use any XML document as a JSP document. The root element of the `books.jspx` example JSP document is `books`.

Although the `jsp:root` element is not required, it is still useful in these cases:

- When you want to identify the document as a JSP document to the JSP container without having to add any configuration attributes to the deployment descriptor or name the document with a `.jspx` extension
- When you want to generate—from a single JSP document—more than one XML document or XML content mixed with non-XML content

The `version` attribute is the only required attribute of the `jsp:root` element. It specifies the JSP specification version that the JSP document is using.

The `jsp:root` element can also include `xmlns` attributes for specifying tag libraries used by the other elements in the page.

The `books.jspx` page does not need a `jsp:root` element and therefore doesn't include one. However, suppose that you want to generate two XML documents from `books.jspx`: one that lists books and another that lists magazines (assuming magazines are in the database). This example is similar to the one in the section Including Directives in a JSP Document (page 163). To do this, you can use this `jsp:root` element:

```
<jsp:root
  xmlns:jsp="http://java.sun.com/JSP/Page" version="2.0" >
  <books>...</books>
  <magazines>...</magazines>
</jsp:root>
```

Notice in this example that `jsp:root` defines the JSP namespace because both the `books` and the `magazines` elements use the elements defined in this namespace.

Using the jsp:output Element

The `jsp:output` element specifies the XML declaration or the document type declaration in the request output of the JSP document.

The XML declaration and document type declaration that are declared by the `jsp:output` element are not interpreted by the JSP container. Instead, the container simply directs them to the request output.

To illustrate this, here is an example of specifying a document type declaration with `jsp:output`:

```
<jsp:output doctype-root-element="books"
            doctype-system="books.dtd" />
```

The resulting output is:

```
<!DOCTYPE books SYSTEM "books.dtd" >
```

Specifying the document type declaration in the `jsp:output` element will not cause the JSP container to validate the JSP document against the `books.dtd`.

If you want the JSP document to be validated against the DTD, you must manually include the document type declaration within the JSP document, just as you would with any XML document.

Table 5–3 shows all the `jsp:output` attributes. They are all optional, but some attributes depend on other attributes occurring in the same `jsp:output` element, as shown in the table. The rest of this section explains more about using jsp:output to generate an XML declaration and a document type declaration.

Table 5–3 jsp:output Attributes

Attribute	What It Specifies
omit-xml-declaration	A value of true or yes omits the XML declaration. A value of false or no generates an XML declaration.
doctype-root-element	Indicates the root element of the XML document in the DOCTYPE. Can be specified only if doctype-system is specified.
doctype-system	Specifies that a DOCTYPE is generated in output and gives the SYSTEM literal.
doctype-public	Specifies the value for the Public ID of the generated DOCTYPE. Can be specified only if doctype-system is specified.

Generating XML Declarations

Here is an example of an XML declaration:

```
<?xml version="1.0" encoding="UTF-8" ?>
```

This declaration is the default XML declaration. It means that if the JSP container is generating an XML declaration, this is what the JSP container will include in the output of your JSP document.

Neither a JSP document nor its request output is required to have an XML declaration. In fact, if the JSP document is not producing XML output then it shouldn't have an XML declaration.

The JSP container will *not* include the XML declaration in the output when either of the following is true:

- You set the omit-xml-declaration attribute of the jsp:output element to either true or yes.
- You have a jsp:root element in your JSP document, and you do not specify omit-xml-declaration="false" in jsp:output.

The JSP container will include the XML declaration in the output when either of the following is true:

- You set the `omit-xml-declaration` attribute of the `jsp:output` element to either `false` or `no`.
- You do not have a `jsp:root` action in your JSP document, and you do not specify the `omit-xml-declaration` attribute in `jsp:output`.

The `books.jspx` JSP document does not include a `jsp:root` action nor a `jsp:output`. Therefore, the default XML declaration is generated in the output.

Generating a Document Type Declaration

A document type declaration (DTD) defines the structural rules for the XML document in which the document type declaration occurs. XML documents are not required to have a DTD associated with them. In fact, the `books` example does not include one.

This section shows you how to use the `jsp:output` element to add a document type declaration to the XML output of `books.jspx`. It also shows you how to enter the document type declaration manually into `books.jspx` so that the JSP container will interpret it and validate the document against the DTD.

As shown in Table 5–3, the `jsp:output` element has three attributes that you use to generate the document type declaration:

- `doctype-root-element`: Indicates the root element of the XML document.
- `doctype-system`: Indicates the URI reference to the DTD.
- `doctype-public`: A more flexible way to reference the DTD. This identifier gives more information about the DTD without giving a specific location. A public identifier resolves to the same actual document on any system even though the location of that document on each system may vary. See the XML 1.0 specification for more information.

The rules for using the attributes are as follows:

- The doctype attributes can appear in any order.
- The `doctype-root` attribute must be specified if the `doctype-system` attribute is specified.
- The `doctype-public` attribute must not be specified unless `doctype-system` is specified.

This syntax notation summarizes these rules:

```
<jsp:output (omit-xmldeclaration=
  "yes"|"no"|"true"|"false"){doctypeDecl} />

doctypeDecl:=(doctype-root-element="rootElement"
     doctype-public="PublicLiteral"
   doctype-system="SystemLiteral")
   | (doctype-root-element="rootElement"
   doctype-system="SystemLiteral")
```

Suppose that you want to reference a DTD, called `books.DTD`, from the output of the `books.jspx` page. The DTD would look like this:

```
<!ELEMENT books (book+) >
<!ELEMENT book (surname, firstname, title, price, year,
                description, inventory) >
<!ATTLIST book id CDATA #REQUIRED >
<!ELEMENT surname (#PCDATA) >
<!ELEMENT firstname (#PCDATA) >
<!ELEMENT title (#PCDATA) >
<!ELEMENT price (#PCDATA) >
<!ELEMENT year (#PCDATA) >
<!ELEMENT description (#PCDATA) >
<!ELEMENT inventory (#PCDATA) >
```

To add a document type declaration that references the DTD to the XML request output generated from `books.jspx`, include this `jsp:output` element in `books.jspx`:

```
<jsp:output doctype-root-element="books"
     doctype-system="books.DTD" />
```

With this `jsp:output` action, the JSP container generates this document type declaration in the request output:

```
<!DOCTYPE books SYSTEM "books.DTD" />
```

The `jsp:output` need not be located before the root element of the document. The JSP container will automatically place the resulting document type declaration before the start of the output of the JSP document.

Note that the JSP container will not interpret anything provided by `jsp:output`. This means that the JSP container will not validate the XML document against the DTD. It only generates the document type declaration in the XML request output. To see the XML output, run `http://localhost:8080/books/books.jspx` in your browser after you have updated `books.WAR` with `books.DTD` and the `jsp:output` element. When using some browsers, you might need to view the source of the page to actually see the output.

Directing the document type declaration to output without interpreting it is useful in situations when another system receiving the output expects to see it. For example, two companies that do business via a web service might use a standard DTD, against which any XML content exchanged between the companies is validated by the consumer of the content. The document type declaration tells the consumer what DTD to use to validate the XML data that it receives.

For the JSP container to validate `books.jspx` against `book.DTD`, you must manually include the document type declaration in the `books.jspx` file rather than use `jsp:output`. However, you must add definitions for all tags in your DTD, including definitions for standard elements and custom tags, such as `jsp:useBean` and `c:forEach`. You also must ensure that the DTD is located in the *<JavaEE_HOME>*`/domains/domain1/config/` directory so that the JSP container will validate the JSP document against the DTD.

Identifying the JSP Document to the Container

A JSP document must be identified as such to the web container so that the container interprets it as an XML document. There are three ways to do this:

- In your application's `web.xml` file, set the `is-xml` element of the `jsp-property-group` element to true.
- Use a Java Servlet Specification version 2.4 `web.xml` file and give your JSP document the `.jspx` extension.
- Include a `jsp:root` element in your JSP document. This method is backward-compatible with JSP 1.2.

6

JavaServer Pages Standard Tag Library

THE JavaServer Pages Standard Tag Library (JSTL) encapsulates core functionality common to many JSP applications. Instead of mixing tags from numerous vendors in your JSP applications, JSTL allows you to employ a single, standard set of tags. This standardization allows you to deploy your applications on any JSP container supporting JSTL and makes it more likely that the implementation of the tags is optimized.

JSTL has tags such as iterators and conditionals for handling flow control, tags for manipulating XML documents, internationalization tags, tags for accessing databases using SQL, and commonly used functions.

This chapter demonstrates JSTL through excerpts from the JSP version of the Duke's Bookstore application discussed in the earlier chapters. It assumes that you are familiar with the material in the Using Custom Tags (page 141) section of Chapter 4.

This chapter does not cover every JSTL tag, only the most commonly used ones. Please refer to the reference pages at `http://java.sun.com/products/jsp/jstl/1.1/docs/tlddocs/index.html` for a complete list of the JSTL tags and their attributes.

The Example JSP Pages

This chapter illustrates JSTL using excerpts from the JSP version of the Duke's Bookstore application discussed in Chapter 4. Here, they are rewritten to replace the JavaBeans component database access object with direct calls to the database via the JSTL SQL tags. For most applications, it is better to encapsulate calls to a database in a bean. JSTL includes SQL tags for situations where a new application is being prototyped and the overhead of creating a bean may not be warranted.

The source for the Duke's Bookstore application is located in the `<INSTALL>/javaeetutorial5/examples/web/bookstore4/` directory created when you unzip the tutorial bundle (see About the Examples, page xxxiv).

To deploy and run the application using NetBeans 5.5, follow these steps:

1. Perform all the operations described in Accessing Databases from Web Applications (page 55).
2. In NetBeans 5.5, select File→Open Project.
3. In the Open Project dialog, navigate to:
   `<INSTALL>/javaeetutorial5/examples/web/`
4. Select the `bookstore4` folder.
5. Select the Open as Main Project checkbox and the Open Required Projects checkbox.
6. Click Open Project Folder.
7. In the Projects tab, right-click the `bookstore4` project, and select Deploy Project.
8. To run the application, open the bookstore URL `http://localhost:8080/bookstore4/books/bookstore`.

To deploy and run the application using Ant, follow these steps:

1. In a terminal window, go to `<INSTALL>/javaeetutorial5/examples/web/bookstore4/`.
2. Run `ant`. This target will spawn any necessary compilations, copy files to the `<INSTALL>/javaeetutorial5/examples/web/bookstore4/build/` directory, and create a WAR file and copy it to the `<INSTALL>/javaeetutorial5/examples/web/bookstore4/dist/` directory.
3. Start the Application Server.

4. Perform all the operations described in Creating a Data Source in the Application Server (page 56).
5. To deploy the example, run `ant deploy`. The deploy target outputs a URL for running the application. Ignore this URL, and instead use the one shown in the next step.
6. To run the application, open the bookstore URL `http://localhost:8080/bookstore4/books/bookstore`.

To learn how to configure the example, refer to the `web.xml` file, which includes the following configurations:

- A `display-name` element that specifies the name that tools use to identify the application.
- A `context-param` element that specifies the JSTL resource bundle base name.
- A set of `servlet` elements that identify the application's JSP files.
- A set of `servlet-mapping` elements that define the aliases to the JSP files.
- Nested inside a `jsp-config` element are two `jsp-property-group` elements, which define the preludes and coda to be included in each page. See Setting JavaBeans Component Properties (page 139) for more information.

See Troubleshooting (page 62) for help with diagnosing common problems.

Using JSTL

JSTL includes a wide variety of tags that fit into discrete functional areas. To reflect this, as well as to give each area its own namespace, JSTL is exposed as multiple tag libraries. The URIs for the libraries are as follows:

- *Core*: `http://java.sun.com/jsp/jstl/core`
- *XML*: `http://java.sun.com/jsp/jstl/xml`
- *Internationalization*: `http://java.sun.com/jsp/jstl/fmt`
- *SQL*: `http://java.sun.com/jsp/jstl/sql`
- *Functions*: `http://java.sun.com/jsp/jstl/functions`

Table 6–1 summarizes these functional areas along with the prefixes used in this tutorial.

Table 6–1 JSTL Tags

Area	Subfunction	Prefix
Core	Variable support	`c`
	Flow control	
	URL management	
	Miscellaneous	
XML	Core	`x`
	Flow control	
	Transformation	
I18N	Locale	`fmt`
	Message formatting	
	Number and date formatting	
Database	SQL	`sql`
Functions	Collection length	`fn`
	String manipulation	

Thus, the tutorial references the JSTL core tags in JSP pages by using the following `taglib` directive:

```
<%@ taglib uri="http://java.sun.com/jsp/jstl/core"
     prefix="c" %>
```

In addition to declaring the tag libraries, tutorial examples access the JSTL API and implementation. In the Application Server, the JSTL TLDs and libraries are distributed in the archive `<`*`JAVAEE_HOME`*`>/lib/appserv-jstl.jar`. This library is automatically loaded into the classpath of all web applications running on the Application Server, so you don't need to add it to your web application.

Tag Collaboration

Tags usually collaborate with their environment in implicit and explicit ways. *Implicit* collaboration is done via a well-defined interface that allows nested tags to work seamlessly with the ancestor tag that exposes that interface. The JSTL conditional tags employ this mode of collaboration.

Explicit collaboration happens when a tag exposes information to its environment. JSTL tags expose information as JSP EL variables; the convention followed by JSTL is to use the name `var` for any tag attribute that exports information about the tag. For example, the `forEach` tag exposes the current item of the shopping cart it is iterating over in the following way:

```
<c:forEach var="item" items="${sessionScope.cart.items}">
  ...
</c:forEach>
```

In situations where a tag exposes more than one piece of information, the name `var` is used for the primary piece of information being exported, and an appropriate name is selected for any other secondary piece of information exposed. For example, iteration status information is exported by the `forEach` tag via the attribute `status`.

When you want to use an EL variable exposed by a JSTL tag in an expression in the page's scripting language (see Chapter 8), you use the standard JSP element `jsp:useBean` to declare a scripting variable.

For example, `bookshowcart.jsp` removes a book from a shopping cart using a scriptlet. The ID of the book to be removed is passed as a request parameter. The value of the request parameter is first exposed as an EL variable (to be used later by the JSTL `sql:query` tag) and then is declared as a scripting variable and passed to the `cart.remove` method:

```
<c:set var="bookId" value="${param.Remove}"/>
<jsp:useBean id="bookId" type="java.lang.String" />
<% cart.remove(bookId); %>
<sql:query var="books"
  dataSource="${applicationScope.bookDS}">
  select * from PUBLIC.books where id = ?
  <sql:param value="${bookId}" />
</sql:query>
```

Core Tag Library

Table 6–2 summarizes the core tags, which include those related to variables and flow control, as well as a generic way to access URL-based resources whose content can then be included or processed within the JSP page.

Table 6–2 Core Tags

Area	Function	Tags	Prefix
Core	Variable support	`remove` `set`	`c`

	Flow control	`choose`
		  `when`
		  `otherwise`
		`forEach`
		`forTokens`
		`if`	

	URL management	`import`
		  `param`
		`redirect`
		  `param`
		`url`
		  `param`	

	Miscellaneous	`catch` `out`	

Variable Support Tags

The `set` tag sets the value of an EL variable or the property of an EL variable in any of the JSP scopes (page, request, session, or application). If the variable does not already exist, it is created.

The JSP EL variable or property can be set either from the attribute `value`:

```
<c:set var="foo" scope="session" value="..."/>
```

or from the body of the tag:

```
<c:set var="foo">
  ...
</c:set>
```

For example, the following sets an EL variable named `bookID` with the value of the request parameter named `Remove`:

```
<c:set var="bookId" value="${param.Remove}"/>
```

To remove an EL variable, you use the `remove` tag. When the bookstore JSP page `bookreceipt.jsp` is invoked, the shopping session is finished, so the `cart` session attribute is removed as follows:

```
<c:remove var="cart" scope="session"/>
```

The `value` attribute of the `set` tag can also take a deferred value expression (See Immediate and Deferred Evaluation Syntax, page 115) so that JavaServer Faces component tags can access the value at the appropriate stage of the page life cycle.

JavaServer Faces technology (see Chapter 9) supports a multiphase life cycle, which includes separate phases for rendering components, validating data, updating model values, and performing other tasks. What this means is that any JavaServer Faces component tags that reference the value set by the `set` tag must have access to this value at different phases of the life cycle, not just during the rendering phase. Consider the following code:

```
<c:set var="bookId" scope="page" value="#{BooksBean.books}"/>
...
<h:inputText id="bookId" value="#{bookId}"/>
...
```

The `value` attribute of the c:set tag uses a deferred value expression, which means that the `bookId` variable it references is available not only during the rendering phase of the JavaServer Faces life cycle but also during the later stages of the life cycle. Therefore, whatever value the user enters into the `bookId` component tag is updated to the external data object during the appropriate stage of the life cycle.

If the expression referenced by the `value` attribute used immediate evaluation syntax then the `bookId` variable would be available only when the component is rendered during the render response phase. This would prevent the value the user enters into the component from being converted, validated, or updated to the external data object during the later phases of the life cycle.

Flow Control Tags

To execute flow control logic, a page author must generally resort to using scriptlets. For example, the following scriptlet is used to iterate through a shopping cart:

```
<%
  Iterator i = cart.getItems().iterator();
  while (i.hasNext()) {
    ShoppingCartItem item =
      (ShoppingCartItem)i.next();
    ...
%>
    <tr>
    <td align="right" bgcolor="#ffffff">
    ${item.quantity}
    </td>
    ...
<%
  }
%>
```

Flow control tags eliminate the need for scriptlets. The next two sections have examples that demonstrate the conditional and iterator tags.

Conditional Tags

The `if` tag allows the conditional execution of its body according to the value of the `test` attribute. The following example from `bookcatalog.jsp` tests whether the request parameter `Add` is empty. If the test evaluates to `true`, the page queries the database for the book record identified by the request parameter and adds the book to the shopping cart:

```
<c:if test="${!empty param.Add}">
  <c:set var="bid" value="${param.Add}"/>
  <jsp:useBean id="bid"  type="java.lang.String" />
   <sql:query var="books"
    dataSource="${applicationScope.bookDS}">
    select * from PUBLIC.books where id = ?
    <sql:param value="${bid}" />
```

```
  </sql:query>
  <c:forEach var="bookRow" begin="0" items="${books.rows}">
    <jsp:useBean id="bookRow" type="java.util.Map" />
    <jsp:useBean id="addedBook"
      class="database.Book" scope="page" />
  ...
  <% cart.add(bid, addedBook); %>
...
</c:if>
```

The choose tag performs conditional block execution by the embedded when subtags. It renders the body of the first when tag whose test condition evaluates to true. If none of the test conditions of nested when tags evaluates to true, then the body of an otherwise tag is evaluated, if present.

For example, the following sample code shows how to render text based on a customer's membership category.

```
<c:choose>
  <c:when test="${customer.category == 'trial'}" >
    ...
  </c:when>
  <c:when test="${customer.category == 'member'}" >
    ...
  </c:when>
    <c:when test="${customer.category == 'preferred'}" >
    ...
  </c:when>
  <c:otherwise>
    ...
  </c:otherwise>
</c:choose>
```

The choose, when, and otherwise tags can be used to construct an if-then-else statement as follows:

```
<c:choose>
  <c:when test="${count == 0}" >
    No records matched your selection.
  </c:when>
  <c:otherwise>
    ${count} records matched your selection.
  </c:otherwise>
</c:choose>
```

Iterator Tags

The forEach tag allows you to iterate over a collection of objects. You specify the collection via the items attribute, and the current item is available through a variable named by the var attribute.

A large number of collection types are supported by forEach, including all implementations of java.util.Collection and java.util.Map. If the items attribute is of type java.util.Map, then the current item will be of type java.util.Map.Entry, which has the following properties:

- key: The key under which the item is stored in the underlying Map
- value: The value that corresponds to the key

Arrays of objects as well as arrays of primitive types (for example, int) are also supported. For arrays of primitive types, the current item for the iteration is automatically wrapped with its standard wrapper class (for example, Integer for int, Float for float, and so on).

Implementations of java.util.Iterator and java.util.Enumeration are supported, but they must be used with caution. Iterator and Enumeration objects are not resettable, so they should not be used within more than one iteration tag. Finally, java.lang.String objects can be iterated over if the string contains a list of comma-separated values (for example: Monday,Tuesday,Wednesday,Thursday,Friday).

Here's the shopping cart iteration from the preceding section, now with the forEach tag:

```
<c:forEach var="item" items="${sessionScope.cart.items}">
  ...
  <tr>
    <td align="right" bgcolor="#ffffff">
    ${item.quantity}
  </td>
  ...
</c:forEach>
```

The forTokens tag is used to iterate over a collection of tokens separated by a delimiter.

Similarly to the value attribute of the c:set tag (see Variable Support Tags, page 180), the items attribute of forEach and forTokens can also take a deferred value expression so that JavaServer Faces tags can be included within these tags.

As described in Variable Support Tags (page 180), JavaServer Faces technology (see Chapter 9) supports a multiphase life cycle. Therefore, any JavaServer Faces component tags that are included in the forEach tag or the forTokens tag must have access to the variable referenced by the items attribute at different phases of the life cycle, not just during the rendering phase. Consider the following code:

```
<c:forEach var="book" items="#{BooksBean.books}">
  ...
  <h:inputText id="quantity" value="#{book.quantity}"/>
  ...
</c:forEach>
```

The items attribute uses a deferred value expression, which means that the book variable it references is available not only during the rendering phase of the JavaServer Faces life cycle but also during the later stages of the life cycle. Therefore, whatever values the user enters into the quantity component tags are updated to the external data object during the appropriate stage of the life cycle.

If the expression referenced by the items attribute used immediate evaluation syntax then the book variable would be available only when the component is rendered during the render response phase. This would prevent the values the user enters into the components from being converted, validated, or updated to the external data object during the later phases of the life cycle. The JavaServer Faces version of Duke's Bookstore includes a forEach tag on its bookcatalog.jsp page.

URL Tags

The jsp:include element provides for the inclusion of static and dynamic resources in the same context as the current page. However, jsp:include cannot access resources that reside outside the web application, and it causes unnecessary buffering when the resource included is used by another element.

In the following example, the transform element uses the content of the included resource as the input of its transformation. The jsp:include element reads the content of the response and writes it to the body content of the enclosing transform element, which then rereads exactly the same content. It would be more efficient if the transform element could access the input source directly and thereby avoid the buffering involved in the body content of the transform tag.

```
<acme:transform>
  <jsp:include page="/exec/employeesList"/>
<acme:transform/>
```

The `import` tag is therefore the simple, generic way to access URL-based resources, whose content can then be included and or processed within the JSP page. For example, in XML Tag Library (page 188), `import` is used to read in the XML document containing book information and assign the content to the scoped variable `xml`:

```
<c:import url="/books.xml" var="xml" />
<x:parse doc="${xml}" var="booklist"
  scope="application" />
```

The `param` tag, analogous to the `jsp:param` tag (see jsp:param Element, page 146), can be used with `import` to specify request parameters.

In Session Tracking (page 91) we discuss how an application must rewrite URLs to enable session tracking whenever the client turns off cookies. You can use the `url` tag to rewrite URLs returned from a JSP page. The tag includes the session ID in the URL only if cookies are disabled; otherwise, it returns the URL unchanged. Note that this feature requires that the URL be *relative*. The `url` tag takes `param` subtags to include parameters in the returned URL. For example, `bookcatalog.jsp` rewrites the URL used to add a book to the shopping cart as follows:

```
<c:url var="url" value="/catalog" >
  <c:param name="Add" value="${bookId}" />
</c:url>
<p><strong><a href="${url}">
```

The `redirect` tag sends an HTTP redirect to the client. The `redirect` tag takes `param` subtags for including parameters in the returned URL.

Miscellaneous Tags

The `catch` tag provides a complement to the JSP error page mechanism. It allows page authors to recover gracefully from error conditions that they can control. Actions that are of central importance to a page should *not* be encapsulated in a catch; in this way their exceptions will propagate instead to an error page. Actions with secondary importance to the page should be wrapped in a catch so that they never cause the error page mechanism to be invoked.

The exception thrown is stored in the variable identified by var, which always has page scope. If no exception occurred, the scoped variable identified by var is removed if it existed. If var is missing, the exception is simply caught and not saved.

The out tag evaluates an expression and outputs the result of the evaluation to the current JspWriter object. The syntax and attributes are as follows:

```
<c:out value="value" [escapeXml="{true|false}"]
  [default="defaultValue"] />
```

If the result of the evaluation is a java.io.Reader object, then data is first read from the Reader object and then written into the current JspWriter object. The special processing associated with Reader objects improves performance when a large amount of data must be read and then written to the response.

If escapeXml is true, the character conversions listed in Table 6–3 are applied.

Table 6–3 Character Conversions

Character	Character Entity Code
<	<
>	>
&	&
'	'
"	"

XML Tag Library

The JSTL XML tag set is listed in Table 6–4.

Table 6–4 XML Tags

Area	Function	Tags	Prefix

XML	Core	`out`
		`parse`
		`set`
			x

	Flow control	`choose`
		`  when`
		`  otherwise`
		`forEach`
		`if`	

	Transformation	`transform` `  param`	

A key aspect of dealing with XML documents is to be able to easily access their content. XPath (see `http://java.sun.com/xml/jaxp`), a W3C recommendation since 1999, provides an easy notation for specifying and selecting parts of an XML document. In the JSTL XML tags, XPath expressions specified using the `select` attribute are used to select portions of XML data streams. Note that XPath is used as a *local* expression language only for the `select` attribute. This means that values specified for `select` attributes are evaluated using the XPath expression language but that values for all other attributes are evaluated using the rules associated with the JSP 2.0 expression language.

In addition to the standard XPath syntax, the JSTL XPath engine supports the following scopes to access web application data within an XPath expression:

- `$foo`
- `$param:`
- `$header:`
- `$cookie:`
- `$initParam:`
- `$pageScope:`
- `$requestScope:`

- `$sessionScope:`
- `$applicationScope:`

These scopes are defined in exactly the same way as their counterparts in the JSP expression language discussed in Implicit Objects (page 130). Table 6–5 shows some examples of using the scopes.

Table 6–5 Example XPath Expressions

XPath Expression	Result
`$sessionScope:profile`	The session-scoped EL variable named `profile`
`$initParam:mycom.productId`	The `String` value of the `mycom.productId` context parameter

The XML tags are illustrated in another version (`bookstore5`) of the Duke's Bookstore application. This version replaces the database with an XML representation of the bookstore database, which is retrieved from another web application. The directions for building and deploying this version of the application are in The Example JSP Document (page 156).

Core Tags

The core XML tags provide basic functionality to easily parse and access XML data.

The `parse` tag parses an XML document and saves the resulting object in the EL variable specified by attribute `var`. In `bookstore5`, the XML document is parsed and saved to a context attribute in `parsebooks.jsp`, which is included by all JSP pages that need access to the document:

```
<c:if test="${applicationScope:booklist == null}" >
  <c:import url="${initParam.booksURL}" var="xml" />
  <x:parse doc="${xml}" var="booklist" scope="application" />
</c:if>
```

The `set` and `out` tags parallel the behavior described in Variable Support Tags (page 180) and Miscellaneous Tags (page 186) for the XPath local expression language. The `set` tag evaluates an XPath expression and sets the result into a

JSP EL variable specified by attribute var. The out tag evaluates an XPath expression on the current context node and outputs the result of the evaluation to the current JspWriter object.

The JSP page bookdetails.jsp selects a book element whose id attribute matches the request parameter bookId and sets the abook attribute. The out tag then selects the book's title element and outputs the result.

```
<x:set var="abook"
  select="$applicationScope.booklist/
    books/book[@id=$param:bookId]" />
  <h2><x:out select="$abook/title"/></h2>
```

As you have just seen, x:set stores an internal XML representation of a *node* retrieved using an XPath expression; it doesn't convert the selected node into a String and store it. Thus, x:set is primarily useful for storing parts of documents for later retrieval.

If you want to store a String, you must use x:out within c:set. The x:out tag converts the node to a String, and c:set then stores the String as an EL variable. For example, bookdetails.jsp stores an EL variable containing a book price, which is later provided as the value of a fmt tag, as follows:

```
<c:set var="price">
  <x:out select="$abook/price"/>
</c:set>
<h4><fmt:message key="ItemPrice"/>:
  <fmt:formatNumber value="${price}" type="currency"/>
```

The other option, which is more direct but requires that the user have more knowledge of XPath, is to coerce the node to a String manually by using XPath's string function.

```
<x:set var="price" select="string($abook/price)"/>
```

Flow Control Tags

The XML flow control tags parallel the behavior described in Flow Control Tags (page 182) for XML data streams.

The JSP page bookcatalog.jsp uses the forEach tag to display all the books contained in booklist as follows:

```
<x:forEach var="book"
  select="$applicationScope:booklist/books/*">
  <tr>
    <c:set var="bookId">
      <x:out select="$book/@id"/>
    </c:set>=
    <td bgcolor="#ffffaa">
      <c:url var="url"
      value="/bookdetails" >
        <c:param name="bookId" value="${bookId}" />
        <c:param name="Clear" value="0" />
      </c:url>
      <a href="${url}">
      <strong><x:out select="$book/title"/> 
      </strong></a></td>
    <td bgcolor="#ffffaa" rowspan=2>
      <c:set var="price">
        <x:out select="$book/price"/>
      </c:set>
      <fmt:formatNumber value="${price}" type="currency"/>
       
    </td>
    <td bgcolor="#ffffaa" rowspan=2>
    <c:url var="url" value="/catalog" >
      <c:param name="Add" value="${bookId}" />
    </c:url>
    <p><strong><a href="${url}"> 
      <fmt:message key="CartAdd"/> </a>
    </td>
  </tr>
  <tr>
    <td bgcolor="#ffffff">
      <fmt:message key="By"/> <em>
      <x:out select="$book/firstname"/> 
      <x:out select="$book/surname"/></em></td></tr>
</x:forEach>
```

Transformation Tags

The transform tag applies a transformation, specified by an XSLT stylesheet set by the attribute xslt, to an XML document, specified by the attribute doc. If the doc attribute is not specified, the input XML document is read from the tag's body content.

I18NThe `param` subtag can be used along with `transform` to set transformation parameters. The attributes name and `value` are used to specify the parameter. The `value` attribute is optional. If it is not specified, the value is retrieved from the tag's body.

Internationalization Tag Library

Chapter 14 covers how to design web applications so that they conform to the language and formatting conventions of client locales. This section describes tags that support the internationalization of JSP pages.

JSTL defines tags for setting the locale for a page, creating locale-sensitive messages, and formatting and parsing data elements such as numbers, currencies, dates, and times in a locale-sensitive or customized manner. Table 6–6 lists the tags.

Table 6–6 Internationalization Tags

Area	Function	Tags	Prefix
I18N	Setting Locale	`setLocale` `requestEncoding`	`fmt`

	Messaging	`bundle`
		`message`
		  `param`
		`setBundle`	

	Number and Date Formatting	`formatNumber`
		`formatDate`
		`parseDate`
		`parseNumber`
		`setTimeZone`
		`timeZone`	

JSTL I18N tags use a localization context to localize their data. A *localization context* contains a locale and a resource bundle instance. To specify the localization context at deployment time, you define the context parameter `javax.servlet.jsp.jstl.fmt.localizationContext`, whose value can be a `javax.servlet.jsp.jstl.fmt.LocalizationContext` or a `String`. A `String` context parameter is interpreted as a resource bundle base name. For the Duke's

Bookstore application, the context parameter is the String messages.BookstoreMessages. When a request is received, JSTL automatically sets the locale based on the value retrieved from the request header and chooses the correct resource bundle using the base name specified in the context parameter.

Setting the Locale

The setLocale tag is used to override the client-specified locale for a page. The requestEncoding tag is used to set the request's character encoding, in order to be able to correctly decode request parameter values whose encoding is different from ISO-8859-1.

Messaging Tags

By default, the capability to sense the browser locale setting is enabled in JSTL. This means that the client determines (via its browser setting) which locale to use, and allows page authors to cater to the language preferences of their clients.

The setBundle and bundle Tags

You can set the resource bundle at runtime with the JSTL fmt:setBundle and fmt:bundle tags. fmt:setBundle is used to set the localization context in a variable or configuration variable for a specified scope. fmt:bundle is used to set the resource bundle for a given tag body.

The message Tag

The message tag is used to output localized strings. The following tag from bookcatalog.jsp is used to output a string inviting customers to choose a book from the catalog.

```
<h3><fmt:message key="Choose"/></h3>
```

The param subtag provides a single argument (for parametric replacement) to the compound message or pattern in its parent message tag. One param tag must be specified for each variable in the compound message or pattern. Parametric replacement takes place in the order of the param tags.

Formatting Tags

JSTL provides a set of tags for parsing and formatting locale-sensitive numbers and dates.

The formatNumber tag is used to output localized numbers. The following tag from bookshowcart.jsp is used to display a localized price for a book.

```
<fmt:formatNumber value="${book.price}" type="currency"/>
```

Note that because the price is maintained in the database in dollars, the localization is somewhat simplistic, because the formatNumber tag is unaware of exchange rates. The tag formats currencies but does not convert them.

Analogous tags for formatting dates (formatDate) and for parsing numbers and dates (parseNumber, parseDate) are also available. The timeZone tag establishes the time zone (specified via the value attribute) to be used by any nested formatDate tags.

In bookreceipt.jsp, a "pretend" ship date is created and then formatted with the formatDate tag:

```
<jsp:useBean id="now" class="java.util.Date" />
<jsp:setProperty name="now" property="time"
  value="${now.time + 432000000}" />
<fmt:message key="ShipDate"/>
<fmt:formatDate value="${now}" type="date"
  dateStyle="full"/>.
```

SQL Tag Library

The JSTL SQL tags for accessing databases listed in Table 6–7 are designed for quick prototyping and simple applications. For production applications, database operations are normally encapsulated in JavaBeans components.

Table 6–7 SQL Tags

Area	Function	Tags	Prefix
Database	Setting the data source	`setDataSource`	`sql`

	SQL	`query`
		  `dateParam`
		  `param`
		`transaction`
		`update`
		  `dateParam`
		  `param`	

The `setDataSource` tag allows you to set data source information for the database. You can provide a JNDI name or `DriverManager` parameters to set the data source information. All of the Duke's Bookstore pages that have more than one SQL tag use the following statement to set the data source:

```
<sql:setDataSource dataSource="jdbc/BookDB" />
```

The `query` tag performs an SQL query that returns a result set. For parameterized SQL queries, you use a nested `param` tag inside the `query` tag.

In `bookcatalog.jsp`, the value of the `Add` request parameter determines which book information should be retrieved from the database. This parameter is saved as the attribute name `bid` and is passed to the `param` tag.

```
<c:set var="bid" value="${param.Add}"/>
<sql:query var="books" >
  select * from PUBLIC.books where id = ?
  <sql:param value="${bid}" />
</sql:query>
```

The `update` tag is used to update a database row. The `transaction` tag is used to perform a series of SQL statements atomically.

The JSP page `bookreceipt.jsp` page uses both tags to update the database inventory for each purchase. Because a shopping cart can contain more than one book, the `transaction` tag is used to wrap multiple queries and updates. First, the page establishes that there is sufficient inventory; then the updates are performed.

```
<c:set var="sufficientInventory" value="true" />
<sql:transaction>
  <c:forEach var="item" items="${sessionScope.cart.items}">
    <c:set var="book" value="${item.item}" />
    <c:set var="bookId" value="${book.bookId}" />

    <sql:query var="books"
      sql="select * from PUBLIC.books where id = ?" >
      <sql:param value="${bookId}" />
    </sql:query>
    <jsp:useBean id="inventory"
      class="database.BookInventory" />
    <c:forEach var="bookRow" begin="0"
      items="${books.rowsByIndex}">
      <jsp:useBean id="bookRow"  type="java.lang.Object[]" />
      <jsp:setProperty name="inventory" property="quantity"
        value="${bookRow[7]}" />

      <c:if test="${item.quantity > inventory.quantity}">
        <c:set var="sufficientInventory" value="false" />
        <h3><font color="red" size="+2">
        <fmt:message key="OrderError"/>
        There is insufficient inventory for
        <i>${bookRow[3]}</i>.</font></h3>
      </c:if>
    </c:forEach>
  </c:forEach>

  <c:if test="${sufficientInventory == 'true'}" />
    <c:forEach var="item" items="${sessionScope.cart.items}">
      <c:set var="book" value="${item.item}" />
      <c:set var="bookId" value="${book.bookId}" />

      <sql:query var="books"
        sql="select * from PUBLIC.books where id = ?" >
        <sql:param value="${bookId}" />
      </sql:query>

      <c:forEach var="bookRow" begin="0"
        items="${books.rows}">
        <sql:update var="books" sql="update PUBLIC.books set
```

```
                inventory = inventory - ? where id = ?" >
                <sql:param value="${item.quantity}" />
                <sql:param value="${bookId}" />
            </sql:update>
        </c:forEach>
    </c:forEach>
    <h3><fmt:message key="ThankYou"/>
        ${param.cardname}.</h3><br>
  </c:if>
</sql:transaction>
```

query Tag Result Interface

The Result interface is used to retrieve information from objects returned from a query tag.

```
public interface Result
  public String[] getColumnNames();
  public int getRowCount()
  public Map[] getRows();
  public Object[][] getRowsByIndex();
  public boolean isLimitedByMaxRows();
```

For complete information about this interface, see the API documentation for the JSTL packages.

The var attribute set by a query tag is of type Result. The getRows method returns an array of maps that can be supplied to the items attribute of a forEach tag. The JSTL expression language converts the syntax ${*result*.rows} to a call to *result*.getRows. The expression ${books.rows} in the following example returns an array of maps.

When you provide an array of maps to the forEach tag, the var attribute set by the tag is of type Map. To retrieve information from a row, use the get("*colname*") method to get a column value. The JSP expression language converts the syntax ${*map*.*colname*} to a call to *map*.get("*colname*"). For example, the expression ${book.title} returns the value of the title entry of a book map.

The Duke's Bookstore page bookdetails.jsp retrieves the column values from the book map as follows.

```
<c:forEach var="book" begin="0" items="${books.rows}">
  <h2>${book.title}</h2>
   <fmt:message key="By"/> <em>${book.firstname}
```

```
    ${book.surname}</em>  
    (${book.year})<br>   <br>
    <h4><fmt:message key="Critics"/></h4>
    <blockquote>${book.description}</blockquote>
    <h4><fmt:message key="ItemPrice"/>:
    <fmt:formatNumber value="${book.price}" type="currency"/>
    </h4>
</c:forEach>
```

The following excerpt from bookcatalog.jsp uses the Row interface to retrieve values from the columns of a book row using scripting language expressions. First, the book row that matches a request parameter (bid) is retrieved from the database. Because the bid and bookRow objects are later used by tags that use scripting language expressions to set attribute values and by a scriptlet that adds a book to the shopping cart, both objects are declared as scripting variables using the jsp:useBean tag. The page creates a bean that describes the book, and scripting language expressions are used to set the book properties from book row column values. Then the book is added to the shopping cart.

You might want to compare this version of bookcatalog.jsp to the versions in Chapter 4 and Chapter 7 that use a book database JavaBeans component.

```
<sql:query var="books"
  dataSource="${applicationScope.bookDS}">
  select * from PUBLIC.books where id = ?
  <sql:param value="${bid}" />
</sql:query>
<c:forEach var="bookRow" begin="0"
      items="${books.rowsByIndex}">
  <jsp:useBean id="bid"  type="java.lang.String" />
  <jsp:useBean id="bookRow" type="java.lang.Object[]" />
  <jsp:useBean id="addedBook" class="database.Book"
    scope="page" >
    <jsp:setProperty name="addedBook" property="bookId"
      value="${bookRow[0]}" />
    <jsp:setProperty name="addedBook" property="surname"
      value="${bookRow[1]}" />
    <jsp:setProperty name="addedBook" property="firstName"
      value="${bookRow[2]}" />
    <jsp:setProperty name="addedBook" property="title"
      value="${bookRow[3]}" />
    <jsp:setProperty name="addedBook" property="price"
      value="${bookRow[4])}" />
    <jsp:setProperty name="addedBook" property="year"
      value="${bookRow[6]}" />
    <jsp:setProperty name="addedBook"
```

```
        property="description"
        value="${bookRow[7]}" />
      <jsp:setProperty name="addedBook" property="inventory"
        value="${bookRow[8]}" />
    </jsp:useBean>
    <% cart.add(bid, addedBook); %>
    ...
  </c:forEach>
```

Functions

Table 6–8 lists the JSTL functions.

Table 6–8 Functions

Area	Function	Tags	Prefix
Functions	Collection length	`length`	`fn`

	String manipulation	`toUpperCase, toLowerCase`
		`substring, substringAfter, substringBefore`
		`trim`
		`replace`
		`indexOf, startsWith, endsWith, contains, containsIgnoreCase`
		`split, join`
		`escapeXml`	

Although the `java.util.Collection` interface defines a `size` method, it does not conform to the JavaBeans component design pattern for properties and so cannot be accessed via the JSP expression language. The `length` function can be applied to any collection supported by the `c:forEach` and returns the length of the collection. When applied to a `String`, it returns the number of characters in the string.

For example, the `index.jsp` page of the `hello1` application introduced in Chapter 2 uses the `fn:length` function and the `c:if` tag to determine whether to include a response page:

```
<%@ taglib uri="http://java.sun.com/jsp/jstl/core"
  prefix="c" %>
<%@ taglib uri="http://java.sun.com/jsp/jstl/functions"
  prefix="fn" %>
<html>
<head><title>Hello</title></head>
...
<input type="text" name="username" size="25">
<p></p>
<input type="submit" value="Submit">
<input type="reset" value="Reset">
</form>

<c:if test="${fn:length(param.username) > 0}" >
  <%@include file="response.jsp" %>
</c:if>
</body>
</html>
```

The rest of the JSTL functions are concerned with string manipulation:

- `toUpperCase`, `toLowerCase`: Changes the capitalization of a string
- `substring`, `substringBefore`, `substringAfter`: Gets a subset of a string
- `trim`: Trims whitespace from a string
- `replace`: Replaces characters in a string
- `indexOf`, `startsWith`, `endsWith`, `contains`, `containsIgnoreCase`: Checks whether a string contains another string
- `split`: Splits a string into an array
- `join`: Joins a collection into a string
- `escapeXml`: Escapes XML characters in a string

Further Information

For further information on JSTL, see the following:

- The tag reference documentation:
  `http://java.sun.com/products/jsp/jstl/1.1/docs/tlddocs/index.html`
- The API reference documentation:
  `http://java.sun.com/products/jsp/jstl/1.1/docs/api/index.html`
- The JSTL 1.1 specification:
  `http://java.sun.com/products/jsp/jstl/downloads/index.html#specs`
- The JSTL web site:
  `http://java.sun.com/products/jsp/jstl`

7

Custom Tags in JSP Pages

THE standard JSP tags simplify JSP page development and maintenance. JSP technology also provides a mechanism for encapsulating other types of dynamic functionality in *custom tags*, which are extensions to the JSP language. Some examples of tasks that can be performed by custom tags include operating on implicit objects, processing forms, accessing databases and other enterprise services such as email and directories, and implementing flow control. Custom tags increase productivity because they can be reused in more than one application.

Custom tags are distributed in a *tag library*, which defines a set of related custom tags and contains the objects that implement the tags. The object that implements a custom tag is called a *tag handler*. JSP technology defines two types of tag handlers: simple and classic. *Simple* tag handlers can be used only for tags that do not use scripting elements in attribute values or the tag body. *Classic* tag handlers must be used if scripting elements are required. Simple tag handlers are covered in this chapter, and classic tag handlers are discussed in Chapter 8.

You can write simple tag handlers using the JSP language or using the Java language. A *tag file* is a source file containing a reusable fragment of JSP code that is translated into a simple tag handler by the web container. Tag files can be used to develop custom tags that are presentation-centric or that can take advantage of existing tag libraries, or by page authors who do not know Java. When the flexibility of the Java programming language is needed to define the tag, JSP technology provides a simple API for developing a tag handler in the Java programming language.

This chapter assumes that you are familiar with the material in Chapter 4, especially the section Using Custom Tags (page 141). For more information about tag libraries and for pointers to some freely available libraries, see

```
http://java.sun.com/products/jsp/taglibraries/index.jsp
```

What Is a Custom Tag?

A custom tag is a user-defined JSP language element. When a JSP page containing a custom tag is translated into a servlet, the tag is converted to operations on a tag handler. The web container then invokes those operations when the JSP page's servlet is executed.

Custom tags have a rich set of features. They can

- Be customized via attributes passed from the calling page.
- Pass variables back to the calling page.
- Access all the objects available to JSP pages.
- Communicate with each other. You can create and initialize a JavaBeans component, create a public EL variable that refers to that bean in one tag, and then use the bean in another tag.
- Be nested within one another and communicate via private variables.

The Example JSP Pages

This chapter describes the tasks involved in defining simple tags. We illustrate the tasks using excerpts from the JSP version of the Duke's Bookstore application discussed in The Example JSP Pages (page 101), rewritten here to take advantage of several custom tags:

- A `catalog` tag for rendering the book catalog
- A `shipDate` tag for rendering the ship date of an order
- A template library for ensuring a common look and feel among all screens and composing screens out of content chunks

The `tutorial-template` tag library defines a set of tags for creating an application template. The template is a JSP page that has placeholders for the parts that need to change with each screen. Each of these placeholders is referred to as a *parameter* of the template. For example, a simple template might include a title parameter for the top of the generated screen and a body parameter to refer to a JSP page for the custom content of the screen. The template is created using a set of nested tags—`definition`, `screen`, and `parameter`—that are used to build a table of screen definitions for Duke's Bookstore. An `insert` tag to insert parameters from the table into the screen.

Figure 7–1 shows the flow of a request through the following Duke's Bookstore web components:

- `template.jsp`, which determines the structure of each screen. It uses the `insert` tag to compose a screen from subcomponents.
- `screendefinitions.jsp`, which defines the subcomponents used by each screen. All screens have the same banner but different title and body content (specified by the JSP Pages column in Figure 4–1).
- `Dispatcher`, a servlet, which processes requests and forwards to `template.jsp`.

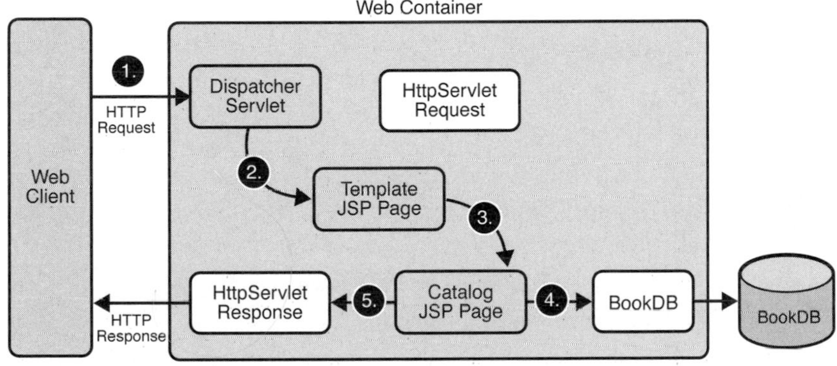

Figure 7–1 Request Flow through Duke's Bookstore Components

The source code for the Duke's Bookstore application is located in the `<INSTALL>/javaeetutorial5/examples/web/bookstore3/` directory created when you unzip the tutorial bundle (see About the Examples, page xxxiv).

To deploy and run the application using NetBeans 5.5, follow these steps:

1. Perform all the operations described in Accessing Databases from Web Applications (page 55).
2. In NetBeans 5.5, select File→Open Project.

3. In the Open Project dialog, navigate to:

   `<INSTALL>/javaeetutorial5/examples/web/`
4. Select the `bookstore3` folder.
5. Select the Open as Main Project checkbox and the Open Required Projects checkbox.
6. Click Open Project Folder.
7. In the Projects tab, right-click the `bookstore3` project, and select Deploy Project.
8. To run the application, open the bookstore URL `http://localhost:8080/bookstore3/bookstore`.

To deploy and run the application using `ant` follow these steps:

1. In a terminal window, go to `<INSTALL>/javaeetutorial5/examples/web/bookstore3/`.
2. Run `ant`. This target will spawn any necessary compilations, copy files to the `<INSTALL>/javaeetutorial5/examples/web/bookstore3/build/` directory, and create a WAR file and copy it to the `<INSTALL>/javaeetutorial5/examples/web/bookstore3/dist/` directory.
3. Start the Application Server.
4. Perform all the operations described in Creating a Data Source in the Application Server (page 56).
5. To deploy the example, run `ant deploy`. The deploy target outputs a URL for running the application. Ignore this URL, and instead use the one shown in the next step.
6. To run the application, open the bookstore URL `http://localhost:8080/bookstore3/bookstore`

To learn how to configure the example, refer to the `web.xml` file, which includes the following configurations:

- A `display-name` element that specifies the name that tools use to identify the application.
- A `context-param` element that specifies the JSTL resource bundle base name.
- A `listener` element that identifies the `ContextListener` class used to create and remove the database access.
- A `servlet` element that identifies the `Dispatcher` instance.

- A set of `servlet-mapping` elements that map `Dispatcher` to URL patterns for each of the JSP pages in the application.
- Nested inside a `jsp-config` element is a `jsp-property-group` element, which sets the properties for the group of pages included in this version of Duke's Bookstore. See Setting Properties for Groups of JSP Pages (page 149) for more information.

To run the example, open the bookstore URL `http://localhost:8080/bookstore3/bookstore`.

See Troubleshooting (page 62) for help with diagnosing common problems.

Types of Tags

Simple tags are invoked using XML syntax. They have a start tag and an end tag, and possibly a body:

```
<tt:tag>
  body
</tt:tag>
```

A custom tag with no body is expressed as follows:

```
<tt:tag /> or <tt:tag></tt:tag>
```

Tags with Attributes

A simple tag can have attributes. Attributes customize the behavior of a custom tag just as parameters customize the behavior of a method. There are three types of attributes:

- Simple attributes
- Fragment attributes
- Dynamic attributes

Simple Attributes

Simple attributes are evaluated by the container before being passed to the tag handler. Simple attributes are listed in the start tag and have the syntax `attr="value"`. You can set a simple attribute value from a `String` constant, or an expression language (EL) expression, or by using a `jsp:attribute` element (see jsp:attribute Element, page 210). The conversion process between the constants and expressions and attribute types follows the rules described for JavaBeans component properties in Setting JavaBeans Component Properties (page 139).

The Duke's Bookstore page `bookcatalog.jsp` calls the `catalog` tag, which has two attributes. The first attribute, a reference to a book database object, is set by an EL expression. The second attribute, which sets the color of the rows in a table that represents the bookstore catalog, is set with a `String` constant.

```
<sc:catalog bookDB ="${bookDB}" color="#cccccc">
```

Fragment Attributes

A *JSP fragment* is a portion of JSP code passed to a tag handler that can be invoked as many times as needed. You can think of a fragment as a template that is used by a tag handler to produce customized content. Thus, unlike a simple attribute which is evaluated by the container, a fragment attribute is evaluated by a tag handler during tag invocation.

To declare a fragment attribute, you use the `fragment` attribute of the `attribute` directive (see Declaring Tag Attributes in Tag Files, page 217) or use the `fragment` subelement of the `attribute` TLD element (see Declaring Tag Attributes for Tag Handlers, page 236). You define the value of a fragment attribute by using a `jsp:attribute` element. When used to specify a fragment attribute, the body of the `jsp:attribute` element can contain only static text and standard and custom tags; it *cannot* contain scripting elements (see Chapter 8).

JSP fragments can be parametrized via expression language (EL) variables in the JSP code that composes the fragment. The EL variables are set by the tag handler, thus allowing the handler to customize the fragment each time it is invoked (see Declaring Tag Variables in Tag Files, page 219, and Declaring Tag Variables for Tag Handlers, page 238).

The `catalog` tag discussed earlier accepts two fragments: `normalPrice`, which is displayed for a product that's full price, and `onSale`, which is displayed for a product that's on sale.

```
<sc:catalog bookDB ="${bookDB}" color="#cccccc">
  <jsp:attribute name="normalPrice">
    <fmt:formatNumber value="${price}" type="currency"/>
  </jsp:attribute>
```

```
  <jsp:attribute name="onSale">
    <strike><fmt:formatNumber value="${price}"
      type="currency"/></strike><br/>
    <font color="red"><fmt:formatNumber value="${salePrice}"
      type="currency"/></font>
  </jsp:attribute>
</sc:catalog>
```

The tag executes the `normalPrice` fragment, using the values for the `price` EL variable, if the product is full price. If the product is on sale, the tag executes the `onSale` fragment using the `price` and `salePrice` variables.

Dynamic Attributes

A *dynamic attribute* is an attribute that is not specified in the definition of the tag. Dynamic attributes are used primarily by tags whose attributes are treated in a uniform manner but whose names are not necessarily known at development time.

For example, this tag accepts an arbitrary number of attributes whose values are colors and outputs a bulleted list of the attributes colored according to the values:

```
<colored:colored color1="red" color2="yellow" color3="blue"/>
```

You can also set the value of dynamic attributes using an EL expression or using the `jsp:attribute` element.

Deferred Value

A *deferred value attribute* is one that accepts deferred value expressions, which are described in Value Expressions (page 117).

Deferred Method

A *deferred method attribute* is one that accepts deferred method expressions, which are described in Method Expressions (page 122).

Dynamic Attribute or Deferred Expression

This kind of attribute can accept a String literal, a scriptlet expression, or an EL expression, including deferred expressions.

jsp:attribute Element

The `jsp:attribute` element allows you to define the value of a tag attribute in the *body* of an XML element instead of in the value of an XML attribute.

For example, the Duke's Bookstore template page `screendefinitions.jsp` uses `jsp:attribute` to use the output of `fmt:message` to set the value of the `value` attribute of `tt:parameter`:

```
...
<tt:screen id="/bookcatalog">
  <tt:parameter name="title" direct="true">
    <jsp:attribute name="value" >
      <fmt:message key="TitleBookCatalog"/>
    </jsp:attribute>
  </tt:parameter>
  <tt:parameter name="banner" value="/template/banner.jsp"
    direct="false"/>
  <tt:parameter name="body" value="/bookcatalog.jsp"
    direct="false"/>
</tt:screen>
...
```

`jsp:attribute` accepts a `name` attribute and a `trim` attribute. The `name` attribute identifies which tag attribute is being specified. The optional `trim` attribute determines whether or not whitespace appearing at the beginning and end of the element body should be discarded. By default, the leading and trailing whitespace is discarded. The whitespace is trimmed when the JSP page is translated. If a body contains a custom tag that produces leading or trailing whitespace, that whitespace is preserved regardless of the value of the `trim` attribute.

An empty body is equivalent to specifying "" as the value of the attribute.

The body of `jsp:attribute` is restricted according to the type of attribute being specified:

- For simple attributes that accept an EL expression, the body can be any JSP content.
- For simple attributes that do not accept an EL expression, the body can contain only static text.
- For fragment attributes, the body must not contain any scripting elements (see Chapter 8).

Tags with Bodies

A simple tag can contain custom and core tags, HTML text, and tag-dependent body content between the start tag and the end tag.

In the following example, the Duke's Bookstore application page bookshowcart.jsp uses the JSTL c:if tag to print the body if the request contains a parameter named Clear:

```
<c:if test="${param.Clear}">
  <font color="#ff0000" size="+2"><strong>
  You just cleared your shopping cart!
  </strong><br> <br></font>
</c:if>
```

jsp:body Element

You can also explicitly specify the body of a simple tag by using the jsp:body element. If one or more attributes are specified with the jsp:attribute element, then jsp:body is the only way to specify the body of the tag. If one or more jsp:attribute elements appear in the body of a tag invocation but you don't include a jsp:body element, the tag has an empty body.

Tags That Define Variables

A simple tag can define an EL variable that can be used within the calling page. In the following example, the iterator tag sets the value of the EL variable departmentName as it iterates through a collection of department names.

```
<tlt:iterator var="departmentName" type="java.lang.String"
    group="${myorg.departmentNames}">
  <tr>
    <td><a href="list.jsp?deptName=${departmentName}">
      ${departmentName}</a></td>
  </tr>
</tlt:iterator>
```

Communication between Tags

Custom tags communicate with each other through shared objects. There are two types of shared objects: public and private.

In the following example, the `c:set` tag creates a public EL variable called `aVariable`, which is then reused by `anotherTag`.

```
<c:set var="aVariable" value="aValue" />
<tt:anotherTag attr1="${aVariable}" />
```

Nested tags can share private objects. In the next example, an object created by `outerTag` is available to `innerTag`. The inner tag retrieves its parent tag and then retrieves an object from the parent. Because the object is not named, the potential for naming conflicts is reduced.

```
<tt:outerTag>
  <tt:innerTag />
</tt:outerTag>
```

The Duke's Bookstore page `template.jsp` uses a set of cooperating tags that share public and private objects to define the screens of the application. These tags are described in A Template Tag Library (page 253).

Encapsulating Reusable Content Using Tag Files

A tag file is a source file that contains a fragment of JSP code that is reusable as a custom tag. Tag files allow you to create custom tags using JSP syntax. Just as a JSP page gets translated into a servlet class and then compiled, a tag file gets translated into a tag handler and then compiled.

The recommended file extension for a tag file is `.tag`. As is the case with JSP files, the tag can be composed of a top file that includes other files that contain either a complete tag or a fragment of a tag file. Just as the recommended extension for a fragment of a JSP file is `.jspf`, the recommended extension for a fragment of a tag file is `.tagf`.

The following version of the Hello, World application introduced in Chapter 2 uses a tag to generate the response. The `response` tag, which accepts two attributes—a greeting string and a name—is encapsulated in `response.tag`:

```
<%@ attribute name="greeting" required="true" %>
<%@ attribute name="name" required="true" %>
<h2><font color="black">${greeting}, ${name}!</font></h2>
```

The highlighted line in the `greeting.jsp` page invokes the `response` tag if the length of the `username` request parameter is greater than `0`:

```
<%@ taglib tagdir="/WEB-INF/tags" prefix="h" %>
<%@ taglib uri="http://java.sun.com/jsp/jstl/core"
  prefix="c" %>
<%@ taglib uri="http://java.sun.com/jsp/jstl/functions"
  prefix="fn" %>
<html>
<head><title>Hello</title></head>
<body bgcolor="white">
<img src="duke.waving.gif">
<c:set var="greeting" value="Hello" />
<h2>${greeting}, my name is Duke. What's yours?</h2>
<form method="get">
<input type="text" name="username" size="25">
<p></p>
<input type="submit" value="Submit">
<input type="reset" value="Reset">
</form>

<c:if test="${fn:length(param.username) > 0}" >
  <h:response greeting="${greeting}"
    name="${param.username}"/>
</c:if>
</body>
</html>
```

To deploy and run the `hello3` application with NetBeans 5.5, follow these steps:

1. In NetBeans 5.5, select File→Open Project.
2. In the Open Project dialog, navigate to:

   `<INSTALL>/javaeetutorial5/examples/web/`
3. Select the `hello3` folder.
4. Select the Open as Main Project checkbox.
5. Click Open Project Folder.
6. In the Projects tab, right-click the `hello3` project, and select Deploy Project.
7. To run the application, open the bookstore URL `http://localhost:8080/hello3`.

To deploy and run the hello3 application with ant, follow these steps:

1. In a terminal window, go to *<INSTALL>*/javaeetutorial5/examples/web/hello3/.
2. Run ant. This target will spawn any necessary compilations, copy files to the *<INSTALL>*/javaeetutorial5/examples/web/hello3/build/ directory, and create a WAR file.
3. Start the Application Server.
4. Run ant deploy.
5. To run the example, open your browser to http://localhost:8080/hello3.

To learn how to configure the example, refer to the deployment descriptor (the web.xml file), which includes the following configurations:

- A display-name element that specifies the name that tools use to identify the application.
- A welcome-file-list element that sets a particular page to be a welcome file.

Tag File Location

Tag files can be placed in one of two locations: in the /WEB-INF/tags/ directory or subdirectory of a web application or in a JAR file (see Packaged Tag Files, page 234) in the /WEB-INF/lib/ directory of a web application. Packaged tag files require a tag library descriptor (see Tag Library Descriptors, page 229), an XML document that contains information about a library as a whole and about each tag contained in the library. Tag files that appear in any other location are not considered tag extensions and are ignored by the web container.

Tag File Directives

Directives are used to control aspects of tag file translation to a tag handler, and to specify aspects of the tag, attributes of the tag, and variables exposed by the tag. Table 7–1 lists the directives that you can use in tag files.

Table 7–1 Tag File Directives

Directive	Description
`taglib`	Identical to `taglib` directive (see Declaring Tag Libraries, page 142) for JSP pages.
`include`	Identical to `include` directive (see Reusing Content in JSP Pages, page 145) for JSP pages. Note that if the included file contains syntax unsuitable for tag files, a translation error will occur.
`tag`	Similar to the `page` directive in a JSP page, but applies to tag files instead of JSP pages. As with the `page` directive, a translation unit can contain more than one instance of the `tag` directive. All the attributes apply to the complete translation unit. However, there can be only one occurrence of any attribute or value defined by this directive in a given translation unit. With the exception of the `import` attribute, multiple attribute or value (re)definitions result in a translation error. Also used for declaring custom tag properties such as display name. See Declaring Tags (page 215).
`attribute`	Declares an attribute of the custom tag defined in the tag file. See Declaring Tag Attributes in Tag Files (page 217).
`variable`	Declares an EL variable exposed by the tag to the calling page. See Declaring Tag Variables in Tag Files (page 219).

Declaring Tags

The `tag` directive is similar to the JSP page's page directive but applies to tag files. Some of the elements in the `tag` directive appear in the `tag` element of a

TLD (see Declaring Tag Handlers, page 234). Table 7–2 lists the tag directive attributes.

Table 7–2 `tag` Directive Attributes

Attribute	Description
`display-name`	(optional) A short name that is intended to be displayed by tools. Defaults to the name of the tag file without the extension `.tag`.
`body-content`	(optional) Provides information on the content of the body of the tag. Can be either `empty`, `tagdependent`, or `scriptless`. A translation error will result if `JSP` or any other value is used. Defaults to `scriptless`. See body-content Attribute (page 217).
`dynamic-attributes`	(optional) Indicates whether this tag supports additional attributes with dynamic names. The value identifies a scoped attribute in which to place a `Map` containing the names and values of the dynamic attributes passed during invocation of the tag. A translation error results if the value of the `dynamic-attributes` of a `tag` directive is equal to the value of a `name-given` of a `variable` directive or the value of a `name` attribute of an `attribute` directive.
`small-icon`	(optional) Relative path, from the tag source file, of an image file containing a small icon that can be used by tools. Defaults to no small icon.
`large-icon`	(optional) Relative path, from the tag source file, of an image file containing a large icon that can be used by tools. Defaults to no large icon.
`description`	(optional) Defines an arbitrary string that describes this tag. Defaults to no description.
`example`	(optional) Defines an arbitrary string that presents an informal description of an example of a use of this action. Defaults to no example.
`language`	(optional) Carries the same syntax and semantics of the `language` attribute of the `page` directive.
`import`	(optional) Carries the same syntax and semantics of the `import` attribute of the `page` directive.

Table 7–2 `tag` Directive Attributes (Continued)

Attribute	Description
`pageEncoding`	(optional) Carries the same syntax and semantics of the `page-Encoding` attribute in the `page` directive.
`isELIgnored`	(optional) Carries the same syntax and semantics of the `isEL-Ignored` attribute of the `page` directive.

body-content Attribute

You specify the type of a tag's body content using the `body-content` attribute:

```
bodycontent="empty | scriptless | tagdependent"
```

You must declare the body content of tags that do not accept a body as `empty`. For tags that have a body there are two options. Body content containing custom and standard tags and HTML text is specified as `scriptless`. All other types of body content—for example, SQL statements passed to the `query` tag—is specified as `tagdependent`. If no attribute is specified, the default is `scriptless`.

Declaring Tag Attributes in Tag Files

To declare the attributes of a custom tag defined in a tag file, you use the `attribute` directive. A TLD has an analogous `attribute` element (see Declaring Tag Attributes for Tag Handlers, page 236). Table 7–3 lists the `attribute` directive attributes.

Table 7–3 `attribute` Directive Attributes

Attribute	Description
`description`	(optional) Description of the attribute. Defaults to no description.
`name`	The unique name of the attribute being declared. A translation error results if more than one `attribute` directive appears in the same translation unit with the same `name`. A translation error results if the value of a `name` attribute of an `attribute` directive is equal to the value of the `dynamic-attributes` attribute of a `tag` directive or the value of a `name-given` attribute of a `variable` directive.
`required`	(optional) Whether this attribute is required (`true`) or optional (`false`). Defaults to `false`.
`rtexprvalue`	(optional) Whether the attribute's value can be dynamically calculated at runtime by an expression. Defaults to `true`. When this element is set to `true` and the attribute definition also includes either a `deferred-value` or `deferred-method` element then the attribute accepts both dynamic and deferred expressions.
`type`	(optional) The runtime type of the attribute's value. Defaults to `java.lang.String`.
`deferred-Value`	(optional) Indicates whether the attribute accepts deferred value expressions. Only one of `deferredValue` or `deferredMethod` can be true. If `deferredValueType` is specified, the default for `deferredValue` is `true`. Causes a translation error if specified in a tag file with a JSP version less than 2.1.
`deferred-ValueType`	(optional) The type resulting from the evaluation of the attribute's value expression. The default is `java.lang.String` if no type is specified. If both `deferredValueType` and `deferredValue` are specified, `deferredValue` must be true. If `deferredValue` is `true`, the default of `deferredValueType` is `java.lang.Object`. Causes a translation error specified in a tag file with a JSP version less than 2.1.

Table 7–3 `attribute` Directive Attributes (Continued)

Attribute	Description
`deferred-Method`	(optional) Indicates whether the tag attribute accepts deferred method expressions. If `deferredMethod` and `deferredMethodSignature` are specified then deferredMethod must be true. The default of deferredMethod is true if `deferredMethodSignature` is specified, otherwise the default of `deferredMethod` is false. The presence of a `deferred-method` element in an attribute definition precludes the inclusion of a `deferred-value` element. Causes a translation error if specified in a tag file with a JSP version less than 2.1.
`deferred-MethodSignature`	(optional) The signature of the method to be invoked by the expression defined by the accompanying `deferredMethod` attribute. If `deferred-Method` is true and this attribute is not specified, the method signature defaults to `void methodName()`. Causes a translation error if specified in a tag file with a JSP version less than 2.1.
`fragment`	(optional) Whether this attribute is a fragment to be evaluated by the tag handler (`true`) or a normal attribute to be evaluated by the container before being passed to the tag handler. If this attribute is `true`: You do not specify the `rtexprvalue` attribute. The container fixes the `rtexprvalue` attribute at `true`. You do not specify the `type` attribute. The container fixes the `type` attribute at `javax.servlet.jsp.tagext.JspFragment`. Defaults to `false`.

Declaring Tag Variables in Tag Files

Tag attributes are used to customize tag behavior much as parameters are used to customize the behavior of object methods. In fact, using tag attributes and EL variables, it is possible to emulate various types of parameters—`IN`, `OUT`, and nested.

To emulate `IN` parameters, use tag attributes. A tag attribute is communicated between the calling page and the tag file when the tag is invoked. No further communication occurs between the calling page and the tag file.

To emulate `OUT` or nested parameters, use EL variables. The variable is not initialized by the calling page but instead is set by the tag file. Each type of parameter is synchronized with the calling page at various points according to the scope of the variable. See Variable Synchronization (page 221) for details.

To declare an EL variable exposed by a tag file, you use the `variable` directive. A TLD has an analogous `variable` element (see Declaring Tag Variables for Tag Handlers, page 238). Table 7–4 lists the `variable` directive attributes.

Table 7–4 `variable` Directive Attributes

Attribute	Description
`description`	(optional) An optional description of this variable. Defaults to no description.
`name-given` | `name-from-attribute`	Defines an EL variable to be used in the page invoking this tag. Either `name-given` or `name-from-attribute` must be specified. If `name-given` is specified, the value is the name of the variable. If `name-from-attribute` is specified, the value is the name of an attribute whose (translation-time) value at the start of the tag invocation will give the name of the variable. Translation errors arise in the following circumstances: 1. Specifying neither `name-given` nor `name-from-attribute` or both. 2. If two `variable` directives have the same `name-given`. 3. If the value of a `name-given` attribute of a `variable` directive is equal to the value of a `name` attribute of an `attribute` directive or the value of a `dynamic-attributes` attribute of a `tag` directive.
`alias`	Defines a variable, local to the tag file, to hold the value of the EL variable. The container will synchronize this value with the variable whose name is given in `name-from-attribute`. Required when `name-from-attribute` is specified. A translation error results if used without `name-from-attribute`. A translation error results if the value of `alias` is the same as the value of a `name` attribute of an `attribute` directive or the `name-given` attribute of a `variable` directive.
`variable-class`	(optional) The name of the class of the variable. The default is `java.lang.String`.

Table 7–4 `variable` Directive Attributes

Attribute	Description
`declare`	(optional) Whether or not the variable is declared. `True` is the default.
`scope`	(optional) The scope of the variable. Can be either `AT_BEGIN`, `AT_END`, or `NESTED`. Defaults to `NESTED`.

Variable Synchronization

The web container handles the synchronization of variables between a tag file and a calling page. Table 7–5 summarizes when and how each object is synchronized according to the object's scope.

Table 7–5 Variable Synchronization Behavior

Tag File Location	`AT_BEGIN`	`NESTED`	`AT_END`
Beginning	Not sync.	Save	Not sync.
Before any fragment invocation via `jsp:invoke` or `jsp:doBody` (see Evaluating Fragments Passed to Tag Files, page 224)	Tag→page	Tag→page	Not sync.
End	Tag→page	Restore	Tag→page

If `name-given` is used to specify the variable name, then the name of the variable in the calling page and the name of the variable in the tag file are the same and are equal to the value of `name-given`.

The `name-from-attribute` and `alias` attributes of the `variable` directive can be used to customize the name of the variable in the calling page while another name is used in the tag file. When using these attributes, you set the name of the variable in the calling page from the value of `name-from-attribute` at the time the tag was called. The name of the corresponding variable in the tag file is the value of `alias`.

Synchronization Examples

The following examples illustrate how variable synchronization works between a tag file and its calling page. All the example JSP pages and tag files reference the JSTL core tag library with the prefix c. The JSP pages reference a tag file located in /WEB-INF/tags with the prefix my.

AT_BEGIN Scope

In this example, the AT_BEGIN scope is used to pass the value of the variable named x to the tag's body and at the end of the tag invocation.

```
<%-- callingpage.jsp --%>
<c:set var="x" value="1"/>
${x} <%-- (x == 1) --%>
<my:example>
  ${x} <%-- (x == 2) --%>
</my:example>
${x} <%-- (x == 4) --%>

<%-- example.tag --%>
<%@ variable name-given="x" scope="AT_BEGIN" %>
${x} <%-- (x == null) --%>
<c:set var="x" value="2"/>
<jsp:doBody/>
${x} <%-- (x == 2) --%>
<c:set var="x" value="4"/>
```

NESTED Scope

In this example, the NESTED scope is used to make a variable named x available only to the tag's body. The tag sets the variable to 2, and this value is passed to the calling page before the body is invoked. Because the scope is NESTED and because the calling page also had a variable named x, its original value, 1, is restored when the tag completes.

```
<%-- callingpage.jsp --%>
<c:set var="x" value="1"/>
${x} <%-- (x == 1) --%>
<my:example>
  ${x} <%-- (x == 2) --%>
</my:example>
${x} <%-- (x == 1) --%>

<%-- example.tag --%>
<%@ variable name-given="x" scope="NESTED" %>
${x} <%-- (x == null) --%>
<c:set var="x" value="2"/>
```

```
<jsp:doBody/>
${x} <%-- (x == 2) --%>
<c:set var="x" value="4"/>
```

AT_END Scope

In this example, the AT_END scope is used to return a value to the page. The body of the tag is not affected.

```
<%-- callingpage.jsp --%>
<c:set var="x" value="1"/>
${x} <%-- (x == 1) --%>
<my:example>
  ${x} <%-- (x == 1) --%>
</my:example>
${x} <%-- (x == 4) --%>

<%-- example.tag --%>
<%@ variable name-given="x" scope="AT_END" %>
${x} <%-- (x == null) --%>
<c:set var="x" value="2"/>
<jsp:doBody/>
${x} <%-- (x == 2) --%>
<c:set var="x" value="4"/>
```

AT_BEGIN and name-from-attribute

In this example the AT_BEGIN scope is used to pass an EL variable to the tag's body and make to it available to the calling page at the end of the tag invocation. The name of the variable is specified via the value of the attribute var. The variable is referenced by a local name, result, in the tag file.

```
<%-- callingpage.jsp --%>
<c:set var="x" value="1"/>
${x} <%-- (x == 1) --%>
<my:example var="x">
  ${x} <%-- (x == 2) --%>
  ${result} <%-- (result == null) --%>
  <c:set var="result" value="invisible"/>
</my:example>
${x} <%-- (x == 4) --%>
${result} <%-- (result == 'invisible') --%>

<%-- example.tag --%>
<%@ attribute name="var" required="true" rtexprvalue="false"%>
<%@ variable alias="result" name-from-attribute="var"
  scope="AT_BEGIN" %>
${x} <%-- (x == null) --%>
```

```
${result} <%-- (result == null) --%>
<c:set var="x" value="ignored"/>
<c:set var="result" value="2"/>
<jsp:doBody/>
${x} <%-- (x == 'ignored') --%>
${result} <%-- (result == 2) --%>
<c:set var="result" value="4"/>
```

Evaluating Fragments Passed to Tag Files

When a tag file is executed, the web container passes it two types of fragments: fragment attributes and the tag body. Recall from the discussion of fragment attributes that fragments are evaluated by the tag handler as opposed to the web container. Within a tag file, you use the `jsp:invoke` element to evaluate a fragment attribute and use the `jsp:doBody` element to evaluate a tag file body.

The result of evaluating either type of fragment is sent to the response or is stored in an EL variable for later manipulation. To store the result of evaluating a fragment to an EL variable, you specify the `var` or `varReader` attribute. If `var` is specified, the container stores the result in an EL variable of type `String` with the name specified by `var`. If `varReader` is specified, the container stores the result in an EL variable of type `java.io.Reader`, with the name specified by `varReader`. The `Reader` object can then be passed to a custom tag for further processing. A translation error occurs if both `var` and `varReader` are specified.

An optional `scope` attribute indicates the scope of the resulting variable. The possible values are `page` (default), `request`, `session`, or `application`. A translation error occurs if you use this attribute without specifying the `var` or `varReader` attribute.

Examples

This section introduces examples that demonstrate using custom tags.

Simple Attribute Example

The Duke's Bookstore `shipDate` tag, defined in `shipDate.tag`, is a custom tag that has a simple attribute. The tag generates the date of a book order according to the type of shipping requested.

```
<%@ taglib prefix="sc" tagdir="/WEB-INF/tags" %>
<h3><fmt:message key="ThankYou"/> ${param.cardname}.</h3><br>
<fmt:message key="With"/>
<em><fmt:message key="${param.shipping}"/></em>,
<fmt:message key="ShipDateLC"/>
<sc:shipDate shipping="${param.shipping}" />
```

The tag determines the number of days until shipment from the `shipping` attribute passed to it by the page `bookreceipt.jsp`. From the number of days, the tag computes the ship date. It then formats the ship date.

```
<%@ attribute name="shipping" required="true" %>

<jsp:useBean id="now" class="java.util.Date" />
<jsp:useBean id="shipDate" class="java.util.Date" />
<c:choose>
  <c:when test="${shipping == 'QuickShip'}">
    <c:set var="days" value="2" />
  </c:when>
  <c:when test="${shipping == 'NormalShip'}">
    <c:set var="days" value="5" />
  </c:when>
  <c:when test="${shipping == 'SaverShip'}">
    <c:set var="days" value="7" />
  </c:when>
</c:choose>
<jsp:setProperty name="shipDate" property="time"
  value="${now.time + 86400000 * days}" />
<fmt:formatDate value="${shipDate}" type="date"
  dateStyle="full"/>.<br><br>
```

Simple and Fragment Attribute and Variable Example

The Duke's Bookstore `catalog` tag, defined in `catalog.tag`, is a custom tag with simple and fragment attributes and variables. The tag renders the catalog of a book database as an HTML table. The tag file declares that it sets variables named `price` and `salePrice` via `variable` directives. The fragment `normalPrice` uses the variable `price`, and the fragment `onSale` uses the variables `price` and `salePrice`. Before the tag invokes the fragment attributes using the `jsp:invoke` element, the web container passes values for the variables back to the calling page.

```
<%@ attribute name="bookDB" required="true"
  type="database.BookDB" %>
<%@ attribute name="color" required="true" %>
<%@ attribute name="normalPrice" fragment="true" %>
<%@ attribute name="onSale" fragment="true" %>

<%@ variable name-given="price" %>
<%@ variable name-given="salePrice" %>

<center>
<table>
<c:forEach var="book" begin="0" items="${bookDB.books}">
  <tr>
  <c:set var="bookId" value="${book.bookId}" />
  <td bgcolor="${color}">
    <c:url var="url" value="/bookdetails" >
      <c:param name="bookId" value="${bookId}" />
    </c:url>
    <a href="${url}"><
      strong>${book.title} </strong></a></td>
  <td bgcolor="${color}" rowspan=2>
  <c:set var="salePrice" value="${book.price * .85}" />
  <c:set var="price" value="${book.price}" />
  <c:choose>
    <c:when test="${book.onSale}" >
      <jsp:invoke fragment="onSale" />
    </c:when>
    <c:otherwise>
      <jsp:invoke fragment="normalPrice"/>
    </c:otherwise>
  </c:choose>

   </td>

...
</table>
</center>
```

The page `bookcatalog.jsp` invokes the `catalog` tag that has the simple attributes `bookDB`, which contains catalog data, and `color`, which customizes the coloring of the table rows. The formatting of the book price is determined by two fragment attributes—`normalPrice` and `onSale`—that are conditionally invoked by the tag according to data retrieved from the book database.

```
<sc:catalog bookDB ="${bookDB}" color="#cccccc">
  <jsp:attribute name="normalPrice">
    <fmt:formatNumber value="${price}" type="currency"/>
  </jsp:attribute>
  <jsp:attribute name="onSale">
    <strike>
    <fmt:formatNumber value="${price}" type="currency"/>
    </strike><br/>
    <font color="red">
    <fmt:formatNumber value="${salePrice}" type="currency"/>
    </font>
  </jsp:attribute>
</sc:catalog>
```

The screen produced by `bookcatalog.jsp` is shown in Figure 7–2. You can compare it to the version in Figure 4–2.

Dynamic Attribute Example

The following code implements the tag discussed in Dynamic Attributes (page 209). An arbitrary number of attributes whose values are colors are stored in a `Map` named by the `dynamic-attributes` attribute of the `tag` directive. The JSTL `forEach` tag is used to iterate through the `Map` and the attribute keys and colored attribute values are printed in a bulleted list.

```
<%@ tag dynamic-attributes="colorMap"%>
<ul>
<c:forEach var="color" begin="0" items="${colorMap}">
  <li>${color.key} =
    <font color="${color.value}">${color.value}</font><li>
</c:forEach>
</ul>
```

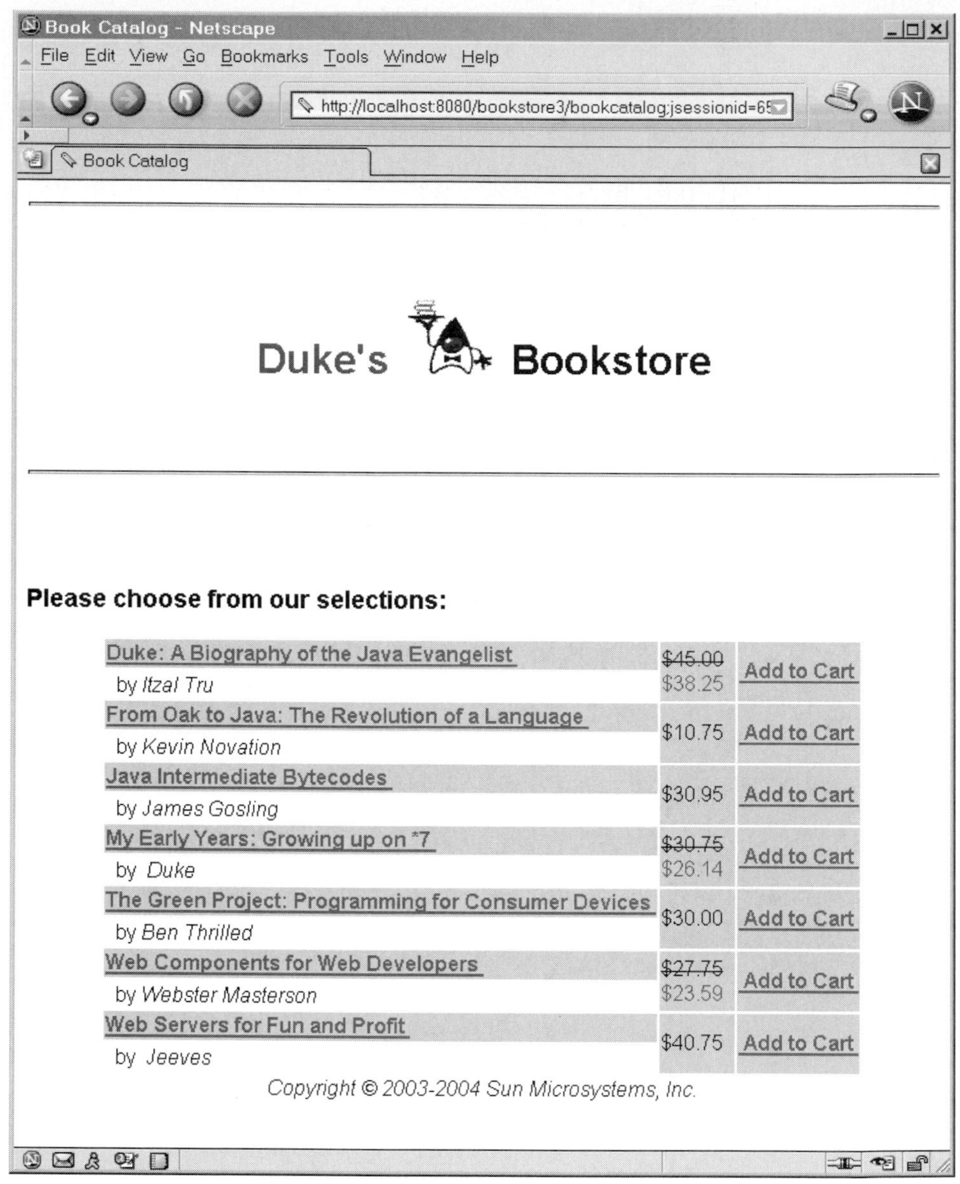

Figure 7–2 Book Catalog

Tag Library Descriptors

If you want to redistribute your tag files or implement your custom tags with tag handlers written in Java, you must declare the tags in a tag library descriptor (TLD). A *tag library descriptor* is an XML document that contains information about a library as a whole and about each tag contained in the library. TLDs are used by a web container to validate the tags and by JSP page development tools.

Tag library descriptor file names must have the extension `.tld` and must be packaged in the `/WEB-INF/` directory or subdirectory of the WAR file or in the `/META-INF/` directory or subdirectory of a tag library packaged in a JAR. If a tag is implemented as a tag file and is packaged in `/WEB-INF/tags/` or a subdirectory, a TLD will be generated automatically by the web container, though you can provide one if you wish.

Most containers set the JSP version of this automatically generated TLD (called an *implicit TLD*) to 2.0. Therefore, in order to take advantage of JSP 2.1 features, you must provide a TLD that sets the JSP version to 2.1 if you don't have a TLD already. This TLD must be named `implicit.tld` and placed into the same directory as the tag files.

You set thc JSP version using the version attribute of the root `taglib` element that of the TLD, as shown here:

```
<taglib
  xsi:schemaLocation=
  "http://java.sun.com/xml/ns/javaee web-
    jsptaglibrary_2_1.xsd"
  xmlns="http://java.sun.com/xml/ns/javaee"|
  xmlns:xsi="http://www.w3.org/2001/XMLSchema-instance"
  version="2.1">
```

Table 7–6 lists the subelements of the `taglib` element.

Table 7–6 `taglib` Subelements

Element	Description
`description`	(optional) A string describing the use of the tag library.
`display-name`	(optional) Name intended to be displayed by tools.
`icon`	(optional) Icon that can be used by tools.
`tlib-version`	The tag library's version.
`short-name`	(optional) Name that could be used by a JSP page-authoring tool to create names with a mnemonic value.
`uri`	A URI that uniquely identifies the tag library.
`validator`	See validator Element (page 231).
`listener`	See listener Element (page 231).
`tag-file | tag`	Declares the tag files or tags defined in the tag library. See Declaring Tag Files (page 231) and Declaring Tag Handlers (page 234). A tag library is considered invalid if a `tag-file` element has a `name` subelement with the same content as a `name` subelement in a `tag` element.
`function`	Zero or more EL functions (see Functions, page 134) defined in the tag library.
`tag-extension`	(optional) Extensions that provide extra information about the tag library for tools.

Top-Level Tag Library Descriptor Elements

This section describes some top-level TLD elements. Subsequent sections describe how to declare tags defined in tag files, how to declare tags defined in tag handlers, and how to declare tag attributes and variables.

validator Element

This element defines an optional tag library validator that can be used to validate the conformance of any JSP page importing this tag library to its requirements. Table 7–7 lists the subelements of the `validator` element.

Table 7–7 `validator` Subelements

Element	Description
`validator-class`	The class implementing `javax.servlet.jsp.tagext.TagLibraryValidator`
`init-param`	(optional) Initialization parameters

listener Element

A tag library can specify some classes that are event listeners (see Handling Servlet Life-Cycle Events, page 63). The listeners are listed in the TLD as `listener` elements, and the web container will instantiate the listener classes and register them in a way analogous to that of listeners defined at the WAR level. Unlike WAR-level listeners, the order in which the tag library listeners are registered is undefined. The only subelement of the `listener` element is the `listener-class` element, which must contain the fully qualified name of the listener class.

Declaring Tag Files

Although not required for tag files, providing a TLD allows you to share the tag across more than one tag library and lets you import the tag library using a URI instead of the `tagdir` attribute.

tag-file TLD Element

A tag file is declared in the TLD using a `tag-file` element. Its subelements are listed in Table 7–8.

Table 7–8 `tag-file` Subelements

Element	Description
`description`	(optional) A description of the tag.
`display-name`	(optional) Name intended to be displayed by tools.
`icon`	(optional) Icon that can be used by tools.
`name`	The unique tag name.
`path`	Where to find the tag file implementing this tag, relative to the root of the web application or the root of the JAR file for a tag library packaged in a JAR. This must begin with `/WEB-INF/tags/` if the tag file resides in the WAR, or `/META-INF/tags/` if the tag file resides in a JAR.
`example`	(optional) Informal description of an example use of the tag.
`tag-extension`	(optional) Extensions that provide extra information about the tag for tools.

Unpackaged Tag Files

Tag files placed in a subdirectory of `/WEB-INF/tags/` do not require a TLD file and don't have to be packaged. Thus, to create reusable JSP code, you simply create a new tag file and place the code inside it.

The web container generates an implicit tag library for each directory under and including `/WEB-INF/tags/`. There are no special relationships between subdirectories; they are allowed simply for organizational purposes. For example, the following web application contains three tag libraries:

```
/WEB-INF/tags/
/WEB-INF/tags/a.tag
/WEB-INF/tags/b.tag
/WEB-INF/tags/foo/
/WEB-INF/tags/foo/c.tag
/WEB-INF/tags/bar/baz/
/WEB-INF/tags/bar/baz/d.tag
```

The implicit TLD for each library has the following values:

- `tlib-version` for the tag library. Defaults to 1.0.
- `short-name` is derived from the directory name. If the directory is `/WEB-INF/tags/`, the short name is simply `tags`. Otherwise, the full directory path (relative to the web application) is taken, minus the `/WEB-INF/tags/` prefix. Then all / characters are replaced with -(hyphen), which yields the short name. Note that short names are not guaranteed to be unique.
- A `tag-file` element is considered to exist for each tag file, with the following subelements:
  - The `name` for each is the filename of the tag file, without the `.tag` extension.
  - The `path` for each is the path of the tag file, relative to the root of the web application.

So, for the example, the implicit TLD for the `/WEB-INF/tags/bar/baz/` directory would be as follows:

```
<taglib>
  <tlib-version>1.0</tlib-version>
  <short-name>bar-baz</short-name>
  <tag-file>
    <name>d</name>
    <path>/WEB-INF/tags/bar/baz/d.tag</path>
  </tag-file>
</taglib>
```

Despite the existence of an implicit tag library, a TLD in the web application can still create additional tags from the same tag files. To accomplish this, you add a `tag-file` element with a `path` that points to the tag file.

Packaged Tag Files

Tag files can be packaged in the `/META-INF/tags/` directory in a JAR file installed in the `/WEB-INF/lib/` directory of the web application. Tags placed here are typically part of a reusable library of tags that can be used easily in any web application.

Tag files bundled in a JAR require a tag library descriptor. Tag files that appear in a JAR but are not defined in a TLD are ignored by the web container.

When used in a JAR file, the `path` subelement of the `tag-file` element specifies the full path of the tag file from the root of the JAR. Therefore, it must always begin with `/META-INF/tags/`.

Tag files can also be compiled into Java classes and bundled as a tag library. This is useful when you wish to distribute a binary version of the tag library without the original source. If you choose this form of packaging, you must use a tool that produces portable JSP code that uses only standard APIs.

Declaring Tag Handlers

When tags are implemented with tag handlers written in Java, each tag in the library must be declared in the TLD with a `tag` element. The `tag` element contains the tag name, the class of its tag handler, information on the tag's attributes, and information on the variables created by the tag (see Tags That Define Variables, page 211).

Each attribute declaration contains an indication of whether the attribute is required, whether its value can be determined by request-time expressions, the type of the attribute, and whether the attribute is a fragment. Variable information can be given directly in the TLD or through a tag extra info class. Table 7–9 lists the subelements of the `tag` element.

Table 7–9 `tag` Subelements

Element	Description
`description`	(optional) A description of the tag.
`display-name`	(optional) name intended to be displayed by tools.
`icon`	(optional) Icon that can be used by tools.
`name`	The unique tag name.
`tag-class`	The fully qualified name of the tag handler class.
`tei-class`	(optional) Subclass of `javax.servlet.jsp.tagext.TagExtraInfo`. See Declaring Tag Variables for Tag Handlers (page 238).
`body-content`	The body content type. See body-content Element (page 235).
`variable`	(optional) Declares an EL variable exposed by the tag to the calling page. See Declaring Tag Variables for Tag Handlers (page 238).
`attribute`	Declares an attribute of the custom tag. See Declaring Tag Attributes for Tag Handlers (page 236).
`dynamic-attributes`	Whether the tag supports additional attributes with dynamic names. Defaults to `false`. If true, the tag handler class must implement the `javax.servlet.jsp.tagext.DynamicAttributes` interface.
`example`	(optional) Informal description of an example use of the tag.
`tag-extension`	(optional) Extensions that provide extra information about the tag for tools.

body-content Element

You specify the type of body that is valid for a tag by using the `body-content` element. This element is used by the web container to validate that a tag invocation has the correct body syntax and is used by page-composition tools to assist the page author in providing a valid tag body. There are three possible values:

- `tagdependent`: The body of the tag is interpreted by the tag implementation itself, and is most likely in a different language, for example, embedded SQL statements.

- `empty`: The body must be empty.
- `scriptless`: The body accepts only static text, EL expressions, and custom tags. No scripting elements are allowed.

Declaring Tag Attributes for Tag Handlers

For each tag attribute, you must specify whether the attribute is required, whether the value can be determined by an expression, the type of the attribute in an `attribute` element (optional), and whether the attribute is a fragment. If the `rtexprvalue` element is `true` or `yes`, then the `type` element defines the return type expected from any expression specified as the value of the attribute. For static values, the type is always `java.lang.String`. An attribute is specified in a TLD in an `attribute` element. Table 7–10 lists the subelements of the `attribute` element.

Table 7–10 `attribute` Subelements

Element	Description
`description`	(optional) A description of the attribute.
`name`	The unique name of the attribute being declared. A translation error results if more than one `attribute` element appears in the same tag with the same `name`.
`required`	(optional) Whether the attribute is required. The default is `false`.
`rtexprvalue`	(optional) Whether the attribute's value can be dynamically calculated at runtime by an EL expression. The default is `false`. When this element is set to `true` and the attribute definition also includes either a `deferred-value` or `deferred-method` element then the attribute accepts both dynamic and deferred expressions.
`type`	(optional) The runtime type of the attribute's value. Defaults to `java.lang.String` if not specified.

Table 7–10 `attribute` Subelements (Continued)

Element	Description
`fragment`	(optional) Whether this attribute is a fragment to be evaluated by the tag handler (`true`) or a normal attribute to be evaluated by the container before being passed to the tag handler. If this attribute is `true`: You do not specify the `rtexprvalue` attribute. The container fixes the `rtexprvalue` attribute at `true`. You do not specify the `type` attribute. The container fixes the `type` attribute at `javax.servlet.jsp.tagext.JspFragment`. Defaults to `false`.
`deferred-value`	(optional) Indicates that the tag attribute accepts deferred value expressions. This element includes an optional `type` child element, which indicates the type of object to which the expression resolves. If no `type` element is included, the type is `java.lang.Object`. Either the `deferred-value` or `deferred-method` element (but not both) can be defined for the same attribute.
`deferred-method`	(optional) Indicates that the tag attribute accepts deferred method expressions. This element includes an optional `method-signature` child element, which indicates the signature of the method that the expression invokes. If no method signature is defined, the method signature default is `void methodName()`. Either the `deferred-value` or `deferred-method` element (but not both) can be defined for the same attribute.

If a tag attribute is not required, a tag handler should provide a default value.

The `tag` element for a tag that outputs its body if a test evaluates to `true` declares that the `test` attribute is required and that its value can be set by a runtime expression.

```
<tag>
  <name>present</name>
     <tag-class>condpkg.IfSimpleTag</tag-class>
  <body-content>scriptless</body-content>
  ...
  <attribute>
    <name>test</name>
    <required>true</required>
```

```
      <rtexprvalue>true</rtexprvalue>
   </attribute>
   ...
</tag>
```

Declaring Tag Variables for Tag Handlers

The example described in Tags That Define Variables (page 211) defines an EL variable `departmentName`:

```
<tlt:iterator var="departmentName" type="java.lang.String"
      group="${myorg.departmentNames}">
   <tr>
      <td><a href="list.jsp?deptName=${departmentName}">
         ${departmentName}</a></td>
   </tr>
</tlt:iterator>
```

When the JSP page containing this tag is translated, the web container generates code to synchronize the variable with the object referenced by the variable. To generate the code, the web container requires certain information about the variable:

- Variable name
- Variable class
- Whether the variable refers to a new or an existing object
- The availability of the variable

There are two ways to provide this information: by specifying the `variable` TLD subelement or by defining a tag extra info class and including the `tei-class` element in the TLD (see TagExtraInfo Class, page 248). Using the `variable` element is simpler but less dynamic. With the `variable` element, the only aspect of the variable that you can specify at runtime is its name (via the `name-from-attribute` element). If you provide this information in a tag extra info class, you can also specify the type of the variable at runtime.

Table 7–11 lists the subelements of the `variable` element.

Table 7–11 `variable` Subelements

Element	**Description**
`description`	(optional) A description of the variable.
`name-given` | `name-from-attribute`	Defines an EL variable to be used in the page invoking this tag. Either `name-given` or `name-from-attribute` must be specified. If `name-given` is specified, the value is the name of the variable. If `name-from-attribute` is specified, the value is the name of an attribute whose (translation-time) value at the start of the tag invocation will give the name of the variable. Translation errors arise in the following circumstances: 1. Specifying neither `name-given` nor `name-from-attribute` or both. 2. If two `variable` elements have the same `name-given`.
`variable-class`	(optional) The fully qualified name of the class of the object. `java.lang.String` is the default.
`declare`	(optional) Whether or not the object is declared. `True` is the default. A translation error results if both `declare` and `fragment` are specified.
`scope`	(optional) The scope of the variable defined. Can be either `AT_BEGIN`, `AT_END`, or `NESTED` (see Table 7–12). Defaults to `NESTED`.

Table 7–12 summarizes a variable's availability according to its declared scope.

Table 7–12 Variable Availability

Value	**Availability**
`NESTED`	Between the start tag and the end tag.
`AT_BEGIN`	From the start tag until the scope of any enclosing tag. If there's no enclosing tag, then to the end of the page.
`AT_END`	After the end tag until the scope of any enclosing tag. If there's no enclosing tag, then to the end of the page.

You can define the following `variable` element for the `tlt:iterator` tag:

```
<tag>
  <variable>
    <name-given>var</name-given>
    <variable-class>java.lang.String</variable-class>
    <declare>true</declare>
    <scope>NESTED</scope>
  </variable>
</tag>
```

Programming Simple Tag Handlers

The classes and interfaces used to implement simple tag handlers are contained in the `javax.servlet.jsp.tagext` package. Simple tag handlers implement the `SimpleTag` interface. Interfaces can be used to take an existing Java object and make it a tag handler. For most newly created handlers, you would use the `SimpleTagSupport` classes as a base class.

The heart of a simple tag handler is a single method—`doTag`—which gets invoked when the end element of the tag is encountered. Note that the default implementation of the `doTag` method of `SimpleTagSupport` does nothing.

A tag handler has access to an API that allows it to communicate with the JSP page. The entry point to the API is the JSP context object (`javax.servlet.jsp.JspContext`). The `JspContext` object provides access to implicit objects. `PageContext` extends `JspContext` with servlet-specific behavior. Through these objects, a tag handler can retrieve all the other implicit objects (request, session, and application) that are accessible from a JSP page. If the tag is nested, a tag handler also has access to the handler (called the *parent*) that is associated with the enclosing tag.

Including Tag Handlers in Web Applications

Tag handlers can be made available to a web application in two basic ways. The classes implementing the tag handlers can be stored in an unpacked form in the `WEB-INF/classes/` subdirectory of the web application. Alternatively, if the library is distributed as a JAR, it is stored in the `WEB-INF/lib/` directory of the web application.

How Is a Simple Tag Handler Invoked?

The SimpleTag interface defines the basic protocol between a simple tag handler and a JSP page's servlet. The JSP page's servlet invokes the setJspContext, setParent, and attribute setting methods before calling doStartTag.

```
ATag t = new ATag();
t.setJSPContext(...);
t.setParent(...);
t.setAttribute1(value1);
t.setAttribute2(value2);
...
t.setJspBody(new JspFragment(...))
t.doTag();
```

The following sections describe the methods that you need to develop for each type of tag introduced in Types of Tags (page 207).

Tag Handlers for Basic Tags

The handler for a basic tag without a body must implement the doTag method of the SimpleTag interface. The doTag method is invoked when the end element of the tag is encountered.

The basic tag discussed in the first section, <tt:basic />, would be implemented by the following tag handler:

```
public HelloWorldSimpleTag extends SimpleTagSupport {
  public void doTag() throws JspException, IOException {
    getJspContext().getOut().write("Hello, world.");
  }
}
```

Tag Handlers for Tags with Attributes

This section describes how to define attributes for a tag handler and how to validate attribute values.

Defining Attributes in a Tag Handler

For each tag attribute, you must define a set method in the tag handler that conforms to the JavaBeans architecture conventions. For example, consider the tag handler for the JSTL c:if tag:

```
<c:if test="${Clear}">
```

This tag handler contains the following method:

```
public void setTest(boolean test) {
  this.test = test;
}
```

As shown by the preceding example, the name of the attribute must match the name of the set method.

Attribute Validation

The documentation for a tag library should describe valid values for tag attributes. When a JSP page is translated, a web container will enforce any constraints contained in the TLD element for each attribute.

The attributes passed to a tag can also be validated at translation time using the validate method of a class derived from TagExtraInfo. This class is also used to provide information about variables defined by the tag (see TagExtraInfo Class, page 248).

The validate method is passed the attribute information in a TagData object, which contains attribute-value tuples for each of the tag's attributes. Because the validation occurs at translation time, the value of an attribute that is computed at request time will be set to TagData.REQUEST_TIME_VALUE.

The tag <tt:twa attr1="value1"/> has the following TLD attribute element:

```
<attribute>
  <name>attr1</name>
  <required>true</required>
  <rtexprvalue>true</rtexprvalue>
</attribute>
```

This declaration indicates that the value of attr1 can be determined at runtime.

The following validate method checks whether the value of attr1 is a valid Boolean value. Note that because the value of attr1 can be computed at runtime, validate must check whether the tag user has chosen to provide a runtime value.

```
public class TwaTEI extends TagExtraInfo {
  public ValidationMessage[] validate(TagData data) {
    Object o = data.getAttribute("attr1");
    if (o != null && o != TagData.REQUEST_TIME_VALUE) {
      if (((String)o).toLowerCase().equals("true") ||
        ((String)o).toLowerCase().equals("false") )
        return null;
      else
        return new ValidationMessage(data.getId(),
          "Invalid boolean value.");
    }
    else
      return null;
  }
}
```

Setting Dynamic Attributes

Simple tag handlers that support dynamic attributes must declare that they do so in the tag element of the TLD (see Declaring Tag Handlers, page 234). In addition, your tag handler must implement the setDynamicAttribute method of the DynamicAttributes interface. For each attribute specified in the tag invocation that does not have a corresponding attribute element in the TLD, the web container calls setDynamicAttribute, passing in the namespace of the attribute (or null if in the default namespace), the name of the attribute, and the value of the attribute. You must implement the setDynamicAttribute method to remember the names and values of the dynamic attributes so that they can be used later when doTag is executed. If the setDynamicAttribute method throws an exception, the doTag method is not invoked for the tag, and the exception must be treated in the same manner as if it came from an attribute setter method.

The following implementation of setDynamicAttribute saves the attribute names and values in lists. Then, in the doTag method, the names and values are echoed to the response in an HTML list.

```
private ArrayList keys = new ArrayList();
private ArrayList values = new ArrayList();

public void setDynamicAttribute(String uri,
```

```
        String localName, Object value ) throws JspException {
        keys.add( localName );
        values.add( value );
    }

    public void doTag() throws JspException, IOException {
        JspWriter out = getJspContext().getOut();
        for( int i = 0; i < keys.size(); i++ ) {
            String key = (String)keys.get( i );
            Object value = values.get( i );
            out.println( "<li>" + key + " = " + value + "</li>" );
        }
    }
```

Setting Deferred Value Attributes and Deferred Method Attributes

For each tag attribute that accepts a deferred value expression or a deferred method expression, the tag handler must have a method to access the value of the attribute.

The methods that access the value of a deferred value attribute method must accept a `ValueExpression` object. The methods that access the value of a deferred method attribute must accept a `MethodExpression` object. These methods take the form setX, where X is the name of the attribute.

The following example shows a method that can be used to access the value of a deferred value attribute called `attributeName`:

```
private javax.el.ValueExpression attributeName = null;

public void setAttributeName(
    javax.el.ValueExpression attributeName)
{
    this.immediate = immediate;
}
```

Deferred value attributes and deferred method attributes are primarily used by JavaServer Faces technology. See Getting the Attribute Values (page 451) for an example of creating a tag handler that processes these attributes for a JavaServer Faces application.

If you have an attribute that is both dynamic and deferred (meaning that the tag attribute definition accepts a deferred expression and has `rtexprvalue` set to true), then the `setX` method that accesses this value must accept an `Object` instance and test if the `Object` instance is a deferred value expression, as shown in this pseudocode:

```
public void setAttr(Object obj) {
  if (obj instance of ValueExpression) {
    // this is a deferred expression
  else {
    // this is an rtexpression
  }
}
```

Tag Handlers for Tags with Bodies

A simple tag handler for a tag with a body is implemented differently depending on whether or not the tag handler needs to manipulate the body. A tag handler manipulates the body when it reads or modifies the contents of the body.

Tag Handler Does Not Manipulate the Body

If a tag handler needs simply to evaluate the body, it gets the body using the `getJspBody` method of `SimpleTag` and then evaluates the body using the `invoke` method.

The following tag handler accepts a `test` parameter and evaluates the body of the tag if the test evaluates to `true`. The body of the tag is encapsulated in a JSP fragment. If the test is `true`, the handler retrieves the fragment using the `getJspBody` method. The `invoke` method directs all output to a supplied writer or, if the writer is `null`, to the `JspWriter` returned by the `getOut` method of the `JspContext` associated with the tag handler.

```
public class IfSimpleTag extends SimpleTagSupport {
  private boolean test;
  public void setTest(boolean test) {
    this.test = test;
  }
  public void doTag() throws JspException, IOException {
    if(test){
      getJspBody().invoke(null);
    }
  }
}
```

Tag Handler Manipulates the Body

If the tag handler needs to manipulate the body, the tag handler must capture the body in a `StringWriter`. The `invoke` method directs all output to a supplied writer. Then the modified body is written to the `JspWriter` returned by the `getOut` method of the `JspContext`. Thus, a tag that converts its body to uppercase could be written as follows:

```
public class SimpleWriter extends SimpleTagSupport {
   public void doTag() throws JspException, IOException {
      StringWriter sw = new StringWriter();
      jspBody.invoke(sw);
      jspContext().
         getOut().println(sw.toString().toUpperCase());
   }
}
```

Tag Handlers for Tags That Define Variables

Similar communication mechanisms exist for communication between JSP page and tag handlers as for JSP pages and tag files.

To emulate `IN` parameters, use tag attributes. A tag attribute is communicated between the calling page and the tag handler when the tag is invoked. No further communication occurs between the calling page and the tag handler.

To emulate `OUT` or nested parameters, use variables with availability `AT_BEGIN`, `AT_END`, or `NESTED`. The variable is not initialized by the calling page but instead is set by the tag handler.

For `AT_BEGIN` availability, the variable is available in the calling page from the start tag until the scope of any enclosing tag. If there's no enclosing tag, then the variable is available to the end of the page. For `AT_END` availability, the variable is available in the calling page after the end tag until the scope of any enclosing tag. If there's no enclosing tag, then the variable is available to the end of the page. For nested parameters, the variable is available in the calling page between the start tag and the end tag.

When you develop a tag handler you are responsible for creating and setting the object referenced by the variable into a context that is accessible from the page. You do this by using the `JspContext().setAttribute(name, value)` or

`JspContext.setAttribute(name, value, scope)` method. You retrieve the page context using the `getJspContext` method of `SimpleTag`.

Typically, an attribute passed to the custom tag specifies the name of the variable and the value of the variable is dependent on another attribute. For example, the `iterator` tag introduced in Chapter 4 retrieves the name of the variable from the `var` attribute and determines the value of the variable from a computation performed on the `group` attribute.

```
public void doTag() throws JspException, IOException {
  if (iterator == null)
    return;
  while (iterator.hasNext()) {
    getJspContext().setAttribute(var, iterator.next());
    getJspBody().invoke(null);
  }
}
public void setVar(String var) {
  this.var = var;
}
public void setGroup(Collection group) {
  this.group = group;
  if(group.size() > 0)
    iterator = group.iterator();
}
```

The scope that a variable can have is summarized in Table 7–13. The scope constrains the accessibility and lifetime of the object.

Table 7–13 Scope of Objects

Name	Accessible From	Lifetime
`page`	Current page	Until the response has been sent back to the user or the request is passed to a new page
`request`	Current page and any included or forwarded pages	Until the response has been sent back to the user
`session`	Current request and any subsequent request from the same browser (subject to session lifetime)	The life of the user's session
`application`	Current and any future request in the same web application	The life of the application

TagExtraInfo Class

In Declaring Tag Variables for Tag Handlers (page 238) we discussed how to provide information about tag variables in the tag library descriptor. Here we describe another approach: defining a tag extra info class. You define a tag extra info class by extending the class `javax.servlet.jsp.tagext.TagExtraInfo`. A `TagExtraInfo` must implement the `getVariableInfo` method to return an array of `VariableInfo` objects containing the following information:

- Variable name
- Variable class
- Whether the variable refers to a new object
- The availability of the variable

The web container passes a parameter of type `javax.servlet.jsp.tagext.TagData` to the `getVariableInfo` method, which contains attribute-value tuples for each of the tag's attributes. These attributes can be used to provide the `VariableInfo` object with an EL variable's name and class.

The following example demonstrates how to provide information about the variable created by the `iterator` tag in a tag extra info class. Because the name (`var`) and class (`type`) of the variable are passed in as tag attributes, they can be retrieved using the `data.getAttributeString` method and can be used to fill in the `VariableInfo` constructor. To allow the variable `var` to be used only within the tag body, you set the scope of the object to `NESTED`.

```
package iterator;
public class IteratorTEI extends TagExtraInfo {
  public VariableInfo[] getVariableInfo(TagData data) {
    String type = data.getAttributeString("type");
    if (type == null)
      type = "java.lang.Object";
    return new VariableInfo[] {
      new VariableInfo(data.getAttributeString("var"),
      type,
      true,
      VariableInfo.NESTED)
    };
  }
}
```

The fully qualified name of the tag extra info class defined for an EL variable must be declared in the TLD in the `tei-class` subelement of the `tag` element. Thus, the `tei-class` element for `IteratorTei` would be as follows:

```
<tei-class>
  iterator.IteratorTEI
</tei-class>
```

Cooperating Tags

Tags cooperate by sharing objects. JSP technology supports two styles of object sharing.

The first style requires that a shared object be named and stored in the page context (one of the implicit objects accessible to JSP pages as well as tag handlers). To access objects created and named by another tag, a tag handler uses the `pageContext.getAttribute(name, scope)` method.

In the second style of object sharing, an object created by the enclosing tag handler of a group of nested tags is available to all inner tag handlers. This form of object sharing has the advantage that it uses a private namespace for the objects, thus reducing the potential for naming conflicts.

To access an object created by an enclosing tag, a tag handler must first obtain its enclosing tag by using the static method `SimpleTagSupport.findAncestorWithClass(from, class)` or the `SimpleTagSupport.getParent` method. The former method should be used when a specific nesting of tag handlers cannot be guaranteed. After the ancestor has been retrieved, a tag handler can access any statically or dynamically created objects. Statically created objects are members of the parent. Private objects can also be created dynamically. Such privately named objects would have to be managed by the tag handler; one approach would be to use a `Map` to store name-object pairs.

The following example illustrates a tag handler that supports both the named approach and the private object approach to sharing objects. In the example, the handler for a query tag checks whether an attribute named `connectionId` has been set. If the `connectionId` attribute has been set, the handler retrieves the connection object from the page context. Otherwise, the tag handler first retrieves the tag handler for the enclosing tag and then retrieves the connection object from that handler.

```
public class QueryTag extends SimpleTagSupport {
  public int doTag() throws JspException {
    String cid = getConnectionId();
    Connection connection;
    if (cid != null) {
    // there is a connection id, use it
      connection =(Connection)pageContext.
        getAttribute(cid);
    } else {
      ConnectionTag ancestorTag =
        (ConnectionTag)findAncestorWithClass(this,
          ConnectionTag.class);
      if (ancestorTag == null) {
        throw new JspTagException("A query without
          a connection attribute must be nested
          within a connection tag.");
      }
      connection = ancestorTag.getConnection();
      ...
    }
  }
}
```

The query tag implemented by this tag handler can be used in either of the following ways:

```
<tt:connection cid="con01" ... >
  ...
</tt:connection>
<tt:query id="balances" connectionId="con01">
  SELECT account, balance FROM acct_table
    where customer_number = ?
  <tt:param value="${requestScope.custNumber}" />
</tt:query>

<tt:connection ... >
  <tt:query cid="balances">
    SELECT account, balance FROM acct_table
    where customer_number = ?
    <tt:param value="${requestScope.custNumber}" />
  </tt:query>
</tt:connection>
```

The TLD for the tag handler uses the following declaration to indicate that the `connectionId` attribute is optional:

```
<tag>
  ...
  <attribute>
    <name>connectionId</name>
    <required>false</required>
  </attribute>
</tag>
```

Examples

The simple tags described in this section demonstrate solutions to two recurring problems in developing JSP applications: minimizing the amount of Java programming in JSP pages and ensuring a common look and feel across applications. In doing so, they illustrate many of the styles of tags discussed in the first part of the chapter.

An Iteration Tag

Constructing page content that is dependent on dynamically generated data often requires the use of flow control scripting statements. By moving the flow control logic to tag handlers, flow control tags reduce the amount of scripting needed in JSP pages. Iteration is a very common flow control function and is easily handled by a custom tag.

The discussion on using tag libraries in Chapter 4 introduced a tag library containing an `iterator` tag. The tag retrieves objects from a collection stored in a JavaBeans component and assigns them to an EL variable. The body of the tag retrieves information from the variable. As long as elements remain in the collection, the `iterator` tag causes the body to be reevaluated. The tag in this example is simplified to make it easy to demonstrate how to program a custom tag. web applications requiring such functionality should use the JSTL `forEach` tag, which is discussed in Iterator Tags (page 184).

JSP Page

The `index.jsp` page invokes the `iterator` tag to iterate through a collection of department names. Each item in the collection is assigned to the `departmentName` variable.

```
<%@ taglib uri="/tlt" prefix="tlt" %>
<html>
  <head>
  <title>Departments</title>
  </head>
  <body bgcolor="white">
  <jsp:useBean id="myorg" class="myorg.Organization"/>
  <table border=2 cellspacing=3 cellpadding=3>
    <tr>
      <td><b>Departments</b></td>
    </tr>
  <tlt:iterator var="departmentName" type="java.lang.String"
      group="${myorg.departmentNames}">
    <tr>
      <td><a href="list.jsp?deptName=${departmentName}">
        ${departmentName}</a></td>
    </tr>
  </tlt:iterator>
  </table>
  </body>
</html>
```

Tag Handler

The collection is set in the tag handler via the group attribute. The tag handler retrieves an element from the group and passes the element back to the page in the EL variable whose name is determined by the var attribute. The variable is accessed in the calling page using the JSP expression language. After the variable is set, the tag body is evaluated with the invoke method.

```
public void doTag() throws JspException, IOException {
  if (iterator == null)
    return;
  while (iterator.hasNext()) {
    getJspContext().setAttribute(var, iterator.next());
    getJspBody().invoke(null);
  }
}
public void setVar(String var) {
  this.var = var;
}
public void setGroup(Collection group) {
  this.group = group;
  if(group.size() > 0)
    iterator = group.iterator();
}
```

A Template Tag Library

A template provides a way to separate the common elements that are part of each screen from the elements that change with each screen of an application. Putting all the common elements together into one file makes it easier to maintain and enforce a consistent look and feel in all the screens. It also makes development of individual screens easier because the designer can focus on portions of a screen that are specific to that screen while the template takes care of the common portions.

The template is a JSP page that has placeholders for the parts that need to change with each screen. Each of these placeholders is referred to as a *parameter* of the template. For example, a simple template might include a title parameter for the top of the generated screen and a body parameter to refer to a JSP page for the custom content of the screen.

The template uses a set of nested tags—`definition`, `screen`, and `parameter`—to define a table of screen definitions and uses an `insert` tag to insert parameters from a screen definition into a specific application screen.

JSP Pages

The template for the Duke's Bookstore example, `template.jsp`, is shown next. This page includes a JSP page that creates the screen definition and then uses the `insert` tag to insert parameters from the definition into the application screen.

```
<%@ taglib uri="/tutorial-template" prefix="tt" %>
<%@ page errorPage="/template/errorinclude.jsp" %>
<%@ include file="/template/screendefinitions.jsp" %>
<html>
<head>
<title>
<tt:insert definition="bookstore" parameter="title"/>
</title>
</head>
<body  bgcolor="#FFFFFF">
  <tt:insert definition="bookstore" parameter="banner"/>
<tt:insert definition="bookstore" parameter="body"/>
<center><em>Copyright &copy; 2004 Sun Microsystems, Inc. </
em></center>
</body>
</html>
```

The `screendefinitions.jsp` page creates a definition for the screen specified by the request attribute `javax.servlet.forward.servlet_path`:

```
<tt:definition name="bookstore"
screen="${requestScope
  ['javax.servlet.forward.servlet_path']}">
  <tt:screen id="/bookstore">
  <tt:parameter name="title" value="Duke's Bookstore"
    direct="true"/>
  <tt:parameter name="banner" value="/template/banner.jsp"
    direct="false"/>
  <tt:parameter name="body" value="/bookstore.jsp"
    direct="false"/>
  </tt:screen>
  <tt:screen id="/bookcatalog">
  <tt:parameter name="title" direct="true">
      <jsp:attribute name="value" >
        <fmt:message key="TitleBookCatalog"/>
      </jsp:attribute>
    </tt:parameter>
    <tt:parameter name="banner" value="/template/banner.jsp"
    direct="false"/>
    <tt:parameter name="body" value="/bookcatalog.jsp"
    direct="false"/>
  </tt:screen>
  ...
</tt:definition>
```

The template is instantiated by the `Dispatcher` servlet. `Dispatcher` first gets the requested screen. `Dispatcher` performs business logic and updates model objects based on the requested screen. For example, if the requested screen is `/bookcatalog`, `Dispatcher` determines whether a book is being added to the cart based on the value of the Add request parameter. It sets the price of the book if it's on sale, and then adds the book to the cart. Finally, the servlet dispatches the request to `template.jsp`:

```
public class Dispatcher extends HttpServlet {
  @Resource
  UserTransaction utx;

  public void doGet(HttpServletRequest request,
    HttpServletResponse response) {
    String bookId = null;
    Book book = null;
    String clear = null;
    BookDBAO bookDBAO =
      (BookDBAO)getServletContext().
        getAttribute("bookDBAO");
    HttpSession session = request.getSession();
    String selectedScreen = request.getServletPath();
```

```
ShoppingCart cart = (ShoppingCart)session.
  getAttribute("cart");
if (cart == null) {
  cart = new ShoppingCart();
  session.setAttribute("cart", cart);
}
if (selectedScreen.equals("/bookcatalog")) {
  bookId = request.getParameter("Add");
  if (!bookId.equals("")) {
    try {
      book = bookDBAO.getBook(bookId);
      if ( book.getOnSale() ) {
        double sale = book.getPrice() * .85;
        Float salePrice = new Float(sale);
        book.setPrice(salePrice.floatValue());
      }
      cart.add(bookId, book);
    } catch (BookNotFoundException ex) {
      // not possible
    }
  }
} else if (selectedScreen.equals("/bookshowcart")) {
  bookId =request.getParameter("Remove");
  if (bookId != null) {
    cart.remove(bookId);
  }
  clear = request.getParameter("Clear");
  if (clear != null && clear.equals("clear")) {
    cart.clear();
  }
} else if (selectedScreen.equals("/bookreceipt")) {
// Update the inventory
  try {
    utx.begin();
    bookDBAO.buyBooks(cart);
    utx.commit();
  } catch (Exception ex) {
    try {
      utx.rollback();
      request.getRequestDispatcher(
        "/bookordererror.jsp").
        forward(request, response);
    } catch(Exception e) {
        System.out.println(
          "Rollback failed: "+e.getMessage());
        e.printStackTrace();
    }
  }
```

```
        }
        try {
            request.
                getRequestDispatcher(
                "/template/template.jsp").
                forward(request, response);
        } catch(Exception ex) {
            ex.printStackTrace();
        }
    }

    public void doPost(HttpServletRequest request,
        HttpServletResponse response) {
        request.setAttribute("selectedScreen",
            request.getServletPath());
        try {
            request.
                getRequestDispatcher(
                "/template/template.jsp").
                forward(request, response);
        } catch(Exception ex) {
            ex.printStackTrace();
        }
    }
}
```

Tag Handlers

The template tag library contains four tag handlers—DefinitionTag, ScreenTag, ParameterTag, and InsertTag—that demonstrate the use of cooperating tags. DefinitionTag, ScreenTag, and ParameterTag constitute a set of nested tag handlers that share private objects. DefinitionTag creates a public object named bookstore that is used by InsertTag.

In doTag, DefinitionTag creates a private object named screens that contains a hash table of screen definitions. A screen definition consists of a screen identifier and a set of parameters associated with the screen. These parameters are loaded when the body of the definition tag, which contains nested screen and parameter tags, is invoked. DefinitionTag creates a public object of class Definition, selects a screen definition from the screens object based on the URL passed in the request, and uses this screen definition to initialize a public Definition object.

```
public int doTag() {
  try {
    screens = new HashMap();
    getJspBody().invoke(null);
    Definition definition = new Definition();
    PageContext context = (PageContext)getJspContext();
    ArrayList params = (ArrayList) screens.get(screenId);
    Iterator ir = null;
    if (params != null) {
      ir = params.iterator();
      while (ir.hasNext())
        definition.setParam((Parameter)ir.next());
    // put the definition in the page context
    context.setAttribute(definitionName, definition,
      context.APPLICATION_SCOPE);
    }
  }
```

The table of screen definitions is filled in by `ScreenTag` and `ParameterTag` from text provided as attributes to these tags. Table 7–14 shows the contents of the screen definitions hash table for the Duke's Bookstore application.

Table 7–14 Screen Definitions

Screen ID	Title	Banner	Body
/bookstore	Duke's Bookstore	/banner.jsp	/bookstore.jsp
/bookcatalog	Book Catalog	/banner.jsp	/bookcatalog.jsp
/bookdetails	Book Description	/banner.jsp	/bookdetails.jsp
/bookshowcart	Shopping Cart	/banner.jsp	/bookshowcart.jsp
/bookcashier	Cashier	/banner.jsp	/bookcashier.jsp
/bookreceipt	Receipt	/banner.jsp	/bookreceipt.jsp

If the URL passed in the request is /bookstore, the Definition object contains the items from the first row of Table 7–14 (see Table 7–15).

Table 7–15 Definition Object Contents for URL /bookstore

Title	Banner	Body
Duke's Bookstore	/banner.jsp	/bookstore.jsp

The parameters for the URL /bookstore are shown in Table 7–16. The parameters specify that the value of the title parameter, Duke's Bookstore, should be inserted directly into the output stream, but the values of banner and body should be included dynamically.

Table 7–16 Parameters for the URL /bookstore

Parameter Name	Parameter Value	isDirect
title	Duke's Bookstore	true
banner	/banner.jsp	false
body	/bookstore.jsp	false

InsertTag inserts parameters of the screen definition into the response. The doTag method retrieves the definition object from the page context and then inserts the parameter value. If the parameter is direct, it is directly inserted into the response; otherwise, the request is sent to the parameter, and the response is dynamically included into the overall response.

```
public void doTag() throws JspTagException {
  Definition definition = null;
  Parameter parameter = null;
  boolean directInclude = false;
  PageContext context = (PageContext)getJspContext();

    // get the definition from the page context
  definition = (Definition)context.getAttribute(
    definitionName, context.APPLICATION_SCOPE);
```

```
    // get the parameter
  if (parameterName != null && definition != null)
    parameter = (Parameter)
      definition.getParam(parameterName);

  if (parameter != null)
    directInclude = parameter.isDirect();

  try {
    // if parameter is direct, print to out
    if (directInclude && parameter  != null)
      context.getOut().print(parameter.getValue());
    // if parameter is indirect,
        include results of dispatching to page
    else {
      if ((parameter != null) &&
        (parameter.getValue() !=  null))
      context.include(parameter.getValue());
    }
  } catch (Exception ex) {
      throw new JspTagException(ex.getMessage());
  }
}
```

8

Scripting in JSP Pages

JSP scripting elements allow you to use Java programming language statements in your JSP pages. Scripting elements are typically used to create and access objects, define methods, and manage the flow of control. Many tasks that require the use of scripts can be eliminated by using custom tag libraries, in particular the JSP Standard Tag Library. Because one of the goals of JSP technology is to separate static data from the code needed to dynamically generate content, very sparing use of JSP scripting is recommended. Nevertheless, there may be some circumstances that require its use.

There are three ways to create and use objects in scripting elements:

- Instance and class variables of the JSP page's servlet class are created in *declarations* and accessed in *scriptlets* and *expressions*.
- Local variables of the JSP page's servlet class are created and used in *scriptlets* and *expressions*.
- Attributes of scope objects (see Using Scope Objects, page 67) are created and used in *scriptlets* and *expressions*.

This chapter briefly describes the syntax and usage of JSP scripting elements.

The Example JSP Pages

This chapter illustrates JSP scripting elements using `webclient`, a version of the `hello1` example introduced in Chapter 2 that accesses a web service.

To deploy and run the `webclient` example using NetBeans 5.5, follow these steps:

1. Build and deploy the JAX-WS web service `MyHelloService` described in Building, Packaging, and Deploying the Service (page 511).
2. In NetBeans 5.5, select File→Open Project.
3. In the Open Project dialog, navigate to:

   `<INSTALL>/javaeetutorial5/examples/jaxws/`
4. Select the `webclient` folder.
5. Select the Open as Main Project checkbox and the Open Required Projects checkbox.
6. Click Open Project Folder.
7. In the Projects tab, right-click the `webclient` project, and select Deploy Project.
8. To run the application, open the bookstore URL `http://localhost:8080/webclient/greeting`.

To deploy and run the `webclient` example using `ant`, follow these steps:

1. Build and deploy the JAX-WS web service `MyHelloService` described in Building, Packaging, and Deploying the Service (page 511).
2. In a terminal window, go to `<INSTALL>/javaeetutorial5/examples/jaxws/webclient/`.
3. Run `ant`. This target will spawn any necessary compilations, will copy files to the `<INSTALL>/javaeetutorial5/examples/jaxws/webclient/build/` directory, will create a WAR file, and will copy it to the `<INSTALL>/javaeetutorial5/examples/jaxws/webclient/dist` directory.
4. Start the Application Server.
5. To deploy the example using `ant`, run the following command:

   ```
   ant deploy
   ```
6. To run the example, open your browser to `http://localhost:8080/webclient/greeting`.

To learn how to configure the example, refer to the deployment descriptor (the web.xml file), which includes the following configurations:

- A display-name element that specifies the name that tools use to identify the application.
- A set of servlet elements that identify the application's JSP file.
- A servlet-mapping element that defines the alias to the JSP file.

Note: The example assumes that the Application Server runs on the default port, 8080. If you have changed the port, you must update the port number in the file <*INSTALL*>/javaeetutorial5/examples/jaxws/webclient/response.jsp before building and running the example.

Using Scripting

JSP technology allows a container to support any scripting language that can call Java objects. If you wish to use a scripting language other than the default, java, you must specify it in the language attribute of the page directive at the beginning of a JSP page:

```
<%@ page language="scripting language" %>
```

Because scripting elements are converted to programming language statements in the JSP page's servlet class, you must import any classes and packages used by a JSP page. If the page language is java, you import a class or package with the import attribute of the page directive:

```
<%@ page import="fully_qualified_classname, packagename.*" %>
```

The webclient JSP page response.jsp uses the following page directive to import the classes needed to access the service classes:

```
<%@ page import=
  "helloservice.endpoint.HelloService,
    helloservice.endpoint.Hello" %>
```

Disabling Scripting

By default, scripting in JSP pages is valid. Because scripting can make pages difficult to maintain, some JSP page authors or page authoring groups may want to follow a methodology in which scripting elements are not allowed.

You can disable scripting for a group of JSP pages in an application in one of two ways:

- Select the Ignore Java Script checkbox in the JSP Property Group node of the NetBeans 5.5 `web.xml` editor.
- Set the `scripting-invalid` element of the application's deployment descriptor to `true`. The `scripting-invalid` element is a child of the `jsp-property-group` element that defines properties for a set of JSP pages.

For information on how to define a group of JSP pages, see Setting Properties for Groups of JSP Pages (page 149). When scripting is invalid, it means that scriptlets, scripting expressions, and declarations will produce a translation error if present in any of the pages in the group. Table 8–1 summarizes the scripting settings and their meanings.

Table 8–1 Scripting Settings

JSP Configuration	Scripting Encountered
Unspecified	Valid
`false`	Valid
`true`	Translation Error

Declarations

A *JSP declaration* is used to declare variables and methods in a page's scripting language. The syntax for a declaration is as follows:

```
<%! scripting language declaration %>
```

When the scripting language is the Java programming language, variables and methods in JSP declarations become declarations in the JSP page's servlet class.

Initializing and Finalizing a JSP Page

You can customize the initialization process to allow the JSP page to read persistent configuration data, initialize resources, and perform any other one-time activities; to do so, you override the `jspInit` method of the `JspPage` interface. You release resources using the `jspDestroy` method. The methods are defined using JSP declarations.

For example, an older version of the Duke's Bookstore application retrieved the object that accesses the bookstore database from the context and stored a reference to the object in the variable `bookDBAO` in the `jspInit` method. The variable definition and the initialization and finalization methods `jspInit` and `jspDestroy` were defined in a declaration:

```
<%!
private BookDBAO bookDBAO;
public void jspInit() {
bookDBAO =
  (BookDBAO)getServletContext().getAttribute("bookDB");
  if (bookDBAO == null)
    System.out.println("Couldn't get database.");
}
%>
```

When the JSP page was removed from service, the `jspDestroy` method released the `BookDBAO` variable.

```
<%!
public void jspDestroy() {
  bookDBAO = null;
}
%>
```

Scriptlets

A *JSP scriptlet* is used to contain any code fragment that is valid for the scripting language used in a page. The syntax for a scriptlet is as follows:

```
<%
  scripting language statements
%>
```

When the scripting language is set to java, a scriptlet is transformed into a Java programming language statement fragment and is inserted into the service method of the JSP page's servlet. A programming language variable created within a scriptlet is accessible from anywhere within the JSP page.

In the web service version of the hello1 application, greeting.jsp contains a scriptlet to retrieve the request parameter named username and test whether it is empty. If the if statement evaluates to true, the response page is included. Because the if statement opens a block, the HTML markup would be followed by a scriptlet that closes the block.

```
<%
  String username = request.getParameter("username");
  if ( username != null && username.length() > 0 ) {
%>
  <%@include file="response.jsp" %>
<%
  }
%>
```

Expressions

A *JSP expression* is used to insert the value of a scripting language expression, converted into a string, into the data stream returned to the client. When the scripting language is the Java programming language, an expression is transformed into a statement that converts the value of the expression into a String object and inserts it into the implicit out object.

The syntax for an expression is as follows:

```
<%= scripting language expression %>
```

Note that a semicolon is not allowed within a JSP expression, even if the same expression has a semicolon when you use it within a scriptlet.

In the web service version of the hello1 application, response.jsp contains the following scriptlet, which gets the proxy that implements the service endpoint interface. It then invokes the `sayHello` method on the proxy, passing the user name retrieved from a request parameter:

```
<%
  String resp = null;
  try {
    Hello hello = new HelloService().getHelloPort();
    resp = hello.sayHello(request.getParameter("username"));
  } catch (Exception ex) {
    resp = ex.toString();
  }
%>
```

A scripting expression is then used to insert the value of `resp` into the output stream:

```
<h2><font color="black"><%= resp %>!</font></h2>
```

Programming Tags That Accept Scripting Elements

Tags that accept scripting elements in attribute values or in the body cannot be programmed as simple tags; they must be implemented as classic tags. The following sections describe the TLD elements and JSP tag extension API specific to classic tag handlers. All other TLD elements are the same as for simple tags.

TLD Elements

You specify the character of a classic tag's body content using the `body-content` element:

```
<body-content>empty | JSP | tagdependent</body-content>
```

You must declare the body content of tags that do not have a body as `empty`. For tags that have a body, there are two options. Body content containing custom and core tags, scripting elements, and HTML text is categorized as `JSP`. All other types of body content—for example, SQL statements passed to the `query` tag—are labeled `tagdependent`.

Tag Handlers

The classes and interfaces used to implement classic tag handlers are contained in the javax.servlet.jsp.tagext package. Classic tag handlers implement either the Tag, the IterationTag, or the BodyTag interface. Interfaces can be used to take an existing Java object and make it a tag handler. For newly created classic tag handlers, you can use the TagSupport and BodyTagSupport classes as base classes. These classes and interfaces are contained in the javax.servlet.jsp.tagext package.

Tag handler methods defined by the Tag and BodyTag interfaces are called by the JSP page's servlet at various points during the evaluation of the tag. When the start element of a custom tag is encountered, the JSP page's servlet calls methods to initialize the appropriate handler and then invokes the handler's doStartTag method. When the end element of a custom tag is encountered, the handler's doEndTag method is invoked for all but simple tags. Additional methods are invoked in between when a tag handler needs to manipulate the body of the tag. For further information, see Tags with Bodies (page 270). To provide a tag handler implementation, you must implement the methods, summarized in Table 8–2, that are invoked at various stages of processing the tag.

Table 8–2 Tag Handler Methods

Tag Type	Interface	Methods
Basic	Tag	doStartTag, doEndTag
Attributes	Tag	doStartTag, doEndTag, setAttribute1,...,N, release
Body	Tag	doStartTag, doEndTag, release
Body, iterative evaluation	IterationTag	doStartTag, doAfterBody, doEndTag, release
Body, manipulation	BodyTag	doStartTag, doEndTag, release, doInitBody, doAfterBody

A tag handler has access to an API that allows it to communicate with the JSP page. The entry points to the API are two objects: the JSP context (javax.servlet.jsp.JspContext) for simple tag handlers and the page context (javax.servlet.jsp.PageContext) for classic tag handlers. JspContext provides access to implicit objects. `PageContext` extends `JspContext` with HTTP-specific behavior. A tag handler can retrieve all the other implicit objects (request, session, and application) that are accessible from a JSP page through these objects. In addition, implicit objects can have named attributes associated with them. Such attributes are accessed using `[set|get]Attribute` methods.

If the tag is nested, a tag handler also has access to the handler (called the *parent*) associated with the enclosing tag.

How Is a Classic Tag Handler Invoked?

The `Tag` interface defines the basic protocol between a tag handler and a JSP page's servlet. It defines the life cycle and the methods to be invoked when the start and end tags are encountered.

The JSP page's servlet invokes the `setPageContext`, `setParent`, and attribute-setting methods before calling `doStartTag`. The JSP page's servlet also guarantees that `release` will be invoked on the tag handler before the end of the page.

Here is a typical tag handler method invocation sequence:

```
ATag t = new ATag();
t.setPageContext(...);
t.setParent(...);
t.setAttribute1(value1);
t.setAttribute2(value2);
t.doStartTag();
t.doEndTag();
t.release();
```

The `BodyTag` interface extends `Tag` by defining additional methods that let a tag handler access its body. The interface provides three new methods:

- `setBodyContent`: Creates body content and adds to the tag handler
- `doInitBody`: Called before evaluation of the tag body
- `doAfterBody`: Called after evaluation of the tag body

A typical invocation sequence is as follows:

```
t.doStartTag();
out = pageContext.pushBody();
t.setBodyContent(out);
// perform any initialization needed after body content is set
t.doInitBody();
t.doAfterBody();
```

```
// while doAfterBody returns EVAL_BODY_AGAIN we
// iterate body evaluation
...
t.doAfterBody();
t.doEndTag();
out = pageContext.popBody();
t.release();
```

Tags with Bodies

A tag handler for a tag with a body is implemented differently depending on whether or not the tag handler needs to manipulate the body. A tag handler manipulates the body when it reads or modifies the contents of the body.

Tag Handler Does Not Manipulate the Body

If the tag handler does not need to manipulate the body, the tag handler should implement the `Tag` interface. If the tag handler implements the `Tag` interface and the body of the tag needs to be evaluated, the `doStartTag` method must return `EVAL_BODY_INCLUDE`; otherwise it should return `SKIP_BODY`.

If a tag handler needs to iteratively evaluate the body, it should implement the `IterationTag` interface. The tag handler should return `EVAL_BODY_AGAIN` from the `doAfterBody` method if it determines that the body needs to be evaluated again.

Tag Handler Manipulates the Body

If the tag handler needs to manipulate the body, the tag handler must implement `BodyTag` (or must be derived from `BodyTagSupport`).

When a tag handler implements the `BodyTag` interface, it must implement the `doInitBody` and the `doAfterBody` methods. These methods manipulate body content passed to the tag handler by the JSP page's servlet.

A `BodyContent` object supports several methods to read and write its contents. A tag handler can use the body content's `getString` or `getReader` method to extract information from the body, and the `writeOut(out)` method to write the body contents to an `out` stream. The writer supplied to the `writeOut` method is obtained using the tag handler's `getPreviousOut` method. This method is used to ensure that a tag handler's results are available to an enclosing tag handler.

If the body of the tag needs to be evaluated, the `doStartTag` method must return `EVAL_BODY_BUFFERED`; otherwise, it should return `SKIP_BODY`.

doInitBody Method

The `doInitBody` method is called after the body content is set but before it is evaluated. You generally use this method to perform any initialization that depends on the body content.

doAfterBody Method

The `doAfterBody` method is called *after* the body content is evaluated. `doAfterBody` must return an indication of whether to continue evaluating the body. Thus, if the body should be evaluated again, as would be the case if you were implementing an iteration tag, `doAfterBody` should return `EVAL_BODY_AGAIN`; otherwise, `doAfterBody` should return `SKIP_BODY`.

The following example reads the content of the body (which contains an SQL query) and passes it to an object that executes the query. Because the body does not need to be reevaluated, `doAfterBody` returns `SKIP_BODY`.

```
public class QueryTag extends BodyTagSupport {
  public int doAfterBody() throws JspTagException {
    BodyContent bc = getBodyContent();
    // get the bc as string
    String query = bc.getString();
    // clean up
    bc.clearBody();
    try {
      Statement stmt = connection.createStatement();
      result = stmt.executeQuery(query);
    } catch (SQLException e) {
      throw new JspTagException("QueryTag: " +
         e.getMessage());
    }
    return SKIP_BODY;
  }
}
```

release Method

A tag handler should reset its state and release any private resources in the `release` method.

Cooperating Tags

Tags cooperate by sharing objects. JSP technology supports two styles of object sharing.

The first style requires that a shared object be named and stored in the page context (one of the implicit objects accessible to JSP pages as well as tag handlers). To access objects created and named by another tag, a tag handler uses the `pageContext.getAttribute(name, scope)` method.

In the second style of object sharing, an object created by the enclosing tag handler of a group of nested tags is available to all inner tag handlers. This form of object sharing has the advantage that it uses a private namespace for the objects, thus reducing the potential for naming conflicts.

To access an object created by an enclosing tag, a tag handler must first obtain its enclosing tag using the static method `TagSupport.findAncestorWithClass(from, class)` or the `TagSupport.getParent` method. The former method should be used when a specific nesting of tag handlers cannot be guaranteed. After the ancestor has been retrieved, a tag handler can access any statically or dynamically created objects. Statically created objects are members of the parent. Private objects can also be created dynamically. Such objects can be stored in a tag handler using the `setValue` method and can be retrieved using the `getValue` method.

The following example illustrates a tag handler that supports both the named approach and the private object approach to sharing objects. In the example, the handler for a query tag checks whether an attribute named `connectionId` has been set. If the `connection` attribute has been set, the handler retrieves the connection object from the page context. Otherwise, the tag handler first retrieves the tag handler for the enclosing tag and then retrieves the connection object from that handler.

```
public class QueryTag extends BodyTagSupport {
  public int doStartTag() throws JspException {
    String cid = getConnectionId();
    Connection connection;
    if (cid != null) {
    // there is a connection id, use it
      connection =(Connection)pageContext.
        getAttribute(cid);
    } else {
      ConnectionTag ancestorTag =
        (ConnectionTag)findAncestorWithClass(this,
          ConnectionTag.class);
```

```
            if (ancestorTag == null) {
               throw new JspTagException("A query without
                  a connection attribute must be nested
                  within a connection tag.");
            }
            connection = ancestorTag.getConnection();
            ...
         }
      }
   }
```

The query tag implemented by this tag handler can be used in either of the following ways:

```
<tt:connection cid="con01" ... >
   ...
</tt:connection>
<tt:query id="balances" connectionId="con01">
   SELECT account, balance FROM acct_table
      where customer_number = ?
   <tt:param value="${requestScope.custNumber}" />
</tt:query>

<tt:connection ... >
   <tt:query cid="balances">
      SELECT account, balance FROM acct_table
      where customer_number = ?
      <tt:param value="${requestScope.custNumber}" />
   </tt:query>
</tt:connection>
```

The TLD for the tag handler use the following declaration to indicate that the `connectionId` attribute is optional:

```
<tag>
   ...
   <attribute>
      <name>connectionId</name>
      <required>false</required>
   </attribute>
</tag>
```

Tags That Define Variables

The mechanisms for defining variables in classic tags are similar to those described in Chapter 7. You must declare the variable in a `variable` element of the TLD or in a tag extra info class. Use `PageContext().setAttribute(name, value)` or `PageContext.setAttribute(name, value, scope)` methods in the tag handler to create or update an association between a name that is accessible in the page context and the object that is the value of the variable. For classic tag handlers, Table 8–3 illustrates how the availability of a variable affects when you may want to set or update the variable's value.

Table 8–3 Variable Availability

Value	Availability	In Methods
`NESTED`	Between the start tag and the end tag	`doStartTag`, `doInitBody`, and `doAfterBody`
`AT_BEGIN`	From the start tag until the end of the page	`doStartTag`, `doInitBody`, `doAfterBody`, and `doEndTag`
`AT_END`	After the end tag until the end of the page	`doEndTag`

A variable defined by a custom tag can also be accessed in a scripting expression. For example, the web service described in the preceding section can be encapsulated in a custom tag that returns the response in a variable named by the `var` attribute, and then `var` can be accessed in a scripting expression as follows:

```
<ws:hello var="response"
     name="<%=request.getParameter("username")%>" />
<h2><font color="black"><%= response %>!</font></h2>
```

Remember that in situations where scripting is not allowed (in a tag body where the `body-content` is declared as `scriptless` and in a page where scripting is specified to be invalid), you wouldn't be able to access the variable in a scriptlet or an expression. Instead, you would have to use the JSP expression language to access the variable.

9

JavaServer Faces Technology

JAVASERVER Faces technology is a server-side user interface component framework for Java technology-based web applications.

The main components of JavaServer Faces technology are as follows:

- An API for representing UI components and managing their state; handling events, server-side validation, and data conversion; defining page navigation; supporting internationalization and accessibility; and providing extensibility for all these features
- Two JavaServer Pages (JSP) custom tag libraries for expressing UI components within a JSP page and for wiring components to server-side objects

The well-defined programming model and tag libraries significantly ease the burden of building and maintaining web applications with server-side UIs. With minimal effort, you can

- Drop components onto a page by adding component tags
- Wire component-generated events to server-side application code
- Bind UI components on a page to server-side data
- Construct a UI with reusable and extensible components
- Save and restore UI state beyond the life of server requests

As shown in Figure 9–1, the user interface you create with JavaServer Faces technology (represented by `myUI` in the graphic) runs on the server and renders back to the client.

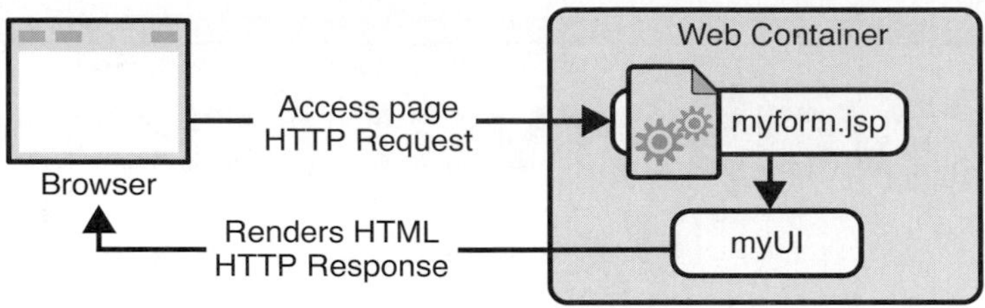

Figure 9–1 The UI Runs on the Server

The JSP page, `myform.jsp`, is a *JavaServer Faces page*, which is a JSP page that includes JavaServer Faces tags. It expresses the user interface components by using custom tags defined by JavaServer Faces technology. The UI for the web application (represented by `myUI` in the figure) manages the objects referenced by the JSP page. These objects include

- The UI component objects that map to the tags on the JSP page
- Any event listeners, validators, and converters that are registered on the components
- The JavaBeans components that encapsulate the data and application-specific functionality of the components

This chapter gives an overview of JavaServer Faces technology. After going over some of the primary benefits of using JavaServer Faces technology and explaining what a JavaServer Faces application is, it describes a simple application and specifies which part of the application the developers of each role work on. It then describes the UI component model, the navigation model, and the backing bean features supported by JavaServer Faces technology. Finally, this chapter uses a page from a simple application to summarize the life cycle of a JavaServer Faces page.

JavaServer Faces Technology Benefits

One of the greatest advantages of JavaServer Faces technology is that it offers a clean separation between behavior and presentation. Web applications built using JSP technology achieve this separation in part. However, a JSP application cannot map HTTP requests to component-specific event handling nor manage UI elements as stateful objects on the server, as a JavaServer Faces application can. JavaServer Faces technology allows you to build web applications that implement the finer-grained separation of behavior and presentation that is traditionally offered by client-side UI architectures.

The separation of logic from presentation also allows each member of a web application development team to focus on his or her piece of the development process, and it provides a simple programming model to link the pieces. For example, page authors with no programming expertise can use JavaServer Faces technology UI component tags to link to server-side objects from within a web page without writing any scripts.

Another important goal of JavaServer Faces technology is to leverage familiar UI-component and web-tier concepts without limiting you to a particular scripting technology or markup language. Although JavaServer Faces technology includes a JSP custom tag library for representing components on a JSP page, the JavaServer Faces technology APIs are layered directly on top of the Servlet API, as shown in Figure 2–2. This layering of APIs enables several important application use cases, such as using another presentation technology instead of JSP pages, creating your own custom components directly from the component classes, and generating output for various client devices.

Most importantly, JavaServer Faces technology provides a rich architecture for managing component state, processing component data, validating user input, and handling events.

What Is a JavaServer Faces Application?

For the most part, a JavaServer Faces application is like any other Java web application. A typical JavaServer Faces application includes the following pieces:

- A set of JSP pages (although you are not limited to using JSP pages as your presentation technology)
- A set of *backing beans*, which are JavaBeans components that define properties and functions for UI components on a page

- An application configuration resource file, which defines page navigation rules and configures beans and other custom objects, such as custom components
- A deployment descriptor (a `web.xml` file)
- Possibly a set of custom objects created by the application developer. These objects might include custom components, validators, converters, or listeners.
- A set of custom tags for representing custom objects on the page

A JavaServer Faces application that includes JSP pages also uses the standard tag libraries defined by JavaServer Faces technology for representing UI components and other objects on the page.

A Simple JavaServer Faces Application

This section describes the general steps involved in developing a simple JavaServer Faces application from the perspective of different development roles. These roles are:

- Page author, who creates pages by using the JavaServer Faces tag libraries.
- Application developer, who programs custom converters, validators, listeners, and backing beans.
- Component author, who creates custom UI components and renderers.
- Application architect, who configures the application, including defining the navigation rules, configuring custom objects, and creating deployment descriptors.

This application is quite simple, and so it does not include any custom components. See chapter 12 to learn about the responsibilities of a component writer.

Steps in the Development Process

Developing a simple JavaServer Faces application usually requires these tasks:

- Mapping the `FacesServlet` instance.
- Creating the pages using the UI component and core tags.
- Defining page navigation in the application configuration resource file.

- Developing the backing beans.
- Adding managed bean declarations to the application configuration resource file.

The example used in this section is the `guessNumber` application, located in the `<INSTALL>/javaeetutorial5/examples/web/` directory. It asks you to guess a number between 0 and 10, inclusive. The second page tells you whether you guessed correctly. The example also checks the validity of your input. The system log prints Duke's number. Figure 9–2 shows what the first page looks like.

Figure 9–2 The `greeting.jsp` Page of the `guessNumber` Application

The source for the `guessNumber` application is located in the `<INSTALL>/javaeetutorial5/examples/web/guessNumber/` dirctory created when you unzip the tutorial bundle (see About the Examples, page xxxiv).

To build, package, deploy, and run this example using NetBeans 5.5, follow these steps:

1. In NetBeans 5.5, select File→Open Project.
2. In the Open Project dialog, navigate to:

   `<INSTALL>/javaeetutorial5/examples/web/`

3. Select the `guessNumber` folder.
4. Select the Open as Main Project checkbox.
5. Click Open Project Folder.

6. In the Projects tab, right-click the `guessNumber` project, and select Deploy Project.
7. To run the application, open the URL `http://localhost:8080/guessNumber` in a browser.

To build, package, and deploy this example using `ant`, follow these steps:

1. Go to `<INSTALL>/javaeetutorial5/examples/web/guessNumber/`.
2. Run `ant`.
3. Start the Application Server.
4. Run `ant deploy`.
5. To run the application, open the URL `http://localhost:8080/guessNumber` in a browser.

To learn how to configure the example, refer to the deployment descriptor (the `web.xml` file), which includes the following configurations:

- A `display-name` element that specifies the name that tools use to identify the application.
- A `servlet` element that identifies the `FacesServlet` instance.
- A `servlet-mapping` element that maps `FacesServlet` to a URL pattern.

Mapping the FacesServlet Instance

All JavaServer Faces applications must include a mapping to the `FacesServlet` instance in their deployment descriptors. The `FacesServlet` instance accepts incoming requests, passes them to the life cycle for processing, and initializes resources. The following piece of the `guessNumber` example's deployment descriptor performs the mapping to the `FacesServlet` instance:

```
<servlet>
  <display-name>FacesServlet</display-name>
  <servlet-name>FacesServlet</servlet-name>
  <servlet-class>javax.faces.webapp.FacesServlet
  </servlet-class>
  <load-on-startup>1</load-on-startup>
</servlet>
<servlet-mapping>
  <servlet-name>FacesServlet</servlet-name>
  <url-pattern>/guess/*</url-pattern>
</servlet-mapping>
```

The mapping to FacesServlet shown above uses a prefix mapping to identify a JSP page as having JavaServer Faces components. Because of this, the URL to the first JSP page of the application must include the mapping. To accomplish this, the guessNumber example includes an HTML page that has the URL to the first JSP page:

```
<a href="guess/greeting.jsp">
```

See Identifying the Servlet for Life Cycle Processing (page 483) for more information on how to map the FacesServlet instance.

Creating the Pages

Creating the pages is the page author's responsibility. This task involves laying out UI components on the pages, mapping the components to beans, and adding tags that register converters, validators, or listeners onto the components.

In this section we'll build the greeting.jsp page, the first page of the guessNumber application. As with any JSP page, you'll need to add the usual HTML and HEAD tags to the page:

```
<HTML xmlns="http://www.w3.org/1999/xhtml"xml:lang="en">
  <HEAD> <title>Hello</title> </HEAD>
  ...
</HTML>
```

You'll also need a page directive that specifies the content type:

```
<%@ page contentType="application/xhtml+xml" %>
```

Declaring the Tag Libraries

In order to use JavaServer Faces components in JSP pages, you need to give your pages access to the two standard tag libraries, the HTML component tag library and the core tag library using taglib declarations:

```
<%@ taglib uri="http://java.sun.com/jsf/html" prefix="h" %>
<%@ taglib uri="http:.//java.sun.com/jsf/core" prefix="f" %>
```

The first taglib declaration declares the HTML component tag library with a prefix, h. All component tags in the page have this prefix. The core tag library is declared with the prefix f. All core tags in the page have this prefix.

User Interface Component Model (page 291) includes a table that lists all the component tags included with JavaServer Faces technology. Adding UI Components to a Page Using the HTML Component Tags (page 326) discusses the tags in more detail.

Adding the view and form Tags

All JavaServer Faces pages are represented by a tree of components, called a *view*. The `view` tag represents the root of the view. All JavaServer Faces component tags must be inside of a `view` tag, which is defined in the core tag library.

The `form` tag represents an input form component, which allows the user to input some data and submit it to the server, usually by clicking a button. All UI component tags that represent editable components (such as text fields and menus) must be nested inside the `form` tag. In the case of the `greeting.jsp` page, some of the tags contained in the form are `outputText`, `inputText`, `commandButton`, and `message`. You can specify an ID for the form tag. This ID maps to the associated form UI component on the server.

With the `view` and `form` tags added, our page looks like this (minus the HTML and HEAD tags):

```
<%@ taglib uri="http://java.sun.com/jsf/html" prefix="h" %>
<%@ taglib uri="http://java.sun.com/jsf/core" prefix="f" %>
<f:view>
  <h:form id="helloForm1">
  </h:form>
</f:view>
```

Adding a Label Component

The `outputText` tag represents a label. The `greeting.jsp` page has two `outputText` tags. One of the tags displays the number 0. The other tag displays the number 10:

```
<h:outputText lang="en_US"
  value="#{UserNumberBean.minimum}"/>
<h:outputText value="#{UserNumberBean.maximum}"/>
```

The `value` attributes of the tags get the values from the `minimum` and `maximum` properties of `UserNumberBean` using *value expressions*, which are used to reference data stored in other objects, such as beans. See Backing Beans (page 304) for more information on value expressions.

With the addition of the outputText tags (along with some static text), the greeting page looks like the following:

```
<%@ taglib uri="http://java.sun.com/jsf/html" prefix="h" %>
<%@ taglib uri="http://java.sun.com/jsf/core" prefix="f" %>
<f:view>
  <h:form id="helloForm1">
    <h2>Hi. My name is Duke. I'm thinking of a number from
    <h:outputText lang="en_US"
      value="#{UserNumberBean.minimum}"/> to
    <h:outputText value="#{UserNumberBean.maximum}"/>.
    Can you guess it?</h2>
  </h:form>
</f:view>
```

Adding an Image

To display images on a page, you use the graphicImage tag. The url attribute of the tag specifies the path to the image file. Let's add Duke to the page using a graphicImage tag:

```
<%@ taglib uri="http://java.sun.com/jsf/html" prefix="h" %>
<%@ taglib uri="http://java.sun.com/jsf/core" prefix="f" %>
<f:view>
  <h:form id="helloForm1">
    <h2>Hi. My name is Duke. I'm thinking of a number from
    <h:outputText lang="en_US"
      value="#{UserNumberBean.minimum}"/> to
    <h:outputText value="#{UserNumberBean.maximum}"/>.
    Can you guess it?</h2>
    <h:graphicImage id="waveImg" url="/wave.med.gif" />
  </h:form>
</f:view>
```

Adding a Text Field

The inputText tag represents a text field component. In the guessNumber example, this text field takes an integer input value. The instance of this tag included in greeting.jsp has three attributes: id, label, and value.

```
<h:inputText id="userNo" label="User Number"
    value="#{UserNumberBean.userNumber}">
    ...
</h:inputText>
```

The `id` attribute corresponds to the ID of the component object represented by this tag. In this case, an `id` attribute is required because the `message` tag (which is used to display validation error messages) needs it to refer to the `userNo` component.

The `label` attribute specifies the name to be used by error messages to refer to the component. In this example, label is set to `"User Number"`. As an example, if a user were to enter 23, the error message that would be displayed is:

```
User Number: Validation Error: Value is greater than allowable
maximum of 10.
```

The `value` attribute binds the `userNo` component value to the bean property `UserNumberBean.userNumber`, which holds the data entered into the text field.

After adding the `inputText` tag, the greeting page looks like the following:

```
<%@ taglib uri="http://java.sun.com/jsf/html" prefix="h" %>
<%@ taglib uri="http://java.sun.com/jsf/core" prefix="f" %>
<f:view>
  <h:form id="helloForm1">
    <h2>Hi. My name is Duke. I'm thinking of a number from
    <h:outputText lang="en_US"
      value="#{UserNumberBean.minimum}"/> to
    <h:outputText value="#{UserNumberBean.maximum}"/>.
    Can you guess it?</h2>
    <h:graphicImage id="waveImg" url="/wave.med.gif" />
    <h:inputText id="userNo" label="User Number"
      value="#{UserNumberBean.userNumber}">
      ...
    </h:inputText>
  </h:form>
</f:view>
```

See Backing Beans (page 304) for more information on creating beans, binding to bean properties, referencing bean methods, and configuring beans.

See Using Text Components (page 331) for more information on the `inputText` tag.

Registering a Validator on a Text Field

By nesting the `validateLongRange` tag within a text field's component's tag, the page author registers a `LongRangeValidator` onto the text field. This validator checks whether the component's local data is within a certain range, defined by the validateLongRange tag's minimum and maximum attributes.

In the case of the greeting page, we want to validate the number the user enters into the text field. So, we add a validateLongRange tag inside the inputText tag. The maximum and minimum attributes of the validateLongRange tag get their values from the minimum and maximum properties of UserNumberBean using the value expressions #{UserNumberBean.minimum} and #{UserNumber-Bean.maximum}. See Backing Beans (page 304) for details on value expressions.

After adding the validateLongRange tag, our page looks like this:

```
<%@ taglib uri="http://java.sun.com/jsf/html" prefix="h" %>
<%@ taglib uri="http://java.sun.com/jsf/core" prefix="f" %>
<f:view>
  <h:form id="helloForm1">
    <h2>Hi. My name is Duke. I'm thinking of a number from
    <h:outputText lang="en_US"
      value="#{UserNumberBean.minimum}"/> to
    <h:outputText value="#{UserNumberBean.maximum}"/>.
    Can you guess it?</h2>
    <h:graphicImage id="waveImg" url="/wave.med.gif" />
    <h:inputText id="userNo" label="User Number"
      value="#{UserNumberBean.userNumber}">
        <f:validateLongRange
          minimum="#{UserNumberBean.minimum}"
          maximum="#{UserNumberBean.maximum}" />
    </h:inputText>
  </h:form>
</f:view>
```

For more information on the standard validators included with JavaServer Faces technology, see Using the Standard Validators (page 369).

Adding a Custom Message

JavaServer Faces technology provides standard error messages that display on the page when conversion or validation fails. In some cases, you might need to override the standard message. For example, if a user were to enter a letter into the text field on greeting.jsp, he or she would see the following error message:

```
User Number: 'm' must be a number between -2147483648 and
2147483647 Example: 9346
```

This is wrong because the field really only accepts values from 0 through 10.

To override this message, you add a converterMessage attribute on the inputText tag. This attribute references the custom error message:

```
<h:inputText id="userNo" label="User Number"
    value="#{UserNumberBean.userNumber}"
        converterMessage="#{ErrMsg.userNoConvert}">
...
</h:inputText>
```

The expression that converterMessage uses references the userNoConvert key of the ErrMsg resource bundle. The application architect needs to define the message in the resource bundle and configure the resource bundle. See Configuring Error Messages (page 289) for more information on this.

See Referencing Error Messages (page 358) for more information on referencing error messages.

Adding a Button

The commandButton tag represents the button used to submit the data entered in the text field. The action attribute specifies an outcome that helps the navigation mechanism decide which page to open next. Defining Page Navigation (page 288) discusses this further.

With the addition of the commandButton tag, the greeting page looks like the following:

```
<%@ taglib uri="http://java.sun.com/jsf/html" prefix="h" %>
<%@ taglib uri="http://java.sun.com/jsf/core" prefix="f" %>
<f:view>
  <h:form id="helloForm1">
    <h2>Hi. My name is Duke. I'm thinking of a number from
    <h:outputText lang="en_US"
      value="#{UserNumberBean.minimum}"/> to
    <h:outputText value="#{UserNumberBean.maximum}"/>.
    Can you guess it?</h2>
    <h:graphicImage id="waveImg" url="/wave.med.gif" />
    <h:inputText id="userNo" label="User Number"
      value="#{UserNumberBean.userNumber}">
        <f:validateLongRange
          minimum="#{UserNumberBean.minimum}"
          maximum="#{UserNumberBean.maximum}" />
    </h:inputText>
```

```
    <h:commandButton id="submit"
      action="success" value="Submit" />
  </h:form>
</f:view>
```

See Using Command Components for Performing Actions and Navigation (page 337) for more information on the commandButton tag.

Displaying Error Messages

A message tag is used to display error messages on a page when data conversion or validation fails after the user submits the form. The message tag in greeting.jsp displays an error message if the data entered in the field does not comply with the rules specified by the LongRangeValidator implementation, whose tag is registered on the text field component.

The error message displays wherever you place the message tag on the page. The message tag's style attribute allows you to specify the formatting style for the message text. Its for attribute refers to the component whose value failed validation, in this case the userNo component represented by the inputText tag in the greeting.jsp page.

Let's put the message tag near the end of the page:

```
<%@ taglib uri="http://java.sun.com/jsf/html" prefix="h" %>
<%@ taglib uri="http://java.sun.com/jsf/core" prefix="f" %>
<f:view>
  <h:form id="helloForm1">
    <h2>Hi. My name is Duke. I'm thinking of a number from
    <h:outputText lang="en_US"
      value="#{UserNumberBean.minimum}"/> to
    <h:outputText value="#{UserNumberBean.maximum}"/>.
    Can you guess it?</h2>
    <h:graphicImage id="waveImg" url="/wave.med.gif" />
    <h:inputText id="userNo" label="User Number"
      value="#{UserNumberBean.userNumber}"
      converterMessage="#{ErrMsg.userNoConvert}">
      <f:validateLongRange
          minimum="#{UserNumberBean.minimum}"
          maximum="#{UserNumberBean.maximum}" />
    </h:inputText>
    <h:commandButton id="submit"
      action="success" value="Submit" />
    <h:message showSummary="true" showDetail="false"
        style="color: red;
        font-family: 'New Century Schoolbook', serif;
```

```
            font-style: oblique;
            text-decoration: overline"
            id="errors1"
            for="userNo"/>
    </h:form>
  </f:view>
```

Now we've completed the greeting page. Assuming we've also done the `response.jsp` page, let's move on to defining the page navigation rules.

Defining Page Navigation

Defining page navigation involves determining which page to go to after the user clicks a button or a hyperlink. Navigation for the application is defined in the application configuration resource file using a powerful rule-based system. Here is one of the navigation rules defined for the `guessNumber` example:

```
<navigation-rule>
  <from-view-id>/greeting.jsp</from-view-id>
  <navigation-case>
    <from-outcome>success</from-outcome>
    <to-view-id>/response.jsp</to-view-id>
  </navigation-case>
</navigation-rule>
<navigation-rule>
  <from-view-id>/response.jsp</from-view-id>
  <navigation-case>
    <from-outcome>success</from-outcome>
    <to-view-id>/greeting.jsp</to-view-id>
  </navigation-case>
</navigation-rule>
```

This navigation rule states that when the button on the greeting page is clicked the application will navigate to `response.jsp` if the navigation system is given a logical outcome of `success`.

In the case of the Guess Number example, the logical outcome is defined by the `action` attribute of the `UICommand` component that submits the form:

```
<h:commandButton id="submit" action="success"
  value="Submit" />
```

To learn more about how navigation works, see Navigation Model (page 302).

Configuring Error Messages

In case the standard error messages don't meet your needs, you can create new ones in resource bundles and configure the resource bundles in your application configuration resource file. The `guessNumber` example has one custom converter message, as described in Adding a Custom Message (page 285).

This message is stored in the resource bundle, `ApplicationMessages.properties`:

```
userNoConvert=The value you entered is not a number.
```

The resource bundle is configured in the application configuration file:

```
<application>
  <resource-bundle>
    <base-name>guessNumber.ApplicationMessages</base-name>
    <var>ErrMsg</var>
  </resource-bundle>
</application>
```

The `base-name` element indicates the fully-qualified name of the resource bundle. The `var` element indicates the name by which page authors refer to the resource bundle with the expression language. Here is the `inputText` tag again:

```
<h:inputText id="userNo" label="User Number"
  value="#{UserNumberBean.userNumber}"
    converterMessage="#{ErrMsg.userNoConvert}">
    ...
</h:inputText>
```

The expression on the `converterMessage` attribute references the `userNoConvert` key of the `ErrMsg` resource bundle.

See Registering Custom Error Messages (page 470) for more information on configuring custom error messages.

Developing the Beans

Developing beans is one responsibility of the application developer. A typical JavaServer Faces application couples a backing bean with each page in the application. The backing bean defines properties and methods that are associated with the UI components used on the page.

The page author binds a component's value to a bean property using the component tag's `value` attribute to refer to the property. Recall that the `userNo` component on the `greeting.jsp` page references the `userNumber` property of `UserNumberBean`:

```
<h:inputText id="userNo" label="User Number"
        value="#{UserNumberBean.userNumber}">
...
</h:inputText>
```

Here is the `userNumber` backing bean property that maps to the data for the `userNo` component:

```
Integer userNumber = null;
...
public void setUserNumber(Integer user_number) {
  userNumber = user_number;
}
public Integer getUserNumber() {
  return userNumber;
}
public String getResponse() {
  if(userNumber != null &&
     userNumber.compareTo(randomInt) == 0) {
        return "Yay! You got it!";
  } else {
     return "Sorry, "+userNumber+" is incorrect.";
  }
}
```

See Backing Beans (page 304) for more information on creating backing beans.

Adding Managed Bean Declarations

After developing the backing beans to be used in the application, you need to configure them in the application configuration resource file so that the JavaServer Faces implementation can automatically create new instances of the beans whenever they are needed.

The task of adding managed bean declarations to the application configuration resource file is the application architect's responsibility. Here is a managed bean declaration for UserNumberBean:

```
<managed-bean>
  <managed-bean-name>UserNumberBean</managed-bean-name>
  <managed-bean-class>
    guessNumber.UserNumberBean
  </managed-bean-class>
  <managed-bean-scope>session</managed-bean-scope>
  <managed-property>
    <property-name>minimum</property-name>
    <property-class>long</property-class>
    <value>0</value>
  </managed-property>
  <managed-property>
    <property-name>maximum</property-name>
    <property-class>long</property-class>
    <value>10</value>
  </managed-property>
</managed-bean>
```

This declaration configures UserNumberBean so that its minimum property is initialized to 0, its maximum property is initialized to 10, and it is added to session scope when it is created.

A page author can use the unified EL to access one of the bean's properties, like this:

```
<h:outputText value="#{UserNumberBean.minimum}"/>
```

For more information on configuring beans, see Configuring a Bean (page 306).

User Interface Component Model

JavaServer Faces UI components are configurable, reusable elements that compose the user interfaces of JavaServer Faces applications. A component can be simple, such as a button, or compound, such as a table, which can be composed of multiple components.

JavaServer Faces technology provides a rich, flexible component architecture that includes the following:

- A set of `UIComponent` classes for specifying the state and behavior of UI components
- A rendering model that defines how to render the components in various ways
- An event and listener model that defines how to handle component events
- A conversion model that defines how to register data converters onto a component
- A validation model that defines how to register validators onto a component

This section briefly describes each of these pieces of the component architecture.

User Interface Component Classes

JavaServer Faces technology provides a set of UI component classes and associated behavioral interfaces that specify all the UI component functionality, such as holding component state, maintaining a reference to objects, and driving event handling and rendering for a set of standard components.

The component classes are completely extensible, allowing component writers to create their own custom components. See Chapter 12 for an example of a custom image map component.

All JavaServer Faces UI component classes extend `UIComponentBase`, which defines the default state and behavior of a UI component. The following set of UI component classes is included with JavaServer Faces technology:

- `UIColumn`: Represents a single column of data in a `UIData` component.
- `UICommand`: Represents a control that fires actions when activated.
- `UIData`: Represents a data binding to a collection of data represented by a `DataModel` instance.
- `UIForm`: Encapsulates a group of controls that submit data to the application. This component is analogous to the `form` tag in HTML.
- `UIGraphic`: Displays an image.
- `UIInput`: Takes data input from a user. This class is a subclass of `UIOutput`.
- `UIMessage`: Displays a localized message.

- `UIMessages`: Displays a set of localized messages.
- `UIOutput`: Displays data output on a page.
- `UIPanel`: Manages the layout of its child components.
- `UIParameter`: Represents substitution parameters.
- `UISelectBoolean`: Allows a user to set a `boolean` value on a control by selecting or deselecting it. This class is a subclass of `UIInput`.
- `UISelectItem`: Represents a single item in a set of items.
- `UISelectItems`: Represents an entire set of items.
- `UISelectMany`: Allows a user to select multiple items from a group of items. This class is a subclass of `UIInput`.
- `UISelectOne`: Allows a user to select one item from a group of items. This class is a subclass of `UIInput`.
- `UIViewRoot`: Represents the root of the component tree.

In addition to extending `UIComponentBase`, the component classes also implement one or more *behavioral interfaces*, each of which defines certain behavior for a set of components whose classes implement the interface.

These behavioral interfaces are as follows:

- `ActionSource`: Indicates that the component can fire an action event. This interface is intended for use with components based on JavaServer Faces technology 1.1_01 and earlier versions.
- `ActionSource2`: Extends `ActionSource`, and therefore provides the same functionality. However, it allows components to use the unified EL when referencing methods that handle action events.
- `EditableValueHolder`: Extends `ValueHolder` and specifies additional features for editable components, such as validation and emitting value-change events.
- `NamingContainer`: Mandates that each component rooted at this component have a unique ID.
- `StateHolder`: Denotes that a component has state that must be saved between requests.
- `ValueHolder`: Indicates that the component maintains a local value as well as the option of accessing data in the model tier.

`UICommand` implements `ActionSource2` and `StateHolder`. `UIOutput` and component classes that extend `UIOutput` implement `StateHolder` and `ValueHolder`. `UIInput` and component classes that extend `UIInput` implement `EditableValueHolder`, `StateHolder`, and `ValueHolder`. `UIComponentBase` implements

StateHolder. See the JavaServer Faces Technology 1.2 API Specification (http://java.sun.com/javaee/javaserverfaces/1.2/docs/api/javax/faces/component/package-summary.html) for more information on these interfaces.

Only component writers will need to use the component classes and behavioral interfaces directly. Page authors and application developers will use a standard UI component by including a tag that represents it on a JSP page. Most of the components can be rendered in different ways on a page. For example, a UICommand component can be rendered as a button or a hyperlink.

The next section explains how the rendering model works and how page authors choose how to render the components by selecting the appropriate tags.

Component Rendering Model

The JavaServer Faces component architecture is designed such that the functionality of the components is defined by the component classes, whereas the component rendering can be defined by a separate renderer. This design has several benefits, including:

- Component writers can define the behavior of a component once but create multiple renderers, each of which defines a different way to render the component to the same client or to different clients.
- Page authors and application developers can change the appearance of a component on the page by selecting the tag that represents the appropriate combination of component and renderer.

A *render kit* defines how component classes map to component tags that are appropriate for a particular client. The JavaServer Faces implementation includes a standard HTML render kit for rendering to an HTML client.

The render kit defines a set of Renderer classes for each component that it supports. Each Renderer class defines a different way to render the particular component to the output defined by the render kit. For example, a UISelectOne component has three different renderers. One of them renders the component as a set of radio buttons. Another renders the component as a combo box. The third one renders the component as a list box.

Each JSP custom tag defined in the standard HTML render kit is composed of the component functionality (defined in the UIComponent class) and the rendering attributes (defined by the `Renderer` class). For example, the two tags in Table 9–1 represent a `UICommand` component rendered in two different ways.

Table 9–1 `UICommand` Tags

Tag	Rendered As
`commandButton`	Login
`commandLink`	hyperlink

The command part of the tags shown in Table 9–1 corresponds to the `UICommand` class, specifying the functionality, which is to fire an action. The button and hyperlink parts of the tags each correspond to a separate `Renderer` class, which defines how the component appears on the page.

The JavaServer Faces implementation provides a custom tag library for rendering components in HTML. It supports all the component tags listed in Table 9–2. To learn how to use the tags in an example, see Adding UI Components to a Page Using the HTML Component Tags (page 326).

Table 9–2 The UI Component Tags

Tag	Functions	Rendered As	Appearance
`column`	Represents a column of data in a `UIData` component.	A column of data in an HTML table	A column in a table

Table 9–2 The UI Component Tags (Continued)

Tag	Functions	Rendered As	Appearance
`commandButton`	Submits a form to the application.	An HTML `<input type=`*`type`*`>` element, where the *`type`* value can be `submit`, `reset`, or `image`	A button
`commandLink`	Links to another page or location on a page.	An HTML `<a href>` element	A hyperlink
`dataTable`	Represents a data wrapper.	An HTML `<table>` element	A table that can be updated dynamically
`form`	Represents an input form. The inner tags of the form receive the data that will be submitted with the form.	An HTML `<form>` element	No appearance
`graphicImage`	Displays an image.	An HTML `<img>` element	An image
`inputHidden`	Allows a page author to include a hidden variable in a page.	An HTML `<input type=hidden>` element	No appearance
`inputSecret`	Allows a user to input a string without the actual string appearing in the field.	An HTML `<input type=password>` element	A text field, which displays a row of characters instead of the actual string entered
`inputText`	Allows a user to input a string.	An HTML `<input type=text>` element	A text field
`inputTextarea`	Allows a user to enter a multiline string.	An HTML `<textarea>` element	A multirow text field
`message`	Displays a localized message.	An HTML `<span>` tag if styles are used	A text string

Table 9–2 The UI Component Tags (Continued)

Tag	Functions	Rendered As	Appearance
`messages`	Displays localized messages.	A set of HTML `<span>` tags if styles are used	A text string
`outputFormat`	Displays a localized message.	Plain text	Plain text
`outputLabel`	Displays a nested component as a label for a specified input field.	An HTML `<label>` element	Plain text
`outputLink`	Links to another page or location on a page without generating an action event.	An HTML `<a>` element	A hyperlink
`outputText`	Displays a line of text.	Plain text	Plain text
`panelGrid`	Displays a table.	An HTML `<table>` element with `<tr>` and `<td>` elements	A table
`panelGroup`	Groups a set of components under one parent.		A row in a table
`selectBoolean Checkbox`	Allows a user to change the value of a Boolean choice.	An HTML `<input type=checkbox>` element.	A checkbox
`selectItem`	Represents one item in a list of items in a `UISelectOne` component.	An HTML `<option>` element	No appearance
`selectItems`	Represents a list of items in a `UISelectOne` component.	A list of HTML `<option>` elements	No appearance

Table 9–2 The UI Component Tags (Continued)

Tag	Functions	Rendered As	Appearance
`selectMany Checkbox`	Displays a set of checkboxes from which the user can select multiple values.	A set of HTML `<input>` elements of type `checkbox`	A set of checkboxes
`selectMany Listbox`	Allows a user to select multiple items from a set of items, all displayed at once.	An HTML `<select>` element	A list box
`selectMany-Menu`	Allows a user to select multiple items from a set of items.	An HTML `<select>` element	A scrollable combo box
`selectOne Listbox`	Allows a user to select one item from a set of items, all displayed at once.	An HTML `<select>` element	A list box
`selectOneMenu`	Allows a user to select one item from a set of items.	An HTML `<select>` element	A scrollable combo box
`selectOneRa-dio`	Allows a user to select one item from a set of items.	An HTML `<input type=radio>` element	A set of radio buttons

Conversion Model

A JavaServer Faces application can optionally associate a component with server-side object data. This object is a JavaBeans component, such as a backing bean. An application gets and sets the object data for a component by calling the appropriate object properties for that component.

When a component is bound to an object, the application has two views of the component's data:

- The model view, in which data is represented as data types, such as `int` or `long`.
- The presentation view, in which data is represented in a manner that can be read or modified by the user. For example, a `java.util.Date` might be represented as a text string in the format mm/dd/yy or as a set of three text strings.

The JavaServer Faces implementation automatically converts component data between these two views when the bean property associated with the component is of one of the types supported by the component's data. For example, if a `UISelectBoolean` component is associated with a bean property of type `java.lang.Boolean`, the JavaServer Faces implementation will automatically convert the component's data from `String` to `Boolean`. In addition, some component data must be bound to properties of a particular type. For example, a `UISelectBoolean` component must be bound to a property of type `boolean` or `java.lang.Boolean`.

Sometimes you might want to convert a component's data to a type other than a standard type, or you might want to convert the format of the data. To facilitate this, JavaServer Faces technology allows you to register a `Converter` implementation on `UIOutput` components and components whose classes subclass `UIOutput`. If you register the `Converter` implementation on a component, the `Converter` implementation converts the component's data between the two views.

You can either use the standard converters supplied with the JavaServer Faces implementation or create your own custom converter.

To create and use a custom converter in your application, three things must happen:

- The application developer must implement the `Converter` class. See Creating a Custom Converter (page 405).
- The application architect must register the `Converter` with the application. See Registering a Custom Converter (page 473).
- The page author must refer to the `Converter` object from the tag of the component whose data must be converted. See Using a Custom Converter (page 384).

Event and Listener Model

The JavaServer Faces event and listener model is similar to the JavaBeans event model in that it has strongly typed event classes and listener interfaces that an application can use to handle events generated by UI components.

An `Event` object identifies the component that generated the event and stores information about the event. To be notified of an event, an application must provide an implementation of the `Listener` class and must register it on the component that generates the event. When the user activates a component, such as by clicking a button, an event is fired. This causes the JavaServer Faces implementation to invoke the listener method that processes the event.

JavaServer Faces technology supports three kinds of events: value-change events, action events, and data-model events.

An *action event* occurs when the user activates a component that implements `ActionSource`. These components include buttons and hyperlinks.

A *value-change* event occurs when the user changes the value of a component represented by `UIInput` or one of its subclasses. An example is selecting a checkbox, an action that results in the component's value changing to `true`. The component types that can generate these types of events are the `UIInput`, `UISelectOne`, `UISelectMany`, and `UISelectBoolean` components. Value-change events are fired only if no validation errors were detected.

Depending on the value of the `immediate` property (see The immediate Attribute, page 328) of the component emitting the event, action events can be processed during the invoke application phase or the apply request values phase, and value-change events can be processed during the process validations phase or the apply request values phase.

A *data-model event* occurs when a new row of a `UIData` component is selected. The discussion of data-model events is an advanced topic. It is not covered in this tutorial but may be discussed in future versions of this tutorial.

There are two ways to cause your application to react to actionevents or value-change events emitted by a standard component:

- Implement an event listener class to handle the event and register the listener on the component by nesting either a `valueChangeListener` tag or an `actionListener` tag inside the component tag.

- Implement a method of a backing bean to handle the event and refer to the method with a method expression from the appropriate attribute of the component's tag.

See Implementing an Event Listener (page 408) for information on how to implement an event listener. See Registering Listeners on Components (page 366) for information on how to register the listener on a component.

See Writing a Method to Handle an Action Event (page 421) and Writing a Method to Handle a Value-Change Event (page 422) for information on how to implement backing bean methods that handle these events.

See Referencing a Backing Bean Method (page 379) for information on how to refer to the backing bean method from the component tag.

When emitting events from custom components, you must implement the appropriate `Event` class and manually queue the event on the component in addition to implementing an event listener class or a backing bean method that handles the event. Handling Events for Custom Components (page 449) explains how to do this.

Validation Model

JavaServer Faces technology supports a mechanism for validating the local data of editable components (such as text fields). This validation occurs before the corresponding model data is updated to match the local value.

Like the conversion model, the validation model defines a set of standard classes for performing common data validation checks. The JavaServer Faces core tag library also defines a set of tags that correspond to the standard `Validator` implementations. See Table 10–7 for a list of all the standard validation classes and corresponding tags.

Most of the tags have a set of attributes for configuring the validator's properties, such as the minimum and maximum allowable values for the component's data. The page author registers the validator on a component by nesting the validator's tag within the component's tag.

The validation model also allows you to create your own custom validator and corresponding tag to perform custom validation. The validation model provides two ways to implement custom validation:

- Implement a `Validator` interface that performs the validation. See Implementing the Validator Interface (page 412) for more information.
- Implement a backing bean method that performs the validation. See Writing a Method to Perform Validation (page 421) for more information.

If you are implementing a `Validator` interface, you must also:

- Register the `Validator` implementation with the application. See Registering a Custom Validator (page 472) for more information.
- Create a custom tag or use a `validator` tag to register the validator on the component. See Creating a Custom Tag (page 416) for more information.

If you are implementing a backing bean method to perform validation, you also must reference the validator from the component tag's `validator` attribute. See Referencing a Method That Performs Validation (page 382) for more information.

Navigation Model

The JavaServer Faces navigation model makes it easy to define page navigation and to handle any additional processing needed to choose the sequence in which pages are loaded.

As defined by JavaServer Faces technology, *navigation* is a set of rules for choosing the next page to be displayed after a button or hyperlink is clicked. These rules are defined by the application architect in the application configuration resource file (see Application Configuration Resource File, page 458) using a small set of XML elements.

To handle navigation in the simplest application, you simply

- Define the rules in the application configuration resource file.
- Refer to an outcome `String` from the button or hyperlink component's `action` attribute. This outcome `String` is used by the JavaServer Faces implementation to select the navigation rule.

The Guess Number example uses this kind of simple navigation. Here is an example navigation rule from the `guessNumber` application described in Defining Page Navigation (page 288):

```
<navigation-rule>
  <from-view-id>/greeting.jsp</from-view-id>
  <navigation-case>
    <from-outcome>success</from-outcome>
    <to-view-id>/response.jsp</to-view-id>
  </navigation-case>
</navigation-rule>
```

This rule states that when the button component on `greeting.jsp` is activated, the application will navigate from the `greeting.jsp` page to the `response.jsp` page if the outcome referenced by the button component's tag is `success`. Here is the `commandButton` tag from `greeting.jsp` that specifies a logical outcome of success:

```
<h:commandButton id="submit" action="success"
    value="Submit" />
```

As the example demonstrates, each `navigation-rule` element defines how to get from one page (specified in the `from-view-id` element) to the other pages of the application. The `navigation-rule` elements can contain any number of `navigation-case` elements, each of which defines the page to open next (defined by `to-view-id`) based on a logical outcome (defined by `from-outcome`).

In more complicated applications, the logical outcome can also come from the return value of an *action method* in a backing bean. This method performs some processing to determine the outcome. For example, the method can check whether the password the user entered on the page matches the one on file. If it does, the method might return `success`; otherwise, it might return `failure`. An outcome of `failure` might result in the logon page being reloaded. An outcome of `success` might cause the page displaying the user's credit card activity to open. If you want the outcome to be returned by a method on a bean, you must refer to the method using a method expression, using the `action` attribute, as shown by this example:

```
<h:commandButton id="submit"
  action="#{userNumberBean.getOrderStatus}" value="Submit" />
```

When the user clicks the button represented by this tag, the corresponding component generates an action event. This event is handled by the default `ActionListener` instance, which calls the action method referenced by the component that triggered the event. The action method returns a logical outcome to the action listener.

The listener passes the logical outcome and a reference to the action method that produced the outcome to the default `NavigationHandler`. The `NavigationHandler` selects the page to display next by matching the outcome or the action method reference against the navigation rules in the application configuration resource file by the following process:

1. The `NavigationHandler` selects the navigation rule that matches the page currently displayed.
2. It matches the outcome or the action method reference it received from the default `ActionListener` with those defined by the navigation cases.
3. It tries to match both the method reference and the outcome against the same navigation case.
4. If the previous step fails, the navigation handler attempts to match the outcome.
5. Finally, the navigation handler attempts to match the action method reference if the previous two attempts failed.

When the `NavigationHandler` achieves a match, the render response phase begins. During this phase, the page selected by the `NavigationHandler` will be rendered.

For more information on how to define navigation rules, see Configuring Navigation Rules (page 474).

For more information on how to implement action methods to handle navigation, see Writing a Method to Handle an Action Event (page 421).

For more information on how to reference outcomes or action methods from component tags, see Referencing a Method That Performs Navigation (page 380).

Backing Beans

A typical JavaServer Faces application includes one or more backing beans, each of which is a JavaServer Faces managed bean that is associated with the UI components used in a particular page. Managed beans are JavaBeans components (see JavaBeans Components, page 136) that you can configure using the managed bean facility, which is described in Configuring Beans, page 459. This section introduces the basic concepts on creating, configuring, and using backing beans in an application.

Creating a Backing Bean Class

In addition to defining a no-arg constructor, as all JavaBeans components must do, a backing bean class also defines a set of UI component properties and possibly a set of methods that perform functions for a component.

Each of the component properties can be bound to one of the following:

- A component's value
- A component instance
- A converter instance
- A listener instance
- A validator instance

The most common functions that backing bean methods perform include the following:

- Validating a component's data
- Handling an event fired by a component
- Performing processing to determine the next page to which the application must navigate.

As with all JavaBeans components, a property consists of a private data field and a set of accessor methods, as shown by this code from the Guess Number example:

```
Integer userNumber = null;
...
public void setUserNumber(Integer user_number) {
  userNumber = user_number;
}
public Integer getUserNumber() {
  return userNumber;
}
public String getResponse() {
  ...
}
```

Because backing beans follow JavaBeans component conventions, you can reference beans you've already written from your JavaServer Faces pages.

When a bean property is bound to a component's value, it can be any of the basic primitive and numeric types or any Java object type for which the application has access to an appropriate converter. For example, a property can be of type `Date` if the application has access to a converter that can convert the `Date` type to a String and back again. See Writing Bean Properties (page 390) for information on which types are accepted by which component tags.

When a bean property is bound to a component instance, the property's type must be the same as the component object. For example, if a `UISelectBoolean` is bound to the property, the property must accept and return a `UISelectBoolean` object.

Likewise, if the property is bound to a converter, validator, or listener instance then the property must be of the appropriate converter, validator, or listener type.

For more information on writing beans and their properties, see Writing Bean Properties (page 390).

Configuring a Bean

JavaServer Faces technology supports a sophisticated managed bean creation facility, which allows application architects to do the following:

- Configure simple beans and more complex trees of beans
- Initialize bean properties with values
- Place beans in a particular scope
- Expose the beans to the unified EL so that page authors can access them

An application architect configures the beans in the application configuration resource file. To learn how to configure a managed bean, see Configuring Beans (page 459). The managed bean configuration used by the Guess Number example is the following:

```
<managed-bean>
  <managed-bean-name>UserNumberBean</managed-bean-name>
  <managed-bean-class>
    guessNumber.UserNumberBean
  </managed-bean-class>
  <managed-bean-scope>session</managed-bean-scope>
  <managed-property>
    <property-name>minimum</property-name>
```

```
            <property-class>long</property-class>
            <value>0</value>
        </managed-property>
        <managed-property>
            <property-name>maximum</property-name>
            <property-class>long</property-class>
            <value>10</value>
        </managed-property>
    </managed-bean>
```

The JavaServer Faces implementation processes this element on application startup time. When UserNumberBean is first referenced from the page, the JavaServer Faces implementation initializes it and sets the values of the properties, maximum and minimum. The bean is then stored in session scope if no instance exists. As such, the bean is available for all pages in the application.

A page author can then access the bean properties from the component tags on the page using the unified EL, as shown here:

```
<h:outputText value="#{UserNumberBean.minimum}"/>
```

The part of the expression before the . matches the name defined by the managed-bean-name element. The part of the expression after the . matches the name defined by the property-name element corresponding to the same managed-bean declaration.

Notice that the application configuration resource file does not configure the userNumber property. Any property that does not have a corresponding managed-property element will be initialized to whatever the constructor of the bean class has the instance variable set to. The next section explains more about using the unified EL to reference backing beans.

For more information on configuring beans using the managed bean creation Facility, see Configuring Beans (page 459).

Using the Unified EL to Reference Backing Beans

To bind UI component values and objects to backing bean properties or to reference backing bean methods from UI component tags, page authors use the unified expression language (EL) syntax defined by JSP 2.1. As explained in

Unified Expression Language (page 113), some of the features this language offers are:

- Deferred evaluation of expressions
- The ability to use a value expression to both read and write data
- Method expressions

These features are all especially important for supporting the sophisticated UI component model offered by JavaServer Faces technology.

Deferred evaluation of expressions is important because the JavaServer Faces life cycle is split into separate phases so that component event handling, data conversion and validation, and data propagation to external objects are all performed in an orderly fashion. The implementation must be able to delay the evaluation of expressions until the proper phase of the life cycle has been reached. Therefore, its tag attributes always use deferred evaluation syntax, which is distinguished by the `#{}` delimiters. The Life Cycle of a JavaServer Faces Page (page 309) describes the life cycle in detail.

In order to store data in external objects, almost all JavaServer Faces tag attributes use lvalue value expressions, which are expressions that allow both getting and setting data on external objects.

Finally, some component tag attributes accept method expressions that reference methods that handle component events, or validate or convert component data.

To illustrate a JavaServer Faces tag using the unified EL, let's suppose that the `userNo` tag of the `guessNumber` application referenced a method rather than using `LongRangeValidator` to perform the validation of user input :

```
<h:inputText id="userNo"
  value="#{UserNumberBean.userNumber}"
  validator="#{UserNumberBean.validate}" />
```

This tag binds the `userNo` component's value to the `UserNumberBean.userNumber` backing bean property using an lvalue expression. It uses a method expression to refer to the `UserNumberBean.validate` method, which performs validation of the component's local value. The local value is whatever the user enters into the field corresponding to this tag. This method is invoked when the expression is evaluated, which is during the process validation phase of the life cycle.

Nearly all JavaServer Faces tag attributes accept value expressions. In addition to referencing bean properties, value expressions can also reference lists, maps, arrays, implicit objects, and resource bundles.

Another use of value expressions is binding a component instance to a backing bean property. A page author does this by referencing the property from the `binding` attribute:

```
<inputText binding="#{UserNumberBean.userNoComponent}" />
```

Those component tags that use method expressions are `UIInput` component tags and `UICommand` component tags. See sections Using Text Components (page 331) and Using Command Components for Performing Actions and Navigation (page 337) for more information on how these component tags use method expressions.

In addition to using expressions with the standard component tags, you can also configure your custom component properties to accept expressions by creating `ValueExpression` or `MethodExpression` instances for them. See Creating Custom Component Classes (page 437) and Enabling Component Properties to Accept Expressions (page 443) for more information on enabling your component's attributes to support expressions.

To learn more about using expressions to bind to backing bean properties, see Binding Component Values and Instances to External Data Sources (page 371).

For information on referencing backing bean methods from component tags, see Referencing a Backing Bean Method (page 379).

The Life Cycle of a JavaServer Faces Page

The life cycle of a JavaServer Faces page is somewhat similar to that of a JSP page: The client makes an HTTP request for the page, and the server responds with the page translated to HTML. However, the JavaServer Faces life cycle differs from the JSP life cycle in that it is split up into multiple phases in order to support the sophisticated UI component model. This model requires that component data be converted and validated, component events be handled, and component data be propagated to beans in an orderly fashion.

A JavaServer Faces page is also different from a JSP page in that it is represented by a tree of UI components, called a *view*. During the life cycle, the JavaServer

Faces implementation must build the view while considering state saved from a previous submission of the page. When the client submits a page, the JavaServer Faces implementation performs several tasks, such as validating the data input of components in the view and converting input data to types specified on the server side.

The JavaServer Faces implementation performs all these tasks as a series of steps in the JavaServer Faces request-response life cycle. Figure 9–3 illustrates these steps.

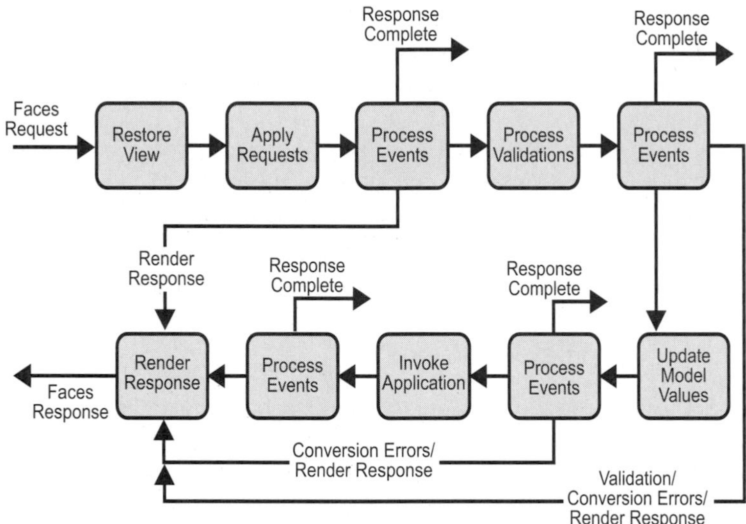

Figure 9–3 JavaServer Faces Standard Request-Response Life Cycle

The life cycle handles both kinds of requests: *initial requests* and *postbacks*. When a user makes an initial request for a page, he or she is requesting the page for the first time. When a user executes a postback, he or she submits the form contained on a page that was previously loaded into the browser as a result of executing an initial request. When the life cycle handles an initial request, it only executes the restore view and render response phases because there is no user input or actions to process. Conversely, when the life cycle handles a postback, it executes all of the phases.

Usually, the first request for a JavaServer Faces pages comes in as a result of clicking a hyperlink on an HTML page that links to the JavaServer Faces page. To render a response that is another JavaServer Faces page, the application creates a new view and stores it in the `FacesContext` instance, which represents all of the contextual information associated with processing an incoming request and creating a response. The application then acquires object references needed by the view and calls `FacesContext.renderResponse`, which forces immediate rendering of the view by skipping to the Render Response Phase (page 314) of the life cycle, as is shown by the arrows labelled Render Response in the diagram.

Sometimes, an application might need to redirect to a different web application resource, such as a web service, or generate a response that does not contain JavaServer Faces components. In these situations, the developer must skip the rendering phase (Render Response Phase, page 314) by calling `FacesContext.responseComplete`. This situation is also shown in the diagram, this time with the arrows labelled Response Complete.

The most common situation is that a JavaServer Faces component submits a request for another JavaServer Faces page. In this case, the JavaServer Faces implementation handles the request and automatically goes through the phases in the life cycle to perform any necessary conversions, validations, and model updates, and to generate the response.

This rest of this section explains each of the life cycle phases using the `guessNumber` example.

The details of the life cycle explained in this section are primarily intended for developers who need to know information such as when validations, conversions, and events are usually handled and what they can do to change how and when they are handled. Page authors don't necessarily need to know the details of the life cycle.

Restore View Phase

When a request for a JavaServer Faces page is made, such as when a link or a button is clicked, the JavaServer Faces implementation begins the restore view phase.

During this phase, the JavaServer Faces implementation builds the view of the page, wires event handlers and validators to components in the view, and saves the view in the `FacesContext` instance, which contains all the information needed to process a single request. All the application's component tags, event handlers, converters, and validators have access to the `FacesContext` instance.

If the request for the page is an initial request, the JavaServer Faces implementation creates an empty view during this phase and the life cycle advances to the render response phase. The empty view will be populated when the page is processed during a postback.

If the request for the page is a postback, a view corresponding to this page already exists. During this phase, the JavaServer Faces implementation restores the view by using the state information saved on the client or the server.

The view for the `greeting.jsp` page of the `guessNumber` example would have the `UIView` component at the root of the tree, with `helloForm` as its child and the rest of the JavaServer Faces UI components as children of `helloForm`.

Apply Request Values Phase

After the component tree is restored, each component in the tree extracts its new value from the request parameters by using its `decode` method. The value is then stored locally on the component. If the conversion of the value fails, an error message associated with the component is generated and queued on `FacesContext`. This message will be displayed during the render response phase, along with any validation errors resulting from the process validations phase.

In the case of the `userNo` component on the `greeting.jsp` page, the value is whatever the user entered in the field. Because the object property bound to the component has an `Integer` type, the JavaServer Faces implementation converts the value from a `String` to an `Integer`.

If any `decode` methods or event listeners called `renderResponse` on the current `FacesContext` instance, the JavaServer Faces implementation skips to the render response phase.

If events have been queued during this phase, the JavaServer Faces implementation broadcasts the events to interested listeners.

If some components on the page have their `immediate` attributes (see The immediate Attribute, page 328) set to `true`, then the validation, conversion, and events associated with these components will be processed during this phase.

At this point, if the application needs to redirect to a different web application resource or generate a response that does not contain any JavaServer Faces components, it can call `FacesContext.responseComplete`.

At the end of this phase, the components are set to their new values, and messages and events have been queued.

Process Validations Phase

During this phase, the JavaServer Faces implementation processes all validators registered on the components in the tree. It examines the component attributes that specify the rules for the validation and compares these rules to the local value stored for the component.

If the local value is invalid, the JavaServer Faces implementation adds an error message to the `FacesContext` instance, and the life cycle advances directly to the render response phase so that the page is rendered again with the error messages displayed. If there were conversion errors from the apply request values phase, the messages for these errors are also displayed.

If any `validate` methods or event listeners called `renderResponse` on the current `FacesContext`, the JavaServer Faces implementation skips to the render response phase.

At this point, if the application needs to redirect to a different web application resource or generate a response that does not contain any JavaServer Faces components, it can call `FacesContext.responseComplete`.

If events have been queued during this phase, the JavaServer Faces implementation broadcasts them to interested listeners.

In the case of the `greeting.jsp` page, the JavaServer Faces implementation processes the standard validator registered on the `userNo` `inputText` tag. It verifies that the data the user entered in the text field is an integer in the range 0 to 10. If the data is invalid or if conversion errors occurred during the apply request values phase, processing jumps to the render response phase, during which the `greeting.jsp` page is rendered again, with the validation and conversion error messages displayed in the component associated with the `message` tag.

Update Model Values Phase

After the JavaServer Faces implementation determines that the data is valid, it can walk the component tree and set the corresponding server-side object properties to the components' local values. The JavaServer Faces implementation will update only the bean properties pointed at by an input component's value attribute. If the local data cannot be converted to the types specified by the bean properties, the life cycle advances directly to the render response phase so that the page is rerendered with errors displayed. This is similar to what happens with validation errors.

If any `updateModels` methods or any listeners called `renderResponse` on the current `FacesContext` instance, the JavaServer Faces implementation skips to the render response phase.

At this point, if the application needs to redirect to a different web application resource or generate a response that does not contain any JavaServer Faces components, it can call `FacesContext.responseComplete`.

If events have been queued during this phase, the JavaServer Faces implementation broadcasts them to interested listeners.

At this stage, the `userNo` property of the `UserNumberBean` is set to the local value of the `userNumber` component.

Invoke Application Phase

During this phase, the JavaServer Faces implementation handles any application-level events, such as submitting a form or linking to another page.

At this point, if the application needs to redirect to a different web application resource or generate a response that does not contain any JavaServer Faces components, it can call `FacesContext.responseComplete`.

If the view being processed was reconstructed from state information from a previous request and if a component has fired an event, these events are broadcast to interested listeners.

The `greeting.jsp` page from the `guessNumber` example has one application-level event associated with the `UICommand` component. When processing this event, a default `ActionListener` implementation retrieves the outcome, `success`, from the component's `action` attribute. The listener passes the outcome to the default `NavigationHandler`. The `NavigationHandler` matches the outcome to the proper navigation rule defined in the application's application configuration resource file to determine which page needs to be displayed next. See Configuring Navigation Rules (page 474) for more information on managing page navigation. The JavaServer Faces implementation then sets the response view to that of the new page. Finally, the JavaServer Faces implementation transfers control to the render response phase.

Render Response Phase

During this phase, the JavaServer Faces implementation delegates authority for rendering the page to the JSP container if the application is using JSP pages. If this is an initial request, the components represented on the page will be added to the component tree as the JSP container executes the page. If this is not an initial request, the components are already added to the tree so they needn't be added again. In either case, the components will render themselves as the JSP container traverses the tags in the page.

If the request is a postback and errors were encountered during the apply request values phase, process validations phase, or update model values phase, the original page is rendered during this phase. If the pages contain `message` or `messages` tags, any queued error messages are displayed on the page.

After the content of the view is rendered, the state of the response is saved so that subsequent requests can access it and it is available to the restore view phase.

In the case of the `guessNumber` example, if a request for the `greeting.jsp` page is an initial request, the view representing this page is built and saved in `FacesContext` during the restore view phase and then rendered during this phase. If a request for the page is a postback (such as when the user enters some invalid data and clicks Submit), the tree is rebuilt during the restore view phase and continues through the request processing life cycle phases.

Further Information

For further information on the technologies discussed in this tutorial see the following web sites:

- The JavaServer Faces 1.2 TLD documentation:

  `http://java.sun.com/javaee/javaserverfaces/1.2/docs/tlddocs/index.html`

- The JavaServer Faces 1.2 standard RenderKit documentation:

  `http://java.sun.com/javaee/javaserverfaces/1.2/docs/renderkitdocs/index.html`

- The JavaServer Faces 1.1 API Specification:

  `http://java.sun.com/javaee/javaserverfaces/1.2/docs/api/index.html`

- The JavaServer Faces 1.1 Specification:

  `http://java.sun.com/javaee/javaserverfaces/download.html`

- The JavaServer Faces web site:

  `http://java.sun.com/javaee/javaserverfaces`

10

Using JavaServer Faces Technology in JSP Pages

THE page author's responsibility is to design the pages of a JavaServer Faces application. This includes laying out the components on the page and wiring them to backing beans, validators, converters, and other server-side objects associated with the page. This chapter uses the Duke's Bookstore application and the Coffee Break application (see Chapter 36) to describe how page authors use the JavaServer Faces tags to perform the following tasks:

- Lay out standard UI components on a page
- Reference localized messages
- Register converters, validators, and listeners on components
- Bind components and their values to server-side objects
- Reference backing bean methods that perform navigation processing, handle events, and perform validation

This chapter also describes how to include custom objects created by application developers and component writers on a JSP page.

The Example JavaServer Faces Application

The JavaServer Faces technology chapters of this tutorial primarily use a rewritten version of the Duke's Bookstore example to illustrate the basic concepts of JavaServer Faces technology. This version of the Duke's Bookstore example includes several JavaServer Faces technology features:

- The JavaServer Faces implementation provides `FacesServlet`, whose instances accept incoming requests and pass them to the implementation for processing. Therefore, the application does not need to include a servlet (such as the `Dispatcher` servlet) that processes request parameters and dispatches to application logic, as do the other versions of Duke's Bookstore.
- A custom image map component that allows you to select the locale for the application.
- Navigation configured in a centralized application configuration resource file. This eliminates the need to calculate URLs, as other versions of the Duke's Bookstore application must do.
- Backing beans associated with the pages. These beans hold the component data and perform other processing associated with the components. This processing includes handling the event generated when a user clicks a button or a hyperlink.
- The table that displays the books from the database and the shopping cart are rendered with the `dataTable` tag, which is used to dynamically render data in a table. The `dataTable` tag on `bookshowcart.jsp` also includes input components.
- The table that displays the books from the database uses a `c:forEach` JSTL tag, demonstrating that you can easily use JavaServer Faces component tags with JSTL tags.
- A custom validator and a custom converter are registered on the credit card field of the `bookcashier.jsp` page.
- A value-change listener is registered on the Name field of `bookcashier.jsp`. This listener saves the name in a parameter so that `bookreceipt.jsp` can access it.

This version of Duke's Bookstore includes the same pages listed in Table 4–1. It also includes the `chooselocale.jsp` page, which displays the custom image map that allows you to select the locale of the application. This page is displayed first and advances directly to the `bookstore.jsp` page after the locale is selected.

The packages of the Duke's Bookstore application are:

- `backing`: Includes the backing bean classes
- `components`: Includes the custom UI component classes
- `converters`: Includes the custom converter class
- `listeners`: Includes the event handler and event listener classes
- `model`: Includes a model bean class
- `renderers`: Includes the custom renderers
- `resources`: Includes custom error messages for the custom converter and validator
- `taglib`: Includes custom tag handler classes
- `util`: Includes a message factory class
- `validators`: Includes a custom validator class

Chapter 11 describes how to program backing beans, custom converters and validators, and event listeners. Chapter 12 describes how to program event handlers, custom components, renderers, and tag handlers.

The source code for the application is located in the *`<INSTALL>`*`/javaeetutorial5/examples/web/bookstore6/` directory.

To deploy and run the application using NetBeans 5.5, follow these steps:

1. Perform all the operations described in Accessing Databases from Web Applications (page 55).
2. In NetBeans 5.5, select File→Open Project.
3. In the Open Project dialog, navigate to:

   `<INSTALL>/javaeetutorial5/examples/web/`
4. Select the `bookstore6` folder.
5. Select the Open as Main Project checkbox and the Open Required Projects checkbox.
6. Click Open Project Folder.
7. In the Projects tab, right-click the `bookstore6` project, and select Deploy Project.
8. To run the application, open the bookstore URL `http://localhost:8080/bookstore6`.

To deploy and run the application using `ant` follow these steps:

1. In a terminal window, go to `<INSTALL>/javaeetutorial5/examples/web/bookstore6/`.
2. Run `ant`. This target will spawn any necessary compilations, copy files to the `<INSTALL>/javaeetutorial5/examples/web/bookstore6/build/` directory, and create a WAR file and copy it to the `<INSTALL>/javaeetutorial5/examples/web/bookstore6/dist/` directory.
3. Start the Application Server.
4. Perform all the operations described in Creating a Data Source in the Application Server (page 56)
5. To deploy the example, run `ant deploy`. The deploy target outputs a URL for running the application. Ignore this URL, and instead use the one shown in the next step.
6. To run the application, open the bookstore URL `http://localhost:8080/bookstore6/`.

To learn how to configure the example, refer to the `web.xml` file, which includes the following elements:

- A `display-name` element that specifies the name that tools use to identify the application.
- A `context-param` element that specifies that the `javax.faces.STATE_SAVING_METHOD` parameter has a value of `client`, meaning that state is saved on the client.
- A `listener` element that identifies the `ContextListener` class used to create and remove the database access.
- A `servlet` element that identifies the `FacesServlet` instance.
- A `servlet-mapping` element that maps `FacesServlet` to a URL pattern.
- Nested inside a `jsp-config` element is a `jsp-property-group` element, which sets the properties for the group of pages included in this version of Duke's Bookstore. See Setting Properties for Groups of JSP Pages (page 149) for more information.

To run the example, open the URL `http://localhost:8080/bookstore6` in a browser.

Setting Up a Page

A typical JavaServer Faces page includes the following elements:

- A set of tag library declarations that declare the two JavaServer Faces tag libraries.
- A view tag
- A form tag

This section tells you how to add these elements to your pages and briefly describes the subview tag for including JavaServer Faces pages inside other pages.

To use the JavaServer Faces UI components in your JSP page, you need to give the page access to the two standard tag libraries: the JavaServer Faces HTML render kit tag library and the JavaServer Faces core tag library. The JavaServer Faces standard HTML render kit tag library defines tags that represent common HTML user interface components. The JavaServer Faces core tag library defines tags that perform core actions and are independent of a particular render kit.

Using these tag libraries is similar to using any other custom tag library. This chapter assumes that you are familiar with the basics of using custom tags in JSP pages (see Using Custom Tags, page 141).

As is the case with any tag library, each JavaServer Faces tag library must have a TLD that describes it. The html_basic TLD describes the The JavaServer Faces standard HTML render kit tag library. The jsf_core TLD describes the JavaServer Faces core tag library.

Please refer to the TLD documentation at http://java.sun.com/javaee/javaserverfaces/1.2/docs/tlddocs/index.html for a complete list of the JavaServer Faces tags and their attributes.

To use any of the JavaServer Faces tags, you need to include these taglib directives at the top of each page containing the tags defined by these tag libraries:

```
<%@ taglib uri="http://java.sun.com/jsf/html" prefix="h" %>
<%@ taglib uri="http://java.sun.com/jsf/core" prefix="f" %>
```

The uri attribute value uniquely identifies the TLD. The prefix attribute value is used to distinguish tags belonging to the tag library. You can use other prefixes rather than the h or f prefixes. However, you must use the prefix you have chosen when including the tag in the page. For example, the form tag must be referenced in the page via the h prefix because the preceding tag library directive uses the h prefix to distinguish the tags defined in html_basic.tld:

```
<h:form ...>
```

A page containing JavaServer Faces tags is represented by a tree of components. At the root of the tree is the UIViewRoot component. The view tag represents this component on the page. Therefore, all component tags on the page must be enclosed in the view tag, which is defined in the jsf_core TLD:

```
<f:view>
  ... other JavaServer Faces tags, possibly mixed with other
  content ...
</f:view>
```

You can enclose other content, including HTML and other JSP tags, within the view tag, but all JavaServer Faces tags must be enclosed within the view tag.

The view tag has four optional attributes:

- A locale attribute. If this attribute is present, its value overrides the Locale stored in the UIViewRoot component. This value is specified as a String and must be of this form:

  :language:[{-,_}:country:[{-,_}:variant]

  The :language:, :country:, and :variant: parts of the expression are as specified in java.util.Locale.
- A renderKitId attribute. A page author uses this attribute to refer to the ID of the render kit used to render the page, therefore allowing the use of custom render kits. If this attribute is not specified, the default HTML render kit is assumed. The process of creating custom render kits is outside the scope of this tutorial.
- A beforePhase attribute. This attribute references a method that takes a PhaseEvent object and returns void, causing the referenced method to be called before each phase (except restore view) of the life cycle begins.
- An afterPhase attribute. This attribute references a method that takes a PhaseEvent object and returns void, causing the referenced method to be called after each phase (except restore view) in the life cycle ends.

An advanced developer might implement the methods referenced by beforePhase and afterPhase to perform such functions as initialize or release resources on a per-page basis. This feature is outside of the scope of this tutorial.

The form tag is nested inside of the view tag. As its name suggests, the form tag represents a form, which is submitted when a button or hyperlink on the page is clicked. For the data of other components on the page to be submitted with the form, the tags representing the components must be nested inside the form tag. See Adding a Form Component (page 330) for more details on using the form tag.

If you want to include a page containing JavaServer Faces tags within another JSP page that includes JavaServer Faces tags, you must enclose the entire nested page in a subview tag. You can add the subview tag on the parent page and nest a jsp:include inside it to include the page:

```
<f:subview id="myNestedPage">
  <jsp:include page="theNestedPage.jsp" />
</f:subview>
```

You can also include the subview tag inside the nested page, but it must enclose all the JavaServer Faces tags on the nested page.

The subview tag has two optional attributes: binding and rendered. The binding attribute binds to a component that implements NamingContainer. One potential use case of binding a subview component to a bean is if you want to dynamically add components to the subview in the backing bean.

The rendered attribute can be set to true or false, indicating whether or not the components nested in the subview tag should be rendered.

In summary, a typical JSP page that uses JavaServer Faces tags will look somewhat like this:

```
<%@ taglib uri="http://java.sun.com/jsf/html" prefix="h" %>
<%@ taglib uri="http://java.sun.com/jsf/core" prefix="f" %>

<f:view>
  <h:form>
    other JavaServer Faces tags and core tags,
    including one or more button or hyperlink components for
    submitting the form
  </h:form>
</f:view>
```

The sections Using the Core Tags (page 324) and Adding UI Components to a Page Using the HTML Component Tags (page 326) describe how to use the core tags from the JavaServer Faces core tag library and the component tags from the JavaServer Faces standard HTML render kit tag library.

Using the Core Tags

The tags included in the JavaServer Faces core tag library are used to perform core actions that are independent of a particular render kit. These tags are listed in Table 10–1.

Table 10–1 The `jsf_core` Tags

Tag Categories	Tags	Functions
Event-handling tags	`actionListener`	Registers an action listener on a parent component
	`phaseListener`	Registers a `PhaseListener` instance on a `UIViewRoot` component
	`setPropertyActionListener`	Registers a special action listener whose sole purpose is to push a value into a backing bean when a form is submitted
	`valueChangeListener`	Registers a value-change listener on a parent component
Attribute configuration tag	`attribute`	Adds configurable attributes to a parent component
Data conversion tags	`converter`	Registers an arbitrary converter on the parent component
	`convertDateTime`	Registers a `DateTime` converter instance on the parent component
	`convertNumber`	Registers a `Number` converter instance on the parent component
Facet tag	`facet`	Signifies a nested component that has a special relationship to its enclosing tag
Localization tag	`loadBundle`	Specifies a `ResourceBundle` that is exposed as a `Map`

Table 10–1 The `jsf_core` Tags (Continued)

Tag Categories	Tags	Functions
Parameter substitution tag	`param`	Substitutes parameters into a `MessageFormat` instance and adds query string name-value pairs to a URL
Tags for representing items in a list	`selectItem`	Represents one item in a list of items in a `UISelectOne` or `UISelectMany` component
	`selectItems`	Represents a set of items in a `UISelectOne` or `UISelect-Many` component
Container tag	`subview`	Contains all JavaServer Faces tags in a page that is included in another JSP page containing JavaServer Faces tags
Validator tags	`validateDoubleRange`	Registers a `DoubleRangeVali-dator` on a component
	`validateLength`	Registers a `LengthValidator` on a component
	`validateLongRange`	Registers a `LongRangeValida-tor` on a component
	`validator`	Registers a custom validator on a component
Output tag	`verbatim`	Generates a `UIOutput` compo-nent that gets its content from the body of this tag
Container for form tags	`view`	Encloses all JavaServer Faces tags on the page

These tags are used in conjunction with component tags and are therefore explained in other sections of this tutorial. Table 10–2 lists the sections that explain how to use specific `jsf_core` tags.

Table 10–2 Where the `jsf_core` Tags Are Explained

Tags	Where Explained
Event-handling tags	Registering Listeners on Components (page 366)
Data conversion tags	Using the Standard Converters (page 359)
`facet`	Using Data-Bound Table Components (page 339) and Laying Out Components with the UIPanel Component (page 344)
`loadBundle`	Rendering Components for Selecting Multiple Values (page 349)
`param`	Displaying a Formatted Message with the outputFormat Tag (page 336)
`selectItem` and `selectItems`	The UISelectItem, UISelectItems, and UISelectItem-Group Components (page 350)
`subview`	Setting Up a Page (page 321)
`verbatim`	Rendering a Hyperlink with the outputLink Tag (page 335)
`view`	Setting Up a Page (page 321)
Validator tags	Using the Standard Validators (page 369) and Creating a Custom Validator (page 411)

Adding UI Components to a Page Using the HTML Component Tags

The tags defined by the JavaServer Faces standard HTML render kit tag library represent HTML form components and other basic HTML elements. These components display data or accept data from the user. This data is collected as part of a form and is submitted to the server, usually when the user clicks a button. This section explains how to use each of the component tags shown in Table 9–2.

The next section explains the more important tag attributes that are common to most component tags. Please refer to the TLD documentation at `http://java.sun.com/javaee/javaserverfaces/1.2/docs/tlddocs/index.html` for a complete list of tags and their attributes.

For each of the components discussed in the following sections, Writing Bean Properties (page 390) explains how to write a bean property bound to a particular UI component or its value.

UI Component Tag Attributes

In general, most of the component tags support these attributes:

- `id`: Uniquely identifies the component
- `immediate`: If set to `true`, indicates that any events, validation, and conversion associated with the component should happen in the apply request values phase rather than a later phase.
- `rendered`: Specifies a condition in which the component should be rendered. If the condition is not satisfied, the component is not rendered.
- `style`: Specifies a Cascading Style Sheet (CSS) style for the tag.
- `styleClass`: Specifies a CSS stylesheet class that contains definitions of the styles.
- `value`: Identifies an external data source and binds the component's value to it.
- `binding`: Identifies a bean property and binds the component instance to it.

All of the UI component tag attributes (except `id`) can accept expressions, as defined by the unified EL described in Unified Expression Language (page 113).

The id Attribute

The `id` attribute is not required for a component tag except in the case when another component or a server-side class must refer to the component. If you don't include an `id` attribute, the JavaServer Faces implementation automatically generates a component ID. Unlike most other JavaServer Faces tag attributes, the id attribute only takes expressions using the immediate evaluation syntax, which uses the `${}` delimiters.

The immediate Attribute

UIInput components and command components (those that implement Action-Source, such as buttons and hyperlinks) can set the immediate attribute to true to force events, validations, and conversions to be processed during the apply request values phase of the life cycle. Page authors need to carefully consider how the combination of an input component's immediate value and a command component's immediate value determines what happens when the command component is activated.

Assume that you have a page with a button and a field for entering the quantity of a book in a shopping cart. If both the button's and the field's immediate attributes are set to true, the new value of the field will be available for any processing associated with the event that is generated when the button is clicked. The event associated with the button and the event, validation, and conversion associated with the field are all handled during the apply request values phase.

If the button's immediate attribute is set to true but the field's immediate attribute is set to false, the event associated with the button is processed without updating the field's local value to the model layer. This is because any events, conversion, or validation associated with the field occurs during its usual phases of the life cycle, which come after the apply request values phase.

The bookshowcart.jsp page of the Duke's Bookstore application has examples of components using the immediate attribute to control which component's data is updated when certain buttons are clicked. The quantity field for each book has its immediate attribute set to false. (The quantity fields are generated by the UIData component. See Using Data-Bound Table Components, page 339, for more information.) The immediate attribute of the Continue Shopping hyperlink is set to true. The immediate attribute of the Update Quantities hyperlink is set to false.

If you click the Continue Shopping hyperlink, none of the changes entered into the quantity input fields will be processed. If you click the Update Quantities hyperlink, the values in the quantity fields will be updated in the shopping cart.

The rendered Attribute

A component tag uses a Boolean JavaServer Faces expression language (EL) expression, along with the rendered attribute, to determine whether or not the component will be rendered. For example, the check commandLink component on the bookcatalog.jsp page is not rendered if the cart contains no items:

```
<h:commandLink id="check"
  ...
  rendered="#{cart.numberOfItems > 0}">
  <h:outputText
    value="#{bundle.CartCheck}"/>
</h:commandLink>
```

Unlike nearly every other JavaServer Faces tag attribute, the rendered attribute is restricted to using rvalue expressions. As explained in Unified Expression Language (page 113), rvalue expressions can only read data; they cannot write the data back to the data source. Therefore, expressions used with rendered attributes can use the arithmetic operators and literals that rvalue expressions can use but lvalue expressions cannot use. For example, the expression in the preceding example uses the > operator.

The style and styleClass Attributes

The style and styleClass attributes allow you to specify Cascading Style Sheets (CSS) styles for the rendered output of your component tags. Displaying Error Messages with the message and messages Tags (page 354) describes an example of using the style attribute to specify styles directly in the attribute. A component tag can instead refer to a CSS stylesheet class. The dataTable tag on the bookcatalog.jsp page of the Duke's Bookstore application references the style class list-background:

```
<h:dataTable id="books"
  ...
  styleClass="list-background"
  value="#{bookDBAO.books}"
  var="book">
```

The stylesheet that defines this class is stylesheet.css, which is included in the application. For more information on defining styles, please the see Cascading Style Sheets Specification at http://www.w3.org/Style/CSS/.

The value and binding Attributes

A tag representing a component defined by UIOutput or a subclass of UIOutput uses value and binding attributes to bind its component's value or instance respectively to an external data source. Binding Component Values and Instances to External Data Sources (page 371) explains how to use these attributes.

Adding a Form Component

A `UIForm` component class represents an input form, which includes child components that contain data that is either presented to the user or submitted with the form.

Figure 10–1 shows a typical login form, in which a user enters a user name and password, and submits the form by clicking the Login button.

User Name: Duke
Password: *********
Login

Figure 10–1 A Typical Form

The `form` tag represents the `UIForm` component on the page and encloses all the components that display or collect data from the user, as shown here:

```
<h:form>
... other JavaServer Faces tags and other content...
</h:form>
```

The `form` tag can also include HTML markup to lay out the components on the page. The `form` tag itself does not perform any layout; its purpose is to collect data and to declare attributes that can be used by other components in the form. A page can include multiple `form` tags, but only the values from the form that the user submits will be included in the postback.

Using Text Components

Text components allow users to view and edit text in web applications. The basic kinds of text components are:

- Label, which displays read-only text.
- Text field, which allows users to enter text, often to be submitted as part of a form.
- Password field, which is one kind of text field that displays a set of characters, such as asterisks, instead of the password that the user enters.
- Text area, which is another kind of text field that allow users to enter multiple lines of text.

Figure 10–2 shows examples of these text components.

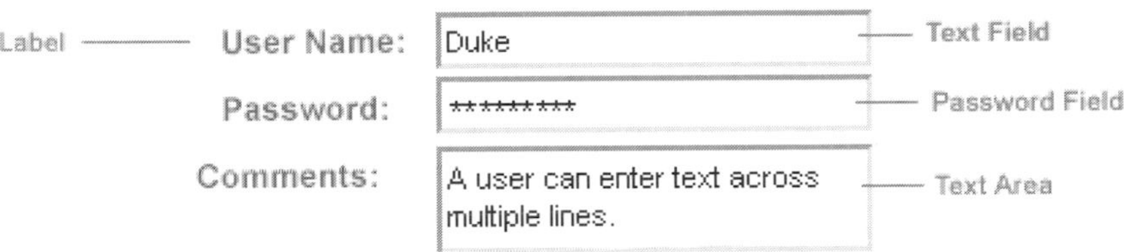

Figure 10–2 Example Text Components

An editable text component in a JavaServer Faces application is represented by a `UIInput` component. One example is a text field. A read-only text component in a JavaServer Faces application is represented by a `UIOutput` component. One example is a label.

The `UIInput` and `UIOutput` components can each be rendered in four ways to display more specialized text components. Table 10–3 lists all the renderers of `UIInput` and `UIOutput` and the tags that represent the component and renderer combination. Recall from Component Rendering Model (page 294) that the name of a tag is composed of the name of the component and the name of the renderer. For example, the inputText tag refers to a UIInput component that is rendered with the Text renderer.

Table 10–3 UIInput and UIOutput Tags

Component	Renderer	Tag	Function
UIInput	Hidden	inputHidden	Allows a page author to include a hidden variable in a page
	Secret	inputSecret	The standard password field: Accepts one line of text with no spaces and displays it as a set of asterisks as it is typed
	Text	inputText	The standard text field: Accepts a text string of one line
	TextArea	inputTextarea	The standard text area: Accepts multiple lines of text
UIOutput	Label	outputLabel	The standard read-only label: Displays a component as a label for a specified input field
	Link	outputLink	Displays an <a href> tag that links to another page without generating an action event
	OutputMessage	outputFormat	Displays a localized message
	Text	outputText	Displays a text string of one line

The UIInput component tags support the following tag attributes in addition to those described at the beginning of Adding UI Components to a Page Using the HTML Component Tags (page 326). This list does not include all the attributes supported by the `UIInput` component tags, just those that page authors will use most often. Please refer to the `html_basic.tld` file for the complete list.

- `converter`: Identifies a converter that will be used to convert the component's local data. See Using the Standard Converters (page 359) for more information on how to use this attribute.
- `converterMessage`: Specifies an error message to display when the converter registered on the component fails.
- `dir`: Specifies the direction of the text displayed by this component. Acceptable values are LTR, meaning left-to-right, and RTL, meaning right-to-left.
- `label`: Specifies a name that can be used to identify this component in error messages.
- `lang`: Specifies the code for the language used in the rendered markup, such as en_US.
- `required`: Takes a `boolean` value that indicates whether or not the user must enter a value in this component.
- `requiredMessage`: Specifies an error message to display when the user does not enter a value into the component.
- `validator`: Identifies a method expression pointing to a backing bean method that performs validation on the component's data. See Referencing a Method That Performs Validation (page 382) for an example of using the `validator` tag.
- `validatorMessage`: Specifies an error message to display when the validator registered on the component fails to validate the component's local value.
- `valueChangeListener`: Identifies a method expression that points to a backing bean method that handles the event of entering a value in this component. See Referencing a Method That Handles a Value-change Event (page 382) for an example of using `valueChangeListener`.

The `UIOutput` component tags support the `converter` tag attribute in addition to those listed in Adding UI Components to a Page Using the HTML Component Tags (page 326). The rest of this section explains how to use selected tags listed in Table 10–3. The other tags are written in a similar way.

Rendering a Text Field with the inputText Tag

The `inputText` tag is used to display a text field. It represents the combination of a `Text` renderer and a `UIInput` component. A similar tag, the `outputText` tag, displays a read-only, single-line string. It represents the combination of a `Text` renderer and a `UIOutput` component. This section shows you how to use the `inputText` tag. The `outputText` tag is written in a similar way.

Here is an example of an `inputText` tag from the `bookcashier.jsp` page:

```
<h:inputText id="name" label="Customer Name" size="50"
  value="#{cashier.name}"
  required="true"
  requiredMessage="#{customMessages.CustomerName}">
  <f:valueChangeListener
    type="com.sun.bookstore6.listeners.NameChanged" />
</h:inputText>
```

The `label` attribute specifies a user-friendly name that will be used in the substitution parameters of error messages displayed for this component.

The `value` attribute refers to the `name` property of `CashierBean`. This property holds the data for the `name` component. After the user submits the form, the value of the `name` property in `CashierBean` will be set to the text entered in the field corresponding to this tag.

The `required` attribute causes the page to reload with errors displayed if the user does not enter a value in the `name` text field. The JavaServer Faces implementation checks whether the value of the component is `null` or is an empty `String`.

If your component must have a non-`null` value or a `String` value at least one character in length, you should add a `required` attribute to your component tag and set it to `true`. If your tag does have a `required` attribute that is set to `true` and the value is `null` or a zero-length string, no other validators registered on the tag are called. If your tag does not have a `required` attribute set to `true`, other validators registered on the tag are called, but those validators must handle the possibility of a `null` or zero-length string.

The `requiredMessage` attribute references an error message from a resource bundle, which is declared in the application configuration file. Refer to Registering Custom Error Messages (page 470) for details on how to declare and reference the resource bundle.

Rendering a Label with the outputLabel Tag

The outputLabel tag is used to attach a label to a specified input field for accessibility purposes. The bookcashier.jsp page uses an outputLabel tag to render the label of a checkbox:

```
<h:selectBooleanCheckbox
  id="fanClub"
  rendered="false"
  binding="#{cashier.specialOffer}" />
<h:outputLabel for="fanClub"
  rendered="false"
  binding="#{cashier.specialOfferText}"  >
  <h:outputText id="fanClubLabel"
    value="#{bundle.DukeFanClub}" />
</h:outputLabel>
...
```

The for attribute of the outputLabel tag maps to the id of the input field to which the label is attached. The outputText tag nested inside the outputLabel tag represents the actual label component. The value attribute on the outputText tag indicates the text that is displayed next to the input field.

Instead of using an outputText tag for the text displayed as a label, you can simply use the outputLabel tag's value attribute. The following code snippet shows what the previous code snippet would look like if it used the value attribute of the outputLabel tag to specify the text of the label.

```
<h:selectBooleanCheckbox
  id="fanClub"
  rendered="false"
  binding="#{cashier.specialOffer}" />
  <h:outputLabel for="fanClub"
    rendered="false"
    binding="#{cashier.specialOfferText}"
    value="#{bundle.DukeFanClub}" />
  </h:outputLabel>
...
```

Rendering a Hyperlink with the outputLink Tag

The outputLink tag is used to render a hyperlink that, when clicked, loads another page but does not generate an action event. You should use this tag instead of the commandLink tag if you always want the URL—specified by the outputLink tag's value attribute—to open and do not have to perform any processing when the user clicks on the link. The Duke's Bookstore application does not utilize this tag, but here is an example of it:

```
<h:outputLink value="javadocs">
  Documentation for this demo
</h:outputLink>
```

The text in the body of the outputLink tag identifies the text the user clicks to get to the next page.

Displaying a Formatted Message with the outputFormat Tag

The outputFormat tag allows a page author to display concatenated messages as a MessageFormat pattern, as described in the API documentation for java.text.MessageFormat (see http://java.sun.com/j2se/1.5.0/docs/api/java/text/MessageFormat.html). Here is an example of an outputFormat tag from the bookshowcart.jsp page of the Duke's Bookstore application:

```
<h:outputFormat value="#{bundle.CartItemCount}">
  <f:param value="#{cart.numberOfItems}"/>
</h:outputFormat>
```

The value attribute specifies the MessageFormat pattern. The param tag specifies the substitution parameters for the message.

In the example outputFormat tag, the value for the parameter maps to the number of items in the shopping cart. When the message is displayed on the page, the number of items in the cart replaces the {0} in the message corresponding to the CartItemCount key in the bundle resource bundle:

```
Your shopping cart contains " + "{0,choice,0#no items|1#one
item|1< {0} items
```

This message represents three possibilities:

- Your shopping cart contains no items.
- Your shopping cart contains one item.
- Your shopping cart contains {0} items.

The value of the parameter replaces the {0} from the message in the sentence in the third bullet. This is an example of a value-expression-enabled tag attribute accepting a complex EL expression.

An outputFormat tag can include more than one param tag for those messages that have more than one parameter that must be concatenated into the message. If you have more than one parameter for one message, make sure that you put the param tags in the proper order so that the data is inserted in the correct place in the message.

A page author can also hardcode the data to be substituted in the message by using a literal value with the value attribute on the param tag.

Rendering a Password Field with the inputSecret Tag

The inputSecret tag renders an <input type="password"> HTML tag. When the user types a string into this field, a row of asterisks is displayed instead of the text the user types. The Duke's Bookstore application does not include this tag, but here is an example of one:

```
<h:inputSecret redisplay="false"
  value="#{LoginBean.password}" />
```

In this example, the redisplay attribute is set to false. This will prevent the password from being displayed in a query string or in the source file of the resulting HTML page.

Using Command Components for Performing Actions and Navigation

The button and hyperlink components are used to perform and action, such as submitting a form, and for navigating to another page.

Command components in JavaServer Faces applications are represented by the UICommand component, which performs an action when it is activated. The UICommand component supports two renderers: Button and Link as UICommand component renderers.

The commandButton tag represents the combination of a UICommand component and a Button renderer and is rendered as a button. The commandLink tag represents the combination of a UICommand component and a Link renderer and is rendered as a hyperlink.

In addition to the tag attributes listed in Adding UI Components to a Page Using the HTML Component Tags (page 326), the commandButton and commandLink tags can use these attributes:

- action, which is either a logical outcome String or a method expression pointing to a bean method that returns a logical outcome String. In either case, the logical outcome String is used by the default NavigationHandler instance to determine what page to access when the UICommand component is activated.
- actionListener, which is a method expression pointing to a bean method that processes an action event fired by the UICommand component.

See Referencing a Method That Performs Navigation (page 380) for more information on using the action attribute.

See Referencing a Method That Handles an Action Event (page 381) for details on using the actionListener attribute.

Rendering a Button with the commandButton Tag

The bookcashier.jsp page of the Duke's Bookstore application includes a commandButton tag. When a user clicks the button, the data from the current page is processed, and the next page is opened. Here is the commandButton tag from bookcashier.jsp:

```
<h:commandButton value="#{bundle.Submit}"
  action="#{cashier.submit}"/>
```

Clicking the button will cause the submit method of CashierBean to be invoked because the action attribute references the submit method of the CashierBean backing bean. The submit method performs some processing and returns a logical outcome. This is passed to the default NavigationHandler, which matches the outcome against a set of navigation rules defined in the application configuration resource file.

The value attribute of the preceding example commandButton tag references the localized message for the button's label. The bundle part of the expression refers to the ResourceBundle that contains a set of localized messages. The Submit part of the expression is the key that corresponds to the message that is displayed on the button. For more information on referencing localized messages, see Rendering Components for Selecting Multiple Values (page 349). See Referencing a Method That Performs Navigation (page 380) for information on how to use the `action` attribute.

Rendering a Hyperlink with the commandLink Tag

The `commandLink` tag represents an HTML hyperlink and is rendered as an HTML <a> element. The `commandLink` tag is used to submit an action event to the application. See Implementing Action Listeners (page 410) for more information on action events.

A `commandLink` tag must include a nested `outputText` tag, which represents the text the user clicks to generate the event. The following tag is from the `chooselocale.jsp` page from the Duke's Bookstore application.

```
<h:commandLink id="NAmerica" action="bookstore"
  actionListener="#{localeBean.chooseLocaleFromLink}">
  <h:outputText value="#{bundle.English}" />
</h:commandLink>
```

This tag will render the following HTML:

```
<a id="_id3:NAmerica" href="#"
  onclick="document.forms['_id3']['_id3:NAmerica'].
  value='_id3:NAmerica';
  document.forms['_id3'].submit();
  return false;">English</a>
```

Note: Notice that the `commandLink` tag will render JavaScript. If you use this tag, make sure your browser is JavaScript-enabled.

Using Data-Bound Table Components

Data-bound table components display relational data in a tabular format. Figure 10–3 shows an example of this kind of table.

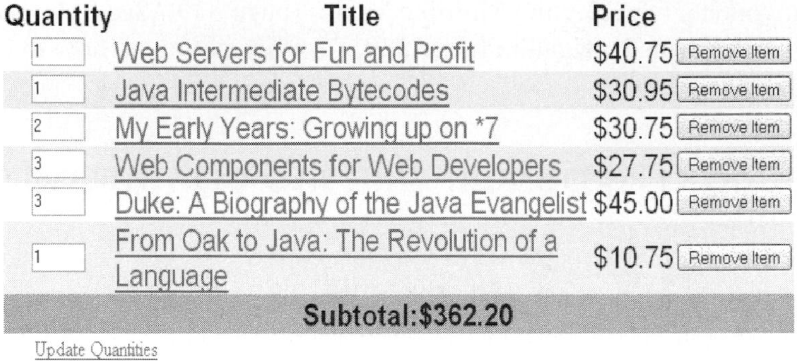

Quantity	Title	Price	
1	Web Servers for Fun and Profit	$40.75	Remove Item
1	Java Intermediate Bytecodes	$30.95	Remove Item
2	My Early Years: Growing up on *7	$30.75	Remove Item
3	Web Components for Web Developers	$27.75	Remove Item
3	Duke: A Biography of the Java Evangelist	$45.00	Remove Item
1	From Oak to Java: The Revolution of a Language	$10.75	Remove Item
	Subtotal:$362.20		

Update Quantities

Figure 10–3 Table on the `bookshowcart.jsp` Page

In a JavaServer Faces application, the `UIData` component supports binding to a collection of data objects. It does the work of iterating over each record in the data source. The standard `Table` renderer displays the data as an HTML table. The `UIColumn` component represents a column of data within the table. Here is a portion of the `dataTable` tag used by the `bookshowcart.jsp` page of the Duke's Bookstore example:

```
<h:dataTable id="items"
  captionClass="list-caption"
  columnClasses="list-column-center, list-column-left,
    list-column-right, list-column-center"
  footerClass="list-footer"
  headerClass="list-header"
  rowClasses="list-row-even, list-row-odd"
  styleClass="list-background"
  summary="#{bundle.ShoppingCart}"
  value="#{cart.items}"
  var="item">
  <h:column headerClass="list-header-left">
    <f:facet name="header">
      <h:outputText value="#{bundle.ItemQuantity}" />
    </f:facet>
    <h:inputText id="quantity" size="4"
      value="#{item.quantity}" >
      ...
    </h:inputText>
    ...
  </h:column>
  <h:column>
    <f:facet name="header">
      <h:outputText value="#{bundle.ItemTitle}"/>
```

```
        </f:facet>
        <h:commandLink action="#{showcart.details}">
            <h:outputText value="#{item.item.title}"/>
        </h:commandLink>
    </h:column>
    ...
    <f:facet name="footer"
        <h:panelGroup>
            <h:outputText value="#{bundle.Subtotal}"/>
            <h:outputText value="#{cart.total}" />
                <f:convertNumber type="currency" />
            </h:outputText>
        </h:panelGroup>
    </f:facet>
    <f:facet name="caption"
        <h:outputText value="#{bundle.Caption}"/>
</h:dataTable>
```

Figure 10–3 shows a data grid that this `dataTable` tag can display.

The example `dataTable` tag displays the books in the shopping cart as well as the quantity of each book in the shopping cart, the prices, and a set of buttons, which the user can click to remove books from the shopping cart.

The `column` tags represent columns of data in a `UIData` component. While the `UIData` component is iterating over the rows of data, it processes the `UIColumn` component associated with each `column` tag for each row in the table.

The `UIData` component shown in the preceding code example iterates through the list of books (`cart.items`) in the shopping cart and displays their titles, authors, and prices. Each time `UIData` iterates through the list of books, it renders one cell in each column.

The `dataTable` and `column` tags use facets to represent parts of the table that are not repeated or updated. These include headers, footers, and captions.

In the preceding example, `column` tags include `facet` tags for representing column headers or footers. The `column` tag allows you to control the styles of these headers and footers by supporting the `headerClass` and `footerClass` attributes. These attributes accept space-separated lists of CSS style classes, which will be applied to the header and footer cells of the corresponding column in the rendered table.

Facets can have only one child, and so a `panelGroup` tag is needed if you want to group more than one component within a `facet`. Because the facet tag representing the footer includes more than one tag, the `panelGroup` is needed to group those tags. Finally, this `dataTable` tag includes a `facet` tag with its `name` attribute set to `caption`, causing a table caption to be rendered below the table.

This table is a classic use case for a `UIData` component because the number of books might not be known to the application developer or the page author at the time the application is developed. The `UIData` component can dynamically adjust the number of rows of the table to accommodate the underlying data.

The `value` attribute of a `dataTable` tag references the data to be included in the table. This data can take the form of

- A list of beans
- An array of beans
- A single bean
- A `javax.faces.model.DataModel`
- A `java.sql.ResultSet`
- A `javax.servlet.jsp.jstl.sql.ResultSet`
- A `javax.sql.RowSet`

All data sources for `UIData` components have a `DataModel` wrapper. Unless you explicitly construct a `DataModel` wrapper, the JavaServer Faces implementation will create one around data of any of the other acceptable types. See Writing Bean Properties (page 390) for more information on how to write properties for use with a `UIData` component.

The `var` attribute specifies a name that is used by the components within the `dataTable` tag as an alias to the data referenced in the `value` attribute of `dataTable`.

In the `dataTable` tag from the `bookshowcart.jsp` page, the `value` attribute points to a list of books. The `var` attribute points to a single book in that list. As the `UIData` component iterates through the list, each reference to `item` points to the current book in the list.

The `UIData` component also has the ability to display only a subset of the underlying data. This is not shown in the preceding example. To display a subset of the data, you use the optional `first` and `rows` attributes.

The `first` attribute specifies the first row to be displayed. The `rows` attribute specifies the number of rows—starting with the first row—to be displayed. For example, if you wanted to display records 2 through 10 of the underlying data, you would set `first` to 2 and `rows` to 9. When you display a subset of the data in your pages, you might want to consider including a link or button that causes subsequent rows to display when clicked. By default, both `first` and `rows` are set to zero, and this causes all the rows of the underlying data to display.

The `dataTable` tag also has a set of optional attributes for adding styles to the table:

- `captionClass`: Defines styles for the table caption
- `columnClasses`: Defines styles for all the columns
- `footerClass`: Defines styles for the footer
- `headerClass`: Defines styles for the header
- `rowClasses`: Defines styles for the rows
- `styleClass`: Defines styles for the entire table

Each of these attributes can specify more than one style. If `columnClasses` or `rowClasses` specifies more than one style, the styles are applied to the columns or rows in the order that the styles are listed in the attribute. For example, if `columnClasses` specifies styles `list-column-center` and `list-column-right` and if there are two columns in the table, the first column will have style `list-column-center`, and the second column will have style `list-column-right`.

If the `style` attribute specifies more styles than there are columns or rows, the remaining styles will be assigned to columns or rows starting from the first column or row. Similarly, if the `style` attribute specifies fewer styles than there are columns or rows, the remaining columns or rows will be assigned styles starting from the first style.

Adding Graphics and Images with the graphicImage Tag

In a JavaServer Faces application, the `UIGraphic` component represents an image. The `graphicImage` tag is used to render a `UIGraphic` component on a page. The Duke's Bookstore application uses a `graphicImage` tag to display the map image on the `chooselocale.jsp` page:

```
<h:graphicImage id="mapImage" url="/template/world.jpg"
  alt="#{bundle.chooseLocale}" usemap="#worldMap" />
```

The `url` attribute specifies the path to the image. It also corresponds to the local value of the `UIGraphic` component so that the URL can be retrieved, possibly from a backing bean. The URL of the example tag begins with a /, which adds the relative context path of the web application to the beginning of the path to the image.

The `alt` attribute specifies the alternative text displayed when the user mouses over the image. In this example, the `alt` attribute refers to a localized message. See Performing Localization (page 402) for details on how to localize your JavaServer Faces application.

The `usemap` attribute refers to the image map defined by the custom component, `MapComponent`, which is on the same page. See Chapter 12 for more information on the image map.

Laying Out Components with the UIPanel Component

In a JavaServer Faces application, you use the `UIPanel` component as a layout container for a set of component components. When you use the renderers from the HTML render kit, `UIPanel` is rendered as an HTML table. This component differs from `UIData` in that `UIData` can dynamically add or delete rows to accommodate the underlying data source, whereas `UIPanel` must have the number of rows predetermined. Table 10–4 lists all the renderers and tags corresponding to the `UIPanel` component.

Table 10–4 `UIPanel` Renderers and Tags

Renderer	Tag	Renderer Attributes	Function
`Grid`	`panelGrid`	`columnClasses`, `columns`, `footerClass`, `headerClass`, `panelClass`, `rowClasses`	Displays a table
`Group`	`panelGroup`	`layout`	Groups a set of components under one parent

The panelGrid tag is used to represent an entire table. The panelGroup tag is used to represent rows in a table. Other UI component tags are used to represent individual cells in the rows.

The panelGrid tag has a set of attributes that specify CSS stylesheet classes: columnClasses, footerClass, headerClass, panelClass, and rowClasses. These stylesheet attributes are optional. The panelGrid tag also has a columns attribute. The columns attribute is required if you want your table to have more than one column because the columns attribute tells the renderer how to group the data in the table.

If the headerClass attribute value is specified, the panelGrid must have a header as its first child. Similarly, if a footerClass attribute value is specified, the panelGrid must have a footer as its last child.

The Duke's Bookstore application includes three panelGrid tags on the bookcashier.jsp page. Here is a portion of one of them:

```
<h:panelGrid columns="3" headerClass="list-header"
  rowClasses="list-row-even, list-row-odd"
  styleClass="list-background"
  title="#{bundle.Checkout}">
  <f:facet name="header">
    <h:outputText value="#{bundle.Checkout}"/>
  </f:facet>
  <h:outputText value="#{bundle.Name}" />
  <h:inputText id="name" size="50"
    value="#{cashier.name}"
    required="true">
    <f:valueChangeListener
      type="listeners.NameChanged" />
  </h:inputText>
  <h:message styleClass="validationMessage" for="name"/>
  <h:outputText value="#{bundle.CCNumber}"/>
  <h:inputText id="ccno" size="19"
    converter="CreditCardConverter" required="true">
    <bookstore:formatValidator
      formatPatterns="9999999999999999|
        9999 9999 9999 9999|9999-9999-9999-9999"/>
  </h:inputText>
  <h:message styleClass="validationMessage"  for="ccno"/>
  ...
</h:panelGrid>
```

This panelGrid tag is rendered to a table that contains components for the customer of the bookstore to input personal information. This panelGrid tag uses stylesheet classes to format the table. The CSS classes are defined in the `stylesheet.css` file in the `<INSTALL>/javaeetutorial5/examples/web/bookstore6/web/` directory. The `list-header` definition is

```
.list-header {
   background-color: #ffffff;
   color: #000000;
   text-align: center;
}
```

Because the `panelGrid` tag specifies a `headerClass`, the `panelGrid` must contain a header. The example `panelGrid` tag uses a `facet` tag for the header. Facets can have only one child, and so a `panelGroup` tag is needed if you want to group more than one component within a `facet`. Because the example `panelGrid` tag has only one cell of data, a `panelGroup` tag is not needed.

The `panelGroup` tag has one attribute, called `layout`, in addition to those listed in UI Component Tag Attributes (page 327). If the `layout` attribute has the value `block` then an HTML `div` element is rendered to enclose the row; otherwise, an HTML `span` element is rendered to enclose the row. If you are specifying styles for the `panelGroup` tag, you should set the `layout` attribute to `block` in order for the styles to be applied to the components within the `panelGroup` tag. This is because styles such as those that set width and height are not applied to inline elements, which is how content enclosed by the `span` element is defined.

A `panelGroup` tag can also be used to encapsulate a nested tree of components so that the tree of components appears as a single component to the parent component.

The data represented by the nested component tags is grouped into rows according to the value of the `columns` attribute of the `panelGrid` tag. The `columns` attribute in the example is set to `"3"`, and therefore the table will have three columns. In which column each component is displayed is determined by the order that the component is listed on the page modulo 3. So if a component is the fifth one in the list of components, that component will be in the 5 modulo 3 column, or column 2.

Rendering Components for Selecting One Value

Another common UI component is one that allows a user to select one value, whether it be the only value available or one of a set of choices. The most common examples of this kind of component are:

- A checkbox, which represents boolean state.
- A set of radio buttons
- A drop-down menu, which displays a scrollable list
- A listbox, which displays an unscrollable list

Figure 10–4 shows examples of these components.

Figure 10–4 Example Select One Components

Displaying a Checkbox Using the selectBooleanCheckbox Tag

The `UISelectBoolean` class defines components that have a `boolean` value. The `selectBooleanCheckbox` tag is the only tag that JavaServer Faces technology provides for representing `boolean` state. The Duke's Bookstore application includes a `selectBooleanCheckbox` tag on the `bookcashier.jsp` page:

```
<h:selectBooleanCheckbox
  id="fanClub"
  rendered="false"
  binding="#{cashier.specialOffer}" />
```

```
<h:outputLabel
  for="fanClub"
  rendered="false"
  binding="#{cashier.specialOfferText}">
  <h:outputText
     id="fanClubLabel"
     value="#{bundle.DukeFanClub}" />
</h:outputLabel>
```

This example tag displays a checkbox to allow users to indicate whether they want to join the Duke Fan Club. The label for the checkbox is rendered by the `outputLabel` tag. The actual text is represented by the nested `outputText` tag. Binding a Component Instance to a Bean Property (page 376) discusses this example in more detail.

Displaying a Menu Using the selectOneMenu Tag

A `UISelectOne` component allows the user to select one value from a set of values. This component can be rendered as a list box, a set of radio buttons, or a menu. This section explains the `selectOneMenu` tag. The `selectOneRadio` and `selectOneListbox` tags are written in a similar way. The `selectOneListbox` tag is similar to the `selectOneMenu` tag except that `selectOneListbox` defines a `size` attribute that determines how many of the items are displayed at once.

The `selectOneMenu` tag represents a component that contains a list of items, from which a user can choose one item. The menu is also commonly known as a drop-down list or a combo box. The following code snippet shows the `selectOneMenu` tag from the `bookcashier.jsp` page of the Duke's Bookstore application. This tag allows the user to select a shipping method:

```
<h:selectOneMenu   id="shippingOption"
  required="true"
  value="#{cashier.shippingOption}">
  <f:selectItem
     itemValue="2"
     itemLabel="#{bundle.QuickShip}"/>
  <f:selectItem
     itemValue="5"
     itemLabel="#{bundle.NormalShip}"/>
  <f:selectItem
     itemValue="7"
     itemLabel="#{bundle.SaverShip}"/>
</h:selectOneMenu>
```

The `value` attribute of the `selectOneMenu` tag maps to the property that holds the currently selected item's value. You are not required to provide a value for the currently selected item. If you don't provide a value, the first item in the list is selected by default.

Like the `selectOneRadio` tag, the `selectOneMenu` tag must contain either a `selectItems` tag or a set of `selectItem` tags for representing the items in the list. The UISelectItem, UISelectItems, and UISelectItemGroup Components (page 350) explains these two tags.

Rendering Components for Selecting Multiple Values

In some cases, you need to allow your users to select multiple values rather than just one value from a list of choices. You can do this using one of the following kinds of components:

- A set of checkboxes
- A drop-down menu
- A listbox

Figure 10–5 shows examples of these components.

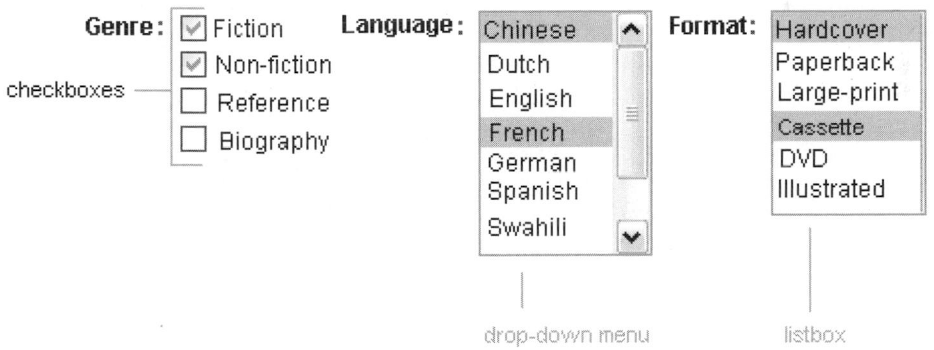

Figure 10–5 Example Select Many Components

The `UISelectMany` class defines a component that allows the user to select zero or more values from a set of values. This component can be rendered as a set of checkboxes, a list box, or a menu. This section explains the `selectManyCheck-`

box tag. The selectManyListbox tag and selectManyMenu tag are written in a similar way.

A list box differs from a menu in that it displays a subset of items in a box, whereas a menu displays only one item at a time when the user is not selecting the menu. The size attribute of the selectManyListbox tag determines the number of items displayed at one time. The list box includes a scrollbar for scrolling through any remaining items in the list.

The selectManyCheckbox tag renders a set of checkboxes, with each checkbox representing one value that can be selected. Duke's Bookstore uses a selectManyCheckbox tag on the bookcashier.jsp page to allow the user to subscribe to one or more newsletters:

```
<h:selectManyCheckbox
  id="newsletters"
  layout="pageDirection"
  value="#{cashier.newsletters}">
  <f:selectItems
    value="#{newsletters}"/>
</h:selectManyCheckbox>
```

The value attribute of the selectManyCheckbox tag identifies the CashierBean backing bean property, newsletters, for the current set of newsletters. This property holds the values of the currently selected items from the set of checkboxes. You are not required to provide a value for the currently selected items. If you don't provide a value, the first item in the list is selected by default.

The layout attribute indicates how the set of checkboxes are arranged on the page. Because layout is set to pageDirection, the checkboxes are arranged vertically. The default is lineDirection, which aligns the checkboxes horizontally.

The selectManyCheckbox tag must also contain a tag or set of tags representing the set of checkboxes. To represent a set of items, you use the selectItems tag. To represent each item individually, you use a selectItem tag for each item. The following subsection explains these two tags in more detail.

The UISelectItem, UISelectItems, and UISelectItemGroup Components

UISelectItem and UISelectItems represent components that can be nested inside a UISelectOne or a UISelectMany component. UISelectItem is associated with a SelectItem instance, which contains the value, label, and description of a single item in the UISelectOne or UISelectMany component.

The UISelectItems instance represents either of the following:

- A set of SelectItem instances, containing the values, labels, and descriptions of the entire list of items
- A set of SelectItemGroup instances, each of which represents a set of SelectItem instances

Figure 10–6 shows an example of a list box constructed with a SelectItems component representing two SelectItemGroup instances, each of which represents two categories of beans. Each category is an array of SelectItem instances.

Figure 10–6 An Example List Box Created Using SelectItemGroup Instances

The selectItem tag represents a UISelectItem component. The selectItems tag represents a UISelectItems component. You can use either a set of selectItem tags or a single selectItems tag within your selectOne or selectMany tag.

The advantages of using the selectItems tag are as follows:

- You can represent the items using different data structures, including Array, Map and Collection. The data structure is composed of SelectItem instances or SelectItemGroup instances.
- You can concatenate different lists together into a single UISelectMany or UISelectOne component and group the lists within the component, as shown in Figure 10–6.
- You can dynamically generate values at runtime.

The advantages of using `selectItem` are as follows:

- The page author can define the items in the list from the page.
- You have less code to write in the bean for the `selectItem` properties.

For more information on writing component properties for the `UISelectItems` components, see Writing Bean Properties (page 390). The rest of this section shows you how to use the `selectItems` and `selectItem` tags.

Using the selectItems Tag

Here is the `selectManyCheckbox` tag from the section Rendering Components for Selecting Multiple Values (page 349):

```
<h:selectManyCheckbox
  id="newsletters"
  layout="pageDirection"
  value="#{cashier.newsletters}">
  <f:selectItems
    value="#{newsletters}"/>
</h:selectManyCheckbox>
```

The `value` attribute of the `selectItems` tag is bound to the `newsletters` managed bean, which is configured in the application configuration resource file. The `newsletters` managed bean is configured as a list:

```
<managed-bean>
  <managed-bean-name>newsletters</managed-bean-name>
  <managed-bean-class>
    java.util.ArrayList</managed-bean-class>
  <managed-bean-scope>application</managed-bean-scope>
  <list-entries>
    <value-class>javax.faces.model.SelectItem</value-class>
    <value>#{newsletter0}</value>
    <value>#{newsletter1}</value>
    <value>#{newsletter2}</value>
    <value>#{newsletter3}</value>
  </list-entries>
</managed-bean>
<managed-bean>
<managed-bean-name>newsletter0</managed-bean-name>
<managed-bean-class>
  javax.faces.model.SelectItem</managed-bean-class>
<managed-bean-scope>none</managed-bean-scope>
<managed-property>
  <property-name>label</property-name>
```

```
    <value>Duke's Quarterly</value>
  </managed-property>
  <managed-property>
    <property-name>value</property-name>
    <value>200</value>
  </managed-property>
  </managed-bean>
  ...
```

As shown in the managed-bean element, the UISelectItems component is a collection of SelectItem instances. See Initializing Array and List Properties (page 466) for more information on configuring collections as beans.

You can also create the list corresponding to a UISelectMany or UISelectOne component programmatically in the backing bean. See Writing Bean Properties (page 390) for information on how to write a backing bean property corresponding to a UISelectMany or UISelectOne component.

The arguments to the SelectItem constructor are:

- An Object representing the value of the item
- A String representing the label that displays in the UISelectMany component on the page
- A String representing the description of the item

UISelectItems Properties (page 397) describes in more detail how to write a backing bean property for a UISelectItems component.

Using the selectItem Tag

The selectItem tag represents a single item in a list of items. Here is the example from Displaying a Menu Using the selectOneMenu Tag (page 348):

```
<h:selectOneMenu
  id="shippingOption" required="true"
  value="#{cashier.shippingOption}">
  <f:selectItem
    itemValue="2"
    itemLabel="#{bundle.QuickShip}"/>
  <f:selectItem
    itemValue="5"
    itemLabel="#{bundle.NormalShip}"/>
```

```
  <f:selectItem
    itemValue="7"
    itemLabel="#{bundle.SaverShip}"/>
</h:selectOneMenu>
```

The `itemValue` attribute represents the default value of the `SelectItem` instance. The `itemLabel` attribute represents the `String` that appears in the drop-down menu component on the page.

The `itemValue` and `itemLabel` attributes are value-binding-enabled, meaning that they can use value-binding expressions to refer to values in external objects. They can also define literal values, as shown in the example `selectOneMenu` tag.

Displaying Error Messages with the message and messages Tags

The `message` and `messages` tags are used to display error messages when conversion or validation fails. The `message` tag displays error messages related to a specific input component, whereas the `messages` tag displays the error messages for the entire page.

Here is an example `message` tag from the `guessNumber` application, discussed in Steps in the Development Process (page 278):

```
<h:inputText id="userNo" value="#{UserNumberBean.userNumber}">
  <f:validateLongRange minimum="0" maximum="10" />
<h:commandButton id="submit"
    action="success" value="Submit" /><p>
<h:message
  style="color: red;
  font-family: 'New Century Schoolbook', serif;
  font-style: oblique;
  text-decoration: overline" id="errors1" for="userNo"/>
```

The `for` attribute refers to the ID of the component that generated the error message. The error message is displayed at the same location that the `message` tag appears in the page. In this case, the error message will appear after the Submit button.

The `style` attribute allows you to specify the style of the text of the message. In the example in this section, the text will be red, New Century Schoolbook, serif font family, and oblique style, and a line will appear over the text. The message and messages tags support many other attributes for defining styles. Please refer to the TLD documentation for more information on these attributes.

Another attribute the `messages` tag supports is the `layout` attribute. Its default value is `list`, which indicates that the messages are displayed in a bulletted list using the HTML `ul` and `li` elements. If you set the attribute to `table`, the messages will be rendered in a table using the HTML `table` element.

The preceding example shows a standard validator is registered on input component. The message tag displays the error message associated with this validator when the validator cannot validate the input component's value. In general, when you register a converter or validator on a component, you are queueing the error messages associated with the converter or validator on the component. The `message` and `messages` tags display the appropriate error messages that are queued on the component when the validators or converters registered on that component fail to convert or validate the component's value.

All the standard error messages that come with the standard converters and validators are listed in section 2.5.4 of the JavaServer Faces specification. An application architect can override these standard messages and supply error messages for custom converters and validators by registering custom error messages with the application via the `message-bundle` element of the application configuration file. Referencing Error Messages (page 358) explains more about error messages.

Using Localized Data

JavaServer Faces applications make use of three different kinds of data that can be localized:

- Static text, such as labels, alternative text, and tool tips
- Error messages, such as those displayed when validation of user input data fails
- Dynamic data, which is data that must be set dynamically by server-side objects, such as by backing beans

This section discusses how to access the first two kinds of data from the page. Performing Localization (page 402) explains how to produce localized error messages as well as how to localize dynamic data. If you are not familiar with the basics of localizing web applications, see Chapter 14.

All data in the Duke's Bookstore application have been localized for Spanish, French, German, and American English. The image map on the first page allows you to select your preferred locale. See Chapter 12 for information on how the image map custom component was created.

All the localized data is stored in resource bundles, which are represented as either `ResourceBundle` classes or text files, usually with the extension `.properties`. For more information about resource bundles, see

```
http://java.sun.com/docs/books/tutorial/i18n/index.html
```

After the application developer has produced a resource bundle, the application architect puts it in the same directory as the application classes. The static text data for the Duke's Bookstore application is stored in a `ResourceBundle` class called `BookstoreMessages`. The error messages are stored in another resource bundle called `ApplicationMessages`. After the resource bundles have been created and before their data can be accessed, they must be made available to the application, as explained in the following section.

Loading a Resource Bundle

To reference error messages or static data from the page, you first need to make available the resource bundle containing the data.

To make available resource bundles that contain static data, you need to do one of two things:

- Register the resource bundle with the application in the configuration file using the `resource-bundle` element, as explained in Registering Custom Localized Static Text (page 471).
- Load the resource bundle into the current view using the `loadBundle` tag.

Here is an example `loadBundle` tag from `bookstore.jsp`:

```
<f:loadBundle var="bundle"
  basename="messages.BookstoreMessages" />
```

The `basename` attribute value specifies the fully-qualified class name of the `ResourceBundle` class, which in this case is located in the `messages` package of the `bookstore` application.

The `var` attribute is an alias to the `ResourceBundle` class. This alias can be used by other tags in the page in order to access the localized messages.

In the case of resource bundles that contain error messages, you need to register the resource bundle with the application in the configuration file using the `message-bundle` element, as explained in Registering Custom Error Messages (page 470). One exception is if you are referencing the error messages from the input component attributes described in Referencing Error Messages (page 358). In that case, you load the resource bundles containing these messages in the same way you load resource bundles containing static text.

Referencing Localized Static Data

To reference static localized data from a resource bundle, you use a value expression from an attribute of the component tag that will display the localized data. You can reference the message from any component tag attribute that is enabled to accept value expressions.

The value expression has the notation `var.message`, in which `var` matches the `var` attribute of the `loadBundle` tag or the `var` element in the configuration file, and `message` matches the key of the message contained in the resource bundle, referred to by the `var` attribute. Here is an example from `bookstore.jsp`:

```
<h:outputText value="#{bundle.Talk}"/>
```

Notice that `bundle` matches the `var` attribute from the `loadBundle` tag and that `Talk` matches the key in the `ResourceBundle`.

Another example is the `graphicImage` tag from `chooselocale.jsp`:

```
<h:graphicImage id="mapImage" url="/template/world.jpg"
  alt="#{bundle.ChooseLocale}"
  usemap="#worldMap" />
```

The `alt` attribute is enabled to accept value expressions. In this case, the `alt` attribute refers to localized text that will be included in the alternative text of the image rendered by this tag.

See Creating Custom Component Classes (page 437) and Enabling Component Properties to Accept Expressions (page 443) for information on how to enable value binding on your custom component's attributes.

Referencing Error Messages

A JavaServer Faces page uses the `message` or `messages` tags to access error messages, as explained in Displaying Error Messages with the message and messages Tags (page 354).

The error messages that these tags access include:

- The standard error messages that accompany the standard converters and validators that ship with the API. See section 2.5.4 of the JavaServer Faces specification, version 1.2, for a complete list of standard error messages.
- Custom error messages contained in resource bundles registered with the application by the application architect using the `message-bundle` element in the configuration file.
- Custom error messages hardcoded in custom converter and validator classes.

When a converter or validator is registered on an input component, the appropriate error message is automatically queued on the component.

A page author can override the error messages queued on a component by using the following attributes of the component's tag:

- `converterMessage`: References the error message to display when the data on the enclosing component can not be converted by the converter registered on this component.
- `requiredMessage`: References the error message to display when no value has been entered into the enclosing component.
- `validatorMessage`: References the error message to display when the data on the enclosing component cannot be validated by the validator registered on this component.

All three attributes are enabled to take literal values and value expressions. If an attribute uses a value expression, this expression references the error message in a resource bundle. This resource bundle must be made available to the application in one of the following ways:

- By the page author using the `loadBundle` tag
- By the application architect using the `resource-bundle` element in the configuration file.

Conversely, the `message-bundle` element must be used to make available to the application those resource bundles containing custom error messages that are queued on the component as a result of a custom converter or validator being registered on the component.

The `bookcashier.jsp` page includes an example of the `requiredMessage` attribute using a value expression to reference an error message:

```
<h:inputText id="ccno" size="19"
  required="true"
  requiredMessage="#{customMessages.ReqMessage}" >
  ...
</h:inputText>
<h:message styleClass="error-message"  for="ccno"/>
```

The value expression that `requiredMessage` is using in this example references the error message with the `ReqMessage` key in the resource bundle, `customMessages`.

This message replaces the corresponding message queued on the component and will display wherever the `message` or `messages` tag is placed on the page.

See Registering Custom Error Messages (page 470) and Registering Custom Localized Static Text (page 471) for information on how to use the `message-bundle` and `resource-bundle` element to register resource bundles that contain error messages.

Using the Standard Converters

The JavaServer Faces implementation provides a set of `Converter` implementations that you can use to convert component data. For more information on the conceptual details of the conversion model, see Conversion Model (page 298).

The standard `Converter` implementations, located in the `javax.faces.convert` package, are as follows:

- `BigDecimalConverter`
- `BigIntegerConverter`
- `BooleanConverter`
- `ByteConverter`
- `CharacterConverter`
- `DateTimeConverter`
- `DoubleConverter`

- FloatConverter
- IntegerConverter
- LongConverter
- NumberConverter
- ShortConverter

Each of these converters has a standard error message associated with them. If you have registered one of these converters onto a component on your page, and the converter is not able to convert the component's value, the converter's error message will display on the page. For example, the error message that displays if BigIntegerConverter fails to convert a value is:

```
{0} must be a number consisting of one or more digits
```

In this case the {0} substitution parameter will be replaced with the name of the input component on which the converter is registered. See section 2.4.5 of the JavaServer Faces specification, version 1.2, for a complete list of error messages.

Two of the standard converters (DateTimeConverter and NumberConverter) have their own tags, which allow you to configure the format of the component data using the tag attributes. Using DateTimeConverter (page 362) discusses using DateTimeConverter. Using NumberConverter (page 364) discusses using NumberConverter. The following section explains how to convert a component's value including how to register the other standard converters with a component.

Converting a Component's Value

To use a particular converter to convert a component's value, you need to register the converter onto the component. You can register any of the standard converters on a component in one of four ways:

- Nest one of the standard converter tags inside the component's tag. These tags are convertDateTime and convertNumber and are described in Using DateTimeConverter (page 362) and Using NumberConverter (page 364), respectively.
- Bind the value of the component to a backing bean property of the same type as the converter.
- Refer to the converter from the component tag's converter attribute.

- Nest a `converter` tag inside of the component tag and use either the `converter` tag's `converterId` attribute or its `binding` attribute to refer to the converter.

As an example of the second approach, if you want a component's data to be converted to an `Integer`, you can simply bind the component's value to a property similar to this:

```
Integer age = 0;
public Integer getAge(){ return age;}
public void setAge(Integer age) {this.age = age;}
```

If the component is not bound to a bean property, you can employ the third technique by using the `converter` attribute on the component tag:

```
<h:inputText
  converter="javax.faces.convert.IntegerConverter" />
```

This example shows the `converter` attribute referring to the fully-qualified class name of the converter. The `converter` attribute can also take the ID of the component. If the converter is a custom converter, the ID is defined in the application configuration resource file (see Application Configuration Resource File, page 458).

The data corresponding to this example `inputText` tag will be converted to a `java.lang.Integer`. Noticc that the `Integer` type is already a supported type of the `NumberConverter`. If you don't need to specify any formatting instructions using the `convertNumber` tag attributes, and if one of the other converters will suffice, you can simply reference that converter using the component tag's `converter` attribute.

Finally, you can nest a `converter` tag within the component tag and use either the converter tag's `converterId` attribute or its `binding` attribute to reference the converter.

The `converterId` attribute must reference the converter's ID. Again, if the converter is a custom converter, the value of `converterID` must match the ID in the application configuration resource file; otherwise it must match the ID as defined in the converter class. Here is an example:

```
<h:inputText value="#{LoginBean.Age}" />
  <f:converter converterId="Integer" />
</h:inputText>
```

Instead of using the converterId attribute, the converter tag can use the binding attribute. The binding attribute must resolve to a bean property that accepts and returns an appropriate Converter instance. See Binding Converters, Listeners, and Validators to Backing Bean Properties (page 378) for more information.

Using DateTimeConverter

You can convert a component's data to a java.util.Date by nesting the convertDateTime tag inside the component tag. The convertDateTime tag has several attributes that allow you to specify the format and type of the data. Table 10–5 lists the attributes.

Here is a simple example of a convertDateTime tag from the bookreceipt.jsp page:

```
<h:outputText id= "shipDate" value="#{cashier.shipDate}">
  <f:convertDateTime dateStyle="full" />
</h:outputText>
```

When binding the DateTime converter to a component, ensure that the backing bean property to which the component is bound is of type java.util.Date. In the case of the preceding example, cashier.shipDate must be of type java.util.Date.

Here is an example of a date and time that the preceding tag can display:

```
Saturday, Feb 22, 2003
```

You can also display the same date and time using this tag:

```
<h:outputText value="#{cashier.shipDate}">
  <f:convertDateTime
    pattern="EEEEEEEE, MMM dd, yyyy" />
</h:outputText>
```

If you want to display the example date in Spanish, you can use the locale attribute:

```
<h:inputText value="#{cashier.shipDate}">
  <f:convertDateTime dateStyle="full"
    locale="Locale.SPAIN"
    timeStyle="long" type="both" />
</h:inputText>
```

This tag would display

```
sabado 23 de septiembre de 2006
```

Please refer to the Customizing Formats lesson of the Java Tutorial at `http://java.sun.com/docs/books/tutorial/i18n/format/simpleDateFormat.html` for more information on how to format the output using the `pattern` attribute of the `convertDateTime` tag..

Table 10–5 `convertDateTime` Tag Attributes

Attribute	Type	Description
`binding`	`DateTimeConverter`	Used to bind a converter to a backing bean property
`dateStyle`	`String`	Defines the format, as specified by `java.text.DateFormat`, of a date or the date part of a `date` string. Applied only if `type` is `date` (or both) and `pattern` is not defined. Valid values: `default`, `short`, `medium`, `long`, and `full`. If no value is specified, `default` is used.
`locale`	`String` or `Locale`	`Locale` whose predefined styles for dates and times are used during formatting or parsing. If not specified, the `Locale` returned by `FacesContext.getLocale` will be used.
`pattern`	`String`	Custom formatting pattern that determines how the date/time string should be formatted and parsed. If this attribute is specified, `dateStyle`, `timeStyle`, and `type` attributes are ignored.
`timeStyle`	`String`	Defines the format, as specified by `java.text.DateFormat`, of a `time` or the time part of a `date` string. Applied only if `type` is time and `pattern` is not defined. Valid values: `default`, `short`, `medium`, `long`, and `full`. If no value is specified, `default` is used.
`timeZone`	`String` or `TimeZone`	Time zone in which to interpret any time information in the `date` string.
`type`	`String`	Specifies whether the string value will contain a `date`, a `time`, or both. Valid values are `date`, `time`, or both. If no value is specified, `date` is used.

Using NumberConverter

You can convert a component's data to a `java.lang.Number` by nesting the `convertNumber` tag inside the component tag. The `convertNumber` tag has several attributes that allow you to specify the format and type of the data. Table 10–6 lists the attributes.

The `bookcashier.jsp` page of Duke's Bookstore uses a `convertNumber` tag to display the total prices of the books in the shopping cart:

```
<h:outputText value="#{cart.total}" >
  <f:convertNumber type="currency"/>
</h:outputText>
```

When binding the `Number` converter to a component, ensure that the backing bean property to which the component is bound is of primitive type or has a type of `java.lang.Number`. In the case of the preceding example, `cart.total` is of type `java.lang.Number`.

Here is an example of a number this tag can display

```
$934
```

This number can also be displayed using this tag:

```
<h:outputText id="cartTotal"
  value="#{cart.Total}" >
  <f:convertNumber pattern="$####" />
</h:outputText>
```

Please refer to the Customizing Formats lesson of the Java Tutorial at
`http://java.sun.com/docs/books/tutorial/i18n/format/decimalFor-`

mat.html for more information on how to format the output using the pattern attribute of the convertNumber tag.

Table 10–6 convertNumber Attributes

Attribute	Type	Description
binding	NumberConverter	Used to bind a converter to a backing bean property
currencyCode	String	ISO4217 currency code, used only when formatting currencies.
currencySymbol	String	Currency symbol, applied only when formatting currencies.
groupingUsed	boolean	Specifies whether formatted output contains grouping separators.
integerOnly	boolean	Specifies whether only the integer part of the value will be parsed.
locale	String or Locale	Locale whose number styles are used to format or parse data.
maxFractionDigits	int	Maximum number of digits formatted in the fractional part of the output.
maxIntegerDigits	int	Maximum number of digits formatted in the integer part of the output.
minFractionDigits	int	Minimum number of digits formatted in the fractional part of the output.
minIntegerDigits	int	Minimum number of digits formatted in the integer part of the output.
pattern	String	Custom formatting pattern that determines how the number string is formatted and parsed.
type	String	Specifies whether the string value is parsed and formatted as a number, currency, or percentage. If not specified, number is used.

Registering Listeners on Components

An application developer can implement listeners as classes or as backing bean methods. If a listener is a backing bean method, the page author references the method from either the component's `valueChangeListener` attribute or its `actionListener` attribute. If the listener is a class, the page author can reference the listener from either a `valueChangeListener` tag or an `actionListener` tag and nest the tag inside the component tag in order to register the listener on the component.

Referencing a Method That Handles an Action Event (page 381) and Referencing a Method That Handles a Value-change Event (page 382) describe how a page author uses the `valueChangeListener` and `actionListener` attributes to reference backing bean methods that handle events.

The Duke's Bookstore application includes a `ValueChangeListener` implementation class but does not use an `ActionListener` implementation class. This section explains how to register the `NameChanged` value-change listener and a hypothetical `LocaleChange` action listener implementation on components. Implementing Value-Change Listeners (page 409) explains how to implement `NameChanged`. Implementing Action Listeners (page 410) explains how to implement the hypothetical `LocaleChange` listener.

Registering a Value-Change Listener on a Component

A page author can register a `ValueChangeListener` implementation on a component that implements `EditableValueHolder` by nesting a `valueChangeListener` tag within the component's tag on the page. The `valueChangeListener` tag supports two attributes:

- `type`: References the fully qualified class name of a `ValueChangeListener` implementation
- `binding`: References an object that implements `ValueChangeListener`

A page author must use one of these attributes to reference the value-change listener. The type attribute accepts a literal or a value expression. The binding attribute only accepts a value expression, which must point to a backing bean property that accepts and returns a `ValueChangeListener` implementation.

Following is the tag corresponding to the name component from the bookcashier.jsp page. It uses the type attribute to reference a value-change listener:

```
<h:inputText  id="name" size="50" value="#{cashier.name}"
  required="true">
  <f:valueChangeListener type="listeners.NameChanged" />
</h:inputText>
```

The type attribute specifies the custom NameChanged listener as the ValueChangeListener implementation to register on the name component.

After this component tag is processed and local values have been validated, its corresponding component instance will queue the ValueChangeEvent associated with the specified ValueChangeListener to the component.

The binding attribute is used to bind a ValueChangeListener implementation to a backing bean property. It works in a similar way to the binding attribute supported by the standard converter tags. Binding Component Values and Instances to External Data Sources (page 371) explains more about binding listeners to backing bean properties.

Registering an Action Listener on a Component

A page author can register an ActionListener implementation on a UICommand component by nesting an actionListener tag within the component's tag on the page. Similarly to the valueChangeListener tag, the actionListener tag supports both the type and binding attributes. A page author must use one of these attributes to reference the action listener.

Duke's Bookstore does not use any ActionListener implementations. Here is one of the commandLink tags on the chooselocale.jsp page, changed to reference an ActionListener implementation rather than a backing bean method:

```
<h:commandLink id="NAmerica" action="bookstore">
   <f:actionListener type="listeners.LocaleChange" />
</h:commandLink>
```

The type attribute of the actionListener tag specifies the fully qualified class name of the ActionListener implementation. Similarly to the valueChangeListener tag, the actionListener tag also supports the binding attribute. Binding Converters, Listeners, and Validators to Backing Bean Properties (page 378) explains more about how to bind listeners to backing bean properties.

When this tag's component is activated, the component's decode method (or its associated Renderer) automatically queues the ActionEvent implementation associated with the specified ActionListener implementation onto the component.

In addition to the actionListener tag that allows you register a custom listener onto a component, the core tag library includes the setPropertyActionListener tag. You use this tag to register a special action listener onto the ActionSource instance associated with a component. When the component is activated, the listener will store the object referenced by the tag's value attribute into the object referenced by the tag's target attribute.

The bookcatalog.jsp page uses setPropertyActionListener with two components: the commandLink component used to link to the bookdetails.jsp page and the commandButton component used to add a book to the cart:

```
<c:forEach items="#{bookDBAO.books}" var="book"
  varStatus="stat">
  <c:set var="book" scope="request" value="${book}"/>
    ...
  <h:commandLink action="#{catalog.details}"
    value="#{book.title}">
    <f:setPropertyActionListener
      target="#{requestScope.book}" value="#{book}"/>
  </h:commandLink>
  ...
  <h:commandButton id="add"
    action="#{catalog.add}" value="#{bundle.CartAdd}">
    <f:setPropertyActionListener
      target="#{requestScope.book}" value="#{book}"/>
  </h:commandButton>
  <c:remove var="book" scope="request"/>
</c:forEach>
```

As shown in the preceding code, the commandLink and commandButton components are within a forEach tag, which iterates over the list of books. The var attribute refers to a single book in the list of books.

The object referenced by the var attribute of a forEach tag is in page scope. However, in this case, you need to put this object into request scope so that when the user activates the commandLink component to go to bookdetails.jsp or activates the commandButton component to go to bookcatalog.jsp, the book data is available to those pages. Therefore, the setPropertyActionListener tag is used to set the current book object into request scope when the commandLink or commandButton component is activated.

In the preceding example, the setPropertyActionListener tag's value attribute references the book object. The setPropertyActionListener tag's target attribute references the value expression requestScope.book, which is where the book object referenced by the value attribute is stored when the commandLink or the commandButton component is activated.

Using the Standard Validators

JavaServer Faces technology provides a set of standard classes and associated tags that page authors and application developers can use to validate a component's data. Table 10–7 lists all the standard validator classes and the tags that allow you to use the validators from the page.

Table 10–7 The Validator Classes

Validator Class	Tag	Function
DoubleRangeValidator	validateDoubleRange	Checks whether the local value of a component is within a certain range. The value must be floating-point or convertible to floating-point.
LengthValidator	validateLength	Checks whether the length of a component's local value is within a certain range. The value must be a java.lang.String.
LongRangeValidator	validateLongRange	Checks whether the local value of a component is within a certain range. The value must be any numeric type or String that can be converted to a long.

All these validator classes implement the Validator interface. Component writers and application developers can also implement this interface to define their own set of constraints for a component's value.

Similarly to the standard converters, each of these validators has one or more standard error messages associated with it. If you have registered one of these validators onto a component on your page, and the validator is not able to validate the component's value, the validator's error message will display on the page. For example, the error message that displays when the component's value exceeds the maximum value allowed by LongRangeValidator is the following:

```
{1}: Validation Error: Value is greater than allowable maximum
of "{0}"
```

In this case the `{1}` substitution parameter is replaced by the component's label or ID, and the `{0}` substitution parameter is replaced with the maximum value allowed by the validator.

See section 2.5.4 of the JavaServer Faces specification for the complete list of error messages. See Displaying Error Messages with the message and messages Tags (page 354) for information on how to display validation error messages on the page when validation fails.

Validating a Component's Value

In order to validate a component's value using a particular validator, you need to register the validator on the component. You have three ways to do this:

- Nest the validator's corresponding tag (shown in Table 10–7) inside the component's tag. Using the LongRangeValidator (page 371) describes how to use the `validateLongRange` tag. You can use the other standard tags in the same way.
- Refer to a method that performs the validation from the component tag's `validator` attribute.
- Nest a `validator` tag inside the component tag and use either the validator tag's `validatorId` attribute or its `binding` attribute to refer to the validator.

See Referencing a Method That Performs Validation (page 382) for more information on using the `validator` attribute.

The `validatorId` attribute works similarly to the converterId attribute of the `converter` tag, as described in Converting a Component's Value (page 360). See Binding Converters, Listeners, and Validators to Backing Bean Properties (page 378) for more information on using the `binding` attribute of the `validator` tag.

Keep in mind that validation can be performed only on components that implement `EditableValueHolder` because these components accept values that can be validated.

Using the LongRangeValidator

The Duke's Bookstore application uses a `validateLongRange` tag on the `quantity` input field of the `bookshowcart.jsp` page:

```
<h:inputText id="quantity" size="4"
  value="#{item.quantity}" >
  <f:validateLongRange minimum="1"/>
</h:inputText>
<h:message for="quantity"/>
```

This tag requires that the user enter a number that is at least 1. The `size` attribute specifies that the number can have no more than four digits. The `validateLongRange` tag also has a `maximum` attribute, with which you can set a maximum value of the input.

The attributes of all the standard validator tags accept value expressions. This means that the attributes can reference backing bean properties rather than specify literal values. For example, the `validateLongRange` tag in the preceding example can reference a backing bean property called `minimum` to get the minimum value acceptable to the validator implementation:

```
<f:validateLongRange minimum="#{ShowCartBean.minimum}" />
```

Binding Component Values and Instances to External Data Sources

As explained in Backing Beans (page 304), a component tag can wire its component's data to a back-end data object by doing one of the following:

- Binding its component's value to a bean property or other external data source
- Binding its component's instance to a bean property

A component tag's `value` attribute uses a value expression to bind the component's value to an external data source, such as a bean property. A component tag's `binding` attribute uses a value expression to bind a component instance to a bean property.

When a component instance is bound to a backing bean property, the property holds the component's local value. Conversely, when a component's value is bound to a backing bean property, the property holds the value stored in the backing bean. This value is updated with the local value during the update model values phase of the life cycle. There are advantages to both of these techniques.

Binding a component instance to a bean property has these advantages:

- The backing bean can programmatically modify component attributes.
- The backing bean can instantiate components rather than let the page author do so.

Binding a component's value to a bean property has these advantages:

- The page author has more control over the component attributes.
- The backing bean has no dependencies on the JavaServer Faces API (such as the UI component classes), allowing for greater separation of the presentation layer from the model layer.
- The JavaServer Faces implementation can perform conversions on the data based on the type of the bean property without the developer needing to apply a converter.

In most situations, you will bind a component's value rather than its instance to a bean property. You'll need to use a component binding only when you need to change one of the component's attributes dynamically. For example, if an application renders a component only under certain conditions, it can set the component's `rendered` property accordingly by accessing the property to which the component is bound.

When referencing the property using the component tag's `value` attribute, you need to use the proper syntax. For example, suppose a backing bean called `MyBean` has this `int` property:

```
int currentOption = null;
int getCurrentOption(){...}
void setCurrentOption(int option){...}
```

The `value` attribute that references this property must have this value-binding expression:

```
#{MyBean.currentOption}
```

In addition to binding a component's value to a bean property, the `value` attribute can specify a literal value or can map the component's data to any primitive (such as `int`), structure (such as an array), or collection (such as a list), independent of a JavaBeans component. Table 10–8 lists some example value-binding expressions that you can use with the `value` attribute.

Table 10–8 Example Value-binding Expressions

Value	Expression
A Boolean	`cart.numberOfItems > 0`
A property initialized from a context `init` parameter	`initParam.quantity`
A bean property	`CashierBean.name`
Value in an array	`books[3]`
Value in a collection	`books["fiction"]`
Property of an object in an array of objects	`books[3].price`

The next two sections explain in more detail how to use the `value` attribute to bind a component's value to a bean property or other external data sources and how to use the `binding` attribute to bind a component instance to a bean property.

Binding a Component Value to a Property

To bind a component's value to a bean property, you specify the name of the bean and the property using the `value` attribute. As explained in Backing Beans (page 304), the value expression of the component tag's `value` attribute must match the corresponding managed bean declaration in the application configuration resource file.

This means that the name of the bean in the value expression must match the `managed-bean-name` element of the managed bean declaration up to the first period (`.`) in the expression. Similarly, the part of the value expression after the period must match the name specified in the corresponding `property-name` element in the application configuration resource file.

For example, consider this managed bean configuration, which configures the `ImageArea` bean corresponding to the North America part of the image map on the `chooselocale.jsp` page of the Duke's Bookstore application:

```
<managed-bean>
  <managed-bean-name> NA </managed-bean-name>
  <managed-bean-class> model.ImageArea </managed-bean-class>
  <managed-bean-scope> application </managed-bean-scope>
  <managed-property>
    <property-name>shape</property-name>
    <value>poly</value>
  </managed-property>
  <managed-property>
    <property-name>alt</property-name>
    <value>NAmerica</value>
  </managed-property>
  ...
</managed-bean>
```

This example configures a bean called `NA`, which has several properties, one of which is called `shape`.

Although the `area` tags on the `chooselocale.jsp` page do not bind to an `ImageArea` property (they bind to the bean itself), to do this, you refer to the property using a value expression from the `value` attribute of the component's tag:

```
<h:outputText value="#{NA.shape}" />
```

Much of the time you will not include definitions for a managed bean's properties when configuring it. You need to define a property and its value only when you want the property to be initialized with a value when the bean is initialized.

If a component tag's `value` attribute must refer to a property that is not initialized in the `managed-bean` configuration, the part of the value-binding expression after the period must match the property name as it is defined in the backing bean.

See Application Configuration Resource File (page 458) for information on how to configure beans in the application configuration resource file.

Writing Bean Properties (page 390) explains in more detail how to write the backing bean properties for each of the component types.

Binding a Component Value to an Implicit Object

One external data source that a `value` attribute can refer to is an implicit object.

The `bookreceipt.jsp` page of the Duke's Bookstore application includes a reference to an implicit object from a parameter substitution tag:

```
<h:outputFormat title="thanks"
value="#{bundle.ThankYouParam}">
  <f:param value="#{sessionScope.name}"/>
</h:outputFormat>
```

This tag gets the name of the customer from the session scope and inserts it into the parameterized message at the key `ThankYouParam` from the resource bundle. For example, if the name of the customer is Gwen Canigetit, this tag will render:

```
Thank you, Gwen Canigetit, for purchasing your books from us.
```

The `name` tag on the `bookcashier.jsp` page has the `NameChanged` listener implementation registered on it. This listener saves the customer's name in the session scope when the `bookcashier.jsp` page is submitted. See Implementing Value-Change Listeners (page 409) for more information on how this listener works. See Registering a Value-Change Listener on a Component (page 366) to learn how the listener is registered on the tag.

Retrieving values from other implicit objects is done in a similar way to the example shown in this section. Table 10–9 lists the implicit objects that a value attribute can refer to. All of the implicit objects except for the scope objects are read-only and therefore should not be used as a value for a UIInput component.

Table 10–9 Implicit Objects

Implicit Object	What It Is
applicationScope	A Map of the application scope attribute values, keyed by attribute name
cookie	A Map of the cookie values for the current request, keyed by cookie name
facesContext	The FacesContext instance for the current request
header	A Map of HTTP header values for the current request, keyed by header name
headerValues	A Map of String arrays containing all the header values for HTTP headers in the current request, keyed by header name
initParam	A Map of the context initialization parameters for this web application
param	A Map of the request parameters for this request, keyed by parameter name
paramValues	A Map of String arrays containing all the parameter values for request parameters in the current request, keyed by parameter name
requestScope	A Map of the request attributes for this request, keyed by attribute name
sessionScope	A Map of the session attributes for this request, keyed by attribute name
view	The root UIComponent in the current component tree stored in the FacesRequest for this request

Binding a Component Instance to a Bean Property

A component instance can be bound to a bean property using a value expression with the binding attribute of the component's tag. You usually bind a component instance rather than its value to a bean property if the bean must dynamically change the component's attributes.

Here are two tags from the bookcashier.jsp page that bind components to bean properties:

```
<h:selectBooleanCheckbox
  id="fanClub"
  rendered="false"
  binding="#{cashier.specialOffer}" />
<h:outputLabel for="fanClub"
  rendered="false"
  binding="#{cashier.specialOfferText}"  >
  <h:outputText id="fanClubLabel"
    value="#{bundle.DukeFanClub}"
  />
</h:outputLabel>
```

The selectBooleanCheckbox tag renders a checkbox and binds the fanClub UISelectBoolean component to the specialOffer property of CashierBean. The outputLabel tag binds the component representing the checkbox's label to the specialOfferText property of CashierBean. If the application's locale is English, the outputLabel tag renders:

```
I'd like to join the Duke Fan Club, free with my purchase of
over $100
```

The rendered attributes of both tags are set to false, which prevents the checkbox and its label from being rendered. If the customer orders more than $100 (or 100 euros) worth of books and clicks the Submit button, the submit method of CashierBean sets both components' rendered properties to true, causing the checkbox and its label to be rendered.

These tags use component bindings rather than value bindings because the backing bean must dynamically set the values of the components' rendered properties.

If the tags were to use value bindings instead of component bindings, the backing bean would not have direct access to the components, and would therefore require additional code to access the components from the FacesContext instance to change the components' rendered properties.

Writing Properties Bound to Component Instances (page 399) explains how to write the bean properties bound to the example components and also discusses how the submit method sets the rendered properties of the components.

Binding Converters, Listeners, and Validators to Backing Bean Properties

As described previously in this chapter, a page author can bind converter, listener, and validator implementations to backing bean properties using the binding attributes of the tags used to register the implementations on components.

This technique has similar advantages to binding component instances to backing bean properties, as described in Binding Component Values and Instances to External Data Sources (page 371). In particular, binding a converter, listener, or validator implementation to a backing bean property yields the following benefits:

- The backing bean can instantiate the implementation instead of allowing the page author to do so.
- The backing bean can programmatically modify the attributes of the implementation. In the case of a custom implementation, the only other way to modify the attributes outside of the implementation class would be to create a custom tag for it and require the page author to set the attribute values from the page.

Whether you are binding a converter, listener, or validator to a backing bean property, the process is the same for any of the implementations:

- Nest the converter, listener, or validator tag within an appropriate component tag.
- Make sure that the backing bean has a property that accepts and returns the converter, listener, or validator implementation class that you want to bind to the property.
- Reference the backing bean property using a value expression from the binding attribute of the converter, listener, or validator tag.

For example, say that you want to bind the standard DateTime converter to a backing bean property because the application developer wants the backing bean to set the formatting pattern of the user's input rather than let the page author do it. First, the page author registers the converter onto the component by nesting the convertDateTime tag within the component tag. Then, the page author references the property with the binding attribute of the convertDateTime tag:

```
<h:inputText value="#{LoginBean.birthDate}">
  <f:convertDateTime binding="#{LoginBean.convertDate}" />
</h:inputText>
```

The convertDate property would look something like this:

```
private DateTimeConverter convertDate;

public DateTimeConverter getConvertDate() {
  ...
  return convertDate;
{

public void setConvertDate(DateTimeConverter convertDate) {
  convertDate.setPattern("EEEEEEEE, MMM dd, yyyy");
  this.convertDate = convertDate;
}
```

See Writing Properties Bound to Converters, Listeners, or Validators (page 401) for more information on writing backing bean properties for converter, listener, and validator implementations.

Referencing a Backing Bean Method

A component tag has a set of attributes for referencing backing bean methods that can perform certain functions for the component associated with the tag. These attributes are summarized in Table 10–10.

Table 10–10 Component Tag Attributes That Reference Backing Bean Methods

Attribute	Function
action	Refers to a backing bean method that performs navigation processing for the component and returns a logical outcome String
actionListener	Refers to a backing bean method that handles action events
validator	Refers to a backing bean method that performs validation on the component's value
valueChangeListener	Refers to a backing bean method that handles value-change events

Only components that implement `ActionSource` can use the `action` and `actionListener` attributes. Only components that implement `EditableValueHolder` can use the `validator` or `valueChangeListener` attributes.

The component tag refers to a backing bean method using a method expression as a value of one of the attributes. The method referenced by an attribute must follow a particular signature, which is defined by the tag attribute's definition in the TLD. For example, the definition of the `validator` attribute of the `inputText` tag in `html_basic.tld` is the following:

```
void validate(javax.faces.context.FacesContext,
  javax.faces.component.UIComponent, java.lang.Object)
```

The following four sections give examples of how to use the four different attributes.

Referencing a Method That Performs Navigation

If your page includes a component (such as a button or hyperlink) that causes the application to navigate to another page when the component is activated, the tag corresponding to this component must include an `action` attribute. This attribute does one of the following

- Specifies a logical outcome `String` that tells the application which page to access next
- References a backing bean method that performs some processing and returns a logical outcome `String`

The `bookcashier.jsp` page of the Duke's Bookstore application has a `commandButton` tag that refers to a backing bean method that calculates the shipping date. If the customer has ordered more than $100 (or 100 euros) worth of books, this method also sets the `rendered` properties of some of the components to `true` and returns `null`; otherwise it returns `receipt`, which causes the `bookreceipt.jsp` page to display. Here is the `commandButton` tag from the `bookcashier.jsp` page:

```
<h:commandButton
  value="#{bundle.Submit}"
  action="#{cashier.submit}" />
```

The `action` attribute uses a method expression to refer to the `submit` method of `CashierBean`. This method will process the event fired by the component corresponding to this tag.

Writing a Method to Handle Navigation (page 419) describes how to implement the `submit` method of `CashierBean`.

The application architect must configure a navigation rule that determines which page to access given the current page and the logical outcome, which is either returned from the backing bean method or specified in the tag. See Configuring Navigation Rules (page 474) for information on how to define navigation rules in the application configuration resource file.

Referencing a Method That Handles an Action Event

If a component on your page generates an action event, and if that event is handled by a backing bean method, you refer to the method by using the component's `actionListener` attribute.

The `chooselocale.jsp` page of the Duke's Bookstore application includes some components that generate action events. One of them is the `NAmerica` component:

```
<h:commandLink id="NAmerica" action="bookstore"
  actionListener="#{localeBean.chooseLocaleFromLink}">
```

The `actionListener` attribute of this component tag references the `chooseLocaleFromLink` method using a method expression. The `chooseLocaleFromLink` method handles the event of a user clicking on the hyperlink rendered by this component.

Writing a Method to Handle an Action Event (page 421) describes how to implement a method that handles an action event.

Referencing a Method That Performs Validation

If the input of one of the components on your page is validated by a backing bean method, you refer to the method from the component's tag using the validator attribute.

The Coffee Break application includes a method that performs validation of the email input component on the checkoutForm.jsp page. Here is the tag corresponding to this component:

```
<h:inputText id="email" value="#{checkoutFormBean.email}"
  size="25" maxlength="125"
  validator="#{checkoutFormBean.validateEmail}"/>
```

This tag references the validate method described in Writing a Method to Perform Validation (page 421) using a method expression.

Referencing a Method That Handles a Value-change Event

If you want a component on your page to generate a value-change event and you want that event to be handled by a backing bean method, you refer to the method using the component's valueChangeListener attribute.

The name component on the bookcashier.jsp page of the Duke's Bookstore application references a ValueChangeListener implementation that handles the event of a user entering a name in the name input field:

```
<h:inputText
  id="name"
  size="50"
  value="#{cashier.name}"
  required="true">
  <f:valueChangeListener type="listeners.NameChanged" />
</h:inputText>
```

For illustration, Writing a Method to Handle a Value-Change Event (page 422) describes how to implement this listener with a backing bean method instead of a listener implementation class. To refer to this backing bean method, the tag uses the `valueChangeListener` attribute:

```
<h:inputText
  id="name"
  size="50"
  value="#{cashier.name}"
  required="true"
  valueChangeListener="#{cashier.processValueChange}" />
</h:inputText>
```

The `valueChangeListener` attribute of this component tag references the `processValueChange` method of `CashierBean` using a method expression. The `processValueChange` method handles the event of a user entering his name in the input field rendered by this component.

Writing a Method to Handle a Value-Change Event (page 422) describes how to implement a method that handles a `ValueChangeEvent`.

Using Custom Objects

As a page author, you might need to use custom converters, validators, or components packaged with the application on your JSP pages.

A custom converter is applied to a component in one of the following ways:

- Reference the converter from the component tag's `converter` attribute
- Nest a `converter` tag inside the component's tag and reference the custom converter from one of the `converter` tag's attributes.

A custom validator is applied to a component in one of the following ways:

- Nest a `validator` tag inside the component's tag and reference the custom validator from the `validator` tag.
- Nest the validator's custom tag (if there is one) inside the component's tag.

To use a custom component, you add the custom tag associated with the component to the page.

As explained in Setting Up a Page (page 321), you must ensure that the TLD that defines any custom tags is packaged in the application if you intend to use the tags in your pages. TLD files are stored in the `WEB-INF` directory or subdirectory of the WAR file or in the `META-INF/` directory or subdirectory of a tag library packaged in a JAR file.

You also need to include a `taglib` declaration in the page so that the page has access to the tags. All custom objects for the Duke's Bookstore application are defined in `bookstore.tld`. Here is the `taglib` declaration that you would include on your page so that you can use the tags from this TLD:

```
<%@ taglib uri="/WEB-INF/bookstore.tld" prefix="bookstore" %>
```

When including the custom tag in the page, you can consult the TLD to determine which attributes the tag supports and how they are used.

The next three sections describe how to use the custom converter, validator, and UI components included in the Duke's Bookstore application.

Using a Custom Converter

As described in the previous section, to apply the data conversion performed by a custom converter to a particular component's value, you must either reference the custom converter from the component tag's `converter` attribute or from a `converter` tag nested inside the component tag.

If you are using the component tag's `converter` attribute, this attribute must reference the `Converter` implementation's identifier or the fully-qualified class name of the converter. The application architect provides this identifier when registering the `Converter` implementation with the application, as explained in Registering a Custom Converter (page 473). Creating a Custom Converter (page 405) explains how a custom converter is implemented.

The identifier for the credit card converter is `CreditCardConverter`. The `CreditCardConverter` instance is registered on the `ccno` component, as shown in this tag from the `bookcashier.jsp` page:

```
<h:inputText id="ccno"
  size="19"
  converter="CreditCardConverter"
  required="true">
  ...
</h:inputText>
```

By setting the `converter` attribute of a component's tag to the converter's identifier or its class name, you cause that component's local value to be automatically converted according to the rules specified in the `Converter` implementation.

Instead of referencing the converter from the component tag's `converter` attribute, you can reference the converter from a `converter` tag nested inside the component's tag. To reference the custom converter using the `converter` tag, you do one of the following:

- Set the `converter` tag's `converterId` attribute to the `Converter` implementation's identifier defined in the application configuration file.
- Bind the `Converter` implementation to a backing bean property using the `converter` tag's `binding` attribute, as described in Binding Converters, Listeners, and Validators to Backing Bean Properties (page 378).

Using a Custom Validator

To register a custom validator on a component, you must do one of the following:

- Nest the validator's custom tag inside the tag of the component whose value you want to be validated.
- Nest the standard `validator` tag within the tag of the component and reference the custom `Validator` implementation from the `validator` tag.

Here is the custom `formatValidator` tag from the `ccno` field on the `bookcashier.jsp` page of the Duke's Bookstore application:

```
<h:inputText id="ccno" size="19"
  ...
  required="true">
  <bookstore:formatValidator
    formatPatterns="9999999999999999|9999 9999 9999 9999|
    9999-9999-9999-9999" />
</h:inputText>
<h:message styleClass="validationMessage"  for="ccno"/>
```

This tag validates the input of the `ccno` field against the patterns defined by the page author in the `formatPatterns` attribute.

You can use the same custom validator for any similar component by simply nesting the custom validator tag within the component tag.

Creating a Custom Validator (page 411) describes how to create the custom validator and its custom tag.

If the application developer who created the custom validator prefers to configure the attributes in the `Validator` implementation rather than allow the page author to configure the attributes from the page, the developer will not create a custom tag for use with the validator.

In this case, the page author must nest the `validator` tag inside the tag of the component whose data needs to be validated. Then the page author needs to do one of the following:

1. Set the `validator` tag's `validatorId` attribute to the ID of the validator that is defined in the application configuration resource file. Registering a Custom Validator (page 472) explains how to configure the validator in the application configuration resource file.
2. Bind the custom `Validator` implementation to a backing bean property using the `validator` tag's `binding` attribute, as described in Binding Converters, Listeners, and Validators to Backing Bean Properties (page 378).

The following tag registers a hypothetical validator on a component using a `validator` tag and references the ID of the validator:

```
<h:inputText id="name" value="#{CustomerBean.name}"
      size="10" ... >
  <f:validator validatorId="customValidator" />
  ...
</h:inputText>
```

Using a Custom Component

In order to use a custom component in a page, you need to declare the tag library that defines the custom tag that renders the custom component, as explained in Using Custom Objects (page 383), and you add the component's tag to the page.

The Duke's Bookstore application includes a custom image map component on the `chooselocale.jsp` page. This component allows you to select the locale for the application by clicking on a region of the image map:

```
...
<h:graphicImage id="mapImage" url="/template/world.jpg"
  alt="#{bundle.chooseLocale}"
  usemap="#worldMap" />
  <bookstore:map id="worldMap" current="NAmericas"
    immediate="true"
    action="bookstore"
    actionListener="#{localeBean.chooseLocaleFromMap}">
    <bookstore:area id="NAmerica" value="#{NA}"
      onmouseover="/template/world_namer.jpg"
      onmouseout="/template/world.jpg"
```

```
      targetImage="mapImage" />
   ...
   <bookstore:area id="France" value="#{fraA}"
      onmouseover="/template/world_france.jpg"
      onmouseout="/template/world.jpg"
      targetImage="mapImage" />
</bookstore:map>
```

The standard `graphicImage` tag associates an image (`world.jpg`) with an image map that is referenced in the `usemap` attribute value.

The custom `map` tag that represents the custom component, `MapComponent`, specifies the image map, and contains a set of `area` tags. Each custom `area` tag represents a custom `AreaComponent` and specifies a region of the image map.

On the page, the `onmouseover` and `onmouseout` attributes specify the image that is displayed when the user performs the actions described by the attributes. The page author defines what these images are. The custom renderer also renders an `onclick` attribute.

In the rendered HTML page, the `onmouseover`, `onmouseout`, and `onclick` attributes define which JavaScript code is executed when these events occur. When the user moves the mouse over a region, the `onmouseover` function associated with the region displays the map with that region highlighted. When the user moves the mouse out of a region, the `onmouseout` function redisplays the original image. When the user clicks a region, the `onclick` function sets the value of a hidden `input` tag to the ID of the selected area and submits the page.

When the custom renderer renders these attributes in HTML, it also renders the JavaScript code. The custom renderer also renders the entire `onclick` attribute rather than let the page author set it.

The custom renderer that renders the `map` tag also renders a hidden `input` component that holds the current area. The server-side objects retrieve the value of the hidden `input` field and set the locale in the `FacesContext` instance according to which region was selected.

Chapter 12 describes the custom tags in more detail and also explains how to create the custom image map components, renderers, and tags.

11

Developing with JavaServer Faces Technology

CHAPTER 10 shows how the page author can bind components to server-side objects by using the component tags and core tags on the JSP page. The application developer's responsibility is to program the server-side objects of a JavaServer Faces application. These objects include backing beans, converters, event handlers, and validators. This chapter uses the Duke's Bookstore application (see The Example JavaServer Faces Application, page 318) to explain all of the application developer's responsibilities, including

- Programming properties and methods of a backing bean
- Localizing an application
- Creating custom converters and validators
- Implementing event listeners
- Writing backing bean methods to perform navigation processing and validation and handle events

Writing Bean Properties

As explained in Backing Beans (page 304), a backing bean property can be bound to one of the following items:

- A component value
- A component instance
- A Converter implementation
- A Listener implementation
- A Validator implementation

These properties follow JavaBeans component conventions (see JavaBeans Components, page 136).

The UI component's tag binds the component's value to a property using its `value` attribute and binds the component's instance to a property using its `binding` attribute, as explained in Binding Component Values and Instances to External Data Sources (page 371). Likewise, all the converter, listener, and validator tags use their `binding` attributes to bind their associated implementations to backing bean properties, as explained in Binding Converters, Listeners, and Validators to Backing Bean Properties (page 378).

To bind a component's value to a backing bean property, the type of the property must match the type of the component's value to which it is bound. For example, if a backing bean property is bound to a `UISelectBoolean` component's value, the property should accept and return a `boolean` value or a `Boolean` wrapper `Object` instance.

To bind a component instance, the property must match the component type. For example, if a backing bean property is bound to a `UISelectBoolean` instance, the property should accept and return `UISelectBoolean`.

Similarly, in order to bind a converter, listener, or validator implementation to a property, the property must accept and return the same type of converter, listener, or validator object. For example, if you are using the `convertDateTime` tag to bind a `DateTime` converter to a property, that property must accept and return a `DateTime` instance.

The rest of this section explains how to write properties that can be bound to component values, to component instances for the component objects described in Adding UI Components to a Page Using the HTML Component Tags (page 326), and to converter, listener, and validator implementations.

Writing Properties Bound to Component Values

To write a backing bean property bound to a component's value, you must know the types that the component's value can be so that you can make the property match the type of the component's value.

Table 11–1 lists all the component classes described in Adding UI Components to a Page Using the HTML Component Tags (page 326) and the acceptable types of their values.

When page authors bind components to properties using the `value` attributes of the component tags, they need to ensure that the corresponding properties match the types of the components' values.

Table 11–1 Acceptable Types of Component Values

Component	Acceptable Types of Component Values
`UIInput`, `UIOutput`, `UISelectItem`, `UISelectOne`	Any of the basic primitive and numeric types or any Java programming language object type for which an appropriate `Converter` implementation is available.
`UIData`	`array` of beans, `List` of beans, single bean, `java.sql.ResultSet`, `javax.servlet.jsp.jstl.sql.Result`, `javax.sql.RowSet`.
`UISelectBoolean`	`boolean` or `Boolean`.
`UISelectItems`	`java.lang.String`, `Collection`, `Array`, `Map`.
`UISelectMany`	`array` or `List`. Elements of the `array` or `List` can be any of the standard types.

UIInput and UIOutput Properties

The following tag binds the name component to the name property of CashierBean.

```
<h:inputText id="name" size="50"
  value="#{cashier.name}"
  required="true">
  <f:valueChangeListener
     type="com.sun.bookstore6.listeners.NameChanged" />
</h:inputText>
```

Here is the bean property bound to the name component:

```
protected String name = null;
public void setName(String name) {
  this.name = name;
}
public String getName() {
  return this.name;
}
```

As Using the Standard Converters (page 359) describes, to convert the value of a UIInput or UIOutput component, you can either apply a converter or create the bean property bound to the component with the desired type. Here is the example tag explained in Using DateTimeConverter (page 362) that displays the date books will be shipped:

```
<h:outputText value="#{cashier.shipDate}">
  <f:convertDateTime dateStyle="full" />
</h:outputText>
```

The application developer must ensure that the property bound to the component represented by this tag has a type of java.util.Date. Here is the shipDate property in CashierBean:

```
protected Date shipDate;
public Date getShipDate() {
  return this.shipDate;
}
public void setShipDate(Date shipDate) {
  this.shipDate = shipDate;
}
```

See Binding Component Values and Instances to External Data Sources (page 371) for more information on applying a `Converter` implementation.

UIData Properties

`UIData` components must be bound to one of the types listed in Table 11–1. The `UIData` component from the `bookshowcart.jsp` page of the Duke's Bookstore example is discussed in the section Using Data-Bound Table Components (page 339). Here is part of the start tag of `dataTable` from that section:

```
<h:dataTable  id="items"
  ...
  value="#{cart.items}"
  var="item" >
```

The value expression points to the `items` property of the `ShoppingCart` bean. The `ShoppingCart` bean maintains a map of `ShoppingCartItem` beans.

The `getItems` method from `ShoppingCart` populates a `List` with `ShoppingCartItem` instances that are saved in the items map from when the customer adds books to the cart:

```
public synchronized List getItems() {
  List results = new ArrayList();
  results.addAll(this.items.values());
  return results;
}
```

All the components contained in the `UIData` component are bound to the properties of the `ShoppingCart` bean that is bound to the entire `UIData` component. For example, here is the `outputText` tag that displays the book title in the table:

```
<h:commandLink action="#{showcart.details}">
  <h:outputText value="#{item.item.title}"/>
</h:commandLink>
```

The book title is actually a hyperlink to the `bookdetails.jsp` page. The `outputText` tag uses the value expression `#{item.item.title}` to bind its `UIOutput` component to the `title` property of the `Book` bean. The first `item` in the expression is the `ShoppingCartItem` instance that the `dataTable` tag is referencing while rendering the current row. The second `item` in the expression refers to the `item` property of `ShoppingCartItem`, which returns a `Book` bean. The `title` part of the expression refers to the `title` property of `Book`. The value of the UIOutput component corresponding to this tag is bound to the title property of the Book bean:

```
private String title = null;

public String getTitle() {
  return this.title;
}
public void setTitle(String title) {
  this.title=title;
}
```

UISelectBoolean Properties

Properties that hold the UISelectBoolean component's data must be of boolean or Boolean type. The example selectBooleanCheckbox tag from the section Rendering Components for Selecting One Value (page 347) binds a component to a property. Here is an example that binds a component value to a property:

```
<h:selectBooleanCheckbox title="#{bundle.receiveEmails}"
  value="#{custFormBean.receiveEmails}" >
</h:selectBooleanCheckbox>
<h:outputText value="#{bundle.receiveEmails}">
```

Here is an example property that can be bound to the component represented by the example tag:

```
protected boolean receiveEmails = false;
   ...
public void setReceiveEmails(boolean receiveEmails) {
   this.receiveEmails = receiveEmails;
}
public boolean getReceiveEmails() {
   return receiveEmails;
}
```

UISelectMany Properties

Because a UISelectMany component allows a user to select one or more items from a list of items, this component must map to a bean property of type List or array. This bean property represents the set of currently selected items from the list of available items.

Here is the example `selectManyCheckbox` tag from Rendering Components for Selecting Multiple Values (page 349):

```
<h:selectManyCheckbox
  id="newsletters"
  layout="pageDirection"
  value="#{cashier.newsletters}">
  <f:selectItems value="#{newsletters}"/>
</h:selectManyCheckbox>
```

Here is a bean property that maps to the `value` of this `selectManyCheckbox` example:

```
protected String newsletters[] = new String[0];

public void setNewsletters(String newsletters[]) {
  this.newsletters = newsletters;
}
public String[] getNewsletters() {
  return this.newsletters;
}
```

As explained in the section Rendering Components for Selecting Multiple Values (page 349), the `UISelectItem` and `UISelectItems` components are used to represent all the values in a `UISelectMany` component. See UISelectItem Properties (page 396) and UISelectItems Properties (page 397) for information on how to write the bean properties for the `UISelectItem` and `UISelectItems` components.

UISelectOne Properties

`UISelectOne` properties accept the same types as `UIInput` and `UIOutput` properties. This is because a `UISelectOne` component represents the single selected item from a set of items. This item can be any of the primitive types and anything else for which you can apply a converter.

Here is the example `selectOneMenu` tag from Displaying a Menu Using the selectOneMenu Tag (page 348):

```
<h:selectOneMenu   id="shippingOption"
  required="true"
  value="#{cashier.shippingOption}">
  <f:selectItem
    itemValue="2"
```

```
      itemLabel="#{bundle.QuickShip}"/>
    <f:selectItem
      itemValue="5"
      itemLabel="#{bundle.NormalShip}"/>
    <f:selectItem
      itemValue="7"
      itemLabel="#{bundle.SaverShip}"/>
</h:selectOneMenu>
```

Here is the property corresponding to this tag:

```
protected String shippingOption = "2";

public void setShippingOption(String shippingOption) {
  this.shippingOption = shippingOption;
}
public String getShippingOption() {
  return this.shippingOption;
}
```

Note that `shippingOption` represents the currently selected item from the list of items in the `UISelectOne` component.

As explained in the section Displaying a Menu Using the selectOneMenu Tag (page 348), the `UISelectItem` and `UISelectItems` components are used to represent all the values in a `UISelectOne` component. See UISelectItem Properties (page 396) and UISelectItems Properties (page 397) for information on how to write the backing bean properties for the `UISelectItem` and `UISelectItems` components.

UISelectItem Properties

A `UISelectItem` component represents one value in a set of values in a `UISelectMany` or `UISelectOne` component. The backing bean property that a `UISelectItem` component is bound to must be of type `SelectItem`. A `SelectItem` object is composed of an `Object` representing the value, along with two `Strings` representing the label and description of the `SelectItem` object.

The Duke's Bookstore application does not use any `UISelectItem` components whose values are bound to backing beans. The example `selectOneMenu` tag from Displaying a Menu Using the selectOneMenu Tag (page 348) contains `selectItem` tags that set the values of the list of items in the page. Here is an example bean property that can set the values for this list in the bean:

```
SelectItem itemOne = null;

SelectItem getItemOne(){
  return itemOne;

}

void setItemOne(SelectItem item) {
  itemOne = item;
}
```

UISelectItems Properties

`UISelectItems` components are children of `UISelectMany` and `UISelectOne` components. Each `UISelectItems` component is composed of either a set of `SelectItem` instances or a set of `SelectItemGroup` instances. As described in Using the selectItems Tag (page 352), a `SelectItemGroup` is composed of a set of `SelectItem` instances. This section describes how to write the properties for `selectItems` tags containing `SelectItem` instances and for `selectItems` tags containing `SelectItemGroup` instances.

Properties for SelectItems Composed of SelectItem Instances

Using the selectItems Tag (page 352) describes how the newsletters list of the Duke's Bookstore application is populated using the application configuration resource file. You can also populate the `SelectItems` with `SelectItem` instances programmatically in the backing bean. This section explains how to do this.

In your backing bean, you create a list that is bound to the `SelectItem` component. Then you define a set of `SelectItem` objects, set their values, and populate the list with the `SelectItem` objects. Here is an example code snippet that shows how to create a `SelectItems` property:

```
import javax.faces.component.SelectItem;
...
protected ArrayList options = null;
protected SelectItem newsletter0 =
  new SelectItem("200", "Duke's Quarterly", "");
...
```

```
//in constructor, populate the list
options.add(newsletter0);
options.add(newsletter1);
options.add(newsletter2);
...
public SelectItem getNewsletter0(){
  return newsletter0;
}

void setNewsletter0(SelectItem firstNL) {
  newsletter0 = firstNL;
}
// Other SelectItem properties

public Collection[] getOptions(){
  return options;
}
public void setOptions(Collection[] options){
  this.options = new ArrayList(options);
}
```

The code first initializes `options` as a list. Each newsletter property is defined with values. Then, each newsletter `SelectItem` is added to the list. Finally, the code includes the obligatory `setOptions` and `getOptions` accessor methods.

Properties for SelectItems Composed of SelectItemGroup Instances

The preceding section explains how to write the bean property for a `SelectItems` component composed of `SelectItem` instances. This section explains how to change the example property from the preceding section so that the `SelectItems` is composed of `SelectItemGroup` instances.

Let's separate the newsletters into two groups: One group includes Duke's newsletters, and the other group includes the *Innovator's Almanac* and *Random Ramblings* newsletters.

In your backing bean, you need a list that contains two `SelectItemGroup` instances. Each `SelectItemGroup` instance contains two `SelectItem` instances, each representing a newsletter:

```
import javax.faces.model.SelectItemGroup;
...
private ArrayList optionsGroup = null;

optionsGroup = new ArrayList(2);
```

```
private static final SelectItem options1[] = {
  new SelectItem("200", "Duke's Quarterly", "");
  new SelectItem("202",
    "Duke's Diet and Exercise Journal", "");
};
private static final SelectItem options2[] = {
  new SelectItem("201", "Innovator's Almanac", "");
  new SelectItem("203", "Random Ramblings", "");
};

SelectItemGroup group1 =
  new SelectItemGroup("Duke's", null, true, options1);
SelectItemGroup group2 =
  new SelectItemGroup("General Interest", null, true,
    options2);

optionsGroup.add(group1);
optionsGroup.add(group2);
...
public Collection getOptionsGroup() {
  return optionsGroup;
}
public void setOptionsGroup(Collection newGroupOptions) {
  optionsGroup = new ArrayList(newGroupOptions);
}
```

The code first initializes `optionsGroup` as a list. The `optionsGroup` list contains two `SelectItemGroup` objects. Each object is initialized with the label of the group appearing in the list or menu; a value; a Boolean indicating whether or not the label is disabled; and an array containing two `SelectItem` instances. Then each `SelectItemGroup` is added to the list. Finally, the code includes the `setOptionsGroup` and `getOptionsGroup` accessor methods so that the tag can access the values. The `selectItems` tag references the `optionsGroup` property to get the `SelectItemGroup` objects for populating the list or menu on the page.

Writing Properties Bound to Component Instances

A property bound to a component instance returns and accepts a component instance rather than a component value. Here are the tags described in Binding a

Component Instance to a Bean Property (page 376) that bind components to backing bean properties:

```
<h:selectBooleanCheckbox
  id="fanClub"
  rendered="false"
  binding="#{cashier.specialOffer}" />
<h:outputLabel for="fanClub"
  rendered="false"
  binding="#{cashier.specialOfferText}"  >
  <h:outputText id="fanClubLabel"
    value="#{bundle.DukeFanClub}" />
</h:outputLabel>
```

As Binding a Component Instance to a Bean Property (page 376) explains, the `selectBooleanCheckbox` tag renders a checkbox and binds the `fanClub` `UISelectBoolean` component to the `specialOffer` property of `CashierBean`. The `outputLabel` tag binds the `fanClubLabel` component (which represents the checkbox's label) to the `specialOfferText` property of `CashierBean`. If the user orders more than $100 (or 100 euros) worth of books and clicks the Submit button, the `submit` method of `CashierBean` sets both components' `rendered` properties to `true`, causing the checkbox and label to display when the page is rerendered.

Because the components corresponding to the example tags are bound to the backing bean properties, these properties must match the components' types. This means that the `specialOfferText` property must be of `UIOutput` type, and the `specialOffer` property must be of `UISelectBoolean` type:

```
UIOutput specialOfferText = null;

public UIOutput getSpecialOfferText() {
  return this.specialOfferText;
}
public void setSpecialOfferText(UIOutput specialOfferText) {
  this.specialOfferText = specialOfferText;
}

UISelectBoolean specialOffer = null;

public UISelectBoolean getSpecialOffer() {
  return this.specialOffer;
}
public void setSpecialOffer(UISelectBoolean specialOffer) {
  this.specialOffer = specialOffer;
}
```

See Backing Beans (page 304) for more general information on component binding.

See Referencing a Method That Performs Navigation (page 380) for information on how to reference a backing bean method that performs navigation when a button is clicked.

See Writing a Method to Handle Navigation (page 419) for more information on writing backing bean methods that handle navigation.

Writing Properties Bound to Converters, Listeners, or Validators

All of the standard converter, listener, and validator tags that are included with JavaServer Faces technology support binding attributes that allow page authors to bind converter, listener, or validator implementations to backing bean properties.

The following example from Binding Converters, Listeners, and Validators to Backing Bean Properties (page 378) shows a standard `convertDateTime` tag using a value expression with its `binding` attribute to bind the `DateTimeConverter` instance to the `convertDate` property of `LoginBean`.:

```
<h:inputText value="#{LoginBean.birthDate}">
  <f:convertDateTime binding="#{LoginBean.convertDate}" />
</h:inputText>
```

The `convertDate` property must therefore accept and return a `DateTimeConverter` object, as shown here:

```
private DateTimeConverter convertDate;

public DateTimeConverter getConvertDate() {
  ...
  return convertDate;
{

public void setConvertDate(DateTimeConverter convertDate) {
  convertDate.setPattern("EEEEEEEE, MMM dd, yyyy");
  this.convertDate = convertDate;
}
```

Because the converter is bound to a backing bean property, the backing bean property is able to modify the attributes of the converter or add new functionality to it. In the case of the preceding example, the property sets the date pattern that the converter will use to parse the user's input into a `Date` object.

The backing bean properties that are bound to validator or listener implementations are written in the same way and have the same general purpose.

Performing Localization

As mentioned in Rendering Components for Selecting Multiple Values (page 349), data and messages in the Duke's Bookstore application have been localized for French, German, Spanish, and American English.

This section explains how to produce the localized error messages as well as how to localize dynamic data and messages.

Rendering Components for Selecting Multiple Values (page 349) describes how page authors access localized data from the page.

If you are not familiar with the basics of localizing web applications, see Chapter 14.

Creating a Resource Bundle

A `ResourceBundle` contains a set of localized messages. To learn how to create a `ResourceBundle`, see

```
http://java.sun.com/docs/books/tutorial/i18n/index.html
```

After you create the `ResourceBundle`, put it in the same directory as your classes. Much of the data for the Duke's Bookstore application is stored in a `ResourceBundle` called `BookstoreMessages`, located in `<INSTALL>/javaeetutorial5/examples/web/bookstore/src/java/com/sun/bookstore/messages/`.

Localizing Dynamic Data

The Duke's Bookstore application has some data that is set dynamically in backing beans. Because of this, the beans must load the localized data themselves; the data can't be loaded from the page.

The `message` method in `AbstractBean` is a general-purpose method that looks up localized data used in the backing beans:

```
protected void message(String clientId, String key) {
   // Look up the requested message text
   String text = null;
   try {
      ResourceBundle bundle =
         ResourceBundle.getBundle("messages.BookstoreMessages",
            context().getViewRoot().getLocale());
      text = bundle.getString(key);
   } catch (Exception e) {
      text = "???" + key + "???";
   }
   // Construct and add a FacesMessage containing it
   context().addMessage(clientId, new FacesMessage(text));
}
```

This method gets the current locale from the `UIViewRoot` instance of the current request and loads the localized data for the messages using the `getBundle` method, passing in the path to the `ResourceBundle` and the current locale.

The other backing beans call this method by using the key to the message that they are trying to retrieve from the resource bundle. Here is a call to the `message` method from `ShowCartBean`:

```
message(null, "Quantities Updated");
```

Localizing Messages

The JavaServer Faces API provides two ways to create messages from a resource bundle:

- You can register the `ResourceBundle` instance with the application configuration resource file and use a message factory pattern to examine the `ResouceBundle` and to generate localized `FacesMessage` instances, which represent single localized messages. The message factory pattern is required to access messages that are registered with the `Application` instance. Instead of writing your own message factory pattern, you can use the one included with the Duke's Bookstore application. It is called `MessageFactory` and is located in `<INSTALL>/javaeetutorial5/examples/web/bookstore6/src/java/com/sun/bookstore6/util/`.

- You can use the `FacesMessage` class to get the localized string directly from the `ResourceBundle` instance.

Registering Custom Error Messages (page 470) includes an example of registering a `ResourceBundle` in the application configuration resource file.

Creating a Message with a Message Factory

To use a message factory to create a message, follow these steps:

1. Register the `ResourceBundle` instance with the application. This is explained in Registering Custom Error Messages (page 470).
2. Create a message factory implementation. You can simply copy the `MessageFactory` class included with the Duke's Bookstore application to your application.
3. Access a message from your application by calling the `getMessage(FacesContext, String, Object)` method of the `MessageFactory` class. The `MessageFactory` class uses the `FacesContext` to access the `Application` instance on which the messages are registered. The `String` argument is the key that corresponds to the message in the `ResourceBundle`. The `Object` instance typically contains the substitution parameters that are embedded in the message. For example, the custom validator described in Implementing the Validator Interface (page 412) will substitute the format pattern for the `{0}` in this error message:

```
Input must match one of the following patterns {0}
```

Implementing the Validator Interface (page 412) gives an example of accessing messages.

Using FacesMessage to Create a Message

Instead of registering messages in the application configuration resource file, you can access the ResourceBundle directly from the code. The validateEmail method from the Coffee Break example does this:

```
...
String message = "";
...
message = CoffeeBreakBean.loadErrorMessage(context,
  CoffeeBreakBean.CB_RESOURCE_BUNDLE_NAME,
    "EMailError");
context.addMessage(toValidate.getClientId(context),
  new FacesMessage(message));
...
```

These lines also call the loadErrorMessage to get the message from the ResourceBundle. Here is the loadErrorMessage method from CoffeeBreakBean:

```
public static String loadErrorMessage(FacesContext context,
  String basename, String key) {
  if ( bundle == null ) {
    try {
      bundle = ResourceBundle.getBundle(basename,
        context.getViewRoot().getLocale());
    } catch (Exception e) {
      return null;
    }
  }
  return bundle.getString(key);
}
```

Creating a Custom Converter

As explained in Conversion Model (page 298), if the standard converters included with JavaServer Faces technology don't perform the data conversion that you need, you can easily create a custom converter to perform this specialized conversion.

All custom converters must implement the Converter interface. This implementation, at a minimum, must define how to convert data both ways between the two views of the data described in Conversion Model (page 298).

This section explains how to implement the `Converter` interface to perform a custom data conversion. To make this implementation available to the application, the application architect registers it with the application, as explained in Registering a Custom Converter (page 473). To use the implementation, the page author must register it on a component, as explained in Registering a Custom Converter (page 473).

The Duke's Bookstore application uses a custom `Converter` implementation, called `CreditCardConverter`, to convert the data entered in the Credit Card Number field on the `bookcashier.jsp` page. It strips blanks and hyphens from the text string and formats it so that a blank space separates every four characters.

To define how the data is converted from the presentation view to the model view, the `Converter` implementation must implement the `getAsObject(FacesContext, UIComponent, String)` method from the `Converter` interface. Here is the implementation of this method from `CreditCardConverter`:

```
public Object getAsObject(FacesContext context,
  UIComponent component, String newValue)
    throws ConverterException {

  String convertedValue = null;
  if ( newValue == null ) {
    return newValue;
  }
  // Since this is only a String to String conversion,
  // this conversion does not throw ConverterException.

  convertedValue = newValue.trim();
  if ( (convertedValue.contains("-")) ||
    (convertedValue.contains(" "))) {
    char[] input = convertedValue.toCharArray();
    StringBuffer buffer = new StringBuffer(input.length);
    for ( int i = 0; i < input.length; ++i ) {
      if ( input[i] == '-' || input[i] == ' '  ) {
        continue;
      } else {
        buffer.append(input[i]);
      }
    }
    convertedValue = buffer.toString();
  }
    return convertedValue;
}
```

During the apply request values phase, when the components' `decode` methods are processed, the JavaServer Faces implementation looks up the component's local value in the request and calls the `getAsObject` method. When calling this method, the JavaServer Faces implementation passes in the current `FacesContext` instance, the component whose data needs conversion, and the local value as a `String`. The method then writes the local value to a character array, trims the hyphens and blanks, adds the rest of the characters to a `String`, and returns the `String`.

To define how the data is converted from the model view to the presentation view, the `Converter` implementation must implement the `getAsString(FacesContext, UIComponent, Object)` method from the `Converter` interface. Here is the implementation of this method from `CreditCardConverter`:

```
public String getAsString(FacesContext context,
  UIComponent component, Object value)
  throws ConverterException {

  String inputVal = null;
  if ( value == null ) {
    return null;
  }
  // value must be of the type that can be cast to a String.
  try {
    inputVal = (String)value;
  } catch (ClassCastException ce) {
    FacesMessage errMsg = MessageFactory.getMessage(
    CONVERSION_ERROR_MESSAGE_ID,
    (new Object[] { value, inputVal }));
    throw new ConverterException(errMsg.getSummary());
  }
  // insert spaces after every four characters for better
  // readability if it doesn't already exist.
  char[] input = inputVal.toCharArray();
  StringBuffer buffer = new StringBuffer(input.length + 3);
  for ( int i = 0; i < input.length; ++i ) {
    if ( (i % 4) == 0 && i != 0) {
      if (input[i] != ' ' || input[i] != '-'){
        buffer.append(" ");
        // if there are any "-"'s convert them to blanks.
      } else if (input[i] == '-') {
        buffer.append(" ");
      }
    }
    buffer.append(input[i]);
```

```
        }
        String convertedValue = buffer.toString();
        return convertedValue;
    }
```

During the render response phase, in which the components' `encode` methods are called, the JavaServer Faces implementation calls the `getAsString` method in order to generate the appropriate output. When the JavaServer Faces implementation calls this method, it passes in the current `FacesContext`, the `UIComponent` whose value needs to be converted, and the bean value to be converted. Because this converter does a `String`-to-`String` conversion, this method can cast the bean value to a `String`.

If the value cannot be converted to a `String`, the method throws an exception, passing the error message from the `ResourceBundle`, which is registered with the application. Registering Custom Error Messages (page 470) explains how to register the error messages with the application. Performing Localization (page 402) explains more about working with localized messages.

If the value can be converted to a `String`, the method reads the `String` to a character array and loops through the array, adding a space after every four characters.

Implementing an Event Listener

As explained in Event and Listener Model (page 300), JavaServer Faces technology supports action events and value-change events.

Action events occur when the user activates a component that implements `ActionSource`. These events are represented by the class `javax.faces.event.ActionEvent`.

Value-change events occur when the user changes the value of a component that implements `EditableValueHolder`. These events are represented by the class `javax.faces.event.ValueChangeEvent`.

One way to handle these events is to implement the appropriate listener classes. Listener classes that handle the action events in an application must implement the interface `javax.faces.event.ActionListener`. Similarly, listeners that handle the value-change events must implement the interface `javax.faces.event.ValueChangeListener`.

This section explains how to implement the two listener classes.

If you need to handle events generated by custom components, you must implement an event handler and manually queue the event on the component as well as implement an event listener. See Handling Events for Custom Components (page 449) for more information.

Note: You need not create an `ActionListener` implementation to handle an event that results solely in navigating to a page and does not perform any other application-specific processing. See Writing a Method to Handle Navigation (page 419) for information on how to manage page navigation.

Implementing Value-Change Listeners

A `ValueChangeListener` implementation must include a `processValueChange(ValueChangeEvent)` method. This method processes the specified value-change event and is invoked by the JavaServer Faces implementation when the value-change event occurs. The `ValueChangeEvent` instance stores the old and the new values of the component that fired the event.

The `NameChanged` listener implementation is registered on the `name` `UIInput` component on the `bookcashier.jsp` page. This listener stores into session scope the name the user entered in the text field corresponding to the `name` component. When the `bookreceipt.jsp` page is loaded, it displays the first name inside the message:

```
"Thank you, {0} for purchasing your books from us."
```

Here is part of the `NameChanged` listener implementation:

```
...
public class NameChanged extends Object implements
  ValueChangeListener {

   public void processValueChange(ValueChangeEvent event)
     throws AbortProcessingException {

     if (null != event.getNewValue()) {
          FacesContext.getCurrentInstance().
           getExternalContext().getSessionMap().
              put("name", event.getNewValue());
     }
  }
}
```

When the user enters the name in the text field, a value-change event is generated, and the processValueChange(ValueChangeEvent) method of the NameChanged listener implementation is invoked. This method first gets the ID of the component that fired the event from the ValueChangeEvent object. Next, it puts the value, along with an attribute name, into the session map of the FacesContext instance.

Registering a Value-Change Listener on a Component (page 366) explains how to register this listener onto a component.

Implementing Action Listeners

An ActionListener implementation must include a processAction(ActionEvent) method. The processAction(ActionEvent) method processes the specified action event. The JavaServer Faces implementation invokes the processAction(ActionEvent) method when the ActionEvent occurs.

The Duke's Bookstore application does not use any ActionListener implementations. Instead, it uses method expressions from actionListener attributes to refer to backing bean methods that handle events. This section explains how to turn one of these methods into an ActionListener implementation.

The chooselocale.jsp page allows the user to select a locale for the application by clicking on one of a set of hyperlinks. When the user clicks one of the hyperlinks, an action event is generated, and the chooseLocaleFromLink(ActionEvent) method of LocaleBean is invoked. Instead of implementing a bean method to handle this event, you can create a listener implementation to handle it. To do this, you do the following:

- Move the chooseLocaleFromLink(ActionEvent) method to a class that implements ActionListener
- Rename the method to processAction(ActionEvent)

The listener implementation would look something like this:

```
...
public class LocaleChangeListener extends Object implements
  ActionListener {

  private HashMap<String, Locale> locales = null;

  public LocaleChangeListener() {
```

```
        locales = new HashMap<String, Locale>(4);
        locales.put("NAmerica", new Locale("en", "US"));
        locales.put("SAmerica", new Locale("es", "MX"));
        locales.put("Germany", new Locale("de", "DE"));
        locales.put("France", new Locale("fr", "FR"));
    }

    public void processAction(ActionEvent event)
        throws AbortProcessingException {

        String current = event.getComponent().getId();
        FacesContext context = FacesContext.getCurrentInstance();
        context.getViewRoot().setLocale((Locale)
        locales.get(current));
    }
}
```

Registering an Action Listener on a Component (page 367) explains how to register this listener onto a component.

Creating a Custom Validator

If the standard validators don't perform the validation checking you need, you can easily create a custom validator to validate user input. As explained in Validation Model (page 301), there are two ways to implement validation code:

- Implement a backing bean method that performs the validation.
- Provide an implementation of the `Validator` interface to perform the validation.

Writing a Method to Perform Validation (page 421) explains how to implement a backing bean method to perform validation. The rest of this section explains how to implement the `Validator` interface.

If you choose to implement the `Validator` interface and you want to allow the page author to configure the validator's attributes from the page, you also must create a custom tag for registering the validator on a component.

If you prefer to configure the attributes in the `Validator` implementation, you can forgo creating a custom tag and instead let the page author register the validator on a component using the `validator` tag, as described in Using a Custom Validator (page 385).

You can also create a backing bean property that accepts and returns the `Validator` implementation you create as described in Writing Properties Bound to Converters, Listeners, or Validators (page 401). The page author can use the `validator` tag's binding attribute to bind the `Validator` implementation to the backing bean property.

Usually, you will want to display an error message when data fails validation. You need to store these error messages in resource bundle, as described in Creating a Resource Bundle (page 402).

After creating the resource bundle, you have two ways to make the messages available to the application. You can queue the error messages onto the `FacesContext` programmatically. Or, you can have the application architect register the error messages using the application configuration resource file, as explained in Registering Custom Error Messages (page 470).

The Duke's Bookstore application uses a general-purpose custom validator (called `FormatValidator`) that validates input data against a format pattern that is specified in the custom validator tag. This validator is used with the Credit Card Number field on the `bookcashier.jsp` page. Here is the custom validator tag:

```
<bookstore:formatValidator
  formatPatterns="9999999999999999|9999 9999 9999 9999|
    9999-9999-9999-9999"/>
```

According to this validator, the data entered in the field must be one of the following:

- A 16-digit number with no spaces
- A 16-digit number with a space between every four digits
- A 16-digit number with hyphens between every four digits

The rest of this section describes how this validator is implemented and how to create a custom tag so that the page author can register the validator on a component.

Implementing the Validator Interface

A `Validator` implementation must contain a constructor, a set of accessor methods for any attributes on the tag, and a `validate` method, which overrides the `validate` method of the `Validator` interface.

The FormatValidator class also defines accessor methods for setting the formatPatterns attribute, which specifies the acceptable format patterns for input into the fields. In addition, the class overrides the validate method of the Validator interface. This method validates the input and also accesses the custom error messages to be displayed when the String is invalid.

The validate method performs the actual validation of the data. It takes the FacesContext instance, the component whose data needs to be validated, and the value that needs to be validated. A validator can validate only data of a component that implements EditableValueHolder.

Here is the validate method from FormatValidator:

```
public void validate(FacesContext context, UIComponent
component, Object toValidate) {

  boolean valid = false;
  String value = null;
  if ((context == null) || (component == null)) {
    throw new NullPointerException();
  }
  if (!(component instanceof UIInput)) {
    return;
  }
  if ( null == formatPatternsList || null == toValidate) {
    return;
  }
  value = toValidate.toString();
  //validate the value against the list of valid patterns.
  Iterator patternIt = formatPatternsList.iterator();
  while (patternIt.hasNext()) {
    valid = isFormatValid(
      ((String)patternIt.next()), value);
    if (valid) {
      break;
    }
  }
  if ( !valid ) {
    FacesMessage errMsg =
      MessageFactory.getMessage(context,
        FORMAT_INVALID_MESSAGE_ID,
          (new Object[] {formatPatterns}));
      throw new ValidatorException(errMsg);
  }
}
```

This method gets the local value of the component and converts it to a `String`. It then iterates over the `formatPatternsList` list, which is the list of acceptable patterns as specified in the `formatPatterns` attribute of the custom validator tag.

While iterating over the list, this method checks the pattern of the component's local value against the patterns in the list. If the pattern of the local value does not match any pattern in the list, this method generates an error message. It then passes the message to the constructor of `ValidatorException`. Eventually the message is queued onto the `FacesContext` instance so that the message is displayed on the page during the render response phase.

The error messages are retrieved from the `Application` instance by `MessageFactory`. An application that creates its own custom messages must provide a class, such as `MessageFactory`, that retrieves the messages from the `Application` instance. When creating your own application, you can simply copy the `MessageFactory` class from the Duke's Bookstore application to your application.

The `getMessage(FacesContext, String, Object)` method of `MessageFactory` takes a `FacesContext`, a static `String` that represents the key into the `Properties` file, and the format pattern as an `Object`. The key corresponds to the static message ID in the `FormatValidator` class:

```
public static final String FORMAT_INVALID_MESSAGE_ID =
  "FormatInvalid";
}
```

When the error message is displayed, the format pattern will be substituted for the `{0}` in the error message, which, in English, is

```
Input must match one of the following patterns {0}
```

JavaServer Faces applications can save the state of validators and components on either the client or the server. Specifying Where State Is Saved (page 487) explains how to configure your application to save state on either the client or the server.

If your JavaServer Faces application saves state on the client (which is the default), you need to make the `Validator` implementation implement `StateHolder` as well as `Validator`. In addition to implementing `StateHolder`, the `Validator` implementation needs to implement the `saveState(FacesContext)` and `restoreState(FacesContext, Object)` methods of `StateHolder`. With these methods, the `Validator` implementation tells the JavaServer Faces implementation which attributes of the `Validator` implementation to save and restore across multiple requests.

To save a set of values, you must implement the `saveState(FacesContext)` method. This method is called during the render response phase, during which the state of the response is saved for processing on subsequent requests. When implementing the `saveState(FacesContext)` method, you need to create an array of objects and add the values of the attributes you want to save to the array. Here is the `saveState(FacesContext)` method from `FormatValidator`:

```
public Object saveState(FacesContext context) {
  Object values[] = new Object[2];
  values[0] = formatPatterns;
  values[1] = formatPatternsList;
  return (values);
}
```

To restore the state saved with the `saveState(FacesContext)` method in preparation for the next postback, the `Validator` implementation implements `restoreState(FacesContext, Object)`. The `restoreState(FacesContext, Object)` method takes the `FacesContext` instance and an `Object` instance, which represents the array that is holding the state for the `Validator` implementation. This method sets the `Validator` implementation's properties to the values saved in the `Object` array. Here is the `restoreState(FacesContext, Object)` method from `FormatValidator`:

```
public void restoreState(FacesContext context, Object state) {
  Object values[] = (Object[]) state;
  formatPatterns = (String) values[0];
  formatPatternsList = (ArrayList) values[1];
}
```

As part of implementing `StateHolder`, the custom `Validator` implementation must also override the `isTransient` and `setTransient(boolean)` methods of `StateHolder`. By default, `transientValue` is false, which means that the `Validator` implementation will have its state information saved and restored. Here are the `isTransient` and `setTransient(boolean)` methods of `FormatValidator`:

```
private boolean transientValue = false;

public boolean isTransient() {
  return (this.transientValue);
}
```

```
public void setTransient(boolean transientValue) {
  this.transientValue = transientValue;
}
```

Saving and Restoring State (page 445) describes how a custom component must implement the `saveState(FacesContext)` and `restoreState(FacesContext, Object)` methods.

Creating a Custom Tag

If you implemented a `Validator` interface rather than implementing a backing bean method that performs the validation, you need to do one of the following:

- Allow the page author to specify the `Validator` implementation to use with the `validator` tag. In this case, the `Validator` implementation must define its own properties. Using a Custom Validator (page 385) explains how to use the `validator` tag.
- Create a custom tag that provides attributes for configuring the properties of the validator from the page. Because the `Validator` implementation from the preceding section does not define its attributes, the application developer must create a custom tag so that the page author can define the format patterns in the tag.

To create a custom tag, you need to do two things:

- Write a tag handler to create and register the `Validator` implementation on the component.
- Write a TLD to define the tag and its attributes.

Using a Custom Validator (page 385) explains how to use the custom validator tag on the page.

Writing the Tag Handler

The tag handler associated with a custom validator tag must extend the `ValidatorELTag` class. This class is the base class for all custom tag handlers that create `Validator` instances and register them on UI components. The `FormatValidatorTag` class registers the `FormatValidator` instance onto the component.

The `FormatValidatorTag` tag handler class does the following:

- Sets the ID of the validator.
- Provides a set of accessor methods for each attribute defined on the tag.
- Implements the `createValidator` method of the `ValidatorELTag` class. This method creates an instance of the validator and sets the range of values accepted by the validator.

The `formatPatterns` attribute of the `fomatValidator` tag supports literals and value expressions. Therefore, the accessor method for this attribute in the `FormatValidatorTag` class must accept and return an instance of `ValueExpression`:

```
protected ValueExpression formatPatterns = null;

public void setFormatPatterns(ValueExpression fmtPatterns){
  formatPatterns = fmtPatterns;
}
```

Finally, the `createValidator` method creates an instance of `FormatValidator`, extracts the value from the `formatPatterns` attribute's value expression and sets the `formatPatterns` property of `FormatValidator` to this value:

the `formatPatterns` property of `FormatValidator` to this value:

```
protected Validator createValidator() throws JspException {

  FacesContext facesContext =
    FacesContext.getCurrentInstance();
  FormatValidator result = null;
  if(validatorID != null){
    result = (FormatValidator) facesContext.getApplication()
      .createValidator(validatorID);
  }
  String patterns = null;
  if (formatPatterns != null) {
    if (!formatPatterns.isLiteralText()) {
      patterns = (String)
      formatPatterns.getValue(facesContext.getELContext());
    } else {
      patterns = formatPatterns.getExpressionString();
    }
```

Writing the Tag Library Descriptor

To define a tag, you declare it in a tag library descriptor (TLD), which is an XML document that describes a tag library. A TLD contains information about a library and each tag contained in it. See Tag Library Descriptors (page 229) for more information about TLDs.

The custom validator tag is defined in `bookstore.tld`, located in `<INSTALL>/javaeetutorial5/examples/web/bookstore6/web/` directory. It contains a tag definition for `formatValidator`:

```
<tag>
  <name>formatValidator</name>
  ...
  <tag-class>
    com.sun.bookstore6.taglib.FormatValidatorTag</tag-class>
  <attribute>
    <name>formatPatterns</name>
    <required>true</required>
    <deferred-value>
      <type>String</type>
    </deferred-value>
  </attribute>
</tag>
```

The `name` element defines the name of the tag as it must be used in the page. The `tag-class` element defines the tag handler class. The attribute elements define each of the tag's attributes. The formatPatterns attribute is the only attribute that the tag supports. The `deferred-value` element indicates that the `formatPatterns` attribute accepts deferred value expressions. The `type` element says that the expression resolves to a property of type `String`.

Writing Backing Bean Methods

Methods of a backing bean perform application-specific functions for components on the page. These functions include performing validation on the component's value, handling action events, handling value-change events, and performing processing associated with navigation.

By using a backing bean to perform these functions, you eliminate the need to implement the `Validator` interface to handle the validation or the `Listener` interface to handle events. Also, by using a backing bean instead of a `Validator` implementation to perform validation, you eliminate the need to create a custom tag for the `Validator` implementation. Creating a Custom Validator (page 411) describes implementing a custom validator. Implementing an Event Listener (page 408) describes implementing a listener class.

In general, it's good practice to include these methods in the same backing bean that defines the properties for the components referencing these methods. The reason is that the methods might need to access the component's data to determine how to handle the event or to perform the validation associated with the component.

This section describes the requirements for writing the backing bean methods.

Writing a Method to Handle Navigation

A backing bean method that handles navigation processing—called an action method—must be a public method that takes no parameters and returns an `Object`, which is the logical outcome that the navigation system uses to determine what page to display next. This method is referenced using the component tag's `action` attribute.

The following action method in `CashierBean` is invoked when a user clicks the Submit button on the `bookcashier.jsp` page. If the user has ordered more than $100 (or 100 euros) worth of books, this method sets the `rendered` properties of the `fanClub` and `specialOffer` components to `true`. This causes them to be displayed on the page the next time the page is rendered.

After setting the components' `rendered` properties to `true`, this method returns the logical outcome `null`. This causes the JavaServer Faces implementation to rerender the `bookcashier.jsp` page without creating a new view of the page. If this method were to return `purchase` (which is the logical outcome to use to advance to `bookcashier.jsp`, as defined by the application configuration resource file), the `bookcashier.jsp` page would rerender without retaining the customer's input. In this case, we want to rerender the page without clearing the data.

If the user does not purchase more than $100 (or 100 euros) worth of books or the `thankYou` component has already been rendered, the method returns `receipt`.

The default `NavigationHandler` provided by the JavaServer Faces implementation matches the logical outcome, as well as the starting page (`bookcashier.jsp`) against the navigation rules in the application configuration resource file to determine which page to access next. In this case, the JavaServer Faces implementation loads the `bookreceipt.jsp` page after this method returns.

```
public String submit() {
  ...
  if(cart().getTotal() > 100.00 &&
     !specialOffer.isRendered())
  {
     specialOfferText.setRendered(true);
     specialOffer.setRendered(true);
     return null;
  } else if (specialOffer.isRendered() &&
     !thankYou.isRendered()){
     thankYou.setRendered(true);
     return null;
  } else {
     clear();
     return ("receipt");
  }
}
```

Typically, an action method will return a `String` outcome, as shown in the previous example. Alternatively, you can define an Enum class that encapsulates all possible outcome strings and then make an action method return an enum constant, which represents a particular String outcome defined by the Enum class. In this case, the value returned by a call to the Enum class's `toString` method must match that specified by the `from-outcome` element in the appropriate navigation rule configuration defined in the application configuration file.

The Duke's Bank example uses an `Enum` class to encapsulate all logical outcomes:

```
public enum Navigation  {
  main, accountHist, accountList, atm, atmAck, transferFunds,
  transferAck, error
}
```

When an action method returns an outcome, it uses the dot notation to reference the outcome from the `Enum` class:

```
public Object submit(){
  ...
  return Navigation.accountHist;
}
```

Referencing a Method That Performs Navigation (page 380) explains how a component tag references this method. Binding a Component Instance to a Bean Property (page 376) discusses how the page author can bind these components to bean properties. Writing Properties Bound to Component Instances (page 399) discusses how to write the bean properties to which the components are bound. Configuring Navigation Rules (page 474) provides more information on configuring navigation rules.

Writing a Method to Handle an Action Event

A backing bean method that handles an action event must be a public method that accepts an action event and returns `void`. This method is referenced using the component tag's `actionListener` attribute. Only components that implement `ActionSource` can refer to this method.

The following backing bean method from `LocaleBean` of the Duke's Bookstore application processes the event of a user clicking one of the hyperlinks on the `chooselocale.jsp` page:

```
public void chooseLocaleFromLink(ActionEvent event) {
  String current = event.getComponent().getId();
  FacesContext context = FacesContext.getCurrentInstance();
  context.getViewRoot().setLocale((Locale)
    locales.get(current));
}
```

This method gets the component that generated the event from the event object. Then it gets the component's ID. The ID indicates a region of the world. The method matches the ID against a `HashMap` object that contains the locales available for the application. Finally, it sets the locale using the selected value from the `HashMap` object.

Referencing a Method That Handles an Action Event (page 381) explains how a component tag references this method.

Writing a Method to Perform Validation

Rather than implement the `Validator` interface to perform validation for a component, you can include a method in a backing bean to take care of validating input for the component.

A backing bean method that performs validation must accept a FacesContext, the component whose data must be validated, and the data to be validated, just as the validate method of the Validator interface does. A component refers to the backing bean method via its validator attribute. Only values of UIInput components or values of components that extend UIInput can be validated.

Here is the backing bean method of CheckoutFormBean from the Coffee Break example:

```
public void validateEmail(FacesContext context,
  UIComponent toValidate, Object value) {

  String message = "";
  String email = (String) value;
  if (email.contains('@')) {
    ((UIInput)toValidate).setValid(false);
    message = CoffeeBreakBean.loadErrorMessage(context,
      CoffeeBreakBean.CB_RESOURCE_BUNDLE_NAME,
      "EMailError");
    context.addMessage(toValidate.getClientId(context),
      new FacesMessage(message));
  }
}
```

The validateEmail method first gets the local value of the component. It then checks whether the @ character is contained in the value. If it isn't, the method sets the component's valid property to false. The method then loads the error message and queues it onto the FacesContext instance, associating the message with the component ID.

See Referencing a Method That Performs Validation (page 382) for information on how a component tag references this method.

Writing a Method to Handle a Value-Change Event

A backing bean that handles a value-change event must be a public method that accepts a value-change event and returns void. This method is referenced using the component's valueChangeListener attribute.

The Duke's Bookstore application does not have any backing bean methods that handle value-change events. It does have a ValueChangeListener implementation, as explained in the Implementing Value-Change Listeners (page 409) section.

For illustration, this section explains how to write a backing bean method that can replace the `ValueChangeListener` implementation.

As explained in Registering a Value-Change Listener on a Component (page 366), the `name` component of the `bookcashier.jsp` page has a `ValueChangeListener` instance registered on it. This `ValueChangeListener` instance handles the event of entering a value in the field corresponding to the component. When the user enters a value, a value-change event is generated, and the `processValueChange(ValueChangeEvent)` method of the `ValueChangeListener` class is invoked.

Instead of implementing `ValueChangeListener`, you can write a backing bean method to handle this event. To do this, you move the `processValueChange(ValueChangeEvent)` method from the `ValueChangeListener` class, called `NameChanged`, to your backing bean.

Here is the backing bean method that processes the event of entering a value in the `name` field on the `bookcashier.jsp` page:

```
public void processValueChange(ValueChangeEvent event)
  throws AbortProcessingException {
  if (null != event.getNewValue()) {
    FacesContext.getCurrentInstance().
      getExternalContext().getSessionMap().
        put("name", event.getNewValue());
  }
}
```

The page author can make this method handle the `ValueChangeEvent` object emitted by a `UIInput` component by referencing this method from the component tag's `valueChangeListener` attribute. See Referencing a Method That Handles a Value-change Event (page 382) for more information.

12

Creating Custom UI Components

JAVASERVER Faces technology offers a basic set of standard, reusable UI components that enable page authors and application developers to quickly and easily construct UIs for web applications. But often an application requires a component that has additional functionality or requires a completely new component. JavaServer Faces technology allows a component writer to extend the standard components to enhance their functionality or create custom components.

In addition to extending the functionality of standard components, a component writer might want to give a page author the ability to change the appearance of the component on the page. Or the component writer might want to render a component to a different client. Enabled by the flexible JavaServer Faces architecture, a component writer can separate the definition of the component behavior from its appearance by delegating the rendering of the component to a separate renderer. In this way, a component writer can define the behavior of a custom component once but create multiple renderers, each of which defines a different way to render the component to a particular kind of client device.

As well as providing a means to easily create custom components and renderers, the JavaServer Faces design also makes it easy to reference them from the page through JSP custom tag library technology.

This chapter uses the image map custom component from the Duke's Bookstore application (see The Example JavaServer Faces Application, page 318) to explain how a component writer can create simple custom components, custom renderers, and associated custom tags, and take care of all the other details associated with using the components and renderers in an application.

If you are creating components intended for use with an IDE such as Sun Java Studio Creator, you might need to take some extra steps—beyond what this chapter details—to get your components to work with the IDE. For information on how to make your custom components work with Sun Java Studio Creator, see the article *Writing Custom Components for Java Studio Creator Part 1: Developing a Component Library*, located at `http://developers.sun.com/prodtech/javatools/jscreator/reference/techart/2/writing_custom_components.html`.

Determining Whether You Need a Custom Component or Renderer

The JavaServer Faces implementation supports a rich set of components and associated renderers, which are enough for most simple applications. This section helps you decide whether you need a custom component or custom renderer or instead can use a standard component and renderer.

When to Use a Custom Component

A component class defines the state and behavior of a UI component. This behavior includes converting the value of a component to the appropriate markup, queuing events on components, performing validation, and other functionality.

You need to create a custom component in these situations:

- You need to add new behavior to a standard component, such as generating an additional type of event.
- You need to aggregate components to create a new component that has its own unique behavior. The new component must be a custom component. One example is a date chooser component consisting of three drop-down lists.
- You need a component that is supported by an HTML client but is not currently implemented by JavaServer Faces technology. The current release does not contain standard components for complex HTML components,

such as frames; however, because of the extensibility of the component architecture, you can use JavaServer Faces technology to create components like these.

- You need to render to a non-HTML client that requires extra components not supported by HTML. Eventually, the standard HTML render kit will provide support for all standard HTML components. However, if you are rendering to a different client, such as a phone, you might need to create custom components to represent the controls uniquely supported by the client. For example, some component architectures for wireless clients include support for tickers and progress bars, which are not available on an HTML client. In this case, you might also need a custom renderer along with the component; or you might need only a custom renderer.

You do not need to create a custom component in these cases:

- You simply need to manipulate data on the component or add application-specific functionality to it. In this situation, you should create a backing bean for this purpose and bind it to the standard component rather than create a custom component. See Backing Beans (page 304) for more information on backing beans.
- You need to convert a component's data to a type not supported by its renderer. See Using the Standard Converters (page 359) for more information about converting a component's data.
- You need to perform validation on the component data. Standard validators and custom validators can be added to a component by using the validator tags from the page. See Using the Standard Validators (page 369) and Creating a Custom Validator (page 411) for more information about validating a component's data.
- You need to register event listeners on components. You can either register event listeners on components using the `valueChangeListener` and `actionListener` tags, or you can point at an event-processing method on a backing bean using the component's `actionListener` or `valueChangeListener` attributes. See Implementing an Event Listener (page 408) and Writing Backing Bean Methods (page 418) for more information.

When to Use a Custom Renderer

If you are creating a custom component, you need to ensure, among other things, that your component class performs these operations:

- **Decoding**: Converting the incoming request parameters to the local value of the component
- **Encoding**: Converting the current local value of the component into the corresponding markup that represents it in the response

The JavaServer Faces specification supports two programming models for handling encoding and decoding:

- **Direct implementation**: The component class itself implements the decoding and encoding.
- **Delegated implementation**: The component class delegates the implementation of encoding and decoding to a separate renderer.

By delegating the operations to the renderer, you have the option of associating your custom component with different renderers so that you can represent the component in different ways on the page. If you don't plan to render a particular component in different ways, it's simpler to let the component class handle the rendering.

If you aren't sure whether you will need the flexibility offered by separate renderers but you want to use the simpler direct-implementation approach, you can actually use both models. Your component class can include some default rendering code, but it can delegate rendering to a renderer if there is one.

Component, Renderer, and Tag Combinations

When you create a custom component, you will usually create a custom renderer to go with it. You will also need a custom tag to associate the component with the renderer and to reference the component from the page.

In rare situations, however, you might use a custom renderer with a standard component rather than a custom component. Or you might use a custom tag without a renderer or a component. This section gives examples of these situations and summarizes what's required for a custom component, renderer, and tag.

You would use a custom renderer without a custom component if you wanted to add some client-side validation on a standard component. You would implement the validation code with a client-side scripting language, such as JavaScript, and then render the JavaScript with the custom renderer. In this situation, you need a custom tag to go with the renderer so that its tag handler can register the renderer on the standard component.

Custom components as well as custom renderers need custom tags associated with them. However, you can have a custom tag without a custom renderer or custom component. For example, suppose that you need to create a custom validator that requires extra attributes on the validator tag. In this case, the custom tag corresponds to a custom validator and not to a custom component or custom renderer. In any case, you still need to associate the custom tag with a server-side object.

Table 12–1 summarizes what you must or can associate with a custom component, custom renderer, or custom tag.

Table 12–1 Requirements for Custom Components, Custom Renderers, and Custom Tags

Custom Item	Must Have	Can Have
Custom component	Custom tag	Custom renderer or standard renderer
Custom renderer	Custom tag	Custom component or standard component
Custom JavaServer Faces tag	Some server-side object, like a component, a custom renderer, or custom validator	Custom component or standard component associated with a custom renderer

Understanding the Image Map Example

Duke's Bookstore includes a custom image map component on the `chooselocale.jsp` page. This image map displays a map of the world. When the user clicks one of a particular set of regions in the map, the application sets the locale on the `UIViewRoot` component of the current `FacesContext` to the language spoken in the selected region. The hotspots of the map are the United States, Spanish-speaking Central and South America, France, and Germany.

Why Use JavaServer Faces Technology to Implement an Image Map?

JavaServer Faces technology is an ideal framework to use for implementing this kind of image map because it can perform the work that must be done on the server without requiring you to create a server-side image map.

In general, client-side image maps are preferred over server-side image maps for several reasons. One reason is that the client-side image map allows the browser to provide immediate feedback when a user positions the mouse over a hotspot. Another reason is that client-side image maps perform better because they don't require round-trips to the server. However, in some situations, your image map might need to access the server to retrieve data or to change the appearance of nonform controls, tasks that a client-side image map cannot do.

Because the image map custom component uses JavaServer Faces technology, it has the best of both styles of image maps: It can handle the parts of the application that need to be performed on the server, while allowing the other parts of the application to be performed on the client side.

Understanding the Rendered HTML

Here is an abbreviated version of the form part of the HTML page that the application needs to render:

```
<form id="_id38" method="post"
  action="/bookstore6/chooselocale.faces" ... >
  ...
  <img id="_id38:mapImage"
    src="/bookstore6/template/world.jpg"
    alt="Choose Your Preferred Locale from the Map"
    usemap="#worldMap" />
    <map name="worldMap">
      <area alt="NAmerica"
        coords="53,109,1,110,2,167,,..."
        shape="poly"
        onmouseout=
          "document.forms[0]['_id_id38:mapImage'].src=
            '/bookstore6/template/world.jpg'"
```

```
            onmouseover=
              "document.forms[0]['_id_id38:mapImage'].src=
                '/bookstore6/template/world_namer.jpg'"
            onclick=
              "document.forms[0]['worldMap_current'].
                value=
                  'NAmerica';document.forms[0].submit()"
        />
        <input type="hidden" name="worldMap_current">
      </map>
      ...
    </form>
```

The img tag associates an image (world.jpg) with the image map referenced in the usemap attribute value.

The map tag specifies the image map and contains a set of area tags.

Each area tag specifies a region of the image map. The onmouseover, onmouseout, and onclick attributes define which JavaScript code is executed when these events occur. When the user moves the mouse over a region, the onmouseover function associated with the region displays the map with that region highlighted. When the user moves the mouse out of a region, the onmouseout function redisplays the original image. If the user clicks on a region, the onclick function sets the value of the input tag to the ID of the selected area and submits the page.

The input tag represents a hidden control that stores the value of the currently selected area between client-server exchanges so that the server-side component classes can retrieve the value.

The server-side objects retrieve the value of worldMap_current and set the locale in the FacesContext instance according to the region that was selected.

Understanding the JSP Page

Here is an abbreviated form of the JSP page that the image map component will use to generate the HTML page shown in the preceding section:

```
<f:view>
  <f:loadBundle basename="messages.BookstoreMessages"
    var="bundle"/>
  <h:form>
    ...
```

```
        <h:graphicImage id="mapImage" url="/template/world.jpg"
          alt="#{bundle.ChooseLocale}"
          usemap="#worldMap" />
        <bookstore:map id="worldMap" current="NAmericas"
          immediate="true" action="bookstore"
          actionListener="#{localeBean.chooseLocaleFromMap}">
          <bookstore:area id="NAmerica" value="#{NA}"
            onmouseover="/template/world_namer.jpg"
            onmouseout="/template/world.jpg"
            targetImage="mapImage" />
          <bookstore:area id="SAmerica" value="#{SA}"
            onmouseover="/template/world_samer.jpg"
            onmouseout="/template/world.jpg"
            targetImage="mapImage" />
          <bookstore:area id="Germany" value="#{gerA}"
            onmouseover="/template/world_germany.jpg"
            onmouseout="/template/world.jpg"
            targetImage="mapImage" />
          <bookstore:area id="France" value="#{fraA}"
            onmouseover="/template/world_france.jpg"
            onmouseout="/template/world.jpg"
            targetImage="mapImage" />
          </bookstore:map>
        ...
      </h:form>
    </f:view>
```

The `alt` attribute of `graphicImage` maps to the localized string `"Choose Your Locale from the Map"`.

The `actionListener` attribute of the `map` tag points at a method in `LocaleBean` that accepts an action event. This method changes the locale according to the area selected from the image map. The way this event is handled is explained more in Handling Events for Custom Components (page 449).

The `action` attribute specifies a logical outcome `String`, which is matched against the navigation rules in the application configuration resource file. For more information on navigation, see the section Configuring Navigation Rules (page 474).

The `immediate` attribute of the `map` tag is set to `true`, which indicates that the default `ActionListener` implementation should execute during the apply request values phase of the request-processing life cycle, instead of waiting for the invoke application phase. Because the request resulting from clicking the map does not require any validation, data conversion, or server-side object updates, it makes sense to skip directly to the invoke application phase.

The `current` attribute of the `map` tag is set to the default area, which is `NAmerica`.

Notice that the `area` tags do not contain any of the JavaScript, coordinate, or shape data that is displayed on the HTML page. The JavaScript is generated by the `AreaRenderer` class. The `onmouseover` and `onmouseout` attribute values indicate the image to be loaded when these events occur. How the JavaScript is generated is explained more in Performing Encoding (page 440).

The coordinate, shape, and alternate text data are obtained through the `value` attribute, whose value refers to an attribute in application scope. The value of this attribute is a bean, which stores the coordinate, shape, and alt data. How these beans are stored in the application scope is explained more in the next section.

Configuring Model Data

In a JavaServer Faces application, data such as the coordinates of a hotspot of an image map is retrieved from the `value` attribute via a bean. However, the shape and coordinates of a hotspot should be defined together because the coordinates are interpreted differently depending on what shape the hotspot is. Because a component's value can be bound only to one property, the `value` attribute cannot refer to both the shape and the coordinates.

To solve this problem, the application encapsulates all of this information in a set of `ImageArea` objects. These objects are initialized into application scope by the managed bean creation facility (see Backing Beans, page 304). Here is part of the managed bean declaration for the `ImageArea` bean corresponding to the South America hotspot:

```
<managed-bean>
  ...
  <managed-bean-name>SA</managed-bean-name>
  <managed-bean-class>
    components.model.ImageArea
  </managed-bean-class>
  <managed-bean-scope>application</managed-bean-scope>
  <managed-property>
    <property-name>shape</property-name>
    <value>poly</value>
  </managed-property>
  <managed-property>
    <property-name>alt</property-name>
    <value>SAmerica</value>
```

```
    </managed-property>
    <managed-property>
        <property-name>coords</property-name>
        <value>89,217,95,100...</value>
    </managed-property>
</managed-bean>
```

For more information on initializing managed beans with the managed bean creation facility, see the section Application Configuration Resource File (page 458).

The `value` attributes of the `area` tags refer to the beans in the application scope, as shown in this `area` tag from `chooselocale.jsp`:

```
<bookstore:area id="NAmerica"
    value="#{NA}"
    onmouseover="/template/world_namer.jpg"
    onmouseout="/template/world.jpg" />
```

To reference the `ImageArea` model object bean values from the component class, you implement a `getValue` method in the component class. This method calls `super.getValue`. The superclass of `AreaComponent`, `UIOutput`, has a `getValue` method that does the work of finding the `ImageArea` object associated with `AreaComponent`. The `AreaRenderer` class, which needs to render the alt, shape, and coords values from the `ImageArea` object, calls the `getValue` method of `AreaComponent` to retrieve the `ImageArea` object.

```
ImageArea iarea = (ImageArea) area.getValue();
```

`ImageArea` is only a simple bean, so you can access the shape, coordinates, and alternative text values by calling the appropriate accessor methods of `ImageArea`. Creating the Renderer Class (page 447) explains how to do this in the `AreaRenderer` class.

Summary of the Application Classes

Table 12–2 summarizes all the classes needed to implement the image map component.

Table 12–2 Image Map Classes

Class	Function
AreaSelectedEvent	The ActionEvent indicating that an AreaComponent from the MapComponent has been selected.
AreaTag	The tag handler that implements the area custom tag.
MapTag	The tag handler that implements the map custom tag.
AreaComponent	The class that defines AreaComponent, which corresponds to the area custom tag.
MapComponent	The class that defines MapComponent, which corresponds to the map custom tag.
AreaRenderer	This Renderer performs the delegated rendering for AreaComponent.
ImageArea	The bean that stores the shape and coordinates of the hotspots.
LocaleBean	The backing bean for the chooselocale.jsp page.

The event and listener classes are located in *<INSTALL>*/javaeetutorial5/examples/web/bookstore6/src/listeners. The tag handlers are located in *<INSTALL>*/javaeetutorial5/examples/web/bookstore6/src/taglib/. The component classes are located in *<INSTALL>*/javaeetutorial5/examples/web/bookstore6/src/components/. The renderer classes are located in *<INSTALL>*/javaeetutorial5/examples/web/bookstore6/src/renderers/. ImageArea is located in *<INSTALL>*/javaeetutorial5/examples/web/bookstore6/src/model/. LocaleBean is located in *<INSTALL>*/javaeetutorial5/examples/web/bookstore6/src/backing/.

Steps for Creating a Custom Component

Before we describe how the image map works, let's summarize the basic steps for creating custom components. You can apply the following steps while developing your own custom component.

1. Create a custom component class that does the following:
   a. Overrides the `getFamily` method to return the component family, which is used to look up renderers that can render the component.
   b. Includes the rendering code or delegates it to a renderer (explained in step 2).
   c. Enables component attributes to accept expressions.
   d. Queues an event on the component if the component generates events.
   e. Saves and restores the component state.
2. Delegate rendering to a renderer if your component does not handle the rendering. To do this:
   a. Create a custom renderer class by extending `javax.faces.render.Renderer`.
   b. Register the renderer to a render kit.
   c. Identify the renderer type in the component tag handler.
3. Register the component.
4. Create an event handler if your component generates events.
5. Write a tag handler class that extends `javax.faces.webapp.UIComponentELTag`. In this class, you need a `getRendererType` method, which returns the type of your custom renderer if you are using one (explained in step 2); a `getComponentType` method, which returns the type of the custom component; and a `setProperties` method, with which you set all the new attributes of your component.
6. Create a tag library descriptor (TLD) that defines the custom tag.

The application architect does the work of registering the custom component and the renderer. See Registering a Custom Converter (page 473) and Registering a Custom Renderer with a Render Kit (page 478) for more information. Using a Custom Component (page 386) discusses how to use the custom component in a JavaServer Faces page.

Creating Custom Component Classes

As explained in When to Use a Custom Component (page 426), a component class defines the state and behavior of a UI component. The state information includes the component's type, identifier, and local value. The behavior defined by the component class includes the following:

- Decoding (converting the request parameter to the component's local value)
- Encoding (converting the local value into the corresponding markup)
- Saving the state of the component
- Updating the bean value with the local value
- Processing validation on the local value
- Queueing events

The `UIComponentBase` class defines the default behavior of a component class. All the classes representing the standard components extend from `UIComponentBase`. These classes add their own behavior definitions, as your custom component class will do.

Your custom component class must either extend `UIComponentBase` directly or extend a class representing one of the standard components. These classes are located in the `javax.faces.component` package and their names begin with `UI`.

If your custom component serves the same purpose as a standard component, you should extend that standard component rather than directly extend `UIComponentBase`. For example, suppose you want to create an editable menu component. It makes sense to have this component extend `UISelectOne` rather than `UIComponentBase` because you can reuse the behavior already defined in `UISelectOne`. The only new functionality you need to define is to make the menu editable.

Whether you decide to have your component extend `UIComponentBase` or a standard component, you might also want your component to implement one or more of these behavioral interfaces:

- `ActionSource`: Indicates that the component can fire an `ActionEvent`.
- `ActionSource2`: Extends `ActionSource` and allows component properties referencing methods that handle action events to use method expressions as defined by the unified EL. This class was introduced in JavaServer Faces Technology 1.2.

- `EditableValueHolder`: Extends `ValueHolder` and specifies additional features for editable components, such as validation and emitting value-change events.
- `NamingContainer`: Mandates that each component rooted at this component have a unique ID.
- `StateHolder`: Denotes that a component has state that must be saved between requests.
- `ValueHolder`: Indicates that the component maintains a local value as well as the option of accessing data in the model tier.

If your component extends `UIComponentBase`, it automatically implements only `StateHolder`. Because all components—directly or indirectly—extend `UIComponentBase`, they all implement `StateHolder`.

If your component extends one of the other standard components, it might also implement other behavioral interfaces in addition to `StateHolder`. If your component extends `UICommand`, it automatically implements `ActionSource2`. If your component extends `UIOutput` or one of the component classes that extend `UIOutput`, it automatically implements `ValueHolder`. If your component extends `UIInput`, it automatically implements `EditableValueHolder` and `ValueHolder`. See the JavaServer Faces API Javadoc to find out what the other component classes implement.

You can also make your component explicitly implement a behavioral interface that it doesn't already by virtue of extending a particular standard component. For example, if you have a component that extends `UIInput` and you want it to fire action events, you must make it explicitly implement `ActionSource2` because a `UIInput` component doesn't automatically implement this interface.

The image map example has two component classes: `AreaComponent` and `MapComponent`. The `MapComponent` class extends `UICommand` and therefore implements `ActionSource2`, which means it can fire action events when a user clicks on the map. The `AreaComponent` class extends the standard component `UIOutput`.

The `MapComponent` class represents the component corresponding to the `map` tag:

```
<bookstore:map id="worldMap" current="NAmericas"
  immediate="true"
  action="bookstore"
  actionListener="#{localeBean.chooseLocaleFromMap}">
```

The AreaComponent class represents the component corresponding to the area tag:

```
<bookstore:area id="NAmerica" value="#{NA}"
  onmouseover="/template/world_namer.jpg"
  onmouseout="/template/world.jpg"
  targetImage="mapImage" />
```

MapComponent has one or more AreaComponent instances as children. Its behavior consists of the following

- Retrieving the value of the currently selected area
- Defining the properties corresponding to the component's values
- Generating an event when the user clicks on the image map
- Queuing the event
- Saving its state
- Rendering the map tag and the input tag

The rendering of the map and input tags is performed by MapRenderer, but MapComponent delegates this rendering to MapRenderer.

AreaComponent is bound to a bean that stores the shape and coordinates of the region of the image map. You'll see how all this data is accessed through the value expression in Creating the Renderer Class (page 447). The behavior of AreaComponent consists of the following

- Retrieving the shape and coordinate data from the bean
- Setting the value of the hidden tag to the id of this component
- Rendering the area tag, including the JavaScript for the onmouseover, onmouseout, and onclick functions

Although these tasks are actually performed by AreaRenderer, AreaComponent must delegate the tasks to AreaRenderer. See Delegating Rendering to a Renderer (page 446) for more information.

The rest of this section describes the tasks that MapComponent performs as well as the encoding and decoding that it delegates to MapRenderer. Handling Events for Custom Components (page 449) details how MapComponent handles events.

Specifying the Component Family

If your custom component class delegates rendering, it needs to override the getFamily method of UIComponent to return the identifier of a *component family*, which is used to refer to a component or set of components that can be rendered by a renderer or set of renderers. The component family is used along with the renderer type to look up renderers that can render the component.

Because MapComponent delegates its rendering, it overrides the getFamily method:

```
public String getFamily() {
  return ("Map");
}
```

The component family identifier, Map, must match that defined by the component-family elements included in the component and renderer configurations in the application configuration resource file. Registering a Custom Renderer with a Render Kit (page 478) explains how to define the component family in the renderer configuration. Registering a Custom Component (page 480) explains how to define the component family in the component configuration.

Performing Encoding

During the render response phase, the JavaServer Faces implementation processes the encoding methods of all components and their associated renderers in the view. The encoding methods convert the current local value of the component into the corresponding markup that represents it in the response.

The UIComponentBase class defines a set of methods for rendering markup: encodeBegin, encodeChildren, and encodeEnd. If the component has child components, you might need to use more than one of these methods to render the component; otherwise, all rendering should be done in encodeEnd.

Because MapComponent is a parent component of AreaComponent, the area tags must be rendered after the beginning map tag and before the ending map tag. To accomplish this, the MapRenderer class renders the beginning map tag in encodeBegin and the rest of the map tag in encodeEnd.

The JavaServer Faces implementation automatically invokes the encodeEnd method of AreaComponent's renderer after it invokes MapRenderer's encodeBegin method and before it invokes MapRenderer's encodeEnd method.

If a component needs to perform the rendering for its children, it does this in the `encodeChildren` method.

Here are the `encodeBegin` and `encodeEnd` methods of `MapRenderer`:

```
public void encodeBegin(FacesContext context,
  UIComponent component) throws IOException {
  if ((context == null)|| (component == null)){
    throw new NullPointerException();
  }
  MapComponent map = (MapComponent) component;
  ResponseWriter writer = context.getResponseWriter();
  writer.startElement("map", map);
  writer.writeAttribute("name", map.getId(),"id");
}

public void encodeEnd(FacesContext context) throws IOException
{
  if ((context == null) || (component == null)){
    throw new NullPointerException();
  }
  MapComponent map = (MapComponent) component;
  ResponseWriter writer = context.getResponseWriter();
  writer.startElement("input", map);
  writer.writeAttribute("type", "hidden", null);
  writer.writeAttribute("name",
    getName(context,map), "clientId");(
  writer.endElement("input");
  writer.endElement("map");
}
```

Notice that `encodeBegin` renders only the beginning `map` tag. The `encodeEnd` method renders the `input` tag and the ending `map` tag.

The encoding methods accept a `UIComponent` argument and a `FacesContext` argument. The `FacesContext` instance contains all the information associated with the current request. The `UIComponent` argument is the component that needs to be rendered.

The rest of the method renders the markup to the `ResponseWriter` instance, which writes out the markup to the current response. This basically involves passing the HTML tag names and attribute names to the `ResponseWriter` instance as strings, retrieving the values of the component attributes, and passing these values to the `ResponseWriter` instance.

The `startElement` method takes a `String` (the name of the tag) and the component to which the tag corresponds (in this case, `map`). (Passing this information to the ResponseWriter instance helps design-time tools know which portions of the generated markup are related to which components.)

After calling startElement, you can call writeAttribute to render the tag's attributes. The writeAttribute method takes the name of the attribute, its value, and the name of a property or attribute of the containing component corresponding to the attribute. The last parameter can be null, and it won't be rendered.

The name attribute value of the map tag is retrieved using the getId method of UIComponent, which returns the component's unique identifier. The name attribute value of the input tag is retrieved using the getName(FacesContext, UIComponent) method of MapRenderer.

If you want your component to perform its own rendering but delegate to a renderer if there is one, include the following lines in the encoding method to check whether there is a renderer associated with this component.

```
if (getRendererType() != null) {
   super.encodeEnd(context);
   return;
}
```

If there is a renderer available, this method invokes the superclass's encodeEnd method, which does the work of finding the renderer. The MapComponent class delegates all rendering to MapRenderer, so it does not need to check for available renderers.

In some custom component classes that extend standard components, you might need to implement other methods in addition to encodeEnd. For example, if you need to retrieve the component's value from the request parameters—to, for example, update a bean's values—you must also implement the decode method.

Performing Decoding

During the apply request values phase, the JavaServer Faces implementation processes the decode methods of all components in the tree. The decode method extracts a component's local value from incoming request parameters and uses a Converter class to convert the value to a type that is acceptable to the component class.

A custom component class or its renderer must implement the `decode` method only if it must retrieve the local value or if it needs to queue events. The `MapRenderer` instance retrieves the local value of the hidden `input` field and sets the `current` attribute to this value by using its `decode` method. The `setCurrent` method of `MapComponent` queues the event by calling `queueEvent`, passing in the `AreaSelectedEvent` instance generated by `MapComponent`.

Here is the `decode` method of `MapRenderer`:

```
public void decode(FacesContext context, UIComponent component)
{
  if ((context == null) || (component == null)) {
    throw new NullPointerException();
  }
  MapComponent map = (MapComponent) component;
  String key = getName(context, map);
  String value = (String)context.getExternalContext().
    getRequestParameterMap().get(key);
  if (value != null)
    map.setCurrent(value);
  }
}
```

The `decode` method first gets the name of the hidden `input` field by calling `getName(FacesContext, UIComponent)`. It then uses that name as the key to the request parameter map to retrieve the current value of the `input` field. This value represents the currently selected area. Finally, it sets the value of the `MapComponent` class's `current` attribute to the value of the `input` field.

Enabling Component Properties to Accept Expressions

Nearly all the attributes of the standard JavaServer Faces tags can accept expressions, whether they are value expressions or a method expressions. It is recommended that you also enable your component attributes to accept expressions because this is what page authors expect, and it gives page authors much more flexibility when authoring their pages.

Creating the Component Tag Handler (page 450) describes how MapTag, the tag handler for the map tag, sets the component's values when processing the tag. It does this by providing the following:

- A method for each attribute that takes either a ValueExpression or MethodExpression object depending on what kind of expression the attribute accepts.
- A setProperties method that stores the ValueExpression or MethodExpression object for each component property so that the component class can retrieve the expression object later.

To retrieve the expression objects that setProperties stored, the component class must implement a method for each property that accesses the appropriate expression object, extracts the value from it and returns the value.

Because MapComponent extends UICommand, the UICommand class already does the work of getting the ValueExpression and MethodExpression instances associated with each of the attributes that it supports.

However, if you have a custom component class that extends UIComponentBase, you will need to implement the methods that get the ValueExpression and MethodExpression instances associated with those attributes that are enabled to accept expressions. For example, if MapComponent extended UIComponentBase instead of UICommand, it would need to include a method that gets the ValueExpression instance for the immediate attribute:

```
public boolean isImmediate() {
  if (this.immediateSet) {
      return (this.immediate);
  }
  ValueExpression ve = getValueExpression("immediate");
  if (ve != null) {
     Boolean value = (Boolean) ve.getValue(
        getFacesContext().getELContext());
     return (value.booleanValue());
  } else {
      return (this.immediate);
  }
}
```

The properties corresponding to the component attributes that accept method expressions must accept and return a MethodExpression object. For example, if MapComponent extended UIComponentBase instead of UICommand, it would need to provide an `action` property that returns and accepts a `MethodExpression` object:

```
public MethodExpression getAction() {
  return (this.action);
}
public void setAction(MethodExpression action) {
  this.action = action;
}
```

Saving and Restoring State

Because component classes implement `StateHolder`, they must implement the `saveState(FacesContext)` and `restoreState(FacesContext, Object)` methods to help the JavaServer Faces implementation save and restore the state of components across multiple requests.

To save a set of values, you must implement the `saveState(FacesContext)` method. This method is called during the render response phase, during which the state of the response is saved for processing on subsequent requests. Here is the method from `MapComponent`:

```
public Object saveState(FacesContext context) {
  Object values[] = new Object[2];
  values[0] = super.saveState(context);
  values[1] = current;
  return (values);
}
```

This method initializes an array, which will hold the saved state. It next saves all of the state associated with `MapComponent`.

A component that implements `StateHolder` must also provide an implementation for `restoreState(FacesContext, Object)`, which restores the state of the component to that saved with the `saveState(FacesContext)` method. The `restoreState(FacesContext, Object)` method is called during the restore view phase, during which the JavaServer Faces implementation checks whether there is any state that was saved during the last render response phase and needs to be restored in preparation for the next postback. Here is the restore-State(FacesContext, Object) method from MapComponent:

```
public void restoreState(FacesContext context, Object state) {
  Object values[] = (Object[]) state;
  super.restoreState(context, values[0]);
  current = (String) values[1];
}
```

This method takes a FacesContext and an Object instance, representing the array that is holding the state for the component. This method sets the component's properties to the values saved in the Object array.

When you implement these methods in your component class, be sure to specify in the deployment descriptor where you want the state to be saved: either client or server. If state is saved on the client, the state of the entire view is rendered to a hidden field on the page.

To specify where state is saved for a particular web application, you need to set the javax.faces.STATE_SAVING_METHOD context parameter to either client or server in your application's deployment descriptor. See Saving and Restoring State (page 445) for more information on specifying where state is saved in the deployment desciptor.

Delegating Rendering to a Renderer

Both MapComponent and AreaComponent delegate all of their rendering to a separate renderer. The section Performing Encoding (page 440) explains how MapRenderer performs the encoding for MapComponent. This section explains in detail the process of delegating rendering to a renderer using AreaRenderer, which performs the rendering for AreaComponent.

To delegate rendering, you perform these tasks:

- Create the Renderer class.
- Register the renderer with a render kit (explained in Registering a Custom Renderer with a Render Kit, page 478).
- Identify the renderer type in the component's tag handler.

Creating the Renderer Class

When delegating rendering to a renderer, you can delegate all encoding and decoding to the renderer, or you can choose to do part of it in the component class. The AreaComponent class delegates encoding to the AreaRenderer class.

To perform the rendering for AreaComponent, AreaRenderer must implement an encodeEnd method. The encodeEnd method of AreaRenderer retrieves the shape, coordinates, and alternative text values stored in the ImageArea bean that is bound to AreaComponent. Suppose that the area tag currently being rendered has a value attribute value of "fraA". The following line from encodeEnd gets the value of the attribute "fraA" from the FacesContext instance.

```
ImageArea ia = (ImageArea)area.getValue();
```

The attribute value is the ImageArea bean instance, which contains the shape, coordinates, and alt values associated with the fraA AreaComponent instance. Configuring Model Data (page 433) describes how the application stores these values.

After retrieving the ImageArea object, it renders the values for shape, coords, and alt by simply calling the associated accessor methods and passing the returned values to the ResponseWriter instance, as shown by these lines of code, which write out the shape and coordinates:

```
writer.startElement("area", area);
writer.writeAttribute("alt", iarea.getAlt(), "alt");
writer.writeAttribute("coords", iarea.getCoords(), "coords");
writer.writeAttribute("shape", iarea.getShape(), "shape");
```

The encodeEnd method also renders the JavaScript for the onmouseout, onmouseover, and onclick attributes. The page author need only provide the path to the images that are to be loaded during an onmouseover or onmouseout action:

```
<bookstore:area id="France" value="#{fraA}"
  onmouseover="/template/world_france.jpg"
  onmouseout="/template/world.jpg" targetImage="mapImage" />
```

The AreaRenderer class takes care of generating the JavaScript for these actions, as shown in the following code from encodeEnd. The JavaScript that

AreaRenderer generates for the onclick action sets the value of the hidden field to the value of the current area's component ID and submits the page.

```
sb = new StringBuffer("document.forms[0]['").
  append(targetImageId).append("'].src='");
sb.append(getURI(context,
  (String) area.getAttributes().get("onmouseout")));
sb.append("'");
writer.writeAttribute("onmouseout", sb.toString(),
  "onmouseout");
sb = new StringBuffer("document.forms[0]['").
  append(targetImageId).append("'].src='");
sb.append(getURI(context,
  (String) area.getAttributes().get("onmouseover")));
sb.append("'");
writer.writeAttribute("onmouseover", sb.toString(),
  "onmouseover");
sb = new StringBuffer("document.forms[0]['");
sb.append(getName(context, area));
sb.append("'].value='");
sb.append(iarea.getAlt());
sb.append("'; document.forms[0].submit()");
writer.writeAttribute("onclick", sb.toString(), "value");
writer.endElement("area");
```

By submitting the page, this code causes the JavaServer Faces life cycle to return back to the restore view phase. This phase saves any state information—including the value of the hidden field—so that a new request component tree is constructed. This value is retrieved by the decode method of the MapComponent class. This decode method is called by the JavaServer Faces implementation during the apply request values phase, which follows the restore view phase.

In addition to the encodeEnd method, AreaRenderer contains an empty constructor. This is used to create an instance of AreaRenderer so that it can be added to the render kit.

Identifying the Renderer Type

During the render response phase, the JavaServer Faces implementation calls the getRendererType method of the component's tag handler to determine which renderer to invoke, if there is one.

The getRendererType method of AreaTag must return the type associated with AreaRenderer. You identify this type when you register AreaRenderer with the render kit, as described in Registering a Custom Renderer with a Render Kit (page 478). Here is the `getRendererType` method from the `AreaTag` class:

```
public String getRendererType() { return ("DemoArea");}
```

Creating the Component Tag Handler (page 450) explains more about the `getRendererType` method.

Handling Events for Custom Components

As explained in Implementing an Event Listener (page 408), events are automatically queued on standard components that fire events. A custom component, on the other hand, must manually queue events from its `decode` method if it fires events.

Performing Decoding (page 442) explains how to queue an event on `MapComponent` using its `decode` method. This section explains how to write the class representing the event of clicking on the map and how to write the method that processes this event.

As explained in Understanding the JSP Page (page 431), the `actionListener` attribute of the `map` tag points to the `chooseLocaleFromMap` method of the bean `LocaleBean`. This method processes the event of clicking the image map. Here is the `chooseLocaleFromMap` method of `LocaleBean`:

```
public void chooseLocaleFromMap(ActionEvent actionEvent) {
  AreaSelectedEvent event = (AreaSelectedEvent) actionEvent;
  String current = event.getMapComponent().getCurrent();
  FacesContext context = FacesContext.getCurrentInstance();
  context.getViewRoot().setLocale((Locale)
    locales.get(current));
}
```

When the JavaServer Faces implementation calls this method, it passes in an `ActionEvent` object that represents the event generated by clicking on the image map. Next, it casts it to an `AreaSelectedEvent` object. Then this method gets the `MapComponent` associated with the event. It then gets the value of the `MapComponent` object's `current` attribute, which indicates the currently selected area. The method then uses the value of the `current` property to get the `Locale` object from a `HashMap` object, which is constructed elsewhere in the `LocaleBean` class. Finally the method sets the locale of the FacesContext instance to the Locale obtained from the HashMap object.

In addition to the method that processes the event, you need the event class itself. This class is very simple to write: You have it extend ActionEvent and provide a constructor that takes the component on which the event is queued and a method that returns the component. Here is the AreaSelectedEvent class used with the image map:

```
public class AreaSelectedEvent extends ActionEvent {
    ...
    public AreaSelectedEvent(MapComponent map) {
        super(map);
    }
    public MapComponent getMapComponent() {
        return ((MapComponent) getComponent());
    }
}
```

As explained in the section Creating Custom Component Classes (page 437), in order for MapComponent to fire events in the first place, it must implement ActionSource. Because MapComponent extends UICommand, it also implements ActionSource.

Creating the Component Tag Handler

Now that you've created your component and renderer classes, you're ready to define how a tag handler processes the tag representing the component and renderer combination. If you've created your own JSP custom tags before, creating a component tag handler should be easy for you.

In JavaServer Faces applications, the tag handler class associated with a component drives the render response phase of the JavaServer Faces life cycle. For more information on the JavaServer Faces life cycle, see The Life Cycle of a JavaServer Faces Page (page 309).

The first thing that the tag handler does is to retrieve the type of the component associated with the tag. Next, it sets the component's attributes to the values given in the page. It then returns the type of the renderer (if there is one) to the JavaServer Faces implementation so that the component's encoding can be performed when the tag is processed. Finally, it releases resources used during the processing of the tag.

The image map custom component includes two tag handlers: `AreaTag` and `MapTag`. To see how the operations on a JavaServer Faces tag handler are implemented, let's take a look at `MapTag`.

The `MapTag` class extends `UIComponentELTag`, which supports `jsp.tagext.Tag` functionality as well as JavaServer Faces-specific functionality. `UIComponentELTag` is the base class for all JavaServer Faces tags that correspond to a component. Tags that need to process their tag bodies should instead subclass `UIComponentBodyELTag`.

Retrieving the Component Type

As explained earlier, the first thing `MapTag` does is to retrieve the type of the component. It does this by using the `getComponentType` operation:

```
public String getComponentType() {
  return ("DemoMap");
}
```

The value returned from `getComponentType` must match the value configured for the component with the `component-type` element of the application's application configuration resource file. Registering a Custom Component (page 480) explains how to configure a component.

Setting Component Property Values

After retrieving the type of the component, the tag handler sets the component's property values to those supplied as tag attributes values in the page. This section assumes that your component properties are enabled to accept expressions, as explained in Enabling Component Properties to Accept Expressions (page 443).

Getting the Attribute Values

Before setting the values in the component class, the `MapTag` handler first gets the attribute values from the page via JavaBeans component properties that correspond to the attributes. The following code shows the property used to access the value of the immediate attribute.

```
private javax.el.ValueExpression immediate = null;

public void setImmediate(javax.el.ValueExpression immediate)
{
  this.immediate = immediate;
}
```

As this code shows, the setImmediate method takes a ValueExpression object. This means that the immediate attribute of the map tag accepts value expressions.

Similarly, the setActionListener and setAction methods take MethodExpression objects, which means that these attributes accept method expressions. The following code shows the properties used to access the values of the actionListener and the action attributes

```
private javax.el.MethodExpression actionListener = null;

public void setActionListener(
  javax.el.MethodExpression actionListener) {

  this.actionListener = actionListener;
}
private javax.el.MethodExpression action = null;

public void setAction(javax.el.MethodExpression action) {
    this.action = action;
}
```

Setting the Component Property Values

To pass the value of the tag attributes to MapComponent, the tag handler implements the setProperties method. The way setProperties passes the attribute values to the component class depends on whether the values are value expressions or method expressions.

Setting Value Expressions on Component Properties

When the attribute value is a value expression, setProperties first checks if it is not a literal expression. If the expression is not a literal, setProperties stores the expression into a collection, from which the component class can retrieve it and resolve it at the appropriate time. If the expression is a literal, `setProperties` performs any required type conversion and then does one of the following:

- If the attribute is renderer-independent, meaning that it is defined by the component class, then `setProperties` calls the corresponding setter method of the component class.
- If the attribute is renderer-dependent, `setProperties` stores the converted value into the component's map of generic renderer attributes.

The following piece of the `MapTag` handler's `setProperties` method sets the renderer-dependent property, `styleClass`, and the renderer-independent property, `immediate`:

```
if (styleClass != null) {
  if (!styleClass.isLiteralText()) {
    map.setValueExpression("styleClass", styleClass);
  } else {
    map.getAttributes().put("styleClass",
      styleClass.getExpressionString());
  }
}
...
if (immediate != null) {
  if (!immediate.isLiteralText()) {
    map.setValueExpression("immediate", immediate);
  } else {
    map.setImmediate(new
      Boolean(immediate.getExpressionString()).
        booleanValue());
  }
}
```

Setting Method Expressions on Component Properties

The process of setting the properties that accept method expressions is done differently depending on the purpose of the method. The `actionListener` attribute uses a method expression to reference a method that handles action events. The `action` attribute uses a method expression to either specify a logical outcome or to reference a method that returns a logical outcome, which is used for navigation purposes.

To handle the method expression referenced by `actionListener`, the `setProperties` method must wrap the expression in a special action listener object called `MethodExpressionActionListener`. This listener executes the method referenced by the expression when it receives the action event. The setProperties method then adds this MethodExpressionActionListener object to the list of listeners to be notified when the event of a user clicking on the map occurs. The following piece of setProperties does all of this:

```
if (actionListener != null) {
  map.addActionListener(
    new MethodExpressionActionListener(actionListener));
}
```

If your component fires value change events, your tag handler's setProperties method does a similar thing, except it wraps the expression in a MethodExpressionValueChangeListener object and adds the listener using the addValueChangeListener method.

In the case of the method expression referenced by the action attribute, the setProperties method uses the setActionExpression method of ActionSource2 to set the corresponding property on MapComponent:

```
if (action != null) {
  map.setActionExpression(action);
}
```

Providing the Renderer Type

After setting the component properties, the tag handler provides a renderer type—if there is a renderer associated with the component—to the JavaServer Faces implementation. It does this using the getRendererType method:

```
public String getRendererType() {return "DemoMap";}
```

The renderer type that is returned is the name under which the renderer is registered with the application. See Delegating Rendering to a Renderer (page 446) for more information.

If your component does not have a renderer associated with it, getRendererType should return null. In this case, the renderer-type element in the application configuration file should also be set to null.

Releasing Resources

It's recommended practice that all tag handlers implement a `release` method, which releases resources allocated during the execution of the tag handler. The release method of `MapTag` as follows:

```
public void release() {
  super.release();
  current = null;
  styleClass = null;
  actionListener = null;
  immediate = null;
  action = null;
}
```

This method first calls the `UIComponentTag.release` method to release resources associated with `UIComponentTag`. Next, the method sets all attribute values to `null`.

Defining the Custom Component Tag in a Tag Library Descriptor

To define a tag, you declare it in a TLD. The web container uses the TLD to validate the tag. The set of tags that are part of the HTML render kit are defined in the `html_basic` TLD.

The custom tags `area` and `map` are defined in `bookstore.tld`. The `bookstore.tld` file defines tags for all the custom components and the custom validator tag described in Creating a Custom Tag (page 416).

All tag definitions must be nested inside the `taglib` element in the TLD. Each tag is defined by a `tag` element. Here is part of the tag definition of the `map` tag:

```
<tag>
  <name>map</name>
  <tag-class>taglib.MapTag</tag-class>
  <attribute>
    <name>binding</name>
    <required>false</required>
    <deferred-value>
      <type>
        javax.faces.component.UIComponent
      </type>
```

```
            </deferred-value>
        </attribute>
        <attribute>
            <name>current</name>
            <required>false</required>
            <deferred-value>
                <type>
                    java.lang.String
                </type>
            </deferred-value>
        </attribute>
        ...
        <attribute>
            <name>actionListener</name>
            <required>false</required>
            <deferred-method>
                <method-signature>
                    void actionListener(javax.faces.event.ActionEvent)
                </method-signature>
            </deferred-method>
            <type>String</type>
        </attribute>
        ...
    </tag>
```

At a minimum, each tag must have a `name` (the name of the tag) and a `tag-class` attribute, which specifies the fully-qualified class name of the tag handler.

Each attribute element defines one of the tag attributes. As described in Defining a Tag Attribute Type (page 123), the attribute element must define what kind of value the attribute accepts, which for JavaServer Faces tags is either a deferred value expression or a method expression.

To specify that an attribute accepts a deferred value expression, you define the type that the corresponding component property accepts using a `type` element nested inside of a `deferred-value` element, as shown for the `binding` and `current` attribute definitions in the preceding code snippet.

To specify that an attribute accepts a method expression, you define the signature of the method that expression references using a `method-signature` element nested inside a `deferred-method` element, as shown by the `actionListener` attribute definition in the preceding code snippet. The actual name of the method is ignored by the runtime.

For more information on defining tags in a TLD, please consult the Tag Library Descriptors (page 229) section of this tutorial.

13

Configuring JavaServer Faces Applications

THE responsibilities of the application architect include the following:

- Registering back-end objects with the application so that all parts of the application have access to them
- Configuring backing beans and model beans so that they are instantiated with the proper values when a page makes reference to them
- Defining navigation rules for each of the pages in the application so that the application has a smooth page flow
- Packaging the application to include all the pages, objects, and other files so that the application can be deployed on any compliant container

This chapter explains how to perform all the responsibilities of the application architect.

Application Configuration Resource File

JavaServer Faces technology provides a portable configuration format (as an XML document) for configuring resources. An application architect creates one or more files, called *application configuration resource files*, that use this format to register and configure objects and to define navigation rules. An application configuration resource file is usually called `faces-config.xml`.

The application configuration resource file must be valid against the schema located at the following URL:

```
http://java.sun.com/xml/ns/javaee/web-facesconfig_1_2.xsd
```

In addition, each file must include the following, in this order:

- The XML version number:

  ```
  <?xml version="1.0"?>
  ```

- A `faces-config` tag enclosing all the other declarations:

  ```
  <faces-config xmlns="http://java.sun.com/xml/ns/javaee"
     xmlns:xsi="http://www.w3.org/2001/XMLSchema-instance"
     xsi:schemaLocation="http://java.sun.com/xml/ns/javaee
     http://java.sun.com/xml/ns/javaee/
        web-facesconfig_1_2.xsd"
     version="1.2">
     ...
  </faces-config>
  ```

You can have more than one application configuration resource file. The JavaServer Faces implementation finds the file or files by looking for the following:

- A resource named `/META-INF/faces-config.xml` in any of the JAR files in the web application's `/WEB-INF/lib/` directory and in parent class loaders. If a resource with this name exists, it is loaded as a configuration resource. This method is practical for a packaged library containing some components and renderers.
- A context initialization parameter, `javax.faces.application.CONFIG_FILES`, that specifies one or more (comma-delimited) paths to multiple configuration files for your web application. This method will most likely be used for enterprise-scale applications that delegate to separate groups the responsibility for maintaining the file for each portion of a big application.

- A resource named `faces-config.xml` in the `/WEB-INF/` directory of your application. This is the way most simple applications will make their configuration files available.

To access resources registered with the application, an application developer uses an instance of the `Application` class, which is automatically created for each application. The `Application` instance acts as a centralized factory for resources that are defined in the XML file.

When an application starts up, the JavaServer Faces implementation creates a single instance of the `Application` class and configures it with the information you configure in the application configuration resource file.

Configuring Beans

To instantiate backing beans and other managed beans used in a JavaServer Faces application and store them in scope, you use the managed bean creation facility. This facility is configured in the application configuration resource file using `managed-bean` XML elements to define each bean. This file is processed at application startup time. When a page references a bean, the JavaServer Faces implementation initializes it according to its configuration in the application configuration resource file.

With the managed bean creation facility, you can:

- Create beans in one centralized file that is available to the entire application, rather than conditionally instantiate beans throughout the application.
- Customize the bean's properties without any additional code.
- Customize the bean's property values directly from within the configuration file so that that it is initialized with these values when it is created.
- Using `value` elements, set the property of one managed bean to be the result of evaluating another value expression.

This section shows you how to initialize beans using the managed bean creation facility. See Writing Bean Properties (page 390) and Writing Backing Bean Methods (page 418) for information on programming backing beans. Binding Component Values and Instances to External Data Sources (page 371) explains how to reference a managed bean from the component tags.

Using the managed-bean Element

You create a bean using a `managed-bean` element, which represents an instance of a bean class that must exist in the application. At runtime, the JavaServer Faces implementation processes the `managed-bean` element. If a page references the bean, the JavaServer Faces implementation instantiates the bean as specified by the element configuration if no instance exists.

Here is an example managed bean configuration from the Duke's Bookstore application:

```
<managed-bean>
  <managed-bean-name> NA </managed-bean-name>
    <managed-bean-class>
      com.sun.bookstore6.model.ImageArea
    </managed-bean-class>
    <managed-bean-scope> application </managed-bean-scope>
    <managed-property>
      <property-name>shape</property-name>
      <value>poly</value>
    </managed-property>
    ...
  </managed-bean-name>
</managed-bean>
```

Using NetBeans 5.5, you can add a managed bean declaration by doing the following:

1. After opening your project in NetBeans 5.5, expand the project node in the Projects pane.
2. Expand the Web Pages and WEB-INF nodes of the project node.
3. Double-click `faces-config.xml`.
4. After `faces-config.xml` opens in the editor pane, right-click in the editor pane.
5. Select JavaServer Faces → Add Managed Bean.
6. In the Add Managed Bean dialog:
   a. Enter the display name of the bean in the Bean Name field.
   b. Click Browse to locate the bean's class.
7. In the Browse Class dialog:
   a. Start typing the name of the class you are looking for in the Class Name field. While you are typing, the dialog will show the matching classes.

   b. Select the class from the Matching Classes box.
   c. Click OK.
8. In the Add Managed Bean dialog:
   a. Select the bean's scope from the Scope menu.
   b. Click Add.
9. In the Projects tab, right-click the `bookstore1` project, and select Deploy Project.

The preceding steps will add the `managed-bean` element and three elements inside of it: a `managed-bean-name` element, a `managed-bean-class` element and a `managed-bean-scope` element. You will need to edit the XML of the configuration file directly to further configure this managed bean.

The `managed-bean-name` element defines the key under which the bean will be stored in a scope. For a component's value to map to this bean, the component tag's `value` attribute must match the `managed-bean-name` up to the first period. For example, this value expression maps to the `shape` property of the `ImageArea` instance, `NA`:

```
value="#{NA.shape}"
```

The part before the period (`.`)matches the `managed-bean-name` of `ImageArea`. Adding UI Components to a Page Using the HTML Component Tags (page 326) has more examples of using the `value` attribute to bind components to bean properties.

The `managed-bean-class` element defines the fully qualified name of the JavaBeans component class used to instantiate the bean. It is the application developer's responsibility to ensure that the class complies with the configuration of the bean in the application configuration resource file. This includes making sure that the types of the properties in the bean match those configured for the bean in the configuration file.

The `managed-bean-scope` element defines the scope in which the bean will be stored. The four acceptable scopes are `none`, `request`, `session`, or `application`. If you define the bean with a `none` scope, the bean is instantiated anew each time it is referenced, and so it does not get saved in any scope. One reason to use a scope of `none` is that a managed bean references another managed bean. The second bean should be in `none` scope if it is supposed to be created only when it is referenced. See Initializing Managed Bean Properties (page 467) for an example of initializing a managed bean property.

If you are configuring a backing bean that is referenced by a component tag's `binding` attribute, you should define the bean with a request scope. If you placed the bean in session or application scope instead, the bean would need to take precautions to ensure thread safety because `UIComponent` instances depend on running inside of a single thread.

The `managed-bean` element can contain zero or more `managed-property` elements, each corresponding to a property defined in the bean class. These elements are used to initialize the values of the bean properties. If you don't want a particular property initialized with a value when the bean is instantiated, do not include a `managed-property` definition for it in your application configuration resource file.

If a `managed-bean` element does not contain other `managed-bean` elements, it can contain one `map-entries` element or `list-entries` element. The `map-entries` element configures a set of beans that are instances of `Map`. The `list-entries` element configures a set of beans that are instances of `List`.

To map to a property defined by a `managed-property` element, you must ensure that the part of a component tag's `value` expression after the period matches the `managed-property` element's `property-name` element. In the earlier example, the `shape` property is initialized with the value `poly`. The next section explains in more detail how to use the `managed-property` element.

Initializing Properties Using the managed-property Element

A `managed-property` element must contain a `property-name` element, which must match the name of the corresponding property in the bean. A `managed-property` element must also contain one of a set of elements (listed in Table 13–1) that defines the value of the property. This value must be of the same type as that defined for the property in the corresponding bean. Which element you use to define the value depends on the type of the property defined in the bean. Table 13–1 lists all the elements used to initialize a value.

Table 13–1 Subelements of `managed-property` Elements That Define Property Values

Element	ValueThat It Defines
`list-entries`	Defines the values in a list
`map-entries`	Defines the values of a map
`null-value`	Explicitly sets the property to `null`
`value`	Defines a single value, such as a `String` or `int`, or a JavaServer Faces EL expression

Using the managed-bean Element (page 460) includes an example of initializing `String` properties using the `value` subelement. You also use the `value` subelement to initialize primitive and other reference types. The rest of this section describes how to use the `value` subelement and other subelements to initialize properties of Java Enum types, `java.util.Map`, `array`, and `Collection`, as well as initialization parameters.

Referencing a Java Enum Type

As of version 1.2 of JavaServer Faces technology, a managed bean property can also be a Java Enum type (see `http://java.sun.com/j2se/1.5.0/docs/api/Enum.html`). In this case, the `value` element of the `managed-property` element must be a `String` that matches one of the `String` constants of the Enum. In other words, the `String` must be one of the valid values that can be returned if you were to call `valueOf(Class, String)` on enum, where `Class` is the `Enum` class and `String` is the contents of the `value` subelement. For example, suppose the managed bean property is the following:

```
public enum Suit { Hearts, Spades, Diamonds, Clubs}
...
public Suit getSuit() { ... return Suit.Hearts; }
```

Assuming that you want to configure this property in the application configuration file, the corresponding managed-property element would look like this:

```
<managed-property>
  <property-name>Suit</property-name>
  <value>Hearts</value>
</managed-property>
```

When the system encounters this property, it iterates over each of the members of the enum and calls toString() on each member until it finds one that is exactly equal to the value from the value element.

Referencing an Initialization Parameter

Another powerful feature of the managed bean creation facility is the ability to reference implicit objects from a managed bean property.

Suppose that you have a page that accepts data from a customer, including the customer's address. Suppose also that most of your customers live in a particular area code. You can make the area code component render this area code by saving it in an implicit object and referencing it when the page is rendered.

You can save the area code as an initial default value in the context initParam implicit object by adding a context parameter to your web application and setting its value in the deployment descriptor. For example, to set a context parameter called defaultAreaCode to 650, add a context-param element to the deployment descriptor, give the parameter the name defaultAreaCode and the value 650.

Next, you write a managed-bean declaration that configures a property that references the parameter:

```
<managed-bean>
  <managed-bean-name>customer</managed-bean-name>
    <managed-bean-class>CustomerBean</managed-bean-class>
    <managed-bean-scope>request</managed-bean-scope>
    <managed-property>
      <property-name>areaCode</property-name>
        <value>#{initParam.defaultAreaCode}</value>
      </managed-property>
      ...
</managed-bean>
```

To access the area code at the time the page is rendered, refer to the property from the area component tag's value attribute:

```
<h:inputText id=area value="#{customer.areaCode}"
```

Retrieving values from other implicit objects is done in a similar way. See Implicit Objects (page 130) for a list of implicit objects.

Initializing Map Properties

The map-entries element is used to initialize the values of a bean property with a type of java.util.Map if the map-entries element is used within a managed-property element. A map-entries element contains an optional key-class element, an optional value-class element, and zero or more map-entry elements.

Each of the map-entry elements must contain a key element and either a null-value or value element. Here is an example that uses the map-entries element:

```
<managed-bean>
  ...
  <managed-property>
    <property-name>prices</property-name>
    <map-entries>
      <map-entry>
        <key>My Early Years: Growing Up on *7</key>
        <value>30.75</value>
      </map-entry>
      <map-entry>
        <key>Web Servers for Fun and Profit</key>
        <value>40.75</value>
      </map-entry>
    </map-entries>
  </managed-property>
</managed-bean>
```

The map that is created from this map-entries tag contains two entries. By default, all the keys and values are converted to java.lang.String. If you want to specify a different type for the keys in the map, embed the key-class element just inside the map-entries element:

```
<map-entries>
  <key-class>java.math.BigDecimal</key-class>
  ...
</map-entries>
```

This declaration will convert all the keys into java.math.BigDecimal. Of course, you must make sure that the keys can be converted to the type that you specify. The key from the example in this section cannot be converted to a java.math.BigDecimal because it is a String.

If you also want to specify a different type for all the values in the map, include the value-class element after the key-class element:

```
<map-entries>
  <key-class>int</key-class>
  <value-class>java.math.BigDecimal</value-class>
  ...
</map-entries>
```

Note that this tag sets only the type of all the value subelements.

The first map-entry in the preceding example includes a value subelement. The value subelement defines a single value, which will be converted to the type specified in the bean.

The second map-entry defines a value element, which references a property on another bean. Referencing another bean from within a bean property is useful for building a system from fine-grained objects. For example, a request-scoped form-handling object might have a pointer to an application-scoped database mapping object. Together the two can perform a form-handling task. Note that including a reference to another bean will initialize the bean if it does not already exist.

Instead of using a map-entries element, it is also possible to assign the entire map using a value element that specifies a map-typed expression.

Initializing Array and List Properties

The list-entries element is used to initialize the values of an array or List property. Each individual value of the array or List is initialized using a value or null-value element. Here is an example:

```
<managed-bean>
  ...
  <managed-property>
    <property-name>books</property-name>
    <list-entries>
      <value-class>java.lang.String</value-class>
      <value>Web Servers for Fun and Profit</value>
      <value>#{myBooks.bookId[3]}</value>
```

```
      <null-value/>
    </list-entries>
  </managed-property>
</managed-bean>
```

This example initializes an `array` or a `List`. The type of the corresponding property in the bean determines which data structure is created. The `list-entries` element defines the list of values in the `array` or `List`. The `value` element specifies a single value in the `array` or `List` and can reference a property in another bean. The `null-value` element will cause the `setBooks` method to be called with an argument of `null`. A `null` property cannot be specified for a property whose data type is a Java primitive, such as `int` or `boolean`.

Initializing Managed Bean Properties

Sometimes you might want to create a bean that also references other managed beans so that you can construct a graph or a tree of beans. For example, suppose that you want to create a bean representing a customer's information, including the mailing address and street address, each of which is also a bean. The following `managed-bean` declarations create a `CustomerBean` instance that has two `AddressBean` properties: one representing the mailing address, and the other representing the street address. This declaration results in a tree of beans with `CustomerBean` as its root and the two `AddressBean` objects as children.

```
<managed-bean>
  <managed-bean-name>customer</managed-bean-name>
  <managed-bean-class>
    com.mycompany.mybeans.CustomerBean
  </managed-bean-class>
  <managed-bean-scope> request </managed-bean-scope>
  <managed-property>
    <property-name>mailingAddress</property-name>
    <value>#{addressBean}</value>
  </managed-property>
  <managed-property>
    <property-name>streetAddress</property-name>
    <value>#{addressBean}</value>
  </managed-property>
  <managed-property>
    <property-name>customerType</property-name>
    <value>New</value>
  </managed-property>
</managed-bean>
<managed-bean>
```

```
    <managed-bean-name>addressBean</managed-bean-name>
    <managed-bean-class>
      com.mycompany.mybeans.AddressBean
    </managed-bean-class>
    <managed-bean-scope> none </managed-bean-scope>
    <managed-property>
      <property-name>street</property-name>
      <null-value/>
    <managed-property>
    ...
  </managed-bean>
```

The first CustomerBean declaration (with the managed-bean-name of customer) creates a CustomerBean in request scope. This bean has two properties: mailingAddress and streetAddress. These properties use the value element to reference a bean named addressBean.

The second managed bean declaration defines an AddressBean but does not create it because its managed-bean-scope element defines a scope of none. Recall that a scope of none means that the bean is created only when something else references it. Because both the mailingAddress and the streetAddress properties reference addressBean using the value element, two instances of AddressBean are created when CustomerBean is created.

When you create an object that points to other objects, do not try to point to an object with a shorter life span because it might be impossible to recover that scope's resources when it goes away. A session-scoped object, for example, cannot point to a request-scoped object. And objects with none scope have no effective life span managed by the framework, so they can point only to other none scoped objects. Table 13–2 outlines all of the allowed connections.

Table 13–2 Allowable Connections between Scoped Objects

An Object of This Scope	May Point to an Object of This Scope
none	none
application	none, application
session	none, application, session
request	none, application, session, request

Be sure not allow cyclical references between objects. For example, neither of the AddressBean objects in the preceding example should point back to the CustomerBean object because CustomerBean already points to the AddressBean objects.

Initializing Maps and Lists

In addition to configuring Map and List properties, you can also configure a Map and a List directly so that you can reference them from a tag rather than referencing a property that wraps a Map or a List.

The Duke's Bookstore application configures a List to initialize the list of free newsletters, from which users can choose a set of newsletters to subscribe to on the bookcashier.jsp page:

```
<managed-bean>
  ...
<managed-bean-name>newsletters</managed-bean-name>
  <managed-bean-class>
    java.util.ArrayList
  </managed-bean-class>
  <managed-bean-scope>application</managed-bean-scope>
  <list-entries>
    <value-class>javax.faces.model.SelectItem</value-class>
    <value>#{newsletter0}</value>
    <value>#{newsletter1}</value>
    <value>#{newsletter2}</value>
    <value>#{newsletter3}</value>
  </list-entries>
</managed-bean>
<managed-bean>
  <managed-bean-name>newsletter0</managed-bean-name>
  <managed-bean-class>
    javax.faces.model.SelectItem
  </managed-bean-class>
  <managed-bean-scope>none</managed-bean-scope>
  <managed-property>
    <property-name>label</property-name>
    <value>Duke's Quarterly</value>
  </managed-property>
  <managed-property>
    <property-name>value</property-name>
```

```
      <value>200</value>
    </managed-property>
  </managed-bean>
  ...
```

This configuration initializes a `List` called `newsletters`. This list is composed of `SelectItem` instances, which are also managed beans. See Using the selectItem Tag (page 353) for more information on `SelectItem`. Note that, unlike the example in Initializing Map Properties (page 465), the newsletters list is not a property on a managed bean. (It is not wrapped with a `managed-property` element.) Instead, the list is the managed bean.

Registering Custom Error Messages

If you create custom error messages (which are displayed by the `message` and `messages` tags) for your custom converters or validators, you must make them available at application startup time. You do this in one of two ways: by queuing the message onto the `FacesContext` instance programmatically (as described in Performing Localization, page 402) or by registering the messages with your application using the application configuration resource file.

Here is the part of the file that registers the messages for the Duke's Bookstore application:

```
<application>
  <message-bundle>
    com.sun.bookstore6.resources.ApplicationMessages
  </message-bundle>
  <locale-config>
    <default-locale>en</default-locale>
    <supported-locale>es</supported-locale>
    <supported-locale>de</supported-locale>
    <supported-locale>fr</supported-locale>
  </locale-config>
</application>
```

This set of elements will cause your `Application` instance to be populated with the messages contained in the specified resource bundle.

The `message-bundle` element represents a set of localized messages. It must contain the fully qualified path to the resource bundle containing the localized messages—in this case, `resources.ApplicationMessages`.

The locale-config element lists the default locale and the other supported locales. The locale-config element enables the system to find the correct locale based on the browser's language settings. Duke's Bookstore manually sets the locale and so it overrides these settings. Therefore, it's not necessary to use locale-config to specify the default or supported locales in Duke's Bookstore.

The supported-locale and default-locale tags accept the lower-case, two-character codes as defined by ISO-639 (see http://www.ics.uci.edu/pub/ietf/http/related/iso639.txt). Make sure that your resource bundle actually contains the messages for the locales that you specify with these tags.

To access the localized message, the application developer merely references the key of the message from the resource bundle. See Performing Localization (page 402) for more information.

Registering Custom Localized Static Text

Any custom localized static text you create that is not loaded into the page using the loadBundle tag must be registered with the application using the resource-bundle element in the application configuration resource file for your pages to have access to the text. Likewise, any custom error messages that are referenced by the converterMessage, requiredMessage, or validatorMessage attributes of an input component tag must also be made available to the application by way of the loadBundle tag or the resource-bundle element of the application configuration file.

Here is the part of the file that registers some custom error messages for the Duke's Bookstore application:

```
<application>
  ...
  <resource-bundle>
    <base-name>
      com.sun.bookstore6.resources.CustomMessages
    </base-name>
    <var>customMessages</var>
  </resource-bundle>
  ...
</application>
```

Similarly to the loadBundle tag, the value of the base-name subelement specifies the fully-qualified class name of the ResourceBundle class, which in this case is located in the resources package of the application.

Also similarly to the var attribute of the loadBundle tag, the var subelement of the resource-bundle element is an alias to the ResourceBundle class. This alias is used by tags in the page to identify the resource bundle.

The locale-config element shown in the previous section also applies to the messages and static text identified by the resource-bundle element. As with resource bundles identified by the message-bundle element, make sure that the resource bundle identified by the resource-bundle element actually contains the messages for the locales that you specify with these locale-config elements.

To access the localized message, the page author uses a value expression to reference the key of the message from the resource bundle. See Performing Localization (page 402) for more information.

Registering a Custom Validator

If the application developer provides an implementation of the Validator interface to perform validation, you must register this custom validator in the application configuration resource file by using the validator XML element:

```
<validator>
  ...
  <validator-id>FormatValidator</validator-id>
  <validator-class>
    com.sun.bookstore6.validators.FormatValidator
  </validator-class>
  <attribute>
    ...
    <attribute-name>formatPatterns</attribute-name>
    <attribute-class>java.lang.String</attribute-class>
  </attribute>
</validator>
```

The validator-id and validator-class elements are required subelements. The validator-id element represents the identifier under which the Validator class should be registered. This ID is used by the tag class corresponding to the custom validator tag.

The validator-class element represents the fully qualified class name of the Validator class.

The attribute element identifies an attribute associated with the Validator implementation. It has required attribute-name and attribute-class subelements. The attribute-name element refers to the name of the attribute as it appears in the validator tag. The attribute-class element identifies the Java type of the value associated with the attribute.

Creating a Custom Validator (page 411) explains how to implement the Validator interface.

Using a Custom Validator (page 385) explains how to reference the validator from the page.

Registering a Custom Converter

As is the case with a custom validator, if the application developer creates a custom converter, you must register it with the application. Here is the converter configuration for CreditCardConverter from the Duke's Bookstore application:

```
<converter>
  <description>
    Converter for credit card
    numbers that normalizes
    the input to a standard format
  </description>
  <converter-id>CreditCardConverter</converter-id>
  <converter-class>
    com.sun.bookstore6.converters.CreditCardConverter
  </converter-class>
</converter>
```

The converter element represents a Converter implementation and contains required converter-id and converter-class elements.

The converter-id element identifies an ID that is used by the converter attribute of a UI component tag to apply the converter to the component's data. Using a Custom Converter (page 384) includes an example of referencing the custom converter from a component tag.

The converter-class element identifies the Converter implementation.

Creating a Custom Converter (page 405) explains how to create a custom converter.

Configuring Navigation Rules

As explained in Navigation Model (page 302), navigation is a set of rules for choosing the next page to be displayed after a button or hyperlink component is clicked. Navigation rules are defined in the application configuration resource file.

Each navigation rule specifies how to navigate from one page to a set of other pages. The JavaServer Faces implementation chooses the proper navigation rule according to which page is currently displayed.

After the proper navigation rule is selected, the choice of which page to access next from the current page depends on two factors:

- The action method that was invoked when the component was clicked
- The logical outcome that is referenced by the component's tag or was returned from the action method.

The outcome can be anything the developer chooses, but Table 13–3 lists some outcomes commonly used in web applications.

Table 13–3 Common Outcome Strings

Outcome	What It Means
`success`	Everything worked. Go on to the next page.
`failure`	Something is wrong. Go on to an error page.
`logon`	The user needs to log on first. Go on to the logon page.
`no results`	The search did not find anything. Go to the search page again.

Usually, the action method performs some processing on the form data of the current page. For example, the method might check whether the user name and password entered in the form match the user name and password on file. If they match, the method returns the outcome `success`. Otherwise, it returns the outcome `failure`. As this example demonstrates, both the method used to process the action and the outcome returned are necessary to determine the proper page to access.

Here is a navigation rule that could be used with the example just described:

```
<navigation-rule>
  <from-view-id>/logon.jsp</from-view-id>
  <navigation-case>
    <from-action>#{LogonForm.logon}</from-action>
    <from-outcome>success</from-outcome>
    <to-view-id>/storefront.jsp</to-view-id>
  </navigation-case>
  <navigation-case>
    <from-action>#{LogonForm.logon}</from-action>
    <from-outcome>failure</from-outcome>
    <to-view-id>/logon.jsp</to-view-id>
    </navigation-case>
</navigation-rule>
```

This navigation rule defines the possible ways to navigate from `logon.jsp`. Each `navigation-case` element defines one possible navigation path from `logon.jsp`. The first `navigation-case` says that if `LogonForm.logon` returns an outcome of `success`, then `storefront.jsp` will be accessed. The second `navigation-case` says that `logon.jsp` will be rerendered if `LogonForm.logon` returns `failure`.

The configuration of an application's page flow consists of a set of navigation rules. Each rule is defined by the `navigation-rule` element in the `faces-config.xml` file.

The navigation rules of the Duke's Bookstore application are very simple. Here are two complex navigation rules that could be used with the Duke's Bookstore application:

```
<navigation-rule>
  <from-view-id>/catalog.jsp</from-view-id>
  <navigation-case>
    <from-outcome>success</from-outcome>
    <to-view-id>/bookcashier.jsp</to-view-id>
  </navigation-case>
  <navigation-case>
    <from-outcome>out of stock</from-outcome>
    <from-action>
      #{catalog.buy}
    </from-action>
    <to-view-id>/outofstock.jsp</to-view-id>
```

```
    </navigation-case>
    <navigation-case>
      <from-outcome>error</from-outcome>
      <to-view-id>/error.jsp</to-view-id>
    </navigation-case>
  </navigation-rule>
```

The first navigation rule in this example says that the application will navigate from `catalog.jsp` to

- `bookcashier.jsp` if the item ordered is in stock
- `outofstock.jsp` if the item is out of stock

The second navigation rule says that the application will navigate from any page to `error.jsp` if the application encountered an error.

Each `navigation-rule` element corresponds to one component tree identifier defined by the optional `from-view-id` element. This means that each rule defines all the possible ways to navigate from one particular page in the application. If there is no `from-view-id` element, the navigation rules defined in the `navigation-rule` element apply to all the pages in the application. The `from-view-id` element also allows wildcard matching patterns. For example, this `from-view-id` element says that the navigation rule applies to all the pages in the books directory:

```
<from-view-id>/books/*</from-view-id>
```

As shown in the example navigation rule, a `navigation-rule` element can contain zero or more `navigation-case` elements. The `navigation-case` element defines a set of matching criteria. When these criteria are satisfied, the application will navigate to the page defined by the `to-view-id` element contained in the same `navigation-case` element.

The navigation criteria are defined by optional `from-outcome` and `from-action` elements. The `from-outcome` element defines a logical outcome, such as `success`. The `from-action` element uses a method expression to refer to an action method that returns a `String`, which is the logical outcome. The method performs some logic to determine the outcome and returns the outcome.

The `navigation-case` elements are checked against the outcome and the method expression in this order:

- Cases specifying both a `from-outcome` value and a `from-action` value. Both of these elements can be used if the action method returns different outcomes depending on the result of the processing it performs.
- Cases specifying only a `from-outcome` value. The `from-outcome` element must match either the outcome defined by the `action` attribute of the `UICommand` component or the outcome returned by the method referred to by the `UICommand` component.
- Cases specifying only a `from-action` value. This value must match the `action` expression specified by the component tag.

When any of these cases is matched, the component tree defined by the `to-view-id` element will be selected for rendering.

Using NetBeans 5.5, you can configure a navigation rule by doing the following:

1. After opening your project in NetBeans 5.5, expand the project node in the Projects pane.
2. Expand the Web Pages and WEB-INF nodes of the project node.
3. Double-click `faces-config.xml`.
4. After `faces-config.xml` opens in the editor pane, right-click in the editor pane.
5. Select JavaServer Faces→Add Navigation Rule.
6. In the Add Navigation Rule dialog:
   a. Enter or browse for the page that represents the starting view for this navigation rule.
   b. Click Add.
7. Right-click again in the editor pane.
8. Select JavaServer Faces → Add Navigation Case.
9. In the Add Navigation Case dialog:
   a. From the From View menu, select the page that represents the starting view for the navigation rule (from step 6a).
   b. (optional) In the From Action field, enter the action method invoked when the component that triggered navigation is activated.
   c. (optional) In the From Outcome field, enter the logical outcome string that the activated component references from its `action` attribute.

d. From the To View menu, select or browse for the page that will be opened if this navigation case is selected by the navigation system.
e. Click Add.

Referencing a Method That Performs Navigation (page 380) explains how to use a component tag's `action` attribute to point to an action method. Writing a Method to Handle Navigation (page 419) explains how to write an action method.

Registering a Custom Renderer with a Render Kit

When the application developer creates a custom renderer, as described in Delegating Rendering to a Renderer (page 446), you must register it using the appropriate render kit. Because the image map application implements an HTML image map, `AreaRenderer` (as well as `MapRenderer`) should be registered using the HTML render kit.

You register the renderer using the `render-kit` element of the application configuration resource file. Here is the configuration of `AreaRenderer` from the Duke's Bookstore application:

```
<render-kit>
  <renderer>
    <component-family>Area</component-family>
    <renderer-type>DemoArea</renderer-type>
    <renderer-class>
      com.sun.bookstore6.renderers.AreaRenderer
    </renderer-class>
    <attribute>
      <attribute-name>onmouseout</attribute-name>
      <attribute-class>java.lang.String</attribute-class>
    </attribute>
    <attribute>
      <attribute-name>onmouseover</attribute-name>
      <attribute-class>java.lang.String</attribute-class>
    </attribute>
    <attribute>
      <attribute-name>styleClass</attribute-name>
      <attribute-class>java.lang.String</attribute-class>
    </attribute>
  </renderer>
  ...
```

The render-kit element represents a RenderKit implementation. If no render-kit-id is specified, the default HTML render kit is assumed. The renderer element represents a Renderer implementation. By nesting the renderer element inside the render-kit element, you are registering the renderer with the RenderKit implementation associated with the render-kit element.

The renderer-class is the fully qualified class name of the Renderer.

The component-family and renderer-type elements are used by a component to find renderers that can render it. The component-family identifier must match that returned by the component class's getFamily method. The component family represents a component or set of components that a particular renderer can render. The renderer-type must match that returned by the getRendererType method of the tag handler class.

By using the component family and renderer type to look up renderers for components, the JavaServer Faces implementation allows a component to be rendered by multiple renderers and allows a renderer to render multiple components.

Each of the attribute tags specifies a render-dependent attribute and its type. The attribute element doesn't affect the runtime execution of your application. Instead, it provides information to tools about the attributes the Renderer supports.

The object that is responsible for rendering a component (be it the component itself or a renderer to which the component delegates the rendering) can use facets to aid in the rendering process. These facets allow the custom component developer to control some aspects of rendering the component. Consider this custom component tag example:

```
<d:dataScroller>
  <f:facet name="header">
    <h:panelGroup>
      <h:outputText value="Account Id"/>
      <h:outputText value="Customer Name"/>
      <h:outputText value="Total Sales"/>
    </h:panelGroup>
  </f:facet>
  <f:facet name="next">
    <h:panelGroup>
      <h:outputText value="Next"/>
      <h:graphicImage url="/images/arrow-right.gif" />
```

```
        </h:panelGroup>
    </f:facet>
        ...
</d:dataScroller>
```

The `dataScroller` component tag includes a component that will render the header and a component that will render the Next button. If the renderer associated with this component renders the facets you can include the following `facet` elements in the `renderer` element:

```
<facet>
  <description>This facet renders as the
    header of the table. It should be a panelGroup
    with the same number of columns as the data
  </description>
  <display-name>header</display-name>
  <facet-name>header</facet-name>
</facet>
<facet>
  <description>This facet renders as the content
    of the "next" button in the scroller. It should be a
    panelGroup that includes an outputText tag that
    has the text "Next" and a right arrow icon.
  </description>
  <display-name>Next</display-name>
  <facet-name>next</facet-name>
</facet>
```

If a component that supports facets provides its own rendering and you want to include `facet` elements in the application configuration resource file, you need to put them in the component's configuration rather than the renderer's configuration.

Registering a Custom Component

In addition to registering custom renderers (as explained in the preceding section), you also must register the custom components that are usually associated with the custom renderers.

Here is the component element from the application configuration resource file that registers AreaComponent:

```
<component>
  <component-type>DemoArea</component-type>
  <component-class>
    com.sun.bookstore6.components.AreaComponent
  </component-class>
  <property>
    <property-name>alt</property-name>
    <property-class>java.lang.String</property-class>
  </property>
  <property>
    <property-name>coords</property-name>
    <property-class>java.lang.String</property-class>
  </property>
  <property>
    <property-name>shape</property-name>
    <property-class>java.lang.String</property-class>
  </property>
</component>
```

The component-type element indicates the name under which the component should be registered. Other objects referring to this component use this name. For example, the component-type element in the configuration for AreaComponent defines a value of DemoArea, which matches the value returned by the AreaTag class's getComponentType method.

The component-class element indicates the fully qualified class name of the component. The property elements specify the component properties and their types.

If the custom component can include facets, you can configure the facets in the component configuration using facet elements, which are allowed after the component-class elements. See Registering a Custom Renderer with a Render Kit (page 478) for further details on configuring facets.

Basic Requirements of a JavaServer Faces Application

In addition to configuring your application, you must satisfy other requirements of JavaServer Faces applications, including properly packaging all the necessary files and providing a deployment descriptor. This section describes how to perform these administrative tasks.

JavaServer Faces applications must be compliant with the Servlet specification, version 2.3 (or later) and the JavaServer Pages specification, version 1.2 (or later). All applications compliant with these specifications are packaged in a WAR file, which must conform to specific requirements in order to execute across different containers. At a minimum, a WAR file for a JavaServer Faces application must contain the following:

- A web application deployment descriptor, called `web.xml`, to configure resources required by a web application
- A specific set of JAR files containing essential classes
- A set of application classes, JavaServer Faces pages, and other required resources, such as image files
- An application configuration resource file, which configures application resources

The WAR file typically has this directory structure:

```
index.html
JSP pages
WEB-INF/
   web.xml
   faces-config.xml
   tag library descriptors (optional)
   classes/
      class files
      Properties files
   lib/
      JAR files
```

The `web.xml` file (or deployment descriptor), the set of JAR files, and the set of application files must be contained in the `WEB-INF` directory of the WAR file. Usually, you will want to use the `ant` build tool to compile the classes. You package the necessary files into the WAR and deploy the WAR file.

The `ant` tool is included in the Application Server. You configure how the `ant` build tool builds your WAR file via a `build.xml` file. Each example in the tutorial has its own build file, to which you can refer when creating your own build file.

Configuring an Application with a Deployment Descriptor

Web applications are configured via elements contained in the web application deployment descriptor. The deployment descriptor for a JavaServer Faces application must specify certain configurations, which include the following:

- The servlet used to process JavaServer Faces requests
- The servlet mapping for the processing servlet
- The path to the configuration resource file if it is not located in a default location

The deployment descriptor can also specify other, optional configurations, including:

- Specifying where component state is saved
- Encrypting state saved on the client.
- Compressing state saved on the client.
- Restricting Access to pages containing JavaServer Faces tags
- Turning on XML validation
- Verifying custom objects

This section gives more details on these configurations. Where appropriate, it also describes how you can make these configurations using NetBeans 5.5.

Identifying the Servlet for Life Cycle Processing

One requirement of a JavaServer Faces application is that all requests to the application that reference previously saved JavaServer Faces components must go through `FacesServlet`. A `FacesServlet` instance manages the request processing life cycle for web applications and initializes the resources required by JavaServer Faces technology.

Before a JavaServer Faces application can launch the first JSP page, the web container must invoke the `FacesServlet` instance in order for the application life cycle process to start. The application life cycle is described in the section The Life Cycle of a JavaServer Faces Page (page 309).

To make sure that the `FacesServlet` instance is invoked, you provide a mapping to it. The mapping to `FacesServlet` can be a prefix mapping, such as `/guess/*`, or an extension mapping, such as `*.faces`. The mapping is used to identify a JSP page as having JavaServer Faces content. Because of this, the URL to the first JSP page of the application must include the mapping.

In the case of prefix mapping, there are two ways to accomplish this:

- The page author can include an HTML page in the application that has the URL to the first JSP page. This URL must include the path to `FacesServlet`, as shown by this tag, which uses the mapping defined in the `guessNumber` application:

  ```
  <a href="guess/greeting.jsp">
  ```

- Users of the application can include the path to `FacesServlet` in the URL to the first page when they enter it in their browser, as shown by this URL that accesses the `guessNumber` application:

  ```
  http://localhost:8080/guessNumber/guess/greeting.jsp
  ```

The second method allows users to start the application from the first JSP page, rather than start it from an HTML page. However, the second method requires users to identify the first JSP page. When you use the first method, users need only enter

```
http://localhost:8080/guessNumber
```

In the case of extension mapping, if a request comes to the server for a JSP page with a `.faces` extension, the container will send the request to the `FacesServlet` instance, which will expect a corresponding JSP page of the same name to exist containing the content. For example, if the request URL is `http://localhost/bookstore6/bookstore.faces`, `FacesServlet` will map it to the `bookstore.jsp` page.

If you are using NetBeans 5.5, the time to map the `FacesServlet` instance is when you create your JavaServer Faces project with NetBeans 5.5:

1. In NetBeans 5.5, select File→New Project.
2. In the New Project dialog, select Web from the Categories tree.
3. Select Web Application from the Projects panel.
4. Click Next.
5. Fill out the information in the Name and Location screen of the wizard.
6. Click Next.
7. Select the JavaServer Faces checkbox in the Framewoks screen.

8. Enter the mapping, such as `*.faces`, to the `FacesServlet` instance in the Servlet URL Mapping field.
9. Click Finish.

After your project is open in NetBeans 5.5, you can change the mapping to the `FacesServlet` instance by doing the following:

1. Expand the node of your project in the Projects pane.
2. Expand the Web Pages and WEB-INF nodes that are under the project node.
3. Double-click `web.xml`.
4. After the `web.xml` file appears in the editor pane, click Servlets at the top of the editor pane. The `FacesServlet` configuration appears in the editor pane.

If you prefer to edit the `web.xml` file directly, perform the following steps to configure a mapping to the `FacesServlet` instance:

1. Include a `servlet` element in the deployment descriptor.
2. Inside the `servlet` element, include a `display-name` element and set it to `FacesServlet`.
3. Also inside the `servlet` element, add a `servlet-name` element and set it to `FacesServlet`.
4. Add a third element, called `servlet-class`, inside the `servlet` element and set it to `javax.faces.webapp.FacesServlet`. This is the fully-qualified class name of the `FacesServlet` class.
5. After the `servlet` element, add a `servlet-mapping` element.
6. Inside the `servlet-mapping` element, add a `servlet-name` element and set it to `FacesServlet`. This must match the name identified by the `servlet-name` element described in step 3.
7. Also inside the `servlet-mapping` element, add a `url-pattern` element and set it to whatever mapping you prefer. This will be the path to `FacesServlet`. Users of the application will include this path in the URL when they access the application. For the `guessNumber` application, the path is `/guess/*`.

Specifying a Path to an Application Configuration Resource File

As explained in Application Configuration Resource File (page 458), an application can have multiple application configuration resource files. If these files are not located in the directories that the implementation searches by default or the files are not named `faces-config.xml`, you need to specify paths to these files.

To specify these paths using NetBeans 5.5, do the following:

1. Expand the node of your project in the Projects pane.
2. Expand the Web Pages and WEB-INF nodes that are under the project node.
3. Double-click `web.xml`.
4. After the `web.xml` file appears in the editor pane, click General at the top of the editor pane.
5. Expand the Context Parameters node.
6. Click Add.
7. In the Add Context Parameter dialog:
   a. Enter `javax.faces.CONFIG_FILES` in the Param Name field.
   b. Enter the path to your configuration file in the Param Value field.
   c. Click OK.
8. Repeat steps 1 through 7 for each configuration file.

To specify paths to the files by editing the deployment descriptor directly follow these steps:

1. Add a `context-param` element to the deployment descriptor.
2. Add a `param-value` element inside the `context-param` element and call it `javax.faces.CONFIG_FILES`.
3. Add a `param-value` element inside the `context-param` element and give it the path to your configuration file. For example, the path to the `guessNumber` application's application configuration resource file is `/WEB-INF/faces-config.xml`
4. Repeat steps 2 and 3 for each application configuration resource file that your application contains.

Specifying Where State Is Saved

When implementing the state-holder methods (described in Saving and Restoring State, page 445), you specify in your deployment descriptor where you want the state to be saved, either client or server. You do this by setting a context parameter in your deployment descriptor.

To specify where state is saved using NetBeans 5.5, do the following:

1. Expand the node of your project in the Projects pane.
2. Expand the Web Pages and WEB-INF nodes that are under the project node.
3. Double-click `web.xml`.
4. After the `web.xml` file appears in the editor pane, click General at the top of the editor pane.
5. Expand the Context Parameters node.
6. Click Add.
7. In the Add Context Parameter dialog:
   a. Enter `javax.faces.STATE_SAVING_METHOD` in the Param Name field.
   b. Enter `client` or `server` in the Param Value field.
   c. Click OK.

To specify where state is saved by editing the deployment descriptor directly follow these steps:

1. Add a `context-param` element to the deployment descriptor.
2. Add a `param-name` element inside the `context-param` element and give it the name `javax.faces.STATE_SAVING_METHOD`.
3. Add a `param-value` element to the `context-param` element and give it the value `client` or `server`, depending on whether you want state saved in the client or the server.

If state is saved on the client, the state of the entire view is rendered to a hidden field on the page. The JavaServer Faces implementation saves the state on the client by default. Duke's Bookstore saves its state in the client.

Encrypting Client State

When you are choosing to save state on the client, you are essentially saying that you want state to be sent over the wire and saved on the client in a hidden field.

Clearly, this opens the door to potential tampering with the state information. To prevent this from happening, you can specify that the state must be encrypted before it is transmitted to the client.

To specify that state must be encrypted using NetBeans 5.5, do the following:

1. Expand the node of your project in the Projects pane.
2. Expand the Web Pages and WEB-INF nodes that are under the project node.
3. Double-click `web.xml`.
4. After the `web.xml` file appears in the editor pane, click References at the top of the editor pane.
5. Expand the Environment Entries node.
6. Click Add.
7. In the Add Environment Entry dialog:
   a. Enter `com.sun.faces.ClientStateSavingPassword` in the Entry Name field.
   b. Select `java.lang.String` from the Entry Type menu.
   c. Click OK.

To specify that state must be encrypted by editing the deployment descriptor directly, do the following:

1. Add an `env-entry` element to your deployment descriptor.
2. Add an `env-entry-name` element to the `env-entry` element and give it the name `com.sun.faces.ClientStateSavingPassword`.
3. Add an `env-entry-value` element to the `env-entry` element, and give it your password. The password that you provide is used to generate keys and ciphers for encryption.
4. Add an `env-entry-type` element and give it the type of your password, which must be `java.lang.String`.

If your deployment descriptor does not contain this environment entry then no encryption of client-side state will occur.

Restricting Access to JavaServer Faces Components

In addition to identifying the `FacesServlet` instance and providing a mapping to it, you should also ensure that all applications use `FacesServlet` to process JavaServer Faces components. You do this by setting a security constraint.

To set a security constraint using NetBeans 5.5, do the following:

1. Expand the node of your project in the Projects pane.
2. Expand the Web Pages and WEB-INF nodes that are under the project node.
3. Double-click `web.xml`.
4. After the `web.xml` file appears in the editor pane, click Security at the top of the editor pane.
5. Click Add Security Constraint.
6. Enter a name for the constraint in the Display Name field.
7. Click Add to add a web resource collection.
8. In the Add Web Resource dialog:
   a. Enter a name for the web resource collection in the Resource Name field.
   b. In the URL pattern field, enter the path to a JSP page to which you want to restrict access, such as `/response.jsp`. Use commas to separate multiple patterns.
   c. Click OK.

To set a security constraint by editing the deployment descriptor directly, add a `security-constraint` element, and inside the `security-constraint` element, add the following:

1. Add a `display-name` element to identify the name of the constraint.
2. Add a `web-resource-collection` element.
3. Inside the `web-resource-collection` element, add a `web-resource-name` element that identifies the purpose of the collection.
4. Add a `url-pattern` element inside the `web-resource-collection` element and enter the path to a JSP page to which you want to restrict access, such as `/response.jsp`.
5. Continue to add URL patterns for all the JSP pages to which you want to restrict access.

Turning On Validation of XML Files

Your application contains one or more application configuration resource files written in XML. You can force the JavaServer Faces implementation to validate the XML of these files by setting the `validateXML` flag to `true`.

To set the flag using NetBeans 5.5, do the following:

1. Expand the node of your project in the Projects pane.
2. Expand the Web Pages and WEB-INF nodes that are under the project node.
3. Double-click `web.xml`.
4. After the `web.xml` file appears in the editor pane, click General at the top of the editor pane.
5. Expand the Context Parameters node.
6. Click Add.
7. In the Add Context Parameter dialog:
   a. Enter `com.sun.faces.validateXml` in the Param Name field.
   b. Enter `true` in the Param Value field.
   c. Click OK.

To set the flag in the deployment descriptor directly, do the following:

1. Add a `context-param` element to the deployment descriptor.
2. Add a `param-name` element inside the `context-param` element and give it the name `com.sun.faces.validateXml`.
3. Add a `param-value` element to the `context-param` element and give it the value `true`. The default value is `false`.

Verifying Custom Objects

If your application includes custom objects, such as custom components, converters, validators, and renderers, you can verify when the application starts that they can be created. To do this, you set the `verifyObjects` flag to `true`.

To set the flag using NetBeans 5.5, do the following:

1. Expand the node of your project in the Projects pane.
2. Expand the Web Pages and WEB-INF nodes that are under the project node.

3. Double-click `web.xml`.
4. After the `web.xml` file appears in the editor pane, click General at the top of the editor pane.
5. Expand the Context Parameters node.
6. Click Add.
7. In the Add Context Parameter dialog:
   a. Enter `com.sun.faces.verifyObjects` in the Param Name field.
   b. Enter `true` in the Param Value field.
   c. Click OK.

To set the flag in the deployment descriptor directly, do the following:

1. Add a `context-param` element to the deployment descriptor.
2. Add a `param-name` element inside the `context-param` element and give it the name `com.sun.faces.verifyObjects`.
3. Add a `param-value` element to the `context-param` element and give it the value `true`. The default value is `false`.

Normally, this flag should be set to `false` during development because it takes extra time to check the objects.

Including the Required JAR Files

JavaServer Faces applications require several JAR files to run properly. These JAR files are as follows:

- `jsf-api.jar` (contains the `javax.faces.*` API classes)
- `jsf-impl.jar` (contains the implementation classes of the JavaServer Faces implementation)
- `jstl.jar` (required to use JSTL tags and referenced by JavaServer Faces implementation classes)
- `standard.jar` (required to use JSTL tags and referenced by JavaServer Faces reference implementation classes)
- `commons-beanutils.jar` (utilities for defining and accessing JavaBeans component properties)
- `commons-digester.jar` (for processing XML documents)

- `commons-collections.jar` (extensions of the Java 2 SDK Collections Framework)
- `commons-logging.jar` (a general-purpose, flexible logging facility to allow developers to instrument their code with logging statements)

The `jsf-api.jar` and the `jsf-impl.jar` files are located in *<JAVAEE_HOME>*`/lib`. The `jstl.jar` file is bundled in `appserv-jstl.jar`. The other JAR files are bundled in the `appserv-rt.jar`, also located in *<JAVAEE_HOME>*`/lib/`.

When packaging and deploying your JavaServer Faces application, you do not need to explicitly package any of the JAR files.

Including the Classes, Pages, and Other Resources

When packaging web applications using the included build scripts, you'll notice that the scripts package resources as described here:

- All JSP pages are placed at the top level of the WAR file.
- The TLD files, the `faces-config.xml` file, and the `web.xml` file are packaged in the `WEB-INF` directory.
- All packages are stored in the `WEB-INF/classes` directory.
- All JAR files are packaged in the `WEB-INF/lib` directory.

When packaging your own applications, you can use NetBeans 5.5 or you can use the build scripts included with the tutorial examples, as explained throughout the preceding chapters. You can modify the build scripts to fit your situation. However, we recommend that you continue to package your WAR files as described in this section because this technique complies with commonly-accepted practice for packaging web applications.

14

Internationalizing and Localizing Web Applications

THE process of preparing an application to support more than one language and data format is called *internationalization. Localization* is the process of adapting an internationalized application to support a specific region or locale. Examples of locale-dependent information include messages and user interface labels, character sets and encoding, and date and currency formats. Although all client user interfaces should be internationalized and localized, it is particularly important for web applications because of the global nature of the web.

Java Platform Localization Classes

In the Java 2 platform, `java.util.Locale` represents a specific geographical, political, or cultural region. The string representation of a locale consists of the international standard two-character abbreviation for language and country and an optional variant, all separated by underscore (_) characters. Examples of locale strings include `fr` (French), `de_CH` (Swiss German), and `en_US_POSIX` (English on a POSIX-compliant platform).

Locale-sensitive data is stored in a `java.util.ResourceBundle`. A resource bundle contains key-value pairs, where the keys uniquely identify a locale-specific object in the bundle. A resource bundle can be backed by a text file (properties resource bundle) or a class (list resource bundle) containing the pairs. You construct resource bundle instance by appending a locale string representation to a base name.

For more details on internationalization and localization in the Java 2 platform, see

```
http://java.sun.com/docs/books/tutorial/i18n/index.html
```

In the web technology chapters, the Duke's Bookstore applications contain resource bundles with the base name `messages.BookstoreMessages` for the locales `en_US`, `fr_FR`, `de_DE`, and `es_MX`.

Providing Localized Messages and Labels

Messages and labels should be tailored according to the conventions of a user's language and region. There are two approaches to providing localized messages and labels in a web application:

- Provide a version of the JSP page in each of the target locales and have a controller servlet dispatch the request to the appropriate page depending on the requested locale. This approach is useful if large amounts of data on a page or an entire web application need to be internationalized.
- Isolate any locale-sensitive data on a page into resource bundles, and access the data so that the corresponding translated message is fetched automatically and inserted into the page. Thus, instead of creating strings directly in your code, you create a resource bundle that contains translations and read the translations from that bundle using the corresponding key.

The Duke's Bookstore applications follow the second approach. Here are a few lines from the default resource bundle `messages.BookstoreMessages.java`:

```
{"TitleCashier", "Cashier"},
{"TitleBookDescription", "Book Description"},
{"Visitor", "You are visitor number "},
{"What", "What We're Reading"},
```

```
{"Talk", " talks about how Web components can transform the way
you develop applications for the Web. This is a must read for
any self respecting Web developer!"},
{"Start", "Start Shopping"},
```

Establishing the Locale

To get the correct strings for a given user, a web application either retrieves the locale (set by a browser language preference) from the request using the `getLocale` method, or allows the user to explicitly select the locale.

The JSTL versions of Duke's Bookstore automatically retrieve the locale from the request and store it in a localization context (see Internationalization Tag Library, page 192). It is also possible for a component to explicitly set the locale via the `fmt:setLocale` tag.

The JavaServer Faces version of Duke's Bookstore allows the user to explicitly select the locale. The user selection triggers a method that stores the locale in the `FacesContext` object. The locale is then used in resource bundle selection and is available for localizing dynamic data and messages (see Localizing Dynamic Data, page 403):

```
<h:commandLink id="NAmerica" action="storeFront"
  actionListener="#{localeBean.chooseLocaleFromLink}">
  <h:outputText value="#{bundle.english}" />
</h:commandLink>

public void chooseLocaleFromLink(ActionEvent event) {
  String current = event.getComponent().getId();
  FacesContext context = FacesContext.getCurrentInstance();
  context.getViewRoot().setLocale((Locale)
    locales.get(current));
}
```

Setting the Resource Bundle

After the locale is set, the controller of a web application typically retrieves the resource bundle for that locale and saves it as a session attribute (see Associating Objects with a Session, page 89) for use by other components:

```
messages = ResourceBundle.
  getBundle("com.sun.bookstore.messages.BookstoreMessages",
    locale);
session.setAttribute("messages", messages);
```

The resource bundle base name for the JSTL versions of Duke's Bookstore is set at deployment time through a context parameter. When a session is initiated, the resource bundle for the user's locale is stored in the localization context. It is also possible to override the resource bundle at runtime for a given scope using the `fmt:setBundle` tag and for a tag body using the `fmt:bundle` tag.

The JavaServer Faces version of Duke's Bookstore uses two methods for setting the resource bundle. One method is letting the JSP pages set the resource bundle using the `f:loadBundle` tag. This tag loads the correct resource bundle according to the locale stored in `FacesContext`.

```
<f:loadBundle basename="messages.BookstoreMessages"
  var="bundle"/>
```

For information on this tag, see Loading a Resource Bundle (page 356).

Another way a JavaServer Faces application sets the resource bundle is by configuring it in the application configuration file. There are two XML elements that you can use to set the resource bundle: `message-bundle` and `resource-bundle`.

If the error messages are queued onto a component as a result of a converter or validator being registered on the component, then these messages are automatically displayed on the page using the `message` or `messages` tag. These messages must be registered with the application using the `message-bundle` tag:

```
<message-bundle>
  resources.ApplicationMessages
</message-bundle>
```

For more information on using this element, see Registering Custom Error Messages (page 470).

Resource bundles containing messages that are explicitly referenced from a JavaServer Faces tag attribute using a value expression must be registered using the resource-bundle element of the configuration file:

```
<resource-bundle>
  <base-
name>com.sun.bookstore6.resources.CustomMessages</base-name>
  <var>customMessages</var>
</resource-bundle>
```

For more information on using this element, see Registering Custom Localized Static Text (page 471)

Retrieving Localized Messages

A web component written in the Java programming language retrieves the resource bundle from the session:

```
ResourceBundle messages =
  (ResourceBundle)session.getAttribute("messages");
```

Then it looks up the string associated with the key Talk as follows:

```
messages.getString("Talk");
```

The JSP versions of the Duke's Bookstore application uses the fmt:message tag to provide localized strings for messages, HTML link text, button labels, and error messages:

```
<fmt:message key="Talk"/>
```

For information on the JSTL messaging tags, see Messaging Tags (page 193).

The JavaServer Faces version of Duke's Bookstore retrieves messages using either the message or messages tag, or by referencing the message from a tag attribute using a value expression.

You can only use a message or messages tag to display messages that are queued onto a component as a result of a converter or validator being registered on the component. The following example shows a message tag that displays the error message queued on the userNo input component if the validator registered on the component fails to validate the value the user enters into the component.

```
<h:inputText id="userNo" value="#{UserNumberBean.userNumber}">
  <f:validateLongRange minimum="0" maximum="10" />
  ...
<h:message
  style="color: red;
  text-decoration: overline" id="errors1" for="userNo"/>
```

For more information on using the message or messages tags, see Displaying Error Messages with the message and messages Tags (page 354).

Messages that are not queued on a component and are therefore not loaded automatically are referenced using a value expression. You can reference a localized message from almost any JavaServer Faces tag attribute.

The value expression that references a message has the same notation whether you loaded the resource bundle with the loadBundle tag or registered it with the resource-bundle element in the configuration file.

The value expression notation is var.message, in which var matches the var attribute of the loadBundle tag or the var element defined in the resource-bundle element of the configuration file, and message matches the key of the message contained in the resource bundle, referred to by the var attribute.

Here is an example from bookstore.jsp:

```
<h:outputText value="#{bundle.Talk}"/>
```

Notice that bundle matches the var attribute from the loadBundle tag and that Talk matches the key in the resource bundle.

For information on using localized messages in JavaServer Faces, see Rendering Components for Selecting Multiple Values (page 349).

Date and Number Formatting

Java programs use the DateFormat.getDateInstance(int, locale) to parse and format dates in a locale-sensitive manner. Java programs use the NumberFormat.get*XXX*Instance(locale) method, where *XXX* can be Currency, Number, or Percent, to parse and format numerical values in a locale-sensitive manner. The servlet version of Duke's Bookstore uses the currency version of this method to format book prices.

JSTL applications use the `fmt:formatDate` and `fmt:parseDate` tags to handle localized dates and use the `fmt:formatNumber` and `fmt:parseNumber` tags to handle localized numbers, including currency values. For information on the JSTL formatting tags, see Formatting Tags (page 194). The JSTL version of Duke's bookstore uses the `fmt:formatNumber` tag to format book prices and the `fmt:formatDate` tag to format the ship date for an order:

```
<fmt:formatDate value="${shipDate}" type="date"
  dateStyle="full"/>.
```

The JavaServer Faces version of Duke's Bookstore uses date/time and number converters to format dates and numbers in a locale-sensitive manner. For example, the same shipping date is converted in the JavaServer Faces version as follows:

```
<h:outputText value="#{cashier.shipDate}">
  <f:convertDateTime dateStyle="full"/>
</h:outputText>
```

For information on JavaServer Faces converters, see Using the Standard Converters (page 359).

Character Sets and Encodings

The following sections describe character sets and character encodings.

Character Sets

A *character set* is a set of textual and graphic symbols, each of which is mapped to a set of nonnegative integers.

The first character set used in computing was US-ASCII. It is limited in that it can represent only American English. US-ASCII contains upper- and lower-case Latin alphabets, numerals, punctuation, a set of control codes, and a few miscellaneous symbols.

Unicode defines a standardized, universal character set that can be extended to accommodate additions. When the Java program source file encoding doesn't support Unicode, you can represent Unicode characters as escape sequences by using the notation \u*XXXX*, where *XXXX* is the character's 16-bit representation in hexadecimal. For example, the Spanish version of the Duke's Bookstore message file uses Unicode for non-ASCII characters:

```
{"TitleCashier", "Cajero"},
{"TitleBookDescription", "Descripci" + "\u00f3" + "n del
Libro"},
{"Visitor", "El visitante" + "\u00fa" + "mero "},
{"What", "Qu" + "\u00e9" + " libros leemos"},
{"Talk", " describe cómo los componentes de software de web
pueden transformar la manera en que desarrollamos las
aplicaciones para la web. Este libro es obligatorio para
cualquier programador de respeto!"},
{"Start", "Empezar a Comprar"},
```

Character Encoding

A *character encoding* maps a character set to units of a specific width and defines byte serialization and ordering rules. Many character sets have more than one encoding. For example, Java programs can represent Japanese character sets using the EUC-JP or Shift-JIS encodings, among others. Each encoding has rules for representing and serializing a character set.

The ISO 8859 series defines 13 character encodings that can represent texts in dozens of languages. Each ISO 8859 character encoding can have up to 256 characters. ISO 8859-1 (Latin-1) comprises the ASCII character set, characters with diacritics (accents, diaereses, cedillas, circumflexes, and so on), and additional symbols.

UTF-8 (Unicode Transformation Format, 8-bit form) is a variable-width character encoding that encodes 16-bit Unicode characters as one to four bytes. A byte in UTF-8 is equivalent to 7-bit ASCII if its high-order bit is zero; otherwise, the character comprises a variable number of bytes.

UTF-8 is compatible with the majority of existing web content and provides access to the Unicode character set. Current versions of browsers and email clients support UTF-8. In addition, many new web standards specify UTF-8 as their character encoding. For example, UTF-8 is one of the two required encodings for XML documents (the other is UTF-16).

See Appendix A for more information on character encodings in the Java 2 platform.

Web components usually use `PrintWriter` to produce responses; `PrintWriter` automatically encodes using ISO 8859-1. Servlets can also output binary data using `OutputStream` classes, which perform no encoding. An application that uses a character set that cannot use the default encoding must explicitly set a different encoding.

For web components, three encodings must be considered:

- Request
- Page (JSP pages)
- Response

Request Encoding

The *request encoding* is the character encoding in which parameters in an incoming request are interpreted. Currently, many browsers do not send a request encoding qualifier with the `Content-Type` header. In such cases, a web container will use the default encoding—ISO-8859-1—to parse request data.

If the client hasn't set character encoding and the request data is encoded with a different encoding from the default, the data won't be interpreted correctly. To remedy this situation, you can use the `ServletRequest.setCharacterEncoding(String enc)` method to override the character encoding supplied by the container. To control the request encoding from JSP pages, you can use the JSTL `fmt:requestEncoding` tag. You must call the method or tag before parsing any request parameters or reading any input from the request. Calling the method or tag once data has been read will not affect the encoding.

Page Encoding

For JSP pages, the *page encoding* is the character encoding in which the file is encoded.

For JSP pages in standard syntax, the page encoding is determined from the following sources:

- The page encoding value of a JSP property group (see Setting Properties for Groups of JSP Pages, page 149) whose URL pattern matches the page.
- The `pageEncoding` attribute of the `page` directive of the page. It is a translation-time error to name different encodings in the `pageEncoding` attribute of the page directive of a JSP page and in a JSP property group.
- The `CHARSET` value of the `contentType` attribute of the `page` directive.

If none of these is provided, ISO-8859-1 is used as the default page encoding.

For JSP pages in XML syntax (JSP documents), the page encoding is determined as described in section 4.3.3 and appendix F.1 of the XML specification.

The `pageEncoding` and `contentType` attributes determine the page character encoding of only the file that physically contains the `page` directive. A web container raises a translation-time error if an unsupported page encoding is specified.

Response Encoding

The *response encoding* is the character encoding of the textual response generated by a web component. The response encoding must be set appropriately so that the characters are rendered correctly for a given locale. A web container sets an initial response encoding for a JSP page from the following sources:

- The `CHARSET` value of the `contentType` attribute of the `page` directive
- The encoding specified by the `pageEncoding` attribute of the `page` directive
- The page encoding value of a JSP property group whose URL pattern matches the page

If none of these is provided, ISO-8859-1 is used as the default response encoding.

The `setCharacterEncoding`, `setContentType`, and `setLocale` methods can be called repeatedly to change the character encoding. Calls made after the servlet response's `getWriter` method has been called or after the response is committed have no effect on the character encoding. Data is sent to the response stream on buffer flushes (for buffered pages) or on encountering the first content on unbuffered pages.

Calls to `setContentType` set the character encoding only if the given content type string provides a value for the `charset` attribute. Calls to `setLocale` set the character encoding only if neither `setCharacterEncoding` nor `setContentType` has set the character encoding before. To control the response encoding from JSP pages, you can use the JSTL `fmt.setLocale` tag.

To obtain the character encoding for a locale, the `setLocale` method checks the locale encoding mapping for the web application. For example, to map Japanese to the Japanese-specific encoding `Shift_JIS`, follow these steps:

1. Select the WAR.
2. Click the Advanced Settings button.
3. In the Locale Character Encoding table, Click the Add button.
4. Enter `ja` in the Extension column.
5. Enter `Shift_JIS` in the Character Encoding column.

If a mapping is not set for the web application, `setLocale` uses a Application Server mapping.

The first application in Chapter 4 allows a user to choose an English string representation of a locale from all the locales available to the Java 2 platform and then outputs a date localized for that locale. To ensure that the characters in the date can be rendered correctly for a wide variety of character sets, the JSP page that generates the date sets the response encoding to UTF-8 by using the following directive:

```
<%@ page contentType="text/html; charset=UTF-8" %>
```

Further Information

For a detailed discussion on internationalizing web applications, see the Java BluePrints for the Enterprise:

```
http://java.sun.com/blueprints/enterprise
```

Part Two: Web Services

PART Two explores web services.

15

Building Web Services with JAX-WS

JAX-WS stands for Java API for XML Web Services. JAX-WS is a technology for building web services and clients that communicate using XML. JAX-WS allows developers to write message-oriented as well as RPC-oriented web services.

In JAX-WS, a web service operation invocation is represented by an XML-based protocol such as SOAP. The SOAP specification defines the envelope structure, encoding rules, and conventions for representing web service invocations and responses. These calls and responses are transmitted as SOAP messages (XML files) over HTTP.

Although SOAP messages are complex, the JAX-WS API hides this complexity from the application developer. On the server side, the developer specifies the web service operations by defining methods in an interface written in the Java programming language. The developer also codes one or more classes that implement those methods. Client programs are also easy to code. A client creates a proxy (a local object representing the service) and then simply invokes methods on the proxy. With JAX-WS, the developer does not generate or parse SOAP messages. It is the JAX-WS runtime system that converts the API calls and responses to and from SOAP messages.

With JAX-WS, clients and web services have a big advantage: the platform independence of the Java programming language. In addition, JAX-WS is not restrictive: a JAX-WS client can access a web service that is not running on the Java platform, and vice versa. This flexibility is possible because JAX-WS uses technologies defined by the World Wide Web Consortium (W3C): HTTP, SOAP, and the Web Service Description Language (WSDL). WSDL specifies an XML format for describing a service as a set of endpoints operating on messages.

Setting the Port

Several files in the JAX-WS examples depend on the port that you specified when you installed the Application Server. The tutorial examples assume that the server runs on the default port, 8080. If you have changed the port, you must update the port number in the following file before building and running the JAX-WS examples:

```
<INSTALL>/javaeetutorial5/examples/jaxws/simpleclient/
HelloClient.java
```

Creating a Simple Web Service and Client with JAX-WS

This section shows how to build and deploy a simple web service and client. The source code for the service is in `<INSTALL>/javaeetutorial5/examples/jaxws/helloservice/` and the client is in `<INSTALL>/javaeetutorial5/examples/jaxws/simpleclient/`.

Figure 15–1 illustrates how JAX-WS technology manages communication between a web service and client.

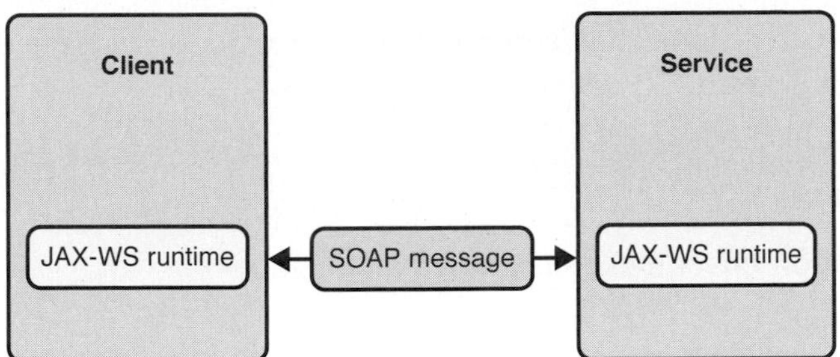

Figure 15–1 Communication between a JAX-WS Web Service and a Client

The starting point for developing a JAX-WS web service is a Java class annotated with the `javax.jws.WebService` annotation. The `@WebService` annotation defines the class as a web service endpoint.

A *service endpoint interface* or *service endpoint implementation* (SEI) is a Java interface or class, respectively, that declares the methods that a client can invoke on the service. An interface is not required when building a JAX-WS endpoint. The web service implementation class implicitly defines an SEI.

You may specify an explicit interface by adding the `endpointInterface` element to the `@WebService` annotation in the implementation class. You must then provide an interface that defines the public methods made available in the endpoint implementation class.

You use the endpoint implementation class and the `wsgen` tool to generate the web service artifacts that connect a web service client to the JAX-WS runtime. For reference documentation on `wsgen`, see the Application Server man pages at `http://docs.sun.com/`.

Together, the `wsgen` tool and the Application Server provide the Application Server's implementation of JAX-WS.

These are the basic steps for creating the web service and client:

1. Code the implementation class.
2. Compile the implementation class.
3. Use `wsgen` to generate the artifacts required to deploy the service.
4. Package the files into a WAR file.
5. Deploy the WAR file. The web service artifacts (which are used to communicate with clients) are generated by the Application Server during deployment.

6. Code the client class.
7. Use `wsimport` to generate and compile the web service artifacts needed to connect to the service.
8. Compile the client class.
9. Run the client.

The sections that follow cover these steps in greater detail.

Requirements of a JAX-WS Endpoint

JAX-WS endpoints must follow these requirements:

- The implementing class must be annotated with either the `javax.jws.WebService` or `javax.jws.WebServiceProvider` annotation.
- The implementing class may explicitly reference an SEI through the `endpointInterface` element of the `@WebService` annotation, but is not required to do so. If no `endpointInterface` is specified in `@WebService`, an SEI is implicitly defined for the implementing class.
- The business methods of the implementing class must be public, and must not be declared `static` or `final`.
- Business methods that are exposed to web service clients must be annotated with `javax.jws.WebMethod`.
- Business methods that are exposed to web service clients must have JAXB-compatible parameters and return types. See Default Data Type Bindings (page 523).
- The implementing class must not be declared `final` and must not be `abstract`.
- The implementing class must have a default public constructor.
- The implementing class must not define the `finalize` method.
- The implementing class may use the `javax.annotation.PostConstruct` or `javax.annotation.PreDestroy` annotations on its methods for life cycle event callbacks.

  The `@PostConstruct` method is called by the container before the implementing class begins responding to web service clients.

  The `@PreDestroy` method is called by the container before the endpoint is removed from operation.

Coding the Service Endpoint Implementation Class

In this example, the implementation class, Hello, is annotated as a web service endpoint using the @WebService annotation. Hello declares a single method named sayHello, annotated with the @WebMethod annotation. @WebMethod exposes the annotated method to web service clients. sayHello returns a greeting to the client, using the name passed to sayHello to compose the greeting. The implementation class also must define a default, public, no-argument constructor.

```
package helloservice.endpoint;

import javax.jws.WebService;

@WebService
public class Hello {
  private String message = new String("Hello, ");

  public void Hello() {}

  @WebMethod
  public String sayHello(String name) {
    return message + name + ".";
  }
}
```

Building, Packaging, and Deploying the Service

You can build, package, and deploy the helloservice application using either NetBeans 5.5 or ant.

Building, Packaging, and Deploying the Service Using NetBeans 5.5

Follow these instructions to build, package, and deploy the `helloservice` example to your Application Server instance using the NetBeans 5.5 IDE.

1. In NetBeans 5.5, select File→Open Project.
2. In the Open Project dialog, navigate to `<INSTALL>/javaeetutorial5/examples/jaxws/`.
3. Select the `helloservice` folder.
4. Select the Open as Main Project checkbox.
5. Click Open Project Folder.
6. In the Projects tab, right-click the `helloservice` project and select Deploy Project.

This builds and packages to application into `helloservice.war`, located in `<INSTALL>/javaeetutorial5/examples/jaxws/helloservice/dist/`, and deploys this WAR file to your Application Server instance.

Building, Packaging, and Deploying the Service Using ant

To build and package `helloservice` using `ant`, in a terminal window, go to the `<INSTALL>/javaeetutorial5/examples/jaxws/helloservice/` directory and type the following:

```
ant
```

This command calls the `default` target, which builds and packages the application into an WAR file, `helloservice.war`, located in the `dist` directory.

To deploy the `helloservice` example, follow these steps:

1. In a terminal window, go to `<INSTALL>/javaeetutorial5/examples/jaxws/helloservice/`.
2. Make sure the Application Server is started.
3. Run `ant deploy`.

You can view the WSDL file of the deployed service by requesting the URL `http://localhost:8080/helloservice/hello?WSDL` in a web browser. Now you are ready to create a client that accesses this service.

Undeploying the Service

At this point in the tutorial, do not undeploy the service. When you are finished with this example, you can undeploy the service by typing this command:

```
ant undeploy
```

The all Task

As a convenience, the `all` task will build, package, and deploy the application. To do this, enter the following command:

```
ant all
```

Testing the Service without a Client

The Application Server Admin Console allows you to test the methods of a web service endpoint. To test the `sayHello` method of `HelloService`, do the following:

1. Open the Admin Console by typing the following URL in a web browser:
   `http://localhost:4848/`
2. Enter the admin user name and password to log in to the Admin Console.
3. Click Web Services in the left pane of the Admin Console.
4. Click Hello.
5. Click Test.
6. Under Methods, enter a name as the parameter to the `sayHello` method.
7. Click the `sayHello` button.
   This will take you to the `sayHello` Method invocation page.
8. Under Method returned, you'll see the response from the endpoint.

A Simple JAX-WS Client

`HelloClient` is a stand-alone Java program that accesses the `sayHello` method of `HelloService`. It makes this call through a port, a local object that acts as a proxy for the remote service. The port is created at development time by the `wsimport` tool, which generates JAX-WS portable artifacts based on a WSDL file.

Coding the Client

When invoking the remote methods on the port, the client performs these steps:

1. Uses the `javax.xml.ws.WebServiceRef` annotation to declare a reference to a web service. `@WebServiceRef` uses the `wsdlLocation` element to specify the URI of the deployed service's WSDL file.

   ```
   @WebServiceRef(wsdlLocation="http://localhost:8080/
        helloservice/hello?wsdl")
   static HelloService service;
   ```

2. Retrieves a proxy to the service, also known as a port, by invoking `getHelloPort` on the service.

   ```
   Hello port = service.getHelloPort();
   ```

   The port implements the SEI defined by the service.

3. Invokes the port's `sayHello` method, passing to the service a name.

   ```
   String response = port.sayHello(name);
   ```

Here is the full source of `HelloClient`, which is located in the `<INSTALL>/javaeetutorial5/examples/jaxws/simpleclient/src/java/` directory.

```
package simpleclient;

import javax.xml.ws.WebServiceRef;
import helloservice.endpoint.HelloService;
import helloservice.endpoint.Hello;

public class HelloClient {
  @WebServiceRef(wsdlLocation="http://localhost:8080/
       helloservice/hello?wsdl")
  static HelloService service;

  public static void main(String[] args) {
    try {
      HelloClient client = new HelloClient();
      client.doTest(args);
    } catch(Exception e) {
      e.printStackTrace();
    }
  }

  public void doTest(String[] args) {
    try {
      System.out.println("Retrieving the port from
           the following service: " + service);
```

```
            Hello port = service.getHelloPort();
            System.out.println("Invoking the sayHello operation
                on the port.");

            String name;
            if (args.length > 0) {
                name = args[0];
            } else {
                name = "No Name";
            }

            String response = port.sayHello(name);
            System.out.println(response);
        } catch(Exception e) {
            e.printStackTrace();
        }
    }
}
```

Building and Running the Client

You can build and run the `simpleclient` application using either NetBeans 5.5 or `ant`. To build the client, you must first have deployed `helloservice`, as described in Building, Packaging, and Deploying the Service (page 511).

Building and Running the Client in NetBeans 5.5

Do the following to build and run `simpleclient`:

1. In NetBeans 5.5, select File→Open Project.
2. In the Open Project dialog, navigate to `<INSTALL>/javaeetutorial5/examples/jaxws/`.
3. Select the `simpleclient` folder.
4. Select the Open as Main Project checkbox.
5. Click Open Project Folder.
6. In the Projects tab ,right-click the `simpleclient` project and select Run Project.

You will see the output of the application client in the Output pane.

Building and Running the Client Using ant

In a terminal navigate to `<INSTALL>/examples/jaxws/simpleclient/` and type the following command:

```
ant
```

This command calls the `default` target, which builds and packages the application into a JAR file, `simpleclient.jar`, located in the `dist` directory.

The run the client, type the following command:

```
ant run
```

Types Supported by JAX-WS

JAX-WS delegates the mapping of Java programming language types to and from XML definitions to JAXB. Application developers don't need to know the details of these mappings, but they should be aware that not every class in the Java language can be used as a method parameter or return type in JAX-WS. For information on which types are supported by JAXB, see Binding between XML Schema and Java Classes (page 519).

Web Services Interoperability and JAX-WS

JAX-WS 2.0 supports the Web Services Interoperability (WS-I) Basic Profile Version 1.1. The WS-I Basic Profile is a document that clarifies the SOAP 1.1 and WSDL 1.1 specifications to promote SOAP interoperability. For links related to WS-I, see Further Information (page 517).

To support WS-I Basic Profile Version 1.1, the JAX-WS runtime supports doc/literal and rpc/literal encodings for services, static ports, dynamic proxies, and DII.

Further Information

For more information about JAX-WS and related technologies, refer to the following:

- Java API for XML Web Services 2.0 specification
  `https://jax-ws.dev.java.net/spec-download.html`
- JAX-WS home
  `https://jax-ws.dev.java.net/`
- Simple Object Access Protocol (SOAP) 1.2 W3C Note
  `http://www.w3.org/TR/SOAP/`
- Web Services Description Language (WSDL) 1.1 W3C Note
  `http://www.w3.org/TR/wsdl`
- WS-I Basic Profile 1.1
  `http://www.ws-i.org`

16

Binding between XML Schema and Java Classes

THE Java™ Architecture for XML Binding (JAXB) provides a fast and convenient way to bind between XML schemas and Java representations, making it easy for Java developers to incorporate XML data and processing functions in Java applications. As part of this process, JAXB provides methods for unmarshalling XML instance documents into Java content trees, and then marshalling Java content trees back into XML instance documents. JAXB also provides a way to generate XML schema from Java objects.

JAXB 2.0 includes several important improvements to JAXB 1.0:

- Support for all W3C XML Schema features. (JAXB 1.0 did not specify bindings for some of the W3C XML Schema features.)
- Support for binding Java-to-XML, with the addition of the `javax.xml.bind.annotation` package to control this binding. (JAXB 1.0 specified the mapping of XML Schema-to-Java, but not Java-to-XML Schema.)
- A significant reduction in the number of generated schema-derived classes.
- Additional validation capabilities through the JAXP 1.3 validation APIs.
- Smaller runtime libraries.

This chapter describes the JAXB architecture, functions, and core concepts. You should read this chapter before proceeding to the examples, which provide example code and step-by-step procedures for using JAXB.

JAXB Architecture

This section describes the components and interactions in the JAXB processing model.

Architectural Overview

Figure 16–1 shows the components that make up a JAXB implementation.

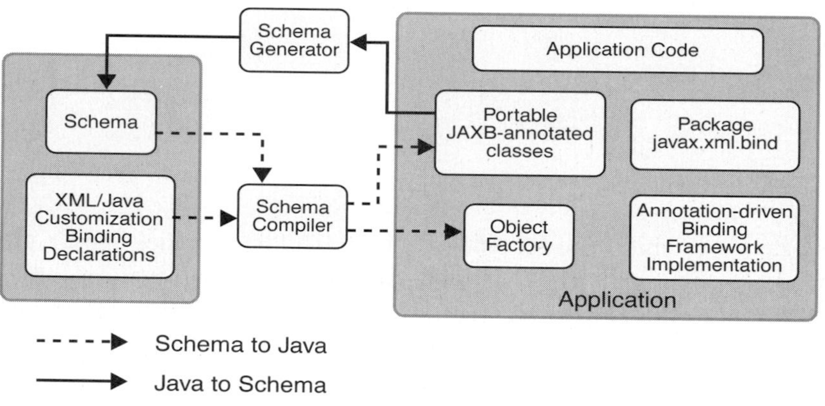

Figure 16–1 JAXB Architectural Overview

A JAXB implementation consists of the following architectural components:

- **Schema compiler**: Binds a source schema to a set of schema-derived program elements. The binding is described by an XML-based binding language.
- **Schema generator**: Maps a set of existing program elements to a derived schema. The mapping is described by program annotations.
- **Binding runtime framework**: Provides unmarshalling (reading) and marshalling (writing) operations for accessing, manipulating, and validating XML content using either schema-derived or existing program elements.

The JAXB Binding Process

Figure 16–2 shows what occurs during the JAXB binding process.

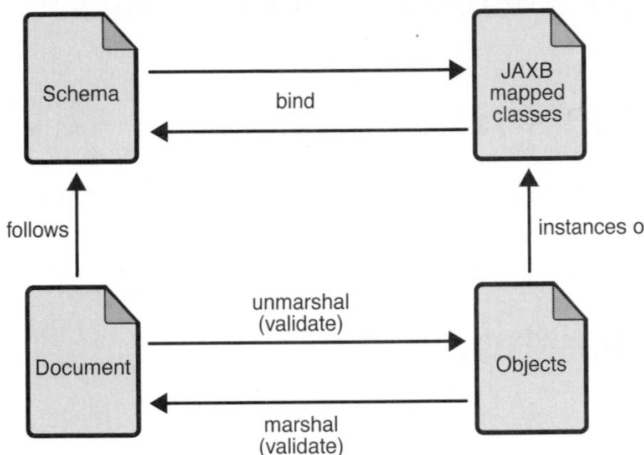

Figure 16–2 Steps in the JAXB Binding Process

The general steps in the JAXB data binding process are:

1. **Generate classes**: An XML schema is used as input to the JAXB binding compiler to generate JAXB classes based on that schema.
2. **Compile classes**: All of the generated classes, source files, and application code must be compiled.
3. **Unmarshal**: XML documents written according to the constraints in the source schema are unmarshalled by the JAXB binding framework. Note that JAXB also supports unmarshalling XML data from sources other than files/documents, such as DOM nodes, string buffers, SAX Sources, and so forth.
4. **Generate content tree**: The unmarshalling process generates a content tree of data objects instantiated from the generated JAXB classes; this content tree represents the structure and content of the source XML documents.
5. **Validate (optional)**: The unmarshalling process optionally involves validation of the source XML documents before generating the content tree. Note that if you modify the content tree in Step 6, below, you can also use the JAXB Validate operation to validate the changes before marshalling the content back to an XML document.

6. **Process content**: The client application can modify the XML data represented by the Java content tree by means of interfaces generated by the binding compiler.
7. **Marshal**: The processed content tree is marshalled out to one or more XML output documents. The content may be validated before marshalling.

More about Unmarshalling

Unmarshalling provides a client application the ability to convert XML data into JAXB-derived Java objects.

More about Marshalling

Marshalling provides a client application the ability to convert a JAXB-derived Java object tree back into XML data.

By default, the `Marshaller` uses UTF-8 encoding when generating XML data.

Client applications are not required to validate the Java content tree before marshalling. There is also no requirement that the Java content tree be valid with respect to its original schema to marshal it back into XML data.

More about Validation

Validation is the process of verifying that an XML document meets all the constraints expressed in the schema. JAXB 1.0 provided validation at unmarshal time and also enabled on-demand validation on a JAXB content tree. JAXB 2.0 only allows validation at unmarshal and marshal time. A web service processing model is to be lax in reading in data and strict on writing it out. To meet that model, validation was added to marshal time so one could confirm that they did not invalidate the XML document when modifying the document in JAXB form.

Representing XML Content

This section describes how JAXB represents XML content as Java objects.

Java Representation of XML Schema

JAXB supports the grouping of generated classes in Java packages. A package consists of the following:

- A Java class name that is derived from the XML element name, or specified by a binding customization.
- An `ObjectFactory` class, which is a factory that is used to return instances of a bound Java class.

Binding XML Schemas

This section describes the default XML-to-Java bindings used by JAXB. All of these bindings can be overridden on global or case-by-case levels by means of a custom binding declaration. See the *JAXB Specification* for complete information about the default JAXB bindings.

Simple Type Definitions

A schema component using a simple type definition typically binds to a Java property. Since there are different kinds of such schema components, the following Java property attributes (common to the schema components) include:

- Base type
- Collection type, if any
- Predicate

The rest of the Java property attributes are specified in the schema component using the `simple` type definition.

Default Data Type Bindings

The following sections explain the default schema-to-Java, `JAXBElement`, and Java-to-schema data type bindings.

Schema-to-Java

The Java language provides a richer set of data type than XML schema. Table 16–1 lists the mapping of XML data types to Java data types in JAXB.

Table 16–1 JAXB Mapping of XML Schema Built-in Data Types

XML Schema Type	Java Data Type
xsd:string	java.lang.String
xsd:integer	java.math.BigInteger
xsd:int	int
xsd.long	long
xsd:short	short
xsd:decimal	java.math.BigDecimal
xsd:float	float
xsd:double	double
xsd:boolean	boolean
xsd:byte	byte
xsd:QName	javax.xml.namespace.QName
xsd:dateTime	javax.xml.datatype.XMLGregorianCalendar
xsd:base64Binary	byte[]
xsd:hexBinary	byte[]
xsd:unsignedInt	long
xsd:unsignedShort	int
xsd:unsignedByte	short
xsd:time	javax.xml.datatype.XMLGregorianCalendar
xsd:date	javax.xml.datatype.XMLGregorianCalendar
xsd:g	javax.xml.datatype.XMLGregorianCalendar

Table 16–1 JAXB Mapping of XML Schema Built-in Data Types (Continued)

XML Schema Type	Java Data Type
`xsd:anySimpleType`	`java.lang.Object`
`xsd:anySimpleType`	`java.lang.String`
`xsd:duration`	`javax.xml.datatype.Duration`
`xsd:NOTATION`	`javax.xml.namespace.QName`

JAXBElement

When XML element information can not be inferred by the derived Java representation of the XML content, a `JAXBElement` object is provided. This object has methods for getting and setting the object name and object value.

Java-to-Schema

Table 16–2 shows the default mapping of Java classes to XML data types.

Table 16–2 JAXB Mapping of XML Data Types to Java Classes

Java Class	XML Data Type
`java.lang.String`	`xs:string`
`java.math.BigInteger`	`xs:integer`
`java.math.BigDecimal`	`xs:decimal`
`java.util.Calendar`	`xs:dateTime`
`java.util.Date`	`xs:dateTime`
`javax.xml.namespace.QName`	`xs:QName`
`java.net.URI`	`xs:string`
`javax.xml.datatype.XMLGregorianCalendar`	`xs:anySimpleType`
`javax.xml.datatype.Duration`	`xs:duration`

Table 16–2 JAXB Mapping of XML Data Types to Java Classes (Continued)

Java Class	XML Data Type
`java.lang.Object`	`xs:anyType`
`java.awt.Image`	`xs:base64Binary`
`javax.activation.DataHandler`	`xs:base64Binary`
`javax.xml.transform.Source`	`xs:base64Binary`
`java.util.UUID`	`xs:string`

Customizing JAXB Bindings

The following sections explain how to customize generated JAXB classes and Java program elements.

Schema-to-Java

Custom JAXB binding declarations also allow you to customize your generated JAXB classes beyond the XML-specific constraints in an XML schema to include Java-specific refinements such as class and package name mappings.

JAXB provides two ways to customize an XML schema:

- As inline annotations in a source XML schema
- As declarations in an external binding customizations file that is passed to the JAXB binding compiler

Code examples that show how to customize JAXB bindings are provided at the end of this chapter.

Java-to-Schema

The JAXB annotations defined in the `javax.xml.bind.annotations` package can be used to customize Java program elements to XML schema mapping.

Table 16–3 summarizes the JAXB annotations that can be used with a Java package.

Table 16–3 JAXB Annotations Associated with a Java Package

Annotation	Description and Default Setting

`@XmlSchema`	Maps a package to an XML target namespace.
	
	Default Settings:
	`@XmlSchema (`
	`  xmlns = {},`
	`  namespace = "",`
	`  elementFormDefault = XmlNsForm.UNSET;`
	`  attributeFormDefault = XmlNsForm.UNSET,`
	`)`

`@XmlAccessorType`	Controls default serialization of fields and properties.
	
	Default Settings:
	`@XmlAccessorType (`
	`  value = AccessType.PUBLIC_MEMBER`
	`)`

`@XmlAccessorOrder`	Controls the default ordering of properties and fields mapped to XML elements.
	
	Default Settings:
	`@XmlAccessorOrder (`
	`  value = AccessorOrder.UNDEFINED`
	`)`

`@XmlSchemaType`	Allows a customized mapping to a XML Schema built-in type.
	
	Default Settings:
	`@XmlSchemaType (`
	`  namespace = "http://www.w3.org/2001/XMLSchema",`
	`  type = DEFAULT.class`
	`)`

`@XmlSchemaTypes`	A container annotation for defining multiple `@XmlSchemaType` annotations. Default Settings: None

Table 16–4 summarizes JAXB annotations that can be used with a Java class.

Table 16–4 JAXB Annotations Associated with a Java Class

Annotation	Description and Default Setting

`@XmlType`	Maps a Java class to a schema type.
	
	Default Settings:
	`@XmlType (`
	`  name = "##default",`
	`  propOrder = {""},`
	`  namespace = "##default" ,`
	`  factoryClass = DEFAULT.class,`
	`  factoryMethod = ""`
	`)`

`@XmlRootElement`	Associates a global element with the schema type to which the class is mapped.
	
	Default Settings:
	`@XmlRootElement (`
	`  name = "##default",`
	`  namespace = "##default"`
	`)`

Table 16–5 summarizes JAXB annotations that can be used with a Java `enum` type.

Table 16–5 JAXB Annotations Associated with a Java `enum` Type

Annotation	Description and Default Setting
`@XmlEnum`	Maps a Java type to a XML simple type. Default Settings: `@XmlEnum ( value = String.class )`
`@XmlEnumValue`	Maps a Java type to an XML simple type. Default Settings: None

Table 16–5 JAXB Annotations Associated with a Java `enum` Type (Continued)

Annotation	Description and Default Setting

`@XmlType`	Maps a Java class to a schema type.
	
	Default Settings:
	`@XmlType (`
	`  name = "##default",`
	`  propOrder = {""},`
	`  namespace = "##default" ,`
	`  factoryClass = DEFAULT.class,`
	`  factoryMethod = ""`
	`)`

`@XmlRootElement`	Associates a global element with the schema type to which the class is mapped.
	
	Default Settings:
	`@XmlRootElement (`
	`  name = "##default",`
	`  namespace = "##default"`
	`)`

Table 16–6 summarizes JAXB annotations that can be used with Java properties and fields.

Table 16–6 JAXB Annotations Associated with Java Properties and Fields

Annotation	Description and Default Setting

`@XmlElement`	Maps a JavaBeans property/field to a XML element derived from a property/field name.
	
	Default Settings:
	`@XmlElement (`
	`  name = "##default",`
	`  nillable = false,`
	`  namespace = "##default",`
	`  type = DEFAULT.class,`
	`  defaultValue = "\u0000"`
	`)`

Table 16–6 JAXB Annotations Associated with Java Properties and Fields (Continued)

Annotation	Description and Default Setting
`@XmlElements`	A container annotation for defining multiple `@XmlElement` annotations. Default Settings: None

`@XmlElementRef`	Maps a JavaBeans property/field to a XML element derived from a property/field's type.
	
	Default Settings:
	`@XmlElementRef (`
	`  name = "##default",`
	`  namespace = "##default",`
	`  type = DEFAULT.class,`
	`)`

`@XmlElementRefs`	A container annotation for defining multiple `@XmlElementRef` annotations. Default Settings: None

`@XmlElementWrapper`	Generates a wrapper element around an XML representation. Typically a wrapper XML element around collections.
	
	Default Settings:
	`@XmlElementWrapper (`
	`  name = "##default",`
	`  namespace = "##default",`
	`  nillable = false`
	`)`

`@XmlAnyElement`	Maps a JavaBeans property to an XML infoset representation and/or JAXB element.
	
	Default Settings:
	`@XmlAnyElement (`
	`  lax = false,`
	`  value = W3CDomHandler.class`
	`)`

Table 16–6 JAXB Annotations Associated with Java Properties and Fields (Continued)

Annotation	Description and Default Setting

`@XmlAttribute`	Maps a JavaBeans property to a XML attribute.
	
	Default Settings:
	`@XmlAttribute (`
	`  name =  ##default,`
	`  required = false,`
	`  namespace = "##default"`
	`)`

`@XmlAnyAttribute`	Maps a JavaBeans property to a map of wildcard attributes. Default Settings: None
`@XmlTransient`	Prevents the mapping of a JavaBeans property to an XML representation. Default Settings: None
`@XmlValue`	Defines mapping of a class to an XML Schema complex type with a `simpleContent` or an XML Schema simple type. Default Settings: None
`@XmlID`	Maps a JavaBeans property to XML ID. Default Settings: None
`@XmlIDREF`	Maps a JavaBeans property to XML IDREF. Default Settings: None
`@XmlList`	Used to map a property to a list simple type. Default Settings: None

Table 16–6 JAXB Annotations Associated with Java Properties and Fields (Continued)

Annotation	Description and Default Setting
`@XmlMixed`	Mark a JavaBeans multi-valued property to support mixed content. Default Settings: None
`@XmlMimeType`	Associates the MIME type that controls the XML representation of the property. Default Settings: None
`@XmlAttachmentRef`	Marks a field/property that its XML form is a URI reference to mime content. Default Settings: None
`@XmlInlineBinaryData`	Disables consideration of XOP encoding for datatypes that are bound to base64-encoded binary data in XML. Default Settings: None

Table 16–7 summarizes the JAXB annotation that can be used with object factories.

Table 16–7 JAXB Annotations Associated with Object Factories

Annotation	Description and Default Setting

`@XmlElementDecl`	Maps a factory method to an XML element.
	
	Default Settings:
	`@XmlElementDecl (`
	`  scope = GLOBAL.class,`
	`  namespace = "##default",`
	`  substitutionHeadNamespace = "##default",`
	`  substitutionHeadName = ""`
	`)`

Table 16–8 summarizes JAXB annotations that can be used with adapters.

Table 16–8 JAXB Annotations Associated with Adapters

Annotation	Description and Default Setting
`@XmlJavaTypeAdapter`	Use the adapter that implements the `@XmlAdapter` annotation for custom marshalling. Default Settings: `@XmlJavaTypeAdapter ( type = DEFAULT.class )`
`@XmlJavaTypeAdapters`	A container annotation for defining multiple `@XmlJavaType-Adapter` annotations at the package level. Default Settings: None

Examples

The sections that follow provide instructions for using the example Java applications that are included in the `<INSTALL>/javaeetutorial5/examples/jaxb/` directory. These examples demonstrate and build upon key JAXB features and concepts. Follow these procedures in the order presented.

After reading this chapter, you should feel comfortable enough with JAXB that you can:

- Generate JAXB Java classes from an XML schema
- Use schema-derived JAXB classes to unmarshal and marshal XML content in a Java application
- Create a Java content tree from scratch using schema-derived JAXB classes
- Validate XML content during unmarshalling and at runtime
- Customize JAXB schema-to-Java bindings

This chapter describes three sets of examples:

- The Basic examples (Modify Marshal, Unmarshal Validate) demonstrate basic JAXB concepts like unmarshalling, marshalling, and validating XML content using default settings and bindings.
- The Customize examples (Customize Inline, Datatype Converter, External Customize) demonstrate various ways of customizing the default binding of XML schemas to Java objects.
- The Java-to-Schema examples show how to use annotations to map Java classes to XML schema.

Note: The Basic and Customize examples are based on a Purchase Order scenario. Each uses an XML document, `po.xml`, written against an XML schema, `po.xsd`. These documents are derived from the W3C XML Schema Part 0: Primer (`http://www.w3.org/TR/xmlschema-0/`), edited by David C. Fallside.

The Basic and Customize example directories contain several base files:

- `po.xsd` is the XML schema you will use as input to the JAXB binding compiler, and from which schema-derived JAXB Java classes will be generated. For the Customize Inline and Datatype Converter examples, this file contains inline binding customizations.
- `po.xml` is the *Purchase Order* XML file containing sample XML content, and is the file you will unmarshal into a Java content tree in each example. This file is almost exactly the same in each example, with minor content differences to highlight different JAXB concepts.
- `Main.java` is the main Java class for each example.
- `build.xml` is an Ant project file provided for your convenience. Use the Ant tool to generate, compile, and run the schema-derived JAXB classes automatically. The `build.xml` file varies across the examples.
- `MyDatatypeConverter.java` in the `inline-customize` example is a Java class used to provide custom datatype conversions.
- `binding.xjb` in the External Customize example is an external binding declarations file that is passed to the JAXB binding compiler to customize the default JAXB bindings.

Table 16–9, Table 16–10, and Table 16–11 briefly describe the Basic, Customize, and Java-to-Schema JAXB examples.

Table 16–9 Basic JAXB Examples

Example Name	Description
Modify Marshal Example	Demonstrates how to modify a Java content tree.
Unmarshal Validate Example	Demonstrates how to enable validation during unmarshalling.

Table 16–10 Customize JAXB Examples

Example Name	Description
Customize Inline Example	Demonstrates how to customize the default JAXB bindings by using inline annotations in an XML schema.
Datatype Converter Example	Similar to the Customize Inline example, this example illustrates alternate, more terse bindings of XML `simpleType` definitions to Java datatypes.
External Customize Example	Illustrates how to use an external binding declarations file to pass binding customizations for a read-only schema to the JAXB binding compiler.

Table 16–11 Java-to-Schema JAXB Examples

Example Name	Description
j2s-create-marshal Example	Illustrates how to marshal and unmarshal JAXB-annotated classes to XML schema. The example also shows how to enable JAXP 1.3 validation at unmarshal time using a schema file that was generated from the JAXB mapped classes.
j2s-xmlAccessorOrder Example	Illustrates how to use the `@XmlAccessorOrder` and `@XmlType.propOrder` mapping annotations in Java classes to control the order in which XML content is marshalled/unmarshalled by a Java type.

Table 16–11 Java-to-Schema JAXB Examples

Example Name	Description
j2s-xmlAdapter-field Example	Illustrates how to use the interface `XmlAdapter` and the annotation `@XmlJavaTypeAdapter` to provide a a custom mapping of XML content into and out of a `HashMap` (field) that uses an `int` as the key and a `String` as the value.
j2s-xmlAttribute-field Example	Illustrates how to use the annotation `@XmlAttribute` to define a property or field to be handled as an XML attribute.
j2s-xmlRootElement Example	Illustrates how to use the annotation `@XmlRootElement` to define an XML element name for the XML schema type of the corresponding class.
j2s-xmlSchemaType-class Example	Illustrates how to use the annotation `@XmlSchemaType` to customize the mapping of a property or field to an XML built-in type.
j2s-xmlType Example	Illustrates how to use the annotation `@XmlType` to map a class or `enum` type to an XML schema type.

JAXB Compiler Options

The JAXB XJC schema binding compiler transforms, or binds, a source XML schema to a set of JAXB content classes in the Java programming language. The compiler, `xjc`, is provided in two flavors in the Application Server: `xjc.sh` (Solaris/Linux) and `xjc.bat` (Windows). Both `xjc.sh` and `xjc.bat` take the same command-line options. You can display quick usage instructions by invoking the scripts without any options, or with the `-help` switch. The syntax is as follows:

```
xjc [-options ...] <schema>
```

Table 16–12 lists the `xjc` command line options.

Table 16–12 `xjc` Command Line Options

Option	Description
`-nv`	Do not perform strict validation of the input schema(s). By default, `xjc` performs strict validation of the source schema before processing. Note that this does not mean the binding compiler will not perform any validation; it simply means that it will perform less-strict validation.
`-extension`	By default, the XJC binding compiler strictly enforces the rules outlined in the Compatibility chapter of the JAXB Specification. In the default (strict) mode, you are also limited to using only the binding customizations defined in the specification. By using the `-extension` switch, you will be allowed to use the JAXB Vendor Extensions.
`-b` *`file`*	Specify one or more external binding files to process. (Each binding file must have its own `-b` switch.) The syntax of the external binding files is extremely flexible. You may have a single binding file that contains customizations for multiple schemas or you can break the customizations into multiple bindings files. In addition, the ordering of the schema files and binding files on the command line does not matter.
`-d` *`dir`*	By default, `xjc` will generate Java content classes in the current directory. Use this option to specify an alternate output directory. The directory must already exist; `xjc` will not create it for you.
`-p` *`package`*	Specify an alternate output directory. By default, the XJC binding compiler will generate the Java content classes in the current directory. The output directory must already exist; the XJC binding compiler will not create it for you.
`-proxy` *`proxy`*	Specify the HTTP/HTTPS proxy. The format is `[user[:password]@]proxyHost[:proxyPort]`. The old `-host` and `-port` options are still supported by the Reference Implementation for backwards compatibility, but they have been deprecated.
`-classpath` *`arg`*	Specify where to find client application class files used by the `<jxb:javaType>` and `<xjc:superClass>` customizations.
`-catalog` *`file`*	Specify catalog files to resolve external entity references. Supports TR9401, XCatalog, and OASIS XML Catalog format. For more information, see the XML Entity and URI Resolvers document or examine the catalog-resolver sample application.

Table 16–12 `xjc` Command Line Options (Continued)

Option	Description
`-readOnly`	Force the XJC binding compiler to mark the generated Java sources read-only. By default, the XJC binding compiler does not write-protect the Java source files it generates.
`-npa`	Suppress the generation of package level annotations into `**/package-info.java`. Using this switch causes the generated code to internalize those annotations into the other generated classes.
`-xmlschema`	Treat input schemas as W3C XML Schema (default). If you do not specify this switch, your input schemas will be treated as W3C XML Schema.
`-quiet`	Suppress compiler output, such as progress information and warnings.
`-help`	Display a brief summary of the compiler switches.
`-version`	Display the compiler version information.
`-Xlocator`	Enable source location support for generated code.
`-Xsync-methods`	Generate accessor methods with the `synchronized` keyword.
`-mark-generated`	Mark the generated code with the `-@javax.annotation.Generated` annotation.

JAXB Schema Generator Option

The JAXB Schema Generator, `schemagen`, creates a schema file for each namespace referenced in your Java classes. The schema generator can be launched using the appropriate `schemagen` shell script in the `bin` directory for your platform. The schema generator processes Java source files only. If your Java sources reference other classes, those sources must be accessible from your system CLASSPATH environment variable, otherwise errors will occur when the schema is generated. There is no way to control the name of the generated schema files.

You can display quick usage instructions by invoking the scripts without any options, or with the `-help` switch. The syntax is as follows:

```
schemagen [-d path] [java_source_files]
```

The `-d path` option specifies the location of the processor- and `javac`-generated class files.

About the Schema-to-Java Bindings

When you run the JAXB binding compiler against the `po.xsd` XML schema used in the basic examples (Unmarshal Read, Modify Marshal, Unmarshal Validate), the JAXB binding compiler generates a Java package named `primer.po` containing 11 classes, making a total of 12 classes in each of the basic examples, as described in Table 16–13.

Table 16–13 Schema-Derived JAXB Classes in the Basic Examples

Class	Description
`primer/po/Comment.java`	Public interface extending `javax.xml.bind.Element`; binds to the global schema `element` named `comment`. Note that JAXB generates element interfaces for all global element declarations.
`primer/po/Items.java`	Public interface that binds to the schema `complexType` named `Items`.
`primer/po/ObjectFactory.java`	Public class extending `com.sun.xml.bind.DefaultJAXBContextImpl`; used to create instances of specified interfaces. For example, the `ObjectFactory createComment()` method instantiates a `Comment` object.
`primer/po/PurchaseOrder.java`	Public interface extending `javax.xml.bind.Element`, and `PurchaseOrderType`; binds to the global schema `element` named `PurchaseOrder`.
`primer/po/PurchaseOrderType.java`	Public interface that binds to the schema `complexType` named `PurchaseOrderType`.
`primer/po/USAddress.java`	Public interface that binds to the schema `complexType` named `USAddress`.
`primer/po/impl/CommentImpl.java`	Implementation of `Comment.java`.
`primer/po/impl/ItemsImpl.java`	Implementation of `Items.java`

Table 16–13 Schema-Derived JAXB Classes in the Basic Examples (Continued)

Class	Description
primer/po/impl/PurchaseOrderImpl.java	Implementation of PurchaseOrder.java
primer/po/impl/PurchaseOrderTypeImpl.java	Implementation of PurchaseOrderType.java
primer/po/impl/USAddressImpl.java	Implementation of USAddress.java

Note: You should never directly use the generated implementation classes—that is, `*Impl.java` in the `<packagename>/impl` directory. These classes are not directly referenceable because the class names in this directory are not standardized by the JAXB specification. The `ObjectFactory` method is the only portable means to create an instance of a schema-derived interface. There is also an `ObjectFactory.newInstance(Class JAXBinterface)` method that enables you to create instances of interfaces.

These classes and their specific bindings to the source XML schema for the basic examples are described in Table 16–14. .

Table 16–14 Schema-to-Java Bindings for the Basic Examples

XML Schema	JAXB Binding
`<xsd:schema xmlns:xsd="http://www.w3.org/2001/XMLSchema">`	
`<xsd:element name="purchaseOrder" type="PurchaseOrderType"/>`	PurchaseOrder.java
`<xsd:element name="comment" type="xsd:string"/>`	Comment.java

Table 16–14 Schema-to-Java Bindings for the Basic Examples (Continued)

XML Schema	JAXB Binding
<xsd:complexType name="PurchaseOrderType"> <xsd:sequence> <xsd:element name="shipTo" type="USAddress"/> <xsd:element name="billTo" type="USAddress"/> <xsd:element ref="comment" minOccurs="0"/> <xsd:element name="items" type="Items"/> </xsd:sequence> <xsd:attribute name="orderDate" type="xsd:date"/> </xsd:complexType>	PurchaseOrderType.java
<xsd:complexType name="USAddress"> <xsd:sequence> <xsd:element name="name" type="xsd:string"/> <xsd:element name="street" type="xsd:string"/> <xsd:element name="city" type="xsd:string"/> <xsd:element name="state" type="xsd:string"/> <xsd:element name="zip" type="xsd:decimal"/> </xsd:sequence> <xsd:attribute name="country" type="xsd:NMTOKEN" fixed="US"/> </xsd:complexType>	USAddress.java
<xsd:complexType name="Items"> <xsd:sequence> <xsd:element name="item" minOccurs="1" maxOccurs="unbounded">	Items.java
<xsd:complexType> <xsd:sequence> <xsd:element name="productName" type="xsd:string"/> <xsd:element name="quantity"> <xsd:simpleType> <xsd:restriction base="xsd:positiveInteger"> <xsd:maxExclusive value="100"/> </xsd:restriction> </xsd:simpleType> </xsd:element> <xsd:element name="USPrice" type="xsd:decimal"/> <xsd:element ref="comment" minOccurs="0"/> <xsd:element name="shipDate" type="xsd:date" minOccurs="0"/> </xsd:sequence> <xsd:attribute name="partNum" type="SKU" use="required"/> </xsd:complexType>	Items.ItemType

Table 16–14 Schema-to-Java Bindings for the Basic Examples (Continued)

XML Schema	JAXB Binding

`    </xsd:element>`
`  </xsd:sequence>`
`</xsd:complexType>`	

`<!-- Stock Keeping Unit, a code for identifying products -->`	

`<xsd:simpleType name="SKU">`
`  <xsd:restriction base="xsd:string">`
`    <xsd:pattern value="\d{3}-[A-Z]{2}"/>`
`  </xsd:restriction>`
`</xsd:simpleType>`	

`</xsd:schema>`	

Schema-Derived JAXB Classes

The sections that follow briefly explain the functions of the following individual classes generated by the JAXB binding compiler for the Basic examples:

- `Comment.java`
- `Items.java`
- `ObjectFactory.java`
- `PurchaseOrder.java`
- `PurchaseOrderType.java`
- `USAddress.java`

Comment.java

In `Comment.java`:

- The `Comment.java` class is part of the `primer.po` package.
- `Comment` is a public interface that extends `javax.xml.bind.Element`.
- Content in instantiations of this class binds to the XML schema element named `comment`.
- The `getValue()` and `setValue()` methods are used to get and set strings representing XML `comment` elements in the Java content tree.

Items.java

In `Items.java`:

- The `Items.java` class is part of the `primer.po` package.
- The class provides public interfaces for `Items` and `ItemType`.
- Content in instantiations of this class binds to the XML ComplexTypes `Items` and its child element `ItemType`.
- `Item` provides the `getItem()` method.
- `ItemType` provides methods for:
  - `getPartNum();`
  - `setPartNum(String value);`
  - `getComment();`
  - `setComment(java.lang.String value);`
  - `getUSPrice();`
  - `setUSPrice(java.math.BigDecimal value);`
  - `getProductName();`
  - `setProductName(String value);`
  - `getShipDate();`
  - `setShipDate(java.util.Calendar value);`
  - `getQuantity();`
  - `setQuantity(java.math.BigInteger value);`

ObjectFactory.java

In `ObjectFactory.java`:

- The `ObjectFactory` class is part of the `primer.po` package.
- `ObjectFactory` provides factory methods for instantiating Java interfaces representing XML content in the Java content tree.
- Method names are generated by concatenating:
  - The string constant `create`.
  - If the Java content interface is nested within another interface, then the concatenation of all outer Java class names.
  - The name of the Java content interface.

For example, in this case, for the Java interface primer.po.Items.ItemType, ObjectFactory creates the method createItemsItemType().

PurchaseOrder.java

In PurchaseOrder.java:

- The PurchaseOrder class is part of the primer.po package.
- PurchaseOrder is a public interface that extends javax.xml.bind.Element and primer.po.PurchaseOrderType.
- Content in instantiations of this class binds to the XML schema element named purchaseOrder.

PurchaseOrderType.java

In PurchaseOrderType.java:

- The PurchaseOrderType class is part of the primer.po package.
- Content in instantiations of this class binds to the XML schema child element named PurchaseOrderType.
- PurchaseOrderType is a public interface that provides the following methods:
    - getItems();
    - setItems(primer.po.Items value);
    - getOrderDate();
    - setOrderDate(java.util.Calendar value);
    - getComment();
    - setComment(java.lang.String value);
    - getBillTo();
    - setBillTo(primer.po.USAddress value);
    - getShipTo();
    - setShipTo(primer.po.USAddress value);

USAddress.java

In `USAddress.java`:

- The `USAddress` class is part of the `primer.po` package.
- Content in instantiations of this class binds to the XML schema element named `USAddress`.
- `USAddress` is a public interface that provides the following methods:
    - `getState();`
    - `setState(String value);`
    - `getZip();`
    - `setZip(java.math.BigDecimal value);`
    - `getCountry();`
    - `setCountry(String value);`
    - `getCity();`
    - `setCity(String value);`
    - `getStreet();`
    - `setStreet(String value);`
    - `getName();`
    - `setName(String value);`

Basic Examples

This section describes the Basic examples (Modify Marshal, Unmarshal Validate) that demonstrate how to:

- Unmarshal an XML document into a Java content tree and access the data contained within it
- Modify a Java content tree
- Use the `ObjectFactory` class to create a Java content tree from scratch and then marshal it to XML data
- Perform validation during unmarshalling
- Validate a Java content tree at runtime

Modify Marshal Example

The Modify Marshal example demonstrates how to modify a Java content tree.

1. The *<INSTALL>*/javaeetutorial5/examples/jaxb/modify-marshal/Main.java class declares imports for three standard Java classes plus four JAXB binding framework classes and primer.po package:

   ```
   import java.io.FileInputStream;
   import java.io.IOException;
   import java.math.BigDecimal;
   import javax.xml.bind.JAXBContext;
   import javax.xml.bind.JAXBException;
   import javax.xml.bind.Marshaller;
   import javax.xml.bind.Unmarshaller;
   import primer.po.*;
   ```

2. A JAXBContext instance is created for handling classes generated in primer.po.

   ```
   JAXBContext jc = JAXBContext.newInstance( "primer.po" );
   ```

3. An Unmarshaller instance is created, and po.xml is unmarshalled.

   ```
   Unmarshaller u = jc.createUnmarshaller();
   PurchaseOrder po =
      (PurchaseOrder)u.unmarshal(
         new FileInputStream( "po.xml" ) );
   ```

4. set methods are used to modify information in the address branch of the content tree.

   ```
   USAddress address = po.getBillTo();
   address.setName( "John Bob" );
   address.setStreet( "242 Main Street" );
   address.setCity( "Beverly Hills" );
   address.setState( "CA" );
   address.setZip( new BigDecimal( "90210" ) );
   ```

5. A Marshaller instance is created, and the updated XML content is marshalled to system.out. The setProperty API is used to specify output encoding; in this case formatted (human readable) XML format.

   ```
   Marshaller m = jc.createMarshaller();
   m.setProperty(Marshaller.JAXB_FORMATTED_OUTPUT,
      Boolean.TRUE);
   m.marshal( po, System.out );
   ```

Building and Running the Modify Marshal Example Using NetBeans 5.5

Follow these instructions to build and run the Modify Marshal example on your Application Server instance using the NetBeans 5.5 IDE.

1. In NetBeans 5.5, select File→Open Project.
2. In the Open Project dialog, navigate to `<INSTALL>/javaeetutorial5/examples/jaxb/`.
3. Select the `modify-marshal` folder.
4. Select the Open as Main Project checkbox.
5. Click Open Project Folder.
6. Right-click the `modify-marshal` project and select Run Project.

Building and Running the Modify Marshal Example Using Ant

To compile and run the Modify Marshal example using Ant, in a terminal window, go to the `<INSTALL>/javaeetutorial5/examples/jaxb/modify-marshal/` directory and type the following:

```
ant runapp
```

Unmarshal Validate Example

The Unmarshal Validate example demonstrates how to enable validation during unmarshalling. Note that JAXB provides functions for validation during unmarshalling but not during marshalling. Validation is explained in more detail in More about Validation (page 522).

1. The `<INSTALL>/javaeetutorial5/examples/jaxb/unmarshal-validate/Main.java` class declares imports for three standard Java classes plus seven JAXB binding framework classes and the `primer.po` package:

```
import java.io.FileInputStream;
import java.io.IOException;
import java.math.BigDecimal;
import javax.xml.bind.JAXBContext;
import javax.xml.bind.JAXBException;
import javax.xml.bind.Marshaller;
```

```
import javax.xml.bind.UnmarshalException;
import javax.xml.bind.Unmarshaller;
import javax.xml.bind.ValidationEvent;
import javax.xml.bind.util.ValidationEventCollector;
import primer.po.*;
```

2. A JAXBContext instance is created for handling classes generated in primer.po.

   ```
   JAXBContext jc = JAXBContext.newInstance( "primer.po" );
   ```

3. An Unmarshaller instance is created.

   ```
   Unmarshaller u = jc.createUnmarshaller();
   ```

4. The default JAXB Unmarshaller ValidationEventHandler is enabled to send to validation warnings and errors to system.out. The default configuration causes the unmarshal operation to fail upon encountering the first validation error.

   ```
   u.setValidating( true );
   ```

5. An attempt is made to unmarshal po.xml into a Java content tree. For the purposes of this example, the po.xml contains a deliberate error.

   ```
   PurchaseOrder po =
      (PurchaseOrder)u.unmarshal(
         new FileInputStream("po.xml"));
   ```

6. The default validation event handler processes a validation error, generates output to system.out, and then an exception is thrown.

   ```
   } catch( UnmarshalException ue ) {
      System.out.println( "Caught UnmarshalException" );
   } catch( JAXBException je ) {
      je.printStackTrace();
   } catch( IOException ioe ) {
      ioe.printStackTrace();
   ```

Building and Running the Unmarshal Validate Example Using NetBeans 5.5

Follow these instructions to build and run the Unmarshal Validate example on your Application Server instance using the NetBeans 5.5 IDE.

1. In NetBeans 5.5, select File→Open Project.
2. In the Open Project dialog, navigate to <*INSTALL*>/javaeetutorial5/examples/jaxb/.
3. Select the unmarshal-validate folder.

4. Select the Open as Main Project checkbox.
5. Click Open Project Folder.
6. Right-click the `unmarshal-validate` project and select Run Project.

Building and Running the Unmarshal Validate Example Using Ant

To compile and run the Unmarshal Validate example using Ant, in a terminal window, go to the `<INSTALL>/javaeetutorial5/examples/jaxb/unmarshal-validate/` directory and type the following:

```
ant runapp
```

Customizing JAXB Bindings

The next part of this chapter describes several examples that build on the concepts demonstrated in the Basic examples.

The goal of this section is to illustrate how to customize JAXB bindings by means of custom binding declarations made in either of two ways:

- As annotations made inline in an XML schema
- As statements in an external file passed to the JAXB binding compiler

Unlike the examples in Basic Examples (page 545), which focus on the Java code in the respective `Main.java` class files, the examples here focus on customizations made to the XML schema *before* generating the schema-derived Java binding classes.

Note: Although JAXB binding customizations must currently be made by hand, it is envisioned that a tool/wizard might eventually be written by Sun or a third party to make this process more automatic. One of the goals of the JAXB technology is to standardize the format of binding declarations, thereby making it possible to create customization tools and to provide a standard interchange format between JAXB implementations.

This section just begins to scratch the surface of customizations you can make to JAXB bindings and validation methods. For more information, refer to the *JAXB Specification* (`http://jcp.org/en/jsr/detail?id=222`).

Why Customize?

In most cases, the default bindings generated by the JAXB binding compiler will be sufficient to meet your needs. There are cases, however, in which you might want to modify the default bindings. Some of these include:

- Creating API documentation for the schema-derived JAXB packages, classes, methods and constants; by adding custom Javadoc tool annotations to your schemas, you can explain concepts, guidelines, and rules specific to your implementation.
- Providing semantically meaningful customized names for cases that the default XML name-to-Java identifier mapping cannot handle automatically; for example:
    - To resolve name collisions (as described in Appendix D.2.1 of the *JAXB Specification*). Note that the JAXB binding compiler detects and reports all name conflicts.
    - To provide names for typesafe enumeration constants that are not legal Java identifiers; for example, enumeration over integer values.
    - To provide better names for the Java representation of unnamed model groups when they are bound to a Java property or class.
    - To provide more meaningful package names than can be derived by default from the target namespace URI.
- Overriding default bindings; for example:
    - Specify that a model group should be bound to a class rather than a list.
    - Specify that a fixed attribute can be bound to a Java constant.
    - Override the specified default binding of XML Schema built-in datatypes to Java datatypes. In some cases, you might want to introduce an alternative Java class that can represent additional characteristics of the built-in XML Schema datatype.

Customization Overview

This section explains some core JAXB customization concepts:

- Inline and external customizations
- Scope, inheritance, and precedence
- Customization syntax
- Customization namespace prefix

Inline and External Customizations

Customizations to the default JAXB bindings are made in the form of *binding declarations* passed to the JAXB binding compiler. These binding declarations can be made in either of two ways:

- As inline annotations in a source XML schema
- As declarations in an external binding customizations file

For some people, using inline customizations is easier because you can see your customizations in the context of the schema to which they apply. Conversely, using an external binding customization file enables you to customize JAXB bindings without having to modify the source schema, and enables you to easily apply customizations to several schema files at once.

Note: You can combine the two types of customizations—for example, you could include a reference to an external binding customizations file in an inline annotation—but you cannot declare both an inline and external customization on the same schema element.

Each of these types of customization is described in more detail below.

Inline Customizations

Customizations to JAXB bindings made by means of inline *binding declarations* in an XML schema file take the form of `<xsd:appinfo>` elements embedded in schema `<xsd:annotation>` elements (`xsd:` is the XML schema namespace prefix, as defined in W3C *XML Schema Part 1: Structures*). The general form for inline customizations is shown below.

```
<xs:annotation>
   <xs:appinfo>
      .
      .
      binding declarations
      .
      .
   </xs:appinfo>
</xs:annotation>
```

Customizations are applied at the location at which they are declared in the schema. For example, a declaration at the level of a particular element would apply to that element only. Note that the XMLSchema namespace prefix must be used with the `<annotation>` and `<appinfo>` declaration tags. In the example above, `xs:` is used as the namespace prefix, so the declarations are tagged `<xs:annotation>` and `<xs:appinfo>`.

External Binding Customization Files

Customizations to JAXB bindings made by means of an external file containing binding declarations take the general form shown below.

```
<jxb:bindings schemaLocation = "xs:anyURI">
   <jxb:bindings node = "xs:string">*
      <binding declaration>
   <jxb:bindings>
</jxb:bindings>
```

- `schemaLocation` is a URI reference to the remote schema
- `node` is an XPath 1.0 expression that identifies the schema node within `schemaLocation` to which the given binding declaration is associated.

For example, the first `schemaLocation/node` declaration in a JAXB binding declarations file specifies the schema name and the root schema node:

```
<jxb:bindings schemaLocation="po.xsd" node="/xs:schema">
```

A subsequent `schemaLocation/node` declaration, say for a `simpleType` element named `ZipCodeType` in the above schema, would take the form:

```
<jxb:bindings node="//xs:simpleType[@name='ZipCodeType']">
```

Binding Customization File Format

Binding customization files should be straight ASCII text. The name or extension does not matter, although a typical extension, used in this chapter, is `.xjb`.

Passing Customization Files to the JAXB Binding Compiler

Customization files containing binding declarations are passed to the JAXB Binding compiler, `xjc`, using the following syntax:

```
xjc -b <file> <schema>
```

where *`<file>`* is the name of binding customization file, and *`<schema>`* is the name of the schema(s) you want to pass to the binding compiler.

You can have a single binding file that contains customizations for multiple schemas, or you can break the customizations into multiple bindings files; for example:

```
xjc schema1.xsd schema2.xsd schema3.xsd -b bindings123.xjb

xjc schema1.xsd schema2.xsd schema3.xsd -b bindings1.xjb -b
bindings2.xjb -b bindings3.xjb
```

Note that the ordering of schema files and binding files on the command line does not matter, although each binding customization file must be preceded by its own `-b` switch on the command line.

For more information about `xjc` compiler options in general, see JAXB Compiler Options (page 536).

Restrictions for External Binding Customizations

There are several rules that apply to binding declarations made in an external binding customization file that do not apply to similar declarations made inline in a source schema:

- The binding customization file must begin with the `jxb:bindings version` attribute, plus attributes for the JAXB and XMLSchema namespaces:

  ```
  <jxb:bindings version="1.0"
    xmlns:jxb="http://java.sun.com/xml/ns/jaxb"
    xmlns:xs="http://www.w3.org/2001/XMLSchema">
  ```

- The remote schema to which the binding declaration applies must be identified explicitly in XPath notation by means of a `jxb:bindings` declaration specifying `schemaLocation` and `node` attributes:
  - `schemaLocation` — URI reference to the remote schema
  - `node` — XPath 1.0 expression that identifies the schema node within `schemaLocation` to which the given binding declaration is associated; in the case of the initial `jxb:bindings` declaration in the binding customization file, this node is typically `"/xs:schema"`

  For information about XPath syntax, see *XML Path Language*, James Clark and Steve DeRose, eds., W3C, 16 November 1999. Available at `http://www.w3.org/TR/1999/REC-xpath-19991116`.

- Similarly, individual nodes within the schema to which customizations are to be applied must be specified using XPath notation; for example:

  ```
  <jxb:bindings node="//xs:complexType[@name='USAddress']">
  ```

In such cases, the customization is applied to the node by the binding compiler as if the declaration was embedded inline in the node's `<xs:appinfo>` element.

To summarize these rules, the external binding element `<jxb:bindings>` is only recognized for processing by a JAXB binding compiler in three cases:

- When its parent is an `<xs:appinfo>` element
- When it is an ancestor of another `<jxb:bindings>` element
- When it is root element of a document—an XML document that has a `<jxb:bindings>` element as its root is referred to as an external binding declaration file

Scope, Inheritance, and Precedence

Default JAXB bindings can be customized or overridden at four different levels, or *scopes*.

Figure 16–3 illustrates the inheritance and precedence of customization declarations. Specifically, declarations towards the top of the pyramid inherit and supersede declarations below them. For example, Component declarations inherit from and supersede Definition declarations; Definition declarations inherit and supersede Schema declarations; and Schema declarations inherit and supersede Global declarations.

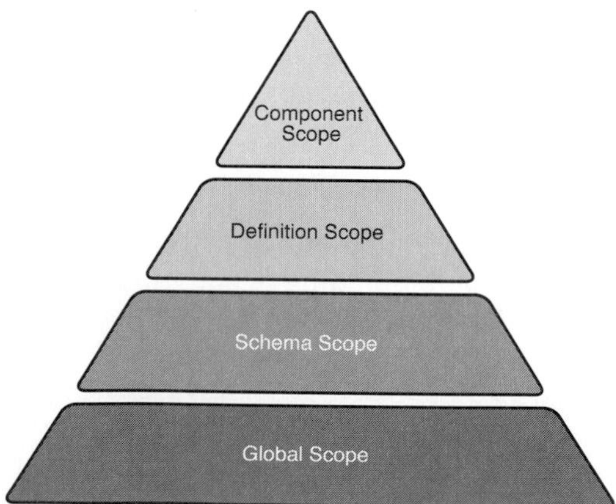

Figure 16–3 Customization Scope Inheritance and Precedence

Customization Syntax

The syntax for the four types of JAXB binding declarations, as well as the syntax for the XML-to-Java datatype binding declarations and the customization namespace prefix, are described below.

- Global binding declarations
- Schema binding declarations
- Class binding declarations
- Property binding declarations
- <javaType> binding declarations
- Typesafe enumeration binding declarations
- <javadoc> binding declarations
- Customization namespace prefix

Global Binding Declarations

Global scope customizations are declared with <globalBindings>. The syntax for global scope customizations is as follows:

```
<globalBindings>
  [ collectionType = "collectionType" ]
  [ fixedAttributeAsConstantProperty= "true" | "false" | "1" | "0" ]
  [ generateIsSetMethod= "true" | "false" | "1" | "0" ]
  [ enableFailFastCheck = "true" | "false" | "1" | "0" ]
  [ choiceContentProperty = "true" | "false" | "1" | "0" ]
  [ underscoreBinding = "asWordSeparator" | "asCharInWord" ]
  [ typesafeEnumBase = "typesafeEnumBase" ]
  [ typesafeEnumMemberName = "generateName" | "generateError" ]
  [ enableJavaNamingConventions = "true" | "false" | "1" | "0" ]
  [ bindingStyle = "elementBinding" | "modelGroupBinding" ]
  [ <javaType> ... </javaType> ]*
</globalBindings>
```

- collectionType can be either indexed or any fully qualified class name that implements java.util.List.
- fixedAttributeAsConstantProperty can be either true, false, 1, or 0. The default value is false.
- generateIsSetMethod can be either true, false, 1, or 0. The default value is false.
- enableFailFastCheck can be either true, false, 1, or 0. If enableFailFastCheck is true or 1 and the JAXB implementation supports this optional checking, type constraint checking is performed when setting a

property. The default value is `false`. Please note that the JAXB implementation does not support failfast validation.

- `choiceContentProperty` can be either `true`, `false`, `1`, or `0`. The default value is `false`. `choiceContentProperty` is not relevant when the `bindingStyle` is `elementBinding`. Therefore, if `bindingStyle` is specified as `elementBinding`, then the `choiceContentProperty` must result in an invalid customization.
- `underscoreBinding` can be either `asWordSeparator` or `asCharInWord`. The default value is `asWordSeparator`.
- `typesafeEnumBase` can be a list of QNames, each of which must resolve to a simple type definition. The default value is `xs:NCName`. See Typesafe Enumeration Binding Declarations (page 560) for information about localized mapping of `simpleType` definitions to Java `typesafe enum` classes.
- `typesafeEnumMemberName` can be either `generateError` or `generateName`. The default value is `generateError`.
- `enableJavaNamingConventions` can be either `true`, `false`, `1`, or `0`. The default value is `true`.
- `bindingStyle` can be either `elementBinding`, or `modelGroupBinding`. The default value is `elementBinding`.
- `<javaType>` can be zero or more javaType binding declarations. For more information, see <javaType> Binding Declarations (page 558).

`<globalBindings>` declarations are only valid in the `annotation` element of the top-level `schema` element. There can only be a single instance of a `<globalBindings>` declaration in any given schema or binding declarations file. If one source schema includes or imports a second source schema, the `<globalBindings>` declaration must be declared in the first source schema.

Schema Binding Declarations

Schema scope customizations are declared with `<schemaBindings>`. The syntax for schema scope customizations is:

```
<schemaBindings>
  [ <package> package </package> ]
  [ <nameXmlTransform> ... </nameXmlTransform> ]*
</schemaBindings>

<package [ name = "packageName" ]
  [ <javadoc> ... </javadoc> ]
</package>
```

```
<nameXmlTransform>
  [ <typeName [ suffix="suffix" ]
              [ prefix="prefix" ] /> ]
  [ <elementName [ suffix="suffix" ]
                 [ prefix="prefix" ] /> ]
  [ <modelGroupName [ suffix="suffix" ]
                    [ prefix="prefix" ] /> ]
  [ <anonymousTypeName [ suffix="suffix" ]
                       [ prefix="prefix" ] /> ]
</nameXmlTransform>
```

As shown above, `<schemaBinding>` declarations include two subcomponents:

- `<package>...</package>` specifies the name of the package and, if desired, the location of the API documentation for the schema-derived classes.
- `<nameXmlTransform>...</nameXmlTransform>` specifies customizations to be applied.

Class Binding Declarations

The `<class>` binding declaration enables you to customize the binding of a schema element to a Java content interface or a Java `Element` interface. `<class>` declarations can be used to customize:

- A name for a schema-derived Java interface
- An implementation class for a schema-derived Java content interface

The syntax for `<class>` customizations is:

```
<class [ name = "className"]
   [ implClass= "implClass" ] >
   [ <javadoc> ... </javadoc> ]
</class>
```

- `name` is the name of the derived Java interface. It must be a legal Java interface name and must not contain a package prefix. The package prefix is inherited from the current value of package.
- `implClass` is the name of the implementation class for `className` and must include the complete package name.
- The `<javadoc>` element specifies the Javadoc tool annotations for the schema-derived Java interface. The string entered here must use `CDATA` or < to escape embedded HTML tags.

Property Binding Declarations

The <property> binding declaration enables you to customize the binding of an XML schema element to its Java representation as a property. The scope of customization can either be at the definition level or component level depending upon where the <property> binding declaration is specified.

The syntax for <property> customizations is:

```
<property[ name = "propertyName"]
  [ collectionType = "propertyCollectionType" ]
  [ fixedAttributeAsConstantProperty = "true" | "false" | "1" | "0" ]
  [ generateIsSetMethod = "true" | "false" | "1" | "0" ]
  [ enableFailFastCheck ="true" | "false" | "1" | "0" ]
  [ <baseType> ... </baseType> ]
  [ <javadoc> ... </javadoc> ]
</property>

<baseType>
  <javaType> ... </javaType>
</baseType>
```

- `name` defines the customization value `propertyName`; it must be a legal Java identifier.
- `collectionType` defines the customization value `propertyCollectionType`, which is the collection type for the property. `propertyCollectionType`. If specified, can be either `indexed` or any fully-qualified class name that implements `java.util.List`.
- `fixedAttributeAsConstantProperty` defines the customization value `fixedAttributeAsConstantProperty`. The value can be either `true`, `false`, `1`, or `0`.
- `generateIsSetMethod` defines the customization value of `generateIsSetMethod`. The value can be either `true`, `false`, `1`, or `0`.
- `enableFailFastCheck` defines the customization value `enableFailFastCheck`. The value can be either `true`, `false`, `1`, or `0`. Please note that the JAXB implementation does not support failfast validation.
- `<javadoc>` customizes the Javadoc tool annotations for the property's getter method.

<javaType> Binding Declarations

The <javaType> declaration provides a way to customize the translation of XML datatypes to and from Java datatypes. XML provides more datatypes than

Java, and so the `<javaType>` declaration lets you specify custom datatype bindings when the default JAXB binding cannot sufficiently represent your schema.

The target Java datatype can be a Java built-in datatype or an application-specific Java datatype. If an application-specific datatype is used as the target, your implementation must also provide parse and print methods for unmarshalling and marshalling data. To this end, the JAXB specification supports a `parseMethod` and `printMethod`:

- The `parseMethod` is called during unmarshalling to convert a string from the input document into a value of the target Java datatype.
- The `printMethod` is called during marshalling to convert a value of the target type into a lexical representation.

If you prefer to define your own datatype conversions, JAXB defines a static class, `DatatypeConverter`, to assist in the parsing and printing of valid lexical representations of the XML Schema built-in datatypes.

The syntax for the `<javaType>` customization is:

```
<javaType name= "javaType"
      [ xmlType= "xmlType" ]
      [ hasNsContext = "true" | "false" ]
      [ parseMethod= "parseMethod" ]
      [ printMethod= "printMethod" ]>
```

- `name` is the Java datatype to which `xmlType` is to be bound.
- `xmlType` is the name of the XML Schema datatype to which `javaType` is to be bound; this attribute is required when the parent of the `<javaType>` declaration is `<globalBindings>`.
- `hasNsContext` allows a namespace context to be specified as a second parameter to a print or a parse method; can be either `true`, `false`, `1`, or `0`. By default, this attribute is `false`, and in most cases you will not need to change it.
- `parseMethod` is the name of the parse method to be called during unmarshalling.
- `printMethod` is the name of the print method to be called during marshalling.

The <javaType> declaration can be used in:

- A <globalBindings> declaration
- An annotation element for simple type definitions, GlobalBindings, and <basetype> declarations
- A <property> declaration

See MyDatatypeConverter Class (page 567) for an example of how <javaType> declarations and the DatatypeConverterInterface interface are implemented in a custom datatype converter class.

Typesafe Enumeration Binding Declarations

The typesafe enumeration declarations provide a localized way to map XML simpleType elements to Java typesafe enum classes. There are two types of typesafe enumeration declarations you can make:

- <typesafeEnumClass> lets you map an entire simpleType class to typesafe enum classes.
- <typesafeEnumMember> lets you map just selected members of a simpleType class to typesafe enum classes.

In both cases, there are two primary limitations on this type of customization:

- Only simpleType definitions with enumeration facets can be customized using this binding declaration.
- This customization only applies to a single simpleType definition at a time. To map sets of similar simpleType definitions on a global level, use the typesafeEnumBase attribute in a <globalBindings> declaration, as described in Global Binding Declarations (page 555).

The syntax for the <typesafeEnumClass> customization is:

```
<typesafeEnumClass[ name = "enumClassName" ]
  [ <typesafeEnumMember> ... </typesafeEnumMember> ]*
  [ <javadoc> enumClassJavadoc </javadoc> ]
</typesafeEnumClass>
```

- name must be a legal Java Identifier, and must not have a package prefix.
- You can have zero or more <typesafeEnumMember> declarations embedded in a <typesafeEnumClass> declaration.
- <javadoc> customizes the Javadoc tool annotations for the enumeration class.

The syntax for the <typesafeEnumMember> customization is:

```
<typesafeEnumMember name = "enumMemberName">
            [ value = "enumMemberValue" ]
  [ <javadoc> enumMemberJavadoc </javadoc> ]
</typesafeEnumMember>
```

- name must always be specified and must be a legal Java identifier.
- value must be the enumeration value specified in the source schema.
- <javadoc> customizes the Javadoc tool annotations for the enumeration constant.

For inline annotations, the <typesafeEnumClass> declaration must be specified in the annotation element of the <simpleType> element. The <typesafeEnumMember> must be specified in the annotation element of the enumeration member. This allows the enumeration member to be customized independently from the enumeration class.

For information about typesafe enum design patterns, see the sample chapter of Joshua Bloch's *Effective Java Programming* on the Java Developer Connection.

<javadoc> Binding Declarations

The <javadoc> declaration lets you add custom Javadoc tool annotations to schema-derived JAXB packages, classes, interfaces, methods, and fields. Note that <javadoc> declarations cannot be applied globally—that is, they are only valid as sub-elements of other binding customizations.

The syntax for the <javadoc> customization is:

```
<javadoc>
  Contents in &lt;b>Javadoc&lt;\b> format.
</javadoc>
```

or

```
<javadoc>
  <<![CDATA[
  Contents in <b>Javadoc<\b> format
  ]]>
</javadoc>
```

Note that documentation strings in <javadoc> declarations applied at the package level must contain <body> open and close tags; for example:

```
<jxb:package name="primer.myPo">
      <jxb:javadoc><![CDATA[<body>Package level documentation
for generated package primer.myPo.</body>]]>
</jxb:javadoc>
     </jxb:package>
```

Customization Namespace Prefix

All standard JAXB binding declarations must be preceded by a namespace prefix that maps to the JAXB namespace URI (`http://java.sun.com/xml/ns/jaxb`). For example, in this sample, `jxb:` is used. To this end, any schema you want to customize with standard JAXB binding declarations *must* include the JAXB namespace declaration and JAXB version number at the top of the schema file. For example, in `po.xsd` for the Customize Inline example, the namespace declaration is as follows:

```
<xsd:schema xmlns:xsd="http://www.w3.org/2001/XMLSchema"
            xmlns:jxb="http://java.sun.com/xml/ns/jaxb"
            jxb:version="1.0">
```

A binding declaration with the `jxb` namespace prefix would then take the form:

```
<xsd:annotation>
   <xsd:appinfo>
      <jxb:globalBindings binding declarations />
      <jxb:schemaBindings>
         .
         .
         binding declarations
         .
         .
      </jxb:schemaBindings>
   </xsd:appinfo>
</xsd:annotation>
```

Note that in this example, the `globalBindings` and `schemaBindings` declarations are used to specify, respectively, global scope and schema scope customizations. These customization scopes are described in more detail in Scope, Inheritance, and Precedence (page 554).

Customize Inline Example

The Customize Inline example illustrates some basic customizations made by means of inline annotations to an XML schema named `po.xsd`. In addition, this example implements a custom datatype converter class, `MyDatatypeConverter.java`, which illustrates print and parse methods in the `<javaType>` customization for handling custom datatype conversions.

To summarize this example:

1. `po.xsd` is an XML schema containing inline binding customizations.
2. `MyDatatypeConverter.java` is a Java class file that implements print and parse methods specified by `<javaType>` customizations in `po.xsd`.
3. `Main.java` is the primary class file in the Customize Inline example, which uses the schema-derived classes generated by the JAXB compiler.

Building and Running the Customize Inline Example Using NetBeans 5.5

Follow these instructions to build and run the Customize Inline example on your Application Server instance using the NetBeans 5.5 IDE.

1. In NetBeans 5.5, select File→Open Project.
2. In the Open Project dialog, navigate to `<INSTALL>/javaeetutorial5/examples/jaxb/`.
3. Select the `inline-customize` folder.
4. Select the Open as Main Project checkbox.
5. Click Open Project Folder.
6. Right-click the `inline-customize` project and select Run Project.

Building and Running the Customize Inline Example Using Ant

To compile and run the Customize Inline example using Ant, in a terminal window, go to the `<INSTALL>/javaeetutorial5/examples/jaxb/inline-customize/` directory and type the following:

```
ant runapp
```

Key customizations in this sample, and the custom MyDatatypeConverter.java class, are described in more detail below.

Customized Schema

The customized schema used in the Customize Inline example is in the file <*JAVA_HOME*>/jaxb/samples/inline-customize/po.xsd. The customizations are in the <xsd:annotation> tags.

Global Binding Declarations

The code below shows the globalBindings declarations in po.xsd:

```
<jxb:globalBindings
        fixedAttributeAsConstantProperty="true"
        collectionType="java.util.Vector"
        typesafeEnumBase="xsd:NCName"
        choiceContentProperty="false"
        typesafeEnumMemberName="generateError"
        bindingStyle="elementBinding"
        enableFailFastCheck="false"
        generateIsSetMethod="false"
        underscoreBinding="asCharInWord"/>
```

In this example, all values are set to the defaults except for collectionType.

- Setting fixedAttributeAsConstantProperty to true indicates that all fixed attributes should be bound to Java constants. By default, fixed attributes are just mapped to either simple or collection property, whichever is more appropriate.
- Setting collectionType to java.util.Vector specifies that all lists in the generated implementation classes should be represented internally as vectors. Note that the class name you specify for collectionType must implement java.util.List and be callable by newInstance.
- If typesafeEnumBase is set to xsd:string, it would be a global way to specify that all simple type definitions deriving directly or indirectly from xsd:string and having enumeration facets should be bound by default to a typesafe enum. If typesafeEnumBase is set to an empty string, "", no simple type definitions would ever be bound to a typesafe enum class by default. The value of typesafeEnumBase can be any atomic simple type definition except xsd:boolean and both binary types.

- The JAXB implementation does not support the `enableFailFastCheck` attribute.

Note: Using `typesafe enum` classes enables you to map schema enumeration values to Java constants, which in turn makes it possible to do compares on Java constants rather than string values.

Schema Binding Declarations

The following code shows the schema binding declarations in `po.xsd`:

```
<jxb:schemaBindings>
      <jxb:package name="primer.myPo">
         <jxb:javadoc>
   <![CDATA[<body> Package level documentation for
generated package primer.myPo.</body>]]>
         </jxb:javadoc>
      </jxb:package>
      <jxb:nameXmlTransform>
          <jxb:elementName suffix="Element"/>
      </jxb:nameXmlTransform>
    </jxb:schemaBindings>
```

- `<jxb:package name="primer.myPo"/>` specifies the `primer.myPo` as the package in which the schema-derived classes should be generated.
- `<jxb:nameXmlTransform>` specifies that all generated Java element interfaces should have `Element` appended to the generated names by default. For example, when the JAXB compiler is run against this schema, the element interfaces `CommentElement` and `PurchaseOrderElement` will be generated. By contrast, without this customization, the default binding would instead generate `Comment` and `PurchaseOrder`.

  This customization is useful if a schema uses the same name in different symbol spaces; for example, in global element and type definitions. In such cases, this customization enables you to resolve the collision with one declaration rather than having to individually resolve each collision with a separate binding declaration.
- `<jxb:javadoc>` specifies customized Javadoc tool annotations for the `primer.myPo` package. Note that, unlike the `<javadoc>` declarations at the class level, below, the opening and closing `<body>` tags must be included when the `<javadoc>` declaration is made at the package level.

Class Binding Declarations

The following code shows the class binding declarations in po.xsd:

```
<xsd:complexType name="PurchaseOrderType">
      <xsd:annotation>
      <xsd:appinfo>
         <jxb:class name="POType">
            <jxb:javadoc>
            A &lt;b>Purchase Order&lt;/b> consists of
addresses and items.
            </jxb:javadoc>
         </jxb:class>
      </xsd:appinfo>
      </xsd:annotation>
      .
      .
      .
</xsd:complexType>
```

The Javadoc tool annotations for the schema-derived POType class will contain the description "A <b>Purchase Order</b> consists of addresses and items." The < is used to escape the opening bracket on the <b> HTML tags.

Note: When a <class> customization is specified in the appinfo element of a complexType definition, as it is here, the complexType definition is bound to a Java content interface.

Later in po.xsd, another <javadoc> customization is declared at this class level, but this time the HTML string is escaped with CDATA:

```
<xsd:annotation>
 <xsd:appinfo>
    <jxb:class>
      <jxb:javadoc>
     <![CDATA[ First line of documentation for a
<b>USAddress</b>.]]>
       </jxb:javadoc>
    </jxb:class>
  </xsd:appinfo>
  </xsd:annotation>
```

Note: If you want to include HTML markup tags in a `<jaxb:javadoc>` customization, you must enclose the data within a `CDATA` section or escape all left angle brackets using `<`. See *XML 1.0 2nd Edition* for more information (`http://www.w3.org/TR/2000/REC-xml-20001006#sec-cdata-sect`).

Property Binding Declarations

Of particular interest here is the `generateIsSetMethod` customization, which causes two additional property methods, `isSetQuantity` and `unsetQuantity`, to be generated. These methods enable a client application to distinguish between schema default values and values occurring explicitly within an instance document.

For example, in `po.xsd`:

```
<xsd:complexType name="Items">
   <xsd:sequence>
      <xsd:element name="item" minOccurs="1"
maxOccurs="unbounded">
         <xsd:complexType>
            <xsd:sequence>
           <xsd:element name="productName" type="xsd:string"/>
            <xsd:element name="quantity" default="10">
            <xsd:annotation>
               <xsd:appinfo>
                  <jxb:property generateIsSetMethod="true"/>
               </xsd:appinfo>
            </xsd:annotation>
         ...
</xsd:complexType>
      </xsd:element>
   </xsd:sequence>
</xsd:complexType>
```

The `@generateIsSetMethod` applies to the `quantity` element, which is bound to a property within the `Items.ItemType` interface. `unsetQuantity` and `isSetQuantity` methods are generated in the `Items.ItemType` interface.

MyDatatypeConverter Class

The class `<INSTALL>/javaeetutorial5/examples/jaxb/inline-customize/MyDatatypeConverter`, shown below, provides a way to customize the translation of XML datatypes to and from Java datatypes by means of a <javaType> customization.

```
package primer;
import java.math.BigInteger;
import javax.xml.bind.DatatypeConverter;

public class MyDatatypeConverter {

  public static short parseIntegerToShort(String value) {
    BigInteger result =
      DatatypeConverter.parseInteger(value);
    return (short)(result.intValue());
  }

  public static String printShortToInteger(short value) {
    BigInteger result = BigInteger.valueOf(value);
    return DatatypeConverter.printInteger(result);
  }

  public static int parseIntegerToInt(String value) {
    BigInteger result =
    DatatypeConverter.parseInteger(value);
  return result.intValue();
  }

  public static String printIntToInteger(int value) {
    BigInteger result = BigInteger.valueOf(value);
    return DatatypeConverter.printInteger(result);
  }
};
```

The following code shows how the `MyDatatypeConverter` class is referenced in a <javaType> declaration in `po.xsd`:

```
<xsd:simpleType name="ZipCodeType">
  <xsd:annotation>
     <xsd:appinfo>
        <jxb:javaType name="int"
parseMethod="primer.MyDatatypeConverter.parseIntegerToInt"
printMethod="primer.MyDatatypeConverter.printIntTo Integer" />
     </xsd:appinfo>
  </xsd:annotation>
  <xsd:restriction base="xsd:integer">
```

```
      <xsd:minInclusive value="10000"/>
      <xsd:maxInclusive value="99999"/>
    </xsd:restriction>
  </xsd:simpleType>
```

In this example, the `jxb:javaType` binding declaration overrides the default JAXB binding of this type to `java.math.BigInteger`. For the purposes of the Customize Inline example, the restrictions on `ZipCodeType`—specifically that legal US ZIP codes are limited to five digits—make it so all valid values can easily fit within the Java primitive datatype `int`. Note also that, because `<jxb:javaType name="int"/>` is declared within `ZipCodeType`, the customization applies to all JAXB properties that reference this `simpleType` definition, including the `getZip` and `setZip` methods.

Datatype Converter Example

The Datatype Converter example is very similar to the Customize Inline example. As with the Customize Inline example, the customizations in the Datatype Converter example are made by using inline binding declarations in the XML schema for the application, `po.xsd`.

The global, schema, and package, and most of the class customizations for the Customize Inline and Datatype Converter examples are identical. Where the Datatype Converter example differs from the Customize Inline example is in the `parseMethod` and `printMethod` used for converting XML data to the Java `int` datatype.

Specifically, rather than using methods in the custom `MyDataTypeConverter` class to perform these datatype conversions, the Datatype Converter example uses the built-in methods provided by `javax.xml.bind.DatatypeConverter`:

```
<xsd:simpleType name="ZipCodeType">
  <xsd:annotation>
     <xsd:appinfo>
        <jxb:javaType name="int"
   parseMethod="javax.xml.bind.DatatypeConverter.parseInt"
   printMethod="javax.xml.bind.DatatypeConverter.printInt"/>
     </xsd:appinfo>
  </xsd:annotation>
  <xsd:restriction base="xsd:integer">
    <xsd:minInclusive value="10000"/>
    <xsd:maxInclusive value="99999"/>
  </xsd:restriction>
</xsd:simpleType>
```

Building and Running the Datatype Converter Example Using NetBeans 5.5

Follow these instructions to build and run the Datatype Converter example on your Application Server instance using the NetBeans 5.5 IDE.

1. In NetBeans 5.5, select File→Open Project.
2. In the Open Project dialog, navigate to `<INSTALL>/javaeetutorial5/examples/jaxb/`.
3. Select the `datatypeconverter` folder.
4. Select the Open as Main Project checkbox.
5. Click Open Project Folder.
6. Right-click the `datatypeconverter` project and select Run Project.

Building and Running the Datatype Converter Example Using Ant

To compile and run the Datatype Converter example using Ant, in a terminal window, go to the `<INSTALL>/javaeetutorial5/examples/jaxb/datatype-converter/` directory and type the following:

```
ant runapp
```

Binding Declaration Files

The following sections provide information about binding declaration files:

- JAXB version, namespace, and schema attributes
- Global and schema binding declarations
- Class declarations

JAXB Version, Namespace, and Schema Attributes

All JAXB binding declarations files must begin with:

- JAXB version number
- Namespace declarations
- Schema name and node

The version, namespace, and schema declarations in `bindings.xjb` are as follows:

```
<jxb:bindings version="1.0"
              xmlns:jxb="http://java.sun.com/xml/ns/jaxb"
              xmlns:xs="http://www.w3.org/2001/XMLSchema">
  <jxb:bindings schemaLocation="po.xsd" node="/xs:schema">
        ...
        <binding_declarations>
        ...
  </jxb:bindings>
<!-- schemaLocation="po.xsd" node="/xs:schema" -->
</jxb:bindings>
```

JAXB Version Number

An XML file with a root element of `<jaxb:bindings>` is considered an external binding file. The root element must specify the JAXB version attribute with which its binding declarations must comply; specifically the root `<jxb:bindings>` element must contain either a `<jxb:version>` declaration or a `version` attribute. By contrast, when making binding declarations inline, the JAXB version number is made as attribute of the `<xsd:schema>` declaration:

```
<xsd:schema xmlns:xsd="http://www.w3.org/2001/XMLSchema"
            xmlns:jxb="http://java.sun.com/xml/ns/jaxb"
            jxb:version="1.0">
```

Namespace Declarations

As shown in JAXB Version, Namespace, and Schema Attributes (page 571), the namespace declarations in the external binding declarations file include both the JAXB namespace and the XMLSchema namespace. Note that the prefixes used in this example could in fact be anything you want; the important thing is to consistently use whatever prefixes you define here in subsequent declarations in the file.

Schema Name and Schema Node

The fourth line of the code in JAXB Version, Namespace, and Schema Attributes (page 571) specifies the name of the schema to which this binding declarations file will apply, and the schema node at which the customizations will first take effect. Subsequent binding declarations in this file will reference specific nodes within the schema, but this first declaration should encompass the schema as a whole; for example, in `bindings.xjb`:

```
<jxb:bindings schemaLocation="po.xsd" node="/xs:schema">
```

Global and Schema Binding Declarations

The global schema binding declarations in `bindings.xjb` are the same as those in `po.xsd` for the Datatype Converter example. The only difference is that because the declarations in `po.xsd` are made inline, you need to embed them in `<xs:appinfo>` elements, which are in turn embedded in `<xs:annotation>` elements. Embedding declarations in this way is unnecessary in the external bindings file.

```
<jxb:globalBindings
    fixedAttributeAsConstantProperty="true"
    collectionType="java.util.Vector"
    typesafeEnumBase="xs:NCName"
    choiceContentProperty="false"
    typesafeEnumMemberName="generateError"
    bindingStyle="elementBinding"
    enableFailFastCheck="false"
    generateIsSetMethod="false"
    underscoreBinding="asCharInWord"/>
<jxb:schemaBindings>
    <jxb:package name="primer.myPo">
        <jxb:javadoc><![CDATA[<body>Package level
documentation for generated package primer.myPo.</body>]]>
        </jxb:javadoc>
    </jxb:package>
    <jxb:nameXmlTransform>
        <jxb:elementName suffix="Element"/>
    </jxb:nameXmlTransform>
</jxb:schemaBindings>
```

By comparison, the syntax used in po.xsd for the Datatype Converter example is:

```
<xsd:annotation>
  <xsd:appinfo>
    <jxb:globalBindings
        ...
        <binding_declarations>
        ...
    <jxb:schemaBindings>
        ...
        <binding_declarations>
        ...
    </jxb:schemaBindings>
  </xsd:appinfo>
</xsd:annotation>
```

Class Declarations

The class-level binding declarations in bindings.xjb differ from the analogous declarations in po.xsd for the Datatype Converter example in two ways:

- As with all other binding declarations in bindings.xjb, you do not need to embed your customizations in schema <xsd:appinfo> elements.
- You must specify the schema node to which the customization will be applied. The general syntax for this type of declaration is:

  ```
  <jxb:bindings node="//<node_type>[@name='<node_name>']">
  ```

For example, the following code shows binding declarations for the complexType named USAddress.

```
<jxb:bindings node="//xs:complexType[@name='USAddress']">
  <jxb:class>
    <jxb:javadoc>
<![CDATA[First line of documentation for a <b>USAddress</b>.]]>
    </jxb:javadoc>
  </jxb:class>

  <jxb:bindings node=".//xs:element[@name='name']">
    <jxb:property name="toName"/>
  </jxb:bindings>

  <jxb:bindings node=".//xs:element[@name='zip']">
```

```
    <jxb:property name="zipCode"/>
  </jxb:bindings>
</jxb:bindings>
<!-- node="//xs:complexType[@name='USAddress']" -->
```

Note in this example that USAddress is the parent of the child elements name and zip, and therefore a </jxb:bindings> tag encloses the bindings declarations for the child elements as well as the class-level javadoc declaration.

External Customize Example

The External Customize example is identical to the Datatype Converter example, except that the binding declarations in the External Customize example are made by means of an external binding declarations file rather than inline in the source XML schema.

The binding customization file used in the External Customize example is <*INSTALL*>/javaeetutorial5/examples/jaxb/external-customize/binding.xjb.

This section compares the customization declarations in bindings.xjb with the analogous declarations used in the XML schema, po.xsd, in the Datatype Converter example. The two sets of declarations achieve precisely the same results.

Building and Running the External Customize Example Using NetBeans 5.5

Follow these instructions to build and run the External Customize example on your Application Server instance using the NetBeans 5.5 IDE.

1. In NetBeans 5.5, select File→Open Project.
2. In the Open Project dialog, navigate to <*INSTALL*>/javaeetutorial5/examples/jaxb/.
3. Select the external-customize folder.
4. Select the Open as Main Project checkbox.
5. Click Open Project Folder.
6. Right-click the external-customize project and select Run Project.

Building and Running the External Customize Example Using Ant

To compile and run the External Customize example using Ant, in a terminal window, go to the *<INSTALL>*/javaeetutorial5/examples/jaxb/external-customize/ directory and type the following:

```
ant runapp
```

Java-to-Schema Examples

The Java-to-Schema examples show how to use annotations to map Java classes to XML schema.

j2s-create-marshal Example

The j2s-create-marshal example illustrates Java-to-schema databinding. It demonstrates marshalling and unmarshalling of JAXB annotated classes and also shows how to enable JAXP 1.3 validation at unmarshal time using a schema file that was generated from the JAXB mapped classes.

The schema file, bc.xsd, was generated with the following commands:

```
% schemagen src/cardfile/*.java
% cp schema1.xsd bc.xsd
```

Note that schema1.xsd, was copied to bc.xsd; schemagen does not allow you to specify a schema name of your choice.

Building and Running the j2s-create-marshal Example Using NetBeans 5.5

Follow these instructions to build and run the j2s-create-marshal example on your Application Server instance using the NetBeans 5.5 IDE.

1. In NetBeans 5.5, select File→Open Project.
2. In the Open Project dialog, navigate to *<INSTALL>*/javaeetutorial5/examples/jaxb/.
3. Select the j2s-create-marshal folder.

4. Select the Open as Main Project checkbox.
5. Click Open Project Folder.
6. Right-click the `j2s-create-marshal` project and select Run Project.

Building and Running the j2s-create-marshal Example Using Ant

To compile and run the `j2s-create-marshal` example using Ant, in a terminal window, go to the `*<INSTALL>*/javaeetutorial5/examples/jaxb/j2s-create-marshal/` directory and type the following:

```
ant runapp
```

j2s-xmlAccessorOrder Example

The `j2s-xmlAccessorOrder` example shows how to use the `@XmlAccessorOrder` and `@XmlType.propOrder` annotations to dictate the order in which XML content is marshalled/unmarshalled by a Java type.

With Java-to-schema mapping, a JavaBean's properties and fields are mapped to an XML Schema type. The class elements are mapped to either an XML Schema complex type or an XML Schema simple type. The default element order for a generated schema type is currently unspecified because Java reflection does not impose a return order. The lack of reliable element ordering negatively impacts application portability. You can use two annotations, `@XmlAccessorOrder` and `@XmlType.propOrder`, to define schema element ordering for applications that need to be portable across JAXB Providers.

Using the @XmlAccessorOrder Annotation to Define Schema Element Ordering

The `@XmlAccessorOrder` annotation imposes one of two element ordering algorithms, `AccessorOrder.UNDEFINED` or `AccessorOrder.ALPHABETICAL`. `AccessorOrder.UNDEFINED` is the default setting. The order is dependent on the system's reflection implementation. `AccessorOrder.ALPHABETICAL` orders the elements in lexicographic order as determined by `java.lang.String.CompareTo(String anotherString)`.

You can define the @XmlAccessorOrder annotation for annotation type ElementType.PACKAGE on a class object. When the @XmlAccessorOrder annotation is defined on a package, the scope of the formatting rule is active for every class in the package. When defined on a class, the rule is active on the contents of that class.

There can be multiple @XmlAccessorOrder annotations within a package. The order of precedence is the innermost (class) annotation takes precedence over the outer annotation. For example, if @XmlAccessorOrder(AccessorOrder.ALPHABETICAL) is defined on a package and @XmlAccessorOrder(AccessorOrder.UNDEFINED) is defined on a class in that package, the contents of the generated schema type for the class would be in an unspecified order and the contents of the generated schema type for every other class in the package would be alphabetical order.

Using the @XmlType Annotation to Define Schema Element Ordering

The @XmlType annotation can be defined for a class. The annotation element propOrder() in the @XmlType annotation allows you to specify the content order in the generated schema type. When you use the @XmlType.propOrder annotation on a class to specify content order, all public properties and public fields in the class must be specified in the parameter list. Any public property or field that you want to keep out of the parameter list must be annotated with @XmlAttribute or @XmlTransient annotation.

The default content order for @XmlType.propOrder is {} or {""}, not active. In such cases, the active @XmlAccessorOrder annotation takes precedence. When class content order is specified by the @XmlType.propOrder annotation, it takes precedence over any active @XmlAccessorOrder annotation on the class or package. If the @XmlAccessorOrder and @XmlType.propOrder(A, B, ...) annotations are specified on a class, the propOrder always takes precedence regardless of the order of the annotation statements. For example, in the code below, the `@XmlAccessorOrder` annotation precedes the `@XmlType.propOrder` annotation.

```
@XmlAccessorOrder(AccessorOrder.ALPHABETICAL)
@XmlType(propOrder={"name", "city"})
public class USAddress {
        .
        .
    public String getCity() {return city;}
    public void setCity(String city) {this.city = city;}

    public String getName() {return name;}
    public void setName(String name) {this.name = name;}
        .
        .
}
```

In the code below, the `@XmlType.propOrder` annotation precedes the `@XmlAccessorOrder` annotation.

```
@XmlType(propOrder={"name", "city"})
@XmlAccessorOrder(AccessorOrder.ALPHABETICAL)
public class USAddress {
        .
        .
public String getCity() {return city;}
    public void setCity(String city) {this.city = city;}

    public String getName() {return name;}
    public void setName(String name) {this.name = name;}
        .
        .
}
```

In both scenarios, `propOrder` takes precedence and the identical schema content shown below will be generated.

```
<xs:complexType name="usAddress">
   <xs:sequence>
      <xs:element name="name" type="xs:string" minOccurs="0"/>
      <xs:element name="city" type="xs:string" minOccurs="0"/>
   </xs:sequence>
</xs:complexType>
```

Schema Content Ordering in the Example

The purchase order code example demonstrates the effects of schema content ordering using the `@XmlAccessorOrder` annotation at the package and class level, and the `@XmlType.propOrder` annotation on a class.

Class `package-info.java` defines `@XmlAccessorOrder` to be `ALPHABETICAL` for the package. The public fields `shipTo` and `billTo` in class `PurchaseOrderType` will be affected in the generated schema content order by this rule. Class `USAddress` defines the `@XmlType.propOrder` annotation on the class. User of this annotation demonstrates user-defined property order superseding `ALPHABETICAL` order in the generated schema.

The generated schema file can be found in the *<INSTALL>*`/javaeetutorial5/examples/jaxb/j2s-xmlAccessorOrder/build/schemas/` directory.

Building and Running the j2s-xmlAccessorOrder Example Using NetBeans 5.5

Follow these instructions to build and run the `j2s-xmlAccessorOrder` example on your Application Server instance using the NetBeans 5.5 IDE.

1. In NetBeans 5.5, select File→Open Project.
2. In the Open Project dialog, navigate to *<INSTALL>*`/javaeetutorial5/examples/jaxb/`.
3. Select the `j2s-xmlAccessorOrder` folder.
4. Select the Open as Main Project checkbox.
5. Click Open Project Folder.
6. Right-click the `j2s-xmlAccessorOrder` project and select Run Project.

Building and Running the j2s-xmlAccessorOrder Example Using Ant

To compile and run the `j2s-xmlAccessorOrder` example using Ant, in a terminal window, go to the *<INSTALL>*`/javaeetutorial5/examples/jaxb/j2s-xmlAccessorOrder/` directory and type the following:

```
ant runapp
```

j2s-xmlAdapter-field Example

The `j2s-xmlAdapter-field` example demonstrates how to use the `XmlAdapter` interface and the `@XmlJavaTypeAdapter` annotation to provide a custom mapping of XML content into and out of a `HashMap` (field) that uses an `int` as the key and a `String` as the value.

Interface `XmlAdapter` and annotation `@XmlJavaTypeAdapter` are used for special processing of datatypes during unmarshalling/marshalling. There are a variety of XML datatypes for which the representation does not map easily into Java (for example, `xs:DateTime` and `xs:Duration`), and Java types which do not map conveniently into XML representations, for example implementations of `java.util.Collection` (such as `List`) and `java.util.Map` (such as `HashMap`) or for non-JavaBean classes.

The `XmlAdapter` interface and the `@XmlJavaTypeAdapter` annotation are provided for cases such as these. This combination provides a portable mechanism for reading/writing XML content into and out of Java applications.

The `XmlAdapter` interface defines the methods for data reading/writing.

```
/*
 *  ValueType - Java class that provides an XML representation
 *              of the data. It is the object that is used for
 *              marshalling and unmarshalling.
 *
 *  BoundType - Java class that is used to process XML content.
 */

public abstract class XmlAdapter<ValueType,BoundType> {
    // Do-nothing constructor for the derived classes.
    protected XmlAdapter() {}

    // Convert a value type to a bound type.
    public abstract BoundType unmarshal(ValueType v);

    // Convert a bound type to a value type.
    public abstract ValueType marshal(BoundType v);
}
```

You can use the `@XmlJavaTypeAdapter` annotation to associate a particular `XmlAdapter` implementation with a `Target` type, `PACKAGE`, `FIELD`, `METHOD`, `TYPE`, or `PARAMETER`.

The `j2s-xmlAdapter-field` example shows how to use an `XmlAdapter` for mapping XML content into and out of a (custom) `HashMap`. The `HashMap` object, `basket`, in class `KitchenWorldBasket`, uses a key of type `int` and a value of type `String`. We want these datatypes to be reflected in the XML content that is read and written. The XML content should look like this.

```
<basket>
     <entry key="9027">glasstop stove in black</entry>
     <entry key="288">wooden spoon</entry>
</basket>
```

The default schema generated for Java type `HashMap` does not reflect the desired format.

```
<xs:element name="basket">
   <xs:complexType>
     <xs:sequence>
       <xs:element name="entry" minOccurs="0"
           maxOccurs="unbounded">
         <xs:complexType>
           <xs:sequence>
             <xs:element name="key" minOccurs="0"
                 type="xs:anyType"/>
             <xs:element name="value" minOccurs="0"
                 type="xs:anyType"/>
           </xs:sequence>
         </xs:complexType>
       </xs:element>
     </xs:sequence>
   </xs:complexType>
</xs:element>
```

In the default `HashMap` schema, key and value are both elements and are of datatype `anyType`. The XML content will look like this:

```
<basket>
     <entry>
        <key>9027</>
        <value>glasstop stove in black</>
     </entry>
     <entry>
        <key>288</>
        <value>wooden spoon</>
     </entry>
</basket>
```

To resolve this issue, we wrote two Java classes, `PurchaseList` and `PartEntry`, that reflect the needed schema format for unmarshalling/marshalling the content. The XML schema generated for these classes is as follows:

```
<xs:complexType name="PurchaseListType">
    <xs:sequence>
        <xs:element name="entry" type="partEntry"
            nillable="true" maxOccurs="unbounded"
            minOccurs="0"/>
    </xs:sequence>
</xs:complexType>

<xs:complexType name="partEntry">
    <xs:simpleContent>
        <xs:extension base="xs:string">
            <xs:attribute name="key" type="xs:int"
                use="required"/>
        </xs:extension>
    </xs:simpleContent>
</xs:complexType>
```

Class `AdapterPurchaseListToHashMap` implements the `XmlAdapter` interface. In class `KitchenWorldBasket`, the `@XmlJavaTypeAdapter` annotation is used to pair `AdapterPurchaseListToHashMap` with field `HashMap basket`. This pairing will cause the marshal/unmarshal method of `AdapterPurchaseListToHashMap` to be called for any corresponding marshal/unmarshal action on `KitchenWorld-Basket`.

Building and Running the j2s-xmlAdapter-field Example Using NetBeans 5.5

Follow these instructions to build and run the `j2s-xmlAdapter-field` example on your Application Server instance using the NetBeans 5.5 IDE.

1. In NetBeans 5.5, select File→Open Project.
2. In the Open Project dialog, navigate to `<INSTALL>/javaeetutorial5/examples/jaxb/`.
3. Select the `j2s-xmlAdapter-field` folder.
4. Select the Open as Main Project checkbox.
5. Click Open Project Folder.
6. Right-click the `j2s-xmlAdapter-field` project and select Run Project.

Building and Running the j2s-xmlAdapter-field Example Using Ant

To compile and run the `j2s-xmlAdapter-field` example using Ant, in a terminal window, go to the *<INSTALL>*`/javaeetutorial5/examples/jaxb/j2s-xmlAdapter-field/` directory and type the following:

```
ant runapp
```

j2s-xmlAttribute-field Example

The `j2s-xmlAttribute-field` example shows how to use the `@XmlAttribute` annotation to define a property or field to be treated as an XML attribute.

The `@XmlAttribute` annotation maps a field or JavaBean property to an XML attribute. The following rules are imposed:

- A static final field is mapped to a XML fixed attribute.
- When the field or property is a collection type, the items of the collection type must map to a schema simple type.
- When the field or property is other than a collection type, the type must map to a schema simple type.

When following the JavaBean programming paradigm, a property is defined by a `get` and `set` prefix on a field name.

```
int zip;
public int getZip(){return zip;}
public void setZip(int z){zip=z;}
```

Within a bean class, you have the choice of setting the `@XmlAttribute` annotation on one of three components: the field, the setter method, or the getter method. If you set the `@XmlAttribute` annotation on the field, the setter method will need to be renamed or there will be a naming conflict at compile time. If you set the `@XmlAttribute` annotation on one of the methods, it must be set on either the setter or getter method, but not on both.

The `j2s-xmlAttribute-field` example shows how to use the `@XmlAttribute` annotation on a static final field, on a field rather than on one of the corresponding bean methods, on a bean property (method), and on a field that is other than a collection type. In class `USAddress`, fields, country, and zip are tagged as attributes. The `setZip` method was disabled to avoid the compile error. Property state was tagged as an attribute on the setter method. You could have used the getter method instead. In class `PurchaseOrderType`, field `cCardVendor` is a non-collection type. It meets the requirement of being a simple type; it is an `enum` type.

Building and Running the j2s-xmlAttribute-field Example Using NetBeans 5.5

Follow these instructions to build and run the `j2s-xmlAttribute-field` example on your Application Server instance using the NetBeans 5.5 IDE.

1. In NetBeans 5.5, select File→Open Project.
2. In the Open Project dialog, navigate to `<INSTALL>/javaeetutorial5/examples/jaxb/`.
3. Select the `j2s-xmlAttribute-field` folder.
4. Select the Open as Main Project checkbox.
5. Click Open Project Folder.
6. Right-click the `j2s-xmlAttribute-field` project and select Run Project.

Building and Running the j2s-xmlAttribute-field Example Using Ant

To compile and run the `j2s-xmlAttribute-field` example using Ant, in a terminal window, go to the `<INSTALL>/javaeetutorial5/examples/jaxb/j2s-xmlAttribute-field/` directory and type the following:

```
ant runapp
```

j2s-xmlRootElement Example

The `j2s-xmlRootElement` example demonstrates the use of the `@XmlRootElement` annotation to define an XML element name for the XML schema type of the corresponding class.

The `@XmlRootElement` annotation maps a class or an `enum` type to an XML element. At least one element definition is needed for each top-level Java type used for unmarshalling/marshalling. If there is no element definition, there is no starting location for XML content processing.

The @XmlRootElement annotation uses the class name as the default element name. You can change the default name by using the annotation attribute name. If you do, the specified name will then be used as the element name and the type name. It is common schema practice for the element and type names to be different. You can use the @XmlType annotation to set the element type name.

The namespace attribute of the @XmlRootElement annotation is used to define a namespace for the element.

Building and Running the j2s-xmlRootElement Example Using NetBeans 5.5

Follow these instructions to build and run the j2s-xmlRootElement example on your Application Server instance using the NetBeans 5.5 IDE.

1. In NetBeans 5.5, select File→Open Project.
2. In the Open Project dialog, navigate to *<INSTALL>*/javaeetutorial5/examples/jaxb/.
3. Select the j2s-xmlRootElement folder.
4. Select the Open as Main Project checkbox.
5. Click Open Project Folder.
6. Right-click the j2s-xmlRootElement project and select Run Project.

Building and Running the j2s-xmlRootElement Example Using Ant

To compile and run the j2s-xmlRootElement example using Ant, in a terminal window, go to the *<INSTALL>*/javaeetutorial5/examples/jaxb/j2s-xmlRootElement/ directory and type the following:

```
ant runapp
```

j2s-xmlSchemaType-class Example

The j2s-xmlSchemaType-class example demonstrates the use of the annotation @XmlSchemaType to customize the mapping of a property or field to an XML built-in type.

The @XmlSchemaType annotation can be used to map a Java type to one of the XML built-in types. This annotation is most useful in mapping a Java type to one of the nine date/time primitive datatypes.

When the @XmlSchemaType annotation is defined at the package level, the identification requires both the XML built-in type name and the corresponding Java type class. An @XmlSchemaType definition on a field or property takes precedence over a package definition.

The j2s-xmlSchemaType-class example shows how to use the @XmlSchemaType annotation at the package level, on a field, and on a property. File TrackingOrder has two fields, orderDate and deliveryDate, which are defined to be of type XMLGregorianCalendar. The generated schema will define these elements to be of XML built-in type gMonthDay. This relationship was defined on the package in the file package-info.java. Field shipDate in file TrackingOrder is also defined to be of type XMLGregorianCalendar, but the @XmlSchemaType annotation statements override the package definition and specify the field to be of type date. Property method getTrackingDuration defines the schema element to be defined as primitive type duration and not Java type String.

Building and Running the j2s-xmlSchemaType-class Example Using NetBeans 5.5

Follow these instructions to build and run the j2s-xmlSchemaType-class example on your Application Server instance using the NetBeans 5.5 IDE.

1. In NetBeans 5.5, select File→Open Project.
2. In the Open Project dialog, navigate to *<INSTALL>*/javaeetutorial5/examples/jaxb/.
3. Select the j2s-xmlSchemaType-class folder.
4. Select the Open as Main Project checkbox.
5. Click Open Project Folder.
6. Right-click the j2s-xmlSchemaType-class project and select Run Project.

Building and Running the j2s-xmlSchemaType-class Example Using Ant

To compile and run the `j2s-xmlSchemaType-class` example using Ant, in a terminal window, go to the *<INSTALL>*`/javaeetutorial5/examples/jaxb/j2s-xmlSchemaType-class/` directory and type the following:

```
ant runapp
```

j2s-xmlType Example

The `j2s-xmlType` example demonstrates the use of the `@XmlType` annotation. The `@XmlType` annotation maps a class or an `enum` type to a XML Schema type.

A class must have either a public zero arg constructor or a static zero arg factory method in order to be mapped by this annotation. One of these methods is used during unmarshalling to create an instance of the class. The factory method may reside within in a factory class or the existing class. There is an order of precedence as to which method is used for unmarshalling:

- If a factory class is identified in the annotation, a corresponding factory method in that class must also be identified and that method will be used.
- If a factory method is identified in the annotation but no factory class is identified, the factory method must reside in the current class. The factory method is used even if there is a public zero arg constructor method present.
- If no factory method is identified in the annotation, the class must contain a public zero arg constructor method.

In this example, a factory class provides zero arg factory methods for several classes. The `@XmlType` annotation on class `OrderContext` references the factory class. The unmarshaller will use the identified factory method in this class.

```
public class OrderFormsFactory {
    public OrderContext newOrderInstance() {
        return new OrderContext()
    }

    public PurchaseOrderType newPurchaseOrderType() {
        return new newPurchaseOrderType();
    }
}
```

```
@XmlType(name="oContext", factoryClass="OrderFormsFactory",
factoryMethod="newOrderInstance")
public class OrderContext {
    public OrderContext(){ ..... }
}
```

In this example, a factory method is defined in a class, which also contains a standard class construct. Because the `factoryMethod` value is defined and no `factoryClass` is defined, the factory method `newOrderInstance` is used during unmarshalling.

```
@XmlType(name="oContext", factoryMethod="newOrderInstance")
 public class OrderContext {

    public OrderContext(){ ..... }

    public OrderContext newOrderInstance() {
        return new OrderContext();
    }
}
```

Building and Running the j2s-xmlType Example Using NetBeans 5.5

Follow these instructions to build and run the `j2s-xmlType` example on your Application Server instance using the NetBeans 5.5 IDE.

1. In NetBeans 5.5, select File→Open Project.
2. In the Open Project dialog, navigate to `<INSTALL>/javaeetutorial5/examples/jaxb/`.
3. Select the `j2s-xmlType` folder.
4. Select the Open as Main Project checkbox.
5. Click Open Project Folder.
6. Right-click the `j2s-xmlType` project and select Run Project.

Building and Running the j2s-xmlType Example Using Ant

To compile and run the `j2s-xmlType` example using Ant, in a terminal window, go to the `<INSTALL>/javaeetutorial5/examples/jaxb/j2s-xmlType/` directory and type the following:

```
ant runapp
```

Further Information

For more information about JAXB, XML, and XML Schema, see:

- Java Community Process page:
  `http://jcp.org/en/jsr/detail?id=222`
- W3C Recommendation "Extensible Markup Language (XML) 1.0":
  `http://www.w3.org/TR/REC-xml`
- XML Information Set:
  `http://www.w3.org/TR/xml-infoset/`
- W3C XML Schema Part 0: Primer, edited by David C. Fallside:
  `http://www.w3.org/TR/xmlschema-0/`
- *XML Path Language*, edited by James Clark and Steve DeRose:
  `http://www.w3.org/TR/1999/REC-xpath-19991116`

17

Streaming API for XML

THIS chapter focuses on the Streaming API for XML (StAX), a streaming Java-based, event-driven, pull-parsing API for reading and writing XML documents. StAX enables you to create bidrectional XML parsers that are fast, relatively easy to program, and have a light memory footprint.

StAX is the latest API in the JAXP family, and provides an alternative to SAX, DOM, TrAX, and DOM for developers looking to do high-performance stream filtering, processing, and modification, particularly with low memory and limited extensibility requirements.

To summarize, StAX provides a standard, bidirectional *pull parser* interface for streaming XML processing, offering a simpler programming model than SAX and more efficient memory management than DOM. StAX enables developers to parse and modify XML streams as events, and to extend XML information models to allow application-specific additions. More detailed comparisons of StAX with several alternative APIs are provided below, in Comparing StAX to Other JAXP APIs (page 594).

Why StAX?

The StAX project was spearheaded by BEA with support from Sun Microsystems, and the JSR 173 specification passed the Java Community Process final approval ballot in March, 2004 (`http://jcp.org/en/jsr/detail?id=173`). The primary goal of the StAX API is to give "parsing control to the programmer by exposing a simple iterator based API. This allows the programmer to ask for the next event (pull the event) and allows state to be stored in procedural fashion." StAX was created to address limitations in the two most prevalent parsing APIs, SAX and DOM.

Streaming versus DOM

Generally speaking, there are two programming models for working with XML infosets: *streaming* and the *document object model* (DOM).

The DOM model involves creating in-memory objects representing an entire document tree and the complete infoset state for an XML document. Once in memory, DOM trees can be navigated freely and parsed arbitrarily, and as such provide maximum flexibility for developers. However, the cost of this flexibility is a potentially large memory footprint and significant processor requirements, because the entire representation of the document must be held in memory as objects for the duration of the document processing. This may not be an issue when working with small documents, but memory and processor requirements can escalate quickly with document size.

Streaming refers to a programming model in which XML infosets are transmitted and parsed serially at application runtime, often in real time, and often from dynamic sources whose contents are not precisely known beforehand. Moreover, stream-based parsers can start generating output immediately, and infoset elements can be discarded and garbage collected immediately after they are used. While providing a smaller memory footprint, reduced processor requirements, and higher performance in certain situations, the primary trade-off with stream processing is that you can only see the infoset state at one location at a time in the document. You are essentially limited to the "cardboard tube" view of a document, the implication being that you need to know what processing you want to do before reading the XML document.

Streaming models for XML processing are particularly useful when your application has strict memory limitations, as with a cellphone running J2ME, or when your application needs to simultaneously process several requests, as with an application server. In fact, it can be argued that the majority of XML business logic can benefit from stream processing, and does not require the in-memory maintenance of entire DOM trees.

Pull Parsing versus Push Parsing

Streaming *pull parsing* refers to a programming model in which a client application calls methods on an XML parsing library when it needs to interact with an XML infoset—that is, the client only gets (pulls) XML data when it explicitly asks for it.

Streaming *push parsing* refers to a programming model in which an XML parser sends (pushes) XML data to the client as the parser encounters elements in an XML infoset—that is, the parser sends the data whether or not the client is ready to use it at that time.

Pull parsing provides several advantages over push parsing when working with XML streams:

- With pull parsing, the client controls the application thread, and can call methods on the parser when needed. By contrast, with push processing, the parser controls the application thread, and the client can only accept invocations from the parser.
- Pull parsing libraries can be much smaller and the client code to interact with those libraries much simpler than with push libraries, even for more complex documents.
- Pull clients can read multiple documents at one time with a single thread.
- A StAX pull parser can filter XML documents such that elements unnecessary to the client can be ignored, and it can support XML views of non-XML data.

StAX Use Cases

The StAX specification defines a number of use cases for the API:

- Data binding
    - Unmarshalling an XML document
    - Marshalling an XML document
    - Parallel document processing
    - Wireless communication

- SOAP message processing
    - Parsing simple predictable structures
    - Parsing graph representations with forward references
    - Parsing WSDL
- Virtual data sources
    - Viewing as XML data stored in databases
    - Viewing data in Java objects created by XML data binding
    - Navigating a DOM tree as a stream of events
- Parsing specific XML vocabularies
- Pipelined XML processing

A complete discussion of all these use cases is beyond the scope of this chapter. Please refer to the StAX specification for further information.

Comparing StAX to Other JAXP APIs

As an API in the JAXP family, StAX can be compared, among other APIs, to SAX, TrAX, and JDOM. Of the latter two, StAX is not as powerful or flexible as TrAX or JDOM, but neither does it require as much memory or processor load to be useful, and StAX can, in many cases, outperform the DOM-based APIs. The same arguments outlined above, weighing the cost/benefits of the DOM model versus the streaming model, apply here.

With this in mind, the closest comparisons can be made between StAX and SAX, and it is here that StAX offers features that are beneficial in many cases; some of these include:

- StAX-enabled clients are generally easier to code than SAX clients. While it can be argued that SAX parsers are marginally easier to write, StAX parser code can be smaller and the code necessary for the client to interact with the parser simpler.
- StAX is a bidirectional API, meaning that it can both read and write XML documents. SAX is read only, so another API is needed if you want to write XML documents.
- SAX is a push API, whereas StAX is pull. The trade-offs between push and pull APIs outlined above apply here.

Table 17–1 summarizes the comparative features of StAX, SAX, DOM, and TrAX (table adapted from "Does StAX Belong in Your XML Toolbox?" at `http://www.developer.com/xml/article.php/3397691` by Jeff Ryan).

Table 17–1 XML Parser API Feature Summary

Feature	StAX	SAX	DOM	TrAX
API Type	Pull, streaming	Push, streaming	In memory tree	XSLT Rule
Ease of Use	High	Medium	High	Medium
XPath Capability	No	No	Yes	Yes
CPU and Memory Efficiency	Good	Good	Varies	Varies
Forward Only	Yes	Yes	No	No
Read XML	Yes	Yes	Yes	Yes
Write XML	Yes	No	Yes	Yes
Create, Read, Update, Delete	No	No	Yes	No

StAX API

The StAX API exposes methods for iterative, event-based processing of XML documents. XML documents are treated as a filtered series of events, and infoset states can be stored in a procedural fashion. Moreover, unlike SAX, the StAX API is bidirectional, enabling both reading and writing of XML documents.

The StAX API is really two distinct API sets: a *cursor* API and an *iterator* API. These two API sets explained in greater detail later in this chapter, but their main features are briefly described below.

Cursor API

As the name implies, the StAX *cursor* API represents a cursor with which you can walk an XML document from beginning to end. This cursor can point to one thing at a time, and always moves forward, never backward, usually one infoset element at a time.

The two main cursor interfaces are XMLStreamReader and XMLStreamWriter. XMLStreamReader includes accessor methods for all possible information retrievable from the XML Information model, including document encoding, element names, attributes, namespaces, text nodes, start tags, comments, processing instructions, document boundaries, and so forth; for example:

```
public interface XMLStreamReader {
  public int next() throws XMLStreamException;
  public boolean hasNext() throws XMLStreamException;
  public String getText();
  public String getLocalName();
  public String getNamespaceURI();
  // ... other methods not shown
}
```

You can call methods on XMLStreamReader, such as getText and getName, to get data at the current cursor location. XMLStreamWriter provides methods that correspond to StartElement and EndElement event types; for example:

```
public interface XMLStreamWriter {
  public void writeStartElement(String localName) \
    throws XMLStreamException;
  public void writeEndElement() \
    throws XMLStreamException;
  public void writeCharacters(String text) \
    throws XMLStreamException;
// ... other methods not shown
}
```

The cursor API mirrors SAX in many ways. For example, methods are available for directly accessing string and character information, and integer indexes can be used to access attribute and namespace information. As with SAX, the cursor API methods return XML information as strings, which minimizes object allocation requirements.

Iterator API

The StAX *iterator* API represents an XML document stream as a set of discrete event objects. These events are pulled by the application and provided by the parser in the order in which they are read in the source XML document.

The base iterator interface is called `XMLEvent`, and there are subinterfaces for each event type listed in Table 17–2. The primary parser interface for reading iterator events is `XMLEventReader`, and the primary interface for writing iterator events is `XMLEventWriter`. The `XMLEventReader` interface contains five methods, the most important of which is `nextEvent`, which returns the next event in an XML stream. `XMLEventReader` implements `java.util.Iterator`, which means that returns from `XMLEventReader` can be cached or passed into routines that can work with the standard Java Iterator; for example:

```
public interface XMLEventReader extends Iterator {
  public XMLEvent nextEvent() throws XMLStreamException;
  public boolean hasNext();
  public XMLEvent peek() throws XMLStreamException;
  ...
}
```

Similarly, on the output side of the iterator API, you have:

```
public interface XMLEventWriter {
  public void flush() throws XMLStreamException;
  public void close() throws XMLStreamException;
  public void add(XMLEvent e) throws XMLStreamException;
  public void add(Attribute attribute) \
    throws XMLStreamException;
  ...
}
```

Iterator Event Types

Table 17–2 lists the `XMLEvent` types defined in the event iterator API.

Table 17–2 `XMLEvent` Types

Event Type	**Description**
`StartDocument`	Reports the beginning of a set of XML events, including encoding, XML version, and standalone properties.
`StartElement`	Reports the start of an element, including any attributes and namespace declarations; also provides access to the prefix, namespace URI, and local name of the start tag.

Table 17–2 `XMLEvent` Types (Continued)

Event Type	Description
`EndElement`	Reports the end tag of an element. Namespaces that have gone out of scope can be recalled here if they have been explicitly set on their corresponding `StartElement`.
`Characters`	Corresponds to XML `CData` sections and `CharacterData` entities. Note that ignorable whitespace and significant whitespace are also reported as `Character` events.
`EntityReference`	Character entities can be reported as discrete events, which an application developer can then choose to resolve or pass through unresolved. By default, entities are resolved. Alternatively, if you do not want to report the entity as an event, replacement text can be substituted and reported as `Characters`.
`ProcessingInstruction`	Reports the target and data for an underlying processing instruction.
`Comment`	Returns the text of a comment.
`EndDocument`	Reports the end of a set of XML events.
`DTD`	Reports as `java.lang.String` information about the DTD, if any, associated with the stream, and provides a method for returning custom objects found in the DTD.
`Attribute`	Attributes are generally reported as part of a `StartElement` event. However, there are times when it is desirable to return an attribute as a standalone `Attribute` event; for example, when a namespace is returned as the result of an `XQuery` or `XPath` expression.
`Namespace`	As with attributes, namespaces are usually reported as part of a `StartElement`, but there are times when it is desirable to report a namespace as a discrete `Namespace` event.

Note that the `DTD`, `EntityDeclaration`, `EntityReference`, `NotationDeclaration`, and `ProcessingInstruction` events are only created if the document being processed contains a DTD.

Example of Event Mapping

As an example of how the event iterator API maps an XML stream, consider the following XML document:

```
<?xml version="1.0"?>
<BookCatalogue xmlns="http://www.publishing.org">
  <Book>
    <Title>Yogasana Vijnana: the Science of Yoga</Title>
    <ISBN>81-40-34319-4</ISBN>
    <Cost currency="INR">11.50</Cost>
  </Book>
</BookCatalogue>
```

This document would be parsed into eighteen primary and secondary events, as shown in Table 17–3. Note that secondary events, shown in curly braces ({}), are typically accessed from a primary event rather than directly.

Table 17–3 Example of Iterator API Event Mapping

#	Element/Attribute	Event
1	`version="1.0"`	`StartDocument`

2	`isCData = false`
	`data = "\n"`
	`IsWhiteSpace = true`
		`Characters`

3	`qname = BookCatalogue:http://www.publishing.org`
	`attributes = null`
	`namespaces = {BookCatalogue" -> http://www.publishing.org"}`
		`StartElement`

4	`qname = Book`
	`attributes = null`
	`namespaces = null`
		`StartElement`

5	`qname = Title`
	`attributes = null`
	`namespaces = null`
		`StartElement`

6	`isCData = false`
	`data = "Yogasana Vijnana: the Science of Yoga\n\t"`
	`IsWhiteSpace = false`
		`Characters`

7	`qname = Title` `namespaces = null`	`EndElement`

Table 17–3 Example of Iterator API Event Mapping (Continued)

#	Element/Attribute	Event

8	`qname = ISBN`
	`attributes = null`
	`namespaces = null`
		`StartElement`

9	`isCData = false`
	`data = "81-40-34319-4\n\t"`
	`IsWhiteSpace = false`
		`Characters`

10	`qname = ISBN` `namespaces = null`	`EndElement`

11	`qname = Cost`
	`attributes = {"currency" -> INR}`
	`namespaces = null`
		`StartElement`

12	`isCData = false`
	`data = "11.50\n\t"`
	`IsWhiteSpace = false`
		`Characters`

13	`qname = Cost` `namespaces = null`	`EndElement`

14	`isCData = false`
	`data = "\n"`
	`IsWhiteSpace = true`
		`Characters`

15	`qname = Book` `namespaces = null`	`EndElement`

16	`isCData = false`
	`data = "\n"`
	`IsWhiteSpace = true`
		`Characters`

17	`qname = BookCatalogue:http://www.publishing.org`
	`namespaces = {BookCatalogue" ->`
	`http://www.publishing.org"}`
		`EndElement`

18		`EndDocument`

There are several important things to note in this example:

- The events are created in the order in which the corresponding XML elements are encountered in the document, including nesting of elements, opening and closing of elements, attribute order, document start and document end, and so forth.

- As with proper XML syntax, all container elements have corresponding start and end events; for example, every `StartElement` has a corresponding `EndElement`, even for empty elements.
- `Attribute` events are treated as secondary events, and are accessed from their corresponding `StartElement` event.
- Similar to `Attribute` events, `Namespace` events are treated as secondary, but appear twice and are accessible twice in the event stream, first from their corresponding `StartElement` and then from their corresponding `EndElement`.
- `Character` events are specified for all elements, even if those elements have no character data. Similarly, `Character` events can be split across events.
- The StAX parser maintains a namespace stack, which holds information about all XML namespaces defined for the current element and its ancestors. The namespace stack, which is exposed through the `javax.xml.namespace.NamespaceContext` interface, can be accessed by namespace prefix or URI.

Choosing between Cursor and Iterator APIs

It is reasonable to ask at this point, "What API should I choose? Should I create instances of `XMLStreamReader` or `XMLEventReader`? Why are there two kinds of APIs anyway?"

Development Goals

The authors of the StAX specification targeted three types of developers:

- **Library and infrastructure developers**: Create application servers, JAXM, JAXB, JAX-RPC and similar implementations; need highly efficient, low-level APIs with minimal extensibility requirements.
- **J2ME developers**: Need small, simple, pull-parsing libraries, and have minimal extensibility needs.
- **Java EE and Java SE developers**: Need clean, efficient pull-parsing libraries, plus need the flexibility to both read and write XML streams, create new event types, and extend XML document elements and attributes.

Given these wide-ranging development categories, the StAX authors felt it was more useful to define two small, efficient APIs rather than overloading one larger and necessarily more complex API.

Comparing Cursor and Iterator APIs

Before choosing between the cursor and iterator APIs, you should note a few things that you can do with the iterator API that you cannot do with cursor API:

- Objects created from the `XMLEvent` subclasses are immutable, and can be used in arrays, lists, and maps, and can be passed through your applications even after the parser has moved on to subsequent events.
- You can create subtypes of `XMLEvent` that are either completely new information items or extensions of existing items but with additional methods.
- You can add and remove events from an XML event stream in much simpler ways than with the cursor API.

Similarly, keep some general recommendations in mind when making your choice:

- If you are programming for a particularly memory-constrained environment, like J2ME, you can make smaller, more efficient code with the cursor API.
- If performance is your highest priority—for example, when creating low-level libraries or infrastructure—the cursor API is more efficient.
- If you want to create XML processing pipelines, use the iterator API.
- If you want to modify the event stream, use the iterator API.
- If you want your application to be able to handle pluggable processing of the event stream, use the iterator API.
- In general, if you do not have a strong preference one way or the other, using the iterator API is recommended because it is more flexible and extensible, thereby "future-proofing" your applications.

Using StAX

In general, StAX programmers create XML stream readers, writers, and events by using the `XMLInputFactory`, `XMLOutputFactory`, and `XMLEventFactory` classes. Configuration is done by setting properties on the factories, whereby implementation-specific settings can be passed to the underlying implementation using the `setProperty` method on the factories. Similarly, implementation-specific settings can be queried using the `getProperty` factory method.

The `XMLInputFactory`, `XMLOutputFactory`, and `XMLEventFactory` classes are described below, followed by discussions of resource allocation, namespace and attribute management, error handling, and then finally reading and writing streams using the cursor and iterator APIs.

StAX Factory Classes

The StAX factory classes. `XMLInputFactory`, `XMLOutputFactory`, and `XMLEventFactory`, let you define and configure implementation instances of XML stream reader, stream writer, and event classes.

XMLInputFactory

The `XMLInputFactory` class lets you configure implementation instances of XML stream reader processors created by the factory. New instances of the abstract class `XMLInputFactory` are created by calling the `newInstance` method on the class. The static method `XMLInputFactory.newInstance` is then used to create a new factory instance.

Deriving from JAXP, the `XMLInputFactory.newInstance` method determines the specific `XMLInputFactory` implementation class to load by using the following lookup procedure:

1. Use the `javax.xml.stream.XMLInputFactory` system property.
2. Use the `lib/xml.stream.properties` file in the J2SE Java Runtime Environment (JRE) directory.
3. Use the Services API, if available, to determine the classname by looking in the `META-INF/services/javax.xml.stream.XMLInputFactory` files in JAR files available to the JRE.
4. Use the platform default `XMLInputFactory` instance.

After getting a reference to an appropriate `XMLInputFactory`, an application can use the factory to configure and create stream instances. Table 17–4 lists the properties supported by XMLInputFactory. See the StAX specification for a more detailed listing.

Table 17–4 javax.xml.stream.XMLInputFactory Properties

Property	Description
isValidating	Turns on implementation-specific validation.
isCoalescing	*(Required)* Requires the processor to coalesce adjacent character data.
isNamespaceAware	Turns off namespace support. All implementations must support namespaces. Support for non-namespace-aware documents is optional.
isReplacingEntityReferences	*(Required)* Requires the processor to replace internal entity references with their replacement value and report them as characters or the set of events that describe the entity.
isSupportingExternalEntities	*(Required)* Requires the processor to resolve external parsed entities.
reporter	*(Required)* Sets and gets the implementation of the XMLReporter interface.
resolver	*(Required)* Sets and gets the implementation of the XMLResolver interface.
allocator	*(Required)* Sets and gets the implementation of the XMLEventAllocator interface.

XMLOutputFactory

New instances of the abstract class XMLOutputFactory are created by calling the newInstance method on the class. The static method XMLOutputFactory.newInstance is then used to create a new factory instance. The algorithm used to obtain the instance is the same as for XMLInputFactory but references the javax.xml.stream.XMLOutputFactory system property.

XMLOutputFactory supports only one property, javax.xml.stream.isRepairingNamespaces. This property is required, and its purpose is to create default prefixes and associate them with Namespace URIs. See the StAX specification for more information.

XMLEventFactory

New instances of the abstract class `XMLEventFactory` are created by calling the `newInstance` method on the class. The static method `XMLEventFactory.newInstance` is then used to create a new factory instance. This factory references the `javax.xml.stream.XMLEventFactory` property to instantiate the factory. The algorithm used to obtain the instance is the same as for `XMLInputFactory` and `XMLOutputFactory` but references the `javax.xml.stream.XMLEventFactory` system property.

There are no default properties for `XMLEventFactory`.

Resources, Namespaces, and Errors

The StAX specification handles resource resolution, attributes and namespace, and errors and exceptions as described below.

Resource Resolution

The `XMLResolver` interface provides a means to set the method that resolves resources during XML processing. An application sets the interface on `XMLInputFactory`, which then sets the interface on all processors created by that factory instance.

Attributes and Namespaces

Attributes are reported by a StAX processor using lookup methods and strings in the cursor interface, and `Attribute` and `Namespace` events in the iterator interface. Note here that namespaces are treated as attributes, although namespaces are reported separately from attributes in both the cursor and iterator APIs. Note also that namespace processing is optional for StAX processors. See the StAX specification for complete information about namespace binding and optional namespace processing.

Error Reporting and Exception Handling

All fatal errors are reported by way of the `javax.xml.stream.XMLStreamException` interface. All nonfatal errors and warnings are reported using the `javax.xml.stream.XMLReporter` interface.

Reading XML Streams

As described earlier in this chapter, the way you read XML streams with a StAX processor—and more importantly, what you get back—varies significantly depending on whether you are using the StAX cursor API or the event iterator API. The following two sections describe how to read XML streams with each of these APIs.

Using XMLStreamReader

The `XMLStreamReader` interface in the StAX cursor API lets you read XML streams or documents in a forward direction only, one item in the infoset at a time. The following methods are available for pulling data from the stream or skipping unwanted events:

- Get the value of an attribute
- Read XML content
- Determine whether an element has content or is empty
- Get indexed access to a collection of attributes
- Get indexed access to a collection of namespaces
- Get the name of the current event (if applicable)
- Get the content of the current event (if applicable)

Instances of `XMLStreamReader` have at any one time a single current event on which its methods operate. When you create an instance of `XMLStreamReader` on a stream, the initial current event is the `START_DOCUMENT` state. The `XMLStreamReader.next` method can then be used to step to the next event in the stream.

Reading Properties, Attributes, and Namespaces

The `XMLStreamReader.next` method loads the properties of the next event in the stream. You can then access those properties by calling the `XMLStreamReader.getLocalName` and `XMLStreamReader.getText` methods.

When the XMLStreamReader cursor is over a StartElement event, it reads the name and any attributes for the event, including the namespace. All attributes for an event can be accessed using an index value, and can also be looked up by namespace URI and local name. Note, however, that only the namespaces declared on the current StartEvent are available; previously declared namespaces are not maintained, and redeclared namespaces are not removed.

XMLStreamReader Methods

XMLStreamReader provides the following methods for retrieving information about namespaces and attributes:

```
int getAttributeCount();
String getAttributeNamespace(int index);
String getAttributeLocalName(int index);
String getAttributePrefix(int index);
String getAttributeType(int index);
String getAttributeValue(int index);
String getAttributeValue(String namespaceUri,
  String localName);
boolean isAttributeSpecified(int index);
```

Namespaces can also be accessed using three additional methods:

```
int getNamespaceCount();
String getNamespacePrefix(int index);
String getNamespaceURI(int index);
```

Instantiating an XMLStreamReader

This example, taken from the StAX specification, shows how to instantiate an input factory, create a reader, and iterate over the elements of an XML stream:

```
XMLInputFactory f = XMLInputFactory.newInstance();
XMLStreamReader r = f.createXMLStreamReader( ... );
while(r.hasNext()) {
  r.next();
}
```

Using XMLEventReader

The XMLEventReader API in the StAX event iterator API provides the means to map events in an XML stream to allocated event objects that can be freely reused, and the API itself can be extended to handle custom events.

`XMLEventReader` provides four methods for iteratively parsing XML streams:

- `next`: Returns the next event in the stream
- `nextEvent`: Returns the next typed XMLEvent
- `hasNext`: Returns true if there are more events to process in the stream
- `peek`: Returns the event but does not iterate to the next event

For example, the following code snippet illustrates the `XMLEventReader` method declarations:

```
package javax.xml.stream;
import java.util.Iterator;
public interface XMLEventReader extends Iterator {
  public Object next();
  public XMLEvent nextEvent() throws XMLStreamException;
  public boolean hasNext();
  public XMLEvent peek() throws XMLStreamException;
...
}
```

To read all events on a stream and then print them, you could use the following:

```
while(stream.hasNext()) {
XMLEvent event = stream.nextEvent();
System.out.print(event);
}
```

Reading Attributes

You can access attributes from their associated `javax.xml.stream.StartElement`, as follows:

```
public interface StartElement extends XMLEvent {
  public Attribute getAttributeByName(QName name);
  public Iterator getAttributes();
}
```

You can use the `getAttributes` method on the `StartElement` interface to use an `Iterator` over all the attributes declared on that `StartElement`.

Reading Namespaces

Similar to reading attributes, namespaces are read using an `Iterator` created by calling the `getNamespaces` method on the `StartElement` interface. Only the namespace for the current `StartElement` is returned, and an application can get the current namespace context by using `StartElement.getNamespaceContext`.

Writing XML Streams

StAX is a bidirectional API, and both the cursor and event iterator APIs have their own set of interfaces for writing XML streams. As with the interfaces for reading streams, there are significant differences between the writer APIs for cursor and event iterator. The following sections describe how to write XML streams using each of these APIs.

Using XMLStreamWriter

The `XMLStreamWriter` interface in the StAX cursor API lets applications write back to an XML stream or create entirely new streams. XMLStreamWriter has methods that let you:

- Write well-formed XML
- Flush or close the output
- Write qualified names

Note that `XMLStreamWriter` implementations are not required to perform well-formedness or validity checks on input. While some implementations may perform strict error checking, others may not. The rules you implement are applied to properties defined in the `XMLOutputFactory` class.

The `writeCharacters` method is used to escape characters such as &, <, >, and ". Binding prefixes can be handled by either passing the actual value for the prefix, by using the `setPrefix` method, or by setting the property for defaulting namespace declarations.

The following example, taken from the StAX specification, shows how to instantiate an output factory, create a writer, and write XML output:

```
XMLOutputFactory output = XMLOutputFactory.newInstance();
XMLStreamWriter writer = output.createXMLStreamWriter( ... );
writer.writeStartDocument();
writer.setPrefix("c","http://c");
writer.setDefaultNamespace("http://c");
writer.writeStartElement("http://c","a");
writer.writeAttribute("b","blah");
writer.writeNamespace("c","http://c");
writer.writeDefaultNamespace("http://c");
```

```
writer.setPrefix("d","http://c");
writer.writeEmptyElement("http://c","d");
writer.writeAttribute("http://c","chris","fry");
writer.writeNamespace("d","http://c");
writer.writeCharacters("Jean Arp");
writer.writeEndElement();
writer.flush();
```

This code generates the following XML (new lines are non-normative):

```
<?xml version='1.0' encoding='utf-8'?>
<a b="blah" xmlns:c="http://c" xmlns="http://c">
<d:d d:chris="fry" xmlns:d="http://c"/>Jean Arp</a>
```

Using XMLEventWriter

The XMLEventWriter interface in the StAX event iterator API lets applications write back to an XML stream or create entirely new streams. This API can be extended, but the main API is as follows:

```
public interface XMLEventWriter {
  public void flush() throws XMLStreamException;
  public void close() throws XMLStreamException;
  public void add(XMLEvent e) throws XMLStreamException;
  // ... other methods not shown.
}
```

Instances of XMLEventWriter are created by an instance of XMLOutputFactory. Stream events are added iteratively, and an event cannot be modified after it has been added to an event writer instance.

Attributes, Escaping Characters, Binding Prefixes

StAX implementations are required to buffer the last StartElement until an event other than Attribute or Namespace is added or encountered in the stream. This means that when you add an Attribute or a Namespace to a stream, it is appended the current StartElement event.

You can use the Characters method to escape characters like &, <, >, and ".

The setPrefix(...) method can be used to explicitly bind a prefix for use during output, and the getPrefix(...) method can be used to get the current prefix. Note that by default, XMLEventWriter adds namespace bindings to its internal namespace map. Prefixes go out of scope after the corresponding EndElement for the event in which they are bound.

Sun's Streaming XML Parser Implementation

Application Server 9.0 PE includes Sun Microsystem's JSR 173 (StAX) implementation, called the Sun Java Streaming XML Parser (referred to as Streaming XML Parser). The Streaming XML Parser is a high-speed, non-validating, W3C XML 1.0 and Namespace 1.0-compliant streaming XML pull parser built upon the Xerces2 codebase.

In Sun's Streaming XML Parser implementation, the Xerces2 lower layers, particularly the Scanner and related classes, have been redesigned to behave in a pull fashion. In addition to the changes in the lower layers, the Streaming XML Parser includes additional StAX-related functionality and many performance-enhancing improvements. The Streaming XML Parser is implemented in the `appserv-ws.jar` and `javaee.jar` files, both of which are located in the `<JAVEE_HOME>/lib/` directory.

Included with this Java EE tutorial are StAX code examples, located in the `<INSTALL>/javaeetutorial5/examples/stax/` directory, that illustrate how Sun's Streaming XML Parser implementation works. These examples are described in Example Code (page 612).

Before you proceed with the example code, there are two aspects of the Streaming XML Parser of which you should be aware:

- Reporting CDATA events
- Streaming XML Parser factories implementation

These topics are discussed below.

Reporting CDATA Events

The `javax.xml.stream.XMLStreamReader` implemented in the Streaming XML Parser does not report CDATA events. If you have an application that needs to receive such events, configure the `XMLInputFactory` to set the following implementation-specific `report-cdata-event` property:

```
XMLInputFactory factory = XMLInptuFactory.newInstance();
factory.setProperty("report-cdata-event", Boolean.TRUE);
```

Streaming XML Parser Factories Implementation

Most applications do not need to know the factory implementation class name. Just adding the `javaee.jar` and `appserv-ws.jar` files to the classpath is sufficient for most applications because these two jars supply the factory implementation classname for various Streaming XML Parser properties under the `META-INF/services` directory—for example, `javax.xml.stream.XMLInputFactory`, `javax.xml.stream.XMLOutputFactory`, and `javax.xml.stream.XMLEventFactory`—which is the third step of a lookup operation when an application asks for the factory instance. See the Javadoc for the `XMLInputFactory.newInstance` method for more information about the lookup mechanism.

However, there may be scenarios when an application would like to know about the factory implementation class name and set the property explicitly. These scenarios could include cases where there are multiple JSR 173 implementations in the classpath and the application wants to choose one, perhaps one that has superior performance, contains a crucial bug fix, or suchlike.

If an application sets the `SystemProperty`, it is the first step in a lookup operation, and so obtaining the factory instance would be fast compared to other options; for example:

```
javax.xml.stream.XMLInputFactory -->
  com.sun.xml.stream.ZephyrParserFactory
javax.xml.stream.XMLOutputFactory -->
  com.sun.xml.stream.ZephyrWriterFactor
javax.xml.stream.XMLEventFactory -->
  com.sun.xml.stream.events.ZephyrEventFactory
```

Example Code

This section steps through the example StAX code included in the Java EE 5 Tutorial bundle. All example directories used in this section are located in the `<INSTALL>/javaeetutorial5/examples/stax/` directory.

The topics covered in this section are as follows:

- Example code organization
- Example XML document
- Cursor example

- Cursor-to-Event example
- Event example
- Filter example
- Read-and-Write example
- Writer example

Example Code Organization

The `<INSTALL>/javaeetutorial5/examples/stax/` directory contains the six StAX example directories:

- **Cursor example**: The `cursor` directory contains `CursorParse.java`, which illustrates how to use the `XMLStreamReader` (cursor) API to read an XML file.
- **Cursor-to-Event example**: The `cursor2event` directory contains `CursorApproachEventObject.java`, which illustrates how an application can get information as an `XMLEvent` object when using cursor API.
- **Event example**: The `event` directory contains `EventParse.java`, which illustrates how to use the `XMLEventReader` (event iterator) API to read an XML file.
- **Filter example**: The `filter` directory contains `MyStreamFilter.java`, which illustrates how to use the StAX Stream Filter APIs. In this example, the filter accepts only `StartElement` and `EndElement` events, and filters out the remainder of the events.
- **Read-and-Write example**: The `readnwrite` directory contains `EventProducerConsumer.java`, which illustrates how the StAX producer/consumer mechanism can be used to simultaneously read and write XML streams.
- **Writer example**: The `writer` directory contains `CursorWriter.java`, which illustrates how to use `XMLStreamWriter` to write an XML file programatically.

All of the StAX examples except for the Writer example use an example XML document, `BookCatalog.xml`.

Example XML Document

The example XML document, `BookCatalog.xml`, used by most of the StAX example classes, is a simple book catalog based on the common `BookCatalogue` namespace. The contents of `BookCatalog.xml` are listed below:

```
<?xml version="1.0" encoding="UTF-8"?>
<BookCatalogue xmlns="http://www.publishing.org">
  <Book>
    <Title>Yogasana Vijnana: the Science of Yoga</Title>
    <author>Dhirendra Brahmachari</Author>
    <Date>1966</Date>
    <ISBN>81-40-34319-4</ISBN>
    <Publisher>Dhirendra Yoga Publications</Publisher>
    <Cost currency="INR">11.50</Cost>
  </Book>
  <Book>
    <Title>The First and Last Freedom</Title>
    <Author>J. Krishnamurti</Author>
    <Date>1954</Date>
    <ISBN>0-06-064831-7</ISBN>
    <Publisher>Harper &amp; Row</Publisher>
    <Cost currency="USD">2.95</Cost>
  </Book>
</BookCatalogue>
```

Cursor Example

Located in the `<INSTALL>/javaeetutorial5/examples/stax/cursor/` directory, `CursorParse.java` demonstrates using the StAX cursor API to read an XML document. In the Cursor example, the application instructs the parser to read the next event in the XML input stream by calling `<code>next()</code>`.

Note that `<code>next()</code>` just returns an integer constant corresponding to underlying event where the parser is positioned. The application needs to call the relevant function to get more information related to the underlying event.

You can imagine this approach as a virtual cursor moving across the XML input stream. There are various accessor methods which can be called when that virtual cursor is at a particular event.

Stepping through Events

In this example, the client application pulls the next event in the XML stream by calling the `next` method on the parser; for example:

```
try
  {
     for(int i = 0 ; i < count ; i++)
       {
          // pass the file name.. all relative entity
          // references will be resolved against this as
          // base URI.
          XMLStreamReader xmlr =
             xmlif.createXMLStreamReader(filename,
                new FileInputStream(filename));
          // when XMLStreamReader is created, it is positioned
          // at START_DOCUMENT event.
          int eventType = xmlr.getEventType();
          printEventType(eventType);
          printStartDocument(xmlr);
          // check if there are more events in the input stream
          while(xmlr.hasNext())
             {
                eventType =xmlr.next();
                printEventType(eventType);
                // these functions print the information about
                // the particular event by calling the relevant
                // function
                printStartElement(xmlr);
                printEndElement(xmlr);
                printText(xmlr);
                printPIData(xmlr);
                printComment(xmlr);
             }
       }
```

Note that `next` just returns an integer constant corresponding to the event underlying the current cursor location. The application calls the relevant function to get more information related to the underlying event. There are various accessor methods which can be called when the cursor is at particular event.

Returning String Representations

Because the next method only returns integers corresponding to underlying event types, you typically need to map these integers to string representations of the events; for example:

```
public final staticString getEventTypeString(inteventType)
{
  switch(eventType)
    {
         case XMLEvent.START_ELEMENT:
            return "START_ELEMENT";
         case XMLEvent.END_ELEMENT:
            return "END_ELEMENT";
         case XMLEvent.PROCESSING_INSTRUCTION:
            return "PROCESSING_INSTRUCTION";
         case XMLEvent.CHARACTERS:
            return "CHARACTERS";
         case XMLEvent.COMMENT:
            return "COMMENT";
         case XMLEvent.START_DOCUMENT:
            return "START_DOCUMENT";
         case XMLEvent.END_DOCUMENT:
            return "END_DOCUMENT";
         case XMLEvent.ENTITY_REFERENCE:
            return "ENTITY_REFERENCE";
         case XMLEvent.ATTRIBUTE:
            return "ATTRIBUTE";
         case XMLEvent.DTD:
            return "DTD";
         case XMLEvent.CDATA:
            return "CDATA";
         case XMLEvent.SPACE:
            return "SPACE";
    }
  return"UNKNOWN_EVENT_TYPE , "+ eventType;
}
```

Building and Running the Cursor Example Using NetBeans 5.5

Follow these instructions to build and run the Cursor example on your Application Server instance using the NetBeans 5.5 IDE.

1. In NetBeans 5.5, select File→Open Project.
2. In the Open Project dialog, navigate to the *<INSTALL>*/javaeetutorial5/examples/stax/ directory.
3. Select the `cursor` folder.
4. Select the Open as Main Project checkbox.
5. Click Open Project Folder.
6. In the Projects tab, right-click the `cursor` project and select Properties. The Project Properties dialog is displayed.
7. Enter the following in the Arguments field:

   ```
   -x 1 BookCatalog.xml
   ```

8. Click OK.
9. Right-click the `cursor` project and select Run Project.

Building and Running the Cursor Example Using Ant

To compile and run the Cursor example using Ant, in a terminal window, go to the *<INSTALL>*/javaeetutorial5/examples/stax/cursor/ directory and type the following:

```
ant run-cursor
```

Cursor-to-Event Example

Located in the *<INSTALL>*/javaeetutorial5/examples/stax/cursor2-event/ directory, `CursorApproachEventObject.java` demonstrates how to get information returned by an `XMLEvent` object even when using the cursor API.

The idea here is that the cursor API's `XMLStreamReader` returns integer constants corresponding to particular events, while the event iterator API's `XMLEventReader` returns immutable and persistent event objects. `XMLStreamReader` is more efficient, but `XMLEventReader` is easier to use, because all the information related to a particular event is encapsulated in a returned XMLEvent object. However, the disadvantage of event approach is the extra overhead of creating objects for every event, which consumes both time and memory.

With this mind, XMLEventAllocator can be used to get event information as an XMLEvent object, even when using the cursor API.

Instantiating an XMLEventAllocator

The first step is to create a new XMLInputFactory and instantiate an XMLEventAllocator:

```
XMLInputFactory xmlif = XMLInputFactory.newInstance();
System.out.println("FACTORY: " + xmlif);
xmlif.setEventAllocator(new XMLEventAllocatorImpl());
allocator = xmlif.getEventAllocator();
XMLStreamReader xmlr = xmlif.createXMLStreamReader(filename,
  new FileInputStream(filename));
```

Creating an Event Iterator

The next step is to create an event iterator:

```
int eventType = xmlr.getEventType();
while(xmlr.hasNext()){
  eventType = xmlr.next();
  //Get all "Book" elements as XMLEvent object
  if(eventType == XMLStreamConstants.START_ELEMENT &&
    xmlr.getLocalName().equals("Book")){
    //get immutable XMLEvent
    StartElement event = getXMLEvent(xmlr).asStartElement();
    System.out.println("EVENT: " + event.toString());
  }
}
```

Creating the Allocator Method

The final step is to create the XMLEventAllocator method:

```
private static XMLEvent getXMLEvent(XMLStreamReader reader)
    throws XMLStreamException {
  return allocator.allocate(reader);
}
```

Building and Running the Cursor-to-Event Example Using NetBeans 5.5

Follow these instructions to build and run the Cursor-to-Event example on your Application Server instance using the NetBeans 5.5 IDE.

1. In NetBeans 5.5, select File→Open Project.
2. In the Open Project dialog, navigate to the *<INSTALL>*/javaeetutorial5/examples/stax/ directory.
3. Select the `cursor2event` folder.
4. Select the Open as Main Project checkbox.
5. Click Open Project Folder.
6. In the Projects tab, right-click the `cursor2event` project and select Properties. The Project Properties dialog is displayed.
7. Enter the following in the Arguments field:

   `BookCatalog.xml`
8. Click OK.
9. Right-click the `cursor2event` project and select Run Project.

   Note how the `Book` events are returned as strings.

Building and Running the Cursor-to-Event Example Using Ant

To compile and run the Cursor-to-Event example using Ant, in a terminal window, go to the *<INSTALL>*/javaeetutorial5/examples/stax/cursor2event/ directory and type the following:

```
ant run-cursor2event
```

Event Example

Located in the *<INSTALL>*/javaeetutorial5/examples/stax/event/ directory, `EventParse.java` demonstrates how to use the StAX event API to read an XML document.

Creating an Input Factory

The first step is to create a new instance of `XMLInputFactory`:

```
XMLInputFactory factory = XMLInputFactory.newInstance();
System.out.println("FACTORY: " + factory);
```

Creating an Event Reader

The next step is to create an instance of `XMLEventReader`:

```
XMLEventReader r = factory.createXMLEventReader(filename,
  new FileInputStream(filename));
```

Creating an Event Iterator

The third step is to create an event iterator:

```
XMLEventReader r = factory.createXMLEventReader(filename,
  new FileInputStream(filename));
while(r.hasNext()) {
  XMLEvent e = r.nextEvent();
  System.out.println(e.toString());
}
```

Getting the Event Stream

The final step is to get the underlying event stream:

```
public final static String getEventTypeString(int eventType)
{
  switch (eventType)
    {
      case XMLEvent.START_ELEMENT:
        return "START_ELEMENT";
      case XMLEvent.END_ELEMENT:
        return "END_ELEMENT";
      case XMLEvent.PROCESSING_INSTRUCTION:
        return "PROCESSING_INSTRUCTION";
      case XMLEvent.CHARACTERS:
        return "CHARACTERS";
      case XMLEvent.COMMENT:
        return "COMMENT";
      case XMLEvent.START_DOCUMENT:
```

```
            return "START_DOCUMENT";
         case XMLEvent.END_DOCUMENT:
            return "END_DOCUMENT";
         case XMLEvent.ENTITY_REFERENCE:
            return "ENTITY_REFERENCE";
         case XMLEvent.ATTRIBUTE:
            return "ATTRIBUTE";
         case XMLEvent.DTD:
            return "DTD";
         case XMLEvent.CDATA:
            return "CDATA";
         case XMLEvent.SPACE:
            return "SPACE";
      }
   return "UNKNOWN_EVENT_TYPE " + "," + eventType;
}
```

Returning the Output

When you run the Event example, the `EventParse` class is compiled, and the XML stream is parsed as events and returned to STDOUT. For example, an instance of the `Author` element is returned as:

```
<['http://www.publishing.org']::Author>
  Dhirendra Brahmachari
</['http://www.publishing.org']::Author>
```

Note in this example that the event comprises an opening and closing tag, both of which include the namespace. The content of the element is returned as a string within the tags.

Similarly, an instance of the `Cost` element is returned as:

```
<['http://www.publishing.org']::Cost currency='INR'>
  11.50
</['http://www.publishing.org']::Cost>
```

In this case, the `currency` attribute and value are returned in the opening tag for the event.

Building and Running the Event Example Using NetBeans 5.5

Follow these instructions to build and run the Event example on your Application Server instance using the NetBeans 5.5 IDE.

1. In NetBeans 5.5, select File→Open Project.
2. In the Open Project dialog, navigate to the *<INSTALL>*/javaeetutorial5/examples/stax/ directory.
3. Select the event folder.
4. Select the Open as Main Project checkbox.
5. Click Open Project Folder.
6. In the Projects tab, right-click the event project and select Properties. The Project Properties dialog is displayed.
7. Enter the following in the Arguments field:

   BookCatalog.xml
8. Click OK.
9. Right-click the event project and select Run Project.

Building and Running the Event Example Using Ant

To compile and run the Event example using Ant, in a terminal window, go to the *<INSTALL>*/javaeetutorial5/examples/stax/event/ directory and type the following:

```
ant run-event
```

Filter Example

Located in the *<INSTALL>*/javaeetutorial5/examples/stax/filter/ directory, MyStreamFilter.java demonstrates how to use the StAX stream filter API to filter out events not needed by your application. In this example, the parser filters out all events except StartElement and EndElement.

Implementing the StreamFilter Class

The `MyStreamFilter` class implements `javax.xml.stream.StreamFilter`:

```
public class MyStreamFilter
  implements javax.xml.stream.StreamFilter{
```

Creating an Input Factory

The next step is to create an instance of `XMLInputFactory`. In this case, various properties are also set on the factory:

```
XMLInputFactory xmlif = null ;
try{
xmlif = XMLInputFactory.newInstance();
xmlif.setProperty(
  XMLInputFactory.IS_REPLACING_ENTITY_REFERENCES,
  Boolean.TRUE);
xmlif.setProperty(
  XMLInputFactory.IS_SUPPORTING_EXTERNAL_ENTITIES,
  Boolean.FALSE);
xmlif.setProperty(XMLInputFactory.IS_NAMESPACE_AWARE,
  Boolean.TRUE);
xmlif.setProperty(XMLInputFactory.IS_COALESCING,
  Boolean.TRUE);
}catch(Exception ex){
  ex.printStackTrace();
}
System.out.println("FACTORY: " + xmlif);
System.out.println("filename = "+ filename);
```

Creating the Filter

The next step is to instantiate a file input stream and create the stream filter:

```
FileInputStream fis = new FileInputStream(filename);

XMLStreamReader xmlr = xmlif.createFilteredReader(
  xmlif.createXMLStreamReader(fis), new MyStreamFilter());

int eventType = xmlr.getEventType();
printEventType(eventType);
while(xmlr.hasNext()){
  eventType = xmlr.next();
  printEventType(eventType);
```

```
    printName(xmlr,eventType);
    printText(xmlr);
    if(xmlr.isStartElement()){
      printAttributes(xmlr);
    }
    printPIData(xmlr);
    System.out.println("-----------------------------");
  }
```

Capturing the Event Stream

The next step is to capture the event stream. This is done in basically the same way as in the Event example.

Filtering the Stream

The final step is to filter the stream:

```
public boolean accept(XMLStreamReader reader) {
  if(!reader.isStartElement() && !reader.isEndElement())
    return false;
  else
    return true;
}
```

Returning the Output

When you run the Filter example, the `MyStreamFilter` class is compiled, and the XML stream is parsed as events and returned to `STDOUT`. For example, an `Author` event is returned as follows:

```
EVENT TYPE(1):START_ELEMENT
HAS NAME: Author
HAS NO TEXT
HAS NO ATTRIBUTES
-----------------------------
EVENT TYPE(2):END_ELEMENT
HAS NAME: Author
HAS NO TEXT
-----------------------------
```

Similarly, a Cost event is returned as follows:

```
EVENT TYPE(1):START_ELEMENT
HAS NAME: Cost
HAS NO TEXT

HAS ATTRIBUTES:
ATTRIBUTE-PREFIX:
ATTRIBUTE-NAMESP: null
ATTRIBUTE-NAME:   currency
ATTRIBUTE-VALUE: USD
ATTRIBUTE-TYPE:  CDATA

-----------------------------
EVENT TYPE(2):END_ELEMENT
HAS NAME: Cost
HAS NO TEXT
-----------------------------
```

See Iterator API (page 596) and Reading XML Streams (page 606) for a more detailed discussion of StAX event parsing.

Building and Running the Filter Example Using NetBeans 5.5

Follow these instructions to build and run the Filter example on your Application Server instance using the NetBeans 5.5 IDE.

1. In NetBeans 5.5, select File→Open Project.
2. In the Open Project dialog, navigate to the *<INSTALL>*/javaeetutorial5/examples/stax/ directory.
3. Select the `filter` folder.
4. Select the Open as Main Project checkbox.
5. Click Open Project Folder.
6. In the Projects tab, right-click the `filter` project and select Properties. The Project Properties dialog is displayed.
7. Enter the following in the Arguments field:

   ```
   -f BookCatalog.xml
   ```
8. Click OK.
9. Right-click the `filter` project and select Run Project.

Building and Running the Filter Example Using Ant

To compile and run the Filter example using Ant, in a terminal window, go to the *<INSTALL>*/javaeetutorial5/examples/stax/filter/ directory and type the following:

```
ant run-filter
```

Read-and-Write Example

Located in the *<INSTALL>*/javaeetutorial5/examples/stax/readnwrite/ directory, EventProducerConsumer.java demonstrates how to use a StAX parser simultaneously as both a producer and a consumer.

The StAX XMLEventWriter API extends from the XMLEventConsumer interface, and is referred to as an *event consumer*. By contrast, XMLEventReader is an *event producer*. StAX supports simultaneous reading and writing, such that it is possible to read from one XML stream sequentially and simultaneously write to another stream.

The Read-and-Write example shows how the StAX producer/consumer mechanism can be used to read and write simultaneously. This example also shows how a stream can be modified and how new events can be added dynamically and then written to a different stream.

Creating an Event Producer/Consumer

The first step is to instantiate an event factory and then create an instance of an event producer/consumer:

```
XMLEventFactory m_eventFactory =
  XMLEventFactory.newInstance();
public EventProducerConsumer() {
}
...
try{
  EventProducerConsumer ms = new EventProducerConsumer();

  XMLEventReader reader =
    XMLInputFactory.newInstance().createXMLEventReader(
      new java.io.FileInputStream(args[0]));
```

```
XMLEventWriter writer =
   XMLOutputFactory.newInstance().createXMLEventWriter(
      System.out);
```

Creating an Iterator

The next step is to create an iterator to parse the stream:

```
while(reader.hasNext())
  {
     XMLEvent event = (XMLEvent)reader.next();
     if(event.getEventType() == event.CHARACTERS)
        {
           writer.add(ms.getNewCharactersEvent(
              event.asCharacters()));
        }
     else
        {
           writer.add(event);
        }
  }
writer.flush();
```

Creating a Writer

The final step is to create a stream writer in the form of a new `Character` event:

```
Characters getNewCharactersEvent(Characters event){
  if(event.getData().equalsIgnoreCase("Name1")){
     return m_eventFactory.createCharacters(
        Calendar.getInstance().getTime().toString());

  }
  //else return the same event
  else return event;
}
```

Returning the Output

When you run the Read-and-Write example, the `EventProducerConsumer` class is compiled, and the XML stream is parsed as events and written back to `STDOUT`. The output is the contents of the `BookCatalog.xml` file described in Example XML Document (page 614).

Building and Running the Read-and-Write Example Using NetBeans 5.5

Follow these instructions to build and run the Read-and-Write example on your Application Server instance using the NetBeans 5.5 IDE.

1. In NetBeans 5.5, select File→Open Project.
2. In the Open Project dialog, navigate to the *<INSTALL>*/`javaeetutorial5/examples/stax/` directory.
3. Select the `readnwrite` folder.
4. Select the Open as Main Project checkbox.
5. Click Open Project Folder.
6. In the Projects tab, right-click the `readnwrite` project and select Properties. The Project Properties dialog is displayed.
7. Enter the following in the Arguments field:

   `BookCatalog.xml`
8. Click OK.
9. Right-click the `readnwrite` project and select Run Project.

Building and Running the Read-and-Write Example Using Ant

To compile and run the Read-and-Write example using Ant, in a terminal window, go to the *<INSTALL>*/`javaeetutorial5/examples/stax/readnwrite/` directory and type the following:

```
ant run-readnwrite
```

Writer Example

Located in the *<INSTALL>*/`javaeetutorial5/examples/stax/writer/` directory, `CursorWriter.java` demonstrates how to use the StAX cursor API to write an XML stream.

Creating the Output Factory

The first step is to create an instance of `XMLOutputFactory`:

```
XMLOutputFactory xof =  XMLOutputFactory.newInstance();
```

Creating a Stream Writer

The next step is to create an instance of `XMLStreamWriter`:

```
XMLStreamWriter xtw = null;
```

Writing the Stream

The final step is to write the XML stream. Note that the stream is flushed and closed after the final `EndDocument` is written:

```
xtw = xof.createXMLStreamWriter(new FileWriter(fileName));
xtw.writeComment(
  "all elements here are explicitly in the HTML namespace");
xtw.writeStartDocument("utf-8","1.0");
xtw.setPrefix("html", "http://www.w3.org/TR/REC-html40");
xtw.writeStartElement(
  "http://www.w3.org/TR/REC-html40","html");
xtw.writeNamespace("html", "http://www.w3.org/TR/REC-html40");
xtw.writeStartElement(
  "http://www.w3.org/TR/REC-html40","head");
xtw.writeStartElement(
  "http://www.w3.org/TR/REC-html40","title");
xtw.writeCharacters("Frobnostication");
xtw.writeEndElement();
xtw.writeEndElement();
xtw.writeStartElement(
  "http://www.w3.org/TR/REC-html40","body");
xtw.writeStartElement("http://www.w3.org/TR/REC-html40","p");
xtw.writeCharacters("Moved to");
xtw.writeStartElement("http://www.w3.org/TR/REC-html40","a");
xtw.writeAttribute("href","http://frob.com");
xtw.writeCharacters("here");
xtw.writeEndElement();
xtw.writeEndElement();
xtw.writeEndElement();
```

```
xtw.writeEndElement();
xtw.writeEndDocument();
xtw.flush();
xtw.close();
```

Returning the Output

When you run the Writer example, the `CursorWriter` class is compiled, and the XML stream is parsed as events and written to a file named `dist/CursorWriter-Output`:

```
<!--all elements here are explicitly in the HTML namespace-->
<?xml version="1.0" encoding="utf-8"?>
<html:html xmlns:html="http://www.w3.org/TR/REC-html40">
<html:head>
<html:title>Frobnostication</html:title></html:head>
<html:body>
<html:p>Moved to <html:a href="http://frob.com">here</html:a>
</html:p>
</html:body>
</html:html>
```

In the actual `dist/CursorWriter-Output` file, this stream is written without any line breaks; the breaks have been added here to make the listing easier to read. In this example, as with the object stream in the Event example, the namespace prefix is added to both the opening and closing HTML tags. Adding this prefix is not required by the StAX specification, but it is good practice when the final scope of the output stream is not definitively known.

Building and Running the Writer Example Using NetBeans 5.5

Follow these instructions to build and run the Writer example on your Application Server instance using the NetBeans 5.5 IDE.

1. In NetBeans 5.5, select File→Open Project.
2. In the Open Project dialog navigate to the `<INSTALL>/javaeetutorial5/examples/stax/` directory.
3. Select the `writer` folder.
4. Select the Open as Main Project checkbox.
5. Click Open Project Folder.

6. In the Projects tab, right-click the `writer` project and select Properties. The Project Properties dialog is displayed.
7. Enter the following in the Arguments field:

   ```
   -f dist/CursorWriter-Output
   ```
8. Click OK.
9. Right-click the `writer` project and select Run Project.

Building and Running the Writer Example Using Ant

To compile and run the Writer example using Ant, in a terminal window, go to the `<INSTALL>/javaeetutorial5/examples/stax/writer/` directory and type the following:

```
ant run-writer
```

Further Information

For more information about StAX, see:

- Java Community Process page:
  `http://jcp.org/en/jsr/detail?id=173`.
- W3C Recommendation “Extensible Markup Language (XML) 1.0”:
  `http://www.w3.org/TR/REC-xml`
- XML Information Set:
  `http://www.w3.org/TR/xml-infoset/`
- JAXB specification:
  `http://java.sun.com/xml/jaxb/`
- JAX-RPC specification:
  `http://java.sun.com/webservices/jaxrpc/`
- W3C Recommendation “Document Object Model”:
  `http://www.w3.org/DOM/`
- SAX “Simple API for XML”:
  `http://www.saxproject.org/`

- DOM "Document Object Model":

  `http://www.w3.org/TR/2002/WD-DOM-Level-3-Core-20020409/core.html#ID-B63ED1A3`

- W3C Recommendation "Namespaces in XML":

  `http://www.w3.org/TR/REC-xml-names/`

For some useful articles about working with StAX, see:

- Jeff Ryan, "Does StAX Belong in Your XML Toolbox?":

  `http://www.developer.com/xml/article.php/3397691`

- Elliotte Rusty Harold, "An Introduction to StAX":

  `http://www.xml.com/pub/a/2003/09/17/stax.html`

- "Tip: Use XML Streaming Parsers: More Efficient XML Parsing with the Streaming API for XML":

  `http://www-128.ibm.com/developerworks/xml/library/x-tipstx/`

18

SOAP with Attachments API for Java

SOAP with Attachments API for Java (SAAJ) is used mainly for the SOAP messaging that goes on behind the scenes in JAX-WS handlers and JAXR implementations. Secondarily, it is an API that developers can use when they choose to write SOAP messaging applications directly rather than use JAX-WS. The SAAJ API allows you to do XML messaging from the Java platform: By simply making method calls using the SAAJ API, you can read and write SOAP-based XML messages, and you can optionally send and receive such messages over the Internet (some implementations may not support sending and receiving). This chapter will help you learn how to use the SAAJ API.

The SAAJ API conforms to the Simple Object Access Protocol (SOAP) 1.1 and 1.2 specifications and the SOAP with Attachments specification. The SAAJ 1.3 specification defines the `javax.xml.soap` package, which contains the API for creating and populating a SOAP message. This package has all the API necessary for sending request-response messages. (Request-response messages are explained in SOAPConnection Objects, page 638.)

Note: The `javax.xml.messaging` package, defined in the Java API for XML Messaging (JAXM) 1.1 specification, is not part of the Java EE platform and is not discussed in this chapter. The JAXM API is available as a separate download from `http://java.sun.com/xml/downloads/jaxm.html`.

This chapter starts with an overview of messages and connections, giving some of the conceptual background behind the SAAJ API to help you understand why certain things are done the way they are. Next, the tutorial shows you how to use the basic SAAJ API, giving examples and explanations of the commonly used features. The code examples in the last part of the tutorial show you how to build an application. The case study in Chapter 36 includes SAAJ code for both sending and consuming a SOAP message.

Overview of SAAJ

This section presents a high-level view of how SAAJ messaging works and explains concepts in general terms. Its goal is to give you some terminology and a framework for the explanations and code examples that are presented in the tutorial section.

The overview looks at SAAJ from two perspectives: messages and connections.

Messages

SAAJ messages follow SOAP standards, which prescribe the format for messages and also specify some things that are required, optional, or not allowed. With the SAAJ API, you can create XML messages that conform to the SOAP 1.1 or 1.2 specification and to the WS-I Basic Profile 1.1 specification simply by making Java API calls.

The Structure of an XML Document

An XML document has a hierarchical structure made up of elements, subelements, subsubelements, and so on. You will notice that many of the SAAJ classes and interfaces represent XML elements in a SOAP message and have the word *element* or *SOAP* (or both) in their names.

An element is also referred to as a *node*. Accordingly, the SAAJ API has the interface `Node`, which is the base class for all the classes and interfaces that represent XML elements in a SOAP message. There are also methods such as `SOAPElement.addTextNode`, `Node.detachNode`, and `Node.getValue`, which you will see how to use in the tutorial section.

What Is in a Message?

The two main types of SOAP messages are those that have attachments and those that do not.

Messages with No Attachments

The following outline shows the very high-level structure of a SOAP message with no attachments. Except for the SOAP header, all the parts listed are required to be in every SOAP message.

I. SOAP message

  A. SOAP part

    1. SOAP envelope

      a. SOAP header (optional)

      b. SOAP body

The SAAJ API provides the `SOAPMessage` class to represent a SOAP message, the `SOAPPart` class to represent the SOAP part, the `SOAPEnvelope` interface to represent the SOAP envelope, and so on. Figure 18–1 illustrates the structure of a SOAP message with no attachments.

Note: Many SAAJ API interfaces extend DOM interfaces. In a SAAJ message, the `SOAPPart` class is also a DOM document. See SAAJ and DOM (page 638) for details.

When you create a new `SOAPMessage` object, it will automatically have the parts that are required to be in a SOAP message. In other words, a new `SOAPMessage` object has a `SOAPPart` object that contains a `SOAPEnvelope` object. The `SOAPEnvelope` object in turn automatically contains an empty `SOAPHeader` object followed by an empty `SOAPBody` object. If you do not need the `SOAPHeader` object, which is optional, you can delete it. The rationale for having it automatically included is that more often than not you will need it, so it is more convenient to have it provided.

The `SOAPHeader` object can include one or more headers that contain metadata about the message (for example, information about the sending and receiving parties). The `SOAPBody` object, which always follows the `SOAPHeader` object if there is one, contains the message content. If there is a `SOAPFault` object (see Using SOAP Faults, page 661), it must be in the `SOAPBody` object.

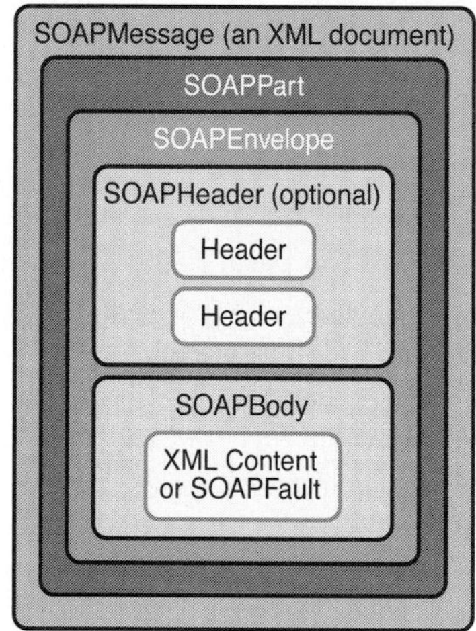

Figure 18–1 `SOAPMessage` Object with No Attachments

Messages with Attachments

A SOAP message may include one or more attachment parts in addition to the SOAP part. The SOAP part must contain only XML content; as a result, if any of the content of a message is not in XML format, it must occur in an attachment part. So if, for example, you want your message to contain a binary file, your message must have an attachment part for it. Note that an attachment part can contain any kind of content, so it can contain data in XML format as well. Figure 18–2 shows the high-level structure of a SOAP message that has two attachments.

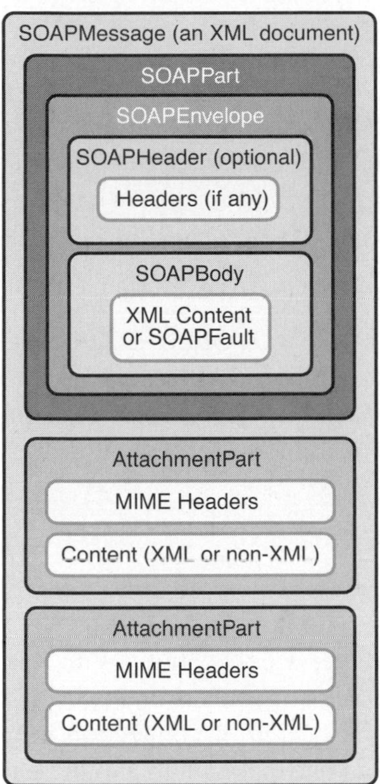

Figure 18–2 `SOAPMessage` Object with Two `AttachmentPart` Objects

The SAAJ API provides the `AttachmentPart` class to represent an attachment part of a SOAP message. A `SOAPMessage` object automatically has a `SOAPPart` object and its required subelements, but because `AttachmentPart` objects are optional, you must create and add them yourself. The tutorial section walks you through creating and populating messages with and without attachment parts.

If a `SOAPMessage` object has one or more attachments, each `AttachmentPart` object must have a MIME header to indicate the type of data it contains. It may also have additional MIME headers to identify it or to give its location. These headers are optional but can be useful when there are multiple attachments. When a `SOAPMessage` object has one or more `AttachmentPart` objects, its `SOAPPart` object may or may not contain message content.

SAAJ and DOM

The SAAJ APIs extend their counterparts in the `org.w3c.dom` package:

- The `Node` interface extends the `org.w3c.dom.Node` interface.
- The `SOAPElement` interface extends both the `Node` interface and the `org.w3c.dom.Element` interface.
- The `SOAPPart` class implements the `org.w3c.dom.Document` interface.
- The `Text` interface extends the `org.w3c.dom.Text` interface.

Moreover, the `SOAPPart` of a `SOAPMessage` is also a DOM Level 2 `Document` and can be manipulated as such by applications, tools, and libraries that use DOM. For details on how to use DOM documents with the SAAJ API, see Adding Content to the SOAPPart Object (page 650) and Adding a Document to the SOAP Body (page 652).

Connections

All SOAP messages are sent and received over a connection. With the SAAJ API, the connection is represented by a `SOAPConnection` object, which goes from the sender directly to its destination. This kind of connection is called a *point-to-point* connection because it goes from one endpoint to another endpoint. Messages sent using the SAAJ API are called *request-response messages*. They are sent over a `SOAPConnection` object with the `call` method, which sends a message (a request) and then blocks until it receives the reply (a response).

SOAPConnection Objects

The following code fragment creates the `SOAPConnection` object `connection` and then, after creating and populating the message, uses `connection` to send the message. As stated previously, all messages sent over a `SOAPConnection` object are sent with the `call` method, which both sends the message and blocks until it receives the response. Thus, the return value for the `call` method is the `SOAPMessage` object that is the response to the message that was sent. The `request` parameter is the message being sent; `endpoint` represents where it is being sent.

```
SOAPConnectionFactory factory =
  SOAPConnectionFactory.newInstance();
SOAPConnection connection = factory.createConnection();
```

```
. . .// create a request message and give it content

java.net.URL endpoint =
  new URL("http://fabulous.com/gizmo/order");
SOAPMessage response = connection.call(request, endpoint);
```

Note that the second argument to the call method, which identifies where the message is being sent, can be a String object or a URL object. Thus, the last two lines of code from the preceding example could also have been the following:

```
String endpoint = "http://fabulous.com/gizmo/order";
SOAPMessage response = connection.call(request, endpoint);
```

A web service implemented for request-response messaging must return a response to any message it receives. The response is a SOAPMessage object, just as the request is a SOAPMessage object. When the request message is an update, the response is an acknowledgment that the update was received. Such an acknowledgment implies that the update was successful. Some messages may not require any response at all. The service that gets such a message is still required to send back a response because one is needed to unblock the call method. In this case, the response is not related to the content of the message; it is simply a message to unblock the call method.

Now that you have some background on SOAP messages and SOAP connections, in the next section you will see how to use the SAAJ API.

Tutorial

This tutorial walks you through how to use the SAAJ API. First, it covers the basics of creating and sending a simple SOAP message. Then you will learn more details about adding content to messages, including how to create SOAP faults and attributes. Finally, you will learn how to send a message and retrieve the content of the response. After going through this tutorial, you will know how to perform the following tasks:

- Creating and sending a simple message
- Adding content to the header
- Adding content to the SOAPPart object
- Adding a document to the SOAP body
- Manipulating message content using SAAJ or DOM APIs
- Adding attachments

- Adding attributes
- Using SOAP faults

In the section Code Examples (page 667), you will see the code fragments from earlier parts of the tutorial in runnable applications, which you can test yourself. To see how the SAAJ API can be used in server code, see the SAAJ part of the Coffee Break case study (SAAJ Coffee Supplier Service, page 1204), which shows an example of both the client and the server code for a web service application.

A SAAJ client can send request-response messages to web services that are implemented to do request-response messaging. This section demonstrates how you can do this.

Creating and Sending a Simple Message

This section covers the basics of creating and sending a simple message and retrieving the content of the response. It includes the following topics:

- Creating a message
- Parts of a message
- Accessing elements of a message
- Adding content to the body
- Getting a `SOAPConnection` object
- Sending a message
- Getting the content of a message

Creating a Message

The first step is to create a message using a `MessageFactory` object. The SAAJ API provides a default implementation of the `MessageFactory` class, thus making it easy to get an instance. The following code fragment illustrates getting an instance of the default message factory and then using it to create a message.

```
MessageFactory factory = MessageFactory.newInstance();
SOAPMessage message = factory.createMessage();
```

As is true of the `newInstance` method for `SOAPConnectionFactory`, the `newInstance` method for `MessageFactory` is static, so you invoke it by calling `MessageFactory.newInstance`.

If you specify no arguments to the `newInstance` method, it creates a message factory for SOAP 1.1 messages. To create a message factory that allows you to create and process SOAP 1.2 messages, use the following method call:

```
MessageFactory factory =
MessageFactory.newInstance(SOAPConstants.SOAP_1_2_PROTOCOL);
```

To create a message factory that can create either SOAP 1.1 or SOAP 1.2 messages, use the following method call:

```
MessageFactory factory =
MessageFactory.newInstance(SOAPConstants.DYNAMIC_SOAP_PROTOCOL
);
```

This kind of factory enables you to process an incoming message that might be of either type.

Parts of a Message

A `SOAPMessage` object is required to have certain elements, and, as stated previously, the SAAJ API simplifies things for you by returning a new `SOAPMessage` object that already contains these elements. When you call `createMessage` with no arguments, the message that is created automatically has the following:

I. A `SOAPPart` object that contains

    A. A `SOAPEnvelope` object that contains

        1. An empty `SOAPHeader` object

        2. An empty `SOAPBody` object

The `SOAPHeader` object is optional and can be deleted if it is not needed. However, if there is one, it must precede the `SOAPBody` object. The `SOAPBody` object can hold either the content of the message or a *fault* message that contains status information or details about a problem with the message. The section Using SOAP Faults (page 661) walks you through how to use `SOAPFault` objects.

Accessing Elements of a Message

The next step in creating a message is to access its parts so that content can be added. There are two ways to do this. The SOAPMessage object message, created in the preceding code fragment, is the place to start.

The first way to access the parts of the message is to work your way through the structure of the message. The message contains a SOAPPart object, so you use the getSOAPPart method of message to retrieve it:

```
SOAPPart soapPart = message.getSOAPPart();
```

Next you can use the getEnvelope method of soapPart to retrieve the SOAPEnvelope object that it contains.

```
SOAPEnvelope envelope = soapPart.getEnvelope();
```

You can now use the getHeader and getBody methods of envelope to retrieve its empty SOAPHeader and SOAPBody objects.

```
SOAPHeader header = envelope.getHeader();
SOAPBody body = envelope.getBody();
```

The second way to access the parts of the message is to retrieve the message header and body directly, without retrieving the SOAPPart or SOAPEnvelope. To do so, use the getSOAPHeader and getSOAPBody methods of SOAPMessage:

```
SOAPHeader header = message.getSOAPHeader();
SOAPBody body = message.getSOAPBody();
```

This example of a SAAJ client does not use a SOAP header, so you can delete it. (You will see more about headers later.) Because all SOAPElement objects, including SOAPHeader objects, are derived from the Node interface, you use the method Node.detachNode to delete header.

```
header.detachNode();
```

Adding Content to the Body

The SOAPBody object contains either content or a fault. To add content to the body, you normally create one or more SOAPBodyElement objects to hold the content. You can also add subelements to the SOAPBodyElement objects by using the addChildElement method. For each element or child element, you add content by using the addTextNode method.

When you create any new element, you also need to create an associated javax.xml.namespace.QName object so that it is uniquely identified.

Note: You can use Name objects instead of QName objects. Name objects are specific to the SAAJ API, and you create them using either SOAPEnvelope methods or SOAPFactory methods. However, the Name interface may be deprecated at a future release.

The SOAPFactory class also lets you create XML elements when you are not creating an entire message or do not have access to a complete SOAPMessage object. For example, JAX-RPC implementations often work with XML fragments rather than complete SOAPMessage objects. Consequently, they do not have access to a SOAPEnvelope object, and this makes using a SOAPFactory object to create Name objects very useful. In addition to a method for creating Name objects, the SOAPFactory class provides methods for creating Detail objects and SOAP fragments. You will find an explanation of Detail objects in Overview of SOAP Faults (page 662) and Creating and Populating a SOAPFault Object (page 663).

QName objects associated with SOAPBodyElement or SOAPHeaderElement objects must be fully qualified; that is, they must be created with a namespace URI, a local part, and a namespace prefix. Specifying a namespace for an element makes clear which one is meant if more than one element has the same local name.

The following code fragment retrieves the SOAPBody object body from message, constructs a QName object for the element to be added, and adds a new SOAPBodyElement object to body.

```
SOAPBody body = message.getSOAPBody();
QName bodyName = new QName("http://wombat.ztrade.com",
  "GetLastTradePrice", "m");
SOAPBodyElement bodyElement = body.addBodyElement(bodyName);
```

At this point, body contains a SOAPBodyElement object identified by the QName object bodyName, but there is still no content in bodyElement. Assuming that you want to get a quote for the stock of Sun Microsystems, Inc., you need to create a child element for the symbol using the addChildElement method. Then you need to give it the stock symbol using the addTextNode method. The QName object for the new SOAPElement object symbol is initialized with only a local name because child elements inherit the prefix and URI from the parent element.

```
QName name = new QName("symbol");
SOAPElement symbol = bodyElement.addChildElement(name);
symbol.addTextNode("SUNW");
```

You might recall that the headers and content in a SOAPPart object must be in XML format. The SAAJ API takes care of this for you, building the appropriate XML constructs automatically when you call methods such as addBodyElement, addChildElement, and addTextNode. Note that you can call the method addTextNode only on an element such as bodyElement or any child elements that are added to it. You cannot call addTextNode on a SOAPHeader or SOAPBody object because they contain elements and not text.

The content that you have just added to your SOAPBody object will look like the following when it is sent over the wire:

```
<SOAP-ENV:Envelope
 xmlns:SOAP-ENV="http://schemas.xmlsoap.org/soap/envelope/">
  <SOAP-ENV:Body>
    <m:GetLastTradePrice xmlns:m="http://wombat.ztrade.com">
      <symbol>SUNW</symbol>
    </m:GetLastTradePrice>
  </SOAP-ENV:Body>
</SOAP-ENV:Envelope>
```

Let's examine this XML excerpt line by line to see how it relates to your SAAJ code. Note that an XML parser does not care about indentations, but they are generally used to indicate element levels and thereby make it easier for a human reader to understand.

Here is the SAAJ code:

```
SOAPMessage message = messageFactory.createMessage();
SOAPHeader header = message.getSOAPHeader();
SOAPBody body = message.getSOAPBody();
```

Here is the XML it produces:

```
<SOAP-ENV:Envelope
 xmlns:SOAP-ENV="http://schemas.xmlsoap.org/soap/envelope/">
  <SOAP-ENV:Header/>
  <SOAP-ENV:Body>
    ...
  </SOAP-ENV:Body>
</SOAP-ENV:Envelope>
```

The outermost element in this XML example is the SOAP envelope element, indicated by `SOAP-ENV:Envelope`. Note that `Envelope` is the name of the element, and `SOAP-ENV` is the namespace prefix. The interface `SOAPEnvelope` represents a SOAP envelope.

The first line signals the beginning of the SOAP envelope element, and the last line signals the end of it; everything in between is part of the SOAP envelope. The second line is an example of an attribute for the SOAP envelope element. Because a SOAP envelope element always contains this attribute with this value, a `SOAPMessage` object comes with it automatically included. `xmlns` stands for "XML namespace," and its value is the URI of the namespace associated with `Envelope`.

The next line is an empty SOAP header. We could remove it by calling `header.detachNode` after the `getSOAPHeader` call.

The next two lines mark the beginning and end of the SOAP body, represented in SAAJ by a `SOAPBody` object. The next step is to add content to the body.

Here is the SAAJ code:

```
QName bodyName = new QName("http://wombat.ztrade.com",
  "GetLastTradePrice", "m");
SOAPBodyElement bodyElement = body.addBodyElement(bodyName);
```

Here is the XML it produces:

```
<m:GetLastTradePrice
 xmlns:m="http://wombat.ztrade.com">
 ...
</m:GetLastTradePrice>
```

These lines are what the `SOAPBodyElement bodyElement` in your code represents. `GetLastTradePrice` is its local name, `m` is its namespace prefix, and `http://wombat.ztrade.com` is its namespace URI.

Here is the SAAJ code:

```
QName name = new QName("symbol");
SOAPElement symbol = bodyElement.addChildElement(name);
symbol.addTextNode("SUNW");
```

Here is the XML it produces:

```
<symbol>SUNW</symbol>
```

The String "SUNW" is the text node for the element <symbol>. This String object is the message content that your recipient, the stock quote service, receives.

The following example shows how to add multiple SOAPElement objects and add text to each of them. The code first creates the SOAPBodyElement object purchaseLineItems, which has a fully qualified name associated with it. That is, the QName object for it has a namespace URI, a local name, and a namespace prefix. As you saw earlier, a SOAPBodyElement object is required to have a fully qualified name, but child elements added to it, such as SOAPElement objects, can have Name objects with only the local name.

```
SOAPBody body = message.getSOAPBody();
QName bodyName = new QName("http://sonata.fruitsgalore.com",
  "PurchaseLineItems", "PO");
SOAPBodyElement purchaseLineItems =
  body.addBodyElement(bodyName);

QName childName = new QName("Order");
SOAPElement order =
  purchaseLineItems.addChildElement(childName);

childName = new QName("Product");
SOAPElement product = order.addChildElement(childName);
product.addTextNode("Apple");

childName = new QName("Price");
SOAPElement price = order.addChildElement(childName);
price.addTextNode("1.56");

childName = new QName("Order");
SOAPElement order2 =
  purchaseLineItems.addChildElement(childName);

childName = new QName("Product");
SOAPElement product2 = order2.addChildElement(childName);
```

```
product2.addTextNode("Peach");

childName = soapFactory.new QName("Price");
SOAPElement price2 = order2.addChildElement(childName);
price2.addTextNode("1.48");
```

The SAAJ code in the preceding example produces the following XML in the SOAP body:

```
<PO:PurchaseLineItems
 xmlns:PO="http://sonata.fruitsgalore.com">
  <Order>
    <Product>Apple</Product>
    <Price>1.56</Price>
  </Order>

  <Order>
    <Product>Peach</Product>
    <Price>1.48</Price>
  </Order>
</PO:PurchaseLineItems>
```

Getting a SOAPConnection Object

The SAAJ API is focused primarily on reading and writing messages. After you have written a message, you can send it using various mechanisms (such as JMS or JAXM). The SAAJ API does, however, provide a simple mechanism for request-response messaging.

To send a message, a SAAJ client can use a SOAPConnection object. A SOAPConnection object is a point-to-point connection, meaning that it goes directly from the sender to the destination (usually a URL) that the sender specifies.

The first step is to obtain a SOAPConnectionFactory object that you can use to create your connection. The SAAJ API makes this easy by providing the SOAPConnectionFactory class with a default implementation. You can get an instance of this implementation using the following line of code.

```
SOAPConnectionFactory soapConnectionFactory =
  SOAPConnectionFactory.newInstance();
```

Now you can use soapConnectionFactory to create a SOAPConnection object.

```
SOAPConnection connection =
  soapConnectionFactory.createConnection();
```

You will use connection to send the message that you created.

Sending a Message

A SAAJ client calls the SOAPConnection method call on a SOAPConnection object to send a message. The call method takes two arguments: the message being sent and the destination to which the message should go. This message is going to the stock quote service indicated by the URL object endpoint.

```
java.net.URL endpoint = new URL(
  "http://wombat.ztrade.com/quotes");

SOAPMessage response = connection.call(message, endpoint);
```

The content of the message you sent is the stock symbol SUNW; the SOAPMessage object response should contain the last stock price for Sun Microsystems, which you will retrieve in the next section.

A connection uses a fair amount of resources, so it is a good idea to close a connection as soon as you are finished using it.

```
connection.close();
```

Getting the Content of a Message

The initial steps for retrieving a message's content are the same as those for giving content to a message: Either you use the Message object to get the SOAPBody object, or you access the SOAPBody object through the SOAPPart and SOAPEnvelope objects.

Then you access the SOAPBody object's SOAPBodyElement object, because that is the element to which content was added in the example. (In a later section you will see how to add content directly to the SOAPPart object, in which case you would not need to access the SOAPBodyElement object to add content or to retrieve it.)

To get the content, which was added with the method SOAPElement.addTextNode, you call the method Node.getValue. Note that getValue returns the value of the immediate child of the element that calls the method. Therefore, in the following code fragment, the getValue method is called on bodyElement, the element on which the addTextNode method was called.

To access bodyElement, you call the getChildElements method on soapBody. Passing bodyName to getChildElements returns a java.util.Iterator object that contains all the child elements identified by the Name object bodyName. You already know that there is only one, so calling the next method on it will return the SOAPBodyElement you want. Note that the Iterator.next method returns a Java Object, so you need to cast the Object it returns to a SOAPBodyElement object before assigning it to the variable bodyElement.

```
SOAPBody soapBody = response.getSOAPBody();
java.util.Iterator iterator =
  soapBody.getChildElements(bodyName);
SOAPBodyElement bodyElement =
  (SOAPBodyElement)iterator.next();
String lastPrice = bodyElement.getValue();
System.out.print("The last price for SUNW is ");
System.out.println(lastPrice);
```

If more than one element had the name bodyName, you would have to use a while loop using the Iterator.hasNext method to make sure that you got all of them.

```
while (iterator.hasNext()) {
  SOAPBodyElement bodyElement =
    (SOAPBodyElement)iterator.next();
  String lastPrice = bodyElement.getValue();
  System.out.print("The last price for SUNW is ");
  System.out.println(lastPrice);
}
```

At this point, you have seen how to send a very basic request-response message and get the content from the response. The next sections provide more detail on adding content to messages.

Adding Content to the Header

To add content to the header, you create a SOAPHeaderElement object. As with all new elements, it must have an associated QName object.

For example, suppose you want to add a conformance claim header to the message to state that your message conforms to the WS-I Basic Profile. The following code fragment retrieves the SOAPHeader object from message and adds a new SOAPHeaderElement object to it. This SOAPHeaderElement object contains the correct qualified name and attribute for a WS-I conformance claim header.

```
SOAPHeader header = message.getSOAPHeader();
QName headerName = new QName(
  "http://ws-i.org/schemas/conformanceClaim/",
  "Claim", "wsi");
SOAPHeaderElement headerElement =
  header.addHeaderElement(headerName);
headerElement.addAttribute(new QName("conformsTo"),
  "http://ws-i.org/profiles/basic/1.1/");
```

At this point, header contains the SOAPHeaderElement object headerElement identified by the QName object headerName. Note that the addHeaderElement method both creates headerElement and adds it to header.

A conformance claim header has no content. This code produces the following XML header:

```
<SOAP-ENV:Header>
  <wsi:Claim
    xmlns:wsi="http://ws-i.org/schemas/conformanceClaim/"
    conformsTo="http://ws-i.org/profiles/basic/1.1/"/>
</SOAP-ENV:Header>
```

For more information about creating SOAP messages that conform to WS-I, see the Conformance Claim Attachment Mechanisms document described in the Conformance section of the WS-I Basic Profile.

For a different kind of header, you might want to add content to headerElement. The following line of code uses the method addTextNode to do this.

```
headerElement.addTextNode("order");
```

Now you have the SOAPHeader object header that contains a SOAPHeaderElement object whose content is "order".

Adding Content to the SOAPPart Object

If the content you want to send is in a file, SAAJ provides an easy way to add it directly to the SOAPPart object. This means that you do not access the SOAPBody object and build the XML content yourself, as you did in the preceding section.

To add a file directly to the SOAPPart object, you use a javax.xml.transform.Source object from JAXP (the Java API for XML Processing). There are three types of Source objects: SAXSource, DOMSource, and StreamSource. A StreamSource object holds an XML document in text form. SAXSource and DOMSource objects hold content along with the instructions for transforming the content into an XML document.

The following code fragment uses the JAXP API to build a DOMSource object that is passed to the SOAPPart.setContent method. The first three lines of code get a DocumentBuilderFactory object and use it to create the DocumentBuilder object builder. Because SOAP messages use namespaces, you should set the NamespaceAware property for the factory to true. Then builder parses the content file to produce a Document object.

```
DocumentBuilderFactory dbFactory =
  DocumentBuilderFactory.newInstance();
dbFactory.setNamespaceAware(true);
DocumentBuilder builder = dbFactory.newDocumentBuilder();
Document document =
  builder.parse("file:///music/order/soap.xml");
DOMSource domSource = new DOMSource(document);
```

The following two lines of code access the SOAPPart object (using the SOAPMessage object message) and set the new Document object as its content. The SOAPPart.setContent method not only sets content for the SOAPBody object but also sets the appropriate header for the SOAPHeader object.

```
SOAPPart soapPart = message.getSOAPPart();
soapPart.setContent(domSource);
```

The XML file you use to set the content of the SOAPPart object must include Envelope and Body elements:

```
<SOAP-ENV:Envelope
xmlns="http://schemas.xmlsoap.org/soap/envelope/">
  <SOAP-ENV:Body>
  ...
  </SOAP-ENV:Body>
</SOAP-ENV:Envelope>
```

You will see other ways to add content to a message in the sections Adding a Document to the SOAP Body (page 652) and Adding Attachments (page 653).

Adding a Document to the SOAP Body

In addition to setting the content of the entire SOAP message to that of a `DOMSource` object, you can add a DOM document directly to the body of the message. This capability means that you do not have to create a `javax.xml.transform.Source` object. After you parse the document, you can add it directly to the message body:

```
SOAPBody body = message.getSOAPBody();
SOAPBodyElement docElement = body.addDocument(document);
```

Manipulating Message Content Using SAAJ or DOM APIs

Because SAAJ nodes and elements implement the DOM `Node` and `Element` interfaces, you have many options for adding or changing message content:

- Use only DOM APIs.
- Use only SAAJ APIs.
- Use SAAJ APIs and then switch to using DOM APIs.
- Use DOM APIs and then switch to using SAAJ APIs.

The first three of these cause no problems. After you have created a message, whether or not you have imported its content from another document, you can start adding or changing nodes using either SAAJ or DOM APIs.

But if you use DOM APIs and then switch to using SAAJ APIs to manipulate the document, any references to objects within the tree that were obtained using DOM APIs are no longer valid. If you must use SAAJ APIs after using DOM APIs, you should set all your DOM typed references to null, because they can become invalid. For more information about the exact cases in which references become invalid, see the SAAJ API documentation.

The basic rule is that you can continue manipulating the message content using SAAJ APIs as long as you want to, but after you start manipulating it using DOM, you should no longer use SAAJ APIs.

Adding Attachments

An `AttachmentPart` object can contain any type of content, including XML. And because the SOAP part can contain only XML content, you must use an `AttachmentPart` object for any content that is not in XML format.

Creating an AttachmentPart Object and Adding Content

The `SOAPMessage` object creates an `AttachmentPart` object, and the message also must add the attachment to itself after content has been added. The `SOAPMessage` class has three methods for creating an `AttachmentPart` object.

The first method creates an attachment with no content. In this case, an `AttachmentPart` method is used later to add content to the attachment.

```
AttachmentPart attachment = message.createAttachmentPart();
```

You add content to `attachment` by using the `AttachmentPart` method `setContent`. This method takes two parameters: a Java `Object` for the content, and a `String` object for the MIME content type that is used to encode the object. Content in the `SOAPBody` part of a message automatically has a `Content-Type` header with the value `"text/xml"` because the content must be in XML. In contrast, the type of content in an `AttachmentPart` object must be specified because it can be any type.

Each `AttachmentPart` object has one or more MIME headers associated with it. When you specify a type to the `setContent` method, that type is used for the header `Content-Type`. Note that `Content-Type` is the only header that is required. You may set other optional headers, such as `Content-Id` and `Content-Location`. For convenience, SAAJ provides `get` and `set` methods for the headers `Content-Type`, `Content-Id`, and `Content-Location`. These headers can be helpful in accessing a particular attachment when a message has multiple attachments. For example, to access the attachments that have particular headers, you can call the `SOAPMessage` method `getAttachments` and pass it a `MIMEHeaders` object containing the MIME headers you are interested in.

The following code fragment shows one of the ways to use the method `setContent`. The Java `Object` in the first parameter can be a `String`, a stream, a `javax.xml.transform.Source` object, or a `javax.activation.DataHandler` object. The Java `Object` being added in the following code fragment is a `String`, which is plain text, so the second argument must be `"text/plain"`. The code also sets a content identifier, which can be used to identify this AttachmentPart object. After you have added content to attachment, you must add it to the SOAPMessage object, something that is done in the last line.

```
String stringContent = "Update address for Sunny Skies " +
  "Inc., to 10 Upbeat Street, Pleasant Grove, CA 95439";

attachment.setContent(stringContent, "text/plain");
attachment.setContentId("update_address");

message.addAttachmentPart(attachment);
```

The attachment variable now represents an AttachmentPart object that contains the string stringContent and has a header that contains the string "text/plain". It also has a Content-Id header with "update_address" as its value. And attachment is now part of message.

The other two SOAPMessage.createAttachment methods create an AttachmentPart object complete with content. One is very similar to the AttachmentPart.setContent method in that it takes the same parameters and does essentially the same thing. It takes a Java Object containing the content and a String giving the content type. As with AttachmentPart.setContent, the Object can be a String, a stream, a javax.xml.transform.Source object, or a javax.activation.DataHandler object.

The other method for creating an AttachmentPart object with content takes a DataHandler object, which is part of the JavaBeans Activation Framework (JAF). Using a DataHandler object is fairly straightforward. First, you create a java.net.URL object for the file you want to add as content. Then you create a DataHandler object initialized with the URL object:

```
URL url = new URL("http://greatproducts.com/gizmos/img.jpg");
DataHandler dataHandler = new DataHandler(url);
AttachmentPart attachment =
  message.createAttachmentPart(dataHandler);
attachment.setContentId("attached_image");

message.addAttachmentPart(attachment);
```

You might note two things about this code fragment. First, it sets a header for Content-ID using the method setContentId. This method takes a String that can be whatever you like to identify the attachment. Second, unlike the other methods for setting content, this one does not take a String for Content-Type. This method takes care of setting the Content-Type header for you, something that is possible because one of the things a DataHandler object does is to determine the data type of the file it contains.

Accessing an AttachmentPart Object

If you receive a message with attachments or want to change an attachment to a message you are building, you need to access the attachment. The SOAPMessage class provides two versions of the getAttachments method for retrieving its AttachmentPart objects. When it is given no argument, the method SOAPMessage.getAttachments returns a java.util.Iterator object over all the AttachmentPart objects in a message. When getAttachments is given a MimeHeaders object, which is a list of MIME headers, getAttachments returns an iterator over the AttachmentPart objects that have a header that matches one of the headers in the list. The following code uses the getAttachments method that takes no arguments and thus retrieves all the AttachmentPart objects in the SOAPMessage object message. Then it prints the content ID, the content type, and the content of each AttachmentPart object.

```
java.util.Iterator iterator = message.getAttachments();
while (iterator.hasNext()) {
  AttachmentPart attachment = (AttachmentPart)iterator.next();
  String id = attachment.getContentId();
  String type = attachment.getContentType();
  System.out.print("Attachment " + id +
     " has content type " + type);
  if (type.equals("text/plain")) {
     Object content = attachment.getContent();
     System.out.println("Attachment contains:\n" + content);
  }
}
```

Adding Attributes

An XML element can have one or more attributes that give information about that element. An attribute consists of a name for the attribute followed immediately by an equal sign (=) and its value.

The SOAPElement interface provides methods for adding an attribute, for getting the value of an attribute, and for removing an attribute. For example, in the following code fragment, the attribute named id is added to the SOAPElement object person. Because person is a SOAPElement object rather than a SOAP-

BodyElement object or SOAPHeaderElement object, it is legal for its QName object to contain only a local name.

```
QName attributeName = new QName("id");
person.addAttribute(attributeName, "Person7");
```

These lines of code will generate the first line in the following XML fragment.

```
<person id="Person7">
  ...
</person>
```

The following line of code retrieves the value of the attribute whose name is id.

```
String attributeValue =
  person.getAttributeValue(attributeName);
```

If you had added two or more attributes to person, the preceding line of code would have returned only the value for the attribute named id. If you wanted to retrieve the values for all the attributes for person, you would use the method getAllAttributes, which returns an iterator over all the values. The following lines of code retrieve and print each value on a separate line until there are no more attribute values. Note that the Iterator.next method returns a Java Object, which is cast to a QName object so that it can be assigned to the QName object attributeName. (The examples in DOMExample.java and DOMSrc-Example.java (page 681) use code similar to this.)

```
Iterator iterator = person.getAllAttributesAsQNames();
while (iterator.hasNext()){
  QName attributeName = (QName) iterator.next();
  System.out.println("Attribute name is " +
    attributeName.toString());
  System.out.println("Attribute value is " +
    element.getAttributeValue(attributeName));
}
```

The following line of code removes the attribute named id from person. The variable successful will be true if the attribute was removed successfully.

```
boolean successful = person.removeAttribute(attributeName);
```

In this section you have seen how to add, retrieve, and remove attributes. This information is general in that it applies to any element. The next section discusses attributes that can be added only to header elements.

Header Attributes

Attributes that appear in a `SOAPHeaderElement` object determine how a recipient processes a message. You can think of header attributes as offering a way to extend a message, giving information about such things as authentication, transaction management, payment, and so on. A header attribute refines the meaning of the header, whereas the header refines the meaning of the message contained in the SOAP body.

The SOAP 1.1 specification defines two attributes that can appear only in `SOAPHeaderElement` objects: `actor` and `mustUnderstand`.

The SOAP 1.2 specification defines three such attributes: `role` (a new name for `actor`), `mustUnderstand`, and `relay`.

The next sections discuss these attributes.

See HeaderExample.java (page 678) for an example that uses the code shown in this section.

The Actor Attribute

The `actor` attribute is optional, but if it is used, it must appear in a `SOAPHeaderElement` object. Its purpose is to indicate the recipient of a header element. The default actor is the message's ultimate recipient; that is, if no actor attribute is supplied, the message goes directly to the ultimate recipient.

An *actor* is an application that can both receive SOAP messages and forward them to the next actor. The ability to specify one or more actors as intermediate recipients makes it possible to route a message to multiple recipients and to supply header information that applies specifically to each of the recipients.

For example, suppose that a message is an incoming purchase order. Its `SOAPHeader` object might have `SOAPHeaderElement` objects with actor attributes that route the message to applications that function as the order desk, the shipping desk, the confirmation desk, and the billing department. Each of these applications will take the appropriate action, remove the `SOAPHeaderElement` objects relevant to it, and send the message on to the next actor.

Note: Although the SAAJ API provides the API for adding these attributes, it does not supply the API for processing them. For example, the actor attribute requires that there be an implementation such as a messaging provider service to route the message from one actor to the next.

An actor is identified by its URI. For example, the following line of code, in which orderHeader is a SOAPHeaderElement object, sets the actor to the given URI.

```
orderHeader.setActor("http://gizmos.com/orders");
```

Additional actors can be set in their own SOAPHeaderElement objects. The following code fragment first uses the SOAPMessage object message to get its SOAPHeader object header. Then header creates four SOAPHeaderElement objects, each of which sets its actor attribute.

```
SOAPHeader header = message.getSOAPHeader();
SOAPFactory soapFactory = SOAPFactory.newInstance();

String nameSpace = "ns";
String nameSpaceURI = "http://gizmos.com/NSURI";

QName order =
  new QName(nameSpaceURI, "orderDesk", nameSpace);
SOAPHeaderElement orderHeader =
  header.addHeaderElement(order);
orderHeader.setActor("http://gizmos.com/orders");

QName shipping =
  new QName(nameSpaceURI, "shippingDesk", nameSpace);
SOAPHeaderElement shippingHeader =
  header.addHeaderElement(shipping);
shippingHeader.setActor("http://gizmos.com/shipping");

QName confirmation =
  new QName(nameSpaceURI, "confirmationDesk", nameSpace);
SOAPHeaderElement confirmationHeader =
  header.addHeaderElement(confirmation);
confirmationHeader.setActor(
  "http://gizmos.com/confirmations");

QName billing =
  new QName(nameSpaceURI, "billingDesk", nameSpace);
SOAPHeaderElement billingHeader =
  header.addHeaderElement(billing);
billingHeader.setActor("http://gizmos.com/billing");
```

The SOAPHeader interface provides two methods that return a java.util.Iterator object over all the SOAPHeaderElement objects that have an actor that matches the specified actor. The first method, `examineHeaderElements`, returns an iterator over all the elements that have the specified actor.

```
java.util.Iterator headerElements =
  header.examineHeaderElements("http://gizmos.com/orders");
```

The second method, `extractHeaderElements`, not only returns an iterator over all the `SOAPHeaderElement` objects that have the specified actor attribute but also detaches them from the `SOAPHeader` object. So, for example, after the order desk application did its work, it would call `extractHeaderElements` to remove all the `SOAPHeaderElement` objects that applied to it.

```
java.util.Iterator headerElements =
  header.extractHeaderElements("http://gizmos.com/orders");
```

Each `SOAPHeaderElement` object can have only one actor attribute, but the same actor can be an attribute for multiple `SOAPHeaderElement` objects.

Two additional `SOAPHeader` methods—`examineAllHeaderElements` and `extractAllHeaderElements`—allow you to examine or extract all the header elements, whether or not they have an actor attribute. For example, you could use the following code to display the values of all the header elements:

```
Iterator allHeaders =
  header.examineAllHeaderElements();
while (allHeaders.hasNext()) {
  SOAPHeaderElement headerElement =
    (SOAPHeaderElement)allHeaders.next();
  QName headerName =
    headerElement.getElementQName();
  System.out.println("\nHeader name is " +
    headerName.toString());
  System.out.println("Actor is " +
    headerElement.getActor());
}
```

The role Attribute

The `role` attribute is the name used by the SOAP 1.2 specification for the SOAP 1.2 `actor` attribute. The `SOAPHeaderElement` methods `setRole` and `getRole` perform the same functions as the `setActor` and `getActor` methods.

The mustUnderstand Attribute

The other attribute that must be added only to a `SOAPHeaderElement` object is `mustUnderstand`. This attribute says whether or not the recipient (indicated by the `actor` attribute) is required to process a header entry. When the value of the `mustUnderstand` attribute is `true`, the actor must understand the semantics of the header entry and must process it correctly to those semantics. If the value is `false`, processing the header entry is optional. A `SOAPHeaderElement` object with no `mustUnderstand` attribute is equivalent to one with a `mustUnderstand` attribute whose value is `false`.

The `mustUnderstand` attribute is used to call attention to the fact that the semantics in an element are different from the semantics in its parent or peer elements. This allows for robust evolution, ensuring that a change in semantics will not be silently ignored by those who may not fully understand it.

If the actor for a header that has a `mustUnderstand` attribute set to `true` cannot process the header, it must send a SOAP fault back to the sender. (See Using SOAP Faults, page 661.) The actor must not change state or cause any side effects, so that, to an outside observer, it appears that the fault was sent before any header processing was done.

For example, you could set the `mustUnderstand` attribute to `true` for the `confirmationHeader` in the code fragment in The Actor Attribute (page 657):

```
QName confirmation =
  new QName(nameSpaceURI, "confirmationDesk", nameSpace);
SOAPHeaderElement confirmationHeader =
  header.addHeaderElement(confirmation);
confirmationHeader.setActor(
  "http://gizmos.com/confirmations");
confirmationHeader.setMustUnderstand(true);
```

This fragment produces the following XML:

```
<ns:confirmationDesk
  xmlns:ns="http://gizmos.com/NSURI"
  SOAP-ENV:actor="http://gizmos.com/confirmations"
  SOAP-ENV:mustUnderstand="1"/>
```

You can use the `getMustUnderstand` method to retrieve the value of the `mustUnderstand` attribute. For example, you could add the following to the code fragment at the end of the preceding section:

```
System.out.println("mustUnderstand is " +
  headerElement.getMustUnderstand());
```

The relay Attribute

The SOAP 1.2 specification adds a third attribute to a `SOAPHeaderElement`, `relay`. This attribute, like `mustUnderstand`, is a boolean value. If it is set to `true`, it indicates that the SOAP header block must not be processed by any node that is targeted by the header block, but must only be passed on to the next targeted node. This attribute is ignored on header blocks whose `mustUnderstand` attribute is set to true or that are targeted at the ultimate receiver (which is the default). The default value of this attribute is `false`.

For example, you could set the `relay` element to `true` for the `billingHeader` in the code fragment in The Actor Attribute (page 657) (also changing `setActor` to `setRole`):

```
QName billing =
  new QName(nameSpaceURI, "billingDesk", nameSpace);
SOAPHeaderElement billingHeader =
  header.addHeaderElement(billing);
billingHeader.setRole("http://gizmos.com/billing");
billingHeader.setRelay(true);
```

This fragment produces the following XML:

```
<ns:billingDesk
  xmlns:ns="http://gizmos.com/NSURI"
  env:relay="true"
  env:role="http://gizmos.com/billing"/>
```

To display the value of the attribute, call `getRelay`:

```
System.out.println("relay is " + headerElement.getRelay());
```

Using SOAP Faults

In this section, you will see how to use the API for creating and accessing a SOAP fault element in an XML message.

Overview of SOAP Faults

If you send a message that was not successful for some reason, you may get back a response containing a SOAP fault element, which gives you status information, error information, or both. There can be only one SOAP fault element in a message, and it must be an entry in the SOAP body. Furthermore, if there is a SOAP fault element in the SOAP body, there can be no other elements in the SOAP body. This means that when you add a SOAP fault element, you have effectively completed the construction of the SOAP body.

A `SOAPFault` object, the representation of a SOAP fault element in the SAAJ API, is similar to an `Exception` object in that it conveys information about a problem. However, a `SOAPFault` object is quite different in that it is an element in a message's `SOAPBody` object rather than part of the `try/catch` mechanism used for `Exception` objects. Also, as part of the `SOAPBody` object, which provides a simple means for sending mandatory information intended for the ultimate recipient, a `SOAPFault` object only reports status or error information. It does not halt the execution of an application, as an `Exception` object can.

If you are a client using the SAAJ API and are sending point-to-point messages, the recipient of your message may add a `SOAPFault` object to the response to alert you to a problem. For example, if you sent an order with an incomplete address for where to send the order, the service receiving the order might put a `SOAPFault` object in the return message telling you that part of the address was missing.

Another example of who might send a SOAP fault is an intermediate recipient, or actor. As stated in the section Adding Attributes (page 655), an actor that cannot process a header that has a `mustUnderstand` attribute with a value of `true` must return a SOAP fault to the sender.

A `SOAPFault` object contains the following elements:

- **Fault code**: Always required. The fault code must be a fully qualified name: it must contain a prefix followed by a local name. The SOAP specifications define a set of fault code local name values, which a developer can extend to cover other problems. (These are defined in section 4.4.1 of the SOAP 1.1 specification and in section 5.4.6 of the SOAP 1.2 specification.) Table 18–1 lists and describes the default fault code local names defined in the specifications.

  A SOAP 1.2 fault code can optionally have a hierarchy of one or more subcodes.

- **Fault string**: Always required. A human-readable explanation of the fault.

- **Fault actor**: Required if the SOAPHeader object contains one or more actor attributes; optional if no actors are specified, meaning that the only actor is the ultimate destination. The fault actor, which is specified as a URI, identifies who caused the fault. For an explanation of what an actor is, see The Actor Attribute, page 657.
- Detail **object**: Required if the fault is an error related to the SOAPBody object. If, for example, the fault code is Client, indicating that the message could not be processed because of a problem in the SOAPBody object, the SOAPFault object must contain a Detail object that gives details about the problem. If a SOAPFault object does not contain a Detail object, it can be assumed that the SOAPBody object was processed successfully.

Creating and Populating a SOAPFault Object

You have seen how to add content to a SOAPBody object; this section walks you through adding a SOAPFault object to a SOAPBody object and then adding its constituent parts.

As with adding content, the first step is to access the SOAPBody object.

```
SOAPBody body = message.getSOAPBody();
```

With the SOAPBody object body in hand, you can use it to create a SOAPFault object. The following line of code creates a SOAPFault object and adds it to body.

```
SOAPFault fault = body.addFault();
```

The SOAPFault interface provides convenience methods that create an element, add the new element to the SOAPFault object, and add a text node, all in one operation. For example, in the following lines of SOAP 1.1 code, the method setFaultCode creates a faultcode element, adds it to fault, and adds a Text node with the value "SOAP-ENV:Server" by specifying a default prefix and the namespace URI for a SOAP envelope.

```
QName faultName =
  new QName(SOAPConstants.URI_NS_SOAP_ENVELOPE, "Server");
fault.setFaultCode(faultName);
fault.setFaultActor("http://gizmos.com/orders");
fault.setFaultString("Server not responding");
```

The SOAP 1.2 code would look like this:

```
QName faultName =
  new QName(SOAPConstants.URI_NS_SOAP_1_2_ENVELOPE,
    "Receiver");
fault.setFaultCode(faultName);
fault.setFaultRole("http://gizmos.com/order");
fault.addFaultReasonText("Server not responding", Locale.US);
```

To add one or more subcodes to the fault code, call the method `fault.appendFaultSubcode`, which takes a `QName` argument.

The `SOAPFault` object `fault`, created in the preceding lines of code, indicates that the cause of the problem is an unavailable server and that the actor at `http://gizmos.com/orders` is having the problem. If the message were being routed only to its ultimate destination, there would have been no need to set a fault actor. Also note that `fault` does not have a `Detail` object because it does not relate to the `SOAPBody` object. (If you use SOAP 1.2, you can use the `setFaultRole` method instead of `setFaultActor`.)

The following SOAP 1.1 code fragment creates a `SOAPFault` object that includes a `Detail` object. Note that a `SOAPFault` object can have only one `Detail` object, which is simply a container for `DetailEntry` objects, but the `Detail` object can have multiple `DetailEntry` objects. The `Detail` object in the following lines of code has two `DetailEntry` objects added to it.

```
SOAPFault fault = body.addFault();

QName faultName =
  new QName(SOAPConstants.URI_NS_SOAP_ENVELOPE, "Client");
fault.setFaultCode(faultName);
fault.setFaultString("Message does not have necessary info");

Detail detail = fault.addDetail();

QName entryName =
  new QName("http://gizmos.com/orders/", "order", "PO");
DetailEntry entry = detail.addDetailEntry(entryName);
entry.addTextNode("Quantity element does not have a value");

QName entryName2 =
  new QName("http://gizmos.com/orders/", "order", "PO");
DetailEntry entry2 = detail.addDetailEntry(entryName2);
entry2.addTextNode("Incomplete address: no zip code");
```

See SOAPFaultTest.java (page 689) for an example that uses code like that shown in this section.

The SOAP 1.1 and 1.2 specifications define slightly different values for a fault code. Table 18–1 lists and describes these values.

Table 18–1 SOAP Fault Code Values

SOAP 1.1	SOAP 1.2	Description
VersionMismatch	VersionMismatch	The namespace or local name for a `SOAP-Envelope` object was invalid.
MustUnderstand	MustUnderstand	An immediate child element of a `SOAP-Header` object had its `mustUnderstand` attribute set to `true`, and the processing party did not understand the element or did not obey it.
Client	Sender	The `SOAPMessage` object was not formed correctly or did not contain the information needed to succeed.
Server	Receiver	The `SOAPMessage` object could not be processed because of a processing error, not because of a problem with the message itself.
N/A	DataEncodingUnknown	A SOAP header block or SOAP body child element information item targeted at the faulting SOAP node is scoped with a data encoding that the faulting node does not support.

Retrieving Fault Information

Just as the `SOAPFault` interface provides convenience methods for adding information, it also provides convenience methods for retrieving that information. The following code fragment shows what you might write to retrieve fault information from a message you received. In the code fragment, `newMessage` is the `SOAPMessage` object that has been sent to you. Because a `SOAPFault` object must be part of the `SOAPBody` object, the first step is to access the `SOAPBody` object. Then the code tests to see whether the `SOAPBody` object contains a `SOAPFault` object. If it does, the code retrieves the `SOAPFault` object and uses it to retrieve its contents. The convenience methods getFaultCode, getFaultString, and getFaultActor make retrieving the values very easy.

```
SOAPBody body = newMessage.getSOAPBody();
if ( body.hasFault() ) {
  SOAPFault newFault = body.getFault();
  QName code = newFault.getFaultCodeAsQName();
  String string = newFault.getFaultString();
  String actor = newFault.getFaultActor();
```

To retrieve subcodes from a SOAP 1.2 fault, call the method newFault.getFaultSubcodes.

Next the code prints the values it has just retrieved. Not all messages are required to have a fault actor, so the code tests to see whether there is one. Testing whether the variable actor is null works because the method getFaultActor returns null if a fault actor has not been set.

```
  System.out.println("SOAP fault contains: ");
  System.out.println("  Fault code = " +
    code.toString());
  System.out.println("  Local name = " + code.getLocalPart());
  System.out.println("  Namespace prefix = " +
    code.getPrefix() + ", bound to " +
    code.getNamespaceURI());
  System.out.println("  Fault string = " + string);

  if ( actor != null ) {
    System.out.println("  Fault actor = " + actor);
  }
```

The final task is to retrieve the Detail object and get its DetailEntry objects. The code uses the SOAPFault object newFault to retrieve the Detail object newDetail, and then it uses newDetail to call the method getDetailEntries. This method returns the java.util.Iterator object entries, which contains all the DetailEntry objects in newDetail. Not all SOAPFault objects are required to have a Detail object, so the code tests to see whether newDetail is null. If it is not, the code prints the values of the DetailEntry objects as long as there are any.

```
Detail newDetail = newFault.getDetail();
if (newDetail != null) {
  Iterator entries = newDetail.getDetailEntries();
  while ( entries.hasNext() ) {
    DetailEntry newEntry = (DetailEntry)entries.next();
```

```
        String value = newEntry.getValue();
        System.out.println("  Detail entry = " + value);
    }
}
```

In summary, you have seen how to add a SOAPFault object and its contents to a message as well as how to retrieve the contents. A SOAPFault object, which is optional, is added to the SOAPBody object to convey status or error information. It must always have a fault code and a String explanation of the fault. A SOAPFault object must indicate the actor that is the source of the fault only when there are multiple actors; otherwise, it is optional. Similarly, the SOAPFault object must contain a Detail object with one or more DetailEntry objects only when the contents of the SOAPBody object could not be processed successfully.

See SOAPFaultTest.java (page 689) for an example that uses code like that shown in this section.

Code Examples

The first part of this tutorial uses code fragments to walk you through the fundamentals of using the SAAJ API. In this section, you will use some of those code fragments to create applications. First, you will see the program Request.java. Then you will see how to run the programs MyUddiPing.java, HeaderExample.java, DOMExample.java, DOMSrcExample.java, Attachments.java, and SOAPFaultTest.java.

Note: Before you run any of the examples, follow the preliminary setup instructions in Building the Examples (page xxxv).

Request.java

The class Request.java puts together the code fragments used in the section Tutorial (page 639) and adds what is needed to make it a complete example of a client sending a request-response message. In addition to putting all the code together, it adds import statements, a main method, and a try/catch block with exception handling.

```
import javax.xml.soap.*;
import javax.xml.namespace.QName;
```

```
import java.util.Iterator;
import java.net.URL;

public class Request {
  public static void main(String[] args){
    try {
      SOAPConnectionFactory soapConnectionFactory =
        SOAPConnectionFactory.newInstance();
      SOAPConnection connection =
        soapConnectionFactory.createConnection();

      MessageFactory factory =
        MessageFactory.newInstance();
      SOAPMessage message = factory.createMessage();

      SOAPHeader header = message.getSOAPHeader();
      SOAPBody body = message.getSOAPBody();
      header.detachNode();

      QName bodyName = new QName("http://wombat.ztrade.com",
        "GetLastTradePrice", "m");
      SOAPBodyElement bodyElement =
        body.addBodyElement(bodyName);

      QName name = new QName("symbol");
      SOAPElement symbol =
        bodyElement.addChildElement(name);
      symbol.addTextNode("SUNW");

      URL endpoint = new URL
        ("http://wombat.ztrade.com/quotes");
      SOAPMessage response =
        connection.call(message, endpoint);

      connection.close();

      SOAPBody soapBody = response.getSOAPBody();

      Iterator iterator =
        soapBody.getChildElements(bodyName);
      bodyElement = (SOAPBodyElement)iterator.next();
      String lastPrice = bodyElement.getValue();

      System.out.print("The last price for SUNW is ");
      System.out.println(lastPrice);

    } catch (Exception ex) {
      ex.printStackTrace();
```

```
        }
    }
}
```

For `Request.java` to be runnable, the second argument supplied to the `call` method would have to be a valid existing URI, and this is not true in this case. However, the application in the next section is one that you can run.

MyUddiPing.java

The program `MyUddiPing.java` is another example of a SAAJ client application. It sends a request to a Universal Description, Discovery and Integration (UDDI) service and gets back the response. A UDDI service is a business registry from which you can get information about businesses that have registered themselves with the registry service. For this example, the MyUddiPing application accesses a private UDDI service registry. Because of this, the number of businesses you can get information about is limited. Nevertheless, MyUddiPing demonstrates a request being sent and a response being received.

The MyUddiPing example is in the following directory:

```
<INSTALL>/javaeetutorial5/examples/saaj/myuddiping/
```

Note: *<INSTALL>* is the directory where you installed the tutorial bundle.

Examining MyUddiPing

We will go through the file `MyUddiPing.java` a few lines at a time, concentrating on the last section. This is the part of the application that accesses only the content you want from the XML message returned by the UDDI registry.

The first lines of code import the interfaces used in the application.

```
import javax.xml.soap.SOAPConnectionFactory;
import javax.xml.soap.SOAPConnection;
import javax.xml.soap.MessageFactory;
import javax.xml.soap.SOAPMessage;
import javax.xml.soap.SOAPHeader;
import javax.xml.soap.SOAPBody;
import javax.xml.soap.SOAPBodyElement;
import javax.xml.soap.SOAPElement;
import javax.xml.namespace.QName;
```

```
import java.net.URL;
import java.util.Properties;
import java.util.Enumeration;
import java.util.Iterator;
import java.util.Locale;
import java.io.FileInputStream;
```

The next few lines begin the definition of the class `MyUddiPing`, which starts with the definition of its `main` method. The following lines create a `java.util.Properties` object that contains the system properties and the properties from the file `uddi.properties`, which is in the `myuddiping` directory.

```
public class MyUddiPing {
  public static void main(String[] args) {
    try {
      Properties myprops = new Properties();
      myprops.load(new FileInputStream(args[0]));

      Properties props = System.getProperties();

      Enumeration propNames = myprops.propertyNames();
      while (propNames.hasMoreElements()) {
        String s = (String) propNames.nextElement();
        props.setProperty(s, myprops.getProperty(s));
      }
```

The next four lines create a `SOAPMessage` object. First, the code gets an instance of `SOAPConnectionFactory` and uses it to create a connection. Then it gets an instance of a SOAP 1.1 `MessageFactory`, using the `MessageFactory` instance to create a message.

```
SOAPConnectionFactory soapConnectionFactory =
  SOAPConnectionFactory.newInstance();
SOAPConnection connection =
  soapConnectionFactory.createConnection();

MessageFactory messageFactory =
  MessageFactory.newInstance();
SOAPMessage message = messageFactory.createMessage();
```

The next lines of code retrieve the `SOAPHeader` and `SOAPBody` objects from the message and remove the header.

```
SOAPHeader header = message.getSOAPHeader();
header.detachNode();
SOAPBody body = message.getSOAPBody();
```

The following lines of code create the UDDI find_business message. The first line creates a SOAPBodyElement with a fully qualified name, including the required namespace for a UDDI version 2 message. The next lines add two attributes to the new element: the required attribute generic, with the UDDI version number 2.0, and the optional attribute maxRows, with the value 100. Then the code adds a child element that has the QName object name and adds the xml:lang attribute set to the default locale. The code then adds text to the element by using the method addTextNode. The added text is the business name you will supply at the command line when you run the application.

```
SOAPBodyElement findBusiness =
  body.addBodyElement(new QName(
    "urn:uddi-org:api_v2", "find_business"));
findBusiness.addAttribute(new QName("generic"), "2.0");
findBusiness.addAttribute(new QName("maxRows"), "100");

SOAPElement businessName =
  findBusiness.addChildElement(new QName("name"));
Locale loc = Locale.getDefault();
businessName.addAttribute(new QName("xml:lang"),
  loc.toString());
  //"en-US");
businessName.addTextNode(args[1]);
```

The next line of code saves the changes that have been made to the message. This method will be called automatically when the message is sent, but it does not hurt to call it explicitly.

```
message.saveChanges();
```

The following lines display the message that will be sent:

```
System.out.println("\n---- Request Message ----\n");
message.writeTo(System.out);
```

The next line of code creates the java.net.URL object that represents the destination for this message. It gets the value of the property named URL from the system properties.

```
URL endpoint = new URL(
  System.getProperties().getProperty("URL"));
```

Next, the message message is sent to the destination that endpoint represents, which is the UDDI test registry. The call method will block until it gets a SOAPMessage object back, at which point it returns the reply.

```
SOAPMessage reply = connection.call(message, endpoint);
```

In the next lines of code, the first line prints a line giving the URL of the sender (the test registry), and the others display the returned message.

```
System.out.println("\n\nReceived reply from: " +
   endpoint);
System.out.println("\n---- Reply Message ----\n");
reply.writeTo(System.out);
```

The returned message is the complete SOAP message, an XML document, as it looks when it comes over the wire. It is a businessList that follows the format specified in http://uddi.org/pubs/DataStructure-V2.03-Published-20020719.htm#_Toc25130802.

As interesting as it is to see the XML that is actually transmitted, the XML document format does not make it easy to see the text that is the message's content. To remedy this, the last part of MyUddiPing.java contains code that prints only the text content of the response, making it much easier to see the information you want.

Because the content is in the SOAPBody object, the first step is to access it, as shown in the following line of code.

```
SOAPBody replyBody = reply.getSOAPBody();
```

Next, the code displays a message describing the content:

```
System.out.println("\n\nContent extracted from " +
   "the reply message:\n");
```

To display the content of the message, the code uses the known format of the reply message. First, it gets all the reply body's child elements named businessList:

```
Iterator businessListIterator =
   replyBody.getChildElements(new QName(
      "urn:uddi-org:api_v2",
      "businessList"));
```

The method `getChildElements` returns the elements in the form of a `java.util.Iterator` object. You access the child elements by calling the method `next` on the `Iterator` object. An immediate child of a `SOAPBody` object is a `SOAPBodyElement` object.

We know that the reply can contain only one `businessList` element, so the code then retrieves this one element by calling the iterator's `next` method. Note that the method `Iterator.next` returns an `Object`, which must be cast to the specific kind of object you are retrieving. Thus, the result of calling `businessListIterator.next` is cast to a `SOAPBodyElement` object:

```
SOAPBodyElement businessList =
   (SOAPBodyElement) businessListIterator.next();
```

The next element in the hierarchy is a single `businessInfos` element, so the code retrieves this element in the same way it retrieved the `businessList`. Children of `SOAPBodyElement` objects and all child elements from this point forward are `SOAPElement` objects.

```
Iterator businessInfosIterator =
   businessList.getChildElements(new QName(
      "urn:uddi-org:api_v2", "businessInfos"));

SOAPElement businessInfos =
   (SOAPElement) businessInfosIterator.next();
```

The `businessInfos` element contains zero or more `businessInfo` elements. If the query returned no businesses, the code prints a message saying that none were found. If the query returned businesses, however, the code extracts the name and optional description by retrieving the child elements that have those names. The method `Iterator.hasNext` can be used in a `while` loop because it returns `true` as long as the next call to the method `next` will return a child element. Accordingly, the loop ends when there are no more child elements to retrieve.

```
Iterator businessInfoIterator =
   businessInfos.getChildElements(
      soapFactory.createName("businessInfo",
         "", "urn:uddi-org:api_v2"));

if (! businessInfoIterator.hasNext()) {
   System.out.println("No businesses found " +
      "matching the name \"" + args[1] + "\".");
} else {
```

```
            while (businessInfoIterator.hasNext()) {
                SOAPElement businessInfo =
                    (SOAPElement) businessInfoIterator.next();

                Iterator nameIterator =
                    businessInfo.getChildElements(new QName(
                        "urn:uddi-org:api_v2", "name"));

                while (nameIterator.hasNext()) {
                    businessName =
                        (SOAPElement)nameIterator.next();
                    System.out.println("Company name: " +
                        businessName.getValue());
                }
                Iterator descriptionIterator =
                    businessInfo.getChildElements(new QName(
                        "urn:uddi-org:api_v2", "description"));

                while (descriptionIterator.hasNext()) {
                    SOAPElement businessDescription =
                        (SOAPElement) descriptionIterator.next();
                    System.out.println("Description: " +
                        businessDescription.getValue());
                }
                System.out.println("");
            }
        }
    }
```

Finally, the program closes the connection:

```
connection.close();
```

Accessing a Registry

Before you can run MyUddiPing, you must install the Java WSDP Registry Server, a private UDDI registry. To install this registry, follow the instructions in Preliminaries: Getting Access to a Registry (page 697).

MyUddiPing will not return any results until you have run some of the examples in Chapter 19.

The file `uddi.properties` contains the URL of the destination. If the Application Server where you install the registry is running on a remote system, open `uddi.properties` in a text editor and replace `localhost` with the name of the remote system.

Building and Running MyUddiPing Using NetBeans 5.5

To build the program using NetBeans 5.5, follow these steps:

1. In NetBeans 5.5, choose Open Project from the File menu.
2. In the Open Project dialog, navigate to `<INSTALL>/javaeetutorial5/examples/saaj/`.
3. Select the `myuddiping` folder.
4. Select the Open as Main Project checkbox.
5. Click Open Project Folder.

   A Reference Problems dialog appears. Click Close.
6. Right-click the `myuddiping` project and choose Resolve Reference Problems.
7. In the Resolve Reference Problems dialog, select the first of the missing JAR files and click Resolve.

   The missing files are `activation.jar`, `javaee.jar`, and `appserv-ws.jar`.
8. Navigate to the `<JAVAEE_HOME>/lib/` directory.
9. Select the missing JAR file (`activation.jar`, for example) and click Open.

   In the Resolve Reference Problems dialog, all the files have green check marks to the left of their names.
10. Click Close.
11. Right-click the project and choose Build Project.

To run the program using NetBeans 5.5, follow these steps:

1. Right-click the `myuddiping` project and choose Properties.
2. Select Run from the Categories tree.
3. In the Arguments field, type the following:

   ```
   uddi.properties the
   ```

   The first argument is the name of the file `uddi.properties`. The second argument represents the first few letters of the name of the business for which you want to get a description.

4. Click OK.
5. Right-click the project and choose Run Project.

The program output depends on the contents of the registry. For example:

```
Content extracted from the reply message:

Company name: The Coffee Break
Description: Purveyor of the finest coffees. Established 1950

Company name: The Coffee Enterprise Bean Break
Description: Purveyor of the finest coffees. Established 1950
```

If the program returns no results, see Troubleshooting MyUddiPing (page 677) for a possible solution.

To remove the generated files, right-click the project and choose Clean Project.

Building and Running MyUddiPing Using Ant

To build and run MyUddiPing using Ant, go to the directory `<INSTALL>/javaeetutorial5/examples/saaj/myuddiping/` and use the `run-ping` target.

The `run-ping` target takes two arguments, but you need to supply only one of them. The first argument is the file `uddi.properties`, which is supplied by a property that is set in `build.xml`. The other argument is the first few letters of the name of the business for which you want to get a description, and you need to supply this argument on the command line. Note that any property set on the command line overrides any value set for that property in the `build.xml` file.

The `run-ping` target depends on the `compile` target, which compiles the source file and places the resulting `.class` file in the directory `build/classes`.

Use a command like the following to run the example:

```
ant run-ping -Dbusiness-name=the
```

The program output depends on the contents of the registry. For example:

```
Content extracted from the reply message:

Company name: The Coffee Break
Description: Purveyor of the finest coffees. Established 1950

Company name: The Coffee Enterprise Bean Break
Description: Purveyor of the finest coffees. Established 1950
```

To remove the generated files, use the following command:

```
ant clean
```

Troubleshooting MyUddiPing

If MyUddiPing returns no matching businesses, even if you know that the registry contains at least one, there may be a mismatch between the default locale setting on your system and the way JAXR stores names and descriptions of objects. This problem is most likely to occur on Windows systems. Look for the part of the output Request Message that contains the `xml:lang` attribute. It may look like this:

```
<name xml:lang="en_US">
```

The default locale setting being used by the program is `en_US`, but JAXR may have stored the business in the registry using the locale setting `en-US`. If you have this problem with your locale, follow these steps:

1. Open the file `src/MyUddiPing.java` in a text editor.
2. Find the following lines:
   ```
   businessName.addAttribute(new QName("xml:lang"),
      loc.toString());
      //"en-US");
   ```
3. Remove the comment characters from the last line and, if necessary, edit the string to specify your own locale.
4. Put comment characters at the beginning of the second line. The result should look something like this:
   ```
   //loc.toString());
   "en-US");
   ```
5. Rebuild and rerun MyUddiPing.

HeaderExample.java

The example `HeaderExample.java`, based on the code fragments in the section Adding Attributes (page 655), creates a message that has several headers. It then retrieves the contents of the headers and prints them. The example generates either a SOAP 1.1 message or a SOAP 1.2 message, depending on arguments you specify. You will find the code for `HeaderExample` in the following directory:

```
<INSTALL>/javaeetutorial5/examples/saaj/headers/src/
```

Building and Running HeaderExample

To build the program using NetBeans 5.5, follow these steps:

1. In NetBeans 5.5, choose Open Project from the File menu.
2. In the Open Project dialog, navigate to `<INSTALL>/javaeetutorial5/examples/saaj/`.
3. Select the `headers` folder.
4. Select the Open as Main Project checkbox.
5. Click Open Project Folder.

   A Reference Problems dialog appears. Click Close.
6. Right-click the `headers` project and choose Resolve Reference Problems.
7. In the Resolve Reference Problems dialog, select the first of the missing JAR files and click Resolve.

   The missing files are `activation.jar`, `javaee.jar`, and `appserv-ws.jar`.
8. Navigate to the `<JAVAEE_HOME>/lib/` directory.
9. Select the missing JAR file (`activation.jar`, for example) and click Open.

   In the Resolve Reference Problems dialog, all the files have green check marks to the left of their names.
10. Click Close.
11. Right-click the project and choose Build Project.

To run the program using NetBeans 5.5, follow these steps:

1. Right-click the `headers` project and choose Properties.
2. Select Run from the Categories tree.
3. In the Arguments field, type the following:

   ```
   1.1
   ```

   This argument specifies the version of SOAP to be used in generating the message.
4. Click OK.
5. Right-click the project and choose Run Project.
6. Right-click the project and choose Properties.
7. Select Run from the Categories tree.
8. In the Arguments field, type the following:

   ```
   1.2
   ```
9. Click OK.
10. Right-click the project and choose Run Project.

To build and run HeaderExample using Ant, go to the directory `<INSTALL>/javaeetutorial5/examples/saaj/headers/`. Use one of the following commands:

```
ant run-headers -Dsoap=1.1
ant run-headers -Dsoap=1.2
```

When you run HeaderExample to generate a SOAP 1.1 message, you will see output similar to the following:

```
----- Request Message ----

<SOAP-ENV:Envelope
xmlns:SOAP-ENV="http://schemas.xmlsoap.org/soap/envelope/">
<SOAP-ENV:Header>
<ns:orderDesk xmlns:ns="http://gizmos.com/NSURI"
SOAP-ENV:actor="http://gizmos.com/orders"/>
<ns:shippingDesk xmlns:ns="http://gizmos.com/NSURI"
SOAP-ENV:actor="http://gizmos.com/shipping"/>
<ns:confirmationDesk xmlns:ns="http://gizmos.com/NSURI"
SOAP-ENV:actor="http://gizmos.com/confirmations"
SOAP-ENV:mustUnderstand="1"/>
<ns:billingDesk xmlns:ns="http://gizmos.com/NSURI"
SOAP-ENV:actor="http://gizmos.com/billing"/>
```

```
</SOAP-ENV:Header><SOAP-ENV:Body/></SOAP-ENV:Envelope>

Header name is {http://gizmos.com/NSURI}orderDesk
Actor is http://gizmos.com/orders
mustUnderstand is false

Header name is {http://gizmos.com/NSURI}shippingDesk
Actor is http://gizmos.com/shipping
mustUnderstand is false

Header name is {http://gizmos.com/NSURI}confirmationDesk
Actor is http://gizmos.com/confirmations
mustUnderstand is true

Header name is {http://gizmos.com/NSURI}billingDesk
Actor is http://gizmos.com/billing
mustUnderstand is false
```

When you run HeaderExample to generate a SOAP 1.2 message, you will see output similar to the following:

```
----- Request Message ----

<env:Envelope
xmlns:env="http://www.w3.org/2003/05/soap-envelope">
<env:Header>
<ns:orderDesk xmlns:ns="http://gizmos.com/NSURI"
env:role="http://gizmos.com/orders"/>
<ns:shippingDesk xmlns:ns="http://gizmos.com/NSURI"
env:role="http://gizmos.com/shipping"/>
<ns:confirmationDesk xmlns:ns="http://gizmos.com/NSURI"
env:mustUnderstand="true"
env:role="http://gizmos.com/confirmations"/>
<ns:billingDesk xmlns:ns="http://gizmos.com/NSURI"
env:relay="true" env:role="http://gizmos.com/billing"/>
</env:Header><env:Body/></env:Envelope>

Header name is {http://gizmos.com/NSURI}orderDesk
Role is http://gizmos.com/orders
mustUnderstand is false
relay is false

Header name is {http://gizmos.com/NSURI}shippingDesk
Role is http://gizmos.com/shipping
mustUnderstand is false
relay is false

Header name is {http://gizmos.com/NSURI}confirmationDesk
```

```
Role is http://gizmos.com/confirmations
mustUnderstand is true
relay is false

Header name is {http://gizmos.com/NSURI}billingDesk
Role is http://gizmos.com/billing
mustUnderstand is false
relay is true
```

DOMExample.java and DOMSrcExample.java

The examples `DOMExample.java` and `DOMSrcExample.java` show how to add a DOM document to a message and then traverse its contents. They show two ways to do this:

- `DOMExample.java` creates a DOM document and adds it to the body of a message.
- `DOMSrcExample.java` creates the document, uses it to create a `DOMSource` object, and then sets the `DOMSource` object as the content of the message's SOAP part.

You will find the code for DOMExample and DOMSrcExample in the following directory:

```
<INSTALL>/javaeetutorial5/examples/saaj/dom/src/
```

Examining DOMExample

DOMExample first creates a DOM document by parsing an XML document. The file it parses is one that you specify on the command line.

```
static Document document;
...
  DocumentBuilderFactory factory =
     DocumentBuilderFactory.newInstance();
  factory.setNamespaceAware(true);
  try {
     DocumentBuilder builder = factory.newDocumentBuilder();
     document = builder.parse( new File(args[0]) );
     ...
```

Next, the example creates a SOAP message in the usual way. Then it adds the document to the message body:

```
SOAPBodyElement docElement = body.addDocument(document);
```

This example does not change the content of the message. Instead, it displays the message content and then uses a recursive method, `getContents`, to traverse the element tree using SAAJ APIs and display the message contents in a readable form.

```
public void getContents(Iterator iterator, String indent) {

  while (iterator.hasNext()) {
    Node node = (Node) iterator.next();
    SOAPElement element = null;
    Text text = null;
    if (node instanceof SOAPElement) {
      element = (SOAPElement)node;
      QName name = element.getElementQName();
      System.out.println(indent + "Name is " +
        name.toString());
      Iterator attrs = element.getAllAttributesAsQNames();
      while (attrs.hasNext()){
        QName attrName = (QName)attrs.next();
        System.out.println(indent + " Attribute name is " +
          attrName.toString());
        System.out.println(indent + " Attribute value is " +
          element.getAttributeValue(attrName));
      }
      Iterator iter2 = element.getChildElements();
      getContents(iter2, indent + " ");
    } else {
      text = (Text) node;
      String content = text.getValue();
      System.out.println(indent +
        "Content is: " + content);
      }
    }
  }
```

Examining DOMSrcExample

DOMSrcExample differs from DOMExample in only a few ways. First, after it parses the document, DOMSrcExample uses the document to create a DOM-

Source object. This code is the same as that of DOMExample except for the last line:

```
static DOMSource domSource;
...
try {
  DocumentBuilder builder = factory.newDocumentBuilder();
  Document document = builder.parse(new File(args[0]));
  domSource = new DOMSource(document);
  ...
```

Then, after DOMSrcExample creates the message, it does not get the header and body and add the document to the body, as DOMExample does. Instead, DOMSrcExample gets the SOAP part and sets the DOMSource object as its content:

```
// Create a message
SOAPMessage message = messageFactory.createMessage();

// Get the SOAP part and set its content to domSource
SOAPPart soapPart = message.getSOAPPart();
soapPart.setContent(domSource);
```

The example then uses the getContents method to obtain the contents of both the header (if it exists) and the body of the message.

The most important difference between these two examples is the kind of document you can use to create the message. Because DOMExample adds the document to the body of the SOAP message, you can use any valid XML file to create the document. But because DOMSrcExample makes the document the entire content of the message, the document must already be in the form of a valid SOAP message, and not just any XML document.

Building and Running DOMExample and DOMSrcExample

When you run DOMExample and DOMSrcExample, you can specify one of several sample XML files in the directory <*INSTALL*>/javaeetutorial5/examples/saaj/dom/:

- domsrc1.xml, an example that has a SOAP header (the contents of the HeaderExample SOAP 1.1 output) and the body of a UDDI query
- domsrc2.xml, an example of a reply to a UDDI query (sample output from the MyUddiPing example), but with spaces added for readability

- `uddimsg.xml`, similar to `domsrc2.xml` except that it is only the body of the message and contains no spaces
- `slide.xml`, another file that consists only of a body but that contains spaces

You can use any of these four files when you run DOMExample. You can use either `domsrc1.xml` or `domsrc2.xml` to run DOMSrcExample.

To build the programs using NetBeans 5.5, follow these steps:

1. In NetBeans 5.5, choose Open Project from the File menu.
2. In the Open Project dialog, navigate to `<INSTALL>/javaeetutorial5/examples/saaj/`.
3. Select the `dom` folder.
4. Select the Open as Main Project checkbox.
5. Click Open Project Folder.

   A Reference Problems dialog appears. Click Close.
6. Right-click the `dom` project and choose Resolve Reference Problems.
7. In the Resolve Reference Problems dialog, select the first of the missing JAR files and click Resolve.

   The missing files are `activation.jar`, `javaee.jar`, and `appserv-ws.jar`.
8. Navigate to the `<JAVAEE_HOME>/lib/` directory.
9. Select the missing JAR file (`activation.jar`, for example) and click Open.

   In the Resolve Reference Problems dialog, all the files have green check marks to the left of their names.
10. Click Close.
11. Right-click the project and choose Build Project.

To run DOMExample using NetBeans 5.5, follow these steps:

1. Right-click the `dom` project and choose Properties.
2. Select Run from the Categories tree.
3. Click Browse next to the Main Class field.
4. In the Browse Main Classes dialog, select `DomExample`.
5. Click Select Main Class.

6. In the Arguments field, type the name of one of the four files:

   `slide.xml`

7. Click OK.
8. Right-click the project and choose Run Project.

To run DOMSrcExample using NetBeans 5.5, follow these steps:

1. Right-click the `dom` project and choose Properties.
2. Select Run from the Categories tree.
3. Click Browse next to the Main Class field.
4. In the Browse Main Classes dialog, select `DomSrcExample`.
5. Click Select Main Class.
6. In the Arguments field, type either `domsrc1.xml` or `domsrc2.xml`:

   `domsrc1.xml`

7. Click OK.
8. Right-click the project and choose Run Project.

To run the examples using Ant, go to the directory `<INSTALL>/javaeetutorial5/examples/saaj/dom/`.

To run DOMExample using Ant, use a command like the following:

```
ant run-dom -Dxml-file=uddimsg.xml
```

To run DOMSrcExample using Ant, use a command like the following:

```
ant run-domsrc -Dxml-file=domsrc2.xml
```

When you run DOMExample using the file `uddimsg.xml`, you will see output that begins like the following:

```
Name is {urn:uddi-org:api_v2}businessList
Attribute name is generic
Attribute value is 2.0
Attribute name is operator
Attribute value is Sun Microsystems Inc.
Attribute name is truncated
Attribute value is false
Attribute name is xmlns
Attribute value is urn:uddi-org:api_v2
...
```

When you run DOMSrcExample using the file `domsrc2.xml`, you will see output that begins like the following:

```
Body contents:
Content is:

Name is {urn:uddi-org:api_v2}businessList
 Attribute name is generic
 Attribute value is 2.0
 Attribute name is operator
 Attribute value is Sun Microsystems Inc.
 Attribute name is truncated
 Attribute value is false
 Attribute name is xmlns
 Attribute value is urn:uddi-org:api_v2
 ...
```

If you run DOMSrcExample with the file `uddimsg.xml` or `slide.xml`, you will see runtime errors.

Attachments.java

The example `Attachments.java`, based on the code fragments in the sections Creating an AttachmentPart Object and Adding Content (page 653) and Accessing an AttachmentPart Object (page 655), creates a message that has a text attachment and an image attachment. It then retrieves the contents of the attachments and prints the contents of the text attachment. You will find the code for Attachments in the following directory:

```
<INSTALL>/javaeetutorial5/examples/saaj/attachments/src/
```

Attachments first creates a message in the usual way. It then creates an `AttachmentPart` for the text attachment:

```
AttachmentPart attachment1 = message.createAttachmentPart();
```

After it reads input from a file into a string named `stringContent`, it sets the content of the attachment to the value of the string and the type to `text/plain` and also sets a content ID.

```
attachment1.setContent(stringContent, "text/plain");
attachment1.setContentId("attached_text");
```

It then adds the attachment to the message:

```
message.addAttachmentPart(attachment1);
```

The example uses a `javax.activation.DataHandler` object to hold a reference to the graphic that constitutes the second attachment. It creates this attachment using the form of the `createAttachmentPart` method that takes a `DataHandler` argument.

```
// Create attachment part for image
URL url = new URL("file:///../xml-pic.jpg");
DataHandler dataHandler = new DataHandler(url);
AttachmentPart attachment2 =
  message.createAttachmentPart(dataHandler);
attachment2.setContentId("attached_image");

message.addAttachmentPart(attachment2);
```

The example then retrieves the attachments from the message. It displays the `contentId` and `contentType` attributes of each attachment and the contents of the text attachment.

Building and Running Attachments

The Attachments example takes a text file as an argument. You can specify any text file. The `attachments` directory contains a file named `addr.txt` that you can use.

To build the program using NetBeans 5.5, follow these steps:

1. In NetBeans 5.5, choose Open Project from the File menu.
2. In the Open Project dialog, navigate to `<INSTALL>/javaeetutorial5/examples/saaj/`.
3. Select the `attachments` folder.
4. Select the Open as Main Project checkbox.
5. Click Open Project Folder.

   A Reference Problems dialog appears. Click Close.

6. Right-click the `attachments` project and choose Resolve Reference Problems.
7. In the Resolve Reference Problems dialog, select the first of the missing JAR files and click Resolve.

The missing files are `activation.jar`, `javaee.jar`, and `appserv-ws.jar`.

8. Navigate to the *<JAVAEE_HOME>*`/lib/` directory.
9. Select the missing JAR file (`activation.jar`, for example) and click Open.

   In the Resolve Reference Problems dialog, all the files have green check marks to the left of their names.
10. Click Close.
11. Right-click the project and choose Build Project.

To run the program using NetBeans 5.5, follow these steps:

1. Right-click the `attachments` project and choose Properties.
2. Select Run from the Categories tree.
3. In the Arguments field, type the name of a text file:

   `addr.txt`
4. Click OK.
5. Right-click the project and choose Run Project.

To run Attachments using Ant, go to the directory *<INSTALL>*`/javaeetutorial5/examples/saaj/attachments/`. Use the following command:

```
ant run-att -Dfile=path_name
```

Specify a text file as the *path_name* argument:

```
ant run-att -Dfile=addr.txt
```

When you run Attachments using this file, you will see output like the following:

```
Running Attachments.
Attachment attached_text has content type text/plain
Attachment contains:
Update address for Sunny Skies, Inc., to
10 Upbeat Street
Pleasant Grove, CA 95439
USA

Attachment attached_image has content type image/jpeg
```

SOAPFaultTest.java

The example `SOAPFaultTest.java`, based on the code fragments in the sections Creating and Populating a SOAPFault Object (page 663) and Retrieving Fault Information (page 665), creates a message that has a `SOAPFault` object. It then retrieves the contents of the `SOAPFault` object and prints them. You will find the code for SOAPFaultTest in the following directory:

```
<INSTALL>/javaeetutorial5/examples/saaj/fault/src/
```

Like HeaderExample, the SOAPFaultTest example contains code that allows you to generate either a SOAP 1.1 or a SOAP 1.2 message.

Running SOAPFaultTest

To build the program using NetBeans 5.5, follow these steps:

1. In NetBeans 5.5, choose Open Project from the File menu.
2. In the Open Project dialog, navigate to `<INSTALL>/javaeetutorial5/examples/saaj/`.
3. Select the `fault` folder.
4. Select the Open as Main Project checkbox.
5. Click Open Project Folder.

   A Reference Problems dialog appears. Click Close.
6. Right-click the `fault` project and choose Resolve Reference Problems.
7. In the Resolve Reference Problems dialog, select the first of the missing JAR files and click Resolve.

   The missing files are `activation.jar`, `javaee.jar`, and `appserv-ws.jar`.
8. Navigate to the `<JAVAEE_HOME>/lib/` directory.
9. Select the missing JAR file (`activation.jar`, for example) and click Open.

   In the Resolve Reference Problems dialog, all the files have green check marks to the left of their names.
10. Click Close.
11. Right-click the project and choose Build Project.

To run the program using NetBeans 5.5, follow these steps:

1. Right-click the `fault` project and choose Properties.
2. Select Run from the Categories tree.
3. In the Arguments field, type the following:

   `1.1`

   This argument specifies the version of SOAP to be used in generating the message.
4. Click OK.
5. Right-click the project and choose Run Project.
6. Right-click the project and choose Properties.
7. Select Run from the Categories tree.
8. In the Arguments field, type the following:

   `1.2`
9. Click OK.
10. Right-click the project and choose Run Project.

To build and run SOAPFaultTest using Ant, go to the directory *<INSTALL>*`/javaeetutorial5/examples/saaj/fault/`. Use one of the following commands:

```
ant run -Dsoap=1.1
ant run -Dsoap=1.2
```

When you run SOAPFaultTest to generate a SOAP 1.1 message, you will see output like the following (line breaks have been inserted in the message for readability):

```
Here is what the XML message looks like:

<SOAP-ENV:Envelope
xmlns:SOAP-ENV="http://schemas.xmlsoap.org/soap/envelope/">
<SOAP-ENV:Header/><SOAP-ENV:Body>
<SOAP-ENV:Fault><faultcode>SOAP-ENV:Client</faultcode>
<faultstring>Message does not have necessary info</faultstring>
<faultactor>http://gizmos.com/order</faultactor>
<detail>
<PO:order xmlns:PO="http://gizmos.com/orders/">
Quantity element does not have a value</PO:order>
<PO:confirmation xmlns:PO="http://gizmos.com/confirm">
Incomplete address: no zip code</PO:confirmation>
```

```
</detail></SOAP-ENV:Fault>
</SOAP-ENV:Body></SOAP-ENV:Envelope>

SOAP fault contains:
 Fault code = {http://schemas.xmlsoap.org/soap/envelope/}Client
 Local name = Client
 Namespace prefix = SOAP-ENV, bound to
http://schemas.xmlsoap.org/soap/envelope/
 Fault string = Message does not have necessary info
 Fault actor = http://gizmos.com/order
 Detail entry = Quantity element does not have a value
 Detail entry = Incomplete address: no zip code
```

When you run SOAPFaultTest to generate a SOAP 1.2 message, the output looks like this:

```
Here is what the XML message looks like:

<env:Envelope
xmlns:env="http://www.w3.org/2003/05/soap-envelope">
<env:Header/><env:Body>
<env:Fault>
<env:Code><env:Value>env:Sender</env:Value></env:Code>
<env:Reason><env:Text xml:lang="en-US">
Message does not have necessary info
</env:Text></env:Reason>
<env:Role>http://gizmos.com/order</env:Role>
<env:Detail>
<PO:order xmlns:PO="http://gizmos.com/orders/">
Quantity element does not have a value</PO:order>
<PO:confirmation xmlns:PO="http://gizmos.com/confirm">
Incomplete address: no zip code</PO:confirmation>
</env:Detail></env:Fault>
</env:Body></env:Envelope>

SOAP fault contains:
 Fault code = {http://www.w3.org/2003/05/soap-envelope}Sender
 Local name = Sender
 Namespace prefix = env, bound to
http://www.w3.org/2003/05/soap-envelope
 Fault reason text = Message does not have necessary info
 Fault role = http://gizmos.com/order
 Detail entry = Quantity element does not have a value
 Detail entry = Incomplete address: no zip code
```

Further Information

For more information about SAAJ, SOAP, and WS-I, see the following:

- SAAJ 1.3 specification, available from
  `http://java.sun.com/xml/downloads/saaj.html`
- SAAJ web site:
  `http://java.sun.com/webservices/saaj/`
- Simple Object Access Protocol (SOAP) 1.1:
  `http://www.w3.org/TR/2000/NOTE-SOAP-20000508/`
- SOAP Version 1.2 Part 0: Primer:
  `http://www.w3.org/TR/soap12-part0/`
- SOAP Version 1.2 Part 1: Messaging Framework:
  `http://www.w3.org/TR/soap12-part1/`
- SOAP Version 1.2 Part 2: Adjuncts:
  `http://www.w3.org/TR/soap12-part2/`
- WS-I Basic Profile:
  `http://www.ws-i.org/Profiles/BasicProfile-1.1.html`
- WS-I Attachments Profile:
  `http://www.ws-i.org/Profiles/AttachmentsProfile-1.0.html`
- SOAP Message Transmission Optimization Mechanism (MTOM):
  `http://www.w3.org/TR/soap12-mtom/`
- XML-binary Optimized Packaging (XOP):
  `http://www.w3.org/TR/xop10/`
- JAXM web site:
  `http://java.sun.com/webservices/jaxm/`

19

Java API for XML Registries

THE Java API for XML Registries (JAXR) provides a uniform and standard Java API for accessing various kinds of XML registries.

After providing a brief overview of JAXR, this chapter describes how to implement a JAXR client to publish an organization and its web services to a registry and to query a registry to find organizations and services. Finally, it explains how to run the examples provided with this tutorial and offers links to more information on JAXR.

Overview of JAXR

This section provides a brief overview of JAXR. It covers the following topics:

- What is a registry?
- What is JAXR?
- JAXR architecture

What Is a Registry?

An XML *registry* is an infrastructure that enables the building, deployment, and discovery of web services. It is a neutral third party that facilitates dynamic and loosely coupled business-to-business (B2B) interactions. A registry is available to organizations as a shared resource, often in the form of a web-based service.

Currently there are a variety of specifications for XML registries. These include

- The ebXML Registry and Repository standard, which is sponsored by the Organization for the Advancement of Structured Information Standards (OASIS) and the United Nations Centre for the Facilitation of Procedures and Practices in Administration, Commerce and Transport (U.N./CEFACT)
- The Universal Description, Discovery, and Integration (UDDI) project, which is being developed by a vendor consortium

A *registry provider* is an implementation of a business registry that conforms to a specification for XML registries.

What Is JAXR?

JAXR enables Java software programmers to use a single, easy-to-use abstraction API to access a variety of XML registries. A unified JAXR information model describes content and metadata within XML registries.

JAXR gives developers the ability to write registry client programs that are portable across various target registries. JAXR also enables value-added capabilities beyond those of the underlying registries.

The current version of the JAXR specification includes detailed bindings between the JAXR information model and both the ebXML Registry and the UDDI version 2 specifications. You can find the latest version of the specification at

```
http://java.sun.com/xml/downloads/jaxr.html
```

At this release of the Application Server, the JAXR provider implements the level 0 capability profile defined by the JAXR specification. This level allows access to both UDDI and ebXML registries at a basic level. At this release, the JAXR provider supports access only to UDDI version 2 registries.

Currently no public UDDI registries exist. However, you can use the Java WSDP Registry Server, a private UDDI version 2 registry that came with release 1.5 of the Java Web Services Developer Pack (Java WSDP).

Service Registry, an ebXML registry and repositry with a JAXR provider, is available as part of the Sun Java Enterprise System.

JAXR Architecture

The high-level architecture of JAXR consists of the following parts:

- **JAXR client**: This is a client program that uses the JAXR API to access a business registry via a JAXR provider.
- **JAXR provider**: This is an implementation of the JAXR API that provides access to a specific registry provider or to a class of registry providers that are based on a common specification.

A JAXR provider implements two main packages:

- `javax.xml.registry`: This package consists of the API interfaces and classes that define the registry access interface.
- `javax.xml.registry.infomodel`: This package consists of interfaces that define the information model for JAXR. These interfaces define the types of objects that reside in a registry and how they relate to each other. The basic interface in this package is the `RegistryObject` interface. Its subinterfaces include `Organization`, `Service`, and `ServiceBinding`.

The most basic interfaces in the `javax.xml.registry` package are

- `Connection`: This interface represents a client session with a registry provider. The client must create a connection with the JAXR provider in order to use a registry.
- `RegistryService`: The client obtains a `RegistryService` object from its connection. The `RegistryService` object in turn enables the client to obtain the interfaces it uses to access the registry.

The primary interfaces, also part of the `javax.xml.registry` package, are

- `BusinessQueryManager`: This interface allows the client to search a registry for information in accordance with the `javax.xml.registry.infomodel` interfaces. An optional interface, `DeclarativeQueryManager`, allows the client to use SQL syntax for queries. (The implementation of JAXR in the Application Server does not implement `DeclarativeQueryManager`.)
- `BusinessLifeCycleManager`: This interface allows the client to modify the information in a registry by either saving it (updating it) or deleting it.

When an error occurs, JAXR API methods throw a `JAXRException` or one of its subclasses.

Many methods in the JAXR API use a `Collection` object as an argument or a returned value. Using a `Collection` object allows operations on several registry objects at a time.

Figure 19–1 illustrates the architecture of JAXR. In the Application Server, a JAXR client uses the capability level 0 interfaces of the JAXR API to access the JAXR provider. The JAXR provider in turn accesses a registry. The Application Server supplies a JAXR provider for UDDI registries.

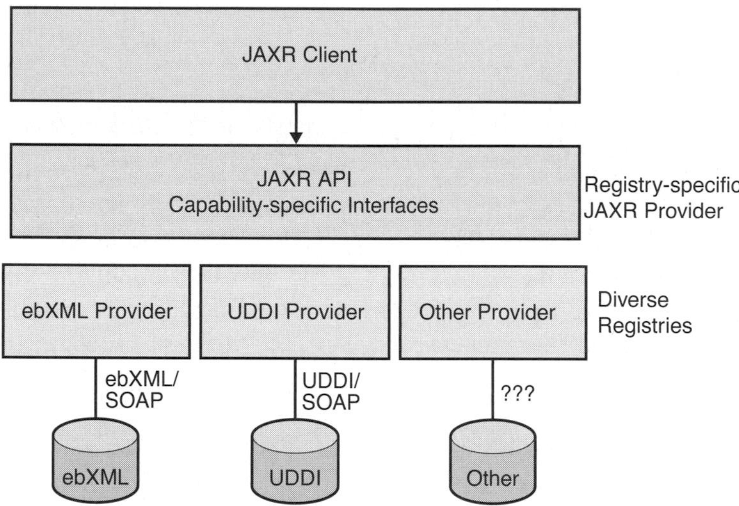

Figure 19–1 JAXR Architecture

Implementing a JAXR Client

This section describes the basic steps to follow in order to implement a JAXR client that can perform queries and updates to a UDDI registry. A JAXR client is a client program that can access registries using the JAXR API. This section covers the following topics:

- Establishing a connection
- Querying a registry
- Managing registry data
- Using taxonomies in JAXR clients

This tutorial does not describe how to implement a JAXR provider. A JAXR provider provides an implementation of the JAXR specification that allows access to an existing registry provider, such as a UDDI or ebXML registry. The implementation of JAXR in the Application Server is an example of a JAXR provider.

The Application Server provides JAXR in the form of a resource adapter using the Java EE Connector architecture. The resource adapter is in the directory `<JAVAEE_HOME>/lib/install/applications/jaxr-ra/`. (`<JAVAEE_HOME>` is the directory where the Application Server is installed.)

This tutorial includes several client examples, which are described in Running the Client Examples (page 720), and a Java EE application example, described in Using JAXR Clients in Java EE Applications (page 733). The examples are in the directory `<INSTALL>/javaeetutorial5/examples/jaxr/`. (`<INSTALL>` is the directory where you installed the tutorial bundle.) Each example directory has a `build.xml` file that refers to targets in the directory `<INSTALL>/javaeetutorial5/examples/bp-project/`.

Establishing a Connection

The first task a JAXR client must complete is to establish a connection to a registry. Establishing a connection involves the following tasks:

- Preliminaries: Getting access to a registry
- Creating or looking up a connection factory
- Creating a connection
- Setting connection properties
- Obtaining and using a `RegistryService` object

Preliminaries: Getting Access to a Registry

To use the Java WSDP Registry Server, a private UDDI version 2 registry, you need to copy some files from the tutorial to the Application Server, then restart the Application Server.

Follow these steps:

1. Stop the Application Server if it is running.
2. Navigate to the directory `<INSTALL>/javaeetutorial5/examples/jaxr/lib/`.

3. Copy the files `RegistryServer.war` and `Xindice.war` to the following directory:

   `<JAVAEE_HOME>/domains/domain1/autodeploy/`

4. Copy the file `commons-logging.jar` to the following directory:

   `<JAVAEE_HOME>/lib/`

5. Start the Application Server.

Any user of a JAXR client can perform queries on a registry. To add data to the registry or to update registry data, however, a user must obtain permission from the registry to access it.

To add or update data in the Java WSDP Registry Server, you can use the default user name and password, `testuser` and `testuser`.

Obtaining a Connection Factory

A client creates a connection from a connection factory. A JAXR provider can supply one or more preconfigured connection factories. Clients can obtain these factories by using resource injection.

At this release of the Application Server, JAXR supplies a connection factory through the JAXR RA, but you need to use a connector resource whose JNDI name is `eis/JAXR` to access this connection factory from a Java EE application. To inject this resource in a Java EE component, use code like the following:

```
import javax.annotation.Resource;.*;
import javax.xml.registry.ConnectionFactory;
...
  @Resource(mappedName="eis/JAXR")
  public ConnectionFactory factory;
```

Later in this chapter you will learn how to create this connector resource.

To use JAXR in a stand-alone client program, you must create an instance of the abstract class `ConnectionFactory`:

```
import javax.xml.registry.ConnectionFactory;
...
ConnectionFactory connFactory =
  ConnectionFactory.newInstance();
```

Creating a Connection

To create a connection, a client first creates a set of properties that specify the URL or URLs of the registry or registries being accessed. For example, the following code provides the URLs of the query service and publishing service for a hypothetical registry. (There should be no line break in the strings.)

```
Properties props = new Properties();
props.setProperty("javax.xml.registry.queryManagerURL",
  "http://localhost:8080/RegistryServer/");
props.setProperty("javax.xml.registry.lifeCycleManagerURL",
  "http://localhost:8080/RegistryServer/");
```

With the Application Server implementation of JAXR, if the client is accessing a registry that is outside a firewall, it must also specify proxy host and port information for the network on which it is running. For queries it may need to specify only the HTTP proxy host and port; for updates it must specify the HTTPS proxy host and port.

```
props.setProperty("com.sun.xml.registry.http.proxyHost",
  "myhost.mydomain");
props.setProperty("com.sun.xml.registry.http.proxyPort",
  "8080");
props.setProperty("com.sun.xml.registry.https.proxyHost",
  "myhost.mydomain");
props.setProperty("com.sun.xml.registry.https.proxyPort",
  "8080");
```

The client then sets the properties for the connection factory and creates the connection:

```
connFactory.setProperties(props);
Connection connection = connFactory.createConnection();
```

The `makeConnection` method in the sample programs shows the steps used to create a JAXR connection.

Setting Connection Properties

The implementation of JAXR in the Application Server allows you to set a number of properties on a JAXR connection. Some of these are standard properties defined in the JAXR specification. Other properties are specific to the implementation of JAXR in the Application Server. Table 19–1 and Table 19–2 list and describe these properties.

Table 19–1 Standard JAXR Connection Properties

Property Name and Description	Data Type	Default Value
`javax.xml.registry.queryManagerURL` Specifies the URL of the query manager service within the target registry provider.	String	None
`javax.xml.registry.lifeCycleManagerURL` Specifies the URL of the life-cycle manager service within the target registry provider (for registry updates).	String	Same as the specified `queryManagerURL` value

`javax.xml.registry.semanticEquivalences`
 	
Specifies semantic equivalences of concepts as one or more tuples of the ID values of two equivalent concepts separated by a comma. The tuples are separated by vertical bars:
`id1,id2|id3,id4`
	String	None

`javax.xml.registry.security.authentica-tionMethod` Provides a hint to the JAXR provider on the authentication method to be used for authenticating with the registry provider.	String	None; `UDDI_GET_AUTHTOKEN` is the only supported value
`javax.xml.registry.uddi.maxRows` The maximum number of rows to be returned by find operations. Specific to UDDI providers.	String	100
`javax.xml.registry.postalAddressScheme` The ID of a `ClassificationScheme` to be used as the default postal address scheme. See Specifying Postal Addresses (page 718) for an example.	String	None

Table 19–2 Implementation-Specific JAXR Connection Properties

Property Name and Description	Data Type	Default Value
`com.sun.xml.registry.http.proxyHost` Specifies the HTTP proxy host to be used for accessing external registries.	String	None
`com.sun.xml.registry.http.proxyPort` Specifies the HTTP proxy port to be used for accessing external registries; usually 8080.	String	None
`com.sun.xml.registry.https.proxyHost` Specifies the HTTPS proxy host to be used for accessing external registries.	String	Same as HTTP proxy host value
`com.sun.xml.registry.https.proxyPort` Specifies the HTTPS proxy port to be used for accessing external registries; usually 8080.	String	Same as HTTP proxy port value
`com.sun.xml.registry.http.proxyUserName` Specifies the user name for the proxy host for HTTP proxy authentication, if one is required.	String	None
`com.sun.xml.registry.http.proxyPassword` Specifies the password for the proxy host for HTTP proxy authentication, if one is required.	String	None
`com.sun.xml.registry.useCache` Tells the JAXR implementation to look for registry objects in the cache first and then to look in the registry if not found.	Boolean, passed in as String	True
`com.sun.xml.registry.userTaxonomyFilenames` For details on setting this property, see Defining a Taxonomy (page 715).	String	None

Obtaining and Using a RegistryService Object

After creating the connection, the client uses the connection to obtain a RegistryService object and then the interface or interfaces it will use:

```
RegistryService rs = connection.getRegistryService();
BusinessQueryManager bqm = rs.getBusinessQueryManager();
BusinessLifeCycleManager blcm =
  rs.getBusinessLifeCycleManager();
```

Typically, a client obtains both a BusinessQueryManager object and a BusinessLifeCycleManager object from the RegistryService object. If it is using the registry for simple queries only, it may need to obtain only a BusinessQueryManager object.

Querying a Registry

The simplest way for a client to use a registry is to query it for information about the organizations that have submitted data to it. The BusinessQueryManager interface supports a number of find methods that allow clients to search for data using the JAXR information model. Many of these methods return a BulkResponse (a collection of objects) that meets a set of criteria specified in the method arguments. The most useful of these methods are as follows:

- findOrganizations, which returns a list of organizations that meet the specified criteria—often a name pattern or a classification within a classification scheme
- findServices, which returns a set of services offered by a specified organization
- findServiceBindings, which returns the *service bindings* (information about how to access the service) that are supported by a specified service

The JAXRQuery program illustrates how to query a registry by organization name and display the data returned. The JAXRQueryByNAICSClassification and JAXRQueryByWSDLClassification programs illustrate how to query a registry using classifications. All JAXR providers support at least the following taxonomies for classifications:

- The North American Industry Classification System (NAICS). For details, see http://www.census.gov/epcd/www/naics.html.
- The Universal Standard Products and Services Classification (UNSPSC). For details, see http://www.eccma.org/unspsc/.

- The ISO 3166 country codes classification system maintained by the International Organization for Standardization (ISO). For details, see `http://www.iso.org/iso/en/prods-services/iso3166ma/index.html`.

The following sections describe how to perform some common queries:

- Finding organizations by name
- Finding organizations by classification
- Finding services and service bindings

Finding Organizations by Name

To search for organizations by name, you normally use a combination of find qualifiers (which affect sorting and pattern matching) and name patterns (which specify the strings to be searched). The `findOrganizations` method takes a collection of `findQualifier` objects as its first argument and takes a collection of `namePattern` objects as its second argument. The following fragment shows how to find all the organizations in the registry whose names begin with a specified string, `qString`, and sort them in alphabetical order.

```
// Define find qualifiers and name patterns
Collection<String> findQualifiers = new ArrayList<String>();
findQualifiers.add(FindQualifier.SORT_BY_NAME_DESC);
Collection<String> namePatterns = new ArrayList<String>();
namePatterns.add(qString);

// Find orgs whose names begin with qString
BulkResponse response =
  bqm.findOrganizations(findQualifiers, namePatterns, null,
     null, null, null);
Collection orgs = response.getCollection();
```

The last four arguments to `findOrganizations` allow you to search using other criteria than the name: classifications, specification concepts, external identifiers, or external links. Finding Organizations by Classification (page 704) describes searching by classification and by specification concept. The other searches are less common and are not described in this tutorial.

A client can use percent signs (%) to specify that the query string can occur anywhere within the organization name. For example, the following code fragment performs a case-sensitive search for organizations whose names contain qString:

```
Collection<String> findQualifiers = new ArrayList<String>();
findQualifiers.add(FindQualifier.CASE_SENSITIVE_MATCH);
Collection<String> namePatterns = new ArrayList<String>();
namePatterns.add("%" + qString + "%");

// Find orgs with names that contain qString
BulkResponse response =
  bqm.findOrganizations(findQualifiers, namePatterns, null,
    null, null, null);
Collection orgs = response.getCollection();
```

Finding Organizations by Classification

To find organizations by classification, you establish the classification within a particular classification scheme and then specify the classification as an argument to the findOrganizations method.

The following code fragment finds all organizations that correspond to a particular classification within the NAICS taxonomy. (You can find the NAICS codes at http://www.census.gov/epcd/naics/naicscod.txt.)The NAICS taxonomy has a well-known universally unique identifier (UUID) that is defined by the UDDI specification. The getRegistryObject method finds an object based upon its key. (See Creating an Organization, page 708 for more information about keys)

```
String uuid_naics =
  "uuid:C0B9FE13-179F-413D-8A5B-5004DB8E5BB2";
ClassificationScheme cScheme =
  (ClassificationScheme) bqm.getRegistryObject(uuid_naics,
    LifeCycleManager.CLASSIFICATION_SCHEME);
InternationalString sn = blcm.createInternationalString(
  "All Other Specialty Food Stores"));
String sv = "445299";
Classification classification =
  blcm.createClassification(cScheme, sn, sv);
Collection<Classification> classifications =
  new ArrayList<Classification>();
classifications.add(classification);
BulkResponse response = bqm.findOrganizations(null, null,
  classifications, null, null, null);
Collection orgs = response.getCollection();
```

You can also use classifications to find organizations that offer services based on technical specifications that take the form of WSDL (Web Services Description Language) documents. In JAXR, a *concept* is used as a proxy to hold the information about a specification. The steps are a little more complicated than in the preceding example, because the client must first find the specification concepts and then find the organizations that use those concepts.

The following code fragment finds all the WSDL specification instances used within a given registry. You can see that the code is similar to the NAICS query code except that it ends with a call to `findConcepts` instead of `findOrganizations`.

```
String schemeName = "uddi-org:types";
ClassificationScheme uddiOrgTypes =
  bqm.findClassificationSchemeByName(null, schemeName);

/*
 * Create a classification, specifying the scheme
 *  and the taxonomy name and value defined for WSDL
 *  documents by the UDDI specification.
 */
Classification wsdlSpecClassification =
  blcm.createClassification(uddiOrgTypes, "wsdlSpec",
     "wsdlSpec");

Collection<Classification> classifications =
  new ArrayList<Classification>();
classifications.add(wsdlSpecClassification);

// Find concepts
BulkResponse br = bqm.findConcepts(null, null,
  classifications, null, null);
```

To narrow the search, you could use other arguments of the `findConcepts` method (search qualifiers, names, external identifiers, or external links).

The next step is to go through the concepts, find the WSDL documents they correspond to, and display the organizations that use each document:

```
// Display information about the concepts found
Collection specConcepts = br.getCollection();
Iterator iter = specConcepts.iterator();
if (!iter.hasNext()) {
  System.out.println("No WSDL specification concepts found");
} else {
  while (iter.hasNext()) {
```

```
        Concept concept = (Concept) iter.next();

        String name = getName(concept);

        Collection links = concept.getExternalLinks();
        System.out.println("\nSpecification Concept:\n\tName: " +
          name + "\n\tKey: " + concept.getKey().getId() +
          "\n\tDescription: " + getDescription(concept));
        if (links.size() > 0) {
          ExternalLink link =
            (ExternalLink) links.iterator().next();
          System.out.println("\tURL of WSDL document: '" +
            link.getExternalURI() + "'");
        }

        // Find organizations that use this concept
        Collection<Concept> specConcepts1 =
          new ArrayList<Concept>();
        specConcepts1.add(concept);
        br = bqm.findOrganizations(null, null, null,
          specConcepts1, null, null);

        // Display information about organizations
        ...
      }
    }
```

If you find an organization that offers a service you wish to use, you can invoke the service using JAX-WS.

Finding Services and Service Bindings

After a client has located an organization, it can find that organization's services and the service bindings associated with those services.

```
Iterator orgIter = orgs.iterator();
while (orgIter.hasNext()) {
  Organization org = (Organization) orgIter.next();
  Collection services = org.getServices();
  Iterator svcIter = services.iterator();
  while (svcIter.hasNext()) {
    Service svc = (Service) svcIter.next();
    Collection serviceBindings =
      svc.getServiceBindings();
    Iterator sbIter = serviceBindings.iterator();
    while (sbIter.hasNext()) {
```

```
            ServiceBinding sb =
              (ServiceBinding) sbIter.next();
        }
    }
}
```

Managing Registry Data

If a client has authorization to do so, it can submit data to a registry, modify it, and remove it. It uses the `BusinessLifeCycleManager` interface to perform these tasks.

Registries usually allow a client to modify or remove data only if the data is being modified or removed by the same user who first submitted the data.

Managing registry data involves the following tasks:

- Getting authorization from the registry
- Creating an organization
- Adding classifications
- Adding services and service bindings to an organization
- Publishing an organization
- Publishing a specification concept
- Removing data from the registry

Getting Authorization from the Registry

Before it can submit data, the client must send its user name and password to the registry in a set of *credentials*. The following code fragment shows how to do this.

```
String username = "testuser";
String password = "testuser";

// Get authorization from the registry
PasswordAuthentication passwdAuth =
  new PasswordAuthentication(username,
    password.toCharArray());
```

```
HashSet<PasswordAuthentication> creds =
  new HashSet<PasswordAuthentication>();
creds.add(passwdAuth);
connection.setCredentials(creds);
```

Creating an Organization

The client creates the organization and populates it with data before publishing it.

An `Organization` object is one of the more complex data items in the JAXR API. It normally includes the following:

- A `Name` object.
- A `Description` object.
- A `Key` object, representing the ID by which the organization is known to the registry. This key is created by the registry, not by the user, and is returned after the organization is submitted to the registry.
- A `PrimaryContact` object, which is a `User` object that refers to an authorized user of the registry. A `User` object normally includes a `PersonName` object and collections of `TelephoneNumber`, `EmailAddress`, and `PostalAddress` objects.
- A collection of `Classification` objects.
- `Service` objects and their associated `ServiceBinding` objects.

For example, the following code fragment creates an organization and specifies its name, description, and primary contact. When a client creates an organization to be published to a UDDI registry, it does not include a key; the registry returns the new key when it accepts the newly created organization. The `blcm` object in the following code fragment is the `BusinessLifeCycleManager` object returned in Obtaining and Using a RegistryService Object (page 702). An `InternationalString` object is used for string values that may need to be localized.

```
// Create organization name and description
InternationalString s =
  blcm.createInternationalString("The Coffee Break");
Organization org = blcm.createOrganization(s);
s = blcm.createInternationalString("Purveyor of the " +
  "finest coffees. Established 1950");
org.setDescription(s);

// Create primary contact, set name
User primaryContact = blcm.createUser();
```

```
PersonName pName = blcm.createPersonName("Jane Doe");
primaryContact.setPersonName(pName);

// Set primary contact phone number
TelephoneNumber tNum = blcm.createTelephoneNumber();
tNum.setNumber("(800) 555-1212");
Collection<TelephoneNumber> phoneNums =
  new ArrayList<TelephoneNumber>();
phoneNums.add(tNum);
primaryContact.setTelephoneNumbers(phoneNums);

// Set primary contact email address
EmailAddress emailAddress =
  blcm.createEmailAddress("jane.doe@TheCoffeeBreak.com");
Collection<EmailAddress> emailAddresses =
  new ArrayList<EmailAddress>();
emailAddresses.add(emailAddress);
primaryContact.setEmailAddresses(emailAddresses);

// Set primary contact for organization
org.setPrimaryContact(primaryContact);
```

Adding Classifications

Organizations commonly belong to one or more classifications based on one or more classification schemes (taxonomies). To establish a classification for an organization using a taxonomy, the client first locates the taxonomy it wants to use. It uses the `BusinessQueryManager` to find the taxonomy. The `findClassificationSchemeByName` method takes a set of `FindQualifier` objects as its first argument, but this argument can be null.

```
// Set classification scheme to NAICS
ClassificationScheme cScheme =
  bqm.findClassificationSchemeByName(null,
    "ntis-gov:naics:1997");
```

The client then creates a classification using the classification scheme and a concept (a taxonomy element) within the classification scheme. For example, the following code sets up a classification for the organization within the NAICS taxonomy. The second and third arguments of the createClassification method are the name and the value of the concept.

```
// Create and add classification
InternationalString sn =
  blcm.createInternationalString(
    "All Other Specialty Food Stores"));
String sv = "445299";
Classification classification =
  blcm.createClassification(cScheme, sn, sv);
Collection<Classification> classifications =
  new ArrayList<Classification>();
classifications.add(classification);
org.addClassifications(classifications);
```

Services also use classifications, so you can use similar code to add a classification to a Service object.

Adding Services and Service Bindings to an Organization

Most organizations add themselves to a registry in order to offer services, so the JAXR API has facilities to add services and service bindings to an organization.

Like an Organization object, a Service object has a name, a description, and a unique key that is generated by the registry when the service is registered. It may also have classifications associated with it.

A service also commonly has *service bindings*, which provide information about how to access the service. A ServiceBinding object normally has a description, an access URI, and a specification link, which provides the linkage between a service binding and a technical specification that describes how to use the service by using the service binding.

The following code fragment shows how to create a collection of services, add service bindings to a service, and then add the services to the organization. It specifies an access URI but not a specification link. Because the access URI is not real and because JAXR by default checks for the validity of any published URI, the binding sets its validateURI property to false.

```
// Create services and service
Collection<Service> services = new ArrayList<Service>();
InternationalString s =
  blcm.createInternationalString("My Service Name"));
```

```
Service service = blcm.createService(s);
s = blcm.createInternationalString("My Service Description");
service.setDescription(is);

// Create service bindings
Collection<ServiceBinding> serviceBindings =
  new ArrayList<ServiceBinding>();
ServiceBinding binding = blcm.createServiceBinding();
s = blcm.createInternationalString("My Service Binding " +
  "Description");
binding.setDescription(is);
// allow us to publish a fictitious URI without an error
binding.setValidateURI(false);
binding.setAccessURI("http://TheCoffeeBreak.com:8080/sb/");
serviceBindings.add(binding);

// Add service bindings to service
service.addServiceBindings(serviceBindings);

// Add service to services, then add services to organization
services.add(service);
org.addServices(services);
```

Publishing an Organization

The primary method a client uses to add or modify organization data is the `saveOrganizations` method, which creates one or more new organizations in a registry if they did not exist previously. If one of the organizations exists but some of the data have changed, the `saveOrganizations` method updates and replaces the data.

After a client populates an organization with the information it wants to make public, it saves the organization. The registry returns the key in its response, and the client retrieves it.

```
// Add organization and submit to registry
// Retrieve key if successful
Collection<Organization> orgs = new ArrayList<Organization>();
orgs.add(org);
BulkResponse response = blcm.saveOrganizations(orgs);
Collection exceptions = response.getException();
if (exceptions == null) {
  System.out.println("Organization saved");

  Collection keys = response.getCollection();
  Iterator keyIter = keys.iterator();
```

```
        if (keyIter.hasNext()) {
            Key orgKey = (Key) keyIter.next();
            String id = orgKey.getId();
            System.out.println("Organization key is " + id);
        }
    }
```

Publishing a Specification Concept

A service binding can have a technical specification that describes how to access the service. An example of such a specification is a WSDL document. To publish the location of a service's specification (if the specification is a WSDL document), you create a `Concept` object and then add the URL of the WSDL document to the `Concept` object as an `ExternalLink` object. The following code fragment shows how to create a concept for the WSDL document associated with the simple web service example in Creating a Simple Web Service and Client with JAX-WS (page 508). First, you call the `createConcept` method to create a concept named `HelloConcept`. After setting the description of the concept, you create an external link to the URL of the `Hello` service's WSDL document, and then add the external link to the concept.

```
Concept specConcept =
    blcm.createConcept(null, "HelloConcept", "");
InternationalString s =
    blcm.createInternationalString(
        "Concept for Hello Service");
specConcept.setDescription(s);
ExternalLink wsdlLink =
    blcm.createExternalLink(
        "http://localhost:8080/hello-jaxws/hello?WSDL",
        "Hello WSDL document");
specConcept.addExternalLink(wsdlLink);
```

Next, you classify the `Concept` object as a WSDL document. To do this for a UDDI registry, you search the registry for the well-known classification scheme `uddi-org:types`, using its key ID. (The UDDI term for a classification scheme is *tModel*.) Then you create a classification using the name and value `wsdlSpec`. Finally, you add the classification to the concept.

```
String uuid_types =
    "uuid:c1acf26d-9672-4404-9d70-39b756e62ab4";
ClassificationScheme uddiOrgTypes =
    (ClassificationScheme) bqm.getRegistryObject(uuid_types,
        LifeCycleManager.CLASSIFICATION_SCHEME);
```

```
Classification wsdlSpecClassification =
    blcm.createClassification(uddiOrgTypes,
      "wsdlSpec", "wsdlSpec");
specConcept.addClassification(wsdlSpecClassification);
```

Finally, you save the concept using the saveConcepts method, similarly to the way you save an organization:

```
Collection<Concept> concepts = new ArrayList<Concept>();
concepts.add(specConcept);
BulkResponse concResponse = blcm.saveConcepts(concepts);
```

After you have published the concept, you normally add the concept for the WSDL document to a service binding. To do this, you can retrieve the key for the concept from the response returned by the saveConcepts method; you use a code sequence very similar to that of finding the key for a saved organization.

```
String conceptKeyId = null;
Collection concExceptions = concResponse.getExceptions();
Key concKey = null;
if (concExceptions == null) {
  System.out.println("WSDL Specification Concept saved");

  Collection keys = concResponse.getCollection();
  Iterator keyIter = keys.iterator();
  if (keyIter.hasNext()) {
    concKey = (Key) keyIter.next();
    conceptKeyId = concKey.getId();
    System.out.println("Concept key is " + conceptKeyId);
  }
}
```

Then you can call the getRegistryObject method to retrieve the concept from the registry:

```
Concept specConcept =
  (Concept) bqm.getRegistryObject(conceptKeyId,
    LifeCycleManager.CONCEPT);
```

Next, you create a SpecificationLink object for the service binding and set the concept as the value of its SpecificationObject:

```
SpecificationLink specLink =
  blcm.createSpecificationLink();
specLink.setSpecificationObject(specConcept);
binding.addSpecificationLink(specLink);
```

Now when you publish the organization with its service and service bindings, you have also published a link to the WSDL document. Now the organization can be found via queries such as those described in Finding Organizations by Classification (page 704).

If the concept was published by someone else and you don't have access to the key, you can find it using its name and classification. The code looks very similar to the code used to search for a WSDL document in Finding Organizations by Classification (page 704), except that you also create a collection of name patterns and include that in your search. Here is an example:

```
// Define name pattern
Collection namePatterns = new ArrayList();
namePatterns.add("HelloConcept");

BulkResponse br = bqm.findConcepts(null, namePatterns,
  classifications, null, null);
```

Removing Data from the Registry

A registry allows you to remove from it any data that you have submitted to it. You use the key returned by the registry as an argument to one of the BusinessLifeCycleManager delete methods: deleteOrganizations, deleteServices, deleteServiceBindings, deleteConcepts, and others.

The JAXRDelete sample program deletes the organization created by the JAXRPublish program. It deletes the organization that corresponds to a specified key string and then displays the key again so that the user can confirm that it has deleted the correct one.

```
String id = key.getId();
System.out.println("Deleting organization with id " + id);
Collection<Key> keys = new ArrayList<Key>();
keys.add(key);
BulkResponse response = blcm.deleteOrganizations(keys);
Collection exceptions = response.getException();
```

```
if (exceptions == null) {
  System.out.println("Organization deleted");
  Collection retKeys = response.getCollection();
  Iterator keyIter = retKeys.iterator();
  Key orgKey = null;
  if (keyIter.hasNext()) {
    orgKey = (Key) keyIter.next();
    id = orgKey.getId();
    System.out.println("Organization key was " + id);
  }
}
```

A client can use a similar mechanism to delete concepts, services, and service bindings.

Using Taxonomies in JAXR Clients

In the JAXR API, a taxonomy is represented by a `ClassificationScheme` object. This section describes how to use the implementation of JAXR in the Application Server to perform these tasks:

- To define your own taxonomies
- To specify postal addresses for an organization

Defining a Taxonomy

The JAXR specification requires that a JAXR provider be able to add user-defined taxonomies for use by JAXR clients. The mechanisms clients use to add and administer these taxonomies are implementation-specific.

The implementation of JAXR in the Application Server uses a simple file-based approach to provide taxonomies to the JAXR client. These files are read at runtime, when the JAXR provider starts up.

The taxonomy structure for the Application Server is defined by the JAXR Predefined Concepts DTD, which is declared both in the file `jaxrconcepts.dtd` and, in XML schema form, in the file `jaxrconcepts.xsd`. The file `jaxrconcepts.xml` contains the taxonomies for the implementation of JAXR in the Application Server. All these files are contained in the *<JAVAEE_HOME>*`/lib/appserv-ws.jar` file. This JAR file also includes files that define the well-known taxonomies used by the implementation of JAXR in the Application Server: `naics.xml`, `iso3166.xml`, and `unspsc.xml`.

The entries in the `jaxrconcepts.xml` file look like this:

```
<PredefinedConcepts>
  <JAXRClassificationScheme id="schId" name="schName">
    <JAXRConcept id="schId/conCode" name="conName"
      parent="parentId" code="conCode">
    </JAXRConcept>
    ...
  </JAXRClassificationScheme>
</PredefinedConcepts>
```

The taxonomy structure is a containment-based structure. The element `PredefinedConcepts` is the root of the structure and must be present. The `JAXRClassificationScheme` element is the parent of the structure, and the `JAXRConcept` elements are children and grandchildren. A `JAXRConcept` element may have children, but it is not required to do so.

In all element definitions, attribute order and case are significant.

To add a user-defined taxonomy, follow these steps.

1. Publish the `JAXRClassificationScheme` element for the taxonomy as a `ClassificationScheme` object in the registry that you will be accessing. To publish a `ClassificationScheme` object, you must set its name. You also give the scheme a classification within a known classification scheme such as `uddi-org:types`. In the following code fragment, the name is the first argument of the `LifeCycleManager.createClassificationScheme` method call.

```
InternationalString sn =
  blcm.createInternationalString("MyScheme");
InternationalString sd = blcm.createInternationalString(
  "A Classification Scheme");
ClassificationScheme postalScheme =
  blcm.createClassificationScheme(sn, sd);
String uuid_types =
  "uuid:c1acf26d-9672-4404-9d70-39b756e62ab4";
ClassificationScheme uddiOrgTypes =
  (ClassificationScheme) bqm.getRegistryObject(uuid_types,
    LifeCycleManager.CLASSIFICATION_SCHEME);
if (uddiOrgTypes != null) {
  Classification classification =
    blcm.createClassification(uddiOrgTypes,
      "postalAddress", "postalAddress" );
  postalScheme.addClassification(classification);
  InternationalString ld =
    blcm.createInternationalString("My Scheme");
```

```
    ExternalLink externalLink =
        blcm.createExternalLink(
            "http://www.mycom.com/myscheme.xml", ld);
    postalScheme.addExternalLink(externalLink);
    Collection<ClassificationScheme> schemes =
        new ArrayList<ClassificationScheme>();
    schemes.add(cScheme);
    BulkResponse br =
        blcm.saveClassificationSchemes(schemes);
}
```

The `BulkResponse` object returned by the `saveClassificationSchemes` method contains the key for the classification scheme, which you need to retrieve:

```
if (br.getStatus() == JAXRResponse.STATUS_SUCCESS) {
    System.out.println("Saved ClassificationScheme");
    Collection schemeKeys = br.getCollection();
    Iterator keysIter = schemeKeys.iterator();
    while (keysIter.hasNext()) {
        Key key = (Key) keysIter.next();
        System.out.println("The postalScheme key is " +
            key.getId());
        System.out.println("Use this key as the scheme" +
            " uuid in the taxonomy file");
    }
}
```

2. In an XML file, define a taxonomy structure that is compliant with the JAXR Predefined Concepts DTD. Enter the `ClassificationScheme` element in your taxonomy XML file by specifying the returned key ID value as the `id` attribute and the name as the `name` attribute. For the foregoing code fragment, for example, the opening tag for the `JAXRClassificationScheme` element looks something like this (all on one line):

   ```
   <JAXRClassificationScheme
   id="uuid:nnnnnnnn-nnnn-nnnn-nnnn-nnnnnnnnnnnn"
   name="MyScheme">
   ```

   The `ClassificationScheme` `id` must be a universally unique identifier (UUID).

3. Enter each `JAXRConcept` element in your taxonomy XML file by specifying the following four attributes, in this order:

   a. `id` is the `JAXRClassificationScheme` `id` value, followed by a / separator, followed by the code of the `JAXRConcept` element.

   b. `name` is the name of the `JAXRConcept` element.

c. `parent` is the immediate parent `id` (either the `ClassificationScheme` `id` or that of the parent `JAXRConcept`).

d. `code` is the `JAXRConcept` element code value.

The first `JAXRConcept` element in the `naics.xml` file looks like this (all on one line):

```
<JAXRConcept
id="uuid:C0B9FE13-179F-413D-8A5B-5004DB8E5BB2/11"
name="Agriculture, Forestry, Fishing and Hunting"
parent="uuid:C0B9FE13-179F-413D-8A5B-5004DB8E5BB2"
code="11"></JAXRConcept>
```

4. To add the user-defined taxonomy structure to the JAXR provider, specify the connection property `com.sun.xml.registry.userTaxonomyFilenames` in your client program. You set the property as follows:

```
props.setProperty
("com.sun.xml.registry.userTaxonomyFilenames",
   "c:\mydir\xxx.xml|c:\mydir\xxx2.xml");
```

Use the vertical bar (`|`) as a separator if you specify more than one file name.

Specifying Postal Addresses

The JAXR specification defines a postal address as a structured interface with attributes for street, city, country, and so on. The UDDI specification, on the other hand, defines a postal address as a free-form collection of address lines, each of which can also be assigned a meaning. To map the JAXR `PostalAddress` format to a known UDDI address format, you specify the UDDI format as a `ClassificationScheme` object and then specify the semantic equivalences between the concepts in the UDDI format classification scheme and the comments in the JAXR `PostalAddress` classification scheme. The JAXR `PostalAddress` classification scheme is provided by the implementation of JAXR in the Application Server.

In the JAXR API, a `PostalAddress` object has the fields `streetNumber`, `street`, `city`, `state`, `postalCode`, and `country`. In the implementation of JAXR in the Application Server, these are predefined concepts in the `jaxrconcepts.xml` file, within the `ClassificationScheme` named `PostalAddressAttributes`.

To specify the mapping between the JAXR postal address format and another format, you set two connection properties:

- The `javax.xml.registry.postalAddressScheme` property, which specifies a postal address classification scheme for the connection
- The `javax.xml.registry.semanticEquivalences` property, which specifies the semantic equivalences between the JAXR format and the other format

For example, suppose you want to use a scheme named `MyPostalAddressScheme`, which you published to a registry with the UUID `uuid:f7922839-f1f7-9228-c97d-ce0b4594736c`.

```
<JAXRClassificationScheme id="uuid:f7922839-f1f7-9228-c97d-
ce0b4594736c" name="MyPostalAddressScheme">
```

First, you specify the postal address scheme using the `id` value from the `JAXRClassificationScheme` element (the UUID). Case does not matter:

```
props.setProperty("javax.xml.registry.postalAddressScheme",
  "uuid:f7922839-f1f7-9228-c97d-ce0b4594736c");
```

Next, you specify the mapping from the `id` of each `JAXRConcept` element in the default JAXR postal address scheme to the `id` of its counterpart in the scheme you published:

```
props.setProperty("javax.xml.registry.semanticEquivalences",
  "urn:uuid:PostalAddressAttributes/StreetNumber," +
  "uuid:f7922839-f1f7-9228-c97d-ce0b4594736c/
StreetAddressNumber|" +
  "urn:uuid:PostalAddressAttributes/Street," +
  "urn:uuid:f7922839-f1f7-9228-c97d-ce0b4594736c/
StreetAddress|" +
  "urn:uuid:PostalAddressAttributes/City," +
  "urn:uuid:f7922839-f1f7-9228-c97d-ce0b4594736c/City|" +
  "urn:uuid:PostalAddressAttributes/State," +
  "urn:uuid:f7922839-f1f7-9228-c97d-ce0b4594736c/State|" +
  "urn:uuid:PostalAddressAttributes/PostalCode," +
  "urn:uuid:f7922839-f1f7-9228-c97d-ce0b4594736c/ZipCode|" +
  "urn:uuid:PostalAddressAttributes/Country," +
  "urn:uuid:f7922839-f1f7-9228-c97d-ce0b4594736c/Country");
```

After you create the connection using these properties, you can create a postal address and assign it to the primary contact of the organization before you publish the organization:

```
String streetNumber = "99";
String street = "Imaginary Ave. Suite 33";
String city = "Imaginary City";
String state = "NY";
String country = "USA";
String postalCode = "00000";
String type = "";
PostalAddress postAddr =
  blcm.createPostalAddress(streetNumber, street, city, state,
    country, postalCode, type);
Collection<PostalAddress> postalAddresses =
  new ArrayList<PostalAddress>();
postalAddresses.add(postAddr);
primaryContact.setPostalAddresses(postalAddresses);
```

If the postal address scheme and semantic equivalences for the query are the same as those specified for the publication, a JAXR query can then retrieve the postal address using `PostalAddress` methods. To retrieve postal addresses when you do not know what postal address scheme was used to publish them, you can retrieve them as a collection of `Slot` objects. The `JAXRQueryPostal.java` sample program shows how to do this.

In general, you can create a user-defined postal address taxonomy for any `PostalAddress` tModels that use the well-known categorization in the `uddi-org:types` taxonomy, which has the tModel UUID `uuid:c1acf26d-9672-4404-9d70-39b756e62ab4` with a value of `postalAddress`. You can retrieve the tModel `overviewDoc`, which points to the technical detail for the specification of the scheme, where the taxonomy structure definition can be found. (The JAXR equivalent of an `overviewDoc` is an `ExternalLink`.)

Running the Client Examples

The simple client programs provided with this tutorial can be run from the command line. You can modify them to suit your needs. They allow you to specify the Java WSDP Registry Server for queries and updates. (To install the Registry Server files, follow the instructions in Preliminaries: Getting Access to a Registry (page 697).

The examples, in the `<INSTALL>/javaeetutorial5/examples/jaxr/simple/src/` directory, are as follows:

- `JAXRQuery.java` shows how to search a registry for organizations.
- `JAXRQueryByNAICSClassification.java` shows how to search a registry using a common classification scheme.
- `JAXRQueryByWSDLClassification.java` shows how to search a registry for web services that describe themselves by means of a WSDL document.
- `JAXRPublish.java` shows how to publish an organization to a registry.
- `JAXRDelete.java` shows how to remove an organization from a registry.
- `JAXRSaveClassificationScheme.java` shows how to publish a classification scheme (specifically, a postal address scheme) to a registry.
- `JAXRPublishPostal.java` shows how to publish an organization with a postal address for its primary contact.
- `JAXRQueryPostal.java` shows how to retrieve postal address data from an organization.
- `JAXRDeleteScheme.java` shows how to delete a classification scheme from a registry.
- `JAXRPublishConcept.java` shows how to publish a concept for a WSDL document.
- `JAXRPublishHelloOrg.java` shows how to publish an organization with a service binding that refers to a WSDL document.
- `JAXRDeleteConcept.java` shows how to delete a concept.
- `JAXRGetMyObjects.java` lists all the objects that you own in a registry.

The `<INSTALL>/javaeetutorial5/examples/jaxr/simple/` directory also contains the following:

- A `build.xml` file for the examples
- A `JAXRExamples.properties` file, in the `src` subdirectory, that supplies string values used by the sample programs
- A file called `postalconcepts.xml` that serves as the taxonomy file for the postal address examples

Before You Compile the Examples

Before you compile the examples, edit the file `<INSTALL>/javaeetutorial5/examples/jaxr/simple/src/JAXRExamples.properties` as follows.

1. If the Application Server where you installed the Registry Server files is running on a system other than your own or if itis using a nondefault HTTP port, change the following lines:

   ```
   query.url=http://localhost:8080/RegistryServer/
   publish.url=http://localhost:8080/RegistryServer/
   ...
   link.uri=http://localhost:8080/hello-jaxws/hello?WSDL
   ...
   wsdlorg.svcbnd.uri=http://localhost:8080/hello-jaxws/hello
   ```

   Specify the fully qualified host name instead of `localhost`, or change `8080` to the correct value for your system.

2. (Optional) Edit the following lines, which contain empty strings for the proxy hosts, to specify your own proxy settings. The proxy host is the system on your network through which you access the Internet; you usually specify it in your Internet browser settings.

   ```
   ## HTTP and HTTPS proxy host and port
   http.proxyHost=
   http.proxyPort=8080
   https.proxyHost=
   https.proxyPort=8080
   ```

   The proxy ports have the value 8080, which is the usual one; change this string if your proxy uses a different port.

   Your entries usually follow this pattern:

   ```
   http.proxyHost=proxyhost.mydomain
   http.proxyPort=8080
   https.proxyHost=proxyhost.mydomain
   https.proxyPort=8080
   ```

   You need to specify a proxy only if you want to specify an external link or service binding that is outside your firewall.

3. Feel free to change any of the organization data in the remainder of the file. This data is used by the publishing and postal address examples.

You can edit the `src/JAXRExamples.properties` file at any time. The Ant targets that run the client examples will use the latest version of the file.

Note: Before you compile any of the examples, follow the preliminary setup instructions in Building the Examples (page xxxv).

Compiling the Examples

You can compile and run the examples using either the NetBeans 5.5 IDE or Ant.

To compile the programs using NetBeans 5.5, follow these steps:

1. In NetBeans 5.5, choose Open Project from the File menu.
2. In the Open Project dialog, navigate to <*INSTALL*>`/javaeetutorial5/examples/jaxr/`.
3. Select the `simple` folder.
4. Select the Open as Main Project checkbox.
5. Click Open Project Folder.

   A Reference Problems dialog appears. Click Close.
6. Right-click the `simple` project and choose Resolve Reference Problems.
7. In the Resolve Reference Problems dialog, select the first of the missing JAR files and click Resolve.

   The missing files are `appserv-ws.jar`, `javaee.jar`, `appserv-rt.jar`, and `commons-logging.jar`.
8. Navigate to the <*JAVAEE_HOME*>`/lib/` directory.
9. Select the missing JAR file (`appserv-ws.jar`, for example) and click Open.

   In the Resolve Reference Problems dialog, all the files have green check marks to the left of their names.
10. Click Close.
11. Right-click the `simple` project and choose Build Project.

To compile the programs using Ant, follow these steps:

1. In a terminal window, go to the following directory:

   ```
   <INSTALL>/javaeetutorial5/examples/jaxr/simple/
   ```
2. Type the following command:

   ```
   ant
   ```

This command uses the default target, which performs the compilation. The Ant targets create subdirectories called `build` and `dist`.

Running the Examples

You must start the Application Server in order to run the examples against the Registry Server. For details, see Starting and Stopping the Application Server (page 27).

Getting a List of Your Registry Objects

To get a list of the objects you own in the registry—organizations, classification schemes, and concepts—run the `JAXRGetMyObjects` program.

To run the program using NetBeans 5.5, follow these steps:

1. Right-click the `simple` project and choose Properties.
2. Select Run from the Categories tree.
3. Click Browse next to the Main Class field.
4. In the Browse Main Classes dialog, select `JAXRGetMyObjects`.
5. Click Select Main Class.
6. Click OK.
7. Right-click the project and choose Run Project.

To run the program using Ant, use the `run-get-objects` target:

```
ant run-get-objects
```

It is a good idea to run this program first to make sure the Registry Server is running properly.

Note: The first time you access the Registry Server, you are likely to see a runtime error. If you run the program a second time, the program should run correctly.

Because you are logged in as the default user, `testuser`, you will see a list of all the objects in the registry when you run this program. Most of these objects are classification schemes.

Running the JAXRPublish Example

To run the `JAXRPublish` program using NetBeans 5.5, follow these steps:

1. Right-click the `simple` project and choose Properties.
2. Select Run from the Categories tree.
3. Click Browse next to the Main Class field.
4. In the Browse Main Classes dialog, select `JAXRPublish`.
5. Click Select Main Class.
6. Click OK.
7. Right-click the project and choose Run Project.

To run the program using Ant, use the `run-publish` target with no command-line arguments:

```
ant run-publish
```

The program output displays the string value of the key of the new organization.

After you run the `JAXRPublish` program but before you run `JAXRDelete`, you can run `JAXRQuery` to look up the organization you published.

Note: When you run any program that publishes an object to the registry, a runtime warning appears in the server log (a `com.sun.xnode.XNodeException`). It is safe to ignore this warning.

Running the JAXRQuery Example

To run the `JAXRQuery` example, specify a string argument on the command line to search the registry for organizations whose names contain that string. Searching is not case-sensitive.

To run the program using NetBeans 5.5, follow these steps:

1. Right-click the `simple` project and choose Properties.
2. Select Run from the Categories tree.
3. Click Browse next to the Main Class field.
4. In the Browse Main Classes dialog, select `JAXRQuery`.
5. Click Select Main Class.
6. In the Arguments field, type the query string value (for example, `coffee`).

7. Click OK.
8. Right-click the project and choose Run Project.

To run the program using Ant, use the `run-query` target. Specify a `query-string` argument on the command line:

```
ant -Dquery-string=coffee run-query
```

Running the JAXRQueryByNAICSClassification Example

After you run the `JAXRPublish` program, you can also run the `JAXRQueryByNAICSClassification` example, which looks for organizations that use the All Other Specialty Food Stores classification, the same one used for the organization created by `JAXRPublish`.

To run the program using NetBeans 5.5, follow these steps:

1. Right-click the `simple` project and choose Properties.
2. Select Run from the Categories tree.
3. Click Browse next to the Main Class field.
4. In the Browse Main Classes dialog, select `JAXRQueryByNAICSClassification`.
5. Click Select Main Class.

   You do not have to remove the argument string left over from the previous program. Since this program takes no arguments, the string will be ignored.
6. Click OK.
7. Right-click the project and choose Run Project.
8. In the output window, find the ID string that follows `Org key id:` and select it.
9. Right-click the selected text and choose Copy.

To run the program using Ant, use the `run-query-naics` target:

```
ant run-query-naics
```

Running the JAXRDelete Example

To run the `JAXRDelete` program, specify the key string for the object you want to delete as input to the program. For example, you can use the key string displayed by the `JAXRQueryByNAICSClassification` program.

To run the program using NetBeans 5.5, follow these steps:

1. Right-click the `simple` project and choose Properties.
2. Select Run from the Categories tree.
3. Click Browse next to the Main Class field.
4. In the Browse Main Classes dialog, select `JAXRDelete`.
5. Click Select Main Class.
6. In the Arguments field, paste the string you copied when you ran the program in the previous section.
7. Click OK.
8. Right-click the project and choose Run Project.

To run the program using Ant, use the `run-delete` target. Specify a `key-string` argument on the command line:

```
ant -Dkey-string=keyString run-delete
```

Publishing a Classification Scheme

To publish organizations with postal addresses, you must first publish a classification scheme for the postal address.

To run the `JAXRSaveClassificationScheme` program using NetBeans 5.5, follow these steps:

1. Right-click the `simple` project and choose Properties.
2. Select Run from the Categories tree.
3. Click Browse next to the Main Class field.
4. In the Browse Main Classes dialog, select `JAXRSaveClassification-Scheme`.
5. Click Select Main Class.
6. Click OK.
7. Right-click the project and choose Run Project.

8. In the output window, find the UUID string that follows the string `The postalScheme key is` and select it.
9. Right-click the selected text and choose Copy.

To run the program using Ant, use the `run-save-scheme` target:

```
ant run-save-scheme
```

You will use the UUID string returned by this program in the next section.

Running the Postal Address Examples

Before you run the postal address examples, perform these steps:

1. In the `simple` directory, open the file `postalconcepts.xml` in an editor.
2. Wherever you see the string `uuid-from-save`, replace it with the UUID string returned by the `JAXRSaveClassificationScheme` program (including the `uuid:` prefix). Make sure there are no leading or trailing spaces in the string.
3. Save and close the file.

For a given registry, you only need to publish the classification scheme and edit `postalconcepts.xml` once. After you perform those steps, you can run the `JAXRPublishPostal` and `JAXRQueryPostal` programs multiple times.

To run the `JAXRPublishPostal` program using NetBeans 5.5, follow these steps:

1. Right-click the `simple` project and choose Properties.
2. Select Run from the Categories tree.
3. Click Browse next to the Main Class field.
4. In the Browse Main Classes dialog, select `JAXRPublishPostal`.
5. Click Select Main Class.
6. In the Arguments field, paste the UUID string returned by the `run-save-scheme` target. The UUID string would look something like this:

   `uuid:938d9ccd-a74a-4c7e-864a-e6e2c6822519`
7. Click OK.
8. Right-click the project and choose Run Project.

To run the `JAXRQueryPostal` program using NetBeans 5.5, follow these steps:

1. Right-click the `simple` project and choose Properties.
2. Select Run from the Categories tree.
3. Click Browse next to the Main Class field.
4. In the Browse Main Classes dialog, select `JAXRQueryPostal`.
5. Click Select Main Class.
6. In the Arguments field, type a query string, then the UUID string returned by the `run-save-scheme` target. The order is important. For example:

   `coffee` *`uuidstring`*

7. Click OK.
8. Right-click the project and choose Run Project.

To run the `JAXRPublishPostal` program using Ant, specify the string you entered in the `postalconcepts.xml` file, including the `uuid:` prefix, as input to the `run-publish-postal` target:

```
ant -Duuid-string=uuidstring run-publish-postal
```

The program output displays the string value of the key of the new organization.

To run the `JAXRQueryPostal` program using Ant, use the `run-query-postal` target. This target specifies the `postalconcepts.xml` file in a `<sysproperty>` tag.

As input to the `run-query-postal` target, specify both a `query-string` argument and a `uuid-string` argument on the command line to search the registry for the organization published by the `run-publish-postal` target:

```
ant -Dquery-string=coffee -Duuid-string=uuidstring
run-query-postal
```

The postal address for the primary contact will appear correctly with the JAXR `PostalAddress` methods. Any postal addresses found that use other postal address schemes will appear as `Slot` lines.

If you want to delete the organization you published, follow the instructions in Running the JAXRDelete Example (page 727).

Deleting a Classification Scheme

To delete the classification scheme you published after you have finished using it, run the `JAXRDeleteScheme` program.

To run the program using NetBeans 5.5, follow these steps:

1. Right-click the `simple` project and choose Properties.
2. Select Run from the Categories tree.
3. Click Browse next to the Main Class field.
4. In the Browse Main Classes dialog, select `JAXRDeleteScheme`.
5. Click Select Main Class.
6. In the Arguments field, paste the UUID string for the postal address scheme.
7. Click OK.
8. Right-click the project and choose Run Project.

To run the program using Ant, use the `run-delete-scheme` target, specifying the UUID string:

```
ant -Duuid-string=uuidstring run-delete-scheme
```

Publishing a Concept for a WSDL Document

The `JAXRPublishConcept` program publishes the location of the WSDL document for the JAX-WS `Hello` service described in Creating a Simple Web Service and Client with JAX-WS (page 508). Normally, you deploy the service before you publish the location of the WSDL document. However, this program runs correctly whether or not the service is deployed.

To run the `JAXRPublishConcept` program using NetBeans 5.5, follow these steps:

1. Right-click the `simple` project and choose Properties.
2. Select Run from the Categories tree.
3. Click Browse next to the Main Class field.
4. In the Browse Main Classes dialog, select `JAXRPublishConcept`.
5. Click Select Main Class.
6. Click OK.
7. Right-click the project and choose Run Project.

8. In the output window, find the UUID string that follows the string `Concept key is` and select it.
9. Right-click the selected text and choose Copy.

To run the program using Ant, use the `run-publish-concept` target:

```
ant run-publish-concept
```

The program output displays the UUID string of the new specification concept, which is named HelloConcept. You will use this string in the next section.

After you run the `JAXRPublishConcept` program, you can run `JAXRPublish-HelloOrg` to publish an organization that uses this concept.

Publishing an Organization with a WSDL Document in Its Service Binding

To run the `JAXRPublishHelloOrg` example, specify the string returned from `JAXRPublishConcept` (including the `uuid:` prefix) as input to the program.

To run the program using NetBeans 5.5, follow these steps:

1. Right-click the `simple` project and choose Properties.
2. Select Run from the Categories tree.
3. Click Browse next to the Main Class field.
4. In the Browse Main Classes dialog, select `JAXRPublishHelloOrg`.
5. Click Select Main Class.
6. In the Arguments field, paste the UUID string for the concept. The *`uuidstring`* would look something like this:

   `uuid:10945f5c-f2e1-0945-2f07-5897ebcfaa35`
7. Click OK.
8. Right-click the project and choose Run Project.

To run the program using Ant, use the `run-publish-hello-org` target:

```
ant -Duuid-string=uuidstring run-publish-hello-org
```

The program output displays the string value of the key of the new organization, which is named Hello Organization.

After you publish the organization, run the `JAXRQueryByWSDLClassification` example to search for it. To delete it, run `JAXRDelete`.

Running the JAXRQueryByWSDLClassification Example

To run the `JAXRQueryByWSDLClassification` example, specify a string argument to search the registry for specification concepts whose names contain that string. Searching is not case-sensitive.

To run the program using NetBeans 5.5, follow these steps:

1. Right-click the `simple` project and choose Properties.
2. Select Run from the Categories tree.
3. Click Browse next to the Main Class field.
4. In the Browse Main Classes dialog, select `JAXRQueryByWSDLClassification`.
5. Click Select Main Class.
6. In the Arguments field, type `helloconcept`.
7. Click OK.
8. Right-click the project and choose Run Project.

To run the program using Ant, use the `run-query-wsdl` target:

```
ant -Dquery-string=helloconcept run-query-wsdl
```

This example finds the concept and organization you published.

Deleting a Concept

To run the `JAXRDeleteConcept` program, specify the UUID string displayed by the `JAXRPublishConcept` program as input to the program. Do not delete the concept until after you have deleted any organizations that refer to it.

To run the program using NetBeans 5.5, follow these steps:

1. Right-click the `simple` project and choose Properties.
2. Select Run from the Categories tree.
3. Click Browse next to the Main Class field.
4. In the Browse Main Classes dialog, select `JAXRDeleteConcept`.

5. Click Select Main Class.
6. In the Arguments field, paste the UUID string for the concept.
7. Click OK.
8. Right-click the project and choose Run Project.

To run the program using Ant, use the `run-delete-concept` target:

```
ant -Duuid-string=uuidString run-delete-concept
```

Other Targets

To remove the `build` and `dist` directories and the class files using NetBeans 5.5, right-click the `simple` project and choose Clean Project.

To perform this task using Ant, type the following command:

```
ant clean
```

To obtain an Ant syntax reminder for all the targets, use the command

```
ant -projecthelp
```

Using JAXR Clients in Java EE Applications

You can create Java EE applications that use JAXR clients to access registries. This section explains how to write, compile, package, deploy, and run a Java EE application that uses JAXR to publish an organization to a registry and then query the registry for that organization. The application in this section uses two components: an application client and a stateless session bean.

The section covers the following topics:

- Coding the application client: `MyAppClient.java`
- Coding the `PubQuery` session bean
- Editing the properties file
- Starting the Application Server
- Creating JAXR resources

- Building, deploying, and running the application using NetBeans 5.5
- Building, deploying, and running the application using Ant

You will find the source files for this section in the directory `<INSTALL>/javaeetutorial5/examples/jaxr/clientsession/`. Path names in this section are relative to this directory.

The example has a `build.xml` file that refers to files in the following directory:

```
<INSTALL>/javaeetutorial5/examples/bp-project/
```

Coding the Application Client: MyAppClient.java

The application client class, `clientsession-app-client/src/java/MyAppClient.java`, accesses the `PubQuery` enterprise bean's remote interface, `clientsession-app-client/src/java/PubQueryRemote.java`. The program calls the bean's two business methods, `executePublish` and `executeQuery`.

Coding the PubQuery Session Bean

The `PubQuery` bean is a stateless session bean that has two business methods. The bean uses remote interfaces rather than local interfaces because it is accessed from the application client.

The remote interface, `clientsession-ejb/src/java/PubQueryRemote.java`, declares two business methods: `executePublish` and `executeQuery`. The bean class, `clientsession-ejb/src/java/PubQueryBean.java`, implements the `executePublish` and `executeQuery` methods and their helper methods `getName`, `getDescription`, and `getKey`. These methods are very similar to the methods of the same name in the simple examples `JAXRQuery.java` and `JAXRPublish.java`. The `executePublish` method uses information in the file `PubQueryBeanExample.properties` to create an organization named The Coffee Enterprise Bean Break. The `executeQuery` method uses the organization name, specified in the application client code, to locate this organization.

The bean class injects a `ConnectionFactory` resource. It implements a `@PostConstruct` method named `makeConnection`, which uses the `ConnectionFactory` to create the `Connection`. Finally, a `@PreDestroy` method named `endConnection` closes the `Connection`.

Editing the Properties File

Before you compile the application, edit the `clientsession-ejb/src/java/PubQueryBeanExamples.properties` file in the same way you edited the `JAXRExamples.properties` file to run the simple examples (see Before You Compile the Examples, page 722). Feel free to change any of the organization data in the file.

Starting the Application Server

To run this example, you need to start the Application Server. Follow the instructions in Starting and Stopping the Application Server (page 27). To verify that the Registry Server is deployed, use the `asadmin` command as follows:

```
% asadmin list-components
Xindice <web-module>
RegistryServer <web-module>
Command list-components executed successfully.
```

Creating JAXR Resources

To use JAXR in a Java EE application that uses the Application Server, you need to access the JAXR resource adapter (see Implementing a JAXR Client, page 696) through a connector connection pool and a connector resource. There are no Ant targets to create these resources, so you need to use either the Admin Console or the `asadmin` command. Using the Admin Console is less likely to result in errors.

If you have not done so, start the Admin Console as described in Starting the Admin Console (page 28).

To create the connector connection pool, perform the following steps:

1. In the tree component, expand the Resources node, then expand the Connectors node.
2. Click Connector Connection Pools.
3. Click New.
4. On the General Settings page:
   a. Type `jaxr-pool` in the Name field.
   b. Choose `jaxr-ra` from the Resource Adapter drop-down list.

   c. Choose `com.sun.connector.jaxr.JaxrConnectionFactory` (the only choice) from the Connection Definition drop-down list.
   d. Click Next.
5. On the next page, click Finish.

To create the connector resource, perform the following steps:

1. Under the Connectors node, click Connector Resources.
2. Click New. The Create Connector Resource page appears.
3. In the JNDI Name field, type `eis/JAXR`.
4. Choose `jaxr-pool` from the Pool Name drop-down list.
5. Click OK.

To create the connection pool using the `asadmin` command, type the following command (all on one line):

```
asadmin create-connector-connection-pool --raname jaxr-ra
--connectiondefinition
com.sun.connector.jaxr.JaxrConnectionFactory jaxr-pool
```

To create the connector resource using the `asadmin` command, type the following command:

```
asadmin create-connector-resource --poolname jaxr-pool eis/JAXR
```

Building, Deploying, and Running the Application Using NetBeans 5.5

To build, deploy, and run the application using NetBeans 5.5, do the following:

1. In NetBeans 5.5, choose Open Project from the File menu.
2. In the Open Project dialog, navigate to `<INSTALL>/javaeetutorial5/examples/jaxr/`.
3. Select the `clientsession` folder.
4. Select the Open as Main Project checkbox and the Open Required Projects checkbox.
5. Click Open Project Folder.
6. Right-click the `clientsession` project and choose Build Project.

This task compiles and packages the session bean and application client, then packages the EAR file.

7. Right-click the project and choose Deploy Project.
8. Right-click the project and choose Run Project.

   This command returns a JAR file named `clientsessionClient.jar` and then executes it.

The output of the application client in the Output pane looks like this:

```
To view the bean output,
 check <install_dir>/domains/domain1/logs/server.log.
```

In the server log, you will find the output from the `executePublish` and `executeQuery` methods, wrapped in logging information.

To undeploy the application, follow these steps:

1. Click the Runtime tab.
2. Expand the Servers node.
3. Expand the Sun Java System Application Server node.
4. Expand the Applications node.
5. Expand the Enterprise Applications node.
6. Right-click `clientsession` and choose Undeploy.

If you wish, you can run the `JAXRDelete` program in the `simple` project to delete the organization that was published.

Building, Deploying, and Running the Application Using Ant

To build the application using Ant, do the following:

1. Start the Application Server, if it is not already running.
2. Go to the following directory:

   `<INSTALL>/javaeetutorial5/examples/jaxr/clientsession/`

3. To compile the source files and package the application, use the following command:

   `ant`

This task does the following:

a. Compiles and packages the session bean
b. Compiles and packages the application client
c. Packages the EAR file, creating a file named `clientsession.ear` in the `dist` directory.

To deploy the application and run the client using Ant, use the following command:

```
ant run
```

Ignore the message that states that the application is deployed at a URL.

The output in the terminal window looks like this:

```
[echo] running application client container.
[exec] To view the bean output,
[exec]  check <install_dir>/domains/domain1/logs/server.log.
```

In the server log, you will find the output from the `executePublish` and `executeQuery` methods, wrapped in logging information.

After you run the example, use the following command to undeploy the application:

```
ant undeploy
```

If you wish, you can use the `run-delete` target in the `simple` directory to delete the organization that was published.

To remove the generated files, use the following command:

```
ant clean
```

Further Information

For more information about JAXR, registries, and web services, see the following:

- Java Specification Request (JSR) 93: JAXR 1.0:
  `http://jcp.org/jsr/detail/093.jsp`
- JAXR home page:
  `http://java.sun.com/xml/jaxr/`
- Universal Description, Discovery and Integration (UDDI) project:
  `http://www.uddi.org/`
- ebXML:
  `http://www.ebxml.org/`
- Service Registry (ebXML Registry/Repository):
  `http://www.sun.com/products/soa/registry/`
- Open Source JAXR Provider for ebXML Registries:
  `http://ebxmlrr.sourceforge.net/jaxr/`
- Java Platform, Enterprise Edition:
  `http://java.sun.com/javaee/`
- Java Technology and XML:
  `http://java.sun.com/xml/`
- Java Technology and Web Services:
  `http://java.sun.com/webservices/`

Part Three: Enterprise Beans

PART Three explores Enterprise JavaBeans.

20

Enterprise Beans

ENTERPRISE beans are Java EE components that implement Enterprise JavaBeans (EJB) technology. Enterprise beans run in the EJB container, a runtime environment within the Application Server (see Container Types, page 10). Although transparent to the application developer, the EJB container provides system-level services such as transactions and security to its enterprise beans. These services enable you to quickly build and deploy enterprise beans, which form the core of transactional Java EE applications.

What Is an Enterprise Bean?

Written in the Java programming language, an *enterprise bean* is a server-side component that encapsulates the business logic of an application. The business logic is the code that fulfills the purpose of the application. In an inventory control application, for example, the enterprise beans might implement the business logic in methods called `checkInventoryLevel` and `orderProduct`. By invoking these methods, clients can access the inventory services provided by the application.

Benefits of Enterprise Beans

For several reasons, enterprise beans simplify the development of large, distributed applications. First, because the EJB container provides system-level services to enterprise beans, the bean developer can concentrate on solving business problems. The EJB container—and not the bean developer—is responsible for system-level services such as transaction management and security authorization.

Second, because the beans—and not the clients—contain the application's business logic, the client developer can focus on the presentation of the client. The client developer does not have to code the routines that implement business rules or access databases. As a result, the clients are thinner, a benefit that is particularly important for clients that run on small devices.

Third, because enterprise beans are portable components, the application assembler can build new applications from existing beans. These applications can run on any compliant Java EE server provided that they use the standard APIs.

When to Use Enterprise Beans

You should consider using enterprise beans if your application has any of the following requirements:

- The application must be scalable. To accommodate a growing number of users, you may need to distribute an application's components across multiple machines. Not only can the enterprise beans of an application run on different machines, but also their location will remain transparent to the clients.
- Transactions must ensure data integrity. Enterprise beans support transactions, the mechanisms that manage the concurrent access of shared objects.
- The application will have a variety of clients. With only a few lines of code, remote clients can easily locate enterprise beans. These clients can be thin, various, and numerous.

Types of Enterprise Beans

Table 20–1 summarizes the two types of enterprise beans. The following sections discuss each type in more detail.

Table 20–1 Enterprise Bean Types

Enterprise Bean Type	Purpose
Session	Performs a task for a client; optionally may implement a web service
Message-Driven	Acts as a listener for a particular messaging type, such as the Java Message Service API

Note: Entity beans have been replaced by Java Persistence API entities. For information about entities, see Chapter 24, Introduction to the Java Persistence API.

What Is a Session Bean?

A *session bean* represents a single client inside the Application Server. To access an application that is deployed on the server, the client invokes the session bean's methods. The session bean performs work for its client, shielding the client from complexity by executing business tasks inside the server.

As its name suggests, a session bean is similar to an interactive session. A session bean is not shared; it can have only one client, in the same way that an interactive session can have only one user. Like an interactive session, a session bean is not persistent. (That is, its data is not saved to a database.) When the client terminates, its session bean appears to terminate and is no longer associated with the client.

For code samples, see Chapter 22.

State Management Modes

There are two types of session beans: stateful and stateless.

Stateful Session Beans

The state of an object consists of the values of its instance variables. In a *stateful* session bean, the instance variables represent the state of a unique client-bean session. Because the client interacts ("talks") with its bean, this state is often called the *conversational state*.

The state is retained for the duration of the client-bean session. If the client removes the bean or terminates, the session ends and the state disappears. This transient nature of the state is not a problem, however, because when the conversation between the client and the bean ends there is no need to retain the state.

Stateless Session Beans

A *stateless* session bean does not maintain a conversational state with the client. When a client invokes the methods of a stateless bean, the bean's instance variables may contain a state specific to that client, but only for the duration of the invocation. When the method is finished, the client-specific state should not be retained. Clients may, however, change the state of instance variables in pooled stateless beans, and this state is held over to the next invocation of the pooled stateless bean. Except during method invocation, all instances of a stateless bean are equivalent, allowing the EJB container to assign an instance to any client. That is, the state of a stateless session bean should apply accross all clients.

Because stateless session beans can support multiple clients, they can offer better scalability for applications that require large numbers of clients. Typically, an application requires fewer stateless session beans than stateful session beans to support the same number of clients.

A stateless session bean can implement a web service, but other types of enterprise beans cannot.

When to Use Session Beans

In general, you should use a session bean if the following circumstances hold:

- At any given time, only one client has access to the bean instance.
- The state of the bean is not persistent, existing only for a short period (perhaps a few hours).
- The bean implements a web service.

Stateful session beans are appropriate if any of the following conditions are true:

- The bean's state represents the interaction between the bean and a specific client.
- The bean needs to hold information about the client across method invocations.
- The bean mediates between the client and the other components of the application, presenting a simplified view to the client.
- Behind the scenes, the bean manages the work flow of several enterprise beans. For an example, see the `AccountControllerBean` session bean in Chapter 37.

To improve performance, you might choose a stateless session bean if it has any of these traits:

- The bean's state has no data for a specific client.
- In a single method invocation, the bean performs a generic task for all clients. For example, you might use a stateless session bean to send an email that confirms an online order.

What Is a Message-Driven Bean?

A *message-driven bean* is an enterprise bean that allows Java EE applications to process messages asynchronously. It normally acts as a JMS message listener, which is similar to an event listener except that it receives JMS messages instead of events. The messages can be sent by any Java EE component—an application client, another enterprise bean, or a web component—or by a JMS application or system that does not use Java EE technology. Message-driven beans can process JMS messages or other kinds of messages.

For a simple code sample, see Chapter 23. For more information about using message-driven beans, see Using the JMS API in a Java EE Application (page 1119) and Chapter 32.

What Makes Message-Driven Beans Different from Session Beans?

The most visible difference between message-driven beans and session beans is that clients do not access message-driven beans through interfaces. Interfaces are described in the section Defining Client Access with Interfaces (page 749). Unlike a session bean, a message-driven bean has only a bean class.

In several respects, a message-driven bean resembles a stateless session bean.

- A message-driven bean's instances retain no data or conversational state for a specific client.
- All instances of a message-driven bean are equivalent, allowing the EJB container to assign a message to any message-driven bean instance. The container can pool these instances to allow streams of messages to be processed concurrently.
- A single message-driven bean can process messages from multiple clients.

The instance variables of the message-driven bean instance can contain some state across the handling of client messages—for example, a JMS API connection, an open database connection, or an object reference to an enterprise bean object.

Client components do not locate message-driven beans and invoke methods directly on them. Instead, a client accesses a message-driven bean through, for example, JMS by sending messages to the message destination for which the message-driven bean class is the `MessageListener`. You assign a message-driven bean's destination during deployment by using Application Server resources.

Message-driven beans have the following characteristics:

- They execute upon receipt of a single client message.
- They are invoked asynchronously.
- They are relatively short-lived.
- They do not represent directly shared data in the database, but they can access and update this data.
- They can be transaction-aware.
- They are stateless.

When a message arrives, the container calls the message-driven bean's `onMessage` method to process the message. The `onMessage` method normally casts the message to one of the five JMS message types and handles it in accordance with the application's business logic. The `onMessage` method can call helper methods, or it can invoke a session bean to process the information in the message or to store it in a database.

A message can be delivered to a message-driven bean within a transaction context, so all operations within the `onMessage` method are part of a single transaction. If message processing is rolled back, the message will be redelivered. For more information, see Chapter 23.

When to Use Message-Driven Beans

Session beans allow you to send JMS messages and to receive them synchronously, but not asynchronously. To avoid tying up server resources, do not to use blocking synchronous receives in a server-side component, and in general JMS messages should not be sent or received synchronously. To receive messages asynchronously, use a message-driven bean.

Defining Client Access with Interfaces

The material in this section applies only to session beans and not to message-driven beans. Because they have a different programming model, message-driven beans do not have interfaces that define client access.

A client can access a session bean only through the methods defined in the bean's business interface. The business interface defines the client's view of a bean. All other aspects of the bean—method implementations and deployment settings—are hidden from the client.

Well-designed interfaces simplify the development and maintenance of Java EE applications. Not only do clean interfaces shield the clients from any complexities in the EJB tier, but they also allow the beans to change internally without affecting the clients. For example, if you change a session bean from a stateless to a stateful session bean, you won't have to alter the client code. But if you were to change the method definitions in the interfaces, then you might have to modify the client code as well. Therefore, it is important that you design the interfaces carefully to isolate your clients from possible changes in the beans.

Session beans can have more than one business interface. Session beans should, but are not required to, implement their business interface or interfaces.

When you design a Java EE application, one of the first decisions you make is the type of client access allowed by the enterprise beans: remote, local, or web service.

Remote Clients

A remote client of an enterprise bean has the following traits:

- It can run on a different machine and a different Java virtual machine (JVM) than the enterprise bean it accesses. (It is not required to run on a different JVM.)
- It can be a web component, an application client, or another enterprise bean.
- To a remote client, the location of the enterprise bean is transparent.

To create an enterprise bean that allows remote access, you must do one of the following:

- Decorate the business interface of the enterprise bean with the `@Remote` annotation:

```
@Remote
public interface InterfaceName {
   ...
}
```

- Decorate the bean class with `@Remote`, specifying the business interface(s):

```
@Remote(InterfaceName.class)
public class BeanName implements InterfaceName {
   ...
}
```

The *remote interface* defines the business and life cycle methods that are specific to the bean. For example, the remote interface of a bean named `BankAccount-Bean` might have business methods named `deposit` and `credit`. Figure 20–1 shows how the interface controls the client's view of an enterprise bean.

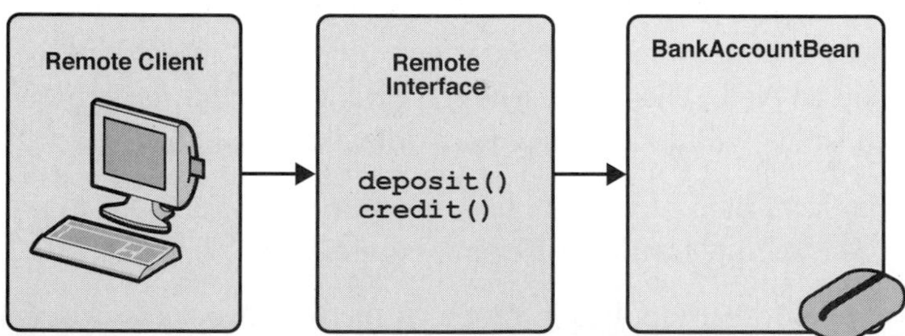

Figure 20–1 Interfaces for an Enterprise Bean with Remote Access

Local Clients

A local client has these characteristics:

- It must run in the same JVM as the enterprise bean it accesses.
- It can be a web component or another enterprise bean.
- To the local client, the location of the enterprise bean it accesses is not transparent.

The *local business interface* defines thc bean's business and life cycle methods. If the bean's business interface is not decorated with `@Local` or `@Remote`, and the bean class does not specify the interface using `@Local` or `@Remote`, the business interface is by default a local interface. To build an enterprise bean that allows only local access, you may, but are not required to do one of the following:

- Annotate the business interface of the enterprise bean as a `@Local` interface. For example:

  ```
  @Local
  public interface InterfaceName {
  ...
  }
  ```

- Specify the interface by decorating the bean class with `@Local` and specify the interface name. For example:

  ```
  @Local(InterfaceName.class)
  public class BeanName implements InterfaceName {
  ...
  }
  ```

Deciding on Remote or Local Access

Whether to allow local or remote access depends on the following factors.

- **Tight or loose coupling of related beans**: Tightly coupled beans depend on one another. For example, if a session bean that processes sales orders calls a session bean that emails a confirmation message to the customer, these beans are tightly coupled. Tightly coupled beans are good candidates for local access. Because they fit together as a logical unit, they typically call each other often and would benefit from the increased performance that is possible with local access.
- **Type of client**: If an enterprise bean is accessed by application clients, then it should allow remote access. In a production environment, these clients

almost always run on different machines than the Application Server. If an enterprise bean's clients are web components or other enterprise beans, then the type of access depends on how you want to distribute your components.

- **Component distribution**: Java EE applications are scalable because their server-side components can be distributed across multiple machines. In a distributed application, for example, the web components may run on a different server than do the enterprise beans they access. In this distributed scenario, the enterprise beans should allow remote access.
- **Performance**: Due to factors such as network latency, remote calls may be slower than local calls. On the other hand, if you distribute components among different servers, you may improve the application's overall performance. Both of these statements are generalizations; actual performance can vary in different operational environments. Nevertheless, you should keep in mind how your application design might affect performance.

If you aren't sure which type of access an enterprise bean should have, choose remote access. This decision gives you more flexibility. In the future you can distribute your components to accommodate the growing demands on your application.

Although it is uncommon, it is possible for an enterprise bean to allow both remote and local access. If this is the case, either the business interface of the bean must be explicitly designated as a business interface by being decorated with the `@Remote` or `@Local` annotations, or the bean class must explicitly designate the business interfaces by using the `@Remote` and `@Local` annotations. The same business interface cannot be both a local and remote business interface.

Web Service Clients

A web service client can access a Java EE application in two ways. First, the client can access a web service created with JAX-WS. (For more information on JAX-WS, see Chapter 15, Building Web Services with JAX-WS, page 507.) Second, a web service client can invoke the business methods of a stateless session bean. Message beans cannot be accessed by web service clients.

Provided that it uses the correct protocols (SOAP, HTTP, WSDL), any web service client can access a stateless session bean, whether or not the client is written in the Java programming language. The client doesn't even "know" what technology implements the service—stateless session bean, JAX-WS, or some other technology. In addition, enterprise beans and web components can be clients of web services. This flexibility enables you to integrate Java EE applications with web services.

A web service client accesses a stateless session bean through the bean's web service endpoint implementation class. By default, all public methods in the bean class are accessible to web service clients. The `@WebMethod` annotation may be used to customize the behavior of web service methods. If the `@WebMethod` annotation is used to decorate the bean class's methods, only those methods decorated with `@WebMethod` are exposed to web service clients.

For a code sample, see A Web Service Example: helloservice (page 780).

Method Parameters and Access

The type of access affects the parameters of the bean methods that are called by clients. The following topics apply not only to method parameters but also to method return values.

Isolation

The parameters of remote calls are more isolated than those of local calls. With remote calls, the client and bean operate on different copies of a parameter object. If the client changes the value of the object, the value of the copy in the bean does not change. This layer of isolation can help protect the bean if the client accidentally modifies the data.

In a local call, both the client and the bean can modify the same parameter object. In general, you should not rely on this side effect of local calls. Perhaps someday you will want to distribute your components, replacing the local calls with remote ones.

As with remote clients, web service clients operate on different copies of parameters than does the bean that implements the web service.

Granularity of Accessed Data

Because remote calls are likely to be slower than local calls, the parameters in remote methods should be relatively coarse-grained. A coarse-grained object contains more data than a fine-grained one, so fewer access calls are required. For the same reason, the parameters of the methods called by web service clients should also be coarse-grained.

The Contents of an Enterprise Bean

To develop an enterprise bean, you must provide the following files:

- **Enterprise bean class**: Implements the methods defined in the business interface and any life cycle callback methods.
- **Business Interfaces**: The business interface defines the methods implemented by the enterprise bean class.
- **Helper classes**: Other classes needed by the enterprise bean class, such as exception and utility classes.

You package the files in the preceding list into an EJB JAR file, the module that stores the enterprise bean. An EJB JAR file is portable and can be used for different applications. To assemble a Java EE application, you package one or more modules—such as EJB JAR files—into an EAR file, the archive file that holds the application. When you deploy the EAR file that contains the bean's EJB JAR file, you also deploy the enterprise bean to the Application Server. You can also deploy an EJB JAR that is not contained in an EAR file. Figure 20–2 shows the contents of an EJB JAR file.

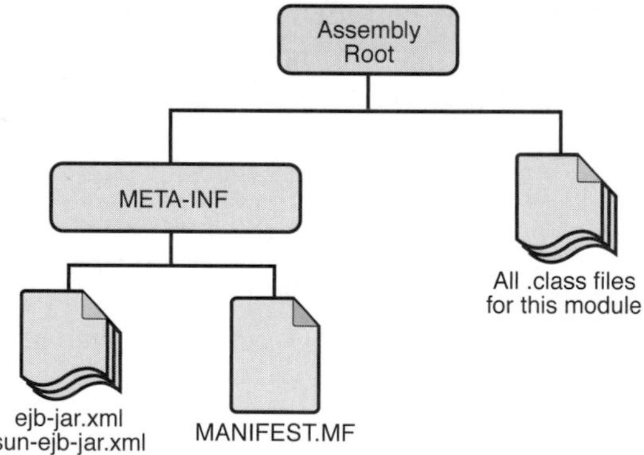

Figure 20–2 Structure of an Enterprise Bean JAR

Naming Conventions for Enterprise Beans

Because enterprise beans are composed of multiple parts, it's useful to follow a naming convention for your applications. Table 20–2 summarizes the conventions for the example beans in this tutorial.

Table 20–2 Naming Conventions for Enterprise Beans

Item	Syntax	Example
Enterprise bean name	`<name>Bean`	`AccountBean`
Enterprise bean class	`<name>Bean`	`AccountBean`
Business interface	`<name>`	`Account`

The Life Cycles of Enterprise Beans

An enterprise bean goes through various stages during its lifetime, or life cycle. Each type of enterprise bean—stateful session, stateless session, or message-driven—has a different life cycle.

The descriptions that follow refer to methods that are explained along with the code examples in the next two chapters. If you are new to enterprise beans, you should skip this section and run the code examples first.

The Life Cycle of a Stateful Session Bean

Figure 20–3 illustrates the stages that a session bean passes through during its lifetime. The client initiates the life cycle by obtaining a reference to a stateful session bean. The container performs any dependency injection and then invokes the method annotated with `@PostConstruct`, if any. The bean is now ready to have its business methods invoked by the client.

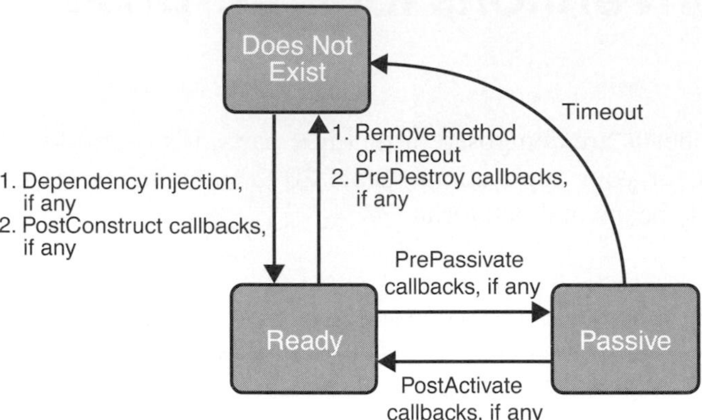

Figure 20–3 Life Cycle of a Stateful Session Bean

While in the ready stage, the EJB container may decide to deactivate, or *passivate*, the bean by moving it from memory to secondary storage. (Typically, the EJB container uses a least-recently-used algorithm to select a bean for passivation.) The EJB container invokes the method annotated `@PrePassivate`, if any, immediately before passivating it. If a client invokes a business method on the bean while it is in the passive stage, the EJB container activates the bean, calls the method annotated `@PostActivate`, if any, and then moves it to the ready stage.

At the end of the life cycle, the client invokes a method annotated `@Remove`, and the EJB container calls the method annotated `@PreDestroy`, if any. The bean's instance is then ready for garbage collection.

Your code controls the invocation of only one life-cycle method: the method annotated `@Remove`. All other methods in Figure 20–3 are invoked by the EJB container. See Chapter 34 for more information.

The Life Cycle of a Stateless Session Bean

Because a stateless session bean is never passivated, its life cycle has only two stages: nonexistent and ready for the invocation of business methods. Figure 20–4 illustrates the stages of a stateless session bean.

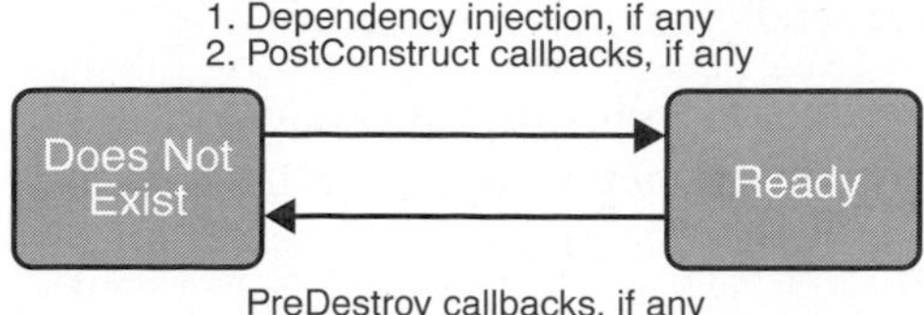

Figure 20–4 Life Cycle of a Stateless Session Bean

The client initiates the life cycle by obtaining a reference to a stateless session bean. The container performs any dependency injection and then invokes the method annotated `@PostConstruct`, if any. The bean is now ready to have its business methods invoked by the client.

At the end of the life cycle, the EJB container calls the method annotated `@PreDestroy`, if any. The bean's instance is then ready for garbage collection.

The Life Cycle of a Message-Driven Bean

Figure 20–5 illustrates the stages in the life cycle of a message-driven bean.

The EJB container usually creates a pool of message-driven bean instances. For each instance, the EJB container performs these tasks:

1. If the message-driven bean uses dependency injection, the container injects these references before instantiating the instance.
2. The container calls the method annotated `@PostConstruct`, if any.

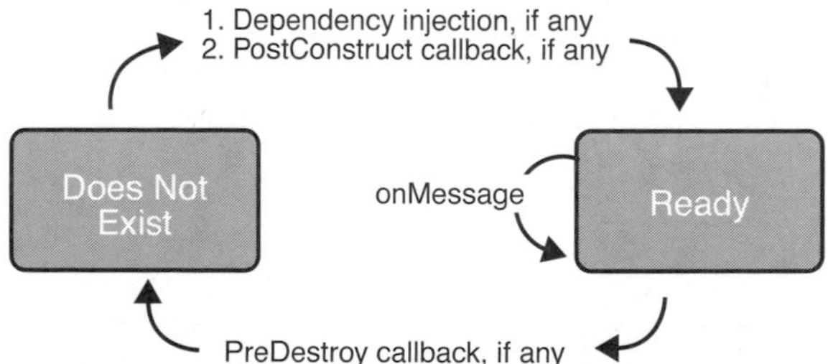

Figure 20–5 Life Cycle of a Message-Driven Bean

Like a stateless session bean, a message-driven bean is never passivated, and it has only two states: nonexistent and ready to receive messages.

At the end of the life cycle, the container calls the method annotated `@PreDestroy`, if any. The bean's instance is then ready for garbage collection.

Further Information

For further information on Enterprise JavaBeans technology, see the following:

- Enterprise JavaBeans 3.0 specification:
  `http://java.sun.com/products/ejb/docs.html`
- The Enterprise JavaBeans web site:
  `http://java.sun.com/products/ejb`

21

Getting Started with Enterprise Beans

THIS chapter shows how to develop, deploy, and run a simple Java EE application named `converter`. The purpose of `converter` is to calculate currency conversions between Japanese yen and Eurodollars. `converter` consists of an enterprise bean, which performs the calculations, and two types of clients: an application client and a web client.

Here's an overview of the steps you'll follow in this chapter:

1. Create the enterprise bean: `ConverterBean`.
2. Create the application client: `ConverterClient`.
3. Create the web client in `converter-war`.
4. Deploy `converter` onto the server.
5. Run the application client.
6. Using a browser, run the web client.

Before proceeding, make sure that you've done the following:

- Read Chapter 1.
- Become familiar with enterprise beans (see Chapter 20).
- Started the server (see Starting and Stopping the Application Server, page 27).

Creating the Enterprise Bean

The enterprise bean in our example is a stateless session bean called ConverterBean. The source code for ConverterBean is in the *<INSTALL>*/javaeetutorial5/examples/ejb/converter/converter-ejb/src/java/ directory.

Creating ConverterBean requires these steps:

1. Coding the bean's business interface and class (the source code is provided)
2. Compiling the source code with the Ant tool

Coding the Enterprise Bean

The enterprise bean in this example needs the following code:

- Remote business interface
- Enterprise bean class

Coding the Business Interface

The *business interface* defines the business methods that a client can call. The business methods are implemented in the enterprise bean class. The source code for the Converter remote business interface follows.

```
package com.sun.tutorial.javaee.ejb;

import java.math.BigDecimal;
import javax.ejb.Remote;

@Remote
public interface Converter {
  public BigDecimal dollarToYen(BigDecimal dollars);
  public BigDecimal yenToEuro(BigDecimal yen);
}
```

Note the @Remote annotation decorating the interface definition. This lets the container know that ConverterBean will be accessed by remote clients.

Coding the Enterprise Bean Class

The enterprise bean class for this example is called `ConverterBean`. This class implements the two business methods (`dollarToYen` and `yenToEuro`) that the `Converter` remote business interface defines. The source code for the `ConverterBean` class follows.

```
package com.sun.tutorial.javaee.ejb;

import java.math.BigDecimal;
import javax.ejb.*;

@Stateless
public class ConverterBean implements Converter {
  private BigDecimal yenRate = new BigDecimal("115.3100");
  private BigDecimal euroRate = new BigDecimal("0.0071");

  public BigDecimal dollarToYen(BigDecimal dollars) {
    BigDecimal result = dollars.multiply(yenRate);
    return result.setScale(2, BigDecimal.ROUND_UP);
  }

  public BigDecimal yenToEuro(BigDecimal yen) {
    BigDecimal result = yen.multiply(euroRate);
    return result.setScale(2, BigDecimal.ROUND_UP);
  }
}
```

Note the `@Stateless` annotation decorating the enterprise bean class. This lets the container know that `ConverterBean` is a stateless session bean.

Compiling and Packaging the converter Example

Now you are ready to compile the remote business interface (`Converter.java`) and the enterprise bean class (`ConverterBean.java`), and package the compiled classes into an enterprise bean JAR.

Compiling and Packaging the converter Example in NetBeans 5.5

Follow these instructions to build and package the `converter` example in NetBeans 5.5.

1. In NetBeans 5.5, select File→Open Project.
2. In the Open Project dialog, navigate to `<INSTALL>/javaeetutorial5/examples/ejb/`.
3. Select the `converter` folder.
4. Select the Open as Main Project and Open Required Projects checkboxes.
5. Click Open Project Folder.
6. In the Projects tab, right-click the `converter` project and select Build Project. You will see the output in the Output tab.

Compiling and Packaging the converter Example Using Ant

To compile and package `converter` using Ant, do the following:

1. In a terminal window, go to this directory:

   ```
   <INSTALL>/javaeetutorial5/examples/ejb/converter/
   ```

2. Type the following command:

   ```
   ant
   ```

This command calls the `default` task, which compiles the source files for the enterprise bean and the application client, placing the class files in the `build` subdirectories (not the `src` directory) of each submodule. Then the default task packages each submodule into the appropriate package file: `converter-app-client.jar` for the application client, `converter-ejb.jar` for the enterprise bean JAR, and `converter-war.war` for the web client. The web client in this example requires no compilation. For more information about the Ant tool, see Building the Examples (page xxxv).

Note: When compiling the code, the preceding `ant` task includes the `javaee.jar` file in the classpath. This file resides in the `lib` directory of your Application Server installation. If you plan to use other tools to compile the source code for Java EE components, make sure that the classpath includes the `javaee.jar` file.

Creating the Application Client

An application client is a program written in the Java programming language. At runtime, the client program executes in a different virtual machine than the Application Server. For detailed information on the `appclient` command-line tool, see the man page at `http://java.sun.com/javaee/5/docs/relnotes/cliref/index.html`.

The application client in this example requires two JAR files. The first JAR file is for the Java EE component of the client. This JAR file contains the client's deployment descriptor and class files; it is created when you run the New Application Client wizard. Defined by the *Java EE Specification*, this JAR file is portable across all compliant application servers.

The second JAR file contains all the classes that are required by the client program at runtime. These classes enable the client to access the enterprise beans that are running in the Application Server. The JAR file is retrieved before you run the application. Because this retrieved JAR file is not covered by the Java EE specification, it is implementation-specific, intended only for the Application Server.

The application client source code is in the `ConverterClient.java` file, which is in this directory:

```
<INSTALL>/javaeetutorial5/examples/ejb/converter/converter-
app-client/src/java/
```

You compiled this code along with the enterprise bean code in the section Compiling and Packaging the converter Example (page 761).

Coding the Application Client

The `ConverterClient.java` source code illustrates the basic tasks performed by the client of an enterprise bean:

- Creating an enterprise bean instance
- Invoking a business method

Creating a Reference to an Enterprise Bean Instance

Java EE application clients refer to enterprise bean instances by annotating static fields with the `@EJB` annotation. The annotated static field represents the enterprise bean's business interface, which will resolve to the session bean instance when the application client container injects the resource references at runtime.

```
@EJB
private static Converter converter;
```

The field is static because the client class runs in a static context.

Invoking a Business Method

Calling a business method is easy: you simply invoke the method on the injected `Converter` object. The EJB container will invoke the corresponding method on the `ConverterBean` instance that is running on the server. The client invokes the `dollarToYen` business method in the following lines of code.

```
BigDecimal param = new BigDecimal ("100.00");
BigDecimal amount = currencyConverter.dollarToYen(param);
```

ConverterClient Source Code

The full source code for the `ConverterClient` program follows.

```
package com.sun.tutorial.javaee.ejb;

import java.math.BigDecimal;
import javax.ejb.EJB;

public class ConverterClient {
  @EJB
  private static Converter converter;

  public ConverterClient(String[] args) {
  }

  public static void main(String[] args) {
    ConverterClient client = new ConverterClient(args);
    client.doConversion();
  }
```

```
    public void doConversion() {
        try {
            BigDecimal param = new BigDecimal("100.00");
            BigDecimal yenAmount = converter.dollarToYen(param);

            System.out.println("$" + param + " is " + yenAmount
                    + " Yen.");
            BigDecimal euroAmount = converter.yenToEuro(yenAmount);
            System.out.println(yenAmount + " Yen is " + euroAmount
                    + " Euro.");

            System.exit(0);
        } catch (Exception ex) {
            System.err.println("Caught an unexpected exception!");
            ex.printStackTrace();
        }
    }
}
```

Compiling the Application Client

The application client files are compiled at the same time as the enterprise bean files, as described in Compiling and Packaging the converter Example (page 761).

Creating the Web Client

The web client is contained in the JSP page *<INSTALL>*/javaeetutorial5/examples/ejb/converter/converter-war/web/index.jsp. A JSP page is a text-based document that contains JSP elements, which construct dynamic content, and static template data, which can be expressed in any text-based format such as HTML, WML, and XML.

Coding the Web Client

The statements (in bold in the following code) for locating the business interface, creating an enterprise bean instance, and invoking a business method are nearly identical to those of the application client. The parameter of the lookup method is the only difference.

The classes needed by the client are declared using a JSP page directive (enclosed within the `<%@ %>` characters). Because locating the business interface and creating the enterprise bean are performed only once, this code appears in a JSP declaration (enclosed within the `<%! %>` characters) that contains the initialization method, `jspInit`, of the JSP page. The declaration is followed by standard HTML markup for creating a form that contains an input field. A scriptlet (enclosed within the `<% %>` characters) retrieves a parameter from the request and converts it to a `BigDecimal` object. Finally, a JSP scriptlet invokes the enterprise bean's business methods, and JSP expressions (enclosed within the `<%= %>` characters) insert the results into the stream of data returned to the client.

```
<%@ page import="converter.ejb.Converter,
        java.math.*, javax.naming.*"%>

<%!
  private Converter converter = null;
  public void jspInit() {
     try {
        InitialContext ic = new InitialContext();
        converter = (Converter)
             ic.lookup(Converter.class.getName());
     } catch (Exception ex) {
        System.out.println("Couldn't create converter bean."+
             ex.getMessage());
     }
  }

  public void jspDestroy() {
     converter = null;
  }
%>
<html>
  <head>
     <title>Converter</title>
  </head>

  <body bgcolor="white">
     <h1>Converter</h1>
     <hr>
     <p>Enter an amount to convert:</p>
     <form method="get">
        <input type="text" name="amount" size="25">
        <br>
        <p>
        <input type="submit" value="Submit">
        <input type="reset" value="Reset">
```

```
      </form>

      <%
         String amount = request.getParameter("amount");
         if ( amount != null && amount.length() > 0 ) {
            BigDecimal d = new BigDecimal(amount);

            BigDecimal yenAmount = converter.dollarToYen(d);
      %>
      <p>
      <%= amount %> dollars are  <%= yenAmount %>  Yen.
      <p>
      <%
            BigDecimal euroAmount =
                converter.yenToEuro(yenAmount);
      %>
      <%= amount %> Yen are <%= euroAmount %>  Euro.
      <%
         }
      %>
   </body>
</html>
```

Compiling the Web Client

The Application Server automatically compiles web clients that are JSP pages. If the web client were a servlet, you would have to compile it.

Deploying the Java EE Application

Now that the Java EE application contains the components, it is ready for deployment. You can deploy the application using either NetBeans 5.5 or Ant.

Deploying the converter Example Using NetBeans 5.5

Follow these instructions to deploy the `converter` example to your Application Server instance using NetBeans 5.5.

1. In NetBeans 5.5, make sure the `converter` application is open.
2. In the Projects tab, right-click the `converter` project and select Deploy Project. You will see the output in the Output tab.

Deploying the converter Example Using Ant

To deploy `converter.ear` using Ant, run the deploy task.

```
ant deploy
```

`converter.ear` will be deployed to the Application Server.

Running the Application Client

When you run the application client, the application client container first injects the resources specified in the client and then runs the client. You can run the application client using either NetBeans 5.5 or Ant.

Running the Application Client Using NetBeans 5.5

Follow these instructions to run the application client using NetBeans 5.5.

1. In NetBeans 5.5, make sure the `converter` application is open.
2. In the Projects tab, right-click the `converter` project and select Run Project. You will see the following output in the Output tab:

```
...
$100.00 is 11258.00 Yen.
11258.00 Yen is 78.81 Euro.
...
```

Running the Application Client Using Ant

To run the application client using Ant, perform the following steps.

1. In a terminal window, go to this directory:

   `<INSTALL>/javaeetutorial5/examples/ejb/converter/`

2. Type the following command:

   ```
   ant run
   ```

   This task will retrieve the application client JAR, `converterClient.jar` and run the retrieved client JAR. `converterClient.jar` contains the application client class and the support classes needed to access `ConverterBean`. Although we are using Ant to run the client, this task is the equivalent of running:

   ```
   appclient -client client-jar/converterClient.jar
   ```

3. In the terminal window, the client displays these lines:

   ```
   ...
   $100.00 is 11531.00 Yen.
   11531.00 Yen is 81.88 Euro.
   ...
   ```

Running the Web Client

To run the web client, point your browser at the following URL. Replace *<host>* with the name of the host running the Application Server. If your browser is running on the same host as the Application Server, you can replace *<host>* with `localhost`.

```
http://<host>:8080/converter
```

After entering `100` in the input field and clicking Submit, you should see the screen shown in Figure 21–1.

Figure 21–1 `converter` Web Client

Modifying the Java EE Application

The Application Server supports iterative development. Whenever you make a change to a Java EE application, you must redeploy the application.

Modifying a Class File

To modify a class file in an enterprise bean, you change the source code, recompile it, and redeploy the application. For example, if you want to change the exchange rate in the `dollarToYen` business method of the `ConverterBean` class, you would follow these steps.

1. Edit `ConverterBean.java`.
2. Recompile `ConverterBean.java`.
   a. In a terminal window, go to the `<INSTALL>/javaeetutorial5/examples/ejb/converter/` subdirectory.
   b. Type `ant`. This runs the `default` task, which repackages the entire application (application client, enterprise bean JAR, and web client).
3. Type `ant deploy`.

To modify the contents of a WAR file, or to modify the application client, follow the preceding steps.

22

Session Bean Examples

SESSION beans provide a simple but powerful way to encapsulate business logic within an application. They can be accessed from remote Java clients, web service clients, and from components running in the same server.

In Chapter 21, you built a stateless session bean named `ConverterBean`. This chapter examines the source code of three more session beans:

- `CartBean`: a stateful session bean that is accessed by a remote client
- `HelloServiceBean`: a stateless session bean that implements a web service
- `TimerSessionBean`: a stateless session bean that sets a timer

The cart Example

The `cart` session bean represents a shopping cart in an online bookstore. The bean's client can add a book to the cart, remove a book, or retrieve the cart's contents. To assemble `cart`, you need the following code:

- Session bean class (`CartBean`)
- Remote business interface (`Cart`)

All session beans require a session bean class. All enterprise beans that permit remote access must have a remote business interface. To meet the needs of a specific application, an enterprise bean may also need some helper classes. The CartBean session bean uses two helper classes (BookException and IdVerifier) which are discussed in the section Helper Classes (page 777).

The source code for this example is in the *<INSTALL>*/javaeetutorial5/examples/ejb/cart/ directory.

The Business Interface

The Cart business interface is a plain Java interface that defines all the business methods implemented in the bean class. If the bean class implements a single interface, that interface is assumed to the business interface. The business interface is a local interface unless it is annotated with the javax.ejb.Remote annotation; the javax.ejb.Local annotation is optional in this case.

The bean class may implement more than one interface. If the bean class implements more than one interface, either the business interfaces must be explicitly annotated either @Local or @Remote, or the business interfaces must be specified by decorating the bean class with @Local or @Remote. However, the following interfaces are excluded when determining if the bean class implements more than one interface:

- java.io.Serializable
- java.io.Externalizable
- Any of the interfaces defined by the javax.ejb package

The source code for the Cart business interface follows:

```
package com.sun.tutorial.javaee.ejb;

import java.util.List;
import javax.ejb.Remote;

@Remote
public interface Cart {
  public void initialize(String person) throws BookException;
  public void initialize(String person, String id)
    throws BookException;
  public void addBook(String title);
```

```
    public void removeBook(String title) throws BookException;
    public List<String> getContents();
    public void remove();
}
```

Session Bean Class

The session bean class for this example is called `CartBean`. Like any stateful session bean, the `CartBean` class must meet these requirements:

- The class is annotated `@Stateful`.
- The class implements the business methods defined in the business interface.

Stateful session beans also may:

- Implement the business interface, a plain Java interface. It is good practice to implement the bean's business interface.
- Implement any optional life cycle callback methods, annotated `@PostConstruct`, `@PreDestroy`, `@PostActivate`, and `@PrePassivate`.
- Implement any optional business methods annotated `@Remove`.

The source code for the `CartBean` class follows.

```
package com.sun.tutorial.javaee.ejb;

import java.util.ArrayList;
import java.util.List;
import javax.ejb.Remove;
import javax.ejb.Stateful;

@Stateful
public class CartBean implements Cart {
    String customerName;
    String customerId;
    List<String> contents;

    public void initialize(String person) throws BookException {
        if (person == null) {
            throw new BookException("Null person not allowed.");
        } else {
            customerName = person;
        }

        customerId = "0";
```

```
        contents = new ArrayList<String>();
    }

    public void initialize(String person, String id)
            throws BookException {
        if (person == null) {
            throw new BookException("Null person not allowed.");
        } else {

            customerName = person;
        }

        IdVerifier idChecker = new IdVerifier();

        if (idChecker.validate(id)) {
            customerId = id;
        } else {
            throw new BookException("Invalid id: " + id);
        }

        contents = new ArrayList<String>();
    }

    public void addBook(String title) {
        contents.add(title);
    }

    public void removeBook(String title) throws BookException {
        boolean result = contents.remove(title);
        if (result == false) {
            throw new BookException(title + " not in cart.");
        }
    }

    public List<String> getContents() {
        return contents;
    }

    @Remove
    public void remove() {
        contents = null;
    }
}
```

Life-Cycle Callback Methods

Methods in the bean class may be declared as a life-cycle callback method by annotating the method with the following annotations:

- `javax.annotation.PostConstruct`
- `javax.annotation.PreDestroy`
- `javax.ejb.PostActivate`
- `javax.ejb.PrePassivate`

Life-cycle callback methods must return `void` and have no parameters.

`@PostConstruct` methods are invoked by the container on newly constructed bean instances after all dependency injection has completed and before the first business method is invoked on the enterprise bean.

`@PreDestroy` methods are invoked after any method annotated `@Remove` has completed, and before the container removes the enterprise bean instance.

`@PostActivate` methods are invoked by the container after the container moves the bean from secondary storage to active status.

`@PrePassivate` methods are invoked by the container before the container passivates the enterprise bean, meaning the container temporarily removes the bean from the environment and saves it to secondary storage.

Business Methods

The primary purpose of a session bean is to run business tasks for the client. The client invokes business methods on the object reference it gets from dependency injection or JNDI lookup. From the client's perspective, the business methods appear to run locally, but they actually run remotely in the session bean. The following code snippet shows how the `CartClient` program invokes the business methods:

```
cart.create("Duke DeEarl", "123");
...
cart.addBook("Bel Canto");
...
List<String> bookList = cart.getContents();
...
cart.removeBook("Gravity's Rainbow");
```

The CartBean class implements the business methods in the following code:

```
public void addBook(String title) {
   contents.addElement(title);
}

public void removeBook(String title) throws BookException {
   boolean result = contents.remove(title);
   if (result == false) {
      throw new BookException(title + "not in cart.");
   }
}

public List<String> getContents() {
   return contents;
}
```

The signature of a business method must conform to these rules:

- The method name must not begin with ejb to avoid conflicts with callback methods defined by the EJB architecture. For example, you cannot call a business method ejbCreate or ejbActivate.
- The access control modifier must be public.
- If the bean allows remote access via a remote business interface, the arguments and return types must be legal types for the Java RMI API.
- If the bean is a web service endpoint, the arguments and return types for the methods annotated @WebMethod must be legal types for JAX-WS.
- The modifier must not be static or final.

The throws clause can include exceptions that you define for your application. The removeBook method, for example, throws the BookException if the book is not in the cart.

To indicate a system-level problem, such as the inability to connect to a database, a business method should throw the javax.ejb.EJBException. The container will not wrap application exceptions such as BookException. Because EJBException is a subclass of RuntimeException, you do not need to include it in the throws clause of the business method.

The Remove Method

Business methods annotated with javax.ejb.Remove in the stateful session bean class can be invoked by enterprise bean clients to remove the bean instance.

The container will remove the enterprise bean after a `@Remove` method completes, either normally or abnormally.

In `CartBean`, the `remove` method is a `@Remove` method:

```
@Remove
public void remove() {
  contents = null;
}
```

Helper Classes

The `CartBean` session bean has two helper classes: `BookException` and `IdVerifier`. The `BookException` is thrown by the `removeBook` method, and the `IdVerifier` validates the `customerId` in one of the `create` methods. Helper classes may reside in the EJB JAR file that contains the enterprise bean class, or in an EAR that contains the EJB JAR.

Building, Packaging, Deploying, and Running the cart Example

You can build, package, deploy, and run the `cart` application using either NetBeans 5.5 or the Ant tool.

Building, Packaging, and Deploying the cart Example Using NetBeans 5.5

Follow these instructions to build, package, and deploy the `cart` example to your Application Server instance using the NetBeans 5.5 IDE.

1. In NetBeans 5.5, select File→Open Project.
2. In the Open Project dialog, navigate to `<INSTALL>/javaeetutorial5/examples/ejb/`.
3. Select the `cart` folder.
4. Select the Open as Main Project and Open Required Projects checkboxes.
5. Click Open Project Folder.
6. In the Projects tab, right-click the `cart` project and select Deploy Project.

This builds and packages the application into `cart.ear`, located in *<INSTALL>*/`javaeetutorial5/examples/ejb/cart/dist/`, and deploys this EAR file to your Application Server instance.

Running the Application Client Using NetBeans 5.5

To run `cart`'s application client, select Run→Run Main Project. You will see the output of the application client in the Output pane:

```
...
Retrieving book title from cart: Infinite Jest
Retrieving book title from cart: Bel Canto
Retrieving book title from cart: Kafka on the Shore
Removing "Gravity's Rainbow" from cart.
Caught a BookException: "Gravity's Rainbow" not in cart.
Java Result: 1
run-cart-app-client:
run-nb:
BUILD SUCCESSFUL (total time: 14 seconds)
```

Building, Packaging, and Deploying the cart Example Using Ant

Now you are ready to compile the remote interface (`Cart.java`), the home interface (`CartHome.java`), the enterprise bean class (`CartBean.java`), the client class (`CartClient.java`), and the helper classes (`BookException.java` and `IdVerifier.java`).

1. In a terminal window, go to this directory:

   <INSTALL>`/javaeetutorial5/examples/ejb/cart/`

2. Type the following command:

   ```
   ant
   ```

   This command calls the `default` target, which builds and packages the application into an EAR file, `cart.ear`, located in the `dist` directory.

3. Type the following command:

   ```
   ant deploy
   ```

   `cart.ear` will be deployed to the Application Server.

Running the Application Client Using Ant

When you run the client, the application client container injects any component references declared in the application client class, in this case the reference to the `Cart` enterprise bean. To run the application client, perform the following steps.

1. In a terminal window, go to this directory:

   `<INSTALL>/javaeetutorial5/examples/ejb/cart/`

2. Type the following command:

   ```
   ant run
   ```

   This task will retrieve the application client JAR, `cartClient.jar` and run the application client. `cartClient.jar` contains the application client class, the helper class `BookException`, and the `Cart` business interface.

   This is the equivalent of running:

   ```
   appclient -client cartClient.jar
   ```

3. In the terminal window, the client displays these lines:

   ```
   [echo] running application client container.
   [exec] Retrieving book title from cart: Infinite Jest
   [exec] Retrieving book title from cart: Bel Canto
   [exec] Retrieving book title from cart: Kafka on the Shore
   [exec] Removing "Gravity's Rainbow" from cart.
   [exec] Caught a BookException: "Gravity's Rainbow" not in
   cart.
   [exec] Result: 1
   ```

The all Task

As a convenience, the `all` task will build, package, deploy, and run the application. To do this, enter the following command:

```
ant all
```

Undeploying the cart Example

To undeploy `cart.ear` using NetBeans 5.5:

1. Click the Runtime tab.
2. Expand the Servers node and locate the Application Server instance to which you deployed `cart`.

3. Expand your Application Server instance node, then Applications→Enterprise Applications.
4. Right-click `cart` and select Undeploy.

To undeploy `cart.ear` using Ant, enter the following command:

```
ant undeploy
```

A Web Service Example: helloservice

This example demonstrates a simple web service that generates a response based on information received from the client. `HelloServiceBean` is a stateless session bean that implements a single method, `sayHello`. This method matches the `sayHello` method invoked by the client described in A Simple JAX-WS Client (page 513).

The Web Service Endpoint Implementation Class

`HelloServiceBean` is the endpoint implementation class. The endpoint implementation class is typically the primary programming artifact for enterprise bean web service endpoints. The web service endpoint implementation class has the following requirements:

- The class must be annotated with either the `javax.jws.WebService` or `javax.jws.WebServiceProvider` annotations.
- The implementing class may explicitly reference an SEI through the `endpointInterface` element of the `@WebService` annotation, but is not required to do so. If no `endpointInterface` is specified in `@WebService`, an SEI is implicitly defined for the implementing class.
- The business methods of the implementing class must be public, and must not be declared `static` or `final`.
- Business methods that are exposed to web service clients must be annotated with `javax.jws.WebMethod`.
- Business methods that are exposed to web service clients must have JAXB-compatible parameters and return types. See Default Data Type Bindings (page 523).

- The implementing class must not be declared `final` and must not be `abstract`.
- The implementing class must have a default public constructor.
- The endpoint class must be annotated `@Stateless`.
- The implementing class must not define the `finalize` method.
- The implementing class may use the `javax.annotation.PostConstruct` or `javax.annotation.PreDestroy` annotations on its methods for life-cycle event callbacks.

  The `@PostConstruct` method is called by the container before the implementing class begins responding to web service clients.

  The `@PreDestroy` method is called by the container before the endpoint is removed from operation.

Stateless Session Bean Implementation Class

The `HelloServiceBean` class implements the `sayHello` method, which is annotated `@WebMethod`. The source code for the `HelloServiceBean` class follows:

```
package com.sun.tutorial.javaee.ejb;

import javax.ejb.Stateless;
import javax.jws.WebMethod;
import javax.jws.WebService;

@Stateless
@WebService
public class HelloServiceBean {
  private String message = "Hello, ";

  public void HelloServiceBean() {}

  @WebMethod
  public String sayHello(String name) {
     return message + name + ".";
  }
}
```

Building, Packaging, Deploying, and Testing the helloservice Example

You can build, package, and deploy the `helloservice` example using either NetBeans 5.5 or Ant. You can then use the Admin Console to test the web service endpoint methods.

Building, Packaging, and Deploying the helloservice Example Using NetBeans 5.5

Follow these instructions to build, package, and deploy the `helloservice` example to your Application Server instance using the NetBeans 5.5 IDE.

1. In NetBeans 5.5, select File→Open Project.
2. In the Open Project dialog, navigate to `<INSTALL>/javaeetutorial5/examples/ejb/`.
3. Select the `helloservice` folder.
4. Select the Open as Main Project and Open Required Projects checkboxes.
5. Click Open Project Folder.
6. In the Projects tab, right-click the `helloservice` project and select Deploy Project.

This builds and packages to application into `helloservice.ear`, located in `<INSTALL>/javaeetutorial5/examples/ejb/helloservice/dist`, and deploys this ear file to your Application Server instance.

Building, Packaging, and Deploying the helloservice Example Using Ant

Follow these instructions to build, package, and deploy the `helloservice` example to your Application Server instance using Ant.

1. In a terminal window, go to the `<INSTALL>/javaeetutorial5/examples/ejb/helloservice/` directory.
2. To build `helloservice`, type the following command:

```
ant
```

This runs the `default` task, which compiles the source files and packages the application into a JAR file located at `<INSTALL>/examples/ejb/helloservice/dist/helloservice.jar`.

3. To deploy `helloservice`, type the following command:

   ```
   ant deploy
   ```

   Upon deployment, the Application Server generates additional artifacts required for web service invocation, including the WSDL file.

Testing the Service without a Client

The Application Server Admin Console allows you to test the methods of a web service endpoint. To test the `sayHello` method of `HelloServiceBean`, do the following:

1. Open the Admin Console by opening the following URL in a web browser:

   ```
   http://localhost:4848/
   ```

2. Enter the admin username and password to log in to the Admin Console.
3. Click Web Services in the left pane of the Admin Console.
4. Click `helloservice`.
5. Click Test.
6. Under Methods, enter a name as the parameter to the `sayHello` method.
7. Click the `sayHello` button.

   This will take you to the `sayHello` Method invocation page.

8. Under Method returned, you'll see the response from the endpoint.

Using the Timer Service

Applications that model business work flows often rely on timed notifications. The timer service of the enterprise bean container enables you to schedule timed notifications for all types of enterprise beans except for stateful session beans. You can schedule a timed notification to occur at a specific time, after a duration of time, or at timed intervals. For example, you could set timers to go off at 10:30 AM on May 23, in 30 days, or every 12 hours.

When a timer expires (goes off), the container calls the method annotated @Timeout in the bean's implementation class. The @Timeout method contains the business logic that handles the timed event.

The Timeout Method

Methods annotated @Timeout in the enterprise bean class must return void and take a javax.ejb.Timer object as the only parameter. They may not throw application exceptions.

```
@Timeout
public void timeout(Timer timer) {
   System.out.println("TimerBean: timeout occurred");
}
```

Creating Timers

To create a timer, the bean invokes one of the createTimer methods of the TimerService interface. (For details on the method signatures, see the TimerService API documentation.) When the bean invokes createTimer, the timer service begins to count down the timer duration.

The bean described in The timersession Example (page 786) creates a timer as follows:

```
Timer timer = timerService.createTimer(intervalDuration,
     "Created new timer");
```

In the timersession example, createTimer is invoked in a business method, which is called by a client.

Timers are persistent. If the server is shut down (or even crashes), timers are saved and will become active again when the server is restarted. If a timer expires while the server is down, the container will call the @Timeout method when the server is restarted.

The Date and long parameters of the createTimer methods represent time with the resolution of milliseconds. However, because the timer service is not intended for real-time applications, a callback to the @Timeout method might not occur with millisecond precision. The timer service is for business applications, which typically measure time in hours, days, or longer durations.

Canceling and Saving Timers

Timers can be canceled by the following events:

- When a single-event timer expires, the EJB container calls the `@Timeout` method and then cancels the timer.
- When the bean invokes the `cancel` method of the `Timer` interface, the container cancels the timer.

If a method is invoked on a canceled timer, the container throws the `javax.ejb.NoSuchObjectLocalException`.

To save a `Timer` object for future reference, invoke its `getHandle` method and store the `TimerHandle` object in a database. (A `TimerHandle` object is serializable.) To reinstantiate the `Timer` object, retrieve the handle from the database and invoke `getTimer` on the handle. A `TimerHandle` object cannot be passed as an argument of a method defined in a remote or web service interface. In other words, remote clients and web service clients cannot access a bean's `TimerHandle` object. Local clients, however, do not have this restriction.

Getting Timer Information

In addition to defining the `cancel` and `getHandle` methods, the `Timer` interface defines methods for obtaining information about timers:

```
public long getTimeRemaining();
public java.util.Date getNextTimeout();
public java.io.Serializable getInfo();
```

The `getInfo` method returns the object that was the last parameter of the `createTimer` invocation. For example, in the `createTimer` code snippet of the preceding section, this information parameter is a `String` object with the value `created timer`.

To retrieve all of a bean's active timers, call the `getTimers` method of the `TimerService` interface. The `getTimers` method returns a collection of `Timer` objects.

Transactions and Timers

An enterprise bean usually creates a timer within a transaction. If this transaction is rolled back, the timer creation is also rolled back. Similarly, if a bean cancels a timer within a transaction that gets rolled back, the timer cancellation is rolled back. In this case, the timer's duration is reset as if the cancellation had never occurred.

In beans that use container-managed transactions, the `@Timeout` method usually has the `Required` or `RequiresNew` transaction attribute to preserve transaction integrity. With these attributes, the EJB container begins the new transaction before calling the `@Timeout` method. If the transaction is rolled back, the container will call the `@Timeout` method at least one more time.

The timersession Example

The source code for this example is in the `<INSTALL>/javaeetutorial5/examples/ejb/timersession/timersession-ejb/src/java/` directory.

`TimerSessionBean` is a stateless session bean that shows how to set a timer. In the source code listing of `TimerSessionBean` that follows, note the `createTimer` and `@Timeout` methods. Because it's a business method, `createTimer` is defined in the bean's remote business interface (`TimerSession`) and can be invoked by the client. In this example, the client invokes `createTimer` with an interval duration of 30,000 milliseconds. The `createTimer` method creates a new timer by invoking the `createTimer` method of `TimerService`. `TimerService` which is injected by the container when the bean is created. Now that the timer is set, the EJB container will invoke the `timeout` method of `TimerSessionBean` when the timer expires—in about 30 seconds. Here's the source code for the `TimerSessionBean` class:

```
package com.sun.tutorial.javaee.ejb;

import java.util.logging.Logger;
import javax.annotation.Resource;
import javax.ejb.Stateless;
import javax.ejb.Timeout;
import javax.ejb.Timer;
import javax.ejb.TimerService;
```

```
@Stateless
public class TimerSessionBean implements TimerSession {
  @Resource
  TimerService timerService;

private static final Logger logger = Logger
    .getLogger("com.sun.tutorial.javaee.ejb.
         timersession.TimerSessionBean");

  public void createTimer(long intervalDuration) {
    Timer timer = timerService.createTimer(intervalDuration,
         "Created new timer");
  }

  @Timeout
  public void timeout(Timer timer) {
    logger.info("Timeout occurred");
  }
}
```

Building, Packaging, Deploying, and Running the timersession Example

You can build, package, deploy, and run the `timersession` example using either NetBeans 5.5 or Ant.

Building, Packaging, Deploying, and Running the timersession Example Using NetBeans 5.5

Follow these instructions to build, package, and deploy the `timersession` example to your Application Server instance using the NetBeans 5.5 IDE.

1. In NetBeans 5.5, select File→Open Project.
2. In the Open Project dialog, navigate to `<INSTALL>/javaeetutorial5/examples/ejb/`.
3. Select the `timersession` folder.
4. Select the Open as Main Project and Open Required Projects checkboxes.
5. Click Open Project Folder.
6. Select Run→Run Main Project.

This builds and packages the application into `timersession.ear`, located in `<INSTALL>/javaeetutorial5/examples/ejb/timersession/dist/`, deploys this EAR file to your Application Server instance, and then runs the application client.

You will see the output from the application client in the Output tab:

```
...
Creating a timer with an interval duration of 3000 ms.
run-timersession-app-client:
run-nb:
BUILD SUCCESSFUL (total time: 16 seconds)
```

The output from the timer is sent to the `server.log` file located in the `<JAVAEE_HOME>/domains/domain1/server/logs/` directory. To view this file:

1. Click the Runtime tab.
2. Right-click your Application Server instance and select View Server Log.

Look for the following line at the bottom of `server.log`:

```
Timeout occurred
```

Building, Packaging, and Deploying the timersession Example Using Ant

Follow these instructions to build, package, and deploy the `timersession` example to your Application Server instance using Ant.

1. In a terminal window, go to the `<INSTALL>/javaeetutorial5/examples/ejb/timersession/` directory.
2. To build `TimerSessionBean`, type the following command:

   ```
   ant build
   ```

   This runs the `default` task, which compiles the source files and packages the application into an EAR file located at `<INSTALL>/examples/ejb/timersession/dist/timersession.ear`.

3. To deploy the application, type the following command:

   ```
   ant deploy
   ```

Running the Application Client Using Ant

To run the application client, perform the following steps.

1. In a terminal window, go to the *<INSTALL>*/javaeetutorial5/examples/ejb/timersession/ directory.
2. Type the following command:

   ```
   ant run
   ```

   This task first retrieves the client JAR, timersessionClient.jar to the dist directory, and then runs the client. This is the equivalent of running:

   ```
   appclient -client TimerSessionAppClient.jar
   ```

3. In the terminal window, the client displays these lines:

   ```
   Creating a timer with an interval duration of 30000 ms.
   ```

The output from the timer is sent to the server.log file located in the *<JAVAEE_HOME>*/domains/domain1/server/logs/ directory.

View the output in the Admin Console:

1. Open the Admin Console by opening the following URL in a web browser:

   ```
   http://localhost:4848/
   ```

2. Enter the admin username and password to log in to the Admin Console.
3. Click Application Server in the navigation pane.
4. Click View Log Files.
5. At the top of the page, you'll see this line in the Message column:

   ```
   Timeout occurred
   ```

Alternatively, you can look at the log file directly. After about 30 seconds, open server.log in a text editor and you will see the following lines:

```
TimerSessionBean: Timeout occurred
```

Handling Exceptions

The exceptions thrown by enterprise beans fall into two categories: system and application.

A *system exception* indicates a problem with the services that support an application. Examples of these problems include the following: a connection to an external resource cannot be obtained or an injected resource cannot be found. If your enterprise bean encounters a system-level problem, it should throw a `javax.ejb.EJBException`. Because the `EJBException` is a subclass of the `RuntimeException`, you do not have to specify it in the `throws` clause of the method declaration. If a system exception is thrown, the EJB container might destroy the bean instance. Therefore, a system exception cannot be handled by the bean's client program; it requires intervention by a system administrator.

An *application exception* signals an error in the business logic of an enterprise bean. Application exceptions are typically exceptions that you've coded yourself, such as the `BookException` thrown by the business methods of the `CartBean` example. When an enterprise bean throws an application exception, the container does not wrap it in another exception. The client should be able to handle any application exception it receives.

If a system exception occurs within a transaction, the EJB container rolls back the transaction. However, if an application exception is thrown within a transaction, the container does not roll back the transaction.

23

A Message-Driven Bean Example

MESSAGE-DRIVEN beans can implement any messaging type. Most commonly, they implement the Java Message Service (JMS) technology. The example in this chapter uses JMS technology, so you should be familiar with basic JMS concepts such as queues and messages. To learn about these concepts, see Chapter 31.

This chapter describes the source code of a simple message-driven bean example. Before proceeding, you should read the basic conceptual information in the section What Is a Message-Driven Bean? (page 747) as well as Using Message-Driven Beans (page 1121) in Chapter 31.

Example Application Overview

The `SimpleMessageApp` application has the following components:

- `SimpleMessageClient`: An application client that sends several messages to a queue
- `SimpleMessageEJB`: A message-driven bean that asynchronously receives and processes the messages that are sent to the queue

Figure 23–1 illustrates the structure of this application. The application client sends messages to the queue, which was created administratively using the

Admin Console. The JMS provider (in this case, the Application Server) delivers the messages to the instances of the message-driven bean, which then processes the messages.

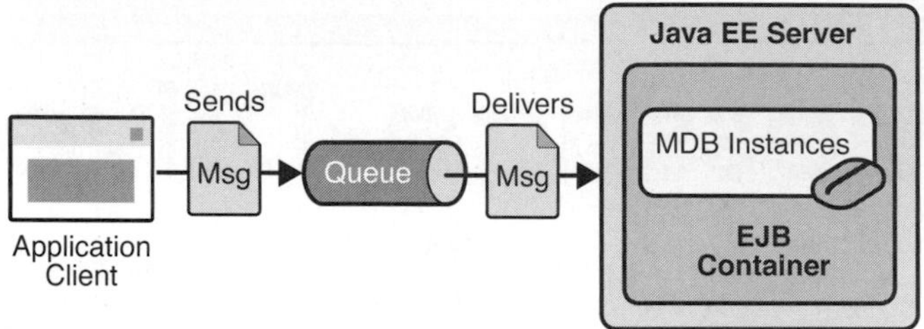

Figure 23–1 The `SimpleMessageApp` Application

The source code for this application is in the `<INSTALL>/javaeetutorial5/examples/ejb/simplemessage/` directory.

The Application Client

The `SimpleMessageClient` sends messages to the queue that the `SimpleMessageBean` listens to. The client starts by injecting the the connection factory and queue resources:

```
@Resource(mappedName="jms/ConnectionFactory")
private static ConnectionFactory connectionFactory;

@Resource(mappedName=”jms/Queue”)
private static Queue queue;
```

Next, the client creates the connection, session, and message producer:

```
connection = connectionFactory.createConnection();
session = connection.createSession(false,
  Session.AUTO_ACKNOWLEDGE);
messageProducer = session.createProducer(queue);
```

Finally, the client sends several messages to the queue:

```
message = session.createTextMessage();

for (int i = 0; i < NUM_MSGS; i++) {
  message.setText("This is message " + (i + 1));
```

```
        System.out.println("Sending message: " +
            message.getText());
        messageProducer.send(message);
    }
```

The Message-Driven Bean Class

The code for the `SimpleMessageBean` class illustrates the requirements of a message-driven bean class:

- It must be annotated with the `@MessageDriven` annotation if it does not use a deployment descriptor.
- The class must be defined as `public`.
- The class cannot be defined as `abstract` or `final`.
- It must contain a public constructor with no arguments.
- It must not define the `finalize` method.

It is recommended, but not required, that a message-driven bean class implement the message listener interface for the message type it supports. A bean that supports the JMS API implements the `javax.jms.MessageListener` interface.

Unlike session beans and entities, message-driven beans do not have the remote or local interfaces that define client access. Client components do not locate message-driven beans and invoke methods on them. Although message-driven beans do not have business methods, they may contain helper methods that are invoked internally by the `onMessage` method.

For the Application Server, the `@MessageDriven` annotation typically contains a `mappedName` element that specifies the JNDI name of the destination from which the bean will consume messages. For complex message-driven beans there can also be an `activationconfig` element containing `@ActivationConfigProperty` annotations used by the bean. See A Java EE Application That Uses the JMS API with a Session Bean (page 1130) for an example.

A message-driven bean can also inject a `MessageDrivenContext` resource. Commonly you use this resource to call the `setRollbackOnly` method to handle exceptions for a bean that uses container-managed transactions.

Therefore, the first few lines of the `SimpleMessageBean` class look like this:

```
@MessageDriven(mappedName="jms/Queue")
public class SimpleMessageBean implements MessageListener {

  @Resource
  private MessageDrivenContext mdc;
  ...
```

The onMessage Method

When the queue receives a message, the EJB container invokes the message listener method or methods. For a bean that uses JMS, this is the `onMessage` method of the `MessageListener` interface.

A message listener method must follow these rules:

- The method must be declared as `public`.
- The method must not be declared as `final` or `static`.

The `onMessage` method is called by the bean's container when a message has arrived for the bean to service. This method contains the business logic that handles the processing of the message. It is the message-driven bean's responsibility to parse the message and perform the necessary business logic.

The `onMessage` method has a single argument: the incoming message.

The signature of the `onMessage` method must follow these rules:

- The return type must be `void`.
- The method must have a single argument of type `javax.jms.Message`.

In the `SimpleMessageBean` class, the `onMessage` method casts the incoming message to a `TextMessage` and displays the text:

```
public void onMessage(Message inMessage) {
  TextMessage msg = null;

  try {
    if (inMessage instanceof TextMessage) {
      msg = (TextMessage) inMessage;
      logger.info("MESSAGE BEAN: Message received: " +
        msg.getText());
    } else {
      logger.warning("Message of wrong type: " +
        inMessage.getClass().getName());
```

```
        }
    } catch (JMSException e) {
        e.printStackTrace();
        mdc.setRollbackOnly();
    } catch (Throwable te) {
        te.printStackTrace();
    }
}
```

Packaging, Deploying, and Running the SimpleMessage Example

To package, deploy and run this example, go to the `<INSTALL>/javaeetutorial5/examples/ejb/simplemessage/` directory.

Creating the Administered Objects

This example requires the following:

- A JMS connection factory resourcc
- A JMS destination resource

If you have run the simple JMS examples in Chapter 31 and have not deleted the resources, you already have these resources and do not need to perform these steps.

You can use Ant targets to create the resources. The Ant targets, which are defined in the `build.xml` file for this example, use the `asadmin` command. To create the resources needed for this example, use the following commands:

```
ant create-cf
ant create-queue
```

These commands do the following:

- Create a connection factory resource named `jms/ConnectionFactory`
- Create a a destination resource named `jms/Queue`

The Ant targets for these commands refer to other targets that are defined in the `<INSTALL>/javaeetutorial5/examples/bp-project/app-server-ant.xml` file.

Building, Deploying, and Running the Application Using NetBeans 5.5

To build, deploy, and run the application using NetBeans 5.5, do the following:

1. In NetBeans 5.5, choose Open Project from the File menu.
2. In the Open Project dialog, navigate to `<INSTALL>/javaeetutorial5/examples/ejb/`.
3. Select the `simplemessage` folder.
4. Select the Open as Main Project checkbox and the Open Required Projects checkbox.
5. Click Open Project Folder.
6. Right-click the `simplemessage` project and choose Build Project.

   This task packages the application client and the message-driven bean, then creates a file named `simplemessage.ear` in the `dist` directory.
7. Right-click the project and choose Deploy Project.
8. Right-click the project and choose Run Project.

   This command returns a JAR file named `simplemessageClient.jar` and then executes it.

The output of the application client in the Output pane looks like this:

```
Sending message: This is message 1
Sending message: This is message 2
Sending message: This is message 3
To see if the bean received the messages,
 check <install_dir>/domains/domain1/logs/server.log.
```

The output from the message-driven bean appears in the server log (`<JAVAEE_HOME>/domains/domain1/logs/server.log`), wrapped in logging information.

```
MESSAGE BEAN: Message received: This is message 1
MESSAGE BEAN: Message received: This is message 2
MESSAGE BEAN: Message received: This is message 3
```

The received messages often appear in a different order from the order in which they were sent.

Undeploy the application after you finish running the client. To undeploy the application, follow these steps:

1. Click the Runtime tab.
2. Expand the Servers node.
3. Expand the Sun Java System Application Server node.
4. Expand the Applications node.
5. Expand the Enterprise Applications node.
6. Right-click `simplemessage` and choose Undeploy.

To remove the generated files, right-click the `simplemessage` project and choose Clean Project.

Building, Deploying, and Running the Application Using Ant

To create and package the application using Ant, use the default target for the `build.xml` file:

```
ant
```

This target packages the application client and the message-driven bean, then creates a file named `simplemessage.ear` in the `dist` directory.

By using resource injection and annotations, you avoid having to create deployment descriptor files for the message-driven bean and application client. You need to use deployment descriptors only if you want to override the values specified in the annotated source files.

To deploy the application and run the client using Ant, use the following command:

```
ant run
```

Ignore the message that states that the application is deployed at a URL.

The output in the terminal window looks like this:

```
running application client container.
Sending message: This is message 1
Sending message: This is message 2
Sending message: This is message 3
To see if the bean received the messages,
 check <install_dir>/domains/domain1/logs/server.log.
```

In the server log file, the following lines should be displayed, wrapped in logging information:

```
MESSAGE BEAN: Message received: This is message 1
MESSAGE BEAN: Message received: This is message 2
MESSAGE BEAN: Message received: This is message 3
```

The received messages often appear in a different order from the order in which they were sent.

Undeploy the application after you finish running the client. Use the following command:

```
ant undeploy
```

To remove the generated files, use the following command:

```
ant clean
```

Removing the Administered Objects

After you run the example, you can use the following Ant targets to delete the connection factory and queue:

```
ant delete-cf
ant delete-queue
```

Creating Deployment Descriptors for Message-Driven Beans

By using resource injection and annotations, you avoid having to create a standard `ejb-jar.xml` deployment descriptor file for a message-driven bean. However, in certain situations you still need a deployment descriptor specific to the Application Server, in the file sun-ejb-jar.xml.

You are likely to need a deployment descriptor if the message-driven bean will consume messages from a remote system. You use the deployment descriptor to specify the connection factory that points to the remote system. The deployment descriptor would look something like this:

```
<sun-ejb-jar>
  <enterprise-beans>
    <ejb>
      <ejb-name>MessageBean</ejb-name>
      <mdb-connection-factory>
        <jndi-name>jms/JupiterConnectionFactory</jndi-name>
      </mdb-connection-factory>
    </ejb>
  </enterprise-beans>
</sun-ejb-jar>
```

The ejb element for the message-driven bean contains the following:

- The ejb-name element contains the package name of the bean class.
- The mdb-connection-factory element contains a jndi-name element that specifies the connection factory for the bean.

For an example of the use of such a deployment descriptor, see An Application Example That Consumes Messages from a Remote Server (page 1146).

Part Four: Persistence

PART Four explores Java Persistence.

24

Introduction to the Java Persistence API

THE Java Persistence API provides an object/relational mapping facility to Java developers for managing relational data in Java applications. Java Persistence consists of three areas:

- The Java Persistence API
- The query language
- Object/relational mapping metadata

Entities

An entity is a lightweight persistence domain object. Typically an entity represents a table in a relational database, and each entity instance corresponds to a row in that table. The primary programming artifact of an entity is the entity class, although entities can use helper classes.

The persistent state of an entity is represented either through persistent fields or persistent properties. These fields or properties use object/relational mapping annotations to map the entities and entity relationships to the relational data in the underlying data store.

Requirements for Entity Classes

An entity class must follow these requirements:

- The class must be annotated with the `javax.persistence.Entity` annotation.
- The class must have a public or protected, no-argument constructor. The class may have other constructors.
- The class must not be declared `final`. No methods or persistent instance variables must be declared `final`.
- If an entity instance be passed by value as a detached object, such as through a session bean's remote business interface, the class must implement the `Serializable` interface.
- Entities may extend both entity and non-entity classes, and non-entity classes may extend entity classes.
- Persistent instance variables must be declared private, protected, or package-private, and can only be accessed directly by the entity class's methods. Clients must access the entity's state through accessor or business methods.

Persistent Fields and Properties in Entity Classes

The persistent state of an entity can be accessed either through the entity's instance variables or through JavaBeans-style properties. The fields or properties must be of the following Java language types:

- Java primitive types
- `java.lang.String`
- Other serializable types including:
    - Wrappers of Java primitive types
    - `java.math.BigInteger`
    - `java.math.BigDecimal`
    - `java.util.Date`
    - `java.util.Calendar`
    - `java.sql.Date`
    - `java.sql.Time`

  - `java.sql.TimeStamp`
  - User-defined serializable types
  - `byte[]`
  - `Byte[]`
  - `char[]`
  - `Character[]`
- Enumerated types
- Other entities and/or collections of entities
- Embeddable classes

Entities may either use persistent fields or persistent properties. If the mapping annotations are applied to the entity's instance variables, the entity uses persistent fields. If the mapping annotations are applied to the entity's getter methods for JavaBeans-style properties, the entity uses persistent properties. You cannot apply mapping annotations to both fields and properties in a single entity.

Persistent Fields

If the entity class uses persistent fields, the Persistence runtime accesses entity class instance variables directly. All fields not annotated `javax.persistence.Transient` or not marked as Java `transient` will be persisted to the data store. The object/relational mapping annotations must be applied to the instance variables.

Persistent Properties

If the entity uses persistent properties, the entity must follow the method conventions of JavaBeans components. JavaBeans-style properties use getter and setter methods that are typically named after the entity class's instance variable names. For every persistent property *property* of type *Type* of the entity, there is a getter method get*Property* and setter method set*Property*. If the property is a boolean, you may use is*Property* instead of get*Property*. For example, if a `Customer` entity uses persistent properties, and has a private instance variable called `firstName`, the class defines a `getFirstName` and `setFirstName` method for retrieving and setting the state of the `firstName` instance variable.

The method signature for single-valued persistent properties are as follows:

```
Type getProperty()
void setProperty(Type type)
```

Collection-valued persistent fields and properties must use the supported Java collection interfaces regardless of whether the entity uses persistent fields or properties. The following collection interfaces may be used:

- `java.util.Collection`
- `java.util.Set`
- `java.util.List`
- `java.util.Map`

If the entity class uses persistent fields, the type in the above method signatures must be one of these collection types. Generic variants of these collection types may also be used. For example, if the `Customer` entity has a persistent property that contains a set of phone numbers, it would have the following methods:

```
Set<PhoneNumber> getPhoneNumbers() {}
void setPhoneNumbers(Set<PhoneNumber>) {}
```

The object/relational mapping annotations for must be applied to the getter methods. Mapping annotations cannot be applied to fields or properties annotated `@Transient` or marked `transient`.

Primary Keys in Entities

Each entity has a unique object identifier. A customer entity, for example, might be identified by a customer number. The unique identifier, or *primary key*, enables clients to locate a particular entity instance. Every entity must have a primary key. An entity may have either a simple or a composite primary key.

Simple primary keys use the `javax.persistence.Id` annotation to denote the primary key property or field.

Composite primary keys must correspond to either a single persistent property or field, or to a set of single persistent properties or fields. Composite primary keys must be defined in a primary key class. Composite primary keys are denoted using the `javax.persistence.EmbeddedId` and `javax.persistence.IdClass` annotations.

The primary key, or the property or field of a composite primary key, must be one of the following Java language types:

- Java primitive types
- Java primitive wrapper types
- `java.lang.String`
- `java.util.Date` (the temporal type should be `DATE`)
- `java.sql.Date`

Floating point types should never be used in primary keys. If you use a generated primary key, only integral types will be portable.

Primary Key Classes

A primary key class must meet these requirements:

- The access control modifier of the class must be `public`.
- The properties of the primary key class must be `public` or `protected` if property-based access is used.
- The class must have a public default constructor.
- The class must implement the `hashCode()` and `equals(Object other)` methods.
- The class must be serializable.
- A composite primary key must be represented and mapped to multiple fields or properties of the entity class, or must be represented and mapped as an embeddable class.
- If the class is mapped to multiple fields or properties of the entity class, the names and types of the primary key fields or properties in the primary key class must match those of the entity class.

The following primary key class is a composite key, the `orderId` and `itemId` fields together uniquely identify an entity.

```
public final class LineItemKey implements Serializable {
  public Integer orderId;
  public int itemId;

  public LineItemKey() {}

  public LineItemKey(Integer orderId, int itemId) {
    this.orderId = orderId;
    this.itemId = itemId;
```

```
    }

    public boolean equals(Object otherOb) {
        if (this == otherOb) {
            return true;
        }
        if (!(otherOb instanceof LineItemKey)) {
            return false;
        }
        LineItemKey other = (LineItemKey) otherOb;
        return (
                (orderId==null?other.orderId==null:orderId.equals
                (other.orderId)
                )
                &&
                (itemId == other.itemId)
            );
    }

    public int hashCode() {
        return (
                (orderId==null?0:orderId.hashCode())
                ^
                ((int) itemId)
            );
    }

    public String toString() {
        return "" + orderId + "-" + itemId;
    }
}
```

Multiplicity in Entity Relationships

There are four types of multiplicities: one-to-one, one-to-many, many-to-one, and many-to-many.

One-to-one: Each entity instance is related to a single instance of another entity. For example, to model a physical warehouse in which each storage bin contains a single widget, `StorageBin` and `Widget` would have a one-to-one relationship. One-to-one relationships use the `javax.persistence.OneToOne` annotation on the corresponding persistent property or field.

One-to-many: An entity instance can be related to multiple instances of the other entities. A sales order, for example, can have multiple line items. In the order application, `Order` would have a one-to-many relationship with `LineItem`. One-to-many relationships use the `javax.persistence.OneToMany` annotation on the corresponding persistent property or field.

Many-to-one: Multiple instances of an entity can be related to a single instance of the other entity. This multiplicity is the opposite of a one-to-many relationship. In the example just mentioned, from the perspective of `LineItem` the relationship to `Order` is many-to-one. Many-to-one relationships use the `javax.persistence.ManyToOne` annotation on the corresponding persistent property or field.

Many-to-many: The entity instances can be related to multiple instances of each other. For example, in college each course has many students, and every student may take several courses. Therefore, in an enrollment application, `Course` and `Student` would have a many-to-many relationship. Many-to-many relationships use the `javax.persistence.ManyToMany` annotation on the corresponding persistent property or field.

Direction in Entity Relationships

The direction of a relationship can be either bidirectional or unidirectional. A bidirectional relationship has both an owning side and an inverse side. A unidirectional relationship has only an owning side. The owning side of a relationship determines how the Persistence runtime makes updates to the relationship in the database.

Bidirectional Relationships

In a *bidirectional* relationship, each entity has a relationship field or property that refers to the other entity. Through the relationship field or property, an entity class's code can access its related object. If an entity has a related field, then we often say that it "knows" about its related object. For example, if `Order` knows what `LineItem` instances it has and if `LineItem` knows what `Order` it belongs to, then they have a bidirectional relationship.

Bidirectional relationships must follow these rules:

- The inverse side of a bidirectional relationship must refer to its owning side by using the `mappedBy` element of the `@OneToOne`, `@OneToMany`, or `@ManyToMany` annotation. The `mappedBy` element designates the property or field in the entity that is the owner of the relationship.

- The many side of many-to-one bidirectional relationships must not define the mappedBy element. The many side is always the owning side of the relationship.
- For one-to-one bidirectional relationships, the owning side corresponds to the side that contains the corresponding foreign key.
- For many-to-many bidirectional relationships either side may be the owning side.

Unidirectional Relationships

In a *unidirectional* relationship, only one entity has a relationship field or property that refers to the other. For example, LineItem would have a relationship field that identifies Product, but Product would not have a relationship field or property for LineItem. In other words, LineItem knows about Product, but Product doesn't know which LineItem instances refer to it.

Queries and Relationship Direction

Java Persistence query language queries often navigate across relationships. The direction of a relationship determines whether a query can navigate from one entity to another. For example, a query can navigate from LineItem to Product but cannot navigate in the opposite direction. For Order and LineItem, a query could navigate in both directions, because these two entities have a bidirectional relationship.

Cascade Deletes and Relationships

Entities that use relationships often have dependencies on the existence of the other entity in the relationship. For example, a line item is part of an order, and if the order is deleted, then the line item should also be deleted. This is called a cascade delete relationship.

Cascade delete relationships are specified using the cascade=REMOVE element specification for @OneToOne and @OneToMany relationships. For example:

```
@OneToMany(cascade=REMOVE, mappedBy="customer")
public Set<Order> getOrders() { return orders; }
```

Entity Inheritance

Entities support class inheritance, polymorphic associations, and polymorphic queries. They can extend non-entity classes, and non-entity classes can extend entity classes. Entity classes can be both abstract and concrete.

The `roster` example application demonstrates entity inheritance, and is described in Entity Inheritance in the roster Application (page 854).

Abstract Entities

An abstract class may be declared an entity by decorating the class with `@Entity`. Abstract entities differ from concrete entities only in that they cannot be instantiated.

Abstract entities can be queried just like concrete queries. If an abstract entity is the target of a query, the query operates on all the concrete subclasses of the abstract entity.

```
@Entity
public abstract class Employee {
  @Id
  protected Integer employeeId;
  ...
}

@Entity
public class FullTimeEmployee extends Employee {
  protected Integer salary;
  ...
}

@Entity
public class PartTimeEmployee extends Employee {
  protected Float hourlyWage;
}
```

Mapped Superclasses

Entities may inherit from superclasses that contain persistent state and mapping information, but are not entities. That is, the superclass is not decorated with the `@Entity` annotation, and is not mapped as an entity by the Java Persistence provider. These superclasses are most often used when you have state and mapping information common to multiple entity classes.

Mapped superclasses are specified by decorating the class with the `javax.persistence.MappedSuperclass` annotation.

```
@MappedSuperclass
public class Employee {
  @Id
  protected Integer employeeId;
  ...
}

@Entity
public class FullTimeEmployee extends Employee {
  protected Integer salary;
  ...
}

@Entity
public class PartTimeEmployee extends Employee {
  protected Float hourlyWage;
  ...
}
```

Mapped superclasses are not queryable, and can't be used in `EntityManager` or `Query` operations. You must use entity subclasses of the mapped superclass in `EntityManager` or `Query` operations. Mapped superclasses can't be targets of entity relationships. Mapped superclasses can be abstract or concrete.

Mapped superclasses do not have any corresponding tables in the underlying datastore. Entities that inherit from the mapped superclass define the table mappings. For instance, in the code sample above the underlying tables would be `FULLTIMEEMPLOYEE` and `PARTTIMEEMPLOYEE`, but there is no `EMPLOYEE` table.

Non-Entity Superclasses

Entities may have non-entity superclasses, and these superclasses can be either abstract or concrete. The state of non-entity superclasses is non-persistent, and any state inherited from the non-entity superclass by an entity class is non-persistent. Non-entity superclasses may not be used in `EntityManager` or `Query` operations. Any mapping or relationship annotations in non-entity superclasses are ignored.

Entity Inheritance Mapping Strategies

You can configure how the Java Persistence provider maps inherited entities to the underlying datastore by decorating the root class of the hierarchy with the `javax.persistence.Inheritance` annotation. There are three mapping strategies that are used to map the entity data to the underlying database:

- A single table per class hierarchy
- A table per concrete entity class
- A "join" strategy, where fields or properties that are specific to a subclass are mapped to a different table than the fields or properties that are common to the parent class

The strategy is configured by setting the `strategy` element of `@Inheritance` to one of the options defined in the `javax.persistence.InheritanceType` enumerated type:

```
public enum InheritanceType {
  SINGLE_TABLE,
  JOINED,
  TABLE_PER_CLASS
};
```

The default strategy is `InheritanceType.SINGLE_TABLE`, and is used if the `@Inheritance` annotation is not specified on the root class of the entity hierarchy.

The Single Table per Class Hierarchy Strategy

With this strategy, which corresponds to the default `InheritanceType.SINGLE_TABLE`, all classes in the hierarchy are mapped to a single table in the database. This table has a *discriminator column*, a column that contains a value that identifies the subclass to which the instance represented by the row belongs.

The discriminator column can be specified by using the `javax.persistence.DiscriminatorColumn` annotation on the root of the entity class hierarchy.

Table 24–1 `@DiscriminatorColumn` Elements

Type	Name	Description
`String`	`name`	The name of the column in the table to be used as the discriminator column. The default is `DTYPE`. This element is optional.
`DiscriminatorType`	`discriminatorType`	The type of the column to be used as a discriminator column. The default is `DiscriminatorType.STRING`. This element is optional.
`String`	`columnDefinition`	The SQL fragment to use when creating the discriminator column. The default is generated by the Persistence provider, and is implementation-specific. This element is optional.
`String`	`length`	The column length for `String`-based discriminator types. This element is ignored for non-`String` discriminator types. The default is 31. This element is optional.

The `javax.persistence.DiscriminatorType` enumerated type is used to set the type of the discriminator column in the database by setting the `discriminatorType` element of `@DiscriminatorColumn` to one of the defined types. `DiscriminatorType` is defined as:

```
public enum DiscriminatorType {
  STRING,
  CHAR,
  INTEGER
};
```

If `@DiscriminatorColumn` is not specified on the root of the entity hierarchy and a discriminator column is required, the Persistence provider assumes a default column name of `DTYPE`, and column type of `DiscriminatorType.STRING`.

The javax.persistence.DiscriminatorValue annotation may be used to set the value entered into the discriminator column for each entity in a class hierarchy. You may only decorate concrete entity classes with @DiscriminatorValue.

If @DiscriminatorValue is not specified on an entity in a class hierarchy that uses a discriminator column, the Persistence provider will provide a default, implemenation-specific value. If the discriminatorType element of @DiscriminatorColumn is DiscriminatorType.STRING, the default value is the name of the entity.

This strategy provides good support for polymorphic relationships between entities and queries that cover the entire entity class hierarchy. However, it requires the columns that contain the state of subclasses to be nullable.

The Table per Concrete Class Strategy

In this strategy, which corresponds to InheritanceType.TABLE_PER_CLASS, each concrete class is mapped to a separate table in the database. All fields or properties in the class, including inherited fields or properties, are mapped to columns in the class's table in the database.

This strategy provides poor support for polymorphic relationships, and usually requires either SQL UNION queries or separate SQL queries for each subclass for queries that cover the entire entity class hierarchy.

Support for this strategy is optional, and may not be supported by all Java Persistence API providers. The default Java Persistence API provider in the Application Server does not support this strategy.

The Joined Subclass Strategy

In this strategy, which corresponds to InheritanceType.JOINED, the root of the class hierarchy is represented by a single table, and each subclass has a separate table that only contains those fields specific to that subclass. That is, the subclass table does not contain columns for inherited fields or properties. The subclass table also has a column or columns that represent its primary key, which is a foreign key to the primary key of the superclass table.

This strategy provides good support for polymorphic relationships, but requires one or more join operations to be performed when instantiating entity subclasses. This may result in poor performance for extensive class hierarchies. Similarly, queries that cover the entire class hierarchy require join operations between the subclass tables, resulting in decreased performance.

Some Java Persistence API providers, including the default provider in the Application Server, require a discriminator column in the table that corresponds to the root entity when using the joined subclass strategy. If you are not using automatic table creation in your application, make sure the database table is set up correctly for the discriminator column defaults, or use the `@DiscriminatorColumn` annotation to match your database schema. For information on discriminator columns, see The Single Table per Class Hierarchy Strategy (page 813).

Managing Entities

Entities are managed by the entity manager. The entity manager is represented by `javax.persistence.EntityManager` instances. Each `EntityManager` instance is associated with a persistence context. A persistence context defines the scope under which particular entity instances are created, persisted, and removed.

The Persistence Context

A persistence context is a set of managed entity instances that exist in a particular data store. The `EntityManager` interface defines the methods that are used to interact with the persistence context.

The EntityManager

The `EntityManager` API creates and removes persistent entity instances, finds entities by the entity's primary key, and allows queries to be run on entities.

Container-Managed Entity Managers

With a *container-managed entity manager*, an `EntityManager` instance's persistence context is automatically propagated by the container to all application components that use the `EntityManager` instance within a single Java Transaction Architecture (JTA) transaction.

JTA transactions usually involve calls across application components. To complete a JTA transaction, these components usually need access to a single persistence context. This occurs when an `EntityManager` is injected into the application components via the `javax.persistence.PersistenceContext` annotation. The persistence context is automatically propagated with the current JTA transaction, and EntityManager references that are mapped to the same persistence unit provide access to the persistence context within that transaction. By automatically propagating the persistence context, application components don't need to pass references to EntityManager instances to each other in order to make changes within a single transaction. The Java EE container manages the life cycle of container-managed entity managers.

To obtain an EntityManager instance, inject the entity manager into the application component:

```
@PersistenceContext
EntityManager em;
```

Application-Managed Entity Managers

With *application-managed entity managers*, on the other hand, the persistence context is not propagated to application components, and the life cycle of EntityManager instances is managed by the application.

Application-managed entity managers are used when applications need to access a persistence context that is not propagated with the JTA transaction across EntityManager instances in a particular persistence unit. In this case, each EntityManager creates a new, isolated persistence context. The EntityManager, and its associated persistence context, is created and destroyed explicitly by the application.

Applications create EntityManager instances in this case by using the createEntityManager method of javax.persistence.EntityManagerFactory.

To obtain an EntityManager instance, you first must obtain an EntityManagerFactory instance by injecting it into the application component via the javax.persistence.PersistenceUnit annotation:

```
@PersistenceUnit
EntityManagerFactory emf;
```

Then, obtain an EntityManager from the EntityManagerFactory instance:

```
EntityManager em = emf.createEntityManager();
```

Finding Entities Using the EntityManager

The `EntityManager.find` method is used to look up entities in the data store by the entity's primary key.

```
@PersistenceContext
EntityManager em;
public void enterOrder(int custID, Order newOrder) {
  Customer cust = em.find(Customer.class, custID);
  cust.getOrders().add(newOrder);
  newOrder.setCustomer(cust);
}
```

Managing an Entity Instance's Life Cycle

You manage entity instances by invoking operations on the entity via an `EntityManager` instance. Entity instances are in one of four states: new, managed, detached, or removed.

New entity instances have no persistent identity and are not yet associated with a persistence context.

Managed entity instances have a persistent identity and are associated with a persistence context.

Detached entity instances have a persistent identify and are not currently associated with a persistence context.

Removed entity instances have a persistent identity, are associated with a persistent context, and are scheduled for removal from the data store.

Persisting Entity Instances

New entity instances become managed and persistent either by invoking the `persist` method, or by a cascading `persist` operation invoked from related entities that have the `cascade=PERSIST` or `cascade=ALL` elements set in the relationship annotation. This means the entity's data is stored to the database when the transaction associated with the `persist` operation is completed. If the entity is already managed, the `persist` operation is ignored, although the `persist` operation will cascade to related entities that have the `cascade` element set to `PERSIST` or `ALL` in the relationship annotation. If `persist` is called on a removed entity instance, it becomes managed. If the entity is detached, `persist` will throw an `IllegalArgumentException`, or the transaction commit will fail.

```
@PersistenceContext
EntityManager em;
...
public LineItem createLineItem(Order order, Product product,
        int quantity) {
    LineItem li = new LineItem(order, product, quantity);
    order.getLineItems().add(li);
    em.persist(li);
    return li;
}
```

The `persist` operation is propagated to all entities related to the calling entity that have the `cascade` element set to `ALL` or `PERSIST` in the relationship annotation.

```
@OneToMany(cascade=ALL, mappedBy="order")
public Collection<LineItem> getLineItems() {
    return lineItems;
}
```

Removing Entity Instances

Managed entity instances are removed by invoking the `remove` method, or by a cascading `remove` operation invoked from related entities that have the `cascade=REMOVE` or `cascade=ALL` elements set in the relationship annotation. If the `remove` method is invoked on a new entity, the `remove` operation is ignored, although `remove` will cascade to related entities that have the `cascade` element set to `REMOVE` or `ALL` in the relationship annotation. If `remove` is invoked on a detached entity it will throw an `IllegalArgumentException`, or the transaction commit will fail. If `remove` is invoked on an already removed entity, it will be ignored. The entity's data will be removed from the data store when the transaction is completed, or as a result of the `flush` operation.

```
public void removeOrder(Integer orderId) {
    try {
        Order order = em.find(Order.class, orderId);
        em.remove(order);
    }...
```

In this example, all `LineItem` entities associated with the order are also removed, as `Order.getLineItems` has `cascade=ALL` set in the relationship annotation.

Synchronizing Entity Data to the Database

The state of persistent entities is synchronized to the database when the transaction with which the entity is associated commits. If a managed entity is in a bidirectional relationship with another managed entity, the data will be persisted based on the owning side of the relationship.

To force synchronization of the managed entity to the data store, invoke the `flush` method of the entity. If the entity is related to another entity, and the relationship annotation has the `cascade` element set to `PERSIST` or `ALL`, the related entity's data will be synchronized with the data store when `flush` is called.

If the entity is removed, calling `flush` will remove the entity data from the data store.

Creating Queries

The `EntityManager.createQuery` and `EntityManager.createNamedQuery` methods are used to query the datastore using Java Persistence query language queries. See Chapter 24 for more information on the query language.

The `createQuery` method is used to create *dynamic queries*, queries that are defined directly within an application's business logic.

```
public List findWithName(String name) {
return em.createQuery(
  "SELECT c FROM Customer c WHERE c.name LIKE :custName")
  .setParameter("custName", name)
  .setMaxResults(10)
  .getResultList();
}
```

The `createNamedQuery` method is used to create *static queries*, queries that are defined in metadata using the `javax.persistence.NamedQuery` annotation. The `name` element of `@NamedQuery` specifies the name of the query that will be used with the `createNamedQuery` method. The `query` element of `@NamedQuery` is the query.

```
@NamedQuery(
  name="findAllCustomersWithName",
  query="SELECT c FROM Customer c WHERE c.name LIKE :custName"
)
```

Here's an example of `createNamedQuery`, which uses the `@NamedQuery` defined above.

```
@PersistenceContext
public EntityManager em;
...
customers = em.createNamedQuery("findAllCustomersWithName")
  .setParameter("custName", "Smith")
  .getResultList();
```

Named Parameters in Queries

Named parameters are parameters in a query that are prefixed with a colon (`:`). Named parameters in a query are bound to an argument by the `javax.persistence.Query.setParameter(String name, Object value)` method. In the following example, the `name` argument to the `findWithName` business method is bound to the `:custName` named parameter in the query by calling `Query.setParameter`.

```
public List findWithName(String name) {
  return em.createQuery(
    "SELECT c FROM Customer c WHERE c.name LIKE :custName")
    .setParameter("custName", name)
    .getResultList();
}
```

Named parameters are case-sensitive, and may be used by both dynamic and static queries.

Positional Parameters in Queries

You may alternately use positional parameters in queries, instead of named parameters. Positional parameters are prefixed with a question mark (?) followed the numeric position of the parameter in the query. The `Query.setParameter(integer position, Object value)` method is used to set the parameter values.

In the following example, the findWithName business method is rewritten to use input parameters:

```
public List findWithName(String name) {
  return em.createQuery(
    "SELECT c FROM Customer c WHERE c.name LIKE ?1")
    .setParameter(1, name)
    .getResultList();
}
```

Input parameters are numbered starting from 1. Input parameters are case-sensitive, and may be used by both dynamic and static queries.

Persistence Units

A persistence unit defines a set of all entity classes that are managed by EntityManager instances in an application. This set of entity classes represents the data contained within a single data store.

Persistence units are defined by the persistence.xml configuration file. The JAR file or directory whose META-INF directory contains persistence.xml is called the root of the persistence unit. The scope of the persistence unit is determined by the persistence unit's root.

Each persistence unit must be identified with a name that is unique to the persistence unit's scope.

Persistent units can be packaged as part of a WAR or EJB JAR file, or can be packaged as a JAR file that can then be included in an WAR or EAR file.

If you package the persistent unit as a set of classes in an EJB JAR file, persistence.xml should be put in the EJB JAR's META-INF directory.

If you package the persistence unit as a set of classes in a WAR file, persistence.xml should be located in the WAR file's WEB-INF/classes/META-INF directory.

If you package the persistence unit in a JAR file that will be included in a WAR or EAR file, the JAR file should be located:

- In the WEB-INF/lib directory of a WAR.
- In the top-level of an EAR file.
- In the EAR file's library directory.

The persistence.xml File

`persistence.xml` defines one or more persistence units. The following is an example `persistence.xml` file.

```
<persistence>
  <persistence-unit name="OrderManagement">
    <description>This unit manages orders and customers.
      It does not rely on any vendor-specific features and can
      therefore be deployed to any persistence provider.
    </description>
    <jta-data-source>jdbc/MyOrderDB</jta-data-source>
    <jar-file>MyOrderApp.jar</jar-file>
    <class>com.widgets.Order</class>
    <class>com.widgets.Customer</class>
  </persistence-unit>
</persistence>
```

This file defines a persistence unit named `OrderManagement`, which uses a JTA-aware data source `jdbc/MyOrderDB`. The `jar-file` and `class` elements specify managed persistence classes: entity classes, embeddable classes, and mapped superclasses. The jar-file element specifies JAR files that are visible to the packaged persistence unit that contain managed persistence classes, while the class element explicitly names managed persistence classes.

The `jta-data-source` (for JTA-aware data sources) and `non-jta-data-source` (non-JTA-aware data sources) elements specify the global JNDI name of the data source to be used by the container.

25

Persistence in the Web Tier

THIS chapter describes how to use the Java Persistence API from web applications. The material here focuses on the source code and settings of an example called bookstore, a web application that manages entities related to a book store. This chapter assumes that you are familiar with the concepts detailed in Chapter 24.

Accessing Databases from Web Applications

Data that is shared between web components and is persistent between invocations of a web application is usually maintained in a database. Web applications use the Java Persistence API (see Chapter 24) to access relational databases.

The Java Persistence API provides a facility for managing the object/relational mapping (ORM) of Java objects to persistent data (stored in a database). A Java object that maps to a database table is called an entity class. It is a regular Java object (also known as a POJO, or plain, old Java object) with properties that map to columns in the database table. The Duke's Bookstore application has one entity class, called Book that maps to WEB_BOOKSTORE_BOOKS.

To manage the interaction of entities with the Java Persistence facility, an application uses the `EntityManager` interface. This interface provides methods that perform common database functions, such as querying and updating the database. The `BookDBAO` class of the Duke's Bookstore application uses the entity manager to query the database for the book data and to update the inventory of books that are sold.

The set of entities that can be managed by an entity manager are defined in a persistence unit. It oversees all persistence operations in the application. The persistence unit is configured by a descriptor file called `persistence.xml`. This file also defines the data source, what type of transactions the application uses, along with other information. For the Duke's Bookstore application, the `persistence.xml` file and the `Book` class are packaged into a separate JAR file and added to the application's WAR file.

As in JDBC technology, a `DataSource` object has a set of properties that identify and describe the real world data source that it represents. These properties include information such as the location of the database server, the name of the database, the network protocol to use to communicate with the server, and so on.

An application that uses the Java Persistence API does not need to explicitly create a connection to the data source, as it would when using JDBC technology exclusively. Still, the DataSource object must be created in the Application Server.

To maintain the catalog of books, the Duke's Bookstore examples described in Chapters 3 through 14 use the Java DB evaluation database included with the Application Server.

To populate the database, follow the instructions in Populating the Example Database (page 56).

To create a data source, follow the instructions in Creating a Data Source in the Application Server (page 56).

This section describes the following:

- Defining a persistence unit
- Creating an entity class
- Obtaining access to an entity manager
- Accessing data from the database
- Updating data in the database

Defining the Persistence Unit

As described in Accessing Databases from Web Applications (page 825), a persistence unit is defined by a `persistence.xml` file, which is packaged with the application WAR file. This file includes the following:

- A `persistence` element that identifies the schema that the descriptor validates against and includes a persistence-unit element.
- A `persistence-unit` element that identifies the name of a persistence unit and the transaction type.
- An optional `description` element.
- A `jta-data-source` element that specifies the global JNDI name of the JTA data source.

The `jta-data-source` element indicates that the transactions in which the entity manager takes part are JTA transactions, meaning that transactions are managed by the container. Alternatively, you can use resource-local transactions, which are transactions controlled by the application itself. In general, web application developers will use JTA transactions so that they don't need to manually manage the life cyle of the `EntityManager` instance.

A resource-local entity manager cannot participate in global transactions. In addition, the web container will not roll back pending transactions left behind by poorly written applications.

Creating an Entity Class

As explained in Accessing Databases from Web Applications (page 825), an entity class is a component that represents a table in the database. In the case of the Duke's Bookstore application, there is only one database table and therefore only one entity class: the `Book` class.

The `Book` class contains properties for accessing each piece of data for a particular book, such as the book's title and author. To make it an entity class that is accessible to an entity manager, you need to do the following:

- Add the `@Entity` annotation to the class.
- Add the `@Id` annotation to the property that represents the primary key of the table.

- Add the `@Table` annotation to the class to identify the name of the database table if it is different from the name of the entity class.
- Optionally make the class `Serializable`.

The following code shows part of the `Book` class:

```
import java.io.Serializable;
import javax.persistence.Entity;
import javax.persistence.Id;
import javax.persistence.Table;

@Entity
@Table(name="WEB_BOOKSTORE_BOOKS")

public class Book implements Serializable {

  private String bookId;
  private String title;

  public Book() { }

  public Book(String bookId, String title, ...) {
    this.bookId = bookId;
    this.title = title;
    ...
  }

  @Id
  public String getBookId() {
    return this.bookId;
  }

  public String getTitle() {
    return this.title;
  }
  ...

  public void setBookId(String id) {
    this.bookId=id;
  }

  public void setTitle(String title) {
    this.title=title;
  }
  ...
}
```

Obtaining Access to an Entity Manager

The `BookDBAO` object of the Duke's Bookstore application includes methods for getting the book data from the database and updating the inventory in the database when books are sold. In order to perform database queries, the `BookDBAO` object needs to obtain an `EntityManager` instance.

The Java Persistence API allows developers to use annotations to identify a resource so that the container can transparently inject it into an object. You can give an object access to an `EntityManager` instance by using the `@PersistenceUnit` annotation to inject an `EntityManagerFactory`, from which you can obtain an `EntityManager` instance.

Unfortunately for the web application developer, resource injection using annotations can only be used with classes that are managed by a Java EE compliant container. Because the web container does not manage JavaBeans components, you cannot inject resources into them. One exception is a JavaServer Faces managed bean. These beans are managed by the container and therefore support resource injection. This is only helpful if your application is a JavaServer Faces application.

You can still use resource injection in a web application that is not a JavaServer Faces application if you can do it in an object that is managed by the container. These objects include servlets and `ServletContextListener` objects. These objects can then give the application's beans access to the resources.

In the case of Duke's Bookstore, the `ContextListener` object creates the `BookDBAO` object and puts it into application scope. In the process, it passes to the `BookDBAO` object the `EntityManagerFactory` object that was injected into `ContextListener`:

```
public final class ContextListener implements
SerlvetContextListener {
...
@PersistenceUnit
private EntityManagerFactory emf;

public void contextInitialized(ServletContexEvent event) {
  context = event.getServletContext();
  ...
  try {
    BookDBAO bookDB = new BookDBAO(emf);
    context.setAttribute("bookDB", bookDB);
  } catch (Exception ex) {
    System.out.println(
```

```
        "Couldn't create bookstore database bean: "
          + ex.getMessage());
    }
  }
}
```

The BookDBAO object can then obtain an EntityManager from the EntityManagerFactory that the ContextListener object passes to it:

```
private EntityManager em;

public BookDBAO (EntityManagerFactory emf) throws Exception {
  em = emf.getEntityManager();
  ...
}
```

The JavaServer Faces version of Duke's Bookstore gets access to the EntityManager instance a little differently. Because managed beans allow resource injection, you can inject the EntityManagerFactory instance into BookDBAO.

In fact, you can bypass injecting EntityManagerFactory and instead inject the EntityManager directly into BookDBAO. This is because thread safety is not an issue with request-scoped beans. Conversely, developers need to be concerned with thread safety when working with servlets and listeners. Therefore, a servlet or listener needs to inject an EntityManagerFactory instance, which is thread-safe, whereas a persistence context is not thread-safe. The following code shows part of the BookDBAO object included in the JavaServer Faces version of Duke's Bookstore:

```
import javax.ejb.*;
import javax.persistence.*;
import javax.transaction.NotSupportedException;

public class BookDBAO {

  @PersistenceContext
  private static EntityManager em;
...
```

As shown in the preceding code, an EntityManager instance is injected into an object using the @PersistenceContext annotation. An EntityManager instance is associated with a persistence context, which is a set of entity instances that the entity manager is tasked with managing.

The annotation may specify the name of the persistence unit with which it is associated. This name must match a persistence unit defined in the application's `persistence.xml` file.

The next section explains how the `BookDBAO` object uses the entity manager instance to query the database.

Accessing Data from the Database

After the `BookDBAO` object obtains an `EntityManager` instance, it can access data from the database. The `getBooks` method of `BookDBAO` calls the `createQuery` method of the `EntityManager` instance to retrieve a list of all books by `bookId`:

```
public List getBooks() throws BooksNotFoundException {
  try {
     return em.createQuery(
        "SELECT bd FROM Book bd ORDER BY bd.bookId").
           getResultList();
  } catch(Exception ex){
     throw new BooksNotFoundException("Could not get books: "
        + ex.getMessage());
  }
}
```

The `getBook` method of `BookDBAO` uses the find method of the `EntityManager` instance to search the database for a particular book and return the associated `Book` instance:

```
public Book getBook(String bookId) throws BookNotFoundException
{
  Book requestedBook = em.find(Book.class, bookId);
  if (requestedBook == null) {
     throw new BookNotFoundException("Couldn't find book: "
        + bookId);
  }
  return requestedBook;
}
```

The next section describes how Duke's Bookstore performs updates to the data.

Updating Data in the Database

In the Duke's Bookstore application, updates to the database involve decrementing the inventory count of a book when the user buys copies of the book. The BookDBAO performs this update in the buyBooks and buyBook methods:

```
public void buyBooks(ShoppingCart cart) throws OrderException{
  Collection items = cart.getItems();
  Iterator i = items.iterator();
  try {
    while (i.hasNext()) {
      ShoppingCartItem sci = (ShoppingCartItem)i.next();
      Book bd = (Book)sci.getItem();
      String id = bd.getBookId();
      int quantity = sci.getQuantity();
      buyBook(id, quantity);
    }
  } catch (Exception ex) {
    throw new OrderException("Commit failed: "
      + ex.getMessage());
  }
}

public void buyBook(String bookId, int quantity)
  throws OrderException {
  try {
    Book requestedBook = em.find(Book.class, bookId);
    if (requestedBook != null) {
      int inventory = requestedBook.getInventory();
      if ((inventory - quantity) >= 0) {
        int newInventory = inventory - quantity;
        requestedBook.setInventory(newInventory);
      } else{
        throw new OrderException("Not enough of "
          + bookId + " in stock to complete order.");
      }
    }
  } catch (Exception ex) {
    throw new OrderException("Couldn't purchase book: "
      + bookId + ex.getMessage());
  }
}
```

In the buyBook method, the find method of the EntityManager instance retrieves one of the books that is in the shopping cart. The buyBook method then updates the inventory on the Book object.

To ensure that the update is processed in its entirety, the call to buyBooks is wrapped in a single transaction. In the JSP versions of Duke's Bookstore, the Dispatcher servlet calls buyBooks and therefore sets the transaction demarcations.

In the following code, the UserTransaction resource is injected into the Dispatcher servlet. UserTransaction is an interface to the underlying JTA transaction manager used to begin a new transaction and end a transaction. After getting the UserTransaction resource, the servlet calls to the begin and commit methods of UserTransaction to mark the boundaries of the transaction. The call to the rollback method of UserTransaction undoes the effects of all statements in the transaction so as to protect the integrity of the data.

```
@Resource
UserTransaction utx;
...
try {
  utx.begin();
  bookDBAO.buyBooks(cart);
  utx.commit();
} catch (Exception ex) {
  try {
     utx.rollback();
  } catch (Exception exe) {
     System.out.println("Rollback failed: "+exe.getMessage());
}
...
```

26

Persistence in the EJB Tier

THIS chapter describes how to use the Java Persistence API from enterprise beans. The material here focuses on the source code and settings of two examples. The first example called `order` is an application that uses a stateful session bean to manage entities related to an ordering system. The second example is `roster`, an application that manages a community sports system. This chapter assumes that you are familiar with the concepts detailed in Chapter 24.

The order Application

The `order` application is a simple inventory and ordering application for maintaining a catalog of parts and placing an itemized order of those parts. It has entities that represent parts, vendors, orders, and line items. These entities are accessed using a stateful session bean that holds the business logic of the application. A simple command-line client adds data to the entities, manipulates the data, and displays data from the catalog.

The information contained in an order can be divided into different elements. What is the order number? What parts are included in the order? What parts make up that part? Who makes the part? What are the specifications for the part? Are there any schematics for the part? `order` is a simplified version of an ordering system that has all these elements.

The order application consists of two modules: order-ejb, an enterprise bean JAR file containing the entities, the support classes, and a stateful session bean that accesses the data in the entities; and order-app-client, the application client that populates the entities with data and manipulates the data, displaying the results in a terminal.

Entity Relationships in the order Application

The order application demonstrates several types of entity relationships: one-to-many, many-to-one, one-to-one, unidirectional, and self-referential relationships.

Self-Referential Relationships

A *self-referential* relationship is a relationship between relationship fields in the same entity. Part has a field bomPart that has a one-to-many relationship with the field parts, which is also in Part. That is, a part can be made up of many parts, and each of those parts has exactly one bill-of-material part.

The primary key for Part is a compound primary key, a combination of the partNumber and revision fields. It is mapped to the PARTNUMBER and REVISION columns in the EJB_ORDER_PART table.

```
...
@ManyToOne
@JoinColumns({
  @JoinColumn(name="BOMPARTNUMBER",
     referencedColumnName="PARTNUMBER"),
  @JoinColumn(name="BOMREVISION",
     referencedColumnName="REVISION")
})
public Part getBomPart() {
  return bomPart;
}
...
@OneToMany(mappedBy="bomPart")
public Collection<Part> getParts() {
  return parts;
}
...
```

One-to-One Relationships

Part has a field, vendorPart, that has a one-to-one relationship with VendorPart's part field. That is, each part has exactly one vendor part, and vice versa.

Here is the relationship mapping in Part:

```
@OneToOne(mappedBy="part")
public VendorPart getVendorPart() {
  return vendorPart;
}
```

Here is the relationship mapping in VendorPart:

```
@OneToOne
@JoinColumns({
  @JoinColumn(name="PARTNUMBER",
     referencedColumnName="PARTNUMBER"),
  @JoinColumn(name="PARTREVISION",
     referencedColumnName="REVISION")
})
public Part getPart() {
  return part;
}
```

Note that, because Part uses a compound primary key, the @JoinColumns annotation is used to map the columns in the EJB_ORDER_VENDOR_PART table to the columns in EJB_ORDER_PART. EJB_ORDER_VENDOR_PART's PARTREVISION column refers to EJB_ORDER_PART's REVISION column.

One-to-Many Relationship Mapped to Overlapping Primary and Foreign Keys

Order has a field, lineItems, that has a one-to-many relationship with LineItem's field order. That is, each order has one or more line item.

LineItem uses a compound primary key that is made up of the orderId and itemId fields. This compound primary key maps to the ORDERID and ITEMID columns in the EJB_ORDER_LINEITEM database table. ORDERID is a foreign key to the ORDERID column in the EJB_ORDER_ORDER table. This means that the ORDERID column is mapped twice: once as a primary key field, orderId; and again as a relationship field, order.

Here's the relationship mapping in Order:

```
@OneToMany(cascade=ALL, mappedBy="order")
  public Collection<LineItem> getLineItems() {
  return lineItems;
}
```

Here is the relationship mapping in LineItem:

```
@ManyToOne
  public Order getOrder() {
  return order;
}
```

Unidirectional Relationships

LineItem has a field, vendorPart, that has a unidirectional many-to-one relationship with VendorPart. That is, there is no field in the target entity in this relationship.

```
@ManyToOne
  public VendorPart getVendorPart() {
  return vendorPart;
}
```

Primary Keys in the order Application

The order application uses several types of primary keys: single-valued primary keys, compound primary keys, and generated primary keys.

Generated Primary Keys

VendorPart uses a generated primary key value. That is, the application does not assign primary key values for the entities, but instead relies on the persistence provider to generate the primary key values. The @GeneratedValue annotation is used to specify that an entity will use a generated primary key.

In VendorPart, the following code specifies the settings for generating primary key values:

```
@TableGenerator(
  name="vendorPartGen",
  table="EJB_ORDER_SEQUENCE_GENERATOR",
  pkColumnName="GEN_KEY",
  valueColumnName="GEN_VALUE",
  pkColumnValue="VENDOR_PART_ID",
  allocationSize=10)
@Id
@GeneratedValue(strategy=GenerationType.TABLE,
  generator="vendorPartGen")
public Long getVendorPartNumber() {
  return vendorPartNumber;
}
```

The @TableGenerator annotation is used in conjunction with @GeneratedValue's strategy=TABLE element. That is, the strategy used to generate the primary keys is use a table in the database. @TableGenerator is used to configure the settings for the generator table. The name element sets the name of the generator, which is vendorPartGen in VendorPart.

The EJB_ORDER_SEQUENCE_GENERATOR table, which has two columns GEN_KEY and GEN_VALUE, will store the generated primary key values. This table could be used to generate other entity's primary keys, so the pkColumnValue element is set to VENDOR_PART_ID to distinguish this entity's generated primary keys from other entity's generated primary keys. The allocationSize element specifies the amount to increment when allocating primary key values In this case, each VendorPart's primary key will increment by 10.

The primary key field vendorPartNumber is of type Long, as the generated primary key's field must be an integral type.

Compound Primary Keys

A compound primary key is made up of multiple fields and follows the requirements described in Primary Key Classes (page 807). To use a compound primary key, you must create a wrapper class.

In order, two entities use compound primary keys: Part and LineItem.

Part uses the PartKey wrapper class. Part's primary key is a combination of the part number and the revision number. PartKey encapsulates this primary key.

`LineItem` uses the `LineItemKey` class. `LineItem`'s primary key is a combination of the order number and the item number. `LineItemKey` encapsulates this primary key. This is the `LineItemKey` compound primary key wrapper class:

```
package order.entity;

public final class LineItemKey implements
      java.io.Serializable {

   private Integer orderId;
   private int itemId;

   public int hashCode() {
      return ((this.getOrderId()==null
               ?0:this.getOrderId().hashCode())
            ^ ((int) this.getItemId()));
   }

   public boolean equals(Object otherOb) {
      if (this == otherOb) {
         return true;
      }
      if (!(otherOb instanceof LineItemKey)) {
         return false;
      }
      LineItemKey other = (LineItemKey) otherOb;
      return ((this.getOrderId()==null
               ?other.orderId==null:this.getOrderId().equals
            (other.orderId)) && (this.getItemId ==
               other.itemId));
   }

   public String toString() {
      return "" + orderId + "-" + itemId;
   }
}
```

The `@IdClass` annotation is used to specify the primary key class in the entity class. In `LineItem`, `@IdClass` is used as follows:

```
@IdClass(order.entity.LineItemKey.class)
@Entity
...
public class LineItem {
...
}
```

The two fields in `LineItem` are tagged with the `@Id` annotation to mark those fields as part of the compound primary key:

```
@Id
public int getItemId() {
  return itemId;
}
...
@Id
@Column(name="ORDERID", nullable=false,
  insertable=false, updatable=false)
public Integer getOrderId() {
  return orderId;
}
```

For `orderId`, we also use the `@Column` annotation to specify the column name in the table, and that this column should not be inserted or updated, as it is an overlapping foreign key pointing at the `EJB_ORDER_ORDER` table's `ORDERID` column (see One-to-Many Relationship Mapped to Overlapping Primary and Foreign Keys, page 837). That is, `orderId` will be set by the `Order` entity.

In `LineItem`'s constructor, the line item number (`LineItem.itemId`) is set using the `Order.getNextId` method.

```
public LineItem(Order order, int quantity, VendorPart
    vendorPart) {
  this.order = order;
  this.itemId = order.getNextId();
  this.orderId = order.getOrderId();
  this.quantity = quantity;
  this.vendorPart = vendorPart;
}
```

`Order.getNextId` counts the number of current line items, adds one, and returns that number.

```
public int getNextId() {
  return this.lineItems.size() + 1;
}
```

Part doesn't require the @Column annotation on the two fields that comprise Part's compound primary key. This is because Part's compound primary key is not an overlapping primary key/foreign key.

```
@IdClass(order.entity.PartKey.class)
@Entity
...
public class Part {
...
  @Id
  public String getPartNumber() {
     return partNumber;
  }
...
  @Id
  public int getRevision() {
     return revision;
  }
...
}
```

Entity Mapped to More Than One Database Table

Part's fields map to more than one database table: EJB_ORDER_PART and EJB_ORDER_PART_DETAIL. The EJB_ORDER_PART_DETAIL table holds the specification and schematics for the part. The @SecondaryTable is used to specify the secondary table.

```
...
@Entity
@Table(name="EJB_ORDER_PART")
@SecondaryTable(name="EJB_ORDER_PART_DETAIL", pkJoinColumns={
  @PrimaryKeyJoinColumn(name="PARTNUMBER",
     referencedColumnName="PARTNUMBER"),
  @PrimaryKeyJoinColumn(name="REVISION",
     referencedColumnName="REVISION")
})
public class Part {
...
}
```

EJB_ORDER_PART_DETAIL shares the same primary key values as EJB_ORDER_PART. The pkJoinColumns element of @SecondaryTable is used to specify that EJB_ORDER_PART_DETAIL's primary key columns are foreign keys to EJB_ORDER_PART. The @PrimaryKeyJoinColumn sets the primary key column names and specifies which column in the primary table the column refers to. In this case, the primary key column names for both EJB_ORDER_PART_DETAIL and EJB_ORDER_PART are the same: PARTNUMBER and REVISION, respectively.

Cascade Operations in the order Application

Entities that have relationships to other entities often have dependencies on the existence of the other entity in the relationship. For example, a line item is part of an order, and if the order is deleted, then the line item should also be deleted. This is called a cascade delete relationship.

In order, there are two cascade delete dependencies in the entity relationships. If the Order to which a LineItem is related is deleted, then the LineItem should also be deleted. If the Vendor to which a VendorPart is related is deleted, then the VendorPart should also be deleted.

You specify the cascade operations for entity relationships by setting the cascade element in the inverse (non-owning) side of the relationship. The cascade element is set to ALL in the case of Order.lineItems. This means that all persistence operations (deletes, updates, and so on) are cascaded from orders to line items.

Here is the relationship mapping in Order:

```
@OneToMany(cascade=ALL, mappedBy="order")
public Collection<LineItem> getLineItems() {
  return lineItems;
}
```

Here is the relationship mapping in LineItem:

```
@ManyToOne
  public Order getOrder() {
  return order;
}
```

BLOB and CLOB Database Types in the order Application

The PARTDETAIL table in the database has a column, DRAWING, of type BLOB. BLOB stands for binary large objects, which are used for storing binary data such as an image. The DRAWING column is mapped to the field Part. drawing of type java.io.Serializable. The @Lob annotation is used to denote that the field is large object.

```
@Column(table="EJB_ORDER_PART_DETAIL")
@Lob
public Serializable getDrawing() {
  return drawing;
}
```

PARTDETAIL also has a column, SPECIFICATION, of type CLOB. CLOB stands for character large objects, which are used to store string data too large to be stored in a VARCHAR column. SPECIFICATION is mapped to the field Part.specification of type java.lang.String. The @Lob annotation is also used here to denote that the field is a large object.

```
@Column(table="EJB_ORDER_PART_DETAIL")
@Lob
public String getSpecification() {
  return specification;
}
```

Both of these fields use the @Column annotation and set the table element to the secondary table.

Temporal Types in the order Application

The Order.lastUpdate persistent property, which is of type java.util.Date, is mapped to the EJB_ORDER_ORDER.LASTUPDATE database field, which is of the SQL type TIMESTAMP. To ensure the proper mapping between these types, you must use the @Temporal annotation with the proper temporal type specified in

@Temporal's element. @Temporal's elements are of type javax.persistence.TemporalType. The possible values are:

- DATE, which maps to java.sql.Date
- TIME, which maps to java.sql.Time
- TIMESTAMP, which maps to java.sql.Timestamp

Here is the relevant section of Order:

```
@Temporal(TIMESTAMP)
public Date getLastUpdate() {
  return lastUpdate;
}
```

Managing the order Application's Entities

The RequestBean stateful session bean contains the business logic and manages the entities of order.

RequestBean uses the @PersistenceContext annotation to retrieve an entity manager instance which is used to manage order's entities in RequestBean's business methods.

```
@PersistenceContext
private EntityManager em;
```

This EntityManager instance is a container-managed entity manager, so the container takes care of all the transactions involved in the managing order's entities.

Creating Entities

The RequestBean.createPart business method creates a new Part entity. The EntityManager.persist method is used to persist the newly created entity to the database.

```
Part part = new Part(partNumber,
  revision,
  description,
  revisionDate,
  specification,
  drawing);
em.persist(part);
```

Finding Entities

The RequestBean.getOrderPrice business method returns the price of a given order, based on the orderId. The EntityManager.find method is used to retrieve the entity from the database.

```
Order order = em.find(Order.class, orderId);
```

The first argument of EntityManager.find is the entity class, and the second is the primary key.

Setting Entity Relationships

The RequestBean.createVendorPart business method creates a VendorPart associated with a particular Vendor. The EntityManager.persist method is used to persist the newly created VendorPart entity to the database, and the VendorPart.setVendor and Vendor.setVendorPart methods are used to associate the VendorPart with the Vendor.

```
PartKey pkey = new PartKey();
pkey.partNumber = partNumber;
pkey.revision = revision;

Part part = em.find(Part.class, pkey);
VendorPart vendorPart = new VendorPart(description, price,
  part);
em.persist(vendorPart);
```

```
Vendor vendor = em.find(Vendor.class, vendorId);
vendor.addVendorPart(vendorPart);
vendorPart.setVendor(vendor);
```

Using Queries

The `RequestBean.adjustOrderDiscount` business method updates the discount applied to all orders. It uses the `findAllOrders` named query, defined in `Order`:

```
@NamedQuery(
  name="findAllOrders",
  query="SELECT o FROM Order o"
)
```

The `EntityManager.createNamedQuery` method is used to run the query. Because the query returns a `List` of all the orders, the `Query.getResultList` method is used.

```
List orders = em.createNamedQuery(
  "findAllOrders")
  .getResultList();
```

The `RequestBean.getTotalPricePerVendor` business method returns the total price of all the parts for a particular vendor. It uses a named parameter, `id`, defined in the named query `findTotalVendorPartPricePerVendor` defined in `VendorPart`.

```
@NamedQuery(
  name="findTotalVendorPartPricePerVendor",
  query="SELECT SUM(vp.price) " +
  "FROM VendorPart vp " +
  "WHERE vp.vendor.vendorId = :id"
)
```

When running the query, the `Query.setParameter` method is used to set the named parameter `id` to the value of `vendorId`, the parameter to `RequestBean.getTotalPricePerVendor`.

```
return (Double) em.createNamedQuery(
  "findTotalVendorPartPricePerVendor")
  .setParameter("id", vendorId)
  .getSingleResult();
```

The `Query.getSingleResult` method is used for this query because the query returns a single value.

Removing Entities

The `RequestBean.removeOrder` business method deletes a given order from the database. It uses the `EntityManager.remove` method to delete the entity from the database.

```
Order order = em.find(Order.class, orderId);
em.remove(order);
```

Building and Running the order Application

This section describes how to build, package, deploy, and run the `order` application. To do this, you will create the database tables in the Java DB server, then build, deploy, and run the example.

Creating the Database Tables in NetBeans 5.5

To create the database tables in Java DB, the database server included with Application Server, you need to create the database connection and execute the SQL commands in `<INSTALL>/examples/common/sql/javadb/tutorial.sql`.

Creating the Database Connection

To create the database connection do the following:

1. Click the Runtime tab.
2. Right-click the Databases node and select New Connection to open the New Connection dialog.
3. Under Name, select Java DB (Network).
4. Set Database URL to the following:

   `jdbc:derby://localhost:1527/sun-appserv-samples`
5. Set User Name to `APP`.
6. Set Password to `APP`.

7. Select the Remember Password during this Session box.
8. Click OK.

Creating the Tables

To create the tutorial tables, do the following:

1. Select File→Open File.
2. Navigate to `<INSTALL>/examples/common/sql/javadb/` and open `tutorial.sql`.
3. In the editor pane, select the connection URL to Java DB:

   ```
   jdbc:derby://localhost:1527/sun-appserv-samples
   ```
4. Click the Run SQL button at the top of the editor pane.

   You will see the output from the SQL commands in the Output tab.

Deleting the Tables

To delete the tutorial tables, do the following:

1. Select File→Open File.
2. Navigate to `<INSTALL>/examples/common/sql/javadb/` and open `delete.sql`.
3. In the editor pane, select the connection URL to Java DB:

   ```
   jdbc:derby://localhost:1527/sun-appserv-samples
   ```
4. Click the Run SQL button at the top of the editor pane.

   You will see the output from the SQL commands in the Output tab.

Creating the Database Tables Using Ant

The database tables are automatically created by the `create-tables` task, which is called before you deploy the application with the `ant deploy` task. To manually create the tables, do the following:

1. In a terminal window, navigate to `<INSTALL>/javaeetutorial5/examples/ejb/order/`.
2. Type the following command:

   ```
   ant create-tables
   ```

Note: The first time the `create-tables` task is run, you will see error messages when the task attempts to remove tables that don't exist. Ignore these error messages. Subsequent calls to `create-tables` will run with no errors and will reset the database tables.

Building, Packaging, Deploying, and Running order In NetBeans 5.5

Follow these instructions to build, package, deploy, and run the `order` example to your Application Server instance using NetBeans 5.5.

1. In NetBeans 5.5, select File→Open Project.
2. In the Open Project dialog, navigate to `<INSTALL>/javaeetutorial5/examples/ejb/`.
3. Select the `order` folder.
4. Select the Open as Main Project and Open Required Projects checkboxes.
5. Click Open Project Folder.
6. In the Projects tab, right-click the `order` project and select Run Project.

You will see the following output from the application client in the Output tab:

```
...
Cost of Bill of Material for PN SDFG-ERTY-BN Rev: 7:  $241.86
Cost of Order 1111:  $664.68
Cost of Order 4312:  $2,011.44

Adding 5% discount
Cost of Order 1111:  $627.75
Cost of Order 4312:  $1,910.87

Removing 7% discount
Cost of Order 1111:  $679.45
Cost of Order 4312:  $2,011.44

Average price of all parts:  $117.55

Total price of parts for Vendor 100:  $501.06

Ordered list of vendors for order 1111
200 Gadget, Inc. Mrs. Smith
100 WidgetCorp Mr. Jones
```

```
Counting all line items
Found 6 line items

Removing Order 4312
Counting all line items
Found 3 line items

Found 1 out of 2 vendors with 'I' in the name:
Gadget, Inc.
run-order-app-client:
run-ant:
run:
BUILD SUCCESSFUL (total time: 22 seconds)
```

Building, Packaging, Deploying, and Running order Using Ant

To build the application components of `order`, enter the following command:

```
ant
```

This runs the `default` task, which compiles the source files and packages the application into an EAR file located at `<INSTALL>/examples/ejb/order/dist/order.ear`.

To deploy the EAR, make sure the Application Server is started, then enter the following command:

```
ant deploy
```

After `order.ear` is deployed, a client JAR, `orderClient.jar`, is retrieved. This contains the application client.

To run the application client, enter the following command:

```
ant run
```

You will see the following output:

```
...
run:
  [echo] Running appclient for Order.

appclient-command-common:
  [exec] Cost of Bill of Material for PN SDFG-ERTY-BN Rev: 7:
```

```
    $241.86
  [exec] Cost of Order 1111:  $664.68
  [exec] Cost of Order 4312:  $2,011.44

  [exec] Adding 5% discount
  [exec] Cost of Order 1111:  $627.75
  [exec] Cost of Order 4312:  $1,910.87

  [exec] Removing 7% discount
  [exec] Cost of Order 1111:  $679.45
  [exec] Cost of Order 4312:  $2,011.44

  [exec] Average price of all parts:  $117.55

  [exec] Total price of parts for Vendor 100:  $501.06

  [exec] Ordered list of vendors for order 1111
  [exec] 200 Gadget, Inc. Mrs. Smith
  [exec] 100 WidgetCorp Mr. Jones

  [exec] Counting all line items
  [exec] Found 6 line items

  [exec] Removing Order 4312
  [exec] Counting all line items
  [exec] Found 3 line items

  [exec] Found 1 out of 2 vendors with 'I' in the name:
  [exec] Gadget, Inc.

BUILD SUCCESSFUL
```

Note: Before re-running the application client, you must reset the database by running the `create-tables` task.

The all Task

As a convenience, the `all` task will build, package, deploy, and run the application. To do this, enter the following command:

```
ant all
```

Undeploying order

To undeploy `order.ear`, enter the following command:

```
ant undeploy
```

The roster Application

The `roster` application maintains the team rosters for players in recreational sports leagues. The application has four components: Java Persistence API entities (`Player`, `Team`, and `League`), a stateful session bean (`RequestBean`), an application client (`RosterClient`), and three helper classes (`PlayerDetails`, `TeamDetails`, and `LeagueDetails`).

Functionally, `roster` is similar to the `order` application described earlier in this chapter with three new features that `order` does not have: many-to-many relationships, entity inheritance, and automatic table creation at deploytime.

Relationships in the roster Application

A recreational sports system has the following relationships:

- A player can be on many teams.
- A team can have many players.
- A team is in exactly one league.
- A league has many teams.

In `roster` this is reflected by the following relationships between the `Player`, `Team`, and `League` entities:

- There is a many-to-many relationship between `Player` and `Team`.
- There is a many-to-one relationship between `Team` and `League`.

The Many-To-Many Relationship in roster

The many-to-many relationship between `Player` and `Team` is specified by using the `@ManyToMany` annotation.

In Team.java, the @ManyToMany annotation decorates the getPlayers method:

```
@ManyToMany
@JoinTable(
  name="EJB_ROSTER_TEAM_PLAYER",
  joinColumns=
    @JoinColumn(name="TEAM_ID", referencedColumnName="ID"),
  inverseJoinColumns=
    @JoinColumn(name="PLAYER_ID", referencedColumnName="ID")
)
public Collection<Player> getPlayers() {
  return players;
}
```

The @JoinTable annotation is used to specify a table in the database that will associate player IDs with team IDs. The entity that specifies the @JoinTable is the owner of the relationship, so in this case the Team entity is the owner of the relationship with the Player entity. Because roster uses automatic table creation at deploytime, the container will create a join table in the database named EJB_ROSTER_TEAM_PLAYER.

Player is the inverse, or non-owning side of the relationship with Team. As one-to-one and many-to-one relationships, the non-owning side is marked by the mappedBy element in the relationship annotation. Because the relationship between Player and Team is bidirectional, the choice of which entity is the owner of the relationship is arbitrary.

In Player.java, the @ManyToMany annotation decorates the getTeams method:

```
@ManyToMany(mappedBy="players")
public Collection<Team> getTeams() {
  return teams;
}
```

Entity Inheritance in the roster Application

The roster application demonstrates how to use entity inheritance, as described in Entity Inheritance (page 811).

The League entity in roster is an abstract entity with two concrete subclasses: SummerLeague and WinterLeague. Because League is an abstract class it cannot be instantiated:

```
...
@Entity
@Table(name = "EJB_ROSTER_LEAGUE")
public abstract class League implements java.io.Serializable {
...
}
```

Instead, SummerLeague or WinterLeague are used by clients when creating a league. SummerLeague and WinterLeague inherit the persistent properties defined in League, and only add a constructor that verifies that the sport parameter matches the type of sport allowed in that seasonal league. For example, here is the SummerLeague entity:

```
...
@Entity
public class SummerLeague extends League
     implements java.io.Serializable {

  /** Creates a new instance of SummerLeague */
  public SummerLeague() {
  }

  public SummerLeague(String id, String name,
       String sport) throws IncorrectSportException {
    this.id = id;
    this.name = name;
    if (sport.equalsIgnoreCase("swimming") ||
         sport.equalsIgnoreCase("soccer") ||
         sport.equalsIgnoreCase("basketball") ||
         sport.equalsIgnoreCase("baseball")) {
      this.sport = sport;
    } else {
      throw new IncorrectSportException(
        "Sport is not a summer sport.");
    }
  }
}
```

The roster application uses the default mapping strategy of InheritanceType.SINGLE_TABLE, so the @Inheritance annotation is not required. If you wanted to use a different mapping strategy, decorate League with @Inheritance and specify the mapping strategy in the strategy element:

```
@Entity
@Inheritance(strategy=JOINED)
@Table(name="EJB_ROSTER_LEAGUE")
public abstract class League implements java.io.Serializable {
  ...
}
```

roster uses the default discriminator column name, so the @DiscriminatorColumn annotation is not required. Because we are using automatic table generation in roster the Persistence provider will create a discriminator column in the EJB_ROSTER_LEAGUE table called DTYPE, which will store the name of the inherited entity used to create the league. If you want to use a different name for the discriminator column, decorate League with @DiscriminatorColumn and set the name element:

```
@Entity
@DiscriminatorColumn(name="DISCRIMINATOR")
@Table(name="EJB_ROSTER_LEAGUE")
public abstract class League implements java.io.Serializable {
  ...
}
```

Automatic Table Generation in the roster Application

At deploytime the Application Server will automatically drop and create the database tables used by roster. This is done by setting the toplink.ddl-generation property to drop-and-create-tables in persistence.xml.

```
<?xml version="1.0" encoding="UTF-8"?>
<persistence xmlns="http://java.sun.com/xml/ns/persistence"
xmlns:xsi="http://www.w3.org/2001/XMLSchema-instance"
xsi:schemaLocation="http://java.sun.com/xml/ns/persistence
http://java.sun.com/xml/ns/persistence/persistence_1_0.xsd"
version="1.0">
  <persistence-unit name="em" transaction-type="JTA">
    <jta-data-source>jdbc/__default</jta-data-source>
    <properties>
      <property name="toplink.ddl-generation"
```

```
                    value="drop-and-create-tables"/>
        </properties>
    </persistence-unit>
</persistence>
```

This feature is specific to the Java Persistence API provider used by the Application Server, and is non-portable across Java EE servers. Automatic table creation is useful for development purposes, however, and the `toplink.ddl-generation` property may be removed from `persistence.xml` when preparing the application for production use, or when deploying to other Java EE servers.

Building and Running the roster Application

This section describes how to build, package, deploy, and run the `roster` application. You can do this using either NetBeans 5.5 or Ant.

Building, Packaging, Deploying, and Running roster in NetBeans 5.5

Follow these instructions to build, package, deploy, and run the `roster` example to your Application Server instance using NetBeans 5.5.

1. In NetBeans 5.5, select File→Open Project.
2. In the Open Project dialog, navigate to `<INSTALL>/javaeetutorial5/examples/ejb/`.
3. Select the `roster` folder.
4. Select the Open as Main Project and Open Required Projects checkboxes.
5. Click Open Project Folder.
6. In the Projects tab, right-click the `roster` project and select Run Project.

You will see the following partial output from the application client in the Output tab:

```
List all players in team T2:
P6 Ian Carlyle goalkeeper 555.0
P7 Rebecca Struthers midfielder 777.0
P8 Anne Anderson forward 65.0
P9 Jan Wesley defender 100.0
P10 Terry Smithson midfielder 100.0
```

```
List all teams in league L1:
T1 Honey Bees Visalia
T2 Gophers Manteca
T5 Crows Orland

List all defenders:
P2 Alice Smith defender 505.0
P5 Barney Bold defender 100.0
P9 Jan Wesley defender 100.0
P22 Janice Walker defender 857.0
P25 Frank Fletcher defender 399.0
...
```

Building, Packaging, Deploying, and Running roster Using Ant

To build the application components of `roster`, enter the following command:

```
ant
```

This runs the `default` task, which compiles the source files and packages the application into an EAR file located at `<INSTALL>/examples/ejb/roster/dist/roster.ear`.

To deploy the EAR, make sure the Application Server is started, then enter the following command:

```
ant deploy
```

The build system will check to see if the Java DB database server is running and start it if it is not running, then deploy `roster.ear`. The Application Server will then drop and create the database tables during deployment, as specified in `persistence.xml`.

After `roster.ear` is deployed, a client JAR, `rosterClient.jar`, is retrieved. This contains the application client.

To run the application client, enter the following command:

```
ant run
```

You will see the output, which begins:

```
[echo] running application client container.
[exec] List all players in team T2:
[exec] P6 Ian Carlyle goalkeeper 555.0
[exec] P7 Rebecca Struthers midfielder 777.0
[exec] P8 Anne Anderson forward 65.0
[exec] P9 Jan Wesley defender 100.0
[exec] P10 Terry Smithson midfielder 100.0

[exec] List all teams in league L1:
[exec] T1 Honey Bees Visalia
[exec] T2 Gophers Manteca
[exec] T5 Crows Orland

[exec] List all defenders:
[exec] P2 Alice Smith defender 505.0
[exec] P5 Barney Bold defender 100.0
[exec] P9 Jan Wesley defender 100.0
[exec] P22 Janice Walker defender 857.0
[exec] P25 Frank Fletcher defender 399.0
...
```

The all Task

As a convenience, the `all` task will build, package, deploy, and run the application. To do this, enter the following command:

```
ant all
```

Undeploying order

To undeploy `roster.ear`, enter the following command:

```
ant undeploy
```

27

The Java Persistence Query Language

THE Java Persistence query language defines queries for entities and their persistent state. The query language allows you to write portable queries that work regardless of the underlying data store.

The query language uses the abstract persistence schemas of entities, including their relationships, for its data model, and it defines operators and expressions based on this data model. The scope of a query spans the abstract schemas of related entities that are packaged in the same persistence unit. The query language uses a SQL-like syntax to select objects or values based on entity abstract schema types and relationships among them.

This chapter relies on the material presented in earlier chapters. For conceptual information, see Chapter 24. For code examples, see Chapters 25 and 26.

Terminology

The following list defines some of the terms referred to in this chapter.

- **Abstract schema**: The persistent schema abstraction (persistent entities, their state, and their relationships) over which queries operate. The query language translates queries over this persistent schema abstraction into queries that are executed over the database schema to which entities are mapped.
- **Abstract schema type**: All expressions evaluate to a type. The abstract schema type of an entity is derived from the entity class and the metadata information provided by Java language annotations.
- **Backus-Naur Form (BNF)**: A notation that describes the syntax of high-level languages. The syntax diagrams in this chapter are in BNF notation.
- **Navigation**: The traversal of relationships in a query language expression. The navigation operator is a period.
- **Path expression**: An expression that navigates to a entity's state or relationship field.
- **State field**: A persistent field of an entity.
- **Relationship field**: A persistent relationship field of an entity whose type is the abstract schema type of the related entity.

Simplified Syntax

This section briefly describes the syntax of the query language so that you can quickly move on to the next section, Example Queries. When you are ready to learn about the syntax in more detail, see the section Full Syntax (page 870).

Select Statements

A select query has six clauses: `SELECT`, `FROM`, `WHERE`, `GROUP BY`, `HAVING`, and `ORDER BY`. The `SELECT` and `FROM` clauses are required, but the `WHERE`, `GROUP BY`, `HAVING`, and `ORDER BY` clauses are optional. Here is the high-level BNF syntax of a query language query:

```
QL_statement ::= select_clause from_clause
[where_clause][groupby_clause][having_clause][orderby_clause]
```

The `SELECT` clause defines the types of the objects or values returned by the query.

The `FROM` clause defines the scope of the query by declaring one or more identification variables, which can be referenced in the `SELECT` and `WHERE` clauses. An identification variable represents one of the following elements:

- The abstract schema name of an entity
- An element of a collection relationship
- An element of a single-valued relationship
- A member of a collection that is the multiple side of a one-to-many relationship

The `WHERE` clause is a conditional expression that restricts the objects or values retrieved by the query. Although it is optional, most queries have a `WHERE` clause.

The `GROUP BY` clause groups query results according to a set of properties.

The `HAVING` clause is used with the `GROUP BY` clause to further restrict the query results according to a conditional expression.

The `ORDER BY` clause sorts the objects or values returned by the query into a specified order.

Update and Delete Statements

Update and delete statements provide bulk operations over sets of entities. They have the following syntax:

```
update_statement :: = update_clause [where_clause]

delete_statement :: = delete_clause [where_clause]
```

The update and delete clauses determine the type of the entities to be updated or deleted. The `WHERE` clause may be used to restrict the scope of the update or delete operation.

Example Queries

The following queries are from the `Player` entity of the `roster` application, which is documented in Chapter 26.

Simple Queries

If you are unfamiliar with the query language, these simple queries are a good place to start.

A Basic Select Query

```
SELECT p
FROM Player p
```

Data retrieved: All players.

Description: The `FROM` clause declares an identification variable named `p`, omitting the optional keyword `AS`. If the `AS` keyword were included, the clause would be written as follows:

```
FROM Player AS p
```

The `Player` element is the abstract schema name of the `Player` entity.

See also: Identification Variables (page 877)

Eliminating Duplicate Values

```
SELECT DISTINCT p
FROM Player p
WHERE p.position = ?1
```

Data retrieved: The players with the position specified by the query's parameter.

Description: The `DISTINCT` keyword eliminates duplicate values.

The `WHERE` clause restricts the players retrieved by checking their `position`, a persistent field of the `Player` entity. The `?1` element denotes the input parameter of the query.

See also: Input Parameters (page 883), The DISTINCT Keyword (page 894)

Using Named Parameters

```
SELECT DISTINCT p
FROM Player p
WHERE p.position = :position AND p.name = :name
```

Data retrieved: The players having the specified positions and names.

Description: The position and name elements are persistent fields of the Player entity. Thc WHERE clause compares the values of these fields with the named parameters of the query, set using the Query.setNamedParameter method. The query language denotes a named input parameter using colon (:) followed by an identifier. The first input parameter is :position, the second is :name.

Queries That Navigate to Related Entities

In the query language, an expression can traverse (or navigate) to related entities. These expressions are the primary difference between the Java Persistence query language and SQL. Queries navigates to related entities, whereas SQL joins tables.

A Simple Query with Relationships

```
SELECT DISTINCT p
FROM Player p, IN(p.teams) t
```

Data retrieved: All players who belong to a team.

Description: The FROM clause declares two identification variables: p and t. The p variable represents the Player entity, and the t variable represents the related Team entity. The declaration for t references the previously declared p variable. The IN keyword signifies that teams is a collection of related entities. The p.teams expression navigates from a Player to its related Team. The period in the p.teams expression is the navigation operator.

You may also use the JOIN statement to write the same query:

```
SELECT DISTINCT p
FROM Player p JOIN p.teams t
```

This query could also be rewritten as:

```
SELECT DISTINCT p
FROM Player p
WHERE p.team IS NOT EMPTY
```

Navigating to Single-Valued Relationship Fields

Use the JOIN clause statement to navigate to a single-valued relationship field:

```
SELECT t
FROM Team t JOIN t.league l
WHERE l.sport = 'soccer' OR l.sport ='football'
```

In this example, the query will return all teams that are in either soccer or football leagues.

Traversing Relationships with an Input Parameter

```
SELECT DISTINCT p
FROM Player p, IN (p.teams) AS t
WHERE t.city = :city
```

Data retrieved: The players whose teams belong to the specified city.

Description: This query is similar to the previous example, but it adds an input parameter. The AS keyword in the FROM clause is optional. In the WHERE clause, the period preceding the persistent variable city is a delimiter, not a navigation operator. Strictly speaking, expressions can navigate to relationship fields (related entities), but not to persistent fields. To access a persistent field, an expression uses the period as a delimiter.

Expressions cannot navigate beyond (or further qualify) relationship fields that are collections. In the syntax of an expression, a collection-valued field is a terminal symbol. Because the teams field is a collection, the WHERE clause cannot specify p.teams.city—an illegal expression.

See also: Path Expressions (page 880)

Traversing Multiple Relationships

```
SELECT DISTINCT p
FROM Player p, IN (p.teams) t
WHERE t.league = :league
```

Data retrieved: The players that belong to the specified league.

Description: The expressions in this query navigate over two relationships. The `p.teams` expression navigates the `Player-Team` relationship, and the `t.league` expression navigates the `Team-League` relationship.

In the other examples, the input parameters are `String` objects, but in this example the parameter is an object whose type is a `League`. This type matches the `league` relationship field in the comparison expression of the `WHERE` clause.

Navigating According to Related Fields

```
SELECT DISTINCT p
FROM Player p, IN (p.teams) t
WHERE t.league.sport = :sport
```

Data retrieved: The players who participate in the specified sport.

Description: The `sport` persistent field belongs to the `League` entity. To reach the `sport` field, the query must first navigate from the `Player` entity to `Team` (`p.teams`) and then from `Team` to the `League` entity (`t.league`). Because the `league` relationship field is not a collection, it can be followed by the `sport` persistent field.

Queries with Other Conditional Expressions

Every `WHERE` clause must specify a conditional expression, of which there are several kinds. In the previous examples, the conditional expressions are comparison expressions that test for equality. The following examples demonstrate some of the other kinds of conditional expressions. For descriptions of all conditional expressions, see the section WHERE Clause (page 881).

The LIKE Expression

```
SELECT p
FROM Player p
WHERE p.name LIKE 'Mich%'
```

Data retrieved: All players whose names begin with "Mich."

Description: The `LIKE` expression uses wildcard characters to search for strings that match the wildcard pattern. In this case, the query uses the `LIKE` expression and the `%` wildcard to find all players whose names begin with the string "Mich." For example, "Michael" and "Michelle" both match the wildcard pattern.

See also: LIKE Expressions (page 885)

The IS NULL Expression

```
SELECT t
FROM Team t
WHERE t.league IS NULL
```

Data retrieved: All teams not associated with a league.

Description: The `IS NULL` expression can be used to check if a relationship has been set between two entities. In this case, the query checks to see if the teams are associated with any leagues, and returns the teams that do not have a league.

See also: NULL Comparison Expressions (page 886), NULL Values (page 890)

The IS EMPTY Expression

```
SELECT p
FROM Player p
WHERE p.teams IS EMPTY
```

Data retrieved*:* All players who do not belong to a team.

Description*:* The `teams` relationship field of the `Player` entity is a collection. If a player does not belong to a team, then the `teams` collection is empty and the conditional expression is `TRUE`.

See also*:* Empty Collection Comparison Expressions (page 886)

The BETWEEN Expression

```
SELECT DISTINCT p
FROM Player p
WHERE p.salary BETWEEN :lowerSalary AND :higherSalary
```

Data retrieved: The players whose salaries fall within the range of the specified salaries.

Description: This BETWEEN expression has three arithmetic expressions: a persistent field (p.salary) and the two input parameters (:lowerSalary and :higherSalary). The following expression is equivalent to the BETWEEN expression:

```
p.salary >= :lowerSalary AND p.salary <= :higherSalary
```

See also: BETWEEN Expressions (page 884)

Comparison Operators

```
SELECT DISTINCT p1
FROM Player p1, Player p2
WHERE p1.salary > p2.salary AND p2.name = :name
```

Data retrieved: All players whose salaries are higher than the salary of the player with the specified name.

Description: The FROM clause declares two identification variables (p1 and p2) of the same type (Player). Two identification variables are needed because the WHERE clause compares the salary of one player (p2) with that of the other players (p1).

See also: Identification Variables (page 877)

Bulk Updates and Deletes

The following examples show how to use the UPDATE and DELETE expressions in queries. UPDATE and DELETE operate on multiple entities according to the condition or conditions set in the WHERE clause. The WHERE clause in UPDATE and DELETE queries follows the same rules as SELECT queries.

Update Queries

```
UPDATE Player p
SET p.status = 'inactive'
WHERE p.lastPlayed < :inactiveThresholdDate
```

Description: This query sets the status of a set of players to `inactive` if the player's last game was longer than the date specified in `inactiveThresholdDate`.

Delete Queries

```
DELETE
FROM Player p
WHERE p.status = 'inactive'
AND p.teams IS EMPTY
```

Description: This query deletes all inactive players who are not on a team.

Full Syntax

This section discusses the query language syntax, as defined in the Java Persistence specification. Much of the following material paraphrases or directly quotes the specification.

BNF Symbols

Table 27–1 describes the BNF symbols used in this chapter.

Table 27–1 BNF Symbol Summary

Symbol	Description
`::=`	The element to the left of the symbol is defined by the constructs on the right.
`*`	The preceding construct may occur zero or more times.
`{...}`	The constructs within the curly braces are grouped together.

Table 27–1 BNF Symbol Summary (Continued)

Symbol	Description
[...]	The constructs within the square brackets are optional.
|	An exclusive OR.
BOLDFACE	A keyword (although capitalized in the BNF diagram, keywords are not case-sensitive).
Whitespace	A whitespace character can be a space, a horizontal tab, or a linefeed.

BNF Grammar of the Java Persistence Query Language

Here is the entire BNF diagram for the query language:

```
QL_statement ::= select_statement | update_statement |
delete_statement
select_statement ::= select_clause from_clause [where_clause]
[groupby_clause][having_clause] [orderby_clause]
update_statement ::= update_clause [where_clause]
delete_statement ::= delete_clause [where_clause]
from_clause ::=
  FROM identification_variable_declaration
    {, {identification_variable_declaration |
      collection_member_declaration}}*
identification_variable_declaration ::=
    range_variable_declaration { join | fetch_join }*
range_variable_declaration ::= abstract_schema_name [AS]
    identification_variable
join ::= join_spec join_association_path_expression [AS]
    identification_variable
fetch_join ::= join_specFETCH join_association_path_expression
association_path_expression ::=
    collection_valued_path_expression |
    single_valued_association_path_expression
join_spec::= [LEFT [OUTER] |INNER] JOIN
join_association_path_expression ::=
    join_collection_valued_path_expression |
    join_single_valued_association_path_expression
join_collection_valued_path_expression::=
  identification_variable.collection_valued_association_field
join_single_valued_association_path_expression::=
```

```
        identification_variable.single_valued_association_field
    collection_member_declaration ::=
        IN (collection_valued_path_expression) [AS]
        identification_variable
    single_valued_path_expression ::=
        state_field_path_expression |
        single_valued_association_path_expression
    state_field_path_expression ::=
      {identification_variable |
      single_valued_association_path_expression}.state_field
    single_valued_association_path_expression ::=
      identification_variable.{single_valued_association_field.}*
      single_valued_association_field
    collection_valued_path_expression ::=
      identification_variable.{single_valued_association_field.}*
      collection_valued_association_field
    state_field ::=
      {embedded_class_state_field.}*simple_state_field
    update_clause ::=UPDATE abstract_schema_name [[AS]
      identification_variable] SET update_item {, update_item}*
    update_item ::= [identification_variable.]{state_field |
      single_valued_association_field} = new_value
    new_value ::=
      simple_arithmetic_expression |
      string_primary |
      datetime_primary |
      boolean_primary |
      enum_primary simple_entity_expression |
      NULL
    delete_clause ::= DELETE FROM abstract_schema_name [[AS]
      identification_variable]
    select_clause ::= SELECT [DISTINCT] select_expression {,
      select_expression}*
    select_expression ::=
      single_valued_path_expression |
      aggregate_expression |
      identification_variable |
      OBJECT(identification_variable) |
      constructor_expression
    constructor_expression ::=
      NEW constructor_name(constructor_item {,
      constructor_item}*)
    constructor_item ::= single_valued_path_expression |
      aggregate_expression
    aggregate_expression ::=
      {AVG |MAX |MIN |SUM} ([DISTINCT]
        state_field_path_expression) |
      COUNT ([DISTINCT] identification_variable |
```

```
    state_field_path_expression |
    single_valued_association_path_expression)
where_clause ::= WHERE conditional_expression
groupby_clause ::= GROUP BY groupby_item {, groupby_item}*
groupby_item ::= single_valued_path_expression
having_clause ::= HAVING conditional_expression
orderby_clause ::= ORDER BY orderby_item {, orderby_item}*
orderby_item ::= state_field_path_expression [ASC |DESC]
subquery ::= simple_select_clause subquery_from_clause
  [where_clause] [groupby_clause] [having_clause]
subquery_from_clause ::=
  FROM subselect_identification_variable_declaration
    {, subselect_identification_variable_declaration}*
subselect_identification_variable_declaration ::=
  identification_variable_declaration |
  association_path_expression [AS] identification_variable |
  collection_member_declaration
simple_select_clause ::= SELECT [DISTINCT]
  simple_select_expression
simple_select_expression::=
  single_valued_path_expression |
  aggregate_expression |
  identification_variable
conditional_expression ::= conditional_term |
  conditional_expression OR conditional_term
conditional_term ::= conditional_factor | conditional_term AND
  conditional_factor
conditional_factor ::= [NOT] conditional_primary
conditional_primary ::= simple_cond_expression |(
  conditional_expression)
simple_cond_expression ::=
  comparison_expression |
  between_expression |
  like_expression |
  in_expression |
  null_comparison_expression |
  empty_collection_comparison_expression |
  collection_member_expression |
  exists_expression
between_expression ::=
  arithmetic_expression [NOT] BETWEEN
    arithmetic_expressionAND arithmetic_expression |
  string_expression [NOT] BETWEEN string_expression AND
    string_expression |
  datetime_expression [NOT] BETWEEN
    datetime_expression AND datetime_expression
in_expression ::=
  state_field_path_expression [NOT] IN (in_item {, in_item}*
```

```
    | subquery)
in_item ::= literal | input_parameter
like_expression ::=
  string_expression [NOT] LIKE pattern_value [ESCAPE
    escape_character]
null_comparison_expression ::=
  {single_valued_path_expression | input_parameter} IS [NOT]
    NULL
empty_collection_comparison_expression ::=
  collection_valued_path_expression IS [NOT] EMPTY
collection_member_expression ::= entity_expression
  [NOT] MEMBER [OF] collection_valued_path_expression
exists_expression::= [NOT] EXISTS (subquery)
all_or_any_expression ::= {ALL |ANY |SOME} (subquery)
comparison_expression ::=
  string_expression comparison_operator {string_expression |
  all_or_any_expression} |
  boolean_expression {= |<> } {boolean_expression |
  all_or_any_expression} |
  enum_expression {= |<> } {enum_expression |
  all_or_any_expression} |
  datetime_expression comparison_operator
    {datetime_expression | all_or_any_expression} |
  entity_expression {= |<> } {entity_expression |
  all_or_any_expression} |
  arithmetic_expression comparison_operator
    {arithmetic_expression | all_or_any_expression}
comparison_operator ::= = |> |>= |< |<= |<>
arithmetic_expression ::= simple_arithmetic_expression |
  (subquery)
simple_arithmetic_expression ::=
  arithmetic_term | simple_arithmetic_expression {+ |- }
    arithmetic_term
arithmetic_term ::= arithmetic_factor | arithmetic_term {* |/ }
  arithmetic_factor
arithmetic_factor ::= [{+ |- }] arithmetic_primary
arithmetic_primary ::=
  state_field_path_expression |
  numeric_literal |
  (simple_arithmetic_expression) |
  input_parameter |
  functions_returning_numerics |
  aggregate_expression
string_expression ::= string_primary | (subquery)
string_primary ::=
  state_field_path_expression |
  string_literal |
  input_parameter |
```

```
  functions_returning_strings |
  aggregate_expression
datetime_expression ::= datetime_primary | (subquery)
datetime_primary ::=
  state_field_path_expression |
  input_parameter |
  functions_returning_datetime |
  aggregate_expression
boolean_expression ::= boolean_primary | (subquery)
boolean_primary ::=
  state_field_path_expression |
  boolean_literal |
  input_parameter
enum_expression ::= enum_primary | (subquery)
enum_primary ::=
  state_field_path_expression |
  enum_literal |
  input_parameter
entity_expression ::=
  single_valued_association_path_expression |
    simple_entity_expression
simple_entity_expression ::=
  identification_variable |
  input_parameter
functions_returning_numerics::=
  LENGTH(string_primary) |
  LOCATE(string_primary, string_primary[,
    simple_arithmetic_expression]) |
  ABS(simple_arithmetic_expression) |
  SQRT(simple_arithmetic_expression) |
  MOD(simple_arithmetic_expression,
    simple_arithmetic_expression) |
  SIZE(collection_valued_path_expression)
functions_returning_datetime ::=
  CURRENT_DATE |
  CURRENT_TIME |
  CURRENT_TIMESTAMP
functions_returning_strings ::=
  CONCAT(string_primary, string_primary) |
  SUBSTRING(string_primary,
    simple_arithmetic_expression,
    simple_arithmetic_expression)|
  TRIM([[trim_specification] [trim_character] FROM]
    string_primary) |
  LOWER(string_primary) |
  UPPER(string_primary)
trim_specification ::= LEADING | TRAILING | BOTH
```

FROM Clause

The FROM clause defines the domain of the query by declaring identification variables.

Identifiers

An identifier is a sequence of one or more characters. The first character must be a valid first character (letter, $, _) in an identifier of the Java programming language (hereafter in this chapter called simply "Java"). Each subsequent character in the sequence must be a valid nonfirst character (letter, digit, $, _) in a Java identifier. (For details, see the J2SE API documentation of the isJavaIdentifierStart and isJavaIdentifierPart methods of the Character class.) The question mark (?) is a reserved character in the query language and cannot be used in an identifier.

A query language identifier is case-sensitive with two exceptions:

- Keywords
- Identification variables

An identifier cannot be the same as a query language keyword. Here is a list of query language keywords:

```
ALL                 FALSE       NOT
AND                 FETCH       NULL
ANY                 FROM        OBJECT
AS                  GROUP       OF
ASC                 HAVING      OUTER
AVG                 IN          OR
BETWEEN             INNER       ORDER
BY                  IS          SELECT
COUNT               JOIN        SOME
CURRENT_DATE        LEFT        SUM
CURRENT_TIME        LIKE        TRIM
CURRENT_TIMESTAMP   MAX         TRUE
DELETE              MEMBER      UNKNOWN
DESC                MIN         UPDATE
DISTINCT            MOD         UPPER
EMPTY               NEW         WHERE
EXISTS
```

It is not recommended that you use a SQL keyword as an identifier, because the list of keywords may expand to include other reserved SQL words in the future.

Identification Variables

An *identification variable* is an identifier declared in the `FROM` clause. Although the `SELECT` and `WHERE` clauses can reference identification variables, they cannot declare them. All identification variables must be declared in the `FROM` clause.

Because an identification variable is an identifier, it has the same naming conventions and restrictions as an identifier with the exception that an identification variables is case-insensitive. For example, an identification variable cannot be the same as a query language keyword. (See the preceding section for more naming rules.) Also, within a given persistence unit, an identification variable name must not match the name of any entity or abstract schema.

The `FROM` clause can contain multiple declarations, separated by commas. A declaration can reference another identification variable that has been previously declared (to the left). In the following `FROM` clause, the variable `t` references the previously declared variable `p`:

```
FROM Player p, IN (p.teams) AS t
```

Even if an identification variable is not used in the `WHERE` clause, its declaration can affect the results of the query. For an example, compare the next two queries. The following query returns all players, whether or not they belong to a team:

```
SELECT p
FROM Player p
```

In contrast, because the next query declares the `t` identification variable, it fetches all players that belong to a team:

```
SELECT p
FROM Player p, IN (p.teams) AS t
```

The following query returns the same results as the preceding query, but the `WHERE` clause makes it easier to read:

```
SELECT p
FROM Player p
WHERE p.teams IS NOT EMPTY
```

An identification variable always designates a reference to a single value whose type is that of the expression used in the declaration. There are two kinds of declarations: range variable and collection member.

Range Variable Declarations

To declare an identification variable as an abstract schema type, you specify a range variable declaration. In other words, an identification variable can range over the abstract schema type of an entity. In the following example, an identification variable named p represents the abstract schema named Player:

```
FROM Player p
```

A range variable declaration can include the optional AS operator:

```
FROM Player AS p
```

In most cases, to obtain objects a query uses path expressions to navigate through the relationships. But for those objects that cannot be obtained by navigation, you can use a range variable declaration to designate a starting point (or *root*).

If the query compares multiple values of the same abstract schema type, then the FROM clause must declare multiple identification variables for the abstract schema:

```
FROM Player p1, Player p2
```

For a sample of such a query, see Comparison Operators (page 869).

Collection Member Declarations

In a one-to-many relationship, the multiple side consists of a collection of entities. An identification variable can represent a member of this collection. To access a collection member, the path expression in the variable's declaration navigates through the relationships in the abstract schema. (For more information on path expressions, see the following section.) Because a path expression can be based on another path expression, the navigation can traverse several relationships. See Traversing Multiple Relationships (page 867).

A collection member declaration must include the IN operator, but it can omit the optional AS operator.

In the following example, the entity represented by the abstract schema named Player has a relationship field called teams. The identification variable called t represents a single member of the teams collection.

```
FROM Player p, IN (p.teams) t
```

Joins

The JOIN operator is used to traverse over relationships between entities, and is functionally similar to the IN operator.

In the following example, the query joins over the relationship between customers and orders:

```
SELECT c
FROM Customer c JOIN c.orders o
WHERE c.status = 1 AND o.totalPrice > 10000
```

The INNER keyword is optional:

```
SELECT c
FROM Customer c INNER JOIN c.orders o
WHERE c.status = 1 AND o.totalPrice > 10000
```

These examples are equivalent to the following query, which uses the IN operator:

```
SELECT c
FROM Customer c, IN(c.orders) o
WHERE c.status = 1 AND o.totalPrice > 10000
```

You can also join a single-valued relationship.

```
SELECT t
FROM Team t JOIN t.league l
WHERE l.sport = :sport
```

A LEFT JOIN or LEFT OUTER JOIN retrieves a set of entities where matching values in the join condition may be absent. The OUTER keyword is optional.

```
SELECT c.name, o.totalPrice
FROM Order o LEFT JOIN o.customer c
```

A FETCH JOIN is a join operation that returns associated entities as a side-effect of running the query. In the following example, the query returns a set of departments, and as a side-effect, the associated employees of the departments, even though the employees were not explicitly retrieved by the SELECT clause.

```
SELECT d
FROM Department d LEFT JOIN FETCH d.employees
WHERE d.deptno = 1
```

Path Expressions

Path expressions are important constructs in the syntax of the query language, for several reasons. First, they define navigation paths through the relationships in the abstract schema. These path definitions affect both the scope and the results of a query. Second, they can appear in any of the main clauses of a query (SELECT, DELETE, HAVING, UPDATE, WHERE, FROM, GROUP BY, ORDER BY). Finally, although much of the query language is a subset of SQL, path expressions are extensions not found in SQL.

Examples

Here, the WHERE clause contains a single_valued_path_expression. The p is an identification variable, and salary is a persistent field of Player.

```
SELECT DISTINCT p
FROM Player p
WHERE p.salary BETWEEN :lowerSalary AND :higherSalary
```

Here, the WHERE clause also contains a single_valued_path_expression. The t is an identification variable, league is a single-valued relationship field, and sport is a persistent field of league.

```
SELECT DISTINCT p
FROM Player p, IN (p.teams) t
WHERE t.league.sport = :sport
```

Here, the WHERE clause contains a collection_valued_path_expression. The p is an identification variable, and teams designates a collection-valued relationship field.

```
SELECT DISTINCT p
FROM Player p
WHERE p.teams IS EMPTY
```

Expression Types

The type of a path expression is the type of the object represented by the ending element, which can be one of the following:

- Persistent field
- Single-valued relationship field
- Collection-valued relationship field

For example, the type of the expression p.salary is double because the terminating persistent field (salary) is a double.

In the expression p.teams, the terminating element is a collection-valued relationship field (teams). This expression's type is a collection of the abstract schema type named Team. Because Team is the abstract schema name for the Team entity, this type maps to the entity. For more information on the type mapping of abstract schemas, see the section Return Types (page 892).

Navigation

A path expression enables the query to navigate to related entities. The terminating elements of an expression determine whether navigation is allowed. If an expression contains a single-valued relationship field, the navigation can continue to an object that is related to the field. However, an expression cannot navigate beyond a persistent field or a collection-valued relationship field. For example, the expression p.teams.league.sport is illegal, because teams is a collection-valued relationship field. To reach the sport field, the FROM clause could define an identification variable named t for the teams field:

```
FROM Player AS p, IN (p.teams) t
WHERE t.league.sport = 'soccer'
```

WHERE Clause

The WHERE clause specifies a conditional expression that limits the values returned by the query. The query returns all corresponding values in the data store for which the conditional expression is TRUE. Although usually specified, the WHERE clause is optional. If the WHERE clause is omitted, then the query returns all values. The high-level syntax for the WHERE clause follows:

```
where_clause ::= WHERE conditional_expression
```

Literals

There are four kinds of literals: string, numeric, Boolean, and enum.

String Literals

A string literal is enclosed in single quotes:

```
'Duke'
```

If a string literal contains a single quote, you indicate the quote by using two single quotes:

```
'Duke''s'
```

Like a Java `String`, a string literal in the query language uses the Unicode character encoding.

Numeric Literals

There are two types of numeric literals: exact and approximate.

An exact numeric literal is a numeric value without a decimal point, such as 65, –233, and +12. Using the Java integer syntax, exact numeric literals support numbers in the range of a Java `long`.

An approximate numeric literal is a numeric value in scientific notation, such as 57., –85.7, and +2.1. Using the syntax of the Java floating-point literal, approximate numeric literals support numbers in the range of a Java `double`.

Boolean Literals

A Boolean literal is either `TRUE` or `FALSE`. These keywords are not case-sensitive.

Enum Literals

The Java Persistence Query Language supports the use of enum literals using the Java enum literal syntax. The enum class name must be specified as fully qualified class name.

```
SELECT e
FROM Employee e
WHERE e.status = com.xyz.EmployeeStatus.FULL_TIME
```

Input Parameters

An input parameter can be either a named parameter or a positional parameter.

A named input parameter is designated by a colon (`:`) followed by a string. For example, `:name`.

A positional input parameter is designated by a question mark (`?`) followed by an integer. For example, the first input parameter is `?1`, the second is `?2`, and so forth.

The following rules apply to input parameters:

- They can be used only in a `WHERE` or `HAVING` clause.
- Positional parameters must be numbered, starting with the integer 1.
- Named parameters and positional parameters may not be mixed in a single query.
- Named parameters are case-sensitive.

Conditional Expressions

A `WHERE` clause consists of a conditional expression, which is evaluated from left to right within a precedence level. You can change the order of evaluation by using parentheses.

Operators and Their Precedence

Table 27–2 lists the query language operators in order of decreasing precedence.

Table 27–2 Query Language Order Precedence

Type	Precedence Order
Navigation	. (a period)
Arithmetic	+ – (unary) * / (multiplication and division) + – (addition and subtraction)

Table 27–2 Query Language Order Precedence (Continued)

Type	Precedence Order
Comparison	= > >= < <= <> (not equal) [NOT] BETWEEN [NOT] LIKE [NOT] IN IS [NOT] NULL IS [NOT] EMPTY [NOT] MEMBER OF
Logical	NOT AND OR

BETWEEN Expressions

A BETWEEN expression determines whether an arithmetic expression falls within a range of values.

These two expressions are equivalent:

```
p.age BETWEEN 15 AND 19
p.age >= 15 AND p.age <= 19
```

The following two expressions are also equivalent:

```
p.age NOT BETWEEN 15 AND 19
p.age < 15 OR p.age > 19
```

If an arithmetic expression has a NULL value, then the value of the BETWEEN expression is unknown.

IN Expressions

An IN expression determines whether or not a string belongs to a set of string literals, or whether a number belongs to a set of number values.

The path expression must have a string or numeric value. If the path expression has a `NULL` value, then the value of the `IN` expression is unknown.

In the following example, if the country is `UK` the expression is `TRUE`. If the country is `Peru` it is `FALSE`.

```
o.country IN ('UK', 'US', 'France')
```

You may also use input parameters:

```
o.country IN ('UK', 'US', 'France', :country)
```

LIKE Expressions

A `LIKE` expression determines whether a wildcard pattern matches a string.

The path expression must have a string or numeric value. If this value is `NULL`, then the value of the `LIKE` expression is unknown. The pattern value is a string literal that can contain wildcard characters. The underscore (_) wildcard character represents any single character. The percent (%) wildcard character represents zero or more characters. The `ESCAPE` clause specifies an escape character for the wildcard characters in the pattern value. Table 27–3 shows some sample `LIKE` expressions.

Table 27–3 `LIKE` Expression Examples

Expression	TRUE	FALSE
`address.phone LIKE '12%3'`	`'123'` `'12993'`	`'1234'`
`asentence.word LIKE 'l_se'`	`'lose'`	`'loose'`
`aword.underscored LIKE '\_%' ESCAPE '\'`	`'_foo'`	`'bar'`
`address.phone NOT LIKE '12%3'`	`'1234'`	`'123'` `'12993'`

NULL Comparison Expressions

A `NULL` comparison expression tests whether a single-valued path expression or an input parameter has a `NULL` value. Usually, the `NULL` comparison expression is used to test whether or not a single-valued relationship has been set.

```
SELECT t
FROM Team t
WHERE t.league IS NULL
```

This query selects all teams where the league relationship is not set. Please note, the following query is *not* equivalent:

```
SELECT t
FROM Team t
WHERE t.league = NULL
```

The comparison with `NULL` using the equals operator (=) always returns an unknown value, even if the relationship is not set. The second query will always return an empty result.

Empty Collection Comparison Expressions

The `IS [NOT] EMPTY` comparison expression tests whether a collection-valued path expression has no elements. In other words, it tests whether or not a collection-valued relationship has been set.

If the collection-valued path expression is `NULL`, then the empty collection comparison expression has a `NULL` value.

Here is an example that finds all orders that do not have any line items:

```
SELECT o
FROM Order o
WHERE o.lineItems IS EMPTY
```

Collection Member Expressions

The `[NOT] MEMBER [OF]` collection member expression determines whether a value is a member of a collection. The value and the collection members must have the same type.

If either the collection-valued or single-valued path expression is unknown, then the collection member expression is unknown. If the collection-valued path expression designates an empty collection, then the collection member expression is FALSE.

The OF keyword is optional.

The following example tests whether a line item is part of an order:

```
SELECT o
FROM Order o
WHERE :lineItem MEMBER OF o.lineItems
```

Subqueries

Subqueries may be used in the WHERE or HAVING clause of a query. Subqueries must be surrounded by parentheses.

The following example find all customers who have placed more than 10 orders:

```
SELECT c
FROM Customer c
WHERE (SELECT COUNT(o) FROM c.orders o) > 10
```

Exists Expressions

The [NOT] EXISTS expression is used with a subquery, and is true only if the result of the subquery consists of one or more values and is false otherwise.

The following example finds all employees whose spouse is also an employee:

```
SELECT DISTINCT emp
FROM Employee emp
WHERE EXISTS (
  SELECT spouseEmp
  FROM Employee spouseEmp
  WHERE spouseEmp = emp.spouse)
```

ALL and ANY Expressions

The ALL expression is used with a subquery, and is true if all the values returned by the subquery are true, or if the subquery is empty.

The ANY expression is used with a subquery, and is true if some of the values returned by the subquery are true. An ANY expression is false if the subquery result is empty, or if all the values returned are false. The SOME keyword is synonymous with ANY.

The ALL and ANY expressions are used with the =, <, <=, >, >=, <> comparison operators.

The following example finds all employees whose salary is higher than the salary of the managers in the employee's department:

```
SELECT emp
FROM Employee emp
WHERE emp.salary > ALL (
  SELECT m.salary
  FROM Manager m
  WHERE m.department = emp.department)
```

Functional Expressions

The query language includes several string and arithmetic functions which may be used in the WHERE or HAVING clause of a query. The functions are listed in the following tables. In Table 27–4, the start and length arguments are of type int. They designate positions in the String argument. The first position in a string is designated by 1. In Table 27–5, the number argument can be either an int, a float, or a double.

Table 27–4 String Expressions

<table>
<tr><th>Function Syntax</th><th>Return Type</th></tr>
<tr><td>CONCAT(String, String)</td><td>String</td></tr>
<tr><td>LENGTH(String)</td><td>int</td></tr>
<tr><td>LOCATE(String, String [, start])</td><td>int</td></tr>
<tr><td>SUBSTRING(String, start, length)</td><td>String</td></tr>
<tr><td>TRIM([[LEADING|TRAILING|BOTH] char) FROM] (String)</td><td>String</td></tr>
<tr><td>LOWER(String)</td><td>String</td></tr>
<tr><td>UPPER(String)</td><td>String</td></tr>
</table>

The CONCAT function concatenates two strings into one string.

The LENGTH function returns the length of a string in characters as an integer.

The LOCATE function returns the positon of a given string within a string. It returns the first position at which the string was found as an integer. The first argument is the string to be located. The second argument is the string to be searched. The optional third argument is an integer that represents the starting string position. By default, LOCATE starts at the beginning of the string. The starting position of a string is 1. If the string cannot be located, LOCATE returns 0.

The SUBSTRING function returns a string that is a substring of the first argument based on the starting position and length.

The TRIM function trims the specified character from the beginning and/or end of a string. If no character is specified, TRIM removes spaces or blanks from the string. If the optional LEADING specification is used, TRIM removes only the leading character(s) from the string. If the optional TRAILING specification is used, TRIM removes only the trailing character(s) from the string. The default is BOTH, which removes the leading and trailing character(s) from the string.

The LOWER and UPPER functions convert a string to lower or upper case, respectively.

Table 27–5 Arithmetic Expressions

Function Syntax	Return Type
ABS(number)	int, float, or double
MOD(int, int)	int
SQRT(double)	double
SIZE(Collection)	int

The ABS function takes a numeric expression and returns a number of the same type as the argument.

The MOD function returns the remainder of the first argument divided by the second.

The SQRT function returns the square root of a number.

The `SIZE` function returns an integer of the number of elements in the given collection.

NULL Values

If the target of a reference is not in the persistent store, then the target is `NULL`. For conditional expressions containing `NULL`, the query language uses the semantics defined by SQL92. Briefly, these semantics are as follows:

- If a comparison or arithmetic operation has an unknown value, it yields a `NULL` value.
- Two `NULL` values are not equal. Comparing two `NULL` values yields an unknown value.
- The `IS NULL` test converts a `NULL` persistent field or a single-valued relationship field to `TRUE`. The `IS NOT NULL` test converts them to `FALSE`.
- Boolean operators and conditional tests use the three-valued logic defined by Table 27–6 and Table 27–7. (In these tables, T stands for `TRUE`, F for `FALSE`, and U for unknown.)

Table 27–6 `AND` Operator Logic

AND	T	F	U
T	T	F	U
F	F	F	F
U	U	F	U

Table 27–7 `OR` Operator Logic

OR	T	F	U
T	T	T	T
F	T	F	U
U	T	U	U

Equality Semantics

In the query language, only values of the same type can be compared. However, this rule has one exception: Exact and approximate numeric values can be compared. In such a comparison, the required type conversion adheres to the rules of Java numeric promotion.

The query language treats compared values as if they were Java types and not as if they represented types in the underlying data store. For example, if a persistent field could be either an integer or a `NULL`, then it must be designated as an `Integer` object and not as an `int` primitive. This designation is required because a Java object can be `NULL` but a primitive cannot.

Two strings are equal only if they contain the same sequence of characters. Trailing blanks are significant; for example, the strings `'abc'` and `'abc '` are not equal.

Two entities of the same abstract schema type are equal only if their primary keys have the same value. Table 27–8 shows the operator logic of a negation, and Table 27–9 shows the truth values of conditional tests.

Table 27–8 `NOT` Operator Logic

NOT Value	Value
T	F
F	T
U	U

Table 27–9 Conditional Test

Conditional Test	T	F	U
Expression `IS TRUE`	T	F	F
Expression `IS FALSE`	F	T	F
Expression is unknown	F	F	T

SELECT Clause

The SELECT clause defines the types of the objects or values returned by the query.

Return Types

The return type of the SELECT clause is defined by the result types of the select expressions contained within it. If multiple expressions are used, the result of the query is an Object[], and the elements in the array correspond to the order of the expressions in the SELECT clause, and in type to the result types of each expression.

A SELECT clause cannot specify a collection-valued expression. For example, the SELECT clause p.teams is invalid because teams is a collection. However, the clause in the following query is valid because the t is a single element of the teams collection:

```
SELECT t
FROM Player p, IN (p.teams) t
```

The following query is an example of a query with multiple expressions in the select clause:

```
SELECT c.name, c.country.name
FROM customer c
WHERE c.lastname = 'Coss' AND c.firstname = 'Roxane'
```

It returns a list of Object[] elements where the first array element is a string denoting the customer name and the second array element is a string denoting the name of the customer's country.

Aggregate Functions in the SELECT Clause

The result of a query may be the result of an aggregate function, listed in Table 27–10.

Table 27–10 Aggregate Functions in Select Statements

Name	Return Type	Description
`AVG`	`Double`	Returns the mean average of the fields.
`COUNT`	`Long`	Returns the total number of results.
`MAX`	the type of the field	Returns the highest value in the result set.
`MIN`	the type of the field	Returns the lowest value in the result set.
`SUM`	`Long` (for integral fields) `Double` (for floating point fields) `BigInteger` (for `BigInteger` fields) `BigDecimal` (for `BigDecimal` fields)	Returns the sum of all the values in the result set.

For select method queries with an aggregate function (`AVG`, `COUNT`, `MAX`, `MIN`, or `SUM`) in the `SELECT` clause, the following rules apply:

- For the `AVG`, `MAX`, `MIN`, and `SUM` functions, the functions return `null` if there are no values to which the function can be applied.
- For the `COUNT` function, if there are no values to which the function can be applied, `COUNT` returns 0.

The following example returns the average order quantity:

```
SELECT AVG(o.quantity)
FROM Order o
```

The following example returns the total cost of the items ordered by Roxane Coss:

```
SELECT SUM(l.price)
FROM Order o JOIN o.lineItems l JOIN o.customer c
WHERE c.lastname = 'Coss' AND c.firstname = 'Roxane'
```

The following example returns the total number of orders:

```
SELECT COUNT(o)
FROM Order o
```

The following example returns the total number of items in Hal Incandenza's order that have prices:

```
SELECT COUNT(l.price)
FROM Order o JOIN o.lineItems l JOIN o.customer c
WHERE c.lastname = 'Incandenza' AND c.firstname = 'Hal'
```

The DISTINCT Keyword

The `DISTINCT` keyword eliminates duplicate return values. If a query returns a `java.util.Collection`—which allows duplicates—then you must specify the `DISTINCT` keyword to eliminate duplicates.

Constructor Expressions

Constructor expressions allow you to return Java instances that store a query result element instead of an `Object[]`.

The following query creates a `CustomerDetail` instance per `Customer` matching the `WHERE` clause. A `CustomerDetail` stores the customer name and customer's country name. So the query returns a `List` of `CustomerDetail` instances:

```
SELECT NEW com.xyz.CustomerDetail(c.name, c.country.name)
FROM customer c
WHERE c.lastname = 'Coss' AND c.firstname = 'Roxane'
```

ORDER BY Clause

As its name suggests, the `ORDER BY` clause orders the values or objects returned by the query.

If the ORDER BY clause contains multiple elements, the left-to-right sequence of the elements determines the high-to-low precedence.

The ASC keyword specifies ascending order (the default), and the DESC keyword indicates descending order.

When using the ORDER BY clause, the SELECT clause must return an orderable set of objects or values. You cannot order the values or objects for values or objects not returned by the SELECT clause. For example, the following query is valid because the ORDER BY clause uses the objects returned by the SELECT clause:

```
SELECT o
FROM Customer c JOIN c.orders o JOIN c.address a
WHERE a.state = 'CA'
ORDER BY o.quantity, o.totalcost
```

The following example is *not* valid because the ORDER BY clause uses a value not returned by the SELECT clause:

```
SELECT p.product_name
FROM Order o, IN(o.lineItems) l JOIN o.customer c
WHERE c.lastname = 'Faehmel' AND c.firstname = 'Robert'
ORDER BY o.quantity
```

The GROUP BY Clause

The GROUP BY clause allows you to group values according to a set of properties.

The following query groups the customers by their country and returns the number of customers per country:

```
SELECT c.country, COUNT(c)
FROM Customer c GROUP BY c.country
```

The HAVING Clause

The HAVING clause is used with the GROUP BY clause to further restrict the returned result of a query.

The following query groups orders by the status of their customer and returns the customer status plus the average totalPrice for all orders where the corresponding customers has the same status. In addition, it considers only customers with status 1, 2, or 3, so orders of other customers are not taken into account:

```
SELECT c.status, AVG(o.totalPrice)
FROM Order o JOIN o.customer c
GROUP BY c.status HAVING c.status IN (1, 2, 3)
```

Part Five: Services

PART Five explores services.

28

Introduction to Security in Java EE

THIS and subsequent chapters discuss how to address security requirements in Java EE, web, and web services applications. Every enterprise that has sensitive resources that can be accessed by many users, or resources that traverse unprotected, open, networks, such as the Internet, needs to be protected.

This chapter introduces basic security concepts and security implementation mechanisms. More information on these concepts and mechanisms can be found in the *Security* chapter of the Java EE 5 specification. This document is available for download online at the following URL:

```
http://www.jcp.org/en/jsr/detail?id=244
```

Other chapters in this tutorial that address security requirements include the following:

- Chapter 29 discusses adding security to Java EE components such as enterprise beans and application clients.
- Chapter 30 discusses and provides examples for adding security to web components such as servlets and JSP pages.

Some of the material in this chapter assumes that you understand basic security concepts. To learn more about these concepts, we recommend that you explore the Java SE security web site before you begin this chapter. The URL for this site is:

```
http://java.sun.com/j2se/1.5.0/docs/guide/security/index.html
```

This tutorial assumes deployment onto the Sun Java System Application Server (hereafter, Application Server) and provides some information regarding configuration of the Application Server. The best source for information regarding configuration of the Application Server, however, is the Application Server *Administration Guide*. The best source for development tips specific to the Application Server is the Application Server *Developer's Guide*. The best source for tips on deploying applications to the Application Server is the Application Server *Application Deployment Guide*.

Overview

Java EE, web, and web services applications are made up of components that can be deployed into different containers. These components are used to build a multitier enterprise application. Security for components is provided by their containers. A container provides two kinds of security: declarative and programmatic security.

- *Declarative security* expresses an application component's security requirements using *deployment descriptors*. Deployment descriptors are external to an application, and include information that specifies how security roles and access requirements are mapped into environment-specific security roles, users, and policies. For more information about deployment descriptors, read Using Deployment Descriptors for Declarative Security (page 910).
- *Programmatic security* is embedded in an application and is used to make security decisions. Programmatic security is useful when declarative security alone is not sufficient to express the security model of an application. For more information about programmatic security, read Using Programmatic Security (page 913).
- *Annotations* (also called *metadata*) are used to specify information about security within a class file. When the application is deployed, this information can either be used by or overridden by the application deployment descriptor. For more information about annotations, read Using Annotations (page 912).

A Simple Example

The security behavior of a Java EE environment may be better understood by examining what happens in a simple application with a web client, a JSP user interface, and enterprise bean business logic.

In the following example, which is taken from the Java EE 5 Specification (JSR-244), the web client relies on the web server to act as its authentication proxy by collecting user authentication data from the client and using it to establish an authenticated session.

Step 1: Initial Request

In the first step of this example, the web client requests the main application URL. This action is shown in Figure 28–1.

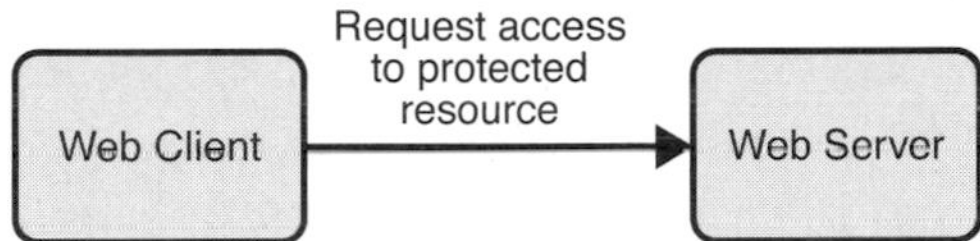

Figure 28–1 Initial Request

Since the client has not yet authenticated itself to the application environment, the server responsible for delivering the web portion of the application (hereafter referred to as *web server*) detects this and invokes the appropriate authentication mechanism for this resource. For more information on these mechanisms, read Security Implementation Mechanisms (page 906).

Step 2: Initial Authentication

The web server returns a form that the web client uses to collect authentication data (for example, user name and password) from the user. The web client forwards the authentication data to the web server, where it is validated by the web server, as shown in Figure 28–2.

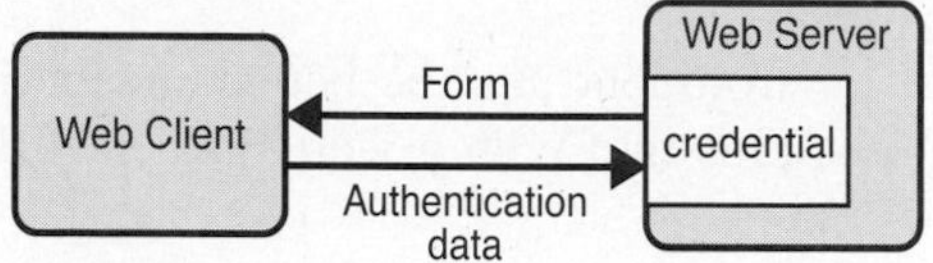

Figure 28–2 Initial Authentication

The validation mechanism may be local to a server, or it may leverage the underlying security services. On the basis of the validation, the web server sets a credential for the user.

Step 3: URL Authorization

The credential is used for future determinations of whether the user is authorized to access restricted resources it may request. The web server consults the security policy (derived from the deployment descriptor) associated with the web resource to determine the security roles that are permitted access to the resource. The web container then tests the user's credential against each role to determine if it can map the user to the role. Figure 28–3 shows this process.

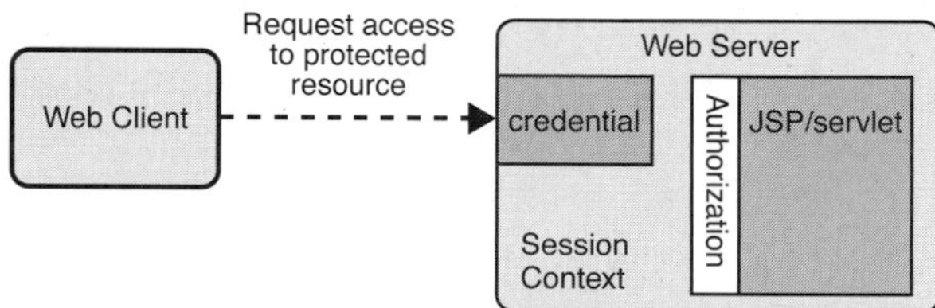

Figure 28–3 URL Authorization

The web server's evaluation stops with an "is authorized" outcome when the web server is able to map the user to a role. A "not authorized" outcome is reached if the web server is unable to map the user to any of the permitted roles.

Step 4: Fulfilling the Original Request

If the user is authorized, the web server returns the result of the original URL request, as shown in Figure 28–4.

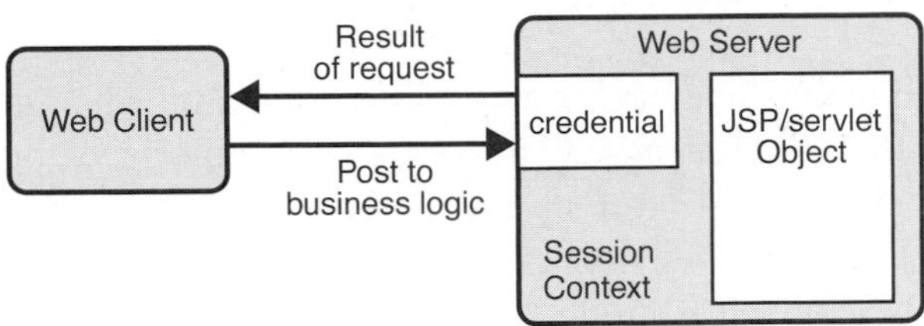

Figure 28–4 Fulfilling the Original Request

In our example, the response URL of a JSP page is returned, enabling the user to post form data that needs to be handled by the business logic component of the application. Read Chapter 30 for more information on protecting web applications.

Step 5: Invoking Enterprise Bean Business Methods

The JSP page performs the remote method call to the enterprise bean, using the user's credential to establish a secure association between the JSP page and the enterprise bean (as shown in Figure 28–5). The association is implemented as two related security contexts, one in the web server and one in the EJB container.

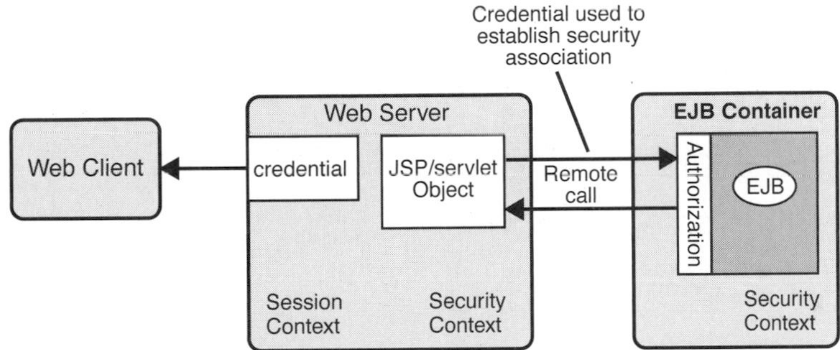

Figure 28–5 Invoking an Enterprise Bean Business Method

The EJB container is responsible for enforcing access control on the enterprise bean method. It consults the security policy (derived from the deployment descriptor) associated with the enterprise bean to determine the security roles that are permitted access to the method. For each role, the EJB container uses the security context associated with the call to determine if it can map the caller to the role.

The container's evaluation stops with an "is authorized" outcome when the container is able to map the caller's credential to a role. A "not authorized" outcome is reached if the container is unable to map the caller to any of the permitted roles. A "not authorized" result causes an exception to be thrown by the container, and propagated back to the calling JSP page.

If the call is authorized, the container dispatches control to the enterprise bean method. The result of the bean's execution of the call is returned to the JSP, and ultimately to the user by the web server and the web client.

Read Chapter 29 for more information on protecting web applications.

Security Functions

A properly implemented security mechanism will provide the following functionality:

- Prevent unauthorized access to application functions and business or personal data
- Hold system users accountable for operations they perform (non-repudiation)
- Protect a system from service interruptions and other breaches that affect quality of service

Ideally, properly implemented security mechanisms will also provide the following functionality:

- Easy to administer
- Transparent to system users
- Interoperable across application and enterprise boundaries

Characteristics of Application Security

Java EE applications consist of components that can contain both protected and unprotected resources. Often, you need to protect resources to ensure that only authorized users have access. *Authorization* provides controlled access to protected resources. Authorization is based on identification and authentication. *Identification* is a process that enables recognition of an entity by a system, and *authentication* is a process that verifies the identity of a user, device, or other entity in a computer system, usually as a prerequisite to allowing access to resources in a system.

Authorization and authentication are not required for an entity to access unprotected resources. Accessing a resource without authentication is referred to as *unauthenticated* or *anonymous* access.

These and several other well-defined characteristics of application security that, when properly addressed, help to minimize the security threats faced by an enterprise, include the following:

- **Authentication**: The means by which communicating entities (for example, client and server) prove to one another that they are acting on behalf of specific identities that are authorized for access. This ensures that users are who they say they are.
- **Authorization**, or **Access Control**: The means by which interactions with resources are limited to collections of users or programs for the purpose of enforcing integrity, confidentiality, or availability constraints. This ensures that users have permission to perform operations or access data.
- **Data integrity**: The means used to prove that information has not been modified by a third party (some entity other than the source of the information). For example, a recipient of data sent over an open network must be able to detect and discard messages that were modified after they were sent. This ensures that only authorized users can modify data.
- **Confidentiality** or **Data Privacy**: The means used to ensure that information is made available only to users who are authorized to access it. This ensures that only authorized users can view sensitive data.
- **Non-repudiation**: The means used to prove that a user performed some action such that the user cannot reasonably deny having done so. This ensures that transactions can be proven to have happened.
- **Quality of Service (QoS)**: The means used to provide better service to selected network traffic over various technologies.
- **Auditing**: The means used to capture a tamper-resistant record of security-related events for the purpose of being able to evaluate the effectiveness of security policies and mechanisms. To enable this, the system maintains a record of transactions and security information.

Security Implementation Mechanisms

The characteristics of an application should be considered when deciding the layer and type of security to be provided for applications. The following sections discuss the characteristics of the common mechanisms that can be used to secure Java EE applications. Each of these mechanisms can be used individually or with others to provide protection layers based on the specific needs of your implementation.

Java SE Security Implementation Mechanisms

Java SE provides support for a variety of security features and mechanisms, including:

- **Java Authentication and Authorization Service (JAAS)**: JAAS is a set of APIs that enable services to authenticate and enforce access controls upon users. JAAS provides a pluggable and extensible framework for programmatic user authentication and authorization. JAAS is a core J2SE 1.5 API and is an underlying technology for Java EE security mechanisms.
- **Java Generic Security Services (Java GSS-API)**: Java GSS-API is a token-based API used to securely exchange messages between communicating applications. The GSS-API offers application programmers uniform access to security services atop a variety of underlying security mechanisms, including Kerberos.
- **Java Cryptography Extension (JCE)**: JCE provides a framework and implementations for encryption, key generation and key agreement, and Message Authentication Code (MAC) algorithms. Support for encryption includes symmetric, asymmetric, block, and stream ciphers. Block ciphers operate on groups of bytes while stream ciphers operate on one byte at a time. The software also supports secure streams and sealed objects.
- **Java Secure Sockets Extension (JSSE)**: JSSE provides a framework and an implementation for a Java version of the SSL and TLS protocols and includes functionality for data encryption, server authentication, message integrity, and optional client authentication to enable secure Internet communications.
- **Simple Authentication and Security Layer (SASL)**: SASL is an Internet standard (RFC 2222) that specifies a protocol for authentication and

optional establishment of a security layer between client and server applications. SASL defines how authentication data is to be exchanged but does not itself specify the contents of that data. It is a framework into which specific authentication mechanisms that specify the contents and semantics of the authentication data can fit.

Java SE also provides a set of tools for managing keystores, certificates, and policy files; generating and verifying JAR signatures; and obtaining, listing, and managing Kerberos tickets.

For more information on Java SE security, visit its web page at `http://java.sun.com/j2se/1.5.0/docs/guide/security/`.

Java EE Security Implementation Mechanisms

Java EE security services are provided by the component container and can be implemented using declarative or programmatic techniques (container security is discussed more in Securing Containers, page 910). Java EE security services provide a robust and easily configured security mechanism for authenticating users and authorizing access to application functions and associated data at many different layers. Java EE security services are separate from the security mechanisms of the operating system.

Application-Layer Security

In Java EE, component containers are responsible for providing application-layer security. Application-layer security provides security services for a specific application type tailored to the needs of the application. At the application layer, application firewalls can be employed to enhance application protection by protecting the communication stream and all associated application resources from attacks.

Java EE security is easy to implement and configure, and can offer fine-grained access control to application functions and data. However, as is inherent to security applied at the application layer, security properties are not transferable to applications running in other environments and only protect data while it is residing in the application environment. In the context of a traditional application, this is not necessarily a problem, but when applied to a web services application, where data often travels across several intermediaries, you would need to use the Java EE security mechanisms along with transport-layer security and message-layer security for a complete security solution.

The advantages of using application-layer security include the following:

- Security is uniquely suited to the needs of the application.
- Security is fine-grained, with application-specific settings.

The disadvantages of using application-layer security include the following:

- The application is dependent on security attributes that are not transferable between application types.
- Support for multiple protocols makes this type of security vulnerable.
- Data is close to or contained within the point of vulnerability.

For more information on providing security at the application layer, read Securing Containers (page 910).

Transport-Layer Security

Transport-layer security is provided by the transport mechanisms used to transmit information over the wire between clients and providers, thus transport-layer security relies on secure HTTP transport (HTTPS) using Secure Sockets Layer (SSL). Transport security is a point-to-point security mechanism that can be used for authentication, message integrity, and confidentiality. When running over an SSL-protected session, the server and client can authenticate one another and negotiate an encryption algorithm and cryptographic keys before the application protocol transmits or receives its first byte of data. Security is "live" from the time it leaves the consumer until it arrives at the provider, or vice versa, even across intermediaries. The problem is that it is not protected once it gets to its destination. One solution is to encrypt the message before sending.

Transport-layer security is performed in a series of phases, which are listed here:

- The client and server agree on an appropriate algorithm.
- A key is exchanged using public-key encryption and certificate-based authentication.
- A symmetric cipher is used during the information exchange.

Digital certificates are necessary when running secure HTTP transport (HTTPS) using Secure Sockets Layer (SSL). The HTTPS service of most web servers will not run unless a digital certificate has been installed. Digital certificates have already been created for the Sun Java Systems Application Server. If you are using a different server, use the procedure outlined in Working with Digital Certificates (page 926) to set up a digital certificate that can be used by your web or application server to enable SSL.

The advantages of using transport-layer security include the following:

- Relatively simple, well understood, standard technology.
- Applies to message body and attachments.

The disadvantages of using transport-layer security include the following:

- Tightly-coupled with transport-layer protocol.
- All or nothing approach to security. This implies that the security mechanism is unaware of message contents, and as such, you cannot selectively apply security to portions of the message as you can with message-layer security.
- Protection is transient. The message is only protected while in transit. Protection is removed automatically by the endpoint when it receives the message.
- Not an end-to-end solution, simply point-to-point.

For more information on transport-layer security, read Establishing a Secure Connection Using SSL (page 922).

Message-Layer Security

In message-layer security, security information is contained within the SOAP message and/or SOAP message attachment, which allows security information to travel along with the message or attachment. For example, a portion of the message may be signed by a sender and encrypted for a particular receiver. When the message is sent from the initial sender, it may pass through intermediate nodes before reaching its intended receiver. In this scenario, the encrypted portions continue to be opaque to any intermediate nodes and can only be decrypted by the intended receiver. For this reason, message-layer security is also sometimes referred to as *end-to-end security*.

The advantages of message-layer security include the following:

- Security stays with the message over all hops and after the message arrives at its destination.
- Security can be selectively applied to different portions of a message (and to attachments if using XWSS).
- Message security can be used with intermediaries over multiple hops.
- Message security is independent of the application environment or transport protocol.

The disadvantage to using message-layer security is that it is relatively complex and adds some overhead to processing.

The Sun Java System Application Server supports message security. It uses Web Services Security (WSS) to secure messages. Because this message security is specific to the Application Server and not a part of the Java EE platform, this tutorial does not discuss using WSS to secure messages. For a link to the Application Server *Administration Guide* and *Developer's Guide*, which discuss this topic, see Further Information (page 934).

Securing Containers

In Java EE, the component containers are responsible for providing application security. A container provides two types of security: declarative and programmatic. The following sections discuss these concepts in more detail.

Using Deployment Descriptors for Declarative Security

Declarative security expresses an application component's security requirements using *deployment descriptors*. A deployment descriptor is an XML document with an `.xml` extension that describes the deployment settings of an application, a module, or a component. Because deployment descriptor information is declarative, it can be changed without the need to modify the source code. At runtime, the Java EE server reads the deployment descriptor and acts upon the application, module, or component accordingly.

This tutorial does not document how to write the deployment descriptors from scratch, only what configurations each example requires its deployment descriptors to define. For help with writing deployment descriptors, you can view the provided deployment descriptors in a text editor. Each example's deployment descriptors are stored at the top layer of each example's directory. Another way to learn how to write deployment descriptors is to read the specification in which the deployment descriptor elements are defined.

Deployment descriptors must provide certain structural information for each component if this information has not been provided in annotations or is not to be defaulted.

Different types of components use different formats, or *schema*, for their deployment descriptors. The security elements of deployment descriptors which are discussed in this tutorial include the following:

- Enterprise JavaBeans components use an EJB deployment descriptor that must be named `META-INF/ejb-jar.xml` and must be contained in the EJB JAR file.

  The schema for enterprise bean deployment descriptors is provided in the EJB 3.0 Specification (JSR-220), Chapter 18.5, *Deployment Descriptor XML Schema*, which can be downloaded from `http://jcp.org/en/jsr/detail?id=220`.

  Security elements for EJB deployment descriptors are discussed in this tutorial in the section Using Enterprise Bean Security Deployment Descriptor Elements (page 958).

- Web Services components use a `jaxrpc-mapping-info` deployment descriptor defined in JSR 109. This deployment descriptor provides deployment-time mapping functionality between Java and WSDL. In conjunction with JSR 181, JAX-WS 2.0 complements this mapping functionality with development-time Java annotations that control mapping between Java and WSDL.

  The schema for web services deployment descriptors is provided in Web Services for Java EE (JSR-109), section 7.1, *Web Services Deployment Descriptor XML Schema*, which can be downloaded from `http://jcp.org/en/jsr/detail?id=109`.

  Schema elements for web application deployment descriptors are discussed in this tutorial in the section Declaring Security Requirements in a Deployment Descriptor (page 1002).

- Web components use a web application deployment descriptor named `web.xml`.

The schema for web component deployment descriptors is provided in the Java Servlet 2.5 Specification (JSR-154), section SRV.13, *Deployment Descriptor*, which can be downloaded from `http://jcp.org/en/jsr/detail?id=154`.

Security elements for web application deployment descriptors are discussed in this tutorial in the section Declaring Security Requirements in a Deployment Descriptor (page 1002).

Using Annotations

Annotations enable a declarative style of programming, and so encompass both the declarative and programmatic security concepts. Users can specify information about security within a class file using annotations. When the application is deployed, this information is used by the Application Server. Not all security information can be specified using annotations, however. Some information must be specified in the application deployment descriptors.

Annotations let you avoid writing boilerplate code under many circumstances by enabling tools to generate it from annotations in the source code. This leads to a declarative programming style, where the programmer says what should be done and tools emit the code to do it. It also eliminates the need for maintaining side files that must be kept up to date with changes in source files. Instead the information can be maintained in the source file.

In this tutorial, specific annotations that can be used to specify security information within a class file are described in the following sections:

- Declaring Security Requirements Using Annotations (page 999)
- Using Enterprise Bean Security Annotations (page 957)

The following are sources for more information on annotations:

- *JSR 175: A Metadata Facility for the Java Programming Language*
- *JSR 181: Web Services Metadata for the Java Platform*
- *JSR 250: Common Annotations for the Java Platform*
- The Java SE discussion of annotations

Links to this information are provided in Further Information (page 934).

Using Programmatic Security

Programmatic security is embedded in an application and is used to make security decisions. Programmatic security is useful when declarative security alone is not sufficient to express the security model of an application. The API for programmatic security consists of two methods of the `EJBContext` interface and two methods of the servlet `HttpServletRequest` interface. These methods allow components to make business logic decisions based on the security role of the caller or remote user.

Programmatic security is discussed in more detail in the following sections:

- Accessing an Enterprise Bean Caller's Security Context (page 940)
- Working with Security Roles (page 989)

Securing the Application Server

This tutorial describes deployment to the Sun Java System Application Server, which provides highly secure, interoperable, and distributed component computing based on the Java EE security model. The Application Server supports the Java EE 5 security model. You can configure the Application Server for the following purposes:

- Adding, deleting, or modifying authorized users. For more information on this topic, read Working with Realms, Users, Groups, and Roles (page 914).
- Configuring secure HTTP and IIOP listeners.
- Configuring secure JMX connectors.
- Adding, deleting, or modifying existing or custom realms.
- Defining an interface for pluggable authorization providers using Java Authorization Contract for Containers (JACC).

  Java Authorization Contract for Containers (JACC) defines security contracts between the Application Server and authorization policy modules. These contracts specify how the authorization providers are installed, configured, and used in access decisions.
- Using pluggable audit modules.
- Setting and changing policy permissions for an application.

The following features are specific to the Application Server:

- Message security
- Single sign-on across all Application Server applications within a single security domain
- Programmatic login

For more information about configuring the Application Server, read the Application Server's *Developer's Guide* and *Administration Guide*. Links to both of these documents are provided in Further Information (page 934).

Working with Realms, Users, Groups, and Roles

You often need to protect resources to ensure that only *authorized users* have access. *Authorization* provides controlled access to protected resources. Authorization is based on identification and authentication. *Identification* is a process that enables recognition of an entity by a system, and *authentication* is a process that verifies the identity of a user, device, or other entity in a computer system, usually as a prerequisite to allowing access to resources in a system. These concepts are discussed in more detail in Characteristics of Application Security (page 904).

This section discusses setting up users so that they can be correctly identified and either given access to protected resources, or denied access if the user is not authorized to access the protected resources. To authenticate a user, you need to follow these basic steps:

1. The Application Developer writes code to prompt the user for their user name and password. The different methods of authentication are discussed in Specifying an Authentication Mechanism (page 1010).
2. The Application Developer communicates how to set up security for the deployed application by use of a deployment descriptor. This step is discussed in Setting Up Security Roles (page 920).
3. The Server Administrator sets up authorized users and groups on the Application Server. This is discussed in Managing Users and Groups on the Application Server (page 918)
4. The Application Deployer maps the application's security roles to users, groups, and principals defined on the Application Server. This topic is discussed in Mapping Roles to Users and Groups (page 921).

What Are Realms, Users, Groups, and Roles?

A realm is defined on a web or application server. It contains a collection of users, which may or may not be assigned to a group, that are controlled by the same authentication policy. Managing users on the Application Server is discussed in Managing Users and Groups on the Application Server (page 918).

An application will often prompt a user for their user name and password before allowing access to a protected resource. After the user has entered their user name and password, that information is passed to the server, which either authenticates the user and sends the protected resource, or does not authenticate the user, in which case access to the protected resource is denied. This type of user authentication is discussed in Specifying an Authentication Mechanism (page 1010).

In some applications, authorized users are assigned to roles. In this situation, the role assigned to the user in the application must be mapped to a group defined on the application server. Figure 28–6 shows this. More information on mapping roles to users and groups can be found in Setting Up Security Roles (page 920).

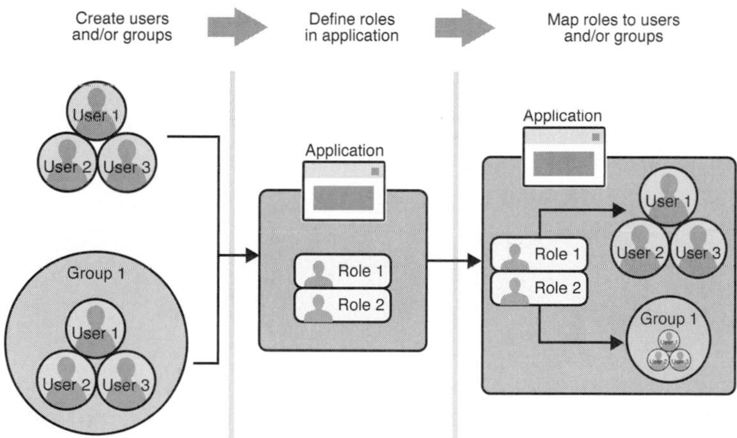

Figure 28–6 Mapping Roles to Users and Groups

The following sections provide more information on realms, users, groups, and roles.

What Is a Realm?

For a web application, a *realm* is a complete database of *users* and *groups* that identify valid users of a web application (or a set of web applications) and are controlled by the same authentication policy.

The Java EE server authentication service can govern users in multiple realms. In this release of the Application Server, the `file`, `admin-realm`, and `certificate` realms come preconfigured for the Application Server.

In the `file` realm, the server stores user credentials locally in a file named `keyfile`. You can use the Admin Console to manage users in the `file` realm.

When using the `file` realm, the server authentication service verifies user identity by checking the `file` realm. This realm is used for the authentication of all clients except for web browser clients that use the HTTPS protocol and certificates.

In the `certificate` realm, the server stores user credentials in a certificate database. When using the `certificate` realm, the server uses certificates with the HTTPS protocol to authenticate web clients. To verify the identity of a user in the `certificate` realm, the authentication service verifies an X.509 certificate. For step-by-step instructions for creating this type of certificate, see Working with Digital Certificates (page 926). The common name field of the X.509 certificate is used as the principal name.

The `admin-realm` is also a `FileRealm` and stores administrator user credentials locally in a file named `admin-keyfile`. You can use the Admin Console to manage users in this realm in the same way you manage users in the `file` realm. For more information, see Managing Users and Groups on the Application Server (page 918).

What Is a User?

A *user* is an individual (or application program) identity that has been defined in the Application Server. In a web application, a user can have a set of *roles* associated with that identity, which entitles them to access all resources protected by those roles. Users can be associated with a group.

A Java EE user is similar to an operating system user. Typically, both types of users represent people. However, these two types of users are not the same. The Java EE server authentication service has no knowledge of the user name and password you provide when you log on to the operating system. The Java EE server authentication service is not connected to the security mechanism of the operating system. The two security services manage users that belong to different realms.

What Is a Group?

A *group* is a set of authenticated *users*, classified by common traits, defined in the Application Server.

A Java EE user of the `file` realm can belong to an Application Server group. (A user in the `certificate` realm cannot.) An Application Server *group* is a category of users classified by common traits, such as job title or customer profile. For example, most customers of an e-commerce application might belong to the `CUSTOMER` group, but the big spenders would belong to the `PREFERRED` group. Categorizing users into groups makes it easier to control the access of large numbers of users.

An Application Server *group* has a different scope from a *role*. An Application Server group is designated for the entire Application Server, whereas a role is associated only with a specific application in the Application Server.

What Is a Role?

A *role* is an abstract name for the permission to access a particular set of resources in an application. A *role* can be compared to a key that can open a lock. Many people might have a copy of the key. The lock doesn't care who you are, only that you have the right key.

Some Other Terminology

The following terminology is also used to describe the security requirements of the Java EE platform:

- **Principal**: A principal is an entity that can be authenticated by an authentication protocol in a security service that is deployed in an enterprise. A principal is identified using a principal name and authenticated using authentication data.
- **Security policy domain** (also known as **security domain** or **realm**): A security policy domain is a scope over which a common security policy is defined and enforced by the security administrator of the security service.

- **Security attributes**: A set of security attributes is associated with every principal. The security attributes have many uses, for example, access to protected resources and auditing of users. Security attributes can be associated with a principal by an authentication protocol.
- **Credential**: A credential contains or references information (security attributes) used to authenticate a principal for Java EE product services. A principal acquires a credential upon authentication, or from another principal that allows its credential to be used.

Managing Users and Groups on the Application Server

Managing users on the Application Server is discussed in more detail in the Application Server's *Administration Guide*. For a link to this guide, see Further Information (page 934).

This tutorial provides steps for managing users that will need to be completed to work through the tutorial examples.

Adding Users to the Application Server

To add users to the Application Server, follow these steps:

1. Start the Application Server if you haven't already done so. Information on starting the Application Server is available in Starting and Stopping the Application Server (page 27).
2. Start the Admin Console if you haven't already done so. You can start the Admin Console by starting a web browser and entering the URL `http://localhost:4848/asadmin`. If you changed the default Admin port during installation, enter the correct port number in place of `4848`.
3. To log in to the Admin Console, enter the user name and password of a user in the `admin-realm` who belongs to the `asadmin` group. The name and password entered during installation will work, as will any users added to this realm and group subsequent to installation.
4. Expand the Configuration node in the Admin Console tree.
5. Expand the Security node in the Admin Console tree.

6. Expand the Realms node.
   - Select the `file` realm to add users you want to enable to access applications running in this realm. (For the example security applications, select the `file` realm.)
   - Select the `admin-realm` to add users you want to enable as system administrators of the Application Server.
   - You cannot enter users into the `certificate` realm using the Admin Console. You can only add certificates to the `certificate` realm. For information on adding (importing) certificates to the `certificate` realm, read Adding Users to the Certificate Realm (page 919).
7. Click the Manage Users button.
8. Click New to add a new user to the realm.
9. Enter the correct information into the User ID, Password, and Group(s) fields.
   - If you are adding a user to the `file` realm, enter the name to identify the user, a password to allow the user access to the realm, and a group to which this user belongs. For more information on these properties, read Working with Realms, Users, Groups, and Roles (page 914).

     For the example security applications, enter a user with any name and password you like, but make sure that the user is assigned to the group of `user`.
   - If you are adding a user to the `admin-realm`, enter the name to identify the user, a password to allow the user access to the Application Server, and enter `asadmin` in the Group field.
10. Click OK to add this user to the list of users in the realm.
11. Click Logout when you have completed this task.

Adding Users to the Certificate Realm

In the `certificate` realm, user identity is set up in the Application Server security context and populated with user data obtained from cryptographically-verified client certificates. For step-by-step instructions for creating this type of certificate, see Working with Digital Certificates (page 926).

Setting Up Security Roles

When you design an enterprise bean or web component, you should always think about the kinds of users who will access the component. For example, a web application for a human resources department might have a different request URL for someone who has been assigned the role of DEPT_ADMIN than for someone who has been assigned the role of DIRECTOR. The DEPT_ADMIN role may let you view employee data, but the DIRECTOR role enables you to modify employee data, including salary data. Each of these *security roles* is an abstract logical grouping of users that is defined by the person who assembles the application. When an application is deployed, the deployer will map the roles to security identities in the operational environment, as shown in Figure 28–6.

For applications, you define security roles in the Java EE deployment descriptor file application.xml, and the corresponding role mappings in the Application Server deployment descriptor file sun-application.xml. For individually deployed web or EJB modules, you define roles in the Java EE deployment descriptor files web.xml or ejb-jar.xml and the corresponding role mappings in the Application Server deployment descriptor files sun-web.xml or sun-ejb-jar.xml.

The following is an example of a security constraint from a web.xml application deployment descriptor file where the role of DEPT-ADMIN is authorized for methods that review employee data and the role of DIRECTOR is authorized for methods that change employee data.

```
<security-constraint>
  <web-resource-collection>
    <web-resource-name>view dept data</web-resource-name>
    <url-pattern>/hr/employee/*</url-pattern>
    <http-method>GET</http-method>
    <http-method>POST</http-method>
  </web-resource-collection>
  <auth-constraint>
    <role-name>DEPT_ADMIN</role-name>
  </auth-constraint>
  <user-data-constraint>
    <transport-guarantee>CONFIDENTIAL</transport-guarantee>
  </user-data-constraint>
</security-constraint>

<security-constraint>
  <web-resource-collection>
    <web-resource-name>change dept data</web-resource-name>
    <url-pattern>/hr/employee/*</url-pattern>
```

```
      <http-method>GET</http-method>
      <http-method>PUT</http-method>
    </web-resource-collection>
    <auth-constraint>
      <role-name>DIRECTOR</role-name>
    </auth-constraint>
    <user-data-constraint>
      <transport-guarantee>CONFIDENTIAL</transport-guarantee>
    </user-data-constraint>
  </security-constraint>
```

The web.xml application deployment descriptor is described in more detail in Declaring Security Requirements in a Deployment Descriptor (page 1002).

After users have provided their login information, and the application has declared what roles are authorized to access protected parts of an application, the next step is to map the security role to the name of a user, or principal. This step is discussed in the following section.

Mapping Roles to Users and Groups

When you are developing a Java EE application, you don't need to know what categories of users have been defined for the realm in which the application will be run. In the Java EE platform, the security architecture provides a mechanism for mapping the roles defined in the application to the users or groups defined in the runtime realm. To map a role name permitted by the application or module to principals (users) and groups defined on the server, use the security-role-mapping element in the runtime deployment descriptor (sun-application.xml, sun-web.xml, or sun-ejb-jar.xml) file. The entry needs to declare a mapping between a security role used in the application and one or more groups or principals defined for the applicable realm of the Application Server. An example for the sun-web.xml file is shown below:

```
<sun-web-app>
  <security-role-mapping>
    <role-name>DIRECTOR</role-name>
    <principal-name>mcneely</principal-name>
  </security-role-mapping>
  <security-role-mapping>
    <role-name>MANAGER</role-name>
    <group-name>manager</group-name>
  </security-role-mapping>
</sun-web-app>
```

The role name can be mapped to either a specific principal (user), a group, or both. The principal or group names referenced must be valid principals or groups in the current default realm of the Application Server. The `role-name` in this example must exactly match the `role-name` in the `security-role` element of the corresponding `web.xml` file or the role name defined in the `@DeclareRoles` or `@RolesAllowed` annotations.

Sometimes the role names used in the application are the same as the group names defined on the Application Server. Under these circumstances, you can enable a default principal-to-role mapping on the Application Server using the Admin Console. From the Admin Console, select Configuration, then Security, then check the enable box beside Default Principal to Role Mapping. If you need more information about using the Admin Console, see Adding Users to the Application Server (page 918).

Establishing a Secure Connection Using SSL

Secure Socket Layer (SSL) technology is security that is implemented at the transport layer (see Transport-Layer Security, page 908, for more information about transport layer security). SSL allows web browsers and web servers to communicate over a secure connection. In this secure connection, the data that is being sent is encrypted before being sent and then is decrypted upon receipt and before processing. Both the browser and the server encrypt all traffic before sending any data. SSL addresses the following important security considerations.

- **Authentication**: During your initial attempt to communicate with a web server over a secure connection, that server will present your web browser with a set of credentials in the form of a server certificate. The purpose of the certificate is to verify that the site is who and what it claims to be. In some cases, the server may request a certificate that the client is who and what it claims to be (which is known as client authentication).
- **Confidentiality**: When data is being passed between the client and the server on a network, third parties can view and intercept this data. SSL responses are encrypted so that the data cannot be deciphered by the third party and the data remains confidential.

- **Integrity**: When data is being passed between the client and the server on a network, third parties can view and intercept this data. SSL helps guarantee that the data will not be modified in transit by that third party.

Installing and Configuring SSL Support

An SSL HTTPS connector is already enabled in the Sun Java System Application Server. For more information on configuring SSL for the Application Server, refer to the *Administration Guide*. See Further Information, page 934, for a link to this document.

If you are using a different application server or web server, an SSL HTTPS connector might or might not be enabled. If you are using a server that needs its SSL connector to be configured, consult the documentation for that server.

As a general rule, to enable SSL for a server, you must address the following issues:

- There must be a `Connector` element for an SSL connector in the server deployment descriptor.
- There must be valid keystore and certificate files.
- The location of the keystore file and its password must be specified in the server deployment descriptor.

You can verify whether or not SSL is enabled by following the steps in Verifying SSL Support (page 925).

Specifying a Secure Connection in Your Application Deployment Descriptor

To specify a requirement that protected resources be received over a protected transport layer connection (SSL), specify a user data constraint in the application deployment descriptor. The following is an example of a `web.xml` application deployment descriptor that specifies that SSL be used:

```
<security-constraint>
  <web-resource-collection>
    <web-resource-name>view dept data</web-resource-name>
    <url-pattern>/hr/employee/*</url-pattern>
    <http-method>GET</http-method>
    <http-method>POST</http-method>
```

```
    </web-resource-collection>
    <auth-constraint>
      <role-name>DEPT_ADMIN</role-name>
    </auth-constraint>
    <user-data-constraint>
      <transport-guarantee>CONFIDENTIAL</transport-guarantee>
    </user-data-constraint>
  </security-constraint>
```

A user data constraint (`<user-data-constraint>` in the deployment descriptor) requires that all constrained URL patterns and HTTP methods specified in the security constraint are received over a protected transport layer connection such as HTTPS (HTTP over SSL). A user data constraint specifies a transport guarantee (`<transport-guarantee>` in the deployment descriptor). The choices for transport guarantee include `CONFIDENTIAL`, `INTEGRAL`, or `NONE`. If you specify `CONFIDENTIAL` or `INTEGRAL` as a security constraint, that type of security constraint applies to all requests that match the URL patterns in the web resource collection and not just to the login dialog box.

The strength of the required protection is defined by the value of the transport guarantee.

- Specify `CONFIDENTIAL` when the application requires that data be transmitted so as to prevent other entities from observing the contents of the transmission.
- Specify `INTEGRAL` when the application requires that the data be sent between client and server in such a way that it cannot be changed in transit.
- Specify `NONE` to indicate that the container must accept the constrained requests on any connection, including an unprotected one.

The user data constraint is handy to use with basic and form-based user authentication. When the login authentication method is set to `BASIC` or `FORM`, passwords are not protected, meaning that passwords sent between a client and a server on an unprotected session can be viewed and intercepted by third parties. Using a user data constraint with the user authentication mechanism can alleviate this concern. Configuring a user authentication mechanism is described in Specifying an Authentication Mechanism (page 1010).

Verifying SSL Support

For testing purposes, and to verify that SSL support has been correctly installed, load the default introduction page with a URL that connects to the port defined in the server deployment descriptor:

```
https://localhost:8181/
```

The `https` in this URL indicates that the browser should be using the SSL protocol. The `localhost` in this example assumes that you are running the example on your local machine as part of the development process. The `8181` in this example is the secure port that was specified where the SSL connector was created. If you are using a different server or port, modify this value accordingly.

The first time that you load this application, the New Site Certificate or Security Alert dialog box displays. Select Next to move through the series of dialog boxes, and select Finish when you reach the last dialog box. The certificates will display only the first time. When you accept the certificates, subsequent hits to this site assume that you still trust the content.

Tips on Running SSL

The SSL protocol is designed to be as efficient as securely possible. However, encryption and decryption are computationally expensive processes from a performance standpoint. It is not strictly necessary to run an entire web application over SSL, and it is customary for a developer to decide which pages require a secure connection and which do not. Pages that might require a secure connection include login pages, personal information pages, shopping cart checkouts, or any pages where credit card information could possibly be transmitted. Any page within an application can be requested over a secure socket by simply prefixing the address with `https:` instead of `http:`. Any pages that absolutely require a secure connection should check the protocol type associated with the page request and take the appropriate action if `https` is not specified.

Using name-based virtual hosts on a secured connection can be problematic. This is a design limitation of the SSL protocol itself. The SSL *handshake*, where the client browser accepts the server certificate, must occur before the HTTP request is accessed. As a result, the request information containing the virtual host name cannot be determined before authentication, and it is therefore not possible to assign multiple certificates to a single IP address. If all virtual hosts on a single IP address need to authenticate against the same certificate, the addition of multiple virtual hosts should not interfere with normal SSL operations on the server. Be aware, however, that most client browsers will compare the server's domain name against the domain name listed in the certificate, if any (this is applicable primarily to official, CA-signed certificates). If the domain names do not match, these browsers will display a warning to the client. In general, only address-based virtual hosts are commonly used with SSL in a production environment.

Working with Digital Certificates

Note: Digital certificates for the Application Server have already been generated and can be found in the directory `<JAVAEE_HOME>/domains/domain1/config/`. These digital certificates are self-signed and are intended for use in a development environment; they are not intended for production purposes. For production purposes, generate your own certificates and have them signed by a CA.

Note: The instructions in this section apply to the PE version of the Application Server. In the EE version of the Application Server, the `certutil` utility is used to create digital certificates. If you are working with the EE version of the Application Server, refer to the EE version of the Administration Guide.

To use SSL, an application or web server must have an associated certificate for each external interface, or IP address, that accepts secure connections. The theory behind this design is that a server should provide some kind of reasonable assurance that its owner is who you think it is, particularly before receiving any sensitive information. It may be useful to think of a certificate as a "digital driver's license" for an Internet address. It states with which company the site is associated, along with some basic contact information about the site owner or administrator.

The digital certificate is cryptographically signed by its owner and is difficult for anyone else to forge. For sites involved in e-commerce or in any other business transaction in which authentication of identity is important, a certificate can be purchased from a well-known certificate authority (CA) such as VeriSign or Thawte. If your server certificate is self-signed, you must install it in the Application Server's keystore file (`keystore.jks`). If your client certificate is self-signed, you should install it in the Application Server's truststore file (`cacerts.jks`).

Sometimes authentication is not really a concern—for example, an administrator might simply want to ensure that data being transmitted and received by the server is private and cannot be snooped by anyone eavesdropping on the connection. In such cases, you can save the time and expense involved in obtaining a CA certificate and simply use a self-signed certificate.

SSL uses *public key cryptography*, which is based on *key pairs*. Key pairs contain one public key and one private key. If data is encrypted with one key, it can be decrypted only with the other key of the pair. This property is fundamental to establishing trust and privacy in transactions. For example, using SSL, the server computes a value and encrypts the value using its private key. The encrypted value is called a *digital signature*. The client decrypts the encrypted value using the server's public key and compares the value to its own computed value. If the two values match, the client can trust that the signature is authentic, because only the private key could have been used to produce such a signature.

Digital certificates are used with the HTTPS protocol to authenticate web clients. The HTTPS service of most web servers will not run unless a digital certificate has been installed. Use the procedure outlined in the next section, Creating a Server Certificate, to set up a digital certificate that can be used by your application or web server to enable SSL.

One tool that can be used to set up a digital certificate is `keytool`, a key and certificate management utility that ships with the Java SE SDK. It enables users to administer their own public/private key pairs and associated certificates for use in self-authentication (where the user authenticates himself or herself to other users or services) or data integrity and authentication services, using digital signatures. It also allows users to cache the public keys (in the form of certificates) of their communicating peers. For a better understanding of `keytool` and public key cryptography, read the `keytool` documentation at `http://java.sun.com/j2se/1.5.0/docs/tooldocs/solaris/keytool.html`.

Creating a Server Certificate

A server certificate has already been created for the Application Server. The certificate can be found in the `<JAVAEE_HOME>/domains/domain1/config/` directory. The server certificate is in `keystore.jks`. The `cacerts.jks` file contains all the trusted certificates, including client certificates.

If necessary, you can use `keytool` to generate certificates. The `keytool` stores the keys and certificates in a file termed a *keystore*, a repository of certificates used for identifying a client or a server. Typically, a keystore is a file that contains one client or one server's identity. It protects private keys by using a password.

If you don't specify a directory when specifying the keystore file name, the keystores are created in the directory from which the `keytool` command is run. This can be the directory where the application resides, or it can be a directory common to many applications.

To create a server certificate, follow these steps:

1. Create the keystore.
2. Export the certificate from the keystore.
3. Sign the certificate.
4. Import the certificate into a *truststore*: a repository of certificates used for verifying the certificates. A truststore typically contains more than one certificate.

Run `keytool` to generate the server keystore, which we will name `keystore.jks`. This step uses the alias `server-alias` to generate a new public/private key pair and wrap the public key into a self-signed certificate inside `keystore.jks`. The key pair is generated using an algorithm of type RSA, with a default password of `changeit`. For more information on `keytool` options, see its online help at `http://java.sun.com/j2se/1.5.0/docs/tooldocs/solaris/keytool.html`.

Note: RSA is public-key encryption technology developed by RSA Data Security, Inc. The acronym stands for Rivest, Shamir, and Adelman, the inventors of the technology.

From the directory in which you want to create the keystore, run `keytool` with the following parameters.

1. Generate the server certificate.

   ```
   <JAVA_HOME>\bin\keytool -genkey -alias server-alias
   -keyalg RSA -keypass changeit -storepass changeit
   -keystore keystore.jks
   ```

   When you press Enter, `keytool` prompts you to enter the server name, organizational unit, organization, locality, state, and country code.

   You must enter the server name in response to `keytool`'s first prompt, in which it asks for first and last names. For testing purposes, this can be `localhost`.

When you run the example applications, the host specified in the keystore must match the host identified in the `javaee.server.name` property specified in the file *<INSTALL>*`/javaeetutorial5/examples/bp-project/build.properties`.

2. Export the generated server certificate in `keystore.jks` into the file `server.cer`.

```
<JAVA_HOME>\bin\keytool -export -alias server-alias
-storepass changeit -file server.cer -keystore keystore.jks
```

3. If you want to have the certificate signed by a CA, read Signing Digital Certificates (page 929) for more information.
4. To create the truststore file `cacerts.jks` and add the server certificate to the truststore, run `keytool` from the directory where you created the keystore and server certificate. Use the following parameters:

```
<JAVA_HOME>\bin\keytool -import -v -trustcacerts
-alias server-alias -file server.cer
-keystore cacerts.jks -keypass changeit
-storepass changeit
```

Information on the certificate, such as that shown next, will display.

```
% keytool -import -v -trustcacerts -alias server-alias
-file server.cer -keystore cacerts.jks -keypass changeit
-storepass changeit
Owner: CN=localhost, OU=Sun Micro, O=Docs, L=Santa Clara,
ST=CA, C=US
Issuer: CN=localhost, OU=Sun Micro, O=Docs, L=Santa Clara,
ST=CA, C=US
Serial number: 3e932169
Valid from: Tue Apr 08
Certificate fingerprints:
MD5: 52:9F:49:68:ED:78:6F:39:87:F3:98:B3:6A:6B:0F:90
SHA1: EE:2E:2A:A6:9E:03:9A:3A:1C:17:4A:28:5E:97:20:78:3F:
Trust this certificate? [no]:
```

5. Enter `yes`, and then press the `Enter` or `Return` key. The following information displays:

```
Certificate was added to keystore
[Saving cacerts.jks]
```

Signing Digital Certificates

After you've created a digital certificate, you will want to have it signed by its owner. After the digital certificate has been cryptographically signed by its owner, it is difficult for anyone else to forge. For sites involved in e-commerce or any other business transaction in which authentication of identity is important, a certificate can be purchased from a well-known certificate authority such as VeriSign or Thawte.

As mentioned earlier, if authentication is not really a concern, you can save the time and expense involved in obtaining a CA certificate and simply use the self-signed certificate.

Obtaining a Digitally Signed Certificate

This example assumes that the keystore is named `keystore.jks`, the certificate file is `server.cer`, and the CA file is `cacerts.jks`. To get your certificate digitally signed by a CA:

1. Generate a Certificate Signing Request (CSR).
   ```
   keytool -certreq -alias server-alias -keyalg RSA
      -file <csr_filename> -keystore cacerts.jks
   ```
2. Send the contents of the *`csr_filename`* for signing.
3. If you are using Verisign CA, go to `http://digitalid.verisign.com/`. Verisign will send the signed certificate in email. Store this certificate in a file.

Using a Different Server Certificate with the Application Server

Follow the steps in Creating a Server Certificate (page 927), to create your own server certificate, have it signed by a CA, and import the certificate into `keystore.jks`.

Make sure that when you create the certificate, you follow these rules:

- When you create the server certificate, `keytool` prompts you to enter your first and last name. In response to this prompt, you must enter the name of your server. For testing purposes, this can be `localhost`.
- The server/host specified in the keystore must match the host identified in the `javaee.server.name` property specified in the `<INSTALL>/javaeetutorial5/examples/bp-project/build.properties` file for running the example applications.
- Your key/certificate password in `keystore.jks` should match the password of your keystore, `keystore.jks`. This is a bug. If there is a mis-

match, the Java SDK cannot read the certificate and you get a "tampered" message.

- If you want to replace the existing `keystore.jks`, you must either change your keystore's password to the default password (`changeit`) or change the default password to your keystore's password.

To specify that the Application Server should use the new keystore for authentication and authorization decisions, you must set the JVM options for the Application Server so that they recognize the new keystore. To use a different keystore than the one provided for development purposes, follow these steps.

1. Start the Application Server if you haven't already done so. Information on starting the Application Server can be found in Starting and Stopping the Application Server (page 27).
2. Start the Admin Console. Information on starting the Admin Console can be found in Starting the Admin Console (page 28).
3. Select Application Server in the Admin Console tree.
4. Select the JVM Settings tab.
5. Select the JVM Options tab.
6. Change the following JVM options so that they point to the location and name of the new keystore. There current settings are shown below:
   ```
   -Djavax.net.ssl.keyStore=${com.sun.aas.instanceRoot}/con-
   fig/keystore.jks
   -Djavax.net.ssl.trustStore=${com.sun.aas.instanceRoot}/con-
   fig/cacerts.jks
   ```
7. If you've changed the keystore password from its default value, you need to add the password option as well:
   ```
   -Djavax.net.ssl.keyStorePassword=your_new_password
   ```
8. Logout of the Admin Console and restart the Application Server.

Miscellaneous Commands for Certificates

To check the contents of a keystore that contains a certificate with an alias `server-alias`, use this command:

```
keytool -list -keystore keystore.jks -alias server-alias -v
```

To check the contents of the `cacerts` file, use this command:

```
keytool -list -keystore cacerts.jks
```

Enabling Mutual Authentication over SSL

This section discusses setting up client-side authentication. When both server-side and client-side authentication are enabled, it is called mutual, or two-way, authentication. In client authentication, clients are required to submit certificates that are issued by a certificate authority that you choose to accept.

There are at least two ways to enable mutual authentication over SSL:

- The preferred method is to set the method of authentication in the `web.xml` application deployment descriptor to `CLIENT-CERT`. This enforces mutual authentication by modifying the deployment descriptor of the given application. By enabling client authentication in this way, client authentication is enabled only for a specific resource controlled by the security constraint, and the check is only performed when the application requires client authentication.
- A less commonly used method is to set the `clientAuth` property in the `certificate` realm to `true` if you want the SSL stack to require a valid certificate chain from the client before accepting a connection. A `false` value (which is the default) will not require a certificate chain unless the client requests a resource protected by a security constraint that uses `CLIENT-CERT` authentication. When you enable client authentication by setting the `clientAuth` property to `true`, client authentication will be required for all the requests going through the specified SSL port. If you turn `clientAuth` on, it is on all of the time, which can severely degrade performance.

When client authentication is enabled in both of these ways, client authentication will be performed twice.

Creating a Client Certificate for Mutual Authentication

If you have a certificate signed by a trusted Certificate Authority (CA) such as Verisign, and the Application Server's `cacerts.jks` file already contains a certificate verified by that CA, you do not need to complete this step. You only need to install your certificate in the Application Server's certificate file when your certificate is self-signed.

From the directory where you want to create the client certificate, run `keytool` as outlined here. When you press Enter, `keytool` prompts you to enter the server name, organizational unit, organization, locality, state, and country code.

You must enter the *server name* in response to keytool's first prompt, in which it asks for first and last names. For testing purposes, this can be localhost. The host specified in the keystore must match the host identified in the javee.server.host variable specified in your <*INSTALL*>/javaeetutorial5/examples/bp-project/build.properties file. If this example is to verify mutual authentication and you receive a runtime error stating that the HTTPS host name is wrong, re-create the client certificate, being sure to use the same host name that you will use when running the example. For example, if your machine name is duke, then enter duke as the certificate CN or when prompted for first and last names. When accessing the application, enter a URL that points to the same location—for example, https://duke:8181/mutualauth/hello. This is necessary because during SSL handshake, the server verifies the client certificate by comparing the certificate name and the host name from which it originates.

To create a keystore named client_keystore.jks that contains a client certificate named client.cer, follow these steps:

1. Create a backup copy of the server truststore file. To do this,
   a. Change to the directory containing the server's keystore and truststore files, <*JAVAEE_HOME*>\domains\domain1\config.
   b. Copy cacerts.jks to cacerts.backup.jks.
   c. Copy keystore.jks to keystore.backup.jks.

   Do not put client certificates in the cacerts.jks file. Any certificate you add to the cacerts file effectively means it can be a trusted root for any and all certificate chains. After you have completed development, delete the development version of the cacerts file and replace it with the original copy.

2. Generate the client certificate. Enter the following command from the directory where you want to generate the client certificate:

```
<JAVA_HOME>\bin\keytool -genkey -alias client-alias -keyalg
RSA -keypass changeit
-storepass changeit -keystore client_keystore.jks
```

3. Export the generated client certificate into the file client.cer.

```
<JAVA_HOME>\bin\keytool -export -alias client-alias
-storepass changeit -file client.cer
-keystore client_keystore.jks
```

4. Add the certificate to the truststore file <*JAVAEE_HOME*>/domains/domain1/config/cacerts.jks. Run keytool from the directory where

you created the keystore and client certificate. Use the following parameters:

```
<JAVA_HOME>\bin\keytool -import -v -trustcacerts
-alias client-alias -file client.cer
-keystore <JAVAEE_HOME>/domains/domain1/config/cacerts.jks
-keypass changeit -storepass changeit
```

The `keytool` utility returns a message like this one:

```
Owner: CN=localhost, OU=Java EE, O=Sun, L=Santa Clara,
ST=CA, C=US
Issuer: CN=localhost, OU=Java EE, O=Sun, L=Santa Clara,
ST=CA, C=US
Serial number: 3e39e66a
Valid from: Thu Jan 30 18:58:50 PST 2005 until: Wed Apr 30
19:58:50 PDT 2005
Certificate fingerprints:
MD5: 5A:B0:4C:88:4E:F8:EF:E9:E5:8B:53:BD:D0:AA:8E:5A
SHA1:90:00:36:5B:E0:A7:A2:BD:67:DB:EA:37:B9:61:3E:26:B3:89:
46:
32
Trust this certificate? [no]: yes
Certificate was added to keystore
```

5. Restart the Application Server.

Further Information

- *Java EE 5 Specification*:

  `http://jcp.org/en/jsr/detail?id=244`

- The *Developer's Guide* for the Application Server PE includes security information for application developers:

  `http://docs.sun.com/doc/819-3659`

- The *Administration Guide* for the Application Server PE includes information on setting security settings for the Application Server:

  `http://docs.sun.com/doc/819-3658`

- The *Application Deployment Guide* for the Application Server PE:

  `http://docs.sun.com/doc/819-3660`

- *EJB 3.0 Specification* (JSR-220):

  `http://jcp.org/en/jsr/detail?id=220`

- *Web Services for Java EE* (JSR-109):

  `http://jcp.org/en/jsr/detail?id=109`

- Java 2 Standard Edition, v.1.5.0 security information:

  `http://java.sun.com/j2se/1.5.0/docs/guide/security/index.html`

- Java Servlet specification:

  `http://jcp.org/en/jsr/detail?id=154`

- *JSR 175: A Metadata Facility for the Java Programming Language*:

  `http://jcp.org/en/jsr/detail?id=175`

- *JSR 181: Web Services Metadata for the Java Platform*:

  `http://jcp.org/en/jsr/detail?id=181`

- *JSR 250: Common Annotations for the Java Platform*:

  `http://jcp.org/en/jsr/detail?id=250`

- The Java SE discussion of annotations:

  `http://java.sun.com/j2se/1.5.0/docs/guide/language/annotations.html`

- The API specification for Java Authorization Contract for Containers:

  `http://jcp.org/en/jsr/detail?id=115`

- Information on SSL specifications:

  `http://wp.netscape.com/eng/security`

29

Securing Java EE Applications

JAVA EE applications are made up of components that can be deployed into different containers. These components are used to build multitier enterprise applications. Security services are provided by the component container and can be implemented using declarative or programmatic techniques. Java EE security services provide a robust and easily configured security mechanism for authenticating users and authorizing access to application functions and associated data. Java EE security services are separate from the security mechanisms of the operating system.

The ways to implement Java EE security services are discussed in a general way in Securing Containers (page 910). This chapter provides more detail and a few examples that explore these security services as they relate to Java EE components. Java EE security services can be implemented in the following ways:

- *Metadata annotations* (or simply, *annotations*) enable a declarative style of programming. Users can specify information about security within a class file using annotations. When the application is deployed, this information can either be used by or overridden by the application deployment descriptor.
- *Declarative security* expresses an application's security structure, including security roles, access control, and authentication requirements in a deployment descriptor, which is external to the application.

Any values explicitly specified in the deployment descriptor override any values specified in annotations.

- *Programmatic security* is embedded in an application and is used to make security decisions. Programmatic security is useful when declarative security alone is not sufficient to express the security model of an application.

Some of the material in this chapter assumes that you have already read Chapter 28.

This chapter includes the following topics:

- Securing enterprise beans
- Securing application clients
- Securing EIS applications

Chapter 30 discusses security specific to web components such as servlets and JSP pages.

Securing Enterprise Beans

Enterprise beans are the Java EE components that implement Enterprise JavaBeans (EJB) technology. Enterprise beans run in the EJB container, a runtime environment within the Application Server, as shown in Figure 29–1.

Although transparent to the application developer, the EJB container provides system-level services such as transactions and security to its enterprise beans. These services enable you to quickly build and deploy enterprise beans, which form the core of transactional Java EE applications.

The following sections describe declarative and programmatic security mechanisms that can be used to protect enterprise bean resources. The protected resources include methods of enterprise beans that are called from application clients, web components, or other enterprise beans. This section assumes that you have read Chapters 20 and 21 before starting this section.

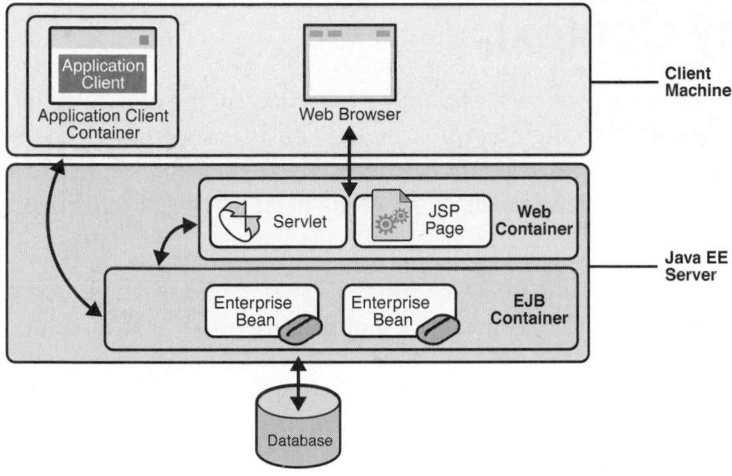

Figure 29–1 Java EE Server and Containers

You can protect enterprise beans by doing the following:

- Accessing an enterprise bean caller's security context
- Declaring security role names referenced from enterprise bean code
- Defining a security view of enterprise beans
- Using enterprise bean security annotations
- Using enterprise bean security deployment descriptor elements
- Configuring IOR security
- Deploying secure enterprise beans

Two example applications demonstrate adding security to enterprise beans. These example applications are discussed in the following sections:

- Example: Securing an Enterprise Bean (page 964)
- Example: Using the isCallerInRole and getCallerPrincipal Methods (page 970)

You should also read *JSR-220: Enterprise JavaBeans 3.0* for more information on this topic. This document can be downloaded from the following URL: `http://jcp.org/en/jsr/detail?id=220`. Chapter 16 of this specification, *Security Management*, discusses security management for enterprise beans.

Accessing an Enterprise Bean Caller's Security Context

In general, security management should be enforced by the container in a manner that is transparent to the enterprise beans' business methods. The security API described in this section should be used only in the less frequent situations in which the enterprise bean business methods need to access the security context information.

The `javax.ejb.EJBContext` interface provides two methods that allow the bean provider to access security information about the enterprise bean's caller.

- `java.security.Principal getCallerPrincipal();`

  The purpose of the `getCallerPrincipal` method is to allow the enterprise bean methods to obtain the current caller principal's name. The methods might, for example, use the name as a key to information in a database.

- `boolean isCallerInRole(String roleName);`

  The purpose of the `isCallerInRole(String roleName)` method is to test whether the current caller has been assigned to a given security role. Security roles are defined by the bean provider or the application assembler, and are assigned to principals or principals groups that exist in the operational environment by the deployer.

The following code sample illustrates the use of the `getCallerPrincipal()` method:

```
@Stateless public class EmployeeServiceBean
        implements EmployeeService{
   @Resource SessionContext ctx;
   @PersistenceContext EntityManager em;

   public void changePhoneNumber(...) {
      ...
      // obtain the caller principal.
      callerPrincipal = ctx.getCallerPrincipal();

      // obtain the caller principal's name.
      callerKey = callerPrincipal.getName();

      // use callerKey as primary key to find EmployeeRecord
      EmployeeRecord myEmployeeRecord =
         em.findByPrimaryKey(EmployeeRecord.class, callerKey);
```

```
        // update phone number
        myEmployeeRecord.setPhoneNumber(...);

        ...
    }
}
```

In the previous example, the enterprise bean obtains the principal name of the current caller and uses it as the primary key to locate an `EmployeeRecord` entity. This example assumes that application has been deployed such that the current caller principal contains the primary key used for the identification of employees (for example, employee number).

The following code sample illustrates the use of the `isCallerInRole(String roleName)` method:

```
@DeclareRoles("payroll")
@Stateless public class PayrollBean implements Payroll {
  @Resource SessionContext ctx;

  public void updateEmployeeInfo(EmplInfo info) {

     oldInfo = ... read from database;

     // The salary field can be changed only by callers
     // who have the security role "payroll"
     if (info.salary != oldInfo.salary &&
        !ctx.isCallerInRole("payroll")) {
          throw new SecurityException(...);
     }
     ...
  }
  ...
}
```

An example application that uses the `getCallerPrincipal` and `isCallerInRole` methods is described in Example: Using the isCallerInRole and getCallerPrincipal Methods (page 970).

Declaring Security Role Names Referenced from Enterprise Bean Code

You can declare security role names used in enterprise bean code using either the `@DeclareRoles` annotation (preferred) or the `security-role-ref` elements of the deployment descriptor. Declaring security role names in this way enables you to link these security role names used in the code to the security roles defined for an assembled application. In the absence of this linking step, any security role name used in the code will be assumed to correspond to a security role of the same name in the assembled application.

A security role reference, including the name defined by the reference, is scoped to the component whose bean class contains the `@DeclareRoles` annotation or whose deployment descriptor element contains the `security-role-ref` deployment descriptor element.

You can also use the `security-role-ref` elements for those references that were declared in annotations and you want to have linked to a `security-role` whose name differs from the reference value. If a security role reference is not linked to a security role in this way, the container must map the reference name to the security role of the same name. See Linking Security Role References to Security Roles (page 946) for a description of how security role references are linked to security roles.

For an example using each of these methods, read the following sections:

- Declaring Security Roles Using Annotations (page 942)
- Declaring Security Roles Using Deployment Descriptor Elements (page 943)

Declaring Security Roles Using Annotations

The `@DeclareRoles` annotation is specified on a bean class, where it serves to declare roles that can be tested by calling `isCallerInRole` from within the methods of the annotated class.

You declare the security roles referenced in the code using the `@DeclareRoles` annotation. When declaring the name of a role used as a parameter to the `isCallerInRole(String roleName)` method, the declared name must be the same as the parameter value. You can optionally provide a description of the named security roles in the description element of the `@DeclareRoles` annotation.

The following code snippet demonstrates the use of the `@DeclareRoles` annotation. In this example, the `@DeclareRoles` annotation indicates that the enterprise bean `AardvarkPayroll` makes the security check using `isCallerInRole("payroll")` to verify that the caller is authorized to change salary data. The security role reference is scoped to the session or entity bean whose declaration contains the `@DeclareRoles` annotation.

```
@DeclareRoles("payroll")
@Stateless public class PayrollBean implements Payroll {
  @Resource SessionContext ctx;

  public void updateEmployeeInfo(EmplInfo info) {

    oldInfo = ... read from database;

    // The salary field can be changed only by callers
    // who have the security role "payroll"
    if (info.salary != oldInfo.salary &&
      !ctx.isCallerInRole("payroll")) {
        throw new SecurityException(...);
    }
    ...
  }
  ...
}
```

The syntax for declaring more than one role is as shown in the following example:

```
@DeclareRoles({"Administrator", "Manager", "Employee"})
```

Declaring Security Roles Using Deployment Descriptor Elements

---

Note: Any values explicitly specified in the deployment descriptor override any values specified in annotations. If a value for a method has not been specified in the deployment descriptor, and a value has been specified for that method by means of the use of annotations, the value specified in annotations will apply. The granularity of overriding is on the per-method basis.

If the @DeclareRoles annotation is not used, you can use the security-role-ref elements of the deployment descriptor to declare the security roles referenced in the code, as follows:

- Declare the name of the security role using the role-name element in the deployment descriptor. The name must be the security role name that is used as a parameter to the isCallerInRole(String roleName) method.
- Optionally provide a description of the security role in the description element.

The following example illustrates how an enterprise bean's references to security roles are declared in the deployment descriptor. In this example, the deployment descriptor indicates that the enterprise bean AardvarkPayroll makes the security check using isCallerInRole("payroll") in its business method. The security role reference is scoped to the session or entity bean whose declaration contains the security-role-ref element.

```
...
<enterprise-beans>
  ...
  <session>
    <ejb-name>AardvarkPayroll</ejb-name>
    <ejb-class>com.aardvark.payroll.PayrollBean</ejb-class>
    ...
    <security-role-ref>
      <description>
        This security role should be assigned to the
        employees of the payroll department who are
        allowed to update employees' salaries.
      </description>
      <role-name>payroll</role-name>
    </security-role-ref>
    ...
  </session>
  ...
</enterprise-beans>
...
```

Defining a Security View of Enterprise Beans

You can define a *security view* of the enterprise beans contained in the ejb-jar file and pass this information along to the deployer. When a security view is passed on to the deployer, the deployer uses this information to define method permissions for security roles. If you don't define a security view, the deployer will have to determine what each business method does to determine which users are authorized to call each method.

A security view consists of a set of *security roles* — a semantic grouping of permissions that a given type of users of an application must have to successfully access the application. Security roles are meant to be logical roles, representing a type of user. You can define *method permissions* for each security role. A method permission is a permission to invoke a specified group of methods of the enterprise beans' business interface, home interface, component interface, and/or web service endpoints. You can specify an authentication mechanism that will be used to verify the identity of a user.

It is important to keep in mind that security roles are used to define the logical security view of an application. They should not be confused with the user groups, users, principals, and other concepts that exist in the Application Server.

The following sections discuss setting up security roles, authentication mechanisms, and method permissions that define a security view:

Defining Security Roles

Use the `@DeclareRoles` and `@RolesAllowed` annotations to define security roles using Java language annotations. The set of security roles used by the application is the total of the security roles defined by the security role names used in the `@DeclareRoles` and `@RolesAllowed` annotations.

You can augment the set of security roles defined for the application by annotations using the `security-role` deployment descriptor element to define security roles, where you use the `role-name` element to define the name of the security role.

The following example illustrates how to define security roles in a deployment descriptor:

```
  ...
<assembly-descriptor>
  <security-role>
    <description>
```

```
            This role includes the employees of the
            enterprise who are allowed to access the
            employee self-service application. This role
            is allowed only to access his/her own
            information.
        </description>
        <role-name>employee</role-name>
    </security-role>

    <security-role>
        <description>
            This role includes the employees of the human
            resources department. The role is allowed to
            view and update all employee records.
        </description>
        <role-name>hr-department</role-name>
    </security-role>

    <security-role>
        <description>
            This role includes the employees of the payroll
            department. The role is allowed to view and
            update the payroll entry for any employee.
        </description>
        <role-name>payroll-department</role-name>
    </security-role>

    <security-role>
        <description>
            This role should be assigned to the personnel
            authorized to perform administrative functions
            for the employee self-service application.
            This role does not have direct access to
            sensitive employee and payroll information.
        </description>
        <role-name>admin</role-name>
    </security-role>
    ...
</assembly-descriptor>
```

Linking Security Role References to Security Roles

The security role references used in the components of the application are linked to the security roles defined for the application. In the absence of any explicit linking, a security role reference will be linked to a security role having the same name.

You can explicitly link all the security role references declared in the `@DeclareRoles` annotation or `security-role-ref` elements for a component to the security roles defined by the use of annotations (as discussed in Defining Security Roles, page 945) and/or in the `security-role` elements.

You use the `role-link` element to link each security role reference to a security role. The value of the `role-link` element must be the name of one of the security roles defined in a `security-role` element, or by the `@DeclareRoles` or `@RolesAllowed` annotations (as discussed in Defining Security Roles, page 945). You do not need to use the `role-link` element to link security role references to security roles when the `role-name` used in the code is the same as the name of the `security-role` to which you would be linking.

The following example illustrates how to link the security role reference name `payroll` to the security role named `payroll-department`:

```
...
<enterprise-beans>
  ...
  <session>
    <ejb-name>AardvarkPayroll</ejb-name>
    <ejb-class>com.aardvark.payroll.PayrollBean</ejb-class>
    ...
    <security-role-ref>
      <description>
        This role should be assigned to the
        employees of the payroll department.
        Members of this role have access to
        anyone's payroll record.
        The role has been linked to the
        payroll-department role.
      </description>
      <role-name>payroll</role-name>
      <role-link>payroll-department</role-link>
    </security-role-ref>
    ...
  </session>
  ...
</enterprise-beans>
...
```

Specifying an Authentication Mechanism

Authentications mechanisms are specified in the runtime deployment descriptor. When annotations, such as the `@RolesAllowed` annotation, are used to protect methods in the enterprise bean, you can configure the Interoperable Object Reference (IOR) to enable authentication for an enterprise application. This is accomplished by adding the `<login-config>` element to the runtime deployment descriptor, `sun-ejb-jar.xml`.

You can use the `USERNAME-PASSWORD` authentication method for an enterprise bean. You can use either the `BASIC` or `CLIENT-CERT` authentication methods for web service endpoints.

For more information on specifying an authentication mechanism, read Configuring IOR Security (page 959) or Example: Securing an Enterprise Bean (page 964).

Specifying Method Permissions

If you have defined security roles for the enterprise beans in the `ejb-jar` file, you can also specify the methods of the business interface, home interface, component interface, and/or web service endpoints that each security role is allowed to invoke.

You can use annotations and/or the deployment descriptor for this purpose. Refer to the following sections for more information on specifying method permissions:

- Specifying Method Permissions Using Annotations (page 948)
- Specifying Method Permissions Using Deployment Descriptors (page 950)

Specifying Method Permissions Using Annotations

The method permissions for the methods of a bean class can be specified on the class, the business methods of the class, or both. Method permissions can be specified on a method of the bean class to override the method permissions value specified on the entire bean class. The following annotations are used to specify method permissions:

- `@RolesAllowed("`*`list_of_roles`*`")`

  The value of the `@RolesAllowed` annotation is a list of security role names to be mapped to the security roles that are permitted to execute the specified method(s). Specifying this annotation on the bean class means that it applies to all applicable business methods of the class.

- `@PermitAll`

  The `@PermitAll` annotation specifies that all security roles are permitted to execute the specified method(s). Specifying this annotation on the bean class means that it applies to all applicable business methods of the class.

- `@DenyAll`

  The `@DenyAll` annotation specifies that no security roles are permitted to execute the specified method(s).

The following example code illustrates the use of these annotations:

```
@RolesAllowed("admin")
public class SomeClass {
  public void aMethod () {...}
  public void bMethod () {...}
  ...
}

@Stateless public class MyBean implements A extends SomeClass {

  @RolesAllowed("HR")
  public void aMethod () {...}

  public void cMethod () {...}
  ...
}
```

In this example, assuming `aMethod`, `bMethod`, and `cMethod` are methods of business interface `A`, the method permissions values of methods `aMethod` and `bMethod` are `@RolesAllowed("HR")` and `@RolesAllowed("admin")` respectively. The method permissions for method `cMethod` have not been specified.

To clarify, the annotations are not inherited by the subclass per se, they apply to methods of the superclass which are inherited by the subclass. Also, annotations do not apply to CMP entity beans.

An example that uses annotations to specify method permissions is described in Example: Securing an Enterprise Bean (page 964).

Specifying Method Permissions Using Deployment Descriptors

Note: Any values explicitly specified in the deployment descriptor override any values specified in annotations. If a value for a method has not been specified in the deployment descriptor, and a value has been specified for that method by means of the use of annotations, the value specified in annotations will apply. The granularity of overriding is on the per-method basis.

You define the method permissions in the deployment descriptor using the `method-permission` elements, as discussed below:

- Each `method-permission` element includes a list of one or more security roles and a list of one or more methods. All the listed security roles are allowed to invoke all the listed methods. Each security role in the list is identified by the `role-name` element. Each method (or set of methods) is identified by the `method` element.
- The method permissions relation is defined as the union of all the method permissions defined in the individual `method-permission` elements.
- A security role or a method can appear in multiple `method-permission` elements.

Here is some other useful information about setting method permissions using deployment descriptors:

- You can specify that all roles are permitted to execute one or more specified methods, which, in effect, indicates that the methods should not be checked for authorization prior to invocation by the container. To specify that all roles are permitted, use the `unchecked` element instead of a role name in a method permission.

  If a method permission specifies both the `unchecked` element for a given method and one or more security roles, all roles are permitted for the specified methods.

- The `exclude-list` element can be used to indicate the set of methods that should not be called. At deployment time, the deployer will know that no access is permitted to any method contained in this list.

  If a given method is specified in both the `exclude-list` element and in a method permission, the deployer should exclude access to this method.

- It is possible that some methods are not assigned to any security roles nor contained in the `exclude-list` element. In this case, the deployer should assign method permissions for all of the unspecified methods, either by assigning them to security roles, or by marking them as unchecked. If the deployer does not assign method permissions to the unspecified methods, those methods must be treated by the container as unchecked.
- The `method` element uses the `ejb-name`, `method-name`, and `method-params` elements to denote one or more methods of an enterprise bean's business interface, home interface, component interface, and/or web service endpoints.

There are three legal styles for composing the `method` element:

- The first style is used for referring to all of the business interface, home interface, component interface, and web service endpoints methods of a specified bean.

```
<method>
  <ejb-name>EJB_NAME</ejb-name>
  <method-name>*</method-name>
</method>
```

- The second style is used for referring to a specified method of the business interface, home interface, component interface, or web service endpoints methods of the specified enterprise bean. If the enterprise bean contains multiple methods with the same overloaded name, the element of this style refers to all of the methods with the overloaded name.

```
<method>
  <ejb-name>EJB_NAME</ejb-name>
  <method-name>METHOD</method-name>
</method>
```

- The third style is used for referring to a specified method within a set of methods with an overloaded name. The method must be defined in the business interface, home interface, component interface, or web service endpoints methods of the specified enterprise bean. If there are multiple methods with the same overloaded name, however, this style refers to all of the overloaded methods. All of the parameters are the fully-qualified Java types, for example, `java.lang.String`.

```
<method>
  <ejb-name>EJB_NAME</ejb-name>
  <method-name>METHOD</method-name>
  <method-params>
    <method-param>PARAMETER_1</method-param>
    <method-param>PARAMETER_2</method-param>
```

```
    </method-params>
  </method>
```

The following example illustrates how security roles are assigned method permissions in the deployment descriptor:

```
...
<method-permission>
  <role-name>employee</role-name>
  <method>
    <ejb-name>EmployeeService</ejb-name>
    <method-name>*</method-name>
  </method>
</method-permission>

<method-permission>
  <role-name>employee</role-name>
  <method>
    <ejb-name>AardvarkPayroll</ejb-name>
    <method-name>findByPrimaryKey</method-name>
  </method>
  <method>
    <ejb-name>AardvarkPayroll</ejb-name>
    <method-name>getEmployeeInfo</method-name>
  </method>
  <method>
    <ejb-name>AardvarkPayroll</ejb-name>
    <method-name>updateEmployeeInfo</method-name>
  </method>
</method-permission>

<method-permission>
  <role-name>payroll-department</role-name>
  <method>
    <ejb-name>AardvarkPayroll</ejb-name>
    <method-name>findByPrimaryKey</method-name>
  </method>
  <method>
    <ejb-name>AardvarkPayroll</ejb-name>
    <method-name>getEmployeeInfo</method-name>
  </method>
  <method>
    <ejb-name>AardvarkPayroll</ejb-name>
    <method-name>updateEmployeeInfo</method-name>
  </method>
  <method>
    <ejb-name>AardvarkPayroll</ejb-name>
    <method-name>updateSalary</method-name>
```

```
    </method>
  </method-permission>

  <method-permission>
    <role-name>admin</role-name>
    <method>
      <ejb-name>EmployeeServiceAdmin</ejb-name>
      <method-name>*</method-name>
    </method>
  </method-permission>
  ...
```

Mapping Security Roles to Application Server Groups

The Application Server assigns users to *principals* or *groups*, rather than to security roles. When you are developing a Java EE application, you don't need to know what categories of users have been defined for the realm in which the application will be run. In the Java EE platform, the security architecture provides a mechanism for mapping the roles defined in the application to the users or groups defined in the runtime realm.

To map a role name permitted by the application or module to principals (users) and groups defined on the server, use the `security-role-mapping` element in the runtime deployment descriptor (`sun-application.xml`, `sun-web.xml`, or `sun-ejb-jar.xml`) file. The entry needs to declare a mapping between a security role used in the application and one or more groups or principals defined for the applicable realm of the Application Server. An example for the `sun-application.xml` file is shown below:

```
<sun-application>
  <security-role-mapping>
    <role-name>CEO</role-name>
    <principal-name>jschwartz</principal-name>
  </security-role-mapping>
  <security-role-mapping>
    <role-name>ADMIN</role-name>
    <group-name>directors</group-name>
  </security-role-mapping>
</sun-application>
```

The role name can be mapped to either a specific principal (user), a group, or both. The principal or group names referenced must be valid principals or groups in the current default realm of the Application Server. The `role-name` in this example must exactly match the `role-name` in the `security-role` element of the corresponding `web.xml` file or the role name defined in the `@DeclareRoles` or `@RolesAllowed` annotations.

Sometimes the role names used in the application are the same as the group names defined on the Application Server. Under these circumstances, you can enable a default principal-to-role mapping on the Application Server using the Admin Console. To enable the default principal-to-role-mapping, follow these steps:

1. Start the Application Server, then the Admin Console.
2. Expand the Configuration node.
3. Select the Security node.
4. On the Security page, check the Enabled box beside Default Principal to Role Mapping.

For an enterprise application, you can specify the security role mapping at the application layer, in `sun-application.xml`, or at the module layer, in `sun-ejb-jar.xml`. When specified at the application layer, the role mapping applies to all contained modules and overrides same-named role mappings at the module layer. The assembler is responsible for reconciling the module-specific role mappings to yield one effective mapping for the application.

Both example applications demonstrate security role mapping. For more information, see Example: Securing an Enterprise Bean (page 964) and Example: Using the isCallerInRole and getCallerPrincipal Methods (page 970).

Propagating Security Identity

You can specify whether a caller's security identity should be used for the execution of specified methods of an enterprise bean, or whether a specific run-as identity should be used.

Figure 29–2 illustrates this concept.

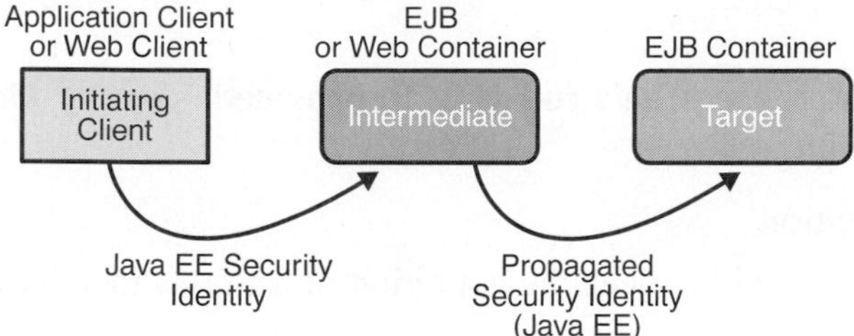

Figure 29–2 Security Identity Propagation

In this illustration, an application client is making a call to an enterprise bean method in one EJB container. This enterprise bean method, in turn, makes a call to an enterprise bean method in another container. The security identity during the first call is the identity of the caller. The security identity during the second call can be any of the following options:

- By default, the identity of the caller of the intermediate component is propagated to the target enterprise bean. This technique is used when the target container trusts the intermediate container.
- A specific identity is propagated to the target enterprise bean. This technique is used when the target container expects access using a specific identity.

  To propagate an identity to the target enterprise bean, configure a run-as identity for the bean as discussed in Configuring a Component's Propagated Security Identity (page 956).

  Establishing a run-as identity for an enterprise bean does not affect the identities of its callers, which are the identities tested for permission to access the methods of the enterprise bean. The run-as identity establishes the identity that the enterprise bean will use when it makes calls.

  The run-as identity applies to the enterprise bean as a whole, including all the methods of the enterprise bean's business interface, home interface, component interface, and web service endpoint interfaces, the message listener methods of a message-driven bean, the time-out callback method of an enterprise bean, and all internal methods of the bean that might be called in turn.

Configuring a Component's Propagated Security Identity

You can configure an enterprise bean's run-as, or propagated, security identity using either of the following:

- The `@RunAs` annotation

  The following example illustrates the definition of a run-as identity using annotations:

  ```
  @RunAs("admin")
  @Stateless public class EmployeeServiceBean
       implements EmployeeService{
     ...
  }
  ```

- The `role-name` element of the `run-as` application deployment descriptor element (`web.xml`, `ejb-jar.xml`)

  The following example illustrates the definition of a `run-as` identity using deployment descriptor elements:

  ```
  ...
  <enterprise-beans>
     ...
     <session>
        <ejb-name>EmployeeService</ejb-name>
        ...
        <security-identity>
           <run-as>
              <role-name>admin</role-name>
           </run-as>
        </security-identity>
        ...
     </session>
     ...
  </enterprise-beans>
  ...
  ```

Alternately, you can use the `use-caller-identity` element to indicate that you want to use the identity of the original caller, as shown in the code below:

```
<security-identity>
  <use-caller-identity />
</security-identity>
```

You must explicitly specify the run-as role name mapping to a given principal in `sun-web.xml` or `sun-ejb-jar.xml` if the given roles associate to more than one user principal.

More detail about the elements contained in deployment descriptors is available in the Application Server's *Application Deployment Guide*, a link to which can be found in Further Information (page 984).

In either case, you will have to map the run-as role name to a given principal defined on the Application Server if the given roles associate to more than one user principal. Mapping roles to principals is described in Mapping Security Roles to Application Server Groups (page 953).

Trust between Containers

When an enterprise bean is designed so that either the original caller identity or a designated identity is used to call a target bean, the target bean will receive the propagated identity only; it will *not* receive any authentication data.

There is no way for the target container to authenticate the propagated security identity. However, because the security identity is used in authorization checks (for example, method permissions or with the `isCallerInRole()` method), it is vitally important that the security identity be authentic. Because there is no authentication data available to authenticate the propagated identity, the target must trust that the calling container has propagated an authenticated security identity.

By default, the Application Server is configured to trust identities that are propagated from different containers. Therefore, there are no special steps that you need to take to set up a trust relationship.

Using Enterprise Bean Security Annotations

Annotations are used in code to relay information to the deployer about security and other aspects of the application. Specifying this information in annotations or in the deployment descriptor helps the deployer set up the appropriate security policy for the enterprise bean application.

Any values explicitly specified in the deployment descriptor override any values specified in annotations. If a value for a method has not been specified in the deployment descriptor, and a value has been specified for that method by means of the use of annotations, the value specified in annotations will apply. The granularity of overriding is on the per-method basis.

The following is a listing of annotations that address security, can be used in an enterprise bean, and are discussed in this tutorial:

- The `@DeclareRoles` annotation declares each security role referenced in the code. Use of this annotation is discussed in Declaring Security Roles Using Annotations (page 942).
- The `@RolesAllowed`, `@PermitAll`, and `@DenyAll` annotations are used to specify method permissions. Use of these annotations is discussed in Specifying Method Permissions Using Annotations (page 948).
- The `@RunAs` metadata annotation is used to configure a component's propagated security identity. Use of this annotation is discussed in Configuring a Component's Propagated Security Identity (page 956).

Using Enterprise Bean Security Deployment Descriptor Elements

Enterprise JavaBeans components use an EJB deployment descriptor that must be named `META-INF/ejb-jar.xml` and must be contained in the EJB JAR file. The role of the deployment descriptor is to relay information to the deployer about security and other aspects of the application. Specifying this information in annotations or in the deployment descriptor helps the deployer set up the appropriate security policy for the enterprise bean application. More detail about the elements contained in deployment descriptors is available in the Application Server's *Application Deployment Guide*, a link to which can be found in Further Information (page 984).

Note: Using annotations is the recommended method for adding security to enterprise bean applications.

Any values explicitly specified in the deployment descriptor override any values specified in annotations. If a value for a method has not been specified in the deployment descriptor, and a value has been specified for that method by means of the use of annotations, the value specified in annotations will apply. The granularity of overriding is on the per-method basis.

The following is a listing of deployment descriptor elements that address security, can be used in an enterprise bean, and are discussed in this tutorial:

- The `security-role-ref` element declares each security role referenced in the code. Use of this element is discussed in Declaring Security Roles Using Deployment Descriptor Elements (page 943).
- The `security-role` element defines broad categories of users, and is used to provide access to protected methods. Use of this element is discussed in Defining Security Roles (page 945).
- The `method-permission` element is used to specify method permissions. Use of these elements is discussed in Specifying Method Permissions Using Deployment Descriptors (page 950).
- The `run-as` element is used to configure a component's propagated security identity. Use of this element is discussed in Configuring a Component's Propagated Security Identity (page 956).

The schema for `ejb-jar` deployment descriptors can be found in section 18.5, *Deployment Descriptor XML Schema*, in the *EJB 3.0 Specification* (JSR-220) at `http://jcp.org/en/jsr/detail?id=220`.

Configuring IOR Security

The EJB interoperability protocol is based on Internet Inter-ORB Protocol (IIOP/GIOP 1.2) and the Common Secure Interoperability version 2 (CSIv2) CORBA Secure Interoperability specification.

Enterprise beans that are deployed in one vendor's server product are often accessed from Java EE client components that are deployed in another vendor's product. CSIv2, a CORBA/IIOP-based standard interoperability protocol, addresses this situation by providing authentication, protection of integrity and confidentiality, and principal propagation for invocations on enterprise beans, where the invocations take place over an enterprise's intranet. CSIv2 configuration settings are specified in the Interoperable Object Reference (IOR) of the target enterprise bean. IOR configurations are defined in Chapter 24 of the CORBA/IIOP specification, *Secure Interoperability*. This chapter can be downloaded from the following URL: `http://www.omg.org/cgi-bin/doc?formal/02-06-60`.

The EJB interoperability protocol is defined in Chapter 14, *Support for Distribution and Interoperability*, of the EJB specification, which can be downloaded from `http://jcp.org/en/jsr/detail?id=220`.

Based on application requirements, IORs are configured in vendor-specific XML files, such as `sun-ejb-jar.xml`, instead of in standard application deployment descriptor files, such as `ejb-jar.xml`.

For a Java EE application, IOR configurations are specified in Sun-specific xml files, for example, `sun-ejb-jar_2_1-1.dtd`. The `ior-security-config` element describes the security configuration information for the IOR. A description of some of the major subelements is provided below.

- `transport-config`

  This is the root element for security between the endpoints. It contains the following elements:

  - `integrity`: This element specifies whether the target supports integrity-protected messages for transport. The values are `NONE`, `SUPPORTED`, or `REQUIRED`.
  - `confidentiality`: This element specifies whether the target supports privacy-protected messages (SSL) for transport. The values are `NONE`, `SUPPORTED`, or `REQUIRED`.
  - `establish-trust-in-target`: This element specifies whether or not the target component is capable of authenticating to a client for transport. It is used for mutual authentication (to validate the server's identity). The values are `NONE`, `SUPPORTED`, or `REQUIRED`.
  - `establish-trust-in-client`: This element specifies whether or not the target component is capable of authenticating a client for transport (target asks the client to authenticate itself). The values are `NONE`, `SUPPORTED`, or `REQUIRED`.

- `as-context`

  This is the element that describes the authentication mechanism (CSIv2 authentication service) that will be used to authenticate the client. If specified, it will be the username-password mechanism.

  In the Duke's Bank example, the `as-context` setting is used to require client authentication (with user name and password) when access to protected methods in the `AccountControllerBean` and `CustomerControllerBean` components is attempted.

  The `as-context` element contains the following elements:

  - `required`: This element specifies whether the authentication method specified is required to be used for client authentication. Setting this field to `true` indicates that the authentication method specified is required. Setting this field to `false` indicates that the method authentication is not required. The element value is either `true` or `false`.

- `auth-method`: This element specifies the authentication method. The only supported value is `USERNAME_PASSWORD`.
- `realm`: This element specifies the realm in which the user is authenticated. Must be a valid realm that is registered in a server configuration.

- `sas-context`

  This element is related to the CSIv2 security attribute service. It describes the `sas-context` fields.

  In the Duke's Bank example, the `sas-context` setting is set to `Supported` for the `AccountBean`, `CustomerBean`, and `TxBean` components, indicating that these target components will accept propagated caller identities.

  The `sas-context` element contains the `caller-propagation` subelement. This element indicates if the target will accept propagated caller identities. The values are `NONE` or `SUPPORTED`.

The following is an example that defines security for an IOR in the `sun ejb-jar.xml` file in the sample application (assuming you installed the samples server) at *<JAVAEE_HOME>*`/samples/webservices/security/ejb/apps/basicAuth/basicAuth-ejb/src/conf/sun-ejb-jar.xml`:

```
<sun-ejb-jar>
  <enterprise-beans>
    <unique-id>1</unique-id>
    <ejb>
      <ejb-name>HelloWorld</ejb-name>
      <jndi-name>HelloWorld</jndi-name>
      <ior-security-config>
        <transport-config>
          <integrity>NONE</integrity>
          <confidentiality>NONE</confidentiality>
          <establish-trust-in-target>
            NONE
          </establish-trust-in-target>
          <establish-trust-in-client>
            NONE
          </establish-trust-in-client>
        </transport-config>
        <as-context>
          <auth-method>USERNAME_PASSWORD</auth-method>
          <realm>default</realm>
          <required>true</required>
        </as-context>
```

```
            <sas-context>
               <caller-propagation>NONE</caller-propagation>
            </sas-context>
         </ior-security-config>
         <webservice-endpoint>
            <port-component-name>HelloIF</port-component-name>
            <endpoint-address-uri>
               service/HelloWorld
            </endpoint-address-uri>
            <login-config>
               <auth-method>BASIC</auth-method>
            </login-config>
         </webservice-endpoint>
      </ejb>
   </enterprise-beans>
</sun-ejb-jar>
```

Deploying Secure Enterprise Beans

The deployer is responsible for ensuring that an assembled application is secure after it has been deployed in the target operational environment. If a security view (security annotations and/or a deployment descriptor) has been provided to the deployer, the security view is mapped to the mechanisms and policies used by the security domain in the target operational environment, which in this case is the Application Server. If no security view is provided, the deployer must set up the appropriate security policy for the enterprise bean application.

Deployment information is specific to a web or application server. Please read the Sun Java System Application Server *Application Deployment Guide* for more information on deploying enterprise beans. A link to this document is provided in Further Information (page 984).

Accepting Unauthenticated Users

Web applications accept unauthenticated web clients and allow these clients to make calls to the EJB container. The EJB specification requires a security credential for accessing EJB methods. Typically, the credential will be that of a generic unauthenticated user. The way you specify this credential is implementation-specific.

In the Application Server, you must specify the name and password that an unauthenticated user will use to log in by modifying the Application Server using the Admin Console:

1. Start the Application Server, then the Admin Console.
2. Expand the Configuration node.
3. Select the Security node.
4. On the Security page, set the Default Principal and Default Principal Password values.

Accessing Unprotected Enterprise Beans

If the deployer has granted full access to a method, any user or group can invoke the method. Conversely, the deployer can deny access to a method.

To modify which role can be used in applications to grant authorization to anyone, specify a value for Anonymous Role. To set the Anonymous Role field, follow these steps:

1. Start the Application Server, then the Admin Console.
2. Expand the Configuration node.
3. Select the Security node.
4. On the Security page, specify the Anonymous Role value.

Enterprise Bean Example Applications

The following example applications demonstrate adding security to enterprise beans applications:

- Example: Securing an Enterprise Bean (page 964) demonstrates adding basic login authentication to an enterprise bean application.
- Example: Using the isCallerInRole and getCallerPrincipal Methods (page 970) demonstrates the use of the `getCallerPrincipal()` and `isCallerInRole(String role)` methods.
- Discussion: Securing the Duke's Bank Example (page 977) provides a brief discussion of how the Duke's Bank example provides security in that application.

Example: Securing an Enterprise Bean

In this section, we discuss how to configure an enterprise bean for username-password authentication. When a bean that is constrained in this way is requested, the server requests a user name and password from the client and verifies that the user name and password are valid by comparing them against a database of authorized users on the Application Server.

If the topic of authentication is new to you, please refer to the section titled Specifying an Authentication Mechanism (page 1010).

For this tutorial, we will add the security elements to an enterprise bean; add security elements to the deployment descriptors; build, package, and deploy the application; and then build and run the client application.

The completed version of this example can be found at `<INSTALL>/javaeetutorial5/examples/ejb/cart-secure/`. This example was developed by starting with the unsecured enterprise bean application, `cart`, which is found in the directory `<INSTALL>/javaeetutorial5/examples/ejb/cart/` and is discussed in The cart Example (page 771). We build on this example by adding the necessary elements to secure the application using username-password authentication.

In general, the following steps are necessary to add username-password authentication to an enterprise bean. In the example application included with this tutorial, many of these steps have been completed for you and are listed here simply to show what needs to be done should you wish to create a similar application.

1. Create an application like the one in The cart Example (page 771). The example in this tutorial starts with this example and demonstrates adding basic authentication of the client to this application. The example application discussed in this section can be found at `<INSTALL>/javaeetutorial5/examples/ejb/cart-secure/`.
2. If you have not already done so, complete the steps in Building the Examples (page xxxv) to configure your system properly for running the tutorial applications.
3. If you have not already done so, add a user to the `file` realm and specify `user` for the group of this new user. Write down the user name and password so that you can use them for testing this application in a later step. Refer to the section Managing Users and Groups on the Application Server (page 918) for instructions on completing this step.

4. Modify the source code for the enterprise bean, `CartBean.java`, to specify which roles are authorized to access which protected methods. This step is discussed in Annotating the Bean (page 965).
5. Modify the runtime deployment descriptor, `sun-ejb-jar.xml`, to map the role used in this application (`CartUser`) to a group defined on the Application Server (`user`) and to add security elements that specify that username-password authentication is to be performed. This step is discussed in Setting Runtime Properties (page 966).
6. Build, package, and deploy the enterprise bean, then build and run the client application by following the steps in Building, Deploying, and Running the Secure Cart Example Using NetBeans 5.5 (page 968) or Building, Deploying, and Running the Secure Cart Example Using Ant (page 969).

Annotating the Bean

The source code for the original `cart` application was modified as shown in the following code snippet (modifications in **bold**, method details removed to save space). The resulting file can be found in `<INSTALL>/javaeetutorial5/examples/ejb/cart-secure/cart-secure-ejb/src/java/cart/secure/ejb/CartBean.java`.

```
package com.sun.tutorial.javaee.ejb;

import java.util.ArrayList;
import java.util.List;
import javax.ejb.Remove;
import javax.ejb.Stateful;
import javax.annotation.security.RolesAllowed;

@Stateful()
public class CartBean implements Cart {

  String customerName;
  String customerId;
  List<String> contents;

  public void initialize(String person) throws BookException {
     ...
    }

  public void initialize(String person, String id) throws
BookException {
     ... }
```

```
    @RolesAllowed("CartUser")
    public void addBook(String title) {
      contents.add(title);
    }

    @RolesAllowed("CartUser")
    public void removeBook(String title) throws BookException {
       ... }
    }

    @RolesAllowed("CartUser")
    public List<String> getContents() {
      return contents;
    }

    @Remove()
      public void remove() {
      contents = null;
    }
}
```

The @RolesAllowed annotation is specified on methods for which we want to restrict access. In this example, only users in the role of CartUser will be allowed to add and remove books from the cart, and to list the contents of the cart. An @RolesAllowed annotation implicitly declares a role that will be referenced in the application, therefore, no @DeclareRoles annotation is required.

Setting Runtime Properties

The role of CartUser has been defined for this application, but there is no group of CartUser defined for the Application Server. To map the role that is defined for the application (CartUser) to a group that is defined on the Application Server (user), add a <security-role-mapping> element to the runtime deployment descriptor, sun-ejb-jar.xml, as shown below. In the original example, there was no need for this deployment descriptor, so it has been added for this example.

To enable username-password authentication for the application, add security elements to the runtime deployment descriptor, sun-ejb-jar.xml. The security element that needs to be added to the deployment descriptor is the <ior-security-config> element. The deployment descriptor is located in *<INSTALL>*/javaeetutorial5/examples/ejb/cart-secure/cart-secure-ejb/src/conf/sun-ejb-jar.xml.

```
<?xml version="1.0" encoding="UTF-8"?>
<!DOCTYPE sun-ejb-jar PUBLIC "-//Sun Microsystems, Inc.//DTD
Application Server 9.0 EJB 3.0//EN" "http://www.sun.com/
software/appserver/dtds/sun-ejb-jar_3_0-0.dtd">
<sun-ejb-jar>
  <security-role-mapping>
    <role-name>CartUser</role-name>
    <group-name>user</group-name>
  </security-role-mapping>
  <enterprise-beans>
    <unique-id>0</unique-id>
    <ejb>
      <ejb-name>CartBean</ejb-name>
      <jndi-name>jacc_mr_CartBean</jndi-name>
      <pass-by-reference>false</pass-by-reference>
      <ior-security-config>
        <transport-config>
          <integrity>supported</integrity>
          <confidentiality>supported</confidentiality>
          <establish-trust-in-target>supported</establish-
trust-in-target>
          <establish-trust-in-client>supported</establish-
trust-in-client>
        </transport-config>
        <as-context>
          <auth-method>username_password</auth-method>
          <realm>default</realm>
          <required>true</required>
        </as-context>
        <sas-context>
          <caller-propagation>supported</caller-
propagation>
        </sas-context>
      </ior-security-config>
      <is-read-only-bean>false</is-read-only-bean>
      <refresh-period-in-seconds>-1</refresh-period-in-
seconds>
      <gen-classes/>
    </ejb>
  </enterprise-beans>
</sun-ejb-jar>
```

For more information on this topic, read Specifying an Authentication Mechanism (page 947) and Configuring IOR Security (page 959).

Building, Deploying, and Running the Secure Cart Example Using NetBeans 5.5

Follow these instructions to build, deploy, and run the `cart-secure` example in your Application Server instance using NetBeans 5.5.

1. In NetBeans 5.5, select File→Open Project.
2. In the Open Project dialog, navigate to `<INSTALL>/javaeetutorial5/examples/ejb/`.
3. Select the `cart-secure` folder.
4. Select the Open as Main Project and Open Required Projects checkboxes.
5. Click Open Project Folder.
6. In the Projects tab, right-click the `cart-secure` project and select Clean and Build Project.
7. In the Projects tab, right-click the `cart-secure` project and select Deploy Project.

   This step builds and packages the application into `cart-secure.ear`, located in `<INSTALL>/javaeetutorial5/examples/ejb/cart-secure/dist/`, and deploys this ear file to your Application Server instance.
8. To run secure cart's application client, select Run→Run Main Project. You will be prompted for your username and password.
9. Enter the username and password of a user that has been entered into the database of users for the file realm and has been assigned to the group of user.

If the username and password you enter are authorized, you will see the output of the application client in the Output pane:

```
...
Retrieving book title from cart: Infinite Jest
Retrieving book title from cart: Bel Canto
Retrieving book title from cart: Kafka on the Shore
Removing "Gravity's Rainbow" from cart.
Caught a BookException: "Gravity's Rainbow" not in cart.
Java Result: 1
run-cart-app-client:
run-nb:
```

Building, Deploying, and Running the Secure Cart Example Using Ant

To build, deploy, and run the secure EJB example using the Ant tool, follow these steps:

1. If you have not already done so, specify properties specific to your installation in the `<INSTALL>/javaeetutorial5/examples/bp-project/build.properties` file and the `<INSTALL>/javaeetutorial5/examples/common/admin-password.txt` file. See Building the Examples (page xxxv) for information on which properties need to be set in which files.
2. If you have not already done so, add a user to the `file` realm and specify `user` for the group of this new user. Refer to the section Managing Users and Groups on the Application Server (page 918) for instructions on completing this step.
3. From a terminal window or command prompt, go to the `<INSTALL>/javaeetutorial5/examples/ejb/cart-secure/` directory.
4. Build, package, and deploy the enterprise application, and build and run the client, by entering the following at the terminal window or command prompt in the `ejb/cart-secure/` directory:

   ```
   ant all
   ```

Note: This step assumes that you have the executable for `ant` in your path; if not, you will need to provide the fully qualified path to the `ant` executable. This command runs the `ant` target named `all` in the `build.xml` file.

A Login for User dialog displays. Enter a user name and password that correspond to a user set up on the Application Server with a group of `user`. Click OK.

If the user name and password are authenticated, the client displays the following output:

```
run:
  [echo] Running appclient for Cart.

appclient-command-common:
  [exec] Infinite Jest
```

```
    [exec] Bel Canto
    [exec] Kafka on the Shore
    [exec] Caught a BookException: "Gravity's Rainbow" not in
cart.
```

If the username and password are *not* authenticated, the client displays the following error:

```
run:
    [echo] Running appclient for Cart.

appclient-command-common:
    [exec] Caught an unexpected exception!
    [exec] javax.ejb.EJBException: nested exception is:
java.rmi.AccessException:
   CORBA NO_PERMISSION 9998 Maybe; nested exception is:
    [exec]     org.omg.CORBA.NO_PERMISSION:
    ----------BEGIN server-side stack trace----------
    [exec] org.omg.CORBA.NO_PERMISSION:   vmcid: 0x2000  minor
code: 1806
```

If you see this response, verify the user name and password of the user that you entered in the login dialog, make sure that user is assigned to the group *user*, and rerun the client application.

Example: Using the isCallerInRole and getCallerPrincipal Methods

This example demonstrates how to use the `getCallerPrincipal()` and `isCallerInRole(String role)` methods with an enterprise bean. This example starts with a very simple EJB application, `converter`, and modifies the methods of the `ConverterBean` so that currency conversion will only occur when the requester is in the role of `BeanUser`.

For this tutorial, we will add the security elements to an enterprise bean; add the security elements to the deployment descriptor; build, package, and deploy the application; and then build and run the client application. The completed version of this example can be found at `<INSTALL>/javaeetutorial5/examples/ejb/converter-secure/`. This example was developed by starting with the unsecured enterprise bean application, `converter`, which is discussed in Chapter 21 and is found in the directory `<INSTALL>/javaeetutorial5/examples/ejb/converter/`. This section builds on this example by adding the necessary elements to secure the application using the `getCallerPrincipal()` and `isCall-`

`erInRole(String role)` methods, which are discussed in more detail in Accessing an Enterprise Bean Caller's Security Context (page 940).

In general, the following steps are necessary when using the `getCallerPrincipal()` and `isCallerInRole(String role)` methods with an enterprise bean. In the example application included with this tutorial, many of these steps have been completed for you and are listed here simply to show what needs to be done should you wish to create a similar application.

1. Create a simple enterprise bean application, such as the `converter` example. See Chapter 21 for more information on creating and understanding this example. This section of the tutorial starts with this unsecured application and demonstrates how to access an enterprise bean caller's security context. The completed example application discussed in this section can be found at `<INSTALL>/javaeetutorial5/examples/ejb/converter-secure/`.
2. If you have not already done so, follow the steps in Building the Examples (page xxxv) to set properties specific to your installation.
3. If you have not already done so, set up a user on the Application Server in the `file` realm. Make sure that the user is included in the group named `user`. For information on adding a user to the `file` realm, read Managing Users and Groups on the Application Server (page 918).
4. Modify `ConverterBean` to add the `getCallerPrincipal()` and `isCallerInRole(String role)` methods. For this example, callers that are in the role of `BeanUser` will be able to calculate the currency conversion. Callers not in the role of `BeanUser` will see a value of zero for the conversion amount. Modifying the `ConverterBean` code is discussed in Modifying ConverterBean (page 972).
5. Modify the `sun-ejb-jar.xml` file to specify a secure connection, username-password login, and security role mapping. Modifying the `sun-ejb-jar.xml` file is discussed in Modifying Runtime Properties for the Secure Converter Example (page 973).
6. Build, package, deploy, and run the application. These steps are discussed in Building, Deploying, and Running the Secure Converter Example Using NetBeans 5.5 (page 975) and Building, Deploying, and Running the Secure Converter Example Using Ant (page 976).
7. If necessary, refer to the tips in Troubleshooting the Secure Converter Application (page 977) for tips on errors you might encounter and some possible solutions.

Modifying ConverterBean

The source code for the original `/converter` application was modified as shown in the following code snippet (modifications in **bold**) to add the `if..else` clause that tests if the caller is in the role of `BeanUser`. If the user is in the correct role, the currency conversion is computed and displayed. If the user is not in the correct role, the computation is not performed, and the application displays the result as `0`. The following code example can be found in `<INSTALL>/javaeetutorial5/examples/ejb/converter-secure/converter-secure-ejb/src/java/converter/secure/ejb/ConverterBean.java`.

```
package converter.secure.ejb;

import java.math.BigDecimal;
import javax.ejb.*;
import java.security.Principal;
import javax.annotation.Resource;
import javax.ejb.SessionContext;
import javax.annotation.security.DeclareRoles;
import javax.annotation.security.RolesAllowed;

@Stateless()
@DeclareRoles("BeanUser")

public class ConverterBean implements
converter.secure.ejb.Converter {
  @Resource SessionContext ctx;

  private BigDecimal yenRate = new BigDecimal("115.3100");
  private BigDecimal euroRate = new BigDecimal("0.0071");

  @RolesAllowed("BeanUser")
   public BigDecimal dollarToYen(BigDecimal dollars) {
    BigDecimal result = new BigDecimal("0.0");
    Principal callerPrincipal = ctx.getCallerPrincipal();

    if (ctx.isCallerInRole("BeanUser")) {
      result = dollars.multiply(yenRate);
      return result.setScale(2, BigDecimal.ROUND_UP);
    }else{
      return result.setScale(2, BigDecimal.ROUND_UP);
    }
    }

  @RolesAllowed("BeanUser")
  public BigDecimal yenToEuro(BigDecimal yen) {
```

```
        BigDecimal result = new BigDecimal("0.0");
        Principal callerPrincipal = ctx.getCallerPrincipal();

         if (ctx.isCallerInRole("BeanUser")) {
            result = yen.multiply(euroRate);
            return result.setScale(2, BigDecimal.ROUND_UP);
        }else{
           return result.setScale(2, BigDecimal.ROUND_UP);
        }
    }
}
```

Modifying Runtime Properties for the Secure Converter Example

Secure connections, username-password login, and the mapping of application roles to Application Server groups and principals are specified in the runtime deployment descriptor file `sun-ejb-jar.xml`. The original `converter` application that did not include any security mechanisms did not have a need for this file: it has been added specifically for this application.

To map the role of `BeanUser` that is defined for this application to the group with the name of `user` in the file realm of the Application Server, specify the `security-role-mapping` element as shown below. Make sure that the `role-name` and `group-name` elements are specified exactly as they are used (the mapping is case-sensitive).

To specify username-password login and a secure connection, use the `ior-security-config` element. The IOR security elements are described in more detail in Configuring IOR Security (page 959).

The following `sun-ejb-jar.xml` file demonstrates how to specify a secure connection, username-password login, and security role mapping. The completed version of this file can be found in `<INSTALL>/javaeetutorial5/examples/ejb/converter-secure/converter-secure-ejb/src/conf/sun-ejb-jar.xml`.

```
<?xml version="1.0" encoding="UTF-8"?>
<!DOCTYPE sun-ejb-jar PUBLIC "-//Sun Microsystems, Inc.//DTD
Application Server 9.0 EJB 3.0//EN" "http://www.sun.com/
software/appserver/dtds/sun-ejb-jar_3_0-0.dtd">
<sun-ejb-jar>

  <security-role-mapping>
```

```
      <role-name>BeanUser</role-name>
      <group-name>user</group-name>
   </security-role-mapping>

   <enterprise-beans>
      <unique-id>0</unique-id>
      <ejb>
         <ejb-name>ConverterBean</ejb-name>
         <jndi-name>ConverterBean</jndi-name>
         <pass-by-reference>false</pass-by-reference>
         <ior-security-config>
            <transport-config>
               <integrity>supported</integrity>
               <confidentiality>supported</confidentiality>
               <establish-trust-in-target>
                  supported
               </establish-trust-in-target>
               <establish-trust-in-client>
                  supported
               </establish-trust-in-client>
               </transport-config>
            <as-context>
               <auth-method>username_password</auth-method>
               <realm>file</realm>
               <required>true</required>
            </as-context>
            <sas-context>
               <caller-propagation>
                  supported
               </caller-propagation>
            </sas-context>
            </ior-security-config>
            <is-read-only-bean>false</is-read-only-bean>
            <refresh-period-in-seconds>
               -1
            </refresh-period-in-seconds>
            <gen-classes/>
         </ejb>
   </enterprise-beans>
</sun-ejb-jar
```

Building, Deploying, and Running the Secure Converter Example Using NetBeans 5.5

Follow these instructions to build, package, and deploy the `converter-secure` example to your Application Server instance using NetBeans 5.5.

1. In NetBeans 5.5, select File→Open Project.
2. In the Open Project dialog, navigate to `<INSTALL>/javaeetutorial5/examples/ejb/`.
3. Select the `converter-secure` folder.
4. Select the Open as Main Project and Open Required Projects checkboxes.
5. Click Open Project Folder.
6. In the Projects tab, right-click the `converter-secure` project and select Clean and Build Project.
7. In the Projects tab, right-click the `converter-secure` project and select Deploy Project.

   This step builds and packages the application into `converter-secure.ear`, located in `<INSTALL>/javaeetutorial5/examples/ejb/converter-secure/dist/`, and deploys this ear file to your Application Server instance.
8. To run the secure converter's application client, select Run→Run Main Project. You will be prompted for your username and password.
9. Enter the username and password of a user that has been entered into the database of users for the file realm and has been assigned to the group of user.

   If the username and password you enter are authorized, you will see the output of the application client in the Output pane:

   ```
   [exec] $100.00 is 11531.00 Yen.
   [exec] 11531.00 Yen is 81.88 Euro.
   ```

Building, Deploying, and Running the Secure Converter Example Using Ant

To build the secure converter enterprise beans and client, package and deploy the enterprise application, and run the client application, follow these steps:

1. Set up your system for running the tutorial examples if you haven't done so already by following the instructions in Building the Examples (page xxxv).
2. From a terminal window or command prompt, go to the `<INSTALL>/javaeetutorial5/examples/ejb/converter-secure/` directory.
3. Build, package, deploy, and run the enterprise application and application client by entering the following at the terminal window or command prompt in the `ejb/converter-secure/` directory:

   ```
   ant all
   ```

Note: This step assumes that you have the executable for `ant` in your path; if not, you will need to provide the fully qualified path to the `ant` executable. This command runs the `ant` target named `all` in the `build.xml` file.

The running application will look like this:

```
appclient-command-common:
```

At this point, a system login dialog will display. Enter the user name and password that correspond to a user in the group *user* on the Application Server. If the user name and password are authenticated, the following text displays in the terminal window or command prompt:

```
appclient-command-common:
  [exec] $100.00 is 11531.00 Yen.
  [exec] 11531.00 Yen is 81.88 Euro.
```

Troubleshooting the Secure Converter Application

Problem: The application displays zero values after authentication, as shown here:

```
appclient-command-common:
  [exec] $100.00 is 0.00 Yen.
  [exec] 0.00 Yen is 0.00 Euro.
```

Solution: Verify that the user name and password that you entered for authentication match a user name and password in the Application Server, and that this user is assigned to the group named *user*. User names and passwords are case-sensitive. Read Adding Users to the Application Server (page 918) for more information on adding users to the `file` realm of the Application Server.

Discussion: Securing the Duke's Bank Example

The Duke's Bank application is an online banking application. Duke's Bank has two clients: an application client used by administrators to manage customers and accounts, and a web client used by customers to access account histories and perform transactions. The clients access the customer, account, and transaction information maintained in a database through enterprise beans. The Duke's Bank application demonstrates the way that many of the component technologies presented in this tutorial—enterprise beans, application clients, and web components—are applied to provide a simple but functional application.

To secure the Duke's Bank example, the following security mechanisms are used:

- Defining security roles
- Specifying form-based user authentication for the web client in a security constraint
- Adding authorized users and groups to the appropriate Application Server realm
- Specifying method permissions for enterprise beans
- Configuring Interoperable Object References (IOR)

Read Chapter 37 for more information on securing the Duke's Bank example.

Securing Application Clients

The Java EE authentication requirements for application clients are the same as for other Java EE components, and the same authentication techniques can be used as for other Java EE application components.

No authentication is necessary when accessing unprotected web resources. When accessing protected web resources, the usual varieties of authentication can be used, namely HTTP basic authentication, SSL client authentication, or HTTP login form authentication. These authentication methods are discussed in Specifying an Authentication Mechanism (page 1010).

Authentication is required when accessing protected enterprise beans. The authentication mechanisms for enterprise beans are discussed in Securing Enterprise Beans (page 938). Lazy authentication can be used.

An application client makes use of an authentication service provided by the application client container for authenticating its users. The container's service can be integrated with the native platform's authentication system, so that a single sign-on capability is employed. The container can authenticate the user when the application is started, or it can use lazy authentication, authenticating the user when a protected resource is accessed.

An application client can provide a class to gather authentication data. If so, the `javax.security.auth.callback.CallbackHandler` interface must be implemented, and the class name must be specified in its deployment descriptor. The application's callback handler must fully support `Callback` objects specified in the `javax.security.auth.callback` package. Gathering authentication data in this way is discussed in the next section, Using Login Modules.

Using Login Modules

An application client can use the Java Authentication and Authorization Service (JAAS) to create *login modules* for authentication. A JAAS-based application implements the `javax.security.auth.callback.CallbackHandler` interface so that it can interact with users to enter specific authentication data, such as user names or passwords, or to display error and warning messages.

Applications implement the `CallbackHandler` interface and pass it to the login context, which forwards it directly to the underlying login modules. A login module uses the callback handler both to gather input (such as a password or smart card PIN) from users and to supply information (such as status information) to users. Because the application specifies the callback handler, an underlying login module can remain independent of the various ways that applications interact with users.

For example, the implementation of a callback handler for a GUI application might display a window to solicit user input. Or the implementation of a callback handler for a command-line tool might simply prompt the user for input directly from the command line.

The login module passes an array of appropriate callbacks to the callback handler's `handle` method (for example, a `NameCallback` for the user name and a `PasswordCallback` for the password); the callback handler performs the requested user interaction and sets appropriate values in the callbacks. For example, to process a `NameCallback`, the `CallbackHandler` might prompt for a name, retrieve the value from the user, and call the `setName` method of the `NameCallback` to store the name.

For more information on using JAAS for login modules for authentication, refer to the following sources:

- *Java Authentication and Authorization Service (JAAS) in Java 2, Standard Edition (J2SE) 1.4*
- *Java Authentication and Authorization Service (JAAS) Reference Guide*
- *Java Authentication and Authorization Service (JAAS): LoginModule Developer's Guide*

Links to this information are provided in Further Information (page 984).

Using Programmatic Login

Programmatic login enables the client code to supply user credentials. If you are using an EJB client, you can use the `com.sun.appserv.security.ProgrammaticLogin` class with their convenient `login` and `logout` methods.

Because programmatic login is specific to a server, information on programmatic login is not included in this document, but is included in the *Sun Java System Application Server Developer's Guide*, a link to which is provided in Further Information (page 984).

Securing EIS Applications

In EIS applications, components request a connection to an EIS resource. As part of this connection, the EIS can require a sign-on for the requester to access the resource. The application component provider has two choices for the design of the EIS sign-on:

- In the container-managed sign-on approach, the application component lets the container take the responsibility of configuring and managing the EIS sign-on. The container determines the user name and password for establishing a connection to an EIS instance. For more information, read Container-Managed Sign-On (page 980).
- In the component-managed sign-on approach, the application component code manages EIS sign-on by including code that performs the sign-on process to an EIS. For more information, read Component-Managed Sign-On (page 981).

You can also configure security for resource adapters. Read Configuring Resource Adapter Security (page 981) for more information.

Container-Managed Sign-On

In container-managed sign-on, an application component does not have to pass any sign-on security information to the `getConnection()` method. The security information is supplied by the container, as shown in the following example.

```
// Business method in an application component
Context initctx = new InitialContext();

// Perform JNDI lookup to obtain a connection factory
javax.resource.cci.ConnectionFactory cxf =
  (javax.resource.cci.ConnectionFactory)initctx.lookup(
  "java:comp/env/eis/MainframeCxFactory");

// Invoke factory to obtain a connection. The security
// information is not passed in the getConnection method
javax.resource.cci.Connection cx = cxf.getConnection();
...
```

Component-Managed Sign-On

In component-managed sign-on, an application component is responsible for passing the needed sign-on security information to the resource to the `getConnection` method. For example, security information might be a user name and password, as shown here:

```
// Method in an application component
Context initctx = new InitialContext();

// Perform JNDI lookup to obtain a connection factory
javax.resource.cci.ConnectionFactory cxf =
  (javax.resource.cci.ConnectionFactory)initctx.lookup(
  "java:comp/env/eis/MainframeCxFactory");

// Get a new ConnectionSpec
com.myeis.ConnectionSpecImpl properties = //..

// Invoke factory to obtain a connection
properties.setUserName("...");
properties.setPassword("...");
javax.resource.cci.Connection cx =
  cxf.getConnection(properties);
...
```

Configuring Resource Adapter Security

A resource adapter is a system-level software component that typically implements network connectivity to an external resource manager. A resource adapter can extend the functionality of the Java EE platform either by implementing one of the Java EE standard service APIs (such as a JDBC driver), or by defining and implementing a resource adapter for a connector to an external application system. Resource adapters can also provide services that are entirely local, perhaps interacting with native resources. Resource adapters interface with the Java EE platform through the Java EE service provider interfaces (Java EE SPI). A resource adapter that uses the Java EE SPIs to attach to the Java EE platform will be able to work with all Java EE products.

To configure the security settings for a resource adapter, you need to edit the `ra.xml` file. If you have installed the samples server, an example of an `ra.xml` file that configures resource adapter security can be found in the sample application file `<JAVAEE_HOME>/samples/connectors/apps/mailconnector/mail-`

`connector-ra/src/conf/ra.xml`. Here is an example of the part of the `ra.xml` file that configures the following security properties for a resource adapter:

```
<authentication-mechanism>
  <authentication-mechanism-type>BasicPassword</
authentication-mechanism-type>
  <credential-interface>
    javax.resource.spi.security.PasswordCredential
  </credential-interface>
</authentication-mechanism>
<reauthentication-support>false</reauthentication-support>
```

You can find out more about the options for configuring resource adapter security by reviewing `<`*`JAVAEE_HOME`*`>/lib/dtds/connector_1_0.dtd`. You can configure the following elements in the resource adapter deployment descriptor file:

- Authentication mechanisms

  Use the `authentication-mechanism` element to specify an authentication mechanism supported by the resource adapter. This support is for the resource adapter and not for the underlying EIS instance.

  There are two supported mechanism types:

  - `BasicPassword:` This mechanism supports the interface `javax.resource.spi.security.PasswordCredential`.
  - `Kerbv5`: This mechanism supports the interface `javax.resource.spi.security.GenericCredential`. The Sun Java System Application Server does not currently support this mechanism type.

- Reauthentication support

  Use the `reauthentication-support` element to specify whether the resource adapter implementation supports re-authentication of existing `Managed- Connection` instanced. Options are `true` or `false`.

- Security permissions

  Use the `security-permission` element to specify a security permission that is required by the resource adapter code. Support for security permissions is optional and is not supported in the current release of the Application Server. You can, however, manually update the `server.policy` file to add the relevant permissions for the resource adapter, as described in the *Developing and Deploying Applications* section of the Application

Server's *Developer's Guide* (see a link to this document in Further Information, page 984).

The security permissions listed in the deployment descriptor are ones that are different from those required by the default permission set as specified in the connector specification.

Refer to the following URL for more information on Sun's implementation of the security permission specification:

```
http://java.sun.com/products/j2se/1.5.0/docs/guide/secu-
rity/PolicyFiles.html#FileSyntax
```

In addition to specifying resource adapter security in the `ra.xml` file, you can create a security map for a connector connection pool to map an application principal or a user group to a back end EIS principal. The security map is usually used in situations where one or more EIS back end principals are used to execute operations (on the EIS) initiated by various principals or user groups in the application. You can find out more about security maps in the *Configuring Security* chapter section of the Application Server's *Administration Guide*. A link to this guide can be found in Further Information (page 984).

Mapping an Application Principal to EIS Principals

When using the Application Server, you can use security maps to map the caller identity of the application (principal or user group) to a suitable EIS principal in container-managed transaction-based scenarios. When an application principal initiates a request to an EIS, the Application Server first checks for an exact principal using the security map defined for the connector connection pool to determine the mapped back end EIS principal. If there is no exact match, then the Application Server uses the wild card character specification, if any, to determine the mapped back-end EIS principal. Security maps are used when an application user needs to execute EIS operations that require to be executed as a specific identity in the EIS.

To work with security maps, use the Admin Console. From the Admin Console, follow these steps to get to the security maps page:

1. Expand the Resources node.
2. Expand the Connectors node.
3. Select the Connector Connection Pools node.

4. Select a Connector Connection Pool by selecting its name from the list of current pools, or create a new connector connection pool by selecting New from the list of current pools
5. Select the Security Maps page.

Example Applications in the Application Server

If you have installed the Application Server's `samples` server, you will have even more example applications to help you in the development of your Java EE applications. The following is a list of a few of the example applications that add security to an application in a way that is not yet covered in this tutorial:

- `<JAVAEE_HOME>/samples/security/ldaprealm/apps/dynamicgroup/docs/index.html`

  The LDAP Dynamic Group Realm sample application consists of an enterprise bean and an application client. The methods of the enterprise bean have been associated with either the `Administrator` role or the `Secret` role in the enterprise bean deployment descriptor. The idea is to associate the `Administrator` role with a dynamic LDAP group, called `ldapdynamicgroup`. Then the application client verifies that user names belonging to `ldapdynamicgroup` have access to methods of the EJB that have been associated with the `Administrator` role, while access to methods not associated with that role will be denied.
- `<JAVAEE_HOME>/samples/security/realms/apps/rdbms/docs/index.html`

  This sample application demonstrates using a custom security realm. You can use any JDBC-compliant relational database server.

Further Information

- *JSR-220: Enterprise JavaBeans 3.0*:

  `http://jcp.org/en/jsr/detail?id=220`
- Chapter 24 of the CORBA/IIOP specification, *Secure Interoperability*:

  `http://www.omg.org/cgi-bin/doc?formal/02-06-60`

- *Java Authentication and Authorization Service (JAAS) in Java 2, Standard Edition (J2SE) 1.4*

  `http://java.sun.com/developer/technicalArticles/Security/jaasv2/index.html`
- *Java Authentication and Authorization Service (JAAS) Reference Guide*

  `http://java.sun.com/j2se/1.5.0/docs/guide/security/jaas/JAASRefGuide.html`
- *Java Authentication and Authorization Service (JAAS): LoginModule Developer's Guide*

  `http://java.sun.com/j2se/1.5.0/docs/guide/security/jaas/JAASLMDevGuide.html`
- *Java EE 5 Specification* at

  `http://jcp.org/en/jsr/detail?id=244`
- Java 2 Standard Edition, v.1.5.0 security information:

  `http://java.sun.com/j2se/1.5.0/docs/guide/security/index.html`
- *JSR 250: Common Annotations for the Java Platform*:

  `http://jcp.org/en/jsr/detail?id=250`
- The API specification for Java Authorization Contract for Containers:

  `http://jcp.org/en/jsr/detail?id=115`
- The *Developer's Guide* for the Application Server includes security information for application developers:

  `http://docs.sun.com/doc/819-3659`
- The *Administration Guide* for the Application Server includes information on setting security settings for the Application Server:

  `http://docs.sun.com/doc/819-3658`
- The *Application Deployment Guide* for the Application Server:

  `http://docs.sun.com/doc/819-3660`

30

Securing Web Applications

WEB applications contain resources that can be accessed by many users. These resources often traverse unprotected, open networks, such as the Internet. In such an environment, a substantial number of web applications will require some type of security.

The ways to implement security for Java EE applications are discussed in a general way in Securing Containers (page 910). This chapter provides more detail and a few examples that explore these security services as they relate to web components. Java EE security services can be implemented for web applications in the following ways:

- *Metadata annotations* (or simply, *annotations*) are used to specify information about security within a class file. When the application is deployed, this information can either be used by or overridden by the application deployment descriptor.
- *Declarative security* expresses an application's security structure, including security roles, access control, and authentication requirements in a deployment descriptor, which is external to the application.

  Any values explicitly specified in the deployment descriptor override any values specified in annotations.

- *Programmatic security* is embedded in an application and is used to make security decisions. Programmatic security is useful when declarative security alone is not sufficient to express the security model of an application.

Some of the material in this chapter assumes that you have already read Chapter 28. This chapter also assumes that you are familiar with the web technologies discussed in Chapters 2, 4, and 9.

Overview

In the Java EE platform, *web components* provide the dynamic extension capabilities for a web server. Web components are either Java servlets, JSP pages, JSF pages, or web service endpoints. The interaction between a web client and a web application is illustrated in Figure 30–1.

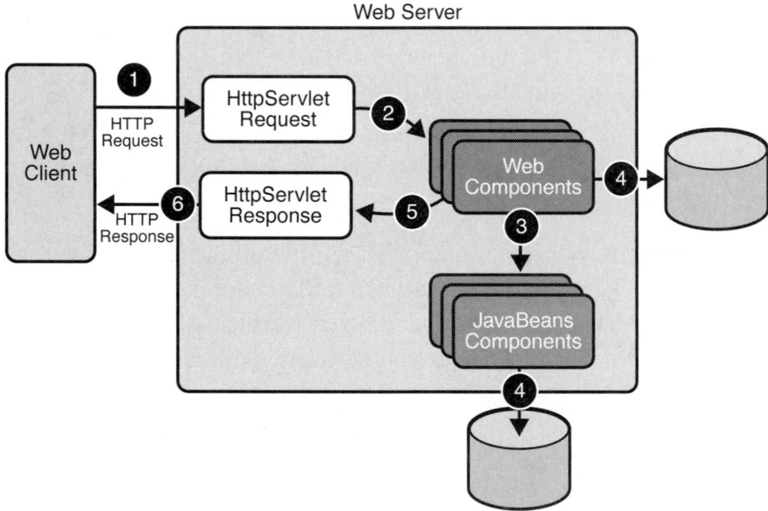

Figure 30–1 Java Web Application Request Handling

Web components are supported by the services of a runtime platform called a *web container*. A web container provides services such as request dispatching, security, concurrency, and life-cycle management.

Certain aspects of web application security can be configured when the application is installed, or *deployed*, to the web container. Annotations and/or deployment descriptors are used to relay information to the deployer about security and other aspects of the application. Specifying this information in annotations or in the deployment descriptor helps the deployer set up the appropriate security policy for the web application. Any values explicitly specified in the deployment descriptor override any values specified in annotations. This chapter provides more information on configuring security for web applications.

For secure transport, most web applications use the HTTPS protocol. For more information on using the HTTPS protocol, read Establishing a Secure Connection Using SSL (page 922).

Working with Security Roles

If you read Working with Realms, Users, Groups, and Roles (page 914), you will remember the following definitions:

- In applications, roles are defined using annotations or in application deployment descriptors such as `web.xml`, `ejb-jar.xml`, and `application.xml`.
  - A *role* is an abstract name for the permission to access a particular set of resources in an application. For more information, read What Is a Role? (page 917).

  For more information on defining roles, see Declaring Security Roles (page 990).

- On the Application Server, the following options are configured using the Admin Console:
  - A *realm* is a complete database of *users* and *groups* that identify valid users of a web application (or a set of web applications) and are controlled by the same authentication policy. For more information, read What Is a Realm? (page 916).
  - A *user* is an individual (or application program) identity that has been defined in the Application Server. On the Application Server, a user generally has a user name, a password, and, optionally, a list of *groups* to which this user has been assigned. For more information, read What Is a User? (page 916).
  - A *group* is a set of authenticated *users*, classified by common traits, defined in the Application Server. For more information, read What Is a Group? (page 917).
  - A *principal* is an entity that can be authenticated by an authentication protocol in a security service that is deployed in an enterprise.

For more information on configuring users on the Application Server, read Managing Users and Groups on the Application Server (page 918).

- During deployment, the deployer takes the information provided in the application deployment descriptor and maps the roles specified for the application to users and groups defined on the server using the Application Server deployment descriptors `sun-web.xml`, `sun-ejb-jar.xml`, or `sun-application.xml`.

  For more information, read Mapping Security Roles to Application Server Groups (page 993).

The example code used in the following sections is taken from the sample application (available only if the samples server is installed) `<AS_INSTALL>/samples/webapps/apps/simple/web`.

Declaring Security Roles

You can declare security role names used in web applications using either the `@DeclareRoles` annotation (preferred) or the `security-role-ref` elements of the deployment descriptor. Declaring security role names in this way enables you to link the security role names used in the code to the security roles defined for an assembled application. In the absence of this linking step, any security role name used in the code will be assumed to correspond to a security role of the same name in the assembled application.

A security role reference, including the name defined by the reference, is scoped to the component whose class contains the `@DeclareRoles` annotation or whose deployment descriptor element contains the `security-role-ref` deployment descriptor element.

You can also use the `security-role-ref` elements for those references that were declared in annotations and you want to have linked to a `security-role` whose name differs from the reference value. If a security role reference is not linked to a security role in this way, the container must map the reference name to the security role of the same name. See Declaring and Linking Role References (page 996) for a description of how security role references are linked to security roles.

For an example using each of these methods, read the following sections:

- Specifying Security Roles Using Annotations (page 991)
- Specifying Security Roles Using Deployment Descriptor Elements (page 992)

Specifying Security Roles Using Annotations

Annotations are the best way to define security roles on a class or a method. The @DeclareRoles annotation is used to define the security roles that comprise the security model of the application. This annotation is specified on a class, and it typically would be used to define roles that could be tested (for example, by calling isUserInRole) from within the methods of the annotated class.

Following is an example of how this annotation would be used. In this example, employee is the only security role specified, but the value of this parameter can include a list of security roles specified by the application.

```
@DeclareRoles("employee")
public class CalculatorServlet {
  //...
}
```

Specifying @DeclareRoles("employee") is equivalent to defining the following in the web.xml:

```
<security-role>
  <role-name>employee</role-name>
</security-role>
```

This annotation is not used to link application roles to other roles. When such linking is necessary, it is accomplished by defining an appropriate security-role-ref in the associated deployment descriptor, as described in Declaring and Linking Role References (page 996).

When a call is made to isUserInRole from the annotated class, the caller identity associated with the invocation of the class is tested for membership in the role with the same name as the argument to isUserInRole. If a security-role-ref has been defined for the argument role-name, the caller is tested for membership in the role mapped to the role-name.

Specifying Security Roles Using Deployment Descriptor Elements

The following snippet of a deployment descriptor is taken from the `simple` sample application. This snippet includes all of the elements needed to specify security roles using deployment descriptors:

```
<servlet>
    ...
    <security-role-ref>
      <role-name>MGR</role-name>
      <!-- role name used in code -->
      <role-link>employee</role-link>
    </security-role-ref>
</servlet>

<security-constraint>
    <web-resource-collection>
      <web-resource-name>Protected Area</web-resource-name>
      <url-pattern>/jsp/security/protected/*</url-pattern>
      <http-method>PUT</http-method>
      <http-method>DELETE</http-method>
      <http-method>GET</http-method>
      <http-method>POST</http-method>
    </web-resource-collection>
    <auth-constraint>
      <role-name>role1</role-name>
      <role-name>employee</role-name>
    </auth-constraint>
</security-constraint>

<!-- Security roles referenced by this web application -->
<security-role>
    <role-name>role1</role-name>
</security-role>
<security-role>
    <role-name>employee</role-name>
</security-role>
```

In this example, the `security-role` element lists all of the security roles used in the application: `role1` and `employee`. This enables the deployer to map all of the roles defined in the application to users and groups defined on the Application Server.

The `auth-constraint` element specifies the roles (`role1`, `employee`) that can access HTTP methods (`PUT`, `DELETE`, `GET`, `POST`) located in the directory specified by the url-pattern element (/jsp/security/protected/*). You could also have used the @DeclareRoles annotation in the source code to accomplish this task.

The security-role-ref element is used when an application uses the HttpServletRequest.isUserInRole(String role) method. The value of the role-name element must be the String used as the parameter to the HttpServletRequest.isUserInRole(String role) method. The role-link must contain the name of one of the security roles defined in the security-role elements. The container uses the mapping of security-role-ref to security-role when determining the return value of the call.

Mapping Security Roles to Application Server Groups

To map security roles to application server principals and groups, use the security-role-mapping element in the runtime deployment descriptor (DD). The runtime deployment descriptor is an XML file that contains information such as the context root of the web application and the mapping of the portable names of an application's resources to the Application Server's resources. The Application Server web application runtime DD is located in /WEB-INF/ along with the web application DD. Runtime deployment descriptors are named sun-web.xml, sun-application.xml, or sun-ejb-jar.xml.

The following example demonstrates how to do this mapping:

```
<sun-web-app>

  <security-role-mapping>
    <role-name>CEO</role-name>
    <principal-name>smcneely</principal-name>
  </security-role-mapping>

  <security-role-mapping>
    <role-name>Admin</role-name>
    <group-name>director</group-name>
  </security-role-mapping>

  ...

</sun-web-app>
```

A role can be mapped to specific principals, specific groups, or both. The principal or group names must be valid principals or groups in the current default realm. The `role-name` element must match the `role-name` in the `security-role` element of the corresponding application deployment descriptor (`web.xml`, `ejb-jar.xml`) or the role name defined in the `@DeclareRoles`.

Sometimes the role names used in the application are the same as the group names defined on the Application Server. Under these circumstances, you can use the Admin Console to define a default principal to role mapping that apply to the entire Application Server instance. From the Admin Console, select Configuration, then Security, then check the enable box beside Default Principal to Role Mapping. For more information, read the Application Server's *Developer's Guide* or *Administration Guid*e (links to which are included in Further Information, page 1049).

Checking Caller Identity Programmatically

In general, security management should be enforced by the container in a manner that is transparent to the web component. The security API described in this section should be used only in the less frequent situations in which the web component methods need to access the security context information.

The `HttpServletRequest` interface provides the following methods that enable you to access security information about the component's caller:

- `getRemoteUser`: Determines the user name with which the client authenticated. If no user has been authenticated, this method returns `null`.
- `isUserInRole`: Determines whether a remote user is in a specific security role. If no user has been authenticated, this method returns `false`. This method expects a `String` user `role-name` parameter.

  You can use either the `@DeclareRoles` annotation or the `<security-role-ref>` element with a `<role-name>` sub-element in the deployment descriptor to pass the role name to this method. Using security role references is discussed in Declaring and Linking Role References (page 996).

- `getUserPrincipal`: Determines the principal name of the current user and returns a `java.security.Principal` object. If no user has been authenticated, this method returns `null`.

Your application can make business logic decisions based on the information obtained using these APIs.

The following is a code snippet from the file *<AS_INSTALL>*`/samples/webapps/apps/simple/web/jsp/security/protected/index.jsp` that uses these methods to access security information about the component's caller. You must have the samples server installed to view this file.

```
<%@ taglib prefix="fmt" uri="http://java.sun.com/jstl/fmt" %>
<fmt:setBundle basename="LocalStrings"/>

<html>
<head>
<title><fmt:message key="index.jsp.title"/>/title>
</head>
<body bgcolor="white">

<fmt:message key="index.jsp.remoteuser"/> <b><%=
request.getRemoteUser() %>
</b><br><br>

<%
  if (request.getUserPrincipal() != null) {
%>
  <fmt:message key="index.jsp.principal"/> <b>
<%= request.getUserPrincipal().getName() %></b><br><br>
<%
  } else {
%>
  <fmt:message key="index.jsp.noprincipal"/>
<%
  }
%>

<%
  String role = request.getParameter("role");
  if (role == null)
    role = "";
  if (role.length() > 0) {
    if (request.isUserInRole(role)) {
%>
       <fmt:message key="index.jsp.granted"/> <b><%= role %></
b><br><br>
<%
    } else {
%>
       <fmt:message key="index.jsp.notgranted"/> <b><%= role
```

```
%></b><br><br>
<%
      }
   }
%>

<fmt:message key="index.jsp.tocheck"/>
<form method="GET">
<input type="text" name="role" value="<%= role %>">
</form>

</body>
</html>
```

Declaring and Linking Role References

A security role is an application-specific logical grouping of users, classified by common traits such as customer profile or job title. When an application is deployed, these roles are mapped to security identities, such as *principals* (identities assigned to users as a result of authentication) or groups, in the runtime environment. Based on this mapping, a user with a certain security role has associated access rights to a web application.

The value passed to the `isUserInRole` method is a `String` representing the role name of the user. A *security role reference* defines a mapping between the name of a role that is called from a web component using `isUserInRole(String role)` and the name of a security role that has been defined for the application. If a `<security-role-ref>` element is not declared in a deployment descriptor, and the `isUserInRole` method is called, the container defaults to checking the provided role name against the list of all security roles defined for the web application. Using the default method instead of using the `<security-role-ref>` element limits your flexibility to change role names in an application without also recompiling the servlet making the call.

For example, during application assembly, the assembler creates security roles for the application and associates these roles with available security mechanisms. The assembler then resolves the security role references in individual servlets and JSP pages by linking them to roles defined for the application. For example, the assembler could map the security role reference `cust` to the security role with the role name `bankCustomer` using the `<security-role-ref>` element of the deployment descriptor.

Declaring Roles Using Annotations

The preferred method of declaring roles referenced in an application is to use the `@DeclareRoles` annotation. The following code sample provides an example that specifies that the roles of `j2ee` and `guest` will be used in the application, and verifies that the user is in the role of `j2ee` before printing out `Hello World`.

```
import java.io.IOException;
import java.io.PrintWriter;

import javax.annotation.security.DeclareRoles;
import javax.servlet.ServletException;
import javax.servlet.http.HttpServlet;
import javax.servlet.http.HttpServletRequest;
import javax.servlet.http.HttpServletResponse;

@DeclareRoles({"j2ee", "guest"})
public class Servlet extends HttpServlet {

  public void service(HttpServletRequest req,
HttpServletResponse resp)
        throws ServletException, IOException {
      resp.setContentType("text/html");
      PrintWriter out = resp.getWriter();

      out.println("<HTML><HEAD><TITLE>Servlet Output</TITLE>
        </HEAD><BODY>");
       if (req.isUserInRole("j2ee") && !req.isUserIn-
Role("guest")) {
        out.println("Hello World");
      } else {
        out.println("Invalid roles");
      }
      out.println("</BODY></HTML>");
  }
}
```

Declaring Roles Using Deployment Descriptor Elements

An example of declaring roles referenced in an application using deployment descriptor elements is shown in the following web.xml deployment descriptor snippet:

```
<servlet>
...
  <security-role-ref>
    <role-name>cust</role-name>
    <role-link>bankCustomer</role-link>
  </security-role-ref>
...
</servlet>
```

When you use the isUserInRole(String role) method, the String role is mapped to the role name defined in the <role-name> element nested within the <security-role-ref> element. The <role-link> element in the web.xml deployment descriptor must match a <role-name> defined in the <security-role> element of the web.xml deployment descriptor, as shown here:

```
<security-role>
  <role-name>bankCustomer</role-name>
</security-role>
```

Defining Security Requirements for Web Applications

Web applications are created by application developers who give, sell, or otherwise transfer the application to an application deployer for installation into a runtime environment. Application developers communicate how the security is to be set up for the deployed application *declaratively* by use of the *deployment descriptor* mechanism or *programmatically* by use of *annotations*. When this information is passed on to the deployer, the deployer uses this information to define method permissions for security roles, set up user authentication, and whether or not to use HTTPS for transport. If you don't define security requirements, the deployer will have to determine the security requirements independently.

If you specify a value in an annotation, and then explicitly specify the same value in the deployment descriptor, the value in the deployment descriptor overrides any values specified in annotations. If a value for a method has not been specified in the deployment descriptor, and a value has been specified for that method by means of the use of annotations, the value specified in annotations will apply. The granularity of overriding is on the per-method basis.

The web application deployment descriptor may contain an attribute of `full` on the `web-app` element. The `full` attribute defines whether the web application deployment descriptor is complete, or whether the class files of the JAR file should be examined for annotations that specify deployment information. When the `full` attribute is not specified, or is set to `false`, the deployment descriptors examine the class files of applications for annotations that specify deployment information. When the `full` attribute is set to `true`, the deployment descriptor ignores any servlet annotations present in the class files of the application. Thus, deployers can use deployment descriptors to customize or override the values specified in annotations.

Many elements for security in a web application deployment descriptor cannot, as yet, be specified as annotations, therefore, for securing web applications, deployment descriptors are a necessity. However, where possible, annotations are the recommended method for securing web components.

Before getting into specifics of securing web applications, annotations and deployment descriptor elements are discussed in the following sections:

- Declaring Security Requirements Using Annotations (below)
- Declaring Security Requirements in a Deployment Descriptor (page 1002)

Declaring Security Requirements Using Annotations

The *Java Metadata Specification* (JSR-175), which is part of J2SE 5.0 and greater, provides a means of specifying configuration data in Java code. Metadata in Java code is more commonly referred to in this document as *annotations*. In Java EE, annotations are used to declare dependencies on external resources and configuration data in Java code without the need to define that data in a configuration file. Several common annotations are specific to specifying security in any Java application. These common annotations are specified in JSR-175, *A Metadata Facility for the Java Programming Language*, and JSR-250, *Common*

Annotations for the Java Platform. Annotations specific to web components are specified in the *Java Servlet 2.5 Specification*.

In servlets, you can use the annotations discussed in the following sections to secure a web application:

- Using the @DeclareRoles Annotation (below)
- Using the @RunAs Annotation (page 1001)

Using the @DeclareRoles Annotation

This annotation is used to define the security roles that comprise the security model of the application. This annotation is specified on a class, and it typically would be used to define roles that could be tested (for example, by calling `isUserInRole`) from within the methods of the annotated class.

Following is an example of how this annotation would be used. In this example, `BusinessAdmin` is the only security role specified, but the value of this parameter can include a list of security roles specified by the application.

```
@DeclareRoles("BusinessAdmin")
public class CalculatorServlet {
  //...
}
```

Specifying `@DeclareRoles("BusinessAdmin")` is equivalent to defining the following in `web.xml`:

```
<web-app>
  <security-role>
    <role-name>BusinessAdmin</role-name>
  </security-role>
</web-app>
```

The syntax for declaring more than one role is as shown in the following example:

```
@DeclareRoles({"Administrator", "Manager", "Employee"})
```

This annotation is not used to link application roles to other roles. When such linking is necessary, it is accomplished by defining an appropriate `security-role-ref` in the associated deployment descriptor, as described in Declaring and Linking Role References (page 996).

When a call is made to `isUserInRole` from the annotated class, the caller identity associated with the invocation of the class is tested for membership in the role with the same name as the argument to `isUserInRole`. If a `security-role-ref` has been defined for the argument `role-name`, the caller is tested for membership in the role mapped to the `role-name`.

For further details on the `@DeclareRoles` annotation, refer to the *Common Annotations for the Java Platform Specification* (JSR-250) and Using Enterprise Bean Security Annotations (page 957) in this tutorial.

Using the @RunAs Annotation

The `@RunAs` annotation defines the role of the application during execution in a Java EE container. It can be specified on a class, allowing developers to execute an application under a particular role. The role must map to the user/group information in the container's security realm. The `value` element in the annotation is the name of a security role of the application during execution in a Java EE container. The use of the `@RunAs` annotation is discussed in more detail in Propagating Security Identity (page 954).

The following is an example that uses the `@RunAs` annotation:

```
@RunAs("Admin")
public class CalculatorServlet {
@EJB private ShoppingCart myCart;
  public void doGet(HttpServletRequest, req,
HttpServletResponse res) {
      //....
      myCart.getTotal();
      //....
  }
}
//....
}
```

The `@RunAs` annotation is equivalent to the `run-as` element in the deployment descriptor.

Declaring Security Requirements in a Deployment Descriptor

Web applications are created by application developers who give, sell, or otherwise transfer the application to an application deployer for installation into a runtime environment. Application developers communicate how the security is to be set up for the deployed application *declaratively* by use of the *deployment descriptor* mechanism. A deployment descriptor enables an application's security structure, including roles, access control, and authentication requirements, to be expressed in a form external to the application.

A web application is defined using a standard Java EE `web.xml` deployment descriptor. A deployment descriptor is an XML schema document that conveys elements and configuration information for web applications. The deployment descriptor must indicate which version of the web application schema (2.4 or 2.5) it is using, and the elements specified within the deployment descriptor must comply with the rules for processing that version of the deployment descriptor. Version 2.5 of the Java Servlet Specification, which can be downloaded at `http://jcp.org/en/jsr/detail?id=154`, *SRV.13, Deployment Descriptor*, contains more information regarding the structure of deployment descriptors.

The following code is an example of the elements in a deployment descriptor that apply specifically to declaring security for web applications or for resources within web applications. This example comes from section SRV.13.5.2, *An Example of Security*, from the Java Servlet Specification 2.5.

```
<?xml version="1.0" encoding="ISO-8859-1"?>
<web-app xmlns="http://java.sun.com/xml/ns/j2ee"
      xmlns:xsi="http://www.w3.org/2001/XMLSchema-instance"
      xsi:schemaLocation="http://java.sun.com/xml/ns/j2ee
      http://java.sun.com/xml/ns/j2ee/web-app_2_5.xsd"
      version="2.5">
   <display-name>A Secure Application</display-name>

   <!-- SERVLET -->
   <servlet>
      <servlet-name>catalog</servlet-name>
      <servlet-class>com.mycorp.CatalogServlet</servlet-class>
      <init-param>
         <param-name>catalog</param-name>
         <param-value>Spring</param-value>
      </init-param>
      <security-role-ref>
         <role-name>MGR</role-name>
```

```
        <!-- role name used in code -->
        <role-link>manager</role-link>
      </security-role-ref>
    </servlet>

    <!-- SECURITY ROLE -->
    <security-role>
      <role-name>manager</role-name>
    </security-role>

    <servlet-mapping>
      <servlet-name>catalog</servlet-name>
      <url-pattern>/catalog/*</url-pattern>
    </servlet-mapping>

    <!-- SECURITY CONSTRAINT -->
    <security-constraint>
      <web-resource-collection>
        <web-resource-name>CartInfo</web-resource-name>
        <url-pattern>/catalog/cart/*</url-pattern>
        <http-method>GET</http-method>
        <http-method>POST</http-method>
      </web-resource-collection>
      <auth-constraint>
        <role-name>manager</role-name>
      </auth-constraint>
      <user-data-constraint>
        <transport-guarantee>CONFIDENTIAL</transport-
guarantee>
      </user-data-constraint>
    </security-constraint>

    <!-- LOGIN CONFIGURATION-->
    <login-config>
      <auth-method>BASIC</auth-method>
    </login-config>
  </web-app>
```

As shown in the preceding example, the <web-app> element is the root element for web applications. The <web-app> element contains the following elements that are used for specifying security for a web application:

- <security-role-ref>

  The *security role reference* element contains the declaration of a security role reference in the web application's code. The declaration consists of an optional description, the security role name used in the code, and an optional link to a security role.

The security *role name* specified here is the security role name used in the code. The value of the role-name element must be the String used as the parameter to the HttpServletRequest.isUserInRole(String role) method. The container uses the mapping of security-role-ref to security-role when determining the return value of the call.

The security *role link* specified here contains the value of the name of the security role that the user may be mapped into. The role-link element is used to link a security role reference to a defined security role. The role-link element must contain the name of one of the security roles defined in the security-role elements.

For more information about security roles, read Working with Security Roles (page 989).

- <security-role>

  A *security role* is an abstract name for the permission to access a particular set of resources in an application. A security role can be compared to a key that can open a lock. Many people might have a copy of the key. The lock doesn't care who you are, only that you have the right key.

  The security-role element is used with the security-role-ref element to map roles defined in code to roles defined for the web application. For more information about security roles, read Working with Security Roles (page 989).

- <security-constraint>

  A *security constraint* is used to define the access privileges to a collection of resources using their URL mapping. Read Specifying Security Constraints (page 1006) for more detail on this element. The following elements can be part of a security constraint:

  - <web-resource-collection> element: *Web resource collections* describe a URL pattern and HTTP method pair that identify resources that need to be protected.
  - <auth-constraint> element: *Authorization constraints* indicate which users in specified roles are permitted access to this resource collection. The role name specified here must either correspond to the role name of one of the <security-role> elements defined for this web application, or be the specially reserved role name "*", which is a compact syntax for indicating all roles in the web application. Role names are case sensitive. The roles defined for the application must be mapped to users and

groups defined on the server. For more information about security roles, read Working with Security Roles (page 989).

- `<user-data-constraint>` element: *User data constraints* specify network security requirements, in particular, this constraint specifies how data communicated between the client and the container should be protected. If a user transport guarantee of INTEGRAL or CONFIDENTIAL is declared, all user name and password information will be sent over a secure connection using HTTP over SSL (HTTPS). Network security requirements are discussed in Specifying a Secure Connection (page 1009).

- `<login-config>`
  The *login configuration* element is used to specify the user authentication method to be used for access to web content, the realm in which the user will be authenticated, and, in the case of form-based login, additional attributes. When specified, the user must be authenticated before access to any resource that is constrained by a security constraint will be granted. The types of user authentication methods that are supported include basic, form-based, digest, and client certificate. Read Specifying an Authentication Mechanism (page 1010) for more detail on this element.

Some of the elements of web application security must be addressed in server configuration files rather than in the deployment descriptor for the web application. Configuring security on the Application Server is discussed in the following sections:

- Securing the Application Server (page 913)
- Managing Users and Groups on the Application Server (page 918)
- Installing and Configuring SSL Support (page 923)
- Deploying Secure Enterprise Beans (page 962)
- *Sun Java System Application Server Administration Guide* (see Further Information, page 1049 for a link to this document)
- *Sun Java System Application Server Developer's Guide* (see Further Information, page 1049 for a link to this document)

The following sections provide more information on deployment descriptor security elements:

- Specifying Security Constraints (page 1006)
- Working with Security Roles (page 989)

- Specifying a Secure Connection (page 1009)
- Specifying an Authentication Mechanism (page 1010)

Specifying Security Constraints

Security constraints are a declarative way to define the protection of web content. A security constraint is used to define access privileges to a collection of resources using their URL mapping. Security constraints are defined in a deployment descriptor. The following example shows a typical security constraint, including all of the elements of which it consists:

```
<security-constraint>
  <display-name>ExampleSecurityConstraint</display-name>
  <web-resource-collection>
    <web-resource-name>
      ExampleWRCollection
    </web-resource-name>
    <url-pattern>/example</url-pattern>
    <http-method>POST</http-method>
    <http-method>GET</http-method>
  </web-resource-collection>
  <auth-constraint>
    <role-name>exampleRole</role-name>
  </auth-constraint>
  <user-data-constraint>
    <transport-guarantee>CONFIDENTIAL</transport-guarantee>
  </user-data-constraint>
</security-constraint>
```

As shown in the example, a security constraint (`<security-constraint>` in deployment descriptor) consists of the following elements:

- *Web resource collection* (`web-resource-collection`)

  A web resource collection is a list of URL patterns (the part of a URL *after* the host name and port which you want to constrain) and HTTP operations (the methods within the files that match the URL pattern which you want to constrain (for example, `POST`, `GET`)) that describe a set of resources to be protected.

- *Authorization constraint* (`auth-constraint`)

  An authorization constraint establishes a requirement for authentication and names the roles authorized to access the URL patterns and HTTP methods declared by this security constraint. If there is no authorization constraint, the container must accept the request without requiring user authentication. If there is an authorization constraint, but no roles are specified within it, the container will not allow access to constrained requests under any circumstances. The wildcard character `"*"` can be used to specify all role names defined in the deployment descriptor. Security roles are discussed in Working with Security Roles (page 989).

- *User data constraint* (`user-data-constraint`)

  A user data constraint establishes a requirement that the constrained requests be received over a protected transport layer connection. This guarantees how the data will be transported between client and server. The choices for type of transport guarantee include `NONE`, `INTEGRAL`, and `CONFIDENTIAL`. If no user data constraint applies to a request, the container must accept the request when received over any connection, including an unprotected one. These options are discussed in Specifying a Secure Connection (page 1009).

Security constraints work only on the original request URI and not on calls made throug a `RequestDispatcher` (which include `<jsp:include>` and `<jsp:forward>`). Inside the application, it is assumed that the application itself has complete access to all resources and would not forward a user request unless it had decided that the requesting user also had access.

Many applications feature unprotected web content, which any caller can access without authentication. In the web tier, you provide unrestricted access simply by not configuring a security constraint for that particular request URI. It is common to have some unprotected resources and some protected resources. In this case, you will define security constraints and a login method, but they will not be used to control access to the unprotected resources. Users won't be asked to log in until the first time they enter a protected request URI.

The Java Servlet specification defines the request URI as the part of a URL *after* the host name and port. For example, let's say you have an e-commerce site with a browsable catalog that you would want anyone to be able to access, and a shopping cart area for customers only. You could set up the paths for your web application so that the pattern `/cart/*` is protected but nothing else is protected. Assuming that the application is installed at context path `/myapp`, the following are true:

- `http://localhost:8080/myapp/index.jsp` is *not* protected.
- `http://localhost:8080/myapp/cart/index.jsp` *is* protected.

A user will not be prompted to log in until the first time that user accesses a resource in the cart/ subdirectory.

Specifying Separate Security Constraints for Different Resources

You can create a separate security constraint for different resources within your application. For example, you could allow users with the role of PARTNER access to the POST method of all resources with the URL pattern /acme/wholesale/*, and allow users with the role of CLIENT access to the POST method of all resources with the URL pattern /acme/retail/*. An example of a deployment descriptor that would demonstrate this functionality is the following:

```
// SECURITY CONSTRAINT #1
<security-constraint>
  <web-resource-collection>
    <web-resource-name>wholesale</web-resource-name>
    <url-pattern>/acme/wholesale/*</url-pattern>
    <http-method>GET</http-method>
    <http-method>POST</http-method>
  </web-resource-collection>
  <auth-constraint>
    <role-name>PARTNER</role-name>
  </auth-constraint>
  <user-data-constraint>
    <transport-guarantee>CONFIDENTIAL</transport-guarantee>
  </user-data-constraint>
</security-constraint>

// SECURITY CONSTRAINT #2
<security-constraint>
  <web-resource-collection>
    <web-resource-name>retail</web-resource-name>
    <url-pattern>/acme/retail/*</url-pattern>
    <http-method>GET</http-method>
    <http-method>POST</http-method>
  </web-resource-collection>
  <auth-constraint>
    <role-name>CLIENT</role-name>
  </auth-constraint>
</security-constraint>
```

When the same url-pattern and http-method occur in multiple security constraints, the constraints on the pattern and method are defined by combining the individual constraints, which could result in unintentional denial of access. Section 12.7.2 of the Java Servlet 2.5 Specification (downloadable from `http://jcp.org/en/jsr/detail?id=154`) gives an example that illustrates the combination of constraints and how the declarations will be interpreted.

Specifying a Secure Connection

A user data constraint (`<user-data-constraint>` in the deployment descriptor) requires that all constrained URL patterns and HTTP methods specified in the security constraint are received over a protected transport layer connection such as HTTPS (HTTP over SSL). A user data constraint specifies a transport guarantee (`<transport-guarantee>` in the deployment descriptor). The choices for transport guarantee include `CONFIDENTIAL`, `INTEGRAL`, or `NONE`. If you specify `CONFIDENTIAL` or `INTEGRAL` as a security constraint, that type of security constraint applies to all requests that match the URL patterns in the web resource collection and not just to the login dialog box. The following security constraint includes a transport guarantee:

```
<security-constraint>
  <web-resource-collection>
    <web-resource-name>wholesale</web-resource-name>
    <url-pattern>/acme/wholesale/*</url-pattern>
    <http-method>GET</http-method>
    <http-method>POST</http-method>
  </web-resource-collection>
  <auth-constraint>
    <role-name>PARTNER</role-name>
  </auth-constraint>
  <user-data-constraint>
    <transport-guarantee>CONFIDENTIAL</transport-guarantee>
  </user-data-constraint>
</security-constraint>
```

The strength of the required protection is defined by the value of the transport guarantee. Specify `CONFIDENTIAL` when the application requires that data be transmitted so as to prevent other entities from observing the contents of the transmission. Specify `INTEGRAL` when the application requires that the data be sent between client and server in such a way that it cannot be changed in transit. Specify `NONE` to indicate that the container must accept the constrained requests on any connection, including an unprotected one.

The user data constraint is handy to use in conjunction with basic and form-based user authentication. When the login authentication method is set to `BASIC` or `FORM`, passwords are not protected, meaning that passwords sent between a client and a server on an unprotected session can be viewed and intercepted by third parties. Using a user data constraint with the user authentication mechanism can alleviate this concern. Configuring a user authentication mechanism is described in Specifying an Authentication Mechanism (page 1010).

To guarantee that data is transported over a secure connection, ensure that SSL support is configured for your server. If your server is the SJS Application Server, SSL support is already configured. If you are using another server, consult the documentation for that server for information on setting up SSL support. More information on configuring SSL support on the Application Server can be found in Establishing a Secure Connection Using SSL (page 922) and in the Application Server's *Administration Guide*. See Further Information (page 1049) for a link to this document.

Note: Good Security Practice: If you are using sessions, after you switch to SSL you should never accept any further requests for that session that are non-SSL. For example, a shopping site might not use SSL until the checkout page, and then it might switch to using SSL to accept your card number. After switching to SSL, you should stop listening to non-SSL requests for this session. The reason for this practice is that the session ID itself was not encrypted on the earlier communications. This is not so bad when you're only doing your shopping, but after the credit card information is stored in the session, you don't want a bad guy trying to fake the purchase transaction against your credit card. This practice could be easily implemented using a filter.

Specifying an Authentication Mechanism

To specify an authentication mechanism for your web application, declare a `login-config` element in the application deployment descriptor. The `login-config` element is used to configure the authentication method and realm name that should be used for this application, and the attributes that are needed by the form login mechanism when form-based login is selected. The sub-element `auth-method` configures the authentication mechanism for the web application. The element content must be either BASIC, DIGEST, FORM, CLIENT-CERT, or a vendor-specific authentication scheme. The `realm-name` element indicates the realm name to use for the authentication scheme chosen for the web application. The `form-login-config` element specifies the login and error pages that should be used when FORM based login is specified.

The authentication mechanism you choose specifies how the user is prompted to login. If the `<login-config>` element is present, and the `<auth-method>` element contains a value other than `NONE`, the user must be authenticated before it can access any resource that is constrained by the use of a `security-constraint` element in the same deployment descriptor (read Specifying Security Constraints, page 1006 for more information on security constraints). If you do not specify an authentication mechanism, the user will not be authenticated.

When you try to access a web resource that is constrained by a `security-constraint` element, the web container activates the authentication mechanism that has been configured for that resource. To specify an authentication method, place the `<auth-method>` element between `<login-config>` elements in the deployment descriptor, like this:

```
<login-config>
  <auth-method>BASIC</auth-method>
</login-config>
```

An example of a deployment descriptor that constrains all web resources for this application (in *`italics`* below) and requires HTTP basic authentication when you try to access that resource (in **`bold`** below) is shown here:

```
<?xml version="1.0" encoding="UTF-8"?>
<web-app version="2.5"
     xmlns="http://java.sun.com/xml/ns/javaee"
     xmlns:xsi="http://www.w3.org/2001/XMLSchema-instance"
     xsi:schemaLocation="http://java.sun.com/xml/ns/j2ee
        http://java.sun.com/xml/ns/javaee/web-app_2_5.xsd">
  <display-name>basicauth</display-name>
  <servlet>
     <display-name>index</display-name>
     <servlet-name>index</servlet-name>
     <jsp-file>/index.jsp</jsp-file>
  </servlet>
  <security-role>
     <role-name>loginUser</role-name>
  </security-role>
  <security-constraint>
     <display-name>SecurityConstraint1</display-name>
     <web-resource-collection>
        <web-resource-name>WRCollection</web-resource-name>
        <url-pattern>/*</url-pattern>
     </web-resource-collection>
     <auth-constraint>
        <role-name>loginUser</role-name>
     </auth-constraint>
```

```
  </security-constraint>
  <login-config>
    <auth-method>BASIC</auth-method>
  </login-config>
</web-app>
```

Before you can authenticate a user, you must have a database of user names, passwords, and roles configured on your web or application server. For information on setting up the user database, refer to Managing Users and Groups on the Application Server (page 918) and the Application Server's *Administration Guide* (for a link to this document, see Further Information, page 1049).

The authentication mechanisms are discussed further in the following sections:

- HTTP Basic Authentication (page 1012)
- Form-Based Authentication (page 1013)
- HTTPS Client Authentication (page 1015)
- Digest Authentication (page 1018)

HTTP Basic Authentication

HTTP Basic Authentication requires that the server request a user name and password from the web client and verify that the user name and password are valid by comparing them against a database of authorized users. When basic authentication is declared, the following actions occur:

1. A client requests access to a protected resource.
2. The web server returns a dialog box that requests the user name and password.
3. The client submits the user name and password to the server.
4. The server authenticates the user in the specified realm and, if successful, returns the requested resource.

Figure 30–2 shows what happens when you specify HTTP basic authentication.

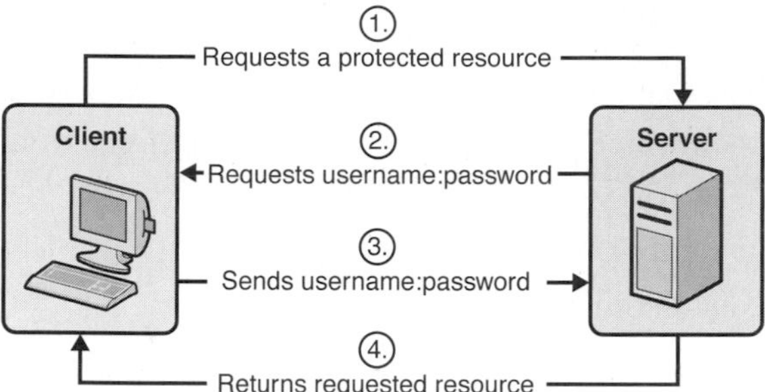

Figure 30–2 HTTP Basic Authentication

The following example shows how to specify basic authentication in your deployment descriptor:

```
<login-config>
  <auth-method>BASIC</auth-method>
</login-config>
```

HTTP basic authentication is not a secure authentication mechanism. Basic authentication sends user names and passwords over the Internet as text that is Base64 encoded, and the target server is not authenticated. This form of authentication can expose user names and passwords. If someone can intercept the transmission, the user name and password information can easily be decoded. However, when a secure transport mechanism, such as SSL, or security at the network level, such as the IPSEC protocol or VPN strategies, is used in conjunction with basic authentication, some of these concerns can be alleviated.

Example: Basic Authentication with JAX-WS (page 1041) is an example application that uses HTTP basic authentication in a JAX-WS service. Example: Using Form-Based Authentication with a JSP Page (page 1020) can be easily modified to demonstrate basic authentication. To do so, replace the text between the `<login-config>` elements with those shown in this section.

Form-Based Authentication

Form-based authentication allows the developer to control the look and feel of the login authentication screens by customizing the login screen and error pages that an HTTP browser presents to the end user. When form-based authentication is declared, the following actions occur:

1. A client requests access to a protected resource.
2. If the client is unauthenticated, the server redirects the client to a login page.
3. The client submits the login form to the server.
4. The server attempts to authenticate the user.
   a. If authentication succeeds, the authenticated user's principal is checked to ensure it is in a role that is authorized to access the resource. If the user is authorized, the server redirects the client to the resource using the stored URL path.
   b. If authentication fails, the client is forwarded or redirected to an error page.

Figure 30–3 shows what happens when you specify form-based authentication.

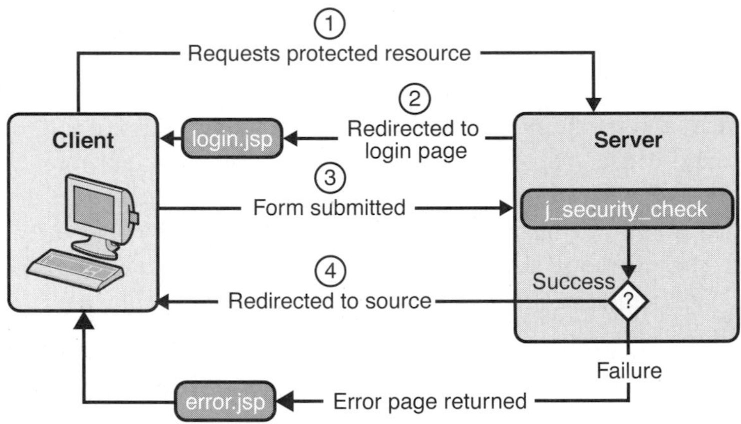

Figure 30–3 Form-Based Authentication

The following example shows how to declare form-based authentication in your deployment descriptor:

```
<login-config>
  <auth-method>FORM</auth-method>
  <realm-name>file</realm-name>
  <form-login-config>
```

```
        <form-login-page>/logon.jsp</form-login-page>
        <form-error-page>/logonError.jsp</form-error-page>
    </form-login-config>
  </login-config>
```

The login and error page locations are specified relative to the location of the deployment descriptor. Examples of login and error pages are shown in Creating the Login Form and the Error Page (page 1021).

Form-based authentication is not particularly secure. In form-based authentication, the content of the user dialog box is sent as plain text, and the target server is not authenticated. This form of authentication can expose your user names and passwords unless all connections are over SSL. If someone can intercept the transmission, the user name and password information can easily be decoded. However, when a secure transport mechanism, such as SSL, or security at the network level, such as the IPSEC protocol or VPN strategies, is used in conjunction with form-based authentication, some of these concerns can be alleviated.

The section Example: Using Form-Based Authentication with a JSP Page (page 1020) is an example application that uses form-based authentication.

Using Login Forms

When creating a form-based login, be sure to maintain sessions using cookies or SSL session information.

As shown in Figure 30–3, for authentication to proceed appropriately, the action of the login form must always be `j_security_check`. This restriction is made so that the login form will work no matter which resource it is for, and to avoid requiring the server to specify the action field of the outbound form. The following code snippet shows how the form should be coded into the HTML page:

```
<form method="POST" action="j_security_check">
<input type="text" name="j_username">
<input type="password" name="j_password">
</form>
```

HTTPS Client Authentication

HTTPS Client Authentication requires the client to possess a *Public Key Certificate (PKC)*. If you specify client authentication, the web server will authenticate the client using the client's public key certificate.

HTTPS Client Authentication is a more secure method of authentication than either basic or form-based authentication. It uses HTTP over SSL (HTTPS), in which the server authenticates the client using the client's Public Key Certificate (PKC). *Secure Sockets Layer* (SSL) technology provides data encryption, server authentication, message integrity, and optional client authentication for a TCP/IP connection. You can think of a public key certificate as the digital equivalent of a passport. It is issued by a trusted organization, which is called a certificate authority (CA), and provides identification for the bearer.

Before using HTTP Client Authentication, you must make sure that the following actions have been completed:

- Make sure that SSL support is configured for your server. If your server is the Sun Java Systems Application Server, SSL support is already configured. If you are using another server, consult the documentation for that server for information on setting up SSL support. More information on configuring SSL support on the application server can be found in Establishing a Secure Connection Using SSL (page 922) and the Application Server's *Administration Guide*. See Further Information (page 1049) for a link to this document.
- Make sure the client has a valid Public Key Certificate. For more information on creating and using public key certificates, read Working with Digital Certificates (page 926).

The following example shows how to declare HTTPS client authentication in your deployment descriptor:

```
<login-config>
  <auth-method>CLIENT-CERT</auth-method>
</login-config>
```

Mutual Authentication

With *mutual authentication*, the server and the client authenticate one another. There are two types of mutual authentication:

- Certificate-based mutual authentication (see Figure 30–4)
- User name- and password-based mutual authentication (see Figure 30–5)

When using certificate-based mutual authentication, the following actions occur:

1. A client requests access to a protected resource.
2. The web server presents its certificate to the client.
3. The client verifies the server's certificate.

4. If successful, the client sends its certificate to the server.
5. The server verifies the client's credentials.
6. If successful, the server grants access to the protected resource requested by the client.

Figure 30–4 shows what occurs during certificate-based mutual authentication.

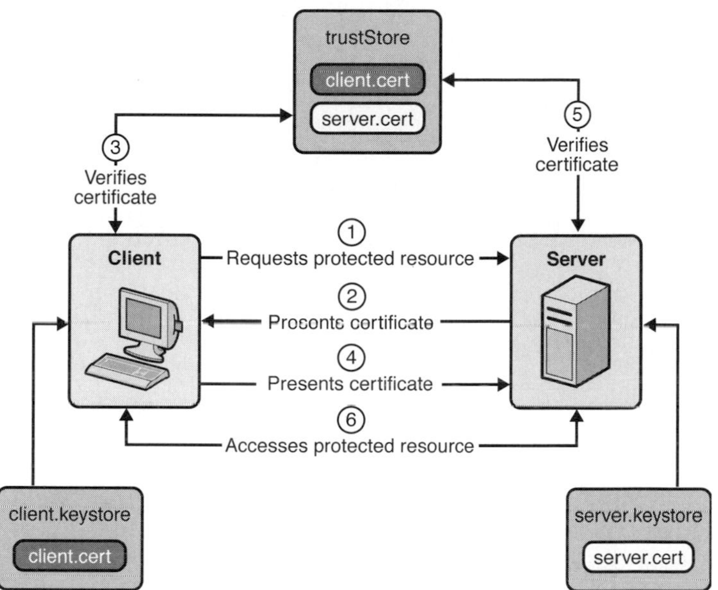

Figure 30–4 Certificate-Based Mutual Authentication

In user name- and password-based mutual authentication, the following actions occur:

1. A client requests access to a protected resource.
2. The web server presents its certificate to the client.
3. The client verifies the server's certificate.
4. If successful, the client sends its user name and password to the server, which verifies the client's credentials.
5. If the verification is successful, the server grants access to the protected resource requested by the client.

Figure 30–5 shows what occurs during user name- and password-based mutual authentication.

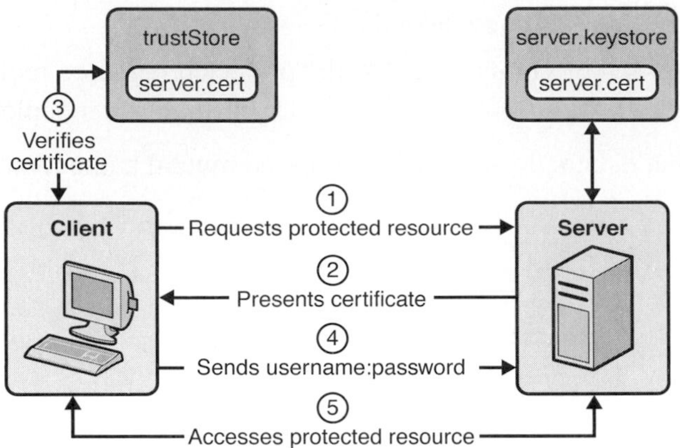

Figure 30–5 User Name- and Password-Based Mutual Authentication

Digest Authentication

Like HTTP basic authentication, *HTTP Digest Authentication* authenticates a user based on a user name and a password. However, the authentication is performed by transmitting the password in an encrypted form which is much more secure than the simple Base64 encoding used by basic authentication. Digest authentication is not currently in widespread use, and is not implemented in the Application Server, therefore, there is no further discussion of it in this document.

Examples: Securing Web Applications

There are several ways in which you can secure web applications. These include the following options:

- You can define a user authentication method for an application in its deployment descriptor. Authentication verifies the identity of a user, device, or other entity in a computer system, usually as a prerequisite to allowing access to resources in a system. When a user authentication method is specified for an application, the web container activates the specified authentication mechanism when you attempt to access a protected resource.

The options for user authentication methods are discussed in Specifying an Authentication Mechanism (page 1010). All of the example security applications use a user authentication method.

- You can define a transport guarantee for an application in its deployment descriptor. Use this method to run over an SSL-protected session and ensure that all message content is protected for confidentiality or integrity. The options for transport guarantees are discussed in Specifying a Secure Connection (page 1009).

  When running over an SSL-protected session, the server and client can authenticate one another and negotiate an encryption algorithm and cryptographic keys before the application protocol transmits or receives its first byte of data.

  SSL technology allows web browsers and web servers to communicate over a secure connection. In this secure connection, the data is encrypted before being sent, and then is decrypted upon receipt and before processing. Both the browser and the server encrypt all traffic before sending any data. For more information, see Establishing a Secure Connection Using SSL (page 922).

  Digital certificates are necessary when running HTTP over SSL (HTTPS). The HTTPS service of most web servers will not run unless a digital certificate has been installed. Digital certificates have already been created for the Application Server.

The following examples use annotations, programmatic security, and/or declarative security to demonstrate adding security to existing web applications:

- Example: Using Form-Based Authentication with a JSP Page (page 1020)
- Example: Basic Authentication with a Servlet (page 1031)
- Example: Basic Authentication with JAX-WS (page 1041)
- Discussion: Securing the Duke's Bank Example (page 977)

The following examples demonstrate adding basic authentication to an EJB endpoint or enterprise bean:

- Example: Securing an Enterprise Bean (page 964)
- Example: Using the isCallerInRole and getCallerPrincipal Methods (page 970)
- Discussion: Securing the Duke's Bank Example (page 977)

Example: Using Form-Based Authentication with a JSP Page

This example discusses how to use form-based authentication with a basic JSP page. With form-based authentication, you can customize the login screen and error pages that are presented to the web client for authentication of their user name and password. When a user submits their name and password, the server determines if the user name and password are those of an authorized user and, if authorized, sends the requested web resource. If the topic of authentication is new to you, please refer to the section Specifying an Authentication Mechanism (page 1010).

In general, the following steps are necessary for adding form-based authentication to an unsecured JSP page, such as the one described in Web Modules (page 38). In the example application included with this tutorial, many of these steps have been completed for you and are listed here simply to show what needs to be done should you wish to create a similar application. The completed version of this example application can be found in the directory `<INSTALL>/javaeetutorial5/examples/web/hello1_formauth/`.

The following steps describe how to set up your system for running the example applications, describe the sample application, and provide the steps for compiling, packaging, deploying, and testing the example application.

1. If you have not already done so, set up your system so that the Ant tool and/or NetBeans 5.5 will run properly. To do this, follow the instructions in Building the Examples (page xxxv). This step is necessary to set the properties that are specific to your installation of the Application Server and Java EE 5 Tutorial.
2. If you have not already done so, add an authorized user to the Application Server. For this example, add users to the `file` realm of the Application Server and assign the user to the group `user`. This topic is discussed more in Adding Authorized Roles and Users (page 1025).
3. Create a web module as described in Web Modules (page 38). The subsequent steps discuss adding security to this basic application. The resulting application is found in the directory `<INSTALL>/javaeetutorial5/examples/web/hello1_formauth/`.
4. Create the login form and login error form pages. Files for the example application can be viewed at `<INSTALL>/javaeetutorial5/examples/web/hello1_formauth/web`. These pages are discussed in Creating the Login Form and the Error Page (page 1021).

5. Create a `web.xml` deployment descriptor and add the appropriate security elements (the application on which this section is based did not originally require a deployment descriptor.) The deployment descriptor for the example application can be viewed at `<INSTALL>/javaeetutorial5/examples/hello1_formauth/web/WEB-INF`. The security elements for the `web.xml` deployment descriptor are described in Specifying a Security Constraint (page 1023).
6. Map the role name defined for this resource (`loginUser`) to a group of users defined on the Application Server. For more information on how to do this, read Mapping Application Roles to Application Server Groups (page 1026).
7. Build, package, deploy, and run the web application by following the steps in Building, Packaging, and Deploying the Form-Based Authentication Example Using NetBeans 5.5 (page 1027) or Building, Packaging, and Deploying the Form-Based Authentication Example Using Ant (page 1027).
8. Test the web client, following the steps in Testing the Form-Based Authentication Web Client (page 1028).

Creating a Web Client for Form-Based Authentication

The web client in this example is a standard JSP page, and annotations are not used in JSP pages because JSP pages are compiled as they are presented to the browser. Therefore, none of the code that adds form-based authentication to the example is included in the web client. The code for the JSP page used in this example, `hello1_formauth/web/index.jsp`, is exactly the same as the code used for the unsecured JSP page from the example application at `<INSTALL>/javaeetutorial5/examples/web/hello1/web/index.jsp`.

The information that adds form-based authentication to this example is specified in the deployment descriptor. This information is discussed in Specifying a Security Constraint (page 1023).

Creating the Login Form and the Error Page

When using form-based login mechanisms, you must specify a page that contains the form you want to use to obtain the user name and password, as well as which page to display if login authentication fails. This section discusses the login form and the error page used in this example. The section Specifying a Security Constraint (page 1023) shows how you specify these pages in the deployment descriptor.

The login page can be an HTML page, a JSP page, or a servlet, and it must return an HTML page containing a form that conforms to specific naming conventions (see the Java Servlet 2.5 specification for more information on these requirements). To do this, include the elements that accept user name and password information between `<form></form>` tags in your login page. The content of an HTML page, JSP page, or servlet for a login page should be coded as follows:

```
<form method=post action="j_security_check" >
  <input type="text"  name= "j_username" >
  <input type="password"  name= "j_password" >
</form>
```

The full code for the login page used in this example can be found at `<INSTALL>/javaeetutorial5/examples/web/hello1_formauth/web/logon.jsp`. An example of the running login form page is shown later in Figure 30–6. Here is the code for this page:

```
<html>
<head>
  <title>Login Page</title>
</head>

<h2>Hello, please log in:</h2>
<br><br>
<form action="j_security_check" method=post>
  <p><strong>Please Enter Your User Name: </strong>
  <input type="text" name="j_username" size="25">
  <p><p><strong>Please Enter Your Password: </strong>
  <input type="password" size="15" name="j_password">
  <p><p>
  <input type="submit" value="Submit">
  <input type="reset" value="Reset">
</form>
</html>
```

The login error page is displayed if the user enters a user name and password combination that is not authorized to access the protected URI. For this example, the login error page can be found at `<INSTALL>/javaeetutorial5/examples/web/hello1_formauth/web/logonError.jsp`. For this example, the login error page explains the reason for receiving the error page and provides a link that will allow the user to try again. Here is the code for this page:

```
<html>
<head>
  <title>Login Error</title>
</head>
<body>
  <c:url var="url" value="/index.jsp"/>
  <h2>Invalid user name or password.</h2>

  <p>Please enter a user name or password that is authorized to
access this application.
  For this application, this means a user that has been created
in the <code>file</code> realm
  and has been assigned to the <em>group</em> of <code>user</
code>.  Click here to
  <a href="${url}">Try Again</a></h2>
</body>
</html>
```

Specifying a Security Constraint

In this example, we are taking a very simple JSP page-based web application and adding form-based security to this application. The JSP page is exactly the same as the JSP page used in the example described in Web Modules (page 38). All security for this example is declared in the deployment descriptor for the application. A security constraint is defined in the deployment descriptor that tells the server to send a login form to collect user data, verify that the user is authorized to access the application, and, if so, display the JSP page to the user.

If this client were a web service endpoint and not a JSP page, we could use annotations to declare security roles and to specify which roles were allowed access to which methods. However, there is no resource injection in JSP pages, so we cannot use annotations and must use the equivalent deployment descriptor elements.

Deployment descriptor elements are described in Declaring Security Requirements in a Deployment Descriptor (page 1002).

The following sample code shows the deployment descriptor used in this example of form-based login authentication, which can be found in *<INSTALL>*/javaeetutorial5/examples/web/hello1_formauth/web/WEB-INF/web.xml.

```
<!-- FORM-BASED LOGIN AUTHENTICATION EXAMPLE -->
<?xml version="1.0" encoding="UTF-8"?>
<web-app xmlns="http://java.sun.com/xml/ns/javaee"
version="2.5"
  xmlns:xsi="http://www.w3.org/2001/XMLSchema-instance"
  xsi:schemaLocation="http://java.sun.com/xml/ns/javaee
  http://java.sun.com/xml/ns/javaee/web-app_2_5.xsd">

  <display-name>hello1_formauth</display-name>
  <servlet>
    <display-name>index</display-name>
    <servlet-name>index</servlet-name>
    <jsp-file>/index.jsp</jsp-file>
  </servlet>
  <security-constraint>
    <display-name>SecurityConstraint</display-name>
    <web-resource-collection>
      <web-resource-name>WRCollection</web-resource-name>
      <url-pattern>/*</url-pattern>
    </web-resource-collection>
    <auth-constraint>
      <role-name>loginUser</role-name>
    </auth-constraint>
    <user-data-constraint>
      <transport-guarantee>NONE</transport-guarantee>
    </user-data-constraint>
  </security-constraint>
  <login-config>
    <auth-method>FORM</auth-method>
    <form-login-config>
      <form-login-page>/logon.jsp</form-login-page>
      <form-error-page>/logonError.jsp</form-error-page>
    </form-login-config>
  </login-config>
  <security-role>
    <role-name>loginUser</role-name>
  </security-role>
</web-app>
```

More description of the elements that declare security in a deployment descriptor can be found in Specifying Security Constraints (page 1006).

Protecting Passwords with SSL

Passwords are not protected for confidentiality with HTTP basic or form-based authentication, meaning that passwords sent between a client and a server on an unprotected session can be viewed and intercepted by third parties. To overcome this limitation, you can run these authentication protocols over an SSL-protected session and ensure that all message content is protected for confidentiality.

A `<transport-guarantee>` element indicates whether or not the protected resources should travel over protected transport. For simplicity, this example does not require protected transport, but in a real world application, you would want to set this value to `CONFIDENTIAL` to ensure that the user name and password are not observed during transmission. When running on protected transport, you can run the application over the secure SSL protocol, `https`, and specify the secure port where your SSL connector is created (the default for the Application Server is `8181`). If you do not specify the HTTPS protocol, the server will automatically redirect the application to the secure port.

Adding Authorized Roles and Users

To authenticate a user and allow that user access to protected resources on the Application Server, you must link the roles defined in the application to the users defined for the Application Server.

- An application may define *security roles*, which are a logical grouping of users, classified by common traits such as customer profile or job title.
- The Application Server has multiple *realms*, each of which generally includes a database of authorized users, their passwords, and the logical group(s) to which the each user belongs.

When an application is deployed, the application-specific security roles are mapped to security identities in the runtime environment, such as *principals* (identities assigned to users as a result of authentication) or *groups*. Based on this mapping, a user who has been assigned a certain security role has associated access rights to a web application deployed onto a server.

As shown in the deployment descriptor for this example application, the security constraint specifies that users assigned to the role of `loginUser` are authorized to access any of the files in the `hello1_formauth` application. In this example, when a resource that is constrained by this same security constraint is accessed, for example, `hello1_formauth/web/index.jsp`, the Application Server sends the login form, receives the login information, and checks to see if the user is in a group that has been mapped to the role of `loginUser`. If the user name and password are those of an authorized user, access to the resource is granted to the requester.

To set up users for this example application, follow these steps:

1. Using the Admin Console, create a user in the `file` realm of the Application Server and assign that user to the group `user`. Make sure to note the user name and password that you enter in this step so that you can use it for testing the application later (these fields are case-sensitive). If you need help with the steps required to accomplish this task, read Managing Users and Groups on the Application Server (page 918) for more information.
2. Map the application security role of `loginUser` to the *group* of `user` that has been configured on the Application Server. For more information on how to do this mapping, read Mapping Application Roles to Application Server Groups (page 1026).

Mapping Application Roles to Application Server Groups

Map the role of `loginUser` defined in the application to the group of `user` defined on the Application Server by adding a `security-role-mapping` element to the `sun-web.xml` runtime deployment descriptor file. To deploy a WAR on the Application Server, the WAR file must contain a runtime deployment descriptor. The runtime deployment descriptor is an XML file that contains information such as the context root of the web application and the mapping of the portable names of an application's resources to the Application Server's resources.

The runtime deployment descriptor for this example, *<INSTALL>*/`javaeetutorial5/examples/web/hello1_formauth/web/WEB-INF/sun-web.xml`, looks like this:

```
<?xml version="1.0" encoding="UTF-8"?>
<!DOCTYPE sun-web-app PUBLIC "-//Sun Microsystems, Inc.//DTD
Application Server 9.0 Servlet 2.5//EN" "http://www.sun.com/
software/appserver/dtds/sun-web-app_2_5-0.dtd">
<sun-web-app>
  <context-root>/hello1_formauth</context-root>
  <security-role-mapping>
    <role-name>loginUser</role-name>
    <group-name>user</group-name>
  </security-role-mapping>
</sun-web-app>
```

Building, Packaging, and Deploying the Form-Based Authentication Example Using NetBeans 5.5

To build, package, and deploy this application using NetBeans 5.5, follow these steps:

1. Follow the instructions in Building the Examples (page xxxv) if you have not already done so. This step is necessary to provide the Ant targets with the location of your tutorial and Application Server installations.
2. Add users to the `file` realm of the Application Server as described in Adding Authorized Roles and Users (page 1025) if you have not already done so.
3. Open the project in NetBeans 5.5 by selecting File→Open Project.
4. Browse to the `<INSTALL>javaeetutorial5/examples/web/hello1_formauth/` directory.
5. Select Open Project Folder.
6. If you are prompted to regenerate the `build-impl.xml` file, select the Regenerate button.
7. Right-click `hello1_formauth` in the Projects pane, then select Clean and Build Project.
8. Right-click `hello1_formauth` in the Projects pane, then select Deploy Project.
9. Follow the steps in Testing the Form-Based Authentication Web Client (page 1028).

Building, Packaging, and Deploying the Form-Based Authentication Example Using Ant

To build, package, and deploy this application using the Ant tool, follow these steps:

1. Follow the instructions in Building the Examples (page xxxv) if you have not already done so. This step is necessary to provide the Ant targets with the location of your tutorial and Application Server installations.

2. Add users to the `file` realm of the Application Server as described in Adding Authorized Roles and Users (page 1025) if you have not already done so.
3. From a terminal window or command prompt, change to the `<INSTALL>/javaeetutorial5/examples/web/hello1_formauth/` directory.
4. Enter the following command at the terminal window or command prompt:

   ```
   ant
   ```

   This target will spawn any necessary compilations, copy files to the `<INSTALL>/javaeetutorial5/examples/web/hello1_formauth/build/` directory, create the WAR file, and copy it to the `<INSTALL>javaeetutorial5/examples/web/hello1_formauth/dist/` directory.
5. Deploy the WAR named `hello1_formauth.war` onto the Application Server using `ant` by entering the following command at the terminal window or command prompt:

   ```
   ant deploy
   ```

6. Follow the steps in Testing the Form-Based Authentication Web Client (page 1028).

Testing the Form-Based Authentication Web Client

To run the web client, follow these steps:

1. Open a web browser.
2. Enter the following URL in your web browser:

   ```
   http://localhost:8080/hello1_formauth
   ```

Note: If you set the transport guarantee to CONFIDENTIAL as discussed in Protecting Passwords with SSL (page 1025), you must load the application in a web browser using `https` for the protocol, the HTTPS port that you specified during installation for the port (by default this port is 8181), and the context name for the application you wish to run. For the form-based authentication example, you could run the example using the following URL: `https://localhost:8181/hello1_formauth`

The login form displays in the browser, as shown in Figure 30–6.

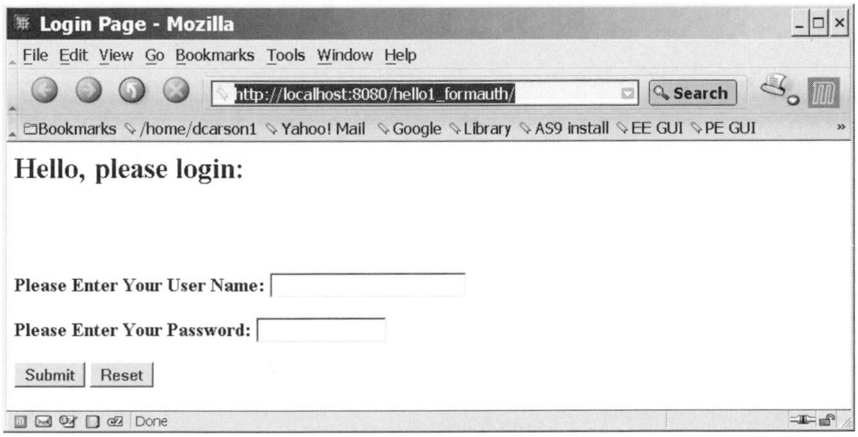

Figure 30–6 Form-Based Login Page

3. Enter a user name and password combination that corresponds to a user that has already been created in the `file` realm of the Application Server and has been assigned to the group of `user`, as discussed in Adding Authorized Roles and Users (page 1025).
4. Click the Submit button. Form-based authentication is case-sensitive for both the user name and password, so enter the user name and password exactly as defined for the Application Server.

   If you entered `My_Name` as the name and `My_Pwd` for the password, the server returns the requested resource if all of the following conditions are met:

   - There is a user defined for the Application Server with the user name of `My_Name`.
   - The user with the user name of `My_Name` has a password of `My_Pwd` defined for the Application Server.
   - The user `My_Name` with the password `My_Pwd` is assigned to the group of `user` on the Application Server.
   - The role of `loginUser`, as defined for the application, is mapped to the group of `user`, as defined for the Application Server.

   When these conditions are met, and the server has authenticated the user, the application will display as shown in Figure 30–7.

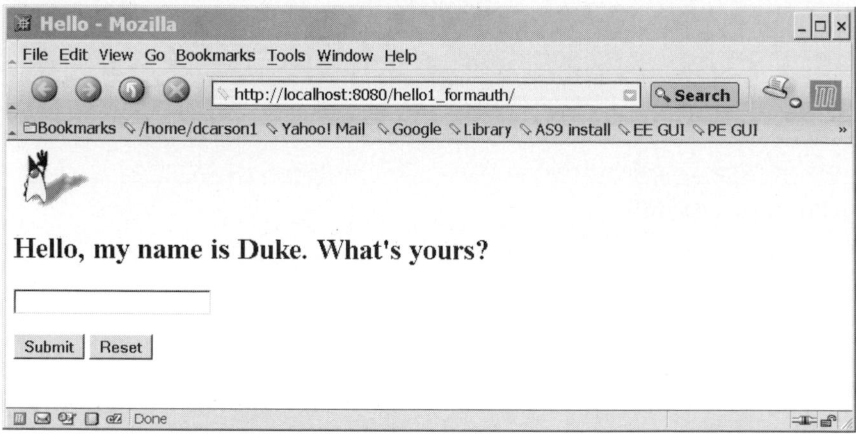

Figure 30–7 Running Web Application

5. Enter your name and click the Submit button. Because you have already been authorized, the name you enter in this step does not have any limitations. You have unlimited access to the application now.

   The application responds by saying "Hello" to you, as shown in Figure 30–8.

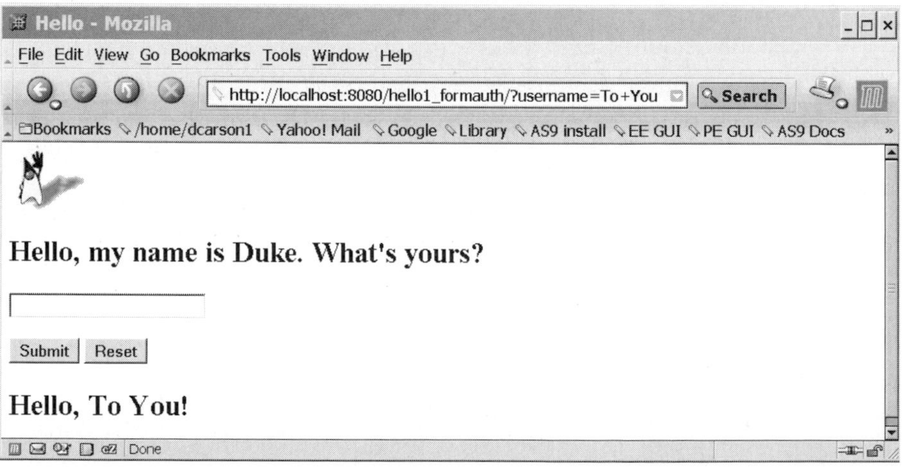

Figure 30–8 The Running Form-Based Authentication Example

Note: For repetitive testing of this example, you may need to close and reopen your browser. You should also run the `ant clean` and `ant undeploy` commands to ensure a fresh build if using the Ant tool, or select Clean and Build Project then Deploy Project if using NetBeans 5.5.

Example: Basic Authentication with a Servlet

This example discusses how to use basic authentication with a servlet. With basic authentication of a servlet, the web browser presents a standard login dialog that is not customizable. When a user submits their name and password, the server determines if the user name and password are those of an authorized user and sends the requested web resource if the user is authorized to view it. If the topic of authentication is new to you, please refer to the section Specifying an Authentication Mechanism (page 1010).

In general, the following steps are necessary for adding basic authentication to an unsecured servlet, such as the one described in Web Modules (page 38). In the example application included with this tutorial, many of these steps have been completed for you and are listed here simply to show what needs to be done should you wish to create a similar application. The completed version of this example application can be found in the directory `<INSTALL>/javaeetutorial5/examples/web/hello2_basicauth/`.

The following steps describe how to set up your system for running the example applications, describe the sample application, and provide the steps for compiling, packaging, deploying, and testing the example application.

1. If you have not already done so, set up your system so that the Ant tool and/or NetBeans 5.5 will run properly. To do this, follow the instructions in Building the Examples (page xxxv). This step is necessary to set the properties that are specific to your installation of the Application Server and Java EE 5 Tutorial.
2. If you have not already done so, add an authorized user to the Application Server. For this example, add users to the `file` realm of the Application Server and assign the user to the group `user`. This topic is discussed more in Adding Authorized Roles and Users (page 1035).
3. Create a web module as described in Web Modules (page 38) for the servlet example, `hello2`. The subsequent steps discuss adding security to this

basic application. The files for this example application are in `<INSTALL>/javaeetutorial5/examples/web/hello2_basicauth/`.

4. Declare the roles that will be used in this application. For this example, this is done by adding the `@DeclareRoles` annotation to `GreetingServlet.java`. This code is shown in Declaring Security Roles (page 1032).
5. Add the appropriate security elements to the `web.xml` deployment descriptor. The deployment descriptor for the example application can be viewed at `<INSTALL>/javaeetutorial5/examples/web/hello2_basicauth/web/WEB-INF/web.xml`. The security elements are described in Specifying the Security Constraint (page 1033).
6. Map the role name defined for this resource (`helloUser`) to a group of users defined on the Application Server. For more information on how to do this, read Mapping Application Roles to Application Server Groups (page 1036).
7. Build, package, and deploy the web application by following the steps in Building, Packaging, and Deploying the Servlet Basic Authentication Example Using NetBeans 5.5 (page 1036) or Building, Packaging, and Deploying the Servlet Basic Authentication Example Using Ant (page 1037).
8. Run the web application by following the steps described in Running the Basic Authentication Servlet (page 1038).
9. If you have any problems running this example, refer to the troubleshooting tips in Troubleshooting the Basic Authentication Example (page 1040).

Declaring Security Roles

There are two annotations that can be used with servlets: `@DeclareRoles` and `@RunAs`. In this example, the `@DeclareRoles` annotation is used to specify which roles are referenced in this example.

The following section of the `<INSTALL>/javaeetutorial5/examples/web/hello2_basicauth/src/servlets/GreetingServlet.java` file contains the code necessary to declare that the role of `helloUser` is used in this application:

```
package servlets;

import java.io.*;
import java.util.*;
import java.sql.*;
```

```
import javax.servlet.*;
import javax.servlet.http.*;
import javax.annotation.security.DeclareRoles;

/**
* This is a simple example of an HTTP Servlet that can only be
accessed
* by an authenticated user.  It responds to the GET
* method of the HTTP protocol.
*/
@DeclareRoles("helloUser")
public class GreetingServlet extends HttpServlet {

  public void doGet (HttpServletRequest request,
    HttpServletResponse response)
      throws ServletException, IOException
```

You could also declare security roles using the `<security-role>` element in the deployment descriptor. If you prefer to declare security roles this way, read Declaring Roles Using Deployment Descriptor Elements (page 998).

Specifying the Security Constraint

In this example, we are taking a very simple servlet-based web application and adding basic authentication to this application. The servlet is basically the same as the servlet used in the example described in Web Modules (page 38), with the exception of the annotations added and discussed in Declaring Security Roles (page 1032).

The security constraint for this example is declared in the application deployment descriptor. The security constraint tells the server or browser to perform the following tasks:

- Send a standard login dialog to collect user name and password data
- Verify that the user is authorized to access the application
- If authorized, display the servlet to the user

Deployment descriptors elements are described in Declaring Security Requirements in a Deployment Descriptor (page 1002).

The following sample code shows the security elements for the deployment descriptor used in this example of basic authentication, which can be found in

<INSTALL>/javaeetutorial5/examples/web/hello2_basicauth/web/WEB-INF/web.xml.

```
<security-constraint>
   <display-name>SecurityConstraint</display-name>
   <web-resource-collection>
      <web-resource-name>WRCollection</web-resource-name>
      <url-pattern>/greeting</url-pattern>
   </web-resource-collection>
   <auth-constraint>
      <role-name>helloUser</role-name>
   </auth-constraint>
   <user-data-constraint>
      <transport-guarantee>NONE</transport-guarantee>
   </user-data-constraint>
</security-constraint>
<login-config>
   <auth-method>BASIC</auth-method>
   <realm-name>file</realm-name>
</login-config>
```

More description of the elements that declare security in a deployment descriptor can be found in Specifying Security Constraints (page 1006).

Protecting Passwords with SSL

Passwords are not protected for confidentiality with HTTP basic or form-based authentication, meaning that passwords sent between a client and a server on an unprotected session can be viewed and intercepted by third parties. To overcome this limitation, you can run these authentication protocols over an SSL-protected session and ensure that all message content is protected for confidentiality.

A `<transport-guarantee>` element indicates whether or not the protected resources should travel over protected transport. For simplicity, this example does not require protected transport, but in a real world application, you would want to set this value to `CONFIDENTIAL` to ensure that the user name and password are not observed during transmission. When running on protected transport, you need to use the secure SSL protocol, `https`, and specify the secure port where your SSL connector is created (the default for the Application Server is `8181`).

Adding Authorized Roles and Users

To authenticate a user and allow that user access to protected resources on the Application Server, you must link the roles defined in the application to the users defined for the Application Server.

- A *security role*, which is defined at the application level, is a logical grouping of users, classified by common traits such as customer profile or job title.
- The Application Server has multiple *realms*, each of which generally includes a database of authorized users, their passwords, and the logical group(s) to which the each user belongs.

When an application is deployed, the application-specific security roles are mapped to security identities in the runtime environment, such as *principals* (identities assigned to users as a result of authentication) or *groups*. Based on this mapping, a user who has been assigned a certain security role has associated access rights to a web application deployed onto a server.

As shown in the deployment descriptor for this example application, the security constraint specifies that users assigned to the role of `helloUser` are authorized to access the URL pattern `/greeting`. In this example, when this resource (because it is constrained by a security constraint) is accessed, the Application Server sends a default login dialog, receives the login information, and checks to see if the user is in a group that has been mapped to the role of `helloUser`. If the user name and password are those of an authorized user, access to the resource is granted to the requester.

To set up users for this example application, follow these steps:

1. If you have not already done so, create a user in the `file` realm of the Application Server and assign that user to the group `user`. Make sure to note the user name and password that you enter in this step so that you can use it for testing the application later. If you need help with the steps required to accomplish this task, read Managing Users and Groups on the Application Server (page 918) for more information.
2. Map the application security role of `helloUser` to the *group* of `user` that has been configured on the Application Server. For more information on how to do this mapping, read Mapping Application Roles to Application Server Groups (page 1036).

Mapping Application Roles to Application Server Groups

Map the role of `helloUser` defined in the application to the group of `user` defined on the Application Server by adding a `security-role-mapping` element to the `sun-web.xml` runtime deployment descriptor file. The runtime deployment descriptor is an XML file that contains information such as the context root of the web application and the mapping of the portable names of an application's resources to the Application Server's resources.

The runtime deployment descriptor for this example, `<INSTALL>/javaeetutorial5/examples/web/hello2_basicauth/web/WEB-INF/sun-web.xml`, looks like this:

```
<sun-web-app>
  <context-root>/hello2_basicauth</context-root>
  <security-role-mapping>
    <role-name>helloUser</role-name>
    <group-name>user</group-name>
  </security-role-mapping>
</sun-web-app>
```

Building, Packaging, and Deploying the Servlet Basic Authentication Example Using NetBeans 5.5

To build, package, and deploy the `web/hello2_basicauth` example application using NetBeans 5.5, follow these steps:

1. If you have not already done so, follow the instructions in Building the Examples (page xxxv). This step is necessary to provide the Ant targets with the location of your tutorial and Application Server installations.
2. If you have not already done so, add authorized users to the `file` realm of the Application Server as described in Adding Authorized Roles and Users (page 1035).
3. Open the project in NetBeans 5.5 by selecting File→Open Project.
4. Browse to the `<INSTALL>javaeetutorial5/examples/web/hello2_basicauth/` directory.
5. Make sure that Open as Main Project is selected.
6. Select Open Project Folder.

7. Right-click `hello2_basicauth` in the Projects pane, then select Clean and Build Project.
8. Right-click `hello2_basicauth` in the Projects pane, then select Deploy Project.
9. To run the servlet, follow the steps in Running the Basic Authentication Servlet (page 1038).

Building, Packaging, and Deploying the Servlet Basic Authentication Example Using Ant

To build, package, and deploy the `web/hello2_basicauth` example using the Ant tool, follow these steps:

1. If you have not already done so, follow the instructions in Building the Examples (page xxxv). This step is necessary to provide the Ant targets with the location of your tutorial and Application Server installations.
2. If you have not already done so, add authorized users to the `file` realm of the Application Server as described in Adding Authorized Roles and Users (page 1035).
3. From a terminal window or command prompt, change to the `<INSTALL>/javaeetutorial5/examples/web/hello2_basicauth/` directory.
4. Build and package the web application by entering the following command at the terminal window or command prompt:

   ```
   ant
   ```

   This command uses `web.xml` and `sun-web.xml` files, located in the `<INSTALL>/javaeetutorial5/examples/web/hello2_basicauth/web/WEB-INF/` directory.

5. To deploy the example using Ant, enter the following command at the terminal window or command prompt:

   ```
   ant deploy
   ```

   The `deploy` target in this case gives you an incorrect URL to run the application. To run the application, please use the URL shown in Running the Basic Authentication Servlet (page 1038).

6. To run the web application, follow the steps in Running the Basic Authentication Servlet (page 1038).

Running the Basic Authentication Servlet

To run the web client, follow these steps:

1. Open a web browser.
2. Enter the following URL in your web browser:

   `http://localhost:8080/hello2_basicauth/greeting`

   If you set the transport guarantee to CONFIDENTIAL as discussed in Protecting Passwords with SSL (page 1034), you must load the application in a web browser using `https` for the protocol, the HTTPS port that you specified during installation for the port (by default this port is 8181), and the context name for the application you wish to run. For the basic authentication example, you could run the example using the following URL: `https://localhost:8181/hello2_basicauth/greeting`.
3. A default login form displays. Enter a user name and password combination that corresponds to a user that has already been created in the `file` realm of the Application Server and has been assigned to the group of `user`, as discussed in Adding Authorized Roles and Users (page 1035).

   Basic authentication is case-sensitive for both the user name and password, so enter the user name and password exactly as defined for the Application Server.

   If you entered `My_Name` as the name and `My_Pwd` for the password, the server returns the requested resource if all of the following conditions are met:

   - There is a user defined for the Application Server with the user name of `My_Name`.
   - The user with the user name of `My_Name` has a password of `My_Pwd` defined for the Application Server.
   - The user `My_Name` with the password `My_Pwd` is assigned to the group of `user` on the Application Server.
   - The role of `helloUser`, as defined for the application, is mapped to the group of `user`, as defined for the Application Server.

   When these conditions are met, and the server has authenticated the user, the application will display as shown in Figure 30–9.

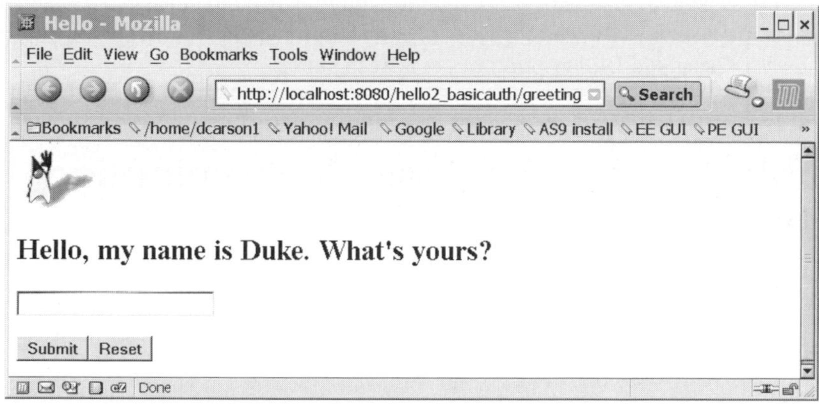

Figure 30–9 Running Web Application

4. Enter your name and click the Submit button. Because you have already been authorized, the name you enter in this step does not have any limitations. You have unlimited access to the application now.

   The application responds by saying "Hello" to you, as shown in Figure 30–10.

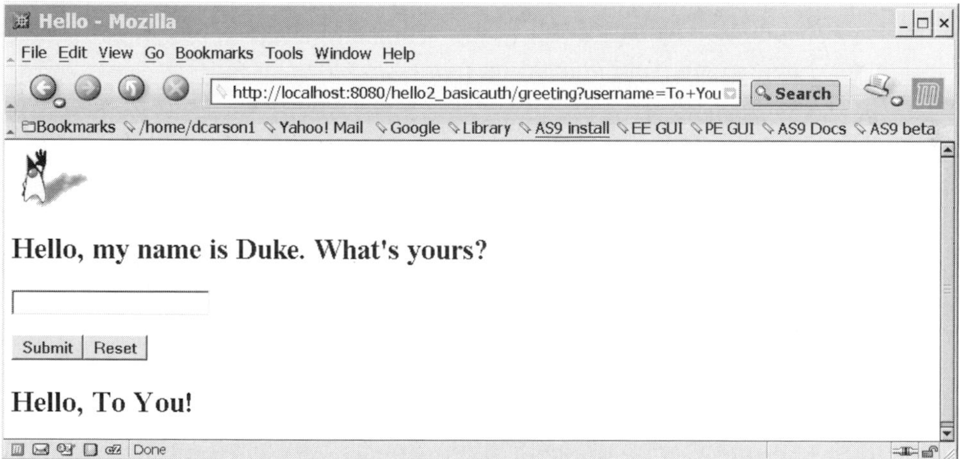

Figure 30–10 The Running Basic Authentication Example

Note: For repetitive testing of this example, you may need to close and reopen your browser. You should also run the `ant clean` and `ant undeploy` targets or the NetBeans 5.5 Clean and Build option to get a fresh start.

Troubleshooting the Basic Authentication Example

When doing iterative development with this web application, follow these steps if you are using NetBeans 5.5:

1. Close your web browser.
2. Clean and recompile the files from the previous build by right-clicking `hello2_basicauth` and selecting Clean and Build Project.
3. Redeploy the application by right-clicking `hello2_basicauth` and selecting Deploy Project.
4. Open your web browser and reload the following URL:

   ```
   http://localhost:8080/hello2_basicauth/greeting
   ```

Follow these steps if you are using the Ant tool:

1. Close your web browser.
2. Undeploy the web application. To undeploy the application, use the following command in the directory:

   ```
   ant undeploy
   ```

3. Clean out files from the previous build, using the following command:

   ```
   ant clean
   ```

4. Recompile, repackage, and redeploy the application, using the following commands:

   ```
   ant
   ant deploy
   ```

5. Open your web browser and reload the following URL:

   ```
   http://localhost:8080/hello2_basicauth/greeting
   ```

Example: Basic Authentication with JAX-WS

In this section, we discuss how to configure a JAX-WS-based web service for HTTP basic authentication. When a service that is constrained by *HTTP basic authentication* is requested, the server requests a user name and password from the client and verifies that the user name and password are valid by comparing them against a database of authorized users.

If the topic of authentication is new to you, please refer to the section titled Specifying an Authentication Mechanism (page 1010). For an explanation of how basic authentication works, see Figure 30–2.

For this tutorial, we will add the security elements to the JAX-WS service and client; build, package, and deploy the service; and then build and run the client application.

This example service was developed by starting with an unsecured service, `helloservice`, which can be found in the directory `<INSTALL>/javaeetutorial5/examples/jaxws/helloservice` and is discussed in Creating a Simple Web Service and Client with JAX-WS (page 508). We build on this simple application by adding the necessary elements to secure the application using basic authentication. The example client used in this application can be found at `<INSTALL>/javaeetutorial5/examples/jaxws/simpleclient-basicauth`, which only varies from the original `simpleclient` application in that it uses the `helloservice-basicauth` endpoint instead of the `helloservice` endpoint. The completed version of the secured service can be found at `<INSTALL>/javaeetutorial5/examples/jaxws/helloservice-basicauth`.

In general, the following steps are necessary to add basic authentication to a JAX-WS web service. In the example application included with this tutorial, many of these steps have been completed for you and are listed here simply to show what needs to be done should you wish to create a similar application.

1. Create an application like the one in Creating a Simple Web Service and Client with JAX-WS (page 508). The example in this tutorial starts with that example and demonstrates adding basic authentication of the client to this application. The completed version of this application is located in the directories `<INSTALL>/javaeetutorial5/examples/jaxws/helloservice-basicauth` and `<INSTALL>/javaeetutorial5/examples/jaxws/simpleclient-basicauth`.

2. If the port value was set to a value other than the default (8080), follow the instructions in Setting the Port (page 508) to update the example files to reflect this change.
3. If you have not already done so, follow the steps in Building the Examples (page xxxv) for information on setting up your system to run the example.
4. If you have not already done so, add a user to the `file` realm and specify `user` for the group of this new user. Write down the user name and password so that you can use them for testing this application in a later step. If you have not already completed this step, refer to the section Managing Users and Groups on the Application Server (page 918) for instructions.
5. Modify the source code for the service, `Hello.java`, to specify which roles are authorized to access the `sayHello (String name)` method. This step is discussed in Annotating the Service (page 1042).
6. Add security elements that specify that basic authentication is to be performed to the application deployment descriptor, `web.xml`. This step is discussed in Adding Security Elements to the Deployment Descriptor (page 1043).
7. Modify the runtime deployment descriptor, `sun-web.xml`, to map the role used in this application (`basicUser`) to a group defined on the Application Server (`user`). This step is discussed in Linking Roles to Groups (page 1045).
8. Build, package, and deploy the web service. See Building and Deploying HelloService with Basic Authentication Using NetBeans 5.5 (page 1045) or Building and Deploying HelloService with Basic Authentication Using Ant (page 1046) for the steps to accomplish this.
9. Build and run the client application. See Building and Running the Client Application for HelloService with Basic Authentication Using NetBeans 5.5 (page 1047) or Building and Running the Client Application for HelloService with Basic Authentication Using Ant (page 1048) for the steps to accomplish this.

Annotating the Service

In this example, annotations are used to specify which users are authorized to access which methods of this service. In this simple example, the `@RolesAllowed` annotation is used to specify that users in the application role of `basicUser` are authorized access to the `sayHello(String name)` method. This application role must be linked to a group of users on the Application Server. Linking the roles to groups is discussed in Linking Roles to Groups (page 1045).

The source code for the original /helloservice application was modified as shown in the following code snippet (modifications in **bold**). This file can be found in *<INSTALL>*/javaeetutorial5/examples/jaxws/helloservice-basicauth/src/java/helloservice/basicauth/endpoint/Hello.java.

```
package helloservice.basicauth.endpoint;

import javax.jws.WebMethod;
import javax.jws.WebService;
import javax.annotation.security.RolesAllowed;

@WebService()
public class Hello {
   private String message = new String("Hello, ");

  @WebMethod()
  @RolesAllowed("basicUser")
  public String sayHello(String name) {
     return message + name + ".";

  }
}
```

The @RolesAllowed annotation specifies that only users in the role of basicUser will be allowed to access the sayHello (String name) method. An @RolesAllowed annotation implicitly declares a role that will be referenced in the application, therefore, no @DeclareRoles annotation is required.

Adding Security Elements to the Deployment Descriptor

To enable basic authentication for the service, add security elements to the application deployment descriptor, web.xml. The security elements that need to be added to the deployment descriptor include the <security-constraint> and <login-config> elements. These security elements are discussed in more detail in Declaring Security Requirements in a Deployment Descriptor (page 1002) and in the Java Servlet Specification. Code in **bold** is added to the original deployment descriptor to enable HTTP basic authentication. The resulting deployment descriptor is located in *<INSTALL>*/javaeetutorial5/examples/jaxws/helloservice-basicauth/web/WEB-INF/web.xml.

```
<?xml version="1.0" encoding="UTF-8"?>
<web-app
  xmlns="http://java.sun.com/xml/ns/javaee" version="2.5"
  xmlns:xsi="http://www.w3.org/2001/XMLSchema"
  xsi:schemaLocation="http://java.sun.com/xml/ns/javaee
  http://java.sun.com/xml/ns/javaee/web-app_2_5.xsd">
  <display-name>HelloService</display-name>
  <listener>
    <listener-class>
      com.sun.xml.ws.transport.http.servlet.WSServletContex-
tListener
    </listener-class>
  </listener>
  <servlet>
    <display-name>HelloService</display-name>
    <servlet-name>HelloService</servlet-name>
    <servlet-class>com.sun.xml.ws.transport.http.serv-
let.WSServlet</servlet-class>
  </servlet>
  <servlet-mapping>
    <servlet-name>HelloService</servlet-name>
    <url-pattern>/hello</url-pattern>
  </servlet-mapping>
  <session-config>
    <session-timeout>30</session-timeout>
  </session-config>
  <security-constraint>
    <display-name>SecurityConstraint</display-name>
    <web-resource-collection>
       <web-resource-name>WRCollection</web-resource-name>
      <url-pattern>/hello</url-pattern>
    </web-resource-collection>
    <auth-constraint>
      <role-name>basicUser</role-name>
    </auth-constraint>
    <user-data-constraint>
      <transport-guarantee>NONE</transport-guarantee>
    </user-data-constraint>
  </security-constraint>
  <login-config>
    <auth-constraint>BASIC</auth-constraint>
    <realm-name>file</realm-name>
  </login-config>
</web-app>
```

Linking Roles to Groups

The role of basicUser has been defined for this application, but there is no group of basicUser defined for the Application Server. To map the role that is defined for the application (basicUser) to a group that is defined on the Application Server (user), add a <security-role-mapping> element to the runtime deployment descriptor, sun-web.xml, as shown below (modifications from the original file are in **bold**). The resulting runtime deployment descriptor is located in *<INSTALL>*/javaeetutorial5/examples/jaxws/helloservice-basicauth/web/WEB-INF/sun-web.xml.

```
<?xml version="1.0" encoding="UTF-8"?>
<!DOCTYPE sun-web-app PUBLIC "-//Sun Microsystems, Inc.//DTD
Application Server 9.0 Servlet 2.5//EN" "http://www.sun.com/
software/appserver/dtds/sun-web-app_2_5-0.dtd">
<sun-web-app error-url="">
  <context-root>/helloservice</context-root>
  <class-loader delegate="true"/>
  <security-role-mapping>
      <role-name>basicUser</role-name>
    <group-name>user</group-name>
  </security-role-mapping>
</sun-web-app>
```

Building and Deploying HelloService with Basic Authentication Using NetBeans 5.5

To build, package, and deploy the jaxws/helloservice-basicauth example using NetBeans 5.5, follow these steps, or the steps described in Building, Packaging, and Deploying the Service (page 511).

1. If you have not already done so, set up your system for running the tutorial examples by following the instructions in Building the Examples (page xxxv).
2. If you haven't already done so, set up an authorized user on the Application Server, assigned to the group user, as described in Managing Users and Groups on the Application Server (page 918).
3. In NetBeans 5.5, select File→Open Project.
4. In the Open Project dialog, navigate to *<INSTALL>*/javaeetutorial5/examples/jaxws/.
5. Select the helloservice-basicauth folder.

6. Check the Open as Main Project and Open Required Projects checkboxes.
7. Click Open Project Folder.
8. In the Projects tab, right-click the `helloservice-basicauth` project and select Clean and Build Project.
9. In the Projects tab, right-click the `helloservice-basicauth` project and select Deploy Project.

   This step builds and packages the application into `helloservice-basicauth.war`, located in `<INSTALL>/javaeetutorial5/examples/jaxws/helloservice-basicauth/dist`, and deploys this war file to your Application Server instance.

Building and Deploying HelloService with Basic Authentication Using Ant

To build, package, and deploy the `jaxws/helloservice-basicauth` example using the Ant tool, follow these steps, or the steps described in Building, Packaging, and Deploying the Service (page 511).

1. If you have not already done so, set up your system for running the tutorial examples by following the instructions in Building the Examples (page xxxv).
2. If you haven't already done so, set up an authorized user on the Application Server, assigned to the group `user`, as described in Managing Users and Groups on the Application Server (page 918).
3. From a terminal window or command prompt, go to the `<INSTALL>/javaeetutorial5/examples/jaxws/helloservice-basicauth/` directory.
4. Build, package, and deploy the JAX-WS service by entering the following at the terminal window or command prompt in the `helloservice-basicauth/` directory:

   ```
   ant all
   ```

   You can test the service by selecting it in the Admin Console and choosing Test. For more information on how to do this, read Testing the Service without a Client (page 513).

Building and Running the Client Application for HelloService with Basic Authentication Using NetBeans 5.5

To build and run the client application, `simpleclient-basicauth`, using NetBeans 5.5, follow these steps. The `helloservice-basicauth` service must be deployed onto the Application Server before compiling the client files. For information on deploying the service, read Building and Deploying HelloService with Basic Authentication Using NetBeans 5.5 (page 1045).

1. In NetBeans 5.5, select File→Open Project.
2. In the Open Project dialog, navigate to `<INSTALL>/javaeetutorial5/examples/jaxws/`.
3. Select the `simpleclient-basicauth` folder.
4. Check the Open as Main Project and Open Required Projects checkboxes.
5. Click Open Project Folder.
6. In the Projects tab, right-click the `simpleclient-basicauth` project and select Clean and Build Project.
7. In the Projects tab, right-click the `simpleclient-basicauth` project and select Run Project.

   You will be prompted for your user name and password.
8. Enter the user name and password of a user that has been entered into the database of users for the file realm and has been assigned to the group of `user`.

   If the username and password you enter are authorized, you will see the output of the application client in the Output pane:

The client displays the following output:

```
[echo] running application client container.
[exec] Retrieving the port from the following service:
helloservice.basicauth.endpoint.HelloSer vice@c8769b
[exec] Invoking the sayHello operation on the port.
[exec] Hello, No Name.
```

Building and Running the Client Application for HelloService with Basic Authentication Using Ant

To build and run the client application, `simpleclient-basicauth`, using the Ant tool, follow these steps. The secured service must be deployed onto the Application Server before you can successfully compile the client application. For more information on deploying the service, read Building and Deploying HelloService with Basic Authentication Using Ant (page 1046).

1. Build the client by changing to the directory `<INSTALL>/examples/jaxws/simpleclient-basicauth/` and entering the following at the terminal window or command prompt:

   ```
   ant
   ```

   This command calls the `default` target, which builds and packages the application into a JAR file, `simpleclient-basicauth.jar`, located in the `/dist` directory.

2. Run the client by entering the following at the terminal window or command prompt:

   ```
   ant run
   ```

   A Login for User dialog displays.

3. Enter a user name and password that correspond to a user set up on the Application Server with a group of `user`. Click OK.

The client displays the following output:

```
[echo] running application client container.
[exec] Retrieving the port from the following service:
helloservice.basicauth.endpoint.HelloService@c8769b
[exec] Invoking the sayHello operation on the port.
[exec] Hello, No Name.
```

Further Information

- *Java EE 5 Specification* at
  `http://jcp.org/en/jsr/detail?id=244`
- Java 2 Standard Edition, v.1.5.0 security information:
  `http://java.sun.com/j2se/1.5.0/docs/guide/security/index.html`
- *JSR 250: Common Annotations for the Java Platform*:
  `http://jcp.org/en/jsr/detail?id=250`
- The *Developer's Guide* for the Application Server:
  `http://docs.sun.com/doc/819-3659`
- The *Administration Guide* for the Application Server:
  `http://docs.sun.com/doc/819-3658`
- The *Application Deployment Guide* for the Application Server:
  `http://docs.sun.com/doc/819-3660`
- *Java Servlet Specification*, Version 2.5:
  `http://jcp.org/en/jsr/detail?id=154`
- Information on SSL specifications:
  `http://wp.netscape.com/eng/security`

31

The Java Message Service API

THIS chapter provides an introduction to the Java Message Service (JMS) API, a Java API that allows applications to create, send, receive, and read messages using reliable, asynchronous, loosely coupled communication. It covers the following topics:

- Overview
- Basic JMS API concepts
- The JMS API programming model
- Writing simple JMS client applications
- Creating robust JMS applications
- Using the JMS API in a Java EE application
- Further information

Overview

This overview of the JMS API answers the following questions.

- What is messaging?
- What is the JMS API?

- When can you use the JMS API?
- How does the JMS API work with the Java EE platform?

What Is Messaging?

Messaging is a method of communication between software components or applications. A messaging system is a peer-to-peer facility: A messaging client can send messages to, and receive messages from, any other client. Each client connects to a messaging agent that provides facilities for creating, sending, receiving, and reading messages.

Messaging enables distributed communication that is *loosely coupled*. A component sends a message to a destination, and the recipient can retrieve the message from the destination. However, the sender and the receiver do not have to be available at the same time in order to communicate. In fact, the sender does not need to know anything about the receiver; nor does the receiver need to know anything about the sender. The sender and the receiver need to know only which message format and which destination to use. In this respect, messaging differs from tightly coupled technologies, such as Remote Method Invocation (RMI), which require an application to know a remote application's methods.

Messaging also differs from electronic mail (email), which is a method of communication between people or between software applications and people. Messaging is used for communication between software applications or software components.

What Is the JMS API?

The Java Message Service is a Java API that allows applications to create, send, receive, and read messages. Designed by Sun and several partner companies, the JMS API defines a common set of interfaces and associated semantics that allow programs written in the Java programming language to communicate with other messaging implementations.

The JMS API minimizes the set of concepts a programmer must learn in order to use messaging products but provides enough features to support sophisticated messaging applications. It also strives to maximize the portability of JMS applications across JMS providers in the same messaging domain.

The JMS API enables communication that is not only loosely coupled but also

- **Asynchronous**: A JMS provider can deliver messages to a client as they arrive; a client does not have to request messages in order to receive them.
- **Reliable**: The JMS API can ensure that a message is delivered once and only once. Lower levels of reliability are available for applications that can afford to miss messages or to receive duplicate messages.

The JMS specification was first published in August 1998. The latest version is Version 1.1, which was released in April 2002. You can download a copy of the specification from the JMS web site: `http://java.sun.com/products/jms/`.

When Can You Use the JMS API?

An enterprise application provider is likely to choose a messaging API over a tightly coupled API, such as remote procedure call (RPC), under the following circumstances.

- The provider wants the components not to depend on information about other components' interfaces, so that components can be easily replaced.
- The provider wants the application to run whether or not all components are up and running simultaneously.
- The application business model allows a component to send information to another and to continue to operate without receiving an immediate response.

For example, components of an enterprise application for an automobile manufacturer can use the JMS API in situations like these:

- The inventory component can send a message to the factory component when the inventory level for a product goes below a certain level so that the factory can make more cars.
- The factory component can send a message to the parts components so that the factory can assemble the parts it needs.
- The parts components in turn can send messages to their own inventory and order components to update their inventories and to order new parts from suppliers.
- Both the factory and the parts components can send messages to the accounting component to update their budget numbers.
- The business can publish updated catalog items to its sales force.

Using messaging for these tasks allows the various components to interact with one another efficiently, without tying up network or other resources. Figure 31–1 illustrates how this simple example might work.

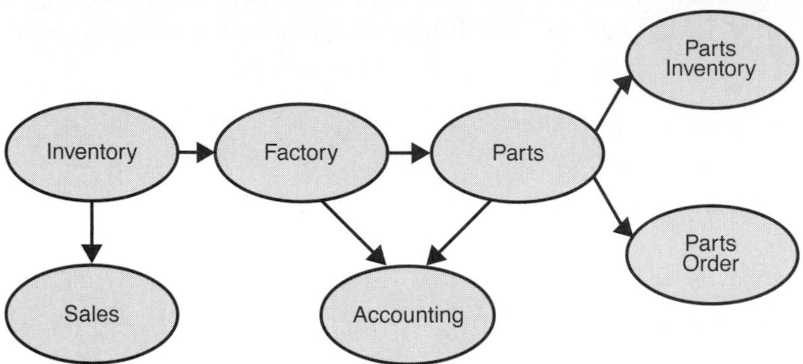

Figure 31–1 Messaging in an Enterprise Application

Manufacturing is only one example of how an enterprise can use the JMS API. Retail applications, financial services applications, health services applications, and many others can make use of messaging.

How Does the JMS API Work with the Java EE Platform?

When the JMS API was introduced in 1998, its most important purpose was to allow Java applications to access existing messaging-oriented middleware (MOM) systems, such as MQSeries from IBM. Since that time, many vendors have adopted and implemented the JMS API, so a JMS product can now provide a complete messaging capability for an enterprise.

Beginning with the 1.3 release of the Java EE platform, the JMS API has been an integral part of the platform, and application developers can use messaging with Java EE components.

The JMS API in the Java EE platform has the following features.

- Application clients, Enterprise JavaBeans (EJB) components, and web components can send or synchronously receive a JMS message. Application clients can in addition receive JMS messages asynchronously. (Applets, however, are not required to support the JMS API.)

- Message-driven beans, which are a kind of enterprise bean, enable the asynchronous consumption of messages. A JMS provider can optionally implement concurrent processing of messages by message-driven beans.
- Message send and receive operations can participate in distributed transactions, which allow JMS operations and database accesses to take place within a single transaction.

The JMS API enhances the Java EE platform by simplifying enterprise development, allowing loosely coupled, reliable, asynchronous interactions among Java EE components and legacy systems capable of messaging. A developer can easily add new behavior to a Java EE application that has existing business events by adding a new message-driven bean to operate on specific business events. The Java EE platform, moreover, enhances the JMS API by providing support for distributed transactions and allowing for the concurrent consumption of messages. For more information, see the Enterprise JavaBeans specification, v3.0.

The JMS provider can be integrated with the application server using the Java EE Connector architecture. You access the JMS provider through a resource adapter. This capability allows vendors to create JMS providers that can be plugged in to multiple application servers, and it allows application servers to support multiple JMS providers. For more information, see the Java EE Connector architecture specification, v1.5.

Basic JMS API Concepts

This section introduces the most basic JMS API concepts, the ones you must know to get started writing simple JMS client applications:

- JMS API architecture
- Messaging domains
- Message consumption

The next section introduces the JMS API programming model. Later sections cover more advanced concepts, including the ones you need to write Java EE applications that use message-driven beans.

JMS API Architecture

A JMS application is composed of the following parts.

- A *JMS provider* is a messaging system that implements the JMS interfaces and provides administrative and control features. An implementation of the Java EE platform includes a JMS provider.
- *JMS clients* are the programs or components, written in the Java programming language, that produce and consume messages. Any Java EE application component can act as a JMS client.
- *Messages* are the objects that communicate information between JMS clients.
- *Administered objects* are preconfigured JMS objects created by an administrator for the use of clients. The two kinds of JMS administered objects are destinations and connection factories, which are described in Administered Objects (page 1060).

Figure 31–2 illustrates the way these parts interact. Administrative tools allow you to bind destinations and connection factories into a JNDI namespace. A JMS client can then use resource injection to access the administered objects in the namespace and then establish a logical connection to the same objects through the JMS provider.

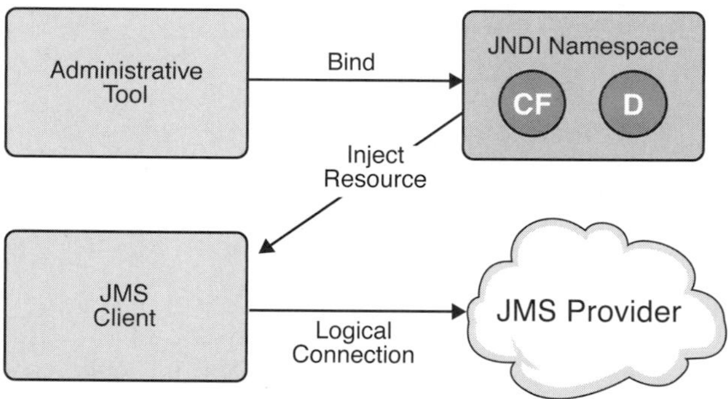

Figure 31–2 JMS API Architecture

Messaging Domains

Before the JMS API existed, most messaging products supported either the *point-to-point* or the *publish/subscribe* approach to messaging. The JMS specification provides a separate domain for each approach and defines compliance for each domain. A stand-alone JMS provider can implement one or both domains. A Java EE provider must implement both domains.

In fact, most implementations of the JMS API support both the point-to-point and the publish/subscribe domains, and some JMS clients combine the use of both domains in a single application. In this way, the JMS API has extended the power and flexibility of messaging products.

The JMS 1.1 specification goes one step further: It provides common interfaces that enable you to use the JMS API in a way that is not specific to either domain. The following subsections describe the two messaging domains and then describe the use of the common interfaces.

Point-to-Point Messaging Domain

A point-to-point (PTP) product or application is built on the concept of message queues, senders, and receivers. Each message is addressed to a specific queue, and receiving clients extract messages from the queues established to hold their messages. Queues retain all messages sent to them until the messages are consumed or until the messages expire.

PTP messaging has the following characteristics and is illustrated in Figure 31–3.

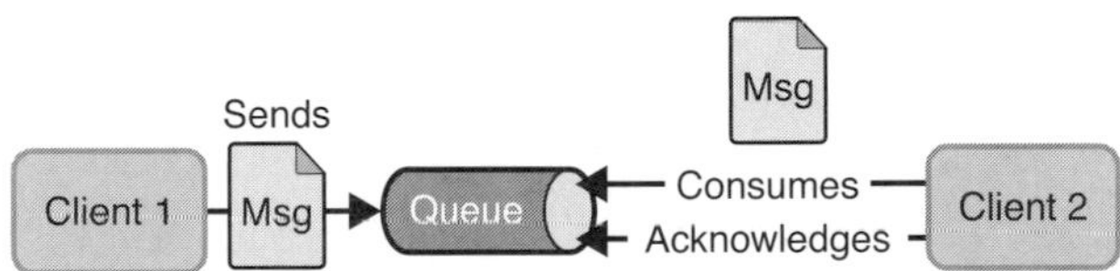

Figure 31–3 Point-to-Point Messaging

- Each message has only one consumer.
- A sender and a receiver of a message have no timing dependencies. The receiver can fetch the message whether or not it was running when the client sent the message.
- The receiver acknowledges the successful processing of a message.

Use PTP messaging when every message you send must be processed successfully by one consumer.

Publish/Subscribe Messaging Domain

In a publish/subscribe (pub/sub) product or application, clients address messages to a *topic*, which functions somewhat like a bulletin board. Publishers and subscribers are generally anonymous and can dynamically publish or subscribe to the content hierarchy. The system takes care of distributing the messages arriving from a topic's multiple publishers to its multiple subscribers. Topics retain messages only as long as it takes to distribute them to current subscribers.

Pub/sub messaging has the following characteristics.

- Each message can have multiple consumers.
- Publishers and subscribers have a timing dependency. A client that subscribes to a topic can consume only messages published after the client has created a subscription, and the subscriber must continue to be active in order for it to consume messages.

The JMS API relaxes this timing dependency to some extent by allowing subscribers to create *durable subscriptions*, which receive messages sent while the subscribers are not active. Durable subscriptions provide the flexibility and reliability of queues but still allow clients to send messages to many recipients. For more information about durable subscriptions, see Creating Durable Subscriptions (page 1106).

Use pub/sub messaging when each message can be processed by zero, one, or many consumers. Figure 31–4 illustrates pub/sub messaging.

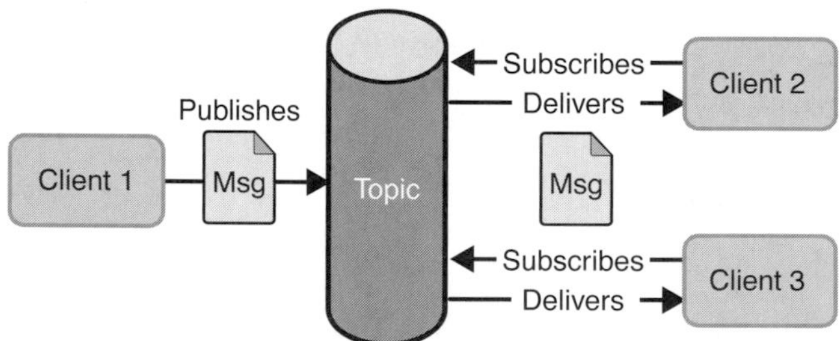

Figure 31–4 Publish/Subscribe Messaging

Programming with the Common Interfaces

Version 1.1 of the JMS API allows you to use the same code to send and receive messages under either the PTP or the pub/sub domain. The destinations that you use remain domain-specific, and the behavior of the application will depend in part on whether you are using a queue or a topic. However, the code itself can be common to both domains, making your applications flexible and reusable. This tutorial describes and illustrates these common interfaces.

Message Consumption

Messaging products are inherently asynchronous: There is no fundamental timing dependency between the production and the consumption of a message. However, the JMS specification uses this term in a more precise sense. Messages can be consumed in either of two ways:

- **Synchronously**: A subscriber or a receiver explicitly fetches the message from the destination by calling the `receive` method. The `receive` method can block until a message arrives or can time out if a message does not arrive within a specified time limit.
- **Asynchronously**: A client can register a *message listener* with a consumer. A message listener is similar to an event listener. Whenever a message arrives at the destination, the JMS provider delivers the message by calling the listener's `onMessage` method, which acts on the contents of the message.

The JMS API Programming Model

The basic building blocks of a JMS application consist of

- Administered objects: connection factories and destinations
- Connections
- Sessions
- Message producers
- Message consumers
- Messages

Figure 31–5 shows how all these objects fit together in a JMS client application.

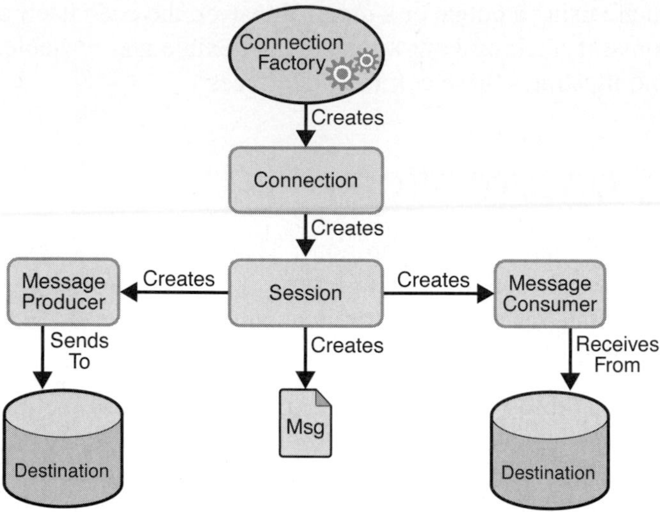

Figure 31–5 The JMS API Programming Model

This section describes all these objects briefly and provides sample commands and code snippets that show how to create and use the objects. The last subsection briefly describes JMS API exception handling.

Examples that show how to combine all these objects in applications appear in later sections. For more details, see the JMS API documentation, which is part of the Java EE API documentation.

Administered Objects

Two parts of a JMS application—destinations and connection factories—are best maintained administratively rather than programmatically. The technology underlying these objects is likely to be very different from one implementation of the JMS API to another. Therefore, the management of these objects belongs with other administrative tasks that vary from provider to provider.

JMS clients access these objects through interfaces that are portable, so a client application can run with little or no change on more than one implementation of the JMS API. Ordinarily, an administrator configures administered objects in a JNDI namespace, and JMS clients then access them by using resource injection.

With Sun Java System Application Server Platform Edition 9, you use the asadmin command or the Admin Console to create JMS administered objects in the form of resources.

Connection Factories

A *connection factory* is the object a client uses to create a connection to a provider. A connection factory encapsulates a set of connection configuration parameters that has been defined by an administrator. Each connection factory is an instance of the ConnectionFactory, QueueConnectionFactory, or TopicConnectionFactory interface. To learn how to create connection factories, see Creating JMS Administered Objects (page 1076).

At the beginning of a JMS client program, you usually inject a connection factory resource into a ConnectionFactory object. For example, the following code fragment specifies a resource whose JNDI name is jms/ConnectionFactory and assigns it to a ConnectionFactory object:

```
@Resource(mappedName="jms/ConnectionFactory")
private static ConnectionFactory connectionFactory;
```

In a Java EE application, JMS administered objects are normally placed in the jms naming subcontext.

Note: The mappedName element of the @Resource annotation is specific to the Application Server.

Destinations

A *destination* is the object a client uses to specify the target of messages it produces and the source of messages it consumes. In the PTP messaging domain, destinations are called queues. In the pub/sub messaging domain, destinations are called topics. A JMS application can use multiple queues or topics (or both). To learn how to create destination resources, see Creating JMS Administered Objects (page 1076).

To create a destination using the Application Server, you create a JMS destination resource that specifies a JNDI name for the destination.

In the Application Server implementation of JMS, each destination resource refers to a physical destination. You can create a physical destination explicitly, but if you do not, the Application Server creates it when it is needed and deletes it when you delete the destination resource.

In addition to injecting a connection factory resource into a client program, you usually inject a destination resource. Unlike connection factories, destinations are specific to one domain or the other. To create an application that allows you to use the same code for both topics and queues, you assign the destination to a `Destination` object.

The following code specifies two resources, a queue and a topic. The resource names are mapped to destinations created in the JNDI namespace.

```
@Resource(mappedName="jms/Queue")
private static Queue queue;

@Resource(mappedName="jms/Topic")
private static Topic topic;
```

With the common interfaces, you can mix or match connection factories and destinations. That is, in addition to using the `ConnectionFactory` interface, you can inject a `QueueConnectionFactory` resource and use it with a `Topic`, and you can inject a `TopicConnectionFactory` resource and use it with a `Queue`. The behavior of the application will depend on the kind of destination you use and not on the kind of connection factory you use.

Connections

A *connection* encapsulates a virtual connection with a JMS provider. A connection could represent an open TCP/IP socket between a client and a provider service daemon. You use a connection to create one or more sessions.

Connections implement the `Connection` interface. When you have a `ConnectionFactory` object, you can use it to create a `Connection`:

```
Connection connection = connectionFactory.createConnection();
```

Before an application completes, you must close any connections that you have created. Failure to close a connection can cause resources not to be released by the JMS provider. Closing a connection also closes its sessions and their message producers and message consumers.

```
connection.close();
```

Before your application can consume messages, you must call the connection's `start` method; for details, see Message Consumers (page 1064). If you want to stop message delivery temporarily without closing the connection, you call the `stop` method.

Sessions

A *session* is a single-threaded context for producing and consuming messages. You use sessions to create the following:

- Message producers
- Message consumers
- Messages
- Queue browsers
- Temporary queues and topics (see Creating Temporary Destinations, page 1105)

Sessions serialize the execution of message listeners; for details, see Message Listeners (page 1065).

A session provides a transactional context with which to group a set of sends and receives into an atomic unit of work. For details, see Using JMS API Local Transactions (page 1111).

Sessions implement the `Session` interface. After you create a `Connection` object, you use it to create a `Session`:

```
Session session = connection.createSession(false,
  Session.AUTO_ACKNOWLEDGE);
```

The first argument means that the session is not transacted; the second means that the session automatically acknowledges messages when they have been received successfully. (For more information, see Controlling Message Acknowledgment, page 1099.)

To create a transacted session, use the following code:

```
Session session = connection.createSession(true, 0);
```

Here, the first argument means that the session is transacted; the second indicates that message acknowledgment is not specified for transacted sessions. For more information on transactions, see Using JMS API Local Transactions (page 1111). For information about the way JMS transactions work in Java EE applications, see Using the JMS API in a Java EE Application (page 1119).

Message Producers

A *message producer* is an object that is created by a session and used for sending messages to a destination. It implements the `MessageProducer` interface.

You use a `Session` to create a `MessageProducer` for a destination. The following examples show that you can create a producer for a `Destination` object, a `Queue` object, or a `Topic` object:

```
MessageProducer producer = session.createProducer(dest);

MessageProducer producer = session.createProducer(queue);

MessageProducer producer = session.createProducer(topic);
```

You can create an unidentified producer by specifying `null` as the argument to `createProducer`. With an unidentified producer, you do not specify a destination until you send a message.

After you have created a message producer, you can use it to send messages by using the `send` method:

```
producer.send(message);
```

You must first create the messages; see Messages (page 1067).

If you created an unidentified producer, use an overloaded `send` method that specifies the destination as the first parameter. For example:

```
MessageProducer anon_prod = session.createProducer(null);

anon_prod.send(dest, message);
```

Message Consumers

A *message consumer* is an object that is created by a session and used for receiving messages sent to a destination. It implements the `MessageConsumer` interface.

A message consumer allows a JMS client to register interest in a destination with a JMS provider. The JMS provider manages the delivery of messages from a destination to the registered consumers of the destination.

For example, you could use a `Session` to create a `MessageConsumer` for a `Destination` object, a `Queue` object, or a `Topic` object:

```
MessageConsumer consumer = session.createConsumer(dest);

MessageConsumer consumer = session.createConsumer(queue);

MessageConsumer consumer = session.createConsumer(topic);
```

You use the `Session.createDurableSubscriber` method to create a durable topic subscriber. This method is valid only if you are using a topic. For details, see Creating Durable Subscriptions (page 1106).

After you have created a message consumer, it becomes active, and you can use it to receive messages. You can use the `close` method for a `MessageConsumer` to make the message consumer inactive. Message delivery does not begin until you start the connection you created by calling its `start` method. (Remember always to call the `start` method; forgetting to start the connection is one of the most common JMS programming errors.)

You use the `receive` method to consume a message synchronously. You can use this method at any time after you call the `start` method:

```
connection.start();
Message m = consumer.receive();

connection.start();
Message m = consumer.receive(1000); // time out after a second
```

To consume a message asynchronously, you use a message listener, described in the next section.

Message Listeners

A *message listener* is an object that acts as an asynchronous event handler for messages. This object implements the `MessageListener` interface, which contains one method, `onMessage`. In the `onMessage` method, you define the actions to be taken when a message arrives.

You register the message listener with a specific `MessageConsumer` by using the `setMessageListener` method. For example, if you define a class named `Listener` that implements the `MessageListener` interface, you can register the message listener as follows:

```
Listener myListener = new Listener();
consumer.setMessageListener(myListener);
```

After you register the message listener, you call the `start` method on the `Connection` to begin message delivery. (If you call `start` before you register the message listener, you are likely to miss messages.)

When message delivery begins, the JMS provider automatically calls the message listener's `onMessage` method whenever a message is delivered. The `onMessage` method takes one argument of type `Message`, which your implementation of the method can cast to any of the other message types (see Message Bodies, page 1069).

A message listener is not specific to a particular destination type. The same listener can obtain messages from either a queue or a topic, depending on the type of destination for which the message consumer was created. A message listener does, however, usually expect a specific message type and format.

Your `onMessage` method should handle all exceptions. It must not throw checked exceptions, and throwing a `RuntimeException` is considered a programming error.

The session used to create the message consumer serializes the execution of all message listeners registered with the session. At any time, only one of the session's message listeners is running.

In the Java EE platform, a message-driven bean is a special kind of message listener. For details, see Using Message-Driven Beans (page 1121).

Message Selectors

If your messaging application needs to filter the messages it receives, you can use a JMS API message selector, which allows a message consumer to specify the messages it is interested in. Message selectors assign the work of filtering messages to the JMS provider rather than to the application. For an example of an application that uses a message selector, see A Java EE Application That Uses the JMS API with a Session Bean (page 1130).

A message selector is a `String` that contains an expression. The syntax of the expression is based on a subset of the SQL92 conditional expression syntax. The message selector in the example selects any message that has a `NewsType` property that is set to the value `'Sports'` or `'Opinion'`:

```
NewsType = 'Sports' OR NewsType = 'Opinion'
```

The `createConsumer`, `createDurableSubscriber` methods allow you to specify a message selector as an argument when you create a message consumer.

The message consumer then receives only messages whose headers and properties match the selector. (See Message Headers, page 1067, and Message Properties, page 1068.) A message selector cannot select messages on the basis of the content of the message body.

Messages

The ultimate purpose of a JMS application is to produce and to consume messages that can then be used by other software applications. JMS messages have a basic format that is simple but highly flexible, allowing you to create messages that match formats used by non-JMS applications on heterogeneous platforms.

A JMS message has three parts: a header, properties, and a body. Only the header is required. The following sections describe these parts:

- Message headers
- Message properties (optional)
- Message bodies (optional)

For complete documentation of message headers, properties, and bodies, see the documentation of the `Message` interface in the API documentation.

Message Headers

A JMS message header contains a number of predefined fields that contain values that both clients and providers use to identify and to route messages. Table 31–1 lists the JMS message header fields and indicates how their values are set. For example, every message has a unique identifier, which is represented in the header field `JMSMessageID`. The value of another header field, `JMSDestination`, represents the queue or the topic to which the message is sent. Other fields include a timestamp and a priority level.

Each header field has associated setter and getter methods, which are documented in the description of the `Message` interface. Some header fields are intended to be set by a client, but many are set automatically by the `send` or the `publish` method, which overrides any client-set values.

Table 31–1 How JMS Message Header Field Values Are Set

Header Field	Set By
`JMSDestination`	`send` or `publish` method
`JMSDeliveryMode`	`send` or `publish` method
`JMSExpiration`	`send` or `publish` method
`JMSPriority`	`send` or `publish` method
`JMSMessageID`	`send` or `publish` method
`JMSTimestamp`	`send` or `publish` method
`JMSCorrelationID`	Client
`JMSReplyTo`	Client
`JMSType`	Client
`JMSRedelivered`	JMS provider

Message Properties

You can create and set properties for messages if you need values in addition to those provided by the header fields. You can use properties to provide compatibility with other messaging systems, or you can use them to create message selectors (see Message Selectors, page 1066). For an example of setting a property to be used as a message selector, see A Java EE Application That Uses the JMS API with a Session Bean (page 1130).

The JMS API provides some predefined property names that a provider can support. The use either of these predefined properties or of user-defined properties is optional.

Message Bodies

The JMS API defines five message body formats, also called message types, which allow you to send and to receive data in many different forms and provide compatibility with existing messaging formats. Table 31–2 describes these message types.

Table 31–2 JMS Message Types

Message Type	Body Contains
`TextMessage`	A `java.lang.String` object (for example, the contents of an XML file).
`MapMessage`	A set of name-value pairs, with names as `String` objects and values as primitive types in the Java programming language. The entries can be accessed sequentially by enumerator or randomly by name. The order of the entries is undefined.
`BytesMessage`	A stream of uninterpreted bytes. This message type is for literally encoding a body to match an existing message format.
`StreamMessage`	A stream of primitive values in the Java programming language, filled and read sequentially.
`ObjectMessage`	A `Serializable` object in the Java programming language.
`Message`	Nothing. Composed of header fields and properties only. This message type is useful when a message body is not required.

The JMS API provides methods for creating messages of each type and for filling in their contents. For example, to create and send a `TextMessage`, you might use the following statements:

```
TextMessage message = session.createTextMessage();
message.setText(msg_text);     // msg_text is a String
producer.send(message);
```

At the consuming end, a message arrives as a generic `Message` object and must be cast to the appropriate message type. You can use one or more getter methods to extract the message contents. The following code fragment uses the getText method:

```
Message m = consumer.receive();
if (m instanceof TextMessage) {
  TextMessage message = (TextMessage) m;
  System.out.println("Reading message: " + message.getText());
} else {
  // Handle error
}
```

Queue Browsers

You can create a QueueBrowser object to inspect the messages in a queue. Messages sent to a queue remain in the queue until the message consumer for that queue consumes them. Therefore, the JMS API provides an object that allows you to browse the messages in the queue and display the header values for each message. To create a QueueBrowser object, use the Session.createBrowser method. For example:

```
QueueBrowser browser = session.createBrowser(queue);
```

See A Simple Example of Browsing Messages in a Queue (page 1087) for an example of the use of a QueueBrowser object.

The createBrowser method allows you to specify a message selector as a second argument when you create a QueueBrowser. For information on message selectors, see Message Selectors (page 1066).

The JMS API provides no mechanism for browsing a topic. Messages usually disappear from a topic as soon as they appear: if there are no message consumers to consume them, the JMS provider removes them. Although durable subscriptions allow messages to remain on a topic while the message consumer is not active, no facility exists for examining them.

Exception Handling

The root class for exceptions thrown by JMS API methods is JMSException. Catching JMSException provides a generic way of handling all exceptions related to the JMS API. The `JMSException` class includes the following subclasses, which are described in the API documentation:

- `IllegalStateException`
- `InvalidClientIDException`
- `InvalidDestinationException`
- `InvalidSelectorException`
- `JMSSecurityException`
- `MessageEOFException`
- `MessageFormatException`
- `MessageNotReadableException`
- `MessageNotWriteableException`
- `ResourceAllocationException`
- `TransactionInProgressException`
- `TransactionRolledBackException`

All the examples in the tutorial catch and handle `JMSException` when it is appropriate to do so.

Writing Simple JMS Client Applications

This section shows how to create, package, and run simple JMS client programs packaged as stand-alone application clients. These clients access a Java EE server. The clients demonstrate the basic tasks that a JMS application must perform:

- Creating a connection and a session
- Creating message producers and consumers
- Sending and receiving messages

In a Java EE application, some of these tasks are performed, in whole or in part, by the container. If you learn about these tasks, you will have a good basis for understanding how a JMS application works on the Java EE platform.

This section covers the following topics:

- An example that uses synchronous message receives
- An example that uses a message listener

- An example that browses messages on a queue
- Running JMS clients on multiple systems

Each example uses two programs: one that sends messages and one that receives them. You can run the programs in NetBeans 5.5 or in two terminal windows.

When you write a JMS application to run in a Java EE application, you use many of the same methods in much the same sequence as you do for a stand-alone application client. However, there are some significant differences. Using the JMS API in a Java EE Application (page 1119) describes these differences, and Chapter 32 provides examples that illustrate them.

The examples for this section are in the following directory:

```
<INSTALL>/javaeetutorial5/examples/jms/simple/
```

The examples are in the following four subdirectories:

```
producer
synchconsumer
asynchconsumer
messagebrowser
```

A Simple Example of Synchronous Message Receives

This section describes the sending and receiving programs in an example that uses the `receive` method to consume messages synchronously. This section then explains how to compile, package, and run the programs using the Application Server.

The following sections describe the steps in creating and running the example:

- Writing the client programs
- Starting the JMS provider
- Creating JMS administered objects
- Compiling and packaging the clients
- Running the clients

Writing the Client Programs

The sending program, `producer/src/java/Producer.java`, performs the following steps:

1. Injects resources for a connection factory, queue, and topic:

```
@Resource(mappedName="jms/ConnectionFactory")
private static ConnectionFactory connectionFactory;

@Resource(mappedName="jms/Queue")
private static Queue queue;

@Resource(mappedName="jms/Topic")
private static Topic topic;
```

2. Retrieves and verifies command-line arguments that specify the destination type and the number of arguments:

```
final int NUM_MSGS;
String destType = args[0];
System.out.println("Destination type is " + destType);
if ( ! ( destType.equals("queue") ||
      destType.equals("topic") ) ) {
    System.err.println("Argument must be \"queue\" or " +
      "\"topic\"");
   System.exit(1);
}
if (args.length == 2){
   NUM_MSGS = (new Integer(args[1])).intValue();
} else {
   NUM_MSGS = 1;
}
```

3. Assigns either the queue or topic to a destination object, based on the specified destination type:

```
Destination dest = null;
try {
   if (destType.equals("queue")) {
      dest = (Destination) queue;
   } else {
      dest = (Destination) topic;
   }
} catch (Exception e) {
   System.err.println("Error setting destination: "+
      e.toString());
   e.printStackTrace();
   System.exit(1);
}
```

4. Creates a `Connection` and a `Session`:

```
Connection connection =
   connectionFactory.createConnection();
Session session = connection.createSession(false,
   Session.AUTO_ACKNOWLEDGE);
```

5. Creates a `MessageProducer` and a `TextMessage`:

```
MessageProducer producer = session.createProducer(dest);
TextMessage message = session.createTextMessage();
```

6. Sends one or more messages to the destination:

```
for (int i = 0; i < NUM_MSGS; i++) {
   message.setText("This is message " + (i + 1));
   System.out.println("Sending message: " +
      message.getText());
   producer.send(message);
}
```

7. Sends an empty control message to indicate the end of the message stream:

```
producer.send(session.createMessage());
```

   Sending an empty message of no specified type is a convenient way to indicate to the consumer that the final message has arrived.

8. Closes the connection in a `finally` block, automatically closing the session and `MessageProducer`:

```
} finally {
   if (connection != null) {
      try {
         connection.close();
      } catch (JMSException e) {
      }
   }
}
```

The receiving program, `synchconsumer/src/java/SynchConsumer.java`, performs the following steps:

1. Injects resources for a connection factory, queue, and topic.
2. Assigns either the queue or topic to a destination object, based on the specified destination type.
3. Creates a `Connection` and a `Session`.
4. Creates a `MessageConsumer`:

```
consumer = session.createConsumer(dest);
```

5. Starts the connection, causing message delivery to begin:

   ```
   connection.start();
   ```

6. Receives the messages sent to the destination until the end-of-message-stream control message is received:

   ```
   while (true) {
      Message m = consumer.receive(1);
      if (m != null) {
         if (m instanceof TextMessage) {
            message = (TextMessage) m;
            System.out.println("Reading message: " +
               message.getText());
         } else {
            break;
         }
      }
   }
   ```

   Because the control message is not a `TextMessage`, the receiving program terminates the `while` loop and stops receiving messages after the control message arrives.

7. Closes the connection in a `finally` block, automatically closing the session and `MessageConsumer`.

The `receive` method can be used in several ways to perform a synchronous receive. If you specify no arguments or an argument of `0`, the method blocks indefinitely until a message arrives:

```
Message m = consumer.receive();

Message m = consumer.receive(0);
```

For a simple client program, this may not matter. But if you do not want your program to consume system resources unnecessarily, use a timed synchronous receive. Do one of the following:

- Call the `receive` method with a timeout argument greater than `0`:

  ```
  Message m = consumer.receive(1); // 1 millisecond
  ```

- Call the `receiveNoWait` method, which receives a message only if one is available:

  ```
  Message m = consumer.receiveNoWait();
  ```

The `SynchConsumer` program uses an indefinite `while` loop to receive messages, calling `receive` with a timeout argument. Calling `receiveNoWait` would have the same effect.

Starting the JMS Provider

When you use the Application Server, your JMS provider is the Application Server. Start the server as described in Starting and Stopping the Application Server (page 27).

Creating JMS Administered Objects

Creating the JMS administered objects for this section involves the following:

- Creating a connection factory
- Creating two destination resources

If you built and ran the `SimpleMessage` example in Chapter 23 and did not delete the resources afterward, you need to create only the topic resource.

You can create these objects using the Ant tool. To create all the resources, do the following:

1. In a terminal window, go to the `producer` directory:

   ```
   cd producer
   ```

2. To create all the resources, type the following command:

   ```
   ant create-resources
   ```

   To create only the topic resource, type the following command:

   ```
   ant create-topic
   ```

These Ant targets use the `asadmin create-jms-resource` command to create the connection factory and the destination resources.

To verify that the resources have been created, use the following command:

```
asadmin list-jms-resources
```

The output looks like this:

```
jms/Queue
jms/Topic
jms/ConnectionFactory
Command list-jms-resources executed successfully.
```

Compiling and Packaging the Clients

The simplest way to run these examples using the Application Server is to package each one in an application client JAR file. The application client JAR file requires a manifest file, located in the `src/conf` directory for each example, along with the `.class` file.

The `build.xml` file for each example contains Ant targets that compile and package the example. The targets place the `.class` file for the example in the `build/jar` directory. Then the targets use the `jar` command to package the class file and the manifest file in an application client JAR file.

To compile and package the `Producer` and `SynchConsumer` examples using NetBeans 5.5, follow these steps:

1. In NetBeans 5.5, choose Open Project from the File menu.
2. In the Open Project dialog, navigate to *<INSTALL>*/javaeetutorial5/examples/jms/simple/.
3. Select the `producer` folder.
4. Select the Open as Main Project checkbox.
5. Click Open Project Folder.
6. Right-click the project and choose Build Project.
7. In NetBeans 5.5, choose Open Project from the File menu.
8. In the Open Project dialog, navigate to *<INSTALL>*/javaeetutorial5/examples/jms/simple/.
9. Select the `synchconsumer` folder.
10. Select the Open as Main Project checkbox.
11. Click Open Project Folder.
12. Right-click the project and choose Build Project.

To compile and package the `Producer` and `SynchConsumer` examples using Ant, follow these steps:

1. In a terminal window, go to the `producer` directory:

   ```
   cd producer
   ```

2. Type the following command:

   ```
   ant
   ```

3. In a terminal window, go to the `synchconsumer` directory:

   ```
   cd ../synchconsumer
   ```

4. Type the following command:

   ```
   ant
   ```

The targets place the application client JAR file in the `dist` directory for each example.

Running the Clients

To run the sample programs using NetBeans 5.5, follow these steps.

1. Run the `Producer` example:
   a. Right-click the `producer` project and choose Properties.
   b. Select Run from the Categories tree.
   c. In the Arguments field, type the following:

      ```
      queue 3
      ```

   d. Click OK.
   e. Right-click the project and choose Run Project.

   The output of the program looks like this:

   ```
   Destination type is queue
   Sending message: This is message 1
   Sending message: This is message 2
   Sending message: This is message 3
   ```

   The messages are now in the queue, waiting to be received.

2. Now run the `SynchConsumer` example:
   a. Right-click the `synchconsumer` project and choose Properties.
   b. Select Run from the Categories tree.

c. In the Arguments field, type the following:

```
queue
```

d. Click OK.

e. Right-click the project and choose Run Project.

The output of the program looks like this:

```
Destination type is queue
Reading message: This is message 1
Reading message: This is message 2
Reading message: This is message 3
```

3. Now try running the programs in the opposite order. Right-click the `synchconsumer` project and choose Run Project.

   The Output pane displays the destination type and then appears to hang, waiting for messages.

4. Right-click the `producer` project and choose Run Project.

   The Output pane shows the output of both programs, in two different tabs.

5. Now run the `Producer` example using a topic instead of a queue.

   a. Right-click the `producer` project and choose Properties.

   b. Select Run from the Categories tree.

   c. In the Arguments field, type the following:

   ```
   topic 3
   ```

   d. Click OK.

   e. Right-click the project and choose Run Project.

   The output of the program looks like this:

   ```
   Destination type is topic
   Sending message: This is message 1
   Sending message: This is message 2
   Sending message: This is message 3
   ```

6. Now run the `SynchConsumer` example using the topic.

   a. Right-click the `synchconsumer` project and choose Properties.

   b. Select Run from the Categories tree.

   c. In the Arguments field, type the following:

   ```
   topic
   ```

   d. Click OK.

   e. Right-click the project and choose Run Project.

The result, however, is different. Because you are using a topic, messages that were sent before you started the consumer cannot be received. (See Publish/Subscribe Messaging Domain, page 1058, for details.) Instead of receiving the messages, the program appears to hang.

7. Run the Producer example again. Right-click the producer project and choose Run Project.

   Now the SynchConsumer example receives the messages:

```
Destination type is topic
Reading message: This is message 1
Reading message: This is message 2
Reading message: This is message 3
```

You can also run the sample programs using the appclient command. Each of the programs takes one or more command-line arguments: a destination type and, for Producer, a number of messages.

To run the clients using the appclient command, follow these steps:

1. In a terminal window, go to the producer/dist directory:

```
cd ../producer/dist
```

2. Run the Producer program, sending three producer to the queue:

```
appclient -client producer.jar queue 3
```

   The output of the program looks like this:

```
Destination type is queue
Sending message: This is message 1
Sending message: This is message 2
Sending message: This is message 3
```

   The messages are now in the queue, waiting to be received.

3. In the same window, go to the synchconsumer/dist directory:

```
cd ../../synchconsumer/dist
```

4. Run the SynchConsumer program, specifying the queue:

```
appclient -client synchconsumer.jar queue
```

   The output of the program looks like this:

```
Destination type is queue
Reading message: This is message 1
Reading message: This is message 2
Reading message: This is message 3
```

5. Now try running the programs in the opposite order. Run the `SynchConsumer` program. It displays the destination type and then appears to hang, waiting for messages.

   ```
   appclient -client synchconsumer.jar queue
   ```

6. In a different terminal window, run the `Producer` program.

   ```
   cd  <INSTALL>/javaeetutorial5/examples/jms/simple/producer/
   dist
   appclient -client producer.jar queue 3
   ```

   When the messages have been sent, the `SynchConsumer` program receives them and exits.

7. Now run the `Producer` program using a topic instead of a queue:

   ```
   appclient -client producer.jar topic 3
   ```

   The output of the program looks like this:

   ```
   Destination type is topic
   Sending message: This is message 1
   Sending message: This is message 2
   Sending message: This is message 3
   ```

8. Now run the `SynchConsumer` program using the topic:

   ```
   appclient -client synchconsumer.jar topic
   ```

   The result, however, is different. Because you are using a topic, messages that were sent before you started the consumer cannot be received. (See Publish/Subscribe Messaging Domain, page 1058, for details.) Instead of receiving the messages, the program appears to hang.

9. Run the `Producer` program again. Now the `SynchConsumer` program receives the messages:

   ```
   Destination type is topic
   Reading message: This is message 1
   Reading message: This is message 2
   Reading message: This is message 3
   ```

Because the examples use the common interfaces, you can run them using either a queue or a topic.

A Simple Example of Asynchronous Message Consumption

This section describes the receiving programs in an example that uses a message listener to consume messages asynchronously. This section then explains how to compile and run the programs using the Application Server.

The following sections describe the steps in creating and running the example:

- Writing the client programs
- Compiling and packaging the `AsynchConsumer` client
- Running the clients

Writing the Client Programs

The sending program is `producer/src/javaProducer.java`, the same program used in the example in A Simple Example of Synchronous Message Receives (page 1072).

An asynchronous consumer normally runs indefinitely. This one runs until the user types the letter `q` or `Q` to stop the program.

The receiving program, `asynchconsumer/src/java/AsynchConsumer.java`, performs the following steps:

1. Injects resources for a connection factory, queue, and topic.
2. Assigns either the queue or topic to a destination object, based on the specified destination type.
3. Creates a `Connection` and a `Session`.
4. Creates a `MessageConsumer`.
5. Creates an instance of the `TextListener` class and registers it as the message listener for the `MessageConsumer`:

   ```
   listener = new TextListener();
   consumer.setMessageListener(listener);
   ```

6. Starts the connection, causing message delivery to begin.
7. Listens for the messages published to the destination, stopping when the user types the character `q` or `Q`:

   ```
   System.out.println("To end program, type Q or q, " +
     "then <return>");
   inputStreamReader = new InputStreamReader(System.in);
   ```

```
while (!((answer == 'q') || (answer == 'Q'))) {
   try {
      answer = (char) inputStreamReader.read();
   } catch (IOException e) {
      System.out.println("I/O exception: " +
         e.toString());
   }
}
```

8. Closes the connection, which automatically closes the session and `MessageConsumer`.

The message listener, `asynchconsumer/src/java/TextListener.java`, follows these steps:

1. When a message arrives, the `onMessage` method is called automatically.
2. The `onMessage` method converts the incoming message to a `TextMessage` and displays its content. If the message is not a text message, it reports this fact:

```
public void onMessage(Message message) {
   TextMessage msg = null;

   try {
      if (message instanceof TextMessage) {
         msg = (TextMessage) message;
         System.out.println("Reading message: " +
            msg.getText());
      } else {
         System.out.println("Message is not a " +
            "TextMessage");
      }
   } catch (JMSException e) {
      System.out.println("JMSException in onMessage(): " +
         e.toString());
   } catch (Throwable t) {
      System.out.println("Exception in onMessage():" +
         t.getMessage());
   }
}
```

You will use the connection factory and destinations you created in Creating JMS Administered Objects (page 1076).

Compiling and Packaging the AsynchConsumer Client

To compile and package the `AsynchConsumer` example using NetBeans 5.5, follow these steps:

1. In NetBeans 5.5, choose Open Project from the File menu.
2. In the Open Project dialog, navigate to `<INSTALL>/javaeetutorial5/examples/jms/simple/`.
3. Select the `asynchconsumer` folder.
4. Select the Open as Main Project checkbox.
5. Click Open Project Folder.
6. Right-click the project and choose Build Project.

To compile and package the `AsynchConsumer` example using Ant, follow these steps:

1. In a terminal window, go to the `asynchconsumer` directory:

   ```
   cd ../../asynchconsumer
   ```

2. Type the following command:

   ```
   ant
   ```

The targets package both the main class and the message listener class in the JAR file and place the file in the `dist` directory for the example.

Running the Clients

To run the programs using NetBeans 5.5, follow these steps.

1. Run the `AsynchConsumer` example:
   a. Right-click the `asynchconsumer` project and choose Properties.
   b. Select Run from the Categories tree.
   c. In the Arguments field, type the following:

      ```
      topic
      ```

   d. Click OK.
   e. Right-click the project and choose Run Project.

The program displays the following lines and appears to hang:

```
Destination type is topic
To end program, type Q or q, then <return>
```

2. Now run the `Producer` example:
   a. Right-click the `producer` project and choose Properties.
   b. Select Run from the Categories tree.
   c. In the Arguments field, type the following:
      ```
      topic 3
      ```
   d. Click OK.
   e. Right-click the project and choose Run Project.

   The output of the program looks like this:

   ```
   Destination type is topic
   Sending message: This is message 1
   Sending message: This is message 2
   Sending message: This is message 3
   ```

   In the other window, the `AsynchConsumer` program displays the following:

   ```
   Destination type is topic
   To end program, type Q or q, then <return>
   Reading message: This is message 1
   Reading message: This is message 2
   Reading message: This is message 3
   Message is not a TextMessage
   ```

   The last line appears because the program has received the non-text control message sent by the `Producer` program.

3. Type `Q` or `q` in the Input field and press Return to stop the program.
4. Now run the programs using a queue. In this case, as with the synchronous example, you can run the `Producer` program first, because there is no timing dependency between the sender and receiver.
   a. Right-click the `producer` project and choose Properties.
   b. Select Run from the Categories tree.
   c. In the Arguments field, type the following:
      ```
      queue 3
      ```
   d. Click OK.
   e. Right-click the project and choose Run Project.

The output of the program looks like this:

```
Destination type is queue
Sending message: This is message 1
Sending message: This is message 2
Sending message: This is message 3
```

5. Run the `AsynchConsumer` program.
   a. Right-click the `asynchconsumer` project and choose Properties.
   b. Select Run from the Categories tree.
   c. In the Arguments field, type the following:

      ```
      queue
      ```

   d. Click OK.
   e. Right-click the project and choose Run Project.

   The output of the program looks like this:

   ```
   Destination type is queue
   To end program, type Q or q, then <return>
   Reading message: This is message 1
   Reading message: This is message 2
   Reading message: This is message 3
   Message is not a TextMessage
   ```

6. Type `Q` or `q` in the Input field and press Return to stop the program.

To run the clients using the `appclient` command, follow these steps:

1. Run the `AsynchConsumer` program, specifying the `topic` destination type.

   ```
   cd dist
   appclient -client asynchconsumer.jar topic
   ```

   The program displays the following lines and appears to hang:

   ```
   Destination type is topic
   To end program, type Q or q, then <return>
   ```

2. In the terminal window where you ran the `Producer` program previously, run the program again, sending three messages. The command looks like this:

   ```
   appclient -client producer.jar topic 3
   ```

   The output of the program looks like this:

   ```
   Destination type is topic
   Sending message: This is message 1
   Sending message: This is message 2
   Sending message: This is message 3
   ```

In the other window, the `AsynchConsumer` program displays the following:

```
Destination type is topic
To end program, type Q or q, then <return>
Reading message: This is message 1
Reading message: This is message 2
Reading message: This is message 3
Message is not a TextMessage
```

The last line appears because the program has received the non-text control message sent by the `Producer` program.

3. Type `Q` or `q` and press Return to stop the program.
4. Now run the programs using a queue. In this case, as with the synchronous example, you can run the `Producer` program first, because there is no timing dependency between the sender and receiver:

```
appclient -client producer.jar queue 3
```

The output of the program looks like this:

```
Destination type is queue
Sending message: This is message 1
Sending message: This is message 2
Sending message: This is message 3
```

5. Run the `AsynchConsumer` program:

```
appclient -client asynchconsumer.jar queue
```

The output of the program looks like this:

```
Destination type is queue
To end program, type Q or q, then <return>
Reading message: This is message 1
Reading message: This is message 2
Reading message: This is message 3
Message is not a TextMessage
```

6. Type `Q` or `q` to stop the program.

A Simple Example of Browsing Messages in a Queue

This section describes an example that creates a `QueueBrowser` object to examine messages on a queue, as described in Queue Browsers (page 1070). This section then explains how to compile, package, and run the example using the Application Server.

The following sections describe the steps in creating and running the example:

- Writing the client program
- Compiling and packaging the `MessageBrowser` client
- Running the clients

Writing the Client Program

To create a `QueueBrowser` for a queue, you call the `Session.createBrowser` method with the queue as the argument. You obtain the messages in the queue as an `Enumeration` object. You can then iterate through the `Enumeration` object and display the contents of each message.

The `messagebrowser/src/java/MessageBrowser.java` program performs the following steps:

1. Injects resources for a connection factory and a queue.
2. Creates a `Connection` and a `Session`.
3. Creates a `QueueBrowser`:

   ```
   QueueBrowser browser = session.createBrowser(queue);
   ```

4. Retrieves the `Enumeration` that contains the messages:

   ```
   Enumeration msgs = browser.getEnumeration();
   ```

5. Verifies that the `Enumeration` contains messages, then displays the contents of the messages:

   ```
   if ( !msgs.hasMoreElements() ) {
      System.out.println("No messages in queue");
   } else {
      while (msgs.hasMoreElements()) {
         Message tempMsg = (Message)msgs.nextElement();
         System.out.println("Message: " + tempMsg);
      }
   }
   ```

6. Closes the connection, which automatically closes the session and `QueueBrowser`.

The format in which the message contents appear is implementation-specific. In the Application Server, the message format looks like this (the message ID is all on one line):

```
Message contents:
Text:   This is message 3
Class:                    com.sun.messaging.jmq.jmsclient.TextMessageImpl
getJMSMessageID():         ID:14-129.148.71.199(f9:86:a2:d5:46:9b)-40814-
1129061034355
getJMSTimestamp():         1129061034355
getJMSCorrelationID():     null
JMSReplyTo:                null
JMSDestination:            PhysicalQueue
getJMSDeliveryMode():      PERSISTENT
getJMSRedelivered():       false
getJMSType():              null
getJMSExpiration():        0
getJMSPriority():          4
Properties:                null
```

You will use the connection factory and queue you created in Creating JMS Administered Objects (page 1076).

Compiling and Packaging the MessageBrowser Client

To compile and package the `MessageBrowser` example using NetBeans 5.5, follow these steps:

1. In NetBeans 5.5, choose Open Project from the File menu.
2. In the Open Project dialog, navigate to `<INSTALL>/javaeetutorial5/examples/jms/simple/`.
3. Select the `messagebrowser` folder.
4. Select the Open as Main Project checkbox.
5. Click Open Project Folder.
6. Right-click the project and choose Build Project.

To compile and package the `MessageBrowser` example using Ant, follow these steps:

1. In a terminal window, go to the `messagebrowser` directory. If you are currently in the `asynchconsumer/dist` directory, you need to go up two levels:

   ```
   cd ../../messagebrowser
   ```

2. Type the following command:

   ```
   ant
   ```

The targets place the application client JAR file in the `dist` directory for the example.

You also need the `Producer` example to send the message to the queue, and one of the consumer programs to consume the messages after you inspect them. If you did not do so already, package these examples.

Running the Clients

To run the programs using NetBeans 5.5, follow these steps.

1. Run the `Producer` program, sending one message to the queue:
   a. Right-click the `producer` project and choose Properties.
   b. Select Run from the Categories tree.
   c. In the Arguments field, type the following:

      ```
      queue
      ```

   d. Click OK.
   e. Right-click the project and choose Run Project.

   The output of the program looks like this:

   ```
   Destination type is queue
   Sending message: This is message 1
   ```

2. Run the `MessageBrowser` program. Right-click the `messagebrowser` project and choose Run Project.

   The output of the program looks like this:

   ```
   Message:
   Text:   This is message 1
   Class:              com.sun.messaging.jmq.jmsclient.TextMessageImpl
   getJMSMessageID():    ID:12-129.148.71.199(8c:34:4a:1a:1b:b8)-40883-
   1129062957611
   getJMSTimestamp():       1129062957611
   getJMSCorrelationID():   null
   JMSReplyTo:              null
   JMSDestination:          PhysicalQueue
   getJMSDeliveryMode():    PERSISTENT
   getJMSRedelivered():     false
   getJMSType():            null
   getJMSExpiration():      0
   getJMSPriority():        4
   ```

```
Properties:              null
Message:
Class:                   com.sun.messaging.jmq.jmsclient.MessageImpl
getJMSMessageID():          ID:13-129.148.71.199(8c:34:4a:1a:1b:b8)-
40883-1129062957616
getJMSTimestamp():       1129062957616
getJMSCorrelationID():   null
JMSReplyTo:              null
JMSDestination:          PhysicalQueue
getJMSDeliveryMode():    PERSISTENT
getJMSRedelivered():     false
getJMSType():            null
getJMSExpiration():      0
getJMSPriority():        4
Properties:              null
```

The first message is the `TextMessage`, and the second is the non-text control message.

3. Run the `SynchConsumer` program to consume the messages.
   a. Right-click the `synchconsumer` project and choose Properties.
   b. Select Run from the Categories tree.
   c. In the Arguments field, type the following:

      ```
      queue
      ```

   d. Click OK.
   e. Right-click the project and choose Run Project.

   The output of the program looks like this:

   ```
   Destination type is queue
   Reading message: This is message 1
   ```

To run the clients using the `appclient` command, follow these steps. You may want to use two terminal windows.

1. Go to the `producer/dist` directory.
2. Run the `Producer` program, sending one message to the queue:

   ```
   appclient -client producer.jar queue
   ```

   The output of the program looks like this:

   ```
   Destination type is queue
   Sending message: This is message 1
   ```

3. Go to the `messagebrowser/dist` directory.

4. Run the `MessageBrowser` program:

   ```
   appclient -client messagebrowser.jar
   ```

   The output of the program looks like this:

   ```
   Message:
   Text:   This is message 1
   Class:              com.sun.messaging.jmq.jmsclient.TextMessageImpl
   getJMSMessageID():    ID:12-129.148.71.199(8c:34:4a:1a:1b:b8)-40883-
   1129062957611
   getJMSTimestamp():      1129062957611
   getJMSCorrelationID():  null
   JMSReplyTo:             null
   JMSDestination:         PhysicalQueue
   getJMSDeliveryMode():   PERSISTENT
   getJMSRedelivered():    false
   getJMSType():           null
   getJMSExpiration():     0
   getJMSPriority():       4
   Properties:             null
   Message:
   Class:                  com.sun.messaging.jmq.jmsclient.MessageImpl
   getJMSMessageID():         ID:13-129.148.71.199(8c:34:4a:1a:1b:b8)-
   40883-1129062957616
   getJMSTimestamp():      1129062957616
   getJMSCorrelationID():  null
   JMSReplyTo:             null
   JMSDestination:         PhysicalQueue
   getJMSDeliveryMode():   PERSISTENT
   getJMSRedelivered():    false
   getJMSType():           null
   getJMSExpiration():     0
   getJMSPriority():       4
   Properties:             null
   ```

   The first message is the `TextMessage`, and the second is the non-text control message.

5. Go to the `synchconsumer/dist` directory.
6. Run the `SynchConsumer` program to consume the messages:

   ```
   appclient -client synchconsumer.jar queue
   ```

   The output of the program looks like this:

   ```
   Destination type is queue
   Reading message: This is message 1
   ```

Running JMS Client Programs on Multiple Systems

JMS client programs using the Application Server can exchange messages with each other when they are running on different systems in a network. The systems must be visible to each other by name—the UNIX host name or the Microsoft Windows computer name—and must both be running the Application Server. You do not have to install the tutorial examples on both systems; you can use the examples installed on one system if you can access its file system from the other system.

Note: Any mechanism for exchanging messages between systems is specific to the Java EE server implementation. This tutorial describes how to use the Application Server for this purpose.

Suppose that you want to run the `Producer` program on one system, `earth`, and the `SynchConsumer` program on another system, `jupiter`. Before you can do so, you need to perform these tasks:

- Create two new connection factories
- Edit the source code for the two examples
- Recompile and repackage the examples

Note: A limitation in the JMS provider in the Application Server may cause a runtime failure to create a connection to systems that use the Dynamic Host Configuration Protocol (DHCP) to obtain an IP address. You can, however, create a connection *from* a system that uses DHCP *to* a system that does not use DHCP. In the examples in this tutorial, `earth` can be a system that uses DHCP, and `jupiter` can be a system that does not use DHCP.

Before you begin, start the server on both systems:

1. Start the Application Server on `earth`.
2. Start the Application Server on `jupiter`.

Creating Administered Objects for Multiple Systems

To run these programs, you must do the following:

- Create a new connection factory on both earth and jupiter
- Create a destination resource on both earth and jupiter

You do not have to install the tutorial on both systems, but you must be able to access the filesystem where it is installed. You may find it more convenient to install the tutorial on both systems if the two systems use different operating systems (for example, Windows and Solaris). Otherwise you will have to edit the file *<INSTALL>*/javaeetutorial5/examples/bp-project/build.properties and change the location of the javaee.home property each time you build or run a program on a different system.

To create a new connection factory on jupiter, perform these steps:

1. From a command shell on jupiter, go to the directory *<INSTALL>*/javaeetutorial5/examples/jms/simple/producer/.
2. Type the following command:

   ```
   ant create-local-factory
   ```

The create-local-factory target, defined in the build.xml file for the Producer example, creates a connection factory named jms/JupiterConnectionFactory.

To create a new connection factory on earth that points to the connection factory on jupiter, perform these steps:

1. From a command shell on earth, go to the directory *<INSTALL>*/javaeetutorial5/examples/jms/simple/producer/.
2. Type the following command:

   ```
   ant create-remote-factory -Dsys=remote_system_name
   ```

   Replace *remote_system_name* with the actual name of the remote system.

The create-remote-factory target, defined in the build.xml file for the Producer example, also creates a connection factory named jms/JupiterConnectionFactory. In addition, it sets the AddressList property for this factory to the name of the remote system.

If you have already been working on either `earth` or `jupiter`, you have the queue and topic on one system. On the system that does not have the queue and topic, type the following command:

```
ant create-resources
```

When you run the programs, they will work as shown in Figure 31–6. The program run on `earth` needs the queue on `earth` only in order that the resource injection will succeed. The connection, session, and message producer are all created on `jupiter` using the connection factory that points to `jupiter`. The messages sent from `earth` will be received on `jupiter`.

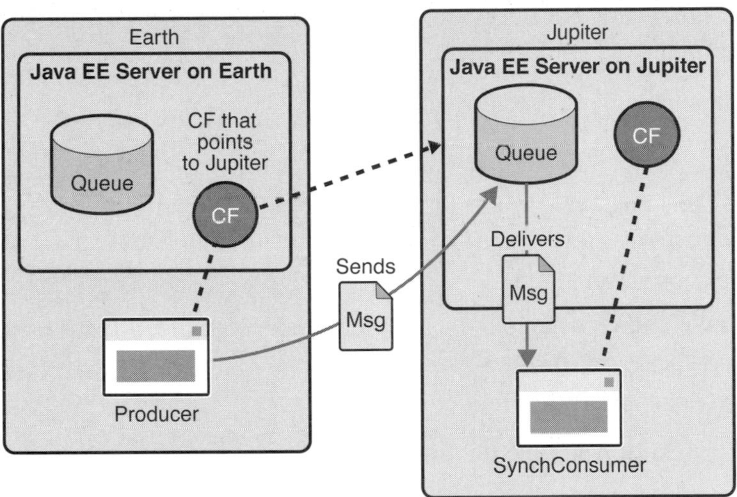

Figure 31–6 Sending Messages from One System to Another

Editing, Recompiling, Repackaging, and Running the Programs

These steps assume that you have the tutorial installed on only one of the two systems you are using and that you are able to access the file system of `jupiter` from `earth` or vice versa.

After you create the connection factories, edit the source files to specify the new connection factory. Then recompile, repackage, and run the programs. Perform the following steps:

1. Open the file `<INSTALL>javaeetutorial5/examples/jms/simple/producer/src/java/Producer.java` in a text editor.
2. Find the following line:

   ```
   @Resource(mappedName="jms/ConnectionFactory")
   ```
3. Change the line to the following:

   ```
   @Resource(mappedName="jms/JupiterConnectionFactory")
   ```
4. Recompile and repackage the `Producer` example on `earth`.

   If you are using NetBeans 5.5, right-click the `producer` project and choose Clean and Build Project.

   If you are using Ant, type the following:

   ```
   ant
   ```
5. Open the file `<INSTALL>javaeetutorial5/examples/jms/simple/synchconsumer/src/java/SynchConsumer.java` in a text editor.
6. Repeat steps 2 and 3.
7. Recompile and repackage the `SynchConsumer` example on `jupiter`.

   If you are using NetBeans 5.5, right-click the `synchconsumer` project and choose Clean and Build Project.

   If you are using Ant, type the following:

   ```
   ant
   ```
8. On `earth`, run `Producer`. If you are using NetBeans 5.5 on `earth`, perform these steps:

   a. Right-click the `producer` project and choose Properties.

   b. Select Run from the Categories tree.

   c. In the Arguments field, type the following:

   ```
   queue 3
   ```

   d. Click OK.

   e. Right-click the project and choose Run Project.

   If you are using the `appclient` command, go to the `producer/dist` directory and type the following:

   ```
   appclient -client producer.jar queue 3
   ```

9. On `jupiter`, run `SynchConsumer`. If you are using NetBeans 5.5 on `jupiter`, perform these steps:
   a. Right-click the `synchconsumer` project and choose Properties.
   b. Select Run from the Categories tree.
   c. In the Arguments field, type the following:
      ```
      queue
      ```
   d. Click OK.
   e. Right-click the project and choose Run Project.

   If you are using the `appclient` command, go to the `synchconsumer/dist` directory and type the following:

   ```
   appclient -client synchconsumer.jar queue
   ```

For examples showing how to deploy Java EE applications on two different systems, see An Application Example That Consumes Messages from a Remote Server (page 1146) and An Application Example That Deploys a Message-Driven Bean on Two Servers (page 1153).

Deleting the Connection Factory and Stopping the Server

You will need the connection factory `jms/JupiterConnectionFactory` in Chapter 32. However, if you wish to delete it, go to the `producer` directory and type the following command:

```
ant delete-remote-factory
```

Remember to delete the connection factory on both systems.

You can also use Ant targets in the `producer/build.xml` file to delete the destinations and connection factories you created in Creating JMS Administered Objects (page 1076). However, we recommend that you keep them, because they will be used in most of the examples in Chapter 32. After you have created them, they will be available whenever you restart the Application Server.

To delete the class and JAR files for each program using NetBeans 5.5, right-click each project and choose Clean Project.

To delete the class and JAR files for each program using Ant, type the following:

```
ant clean
```

You can also stop the Application Server, but you will need it to run the sample programs in the next section.

Creating Robust JMS Applications

This section explains how to use features of the JMS API to achieve the level of reliability and performance your application requires. Many people choose to implement JMS applications because they cannot tolerate dropped or duplicate messages and require that every message be received once and only once. The JMS API provides this functionality.

The most reliable way to produce a message is to send a `PERSISTENT` message within a transaction. JMS messages are `PERSISTENT` by default. A *transaction* is a unit of work into which you can group a series of operations, such as message sends and receives, so that the operations either all succeed or all fail. For details, see Specifying Message Persistence (page 1103) and Using JMS API Local Transactions (page 1111).

The most reliable way to consume a message is to do so within a transaction, either from a queue or from a durable subscription to a topic. For details, see Creating Temporary Destinations (page 1105), Creating Durable Subscriptions (page 1106), and Using JMS API Local Transactions (page 1111).

For other applications, a lower level of reliability can reduce overhead and improve performance. You can send messages with varying priority levels—see Setting Message Priority Levels (page 1104)—and you can set them to expire after a certain length of time (see Allowing Messages to Expire, page 1105).

The JMS API provides several ways to achieve various kinds and degrees of reliability. This section divides them into two categories:

- Using basic reliability mechanisms
- Using advanced reliability mechanisms

The following sections describe these features as they apply to JMS clients. Some of the features work differently in Java EE applications; in these cases, the differences are noted here and are explained in detail in Using the JMS API in a Java EE Application (page 1119).

This section includes three sample programs, which you can find in the directory `<INSTALL>/javaeetutorial5/examples/jms/advanced/`. Each sample uses a utility class called `SampleUtilities.java`.

Using Basic Reliability Mechanisms

The basic mechanisms for achieving or affecting reliable message delivery are as follows:

- **Controlling message acknowledgment**: You can specify various levels of control over message acknowledgment.
- **Specifying message persistence**: You can specify that messages are persistent, meaning that they must not be lost in the event of a provider failure.
- **Setting message priority levels**: You can set various priority levels for messages, which can affect the order in which the messages are delivered.
- **Allowing messages to expire**: You can specify an expiration time for messages so that they will not be delivered if they are obsolete.
- **Creating temporary destinations**: You can create temporary destinations that last only for the duration of the connection in which they are created.

Controlling Message Acknowledgment

Until a JMS message has been acknowledged, it is not considered to be successfully consumed. The successful consumption of a message ordinarily takes place in three stages.

1. The client receives the message.
2. The client processes the message.
3. The message is acknowledged. Acknowledgment is initiated either by the JMS provider or by the client, depending on the session acknowledgment mode.

In transacted sessions (see Using JMS API Local Transactions, page 1111), acknowledgment happens automatically when a transaction is committed. If a transaction is rolled back, all consumed messages are redelivered.

In nontransacted sessions, when and how a message is acknowledged depend on the value specified as the second argument of the `createSession` method. The three possible argument values are as follows:

- `Session.AUTO_ACKNOWLEDGE`: The session automatically acknowledges a client's receipt of a message either when the client has successfully returned from a call to `receive` or when the `MessageListener` it has called to process the message returns successfully. A synchronous receive in an `AUTO_ACKNOWLEDGE` session is the one exception to the rule that message consumption is a three-stage process as described earlier.

In this case, the receipt and acknowledgment take place in one step, followed by the processing of the message.

- `Session.CLIENT_ACKNOWLEDGE`: A client acknowledges a message by calling the message's `acknowledge` method. In this mode, acknowledgment takes place on the session level: Acknowledging a consumed message automatically acknowledges the receipt of *all* messages that have been consumed by its session. For example, if a message consumer consumes ten messages and then acknowledges the fifth message delivered, all ten messages are acknowledged.
- `Session.DUPS_OK_ACKNOWLEDGE`: This option instructs the session to lazily acknowledge the delivery of messages. This is likely to result in the delivery of some duplicate messages if the JMS provider fails, so it should be used only by consumers that can tolerate duplicate messages. (If the JMS provider redelivers a message, it must set the value of the `JMSRedelivered` message header to `true`.) This option can reduce session overhead by minimizing the work the session does to prevent duplicates.

If messages have been received from a queue but not acknowledged when a session terminates, the JMS provider retains them and redelivers them when a consumer next accesses the queue. The provider also retains unacknowledged messages for a terminated session that has a durable `TopicSubscriber`. (See Creating Durable Subscriptions, page 1106.) Unacknowledged messages for a nondurable `TopicSubscriber` are dropped when the session is closed.

If you use a queue or a durable subscription, you can use the `Session.recover` method to stop a nontransacted session and restart it with its first unacknowledged message. In effect, the session's series of delivered messages is reset to the point after its last acknowledged message. The messages it now delivers may be different from those that were originally delivered, if messages have expired or if higher-priority messages have arrived. For a nondurable `TopicSubscriber`, the provider may drop unacknowledged messages when its session is recovered.

The sample program in the next section demonstrates two ways to ensure that a message will not be acknowledged until processing of the message is complete.

A Message Acknowledgment Example

The `AckEquivExample.java` program shows how both of the following two scenarios ensure that a message will not be acknowledged until processing of it is complete:

- Using an asynchronous message consumer—a message listener—in an `AUTO_ACKNOWLEDGE` session
- Using a synchronous receiver in a `CLIENT_ACKNOWLEDGE` session

With a message listener, the automatic acknowledgment happens when the `onMessage` method returns—that is, after message processing has finished. With a synchronous receiver, the client acknowledges the message after processing is complete. (If you use `AUTO_ACKNOWLEDGE` with a synchronous receive, the acknowledgment happens immediately after the `receive` call; if any subsequent processing steps fail, the message cannot be redelivered.)

The program is in the following directory:

```
<INSTALL>/javaeetutorial5/examples/jms/advanced/
ackequivexample/src/java/
```

The program contains a `SynchSender` class, a `SynchReceiver` class, an `AsynchSubscriber` class with a `TextListener` class, a `MultiplePublisher` class, a `main` method, and a method that runs the other classes' threads.

The program uses the following objects:

- `jms/ConnectionFactory`, `jms/Queue`, and `jms/Topic`: resources that you created in Creating JMS Administered Objects (page 1076)
- `jms/ControlQueue`: an additional queue
- `jms/DurableConnectionFactory`: a connection factory with a client ID (see Creating Durable Subscriptions, page 1106, for more information)

To create the new queue and connection factory, you can use Ant targets defined in the file `<INSTALL>/javaeetutorial5/examples/jms/advanced/ackequivexample/build.xml`.

To run this example, follow these steps:

1. In a terminal window, go to the following directory:

   `<INSTALL>/javaeetutorial5/examples/jms/advanced/ackequivexample/`

2. To create the objects needed in this example, type the following commands:

   ```
   ant create-control-queue
   ant create-durable-cf
   ```

3. To compile and package the program using NetBeans 5.5, follow these steps:

   a. In NetBeans 5.5, choose Open Project from the File menu.

   b. In the Open Project dialog, navigate to `<INSTALL>/javaeetutorial5/examples/jms/advanced/`.

   c. Select the `ackequivexample` folder.

   d. Select the Open as Main Project checkbox.

   e. Click Open Project Folder.

   f. Right-click the project and choose Build Project.

   To compile and package the program using Ant, type the following command:

   ```
   ant
   ```

4. To run the program using NetBeans 5.5, right-click the `ackequivexample` project and choose Run Project.

   To run the program from the command line, follow these steps:

   a. Go to the `dist` directory:

   ```
   cd dist
   ```

   b. Type the following command:

   ```
   appclient -client ackequivexample.jar
   ```

The program output looks something like this:

```
Queue name is jms/ControlQueue
Queue name is jms/Queue
Topic name is jms/Topic
Connection factory name is jms/DurableConnectionFactory
  SENDER: Created client-acknowledge session
  SENDER: Sending message: Here is a client-acknowledge message
  RECEIVER: Created client-acknowledge session
  RECEIVER: Processing message: Here is a client-acknowledge
message
  RECEIVER: Now I'll acknowledge the message
SUBSCRIBER: Created auto-acknowledge session
SUBSCRIBER: Sending synchronize message to control queue
PUBLISHER: Created auto-acknowledge session
```

```
PUBLISHER: Receiving synchronize messages from control queue;
count = 1
PUBLISHER: Received synchronize message;  expect 0 more
PUBLISHER: Publishing message: Here is an auto-acknowledge
message 1
PUBLISHER: Publishing message: Here is an auto-acknowledge
message 2
SUBSCRIBER: Processing message: Here is an auto-acknowledge
message 1
PUBLISHER: Publishing message: Here is an auto-acknowledge
message 3
SUBSCRIBER: Processing message: Here is an auto-acknowledge
message 2
SUBSCRIBER: Processing message: Here is an auto-acknowledge
message 3
```

After you run the program, you can delete the destination resource `jms/ControlQueue`. Go to the directory `<INSTALL>/javaeetutorial5/examples/jms/advanced/ackequivexample/` and type the following command:

```
ant delete-control-queue
```

You will need the other resources for other examples.

To delete the class and JAR files for the program using NetBeans 5.5, right-click the project and choose Clean Project.

To delete the class and JAR files for the program using Ant, type the following:

```
ant clean
```

Specifying Message Persistence

The JMS API supports two delivery modes for messages to specify whether messages are lost if the JMS provider fails. These delivery modes are fields of the `DeliveryMode` interface.

- The `PERSISTENT` delivery mode, which is the default, instructs the JMS provider to take extra care to ensure that a message is not lost in transit in case of a JMS provider failure. A message sent with this delivery mode is logged to stable storage when it is sent.
- The `NON_PERSISTENT` delivery mode does not require the JMS provider to store the message or otherwise guarantee that it is not lost if the provider fails.

You can specify the delivery mode in either of two ways.

- You can use the `setDeliveryMode` method of the `MessageProducer` interface to set the delivery mode for all messages sent by that producer. For example, the following call sets the delivery mode to `NON_PERSISTENT` for a producer:

  ```
  producer.setDeliveryMode(DeliveryMode.NON_PERSISTENT);
  ```

- You can use the long form of the `send` or the `publish` method to set the delivery mode for a specific message. The second argument sets the delivery mode. For example, the following `send` call sets the delivery mode for `message` to `NON_PERSISTENT`:

  ```
  producer.send(message, DeliveryMode.NON_PERSISTENT, 3,
    10000);
  ```

  The third and fourth arguments set the priority level and expiration time, which are described in the next two subsections.

If you do not specify a delivery mode, the default is `PERSISTENT`. Using the `NON_PERSISTENT` delivery mode may improve performance and reduce storage overhead, but you should use it only if your application can afford to miss messages.

Setting Message Priority Levels

You can use message priority levels to instruct the JMS provider to deliver urgent messages first. You can set the priority level in either of two ways.

- You can use the `setPriority` method of the `MessageProducer` interface to set the priority level for all messages sent by that producer. For example, the following call sets a priority level of 7 for a producer:

  ```
  producer.setPriority(7);
  ```

- You can use the long form of the `send` or the `publish` method to set the priority level for a specific message. The third argument sets the priority level. For example, the following `send` call sets the priority level for `message` to 3:

  ```
  producer.send(message, DeliveryMode.NON_PERSISTENT, 3,
    10000);
  ```

The ten levels of priority range from 0 (lowest) to 9 (highest). If you do not specify a priority level, the default level is 4. A JMS provider tries to deliver higher-priority messages before lower-priority ones but does not have to deliver messages in exact order of priority.

Allowing Messages to Expire

By default, a message never expires. If a message will become obsolete after a certain period, however, you may want to set an expiration time. You can do this in either of two ways.

- You can use the `setTimeToLive` method of the `MessageProducer` interface to set a default expiration time for all messages sent by that producer. For example, the following call sets a time to live of one minute for a producer:

  ```
  producer.setTimeToLive(60000);
  ```

- You can use the long form of the `send` or the `publish` method to set an expiration time for a specific message. The fourth argument sets the expiration time in milliseconds. For example, the following `send` call sets a time to live of 10 seconds:

  ```
  producer.send(message, DeliveryMode.NON_PERSISTENT, 3,
    10000);
  ```

If the specified `timeToLive` value is `0`, the message never expires.

When the message is sent, the specified `timeToLive` is added to the current time to give the expiration time. Any message not delivered before the specified expiration time is destroyed. The destruction of obsolete messages conserves storage and computing resources.

Creating Temporary Destinations

Normally, you create JMS destinations—queues and topics—administratively rather than programmatically. Your JMS provider includes a tool that you use to create and remove destinations, and it is common for destinations to be long-lasting.

The JMS API also enables you to create destinations—`TemporaryQueue` and `TemporaryTopic` objects—that last only for the duration of the connection in which they are created. You create these destinations dynamically using the `Session.createTemporaryQueue` and the `Session.createTemporaryTopic` methods.

The only message consumers that can consume from a temporary destination are those created by the same connection that created the destination. Any message producer can send to the temporary destination. If you close the connection that a temporary destination belongs to, the destination is closed and its contents are lost.

You can use temporary destinations to implement a simple request/reply mechanism. If you create a temporary destination and specify it as the value of the JMSReplyTo message header field when you send a message, then the consumer of the message can use the value of the JMSReplyTo field as the destination to which it sends a reply. The consumer can also reference the original request by setting the JMSCorrelationID header field of the reply message to the value of the JMSMessageID header field of the request. For example, an onMessage method can create a session so that it can send a reply to the message it receives. It can use code such as the following:

```
producer = session.createProducer(msg.getJMSReplyTo());
replyMsg = session.createTextMessage("Consumer " +
  "processed message: " + msg.getText());
replyMsg.setJMSCorrelationID(msg.getJMSMessageID());
producer.send(replyMsg);
```

For more examples, see Chapter 32.

Using Advanced Reliability Mechanisms

The more advanced mechanisms for achieving reliable message delivery are the following:

- **Creating durable subscriptions**: You can create durable topic subscriptions, which receive messages published while the subscriber is not active. Durable subscriptions offer the reliability of queues to the publish/subscribe message domain.
- **Using local transactions**: You can use local transactions, which allow you to group a series of sends and receives into an atomic unit of work. Transactions are rolled back if they fail at any time.

Creating Durable Subscriptions

To ensure that a pub/sub application receives all published messages, use PERSISTENT delivery mode for the publishers. In addition, use durable subscriptions for the subscribers.

The `Session.createConsumer` method creates a nondurable subscriber if a topic is specified as the destination. A nondurable subscriber can receive only messages that are published while it is active.

At the cost of higher overhead, you can use the `Session.createDurableSubscriber` method to create a durable subscriber. A durable subscription can have only one active subscriber at a time.

A durable subscriber registers a durable subscription by specifying a unique identity that is retained by the JMS provider. Subsequent subscriber objects that have the same identity resume the subscription in the state in which it was left by the preceding subscriber. If a durable subscription has no active subscriber, the JMS provider retains the subscription's messages until they are received by the subscription or until they expire.

You establish the unique identity of a durable subscriber by setting the following:

- A client ID for the connection
- A topic and a subscription name for the subscriber

You set the client ID administratively for a client-specific connection factory using the Admin Console.

After using this connection factory to create the connection and the session, you call the `createDurableSubscriber` method with two arguments: the topic and a string that specifies the name of the subscription:

```
String subName = "MySub";
MessageConsumer topicSubscriber =
  session.createDurableSubscriber(myTopic, subName);
```

The subscriber becomes active after you start the `Connection` or `TopicConnection`. Later, you might close the subscriber:

```
topicSubscriber.close();
```

The JMS provider stores the messages sent or published to the topic, as it would store messages sent to a queue. If the program or another application calls `createDurableSubscriber` using the same connection factory and its client ID, the same topic, and the same subscription name, the subscription is reactivated, and the JMS provider delivers the messages that were published while the subscriber was inactive.

To delete a durable subscription, first close the subscriber, and then use the unsubscribe method, with the subscription name as the argument:

```
topicSubscriber.close();
session.unsubscribe("MySub");
```

The unsubscribe method deletes the state that the provider maintains for the subscriber.

Figure 31–7 and Figure 31–8 show the difference between a nondurable and a durable subscriber. With an ordinary, nondurable subscriber, the subscriber and the subscription begin and end at the same point and are, in effect, identical. When a subscriber is closed, the subscription also ends. Here, create stands for a call to Session.createConsumer with a Topic argument, and close stands for a call to MessageConsumer.close. Any messages published to the topic between the time of the first close and the time of the second create are not consumed by the subscriber. In Figure 31–7, the subscriber consumes messages M1, M2, M5, and M6, but messages M3 and M4 are lost.

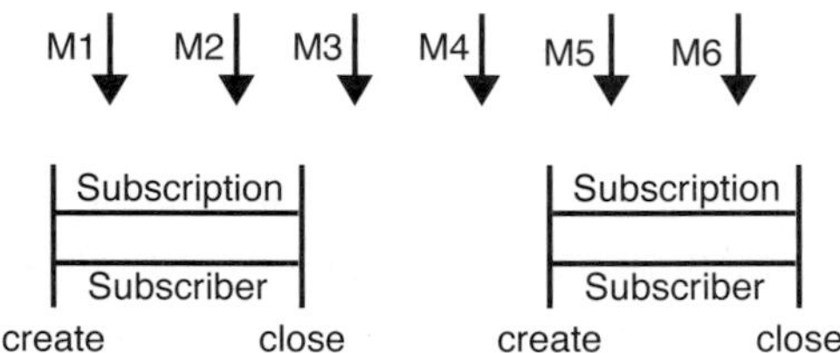

Figure 31–7 Nondurable Subscribers and Subscriptions

With a durable subscriber, the subscriber can be closed and re-created, but the subscription continues to exist and to hold messages until the application calls the unsubscribe method. In Figure 31–8, create stands for a call to Session.createDurableSubscriber, close stands for a call to MessageConsumer.close, and unsubscribe stands for a call to Session.unsubscribe. Messages published while the subscriber is closed are received when the subscriber is created again. So even though messages M2, M4, and M5 arrive while the subscriber is closed, they are not lost.

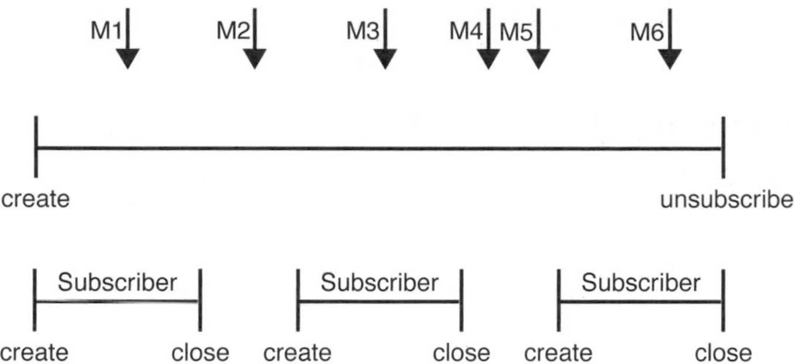

Figure 31–8 A Durable Subscriber and Subscription

See A Java EE Application That Uses the JMS API with a Session Bean (page 1130) for an example of a Java EE application that uses durable subscriptions. See A Message Acknowledgment Example (page 1101) and the next section for examples of client applications that use durable subscriptions.

A Durable Subscription Example

The `DurableSubscriberExample.java` program shows how durable subscriptions work. It demonstrates that a durable subscription is active even when the subscriber is not active. The program contains a `DurableSubscriber` class, a `MultiplePublisher` class, a `main` method, and a method that instantiates the classes and calls their methods in sequence.

The program is in the following directory:

```
<INSTALL>/javaeetutorial5/examples/jms/advanced/
durablesubscriberexample/src/java/
```

The program begins in the same way as any publish/subscribe program: The subscriber starts, the publisher publishes some messages, and the subscriber receives them. At this point, the subscriber closes itself. The publisher then publishes some messages while the subscriber is not active. The subscriber then restarts and receives the messages.

Before you run this program, compile and package the source file and create a connection factory that has a client ID. Perform the following steps:

1. To compile and package the program using NetBeans 5.5, follow these steps:
   a. In NetBeans 5.5, choose Open Project from the File menu.

b. In the Open Project dialog, navigate to `<INSTALL>/javaeetutorial5/examples/jms/advanced/`.
c. Select the `durablesubscriberexample` folder.
d. Select the Open as Main Project checkbox.
e. Click Open Project Folder.
f. Right-click the project and choose Build Project.

To compile and package the program using Ant, follow these steps:

a. Go to the following directory:

`<INSTALL>/javaeetutorial5/examples/jms/advanced/durablesubscriberexample/`

b. Type the following command:

```
ant
```

2. If you did not do so for A Message Acknowledgment Example (page 1101), create a connection factory named `jms/DurableConnectionFactory`:

```
ant create-durable-cf
```

To run the program using NetBeans 5.5, right-click the `durablesubscriberexample` project and choose Run Project.

To run the program from the command line, follow these steps:

1. Go to the `dist` directory:

```
cd dist
```

2. Type the following command:

```
appclient -client durablesubscriberexample.jar
```

The output looks something like this:

```
Connection factory without client ID is jms/ConnectionFactory
Connection factory with client ID is jms/
DurableConnectionFactory
Topic name is jms/Topic
Starting subscriber
PUBLISHER: Publishing message: Here is a message 1
SUBSCRIBER: Reading message: Here is a message 1
PUBLISHER: Publishing message: Here is a message 2
SUBSCRIBER: Reading message: Here is a message 2
PUBLISHER: Publishing message: Here is a message 3
SUBSCRIBER: Reading message: Here is a message 3
Closing subscriber
```

```
PUBLISHER: Publishing message: Here is a message 4
PUBLISHER: Publishing message: Here is a message 5
PUBLISHER: Publishing message: Here is a message 6
Starting subscriber
SUBSCRIBER: Reading message: Here is a message 4
SUBSCRIBER: Reading message: Here is a message 5
SUBSCRIBER: Reading message: Here is a message 6
Closing subscriber
Unsubscribing from durable subscription
```

After you run the program, you can delete the connection factory `jms/DurableConnectionFactory`. Go to the directory `<INSTALL>/javaeetutorial5/examples/jms/advanced/durablesubscriberexample/` and type the following command:

```
ant delete-durable-cf
```

To delete the class and JAR files for the program using NetBeans 5.5, right-click the project and choose Clean Project.

To delete the class and JAR files for the program using Ant, type the following:

```
ant clean
```

Using JMS API Local Transactions

You can group a series of operations into an atomic unit of work called a transaction. If any one of the operations fails, the transaction can be rolled back, and the operations can be attempted again from the beginning. If all the operations succeed, the transaction can be committed.

In a JMS client, you can use local transactions to group message sends and receives. The JMS API `Session` interface provides `commit` and `rollback` methods that you can use in a JMS client. A transaction commit means that all produced messages are sent and all consumed messages are acknowledged. A transaction rollback means that all produced messages are destroyed and all consumed messages are recovered and redelivered unless they have expired (see Allowing Messages to Expire, page 1105).

A transacted session is always involved in a transaction. As soon as the `commit` or the `rollback` method is called, one transaction ends and another transaction begins. Closing a transacted session rolls back its transaction in progress, including any pending sends and receives.

In an Enterprise JavaBeans component, you cannot use the `Session.commit` and `Session.rollback` methods. Instead, you use distributed transactions, which are described in Using the JMS API in a Java EE Application (page 1119).

You can combine several sends and receives in a single JMS API local transaction. If you do so, you need to be careful about the order of the operations. You will have no problems if the transaction consists of all sends or all receives or if the receives come before the sends. But if you try to use a request/reply mechanism, whereby you send a message and then try to receive a reply to the sent message in the same transaction, the program will hang, because the send cannot take place until the transaction is committed. The following code fragment illustrates the problem:

```
// Don't do this!
outMsg.setJMSReplyTo(replyQueue);
producer.send(outQueue, outMsg);
consumer = session.createConsumer(replyQueue);
inMsg = consumer.receive();
session.commit();
```

Because a message sent during a transaction is not actually sent until the transaction is committed, the transaction cannot contain any receives that depend on that message's having been sent.

In addition, the production and the consumption of a message cannot both be part of the same transaction. The reason is that the transactions take place between the clients and the JMS provider, which intervenes between the production and the consumption of the message. Figure 31–9 illustrates this interaction.

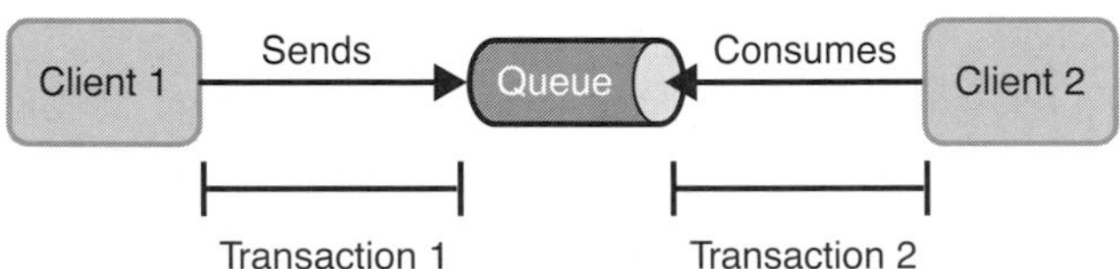

Figure 31–9 Using JMS API Local Transactions

The sending of one or more messages to one or more destinations by client 1 can form a single transaction, because it forms a single set of interactions with the JMS provider using a single session. Similarly, the receiving of one or more messages from one or more destinations by client 2 also forms a single transaction using a single session. But because the two clients have no direct interaction and are using two different sessions, no transactions can take place between them.

Another way of putting this is that the act of producing and/or consuming messages in a session can be transactional, but the act of producing and consuming a specific message across different sessions cannot be transactional.

This is the fundamental difference between messaging and synchronized processing. Instead of tightly coupling the sending and receiving of data, message producers and consumers use an alternative approach to reliability, one that is built on a JMS provider's ability to supply a once-and-only-once message delivery guarantee.

When you create a session, you specify whether it is transacted. The first argument to the `createSession` method is a `boolean` value. A value of `true` means that the session is transacted; a value of `false` means that it is not transacted. The second argument to this method is the acknowledgment mode, which is relevant only to nontransacted sessions (see Controlling Message Acknowledgment, page 1099). If the session is transacted, the second argument is ignored, so it is a good idea to specify `0` to make the meaning of your code clear. For example:

```
session = connection.createSession(true, 0);
```

The `commit` and the `rollback` methods for local transactions are associated with the session. You can combine queue and topic operations in a single transaction if you use the same session to perform the operations. For example, you can use the same session to receive a message from a queue and send a message to a topic in the same transaction.

You can pass a client program's session to a message listener's constructor function and use it to create a message producer. In this way, you can use the same session for receives and sends in asynchronous message consumers.

The next section provides an example of the use of JMS API local transactions.

A Local Transaction Example

The `TransactedExample.java` program demonstrates the use of transactions in a JMS client application. The program is in the following directory:

```
<INSTALL>/javaeetutorial5/examples/jms/advanced/
transactedexample/src/java/
```

This example shows how to use a queue and a topic in a single transaction as well as how to pass a session to a message listener's constructor function. The program represents a highly simplified e-commerce application in which the following things happen.

1. A retailer sends a `MapMessage` to the vendor order queue, ordering a quantity of computers, and waits for the vendor's reply:

   ```
   producer =
     session.createProducer(vendorOrderQueue);
   outMessage = session.createMapMessage();
   outMessage.setString("Item", "Computer(s)");
   outMessage.setInt("Quantity", quantity);
   outMessage.setJMSReplyTo(retailerConfirmQueue);
   producer.send(outMessage);
   System.out.println("Retailer: ordered " +
     quantity + " computer(s)");

   orderConfirmReceiver =
     session.createConsumer(retailerConfirmQueue);
   connection.start();
   ```

2. The vendor receives the retailer's order message and sends an order message to the supplier order topic in one transaction. This JMS transaction uses a single session, so we can combine a receive from a queue with a send to a topic. Here is the code that uses the same session to create a consumer for a queue and a producer for a topic:

   ```
   vendorOrderReceiver =
     session.createConsumer(vendorOrderQueue);
   supplierOrderProducer =
     session.createProducer(supplierOrderTopic);
   ```

   The following code receives the incoming message, sends an outgoing message, and commits the session. The message processing has been removed to keep the sequence simple:

   ```
   inMessage = vendorOrderReceiver.receive();
   // Process the incoming message and format the outgoing
   // message
   ...
   supplierOrderProducer.send(orderMessage);
   ...
   session.commit();
   ```

3. Each supplier receives the order from the order topic, checks its inventory, and then sends the items ordered to the queue named in the order message's `JMSReplyTo` field. If it does not have enough in stock, the supplier

sends what it has. The synchronous receive from the topic and the send to the queue take place in one JMS transaction.

```
receiver = session.createConsumer(orderTopic);
...
inMessage = receiver.receive();
if (inMessage instanceof MapMessage) {
  orderMessage = (MapMessage) inMessage;
}
// Process message
MessageProducer producer =
  session.createProducer((Queue)
    orderMessage.getJMSReplyTo());
outMessage = session.createMapMessage();
// Add content to message
producer.send(outMessage);
// Display message contents
session.commit();
```

4. The vendor receives the replies from the suppliers from its confirmation queue and updates the state of the order. Messages are processed by an asynchronous message listener; this step shows the use of JMS transactions with a message listener.

```
MapMessage component = (MapMessage) message;
...
orderNumber = component.getInt("VendorOrderNumber");
Order order =
  Order.getOrder(orderNumber).processSubOrder(component);
session.commit();
```

5. When all outstanding replies are processed for a given order, the vendor message listener sends a message notifying the retailer whether it can fulfill the order.

```
Queue replyQueue = (Queue) order.order.getJMSReplyTo();
MessageProducer producer =
  session.createProducer(replyQueue);
MapMessage retailerConfirmMessage =
  session.createMapMessage();
// Format the message
producer.send(retailerConfirmMessage);
session.commit();
```

6. The retailer receives the message from the vendor:

```
inMessage =
  (MapMessage) orderConfirmReceiver.receive();
```

Figure 31–10 illustrates these steps.

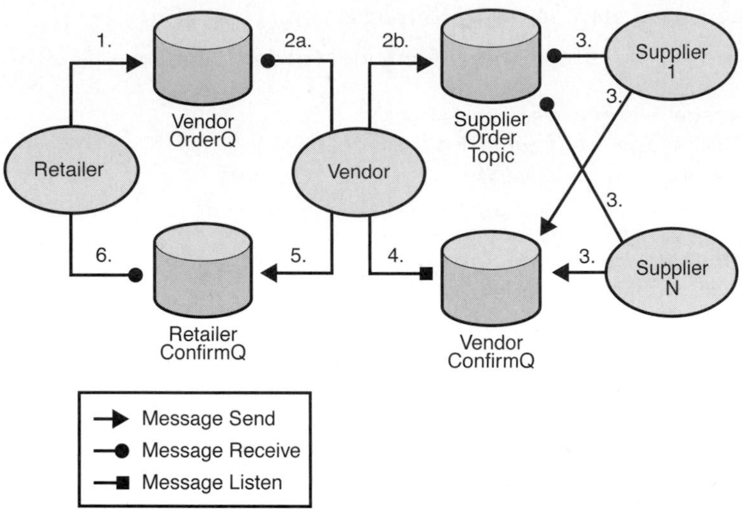

Figure 31–10 Transactions: JMS Client Example

The program contains five classes: `Retailer`, `Vendor`, `GenericSupplier`, `VendorMessageListener`, and `Order`. The program also contains a `main` method and a method that runs the threads of the `Retailer`, `Vendor`, and two supplier classes.

All the messages use the `MapMessage` message type. Synchronous receives are used for all message reception except for the case of the vendor processing the replies of the suppliers. These replies are processed asynchronously and demonstrate how to use transactions within a message listener.

At random intervals, the `Vendor` class throws an exception to simulate a database problem and cause a rollback.

All classes except `Retailer` use transacted sessions.

The program uses three queues named `jms/AQueue`, `jms/BQueue`, and `jms/CQueue`, and one topic named `jms/OTopic`. Before you run the program, do the following:

1. In a terminal window, go to the following directory:

   ```
   <INSTALL>/javaeetutorial5/examples/jms/advanced/transacte-
   dexample/
   ```

2. Create the necessary resources using the following command:

   ```
   ant create-resources
   ```

This command creates three destination resources with the names `jms/AQueue`, `jms/BQueue`, and `jms/CQueue`, all of type `javax.jms.Queue`, and one destination resource with the name `jms/OTopic`, of type `javax.jms.Topic`.

3. To compile and package the program using NetBeans 5.5, follow these steps:
   a. In NetBeans 5.5, choose Open Project from the File menu.
   b. In the Open Project dialog, navigate to `<INSTALL>/javaeetutorial5/examples/jms/advanced/`.
   c. Select the `transactedexample` folder.
   d. Select the Open as Main Project checkbox.
   e. Click Open Project Folder.
   f. Right-click the project and choose Build Project.

   To compile and package the program using Ant, follow these steps:

   a. Go to the following directory:

   ```
   <INSTALL>/javaeetutorial5/examples/jms/advanced/
   transactedexample/
   ```

   b. Type the following command:

   ```
   ant
   ```

To run the program using NetBeans 5.5, right-click the `transactedexample` project and choose Run Project.

   a. Right-click the `transactedexample` project and choose Properties.
   b. Select Run from the Categories tree.
   c. In the Arguments field, type a number that specifies the number of computers to order:

   ```
   3
   ```

   d. Click OK.
   e. Right-click the project and choose Run Project.

To run the program from the command line, follow these steps:

1. Go to the `dist` directory:

```
cd dist
```

2. Use a command like the following to run the program. The argument specifies the number of computers to order:

   ```
   appclient -client transactedexample.jar 3
   ```

The output looks something like this:

```
Quantity to be ordered is 3
Retailer: ordered 3 computer(s)
Vendor: Retailer ordered 3 Computer(s)
Vendor: ordered 3 monitor(s) and hard drive(s)
Monitor Supplier: Vendor ordered 3 Monitor(s)
Monitor Supplier: sent 3 Monitor(s)
  Monitor Supplier: committed transaction
  Vendor: committed transaction 1
Hard Drive Supplier: Vendor ordered 3 Hard Drive(s)
Hard Drive Supplier: sent 1 Hard Drive(s)
Vendor: Completed processing for order 1
  Hard Drive Supplier: committed transaction
Vendor: unable to send 3 computer(s)
  Vendor: committed transaction 2
Retailer: Order not filled
Retailer: placing another order
Retailer: ordered 6 computer(s)
Vendor: JMSException occurred: javax.jms.JMSException:
Simulated database concurrent access exception
javax.jms.JMSException: Simulated database concurrent access
exception
        at TransactedExample$Vendor.run(Unknown Source)
  Vendor: rolled back transaction 1
Vendor: Retailer ordered 6 Computer(s)
Vendor: ordered 6 monitor(s) and hard drive(s)
Monitor Supplier: Vendor ordered 6 Monitor(s)
Hard Drive Supplier: Vendor ordered 6 Hard Drive(s)
Monitor Supplier: sent 6 Monitor(s)
  Monitor Supplier: committed transaction
Hard Drive Supplier: sent 6 Hard Drive(s)
  Hard Drive Supplier: committed transaction
  Vendor: committed transaction 1
Vendor: Completed processing for order 2
Vendor: sent 6 computer(s)
Retailer: Order filled
  Vendor: committed transaction 2
```

After you run the program, you can delete the physical destinations and the destination resources. Go to the directory `<INSTALL>/javaeetutorial5/examples/jms/advanced/transactedexample/` and type the following command:

```
ant delete-resources
```

Use the following command to remove the class and JAR files:

```
ant clean
```

Using the JMS API in a Java EE Application

This section describes the ways in which using the JMS API in a Java EE application differs from using it in a stand-alone client application:

- Using `@Resource` annotations in Java EE components
- Using session beans to produce and to synchronously receive messages
- Using message-driven beans to receive messages asynchronously
- Managing distributed transactions
- Using the JMS API with application clients and web components

A general rule in the Java EE platform specification applies to all Java EE components that use the JMS API within EJB or web containers:

> Application components in the web and EJB containers must not attempt to create more than one active (not closed) `Session` object per connection.

This rule does not apply to application clients.

Using @Resource Annotations in Java EE Components

When you use the `@Resource` annotation in an application client component, you normally declare the JMS resource static:

```
@Resource(mappedName="jms/ConnectionFactory")
private static ConnectionFactory connectionFactory;

@Resource(mappedName="jms/Queue")
private static Queue queue;
```

However, when you use this annotation in a session bean, a message-driven bean, or a web component, do *not* declare the resource static:

```
@Resource(mappedName="jms/ConnectionFactory")
private ConnectionFactory connectionFactory;

@Resource(mappedName="jms/Topic")
private Topic topic;
```

If you declare the resource static, runtime errors will result.

Using Session Beans to Produce and to Synchronously Receive Messages

A Java EE application that produces messages or synchronously receives them can use a session bean to perform these operations. The example in A Java EE Application That Uses the JMS API with a Session Bean (page 1130) uses a stateless session bean to publish messages to a topic.

Because a blocking synchronous receive ties up server resources, it is not a good programming practice to use such a `receive` call in an enterprise bean. Instead, use a timed synchronous receive, or use a message-driven bean to receive messages asynchronously. For details about blocking and timed synchronous receives, see Writing the Client Programs (page 1073).

Using the JMS API in a Java EE application is in many ways similar to using it in a stand-alone client. The main differences are in resource management and transactions.

Resource Management

The JMS API resources are a JMS API connection and a JMS API session. In general, it is important to release JMS resources when they are no longer being used. Here are some useful practices to follow.

- If you wish to maintain a JMS API resource only for the life span of a business method, it is a good idea to close the resource in a `finally` block within the method.
- If you would like to maintain a JMS API resource for the life span of an enterprise bean instance, it is a good idea to use a `@PostConstruct` callback method to create the resource and to use a `@PreDestroy` callback method to close the resource. If you use a stateful session bean and you wish to maintain the JMS API resource in a cached state, you must close the resource in a `@PrePassivate` callback method and set its value to `null`, and you must create it again in a `@PostActivate` callback method.

Transactions

Instead of using local transactions, you use container-managed transactions for bean methods that perform sends or receives, allowing the EJB container to handle transaction demarcation. Because container-managed transactions are the default, you do not have to use an annotation to specify them.

You can use bean-managed transactions and the `javax.transaction.UserTransaction` interface's transaction demarcation methods, but you should do so only if your application has special requirements and you are an expert in using transactions. Usually, container-managed transactions produce the most efficient and correct behavior. This tutorial does not provide any examples of bean-managed transactions.

Using Message-Driven Beans

As we noted in What Is a Message-Driven Bean? (page 747) and How Does the JMS API Work with the Java EE Platform? (page 1054), the Java EE platform supports a special kind of enterprise bean, the message-driven bean, which allows Java EE applications to process JMS messages asynchronously. Session beans allow you to send messages and to receive them synchronously but not asynchronously.

A message-driven bean is a message listener that can reliably consume messages from a queue or a durable subscription. The messages can be sent by any Java EE component—from an application client, another enterprise bean, or a web component—or from an application or a system that does not use Java EE technology.

Like a message listener in a stand-alone JMS client, a message-driven bean contains an `onMessage` method that is called automatically when a message arrives. Like a message listener, a message-driven bean class can implement helper methods invoked by the `onMessage` method to aid in message processing.

A message-driven bean, however, differs from a stand-alone client's message listener in the following ways:

- Certain setup tasks are performed by the EJB container.
- The bean class uses the `@MessageDriven` annotation to specify properties for the bean or the connection factory, such as a destination type, a durable subscription, a message selector, or an acknowledgment mode. The examples in Chapter 32 show how the JMS resource adapter works in the Application Server.

The EJB container automatically performs several setup tasks that a stand-alone client has to do:

- Creating a message consumer to receive the messages. Instead of creating a message consumer in your source code, you associate the message-driven bean with a destination and a connection factory at deployment time. If you want to specify a durable subscription or use a message selector, you do this at deployment time also.
- Registering the message listener. You must not call `setMessageListener`.
- Specifying a message acknowledgment mode. The default mode, `AUTO_ACKNOWLEDGE`, is used unless it is overriden by a property setting.

If JMS is integrated with the application server using a resource adapter, the JMS resource adapter handles these tasks for the EJB container.

Your message-driven bean class must implement the `javax.jms.MessageListener` interface and the `onMessage` method.

It may implement a `@PostConstruct` callback method to create a connection, and a `@PreDestroy` callback method to close the connection. Typically, it implements these methods if it produces messages or does synchronous receives from another destination.

The bean class commonly injects a `MessageDrivenContext` resource, which provides some additional methods that you can use for transaction management.

The main difference between a message-driven bean and a session bean is that a message-driven bean has no local or remote interface. Instead, it has only a bean class.

A message-driven bean is similar in some ways to a stateless session bean: Its instances are relatively short-lived and retain no state for a specific client. The instance variables of the message-driven bean instance can contain some state across the handling of client messages—for example, a JMS API connection, an open database connection, or an object reference to an enterprise bean object.

Like a stateless session bean, a message-driven bean can have many interchangeable instances running at the same time. The container can pool these instances to allow streams of messages to be processed concurrently. The container attempts to deliver messages in chronological order when it does not impair the concurrency of message processing, but no guarantees are made as to the exact order in which messages are delivered to the instances of the message-driven bean class. Because concurrency can affect the order in which messages are delivered, you should write your applications to handle messages that arrive out of sequence.

For example, your application could manage conversations by using application-level sequence numbers. An application-level conversation control mechanism with a persistent conversation state could cache later messages until earlier messages have been processed.

Another way to ensure order is to have each message or message group in a conversation require a confirmation message that the sender blocks on receipt of. This forces the responsibility for order back on the sender and more tightly couples senders to the progress of message-driven beans.

To create a new instance of a message-driven bean, the container does the following:

- Instantiates the bean
- Performs any required resource injection
- Calls the `@PostConstruct` callback method, if it exists

To remove an instance of a message-driven bean, the container calls the `@PreDestroy` callback method.

Figure 31–11 shows the life cycle of a message-driven bean.

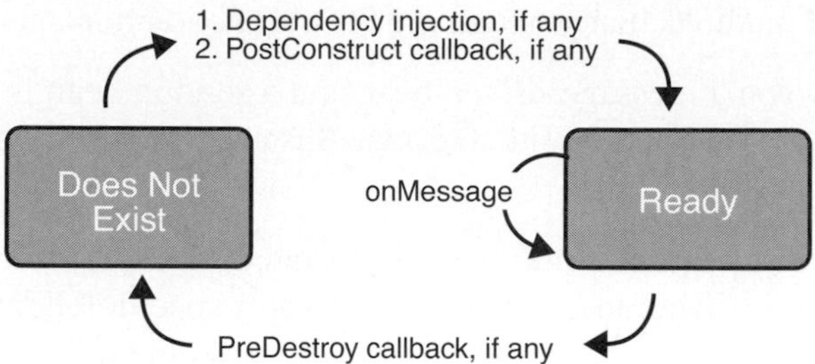

Figure 31–11 Life Cycle of a Message-Driven Bean

Managing Distributed Transactions

JMS client applications use JMS API local transactions (described in Using JMS API Local Transactions, page 1111), which allow the grouping of sends and receives within a specific JMS session. Java EE applications commonly use distributed transactions to ensure the integrity of accesses to external resources. For example, distributed transactions allow multiple applications to perform atomic updates on the same database, and they allow a single application to perform atomic updates on multiple databases.

In a Java EE application that uses the JMS API, you can use transactions to combine message sends or receives with database updates and other resource manager operations. You can access resources from multiple application components within a single transaction. For example, a servlet can start a transaction, access multiple databases, invoke an enterprise bean that sends a JMS message, invoke another enterprise bean that modifies an EIS system using the Connector architecture, and finally commit the transaction. Your application cannot, however, both send a JMS message and receive a reply to it within the same transaction; the restriction described in Using JMS API Local Transactions (page 1111) still applies.

Distributed transactions within the EJB container can be either of two kinds:

- **Container-managed transactions**: The EJB container controls the integrity of your transactions without your having to call `commit` or `rollback`. Container-managed transactions are recommended for Java EE applications that use the JMS API. You can specify appropriate transaction attributes for your enterprise bean methods.

  Use the `Required` transaction attribute (the default) to ensure that a method is always part of a transaction. If a transaction is in progress when the method is called, the method will be part of that transaction; if not, a new transaction will be started before the method is called and will be committed when the method returns.

- **Bean-managed transactions**: You can use these in conjunction with the `javax.transaction.UserTransaction` interface, which provides its own `commit` and `rollback` methods that you can use to delimit transaction boundaries. Bean-managed transactions are recommended only for those who are experienced in programming transactions.

You can use either container-managed transactions or bean-managed transactions with message-driven beans. To ensure that all messages are received and handled within the context of a transaction, use container-managed transactions and use the `Required` transaction attribute (the default) for the `onMessage` method. This means that if there is no transaction in progress, a new transaction will be started before the method is called and will be committed when the method returns.

When you use container-managed transactions, you can call the following `MessageDrivenContext` methods:

- `setRollbackOnly`: Use this method for error handling. If an exception occurs, `setRollbackOnly` marks the current transaction so that the only possible outcome of the transaction is a rollback.
- `getRollbackOnly`: Use this method to test whether the current transaction has been marked for rollback.

If you use bean-managed transactions, the delivery of a message to the `onMessage` method takes place outside the distributed transaction context. The transaction begins when you call the `UserTransaction.begin` method within the `onMessage` method, and it ends when you call `UserTransaction.commit` or `UserTransaction.rollback`. Any call to the `Connection.createSession` method must take place within the transaction. If you call `UserTransaction.rollback`, the message is not redelivered, whereas calling `setRollbackOnly` for container-managed transactions does cause a message to be redelivered.

Neither the JMS API specification nor the Enterprise JavaBeans specification (available from `http://java.sun.com/products/ejb/`) specifies how to handle calls to JMS API methods outside transaction boundaries. The Enterprise JavaBeans specification does state that the EJB container is responsible for acknowledging a message that is successfully processed by the `onMessage` method of a message-driven bean that uses bean-managed transactions. Using bean-managed transactions allows you to process the message by using more than one transaction or to have some parts of the message processing take place outside a transaction context. In most cases, however, container-managed transactions provide greater reliability and are therefore preferable.

When you create a session in an enterprise bean, the container ignores the arguments you specify, because it manages all transactional properties for enterprise beans. It is still a good idea to specify arguments of `true` and `0` to the `createSession` method to make this situation clear:

```
session = connection.createSession(true, 0);
```

When you use container-managed transactions, you normally use the `Required` transaction attribute (the default) for your enterprise bean's business methods.

You do not specify a message acknowledgment mode when you create a message-driven bean that uses container-managed transactions. The container acknowledges the message automatically when it commits the transaction.

If a message-driven bean uses bean-managed transactions, the message receipt cannot be part of the bean-managed transaction, so the container acknowledges the message outside the transaction.

If the `onMessage` method throws a `RuntimeException`, the container does not acknowledge processing the message. In that case, the JMS provider will redeliver the unacknowledged message in the future.

Using the JMS API with Application Clients and Web Components

An application client in a Java EE application can use the JMS API in much the same way that a stand-alone client program does. It can produce messages, and it can consume messages by using either synchronous receives or message listeners. See Chapter 23 for an example of an application client that produces messages. For an example of using an application client to produce and to consume messages, see An Application Example That Deploys a Message-Driven Bean on Two Servers (page 1153).

The Java EE platform specification does not impose strict constraints on how web components should use the JMS API. In the Application Server, a web component—one that uses either the Java Servlet API or JavaServer Pages (JSP) technology—can send messages and consume them synchronously but cannot consume them asynchronously.

Because a blocking synchronous receive ties up server resources, it is not a good programming practice to use such a `receive` call in a web component. Instead, use a timed synchronous receive. For details about blocking and timed synchronous receives, see Writing the Client Programs (page 1073).

Further Information

For more information about JMS, see the following:

- Java Message Service web site:
  `http://java.sun.com/products/jms/`
- Java Message Service specification, version 1.1, available from
  `http://java.sun.com/products/jms/docs.html`

32

Java EE Examples Using the JMS API

THIS chapter provides examples that show how to use the JMS API within a Java EE application in the following ways:

- Using a session bean to send messages that are consumed by a message-driven bean using a message selector and a durable subscription
- Using an application client to send messages that are consumed by two message-driven beans; the information from them is stored in a Java Persistence API entity
- Using an application client to send messages that are consumed by a message-driven bean on a remote server
- Using an application client to send messages that are consumed by message-driven beans on two different servers

The examples are in the following directory:

```
<INSTALL>/javaeetutorial5/examples/jms/
```

To build and run the examples, you will do the following:

1. Use NetBeans 5.5 or the Ant tool to compile and package the example.
2. Use the Ant tool to create resources.

3. Use NetBeans 5.5 or the Ant tool to deploy the example.
4. Use NetBeans 5.5 or the Ant tool to run the client.

Each example has a `build.xml` file that refers to files in the following directory:

```
<INSTALL>/javaeetutorial5/examples/bp-project/
```

See Chapter 23 for a simpler example of a Java EE application that uses the JMS API.

A Java EE Application That Uses the JMS API with a Session Bean

This section explains how to write, compile, package, deploy, and run a Java EE application that uses the JMS API in conjunction with a session bean. The application contains the following components:

- An application client that invokes a session bean
- A session bean that publishes several messages to a topic
- A message-driven bean that receives and processes the messages using a durable topic subscriber and a message selector

The section covers the following topics:

- Writing the application components
- Creating resources for the application
- Building, deploying, and running the application using NetBeans 5.5
- Building, deploying, and running the application using Ant

You will find the source files for this section in the directory `<INSTALL>/javaeetutorial5/examples/jms/clientsessionmdb/`. Path names in this section are relative to this directory.

Writing the Application Components

This application demonstrates how to send messages from an enterprise bean—in this case, a session bean—rather than from an application client, as in the example in Chapter 23. Figure 32–1 illustrates the structure of this application.

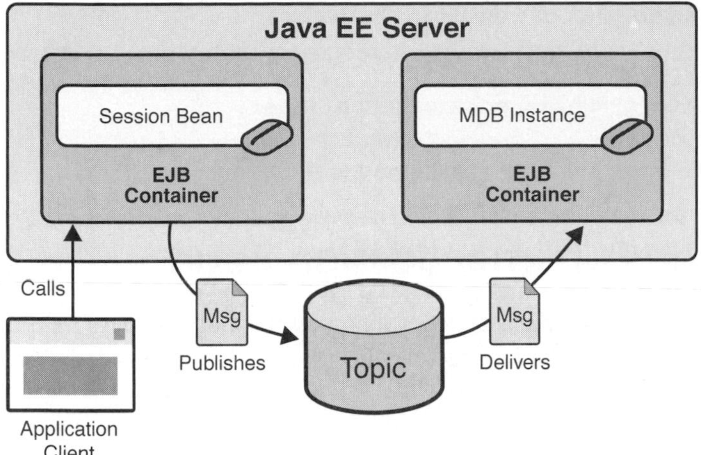

Figure 32–1 A Java EE Application: Client to Session Bean to Message-Driven Bean

The Publisher enterprise bean in this example is the enterprise-application equivalent of a wire-service news feed that categorizes news events into six news categories. The message-driven bean could represent a newsroom, where the sports desk, for example, would set up a subscription for all news events pertaining to sports.

The application client in the example injects the Publisher enterprise bean's remote home interface and then calls the bean's business method. The enterprise bean creates 18 text messages. For each message, it sets a `String` property randomly to one of six values representing the news categories and then publishes the message to a topic. The message-driven bean uses a message selector for the property to limit which of the published messages it receives.

Writing the components of the application involves the following:

- Coding the application client: `MyAppClient.java`
- Coding the Publisher session bean
- Coding the message-driven bean: `MessageBean.java`

Coding the Application Client: MyAppClient.java

The application client program, `clientsessionmdb-app-client/src/java/MyAppClient.java`, performs no JMS API operations and so is simpler than the client program in Chapter 23. The program uses dependency injection to obtain the Publisher enterprise bean's business interface:

```
@EJB(name="PublisherRemote")
static private PublisherRemote publisher;
```

The program then calls the bean's business method twice.

Coding the Publisher Session Bean

The Publisher bean is a stateless session bean that has one business method. The Publisher bean uses a remote interface rather than a local interface because it is accessed from the application client.

The remote interface, `clientsessionmdb-ejb/src/java/sb/PublisherRemote.java`, declares a single business method, `publishNews`.

The bean class, `clientsessionmdb-ejb/src/java/sb/PublisherBean.java`, implements the `publishNews` method and its helper method `chooseType`. The bean class also injects `SessionContext`, `ConnectionFactory`, and `Topic` resources and implements `@PostConstruct` and `@PreDestroy` callback methods. The bean class begins as follows:

```
@Stateless
@Remote({PublisherRemote.class})
public class PublisherBean implements PublisherRemote {

  @Resource
  private SessionContext sc;

  @Resource(mappedName="jms/ConnectionFactory")
  private ConnectionFactory connectionFactory;

  @Resource(mappedName="jms/Topic")
  private Topic topic;
  ...
```

The `@PostConstruct` callback method of the bean class, `makeConnection`, creates the `Connection` used by the bean. The business method `publishNews` creates a `Session` and a `MessageProducer` and publishes the messages.

The `@PreDestroy` callback method, `endConnection`, deallocates the resources that were allocated by the `@PostConstruct` callback method. In this case, the method closes the `Connection`.

Coding the Message-Driven Bean: MessageBean.java

The message-driven bean class, `clientsessionmdb-ejb/src/java/mdb/MessageBean.java`, is almost identical to the one in Chapter 23. However, the `@MessageDriven` annotation is different, because instead of a queue the bean is using a topic with a durable subscription, and it is also using a message selector. Therefore, the annotation sets the activation config properties `messageSelector`, `subscriptionDurability`, `clientId`, and `subscriptionName`, as follows:

```
@MessageDriven(mappedName="jms/Topic",
activationConfig=
{ @ActivationConfigProperty(propertyName="messageSelector",
    propertyValue="NewsType = 'Sports' OR NewsType = 'Opinion'"),
@ActivationConfigProperty(
    propertyName="subscriptionDurability",
    propertyValue="Durable"),
@ActivationConfigProperty(propertyName="clientId",
    propertyValue="MyID"),
@ActivationConfigProperty(propertyName="subscriptionName",
    propertyValue="MySub")
})
```

The JMS resource adapter uses these properties to create a connection factory for the message-driven bean that allows the bean to use a durable subscriber.

Creating Resources for the Application

This example uses the topic named `jms/Topic` and the connection factory `jms/ConnectionFactory`, which you created in Creating JMS Administered Objects (page 1076). If you deleted the connection factory or topic, you can create them again using targets in the `build.xml` file for this example. Use the following commands to create the resources:

```
ant create-cf
ant create-topic
```

Building, Deploying, and Running the Application Using NetBeans 5.5

To build, deploy, and run the application using NetBeans 5.5, do the following:

1. Start the Application Server, if it is not already running.
2. In NetBeans 5.5, choose Open Project from the File menu.
3. In the Open Project dialog, navigate to `<INSTALL>/javaeetutorial5/examples/jms/`.
4. Select the `clientsessionmdb` folder.
5. Select the Open as Main Project checkbox and the Open Required Projects checkbox.
6. Click Open Project Folder.
7. Right-click the `clientsessionmdb` project and choose Build Project.

   This task creates the following:

   - An application client JAR file that contains the client class file and the session bean's remote interface, along with a manifest file that specifies the main class
   - An EJB JAR file that contains both the session bean and the message-driven bean
   - An application EAR file that contains the two JAR files
8. Right-click the project and choose Deploy Project.
9. Right-click the project and choose Run Project.

   This command returns a JAR file named `clientsessionmdbClient.jar` and then executes it.

The output of the application client in the Output pane looks like this:

```
To view the bean output,
 check <install_dir>/domains/domain1/logs/server.log.
```

The output from the enterprise beans appears in the server log (`<JAVAEE_HOME>/domains/domain1/logs/server.log`), wrapped in logging information. The Publisher session bean sends two sets of 18 messages numbered 0 through 17. Because of the message selector, the message-driven bean receives only the messages whose `NewsType` property is `Sports` or `Opinion`.

Undeploy the application after you finish running the client. To undeploy the application, follow these steps:

1. Click the Runtime tab.
2. Expand the Servers node.
3. Expand the Sun Java System Application Server node.
4. Expand the Applications node.
5. Expand the Enterprise Applications node.
6. Right-click `clientsessionmdb` and choose Undeploy.

To remove the generated files, right-click the `clientsessionmdb` project and choose Clean Project.

Building, Deploying, and Running the Application Using Ant

To build the application using Ant, do the following:

1. Start the Application Server, if it is not already running.
2. Go to the following directory:

   ```
   <INSTALL>/javaeetutorial5/examples/jms/clientsessionmdb/
   ```

3. To compile the source files and package the application, use the following command:

   ```
   ant
   ```

The `ant` command creates the following:

- An application client JAR file that contains the client class file and the session bean's remote interface, along with a manifest file that specifies the main class
- An EJB JAR file that contains both the session bean and the message-driven bean
- An application EAR file that contains the two JAR files

The `clientsessionmdb.ear` file is created in the `clientsessionmdb/dist` directory.

To deploy the application and run the client, use the following command:

```
ant run
```

Ignore the message that states that the application is deployed at a URL.

The client displays these lines:

```
running application client container.
To view the bean output,
 check <install_dir>/domains/domain1/logs/server.log.
```

The output from the enterprise beans appears in the server log (`<JAVAEE_HOME>/domains/domain1/logs/server.log`), wrapped in logging information. The Publisher session bean sends two sets of 18 messages numbered 0 through 17. Because of the message selector, the message-driven bean receives only the messages whose `NewsType` property is `Sports` or `Opinion`.

Undeploy the application after you finish running the client. Use the following command:

```
ant undeploy
```

To remove the generated files, use the following command:

```
ant clean
```

A Java EE Application That Uses the JMS API with an Entity

This section explains how to write, compile, package, deploy, and run a Java EE application that uses the JMS API with an entity. The application uses the following components:

- An application client that both sends and receives messages
- Two message-driven beans
- An entity class

This section covers the following topics:

- Overview of the human resources application
- Writing the application components
- Creating resources for the application
- Building, deploying, and running the application using NetBeans 5.5
- Building, deploying, and running the application using Ant

You will find the source files for this section in the directory `<INSTALL>/javaeetutorial5/examples/jms/clientmdbentity/`. Path names in this section are relative to this directory.

Overview of the Human Resources Application

This application simulates, in a simplified way, the work flow of a company's human resources (HR) department when it processes a new hire. This application also demonstrates how to use the Java EE platform to accomplish a task that many JMS client applications perform.

A JMS client must often wait for several messages from various sources. It then uses the information in all these messages to assemble a message that it then sends to another destination. The common term for this process is *joining messages*. Such a task must be transactional, with all the receives and the send as a single transaction. If not all the messages are received successfully, the transaction can be rolled back. For a client example that illustrates this task, see A Local Transaction Example (page 1113).

A message-driven bean can process only one message at a time in a transaction. To provide the ability to join messages, a Java EE application can have the message-driven bean store the interim information in an entity. The entity can then determine whether all the information has been received; when it has, the entity can report this back to one of the message-driven beans, which then creates and sends the message to the other destination. After it has completed its task, the entity can be removed.

The basic steps of the application are as follows.

1. The HR department's application client generates an employee ID for each new hire and then publishes a message (M1) containing the new hire's name, employee ID, and position. The client then creates a temporary queue, `ReplyQueue`, with a message listener that waits for a reply to the message. (See Creating Temporary Destinations, page 1105, for more information.)
2. Two message-driven beans process each message: One bean, `OfficeMDB`, assigns the new hire's office number, and the other bean, `EquipmentMDB`, assigns the new hire's equipment. The first bean to process the message creates and persists an entity named `SetupOffice`, then calls a business method of the entity to store the information it has generated. The second

bean locates the existing entity and calls another business method to add its information.

3. When both the office and the equipment have been assigned, the entity business method returns a value of `true` to the message-driven bean that called the method. The message-driven bean then sends to the reply queue a message (M2) describing the assignments. Then it removes the entity. The application client's message listener retrieves the information.

Figure 32–2 illustrates the structure of this application. Of course, an actual HR application would have more components; other beans could set up payroll and benefits records, schedule orientation, and so on.

Figure 32–2 assumes that `OfficeMDB` is the first message-driven bean to consume the message from the client. `OfficeMDB` then creates and persists the `SetupOffice` entity and stores the office information. `EquipmentMDB` then finds the entity, stores the equipment information, and learns that the entity has completed its work. `EquipmentMDB` then sends the message to the reply queue and removes the entity.

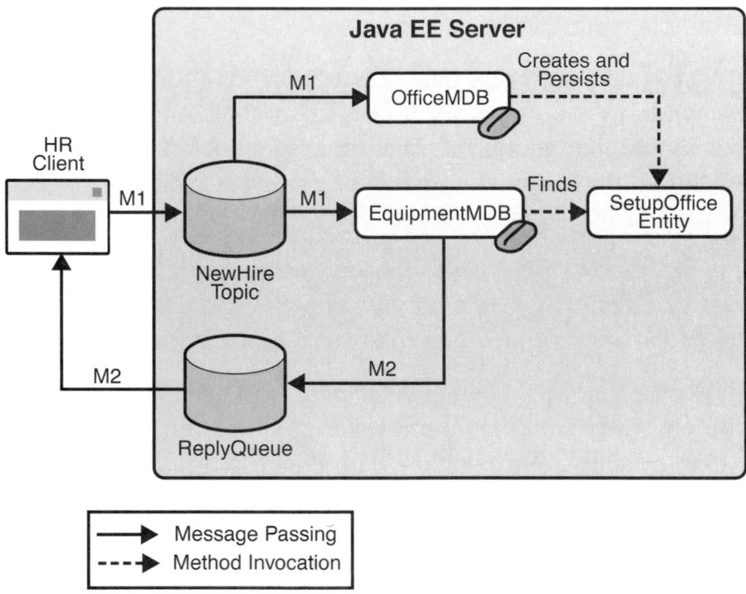

Figure 32–2 A Java EE Application: Client to Message-Driven Beans to Entity

Writing the Application Components

Writing the components of the application involves the following:

- Coding the application client: `HumanResourceClient.java`
- Coding the message-driven beans
- Coding the entity class

Coding the Application Client: HumanResourceClient.java

The application client program, `clientmdbentity-app-client/src/java/HumanResourceClient.java`, performs the following steps:

1. Injects `ConnectionFactory` and `Topic` resources
2. Creates a `TemporaryQueue` to receive notification of processing that occurs, based on new-hire events it has published
3. Creates a `MessageConsumer` for the `TemporaryQueue`, sets the `MessageConsumer`'s message listener, and starts the connection
4. Creates a `MessageProducer` and a `MapMessage`
5. Creates five new employees with randomly generated names, positions, and ID numbers (in sequence) and publishes five messages containing this information

The message listener, `HRListener`, waits for messages that contain the assigned office and equipment for each employee. When a message arrives, the message listener displays the information received and determines whether all five messages have arrived. When they have, the message listener notifies the main program, which then exits.

Coding the Message-Driven Beans

This example uses two message-driven beans:

- `clientmdbentity-ejb/src/java/EquipmentMDB.java`
- `clientmdbentity-ejb/src/java/OfficeMDB.java`

The beans take the following steps.

1. They inject `MessageDrivenContext` and `ConnectionFactory` resources.
2. The `onMessage` method retrieves the information in the message. The `EquipmentMDB`'s `onMessage` method chooses equipment, based on the new hire's position; the `OfficeMDB`'s `onMessage` method randomly generates an office number.
3. After a slight delay to simulate real world processing hitches, the `onMessage` method calls a helper method, `compose`.
4. The `compose` method takes the following steps:
   a. It either creates and persists the `SetupOffice` entity or finds it by primary key.
   b. It uses the entity to store the equipment or the office information in the database, calling either the `doEquipmentList` or the `doOfficeNumber` business method.
   c. If the business method returns `true`, meaning that all of the information has been stored, it creates a connection and a session, retrieves the reply destination information from the message, creates a `MessageProducer`, and sends a reply message that contains the information stored in the entity.
   d. It removes the entity.

Coding the Entity Class

The `SetupOffice` class, `SetupOffice.java`, is an entity class. The entity and the message-driven beans are packaged together in an EJB JAR file. The entity class is declared as follows:

```
@Entity
public class SetupOffice implements Serializable {
```

The class contains a no-argument constructor and a constructor that takes two arguments, the employee ID and name. It also contains getter and setter methods for the employee ID, name, office number, and equipment list. The getter method for the employee ID has the `@Id` annotation to indicate that this field is the primary key:

```
@Id public String getEmployeeId() {
  return id;
}
```

The class also implements the two business methods, `doEquipmentList` and `doOfficeNumber`, and their helper method, `checkIfSetupComplete`.

The message-driven beans call the business methods and the getter methods.

The `persistence.xml` file for the entity specifies the most basic settings:

```
<persistence>
  <persistence-unit name="clientmdbentity">
    <jta-data-source>jdbc/__default</jta-data-source>
    <class>eb.SetupOffice</class>
    <properties>
      <property name="toplink.ddl-generation"
        value="drop-and-create-tables"/>
    </properties>
  </persistence-unit>
</persistence>
```

Creating Resources for the Application

This example uses the connection factory `jms/ConnectionFactory` and the topic `jms/Topic`, both of which you used in A Java EE Application That Uses the JMS API with a Session Bean. It also uses the JDBC resource named `jdbc/__default`, which is enabled by default when you start the Application Server.

If you deleted the connection factory or topic, you can create them again using targets in the `build.xml` file for this example. Use the following commands to create the resources:

```
ant create-cf
ant create-topic
```

Building, Deploying, and Running the Application Using NetBeans 5.5

To build, deploy, and run the application using NetBeans 5.5, do the following:

1. Start the Application Server, if it is not already running.
2. Start the database server as described in Starting and Stopping the Java DB Database Server (page 29), if it is not already running.
3. In NetBeans 5.5, choose Open Project from the File menu.

4. In the Open Project dialog, navigate to `<INSTALL>/javaeetutorial5/examples/jms/`.
5. Select the `clientmdbentity` folder.
6. Select the Open as Main Project checkbox and the Open Required Projects checkbox.
7. Click Open Project Folder.
8. Right-click the `clientmdbentity` project and choose Build Project.

   This task creates the following:

   - An application client JAR file that contains the client class and listener class files, along with a manifest file that specifies the main class
   - An EJB JAR file that contains the message-driven beans and the entity class, along with the `persistence.xml` file
   - An application EAR file that contains the two JAR files along with an `application.xml` file

9. Right-click the project and choose Deploy Project.
10. Right-click the project and choose Run Project.

    This command returns a JAR file named `clientmdbentityClient.jar` and then executes it.

The output of the application client in the Output pane looks something like this:

```
PUBLISHER: Setting hire ID to 25, name Gertrude Bourbon,
position Senior Programmer
PUBLISHER: Setting hire ID to 26, name Jack Verdon, position
Manager
PUBLISHER: Setting hire ID to 27, name Fred Tudor, position
Manager
PUBLISHER: Setting hire ID to 28, name Fred Martin, position
Programmer
PUBLISHER: Setting hire ID to 29, name Mary Stuart, position
Manager
Waiting for 5 message(s)
New hire event processed:
  Employee ID: 25
  Name: Gertrude Bourbon
  Equipment: Laptop
  Office number: 183
Waiting for 4 message(s)
New hire event processed:
  Employee ID: 26
  Name: Jack Verdon
  Equipment: Pager
```

```
  Office number: 20
Waiting for 3 message(s)
New hire event processed:
  Employee ID: 27
  Name: Fred Tudor
  Equipment: Pager
  Office number: 51
Waiting for 2 message(s)
New hire event processed:
  Employee ID: 28
  Name: Fred Martin
  Equipment: Desktop System
  Office number: 141
Waiting for 1 message(s)
New hire event processed:
  Employee ID: 29
  Name: Mary Stuart
  Equipment: Pager
  Office number: 238
```

The output from the message-driven beans and the entity class appears in the server log, wrapped in logging information.

For each employee, the application first creates the entity and then finds it. You may see runtime errors in the server log, and transaction rollbacks may occur. The errors occur if both of the message-driven beans discover at the same time that the entity does not yet exist, so they both try to create it. The first attempt succeeds, but the second fails because the bean already exists. After the rollback, the second message-driven bean tries again and succeeds in finding the entity. Container-managed transactions allow the application to run correctly, in spite of these errors, with no special programming.

You can run the application client repeatedly.

Undeploy the application after you finish running the client. To undeploy the application, follow these steps:

1. Click the Runtime tab.
2. Expand the Servers node.
3. Expand the Sun Java System Application Server node.
4. Expand the Applications node.
5. Expand the Enterprise Applications node.
6. Right-click `clientmdbentity` and choose Undeploy.

To remove the generated files, right-click the `clientmdbentity` project and choose Clean Project.

Building, Deploying, and Running the Application Using Ant

To create and package the application using Ant, perform these steps:

1. Start the Application Server, if it is not already running.
2. Start the database server as described in Starting and Stopping the Java DB Database Server (page 29).
3. Go to the following directory:

   `<INSTALL>/javaeetutorial5/examples/jms/clientmdbentity/`
4. To compile the source files and package the application, use the following command:

   ```
   ant
   ```

The `ant` command creates the following:

- An application client JAR file that contains the client class and listener class files, along with a manifest file that specifies the main class
- An EJB JAR file that contains the message-driven beans and the entity class, along with the `persistence.xml` file
- An application EAR file that contains the two JAR files along with an `application.xml` file

To deploy the application and run the client, use the following command:

```
ant run
```

Ignore the message that states that the application is deployed at a URL.

The program output in the terminal window looks something like this:

```
running application client container.
PUBLISHER: Setting hire ID to 25, name Gertrude Bourbon,
position Senior Programmer
PUBLISHER: Setting hire ID to 26, name Jack Verdon, position
Manager
PUBLISHER: Setting hire ID to 27, name Fred Tudor, position
Manager
PUBLISHER: Setting hire ID to 28, name Fred Martin, position
```

```
Programmer
PUBLISHER: Setting hire ID to 29, name Mary Stuart, position
Manager
Waiting for 5 message(s)
New hire event processed:
  Employee ID: 25
  Name: Gertrude Bourbon
  Equipment: Laptop
  Office number: 183
Waiting for 4 message(s)
New hire event processed:
  Employee ID: 26
  Name: Jack Verdon
  Equipment: Pager
  Office number: 20
Waiting for 3 message(s)
New hire event processed:
  Employee ID: 27
  Name: Fred Tudor
  Equipment: Pager
  Office number: 51
Waiting for 2 message(s)
New hire event processed:
  Employee ID: 28
  Name: Fred Martin
  Equipment: Desktop System
  Office number: 141
Waiting for 1 message(s)
New hire event processed:
  Employee ID: 29
  Name: Mary Stuart
  Equipment: Pager
  Office number: 238
```

The output from the message-driven beans and the entity class appears in the server log, wrapped in logging information.

For each employee, the application first creates the entity and then finds it. You may see runtime errors in the server log, and transaction rollbacks may occur. The errors occur if both of the message-driven beans discover at the same time that the entity does not yet exist, so they both try to create it. The first attempt succeeds, but the second fails because the bean already exists. After the rollback, the second message-driven bean tries again and succeeds in finding the entity. Container-managed transactions allow the application to run correctly, in spite of these errors, with no special programming.

To run the client again, use the run target:

```
ant run
```

Undeploy the application after you finish running the client:

```
ant undeploy
```

To remove the generated files, use the following command:

```
ant clean
```

An Application Example That Consumes Messages from a Remote Server

This section and the following section explain how to write, compile, package, deploy, and run a pair of Java EE modules that run on two Java EE servers and that use the JMS API to interchange messages with each other. It is a common practice to deploy different components of an enterprise application on different systems within a company, and these examples illustrate on a small scale how to do this for an application that uses the JMS API.

However, the two examples work in slightly different ways. In this first example, the deployment information for a message-driven bean specifies the remote server from which it will *consume* messages. In the next example, the same bean is deployed on two different servers, so it is the client module that specifies the servers (one local, one remote) to which it is *sending* messages.

This first example divides the example in Chapter 23 into two modules (not applications): one containing the application client, and the other containing the message-driven bean.

This section covers the following topics:

- Overview of the modules
- Writing the module components
- Creating resources for the modules
- Using two application servers

- Building, deploying, and running the modules using NetBeans 5.5
- Building, deploying, and running the modules using Ant

You will find the source files for this section in `<INSTALL>/javaeetutorial5/examples/jms/consumeremote/`. Path names in this section are relative to this directory.

Overview of the Modules

Except for the fact that it is packaged as two separate modules, this example is very similar to the one in Chapter 23:

- One module contains the application client, which runs on the remote system and sends three messages to a queue.
- The other module contains the message-driven bean, which is deployed on the local server and consumes the messages from the queue on the remote server.

The basic steps of the modules are as follows.

1. The administrator starts two Java EE servers, one on each system.
2. On the local server, the administrator deploys the message-driven bean module, which uses a connection factory that specifies the remote server where the client is deployed.
3. On the remote server, the administrator places the client JAR file.
4. The client module sends three messages to a queue.
5. The message-driven bean consumes the messages.

Figure 32–3 illustrates the structure of this application. You can see that it is almost identical to Figure 23–1 except that there are two Java EE servers. The queue used is the one on the remote server; the queue must also exist on the local server for resource injection to succeed.

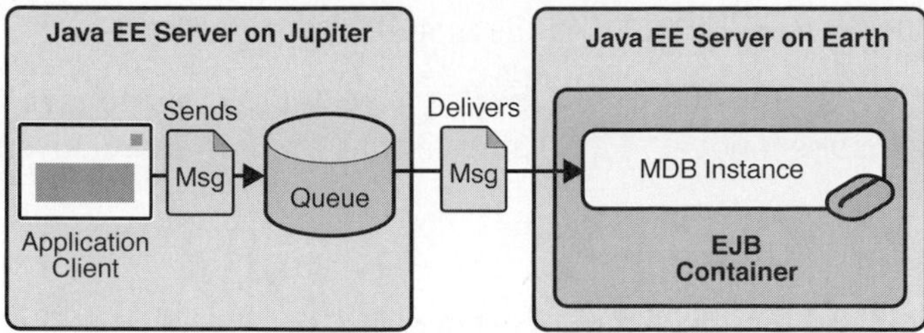

Figure 32–3 A Java EE Application That Consumes Messages from a Remote Server

Writing the Module Components

Writing the components of the modules involves

- Coding the application client
- Coding the message-driven bean

The application client, `jupiterclient/src/java/SimpleClient.java`, is almost identical to the one in The Application Client (page 792).

Similarly, the message-driven bean, `earthmdb/src/java/MessageBean.java`, is almost identical to the one in The Message-Driven Bean Class (page 793).

The only major difference is that the client and the bean are packaged in two separate modules.

Creating Resources for the Application

For this example, the message-driven bean uses the connection factory named `jms/JupiterConnectionFactory`, which you created in Creating Administered Objects for Multiple Systems (page 1094). Use the Admin Console to verify that the connection factory still exists and that its `AddressList` property is set to the name of the remote system. Because this bean must use a specific connection factory, the connection factory is specified in the `mdb-connection-factory` element of the `sun-ejb-jar.xml` file.

If you deleted the connection factory, you can recreate it as follows:

1. Go to the following directory:

   `<INSTALL>/javaeetutorial5/examples/jms/consumeremote/earth-mdb/`

2. Type the following command:

   ```
   ant create-remote-factory -Dsys=remote_system_name
   ```

   Replace `remote_system_name` with the actual name of the remote system.

The application client can use any connection factory that exists on the remote server; it uses `jms/ConnectionFactory`. Both components use the queue named `jms/Queue`, which you created in Creating JMS Administered Objects (page 1076).

Using Two Application Servers

We'll assume, as we did in Running JMS Client Programs on Multiple Systems (page 1093), that the two servers are named `earth` and `jupiter`.

The Application Server must be running on both systems.

Which system you use to package and deploy the modules and which system you use to run the client depend on your network configuration—which file system you can access remotely. These instructions assume that you can access the file system of `jupiter` from `earth` but cannot access the file system of `earth` from `jupiter`. (You can use the same systems for `jupiter` and `earth` that you used in Running JMS Client Programs on Multiple Systems, page 1093.)

You can package both modules on `earth` and deploy the message-driven bean there. The only action you perform on `jupiter` is running the client module.

Building, Deploying, and Running the Modules Using NetBeans 5.5

To package the modules using NetBeans 5.5, perform these steps:

1. In NetBeans 5.5, choose Open Project from the File menu.
2. In the Open Project dialog, navigate to `<INSTALL>/javaeetutorial5/examples/jms/consumeremote/`.
3. Select the `earthmdb` folder.
4. Select the Open as Main Project checkbox.
5. Click Open Project Folder.
6. Right-click the `earthmdb` project and choose Build Project.

This command creates a JAR file that contains the bean class file and the sun-ejb-jar.xml deployment descriptor file.

7. Choose Open Project from the File menu.
8. Select the jupiterclient folder.
9. Select the Open as Main Project checkbox.
10. Click Open Project Folder.
11. Right-click the jupiterclient project and choose Build Project.

    This target creates a JAR file that contains the client class file and a manifest file.

To deploy the earthmdb module and run the application client, perform these steps:

1. Right-click the earthmdb project and choose Set Main Project.
2. Right-click the earthmdb project and choose Deploy Project.
3. Copy the jupiterclient module to the remote system (jupiter):
    a. In a terminal window, change to the directory jupiterclient/dist:
    ```
    cd ../jupiterclient/dist
    ```
    b. Type a command like the following:
    ```
    cp jupiterclient.jar F:/
    ```
    That is, copy the client JAR file to a location on the remote filesystem.
4. Go to the directory on the remote system where you copied the client JAR file.
5. Use the following command:
    ```
    appclient -client jupiterclient.jar
    ```

On jupiter, the output of the appclient command looks like this:

```
Sending message: This is message 1
Sending message: This is message 2
Sending message: This is message 3
```

On earth, the output in the server log looks something like this (wrapped in logging information):

```
MESSAGE BEAN: Message received: This is message 1
MESSAGE BEAN: Message received: This is message 2
MESSAGE BEAN: Message received: This is message 3
```

Undeploy the message-driven bean after you finish running the client. To undeploy the `earthmdb` module, perform these steps:

1. Click the Runtime tab.
2. Expand the Servers node.
3. Expand the Sun Java System Application Server node.
4. Expand the Applications node.
5. Expand the EJB Modules node.
6. Right-click `earthmdb` and choose Undeploy.

To remove the generated files, follow these steps:

1. Right-click the `earthmdb` project and choose Clean Project.
2. In the command line window from which you copied the client JAR file, go to a directory other than the `jupiterclient/dist` directory.
3. Right-click the `jupiterclient` project and choose Clean Project.

You can also delete the `jupiterclient.jar` file from the remote filesystem.

Building, Deploying, and Running the Modules Using Ant

To package the modules using Ant, perform these steps:

1. Go to the following directory:

   ```
   <INSTALL>/javaeetutorial5/examples/jms/consumeremote/earth-
   mdb/
   ```

2. Type the following command:

   ```
   ant
   ```

   This command creates a JAR file that contains the bean class file and the `sun-ejb-jar.xml` deployment descriptor file.

3. Go to the `jupiterclient` directory:

   ```
   cd ../jupiterclient
   ```

4. Type the following command:

   ```
   ant
   ```

   This target creates a JAR file that contains the client class file and a manifest file.

To deploy the `earthmdb` module, perform these steps:

1. Change to the directory `earthmdb`:

   ```
   cd ../earthmdb
   ```

2. Type the following command:

   ```
   ant deploy
   ```

To copy the `jupiterclient` module to the remote system, perform these steps:

1. Change to the directory `jupiterclient/dist`:

   ```
   cd ../jupiterclient/dist
   ```

2. Type a command like the following:

   ```
   cp jupiterclient.jar F:/
   ```

   That is, copy the client JAR file to a location on the remote filesystem.

To run the client, perform the following steps:

1. Go to the directory on the remote system (`jupiter`) where you copied the client JAR file.
2. Use the following command:

   ```
   appclient -client jupiterclient.jar
   ```

On `jupiter`, the output of the `appclient` command looks like this:

```
Sending message: This is message 1
Sending message: This is message 2
Sending message: This is message 3
```

On `earth`, the output in the server log looks something like this (wrapped in logging information):

```
MESSAGE BEAN: Message received: This is message 1
MESSAGE BEAN: Message received: This is message 2
MESSAGE BEAN: Message received: This is message 3
```

Undeploy the message-driven bean after you finish running the client. To undeploy the `earthmdb` module, perform these steps:

1. Change to the directory `earthmdb`.
2. Type the following command:

   ```
   ant undeploy
   ```

You can also delete the `jupiterclient.jar` file from the remote filesystem.

To remove the generated files, use the following command in both the `earthmdb` and `jupiterclient` directories:

```
ant clean
```

An Application Example That Deploys a Message-Driven Bean on Two Servers

This section, like the preceding one, explains how to write, compile, package, deploy, and run a pair of Java EE modules that use the JMS API and run on two Java EE servers. The modules are slightly more complex than the ones in the first example.

The modules use the following components:

- An application client that is deployed on the local server. It uses two connection factories—one ordinary one and one that is configured to communicate with the remote server—to create two publishers and two subscribers and to publish and to consume messages.
- A message-driven bean that is deployed twice: once on the local server, and once on the remote one. It processes the messages and sends replies.

In this section, the term *local server* means the server on which both the application client and the message-driven bean are deployed (`earth` in the preceding example). The term *remote server* means the server on which only the message-driven bean is deployed (`jupiter` in the preceding example).

The section covers the following topics:

- Overview of the modules
- Writing the module components
- Creating resources for the modules
- Using two application servers
- Building, deploying, and running the modules using NetBeans 5.5
- Building, deploying, and running the modules using Ant

You will find the source files for this section in `<INSTALL>/javaeetutorial5/examples/jms/sendremote/`. Path names in this section are relative to this directory.

Overview of the Modules

This pair of modules is somewhat similar to the modules in An Application Example That Consumes Messages from a Remote Server (page 1146) in that the only components are a client and a message-driven bean. However, the modules here use these components in more complex ways. One module consists of the application client. The other module contains only the message-driven bean and is deployed twice, once on each server.

The basic steps of the modules are as follows.

1. You start two Java EE servers, one on each system.
2. On the local server (`earth`), you create two connection factories: one local and one that communicates with the remote server (`jupiter`). On the remote server, you create a connection factory that has the same name.
3. The application client looks up the two connection factories—the local one and the one that communicates with the remote server—to create two connections, sessions, publishers, and subscribers. The subscribers use a message listener.
4. Each publisher publishes five messages.
5. Each of the local and the remote message-driven beans receives five messages and sends replies.
6. The client's message listener consumes the replies.

Figure 32–4 illustrates the structure of this application. M1 represents the first message sent using the local connection factory, and RM1 represents the first reply message sent by the local MDB. M2 represents the first message sent using the remote connection factory, and RM2 represents the first reply message sent by the remote MDB.

Writing the Module Components

Writing the components of the modules involves two tasks:

- Coding the application client: `MultiAppServerClient.java`
- Coding the message-driven bean: `ReplyMsgBean.java`

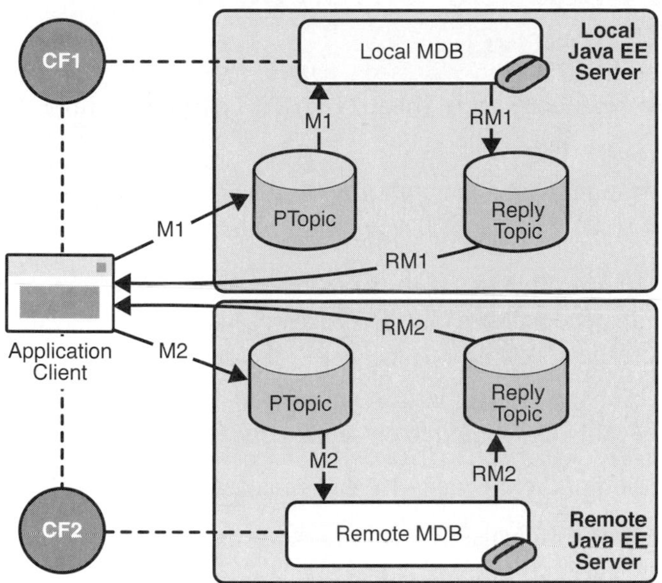

Figure 32–4 A Java EE Application That Sends Messages to Two Servers

Coding the Application Client: MultiAppServerClient.java

The application client class, `multiclient/src/java/MultiAppServer-Client.java`, does the following.

1. It injects resources for two connection factories and a topic.
2. For each connection factory, it creates a connection, a publisher session, a publisher, a subscriber session, a subscriber, and a temporary topic for replies.
3. Each subscriber sets its message listener, `ReplyListener`, and starts the connection.
4. Each publisher publishes five messages and creates a list of the messages the listener should expect.
5. When each reply arrives, the message listener displays its contents and removes it from the list of expected messages.
6. When all the messages have arrived, the client exits.

Coding the Message-Driven Bean: ReplyMsgBean.java

The message-driven bean class, `replybean/src/ReplyMsgBean.java`, does the following:

1. Uses the `@MessageDriven` annotation:

   ```
   @MessageDriven(mappedName="jms/Topic")
   ```

2. Injects resources for the `MessageDrivenContext` and for a connection factory. It does not need a destination resource because it uses the value of the incoming message's `JMSReplyTo` header as the destination.
3. Uses a `@PostConstruct` callback method to create the connection, and a `@PreDestroy` callback method to close the connection.

The `onMessage` method of the message-driven bean class does the following:

1. Casts the incoming message to a `TextMessage` and displays the text
2. Creates a connection, a session, and a publisher for the reply message
3. Publishes the message to the reply topic
4. Closes the connection

On both servers, the bean will consume messages from the topic `jms/Topic`.

Creating Resources for the Modules

This example uses the connection factory named `jms/ConnectionFactory` and the topic named `jms/Topic`. These objects must exist on both the local and the remote servers.

This example uses an additional connection factory, `jms/JupiterConnectionFactory`, which communicates with the remote system; you created it in Creating Administered Objects for Multiple Systems (page 1094). This connection factory must exist on the local server.

The `build.xml` file for the `multiclient` module contains targets that you can use to create these resources if you deleted them previously.

Using Two Application Servers

The Application Server must be running on both systems. You package, deploy, and run the modules from the local system.

If you are using NetBeans 5.5, you need to add the remote server in order to deploy the message-driven bean there. To do so, perform these steps:

1. In NetBeans 5.5, click the Runtime tab.
2. Right-click the Servers node and choose Add Server. In the Add Server Instance dialog, perform these steps:
   a. Select Sun Java System Application Server (the default) from the Server list.
   b. Accept the default name, which is typically `Sun Java System Application Server (1)`.
   c. Click Next.
   d. For the Platform Folder location, you can either browse to the location of the Application Server on the remote system or, if that location is not visible from the local system, use the default location on the local system.
   e. Select the Register Remote Domain radio button.
   f. Click Next.
   g. Type the system name of the host in the Host field.
   h. Click Next.
   i. Type the administrative username and password for the remote system in the Admin Username and Admin Password fields.
   j. Click Finish.

There may be a delay while NetBeans 5.5 registers the remote domain.

Building, Deploying, and Running the Modules Using NetBeans 5.5

To package the modules using NetBeans 5.5, perform these steps:

1. In NetBeans 5.5, choose Open Project from the File menu.
2. In the Open Project dialog, navigate to `<INSTALL>/javaeetutorial5/examples/jms/sendremote/`.

3. Select the `replybean` folder.
4. Select the Open as Main Project checkbox.
5. Click Open Project Folder.
6. Right-click the `replybean` project and choose Build Project.

   This command creates a JAR file that contains the bean class file.
7. Choose Open Project from the File menu.
8. Select the `multiclient` folder.
9. Select the Open as Main Project checkbox.
10. Click Open Project Folder.
11. Right-click the `multiclient` project and choose Build Project.

    This command creates a JAR file that contains the client class file and a manifest file.

To deploy the `multiclient` module on the local server, perform these steps:

1. Right-click the `multiclient` project and choose Properties.
2. Select Run from the Categories tree.
3. From the Server list, select Sun Java System Application Server (the local server).
4. Click OK.
5. Right-click the `multiclient` project and choose Deploy Project.

To deploy the `replybean` module on the local and remote servers, perform these steps:

1. Right-click the `replybean` project and choose Properties.
2. Select Run from the Categories tree.
3. From the Server list, select Sun Java System Application Server (the local server).
4. Click OK.
5. Right-click the `replybean` project and choose Deploy Project.
6. Right-click the `replybean` project again and choose Properties.
7. Select Run from the Categories tree.
8. From the Server list, select Sun Java System Application Server (1) (the remote server).
9. Click OK.
10. Right-click the `replybean` project and choose Deploy Project.

You can use the Runtime tab to verify that `multiclient` is deployed as an App Client Module on the local server and that `replybean` is deployed as an EJB Module on both servers.

To run the application client, right-click the `multiclient` project and choose Run Project.

This command returns a JAR file named `multiclientClient.jar` and then executes it.

On the local system, the output of the `appclient` command looks something like this:

```
running application client container.
Sent message: text: id=1 to local app server
Sent message: text: id=2 to remote app server
ReplyListener: Received message: id=1, text=ReplyMsgBean
processed message: text: id=1 to local app server
Sent message: text: id=3 to local app server
ReplyListener: Received message: id=3, text=ReplyMsgBean
processed message: text: id=3 to local app server
ReplyListener: Received message: id=2, text=ReplyMsgBean
processed message: text: id=2 to remote app server
Sent message: text: id=4 to remote app server
ReplyListener: Received message: id=4, text=ReplyMsgBean
processed message: text: id=4 to remote app server
Sent message: text: id=5 to local app server
ReplyListener: Received message: id=5, text=ReplyMsgBean
processed message: text: id=5 to local app server
Sent message: text: id=6 to remote app server
ReplyListener: Received message: id=6, text=ReplyMsgBean
processed message: text: id=6 to remote app server
Sent message: text: id=7 to local app server
ReplyListener: Received message: id=7, text=ReplyMsgBean
processed message: text: id=7 to local app server
Sent message: text: id=8 to remote app server
ReplyListener: Received message: id=8, text=ReplyMsgBean
processed message: text: id=8 to remote app server
Sent message: text: id=9 to local app server
ReplyListener: Received message: id=9, text=ReplyMsgBean
processed message: text: id=9 to local app server
Sent message: text: id=10 to remote app server
ReplyListener: Received message: id=10, text=ReplyMsgBean
processed message: text: id=10 to remote app server
Waiting for 0 message(s) from local app server
```

```
Waiting for 0 message(s) from remote app server
Finished
Closing connection 1
Closing connection 2
```

On the local system, where the message-driven bean receives the odd-numbered messages, the output in the server log looks like this (wrapped in logging information):

```
ReplyMsgBean: Received message: text: id=1 to local app server
ReplyMsgBean: Received message: text: id=3 to local app server
ReplyMsgBean: Received message: text: id=5 to local app server
ReplyMsgBean: Received message: text: id=7 to local app server
ReplyMsgBean: Received message: text: id=9 to local app server
```

On the remote system, where the bean receives the even-numbered messages, the output in the server log looks like this (wrapped in logging information):

```
ReplyMsgBean: Received message: text: id=2 to remote app server
ReplyMsgBean: Received message: text: id=4 to remote app server
ReplyMsgBean: Received message: text: id=6 to remote app server
ReplyMsgBean: Received message: text: id=8 to remote app server
ReplyMsgBean: Received message: text: id=10 to remote app server
```

Undeploy the modules after you finish running the client. To undeploy the modules, perform these steps:

1. Click the Runtime tab.
2. Expand the Servers node.
3. Expand the Sun Java System Application Server node (the local system).
4. Expand the Applications node.
5. Expand the EJB Modules node.
6. Right-click `replybean` and choose Undeploy.
7. Expand the App Client Modules node.
8. Right-click `multiclient` and choose Undeploy.
9. Expand the Sun Java System Application Server (1) node (the remote system).
10. Expand the Applications node.
11. Expand the EJB Modules node.
12. Right-click `replybean` and choose Undeploy.

To remove the generated files, follow these steps:

1. Right-click the `replybean` project and choose Clean Project.
2. Right-click the `multiclient` project and choose Clean Project.

Building, Deploying, and Running the Modules Using Ant

To package the modules, perform these steps:

1. Go to the following directory:

   ```
   <INSTALL>/javaeetutorial5/examples/jms/sendremote/multicli-
   ent/
   ```
2. Type the following command:

   ```
   ant
   ```

   This command creates a JAR file that contains the client class file and a manifest file.
3. Change to the directory `replybean`:

   ```
   cd ../replybean
   ```
4. Type the following command:

   ```
   ant
   ```

   This command creates a JAR file that contains the bean class file.

To deploy the `replybean` module on the local and remote servers, perform the following steps:

1. Verify that you are still in the directory `replybean`.
2. Type the following command:

   ```
   ant deploy
   ```

   Ignore the message that states that the application is deployed at a URL.
3. Type the following command:

   ```
   ant deploy-remote -Dsys=remote_system_name
   ```

   Replace *`remote_system_name`* with the actual name of the remote system.

To deploy and run the client, perform these steps:

1. Change to the directory `multiclient`:

   ```
   cd ../multiclient
   ```

2. Type the following command:

   ```
   ant run
   ```

On the local system, the output looks something like this:

```
running application client container.
Sent message: text: id=1 to local app server
Sent message: text: id=2 to remote app server
ReplyListener: Received message: id=1, text=ReplyMsgBean
processed message: text: id=1 to local app server
Sent message: text: id=3 to local app server
ReplyListener: Received message: id=3, text=ReplyMsgBean
processed message: text: id=3 to local app server
ReplyListener: Received message: id=2, text=ReplyMsgBean
processed message: text: id=2 to remote app server
Sent message: text: id=4 to remote app server
ReplyListener: Received message: id=4, text=ReplyMsgBean
processed message: text: id=4 to remote app server
Sent message: text: id=5 to local app server
ReplyListener: Received message: id=5, text=ReplyMsgBean
processed message: text: id=5 to local app server
Sent message: text: id=6 to remote app server
ReplyListener: Received message: id=6, text=ReplyMsgBean
processed message: text: id=6 to remote app server
Sent message: text: id=7 to local app server
ReplyListener: Received message: id=7, text=ReplyMsgBean
processed message: text: id=7 to local app server
Sent message: text: id=8 to remote app server
ReplyListener: Received message: id=8, text=ReplyMsgBean
processed message: text: id=8 to remote app server
Sent message: text: id=9 to local app server
ReplyListener: Received message: id=9, text=ReplyMsgBean
processed message: text: id=9 to local app server
Sent message: text: id=10 to remote app server
ReplyListener: Received message: id=10, text=ReplyMsgBean
processed message: text: id=10 to remote app server
Waiting for 0 message(s) from local app server
Waiting for 0 message(s) from remote app server
Finished
Closing connection 1
Closing connection 2
```

On the local system, where the message-driven bean receives the odd-numbered messages, the output in the server log looks like this (wrapped in logging information):

```
ReplyMsgBean: Received message: text: id=1 to local app server
ReplyMsgBean: Received message: text: id=3 to local app server
ReplyMsgBean: Received message: text: id=5 to local app server
ReplyMsgBean: Received message: text: id=7 to local app server
ReplyMsgBean: Received message: text: id=9 to local app server
```

On the remote system, where the bean receives the even-numbered messages, the output in the server log looks like this (wrapped in logging information):

```
ReplyMsgBean: Received message: text: id=2 to remote app server
ReplyMsgBean: Received message: text: id=4 to remote app server
ReplyMsgBean: Received message: text: id=6 to remote app server
ReplyMsgBean: Received message: text: id=8 to remote app server
ReplyMsgBean: Received message: text: id=10 to remote app server
```

Undeploy the modules after you finish running the client. To undeploy the `multiclient` module, perform these steps:

1. Verify that you are still in the directory `multiclient`.
2. Type the following command:

   ```
   ant undeploy
   ```

To undeploy the `replybean` module, perform these steps:

1. Change to the directory `replybean`:

   ```
   cd ../replybean
   ```

2. Type the following command:

   ```
   ant undeploy
   ```

3. Type the following command:

   ```
   ant undeploy-remote -Dsys=remote_system_name
   ```

   Replace *`remote_system_name`* with the actual name of the remote system.

To remove the generated files, use the following command in both the `replybean` and `multiclient` directories:

```
ant clean
```

33

Transactions

A typical enterprise application accesses and stores information in one or more databases. Because this information is critical for business operations, it must be accurate, current, and reliable. Data integrity would be lost if multiple programs were allowed to update the same information simultaneously. It would also be lost if a system that failed while processing a business transaction were to leave the affected data only partially updated. By preventing both of these scenarios, software transactions ensure data integrity. Transactions control the concurrent access of data by multiple programs. In the event of a system failure, transactions make sure that after recovery the data will be in a consistent state.

What Is a Transaction?

To emulate a business transaction, a program may need to perform several steps. A financial program, for example, might transfer funds from a checking account to a savings account using the steps listed in the following pseudocode:

```
begin transaction
   debit checking account
   credit savings account
   update history log
commit transaction
```

Either all three of these steps must complete, or none of them at all. Otherwise, data integrity is lost. Because the steps within a transaction are a unified whole, a *transaction* is often defined as an indivisible unit of work.

A transaction can end in two ways: with a commit or with a rollback. When a transaction commits, the data modifications made by its statements are saved. If a statement within a transaction fails, the transaction rolls back, undoing the effects of all statements in the transaction. In the pseudocode, for example, if a disk drive were to crash during the `credit` step, the transaction would roll back and undo the data modifications made by the `debit` statement. Although the transaction fails, data integrity would be intact because the accounts still balance.

In the preceding pseudocode, the `begin` and `commit` statements mark the boundaries of the transaction. When designing an enterprise bean, you determine how the boundaries are set by specifying either container-managed or bean-managed transactions.

Container-Managed Transactions

In an enterprise bean with *container-managed transaction demarcation*, the EJB container sets the boundaries of the transactions. You can use container-managed transactions with any type of enterprise bean: session, or message-driven. Container-managed transactions simplify development because the enterprise bean code does not explicitly mark the transaction's boundaries. The code does not include statements that begin and end the transaction.

By default if no transaction demarcation is specified enterprise beans use container-managed transaction demarcation.

Typically, the container begins a transaction immediately before an enterprise bean method starts. It commits the transaction just before the method exits. Each method can be associated with a single transaction. Nested or multiple transactions are not allowed within a method.

Container-managed transactions do not require all methods to be associated with transactions. When developing a bean, you can specify which of the bean's methods are associated with transactions by setting the transaction attributes.

Enterprise beans that use container-managed transaction demarcation must not use any transaction management methods that interfere with the container's transaction demarcation boundries. Examples of such methods are the `commit`, `setAutoCommit`, and `rollback` methods of `java.sql.Connection` or the `commit` and `rollback` methods of `javax.jms.Session`. If you require control over the transaction dermarcation, you must use application-managed transaction demarcation.

Enterprise beans that use container-managed transaction demarcation also must not use the `javax.transaction.UserTransaction` interface.

Transaction Attributes

A *transaction attribute* controls the scope of a transaction. Figure 33–1 illustrates why controlling the scope is important. In the diagram, `method-A` begins a transaction and then invokes `method-B` of `Bean-2`. When `method-B` executes, does it run within the scope of the transaction started by `method-A`, or does it execute with a new transaction? The answer depends on the transaction attribute of `method-B`.

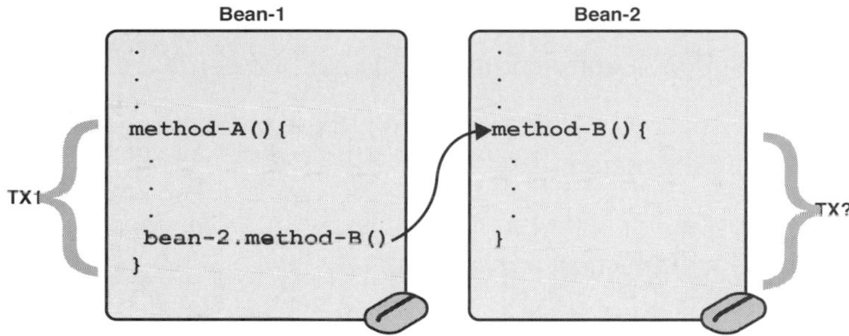

Figure 33–1 Transaction Scope

A transaction attribute can have one of the following values:

- `Required`
- `RequiresNew`
- `Mandatory`
- `NotSupported`
- `Supports`
- `Never`

Required

If the client is running within a transaction and invokes the enterprise bean's method, the method executes within the client's transaction. If the client is not associated with a transaction, the container starts a new transaction before running the method.

The `Required` attribute is the implicit transaction attribute for all enterprise bean methods running with container-managed transaction demarcation. You typically do not set the `Required` attribute unless you need to override another transaction attribute. Because transaction attributes are declarative, you can easily change them later.

RequiresNew

If the client is running within a transaction and invokes the enterprise bean's method, the container takes the following steps:

1. Suspends the client's transaction
2. Starts a new transaction
3. Delegates the call to the method
4. Resumes the client's transaction after the method completes

If the client is not associated with a transaction, the container starts a new transaction before running the method.

You should use the `RequiresNew` attribute when you want to ensure that the method always runs within a new transaction.

Mandatory

If the client is running within a transaction and invokes the enterprise bean's method, the method executes within the client's transaction. If the client is not associated with a transaction, the container throws the `TransactionRequiredException`.

Use the `Mandatory` attribute if the enterprise bean's method must use the transaction of the client.

NotSupported

If the client is running within a transaction and invokes the enterprise bean's method, the container suspends the client's transaction before invoking the method. After the method has completed, the container resumes the client's transaction.

If the client is not associated with a transaction, the container does not start a new transaction before running the method.

Use the `NotSupported` attribute for methods that don't need transactions. Because transactions involve overhead, this attribute may improve performance.

Supports

If the client is running within a transaction and invokes the enterprise bean's method, the method executes within the client's transaction. If the client is not associated with a transaction, the container does not start a new transaction before running the method.

Because the transactional behavior of the method may vary, you should use the `Supports` attribute with caution.

Never

If the client is running within a transaction and invokes the enterprise bean's method, the container throws a `RemoteException`. If the client is not associated with a transaction, the container does not start a new transaction before running the method.

Summary of Transaction Attributes

Table 33–1 summarizes the effects of the transaction attributes. Both the T1 and the T2 transactions are controlled by the container. A T1 transaction is associated with the client that calls a method in the enterprise bean. In most cases, the client is another enterprise bean. A T2 transaction is started by the container just before the method executes.

In the last column of Table 33–1, the word *None* means that the business method does not execute within a transaction controlled by the container. However, the database calls in such a business method might be controlled by the transaction manager of the DBMS.

Table 33–1 Transaction Attributes and Scope

Transaction Attribute	Client's Transaction	Business Method's Transaction
`Required`	None	T2
	T1	T1
`RequiresNew`	None	T2
	T1	T2
`Mandatory`	None	error
	T1	T1
`NotSupported`	None	None
	T1	None
`Supports`	None	None
	T1	T1
`Never`	None	None
	T1	Error

Setting Transaction Attributes

Transaction attributes are specified by decorating the enterprise bean class or method with a `javax.ejb.TransactionAttribute` annotation, and setting it to one of the `javax.ejb.TransactionAttributeType` contants.

If you decorate the enterprise bean class with `@TransactionAttribute`, the specified `TransactionAttributeType` is applied to all the business methods in the class. Decoration a business method with `@TransactionAttribute` applies the `TransactionAttributeType` only to that method. If a `@TransactionAttribute` annotation decorates both the class and the method, the method `TransactionAttributeType` overrides the class `TransactionAttributeType`.

The TransactionAttributeType constants encapsulate the transaction attributes described earlier in this section.

- Required: TransactionAttributeType.REQUIRED
- RequiresNew: TransactionAttributeType.REQUIRES_NEW
- Mandatory: TransactionAttributeType.MANDATORY
- NotSupported: TransactionAttributeType.NOT_SUPPORTED
- Supports: TransactionAttributeType.SUPPORTS
- Never: TransactionAttributeType.NEVER

The following code snippet demonstrates how to use the @TransactionAttribute annotation:

```
@TransactionAttribute(NOT_SUPPORTED)
@Stateful
public class TransactionBean implements Transaction {
...
  @TransactionAttribute(REQUIRES_NEW)
  public void firstMethod() {...}

  @TransactionAttribute(REQUIRED)
  public void secondMethod() {...}

  public void thirdMethod() {...}

  public void fourthMethod() {...}
}
```

In this example, the TransactionBean class's transaction attribute has been set to NotSupported. firstMethod has been set to RequiresNew, and secondMethod has been set to Required. Because a @TransactionAttribute set on a method overrides the class @TransactionAttribute, calls to firstMethod will create a new transaction, and calls to secondMethod will either run in the current transaction, or start a new transaction. Calls to thirdMethod or fourthMethod do not take place within a transaction.

Rolling Back a Container-Managed Transaction

There are two ways to roll back a container-managed transaction. First, if a system exception is thrown, the container will automatically roll back the transaction. Second, by invoking the setRollbackOnly method of the EJBContext interface, the bean method instructs the container to roll back the transaction. If the bean throws an application exception, the rollback is not automatic but can be initiated by a call to `setRollbackOnly`.

Synchronizing a Session Bean's Instance Variables

The `SessionSynchronization` interface, which is optional, allows stateful session bean instances to receive transaction synchronization notifications. For example, you could synchronize the instance variables of an enterprise bean with their corresponding values in the database. The container invokes the `SessionSynchronization` methods—`afterBegin`, `beforeCompletion`, and `afterCompletion`—at each of the main stages of a transaction.

The `afterBegin` method informs the instance that a new transaction has begun. The container invokes `afterBegin` immediately before it invokes the business method.

The container invokes the `beforeCompletion` method after the business method has finished, but just before the transaction commits. The `beforeCompletion` method is the last opportunity for the session bean to roll back the transaction (by calling `setRollbackOnly`).

The `afterCompletion` method indicates that the transaction has completed. It has a single `boolean` parameter whose value is `true` if the transaction was committed and `false` if it was rolled back.

Methods Not Allowed in Container-Managed Transactions

You should not invoke any method that might interfere with the transaction boundaries set by the container. The list of prohibited methods follows:

- The `commit`, `setAutoCommit`, and `rollback` methods of `java.sql.Connection`
- The `getUserTransaction` method of `javax.ejb.EJBContext`
- Any method of `javax.transaction.UserTransaction`

You can, however, use these methods to set boundaries in application-managed transactions.

Bean-Managed Transactions

In *bean-managed transaction demarcation*, the code in the session or message-driven bean explicitly marks the boundaries of the transaction. Although beans with container-managed transactions require less coding, they have one limitation: When a method is executing, it can be associated with either a single transaction or no transaction at all. If this limitation will make coding your bean difficult, you should consider using bean-managed transactions.

The following pseudocode illustrates the kind of fine-grained control you can obtain with application-managed transactions. By checking various conditions, the pseudocode decides whether to start or stop different transactions within the business method.

```
begin transaction
...
update table-a
...
if (condition-x)
   commit transaction
else if (condition-y)
   update table-b
   commit transaction
else
   rollback transaction
   begin transaction
   update table-c
   commit transaction
```

When coding a application-managed transaction for session or message-driven beans, you must decide whether to use JDBC or JTA transactions. The sections that follow discuss both types of transactions.

JTA Transactions

JTA is the abbreviation for the Java Transaction API. This API allows you to demarcate transactions in a manner that is independent of the transaction manager implementation. The Application Server implements the transaction manager with the Java Transaction Service (JTS). But your code doesn't call the JTS methods directly. Instead, it invokes the JTA methods, which then call the lower-level JTS routines.

A *JTA transaction* is controlled by the Java EE transaction manager. You may want to use a JTA transaction because it can span updates to multiple databases from different vendors. A particular DBMS's transaction manager may not work with heterogeneous databases. However, the Java EE transaction manager does have one limitation: it does not support nested transactions. In other words, it cannot start a transaction for an instance until the preceding transaction has ended.

To demarcate a JTA transaction, you invoke the `begin`, `commit`, and `rollback` methods of the `javax.transaction.UserTransaction` interface.

Returning without Committing

In a stateless session bean with bean-managed transactions, a business method must commit or roll back a transaction before returning. However, a stateful session bean does not have this restriction.

In a stateful session bean with a JTA transaction, the association between the bean instance and the transaction is retained across multiple client calls. Even if each business method called by the client opens and closes the database connection, the association is retained until the instance completes the transaction.

In a stateful session bean with a JDBC transaction, the JDBC connection retains the association between the bean instance and the transaction across multiple calls. If the connection is closed, the association is not retained.

Methods Not Allowed in Bean-Managed Transactions

Do not invoke the `getRollbackOnly` and `setRollbackOnly` methods of the `EJBContext` interface in bean-managed transactions. These methods should be used only in container-managed transactions. For bean-managed transactions, invoke the `getStatus` and `rollback` methods of the `UserTransaction` interface.

Transaction Timeouts

For container-managed transactions, you control the transaction timeout interval by setting the value of the `timeout-in-seconds` property in the `domain.xml` file, which is in the `config` directory of your Application Server installation. For example, you would set the timeout value to 5 seconds as follows:

```
timeout-in-seconds=5
```

With this setting, if the transaction has not completed within 5 seconds, the EJB container rolls it back.

When the Application Server is first installed, the timeout value is set to 0:

```
timeout-in-seconds=0
```

If the value is 0, the transaction will not time out.

Only enterprise beans with container-managed transactions are affected by the `timeout-in-seconds` property. For enterprise beans with bean-managed JTA transactions, you invoke the `setTransactionTimeout` method of the `UserTransaction` interface.

Updating Multiple Databases

The Java EE transaction manager controls all enterprise bean transactions except for bean-managed JDBC transactions. The Java EE transaction manager allows an enterprise bean to update multiple databases within a transaction. The figures that follow show two scenarios for updating multiple databases in a single transaction.

In Figure 33–2, the client invokes a business method in `Bean-A`. The business method begins a transaction, updates Database X, updates Database Y, and invokes a business method in `Bean-B`. The second business method updates Database Z and returns control to the business method in `Bean-A`, which commits the transaction. All three database updates occur in the same transaction.

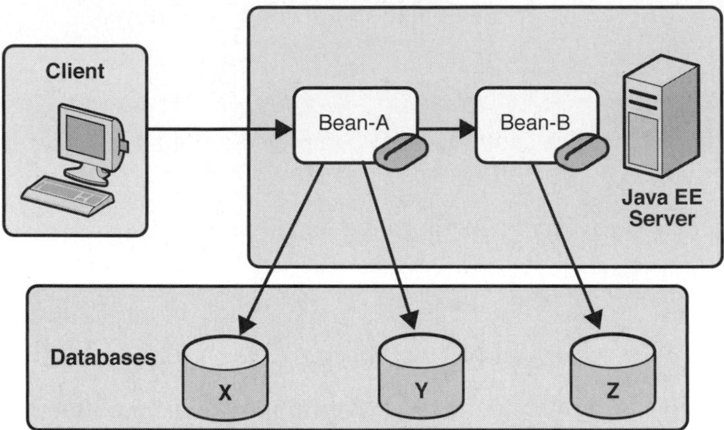

Figure 33–2 Updating Multiple Databases

In Figure 33–3, the client calls a business method in `Bean-A`, which begins a transaction and updates Database X. Then `Bean-A` invokes a method in `Bean-B`, which resides in a remote Java EE server. The method in `Bean-B` updates Database Y. The transaction managers of the Java EE servers ensure that both databases are updated in the same transaction.

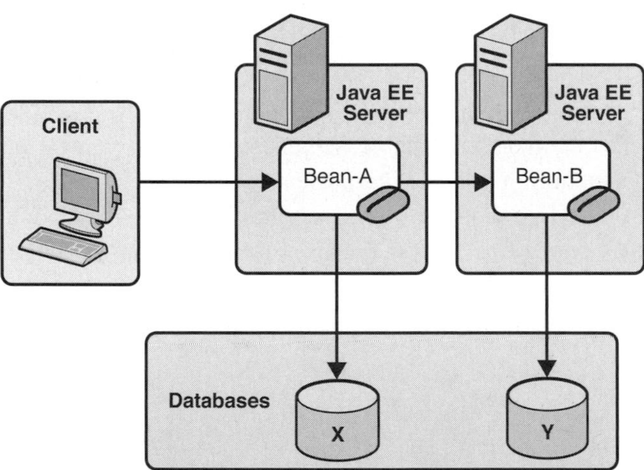

Figure 33–3 Updating Multiple Databases across Java EE Servers

Transactions in Web Components

You can demarcate a transaction in a web component by using either the `java.sql.Connection` or `javax.transaction.UserTransaction` interface. These are the same interfaces that a session bean with bean-managed transactions can use. Transactions demarcated with the `UserTransaction` interface are discussed in the section JTA Transactions (page 1173). For an example of a web component using transactions, see Accessing Databases (page 69).

34

Resource Connections

JAVA EE components can access a wide variety of resources, including databases, mail sessions, Java Message Service objects, JAXR connection factories, and URLs. The Java EE 5 platform provides mechanisms that allow you to access all these resources in a similar manner. This chapter describes how to get connections to several types of resources.

Resources and JNDI Naming

In a distributed application, components need to access other components and resources such as databases. For example, a servlet might invoke remote methods on an enterprise bean that retrieves information from a database. In the Java EE platform, the Java Naming and Directory Interface (JNDI) naming service enables components to locate other components and resources.

A resource is a program object that provides connections to systems, such as database servers and messaging systems. (A JDBC resource is sometimes referred to as a data source.) Each resource object is identified by a unique, people-friendly name, called the JNDI name.

For example, the JNDI name of the JDBC resource for the Java DB database that is shipped with the Application Server is `jdbc/__default`.

An administrator creates resources in a JNDI namespace. In the Application Server, you can use either the Admin Console or the `asadmin` command to create resources. Applications then use annotations to inject the resources. If an application uses resource injection, the Application Server invokes the JNDI API, and the application is not required to do so. However, it is also possible for an application to locate resources by making direct calls to the JNDI API.

A resource object and its JNDI name are bound together by the naming and directory service. To create a new resource, a new name-object binding is entered into the JNDI namespace.

For information on creating Java Message Service (JMS) resources, see Creating JMS Administered Objects (page 1076). For information on creating Java API for XML Registries (JAXR) resources, see Creating JAXR Resources (page 735). For an example of creating a JDBC resource, see Creating a Data Source in the Application Server (page 56).

You inject resources by using the `@Resource` annotation in an application. For information on resource injection, see the following sections of this Tutorial:

- Declaring Resource References (page 52)
- Obtaining a Connection Factory (page 698), for information on injecting a JAXR connection factory resource (actually a connector resource)
- Updating Data in the Database (page 832), for information on injecting a `UserTransaction` resource
- Connection Factories (page 1061), Destinations (page 1061), and Using @Resource Annotations in Java EE Components (page 1120), for information on injecting JMS resources

You can use a deployment descriptor to override the resource mapping that you specify in an annotation. Using a deployment descriptor allows you to change an application by repackaging it, rather than by both recompiling the source files and repackaging. However, for most applications, a deployment descriptor is not necessary.

DataSource Objects and Connection Pools

To store, organize, and retrieve data, most applications use a relational database. Java EE 5 components may access relational databases through the JDBC API. For information on this API, see:

```
http://java.sun.com/products/jdbc
```

In the JDBC API, databases are accessed by using `DataSource` objects. A `DataSource` has a set of properties that identify and describe the real world data source that it represents. These properties include information such as the location of the database server, the name of the database, the network protocol to use to communicate with the server, and so on. In the Application Server, a data source is called a JDBC resource.

Applications access a data source using a connection, and a `DataSource` object can be thought of as a factory for connections to the particular data source that the `DataSource` instance represents. In a basic `DataSource` implementation, a call to the `getConnection` method returns a connection object that is a physical connection to the data source.

If a `DataSource` object is registered with a JNDI naming service, an application can use the JNDI API to access that `DataSource` object, which can then be used to connect to the data source it represents.

`DataSource` objects that implement connection pooling also produce a connection to the particular data source that the `DataSource` class represents. The connection object that the `getConnection` method returns is a handle to a `PooledConnection` object rather than being a physical connection. An application uses the connection object in the same way that it uses a connection. Connection pooling has no effect on application code except that a pooled connection, like all connections, should always be explicitly closed. When an application closes a connection that is pooled, the connection is returned to a pool of reusable connections. The next time `getConnection` is called, a handle to one of these pooled connections will be returned if one is available. Because connection pooling avoids creating a new physical connection every time one is requested, applications can run significantly faster.

A JDBC connection pool is a group of reusable connections for a particular database. Because creating each new physical connection is time consuming, the server maintains a pool of available connections to increase performance. When an application requests a connection, it obtains one from the pool. When an application closes a connection, the connection is returned to the pool.

Applications that use the Persistence API specify the `DataSource` object they are using in the `jta-data-source` element of the `persistence.xml` file.

```
<jta-data-source>jdbc/MyOrderDB</jta-data-source>
```

This is typically the only reference to a JDBC object for a persistence unit. The application code does not refer to any JDBC objects. For more details, see Persistence Units (page 822).

Resource Injection

The `javax.annotation.Resource` annotation is used to declare a reference to a resource. `@Resource` can decorate a class, a field, or a method. The container will inject the resource referred to by `@Resource` into the component either at runtime or when the component is initialized, depending on whether field/method injection or class injection is used. With field and method-based injection, the container will inject the resource when the application is initialized. For class-based injection, the resource is looked up by the application at runtime.

`@Resource` has the following elements:

- `name`: The JNDI name of the resource
- `type`: The Java language type of the resource
- `authenticationType`: The authentication type to use for the resource
- `shareable`: Indicates whether the resource can be shared
- `mappedName`: A non-portable, implementation-specific name to which the resource should be mapped
- `description`: The description of the resource

The `name` element is the JNDI name of the resource, and is optional for field- and method-based injection. For field-based injection, the default `name` is the field name qualified by the class name. For method-based injection, the default `name` is the JavaBeans property name based on the method qualified by the class name. The `name` element must be specified for class-based injection.

The type of resource is determined by one of the following:

- The type of the field the `@Resource` annotation is decorating for field-based injection
- The type of the JavaBeans property the `@Resource` annotation is decorating for method-based injection
- The `type` element of `@Resource`

For class-based injection, the `type` element is required.

The `authenticationType` element is used only for connection factory resources, and can be set to one of the `javax.annotation.Resource.AuthenticationType` enumerated type values: `CONTAINER`, the default, and `APPLICATION`.

The `shareable` element is used only for ORB instance resources or connection factory resource. It indicates whether the resource can be shared between this component and other components, and may be set to `true`, the default, or `false`.

The `mappedName` element is a non-portable, implementation-specific name that the resource should be mapped to. Because the `name` element, when specified or defaulted, is local only to the application, many Java EE servers provide a way of referring to resources across the application server. This is done by setting the `mappedName` element. Use of the `mappedName` element is non-portable across Java EE server implementations.

The `description` element is the description of the resource, typically in the default language of the system on which the application is deployed. It is used to help identify resources, and to help application developers choose the correct resource.

Field-Based Injection

To use field-based resource injection, declare a field and decorate it with the `@Resource` annotation. The container will infer the name and type of the resource if the name and type elements are not specified. If you do specify the type element, it must match the field's type declaration.

```
package com.example;

public class SomeClass {
  @Resource
  private javax.sql.DataSource myDB;
...
}
```

In the code above, the container infers the name of the resource based on the class name and the field name: com.example.SomeClass/myDB. The inferred type is javax.sql.DataSource.class.

```
package com.example;

public class SomeClass {
  @Resource(name="customerDB")
  private javax.sql.DataSource myDB;
...
}
```

In the code above, the JNDI name is customerDB, and the inferred type is javax.sql.DataSource.class.

Method-Based Injection

To use method-based injection, declare a setter method and decorate it with the @Resource annotation. The container will infer the name and type of the resource if the name and type elements are not specified. The setter method must follow the JavaBeans conventions for property names: the method name must begin with set, have a void return type, and only one parameter. If you do specify the type element, it must match the field's type declaration.

```
package com.example;

public class SomeClass {

  private javax.sql.DataSource myDB;
...
  @Resource
  private void setMyDB(javax.sql.DataSource ds) {
```

```
        myDB = ds;
    }
...
}
```

In the code above, the container infers the name of the resource based on the class name and the field name: com.example.SomeClass/myDB. The inferred type is javax.sql.DataSource.class.

```
package com.example;

public class SomeClass {

    private javax.sql.DataSource myDB;
...
    @Resource(name="customerDB")
    private void setMyDB(javax.sql.DataSource ds) {
        myDB = ds;
    }
...
}
```

In the code above, the JNDI name is customerDB, and the inferred type is javax.sql.DataSource.class.

Class-Based Injection

To use class-based injection, decorate the class with a @Resource annotation, and set the required name and type elements.

```
@Resource(name="myMessageQueue",
          type="javax.jms.ConnectionFactory")
public class SomeMessageBean {
...
}
```

Declaring Multiple Resources

The `@Resources` annotation is used to group together multiple `@Resource` declarations for class-based injection.

```
@Resources({
  @Resource(name="myMessageQueue",
            type="javax.jms.ConnectionFactory"),
  @Resource(name="myMailSession",
            type="javax.mail.Session")
})
public class SomeMessageBean {
...
}
```

The code above shows the `@Resources` annotation containing two `@Resource` declarations. One is a JMS message queue, and the other is a JavaMail session.

The confirmer Example Application

The `confirmer` example application demonstrates how to use an injected JavaMail session to send a confirmation email.

If you've ever ordered a product from a web site, you've probably received an email confirming your order. The `ConfirmerBean` class demonstrates how to send email from an enterprise bean.

Like a database connection, a mail session is a resource. In the Application Server, a mail session is called a JavaMail resource. The resource is injected into the class using `@Resource` and specifying the JNDI name of the resource. The type of the `session` field is `javax.mail.Session`.

```
@Resource(name="mail/myMailSession")
private Session session;
```

After calling several `set` methods on the `Message` object, `sendNotice` invokes the `send` method of the `javax.mail.Transport` class to send the message. The source code for the `sendNotice` method follows.

```
public void sendNotice(String recipient) {
  try {
    Message message = new MimeMessage(session);
    message.setFrom();
```

```
        message.setRecipients(Message.RecipientType.TO,
            InternetAddress.parse(recipient, false));
        message.setSubject("Test Message from ConfirmerBean");
        DateFormat dateFormatter = DateFormat
            .getDateTimeInstance(DateFormat.LONG,
            DateFormat.SHORT);
        Date timeStamp = new Date();

        String messageText = "Thank you for your order." + '\n'
            + "We received your order on "
            + dateFormatter.format(timeStamp) + ".";
        message.setText(messageText);

        message.setHeader("X-Mailer", mailer);
        message.setSentDate(timeStamp);

        // Send message
        Transport.send(message);
        logger.info("Mail sent to " + recipient + ".");
    } catch (MessagingException ex) {
        ex.printStackTrace();
        logger.info("Error in ConfirmerBean for " + recipient);
    }
}
```

Running the confirmer Example Application

To run the `confirmer` example, follow these steps, as described in the following sections:

1. Create a mail session in the Admin Console.
2. Build the example.
3. Deploy the example.
4. Retrieve the client JAR.
5. Run the client JAR.

Creating a Mail Session

To create a mail session in the Application Server using the Admin Console, follow these steps:

1. Open the URL `http://localhost:4848/asadmin` in a browser.

2. Select the JavaMail Sessions node.
3. Click New.
4. Type `mail/myMailSession` in the JNDI Name field.
5. Type the name of the host running your mail server in the Mail Host field.
6. Type the destination email address in the Default User field.
7. Type your email address in the Default Return Address field.
8. Click OK.

   Note that `mail/myMailSession` is listed under the JavaMail Sessions node.

Building, Packaging, and Deploying confirmer in NetBeans 5.5

Follow these instructions to build, package, and deploy the `confirmer` example to your Application Server instance using the NetBeans 5.5 IDE.

1. In NetBeans 5.5, select File→Open Project.
2. In the Open Project dialog, navigate to `<INSTALL>/javaeetutorial5/examples/ejb/`.
3. Select the `confirmer` folder.
4. Select the Open as Main Project and Open Required Projects checkboxes.
5. Click Open Project Folder.
6. In the Projects tab, right-click the `confirmer` project and select Deploy Project.

This builds and packages the application into `confirmer.ear`, located in `<INSTALL>/javaeetutorial5/examples/ejb/confirmer/dist`, and deploys this EAR file to your Application Server instance.

Building, Packaging, and Deploying confirmer Using Ant

To build and package the `confirmer` example, do the following:

1. In a terminal window, go to `<INSTALL>/examples/ejb/confirmer`.
2. Enter the following command:

```
ant
```

This compiles the source code and creates an EAR file, `confirmer.ear`, in the `dist` directory.

To deploy `confirmer.ear`, type the following command in a terminal window:

```
ant deploy
```

Running the Client in NetBeans 5.5

By default, the client sends a message to `pig.bodine@example.com`, a fictional email address. To change the email address in NetBeans 5.5, do the following:

1. Right-click the `confirmer` project in the Projects pane and select Properties.
2. Click the Run category.
3. In the Client Information area, under Arguments, enter the email address to which you want the message sent.
4. Click OK.

To run the client in NetBeans 5.5, right-click the confirmer project in the Projects pane and select Run Project. You should see the following line when the client has successfully sent the test message:

```
...
Message sent to pig.bodine@example.com.
...
```

Running the Client Using Ant

By default, the client sends a message to `pig.bodine@example.com`, a fictional email address. To change the email address, set the `app-client.args` property in `<INSTALL>/examples/ejb/confirmer/nbproject/project.properties` to the email address to which you'd like the test message sent. For example:

```
app-client.args=duke@example.com
```

To retrieve the client JAR and run the client, enter the following command in a terminal:

```
ant run
```

You should see the following line when the client has successfully sent the test message:

```
[exec] Message sent to pig.bodine@example.com.
```

If you changed the target email address, the test message should arrive in the user's inbox in a few moments.

Further Information

For more information about resources and annotations, see the following:

- Common Annotations for the Java Platform (JSR 250):
  `http://www.jcp.org/en/jsr/detail?id=250`
- The Java EE 5 Platform Specification (JSR 244):
  `http://www.jcp.org/en/jsr/detail?id=244`
- The Enterprise JavaBeans (EJB) 3.0 specification (JSR 220):
  `http://www.jcp.org/en/jsr/detail?id=220`

35 Connector Architecture

THE Connector architecture enables Java EE components to interact with enterprise information systems (EISs) and EISs to interact with Java EE components. EIS software includes various types of systems: enterprise resource planning (ERP), mainframe transaction processing, and nonrelational databases, among others. Connector architecture simplifies the integration of diverse EISs. Each EIS requires only one implementation of the Connector architecture. Because an implementation adheres to the Connector specification, it is portable across all compliant Java EE servers.

About Resource Adapters

A *resource adapter* is a Java EE component that implements the Connector architecture for a specific EIS. As illustrated in Figure 35–1, the resource adapter facilitates communication between a Java EE application and an EIS.

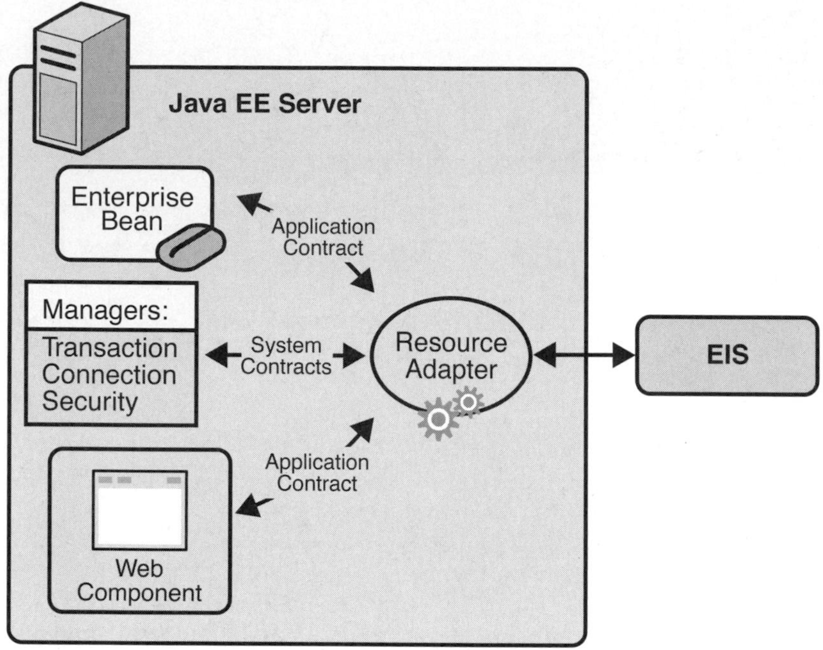

Figure 35–1 Resource Adapter Contracts

Stored in a Resource Adapter Archive (RAR) file, a resource adapter can be deployed on any Java EE server, much like the EAR file of a Java EE application. An RAR file may be contained in an EAR file, or it may exist as a separate file. See Figure 35–2 for the structure of a resource adapter module.

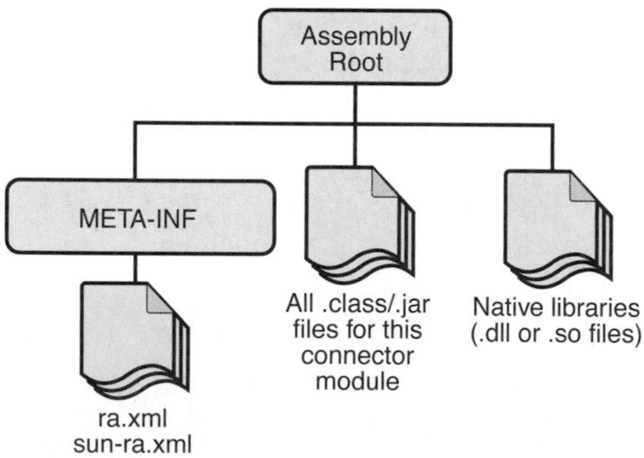

Figure 35–2 Resource Adapter Module Structure

A resource adapter is analogous to a JDBC driver. Both provide a standard API through which an application can access a resource that is outside the Java EE server. For a resource adapter, the outside resource is an EIS; for a JDBC driver, it is a DBMS. Resource adapters and JDBC drivers are rarely created by application developers. In most cases, both types of software are built by vendors that sell products such as tools, servers, or integration software.

Resource Adapter Contracts

The resource adapter mediates communication between the Java EE server and the EIS via contracts. The application contract defines the API through which a Java EE component such as an enterprise bean accesses the EIS. This API is the only view that the component has of the EIS. The system contracts link the resource adapter to important services that are managed by the Java EE server. The resource adapter itself and its system contracts are transparent to the Java EE component.

Management Contracts

The J2EE Connector architecture defines system contracts that enable resource adapter life cycle and thread management.

Life-Cycle Management

The Connector architecture specifies a *life-cycle management contract* that allows an application server to manage the life cycle of a resource adapter. This contract provides a mechanism for the application server to bootstrap a resource adapter instance during the instance's deployment or application server startup. It also provides a means for the application server to notify the resource adapter instance when it is undeployed or when an orderly shutdown of the application server takes place.

Work Management Contract

The Connector architecture *work management contract* ensures that resource adapters use threads in the proper, recommended manner. It also enables an application server to manage threads for resource adapters.

Resource adapters that improperly use threads can create problems for the entire application server environment. For example, a resource adapter might create too many threads or it might not properly release threads it has created. Poor thread handling inhibits application server shutdown. It also impacts the application server's performance because creating and destroying threads are expensive operations.

The work management contract establishes a means for the application server to pool and reuse threads, similar to pooling and reusing connections. By adhering to this contract, the resource adapter does not have to manage threads itself. Instead, the resource adapter has the application server create and provide needed threads. When the resource adapter is finished with a given thread, it returns the thread to the application server. The application server manages the thread: It can return the thread to a pool and reuse it later, or it can destroy the thread. Handling threads in this manner results in increased application server performance and more efficient use of resources.

In addition to moving thread management to the application server, the Connector architecture provides a flexible model for a resource adapter that uses threads:

- The requesting thread can choose to block—stop its own execution—until the work thread completes.
- Or the requesting thread can block while it waits to get the thread. When the application server provides a work thread, the requesting thread and the work thread execute in parallel.
- The resource adapter can opt to submit the work for the thread to a queue. The thread executes the work from the queue at some later point. The resource adapter continues its own execution from the point it submitted the work to the queue, no matter of when the thread executes it.

With the latter two approaches, the resource adapter and the thread may execute simultaneously or independently from each other. For these approaches, the contract specifies a listener mechanism to notify the resource adapter that the thread has completed its operation. The resource adapter can also specify the execution context for the thread, and the work management contract controls the context in which the thread executes.

Outbound Contracts

The Connector architecture defines system-level contracts between an application server and an EIS that enable outbound connectivity to an EIS: connection management, transaction management, and security.

The *connection management contract* supports connection pooling, a technique that enhances application performance and scalability. Connection pooling is transparent to the application, which simply obtains a connection to the EIS.

The *transaction management contract* between the transaction manager and an EIS supports transactional access to EIS resource managers. This contract lets an application server use a transaction manager to manage transactions across multiple resource managers. This contract also supports transactions that are managed inside an EIS resource manager without the necessity of involving an external transaction manager. Because of the transaction management contract, a call to the EIS may be enclosed in an XA transaction (a transaction type defined by the distributed transaction processing specification created by The Open Group). XA transactions are global: they can contain calls to multiple EISs, databases, and enterprise bean business methods. Although often appropriate, XA transactions are not mandatory. Instead, an application can use local transactions, which are managed by the individual EIS, or it can use no transactions at all.

The *security management contract* provides mechanisms for authentication, authorization, and secure communication between a J2EE server and an EIS to protect the information in the EIS.

Inbound Contracts

The J2EE Connector architecture defines system contracts between a Java EE server and an EIS that enable inbound connectivity from the EIS: pluggability contracts for message providers and contracts for importing transactions.

Messaging Contracts

To enable external systems to connect to a Java EE application server, the Connector architecture extends the capabilities of message-driven beans to handle messages from any message provider. That is, message-driven beans are no longer limited to handling JMS messages. Instead, EISs and message providers can plug any message provider, including their own custom or proprietary message providers, into a Java EE server.

To provide this feature, a message provider or an EIS resource adapter implements the *messaging contract*, which details APIs for message handling and message delivery. A conforming resource adapter is assured of the ability to send messages from any provider to a message-driven bean, and it also can be plugged into a Java EE server in a standard manner.

Transaction Inflow

The Connector architecture supports importing transactions from an EIS to a Java EE server. The architecture specifies how to propagate the transaction context from the EIS. For example, a transaction can be started by the EIS, such as the Customer Information Control System (CICS). Within the same CICS transaction, a connection can be made through a resource adapter to an enterprise bean on the application server. The enterprise bean does its work under the CICS transaction context and commits within that transaction context.

The Connector architecture also specifies how the container participates in transaction completion and how it handles crash recovery to ensure that data integrity is not lost.

Common Client Interface

This section describes how components use the Connector architecture Common Client Interface (CCI) API and a resource adapter to access data from an EIS.

Defined by the J2EE Connector architecture specification, the CCI defines a set of interfaces and classes whose methods allow a client to perform typical data access operations. The CCI interfaces and classes are as follows:

- `ConnectionFactory`: Provides an application component with a `Connection` instance to an EIS.
- `Connection`: Represents the connection to the underlying EIS.
- `ConnectionSpec`: Provides a means for an application component to pass connection-request-specific properties to the `ConnectionFactory` when making a connection request.
- `Interaction`: Provides a means for an application component to execute EIS functions, such as database stored procedures.

- `InteractionSpec`: Holds properties pertaining to an application component's interaction with an EIS.
- `Record`: The superclass for the various kinds of record instances. Record instances can be `MappedRecord`, `IndexedRecord`, or `ResultSet` instances, all of which inherit from the `Record` interface.
- `RecordFactory`: Provides an application component with a `Record` instance.
- `IndexedRecord`: Represents an ordered collection of `Record` instances based on the `java.util.List` interface.

A client or application component that uses the CCI to interact with an underlying EIS does so in a prescribed manner. The component must establish a connection to the EIS's resource manager, and it does so using the `ConnectionFactory`. The `Connection` object represents the actual connection to the EIS and is used for subsequent interactions with the EIS.

The component performs its interactions with the EIS, such as accessing data from a specific table, using an `Interaction` object. The application component defines the `Interaction` object using an `InteractionSpec` object. When the application component reads data from the EIS (such as from database tables) or writes to those tables, it does so using a particular type of `Record` instance: either a `MappedRecord`, an `IndexedRecord`, or a `ResultSet` instance. Just as the `ConnectionFactory` creates `Connection` instances, a `RecordFactory` creates `Record` instances.

Note, too, that a client application that relies on a CCI resource adapter is very much like any other Java EE client that uses enterprise bean methods.

Further Information

For further information on the Connector architecture, see:

- Connector 1.5 specification
  `http://java.sun.com/j2ee/connector/download.html`
- The Connector web site
  `http://java.sun.com/j2ee/connector`

Part Six: Case Studies

PART Six presents the case studies.

36 The Coffee Break Application

THIS chapter describes the Coffee Break application, a set of web applications that demonstrate how to use several of the Java Web services APIs together. The Coffee Break sells coffee on the Internet. Customers communicate with the Coffee Break server to order coffee online. The server uses JavaServer Faces technology as well as Java servlets, JSP pages, and JavaBeans components. When using the server a customer enters the quantity of each coffee to order and clicks the Submit button to send the order.

The Coffee Break does not maintain any inventory. It handles customer and order management and billing. Each order is filled by forwarding suborders to one or more coffee suppliers.

The Coffee Break server obtains the coffee varieties and their prices by querying suppliers at startup and on demand.

1. The Coffee Break server uses SAAJ messaging to communicate with one of the suppliers. The Coffee Break has been dealing with this supplier for some time and has previously made the necessary arrangements for doing request-response SAAJ messaging. The two parties have agreed to exchange four kinds of XML messages and have set up the DTDs those messages will follow.
2. The Coffee Break server requests price lists from each of the coffee suppliers. The server makes the appropriate remote web service calls and

waits for the response, which is a JavaBeans component representing a price list. The SAAJ supplier returns price lists as XML documents.

3. Upon receiving the responses, the Coffee Break server processes the price lists from the JavaBeans components returned by calls to the suppliers.
4. The Coffee Break server creates a local database of suppliers.
5. When an order is placed, suborders are sent to one or more suppliers using the supplier's preferred protocol.

Common Code

The Coffee Break servers share the `CoffeeBreak.properties` file, which contains the URLs exposed by the JAX-WS and SAAJ suppliers; the `URLHelper` class, which is used by the server and client classes to retrieve the URLs; the `DateHelper` utility class; and several generated JavaBeans components, described in JAX-WS Coffee Supplier Service (page 1202). These JavaBeans components are generated from the `cb-jaxws` JAX-WS web service by the `wsimport` tool.

The source code for the shared files is in the `<INSTALL>/javaeetutorial5/examples/coffeebreak/cb-common/src/java/com/sun/cb/common/` directory.

JAX-WS Coffee Supplier Service

The Coffee Break servers are clients of the JAX-WS coffee supplier service. The service code consists of the service implementation class, and several JavaBeans components that are used for method parameters and return types. The JavaBeans components are:

- `AddressBean`: shipping information for customer
- `ConfirmationBean`: order ID and ship date
- `CustomerBean`: customer contact information
- `LineItemBean`: order item
- `OrderBean`: order ID, customer, address, list of line items, total price
- `PriceItemBean`: price list entry (coffee name and wholesale price)
- `PriceListBean`: price list

These JavaBeans components are propagated to the clients by means of the wsimport tool.

Service Implementation

The Supplier class implements the placeOrder and getPriceList methods. So that you can focus on the code related to JAX-WS, these methods are short and simplistic. In a real world application, these methods would access databases and would interact with other services, such as shipping, accounting, and inventory.

The placeOrder method accepts as input a coffee order and returns a confirmation for the order. To keep things simple, the placeOrder method confirms every order and sets the ship date in the confirmation to the next day. The source code for the placeOrder method follows:

```
public ConfirmationBean placeOrder(OrderBean order) {

  Date tomorrow = DateHelper.addDays(new Date(), 1);
  ConfirmationBean confirmation =
    new ConfirmationBean(order.getId(),
      DateHelper.dateToCalendar(tomorrow));
  return confirmation;
}
```

The getPriceList method returns a PriceListBean object, which lists the name and price of each type of coffee that can be ordered from this service. The getPriceList method creates the PriceListBean object by invoking a private method named loadPrices. In a production application, the loadPrices method would fetch the prices from a database. However, our loadPrices method takes a shortcut by getting the prices from the SupplierPrices.properties file. Here are the getPriceList and loadPrices methods:

```
public PriceListBean getPriceList() {

  PriceListBean priceList = loadPrices();
  return priceList;
}

private PriceListBean loadPrices() {

  String propsName = "com.sun.cb.ws.server.SupplierPrices";
  Date today = new Date();
  Date endDate = DateHelper.addDays(today, 30);
```

```
        PriceItemBean[] priceItems =
            PriceLoader.loadItems(propsName);
        PriceListBean priceList =
            new PriceListBean(DateHelper.dateToCalendar(today),
                DateHelper.dateToCalendar(endDate), priceItems);

        return priceList;
    }
```

SAAJ Coffee Supplier Service

The SAAJ supplier service implements the arrangements that the supplier and the Coffee Break have made regarding their exchange of XML documents. These arrangements include the kinds of messages they will send, the form of those messages, and the kind of messaging they will do. They have agreed to do request-response messaging using the SAAJ API (the `javax.xml.soap` package).

The Coffee Break servers send two kinds of messages:

- Requests for current wholesale coffee prices
- Customer orders for coffee

The SAAJ coffee supplier responds with two kinds of messages:

- Current price lists
- Order confirmations

All the messages they send conform to an agreed-upon XML structure, which is specified in a DTD for each kind of message. This allows them to exchange messages even though they use different document formats internally.

The four kinds of messages exchanged by the Coffee Break servers and the SAAJ supplier are specified by the following DTDs:

- `request-prices.dtd`
- `price-list.dtd`
- `coffee-order.dtd`
- `confirm.dtd`

These DTDs can be found at `<INSTALL>/javaeetutorial5/examples/coffeebreak/cb-saaj/dtds/`. The `dtds` directory also contains a sample of what the XML documents specified in the DTDs might look like. The corresponding XML files for the DTDs are as follows:

- `request-prices.xml`
- `price-list.xml`
- `coffee-order.xml`
- `confirm.xml`

Because of the DTDs, both parties know ahead of time what to expect in a particular kind of message and can therefore extract its content using the SAAJ API.

Code for the client and server applications is in this directory:

```
<INSTALL>/javaeetutorial5/examples/coffeebreak/cb-saaj/src/
java
```

SAAJ Client

The Coffee Break server, which is a SAAJ client in this scenario, sends requests to the SAAJ supplier. The SAAJ client application uses the `SOAPConnection` method `call` to send messages.

```
SOAPMessage response = con.call(request, endpoint);
```

Accordingly, the client code has two major tasks. The first is to create and send the request; the second is to extract the content from the response. These tasks are handled by the classes `PriceListRequest` and `OrderRequest`.

Sending the Request

This section covers the code for creating and sending the request for an updated price list. This is done in the `getPriceList` method of `PriceListRequest`, which follows the DTD `price-list.dtd`.

The `getPriceList` method begins by creating the connection that will be used to send the request. Then it gets the default `MessageFactory` object to be used for creating the `SOAPMessage` object `msg`.

```
SOAPConnectionFactory scf =
  SOAPConnectionFactory.newInstance();
SOAPConnection con = scf.createConnection();
SOAPFactory soapFactory = SOAPFactory.newInstance();

MessageFactory mf = MessageFactory.newInstance();
SOAPMessage msg = mf.createMessage();
```

The next step is to access the message's `SOAPBody` object, to which the message's content will be added.

```
SOAPBody body = msg.getSOAPBody();
```

The file `price-list.dtd` specifies that the topmost element inside the body is `request-prices` and that it contains the element `request`. The text node added to `request` is the text of the request being sent. Every new element that is added to the message must have a `QName` object to identify it. The following lines of code create the top-level element in the `SOAPBody` object `body`. The first element created in a `SOAPBody` object is always a `SOAPBodyElement` object.

```
Name bodyName = new QName("http://sonata.coffeebreak.com",
  "request-prices", "RequestPrices");
SOAPBodyElement requestPrices =
  body.addBodyElement(bodyName);
```

In the next few lines, the code adds the element `request` to the element `request-prices` (represented by the `SOAPBodyElement requestPrices`). Then the code adds a text node containing the text of the request. Next, because there are no other elements in the request, the code calls the method `saveChanges` on the message to save what has been done.

```
QName requestName = new QName("request");
SOAPElement request =
  requestPrices.addChildElement(requestName);
request.addTextNode("Send updated price list.");

msg.saveChanges();
```

With the creation of the request message completed, the code sends the message to the SAAJ coffee supplier. The message being sent is the `SOAPMessage` object msg, to which the elements created in the previous code snippets were added. The endpoint is the URI for the SAAJ coffee supplier, http://localhost:8080/saaj-coffee-supplier/getPriceList. The SOAPConnection object con is used to send the message, and because it is no longer needed, it is closed.

```
URL endpoint = new URL(url);
SOAPMessage response = con.call(msg, endpoint);
con.close();
```

When the call method is executed, the Application Server executes the servlet PriceListServlet. This servlet creates and returns a SOAPMessage object whose content is the SAAJ supplier's price list. (PriceListServlet is discussed in Returning the Price List, page 1213.) The Application Server knows to execute PriceListServlet because we map the given endpoint to that servlet.

Extracting the Price List

This section demonstrates (1) retrieving the price list that is contained in response, the SOAPMessage object returned by the method call, and (2) returning the price list as a PriceListBean.

The code creates an empty Vector object that will hold the coffee-name and price elements that are extracted from response. Then the code uses response to access its SOAPBody object, which holds the message's content.

```
Vector<String> list = new Vector<String>();

SOAPBody responseBody = response.getSOAPBody();
```

The next step is to retrieve the SOAPBodyElement object. The method getChildElements returns an Iterator object that contains all the child elements of the element on which it is called, so in the following lines of code, it1 contains the SOAPBodyElement object bodyEl, which represents the price-list element.

```
Iterator it1 = responseBody.getChildElements();
while (it1.hasNext()) {
  SOAPBodyElement bodyEl = (SOAPBodyElement)it1.next();
```

The Iterator object it2 holds the child elements of bodyEl, which represent coffee elements. Calling the method next on it2 retrieves the first coffee element in bodyEl. As long as it2 has another element, the method next will return the next coffee element.

```
    Iterator it2 = bodyEl.getChildElements();
    while (it2.hasNext()) {
       SOAPElement child2 = (SOAPElement)it2.next();
```

The next lines of code drill down another level to retrieve the coffee-name and price elements contained in it3. Then the message getValue retrieves the text (a coffee name or a price) that the SAAJ coffee supplier added to the coffee-name and price elements when it gave content to response. The final line in the following code fragment adds the coffee name or price to the Vector object list. Note that because of the nested while loops, for each coffee element that the code retrieves, both of its child elements (the coffee-name and price elements) are retrieved.

```
       Iterator it3 = child2.getChildElements();
       while (it3.hasNext()) {
          SOAPElement child3 = (SOAPElement)it3.next();
          String value = child3.getValue();
          list.addElement(value);
       }
    }
 }
```

The final code fragment adds the coffee names and their prices (as a PriceListItem) to the ArrayList priceItems, and prints each pair on a separate line. Finally it constructs and returns a PriceListBean.

```
ArrayList<PriceItemBean> items =
  new ArrayList<PriceItemBean>();
for (int i = 0; i < list.size(); i = i + 2) {
  PriceItemBean pib = new PriceItemBean();
  pib.setCoffeeName(list.elementAt(i).toString());
  pib.setPricePerPound(new BigDecimal(
     list.elementAt(i + 1).toString()));
  items.add(pib);
  System.out.print(list.elementAt(i) + "        ");
  System.out.println(list.elementAt(i + 1));
}

Date today = new Date();
Date endDate = DateHelper.addDays(today, 30);
GregorianCalendar todayCal = new GregorianCalendar();
todayCal.setTime(today);
```

```
GregorianCalendar cal = new GregorianCalendar();
cal.setTime(endDate);
plb = new PriceListBean();
plb.setStartDate(DatatypeFactory.newInstance()
  .newXMLGregorianCalendar(todayCal));

List<PriceItemBean> priceItems =
  new ArrayList<PriceItemBean>();
Iterator<PriceItemBean> i = items.iterator();
while (i.hasNext()) {
  PriceItemBean pib = i.next();
  plb.getPriceItems().add(pib);
}

plb.setEndDate(DatatypeFactory.newInstance()
  .newXMLGregorianCalendar(cal));
```

Ordering Coffee

The other kind of message that the Coffee Break servers can send to the SAAJ supplier is an order for coffee. This is done in the `placeOrder` method of `OrderRequest`, which follows the DTD `coffee-order.dtd`.

Creating the Order

As with the client code for requesting a price list, the `placeOrder` method starts by creating a `SOAPConnection` object and a `SOAPMessage` object and accessing the message's `SOAPBody` object.

```
SOAPConnectionFactory scf =
  SOAPConnectionFactory.newInstance();
SOAPConnection con = scf.createConnection();

MessageFactory mf = MessageFactory.newInstance();
SOAPMessage msg = mf.createMessage();

SOAPBody body = msg.getSOAPBody();
```

Next, the code creates and adds XML elements to form the order. As is required, the first element is a `SOAPBodyElement`, which in this case is `coffee-order`.

```
QName bodyName = new QName("http://sonata.coffeebreak.com",
  "coffee-order", "PO");
SOAPBodyElement order = body.addBodyElement(bodyName);
```

The application then adds the next level of elements, the first of these being orderID. The value given to orderID is extracted from the OrderBean object passed to the OrderRequest.placeOrder method.

```
QName orderIDName = new QName("orderID");
SOAPElement orderID = order.addChildElement(orderIDName);
orderID.addTextNode(orderBean.getId());
```

The next element, customer, has several child elements that give information about the customer. This information is also extracted from the Customer component of OrderBean.

```
QName childName = new QName("customer");
SOAPElement customer = order.addChildElement(childName);

childName = new QName("last-name");
SOAPElement lastName = customer.addChildElement(childName);
lastName.addTextNode(orderBean.getCustomer().getLastName());

childName = new QName("first-name");
SOAPElement firstName = customer.addChildElement(childName);
firstName.addTextNode(orderBean.getCustomer().getFirstName());

childName = new QName("phone-number");
SOAPElement phoneNumber = customer.addChildElement(childName);
phoneNumber.addTextNode(
  orderBean.getCustomer().getPhoneNumber());

childName = new QName("email-address");
SOAPElement emailAddress =
  customer.addChildElement(childName);
emailAddress.addTextNode(
  orderBean.getCustomer().getEmailAddress());
```

The address element, added next, has child elements for the street, city, state, and zip code. This information is extracted from the Address component of OrderBean.

```
childName = new QName("address");
SOAPElement address = order.addChildElement(childName);

childName = new QName("street");
SOAPElement street = address.addChildElement(childName);
street.addTextNode(orderBean.getAddress().getStreet());

childName = new QName("city");
```

```
SOAPElement city = address.addChildElement(childName);
city.addTextNode(orderBean.getAddress().getCity());

childName = new QName("state");
SOAPElement state = address.addChildElement(childName);
state.addTextNode(orderBean.getAddress().getState());

childName = new QName("zip");
SOAPElement zip = address.addChildElement(childName);
zip.addTextNode(orderBean.getAddress().getZip());
```

The element `line-item` has three child elements: `coffeeName`, `pounds`, and `price`. This information is extracted from the `LineItems` list contained in `OrderBean`.

```
List<LineItemBean> lineItems = orderBean.getLineItems();
Iterator<LineItemBean> i = lineItems.iterator();
while (i.hasNext()) {
  LineItemBean lib = i.next();

  childName = new QName("line-item");
  SOAPElement lineItem = order.addChildElement(childName);

  childName = new QName("coffeeName");
  SOAPElement coffeeName =
    lineItem.addChildElement(childName);
  coffeeName.addTextNode(lib.getCoffeeName());

  childName = new QName("pounds");
  SOAPElement pounds = lineItem.addChildElement(childName);
  pounds.addTextNode(lib.getPounds().toString());

  childName = new QName("price");
  SOAPElement price = lineItem.addChildElement(childName);
  price.addTextNode(lib.getPrice().toString());
}

// total
childName = new QName("total");
SOAPElement total = order.addChildElement(childName);
total.addTextNode(orderBean.getTotal().toString());
```

With the order complete, the application sends the message to the endpoint `http://localhost:8080/saaj-coffee-supplier/orderCoffee` and closes the connection.

```
URL endpoint = new URL(url);
SOAPMessage reply = con.call(msg, endpoint);
con.close();
```

Because we map the given endpoint to `ConfirmationServlet`, the Application Server executes that servlet (discussed in Returning the Order Confirmation, page 1218) to create and return the `SOAPMessage` object `reply`.

Retrieving the Order Confirmation

The rest of the `placeOrder` method retrieves the information returned in `reply`. The client knows what elements are in it because they are specified in `confirm.dtd`. After accessing the `SOAPBody` object, the code retrieves the `confirmation` element and gets the text of the `orderID` and `ship-date` elements. Finally, it constructs and returns a `ConfirmationBean` with this information.

```
SOAPBody sBody = reply.getSOAPBody();
Iterator bodyIt = sBody.getChildElements();
SOAPBodyElement sbEl = (SOAPBodyElement)bodyIt.next();
Iterator bodyIt2 = sbEl.getChildElements();

SOAPElement ID = (SOAPElement)bodyIt2.next();
String id = ID.getValue();

SOAPElement sDate = (SOAPElement)bodyIt2.next();
String shippingDate = sDate.getValue();

SimpleDateFormat df =
  new SimpleDateFormat("EEE MMM dd HH:mm:ss z yyyy");
Date date = df.parse(shippingDate);
GregorianCalendar cal = new GregorianCalendar();
cal.setTime(date);
cb = new ConfirmationBean();
cb.setOrderId(id);
cb.setShippingDate(DatatypeFactory.newInstance()
  .newXMLGregorianCalendar(cal));
```

SAAJ Service

The SAAJ coffee supplier—the SAAJ server in this scenario—provides the response part of the request-response paradigm. When SAAJ messaging is being used, the server code is a servlet. The core part of each servlet is made up of three `javax.servlet.HttpServlet` methods: `init`, `doPost`, and `onMessage`. The `init` and `doPost` methods set up the response message, and the `onMessage` method gives the message its content.

Returning the Price List

This section takes you through the servlet `PriceListServlet`. This servlet creates the message containing the current price list that is returned to the method `call`, invoked in `PriceListRequest`.

Any servlet extends a `javax.servlet` class. Being part of a web application, this servlet extends `HttpServlet`. It first creates a static `MessageFactory` object that will be used later to create the `SOAPMessage` object that is returned.

```
public class PriceListServlet extends HttpServlet {
  static final Logger logger =
    Logger.getLogger("com.sun.cb.saaj.PriceListServlet");
  static MessageFactory messageFactory = null;

  static {
    try {
      messageFactory = MessageFactory.newInstance();
    } catch (Exception ex) {
      logger.severe("Exception: " + ex.toString());
    }
  };
```

Every servlet has an `init` method. This `init` method initializes the servlet with the configuration information that the Application Server passed to it.

```
public void init(ServletConfig servletConfig)
    throws ServletException {
  super.init(servletConfig);
}
```

The next method defined in `PriceListServlet` is `doPost`, which does the real work of the servlet by calling the `onMessage` method. (The `onMessage` method is discussed later in this section.) The Application Server passes the `doPost` method two arguments. The first argument, the `HttpServletRequest` object req, holds the content of the message sent in PriceListRequest. The doPost method gets the content from req and puts it in the SOAPMessage object msg so that it can pass it to the onMessage method. The second argument, the HttpServletResponse object resp, will hold the message generated by executing the method onMessage.

In the following code fragment, doPost calls the methods getHeaders and putHeaders, defined immediately after doPost, to read and write the headers in req. It then gets the content of req as a stream and passes the headers and the input stream to the method MessageFactory.createMessage. The result is that the SOAPMessage object msg contains the request for a price list. Note that in this case, msg does not have any headers because the message sent in PriceListRequest did not have any headers.

```
public void doPost(HttpServletRequest req,
      HttpServletResponse resp)
      throws ServletException, IOException {
   try {
      // Get all the headers from the HTTP request
      MimeHeaders headers = getHeaders(req);

      // Get the body of the HTTP request
      InputStream is = req.getInputStream();

      // Now internalize the contents of the HTTP request
      // and create a SOAPMessage
      SOAPMessage msg =
         messageFactory.createMessage(headers, is);
```

Next, the code declares the SOAPMessage object reply and populates it by calling the method onMessage.

```
      SOAPMessage reply = null;
      reply = onMessage(msg);
```

If reply has anything in it, its contents are saved, the status of resp is set to OK, and the headers and content of reply are written to resp. If reply is empty, the status of resp is set to indicate that there is no content.

```
      if (reply != null) {

         /*
          * Need to call saveChanges because we're
          * going to use the MimeHeaders to set HTTP
          * response information. These MimeHeaders
```

```
          * are generated as part of the save.
          */
         if (reply.saveRequired()) {
            reply.saveChanges();
         }

         resp.setStatus(HttpServletResponse.SC_OK);
         putHeaders(reply.getMimeHeaders(), resp);

         // Write out the message on the response stream
         logger.info("Reply message:");
         OutputStream os = resp.getOutputStream();
         reply.writeTo(os);
         os.flush();
      } else {
         resp.setStatus(
            HttpServletResponse.SC_NO_CONTENT);
      }
   } catch (Exception ex) {
      throw new ServletException( "SAAJ POST failed: " +
         ex.getMessage());
   }
}
```

The methods `getHeaders` and `putHeaders` are not standard methods in a servlet, as `init`, `doPost`, and `onMessage` are. The method `doPost` calls `getHeaders` and passes it the `HttpServletRequest` object `req` that the Application Server passed to it. It returns a `MimeHeaders` object populated with the headers from `req`.

```
static MimeHeaders getHeaders(HttpServletRequest req) {

   Enumeration headerNames = req.getHeaderNames();
   MimeHeaders headers = new MimeHeaders();

   while (headerNames.hasMoreElements()) {
      String headerName = (String)headerNames.nextElement();
      String headerValue = req.getHeader(headerName);

      StringTokenizer values =
         new StringTokenizer(headerValue, ",");
      while (values.hasMoreTokens()) {
         headers.addHeader(headerName,
            values.nextToken().trim());
      }
   }
   return headers;
}
```

The doPost method calls putHeaders and passes it the MimeHeaders object headers, which was returned by the method getHeaders. The method putHeaders writes the headers in headers to res, the second argument passed to it. The result is that res, the response that the Application Server will return to the method call, now contains the headers that were in the original request.

```
static void putHeaders(MimeHeaders headers,
    HttpServletResponse res) {

  Iterator it = headers.getAllHeaders();
  while (it.hasNext()) {
    MimeHeader header = (MimeHeader)it.next();

    String[] values = headers.getHeader(header.getName());
    if (values.length == 1)
      res.setHeader(header.getName(), header.getValue());
    else {
      StringBuffer concat = new StringBuffer();
      int i = 0;
      while (i < values.length) {
        if (i != 0) {
          concat.append(',');
        }
        concat.append(values[i++]);
      }
      res.setHeader(header.getName(), concat.toString());
    }
  }
}
```

The method onMessage is the application code for responding to the message sent by PriceListRequest and internalized into msg. It uses the static MessageFactory object messageFactory to create the SOAPMessage object message and then populates it with the supplier's current coffee prices.

The method doPost invokes onMessage and passes it msg. In this case, onMessage does not need to use msg because it simply creates a message containing the supplier's price list. The onMessage method in ConfirmationServlet (see Returning the Order Confirmation, page 1218), on the other hand, uses the message passed to it to get the order ID.

```
public SOAPMessage onMessage(SOAPMessage msg) {
  SOAPMessage message = null;


  try {
```

```
message = messageFactory.createMessage();

SOAPBody body = message.getSOAPBody();

QName bodyName =
   new QName("http://sonata.coffeebreak.com",
      "price-list", "PriceList");
SOAPBodyElement list = body.addBodyElement(bodyName);

QName coffeeN = new QName("coffee");
SOAPElement coffee = list.addChildElement(coffeeN);

QName coffeeNm1 = new QName("coffee-name");
SOAPElement coffeeName =
   coffee.addChildElement(coffeeNm1);
coffeeName.addTextNode("Arabica");

QName priceName1 = new QName("price");
SOAPElement price1 = coffee.addChildElement(priceName1);
price1.addTextNode("4.50");

QName coffeeNm2 = new QName("coffee-name");
SOAPElement coffeeName2 =
   coffee.addChildElement(coffeeNm2);
coffeeName2.addTextNode("Espresso");

QName priceName2 = new QName("price");
SOAPElement price2 = coffee.addChildElement(priceName2);
price2.addTextNode("5.00");

QName coffeeNm3 = new QName("coffee-name");
SOAPElement coffeeName3 =
   coffee.addChildElement(coffeeNm3);
coffeeName3.addTextNode("Dorada");

QName priceName3 = new QName("price");
SOAPElement price3 = coffee.addChildElement(priceName3);
price3.addTextNode("6.00");

QName coffeeNm4 = snew QName("coffee-name");
SOAPElement coffeeName4 =
   coffee.addChildElement(coffeeNm4);
coffeeName4.addTextNode("House Blend");

QName priceName4 = new QName("price");
SOAPElement price4 = coffee.addChildElement(priceName4);
price4.addTextNode("5.00");
```

```
        message.saveChanges();

      } catch(Exception e) {
        logger.severe("onMessage: Exception: " + e.toString());
      }
      return message;
    }
```

Returning the Order Confirmation

ConfirmationServlet creates the confirmation message that is returned to the call method that is invoked in OrderRequest. It is very similar to the code in PriceListServlet except that instead of building a price list, its onMessage method builds a confirmation containing the order number and shipping date.

The onMessage method for this servlet uses the SOAPMessage object passed to it by the doPost method to get the order number sent in OrderRequest. Then it builds a confirmation message containing the order ID and shipping date. The shipping date is calculated as today's date plus two days.

```
public SOAPMessage onMessage(SOAPMessage message) {
  logger.info("onMessage");
  SOAPMessage confirmation = null;

  try {

    // Retrieve orderID from message received
    SOAPBody sentSB = message.getSOAPBody();
    Iterator sentIt = sentSB.getChildElements();
    SOAPBodyElement sentSBE = (SOAPBodyElement)sentIt.next();
    Iterator sentIt2 = sentSBE.getChildElements();
    SOAPElement sentSE = (SOAPElement)sentIt2.next();

    // Get the orderID test to put in confirmation
    String sentID = sentSE.getValue();

    // Create the confirmation message
    confirmation = messageFactory.createMessage();
    SOAPBody sb = message.getSOAPBody();

    QName newBodyName =
      new QName("http://sonata.coffeebreak.com",
        "confirmation", "Confirm");
    SOAPBodyElement confirm = sb.addBodyElement(newBodyName);

    // Create the orderID element for confirmation
```

```
        QName newOrderIDName = new QName("orderId");
        SOAPElement newOrderNo =
          confirm.addChildElement(newOrderIDName);
        newOrderNo.addTextNode(sentID);

        // Create ship-date element
        QName shipDateName = new QName("ship-date");
        SOAPElement shipDate =
          confirm.addChildElement(shipDateName);

        // Create the shipping date
        Date today = new Date();
        long msPerDay = 1000 * 60 * 60 * 24;
        long msTarget = today.getTime();
        long msSum = msTarget + (msPerDay * 2);
        Date result = new Date();
        result.setTime(msSum);
        String sd = result.toString();
        shipDate.addTextNode(sd);

        confirmation.saveChanges();

      } catch (Exception ex) {
        ex.printStackTrace();
      }
      return confirmation;
    }
```

Coffee Break Server

The Coffee Break server uses JavaServer Faces technology to build its user interface. The JSP pages use JavaServer Faces UI component tags to represent widgets, such as text fields and tables. All the JSP pages use preludes and codas to achieve a common look and feel among the HTML pages, and many of the JSTL custom tags discussed in Chapter 6.

The Coffee Break server implementation is organized along the Model-View-Controller design pattern. A `FacesServlet` instance (included with the JavaServer Faces API) acts as the controller. It examines the request URL, creates and initializes model JavaBeans components, and dispatches requests to view JSP pages. The JavaBeans components contain the business logic for the application; they call the web services and perform computations on the data returned from the services. The JSP pages format the data stored in the JavaBeans components.

The mapping between JavaBeans components and pages is summarized in Table 36–1.

Table 36–1 Model and View Components

Function	JSP Page	JavaBeans Component
Update order data	`orderForm`	`ShoppingCart`
Update delivery and billing data	`checkoutForm`	`CheckoutFormBean`
Display order confirmation	`checkoutAck`	`OrderConfirmations`

JSP Pages

orderForm

`orderForm` displays the current contents of the shopping cart. The first time the page is requested, the quantities of all the coffees are 0 (zero). Each time the customer changes the coffee amounts and clicks the Update button, the request is posted back to `orderForm`.

The `CoffeeBreakBean` bean component updates the values in the shopping cart, which are then redisplayed by `orderForm`. When the order is complete, the customer proceeds to the `checkoutForm` page by clicking the Checkout button.

The table of coffees displayed on the `orderForm` is rendered using one of the JavaServer Faces component tags, `dataTable`. Here is part of the `dataTable` tag from `orderForm`:

```
<h:dataTable id="table"
  columnClasses="list-column-center,list-column-right,
    list-column-center, list-column-right"
  headerClass="list-header" rowClasses="list-row"
  footerClass="list-column-right"
  styleClass="list-background-grid"
  value="#{CoffeeBreakBean.cart.items}" var="sci">
  <f:facet name="header">
    <h:outputText  value="#{CBMessages.OrderForm}"/>
  </f:facet>
  <h:column>
    <f:facet name="header">
```

```
            <h:outputText  value="Coffee"/>
         </f:facet>
         <h:outputText id="coffeeName"
            value="#{sci.item.coffeeName}"/>
      </h:column>
      ...
   </h:dataTable>
```

When this tag is processed, a `UIData` component and a `Table` renderer are created on the server side. The `UIData` component supports a data binding to a collection of data objects. The `Table` renderer takes care of generating the HTML markup. The `UIData` component iterates through the list of coffees, and the `Table` renderer renders each row in the table.

This example is a classic use case for a `UIData` component because the number of coffees might not be known to the application developer or the page author at the time the application is developed. Also, the `UIData` component can dynamically adjust the number of rows in the table to accommodate the underlying data.

For more information on `UIData`, please see Using Data-Bound Table Components (page 339).

checkoutForm

`checkoutForm` is used to collect delivery and billing information from the customer. When the Submit button is clicked, an `ActionEvent` is generated. This event is first handled by the `submit` method of the `checkoutFormBean`. This method acts as a listener for the event because the tag corresponding to the submit button references the `submit` method with its `action` attribute:

```
<h:commandButton value="#{CBMessages.Submit}"
  action="#{checkoutFormBean.submit}"/>
```

The `submit` method submits the suborders to each supplier and stores the result in the request-scoped `OrderConfirmations` bean.

The `checkoutForm` page has standard validators on several components and a custom validator on the email component. Here is the tag corresponding to the `firstName` component, which holds the customer's first name:

```
<h:inputText id="firstName"
  value="#{checkoutFormBean.firstName}"
  size="15" maxlength="20" required="true"/>
```

With the required attribute set to true, the JavaServer Faces implementation will check whether the user entered something in the First Name field.

The email component has a custom validator registered on it. Here is the tag corresponding to the email component:

```
<h:inputText id="email" value="#{checkoutFormBean.email}"
  size="25" maxlength="125"
  validator="#{checkoutFormBean.validateEmail}"/>
```

The validator attribute refers to the validateEmail method on the CheckoutFormBean class. This method ensures that the value the user enters in the email field contains an @ character.

If the validation does not succeed, the checkoutForm is re-rendered, with error notifications in each invalid field. If the validation succeeds, checkoutFormBean submits suborders to each supplier and stores the result in the request-scoped OrderConfirmations JavaBeans component and control is passed to the checkoutAck page.

checkoutAck

checkoutAck simply displays the contents of the OrderConfirmations JavaBeans component, which is a list of the suborders constituting an order and the ship dates of each suborder. This page also uses a UIData component. Again, the number of coffees the customer ordered is not known before runtime. The UIData component dynamically adds rows to accommodate the order.

The checkoutAck.jsp page also makes use of a custom converter that converts the shipping date into an XMLGregorianCalendar type:

```
<h:outputText id="coffeeName"
  value="#{oc.confirmationBean.shippingDate}">
  <f:converter converterId="XMLGregorianCalendarConverter" /
</h:outputText>
```

The custom converter is implemented by XMLGregorianCalendarConverter.java.

JavaBeans Components

RetailPriceList

RetailPriceList is a list of retail price items. A retail price item contains a coffee name, a wholesale price per pound, a retail price per pound, and a supplier. This data is used for two purposes: it contains the price list presented to the end user and is used by CheckoutFormBean when it constructs the suborders dispatched to coffee suppliers.

RetailPriceList first calls the URLHelper.getEndpointURL method to determine the JAX-WS service endpoint. It then queries the JAX-WS service for a coffee price list. Finally it queries the SAAJ service for a price list. The two price lists are combined and a retail price per pound is determined by adding a markup of 35% to the wholesale prices.

ShoppingCart

ShoppingCart is a list of shopping cart items. A ShoppingCartItem contains a retail price item, the number of pounds of that item, and the total price for that item.

OrderConfirmations

OrderConfirmations is a list of order confirmation objects. An OrderConfirmation contains order and confirmation objects, as discussed in Service Implementation (page 1203).

CheckoutFormBean

CheckoutFormBean checks the completeness of information entered into checkoutForm. If the information is incomplete, the bean populates error messages, and redisplays checkoutForm with the error messages. If the information is complete, order requests are constructed from the shopping cart and the information supplied to checkoutForm, and these orders are sent to each supplier. As each confirmation is received, an order confirmation is created and added to OrderConfirmations.

Several of the tags on the checkoutForm page have their required attributes set to true. This will cause the implementation to check whether the user enters values in these fields. The tag corresponding to the email component registers a custom validator on the email component, as explained in checkoutForm (page 1221). The code that performs the validation is the validateEmail method:

```
public void validateEmail(FacesContext context,
  UIComponent toValidate, Object value) {
  String message = "";
  String email = (String) value;
  if (email.indexOf('@') == -1) {
    ((UIInput)toValidate).setValid(false);
    message = CoffeeBreakBean.loadErrorMessage(context,
      CoffeeBreakBean.CB_RESOURCE_BUNDLE_NAME,
        "EMailError");
    context.addMessage(toValidate.getClientId(context),
      new FacesMessage(message));
  }
}
```

CoffeeBreakBean

CoffeeBreakBean acts as the backing bean to the JSP pages. See Backing Beans (page 304) for more information on backing beans. CoffeeBreakBean creates the ShoppingCart object, which defines the model data for the components on the orderForm page that hold the data about each coffee. CoffeeBreakBean also loads the RetailPriceList object. In addition, it provides the methods that are invoked when the buttons on the orderForm and checkoutAck are clicked. For example, the checkout method is invoked when the Checkout button is clicked because the tag corresponding to the Checkout button refers to the checkout method via its action attribute:

```
<h:commandButton id="checkoutLink"
  value="#{CBMessages.Checkout}"
  action="#{CoffeeBreakBean.checkout}" />
```

The checkout method returns a String, which the JavaServer Faces page navigation system matches against a set of navigation rules to determine what page to access next. The navigation rules are defined in a separate XML file, described in Resource Configuration (page 1225).

RetailPriceListServlet

RetailPriceListServlet responds to requests to reload the price list via the URL /loadPriceList. It simply creates a new RetailPriceList and a new ShoppingCart.

Because this servlet would be used by administrators of the Coffee Break server, it is a protected web resource. To load the price list, a user must authenticate (using basic authentication), and the authenticated user must be in the admin role.

Resource Configuration

A JavaServer Faces application usually includes an XML file that configures resources for the application. These resources include JavaBeans components, navigation rules, and others.

Two of the resources configured for the JavaServer Faces version of the Coffee Break server are the CheckoutForm bean and navigation rules for the orderForm page:

```
<managed-bean>
  <managed-bean-name>checkoutFormBean</managed-bean-name>
  <managed-bean-class>
    com.sun.cb.CheckoutFormBean
  </managed-bean-class>
  <managed-bean-scope>request</managed-bean-scope>
    <managed-property>
      <property-name>firstName</property-name>
      <value>Coffee</value>
    </managed-property>
    <managed-property>
      <property-name>lastName</property-name>
      <value>Lover</value>
    </managed-property>
    <managed-property>
      <property-name>email</property-name>
      <value>jane@home</value>
    </managed-property>
    ...
  </managed-bean>
```

```
<navigation-rule>
  <from-view-id>/orderForm.jsp</from-view-id>
  <navigation-case>
    <from-outcome>checkout</from-outcome>
    <to-view-id>/checkoutForm.jsp</to-view-id>
  </navigation-case>
</navigation-rule>
```

As shown in the managed-bean element, the checkoutForm bean properties are initialized with the values for the user, Coffee Lover. In this way, the hyperlink tag from orderForm is not required to submit these values in the request parameters.

As shown in the navigation-rule element, when the String, checkout, is returned from a method referred to by a component's action attribute, the checkoutForm page displays.

Building, Packaging, Deploying, and Running the Application

The source code for the Coffee Break application is located in the directory <*INSTALL*>/javaeetutorial5/examples/coffeebreak/. Within the cb directory are subdirectories for each web application—cb, cb-saaj, and cb-jaxws—and a directory, cb-common, for classes shared by the web applications. Each subdirectory contains a build.xml file. The web application subdirectories in turn contain a src subdirectory for Java classes and configuration files, and a web subdirectory for web resources.

Setting the Port

The JAX-WS and SAAJ services in the Coffee Break application run at the port that you specified when you installed the Application Server. The tutorial examples assume that the Application Server runs on the default port, 8080. If you have changed the port, you must update the port number in the following files before building and running the examples:

- *<INSTALL>*`/javaeetutorial5/examples/coffeebreak/cb-common/src/com/sun/cb/common/CoffeeBreak.properties`. Update the port in the following URLs:
  - `endpoint.url=http://localhost:8080/jaxws-coffee-supplier/jaxws`
  - `saaj.url=http://localhost:8080/saaj-coffee-supplier`

Building, Packaging, and Deploying the JAX-WS Service

To build the JAX-WS service and client library and to package and deploy the JAX-WS service using NetBeans 5.5, follow these steps:

1. In NetBeans 5.5, choose Open Project from the File menu.
2. In the Open Project dialog, navigate to *<INSTALL>*`/javaeetutorial5/examples/coffeebreak/`.
3. Select the `cb-jaxws` folder.
4. Select the Open as Main Project and Open Required Projects checkboxes.
5. Click Open Project Folder.
6. Right-click the `cb-jaxws` project and choose Build Project.
7. Right-click the `cb-jaxws` project and choose Deploy Project.

To build the JAX-WS service and client library and to package and deploy the JAX-WS service using Ant, follow these steps:

1. In a terminal window, go to *<INSTALL>*`/javaeetutorial5/examples/coffeebreak/cb-jaxws/`.
2. Run `ant`. This task calls the `default` target, which compiles the source files of the JAX-WS service.

   Ignore the error issued by the `wsimport-client-generate` target.
3. Make sure the Application Server is running.
4. Deploy the JAX-WS service:

   ```
   ant deploy
   ```

Building, Packaging, and Deploying the SAAJ Service

To build the SAAJ service and client library and to package and deploy the SAAJ service using NetBeans 5.5, follow these steps:

1. In NetBeans 5.5, choose Open Project from the File menu.
2. In the Open Project dialog, navigate to `<INSTALL>/javaeetutorial5/examples/coffeebreak/`.
3. Select the `cb-saaj` folder.
4. Select the Open as Main Project and Open Required Projects checkboxes.
5. Click Open Project Folder.
6. Right-click the `cb-saaj` project and choose Build Project.
7. Right-click the `cb-saaj` project and choose Deploy Project.

To build the SAAJ service and client library and to package and deploy the SAAJ service using Ant, follow these steps:

1. In a terminal window, go to `<INSTALL>/javaeetutorial5/examples/coffeebreak/cb-saaj/`.
2. Run `ant`. This task calls the `default` target, which creates the client library and compiles the SAAJ service classes.
3. Make sure the Application Server is started.
4. Deploy the SAAJ service:
   ```
   ant deploy
   ```

Building, Packaging, and Deploying the Coffee Break Server

To build, package, and deploy the Coffee Break server using NetBeans 5.5, follow these steps:

1. In NetBeans 5.5, choose Open Project from the File menu.
2. In the Open Project dialog, navigate to `<INSTALL>/javaeetutorial5/examples/coffeebreak/`.
3. Select the `cb` folder.
4. Select the Open as Main Project and Open Required Projects checkboxes.
5. Click Open Project Folder.

6. Right-click the cb project and choose Build Project.
7. Right-click the cb project and choose Deploy Project.

To build, package, and deploy the Coffee Break server using Ant, follow these steps:

1. In a terminal window, go to `<INSTALL>/javaeetutorial5/examples/coffeebreak/cb/`.
2. Run `ant`. This task calls the `default` target, which compiles the server classes.
3. Make sure the Application Server is started.
4. Deploy the Coffee Break server:

   ```
   ant deploy
   ```

Running the Coffee Break Client

After you have installed all the web applications, check that all the applications are running in the Admin Console. You should see `cb`, `cb-saaj`, and `cb-jaxws` in the list of applications.

You can run the Coffee Break client by opening this URL in a web browser:

```
http://localhost:8080/cbserver/
```

A page appears with the following message:

```
Redirecting to CoffeeBreak demo...click here otherwise.
```

In a few seconds, you should see a page like the one shown in Figure 36–1.

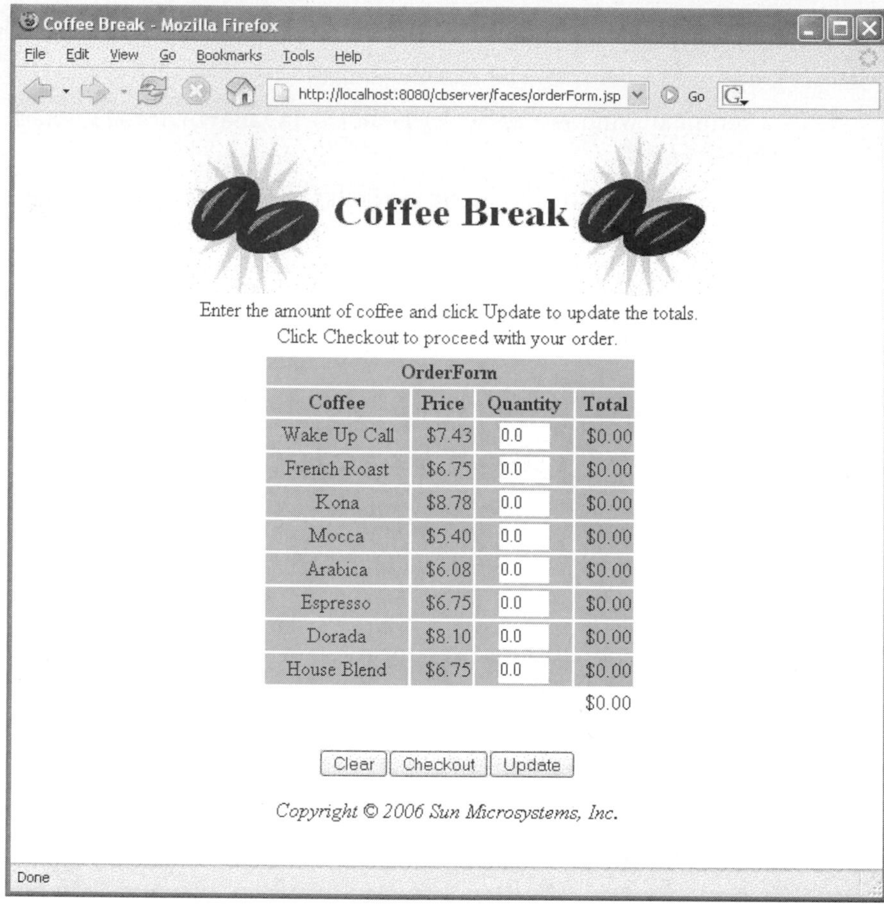

Figure 36–1 Order Form

After you have gone through the application screens, you will get an order confirmation that looks like the one shown in Figure 36–2.

Figure 36–2 Order Confirmation

Removing the Coffee Break Application

To remove the Coffee Break application, perform the following steps:

1. Undeploy the JAX-WS service, SAAJ service, and the Coffee Break server using the Admin Console or by running `ant undeploy` in their respective directories.
2. Stop the Application Server.

If you want to remove the `build` and `dist` directories, run `ant clean` in each directory, including `<INSTALL>/javaeetutorial5/examples/coffeebreak/cb-common/`.

37

The Duke's Bank Application

THIS chapter describes the Duke's Bank application, an online banking application. Duke's Bank has two clients: an application client used by administrators to manage customers and accounts, and a web client used by customers to access account histories and perform transactions. The web client is built using JavaServer Faces technology (see Chapter 9). The clients access the customer, account, and transaction information maintained in a database through enterprise beans. The Duke's Bank application demonstrates the way that many of the component technologies presented in this tutorial—enterprise beans, application clients, and web components—are applied to provide a simple but functional application.

Figure 37–1 gives a high-level view of how the components interact. This chapter looks at each of the component types in detail and concludes with a discussion of how to build, deploy, and run the application.

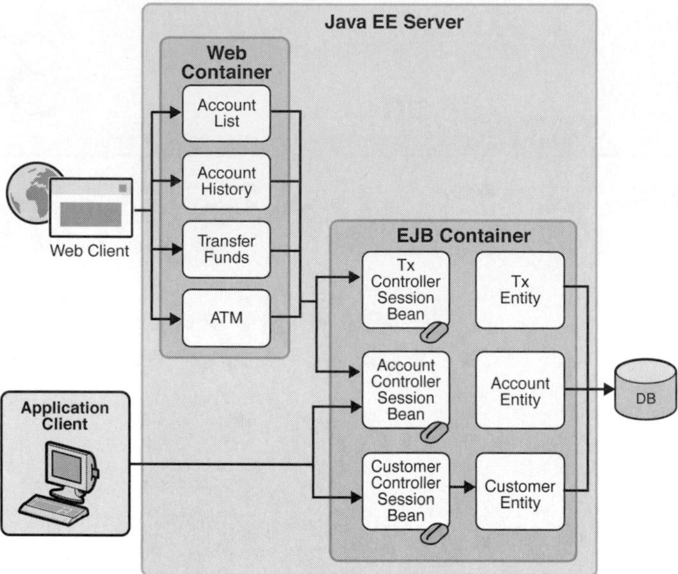

Figure 37–1 Duke's Bank Application

Enterprise Beans

Let's take a closer look at the access paths between the clients, enterprise beans, and database tables. As you can see, the end-user clients (web and application clients) access only the session beans. Within the enterprise bean tier, the session beans use Java Persistence entities. On the back end of the application, the entities access the database tables that store the entity states.

Note: The source code for these enterprise beans is in the *<INSTALL>*/`javaeetutorial5/examples/dukesbank/src/com/sun/ebank/ejb/` directory.

Session Beans

The Duke's Bank application has three session beans: `AccountControllerBean`, `CustomerControllerBean`, and `TxControllerBean`. (`Tx` stands for a business transaction, such as transferring funds.) These session beans provide a client's view of the application's business logic. Hidden from the clients are the server-side routines that implement the business logic, access databases, manage relationships, and perform error checking.

AccountControllerBean

The business methods of the `AccountControllerBean` session bean perform tasks that fall into the following categories: creating and removing entities, managing the account-customer relationship, and getting the account information.

The following methods create and remove entities:

- `createAccount`
- `removeAccount`

These methods of the `AccountControllerBean` session bean call the `create` and `remove` methods of the `Account` entity. The `createAccount` and `removeAccount` methods throw application exceptions to indicate invalid method arguments. The `createAccount` method throws an `IllegalAccountTypeException` if the `type` argument is neither `Checking`, `Savings`, `Credit`, nor `Money Market`. The `createAccount` method also looks up the specified customer exists by invoking the `EntityManager.find` method. If the result of this verification is `null`, the `createAccount` method throws a `CustomerNotFoundException`.

The following methods manage the account-customer relationship:

- `addCustomerToAccount`
- `removeCustomerFromAccount`

The `Account` and `Customer` entities have a many-to-many relationship. A bank account can be jointly held by more than one customer, and a customer can have multiple accounts.

In the Duke's Bank application, the `addCustomerToAccount` and `removeCustomerFromAccount` methods of the `AccountControllerBean` session bean manage the account-customer relationship. The `addCustomerToAccount` method, for example, starts by verifying that the customer exists. To create the relationship, the `addCustomerToAccount` method first looks up the `Customer` and `Account` entities using the `EntityManager.find` method, then it calls the `Account.addCustomer` method to associate the customer with the account.

The following methods get the account information:

- `getAccountsOfCustomer`
- `getDetails`

The AccountControllerBean session bean has two get methods. The getAccountsOfCustomer method returns all of the accounts of a given customer by invoking the getAccounts method of the Account entity. Instead of implementing a get method for every instance variable, the AccountControllerBean has a getDetails method that returns an object (AccountDetails) that encapsulates the entire state of an Account entity. Because it can invoke a single method to retrieve the entire state, the client avoids the overhead associated with multiple remote calls.

CustomerControllerBean

A client creates a Customer entity by invoking the createCustomer method of the CustomerControllerBean session bean. To remove a customer, the client calls the removeCustomer method, which invokes the EntityManager.remove method of Customer.

The CustomerControllerBean session bean has two methods that return multiple customers: getCustomersOfAccount and getCustomersOfLastName. getCustomersOfAccount calls the getCustomers method of the Account entity. getCustomersOfLastName uses the Customer.FindByLastName named query to search the database for customers with a matching last name, which is a named parameter to the query.

TxControllerBean

The TxControllerBean session bean handles bank transactions. In addition to its get methods, getTxsOfAccount and getDetails, the TxControllerBean bean has several methods that change the balances of the bank accounts:

- withdraw
- deposit
- makeCharge
- makePayment
- transferFunds

These methods access an Account entity to verify the account type and to set the new balance. The withdraw and deposit methods are for standard accounts, whereas the makeCharge and makePayment methods are for accounts that include a line of credit. If the type method argument does not match the account, these methods throw an IllegalAccountTypeException. If a withdrawal were to result in a negative balance, the withdraw method throws an Insufficient-

FundsException. If a credit charge attempts to exceed the account's credit line, the makeCharge method throws an InsufficientCreditException.

The transferFunds method also checks the account type and new balance; if necessary, it throws the same exceptions as the withdraw and makeCharge methods. The transferFunds method subtracts from the balance of one Account instance and adds the same amount to another instance. Both of these steps must complete to ensure data integrity. If either step fails, the entire operation is rolled back and the balances remain unchanged. The transferFunds method, like all methods in session beans that use container-managed transaction demarcation, has an implicit Required transaction attribute. That is, you don't need to explicitly decorate the method with a @TransactionAttribute annotation.

Java Persistence Entities

For each business entity represented in our simple bank, the Duke's Bank application has a matching Java Persistence API entity:

- Account
- Customer
- Tx

The purpose of these entities is to provide an object view of these database tables: bank_account, bank_customer, and bank_tx. For each column in a table, the corresponding entity has an instance variable. Because they use the Java Persistence API, the entities contain no SQL statements that access the tables. The enterprise bean container manages all data in the underlying data source, including adding, updating, and deleting data from the database tables.

Unlike the session beans, the entities do not validate method parameters. During the design phase, we decided that the session beans would check the parameters and throw the application exceptions, such as CustomerNotInAccountException and IllegalAccountTypeException. Consequently, if some other application were to include these entities, its session beans would also have to validate the method parameters. We could have added validation code to the entity's methods, but decided not to in order to keep the business logic separate from the entity data.

Helper Classes

The EJB JAR files include several helper classes that are used by the enterprise beans. The source code for these classes is in the `<INSTALL>/javaeetutorial5/examples/dukesbank/dukesbank-ejb/src/java/com/sun/tutorial/javaee/dukesbank/util/` directory. Table 37–1 briefly describes the helper classes.

Table 37–1 Helper Classes for the Application's Enterprise Beans

Class Name	Description
`AccountDetails`	Encapsulates the state of an `Account` instance. Returned by the `getDetails` method of `AccountControllerBean`.
`CustomerDetails`	Encapsulates the state of a `Customer` instance. Returned by the `getDetails` method of `CustomerControllerBean`.
`Debug`	Has simple methods for printing a debugging message from an enterprise bean. These messages appear on the standard output of the Application Server when it's run with the `--verbose` option and in the server log.
`DomainUtil`	Contains validation methods: `getAccountTypes`, `checkAccountType`, and `isCreditAccount`.
`TxDetails`	Encapsulates the state of a `Tx` instance. Returned by the `getDetails` method of `TxControllerBean`.

Database Tables

A database table of the Duke's Bank application can be categorized by its purpose: representing business entities.

Tables Representing Business Entities

Figure 37–2 shows the relationships between the database tables. The `bank_customer` and `bank_account` tables have a many-to-many relationship: A customer can have several bank accounts, and each account can be owned by more than one customer. This many-to-many relationship is implemented by the cross–reference table named `bank_customer_account_xref`. The tables named bank_account and bank_tx have a one-to-many relationship: A bank account can have many transactions, but each transaction refers to a single account.

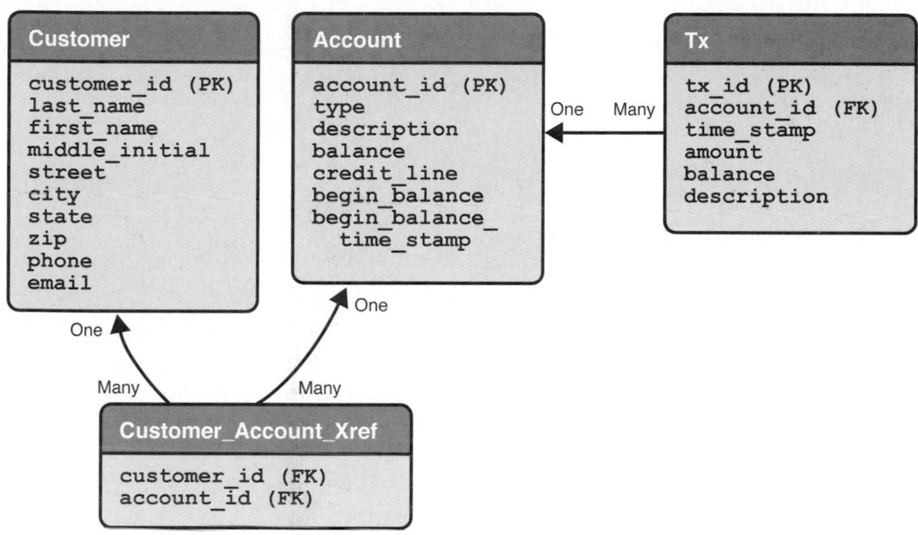

Figure 37–2 Database Tables

Figure 37–2 uses several abbreviations. PK stands for primary key, the value that uniquely identifies a row in a table. FK is an abbreviation for foreign key, which is the primary key of the related table. Tx is short for transaction, such as a deposit or withdrawal.

Protecting the Enterprise Beans

In the Java EE platform, you protect an enterprise bean by specifying the security roles that can access its methods. In the Duke's Bank application, you define two roles—bankCustomer and bankAdmin—because two categories of operations are defined by the enterprise beans.

A user in the bankAdmin role will be allowed to perform administrative functions: creating or removing an account, adding a customer to or removing a customer from an account, setting a credit line, and setting an initial balance. A user in the bankCustomer role will be allowed to deposit, withdraw, and transfer funds, make charges and payments, and list the account's transactions. Notice that there is no overlap in functions that users in either role can perform.

The system restricts access to these functions to the appropriate role by setting method permissions on selected methods of the `CustomerControllerBean`, `AccountControllerBean`, and `TxControllerBean` enterprise beans. For example, by allowing only users in the `bankAdmin` role to access the `createAccount` method in the `AccountControllerBean` enterprise bean, you deny users in the `bankCustomer` role (or any other role) permission to create bank accounts.

Application Client

Sometimes, enterprise applications use a stand-alone client application for handling tasks such as system or application administration. For example, the Duke's Bank application uses an application client to administer customers and accounts. This capability is useful in the event that the site becomes inaccessible for any reason or if a customer prefers to communicate things such as changes to account information by phone.

The application client shown in Figure 37–3 handles basic customer and account administration for the banking application through a Swing user interface. The bank administrator can perform any of the following functions on the respective tabs.

Customer Info tab:

- View customer information
- Add a new customer to the database
- Update customer information
- Remove a customer
- Find a customer's ID

Account administration:

- Create a new account
- Add a new customer to an existing account
- Remove a customer from an existing account
- View account information
- Remove an account from the database

Error and informational messages appear in the bottom under `Messages`.

Figure 37–3 Application Client

The Classes and Their Relationships

The source code for the application client is in the *<INSTALL>*/`javaeetutorial5/examples/dukesbank/dukesbank-appclient/src/java/com/sun/tutorial/javaee/dukesbank/client/` directory. The application client is consists of a single class: `BankAdmin`.

BankAdmin Class

The `BankAdmin` class, which creates the user interface, is a Swing class that provides action methods that are called when certain events occur in the application, and methods that call the controller session beans. It was created using the NetBeans 5.5 Swing editor, Matisse.

Note: Although `BankAdmin` was written using NetBeans 5.5, you do not need to have NetBeans installed in order to run the application. If you want to alter the user interface, however, you do need to use NetBeans.

Constructor

The `BankAdmin` constructor creates the initial user interface, which consists of a menu bar, two tabs, and a message pane, by calling the `initComponents` method. The menu bar contains the standard File and Edit menus, the left tab is for viewing and updating customer information, the right tab is for viewing and updating account information, and the message pane contains a message area.

The `initComponents` method is automatically generated by NetBeans. It creates all the user interface elements visible in `BankAdmin`.

Class Methods

The `BankAdmin` class provides methods that other objects call when they need to update the user interface. These methods are as follows:

- `setCustomerTextFields`: When true enables the user to enter or change information in the customer tab. When false, the fields are disabled.
- `fillCustomerTextFields`: Uses a `CustomerDetails` object to display customer information in the customer tab
- `clearCustomerTextFields`: Clears the contents of the customer fields in the customer tab
- `setAccountTextFields`: When true enables the user to enter or change information in the account tab. When false, the fields are disabled.
- `fillAccountTextFields`: Uses an `AccountDetails` object to display account information in the account tab
- `clearAccountTextFields`: Clears the contents of the account fields in the account tab
- `resetAll`: Calls `setCustomerTextFields` and `setAccountFields`, setting all the fields to disabled

The following methods interact with the controller session beans to create and update customer and account information:

- `createAccount`: uses an `AccountDetails` object to create a new account
- `updateAccount`: uses an `AccountDetails` object to update an account information
- `createCustomer`: uses a `CustomerDetails` object to create a new customer
- `updateCustomer`: uses a `CustomerDetails` object to update a customer's information

The `<UI Element>MouseReleased` methods are linked to the GUI controls in `BankAdmin`. They call the previous methods to enable/disable the GUI fields, and create/update accounts and customers.

Web Client

In the Duke's Bank application, the web client is used by customers to access account information and perform operations on accounts. Table 37–2 lists the functions the client supports, the JSP pages the customer uses to perform the functions, and the backing beans ad other JavaBeans components that implement the functions. Figure 37–4 shows an account history screen.

Note: The source code for the web client is in the `<INSTALL>/javaeetutorial5/examples/dukesbank/dukesbank-war/` directory.

Table 37–2 Web Client

Function	**JSP Pages**	**JavaBeans Components**
Home page	`main.jsp`	`CustomerBean`

Log on to or off of the application	`logon.jsp`
	`logonError.jsp`
	`logoff.jsp`
		`CustomerBean`

List accounts	`accountList.jsp`	`CustomerBean`, `AccountHistoryBean`
List the history of an account	`accountHist.jsp`	`CustomerBean`, `AccountHistoryBean`
Transfer funds between accounts	`transferFunds.jsp` `transferAck.jsp`	`CustomerBean`, `Transfer-` `Bean`
Withdraw and deposit funds	`atm.jsp` `atmAck.jsp`	`CustomerBean`, `ATMBean`
Error handling	`error.jsp`	

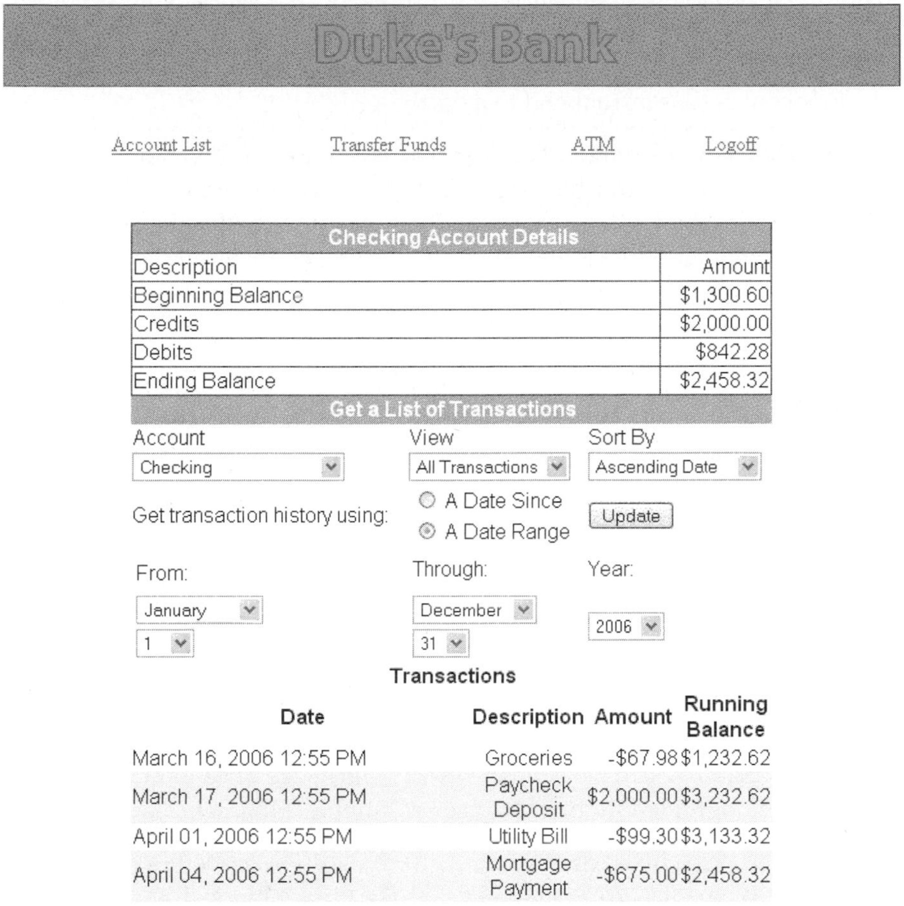

Duke's Bank

Account List Transfer Funds ATM Logoff

Checking Account Details	
Description	Amount
Beginning Balance	$1,300.60
Credits	$2,000.00
Debits	$842.28
Ending Balance	$2,458.32

Get a List of Transactions

Account: Checking
View: All Transactions
Sort By: Ascending Date

Get transaction history using: A Date Since / A Date Range
Update

From: January 1
Through: December 31
Year: 2006

Transactions

Date	Description	Amount	Running Balance
March 16, 2006 12:55 PM	Groceries	-$67.98	$1,232.62
March 17, 2006 12:55 PM	Paycheck Deposit	$2,000.00	$3,232.62
April 01, 2006 12:55 PM	Utility Bill	-$99.30	$3,133.32
April 04, 2006 12:55 PM	Mortgage Payment	-$675.00	$2,458.32

Figure 37–4 Account History

Design Strategies

The main job of the JSP pages in the Duke's Bank application is presentation. They use JavaServer Faces tags to represent UI components on the page, to bind the components to server-side data stored in backing beans, and wire the components to event-handling code. To maintain the separation of presentation and application behavior, most dynamic processing tasks are delegated to enterprise beans, custom tags, and JavaBeans components, including backing beans (see Backing Beans, page 304).

In the Duke's Bank application, the JSP pages rely on backing beans and other JavaBeans components for interactions with the enterprise beans. In the Duke's Bookstore application, discussed in Chapters 2 to 14, the `BookDB` JavaBeans component acts as a front end to a database.

In the Duke's Bank application, `CustomerBean` acts as a facade to the enterprise beans. Through it, the backing beans can invoke methods on the enterprise beans. For example, `TransferFundsBean` can indirectly invoke the `transferFunds` method of the `TxControllerBean` enterprise bean by first calling `getTxController` on `CustomerBean` on then calling `transferFunds` on the `TxController` interface.

The other backing beans have much richer functionality. `ATMBean` sets acknowledgment strings according to customer input, and `AccountHistoryBean` massages the data returned from the enterprise beans in order to present the view of the data required by the customer.

The web client uses a template mechanism implemented by custom tags (discussed in A Template Tag Library, page 253) to maintain a common look across all the JSP pages. The template mechanism consists of three components:

- `template.jsp` determines the structure of each screen. It uses the `insert` tag to compose a screen from subcomponents.
- `screendefinitions.jspf` defines the subcomponents used by each screen. All screens have the same banner, but different title and body content (specified in the JSP Pages column in Table 37–2).

Finally, the web client uses logic tags from the JSTL `core` tag library to perform flow control and tags from the JSTL `fmt` tag library to localize messages and format currency.

Client Components

All the JavaBeans components used in the web client are instantiated by the managed bean facility (see Configuring a Bean, page 306) when they are encountered in the page, such as when an EL expression references the component. The managed bean facility is configured in the `faces-config.xml` file. The following `managed-bean` elements from the `faces-config.xml` file specify how AccountHistoryBean and CustomerBean are to be instantiated and stored in scope:

```
<managed-bean>
  <managed-bean-name>accountHistoryBean</managed-bean-name>
  <managed-bean-class>
    com.sun.tutorial.javaee.dukesbank.web.AccountHistoryBean
  </managed-bean-class>
  <managed-bean-scope>request</managed-bean-scope>
  ...
  <managed-property>
    <property-name>accountId</property-name>
    <value>#{param.accountId}</value>
  </managed-property>
  <managed-property>
  ...
</managed-bean>

<managed-bean>
  <managed-bean-name>customerBean</managed-bean-name>
  <managed-bean-class>
    com.sun.tutorial.javaee.dukesbank.web.CustomerBean
  </managed-bean-class>
  <managed-bean-scope>session</managed-bean-scope>
</managed-bean>
```

As shown by the preceding configurations, an AccountHistoryBean instance is saved into request scope under the name accountHistoryBean, and a CustomerBean instance is saved into session scope under the name customerBean. EL expressions use these names to reference the beans from a page. The managed bean configurations can also initialize bean properties with values. As shown in the preceding configuration, the accountId property of AccountHistoryBean is set to the expression #{param.accountId} when an instance of AccountHistoryBean is created. This expression references the accountId variable in the request parameter map. This is so that other pages in the application can pass the account ID to AccountHistoryBean and therefore make it available to the accountHist.jsp page.

Responsibility for managing the enterprise beans used by the web client rests with CustomerBean. It creates account and transaction controller enterprise beans and provides methods for retrieving the beans.

When instantiated, the `CustomerBean` component uses `@EJB` annotations to inject references to the enterprise beans. Because these enterprise beans apply to a particular customer or session, `CustomerBean` is stored in session.

```
public class CustomerBean {

    @EJB
    private AccountController accountController;

    @EJB
    private TxController txController;
    ...
}
```

`CustomerBean` also does the following:

- Maintains the customer ID
- Retrieves the list of accounts from the database
- Gets detailed information about a particular account
- Invalidates a session to allow a customer to log out.

Because `CustomerBean` is in session, it is a convenient place to keep account information so that the backing beans and their associated pages can pass this information between themselves.

The page fragment `template/links.jsp` generates the list of bank function links at the top of every page. Notice that the customer is retrieved from the `userPrincipal` object, which is set when the customer logs in (see Protecting the Web Client Resources, page 1251). After the customer is set, the page can retrieve the collection of accounts from `CustomerBean`.

As shown by the following code from `links.jsp`, the ID of the first account in the collection of accounts is set into request scope. The `setPropertyActionListener` tag is nested inside the `commandLink` tag, which represents the hyperlink that launches the `atm.jsp` page. This `setPropertyActionListener` tag causes the account ID to be set in request scope when the hyperlink is clicked.

```
...
  <c:set var="accountId" scope="request"
      value="${customerBean.accounts[0].accountId}"/>
  <h:commandLink value="#{bundle.ATM}" action="atm">
    <f:setPropertyActionListener
```

```
            target="#{requestScope.accountId}"
            value="#{customerBean.accounts[0].accountId}"/>
      </h:commandLink>
   ...
```

Request Processing

When a user clicks on a button or a hyperlink, the application navigates to a new page or reloads the current page. Navigation to all pages listed in Table 37–2 is configured in the `web/WEB-INF/faces-config.xml` file using a set of navigation rules.

As described in Configuring Navigation Rules (page 474), the JavaServer Faces navigation mechanism matches a logical outcome `String` or an action method to one of the navigation rules to determine which page to open next. The button or hyperlink that the user clicks specifies the logical outcome `String` or action method with its `action` attribute.

Although it's not necessary to do so, the web client of Duke's Bank uses an Java SE `Enum` class to encapsulate all the possible logical outcomes for the application:

```
public enum Navigation  {
   main,
   accountHist,
   accountList,
   atm,
   atmAck,
   transferFunds,
   transferAck,
   error,
   logout;

   public Object action() {
      return this;
   }
}
```

If you are not familiar with enums, see `http://java.sun.com/j2se/1.5.0/docs/guide/language/enums.html`.

A managed bean is needed to expose the enum to the expression language so that a page can access its logical outcomes. In this case, the `Navigation` enum class is accessed through the `NavigationEnumBean`:

```
public class NavigationEnumBean extends EnumManagedBean {
  public NavigationEnumBean() {
    super(Util.Navigation.class);
  }
}
```

`NavigationEnumBean` extends a special bean class that includes a method to return an enum constant, which represents a logical outcome:

```
public Enum getEnum(String enumName) {
  return Enum.valueOf(e, enumName);
}
```

The application also includes a custom EL resolver, `EnumResolver`, which resolves expressions that reference an instance of this bean class. You create a resolver if you want expressions to particular kinds of objects resolved in a special way that is not already supported by the EL mechanism. See Resolving Expressions (page 127) for more information on EL resolvers.

The resolver calls the bean's `getEnum` method from its `getValue` method to return the enum constant:

```
public Object getValue(ELContext elContext, Object base, Object
property) {
  if ((base != null && property != null)
    && base instanceof EnumManagedBean) {
      elContext.setPropertyResolved(true);
      return
        ((EnumManagedBean)base)
          .getEnum(property.toString());
  }
  return null;
}
```

A tag's `action` attribute references a particular constant of the enum to specify a logical outcome. The following `commandLink` tag appears on the `links.jsp` page:

```
<h:commandLink value="#{bundle.Logoff}"
  action="#{navigation.logout.action}"/>
```

The `action` attribute has the expression `#{navigation.logout.action}` to invoke the `action` method of the `Navigation` enum. This returns the enum constant, representing the logical outcome, `logout`.

The following piece of a navigation rule configuration in the `faces-config.xml` file corresponds to the `action` attribute expression of the preceding `commandLink` tag. It causes the `logoff.jsp` page to open if the `logout` logical outcome is returned.

```
<navigation-rule>
  ...
  <navigation-case>
    <description>
      Any action that returns "logout" should go to the
      logoff page and invalidate the session.
    </description>
    <from-action>logout</from-action>
    <to-view-id>/logoff.jsp</to-view-id>
</navigation-rule>
```

When a page in the application is rendered, it is constructed with the aid of a template mechanism. Every page includes the `template.jsp` page, which in turn includes certain subcomponents, such as `banner.jsp`, into the page depending on which page is being rendered. The `screendefinitions.jspf` page, included in `template.jsp`, determines which page to render based on the current view ID, which identifies the UI component tree that represents the page to be rendered. The `screendefinitions.jspf` page accesses the view ID with this expression from its definition tag:

```
<tt:definition name="bank"
    screen="${facesContext.viewRoot.viewId}">
```

Based on the view ID, the templating mechanism will include specific components into the page.

Protecting the Web Client Resources

In the JavaEE platform, you protect a web resource from anonymous access by specifying which security roles can access the resource. The web container guarantees that only certain users acting in those roles can access the resource. For the web container to enforce the security constraint, the application must specify a means for users to identify themselves, and the web container must support mapping a role to a user.

In the Duke's Bank web client, you restrict all the URLs listed in Table 37–2 to the security role bankCustomer. The application requires users to identify themselves via the form-based login mechanism. When a customer tries to access a web client URL and has not been authenticated, the web container displays the JSP page logon.jsp. This page contains an HTML form that requires a customer to enter an identifier and password. This form is rendered by a JavaServer Faces custom component. A custom tag represents the component on the page. In the following piece of logon.jsp, the <db:formBasedLogin> tag represents the custom component:

```
<f:view>
...
<h:outputText value="#{bundle.Logon}"/>
<h:outputText value="#{bundle.Submit}"/>.</h3>
<br><br>
<db:formBasedLogin  />
</f:view>
```

Note that there is no h:form tag. This is because the custom component renders the form tag along with the complete HTML form that customers use to log in:

```
<form action="j_security_check" method=post>
<table>
<tr>
  <td align="center" >
  <table border="0">
  <tr>
  <td><b><fmt:message key="CustomerId"/></b></td>
  <td>
    <input type="text" size="15" name="j_username">
  </td>
  </tr>
  <tr>
  <td><b><fmt:message key="Password"/></b></td>
  <td>
    <input type="password" size="15" name="j_password">
  </td>
  ...
</form>
```

Note that the action invoked by the form, j_security_check, is specified by the Java Servlet specification, as are the request parameters j_username and j_password. The web container retrieves this information, maps it to a security role, and verifies that the role matches that specified in the security constraint. In order for the web container to check the validity of the authentication information and perform the mapping, you must perform these two steps when you deploy the application:

1. Add the customer's group, ID, and password to the default realm of the container using the Admin Console.
2. Map the `bankCustomer` role to the customer *or* the customer's group in the deployment descriptor.

After the customer has been authenticated, the identifier provided by the customer is used as a key to identify the customer's accounts. The identifier is retrieved from the `FacesContext` object by the `CustomerBean` constructor, which saves it into the `customerId` property:

```
customerId = Long.parseLong(FacesContext.getCurrentInstance()
  .getExternalContext().getUserPrincipal().getName());
```

Building, Packaging, Deploying, and Running the Application

To build the Duke's Bank application, you must have installed the tutorial bundle as described in . When you install the bundle, the Duke's Bank application files are located in the `<INSTALL>/javaeetutorial5/examples/dukesbank/` directory. This directory contains the configuration files for creating the EAR, `dukesbank.ear`. The EAR consists of the following three modules:

- `dukesbank-appclient`: The application client
- `dukesbank-ejb`: The enterprise beans and persistence entities
- `dukesbank-war`: The web client

After you build the source code, all the submodules will be built into their respective module packages, and the resulting EAR file will reside in the `<INSTALL>/javaeetutorial5/examples/dukesbank/dist/` directory.

Setting Up the Servers

Before you can package, deploy, and run the example, you must first set up the Java DB database server with customer and account data, and you must add some resources to the Application Server.

Starting the Application Server

Before you can start this tutorial, the Application Server must be running. For information on starting the Application Server, see Starting and Stopping the Application Server (page 27).

Creating the Bank Database in NetBeans 5.5

To create the database tables used in Duke's Bank, follow the instructions in Creating the Database Tables in NetBeans 5.5 (page 848).

Creating the Bank Database Using Ant

In Duke's Bank, the database tables will be created and populated before deploying the application. This happens automatically when you run the `deploy` task. You can manually reset the database to its original state by following these steps:

1. In a terminal window or command prompt, go to the `<INSTALL>/javaeetutorial5/examples/dukesbank/` directory.
2. Execute the following command:

   ```
   ant create-tables
   ```

This task executes the SQL commands contained in `<INSTALL>/javaeetutorial5/examples/common/sql/javadb/tutorial.sql`. The SQL commands delete any existing tables, create new tables, and insert the initial data in the tables.

Adding Users and Groups to the File Realm

To enable the Application Server to determine which users can access enterprise bean methods and resources in the web client, add users and groups to the server's file security realm using the Admin Console following the procedures described in Managing Users and Groups on the Application Server (page 918). Add the users and groups listed in Table 37–3.

Table 37–3 Duke's Bank Users and Groups

User	Password	Group
200	javaee	bankCustomer
bankadmin	javaee	bankAdmin

Building, Packaging, and Deploying Duke's Bank Using NetBeans 5.5

Follow these instructions to build, package, deploy, and run the Duke's Bank example application to your Application Server instance using NetBeans 5.5.

1. In NetBeans 5.5, select File→Open Project.
2. In the Open Project dialog, navigate to `<INSTALL>/javaeetutorial5/examples/`.
3. Select the `dukesbank` folder.
4. Select the Open as Main Project and Open Required Projects checkboxes.
5. Click Open Project Folder.
6. In the Projects tab, right-click the `dukesbank` project and select Deploy Project.

   You will see the output in the Output tab.

Building, Packaging, and Deploying Duke's Bank Using Ant

To compile and package the enterprise beans, application client, and web client into `dukesbank.ear`, go to the `<INSTALL>/javaeetutorial5/examples/dukesbank/` directory of the tutorial distribution and execute the command:

```
ant
```

Run the following command to deploy dukesbank.ear:

```
ant deploy
```

This task calls the create-tables task to initialize the database tables.

Running the Application Client Using NetBeans 5.5

To run the application client in NetBeans 5.5, follow these steps:

1. In NetBeans 5.5, select the dukesbank project in the Projects pane.
2. Right-click dukesbank and select Run Project.
3. At the login prompts, type bankadmin for the user name and javaee for the password. You should see the application client, as shown in Figure 37–5.

   You can now create customers and accounts using the application client.

Running the Application Client Using Ant

To run the application client, follow these steps:

1. In a terminal window, go to *<INSTALL>*/javaeetutorial5/examples/dukesbank/.
2. Enter the following command:

   ```
   ant run
   ```

3. At the login prompts, type bankadmin for the user name and javaee for the password. You should see the application client, as shown in Figure 37–5.

   You can now create customers and accounts using the application client.

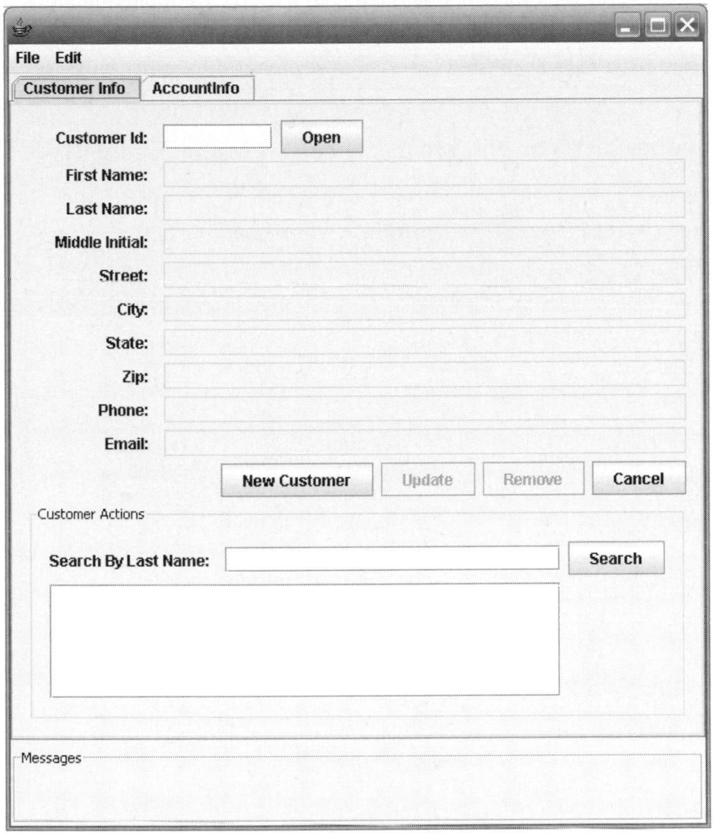

Figure 37–5 `BankAdmin` Application Client

Running the Web Client

To run the web client, follow these steps:

1. Open the bank URL, `http://localhost:8080/bank/main.faces`, in a web browser.
2. The application displays the login page. Enter `200` for the customer ID and `javaee` for the password. Click Submit.
3. Select an application function: Account List, Transfer Funds, ATM, or Logoff. When you have a list of accounts, you can get an account history by selecting an account link.

Note: The first time you select a new page, particularly a complicated page such as an account history, it takes some time to display because the Application Server must translate the page into a servlet class and compile and load the class.

If you select Account List, you will see the screen shown in Figure 37–6.

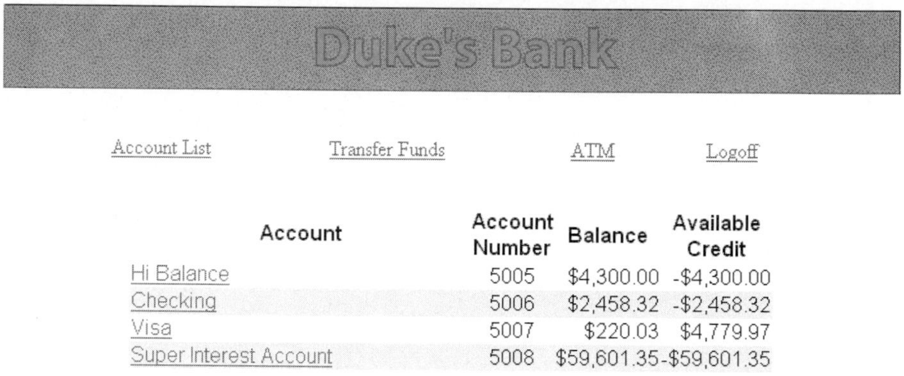

Duke's Bank

Account List Transfer Funds ATM Logoff

Account	Account Number	Balance	Available Credit
Hi Balance	5005	$4,300.00	-$4,300.00
Checking	5006	$2,458.32	-$2,458.32
Visa	5007	$220.03	$4,779.97
Super Interest Account	5008	$59,601.35	-$59,601.35

Figure 37–6 Account List

A

Java Encoding Schemes

THIS appendix describes the character-encoding schemes that are supported by the Java platform.

US-ASCII

US-ASCII is a 7-bit character set and encoding that covers the English-language alphabet. It is not large enough to cover the characters used in other languages, however, so it is not very useful for internationalization.

ISO-8859-1

ISO-8859-1 is the character set for Western European languages. It's an 8-bit encoding scheme in which every encoded character takes exactly 8 bits. (With the remaining character sets, on the other hand, some codes are reserved to signal the start of a multibyte character.)

UTF-8

UTF-8 is an 8-bit encoding scheme. Characters from the English-language alphabet are all encoded using an 8-bit byte. Characters for other languages are encoded using 2, 3, or even 4 bytes. UTF-8 therefore produces compact documents for the English language, but for other languages, documents tend to be half again as large as they would be if they used UTF-16. If the majority of a document's text is in a Western European language, then UTF-8 is generally a good choice because it allows for internationalization while still minimizing the space required for encoding.

UTF-16

UTF-16 is a 16-bit encoding scheme. It is large enough to encode all the characters from all the alphabets in the world. It uses 16 bits for most characters but includes 32-bit characters for ideogram-based languages such as Chinese. A Western European-language document that uses UTF-16 will be twice as large as the same document encoded using UTF-8. But documents written in far Eastern languages will be far smaller using UTF-16.

Note: UTF-16 depends on the system's byte-ordering conventions. Although in most systems, high-order bytes follow low-order bytes in a 16-bit or 32-bit "word," some systems use the reverse order. UTF-16 documents cannot be interchanged between such systems without a conversion.

Further Information

The character set and encoding names recognized by Internet authorities are listed in the IANA character set registry:

```
http://www.iana.org/assignments/character-sets
```

The Java programming language represents characters internally using the Unicode character set, which provides support for most languages. For storage and transmission over networks, however, many other character encodings are used. The Java 2 platform therefore also supports character conversion to and from other character encodings. Any Java runtime must support the Unicode transformations UTF-8, UTF-16BE, and UTF-16LE as well as the ISO-8859-1 character encoding, but most implementations support many more. For a complete list of the encodings that can be supported by the Java 2 platform, see

```
http://java.sun.com/j2se/1.4/docs/guide/intl/encoding.doc.html
```

B

Preparation for Java EE Certification Exams

SUN Microsystems provides certification examinations for Solaris administrators and different types of Java programmers. Sun also offers a learning path, consisting of training classes and practice exams, for each type of certification.

The Java EE learning path focuses on providing Java EE training for architects and for Web component, business component, and integration developers. Java EE training can lead to one of three certifications: Sun Certified Web Component Developer (SCWCD), Sun Certified Business Component Developer (SCBCD), or Sun Certified Enterprise Architect (SCEA).

You can use the *Java EE Tutorial* as preparation for the certification exams. This appendix provides details about how the sections of the exams map to chapters of the tutorial. Exam objectives change over time, and potential certification candidates should check `http://www.sun.com/training/certification` for the most up-to-date list of certification exam objectives.

Note: This tutorial is not intended as a primer for the certification exams: it does not cover every subject to the depth that will be on the exam. The links below are presented so that you can use this tutorial as one of many sources for exam preparation.

This appendix provides information relating to the following certification exam:

- CX-310-081: Sun Certified Web Component Developer

This appendix provides information relating to the following course:

- SL-351: Business Component Development with Enterprise JavaBeans™ Technology

CX-310-081: Sun Certified Web Component Developer

The certification exam, *CX-310-081: Sun Certified Web Component Developer*, is for Sun Certified Programmers (any edition) who are using the Java technology servlet and JavaServer Pages (JSP) application program interface (APIs) to develop Web applications.

Section 1: The Servlet Technology Model

- Chapter 3, Java Servlet Technology (page 59)

Section 2: The Structure and Deployment of Web Applications

- Chapter 2, Getting Started with Web Applications (page 33)

Section 3: The Web Container Model

- Chapter 2, Getting Started with Web Applications (page 33)
- Chapter 3, Java Servlet Technology (page 59)

Section 4: Session Management

- Chapter 2, Getting Started with Web Applications (page 33)
- Chapter 3, Java Servlet Technology (page 59)
- Chapter 4, JavaServer Pages Technology (page 97)

Section 5: Web Application Security

- Chapter 30, Securing Web Applications (page 987)

Section 6: The JavaServer Pages (JSP) Technology Model

- Chapter 4, JavaServer Pages Technology (page 97)

Section 8: Building JSP Pages Using Standard Actions

- Chapter 4, JavaServer Pages Technology (page 97)

Section 9: Building JSP Pages Using Tag Libraries

- Chapter 6, JavaServer Pages Standard Tag Library (page 175)

Section 10: Building a Custom Tag Library

- Chapter 7, Custom Tags in JSP Pages (page 203)

SL-351: Business Component Development with Enterprise JavaBeans™ Technology

The course *SL-351: Business Component Development with Enterprise JavaBeans™ Technology* provides students with advanced concepts and skills in designing, developing, and deploying EJB applications for the business tier.

Module 1: Examine EJB Applications

- Chapter 20, Enterprise Beans (page 743)
- Chapter 21, Getting Started with Enterprise Beans (page 759)

Module 3: Examine session beans

- Chapter 21, Getting Started with Enterprise Beans (page 759)
- Chapter 22, Session Bean Examples (page 771)

Module 4: Examine Java Persistence API

- Chapter 24, Introduction to the Java Persistence API (page 803)
- Chapter 26, Persistence in the EJB Tier (page 835)

Module 5: Model data association relationships using persistence entities

- Chapter 24, Introduction to the Java Persistence API (page 803)
- Chapter 26, Persistence in the EJB Tier (page 835)

Module 6: Model inheritance and composition relationships using persistence entities

- Chapter 24, Introduction to the Java Persistence API (page 803)
- Chapter 26, Persistence in the EJB Tier (page 835)

Module 7: Examine the Java Persistence query language

- Chapter 24, Introduction to the Java Persistence API (page 803)
- Chapter 27, The Java Persistence Query Language (page 861)

Module 8: Examine Java Messaging API

- Chapter 31, The Java Message Service API (page 1051)
- Chapter 32, Java EE Examples Using the JMS API (page 1129)

Module 9: Examine message-driven beans

- Chapter 20, Enterprise Beans (page 743)
- Chapter 23, A Message-Driven Bean Example (page 791)

Module 11: Examine EJB transactions

- Chapter 20, Enterprise Beans (page 743)
- Chapter 33, Transactions (page 1165)

Module 12: Examine exception handling in an EJB application

- Chapter 20, Enterprise Beans (page 743)

Module 13: Use timer services

- Chapter 22, Session Bean Examples (page 771)

Module 14: Examine Java EE security

- Chapter 28, Introduction to Security in Java EE (page 899)
- Chapter 29, Securing Java EE Applications (page 937)

About the Authors

Java Architecture for XML Binding

Eric Jendrock is a staff writer at Sun Microsystems, where he leads the Java EE Tutorial and the Java WSIT Tutorial. Previously, he documented middleware products and standards. Currently, he writes about the Java Web Services Interoperability Technologies, the Java Architecture for XML Binding (JAXB), and security in the Java EE platform.

JavaServer Faces Technology, Web-Tier Technologies

Jennifer Ball is a staff writer at Sun Microsystems, where she documents JavaServer Faces technology. Previously she documented the Java2D API, `deploytool`, and JAXB. She holds an M.A. degree in Interdisciplinary Computer Science from Mills College.

Security

Debbie Carson is a staff writer at Sun Microsystems, where she documents the Java EE, Java SE, and Java Web Services Interoperability Technologies platforms. In previous positions she documented creating database applications using C++ and Java technologies and creating distributed applications using Java technology.

Java API for XML Web Services, Enterprise JavaBeans Technology, Java Persistence API

Ian Evans is a staff writer at Sun Microsystems, where he documents the Java EE and Java Web Services platforms and edits the Java EE platform specifications. In previous positions he documented programming tools, CORBA middleware, and Java application servers, and taught classes on UNIX, web programming, and server-side Java development.

Streaming API for XML, Java Architecture for XML Binding

Scott Fordin is a senior staff writer, illustrator, and online help specialist in the Java and XML Technology groups at Sun Microsystems. He has written numerous articles on Java, XML, and web service technologies. Scott has also written many developer guides, administrator guides, user guides (including the *JAXB User's Guide*), specifications, white papers, and tutorials for a wide range of products. Some of his most recent work includes writing about the StAX APIs, Application Server troubleshooting, and Application Server error messages.

Java API for XML Registries, SOAP with Attachments API for Java, Java Message Service API

Kim Haase is a staff writer at Sun Microsystems, where she documents the Java EE platform and Java Web Services. In previous positions she documented compilers, debuggers, and floating-point programming. She currently writes about the Java Message Service, the Java API for XML Registries, SOAP with Attachments API for Java, the Java DB database, and Service Registry.

Index

A

B

C

D

E

H

I

N

Q

U

V

W

X

The Java™ Series

ISBN 0-201-63456-2

ISBN 0-201-70433-1

ISBN 0-201-31005-8

ISBN 0-321-24575-X

ISBN 0-201-70393-9

ISBN 0-201-48558-3

ISBN 0-201-74622-0

ISBN 0-201-75280-8

ISBN 0-201-76810-0

ISBN 0-201-31002-3

ISBN 0-201-31003-1

ISBN 0-201-48552-4

ISBN 0-201-71102-8

ISBN 0-201-70329-7

ISBN 0-201-30955-6

ISBN 0-201-31008-2

ISBN 0-201-78472-6

ISBN 0-201-78791-1

ISBN 0-201-31009-0

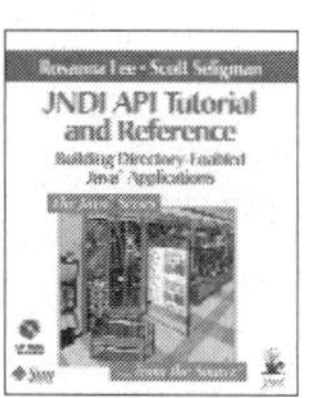

ISBN 0-201-70502-8

ISBN 0-201-32577-2

ISBN 0-201-43294-3

ISBN 0-201-91466-2

ISBN 0-321-19801-8

ISBN 0-201-74627-1

ISBN 0-201-70456-0

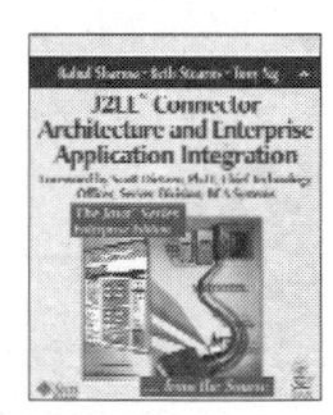

ISBN 0-201-77580-8

ISBN 0-201-78790-3

ISBN 0-201-77582-4

ISBN 0-201-91467-0

ISBN 0-201-70969-4

ISBN 0-321-17384-8

Visit www.awprofessional.com/javaseries for more information on these titles.

THIS BOOK IS SAFARI ENABLED

INCLUDES FREE 45-DAY ACCESS TO THE ONLINE EDITION

The Safari® Enabled icon on the cover of your favorite technology book means the book is available through Safari Bookshelf. When you buy this book, you get free access to the online edition for 45 days.

Safari Bookshelf is an electronic reference library that lets you easily search thousands of technical books, find code samples, download chapters, and access technical information whenever and wherever you need it.

TO GAIN 45-DAY SAFARI ENABLED ACCESS TO THIS BOOK:

- Go to **http://www.awprofessional.com/safarienabled**
- Complete the brief registration form
- Enter the coupon code found in the front of this book on the "Copyright" page

If you have difficulty registering on Safari Bookshelf or accessing the online edition, please e-mail customer-service@safaribooksonline.com.

CD-ROM Warranty

Addison-Wesley Professional warrants the enclosed CD-ROM to be free of defects in materials and faulty workmanship under normal use for a period of ninety days after purchase (when purchased new). If a defect is discovered in the CD-ROM during this warranty period, a replacement CD-ROM can be obtained at no charge by sending the defective CD-ROM, postage prepaid, with proof of purchase to:

Disc Exchange
Addison-Wesley Professional
Pearson Technology Group
75 Arlington Street, Suite 300
Boston, MA 02116
Email: AWPro@aw.com

Addison-Wesley Professional makes no warranty or representation, either expressed or implied, with respect to this software, its quality, performance, merchantability, or fitness for a particular purpose. In no event will Addison-Wesley Professional, its distributors, or dealers be liable for direct, indirect, special, incidental, or consequential damages arising out of the use or inability to use the software. The exclusion of implied warranties is not permitted in some states. Therefore, the above exclusion may not apply to you. This warranty provides you with specific legal rights. There may be other rights that you may have that vary from state to state. The contents of this CD-ROM are intended for personal use only.

More information and updates are available at:
http://www.awprofessional.com/

The Java EE 5 Tutorial CD

THE CD that accompanies this book is loaded with the latest Java EE software and documentation, including the content and code of this book.

Product	Version	Notes
Java EE 5 SDK	5.0 FCS	This bundle, originally released on `http://java.sun.com/javaee/downloads/`, includes Sun Java System Platform Edition 9, Java EE 5 Samples, J2SE 5.0 Update 6, Java BluePrints, and API documentation.
The Java EE 5 Tutorial	September 2006 build	The latest tutorial is available on `http://java.sun.com/javaee/5/docs/tutorial/doc/`.
Netbeans 5.5 IDE	Q-Build 200609062200	The latest version of NetBeans 5.5 is available at `http://netbeans.org/downloads/`.

The `README.html` file on the CD is the central HTML page that links you to all the contents. To view this page, use the Open File command or its equivalent in your Intenet browser. On most platforms, you can double-click the HTML file to launch it in your browser.

The following resources offer useful information and help:

- The Sun Developer Network (SDN) offers free developer tools, newsletters, forums, and more, at `http://developers.sun.com/`.
- `http://java.net/` includes technical forums, blogs, and early releases of Java software.